Fodor's
UpCLOSE

D0367906

ITALY

the complete guide, thoroughly up-to-date

SAVVY TRAVELING: WHERE TO SPEND, HOW TO SAVE

packed with details that will make your trip

CULTURAL TIPS: ESSENTIAL LOCAL DO'S AND TABOOS

must-see sights, on and off the beaten path

INSIDER SECRETS: WHAT'S HIP AND WHAT TO SKIP

the buzz on restaurants, the lowdown on lodgings

FIND YOUR WAY WITH CLEAR AND EASY-TO-USE MAPS

FODOR'S TRAVEL PUBLICATIONS
NEW YORK • TORONTO • LONDON • SYDNEY • AUCKLAND
www.fodors.com

Second Edition

ISBN 0-679-00381-9

ISSN 1527-2745

FODOR'S UPCLOSE ITALY

Editor: Nancy van Itallie

Editorial Contributors: Robert Andrews, Sarah Attia, Gregory Bailey, Sarah Bremer, Mary Benedicta Cipolla, Jon Eldan, Robert Fisher, Jeanine Gade, Robin Goldstein, Valerie Hamilton, Jeffrey Kennedy, James Kwak, Rebecca Lim, Carla Lionello, Lauren Myers, Norman Roberson, Patricia Rucidlo, Helayne Schiff

Editorial Production: Linda K. Schmidt

Maps: David Lindroth, *cartographer*; Rebecca Baer, *map editor*

Design: Fabrizio La Rocca, *creative director*; Allison Saltzman, *cover and text design*; Jolie Novak, *photo editor*

Production/Manufacturing: Robert Shields

Cover Art: Tatsuhiko Shimada/Photonica

SPECIAL SALES

CONTENTS

7. BOLOGNA AND EMILIA-ROMAGNA 165

8. FLORENCE AND TUSCANY 196

9. UMBRIA AND LE MARCHE 253

10. ROME 281

Bene Cipolla went to Italy on a Fulbright grant in 1995 and never left. She currently works as a broadcast journalist in Rome, spinning out freelance pieces on everything from baseball to immigration on the side. She spends much of her free time eating, drinking, and making friends with restaurateurs and wine-bar owners.

Writer **Mary Jane Cryan,** after more than 30 years in Italy, is still living "la dolce vita" outside Rome in a palazzo that she has restored.

Jon Eldan—our middle-of-the-boot sleuth—studied history and baked bread in Berkeley, California, before traveling to Europe in 1994. He lives in Rome.

Fresh pesto, fishing villages, and soccer lured **Robin Goldstein** from his grandmotherly roots in Calabria and Apulia to Genoa, on the shores of the Italian Riviera, where he teaches and writes for Fodor's.

Freelance writer **Jeffrey Kennedy** has been living in Rome for the past 15 years, where he researches and creates scripts for digital audioguides to Italian museums and other historic sights.

Carla Lionello grew up in Venice but now lives in Rome. Although she still hasn't learned to drive, that doesn't stop her from traveling all over Italy in search of endangered pastry.

Norman M. Roberson, an etruscologist, tour guide, and freelance writer who has lived in Rome for nearly 20 years, also works at the American Academy in Rome.

Patricia Rucidlo lives in Florence. Although she has master's degrees in Italian Renaissance history and art history, her true love is Italian food.

A SEND-OFF

Always call ahead. We knock ourselves out to check all the facts, but everything changes all the time, in ways that none of us can ever fully anticipate. Whenever you're making a special trip to a special place, as opposed to merely wandering, always call ahead. Trust us on this.

And then, if something doesn't go quite right—as inevitably happens with even the best-laid plans—stay cool. Missed your train? Stuck in the airport? Use the time to study the people. Strike up a conversation with a stranger. Study the newsstands or flip through the local press. Take a walk. Find the silver lining in the clouds, whatever it is. And do send us a postcard to tell us what went wrong and what went right. You can e-mail us at editors@fodors.com (specify the name of the book on the subject line), or write the Italy editor at Fodor's upCLOSE, 201 East 50th Street, New York, NY 10022. We'll put your ideas to good use and let other travelers benefit from your experiences. In the mean time, *buon viaggio*!

INTRODUCTION

The turmoil that characterizes life in Italy may not be apparent when you first arrive. It's easy to be seduced by the country's beautiful and varied scenery, incredible food and wine, warm people and climate, and stunning architecture and fashion—not to mention the most concentrated collection of artistic masterpieces in the world. Countless others have "discovered," over the centuries, the pleasure of that first bite of tiramisù or that first view of Florence's red rooftops—a 16th-century writer even warned "guileless youth against the irresistible seductions of Italy." You'll find no such warnings here, but be advised that you *will* discover the downside of Italy, perhaps on a sweltering summer afternoon, thirsty and tired, as you consider the many contrasts of 20th-century life here: traffic jams, ancient ruins, curious stares from the locals, pollution, Baroque cathedrals, and Vespa drivers swerving through narrow streets as they chat on cellular phones. Ironically, the country that produced the likes of Michelangelo, Dante, and Galileo also perfected *dolce far niente* (the sweet art of idleness). These contradictions have led Italians to raise difficult questions about the clash between past and present. When subway construction hits underground ruins, does digging stop? And should a country accept, or even exploit, its role as a cultural theme park? Italy, the country that gave us Fiat, fashion, and Fellini films, is still a nation searching to define itself at the turn of the 21st century.

In a period spanning 3,000 years, the narrow peninsula and its islands have supported a series of sophisticated peoples from a nearly endless variety of ethnic, religious, and philosophical backgrounds. These invasions kept the country in constant flux, contributing to Italy's inability to maintain political and social order. Early societies like those of the Carthaginians, Etruscans, and Greeks built magnificent cities throughout Italy, edging out indigenous tribes. In the 6th century BC, Italy's most indefatigable ruler, the Roman Republic, laid claim to the area. Even after the founding of the nearly impenetrable Roman Empire in 27 BC, invasions from north, south, east, and west continued to pummel the land. Roman territory expanded nonetheless, and a succession of ambitious, often maniacal emperors put together the largest, most powerful force in the west. But eventually the Romans spread themselves too thin, and the schism that developed between the eastern and western sides of the Roman Empire led to its downfall.

In the 1300s, semiautonomous city-states emerged throughout Italy, ruled by inbred autocrats and dominating dynasties. Art, literature, and trade thrived in this secular, commercialized environment, but fighting between the states made life in the early Renaissance far from idyllic. In the centuries that followed, dynasties such as the Austrian Hapsburgs and the Spanish Bourbons laid claim to parts of Italy, leaving behind a mixture of languages, architectural styles, and culinary treats. It wasn't until 1861 that Turinese nobleman Camillo Cavour—together with an idealistic rabble-rouser by the name of Giuseppe Garibaldi and his thousand-man army—succeeded in unifying the Kingdom of Italy.

Unfortunately, the Risorgimento (unification) didn't bring cohesion and order, and the country's inability to organize itself ultimately paid off for the Allies in World War II. The Italian Fascist party under Il Duce, Benito Mussolini, entered the war unprepared and with dated equipment. For four years the Italians were enmeshed in countless bloody battles, first alongside the Axis powers, then the Allied powers, and finally the partisan revolutionaries. In the end, Mussolini was overthrown by his own compatriots and assassinated, his body left hanging in a piazza in Milan.

Though Il Duce's obsession with streamlined services and orderly government changed things temporarily, his dream of an efficient, stable Italy died with him. In the years following World War II, more than 50 governments have tried to comb Italy's unruly hair. Until 1993, government control alternated between the right-wing Democrazia Cristiana and the left-wing Partito Socialista Italiano, but neither group did a stellar job of presenting to the outside world an Italy on the economic and cultural rise. As money poured into the north through companies such as Olivetti and Fiat, the money sent to the impoverished Mezzogiorno (southern Italy) took a detour into the pockets of organized crime and corrupt politicians. This disparity continues to affect Italians today: many northerners consider those from the south to be ignorant, and southerners often complain of the northerners' coldness and obsession with money.

Ironically, the least chaotic aspect of Italy is crime. Known as the 'ndragheta in Calabria, la camorra in Naples, and just plain Mafia in Sicily, organized crime has been the subject of graphic movies, novels, and news reports for decades. Whether Mafia bosses are a holdover from the time of feudal lords or a surrogate power for a country where elected politicians are paralyzed by red tape is a moot point. The efforts of Mussolini, the only political figure in Italy's history to damage the organization, were thwarted by the Allies during their occupation of Sicily at the end of World War II. The Mafia, obviously anti-Mussolini, provided the Allies with their only organized source of intelligence. In turn, the Allies entrusted responsibility for 62 of Sicily's 66 towns to men with Mafia connections, tacitly allowing the organization to flourish yet again. The 1990s saw a revival of the war on organized crime, but the Mafia proves ever-resistant to these attacks, as evidenced by their devastating, brutal assassinations in the early 1990s of hardline Mafia prosecutors Giovanni Falcone and Paolo Borsellino. In May 1996, top Mafia boss Giovanni Brusca, the man charged with detonating the bomb that killed Falcone, was caught. Wearing masks to protect their identities, the arresting officers demonstrated the still-pervasive fear of the Mafia, whose contacts penetrate to the highest echelons of Italian government and finance.

While the spruced-up Italy that greets the millennium may not have a clear direction or purpose, even the most jaded cynic cannot mistake Rome, Florence, Naples, or Venice for anything other than what they are—at once extravagant, antiquated, and quintessentially Italian. Whether your images of Italy are of frescoed villas or chronically late trains, the reasons for coming here are as compelling as ever. Despite the political and economic woes of their homeland, Italians know how to make the most of everything—and luckily for us, their passion and appetite for life are contagious.

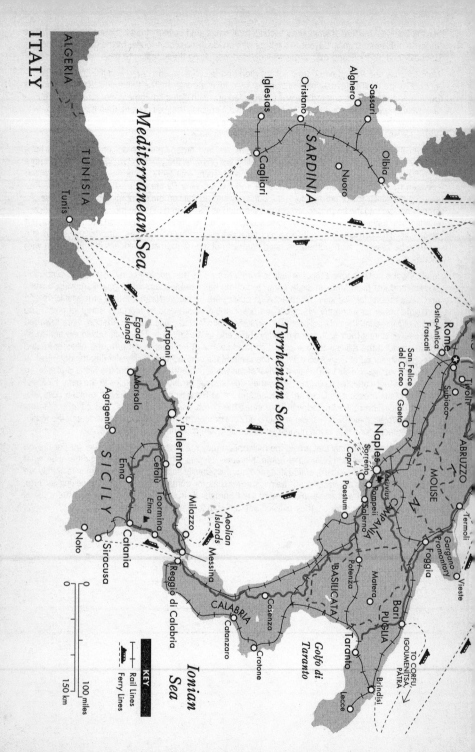

ITALY

ALGERIA

TUNISIA

TUNISIA

Tunis

Mediterranean Sea

Iglesias
Oristano
Alghero
Sassari
Olbia
Nuoro
Cagliari

SARDINIA

Tyrrhenian Sea

Egadi
Islands

Trapani
Marsala
Agrigento
Noto

S I C I L Y

Enna
Cefalù
Palermo
Taormina
Etna
Milazzo

Aeolian
Islands

Catania
Siracusa
Reggio di Calabria
Messina

CALABRIA

Cosenza
Catanzaro
Crotone

*Ionian
Sea*

Rome
Ostia-Antica
Frascati
Tivoli
Subiaco
San Felice
del Circeo
Gaeta

ABRUZZO

MOLISE

Termoli

Naples
Sorrento
Vesuvius
Pompeii
Capri
Paestum
Salerno

CAMPANIA

Gargano
Promontory

Foggia
Vieste

BASILICATA

Potenza
Matera
Bari

PUGLIA

Taranto

*Golfo di
Taranto*

Brindisi
Lecce

TO CORFU,
IGOUMENITSA,
PATRA

KEY

Rail Lines
Ferry Lines

0   100 miles
0   150 km

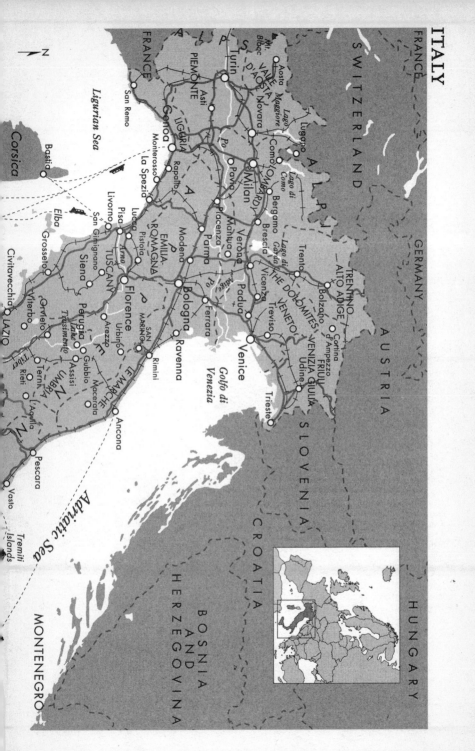

BASICS

I

f you've ever traveled with anyone before, you know that there are two types of people in the world—the planners and the nonplanners. Travel brings out the worst in both groups. Left to their own devices, the planners will have you goose-stepping from attraction to attraction on a cultural blitzkrieg, while the nonplanners will invariably miss the flight, the bus, and maybe even the point. This chapter offers you a middle ground; we hope it provides enough information to help you plan your trip to Italy without nailing you down. Keep flexible and remember that the most hair-raising situations turn into the best travel stories back home.

AIR TRAVEL

BOOKING YOUR FLIGHT

When you book **look for nonstop flights** and **remember that "direct" flights stop at least once.** Try to avoid connecting flights, which require a change of plane.

CARRIERS

MAJOR AIRLINES • From the U.S.: **Alitalia** (tel. 800/223– 5730) to Rome, Milan, and Venice. **American** (tel. 800/433–7300) to Milan. **Continental** (tel. 800/231–0856) to Rome and Milan. **Delta** (tel. 800/241–4141) to Rome and Milan. **Northwest** (tel. 800/225–2525) to Milan. **TWA** (tel. 800/892–4141) to Rome and Milan. **United** (tel. 800/538–2929) to Milan. **US Airways** (tel. 800/428–4322) to Rome. From Canada: **Canadian Air** (tel. 800/426– 7000). From the U.K.: **Alitalia** (tel. 0171/602–7111 or 0990/448– 259). **British Airways** (tel. 0345/222–111). **Meridiana** (tel. 0171/839–2222).

CHECK-IN & BOARDING

Assuming that not everyone with a ticket will show up, airlines routinely overbook planes. When that happens, airlines ask for volunteers to give up their seats. In return these volunteers usually get a certificate for a free flight and are rebooked on the next flight out. If there are not enough volunteers, the airline must choose who will be denied boarding. The first to get bumped are passengers who checked in late and those flying on discounted tickets, so **get to the gate and check in as early as possible,** especially during peak periods.

Always **bring a government-issued photo I.D. to the airport.** You may be asked to show it before you are allowed to check in.

CUTTING COSTS

The least-expensive airfares to Italy must usually be purchased in advance and are non-refundable. It's smart to **call a number of airlines, and when you are quoted a good price, book it on the spot**—the same fare may not be available the next day. Always **check different routings** and look into using different airports. Travel agents, especially low-fare specialists (*see* Discounts & Deals, *below*), are helpful.

Consolidators are another good source. They buy tickets for scheduled international flights at reduced rates from the airlines, then sell them at prices that beat the best fare available directly from the airlines, usually without restrictions. Sometimes you can even get your money back if you need to return the ticket. Carefully read the fine print detailing penalties for changes and cancellations, and **confirm your consolidator reservation with the airline.**

When you **fly as a courier** you trade your checked-luggage space for a ticket deeply subsidized by a courier service. There are restrictions on when you can book and how long you can stay.

CONSOLIDATORS • Airfare Busters (tel. 713/961–5109 or 800/232–8783). **Cheap Tickets** (tel. 800/377–1000). **Discount Airline Ticket Service** (tel. 800/576–1600). **Globe Travel** (tel. 212/843–9885 or 800/969–4562). **Payless Travel** (tel. 202/822–8018 or 800/822–0204). **United States Air Consolidators Association** (tel. 916/441–4166). **Unitravel** (tel. 800/325–2222). **Up & Away Travel** (tel. 212/889–2345 or 800/275–8001). **World Travel Network** (tel. 800/409–6753). In the U.K., **Air Travel Advisory Bureau** (tel. 0171/636–5000, in Manchester 0161/832–2000).

COURIERS • Air Courier Associaton (15000 W. 6th Ave. Suite 203, Golden, CO 80401, tel. 800/282–1202; www.aircourier.org). **Discount Travel International** (169 W. 81st St., New York, NY 10024, tel. 212/362–3636, fax 212/362–3236). **International Association of Air Travel Couriers** (PO Box 1349, Lake Worth, FL 33460, tel. 561/582–8320; www.courier.org. **Now Voyager** (74 Varick St., New York, NY, tel. 212/431–1616, fax 212/334–5243).

ENJOYING THE FLIGHT

For more legroom **request an emergency-aisle seat.** Don't sit in the row in front of the emergency aisle or in front of a bulkhead, where seats may not recline. If you have dietary concerns, **ask for special meals when booking.** These can be vegetarian, low-cholesterol, or kosher, for example. On long flights, try to maintain a normal routine, to help fight jetlag. At night **get some sleep.** By day **eat light meals, drink water** (not alcohol), and **move around the cabin** to stretch your legs.

FLYING WITHIN ITALY

Between getting to the airport, waiting for the plane, flying, and getting to the town center, flying within the country saves you little time and costs a lot of money. **Alitalia** is the main domestic airline, but there are several others. If you must book a flight within the country, go to a travel agent, who might be able to find you a better deal than the airlines' quoted fares.

FLYING TIMES

Flying time to Rome is 7½–8½ hours from New York, 11–12 hours from Chicago, and 15–16 hours from Los Angeles.

HOW TO COMPLAIN

If your baggage goes astray or your flight goes awry, complain to the airline right away. Most carriers require that you **file a claim immediately.**

AIRLINE COMPLAINTS • U.S. Department of Transportation Aviation Consumer Protection Division (C-75, Room 4107, Washington, DC 20590, tel. 202/366–2220). **Federal Aviation Administration Consumer Hotline** (tel. 800/322–7873).

RECONFIRMING

Check with your airline before you leave home to find out whether you must reconfirm your return flight a certain number of hours before departure.

AIRPORTS

The major gateways to Italy include Rome's Leonardo da Vinci Airport, better known as Fiumicino, and Milan's Malpensa Airport.

AIRPORT INFORMATION • Rome: Leonardo da Vinci Airport, called Fiumicino (30 km/19 mi southwest of Rome, tel. 06/65953640). **Milan:** Malpensa and Linate airports (tel. 02/74852200). **Venice:** Marco Polo Airport (Tessera, about 10 km/6 mi north of Venice, tel. 041/2609260). **Florence:** A.

Vespucci Airport, called Peretola (10 km/6 mi northwest of Florence, tel. 055/373498). **Pisa**: Galileo Galilei Airport (80 km/50 mi west of Florence, tel. 050/500707). **Bologna**: Guglielmo Marconi (Borgo Panigale, 7 km/4 mi from Bologna, tel. 051/6479615). **Naples**: Capodichino Airport (8 km/5 mi north of Naples, tel. 081/7896111). **Palermo:** Punta Raisi Airport (32 km/20 mi west of Palermo, tel. 091/591698).

DUTY-FREE SHOPPING
Duty-free shopping is no longer an option within the EU.

BIKE TRAVEL
If maneuvering a pint-size car through twisty roads at white- knuckle speed sounds too intimidating, **consider renting a road or mountain bike for day trips or taking a cycling tour.** Mountain-bike touring is becoming increasingly popular, and it can be very arduous in some areas. Get in shape and know your limits before signing up for a 10-day tour of Tuscany—some hills are killers. Check with your hotel for local rental shops. *See also* Tours & Packages, *below.*

BIKES IN FLIGHT
Most airlines accommodate bikes as luggage, provided they are dismantled and boxed. For bike boxes, often free at bike shops, you'll pay about $5 (at least $100 for bike bags) from airlines. International travelers can sometimes substitute a bike for a piece of checked luggage at no charge; otherwise, the cost is about $100. Domestic and Canadian airlines charge $25–$50.

BOAT & FERRY TRAVEL
Hydrofoils are faster but costlier; ferries are still the primary mode of transport to and between Italian islands. There's daily service to Corsica from Piombino, to Sardinia from Genoa, Livorno, Civitavecchia, Naples, Palermo, and Trapani, to Greece from Ancona, Bari, and Brindisi, and to Palermo from Genoa and Naples. Ferries are usually priced according to day of week and time of year; weekends in July or August are generally the most expensive.

FARES & SCHEDULES
BOAT & FERRY INFORMATION • Adriatica (Rome, tel. 06/4818341). **Ali Lauro** (Naples, tel. 081/7611044). **FS** (tel. 0766/23273). **Navarma** (Elba, tel. 0565/225211). **Navigazione Laghi** (Milan for the lakes, tel. 02/865578). **Tirrenia** (Rome, tel. 06/4742041; Genoa, tel. 010/2758041; Palermo, tel. 091/333300). **Toremar** (Elba, tel. 0565/3110; Livorno, tel. 586/896113).

BUS TRAVEL
Italy's bus network is pretty thorough, though often undermined by the low cost of train travel. Some schedules can be sketchy on weekends. Buses can be faster and more direct than local trains, and they can be the only way to get around mountainous, hilly, and remote areas; it's always a good idea to **compare bus and train schedules.**

Buy local tickets at tobacco shops (marked TABACCHI), newsstands, or bars near bus stops, and long-distance tickets at the bus station (if the town has one) or on the bus. The word to be afraid of is *sciopero* (strike), which you'll see posted at bus stops quite often. Drivers go on strike nearly every couple of weeks, par for the course in Italy.

LONG-DISTANCE BUSES
Taking a long-distance bus can be incredibly complicated; you'll often have to get off in an obscure town to switch lines, and sometimes you'll have to suffer an ungodly long wait. Buses often cost less (though sometimes more), run more frequently, and go more places than trains. Towns in the hills and mountains are especially likely to be served by bus only.

LOCAL & CITY BUSES
Tickets must be punched on the bus, usually in a metal box near the door. Occasionally conductors will get on board and check tickets, and if you don't have one or haven't punched it, you face big fines.

BUSINESS HOURS

Business hours in Italy will inevitably irritate and confound you. The average business is open weekdays or Monday–Saturday from around 9 to about 7:30. But many businesses shut down for a few hours between noon and 4—right when you wanted to go out and buy, eat, or see something.

BANKS & OFFICES

Italian banks have the most absurd hours of all: weekdays 8:30–1 and about 3:30–4:15. Businesses will often post both *feriale* (Monday–Saturday) and *festivo* (Sunday, weekends, and holidays) hours. *Ferragosto* refers to the weeks around August 15, when most Italians take their vacation. When in doubt, **try to call ahead.**

MUSEUMS & SIGHTS

Be aware that many museums (except in major tourist cities like Florence, Venice, or Rome) open only in the morning from about 9 to about 12:30, and some close on Monday.

SHOPS

Restaurants are open for lunch and dinner with siesta in between (*see* Dining, *below*), and most take off one day per week. All shops close down on Sunday, so go to the market on Saturday unless you want to end up at a touristy trattoria or an overpriced convenience store.

CAMERAS & PHOTOGRAPHY

PHOTO HELP • Kodak Information Center (tel. 800/242– 2424). *Kodak Guide to Shooting Great Travel Pictures,* available in bookstores or from Fodor's Travel Publications (tel. 800/533–6478; $16.50 plus $4 shipping).

EQUIPMENT PRECAUTIONS

Always **keep your film and tape out of the sun.** Carry an extra supply of batteries, and **be prepared to turn on your camera or camcorder** to prove to security personnel that the device is real. Always **ask for hand inspection of film,** which becomes clouded after successive exposures to airport X-ray machines, and **keep videotapes away from metal detectors.**

CAR RENTAL

Rates in Rome begin at about $65 a day and $250 a week for an economy car with air-conditioning, manual transmission, unlimited mileage, and insurance. This includes the tax on car rentals, which is 20%. Note that recent Italian legislation now permits certain rental wholesalers, such as Auto Europe (*see below*), to drop the VAT tax. Many companies impose mandatory theft insurance on all rentals, which is usually included in the rental fee. If it isn't, coverage costs about $12–$18 a day. To save money, plan your getaway for the weekend, when most agencies offer discount rates.

MAJOR AGENCIES • Alamo (tel. 800/522–9696; 0181/759–6200 in the U.K.). **Avis** (tel. 800/331–1084; 800/879–2847 in Canada; 02/9353–9000 in Australia; 09/525–1982 in New Zealand). **Budget** (tel. 800/527– 0700; 0144/227–6266 in the U.K.). **Dollar** (tel. 800/800–6000; 0181/897–0811 in the U.K., where it is known as Eurodollar; 02/9223–1444 in Australia). **Hertz** (tel. 800/654–3001; 800/263–0600 in Canada; 0990/90–60–90 in the U.K.; 02/9669–2444 in Australia; 03/358–6777 in New Zealand). **Maggiore** (tel. 800/521– 0643 in the U.S.). **National Car Rental** (tel. 800-CAR-RENT in the U.S., 800/387–4747 in Canada). **National InterRent** (tel. 800/227–3876; 0345/222525 in the U.K., where it is known as Europcar InterRent).

CUTTING COSTS

To get the best deal **book through a travel agent who will shop around.** Also **price local car-rental companies,** although the service and maintenance may not be as good as those of a major player. Remember to ask about required deposits, cancellation penalties, and drop-off charges if you're planning to pick up the car in one city and leave it in another. If you're traveling during a holiday period, also make sure that a confirmed reservation guarantees you a car.

Do **look into wholesalers,** companies that do not own fleets but rent in bulk from those that do and often offer better rates than traditional car-rental operations. Payment must be made before you leave home.

WHOLESALERS • Auto Europe (tel. 207/842–2000 or 800/223–5555, fax 800/235– 6321). **DER Travel Services** (9501 W. Devon Ave., Rosemont, IL 60018, tel. 800/782–2424, fax 800/282–7474 for information; 800/860–9944 for brochures). **Europe by Car** (tel. 212/581–3040 or 800/223–1516, fax 212/246–1458). **Kemwel Holiday Autos** (tel. 914/825–3000 or 800/678–0678, fax 914/381–8847).

INSURANCE

When driving a rented car you are generally responsible for damage to or loss of the vehicle. Before you rent see what coverage your personal auto-insurance policy and credit cards already provide.

Collision policies that car-rental companies sell for European rentals usually do not include stolen-vehicle coverage. Before you buy it, check your existing policies—you may already be covered. Note that in Italy all car-rental companies make you buy theft-protection policies.

REQUIREMENTS & RESTRICTIONS

In Italy your own driver's license is acceptable. An international driver's permit is a good idea; it's available from the American or Canadian automobile association, or in the United Kingdom, from the Automobile Association or Royal Automobile Club.

SURCHARGES

Before you pick up a car in one city and leave it in another **ask about drop-off charges or one-way service fees,** which can be substantial. Note, too, that some rental agencies charge extra if you return the car before the time specified in your contract. To avoid a hefty refueling fee **fill the tank just before you turn in the car,** but be aware that gas stations near the rental outlet may overcharge.

CAR TRAVEL

You've probably heard stories about Italian drivers and their reckless, maniacal ways: they're all true. If you drive on Italian roads, expect tailgaters and people who pass on impossibly narrow roads. And that's just in the country. In the city, you'll face hellish traffic circles where you'll be sitting for hours if you wait for someone to yield the right of way. Defensive driving is a nice idea, but your caution could be met by shrill horn blasts and dirty looks.

Still, there may be times when you'll want a car, especially in parts of southern Italy and the mountainous north, where trains and buses are few and far between. With a group of three or four people, renting a car isn't such a big expense. You'll still have to deal with exorbitant tolls on the highways (L7,600 per 100 km/62 mi) and some of the highest gas prices in Europe (around L1,850 per liter, or L7,000 per gallon). It's vital to **carry a map** for navigating poorly marked roads. A red sign with a horizontal white stripe through it means do not enter; a blue circular sign with a red slash or an X means no parking, as do the signs VIETATO SOSTARE, VIETATO DI SOSTA, and NON PARCHEGGIARE.

The Automobile Club d'Italia (ACI) is affiliated with AAA and provides a varying range of services to members. The ACI offers free emergency auto services, maps, and general tour info to members.

AUTO CLUBS

IN AUSTRALIA • Australian Automobile Association (tel. 02/6247–7311).

IN CANADA • Canadian Automobile Association (CAA, tel. 613/247–0117).

IN NEW ZEALAND • New Zealand Automobile Association (tel. 09/377–4660).

IN THE U.K. • Automobile Association (AA, tel. 0990/500– 600). **Royal Automobile Club** (RAC, tel. 0990/722–722 for membership; 0345/121–345 for insurance).

IN THE U.S. • American Automobile Association (tel. 800/564– 6222).

EMERGENCIES

Dial 116 for towing and repairs; breakdown service (emergency repairs and towing on an autostrada) is free for tourists with foreign license plates or with cars rented in Italy that have breakdown insurance. Dial 113 for an ambulance and highway police.

CONTACTS • Automobile Club d'Italia (ACI; V. Marsala 8, 00185 Roma, tel. 116 for emergency assistance, 06/4477 for 24-hour info, fax 06/4452702).

GASOLINE

Gas costs the equivalent of more than $4 per U.S. gallon, or about L1,900 per liter. Except on the autostrade, most gas stations are closed Sunday; they also close from 12:30 PM to 3:30 PM and at 7 PM for the night. Most gas stations do not accept credit cards. Self-service pumps, which usually accept only L10,000 notes, can be found in most cities and towns.

ROAD CONDITIONS

In addition to its autostrada (toll superhighway) network connecting all major towns, Italy has often narrow but well-maintained, toll-free *superstrade* (express highways), *strade statali* (main roads), and *strade provinciali* (secondary roads). All are signposted and numbered, not always clearly. The ticket issued on entering an autostrada must be returned on leaving, along with the toll. On some shorter autostrade, mainly connections, the toll is payable on entering. Have small bills and change handy for tolls; shortchanging is a risk, so always count your change before leaving the toll booth. If you will be using autostrade extensively, buy a Viacard—an automatic toll card—for L50,000 or L100,000 at autostrada locations. Some automatic booths also take an array of credit cards. Large double trailer trucks are a hazard on Italian roads.

RULES OF THE ROAD

Driving is on the right. The speed limit on an autostrada is 130 kph (81 mph). It is 110 kph (70 mph) on state and provincial roads, unless otherwise marked. The police have the power to levy severe on-the-spot fines. Italians drive fast and impatiently; don't be surprised when, on a winding two-lane highway, drivers zip into the oncoming-traffic lane to pass you if you are going too slowly.

CHILDREN IN ITALY

Italy is one of the most welcoming places in the world for children; walk into a restaurant with a cute two-year-old and the waiter is likely to make friends with the little one and then disappear into the kitchen with him/her so that the rest of the staff can admire the prodigy. If you are renting a car don't forget to **arrange for a car seat** when you reserve.

FLYING

If your children are two or older **ask about children's airfares.** As a general rule, infants under two not occupying a seat fly at greatly reduced fares or even for free. When booking, **confirm carry-on allowances** if you're traveling with infants. In general, for babies charged 10% of the adult fare you are allowed one carry-on bag and a collapsible stroller; if the flight is full the stroller may have to be checked or you may be limited to less.

Experts agree that it's a good idea to use safety seats aloft for children weighing less than 40 pounds. Airlines set their own policies: U.S. carriers usually require that the child be ticketed, even if he or she is young enough to ride free, since the seats must be strapped into regular seats. Do **check your airline's policy about using safety seats during takeoff and landing.** And since safety seats are not allowed just everywhere in the plane, get your seat assignments early.

When reserving, **request children's meals or a freestanding bassinet** if you need them. But note that bulkhead seats, where you must sit to use the bassinet, may lack an overhead bin or storage space on the floor.

LODGING

Most hotels in Italy allow children under a certain age to stay in their parents' room at no extra charge, but others charge for them as extra adults; be sure to **find out the cutoff age for children's discounts.**

CONSUMER PROTECTION

Whenever you're shopping or buying travel services in Italy, **pay with a major credit card** so you can cancel payment or be reimbursed if there's a problem. If you're doing business with a particular company for the first time, **contact your local Better Business Bureau and the attorney general's offices** in your state and the company's home state, as well. Have any complaints been filed? Finally, if you're buying a package or tour, always **consider travel insurance** that includes default coverage (*see* Insurance, *below*).

LOCAL BBBS • Council of Better Business Bureaus (4200 Wilson Blvd., Suite 800, Arlington, VA 22203, tel. 703/276–0100, fax 703/525–8277).

CUSTOMS & DUTIES

When shopping, **keep receipts** for all purchases. Upon reentering your home country **be ready to show customs officials what you've bought.** If you feel a duty is incorrect or object to the way your clearance was handled, note the inspector's badge number and ask to see a supervisor. If the problem isn't resolved, write to the appropriate authorities, beginning with the port director at your point of entry.

IN AUSTRALIA

Australian residents who are 18 or older may bring home $A400 worth of souvenirs and gifts (including jewelry), 250 cigarettes or 250 grams of tobacco, and 1,125 ml of alcohol (including wine, beer, and spirits). Residents under 18 may bring back $A200 worth of goods. Prohibited items include meat products. Seeds, plants, and fruits need to be declared upon arrival.

INFORMATION • Australian Customs Service (Regional Director, Box 8, Sydney, NSW 2001, tel. 02/9213–2000, fax 02/9213–4000).

IN CANADA

Canadian residents who have been out of Canada for at least 7 days may bring home C$500 worth of goods duty-free. If you've been away less than 7 days but more than 48 hours, the duty-free allowance drops to C$200; if your trip lasts 24–48 hours, the allowance is C$50. You may not pool allowances with family members. Goods claimed under the C$500 exemption may follow you by mail; those claimed under the lesser exemptions must accompany you. Alcohol and tobacco products may be included in the 7-day and 48-hour exemptions but not in the 24-hour exemption. If you meet the age requirements of the province or territory through which you reenter Canada, you may bring in, duty-free, 1.14 liters (40 imperial ounces) of wine or liquor or 24 12-ounce cans or bottles of beer or ale. If you are 16 or older you may bring in, duty-free, 200 cigarettes and 50 cigars. Check ahead of time with Revenue Canada or the Department of Agriculture for policies regarding meat products, seeds, plants, and fruits.

You may send an unlimited number of gifts worth up to C$60 each duty-free to Canada. Label the package UNSOLICITED GIFT—VALUE UNDER $60. Alcohol and tobacco are excluded.

INFORMATION • Revenue Canada (2265 St. Laurent Blvd. S, Ottawa, Ontario K1G 4K3, tel. 613/993–0534; 800/461–9999 in Canada).

IN ITALY

For goods obtained anywhere outside the European Union (EU), the allowances are: (1) 200 cigarettes or 100 cigarillos or 50 cigars or 250 grams of tobacco; (2) 2 liters of still table wine or 1 liter of spirits over 22% volume or 2 liters of spirits under 22% volume or 2 liters of fortified and sparkling wines; (3) 50 milliliters of perfume and 250 milliliters of toilet water; (4) 500 grams of coffee.

For goods obtained within another EU country, the allowances are: (1) 800 cigarettes or 400 cigarillos or 400 cigars or 1 kilogram of tobacco; (2) 90 liters of still table wine; plus (3) 10 liters of spirits over 22% volume plus 20 liters of spirits under 22% volume plus 60 liters of sparkling wines plus 110 liters of beer.

IN NEW ZEALAND

Homeward-bound residents 17 or older may bring back $700 worth of souvenirs and gifts. Your duty-free allowance also includes 4.5 liters of wine or beer; one 1,125-ml bottle of spirits; and either 200 cigarettes, 250 grams of tobacco, 50 cigars, or a combination of the three up to 250 grams. Prohibited items include meat products, seeds, plants, and fruits.

INFORMATION • New Zealand Customs (Custom House, 50 Anzac Ave., Box 29, Auckland, New Zealand, tel. 09/359–6655, fax 09/359–6732).

IN THE U.K.

If you are a U.K. resident and your journey was wholly within the European Union (EU), you won't have to pass through customs when you return to the United Kingdom. If you plan to bring back large quantities of alcohol or tobacco, check EU limits beforehand.

INFORMATION • HM Customs and Excise (Dorset House, Stamford St., Bromley Kent BR1 1XX, tel. 0171/202–4227).

IN THE U.S.

U.S. residents who have been out of the country for at least 48 hours (and who have not used the $400 allowance or any part of it in the past 30 days) may bring home $400 worth of foreign goods duty-free.

CAFFÈ CULTURE

Even if you're a seasoned coffee drinker back home, you'll find both the selection of coffee drinks and the etiquette of imbibing them a bit different in Italy. First off, the word "bar" indicates a place to drink coffee. Although alcoholic beverages are available, most folks come to a bar for a jolt of caffeine. Second, espresso—often heavily laden with sugar—is not to be savored; locals knock it back quickly while standing. If you do choose to sit at one of the tables sometimes provided in larger bars, expect to pay up to twice as much for your drink. At most places, it is customary to pay the cashier first, then bring your scontrino (receipt) to the counter and repeat your order. It's also a good idea to leave a L100–L200 tip when you return the receipt. Here are a few of the most commonly ordered drinks, though the possibilities are nearly endless.

CAFFÈ: a single espresso. A good choice any time of day, but most commonly taken at the end of a meal.

CAPPUCCINO: espresso topped with steamed whole milk, foam, and powdered chocolate (never cinnamon!). Considered a morning drink and only a morning drink in Italy—don't reveal your tourist status by ordering cappuccino with a meal.

CAFFÈ MACCHIATO: "stained" espresso, or espresso with a drop of steamed milk. Taken in the same manner as a caffè.

CAFFÈ CORRETTO: espresso "corrected" with a healthy dose of liquor, curiously more popular with older men.

CAFFÈ LATTE: not as popular in Italy as you might think, this morning drink is mostly steamed milk, with the addition of a shot of espresso.

U.S. residents 21 and older may bring back 1 liter of alcohol duty-free. In addition, regardless of your age, you are allowed 200 cigarettes and 100 non-Cuban cigars. Antiques, which the U.S. Customs Service defines as objects more than 100 years old, enter duty-free, as do original works of art done entirely by hand, including paintings, drawings, and sculptures.

You may also send packages home duty-free: up to $200 worth of goods for personal use, with a limit of one parcel per addressee per day (and no alcohol or tobacco products or perfume worth more than $5); label the package PERSONAL USE and attach a list of its contents and their retail value. Do not label the package UNSOLICITED GIFT or your duty-free exemption will drop to $100. Mailed items do not affect your duty-free allowance on your return.

INFORMATION • U.S. Customs Service (inquiries, 1300 Pennsylvania Ave. NW, Washington, DC 20229, tel. 202/927–6724; complaints, Office of Regulations and Rulings, 1300 Pennsylvania Ave. NW, Washington, DC 20229; registration of equipment, Registration Information, 1300 Pennsylvania Ave. NW, Washington, DC 20229, tel. 202/927–0540).

DINING

Italian food is all about yummy plates of pasta, cheap local wine, and potent cappuccino—a delectable triumvirate that even backpackers can enjoy without breaking the bank. However, **think twice before entering a *ristorante*** (restaurant), often more expensive and stuffy than a family-run neighborhood *trattoria,* or the even cheaper alternative, a *tavola calda* (cafeteria-style restaurant). For a fast, cheap, and tasty meal, there are places that sell squares of pizza to be eaten while standing; look for signs saying *pizza a taglio* or *rustica.* A true *osteria* is nothing more than a basic food-serving wine shop; a place might call itself an osteria, but it could be a costly restaurant competing for your tourist dollars. *Paninoteche* serve simple sandwiches, *gastronomie* dish out prepared food to be taken home with you. Find bread at a *panificio* or a *forno* and pastries and sweets at a *pasticceria.* There are also *rosticcerie,* which roast and sell meat. An even cheaper way to eat is to cook for yourself. Italy has incredible fish and meat markets, and fruit and veggie stands, called *bancarelle* or *fruttivendoli,* are scattered throughout most towns.

Breakfast in Italy will never include hash browns and pancakes; more likely you'll find yourself standing at a coffee bar with a pastry and cappuccino in hand. The *cornetto* (a croissant either plain or filled with jam or pastry cream), also called brioche, is one of the more popular breakfast treats. Be aware that sitting at a café table may double the price of your order; so when in Rome, do as do the Romans: **enjoy an espresso or snack standing up at a local caffè.** When it comes to lunch and dinner, the easiest way to keep costs down is by *not* ordering a full, three-course meal. The *primi piatti,* or *primi* (first courses), are plates of pasta, risotto, or soup. They're so filling you may not need to order the more expensive *secondi* (second courses), usually chicken, beef, or fish accompanied by a *contorno* (side dish) of vegetables or salad. Of course, don't skip out on a predinner trip to the *antipasti* table for appetizers. Bread is usually included in the cover charge, and bottled water costs L2000–L3000. Bottled water comes two ways: without bubbles is *acqua naturale* or *acqua senza gas,* with bubbles is *acqua gassata.* If you don't want to pay extra for water, ask for tap water, called *acqua semplice, acqua di Roma,* or *acqua di Milano,* depending on the region. Wine by the bottle can double your bill, so stick with the house red or white, which is usually decent. The high price of desserts, espresso, and after-dinner drinks will surprise you, especially in tourist-oriented restaurants. It's almost always cheaper to **go to a bar or a gelateria for dessert and coffee.**

Vegetarians need not fear: Pasta, tomatoes, and vegetables are staples in Italy. Note that red sauce and risotto are often made with chicken or meat broth. Specify magro or senza carne to avoid surprise appearances of flesh.

Most restaurants serve the same menu for lunch and dinner, so don't expect lunch to be cheaper. At lunch, though, waiters are less likely to sneer at you for not ordering a secondo.

MEALS & SPECIALTIES

In northern Italy, menus offer more cream-based pastas, polenta, and slabs of meat. As you move south and toward coastal areas, menus lighten up a bit with the addition of fresh fish, simple tomato-based pasta sauces, and fewer cholesterol-laden dishes, although you can usually find some combination of all of these on a menu. Even so, Italian cuisine is highly regional. Restaurants in Trentino–Alto Adige serve a killer *Knödel* (dumplings with wine or tomato sauce), almost as heavy as their *Würstel* (sausage). Lombard specialties include risotto *alla milanese* (with chicken stock and saffron), *osso buco alla milanese* (veal shanks with risotto milanese), and *tortelli di zucca* (pumpkin-stuffed pasta), a typical Mantovan dish. Also try the rich, piquant Gorgonzola straight from the source and panettone, a cake with raisins and candied fruit, both from Milan. The cuisine of the French-influenced Valle d'Aosta features sausage, mountain cheeses, and venison. The favorite form of pasta here is *agnolotti,* yet another stuffed pasta. Also try *bagna cauda,* a spicy dipping sauce of olive oil, anchovies, garlic, and butter.

In the Veneto you'll see plenty of polenta, as well as pasta *alla seppia nera* (with squid-ink sauce) or with a tangy *tonno* (tuna) sauce. The best dessert is tiramisu, a decadent sweet from Treviso made with ladyfingers, liqueur, espresso, and creamy mascarpone. Emilia-Romagna is considered the food capital of Italy, renowned for its tortellini and pasta *al ragù* (with a hearty meat sauce). The city of Parma is famous for prosciutto and for the king of Italian cheeses: Parmigiano Reggiano. Liguria's coastal position and Mediterranean climate account for the production of fabulous olive oil. Its capital, Genoa, is the birthplace of pesto, the sauce of basil, olive oil, pine nuts, garlic, and Parmesan now on yuppie tables everywhere. Umbria and Marche are known for truffles—try *strozzapreti al tartufo* (pasta with truffles)—and delicacies produced in the area's many monasteries, like honey and liqueurs. Dishes typical of

Lazio include *bucatini all'amatriciana* (pasta with tomatoes, sheep's-milk cheese, and bacon) and *stracciatella* (egg-drop soup). Tuscan delicacies include *bistecca alla fiorentina* (steak served very rare), thick soups, and tasty bean dishes (Tuscans are known as *mangiafagioli,* or bean eaters). Naples, in Campania, is famous for pizza; you can find this staple in every little town, but nowhere is it made better than here, in its reputed home. Sicily benefits from its island status with tuna, *pesce spada* (swordfish), and pasta *con le sarde* (with sardines, olive oil, anchovies, raisins, and pine nuts). Arabic influence in Sicily extends to the culinary realm, so you'll find many dishes that incorporate couscous and chickpeas. Also try caponata, an antipasto of eggplant, capers, and olives. The island of Sardinia proffers *pane carasau,* a shepherd's cracker usually slathered with olive oil and salt, *malloreddus* (chewy handmade noodles in a spicy tomato-sausage sauce), and pasta with fresh seafood.

MEALTIMES

In Rome lunch is served roughly from 1 to 3, dinner from 8 to 10:30, sometimes later in summer months. Both are meant to be lingered over with wine, coffee, and conversation—Italians don't like to rush a meal. This attitude often transforms an evening bite into a full-blown feast. Service begins and ends a half hour earlier in Florence and Venice and later in the south. Practically all restaurants close one day a week; some close for winter or summer vacations.

PAYING

Restaurants throughout Italy charge a *coperto* (cover charge) in addition to the *servizio* (service charge). Covers range from L1,000 to L5,000 per person, the service charge from 10% to 15% of the bill. **Be careful in tourist traps,** as the prices are often low but are offset by high servizio and coperto charges. **Ask to see a menu before entering an eatery** to see the price of a coperto—it's listed at the bottom. Unless you limit yourself to coffee bars and pizzerias, there's no way around the coperto, but the price of a *menu turistico* (tourist menu) typically includes tax and service.

RESERVATIONS & DRESS

Reservations are always a good idea: we mention them only when they're essential or are not accepted. Book as far ahead as you can, and reconfirm as soon as you arrive. We mention dress only when men are required to wear a jacket or a jacket and tie.

WINE, BEER, & SPIRITS

Roman poets once called Italy *Oenotria Tellus* (the Land of Wine), and with good reason. If you're an undemanding vino consumer, Italy has plenty of bargain-priced reds and whites. If you've made the jump to amateur connoisseur, prepare yourself for quality vintages ranging from moderate to high in price.

In Italy wine comes in *bianco* (white), *rosato* (rosé), and *rosso* (red), and even the cheap stuff is good by American standards. House wine can be ordered by the quarter liter (slightly more than a glass), half liter, and full liter, priced at about L5,000, L7,000, and L10,000, respectively. *Vini della casa* (house wines) usually arrive in an open decanter, though occasionally they do come in bottles. Expect to pay L5,000–L8,000 for a decent bottle in a wine shop. A good rule of thumb for the budget traveler is to **stick to drinking local regional wines.** You not only get the best vino for the buck, but regional cuisine is best accompanied by regional wine.

Italy's Veneto produces the dry, white Soave, sparkling Prosecco, and many varieties of valpolicella. The northwest is home to full-bodied reds, such as Barbaresco and Barolo of Piemonte. If you prefer a lighter wine, try Dolcetto or Grignolino, or Asti Spumante, a semisweet sparkling wine. Emilia-Romagna's crisp, dry wines are less complex, meant more for comsumption with local cuisine. Try Sangiovese di Romagna and the sweet, fizzy Lambrusco. Italy's top wine exports are Tuscany's Chianti Classico and Umbria's Orvieto Secco; also popular worldwide are white Trebbiano and Abruzzo's red Montepulciano, as well as the clean, fruity wines of Lazio, Colli Albani, and Frascati. Sicily alone produces more vino than some wine-producing countries, but in general, the wines of the deep south are underappreciated. Sweet, heavy Malvasia and marsala varieties go well with dessert.

DISABILITIES & ACCESSIBILITY

Italy has only recently begun to provide for travelers with disabilities, and facilities such as ramps and appropriately equipped bathrooms and telephones are still the exception rather than the rule. Throughout your trip, cobblestone streets, old buildings, and winding staircases will present constant challenges.

LOCAL RESOURCES • ENIT offices (*see* Visitor Information, *below*) can provide lists of accessible hotels as well as addresses of Italian associations for people with disabilities. They also distribute a fantastic book called *Roma Accessibile: Turismo e Barriere Architettoniche* (*Accessible Rome: Tourism and Structural Obstacles*), with extensive info on the availibility of public transport, hotels, restaurants, museums, and other places in Rome.

LODGING

Though not often reviewed in this book, large three- and four-star hotels are much more likely to have elevators and wheelchair-accessible bathrooms; call the U.S. toll-free numbers of such major upscale hotel chains, in most major Italian cities. Always **call hotels ahead to find out about facilities.**

When discussing accessibility with an operator or reservations agent **ask hard questions.** Are there any stairs, inside *or* out? Are there grab bars next to the toilet *and* in the shower/tub? How wide is the doorway to the room? To the bathroom? For the most extensive facilities meeting the latest legal specifications **opt for newer accommodations.**

COMPLAINTS • Disability Rights Section (U.S. Department of Justice, Civil Rights Division, Box 66738, Washington, DC 20035-6738, tel. 202/514–0301; 800/514–0301; 202/514–0301 TTY; 800/514–0301 TTY, fax 202/307–1198) for general complaints. **Aviation Consumer Protection Division** (*see* Air Travel, *above*) for airline-related problems. **Civil Rights Office** (U.S. Department of Transportation, Departmental Office of Civil Rights, S-30, 400 7th St. SW, Room 10215, Washington, DC 20590, tel. 202/366–4648, fax 202/366–9371) for problems with surface transportation.

TRAVEL AGENCIES

In the United States, although the Americans with Disabilities Act requires that travel firms serve the needs of all travelers, some agencies specialize in working with people with disabilities.

TRAVELERS WITH MOBILITY PROBLEMS • Access Adventures (206 Chestnut Ridge Rd., Rochester, NY 14624, tel. 716/889–9096). **Accessible Journeys** (35 W. Sellers Ave. Ridley Park, PA 19078, tel. 610/521–0339 or 800/846–4537, fax 610/521–6959). **Accessible Vans of the Rockies, Activity and Travel Agency** (2040 W. Hamilton Pl., Sheridan, CO 80110, tel. 303/806–5047 or 888/837–0065, fax 303/781–2329). **Accessible Vans of Hawaii, Activity and Travel Agency** (186 Mehani Circle, Kihei, HI 96753, tel. 808/879–5521 or 800/303–3750, fax 808/879–0649). **CareVacations** (5-5110 50th Ave., Leduc, Alberta T9E 6V4, tel. 780/986–6404 or 877/478–7827, fax 780/986–8332). **Flying Wheels Travel** (143 W. Bridge St., Box 382, Owatonna, MN 55060, tel. 507/451–5005 or 800/535–6790, fax 507/451–1685). **Hinsdale Travel Service** (201 E. Ogden Ave., Suite 100, Hinsdale, IL 60521, tel. 630/325–1335, fax 630/325–1342).

DISCOUNTS & DEALS

Be a smart shopper and **compare all your options** before making decisions. A plane ticket bought with a promotional coupon from travel clubs, coupon books, and direct-mail offers may not be cheaper than the least expensive fare from a discount ticket agency. And always keep in mind that what you get is just as important as what you save.

DISCOUNT RESERVATIONS

To save money **look into discount-reservations services** with toll-free numbers, which use their buying power to get a better price on hotels, airline tickets, even car rentals. When booking a room, always **call the hotel's local toll-free number** (if one is available) rather than the central reservations number—you'll often get a better price. Always ask about special packages or corporate rates.

You can **find discount airfare and hotel deals on the Web.** At most sites you type in how much you want to spend, and the search engine comes up with available offerings in your price range. Some sites act like an auction, where you enter into a bidding war with other people who are logged on at that moment. Be sure to read the fine print before you agree to book anything, since the majority of the air tickets are non-refundable, and most are not eligible for frequent flyer miles. Also check to see if the site offers secure payment with a credit card.

When shopping for the best deal on hotels and car rentals **look for guaranteed exchange rates,** which protect you against a falling dollar. With your rate locked in, you won't pay more, even if the price goes up in the local currency.

AIRLINE TICKETS • Tel. 800/Fly–4–Less. Tel. 800/Fly– Asap.

WEB SITES OFFERING DISCOUNT AIRLINE TICKETS AND CHEAP HOTEL PRICES • www.priceline.com, www.hotfares.com, www.thefarebusters.com; in the UK, www.cheapflights.co.uk. **HOTEL ROOMS** • **International Marketing & Travel Concepts** (tel. 800/790–4682). **Steigenberger Reservation Service** (tel. 800/223–5652). **Travel Interlink** (tel. 800/888–5898).

PACKAGE DEALS

Don't confuse packages and guided tours. When you buy a package, you travel on your own, just as though you had planned the trip yourself. Fly/drive packages, which combine airfare and car rental, are often a good deal. If you **buy a rail/drive pass** you may save on train tickets and car rentals. All Eurail- and Europass holders get a discount on Eurostar fares through the Channel Tunnel.

ELECTRICITY

To use your U.S.-purchased electric-powered equipment **bring a converter and adapter.** The electrical current in Italy is 220 volts, 50 cycles alternating current (AC); wall outlets take Continental-type plugs, with two round prongs.

If your appliances are dual-voltage you'll need only an adapter. Don't use 110-volt outlets, marked FOR SHAVERS ONLY, for high-wattage appliances such as blow-dryers. Most laptops operate equally well on 110 and 220 volts and so require only an adapter.

EMBASSIES

AUSTRALIA • C. Trieste 25/C, Rome, tel. 06/852721.

CANADA • V. Zara 30, Rome, tel. 06/445981.

IRELAND • P. Campitelli 3, Rome, tel. 06/6979121.

NEW ZEALAND • V. Zara 28, Rome, tel. 06/4402928.

SOUTH AFRICA • V. Tanaro 14, Rome, tel. 06/852541.

UNITED KINGDOM • V. XX (pronounced "Venti") Settembre 80a, tel. 06/4825441.

UNITED STATES • V. Veneto 121, Rome, tel. 06/46741.

EMERGENCIES

Emergency assistance is available 24 hours.

GENERAL EMERGENCY ASSISTANCE • Tel. 113.

CARABINIERI • Military police, tel. 112.

DRIVING • Italian Automobile Club, tel. 116.

FIRE • Tel. 115.

MEDICAL EMERGENCY AND AMBULANCE • Tel. 118.

GAY & LESBIAN TRAVEL

Because Italians are affectionate in general, some same-sex hugging won't attract attention. But Italy is also a Catholic country with a strong dose of machismo, and obvious displays of homosexual affection could get you in trouble—with the police in some places. **Be subtle in small towns and in the south, and live it up in the thriving gay scenes of Bologna, Milan, Florence, and Rome.**

Bologna is the headquarters of the national gay organization ARCIGay. Their organization for lesbians, ARCILesbica, publishes the networking newsletter *Bolletino del Collegamento tra le Lesbiche Italiane.* A national lesbian infoline in Rome takes calls Thursdays 8:30 PM–10:30 PM. The monthly gay and lesbian magazine *Babilonia,* available in all big towns, comes out of Milan.

LOCAL RESOURCES • **ARCIGay** and **ARCILesbica**(P. di Porta Saragozza 2, Box 691, 40123 Bologna, tel. 051/6447054, fax 051/6446722). **National lesbian infoline** (tel. 06/41609240). **Babilonia** (Babilonia Edizioni, V. Ebro 11, 20142 Milan, tel. 02/5696468, fax 02/55213419, www.babilonia.it).

GAY- AND LESBIAN-FRIENDLY TRAVEL AGENCIES • **Different Roads Travel** (8383 Wilshire Blvd., Suite 902, Beverly Hills, CA 90211, tel. 323/651–5557 or 800/429–8747, fax 323/651–3678).

Kennedy Travel (314 Jericho Turnpike, Floral Park, NY 11001, tel. 516/352–4888 or 800/237–7433, fax 516/354–8849). **Now Voyager** (4406 18th St., San Francisco, CA 94114, tel. 415/626–1169 or 800/255–6951, fax 415/626–8626). **Skylink Travel and Tour** (1006 Mendocino Ave., Santa Rosa, CA 95401, tel. 707/546–9888 or 800/225–5759, fax 707/546–9891), serving lesbian travelers.

HOLIDAYS

Most businesses and sometimes entire towns close on the following dates: January 1 (New Year's Day), January 6 (Epiphany), Easter Monday, April 25 (Liberation Day), May 1 (Labor Day), August 15 (Assumption of the Virgin), November 1 (All Saints' Day), December 8 (Feast of the Immaculate Conception), December 25 (Christmas Day), and December 26 (St. Stephen's Day). Many towns also close down—to celebrate, of course—on the feast day of their patron saint.

INSURANCE

The most useful travel insurance plan is a comprehensive policy that includes coverage for trip cancellation and interruption, default, trip delay, and medical expenses (with a waiver for preexisting conditions).

Without insurance you will lose all or most of your money if you cancel your trip, regardless of the reason. Default insurance covers you if your tour operator, airline, or cruise line goes out of business. Trip-delay covers expenses that arise because of bad weather or mechanical delays. Study the fine print when comparing policies.

If you're traveling internationally, a key component of travel insurance is coverage for medical bills incurred if you get sick on the road. Such expenses are not generally covered by Medicare or private policies. U.K. residents can buy a travel-insurance policy valid for most vacations taken during the year in which it's purchased (but check pre-existing-condition coverage). British and Australian citizens need extra medical coverage when traveling overseas.

Always **buy travel policies directly from the insurance company**; if you buy insurance from a cruise line, airline, or tour operator that goes out of business you probably will not be covered for the agency or operator's default, a major risk. Before you make any purchase **review your existing health and home-owner's policies** to find what they cover away from home.

TRAVEL INSURERS • In the U.S. **Access America** (6600 W. Broad St., Richmond, VA 23230, tel. 804/285–3300 or 800/284–8300), **Travel Guard International** (1145 Clark St., Stevens Point, WI 54481, tel. 715/345–0505 or 800/826–1300). In Canada **Voyager Insurance** (44 Peel Center Dr., Brampton, Ontario L6T 4M8, tel. 905/791–8700; 800/668–4342 in Canada).

INSURANCE INFORMATION • In the U.K. the **Association of British Insurers** (51–55 Gresham St., London EC2V 7HQ, tel. 0171/600–3333, fax 0171/696–8999). In Australia the **Insurance Council of Australia** (tel. 03/9614–1077, fax 03/9614–7924).

LANGUAGE

Italians are not French and therefore will be impressed by and receptive to your attempts to speak their language. Although most people who work in the tourist industry (hotels, tourist offices) speak English, the average person on the street probably does not. Italians all speak Italian—developed in Tuscany and officially sanctioned as the national language by Mussolini—as well as diverse regional dialects and languages. Signs and menus in the Valle d'Aosta, for example, are written in French and Italian, while in Alto Adige, you'll see Italian and German. For help with basic communication, **check out the glossary in the back of this book.**

LANGUAGES FOR TRAVELERS

A phrase book and language-tape set can help get you started.

PHRASE BOOKS & LANGUAGE-TAPE SETS • *Fodor's Italian for Travelers* (tel. 800/733–3000 in the U.S.; 800/668–4247 in Canada; $7 for phrasebook, $16.95 for audio set).

LAUNDRY

Coin-ops aren't too hard to come by in touristed areas, but they'll set you back about L6,000 per load. For the average person, hotel rooms are the best and cheapest place to do laundry. A bring-your-own laundry service includes: a plastic bottle of liquid detergent (powder doesn't break down as well), about 6 ft of clothesline (enough to tie to two stable objects), and some plastic clips (bobby pins or paper clips can substitute). Porch railings, shower-curtain rods, bathtubs, and faucets can all serve as wet-laundry hangers if you forget the clothesline, and plain old bar soap, dishwashing liquid, or liquid soap gets clothes clean in a pinch. In hot areas, your clothes will dry overnight. A hair dryer can double as a clothes dryer, not as effectively, but it can at least make damp things wearable. A universal sink plug will come in handy; lacking that, a sock or plastic bag in the drain will do the trick. Use an extra plastic bag for still-damp laundry and dirty clothes.

LODGING

Whenever possible, **reserve a room in advance** when visiting a big city, a popular tourist town, or any place in high season. If you arrive somewhere without a reservation, tourist offices will provide lists of hotels and will sometimes call one or more for you or recommend accommodations.

Hotels in Italy are classified by the government in categories ranging from one to five stars. Most hotels reviewed in this book are one- and two-star establishments. One-star hotels vary from gross to charming, with most falling into the clean-but-generic category. Two-star establishments are usually a bit nicer and have more rooms with private baths, but this is not always the case. In small or out-of-the-way towns, a two-star hotel can be affordable. Budget hotels are usually clustered around the train station. The words *albergo, pensione,* and *locanda* all basically mean hotel and are interchangeable for our purposes. Unless specified, prices listed in this book are for double rooms without bath.

The price for a single hotel room—even in a dive—starts at around L30,000, but if you're traveling in a group, hotels become more appealing. Doubles without bath cost L40,000–L90,000, with bath L80,000–L140,000. In reviews, "full pension" means you get full room and board, and "half pension" means you get a room, breakfast, and either lunch or dinner. When checking into a hotel, **always ask if breakfast is included** in the price (often hotels charge L6,000 or so for a watery coffee and a packaged croissant). If it is included, see if you can get them to deduct the cost of breakfast; you're almost always better off going to a café down the street.

AFFITTACAMERE

Affittacamera means "rent a room," and lots of Italians do exactly that in their own homes, especially during high season. Sometimes affittacamere are listed in the lodging pamphlets at tourist offices; otherwise, look for AFFITACAMERA signs around town or ask around in cafés. Double rooms cost about L60,000–L80,000; you might be able to negotiate in the off-season.

AGRITURISMO

Agriturismo is the practice of renting out rooms in rural homes. This is an excellent way to get an unusual taste of Italy. Prices are about the same as a cheap hotel (L50,000 a night), but you may get to eat farm-fresh food cooked in an Italian kitchen by an adept *madre*. Getting to the farms on public transportation may be difficult—having a car will help a lot. The best places for agriturismo are out-of-the-way locales like Puglia and inland Sardinia. Inquire at the main office, Agriturist, which is open weekdays 10–noon and also 3:30–7:30 Tuesday–Thursday. Or check out the local tourist office for comprehensive lists of participating farms. Some agriturismo stays are reviewed in the specific chapters.

INFORMATION • Agriturist (C. Vittorio Emanuele 89, 00186 Rome, tel. 06/6852342, fax 06/6852424, www.agriturismo.com).

APARTMENT & VILLA RENTALS

If you want a home base that's roomy enough for a family and comes with cooking facilities **consider a furnished rental.** These can save you money, especially if you're traveling with a group. Home-exchange directories sometimes list rentals as well as exchanges.

INTERNATIONAL AGENTS • Drawbridge to Europe (5456 Adams Rd., Talent, OR 97540, tel. 541/512–8927 or 888/268–1148, fax 541/512–0978).**Eurovillas** (1398 55th St., Emeryville, CA 94608, tel. and fax 707/648–2066). **Hideaways International** (767 Islington St., Portsmouth, NH 03801, tel. 603/430–4433 or 800/843–4433, fax 603/430–4444; membership $99). **Hometours International** (Box 11503, Knoxville, TN 37939, tel. 423/690- -8484 or 800/367–4668). **Interhome** (1990 N.E. 163rd St., Suite 110, N. Miami Beach, FL 33162, tel. 305/940–2299 or 800/882–6864, fax 305/940–2911). **The**

Parker Company (Lynn, MA 01902, tel. 781/596–8282 or 800/280–2811, fax 781/596–3125. **Rentals in Italy and Elsewhere** (1742 Calle Corva, Camarillo, CA 93010, tel. 805/987–5278 or 800/726–6702, fax 805/482–7976). **Vacation Home Rentals Worldwide** (235 Kensington Ave., Norwood, NJ 07648, tel. 201/767– 9393 or 800/633–3284, fax 201/767–5510). **Villas International** (950 North Gate Dr., Suite 206, San Rafael, CA 94903, tel. 415/281–0910 or 800/221–2260, fax 415/499–9491).

CAMPING

Campgrounds near cities are often big, ugly affairs—a plot of roadside dirt with tents. Camping is usually the cheapest option, at L7,000–L15,000 per person, though some big campgrounds charge as much as L24,000 for a site. Be prepared for long bus rides out of town. The best places to camp are in nature areas like the Valle d'Aosta and the Dolomites. Campgrounds range from simple, green areas to recreation parks replete with camper vans, water slides, and a full bar. Federazione Italiana del Campeggio, a.k.a. Federcampeggio, issues a free complete list of campgrounds and a map.

INFORMATION • Federazione Italiana del Campeggio (Federcampeggio, Box 23, Calenzano, Florence 50041, tel. 055/882391).

CONVENTS & MONASTERIES

If you want peaceful surroundings, convents and monasteries provide a unique lodging experience and are often less expensive than hotels. Though guests are expected to make their own beds, the cleanliness and beauty of the buildings usually make up for any inconvenience. Some places house only Catholics, but many are flexible. Others might only take women or same-sex groups, depending on the church. Ask every time to be sure. A letter from your priest, pastor, or rabbi may be helpful. Inquire in advance by letter at the tourist offices in major towns for availability. If you're Catholic or Catholic-friendly and plan to stay in one town for an extended period, you can often contact the local parish either directly or through the tourist office.

HOME EXCHANGES

If you would like to exchange your home for someone else's **join a home-exchange organization,** which will send you its updated listings of available exchanges for a year and will include your own listing in at least one of them. It's up to you to make specific arrangements.

EXCHANGE CLUBS • HomeLink International (Box 650, Key West, FL 33041, tel. 305/294–7766 or 800/638–3841, fax 305/294–1448; $93 per year). **Intervac U.S.** (Box 590504, San Francisco, CA 94159, tel. 800/756–4663, fax 415/435–7440; $83 for catalogues.

HOSTELS

No matter what your age you can **save on lodging costs by staying at hostels.** In some 5,000 locations in more than 70 countries around the world, Hostelling International (HI), the umbrella group for a number of national youth-hostel associations, offers single-sex, dorm-style beds and, at many hostels, couples rooms and family accommodations. Membership in any HI national hostel association, open to travelers of all ages, allows you to stay in HI-affiliated hostels at member rates (one-year membership is about $25 for adults; hostels run about $10–$25 per night). Members also have priority if the hostel is full; in Italy, members enjoy discounts on 2nd- and 3rd-class train travel and special rental car rates.

An international hostel directory covers Europe and the Mediterranean ($13.95). Hostels with decent amenities are available all over Italy, in cities and usually on the outskirts of smaller towns. HI membership cards are often necessary; although you can usually buy them on the spot, you'll save money if you have one.

ORGANIZATIONS • AIG B Italian Youth Hostel Association (via Cavour 44, Rome 00184, tel. 06/4871152, fax 06/4880492). **Australian Youth Hostels Association** (YHA; Level 3, 10 Mallett St., Camperdown, New South Wales 2050, tel. 02/9565–1699, fax 02/9565–1325). **Hostelling International—American Youth Hostels** (733 15th St. NW, Suite 840, Washington, DC 20005, tel. 202/783–6161, fax 202/783–6171). **Hostelling International—Canada** (400–205 Catherine St., Ottawa, Ontario K2P 1C3, tel. 613/237–7884, fax 613/237–7868). **Irish Youth Hostel Association** (61 Mountjoy Street, Dublin 7, tel. 01/830–4555, fax 01/830–5808). **Scottish Youth Hostels Association** (7 Glebe Crescent, Stirling FK8 2JA, tel. 01786/891400, fax 01786/891333). **Youth Hostel Association of England and Wales** (Trevelyan House, 8 St. Stephen's Hill, St. Albans, Hertfordshire AL1 2DY, tel. 01727/855215 or 01727/845047, fax 01727/844126). **Youth Hostels Association of New Zealand** (Box 436, Christchurch, New Zealand, tel. 03/379–9970, fax 03/365–4476). Membership in the U.S. $25, in Canada C$26.75, in the U.K. £9.30, in Australia $44, in New Zealand $24.

RIFUGI

The Dolomites and other mountain groups are scattered with huts called *rifugi*. Rifugi are sometimes free; most, however, cost about the same as a hostel or a cheap hotel (L20,000–L50,000). Amenities are generally few. Some have cots rather than beds, although running water is almost always provided. Definitely inquire about availability in your prospective rifugio before trudging up a mountain to find no beds available—though in many cases they will make space, especially in far-flung rifugi. Tourist boards in towns at the base of the mountains will provide you with a list of rifugi and usually call them for you. Club Alpino Italiano owns hundreds of rifugi and publishes a free annual guide with information on access, prices, and equipment. The Touring Club Italiano also publishes guides describing hikes that pass by these mountain huts.

INFORMATION • Club Alpinisti Italiani (CAI; V. Ugo Foscolo 3, 20122 Milan, tel. 02/72023085. **Touring Club Italiano** (TCI; C. Italia 10, 20122 Milan, tel. 02/85261, fax 02/8526362).

MAIL & SHIPPING

Italian mail is notoriously slow (letters to the United States take about 10 days to arrive) and not too reliable, so **don't send valuables in the mail.** Postcards are low priority and take longer than letters.

POSTAL RATES

Stamps, sold at post offices and tobacco shops (labeled TABACCHI) everywhere, cost L1,300 for a postcard or letter up to 19 grams to the United States. Letters and postcards within the EU cost L800.

RECEIVING MAIL

Letters from the United States will take 10–15 days to arrive; packages take a little longer. The main post offices in cities and major towns all accept *fermo posta* (held mail). Have your pen pals address correspondence to you c/o Posta Centrale, with the name of the city, postal code, the words *fermo posta,* and your passport number. **Bring your passport to pick up mail** and expect to pay up to L1,500 per piece. The post offices can be unreliable, however; have your mail held at the nearest American Express office if you are a cardholder.

TELEGRAMS & FAXES

Either a city's main post office will have telegram and fax facilities on-site or there will be a telegram office nearby. Receiving a fax in Italy from the United States will cost L2,000 for the first page and L500 for each subsequent page; in the other direction, it's L5,320 for the first page and L4,720 for subsequent pages. Faxing within Italy will run you L2,500 per page. Some Telecom offices have self-service fax machines that cost only L2,000 plus the price of the phone call.

MONEY MATTERS

Thanks to Italy's unsteady economy, the lira has weakened against other currencies in the last few years; prices, however, continue to rise. Hostels are inexpensive, but a hotel will seem mighty nice should your hostel be overtaken by preteens; pizza for dinner is tasty, but so is a three-course meal; and admission to churches is free, but you'll still want to check out the many excellent museums here, despite steep entrance fees.

For the most part, the north is more expensive than the south. If you're strapped for cash, stay in smaller, less-touristed towns near the cities you wish to visit, such as Padua instead of Venice. You can travel in Italy on about $50–$60 a day if you're careful—and on even less if you're really frugal. Prices throughout this guide are given for adults through middle age. Substantially reduced fees are almost always available for children, students, and senior citizens. For information on taxes, *see* Taxes, *below*.

ATMS

To increase your chances of happy encounters with cash machines in Italy, before leaving home, **make sure that your card has been programmed for ATM use there**—ATMs in Italy accept PINs of four digits only; if your PIN is longer, change it through your bank. If you know your PIN as a word, learn the numerical equivalent since most Italian ATM keypads show numbers only, no letters. You should also have your credit card programmed for ATM use (note that Discover is accepted primarily in the United States); a Visa or MasterCard can also be used to access cash through certain ATMs, although fees may be steep and the charge may begin to accrue interest immediately even if your monthly bills are paid up. Local bank cards often do not work overseas or may access only your checking account; **ask your bank about a MasterCard/Cirrus or Visa debit card,** which works like a bank card but can be used at any store or ATM displaying a MasterCard/Cirrus or Visa logo. These cards, too, may tap only your checking account; check with your bank about their policy.

ATM LOCATIONS AND CUSTOMER SERVICE • Mastercard/Cirrus (www.mastercard.com; in the U.S. and Canada, tel. 800/307–7309; in the U.K., tel. 0800/964–767; in Australia, tel. 800/120–113; in Italy, tel. 800/870–866). **Visa** (www.visa.com for ATM locations; tel. 800/819–014 for emergency assistance).

CREDIT CARDS

In this guide the words "cash only" in the service information indicate that a property does not accept credit cards.

REPORTING LOST CARDS • American Express (tel. 336/668–5110 international collect). **Diner's Club** (tel. 702/797–5532 collect). **Master Card** (tel. 1678/70866 toll-free). **Visa** (tel. 1678/177232).

CURRENCY

The unit of currency in Italy is the lira. Lire (plural) come in notes of 1,000, 5,000, 10,000, 50,000, 100,000, and 500,000. Coins come in denominations of 50, 100, 200, 500, and 1,000. Throughout the text, lire are noted with a capital *L* preceding the number (for example, L5,000). At press time, the exchange rate was about L1,810 lire to the U.S. dollar, L2,927 to the pound sterling, L1,196 to the Canadian dollar, L1,145 to the Australian dollar, L2,459 to the Irish punt, L957 to the New Zealand dollar, and L293 to the South African rand.

CURRENCY EXCHANGE

You'll get a better deal buying lire in Italy than at home. Nonetheless, it's a good idea to exchange a bit of money into lire before you arrive in Italy in case the exchange booth at the train station or airport at which you arrive is closed or has a long line. At other times, for the most favorable rates, **change money at banks.** Although fees charged for ATM transactions may be higher abroad than at home, Cirrus and Plus exchange rates are excellent because they are based on wholesale rates offered only by major banks. In big cities, small exchange offices often offer competitive rates, low fees, more convenient hours, and shorter lines. Just be sure to read the fine print before exchanging any money. You won't do as well at exchange booths in airports or rail and bus stations, hotels, restaurants, or stores. Thomas Cook handles telephone orders and has retail locations worldwide; International Currency Express also handles telephone orders.

EXCHANGE SERVICES • International Currency Express (tel. 888/842–0880 on East Coast; 888/278–6628 on West Coast). **Thomas Cook Currency Services** (tel. 800/287–7362 for telephone orders and retail locations).

TRAVELER'S CHECKS

Do you need traveler's checks? It depends on where you're headed. If you're going to rural areas and small towns, go with cash; traveler's checks are best used in cities. Lost or stolen checks can usually be replaced within 24 hours. To ensure a speedy refund, buy your own traveler's checks—don't let someone else pay for them: irregularities like this can cause delays. The person who bought the checks should make the call to request a refund.

PACKING

You will find that Italians are elegant dressers—and dress much more formally than do Americans; keep your sweatshirts, tank tops, and Nikes at home if you want to dress to kill. If you don't want your appearance to scream tourist (Naples especially!), **try to strike a balance between style and comfort.** If you're traveling to Italy in summer, you can get away with packing very lightly. Bring comfortable, light, and easy-to-clean clothes. Black hides dirt but also absorbs heat. Artificial fabrics don't breathe and will make you hot, so go with light cottons instead. Bring several T-shirts or light shirts, a sweater for cool nights, and a light nylon shell or jacket for rainy weather. All churches appreciate modesty, and some enforce it: tank tops, shorts above mid-thigh, miniskirts, and plunging necklines are not appropriate. And shorts, if not frowned upon, will almost certainly brand you a foreigner.

If you come during winter—it gets surprisingly cold throughout Italy—bring a good coat and an extra sweater or two. A good pair of hiking boots or sneakers will keep your feet happy. But be forewarned:

hiking boots are cumbersome and often too hot to wear in the summer, and wearing them in Italy displays an unrefined fashion sense (again, if you care about that sort of thing). A sturdy pair of walking shoes weighs less and may help you blend in with the generally more formal Italians.

You've heard it a million times. Now you'll hear it once again: **Pack lightly.** The heaviness of your luggage is always directly proportional to how many days you've been carrying it around. Better yet, join the masses and get a suitcase with wheels and a retractable handle, which makes carrying luggage a breeze.

In your carry-on luggage **bring an extra pair of eyeglasses or contact lenses** and **enough of any medication you take** to last the entire trip. You may also want your doctor to write a spare prescription using the drug's generic name, as brand names may vary from country to country. In luggage to be checked, **never pack prescription drugs or valuables.** To avoid customs delays, carry medications in their original packaging. And don't forget to copy down and carry addresses of offices that handle refunds of lost traveler's checks.

CHECKING LUGGAGE

How many carry-on bags you can bring with you is up to the airline. Most allow two, but not always, so make sure that everything you carry aboard will fit under your seat, and get to the gate early. Note that if you have a seat at the back of the plane, you'll probably board first, while the overhead bins are still empty.

If you are flying internationally, note that baggage allowances may be determined not by piece but by weight—generally 88 pounds (40 kilograms) in first class, 66 pounds (30 kilograms) in business class, and 44 pounds (20 kilograms) in economy.

Airline liability for baggage is limited to $1,250 per person on flights within the United States. On international flights it amounts to $9.07 per pound or $20 per kilogram for checked baggage (roughly $640 per 70-pound bag) and $400 per passenger for unchecked baggage. You can buy additional coverage at check-in for about $10 per $1,000 of coverage, but it excludes a rather extensive list of items, shown on your airline ticket.

Before departure **itemize your bags' contents** and their worth, and label the bags with your name, address, and phone number. (If you use your home address, cover it so that potential thieves can't see it readily.) Inside each bag **pack a copy of your itinerary.** At check-in **make sure that each bag is correctly tagged** with the destination airport's three-letter code. If your bags arrive damaged or fail to arrive at all, file a written report with the airline before leaving the airport.

PASSPORTS & VISAS

When traveling internationally **carry a passport even if you don't need one** (it's always the best form of ID), and **make two photocopies of the data page** (one for someone at home and another for you, carried separately from your passport). If you lose your passport, promptly call the nearest embassy or consulate and the local police.

ENTERING ITALY

You need only a valid passport to enter Italy for stays of up to 90 days.

PASSPORT OFFICES

The best time to apply for a passport or to renew is during the fall and winter. Before any trip, check your passport's expiration date, and, if necessary, renew it as soon as possible.

AUSTRALIAN CITIZENS • Australian Passport Office (tel. 131–232).

CANADIAN CITIZENS • Passport Office (tel. 819/994–3500 or 800/567–6868).

NEW ZEALAND CITIZENS • New Zealand Passport Office (tel. 04/494–0700 for information on how to apply; 04/474–8000 or 0800/225–050 in New Zealand for information on applications already submitted).

U.K. CITIZENS • London Passport Office (tel. 0990/210–410).

U.S. CITIZENS • Nantional Passport Inormation Center (tel. 900/225–5674; calls cost 35¢ per minute for automated service, $1.05 per minute for operator service).

TOURS & PACKAGES

BUYER BEWARE

Each year consumers are stranded or lose their money when tour operators—even large ones with excellent reputations—go out of business. So **check out the operator.** Ask several travel agents about its reputation, and try to **book with a company that has a consumer-protection program.** (Look for information in the company's brochure.) In the United States, members of the National Tour Association and United States Tour Operators Association are required to set aside funds to cover your payments and travel arrangements in case the company defaults. It's also a good idea to choose a company that participates in the American Society of Travel Agents' Tour Operator Program (TOP); ASTA will act as mediator in any disputes between you and your tour operator.

Remember that the more your package or tour includes the better you can predict the ultimate cost of your vacation. Make sure you know exactly what is covered, and **beware of hidden costs.** Are taxes, tips, and transfers included? Entertainment and excursions? These can add up.

TOUR-OPERATOR RECOMMENDATIONS • American Society of Travel Agents (*see* Travel Agencies, *below*). **National Tour Association** (NTA, 546 E. Main St., Lexington, KY 40508, tel. 606/226–4444 or 800/682–8886). **United States Tour Operators Association** (USTOA, 342 Madison Ave., Suite 1522, New York, NY 10173, tel. 212/599–6599 or 800/468–7862, fax 212/599–6744).

PACKAGES

AIR/HOTEL • American Airlines Vacations (tel. 800/321– 2121). **Delta Vacations** (tel. 800/654–6559). **DER Tours** (9501 W. Devon Ave., Rosemont, IL 60018, tel. 888/337–7350, fax 800/282–7474). **4th Dimension Tours** (7101 S.W. 99th Ave., #105, Miami, FL 33173, tel. 305/279–0014 or 800/343–0020, fax 305/273–9777. **United Vacations** (tel. 800/377–1816).

FLY/DRIVE • American Airlines Vacations (tel. 800/321– 2121). **Delta Vacations** (tel. 800/654–6559).

FROM THE U.K. • Italian Escapades (227 Shepherds Bush Rd., London W6 7AS, tel. 0181/748–2661). **Page and Moy Holidays** (136–140 London Rd., Leicester LE2 1EN, tel. 0116/250–7676). **Care-free Italy** (Allied Dunbar House, East Park, Crawley, West Sussex RH10 6AJ, tel. 01293/552–277).

THEME GROUP TOURS

See also Volunteering, *below.*

Omega Travel (Suite 305-308, Radnor House, 93/97 Regent Street, London W1R 7TG, tel. 0171/439–6688, fax 0171/439–6699) represents over 700 agents and tour operators in the UK.

ADVENTURE • Adventure Center (1311 63rd St., No. 200, Emeryville, CA 94608, tel. 510/654–1879 or 800/227–8747, fax 510/654–4200). **Himalayan Travel** (110 Prospect St., Stamford, CT 06901, tel. 203/359–3711 or 800/225–2380, fax 203/359–3669).

ART AND ARCHITECTURE • Amelia Tours International (28 East Old Country Rd., Hicksville, NY 11801, tel. 516/433–0696 or 800/742–4591, fax 516/822–6220). **ArchaeoExpeditions** (Cultural Expeditions MEC Canada Inc., Westgate P.O. Box 35012, Ottawa, Ontario K1Z 1AZ, tel. 819/682–0562, fax 819/682–0562). **Archeological Tours** (271 Madison Ave., Suite 904, New York, NY 10016, tel. 212/986–3054, fax 212/370–1561). **Endless Beginnings Tours** (12650 Sabre Springs Pkwy., Suite 207-105, San Diego, CA 92128, tel. 619/566–5595 or 800/822–7855, fax 619/566–5014).

BIKING • Backroads (801 Cedar St., Berkeley, CA 94710-1800, tel. 510/527–1555 or 800/462–2848, fax 510/527–1444). **Bike Riders** (Box 130254, Boston, MA 02113, tel. 617/723–2354 or 800/473–7040, fax 617/723–2355). **Ciclismo Classico** (13 Marathon St., Arlington, MA 02174, tel. 781/646–3377 or 800/866–7314, fax 781/641–1512). **Club Toscana** (477 Mount Pleasant Rd., Suite 105, Toronto, Ontario M4s 2L9, tel. 416/482–8610 or 800/510–9963, fax 416/482–6113. **Euro Bike and Walking Tours** (Box 990, De Kalb, IL 60115, tel. 800/321–6060, fax 815/758–8851). **Europeds** (761 Lighthouse Ave., Monterey, CA 93940, tel. 831/646–4920 or 800/321–9552, fax 408/655–4501). **Uniquely Europe** (2819 1st Ave., Suite 280, Seattle, WA 98121- 1113, tel. 206/441–8682 or 800/426–3615, fax 206/441–8862).

LEARNING • Earthwatch (Box 9104, 680 Mount Auburn St., Watertown, MA 02272, tel. 617/926–8200 or 800/776–0188, fax 617/926–8532) for research expeditions. **Smithsonian Study Tours and Seminars** (1100 Jefferson Dr. SW, Room 3045, MRC 702, Washington, DC 20560, tel. 202/357–4700, fax 202/633–9250).

THE TRAINS EXPLAINED

The fastest Italian train, the pendolino, runs between major cities only and is prohibitively expensive. Eurocity (EC) and InterCity (IC) are next in terms of speed, for which you pay a supplemento (extra charge) of up to 50%, although the supplement is waived for Eurailpass holders. Rapido, diretto, and espresso trains make a few more stops and are usually a little slower, but you don't have to pay a supplemento. Regionale and locale trains are as slow as molasses,

WALKING/HIKING • Above the Clouds Trekking (Box 398, Worcester, MA 01602-0398, tel. 508/799–4499 or 800/233–4499, fax 508/797–4779). **Backroads** (*see* Biking, *above*). **Ciclismo Classico** (*see* Biking, *above*). **Country Walkers** (Box 180, Waterbury, VT 05676-0180, tel. 802/244–1387 or 800/464–9255, fax 802/244–5661). **Euro-Bike Tours** (*see* Biking, *above*). **Mountain Travel Sobek** (6420 Fairmount Ave., El Cerrito, CA 94530, tel. 510/527–8100 or 888/527–8100, fax 510/525–7710; in the U.K., tel. 01494/448–901; in Australia, tel. 02/9264–5710). **Uniquely Europe** (*see* Biking, *above*). **Wilderness Travel** (1102 Ninth St., Berkeley, CA 94710, tel. 510/558C2488 or 800/368–2794, fax 510/558–2489).

TRAIN TRAVEL

In general, Italian trains are clean, affordable, and run on schedule. **Guard your bags and your body on overnight trains,** though, especially south of Rome—you might want to padlock your bag to the overhead rack. Always **make a reservation for long rides.** Sitting in the aisle for several grueling hours is no picnic.

Most stations have a *biglietteria* (ticket office) where you buy your ticket. Some have separate lines for reservations and *couchettes* (bunk beds for overnight trains). If a station is so small it has no biglietteria, you can buy your ticket on the train. Otherwise, buying your ticket on board costs about L10,000 more than in the station. Remember to stamp your ticket in the yellow box in the station or on the platform, or you may be fined. Tickets are quite reasonable; a fare on a somewhat slow train from Florence to Rome costs only about L25,000. First-class tickets usually cost at least 50% more and are not worth the money. Round-trip fares cost as much as two one-way tickets; the only penalty for not buying a round-trip ticket is having to wait in line twice at the ticket counters. Many stations now have computerized ticket sellers (usually broken) and trip planners (also usually broken) that will tell you when the next train is coming and where to change trains. The state railway offers a variety of discounted train tickets (*see* Rail Passes, *below*).

An often-overlooked option for budget travelers *without* a rail pass is the Billet International de Jeunesse (International Youth Ticket), usually known as a BIJ or BIGE ticket. Here's how it works: travelers under the age of 26 can purchase a second-class ticket between two far-flung European cities at a 30% savings and then make unlimited stops along the way for up to two months. BIJ tickets are available throughout Europe at budget travel agencies; try the European offices of STA and Council Travel (*see* Students in Italy, *above*). Also, ask about the Cartaverde, good for 20% off most train trips and valid for one year (*see* Train Passes, *below*).

CUTTING COSTS

If you plan to ride the rails, **compare costs for rail passes and individual tickets.** If you plan to cover a lot of ground in a short period, rail passes may be worth your while; they also spare you the time waiting in lines to buy tickets. If you're under 26 on your first day of travel, you're eligible for a youth pass, valid for second-class travel only. Otherwise, passes are valid for first-class travel and can be pricey; it might cost you less to buy individual tickets, especially if your tastes and budget call for second-class travel. Be sure to **buy your rail pass before leaving the United States**; Eurailpasses are not available in Europe (although you might be able to buy one for a slightly inflated price at some questionable European travel agencies). Finally, **don't assume that your rail pass guarantees you a seat on every train**—seat reservations are required on some trains including some express and overnight trains. Also note that many rail passes entitle you to free or reduced fares for the lowest-cost seats on some ferries; you still have to **make seat reservations in advance.**

Also consider Italian rail passes (*see below*). If you're a European resident or have lived in an EU country for longer than six months, inquire about InterRail passes (*see below*).

EURAILPASSES

The Eurailpass is valid for unlimited first-class train travel through 17 European countries, England (and Scotland) notably excluded. The standard Eurailpass is available for periods of 15 days ($554), 21 days ($718), one month ($890), two months ($1,260), and three months ($1,558).

A Eurail Saverpass, which costs a little less than a comparable EurailPass, is intended for couples and small groups. A pass good for 15 days of first-class travel is $470, for 21 days $610, for one month $756, for two months $1,072, and for three months $1,324. The pass requires that a minimum of two and maximum of five people each buy a Saverpass and travel together at all times.

Unlike the EurailPass and Eurail Youthpass (*see below*), good for unlimited travel for a certain period of time, the Eurail Flexipass allows you to travel for 10 or 15 days within a two-month period. The Flexipass is valid in the same 17 countries as the EurailPass and costs $654 for 10 days and $862 for 15 days. If you're under 26, the second-class Eurail Youth Flexipass is a better deal. Within a two-month period it entitles you to 10 days ($458) or 15 days ($599) of travel.

For travel in France, Germany, Italy, Spain, and Switzerland, consider the Europass (first-class) or Europass Youth (second-class). The basic Europass is good for five days of travel in any of the above-named countries. The five-day pass costs $348 (first-class) or $233 (second-class). The six-, eight-, nine-, 10-, and 15-day passes cost $253/$368, $313/$448, $363/$528, and $513/$728. In all cases the days of travel can be spread out over two calendar months. Call Rail Europe for details on adding extra travel days, buying a discounted pass for your companion, or expanding the reach of your pass to Austria, Belgium, Greece, Luxembourg, and Portugal.

The very first time you use any Eurailpass, you must have it validated at a European station ticket window; otherwise you may be asked to get off the train or be fined. Another pitfall to avoid is losing your pass or having it stolen; **keep the receipts for any train tickets you purchase.** The only real safeguard is Eurail's Pass Protection Plan, which costs $12 and must be arranged at the time of purchase. If you bought the protection plan and your pass mysteriously disappears, file a police report within 24 hours. Then, upon your return home, send a copy of the report and receipts to Eurail. For your trouble you get a 100% refund on the *unused* portion of your stolen or lost pass.

AGENTS • **Rail Europe** (New York, 226–230 Westchester Ave., White Plains, NY 10604, tel. 914/682C5172, 800/438–7245, or 877/456–7245 for a list of travel agents selling Eurail passes; Canada, 2087 Dundas E, Suite 105, Mississauga, Ontario L4X 1M2, tel. 416/602–4195 or 800/361–7245 for the travel agent nearest you). **DER Tours** (9501 W. Devon Ave., Rosemont, IL 60018, tel. 888/337–7350, fax 800/282–7474). **CIT** (342 Madison Ave., Suite 207, New York, NY 10173, tel. 212/697–2100, 800/248–8687, 800/248–7245 western U.S.).

YOUTHPASS

If you're under 26, the Eurail Youthpass is a much better deal. One or two months of unlimited second-class train travel costs $623 or $882, respectively. For 15 consecutive days of travel you pay $388.

ITALIAN PASSES

The Italian train system offers three main types of passes, available at train stations throughout Italy; for information about each and to purchase rail passes, call CIT. The **Italy Flexi Railcard** costs $144 for four days of second-class ($216 for first-class) travel taken within one month, $202/$316 for eight days of travel within one month, and $259/$389 for 12 days of travel within one month. The **Italy Railcard** allows unlimited use of all trains for eight days ($182/$273), 15 days ($228/$341), 21 days ($264/$396), and 30 days ($318/$478). The **Italian Kilometric Ticket** is valid for two months and can be used by as many as five people to travel a total of 3,000 km (1,860 mi) first or second class (you'll have a hard time using it up unless you're traveling with at least two companions). This pass costs L338,000(first class) and L206,000 (second class). The **Carta Verde** saves youths under 26 years 20% for first- or second-class rail travel within a year, so it isn't worthwhile for short-term travel. It's about L40,000 and must be purchased in Italy.

THE HIGHS AND THE LOWS

Average daily temps in degrees Fahrenheit and Celsius stack up as follows:

MILAN

Jan.	40F	5C	May	74F	23C	Sept.	75F	24C
	32	0		57	14		61	16
Feb.	46F	8C	June	80F	27C	Oct.	63F	17C
	35	2		63	17		52	11
Mar.	56F	13C	July	84F	29C	Nov.	51F	10C
	43	6		67	20		43	6
Apr.	65F	18C	Aug.	82F	28C	Dec.	43F	6C
	49	10		66	19		35	2

ROME

Jan.	52F	11C	May	74F	23C	Sept.	79F	26C
	40	5		56	13		62	17
Feb.	55F	13C	June	82F	28C	Oct.	71F	22C
	42	6		63	17		55	13
Mar.	59F	15C	July	87F	30C	Nov.	61F	16C
	45	7		67	20		49	10
Apr.	66F	19C	Aug.	86F	30C	Dec.	55F	13C
	50	10		67	20		44	6

VENICE

Jan.	42F	6C	May	70F	21C	Sept.	75F	24C
	33	1		56	13		61	16
Feb.	46F	8C	June	76F	25C	Oct.	65F	19C
	35	2		63	17		53	12
Mar.	53F	12C	July	81F	27C	Nov.	53F	12C
	41	5		66	19		44	7
Apr.	62F	17C	Aug.	80F	27C	Dec.	46F	8C
	49	10		65	19		37	3

ITALIAN RAIL PASS AGENT • Italian State Railways (CIT representative, 15 W. 44th St., 10th floor, New York, NY 10036, tel. 212/730–2888 or 800/248–7245, fax 212/730–4544; in Canada, tel. 800/387–0711).

INTERRAIL

European citizens and anyone who has lived in the EU for at least six months can purchase an **InterRail Pass,** valid for 22 days or one month's travel in 29 countries, divided up into 8 zones. It works much like Eurail, except you get only a 50% reduction on train travel in the zone or zones you choose. Be prepared to prove EU citizenship or six months of continuous residency. InterRail can only be purchased in Europe at rail stations and some budget travel agencies; try the European branches of STA or Council Travel (*see* Students in Italy, *above*).

FARES & SCHEDULES

A new fare schedule was to go into effect in fall 1999; ticket prices quoted in this book may no longer be accurate.

TRAIN INFORMATION • The national toll-free train information number in Italy is 1478/88088.

TRAVEL AGENCIES

A good travel agent puts your needs first. Look for an agency that has been in business at least five years, emphasizes customer service, and has someone on staff who specializes in your destination. In addition **make sure the agency belongs to a professional trade organization.** The American Society of Travel Agents (ASTA), with 27,000 agents in some 170 countries, is the largest and most influential in the field. Operating under the motto "Integrity in Travel," it maintains and enforces a strict code of ethics and will step in to help mediate any agent-client disputes if necessary. ASTA also maintains a Web site that includes a directory of agents. (Note that if a travel agency is also acting as your tour operator, *see* Buyer Beware *in* Tours & Packages, *above*.)

LOCAL AGENT REFERRALS • American Society of Travel Agents (ASTA, tel. 800/965–2782 24-hr hot line, fax 703/684–8319, www.astanet.com). **Association of British Travel Agents** (68–271 Newman St., London W1P 4AH, tel. 0171/637–2444, fax 0171/637–0713). **Association of Canadian Travel Agents** (1729 Bank St., Suite 201, Ottawa, Ontario K1V 7Z5, tel. 613/521–0474, fax 613/521–0805). **Australian Federation of Travel Agents** (Level 3, 309 Pitt St., Sydney 2000, tel. 02/9264–3299, fax 02/9264–1085). **Travel Agents' Association of New Zealand** (Box 1888, Wellington 10033, tel. 04/499–0104, fax 04/499–0786).

VISITOR INFORMATION

TOURIST INFORMATION • Italian Government Tourist Board (ENIT): New York (630 5th Ave., Suite 1565, New York, NY 10111, tel. 212/245–4822, fax 212/586–9249). **Chicago** (500 N. Michigan Ave., Chicago, IL 60611, tel. 312/644–0990, fax 312/644–3019). **Los Angeles** (12400 Wilshire Blvd., Suite 550, Los Angeles, CA 90025, tel. 310/820–2977, fax 310/820–6357). **Canada** (1 Pl. Ville Marie, Suite 1914, Montreal, Québec H3B 2C3, tel. 514/866–7667, fax 514/392–1429). **U.K.** (1 Princess St., London W1R 9AY-1, tel. 0171/408–1254, fax 0171/493–6695).

CHECK WITH TOURIST OFFICES IN ITALY

An Azienda di Promozione Turismo (APT) or Ente Provinciale per Il Turismo (EPT) office is in every city and almost every small town (*see* individual city and regional chapters); they can be excellent resources for hotels, restaurants, sites, and local tour information. All APT and EPT offices are run by the main EPT office in Rome.

LOCAL CITY OFFICES • Rome (EPT; V. Marghera 2, 00185 Rome, tel. 06/49711, fax 06/4463379).

U.S. GOVERNMENT ADVISORIES • U.S. Department of State (Overseas Citizens Services Office, Room 4811 N.S., 2201 C St. NW, Washington, DC 20520; tel. 202/647–5225 for interactive hot line; tel. 301/946–4400 for computer bulletin board; fax 202/647–3000 for interactive hot line); enclose a self-addressed, stamped, business-size envelope.

VOLUNTEERING

A variety of volunteer programs is available. Council (*see* Students, *above*) is a key player, running its own roster of projects and publishing a directory that lists other sponsor organizations: *Volunteer! The Comprehensive Guide to Voluntary Service in the U.S. and Abroad* ($12.95, plus $1.50 postage). Service Civil International (SCI), International Voluntary Service (IVS), and Volunteers for Peace (VFP) run two- and three-week short work camps; VFP also publishes the *International Workcamp Directory* (included with a $15 membership contribution, $20 if outside North America). Global Volunteers runs two-week teaching programs.

RESOURCES • Global Volunteers (East Little Canada Road, St. Paul, MN 55117-1627, tel. 651/407–6100 or 800/487–1074, fax 651/482C0915). **SCI/IVS** (814 40th St., Seattle, WA 98105, tel./fax 206/545–6585). **VFP** (1034 Tiffany Rd., Belmont, VT 05730, tel. 802/259–2759, fax 802/259–2922).

WEB SITES

Do **check out the World Wide Web** when you're planning. You'll find everything from up-to-date weather forecasts to virtual tours of famous cities. Fodor's Web site—www.fodors.com—is a great place to start your online travels. For more information specifically on Italy, visit: www.italyemb.org, www.enit.it, www.wel.it, or www.jubil2000.org.

WHEN TO GO

Anytime is a good time to visit, except during *ferragosto,* the August 15 holiday when almost all Italians begin their big vacation. At that time, large cities and inland villages suddenly resemble ghost towns, while beach, mountain, and lake retreats are filled to the brim. Not surprisingly, hordes of foreigners flock to Italy in summer, and prices swell along the coast and on the islands. With winter come prime skiing in the Alps and amazingly empty streets, even in Florence and Venice, except during Venice's Carnevale in February. Most experienced travelers to Italy will tell you that late fall and early spring— when you can usually find relative solitude and mild weather—are the best times to go. If you don't like crowds, avoid Easter in Rome.

CLIMATE

FORECASTS • Weather Channel Connection (tel. 900/932– 8437), 95¢ per minute from a Touch-Tone phone.

FESTIVALS

Each big city and tiny town has its share of traditional festivals. Details are sometimes covered in the individual chapters, but a list of some of the biggies follows. It's worth making the effort to attend these festivals; just be sure to book a hotel far in advance.

During the Christmas period culminating on Epiphany, January 6, citizens of Rome crowd Piazza Navona, drawn by the promise of sweets, toys, and presents. On May 1 in Cagliari, the costumed procession of Sagra di Sant'Efisio (Feast of St. Efisio) centers around the effigy of Christ on the cross. For Pisa's Gioco del Ponte (Battle of the Bridge), costumed participants reenact a medieval battle on the first Sunday in June. In Fiesole, the enchanting ancient village overlooking Florence, the Estate Fiesolana festival lasts all summer long and celebrates music, dance, theater, and film. Siena's Il Palio, a highly competitive, frenetic bareback horse race dating from the Middle Ages, explodes every July 2 and August 16 in the Piazza del Campo. The Festa di San Gennaro on September 19 toasts the patron saint of Naples. Venice is a festival capital, with its Carnevale, regattas, and celeb-magnets the Biennale and International Film Festival.

WORKING IN ITALY

Before coming to Italy, in order to work in most jobs Americans must acquire a work permit from their prospective employer and a work visa from the Italian Consulate. It's also possible to get a permit in Italy from your employer once you've been hired. To get the work permit, your prospective employer must claim that you would fill a position that Italian citizens aren't qualified or available for and must clear you with the provincial employment office. Once you have a work permit, you can apply for an entry visa. With your valid Italian visa and work permit, go to the *questura* (police station) upon arrival to apply for residence in Italy. Residents of EU countries can work in Italy without these hassles.

The Council on International Educational Exchange (a.k.a. Council; *see* Students in Italy, *above*) publishes two excellent resource books with complete details on work/travel opportunities, including the valuable *Work, Study, Travel Abroad: The Whole World Handbook* and *The High School Student's Guide to Study, Travel, and Adventure Abroad* ($13.95 each, plus $3 first-class postage). The U.K.-based Vacation Work Press publishes *Directory of Overseas Summer Jobs* ($14.95) and Susan Griffith's *Work Your Way Around the World* ($17.95). The first lists more than 45,000 jobs worldwide; the latter, though with fewer listings, makes a more interesting read.

RESOURCES • Italian Consulate (690 Park Ave., New York, NY 10021, tel. 212/737–9100; 12400 Wilshire Blvd., Suite 300, Los Angeles, CA 90025, tel. 310/820–0622; 2590 Webster St., San Francisco, CA 94115, tel. 415/931–4924; www.italyemb.org). **Vacation Work Press** (c/o Peterson's, 202 Carnegie Center, Princeton, NJ 05843, tel. 609/243–9111). **Association for International Practical Training** (10400 Little Patuxent Parkway, Suite 250, Columbia, MD 21044-3510, tel. 410/997–2200, fax 410/992–3924).

VENICE AND THE VENETO 2

BY JEANINE GADE

UPDATED BY ROBERT ANDREWS

or hundreds of years, the cities of the Veneto came when Venice whistled. The region's architectural styles, ubiquitous statues of the winged lion—the symbol of Venice—and echoes of the nasal Venetian dialect in the "vowelly" Veneto accents are all remnants of Venetian dominance of the province. This stretch of land, which sprawls east–west between Venice and Verona and reaches far north to the edge of the Dolomites, is much more than just a suburb of the Canaled One, though. While the Venetian republic was looking to the East, with its eyes on the prize of Constantinople, the rest of Veneto was developing under the thumb of more traditional medieval dynasties: evil landlord Ezzelino da Romano and his progeny snagged prime land in the areas around Padua and Bassano del Grappa, and the della Scala family dominated Verona, while the Milanese Visconti clan was conquering towns all over northern Italy. The hundreds of castles and monuments to themselves these families left behind give the Veneto a visage different from Venice, its big sister, which governed itself as a republic for a thousand years. When Venice finally decided it was time to take over the nearby mainland at the end of the 14th century, most cities, including Verona, Vicenza, Padua, and Treviso, had already formed civic centers, a university, and distinct personalities.

Today the province is among the most expensive in Italy, populated by dress-for-excess members of the upper middle class. But rumors of snobbery don't deflect the annual flood of travelers who come to ponder Palladian villas, peaceful green hill towns, and paintings by locals Titian, Tintoretto, and Giorgione. And despite tourism, local traditions and fare—everything from horsemeat to squid ink—have kept their place among the newer generations of money. The province's biggest share of land is used for agriculture; farmers grow corn for polenta and grapes to make wines such as Valpolicella and Soave, as well as grappa.

VENICE

Pink palazzi, green canals, the blue Adriatic Sea, yellow signs pointing to Piazza San Marco, and too many red-faced tourists swirl together to form Venice (Venezia)—no wonder the city's Renaissance artists were into color over form. Ethereally beautiful, culturally vigorous, grossly overpriced, and infuriatingly crowded, Venice prods you into forming a strong opinion. Avoid Venice in July or August, when

COME HELL
OR HIGH WATER

Get out those rubber hip boots. The acque alte *(high waters) that periodically flood parts of Venice are getting higher and more frequent every year. Debris from factories in nearby Marghera, with help from natural causes, has stopped up the lagoon and backed up the tides, which rise higher every year during the flood season, from November through April.*

The lowest part of the city—and the tourist hub—is Piazza San Marco, its buildings wading in about 3 ft of water every time it floods. When water rises higher than that, the precious artwork and the building foundations are in danger.

The most absurd solution to the flooding yet proposed was a series of massive water walls to be set into the lagoon's sludge between the islands and the mainland—during exceptionally high tides, these slabs of metal would have mechanically popped up and literally stopped the flow of the Adriatic. The project was shelved when the government realized—after 19 years of development—that it's too darn difficult for humans to stop the sea. Until a new plan arises, Venetians must content themselves with carrying their work shoes and balancing on the planks laid across flooded squares.

trails to Piazza San Marco look like human conveyor belts, and the only food and lodging you'll end up with may be a cardboard pizza and the last *pensione* room available in Venice.

Venice's other problem, is, er, pigeon droppings, which coat the city with a film of corrosive guano. Sentimental pigeon lovers have joined forces with the animal rights lobby to prevent poisoning or shooting the critters, and in the meantime, there's a full-time team of inspectors to map out the most seriously affected sites until a decision is made. If you see a civil servant in a long mac examining the stuff, you'll know what he's up to.

Thanks to mass tourism, scant vestiges of local flavor are left in Venice. Come to study the high culture, as the city is home to some stupendous art and diverse churches. Beyond the striking canvases and structures, the city itself is a visual masterpiece. Built on 100-something islands crisscrossed by palazzo-lined canals, Venice's echoey, tiny walkways are so tranquil and easy on the eye that you can see why the Republic of Venice was dubbed *La Serenissima* (the Most Serene).

Venice was established in the 5th and 6th centuries by mainlanders trying to avoid marauding Huns and Lombards. By the 8th century, when the rest of Europe was snoozing through the Dark Ages, Venice had become a port town dominated by the Byzantine Empire. You can see the Byzantine thumbprint everywhere, especially in the onion domes and opulent gold mosaics in the Basilica di San Marco. After a few hundred years of foreign rule, the city's residents decided that although they liked being rich, they'd like self-government even better. They elected the first doge (chief administrator), and in 828 the symbolic and kooky theft of the body of St. Mark (*see* Worth Seeing, *below*) severed Venice's ties to anything but filthy lucre. In the following centuries, the city traded with and conquered much of the East, and it's still peppered with war spoils, most notably in the gold-dripping, jewel-encrusted Basilica di San Marco. Venice peaked in the 13th–15th centuries, when merchants commissioned scores of ostentatious Venetian-Gothic palazzi, visible today along the Canal Grande (Grand Canal).

The rise of Spanish and Portuguese naval power and the exploration of the New World in the 15th century marked the beginning of the end of Venice's power. In 1508, during the War of the League of Cambrai, jealous Milanese, Austrians, and Turks bullied Venice and bled it of treasure. The city's trade with the East stayed profitable for another century or two, but the Eastern market eventually bottomed out in favor of the West. When Napoléon came through at the end of the 18th century, slicing up Venice's territory, the city was lost. Batted around by major powers for a few decades, it finally, and not without reservations, joined the new nation of Italy in 1866.

So what's a landless, beautiful city with a reputation for debauchery to do to make a little money? Desperate, Venice turned to tourism in the late 19th century. The Lido island became the hot spot for the pre–jet set, glamorized by Byron long before Thomas Mann. The city is now largely dependent on tourism, which has helped raise the cost of living enough to force many locals to leave. Most moved across the lagoon to Mestre, a brutal industrial city founded in the 20th century to boost the regional economy. Some speculate that Venice will sink into the lagoon before the tension between tourism and factories is resolved—such an ironic end to a city whose riches and beauty all depend on water.

BASICS

AMERICAN EXPRESS

The office near Piazza San Marco (San Marco 1471, on Salizzada San Moisè, tel. 041/5200844; open weekdays 9–5:30, Sat. 9–12:30) performs all the usual money magic, exchanging at bad rates but without commission. Cardholder services include holding mail and cashing personal checks.

CHANGING MONEY

Use foresight and change your money in Padua or wherever else you came from—Venice is *not* where you get the most for your money. Crummy rates and 9.8% commissions abound. Banks cluster on the east side of the Ponte di Rialto and on Calle Larga XXII Marzo en route from Piazza San Marco to the Ponte dell'Accademia. Cirrus is everywhere but Plus a little less common; machines that accept Plus cards include **Banca Nazionale del Lavoro,** on Campo Rusolo/San Gallo (from the Procuratie Vecchie in Piazza San Marco, take the middle arch over Ponte del Cavalletto—it's on your left), **Banca Commerciale Italiana,** and **Banca Populare di Novara.** The train station has many exchange booths, all with hideous rates but usually without commission. The one in the info office is open 7:15 AM–9:20 PM, 8:30 AM–7:40 PM in winter, but the line can be hell.

CONSULATES

The **U.K.** consulate (Dorsoduro 1051, tel. 041/5227207) is on the Canal Grande just west of the Ponte dell'Accademia. U.S., Australian, and Canadian, citizens should contact their consulates in Milan (*see* Basics *in* Chapter 4); the closest consulate for New Zealanders is in Rome.

DISCOUNT TRAVEL AGENCIES

Centro Turistico Studentesco (CTS) is the easiest place in the Veneto to get youth and student discount tickets for boat, plane, and international train rides. *Dorsoduro 3252, on Fondamenta Tagliapietra across from university, tel. 041/5205660. From Ca' Foscari, take Calle Larga Foscari, make a hard left on Fondamenta Tagliapietra before bridge. Open weekdays 9:30–1:30 and 5–7.*

The little **Transalpino** booth at the train station specializes in tours and has deals on rail trips to the rest of Europe. *Staz. Santa Lucia, to right as you exit, tel. 041/716600. Open weekdays 8:30–12:30 and 3–7; Sat. 8:30 AM–12:30 PM.*

EMERGENCIES

The general panic number (police, ambulance, fire) is 113; **local police** (041/2715511); **fire** (115); **ambulance** (041/5230000); **emergency care** (041/5294517); **Red Cross First Aid Station** (P. San Marco 52, near Caffè Florian, tel. 041/5286346).

ENGLISH-LANGUAGE BOOKS AND NEWSPAPERS

Find the *International Herald Tribune* and other English- language periodicals at the kiosks by the train station, the Galleria dell'Accademia, and on Piazza San Marco. Spring for a paperback in your mother tongue at **Cafoscarina,** a well- stocked foreign language branch of the university bookshop. *Dorsoduro 3258, tel. 041/5229602. On Campiello degli Squelini behind Ca' Foscari. Open weekdays 9–7, Sat. 9–12:30.*

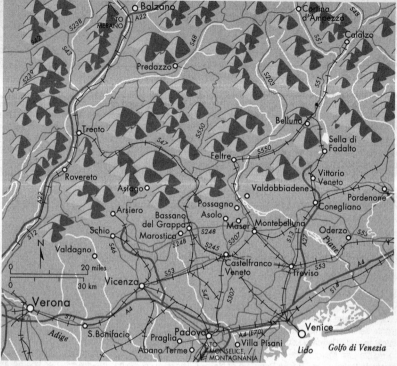

LAUNDRY

Ai Tre Ponti. Ouch: L5000–L7000 for a shirt, L7000–L9000 for a jacket—prices vary according to the load, but count on high prices for machine- or hand-washes. Sadly, Venice has no self-service laundromats, so you'll have to hand over your gear and watch it being assessed piece by piece. *Santa Croce 274, on Fondamenta di Piazzale Roma, tel.041/710654. Open weekdays 8:30–12:30 and 3:30–7:30.*

MAIL

Several post offices around the city sell stamps and send packages weekdays 8:15–1:30. At the central **Poste e Telecommunicazioni,** you can buy *francobolli* (stamps) weekdays 8:15–6:45, pick up *fermo posta* (held mail; postal code is 30100) weekdays 8:15–1:30, and send faxes or telegrams 24 hours a day, seven days a week. *San Marco 5555, tel. 041/2717111. Facing Canal Grande just north of Ponte di Rialto.*

MEDICAL AID

Try to avoid falling ill in Venice—the **Ospedale Civile di Venezia** was installed in the 15th-century Scuola di San Marco by Napoléon, and little has seen modernization since. Very few of the staff speak English. *Tel. 041/5294111. On Fondamenta Nuova east of Ponte di Rialto, next to Chiesa SS Giovanni e Paolo.*

PHARMACIES • Call 041/5311592 (7:30 PM–8:30 AM, 24 hrs Sun.) to find out which **pharmacies** are open all night, as they rotate on a biweekly basis. All pharmacies have the address of the closest night pharmacy posted on their doors. The folks at **Farmacia Italo-Inglese** (San Marco 3717, tel. 041/5224837; open weekdays 8:15–1:30 and 4–7:30) speak some English; they're on Calle de la Cortesa, across the bridge from Campo Manin on the Ponte di Rialto–Ponte dell'Accademia route.

PHONES

Buy *carte telefoniche* (phone cards) in the central post office, at tobacco shops, or from vending machines in the pay-phone room in the train station.

VISITOR INFORMATION

The **APT** runs two offices in Venice. The first is a small, hectic desk at the train station (tel. 041/5298727; open daily 8:10–6:50). The roomier **main office** is on Piazza San Marco. Both offices give out maps and museum, train, gondola, and concert listings. The station office also makes hotel reservations. *Main office: San Marco 71/G, tel. 041/5226356. At end of Procuratie Nuove on P. San Marco. Open daily 9:40–3:20.*

GAY AND LESBIAN RESOURCES • Gay and lesbian travelers can contact the **ARCI Gay/ARCI Lesbica** office (Cannaregio 883A, tel. 041/721197).

COMING AND GOING

BY TRAIN

The **Venezia–Santa Lucia station** is named for the church that was sacrificed so visitors could step off their trains and practically into the Canal Grande. Remember to stay aboard at Venezia-Mestre, the stop before Venice proper. Ticket windows at the Santa Lucia station are open daily 5:50 AM–9:30 PM; the reservation windows, where you can book couchettes and international trains, are open daily 5:50 AM–8:30 PM; and the train info office (tel. 147/888088 toll-free) is open daily 7 AM–9 PM. The station itself is closed 12:30 AM–3:45 AM; luggage storage (L5000 per bag per 12 hrs) is closed 12:30 AM–3:45 AM. When you're trying to find your way back to the station, look for signs for FERROVIA or FS.

Locals use Venice's twisty alleys for real business, and working their way through throngs of tourists is a great annoyance to them. Pausing in the middle of a bridge to consult your map is like jerking a car to a stop in a busy intersection to read a street sign.

Every hour, trains head to Bassano del Grappa (1⅛ hrs, L6,300), Bologna (2 hrs, L14,000), Milan (4 hrs, L22,000), Padua (30 min, L4,100), Treviso (30 min, L4,100), Verona (1½ hrs, L10,400), and Vicenza (50 min, L6,300). Trains also go to Florence (8 daily, 2¾ hrs, L43,500), Rome (7 daily, 5 hrs, L77,000), Geneva (2 daily, 8 hrs, L125,000), Paris (1 daily, 12½ hrs, L190,000), and Vienna (4 daily, 8 hrs, L130,000).

BY BUS

There is no real reason to travel to Venice by bus, but if you do, you'll be deposited at **Piazzale Roma** (the city's only parking lot), just across the Canal Grande from the train station. You can take ACTV (tel. 041/5287886) Bus 2, 4, 7, or 12 from here to Mestre, if you decide to stay there. Buy your ticket (L1,500) from the kiosks on the piazzale.

BY PLANE

International and domestic flights go through the tiny mainland **Aeroporto Marco Polo** (041/2609260), on the lagoon to the north of the city. If you're coming from the United States, flying into Venice doesn't always cost that much more than flying into Milan or Rome (though you'll probably have to change planes in Milan). In the airport, a **luggage storage desk** (open daily 6 AM–9 PM) will stow stuff for L3,500 per item per day.

AIRPORT TRANSIT • To get from the airport to Piazzale Roma, your two cheapest options are to take the functional blue **ATVO** bus (20 min, L5,000) or the often-crowded orange **ACTV** Bus 5 (30 min, L1,500). A more stylish way of arriving in town is to take a seat on a **Cooperativa San Marco** (tel. 041/5415084) water bus, which makes the 70- minute trip from the airport to Piazza San Marco hourly (L17,000 per person, baggage included).

GETTING AROUND

There has been only a single attempt in Venice's history to reorganize and simplify the city's meandering narrow streets, and that was the arrow-straight Strada Nova and Via Garibaldi, created by the Habsburgs in the early 19th century. This meager attempt was positively futile—you *will* get lost in this medieval metropolis. A map is essential for orientation, but there is no such thing as a good map of Venice. After coughing up the L4,000 for a map from any tobacco shop (the APT offers two maps—one they're always out of, and the other a shameful waste of a tree), the best thing to do is wander about and pay attention to landmarks—try to enjoy getting lost.

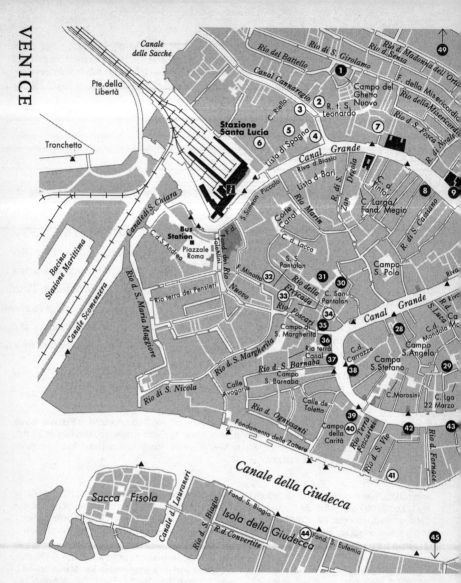

VENICE

Canale delle Sacche

Pte. della Libertà

Tronchetto

Stazione Santa Lucia

Canale di S. Chiara

Bus Station

Piazzale Roma

Bacino Stazione Marittima

Canale Scomenzera

Canale della Giudecca

Sacca Fisola

Isola della Giudecca

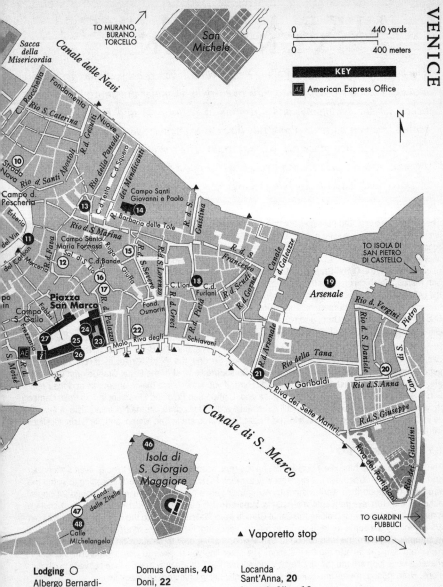

TO MURANO,
BURANO,
TORCELLO

San
Michele

| 0 | | 440 yards |
| 0 | | 400 meters |

KEY

AE American Express Office

Sacca
della
Misericordia

Canale delle Navi

N

Canale delle Navi

C. Racchetta

Fondamenta

Rio S. Caterina

R. d. Gesuiti Nuove

Rio d. Santi Apostoli

Strada
Nova

10

Campo d.
Pescheria

R. d. Testa

Rio della Panada

C. d. Squero

dei Mendicanti

Campo Santi
Giovanni e Paolo

13

R. Barbara delle Tole

14

R. d. S. Marina

R. d. S.
Giustina

R. S. Severo

R. d. S.
Francesco

Erberia

del Vin

11

Campo Santa
Maria Formosa

Ruga

Mercerie

R. d. Fava

12

Sal. S. Lio

C. d. Bande

15

R. S. Lorenzo

R. d. Greci

R. d. Giuffa

C. lion

18

C. d.
Furlani

R. d. Scudi

R. d. Gorne

Canale
d. Galeazze

TO ISOLA DI
SAN PIETRO
DI CASTELLO

19

Arsenale

Rio d. Vergini

del Corbon

po
in

Campo
S. Gallo

Frezzaria

Piazza
San Marco

27

AE

Fabbri

16

17

R. d. Palazzo

Fond.
Osmarin

R. d. Pietà

Schiavoni

22

Riva degli

Molo

24

25

23

26

R. d.
S. Moisé

Rio d. S. Daniele

Rio d. Vergini

21

V. Garibaldi

Riva dei Sette Martiri

Rio della Tana

S. di Pietro

20

Rio d. S. Anna

R. d. S. Giuseppe

Canale di S. Marco

46

Isola di
S. Giorgio
Maggiore

Ci

Fond.
delle Zitelle

47

48

Calle
Michelangelo

TO GIARDINI
PUBBLICI

TO LIDO

▲ Vaporetto stop

Riva dei Partigiani

Rio di Giardini

LIKE A ROLLING VENETIAN

The best deal in town is the Rolling Venice card. If you're between the ages of 14 and 29, L5,000 entitles you to reduced entry to all major museums; half-price tickets for the symphony; and discounts at restaurants and hotels, on bike rentals, even on haircuts. From July through September, you can buy the card in the train station office (tel. 041/5242904). The rest of the year, buy cards at Agenzia Arte e Storia (Santa Croce 659, Campo della Luna, tel. 041/5240232) or Ital-Travel, San Marco 71/G, tel. 041/5229111.

The words for streets and passages are different in Venice from those in every other city in Italy: A street is a *calle*, a covered passage a *sottoportego*, a filled canal a *rio terrà*, a street running along a canal a *fondamenta*, and a square is called a *campo*—the only piazza in Venice is San Marco. The city's skinny alleyways twist in a hopeless maze, randomly dead-ending at canals or residences. Venice's essential reference point, the **Canal Grande**, cuts through the city in a backward *S* from the train station to Piazza San Marco, which means that the canal can lie on three sides of you at once. And if that isn't enough, the numbers painted above each door are useless as guides—they're assigned according to their district and not in a strict numerical progression—in other words, "6867 Dorsoduro" means that it is the 6867th doorway in Dorsoduro, and No. 8738 is just around the corner.

But there is a slight method to the madness. First, the Canal Grande is bridged in only three places: the Ponte di Scalzi in front of the train station, the Ponte di Rialto in the dead center of the city and the canal, and the Ponte dell'Accademia to the southeast. Second, the six *sestieri* (districts) can help you to get oriented a bit: **Santa Croce, San Polo,** and **Dorsoduro** lie west of the Canal Grande, and **Cannaregio, San Marco,** and **Castello** are to the east. Third, if you know some major landmarks and their relation to each neighborhood, you'll start to get a grip: Campo San Polo and I Frari are in San Polo; Campo di Santa Margherita and the Galleria dell'Accademia are in Dorsoduro; Strada Nova and Lista di Spagna lie in Cannaregio; Campo Sant'Angelo and Piazza San Marco are in San Marco; and Via Garibaldi slices through the Castello district.

BY VAPORETTO

The vaporetto, something like a boat-bus, is an easy and scenic way to traverse the city, even if it's pricey and sometimes crowded. It's the quickest way to reach Piazza San Marco. Besides getting to watch the vaporetto dudes do their work without mussing their gelled hair, you can use the vaporetti 24 hours, although they run less frequently after 10 PM. **Vaporetto 1** is called the *accelerato* (accelerated), though it makes almost every stop along the Canal Grande from Piazzale Roma to the Lido. **Vaporetto 82** covers essentially the same route. If you're in a rush, Vaporetto 3, the *direttissimo* (extremely direct), runs in summer only from the train station to San Marco, making only three stops on the way; **Vaporetto 4** runs from San Zaccaria to the train station. The other line you're likely to use is **Vaporetto 52,** which makes a huge loop around the city. Note: Vaporetti marked LIMITATO only make a loop between two major stops. Note too that routes and numbers are currently being changed, so check first.

Buy tickets for vaporetti at kiosks by the *fermate* (stops) or on board if the kiosk is closed. A one-way ticket is L6,000. You can also get 24-hour (L18,000), 72-hour (L35,000), and one-week (L60,000) tickets. Stamp your ticket in the yellow boxes near the stops before boarding; if you're caught without a validated ticket, you will have to pay a L26,000 fine. Of course, the worst penalty is the embarrassing lecture you get when you decide to play dumb tourist. For bus and boat info dial 041/5287886; lost and found is 041/2722179.

BY TRAGHETTO

Only three bridges span the Canal Grande, but during the day another eight *traghetti* (stripped-down gondolas used as ferries) take people—mostly Venetians on their morning commutes—across at points in between. The idea is simple: Board a traghetto at a designated station (usually noted by a yellow sign with a little gondola and an arrow), pay L800, walk to the back of the gondola, and turn around so that you have your back to the water. (This will show you're in the know, because the gondola will swing out of the dock and turn 180 degrees, giving you a forward-facing view.) The traghetti run from about 8 until 7, except when it's rainy, breezy, chilly, lunchtime, or the gondoliers are busy gossiping.

BY GONDOLA

Picture, if you will, a fat man paddling bedraggled tourists up and down a stumpy stretch of the Canal Grande; the former is serenading Naples's greatest hits, while the latter are shelling out an outrageous L120,000 for 50 minutes of gondola time. Such is the sad story of the famed Venetian skiff. If you do decide to take a ride, drive a hard bargain with your gondolier before boarding—make sure that the ride is a full 50 minutes and that the price is set. Don't take a gondola from San Marco, because you might end up spending all your time in boat traffic. Leave instead from the less congested Trinità station (tel. 041/5231837), next to Campo San Moisè on the San Marco–Ponte dell'Accademia route. But really, save your cash—and dignity—and hop a traghetto (see above) instead for that strapping-young-buck-rowing-across-the-canal experience.

BY WATER TAXI

The wooden-hulled beauties you see cruising by as you chug along in a vaporetto are *motoscafi* (water taxis), Venice's expensive modern-day answer to the gondola. The official rate isn't terrible—about L35,000 from the Lido to San Marco and L130,000 from the airport—especially if you split it with friends, but the rate you actually get can be two or three times the official one, so be careful. If you decide to go for it, either flag a taxi down or call 041/5222303 or 041/5228538. There are taxi stations at Piazza San Marco, the train station, and Ponte di Rialto.

The job of gondolier is coveted. The absurdly lucrative occupation is open only to the descendants of gondoliers, and their union is one of Venice's most powerful ones. They seem to spend more time manning their telefonini (cell phones) than their oars.

ON FOOT

The easiest and quickest—these terms are used relatively— way to get around Venice is on foot. Several well-traveled routes usually marked by large signs with arrows cut through the city. Two trails start at the train station and go to Piazza San Marco; follow signs marked PER SAN MARCO. One basically hugs the Canal Grande, traversing the Lista di Spagna and the Strada Nova in Cannaregio; the other leads you across the Ponte di Scalzi, through Santa Croce and San Polo to the Rialto Bridge, and then to the piazza. The trail from the train station to Dorsoduro, which passes I Frari and Campo di Santa Margherita, also starts at the Ponte di Scalzi. Turn right after the bridge, then left before the bridge to Piazzale Roma before wandering maniacally through the back streets.

WHERE TO SLEEP

Staying in Venice will cost you. Every other building here is a hotel, but the best deals need to be reserved at least a month in advance. Reservations are especially important from June to September— if your Italian isn't so hot, take advantage of the **hotel reservation desk** (tel. 041/715288; open June– Sept., daily 8 AM–10 PM; Oct.–May, 8 AM–9 PM) at the train station, where for L1,000 they'll make a reservation for you and take a deposit that will be deducted from the price of your room. But be warned— they may try to bump you up a price class. If Venice is absòlutely full, venture out into the soul-less heart of Mestre for an L80,000 double at the Hotel Cortina (V. Piave 153, tel. 041/929206), to the right of the train station. Day-tripping to Venice from Padua or another nearby Veneto town is another possibility, but train rides are energy-sapping, and you miss out on the beauty of the city at night.

You can find inexpensive hotels near the train station in Cannaregio and way out in Castello, but it is worth the effort to hunt down a nice place in Santa Croce or Dorsoduro. If you're a Rolling Venice card-holder, check their map for the hotels that offer discounts. A virtual lack of crime in Venice promises crime-free budget hotels; the worst you'll encounter is smell or noise. Many budget hotels lock the door sometime between 11 PM and 2 AM; you can often ask for a key. Many close for a few weeks in November for minor repairs and at the end of December and most of January for the holidays. In other words, call ahead. Hostels and other dorm accommodations are the cheapest sleeps, but most don't take phone reservations, and many have strict curfews. Hostels run by nuns often accept only women.

CANNAREGIO

This neighborhood is conveniently close to the train station, but a million and three tourists make it one of the noisiest in Venice, and it's not exactly next door to most sights. Still, it's crammed with cheap sleeps.

UNDER L75,000 • Casa Gerotto Calderan. One of the best values in Venice, this spanking-clean hotel on two floors has good, hot showers and is run by the most darling mother-and-son team in Italy. Doubles go for L70,000; singles L40,000; and dorm beds L30,000. *Cannaregio 283, 30121, tel. and fax 041/715361. From Lista di Spagna, left on Campo San Geremia and look for CALDERAN sign. 29 rooms, 5 with bath.*

Archie's House. With private rooms at L64,000 a double and dormitory accommodation under L30,000 a bed, you can't complain if the rooms are a trifle dowdy. However, the entrance hall looks nattier, with its show of gaudy mirrors. The owner speaks excellent English, and forbids alcohol. *Cannaregio 1814, 30121, tel. 041/720884. Cross Ponte de Cannaregio a.k.a. Ponte Guglie, follow Rio Terrà San Leonardo and turn right into Rio Terrà del Cristo. 7 rooms, 1 with bath. Cash only.*

UNDER L95,000 • Hotel Marte. This clean, comfy hotel is run by cordial but shrewd businessfolk who know their job—squeezing lire out of exhausted travelers. Watch out or you may be switched to a pricier room. Doubles go from L90,000; singles L35,000–L55,000. If they're full, they'll send you to the similarly priced **Biasin,** across the canal. *Cannaregio 338, 30121, tel. 041/716351, fax 041/720642. Take Lista di Spagna to Ponte Guglie and turn left just before bridge. 14 rooms, 13 with bath.*

UNDER L105,000 • Hotel Villa Rosa. Here you don't get ambience, just mass-produced furniture and bare walls. But L100,000 does buy you hot water backed by high pressure, clean bathrooms, and breakfast. *Cannaregio 389, 30121, tel. 041/716569. From Lista di Spagna, turn left on Calle della Misericordia. 33 rooms with showers.*

Albergo Rossi. Follow the tiny alley to this hotel to find impeccably clean rooms and a friendly management who will proudly show you their hotel. Modern doubles (L100,000) include breakfast. *Cannaregio 262, 30121, tel. 041/715164. From Lista di Spagna, go left onto Calle delle Procuratie. 14 rooms, 12 with bath.*

UNDER L135,000 • Albergo Bernardi-Semenzato. The doubles—starting at L130,000 in high season—are a great deal, but book in advance to ensure a place in the *dipendenza* (annex), a bizarre old palazzo with a canal and a garden. *Cannaregio 4363/66, 30121, on Calle dell'Oca, tel. 041/5227257. At east end of Strada Nova, turn left at church of SS Apostoli onto Campiello Salizzada Pistor, and then left on Calle dell'Oca. 15 rooms, 9 with bath. Luggage storage.*

DORSODURO

The presence of the university means you'll find students and casual cafés and trattorias here. It's a great area if you want to be slightly off the tourist track and stay a while.

UNDER L85,000 • La Calcina. A spacious hotel that manages to be both comfortable and funky, this is the place to splurge. Once the residence of English critic John Ruskin, the building is right on the Giudecca Canal. If you add L20,000 onto the L80,000 price of a double (without breakfast or bath in the room), you get a perfect view of Il Redentore across the water. Reservations are advised. *Dorsoduro 780, 30123, tel. 041/5206466. From Zattere vaporetto stop, walk down Fondamenta delle Zattere. 39 rooms, 29 with shower.*

Domus Cavanis. This place is a steal at L65,000 for well- kept doubles, L45,000 for singles, in a prime location between the Accademia and the Zattere promenade. It's run by a warm woman who means business, especially about the curfew. *Dorsoduro 912, 30123, tel. 041/5287374. From Ponte dell'Accademia, turn right on Rio Terrà Foscarini. 25 rooms, 10 with bath. Cash only. Midnight curfew. Closed Oct.–mid-June.*

UNDER L105,000 • Locanda Ca' Foscari. The singles are a pricey L85,000, but the L105,000 doubles are well worth it. The English-speaking owner will proudly show you to your surprisingly well-decorated room, probably with a view and definitely with breakfast. Of course, the best deal is the L168,000 showerless quad. *Dorsoduro 3887/B, 30123, on Calle della Frescada, tel. 041/710401, fax 041/710817. 11 rooms, 5 with bath. Curfew 1 AM.*

CASTELLO

As the Castello butts up against Piazza San Marco, its hotels are predictably expensive. But it's close to major sights, and things simmer down if you dig deep into the district.

UNDER L125,000 • Doni. Once a palace and right on a canal, it has rooms at the front that overlook gondolas through ogee windows. The hotel, now family-run, has solid brown furniture and old-fashioned wallpaper to match, although some rooms have frescoed ceilings and chandeliers. Doubles at L120,000 (without bath) include breakfast. *Castello 4656, 30122, on Fondamenta del Vin, tel. and fax 041/5224267. Walk canal side past San Marco, turn left into Campellio del Vin, left into Ramo del Vin and right into Fondamenta del Vin. 13 rooms, 3 with bath. Closed Jan.*

Caneva. Rooms with a view of the sometimes well-kept courtyard go for L100,000, including breakfast. Prices fall off-season, and plastic is accepted, but you'll pay extra for the privilege. *Castello 5518, 30122, on Ramo dietro la Fava, tel. 041/5228118. From Ponte di Rialto, walk past Campo San Bartolomeo to Calle Stagnieri, cross bridge to Campo della Fava; Ramo dietro la Fava is on right. 23 rooms, 15 with bath.*

Locanda Canal. Big, bright doubles that aren't dank— something to consider in watery Venice—cost L120,000, complete with breakfast and barely functioning furniture. *Castello 4422/C, 30122, on Fondamenta Remedio, tel. 041/5234538. From Campo Santa Maria Formosa, walk behind church to Campiello Querini and veer right to Fondamenta Remedio. 7 rooms, 5 with bath. Cash only.*

Locanda Silva. The staff is bored but helpful; some of the L110,000 doubles have canal views; all are clean and come with breakfast. *Castello 4423, 30122, on Fondamenta Remedio, tel. 041/5227643. See directions to Locanda Canal, above. 25 rooms, 13 with bath. Curfew 2 AM. Cash only.*

Locanda Sant'Anna. Way out in the *popolare* (working-class) section of Castello past the Arsenale, this is more like a strange old apartment than a hotel. The worn, grandmotherly furniture and backyardish courtyard enhance the effect. Doubles go for L110,000 with breakfast. *Castello 269, 30122, on Corte del Bianco, tel. and fax 041/5286466. From west end of V. Garibaldi, veer right on Fondamenta Sant'Anna, turn left on 2nd bridge, right onto Corte del Bianco. 8 rooms, 5 with bath. Curfew 12:30.*

The 4 palazzi-lined km of the Canal Grande—Venice's center stage, Main Street, loading dock, and open sewer all rolled into one—make up the world's grandest thoroughfare. After dark, treat yourself to a leisurely tour on Vaporetto 1 or 82.

SANTA CROCE

Smack-dab in the middle of it all, this 'hood is on the way to everything and a good place for a siesta or a snack.

UNDER L120,000 • Casa Peron. Clean L110,000 doubles include breakfast, and the staff won't blink while you chat with the parrot in the lobby. This is in a nice location, central to Dorsoduro, the train station, and San Marco. They also have the *best* map in town. *Santa Croce 84, 30135, on Salizzada San Pantalon, tel. 041/710021, fax 041/711038. From train station, cross Ponte di Scalzi, go right on Fondamenta San Simeòn Piccolo, then left on Fondamenta Tolentini, right on Fondamenta Minotto, which becomes Salizzada San Pantalon. 11 rooms, 7 with bath.*

Hotel dalla Mora. Well located between Santa Croce and Dorsoduro, this hotel has quiet rooms and a casual staff. Breakfast comes with the L100,000 doubles. *Santa Croce 42/A, 30135, tel. 041/710703, fax 041/723006. From train station, cross Ponte Scalzi and turn right on San Simeòn Piccolo, left on Fondamenta dei Tolentini, right on Fondamenta Minotto, right at Dalla Mora sign. 15 rooms, 7 with bath.*

HOSTELS

Venice has one perennially packed HI hostel, but there are enough dormlike places (often called *foresterie*) to ensure that you get a cheap bed for the night. If the places below are full, try **L. Murialdo** (Cannaregio 3512, tel. 041/719933), **Patronato Salesiano Leone XIII** (Castello 1281, tel. 041/5287299), **Ostello Santa Fosca** (Cannaregio 2372, tel. 041/715775), or the basic dorm beds at Casa Gerotto Calderan (*see* Cannaregio, *above*). For a taste of strict convent life, at L21,000, women can try **Istituto Canossiano** (tel. 041/5222157). The APT office has a list of other hostels, as does the Rolling Venice map (*see box* Like a Rolling Venetian, *above*).

Foresteria Valdese. The dorms may recall scouting memories, but the room with a kitchen is a deal if you pack it with six people. Beds cost L31,000 the first night, L30,000 thereafter, breakfast included. *Castello 5170, 30122, tel. 041/5286797. From Campo S. Maria Formosa, take Calle Lunga S. Maria Formosa until it ends, then cross bridge to Protestant church; it's on right. 48 beds. No curfew, no lockout (ask for key). Reception open Mon.–Sat. 9–1 and 6–8, Sun. 9–1.*

Ostello della Gioventù Venezia (HI). Good luck trying to get a bed here in summer; try to ensure a place by paying in advance at another hostel on the IBN network (*see* Lodging *in* Chapter 1); otherwise show up very early and stand in line. With a mandatory HI card you'll get a bunk and breakfast for L27,000; you can register and buy the mandatory cards (L30,000) anytime. The common room opens at 1:30 PM. *Giudecca 86, 30123, on Fondamenta della Croce, tel. 041/5238211. Vaporetto 82 to Zitelle/Ostello stop and turn right. 260 beds. Curfew 11:30, lockout 9:30–1:30. Closed last 2 wks Jan.*

CAMPING

Trying to camp in Venice is a little like trying to camp in downtown Los Angeles. There are no campgrounds in Venice proper, unless you count the Lido, which is actually one of the more beautiful, quiet, and convenient camping areas in all of Italy. You'll find **Europa Cavallino** (tel. 041/968069; closed Oct.–Easter) on the Adriatic side of the Lido on the island Litorale del Cavallino. Camping costs L12,000–L25,000 per tent, L5,500–L10,000 per person, according to season. Take Vaporetto 14 to Punta Sabbioni. **Camping Jolly delle Querche** (V. A. de Marchi 7, Marghera, tel. 041/920312; closed Oct.–Easter), a mainland site, is well equipped and only costs about L8,500 per person, L18,000 including tent, but it's a pain to reach and none too scenic. From Piazzale Roma, take Bus 6, get off at Piazza Foscori, and follow the signs.

WHERE TO EAT

Cheap, good restaurants exist in Venice, but they're gems in a sea of sewage—prepare for a treasure hunt. Even when Venice is at its cheapest, it's still not cheap—remember, all your little gnocchi, eggplants, and cappuccino cups had to get here by boat. Venice's reputation for having the least satisfactory food in Italy is especially justified if you can't pull yourself out of the quagmires of San Marco and Cannaregio, where quadrilingual menus and compact-disc-sized pizzas are the rule. But if you wander through the back streets of Dorsoduro and San Polo, you can find excellent meals at relatively low prices.

While in town, try the unofficial dish of Venice, *seppia nera* (tender pieces of squid smothered in a rich sauce made from squid ink), usually served with grilled polenta. Other local specialties include spaghetti *alle vongole* (with clams in a butter-herb sauce) and risotto *alle vongole nere* (with black clams). If you want to construct a meal of your own, you'll find that fruits and vegetables aren't that expensive as long as you stay away from the stalls on the streets between the Ponte dell'Accademia, the Ponte di Rialto, and the train station. The largest market is the daily **Mercato di Rialto,** which begins at the tourist stalls on the San Polo side of the Ponte di Rialto. To the left, past the butcher shops and cafés, is the **Erberia** (fruit and vegetable market), the largest and perhaps cheapest place to buy fresh produce. The arcaded building at the end of the Erberia holds the **Pescheria,** or fish market. Otherwise the most thrilling place in Venice to buy your tomatoes is from the **vegetable boat** next to Campo San Barnaba, on the route from the Ponte dell'Accademia to Campo di Santa Margherita. It stays afloat Monday through Saturday. On Strada Nova, **Standa** (Cannaregio 3659; open daily 8:30 AM–7:20 PM), a combination supermarket/department store, sells everything from slippers to chocolate.

CANNAREGIO

Avoid eating anywhere near the train station and push on into the narrow streets north of Strada Nova—you'll thank yourself later.

UNDER L25,000 • Osteria Ai Canottieri. This informal eatery is tucked away on the Canale di Cannaregio, with outside tables right on the water. The inside is cool, with mainstream rock tunes, occasionally live. The food and service have a crude charm, but tasty seafood dishes change regularly, and there's a L18,000 fixed-price lunch. Drinks can be pricey: A liter of wine is L10,000, and beer is L4,000–L6,000. *Cannaregio 690, on Fondamenta di San Giobbe, tel. 041/717999. From train station take San Marco route that starts on left, turn right on Fondamenta Venier just before Ponte delle Guglie; Venier turns into Fondamenta di San Giobbe. Cash only. Closed Sun.*

Sahara. You'll get excellent home cooking at this small and simple little place. The cuisine is Syrian and you'll get couscous of course, but have a go at the shawarma (L12,000) or baba ghannoug (L15,000) and see what you get. *Cannaregio 2519, Fondamenta della Misericordia, tel. 041/721077. From train station, cross Ponte di Cannaregio a.k.a. Ponte Guglie, follow Rio Terrà San Leonardo, then turn left at Campo Santa Fosca into Calle Zancani, cross three bridges until you reach Fondamenta della Misericordia: restaurant is 10 m on left. Closed Mon.*

SAN POLO AND SANTA CROCE

Not many tourists make it into the winding streets of San Polo and Santa Croce—good news for you, as food tends to be better and cheaper here, but bad news, too—you'll have to do some tricky navigating. Be persistent.

UNDER L10,000 • Alle Oche. This renowned pizza joint offers more than 80 different kinds of yummy, massive pizzas. The preferred pie is the Inferno, with spicy salami, hot peppers, and mozzarella. If you don't see exactly what you want, ask nicely if you can mix and match ingredients. *Santa Croce 1552/A, tel. 041/5241161. From Campo San Polo, take Calle Bernardo, cross bridge and continue, take 1st left on Rio Terrà Secondo, then right on Rio Terrà Primo Perrucchetta, cross 1st bridge, and it's on left.*

La Perla d'Oriente. This place would do San Francisco's Chinatown proud, with tasty hot-and-sour soup and tofu in chili sauce. It's the only restaurant on the Campo dei Frari, and the outdoor tables have views of the church's profile. *San Polo 3004, Campo dei Frari, tel. 041/5237229.*

UNDER L15,000 • Due Colonne. The best pizzeria in Venice is named after the two interior stone pillars that purportedly hold the place up. The pizzas are large, fresh, and good—look for specials like mozzarella *di bufala* (made from water-buffalo milk) and tomatoes topped with fresh *rucola* (arugula). The tables on the campo make for beautiful summer meals; be sure to call in the morning to reserve a table. *San Polo 2343, on Campo San Agostin, tel. 041/5240685. From northeast edge of Campo San Polo, take Calle Bernardo, cross bridge, go left on Rio Terrà Secondo, and continue straight to Campo San Agostin. Closed Sun.*

Rule of thumb: panifici *(bakeries),* salumerie *(delis), and all other food stores and stands are closed all day Sunday and on Wednesday afternoon in Venice.*

DORSODURO

Many restaurants here have gardens in back or tables out on quiet *campi,* making this one of Venice's more pleasant places to dine. The presence of a university means plenty of cheap, honest food, though a few places do cater to tourists.

UNDER L10,000 • Al Pantalon. This family-run restaurant offers shoot-from-the-hip food at rock-bottom prices. Your choice of pasta with pesto, *ragù* (meat sauce), or tomato sauce is a wee L6,000. The student menu (you need not actually be a student) gets you pasta, vegetables, beverage, and handles the cover for L15,000; add a meaty *secondo* for L6,000 more. *Dorsoduro 3958, on Salizzada San Rocco, tel. 041/710849. Just southwest of Campo dei Frari off Campo San Rocco. Cash only. Closed Sun.*

Al Profeta. There are similarly priced pizzerias in Dorsoduro, but the pies here taste better than most, especially when eaten in the back garden. Pizza prices swell to L28,000 for the huge, densely topped, and completely shareable Maxipizza. *Dorsoduro 2671, tel. 041/5237466. From southeast corner of Campo San Barnaba, go west on Calle Lunga San Barnaba. Closed Mon. in winter.*

Arca. Run by a friendly family, this place does reasonable pasta and cheap pizzas like *biancaneve* (mozzarella and basil; L6,000). There's a tourist menu at L22,000, or try the tasty sardines with polenta for L13,000. *Dorsoduro 37573761, on Calle San Pantalon, tel. 041/5242189. Along Campo di Santa Margherita–I Frari route. Closed Sun. in winter.*

Iguana. Come here if you simply must have something you know and need, like a burrito. Here, at tables by the Giudecca Canal, you can get a bursting meat or veggie one smothered in fresh guacamole and washed down with a Corona. They make their own salsa and tortillas—obviously concocted by gringos. Reservations are a good idea. A second branch of Venice's only Mexican restaurant can be found at Cannaregio, on Fondamenta della Misericordia (tel. 041/716722). *Giudecca 68–71, on Fondamenta della Croce, tel. 041/5230004. Cash only. Closed Tues.*

UNDER L15,000 • Taverna San Trovaso. This is the best modestly priced restaurant in all of Venice, where the L12,000–L18,000 *piatti secondi* (second courses) are exquisite. Try the spaghetti *alla pirata* with sweet peppers, tomatoes, and mussels; side orders of either *spinaci* (spinach) or zucchini are uninspired. Reservations are paramount, especially if you want a table in the brick-vaulted rooms downstairs. *Dorsoduro 1016, on Fondamenta Priuli, tel. 041/5203703. From northwest edge of Galleria dell'Accademia, go right on Calle Gambara and left on Fondamenta Priuli. Closed Mon.*

LA SERENISSIMA

The Republic of Venice took the nickname La Serenissima, or the Most Serene, because of its history of political stability—only once in the republic's nearly 10 centuries was there anything close to a popular uprising. This unusual respect Venetians had for their government came from the practice of voting for each and every one of the doges, or dukes. To avoid ballot stuffing, the Signoria (the state council) devised a complicated process to elect the doge. After praying in the basilica, the youngest member of the council took the first boy he saw with him to the Palazzo Ducale to become the ballot counter, in the hope that the selection would be as random as possible.

In the end, becoming the doge was more of an honorable burden than anything else—the tradition of tossing coins to the citizens gathered in Piazza San Marco on inauguration day almost bankrupted a few dukes. The "democratic" election, rather than the "divine right" of the doge is why the Palazzo Ducale is more of a public building than a formidable noble residence, why no single family has dominated Venice's history like Florence's Medici, and why Venice was the world's longest-running "republic."

UNDER L20,000 • Trattoria Antico Capon. In one of the greatest people-watching spots in Venice, this joint has a large selection of pastas and pizzas within crawling distance of Campo di Santa Margherita's bars. The *tagliolini* (paper-thin ribbon-shaped pasta) with salmon and cream sauce (L18,000) is glorious. There's a three-course tourist menu for L25,000. *Dorsoduro 3004, on Campo di Santa Margherita, tel. 041/5285252.*

UNDER L25,000 • L'Incontro. Here you'll find creative, fresh, and excellent *primi piatti* (first courses), like gnocchi *al sugo d'anatra* (with a duck sauce). The selection of second courses (around L20,000) depends on what fish were brought in that morning. Reserve in advance, especially if you want a table on the campo. *Dorsoduro 3062/A, Rio Terrà Canal, tel. 041/5222404. On northeast edge of Campo di Santa Margherita toward Ponte dell'Accademia. Closed Mon., 2–3 wks in Jan., and 1 wk in Aug.*

SAN MARCO

As a rule, stay away from the restaurants in San Marco, unless you *want* to sample the most expensive and tasteless food in town. An exception follows.

UNDER L20,000 • Vino, Vino. When your blood sugar drops, this relaxing wine bar–cum–restaurant welcomes you with its cool, dark interior. The menu changes often; pasta of the day is a good bet and *insalata dei polpi* (marinated squid salad; L16,000) is an indulgent complement to your wine. *San Marco 2007/A, Ponte delle Veste, tel. 041/5237027. From P. San Marco, take Salizzada San Moisè, cross Campo San Moisè to Calle Larga XXII Marzo, right onto Calle delle Veste. Closed Tues.*

CASTELLO

Stay away from the back side of San Marco, and you'll do fine in Castello. Via Garibaldi has all kinds of cheap, decent pizzerias and trattorias.

UNDER L15,000 • Trattoria alla Fonte. If you're starving in San Marco, take a short walk to this trattoria for pizza or pasta, like the gnocchi *ai quattro formaggi* (with four cheeses). *Castello 3820, on Campo Bandiera e Moro, tel. 041/5238698. From P. San Marco, left on Riva degli Schiavoni (along lagoon); after Chiesa della Pietà, left onto Calle di Dose, which becomes Campo Bandiera e Moro. Closed Wed.*

CAFÉS AND GELATERIE

Once you've had good gelato, it's hard to stay away. But, hey, a sugar boost is always in order. A few words of warning: avoid the cafés around San Marco and Cannaregio, which tend to design their sandwiches based on how long they will last in a window rather than how they will taste. And if you attempt sitting in one of the piazza's outdoor cafés, be warned that your cappuccino might turn into a L12,000 affair.

Bar da Gino. This casual sidewalk café has what is probably the best cappuccino (L2,500) in the entire Veneto. The staff is friendly, even when busy, and the foam artiste is a darling man with a fantastic belly who serves everyone—octogenarians, art students, tourists—with astonishing grace. *Dorsoduro 853, on Accademia-Guggenheim route, tel. 041/5285276. For directions, see* Collezione Peggy Guggenheim *in* Worth Seeing, *below. Closed Sun.*

Bar Rosso. Definitely the slickest hangout spot in Venice, this bar, with its fire-engine-red sign screaming CAFFE, attracts a mix of student and artsy types without being pretentious. Morning coffee, an afternoon spritzer *all'aperol* (*see box* Cocktails Venetian Style, *below*), and occasional nighttime jazz quartets might make you never want to leave. As usual, prices are higher if you sit. *Dorsoduro 2963, on Campo di Santa Margherita, tel. 041/5287998. Closed Sun.*

Il Doge. This is some serious can't-miss gelato right on Campo di Santa Margherita, with clusters of student types savoring heavenly flavors like kiwi, *frutti di bosco* (berry), or tiramisu. It's open late. *Dorsoduro 3058/A, on Campo di Santa Margherita, tel. 041/5234607.*

Mille Voglie. Pundits argue whether this place (better known among locals as I Frari) or Il Doge is Venice's best. Exquisite creams, like ultrasmooth banana or *bacio* (kiss—chocolate-hazelnut) at L1,500 a scoop, will have you pondering the question yourself. *San Polo 3033–3034, Salizzada San Rocco, behind apse of I Frari, tel. 041/5244667.*

Why do all windows in Venice have a box of pretty geraniums? They repel the mosquitoes that emerge from the canals. Geranium oil is a nontoxic repellent you can buy in any erboristeria *(herb store); there's a good one in Campo di Santa Margherita.*

WORTH SEEING

With dazzling architecture, shady alleys, and art as colorful as its buildings' peeling paint, Venice can easily be considered the most beautiful city in the world. And without marathon distances or car traffic, almost every inch of the city is open to exploration; the only things to overcome are tourist hordes and the likelihood of getting lost. Cramming everything into one day means visual overload and sore feet; allow time to really look at things and savor the spectacular art in the cool churches.

Museums can be expensive, but many places honor Rolling Venice cards. Museum opening hours and admission costs change constantly. During summer madness, it's not a bad idea to visit a museum at lunchtime (all the biggies stay open), when most stores are closed and the crowded streets are most miserable. Relatively few people venture out to the islands of the **Lagoon** (*see* Near Venice, *below*), but it's worth it for the chance to see a slightly different, and perhaps more complete, side of Venice.

PIAZZA SAN MARCO

The heart of Venice, Piazza San Marco—probably the most heavily visited spot in Italy—teems with tourists. Prepare to be overwhelmed, both by the almost gaudy majesty of the buildings and the definitely gaudy tourist fanfare: where else can you watch people pay hard-earned money to feed, touch, and take pictures of scads of disgusting pigeons? If you can, avoid the piazza until evening, when the true spirit of the place almost returns to the square.

The doge's backyard from the 9th to the 19th centuries, the piazza has historically been the seat of the municipal government. The **Procuratie,** the two long buildings stretching out from the basilica, were the offices of the procurators, who tended to the more mundane aspects of running the city while the doge was out a-conquering. The Procuratie Vecchie start at the **Torre dell'Orologio** (Clock Tower), where bronze "Moors" strike the hour on the roof; the Procuratie Nuove stand opposite. Two famous cafés, **Quadri** on the Vecchie and **Florian** on the Nuove, also played a part in history. During the Risorgimento of the 18th and 19th centuries, those who backed Italy conspired in Florian, while supporters of Austria plotted in Quadri. Now they plot together to ream tourists—L10,000 for *caffè* when the bands are playing. Napoléon used the buildings as his palace before he turned Venice over to Austria. Directly across from the Palazzo Ducale (*see below*) is the **Libreria Sansoviniana,** which Jacopo Sansovino, Venice's greatest Renaissance architect, designed to hold the doge's collection of Greek and Latin texts. Though it's supposedly one of the city's architectural masterpieces, the building is closed to the public indefinitely.

BASILICA DI SAN MARCO • This huge hallucination of a basilica has a history as bizarre as its architecture. Originally, Venice's patron saint was Teodoro, the saint of the ruling Byzantine Empire. In AD 828, however, two Venetian merchants stole St. Mark's body and placed it in a shipment of pork—so the Muslim customs officials wouldn't inspect it—bound for Venice. As the story goes, an angel had appeared to St. Mark while he was visiting the lagoon, saying, "Peace to you, Mark, my messenger. Your body will rest here"—a likely embellishment so Venice and the merchants could rest easy believing that their Great Corpse Robbery was divinely ordained. Though the angel's greeting is written in Latin on every statue of the winged lion of St. Mark, secular motives lurked behind the theft. By declaring a new patron saint for the city, the increasingly powerful doges symbolically proclaimed their independence from Constantinople. In fact, Mark's remains were handed directly to the doge of the day, who erected the first basilica in 829. In 932 the basilica was burned to the ground in an uprising against this new power; the structure you see today dates from 1094. Used as the doge's private church for centuries, it didn't become the official cathedral of Venice until 1807, when doges were phased out.

As opposed as they were to Byzantine rule, the builders of the church were still smitten with Byzantine architecture; domes and gold mosaics abound. But the Venetians couldn't leave the thing alone, so the interior is a confusing and wonderful hodgepodge of Byzantine, Gothic, and Renaissance styles mixed with booty from around the world. Sunlight is scarce in the naves and abundant under the domes to enhance the feeling of divine enlightenment. On the Ascension dome in the middle, Christ gives his blessing while being borne toward the light by four angels; on the left side of the basilica's exterior is a 12th-century depiction of the corpse theft story. Take a free guided tour of the basilica, with explanations of the mosaics, at 11 or 3 weekdays; tours start at the entrance hall.

Don't bother paying to see the treasury, but by all means pay the L3,000 admission to the **Pala d'Oro;** this altar screen is covered with more than 2,000 jewels and, of course, lots of *oro* (gold). The treasure is proof of Venetian dominance in the 12th to 14th centuries. You have to share the **loggia** (a.k.a. the Marciano Museum) with a swarm of tourists, but it's the only way to get up close and personal with any of the mosaics. The four merry-go-roundish horses inside (the ones outside are copies) were stolen from Chios by Constantine and swiped by Venice during the Fourth Crusade in 1204. Napoléon took them to Paris in 1797, where they stayed until they were finally returned to the basilica in 1815. *P. San Marco, tel. 041/5225205. From train station, take Vaporetto 1, 82, or 2. Admissions: Basilica free, Pala d'Oro L3,000 (includes admission to treasury), loggia L4,000. Basilica and loggia open daily 9:45–4:30; Treasury and Pala d'Oro open Mon.–Sat. 9:30–5, Sun. 1:30–5.*

PALAZZO DUCALE • The doges' private residence and the site of courts, prisons, and political intrigues, the pink-checkerboard Palazzo Ducale is a perfect example of Venetian-Gothic architecture. The building was a moat-surrounded fortress in 810, and in 1340 it took on the delicate form it has today. Thick columns support the portico, but arcades, pastel marble, and intricate crenellation on the roof alleviate any heaviness. The new design also created an inside courtyard, where anybody in Venice could drink from the wells or crash under the porticoes at night.

The main entrance, called the **Porta della Carta** (Door of the Charter) because public notices were posted there, contains sculptures of the four Virtues, St. Mark, and Justice, all by the Bon family. The **Scala dei Giganti** (Giants' Staircase) leads up to two statues by Jacopo Sansovino: Mars (god of war) and Neptune (god of the sea), both symbols of the Venetian republic. New doges would swear their loyalty to Venice standing between the two. Continue up the Sansovinian **Scala d'Oro** (Golden Staircase) to the major rooms of the palazzo; almost all are covered with paintings by Tintoretto, Veronese, Tiepolo, Titian, and other Venetian masters. The best paintings hang in the Sala di Maggior Consiglio: Veronese's virile *Apotheosis of Venice* stoked the doge's ego every time he looked up, and a whole wall is covered with a *Paradiso* by Tintoretto. From the Great Council Hall, walk down to the **Ponte di Sospiri** (Bridge of Sighs), which leads to part of the prisons. To see the best prisons, including the torture chamber and the maximum-security cells, take the tour called **Itinerari Segreti del Palazzo Ducale** (Secret Intineraries of the Doge's Palace). The L24,000 tour (at 10 and noon, except Wed.) is in Italian only, but it's the only way to see Venice's most sinister side. Call 041/5204287 a day in advance to make tour reservations. *P. San Marco, next to Basilica di San Marco, tel. 041/5224951. Admission L17,000, includes Museo Civico Correr (see below). Open daily 9–7, 5 in winter; last tickets at 5:30, 3:30 in winter.*

MUSEO CIVICO CORRER • This museum is a crash course in Venetian history, putting all those paintings, palazzi, and canals into context. The galleries hold treasures like Ottoman banners captured centuries ago and a dubious but functional-looking chastity belt. On the way out is a display of everyday objects through the ages, including board games and 2-foot-high platform shoes that would make Elton jealous. *P. San Marco, tel. 041/5225625. Admission L17,000, includes Palazzo Ducale (see above). Open daily 9–7, 5 in winter.*

CAMPANILE DI SAN MARCO • Oddly enough, this bell tower is a reconstruction. After 11 centuries of standing strong as a watchtower and lighthouse, the 300-ft tower suddenly and inexplicably collapsed into a pile of rubble in 1902. The city quickly rebuilt it using as many of the old bricks as possible, and the tower you see today looks and functions exactly like its predecessor—right down to its five deafening bells. Take an elevator to the top (admission L8,000) for an unrivaled view of Venice's canals, terraces, and winding *calli. Open daily 9:30–10, 4:30 Oct.–May. Closed 2 weeks in Jan.*

PIAZZETTA AND THE DUE COLONNE • The small, open area surrounded by the Palazzo Ducale, Piazza San Marco, and the lagoon is known as the Piazzetta. The dominating elements here are the Due Colonne, two red Egyptian granite columns next to the fondamenta by the lagoon. The columns were raised in the 12th century, and symbols of the two patron saints of Venice were plopped on top. The replica statue on the right (facing the canal) portrays San Teodoro—who was worshiped when Venice still took orders from Constantinople—as a dragon slayer (no, that's not a crocodile he's standing on). The original statue stands in the Palazzo Ducale. The more famous bronze statue, dating from between the 5th and 4th centuries BC, is the winged lion, St. Mark's trademark.

Two major activities took place between the columns in the Piazzetta: gambling and executions. Because of the latter, it's still considered bad luck to walk between the columns.

GALLERIA DELL'ACCADEMIA

Possibly the only good to have come from Napoléon's repression of churches and schools in Venice is the Galleria dell'Accademia, a collection founded in 1807 to preserve salvaged canvases for study by the Accademia's art students. The collection quickly grew into the single most stunning and extensive gathering of Venetian art. In the 1940s, modern architecture whiz Carlo Scarpa arranged the 24 rooms to display the collection in roughly chronological order—from 14th-century gold-gilt altarpieces to 18th-century bucolic fantasies. It takes an hour to give the place a once-over, though you'll have to stay at least three to render the paintings their due.

The first room you stumble into is **Room 4,** where several Madonnas by 15th-century artist Gentile Bellini look too elegant to have been painted by a human. The revered **Room 5** has the tiny, enigmatic *Tempest,* by the equally enigmatic Giorgione—nobody can tell what's going on in the canvas, and scholars have decided that several additional figures were covered up soon after they were painted. The grandest is **Room 10,** with some of the greatest works by Veronese and Tintoretto. Veronese's massive *Feast at the House of Levi* was too long to fit on the gallery wall, so Scarpa carved out a few accommodating inches of the building. The painting was originally intended to be of the Last Supper, but outraged church officials threatened to excommunicate Veronese for depicting Christ in the company of African slaves, dwarves, a monkey, and a guy with a bloody nose. The artist responded by simply changing the painting's name. On the adjacent wall is Tintoretto's cycle narrating the abduction of St. Mark's body from Alexandria. Here the painter is at his nightmarish best, perversely depicting what is mythically Venice's greatest moment as something psychedelic and dark. **Room 17** has portraits by Rosalba Carriera (1675–1757), known as one of the first independent women artists. A cycle of paintings by Carpaccio tells one of the stranger tales in Catholic lore: a beautiful Breton princess agrees to marry an English prince only after he converts to Christianity and travels with her to Rome with 10,000 virgins in tow—only everybody is slaughtered on the way home. It just goes to show you. *Dorsoduro, tel. 041/5222247. Admission L12,000. Open Tues.–Sat. 9–7, Sun. and Mon. 9–2.*

COLLEZIONE PEGGY GUGGENHEIM

In 1949 American heiress Peggy Guggenheim (not to be confused with her uncle Solomon of Manhattan) came to Venice to avoid the New York City scene. She died 30 years later, leaving behind her 18th-century canalside palazzo and 300 or so works that now make up Italy's most important collection of modern art. Pieces by Pollock, Klee, Picasso, Man Ray, Giacometti, and Kandinsky are beautifully installed in the smallish rooms. A few works have personal import, such as Max Ernst's *The Antipope,* said to be a partial portrait of Peggy—they were once married—and the silver headboard sculpted for her by Alexander Calder. Aside from the superb collection, there's a sculpture garden, a café, a museum shop, the tomb of Peggy's "babies"—actually departed canines—and a staff of chatty English-speaking students. *Dorsoduro 701, on Fondamenta Venier dai Leoni, tel. 041/5206288. From Ponte dell'Accad-*

emia, turn left on Rio Terrà Foscarini, take 1st left on Calle Nuova Sant'Agnese and cross bridge; continue on Calle della Chiesa, which becomes Fondamenta Venier dai Leoni. Admission L12,000. Open Wed.–Mon. 11–6.

SCUOLA GRANDE DI SAN ROCCO

Back in the mid-16th century, the wealthy patrons of the Scuola Grande di San Rocco called on the greatest Venetian painters of their time to submit proposals for a cycle of canvases exalting both San Rocco, a saint thought to be effective against the plague, and the school itself. Most artists, including the favored Veronese, duly prepared detailed drawings. But obsessive Jacopo Tintoretto outshone them all by frantically painting an actual canvas, sneaking into the building, and installing his work in the middle of the night—a gutsy move that was entirely against the rules. The fathers of the *scuola* were impressed enough to offer him the commission over the objections of the other painters. For the next 23 years Tintoretto kept busy producing more than 50 canvases, and the result is stunning. Here you see the full range of Tintoretto's abilities, especially the masterful lighting in apocalyptic backgrounds composed of a dozen shades of black. *San Polo 3052, Campo San Rocco, tel. 041/5234864. Behind I Frari's apse. Admission L8,000. Open Apr.–Oct. daily 9–5:30; Dec.–Feb., Mon.–Fri. 10–1, weekends 10–4; Mar. and Nov. daily 10–4.*

PONTE DI RIALTO

Large, clunky, and white, the 16th-century Ponte di Rialto is one of Venice's most recognizable and infuriatingly crowded structures. There's been a bridge between San Marco and San Polo at this spot since 1172—in fact this was the only place to cross the Canal Grande until the 19th century. The original was a wooden drawbridge, which was replaced by a larger wooden bridge. By 1551 the wood had rotted, so a competition was held to decide who would design a replacement. The proposals by Palladio, Sansovino, and Michelangelo were rejected—you can almost hear the architecture historians groan—in favor of the single-arch scheme by a nobody named Da Ponte, a name that means, of all things, "of the bridge." To his credit, the bridge was an engineering feat, since it needed to be high enough for galleys to pass under it but not so steep as to make crossing on foot difficult—and all this out of stone. Today the Ponte di Rialto is crowded with stands selling sunglasses and gawking tourists. *Follow signs from left of train station or P. San Marco (facing away from canal, look right).*

DISTRICTS

Besides major sights, there are a number of lesser-known jewels—museums, churches, and palazzi strewn through Venice's sestieri (districts), which you could spend weeks exploring. Many aren't on the main tourist circuit, so you can get to know Venice without being forced to get to know those folks visiting from Tokyo or Cincinnati.

CANNAREGIO

The neon signs and fierce tourist traffic of the Cannaregio district will be your introduction to what is really a gracious city; a few choice turns off the infested streets near the Canal Grande, and the story changes dramatically. Here you'll find the **Ghetto Ebreo** (Jewish Ghetto; *see below*), still-functioning convents, and the wide, straight canals that are characteristic of Cannaregio.

CA' D'ORO • The finest surviving example of Venetian-Gothic palatial architecture, this ornate early 15th-century house earned its name "House of Gold" from the gilt that once covered its lacy front. The building was brutally renovated in 1847, and only the nongold part of the facade escaped complete dismemberment. The rooms are filled with minor art, with the exception of a gorgeous full-size fresco of St. Sebastian by Mantegna and a *Venus* by Titian. If you don't feel compelled to see every Titian in town, settle for a gander at the elaborate facade as you chug by on a vaporetto. *Cannaregio 3932, tel. 041/5238790. From train station, Vaporetto 1 to Ca' d'Oro stop; or follow San Marco trail, mid-Strada Nova, turn right on Calle Ca' d'Oro. Admission L6,000. Open daily 9–2.*

CHIESA DELLA MADONNA DELL'ORTO • It's not mentioned in your history books, but this quiet church is a good break from the crowds. Marble Gothic tracery and statues of apostles make a fine facade, but the draw of this 15th-century church is the Tintorettos you'll find inside. Not only are there some striking earlier works, but the painter himself (or rather his remains) are in the chapel to the right of the choir. *Campo Madonna dell'Orto. Admission L3,000. Open Mon.–Sat. 10–5, Sun. 1–5.*

GHETTO EBREO • A symbol of oppression, and at times tolerance, the Jewish Ghetto holds an uneasy place in Venice's history. Jews were first allowed to live in the city in 1381, when the policy makers in the Palazzo Ducale ignored the objections of priests and welcomed them. Many were merchants with money, and Venice badly needed funds to defend the lagoon against an invading navy from Pisa. The opposition never fully ceased, however, and in 1516 all Jews were moved into an area called the Ghetto—actually an island separated from the rest of Cannaregio by canals. The neighborhood was locked at night as much to keep the Jews in as to keep looters out: Before you cross the bridge into the Campo Ghetto Nuovo, look for holes cut into the paving stones for the old gates. The neighborhood was allowed to expand twice, but with the densest population in the city, there still wasn't room for everyone (notice the nine-story buildings—the tallest apartment blocks in Venice). In 1797 the gates were finally torn down by Napoléon, but the Jews didn't move out—partially because of habit, partially because nobody would sell them property anywhere else—until the fascists deported them to Germany during World War II. A series of bas-relief plaques in the Campo del Ghetto Nuovo is dedicated to the Venetian Jews murdered by the Nazis in concentration camps. Today you can enjoy the hip neighborhood's friendly synagogue and good restaurants.

The **Museo Communità Ebraica** houses a small collection of Torah screens and other Judaica; there's also an hourly guided tour (L10,000) of the five beautiful synagogues still in use. *Cannaregio 2902/B, on Campo del Ghetto Nuovo, tel. 041/715359. On train station–Ponte di Rialto route, cross 1st bridge, turn left on Fondamenta di Cannaregio, right on Calle del Ghetto Vecchio, and continue over bridge into Campo Ghetto Nuovo. Admission L5,000. Open Sun.–Fri. 10–5:30.*

> *Venice could be described as a mix of Paul Klee's Magic Garden and Jackson Pollock's Eyes in the Heat. Check out the artists' versions for yourself at the Collezione Peggy Guggenheim.*

SANTA CROCE

This mostly working-class neighborhood was eaten up in the last century by the nasty necessities of modernity: Santa Croce is home to the city's only parking lot, the railroad service yard, the **Stazione Marittima** (the commercial and cruise-ship port), and numerous touristy hotels and restaurants. The only reason to come here is to visit the neglected stepsister of the Collezione Peggy Guggenheim, **Ca' Pesaro** (Fondamenta Pesaro, tel. 041/721127; admission L5,000), Venice's *other* museum of modern art. It's fairly dull except for a few good pieces and the occasional traveling exhibition. At press time, it was closed for restoration until 2001.

SAN POLO

Separated by the Canal Grande, the districts of San Polo and San Marco have always enjoyed an intense rivalry. Until the Ponte di Rialto was rebuilt, the drawbridge of the old wooden structure was raised at night to prevent easy comings and goings between the two districts. Although the lesser-known San Polo doesn't have the spectacle of its haughty neighbor across the canal, it does have fewer tourists, a handful of palazzi on **Campo San Polo,** and some of the city's greatest works of art in the **Scuola Grande di San Rocco** (*see* Worth Seeing, *above*). San Polo's **Mercato di Rialto** (*see* Where to Eat, *above*) has been Venice's marketplace since the first Italians forsook the mainland for the lagoon. Before you leave San Polo, pop into the 17th-century **Chiesa di San Pantalon** (Campo San Pantalon, across bridge from Campo di Santa Margherita). Look up at the ceiling to see the largest canvas painting ever, an over-the-top trompe l'oeil masterpiece that took 24 years to paint. The artist, Fumiani, had just finished the painting when he fell off the scaffoldings to his death.

SANTA MARIA GLORIOSA DEI FRARI • The bulky brick frame of Venice's largest church—called I Frari—is balanced by the delicate art inside: the interior walls are covered with countless canvases and panels, including works by Titian and Bellini. This is also where Titian, Canova, Monteverdi (who composed *Orfeo,* the world's first opera), and a handful of doges are engaged in their big sleeps. The present incarnation dates from the early 15th century, when the gargantuan church was erected on a campo so small that it's impossible to get a full view of the church from the outside. *Campo dei Frari, tel. 041/5222637. From San Polo side of Ponte di Scalzi, walk down Fondamenta San Simeòn Piccolo to Chiesa di San Simeòn Piccolo and follow San Marco trail. Admission L3,000, free Sun. Open Mon.–Sat. 10–5:30, Sun. 1– 5:30, 3–5:30 in winter.*

DORSODURO

Often called "the Greenwich Village of Venice," the Dorsoduro has the bulk of students and grunge types, galleries, trinket stores, and bookshops, mostly thanks to the presence of the 15th-century **Ca' Foscari,** the main building of the **Università di Venezia.** Despite the presence of the big-name **Galleria dell'Accademia** and **Collezione Peggy Guggenheim** (*see* Worth Seeing, *above*), streets here are populated more by Venetians than anybody else. Catch a cross section of the locals in triangular **Campo di Santa Margherita,** which has outdoor cafés, book stalls, wine shops, restaurants, and two trees. The campo comes into its own at dusk, when everybody arrives to drink an aperitif, get in some quick shopping, and watch little kids practicing the futile art of biking.

CA' REZZONICO • The home of Venice's museum of the *settecento* (1700s) is an ornate late-17th-century palazzo jammed with so many whirling moldings, carved tables, and fluttery sconces that you'd think they didn't know how to draw a straight line back then. Tiepolo, Venice's last great painter, is well represented here, though after viewing his swirly paintings in their equally fluffy context, you may need to head to the Guggenheim Collection for a strong dose of cubism. *Dorsoduro 3136, on Fondamenta Rezzonico, tel. 041/2418506. Vaporetto 1 to Ca' Rezzonico. Admission L12,000. Open Mon.–Thurs. and Sat. 10–4. At press time the museum was closed for restoration.*

GIUDECCA • Though officially a part of the Dorsoduro, the islands of the Giudecca, with working-class populations and public housing, feel as if they should be out of sight in the lagoon. The islands were first inhabited by noble families who were dishonored enough to be banished but important enough to stay in Venice. These nobles-in-exile developed a sort of upper-class suburb, complete with villas and gardens, where they entertained the likes of Michelangelo and commissioned two churches by Palladio. The 16th-century **Zitelle** (Fondamenta delle Zitelle; open weekdays 9–noon) has been converted into a contemporary culture factory with enough galleries to mount several exhibitions simultaneously. Most shows are fairly interesting and free (look for posters around town). **Il Redentore** (Fondamenta San Giacomo; open daily 8–noon and 4- -6), also designed by Palladio, was built in 1577 to hold all the people the government promised to bring before God each year to commemorate the city's redemption from the plague. Little did Palladio know that the event would be the excuse for some seriously secular partying in the **Festa del Redentore** (*see* Festivals, *below*).

SANTA MARIA DELLA SALUTE • Despite the popular preoccupation with the Basilica di San Marco, this church's soaring domes and twirling buttresses will probably make a longer-lasting impression on you. Santa Maria della Salute (St. Mary of Health) was built in the 17th century as a thank-you to the Virgin Mary for saving Venice from yet another plague, although half of the city's population died anyway. The half of Venice still around spared no expense, tirelessly hammering 1,156,627 timber piles into the lagoon sludge for the church's foundation and lavishly decorating the building both inside and out. It was dedicated in 1687, and every November 21 the city lights candles and organizes a boat-bridge to the church (*see* Festivals, *below*). The highlight is the **sacristy,** home to some of Titian's major works and Tintoretto's amazing *The Wedding at Cana. Campo della Salute, tel. 041/5225558. Vaporetto 1 to Campo della Salute; or from Collezione Peggy Guggenheim, follow Calle San Cristoforo, cross 3 bridges to campo. Suggested donation: L2,000. Open daily 9–noon and 3–5:30.*

SAN MARCO

The Piazza San Marco (*see* Worth Seeing, *above*) is an unavoidable must-see, but if you have the energy, spend some time wandering the more subdued parts of the district.

PALAZZO FORTUNY • Mariano Fortuny y Madrazo, painter, photographer, architect, engraver, and filthy-rich fabric designer, bought the early 15th-century Palazzo Pesaro in 1889 and turned the place into a school of design, with stores and workshops on the first floor, a chemist's studio on the second, silks on the walls, and artsy people doing artsy things in every nook and cranny. The products produced here demanded an amazing amount of craftsmanship: some of the fabrics were sewn with Murano glass beads and some embroidered with gold thread, while unbleached velvets were brushed with rare pigments. The odd and luxurious stuff Fortuny came up with is all on display, but the palazzo is best when a traveling exhibition—usually photography—passes through. *San Marco 3780, on Campo San Benedetto, tel. 041/5200995. On Ponte dell'Accademia–Ponte di Rialto route, left after Campo Sant'Angelo on Salizzada Chiesa e Teatro, which spills into Campo San Benedetto. Admission L6,000. Open Tues.–Sun. 9–7.*

PALAZZO GRASSI • The last palazzo built on the Canal Grande, Palazzo Grassi was converted into a gallery for traveling shows in 1986 by Gae Aulenti, architect of the Musée d'Orsay in Paris. The massive 18th-century palazzo is now *the* premier space for temporary exhibitions in Italy- –whatever's inside will probably blow you away. *San Marco 3231, on Campo San Samuele, tel. 041/5231680. Vaporetto 2 to San Samuele; or from Campo Sant'Angelo, west on Calle dei Frati, right on Calle delle Botteghe, which becomes Calle Lungo Crosera, and left on Salizzada San Samuele, which leads to Campo San Samuele. Admission L12,000–L14,000—varies with exhibitions. Open daily 10–7.*

SAN GIORGIO MAGGIORE • The best example of Palladian "harmony" and "purity" is the facade of this church on the Isola di San Giorgio, just east of Giudecca. In the 1400s, the architects of Florence had decided on the perfect proportions for the interior of a church, but what looked good on the inside could be viewed as a blocky square set on a squat rectangle on the outside. Palladio succeeded not only in synthesizing the two awkward parts of the exterior but in unifying the facade with the interior. If all that doesn't float your boat, the church has some great Tintorettos, a far-reaching view of the lagoon from the tower, and a quiet old monk who sells jars of honey next to the transept. *Isola di San Giorgio Maggiore, tel. 041/5227827. From San Zaccaria, Vaporetto 82 to San Giorgio. Open Mon.–Sat. 10–12:30 and 2:30–4, Sun. 9.30–10:30 and 2.30–4.30.*

TEATRO LA FENICE • Tucked away to the side of the small Campo San Fantin, La Fenice—once one of the world's finest opera houses—is now a web of scaffolding and charred innards. Proving lightning (in this case a spark) does strike the same place twice, La Fenice burned down for the second time (it was rebuilt in 1837 after the first fire) in the middle of the night in January 1996. Along with La Scala in Milan, it was once the fulcrum of 19th-century Italian opera, premiering some of Verdi's works. Rossini, Bellini, and Donizetti had all composed operas for the first Fenice. As Venice lost its gilt and glory, La Fenice declined in importance, presenting a series of responsible, uninspiring operas to local devotees. But the 1990s fire has, shall we say, rekindled interest, and the grand benefit concerts sometimes outshine the operas. Opera season, by the way, can't be stopped by a meager flame. Performances continue to be held at **Pala La Fenice**, a large tentlike temporary stage set up in the Tronchetto (accessible by Vaporetto 4 or 82 or a special *FeniceBus* from P. Roma). Pick up tickets (from about L25,000) from Cassa di Risparmio (Campo San Luca near San Marco, tel. 041/5210161) and grab a schedule from the APT. If you can't afford tickets, show your support by indulging in a cocktail for a mere L2,500 at **Bar La Fenice** (Campo San Fantin; open Mon.–Sat. until 2 AM), the glammed-out still-open theater bar and the only legal place to buy cigarettes in Venice after 8 PM.

> *The word ghetto is Venetian in origin—it comes from the ghetti, or metal foundries, that once stood in the area.*

CASTELLO

The Castello has two faces—one expresses the glamorous artistic and political traditions of Venice, while the other is calm and almost without history. The first part of Castello, comprising the streets and canals extending eastward out of San Marco, is home to stunning churches like 15th-century **San Zaccaria** (just off Riva degli Schiavoni, not far from the San Marco border), grand palazzi, and overpriced pizza joints and plastic gondola stands that cater to tourists. By the time you've wandered out by the **Arsenale** (*see below*), however, anybody who isn't Venetian is either lost or a serious explorer. On **Via Garibaldi** you'll find fruit stalls, low-budget trattorias, and old men and women who do nothing but smoke, chat, shop, and drink wine all day.

ARSENALE • In the 12th century, Venice constructed a walled port and dry dock as a place to build war galleys. Called the Arsenale, it became the most important ship factory in Europe: Dante raved about it in Canto XXI of *L'Inferno,* and one of Columbus's ships was built here. The Arsenale was in its heyday in the 14th and 15th centuries, when it produced at least one ship per day and the Venetian navy was the world's most powerful. It's still a base for the Italian navy, so most of the Arsenale is closed to the public, but check out the facade for the best lion sculptures in Venice. Near the Arsenale, the **Museo Storico Navale** (Castello 2148, on Riva degli Schiavoni, tel. 041/5200276; admission L2,000) has model warships and re-creations of the Republic's naval battles, not to mention Peggy Guggenheim's gondola (she was the last person in Venice to have a private gondolier). *Vaporetto 1 to Arsenale; or from P. San Marco, left on Riva degli Schiavoni, cross 5 bridges, and left on Fondamenta dell'Arsenale. Open Mon.–Sat. 8:45–1.*

SANTI GIOVANNI E PAOLO • This enormous, dusty 13th-century Gothic creation is not just a church but a warehouse of body parts. Its collection includes the foot of Santa Caterina of Siena; the skin of Marcantonio Bragdin, a war hero flayed alive by the Turks in 1571 (the urn is in the right aisle just after the entrance); and the remains of no fewer than 25 doges. Like I Frari, this church has both schlock and masterpieces strewn across its walls—some of the more interesting pieces are Giovanni Bellini's elegant *Polyptych of San Vicenzo* and a New Testament cycle by Veronese. *Campo SS Giovanni e Paolo, tel. 041/5235913. From train station–Ponte di Rialto route, walk to Chiesa di SS Apostoli and follow the blue OSPEDALE signs. Open Mon.–Sat. 7:30–12:30 and 3–6, Sun. 3–5:30.*

SCUOLA DI SAN GIORGIO DEGLI SCHIAVONI • In 1451 the Senate granted the Venetian Schiavoni (Slavs) the right to build their own *scuola* (a kind of guild). At the time, Venice, Hungary, and the Ottomans were all coveting the Dalmatian coast, the eastern part of the Adriatic in Croatia. By bringing the Slavs into the fold, Venice hoped to gain their voluntary subjugation; they responded favorably, commissioning Carpaccio to paint a cycle of paintings about St. George and the Dragon and St. Jerome and the Lion. The building hasn't been touched since the 1600s, and the dark, hushed downstairs room helps you imagine what the meetings of the scuola must have been like. *Castello, on Ponte dei Greci, tel. 041/5228828. From P. San Marco, walk east on Fondamenta degli Schiavoni, cross 4 bridges, take 1st left, cross Campo Bandiera e Moro to Salizzada San Antonin, veer left, and continue straight. Admission L5,000. Open Tues.–Sat. 10–12:30 and 3–6:30, Sun. 10–12:30.*

CHEAP THRILLS

When little man Bonaparte occupied Venice, he decided the city needed a proper bourgeois, pseudo-Parisian park. He ordered buildings destroyed—that they were the very monasteries, churches, and *scuole* that most resisted his rule didn't hurt—and in 1810 Venice sprouted the **Giardini Pubblici,** a good place to rediscover trees after days spent wandering through the glories of the Renaissance. Every other year, the park hosts the **Biennale** (*see* Festivals, *below*). To get here, take Vaporetto 1, 52, or 82 to the Giardini stop, or from Piazza San Marco, turn left on Riva degli Schiavoni and keep on walking past the giant cement sculpture of a hand until you run smack into green.

If you're feeling broke but very suave, skip the clunky vaporetti and cruise over to the Giudecca on the private launch with the HOTEL CIPRIANI sign; it's next to the Giardini Ex Reali on the fondamenta behind Piazza San Marco. Just be somewhat well-dressed and -coiffed, with an attitude. Along the same lines, you can catch a glimpse of Venice's former grandeur by popping into the 14th-century Palazzo Dandolo, now the four-star Hotel Danieli (Fondamenta degli Schiavoni, 1 bridge east of P. San Marco). Take a peek at the elegant Gothic staircase and its marble paneling, then leave quietly.

FESTIVALS

Every other summer for the last 100 years, the art world has attended the **Biennale di Venezia,** a huge schmooze fest where 30-odd nations display the works of fairly avant-garde artists in little pavilions in the back of the Giardini Pubblici. Although artsy insiders lament the dearth of creativity, the unique pavilions and their bucolic setting make it worth the vaporetto ride and the L18,000 entrance fee. The next Biennale is in 2001, but at press time, it was too early for any specifics; it's usually held from mid-June to the end of September. Call 041/5218711 and an English-speaking staff will give you the scoop, or check the Web site, www.labiennale.org—also check posters in town.

FEBRUARY AND MARCH

Carnevale in Venice is a week-long costume party featuring drunken revelers in outfits that have been planned for months. Parades and performances incorporating the traditional Venetian versions of commedia dell'arte masks and costumes are held more or less daily. Though the costumes are traditional, the modern Carnevale has only been celebrated for about 15 years. The more cynical see it as a ploy to lure tourists here in the off-season, but locals seem to enjoy themselves anyway. The date varies, but it's always in February or at the beginning of March, right before the start of Lent. Merrymaking—wine, kisses, hidden identities—flows throughout the city but not surprisingly always seems to wind its way back to Piazza San Marco.

MAY

Also a recently cultivated event, the **volgalonga** is a 32-km (20-mi) rowing marathon open to anyone with a boat. Participants—some in wildly decorated craft, some in sleek high-tech machines, and others in tubs that barely float—row their way from San Marco to Burano (*see* Near Venice, *below*) and back. The event usually falls on Ascension Sunday, in May or June, when the mayor performs the ritual of La Sensa. Formerly a solemn, symbolic procession during which the doge would toss a ring into the water to celebrate Venice's "marriage" to the sea, it's now a tourist mess that's better avoided.

JULY

On the third Sunday in July, Venice holds the **Festa del Redentore,** an offer of thanks to Jesus for ending a plague back in the 1500s. A makeshift pontoon bridge is built from Venice's main island to the church of Il Redentore on the Giudecca (*see* Districts, *above*). The real fun comes at night, when an unbelievable fireworks display explodes over thousands of inebriated Venetians clamoring from streamer-covered cargo launches and trash barges turned into floating dinner parties; it starts at about 11:15 PM and lasts until midnight. Sweet-talk your way—it ain't too hard—onto a local's boat, or watch the show from the Giudecca's fondamenta.

AUGUST AND SEPTEMBER

In late August and September, Venice's **International Film Festival** (tel. 041/5241320) is *the* film industry kiss-up and show-off party, second only to Cannes. Films are generally shown on the Lido, and tickets—if you can get them—are worth the usually excellent offerings. Call the Biennale's office (tel. 041/5218711), or ask at the tourist office for info, or check it out at www.film festivals.com/list/. The best of foreign and Italian films are shown at the **Palazzo del Cinema** (tel. 041/5260188) and the **Astra** (V. Corfù, tel. 041/5260289). Admission is around L10,000, unless it's the opening-night gala (about L25,000); expect long lines.

On the first Sunday in September, Venice holds the **Regatta Storica**—half boat race, half waterborne parade—with a procession of historically evocative boats toting people dressed as the doge and his entourage. The race is only for experts—usually burly gondoliers—so it's a lot more exciting to watch than the everyone-wins volgalonga.

The church of Santa Maria dei Miracoli, in Cannaregio, is famous throughout the Catholic world for its unspectacular painting of the Madonna, supposedly endowed with the power to raise the dead and perform sundry other divine acts.

NOVEMBER

Yet another plague festival, the **Salute,** on November 21, is a more somber event than the Redentore. The pious light candles and pray, and a string of boats crosses the Canal Grande from San Marco to the church of Santa Maria della Salute.

SHOPPING

The likelihood of having money left over after paying to sleep, eat, and be culturally enriched in Venice might be very slim, but good deals can be ferreted out. The most blatantly commercial area is the **Mercerie,** which starts behind the Torre dell'Orologio in Piazza San Marco; stores here sell mostly clothing and expensive crafts. On **Strada Nova,** in Cannaregio, the shops are a lot cheaper. Venice is famous for its glass and masks, both of which range from cheap schlock to astoundingly expensive art. Almost anyone who sells these things will ship them home for you or package them so that you can get them home with a little care. Most shops stay open until around 7 or 8 and take credit cards.

GLASS

There are a lot of tchotchkes to wade through—like gaudy animal trinkets and chandeliers—but some stuff is tasteful and artistic. Venice's shops, like **Quattro D** (Cannaregio 326, on Ponte delle Guglie, tel. 041/717444), have a decent selection, but your best bet is to head to Murano (*see* Near Venice, *below*), where the glass is actually made. Here you'll find more artistic pieces and better prices. **G.D. Furlan Export** (Fondamenta Navagero 41/A, Murano, tel. 041/739842) has funky bottles in bright colors for L50,000 (expect to pay L95,000 in Venice). **Artisiano Vetraio** (Fondamenta Manin 56, Murano, tel. 041/739454) has glass that ranges from unusual L12,000 rings to beautiful L100,000 jars.

LACE

Venice's shops are pricey, and Burano (the "lace island"; *see* Near Venice, *below*) makes your head swim, but the lace is beautiful, less expensive, and easy to pack. Take note that much of the lace and embroidered linen sold in Venice and on Burano are really made in China or Taiwan. Expect to pay around L50,000 for shirts, L150,000–L200,000 for tablecloths, and a mere L2,000 for doilies. At **Norelene** (Calle de la Chiesa 727, near the Accademia, tel. 041/5237605) you'll find wonderful hand-printed fabrics.

MASKS

Carnevale's (*see above*) commedia dell'arte masks and costumes are elaborate and beautiful. For purchasing or just browsing, try **Mondo Novo** (Dorsoduro 3063, near Campo di Santa Margherita, tel. 041/5231607) for pure art. **La Venexiana Atelier** (San Marco 1135, on Frezzeria San Marco, tel. 041/5286888) has lushly decorated costumes and masks and books on the carnival.

COCKTAILS
VENETIAN STYLE

Forget that martini or cosmopolitan and see how it's done in Venice. The Bellini, peach juice with champagne or Prosecco, is heavenly at Harry's Bar (Calle Vallaresso 1323, tel. 041/5285777), where it was perfected by bartender Claudio Ponzio, or at Ai Sportivi (Campo di Santa Margherita, tel. 041/5211598). Fragolino is a Veneto specialty—a sweet, spicy, nectarlike wine, usually red. After dinner, indulge in an exquisite sgroppino, a whip of lemon sorbet and vodka, at Haig's American Bar (San Marco 2477/B, tel. 041/5232368). But the true Venetian drink is the spritzer, white wine and seltzer water ordered bitter (with Campari) or all'aperol, with orange bitters. You haven't lived the good life until you've sipped a spritzer at Bar Rosso (see Caffè and Gelaterie in Where to Eat, above).

The wineshop Casa Mattiazzi Vini e Spumanti sells excellent, cheap wine by the liter. Grab an empty bottle, jar, or laundry tub and bring it in; they'll fill it up with red, white, or sparkling wines from their wooden vats. There are locations in Campo di Santa Margherita (tel. 041/5231979), in Castello (on V. Garibaldi, tel. 041/5224893), and at Castello 5179 (on Calle Lunga near Santa Maria Formosa, tel. 041/5237592).

PAPER

The marbled paper you see everywhere—on boxes, pencils, even portfolios—is the signature stationery of Venice. **Carta e Penna** (San Marco 4340, on Calle dei Fuseri, tel. 041/5223055) sells stationery sets (L15,000). **Il Pavone** (San Polo 1478, on Campiello dei Meori, tel. 041/5224296) has elegant, hand-inked journals for L20,000–L40,000 and artists at work next to the cash register.

AFTER DARK

You love the nightlife. You've got to boogie. Not in this town, baby. If you want to go clubbing in summer, you have to go to Mestre or the Lido, but if you're looking to get tipsy while listening to music, you won't be too disappointed. Classical music is the real scene here—check with the APT for a list of current concerts.

The most happening *passeggiata* (social evening stroll) locations are Campo San Polo, the Zattere, and Campo di Santa Margherita. Campo San Polo hosts an **open-air cinema** from mid-June to the end of the International Film Festival (*see* Festivals, *above*) in September. Films are mostly Italian-dubbed Hollywood blockbusters that cost around L9,000, but watching them from the campo, you'll be reminded more of *Cinema Paradiso* than *The English Patient.* Pick up "Cinema all'Aperto" from the APT for screening times. **Cinema Olimpia** (San Marco 1094, in Campo San Gallo, tel. 041/5205439) runs two weekly screenings in English. Don't expect art films.

BARS

The Venetian version of a pub crawl is called a *giro (tour) di ombra.* An ombra is a tiny glass of wine, drunk in a gulp, that costs around L2,000; you're not supposed to drink more than one in any one place. The name comes from the traditional way wine was sold—big vats of the stuff were sold outdoors in the ombra (shade) of buildings. *See box* Cocktails Venetian Style, *above,* for an explanation of other traditional Venetian drinks and the bars where you can sample them.

Most bars in Venice close between 10 PM and midnight, though the ones listed below stay open a little later. Bars cluster along Fondamenta della Misericordia in Cannaregio and Campo di Santa Margherita in Dorsoduro.

Caffè Blu. This comfortable, popular bar has loud music (sometimes live) and beers starting at L4,000. Happy hour is actually one hour, 8:30–9:30, and you'll hear it before you see it. *Dorsoduro 3778, on Salizzada San Pantalon, tel. 041/5237227. Closed Sun.*

Devil's Forest Pub. This is a favored hangout for many young Venetians. *Calle dei Stagneri 5185, off Campo San Bartolomeo, tel. 041/5200623. Closed Mon.*

Paradiso Perduto. The most popular bar on the Misericordia is home base for traveling hipsters, though things are much more low-key in winter. The package includes occasional live jazz, a goateed clientele, and gruff, ponytailed bartenders. The food here is excellent and not too expensive. Drinks run L2,000– L7,000, but the price goes up when the band plays. *Cannaregio 2540, on Fondamenta della Misericordia, tel. 041/720581. From Ghetto, cross Rio di San Girolamo and turn right. Closed Wed.*

MUSIC

Venice has little to offer in the way of rock music; check the ubiquitous posters for concerts that are staged on the Lido and in Mestre. For jazz, you'll have to catch a weekly performance at Paradiso Perduto (*see above*). The real music scene in Venice is **classical.** Many churches, especially I Frari (*see* Districts, *above*), hold classical concerts, though the choice of music tends toward the solemn. **Santa Maria della Pietà** (Riva degli Schiavoni), called Chiesa Vivaldi, holds frequent concerts with music by Vivaldi and others. **Teatro La Fenice** (San Marco 1965, tel. 041/5210161) was famous for its opera and concerts—during its restoration (a result of the fire in 1996),

According to legend, Lucifer himself can be seen at the banisterless Devil's Bridge on Torcello. The bridge received its name when people fell off it after a night in a pub, later claiming, "The devil made me do it!"

performances are being held in a temporary outdoor tent (*see* Districts, *above*). **Teatro Goldoni** (San Marco 4650/B, tel. 041/5205422) hosts a range of concerts and puts on several Italian plays. Check posters or with the tourist office for upcoming events.

NEAR VENICE

The tourist office tries to sell the islands of Venice's lagoon as just another shopping venue, but in reality they're uncrowded, cool little places to explore—just a short, relaxing boat ride from Venice. The **Lido** is its own multi-island entity, but **Murano, Burano,** and **Torcello** together make an excellent day trip. Vaporetto 12 stops in Murano and Burano; Vaporetto 14 goes to two Lido stops (Punta Sabbioni and Treporti), Burano, and Torcello; and Vaporetti 23 and 52 go between San Zaccaria and Murano, sometimes stopping at the Lido and San Michele. Most tickets to the lagoon are the standard price (L6,000 one-way, L10,000 round-trip).

MURANO

This island, most famous for its glassworks, really has little else to offer: glass factories just aren't all that scenic. But the blowing process is something to behold. Look for FORNACE signs to witness artists at work. From the vaporetto stop, cross the bridge to Fondamenta Venier to get the best deals on glass goods. At the **Museo Vetrario di Murano** (Fondamenta Giustinian 8, tel. 041/739586; open Thurs.–Tues. 10–5, 4 in winter), pay L8,000 (combined ticket L17,000 also admits you to Museo Correr, Palazzo Ducale, and Scuola di Merletti—*see above*) to see a nifty exhibit of glass through the ages. The church of **Santi Maria e Donato** (behind the Fondamenta Venier, tel. 041/739056; open daily 8–noon and 4–7) has an old, prime example of a mosaic floor. The intricate floor was assembled in the 12th century, when the Byzantine church was rebuilt after a fire. If your stomach calls, you'll find a lot of cheap, authentic restaurants here. For some local color head for **Osteria La Perla ai Bisatei** (Campo San Bernardo 1, tel. 041/ 739528; closed Wed.). Everyone from stolid grandfathers to punks gathers here for filling meals that average L20,000 (with wine). There's no menu, but your waitperson will happily give you the rundown.

BURANO

"Lace island" probably isn't a compelling enough description of Burano to make you want to visit, but this old fishing community is extremely pretty and tranquil. The island's bright pink and red houses look like they were conjured up in somebody's dream, and the delicate cookies baked here make Burano everyone's favorite lagoon island. The tradition of lacemaking has been revived for the tourists, so you'll see a lot of stout old women making lace by hand in chairs in shops. The **Scuola di Merletti di Burano** (P. Galuppi, tel. 041/730034; open Wed.–Mon. 9–5, 10–4 in winter) has lace dating from the 16th century. Admission is L8,000 (for combined L17,000 ticket, *see above*), and you can see workers do their thing 9–1 and 2:30–6. Burano's main street leads to a grassy, tree-shaded area facing the sea. Bring a picnic to avoid having to buy food in the overpriced restaurants and *alimentari* (small grocery stores). If you do decide to eat here, the restaurants along Fondamenta Galuppi serve seafood dishes for L17,000–L22,000.

TORCELLO

You'd never know it now, but this deserted, swampy island was once the most thickly populated in the lagoon—about 200,000 people lived here in its heyday, though only a handful remain. One of the only remnants of Torcello's 15 minutes of fame is the **Cattedrale di Torcello**, a.k.a. Santa Maria Assunta (follow route from vaporetto stop, tel. 041/730084; admission L4,000, open 10:30–12:30 and 2–5). Built in the 7th century and rebuilt in the 9th, the church has astonishing 11th- and 12th-century mosaics that are simpler than those in San Marco. Especially beautiful is the 12th-century *Madonna col Bambino* in the apse. The hulking **Chair of Attila** in the square belonged to the notorious Hun. If you have time, walk down to the swampy parts of the island (off the main walkway) and search for pottery shards dating from who knows when, or get prepackaged shards from the archaeological museum, **Museo dell'Estuario** (in the Palazzo del Consiglio, tel. 041/730761; admission L3000), open Tuesday–Sunday 10:30–12:30 and 2–6.

SAN MICHELE

Even when dead in Venice, it's tough to find digs. San Michele, the cemetery island for Venice since the Napoleonic era, is packed with bureau-drawer crypts, with bodies stacked five high in some places. Even so, the price of resting your body here is so high that most Venetian families buy leases for their deceased, whose bones are moved to an ossuary years later—Igor Stravinsky and Ezra Pound get to stay, though. The cemetery is overgrown and decrepit, and the spookiest part is the old caretaker who lives here among all the tombstones. The first Renaissance church in Venice, **San Michele in Isola**, and its baptistery stand alone here. The cemetery is open 7:30–4.

THE LIDO

The tragic elegance of the Lido (Litorale di Lido) in Thomas Mann's *Death in Venice* is now the tragic scuzzy aftermath of too much pollution and not enough sand. Nevertheless, many Venetians still come here in summer to escape the throngs. If looking at water all day has also made you desperate for a swim, **Blue Moon** (down V. Santa Maria Elizabeth from the vaporetto stop), the free public beach, is less toxic than the canals. Rent bikes at **Lazzari Bruno** (Gran V. Santa Maria Elisabetta 21/B, tel. 041/5268019) daily 8:30–8 for about L5,000 an hour, L15,000 per day. Near San Nicolò on Via Cipro (go left from the vaporetto stop and right on V. Cipro) is the **Cimitero Ebraico** (Jewish Cemetery), a quiet, green place on the grounds of the church of San Nicolò. The gravestones tell the history of the Venetian Jewish community since the cemetery's founding in 1386; also *see* Ghetto Ebreo *in* Districts, *above*. Northeast of the Litorale di Lido, the island **Litorale di Cavallino** is full of cheap hotels that might have space in the summer (ask at the APT office in the train station), but the resorty island called **Lido di Jesolo**, to the east of Cavallino, has better public beaches. To reach the main Lido island, take **ACVO** buses (L7,000) from Piazzale Roma (they get ferried to the Lido), or take Vaporetto 14 to Punta Sabbioni on Litorale del Cavallino and catch the bus from there.

VENETO

Venice's influence can be felt throughout the Veneto, but if you escape the wealthy, boutique-filled city centers, you'll find that each Veneto town has a distinct personality and plenty of local flavor. Marble-covered **Verona** has an excess of charisma and architecture dating from Roman times. The university city of **Padua** has Giotto's Cappella degli Scrovegni, as well as a schizophrenic mix of Veneto snobbery and uni-

versity worldliness. Slick **Vicenza** had Andrea Palladio in charge of its 16th-century urban renewal. **Treviso** is the home of the mighty tiramisu, known to fantasy-dessert lovers everywhere. Towns like the snazzy ski resort of **Cortina D'Ampezzo** are full of look-at-me *Veneti* on vacation, but if you stick to the less advertised cities, you can enjoy fields of sunflowers and tap into local legends like the *Alice in Wonderland*-style chess match— though no Kasparov–versus–Deep Blue matchup—in Marostica. Regional specialties, such as cream-filled meringues, Bassano del Grappa's legendary grappa, and the sparkling, champagnelike Prosecco are reason enough to wander through these parts. A wine better known locally, Valpolicella, will turn you as pink as the namesake marble that coats the province in rosy hues.

PADUA

A city of both high-rises and history, Padua (Padova) is not as beautiful as its counterparts in the Veneto but it's cheaper, more convenient, and mellower. The main reason for the city's laid-back attitude is its university, the second oldest in Italy. Built in the 13th century, it was frequented by brainy types like Dante and Galileo. Most students commute to school, so you won't see them between July and September or on weekends, but they leave their legacy behind in cheap restaurants, theme bars, and English-language bookstores. Because of the university, Padua was a target for bombs during World War II. For the next 20-odd years, the government gave developers free rein to smash churches and replace them with ugly-but-functional buildings. Still, the heart of the city remains dominated by arcaded walkways and Gothic structures. Here you'll find the snooty shopping-bag-and-scooter set—the sons and daughters of Padua's nouveaux riches. You'll notice they share the town with a friendlier mix of intellectuals and street punks.

BASICS

The friendly **APT** office (tel. 049/8752077; open summer, Mon.–Sat. 9–7, Sun. 8:30–12:30; winter, Mon.–Sat. 9:15–5:45, Sun. 9–noon) in the train station stocks the most comprehensive source of info, the free *Padova Today;* it's a toned-down version of the booklet they want money for. For a $3 charge, they'll exchange money and cash traveler's checks. The best place to change your money is **Banca Antoniana** (P. Frutte 39 tel. 049/839111; open weekdays 8:20- -1:20 and 2:35–3:35), where you get the highest rates anywhere with no commission. An **American Express** representative is at Tiarè Viaggi (V. Risorgimento 20, tel. 049/666133; open weekdays 9–1 and 3–7). They won't change money, but if you're a cardholder and need an advance of up to $1,000 on a personal check, write it here, and they'll give you a slip to take to the bank for cash.

COMING AND GOING

The large **train station** (P. Stazione Ferrovia, tel. 147/888088) has trains to Venice (every 15–30 min, 30 min, L4,100), Milan (hourly, 3 hrs, L31,500), Rome (8 daily, 6 hrs, L59,500), Florence (every 2 hrs, 3 hrs, L28,500), Bologna (hourly, 1½ hrs, L16,60), and Bassano del Grappa (10 daily, 1 hr, L4,800). The luggage office (closed 1:30 AM–4:40 AM) charges L5,000 per piece for 12 hours.

The **SITA** station (Piazzale Boschetti, tel. 049/8206844) has buses to Bassano del Grappa (every 30 min, L6,000), Montagnana (hourly, L6,000), and Venice (hourly, L5,500). From the train station, walk up Corso del Popolo and turn left on Via Trieste.

GETTING AROUND

The walled city center—tiny one-way streets, piazza after piazza, and arcaded walkways that look eerily alike—can be covered on foot in about an hour. There's one main street through the center, but it changes names frequently, starting at the train station as **Corso del Popolo,** becoming Corso Garibaldi, Via Cavour, Via VIII Febbraio, Via Roma, and finally Via Umberto I. Via Umberto I runs to the gigantic ugly oval at the south end of the center, **Prato della Valle** (which you should avoid at night). The main piazzas (**Erbe, Frutte,** and **Signori**) are west of this main street. The **university** district lies to the east.

Though it's walkable, the 20-minute tramp from the train station into town is dull and a little taxing with luggage—save yourself and take the bus. The main **ACAP** bus station (V. Risomondo 28, tel.049/8241111) is a bit outside the city walls, past the *fiera* (fairgrounds), but most buses stop at the train station. To reach the center of town or Prato della Valle from the bus station, take Bus 3, 8, or 18 (L1,400); you can buy tickets from the *biglietteria* (ticket office) in front of the station.

WHERE TO SLEEP

If you can handle the 11 PM curfew, the hostel is the cheapest deal in Padua. Hotels fill up in July and August as people seeking hotels in Venice become disillusioned. The local hotels' habit of closing a few weeks in August doesn't help. Beware June 13, the Feast of St. Anthony; it brings traffic and is a sure-fire hotel filler. If the following are full, the APT office in the station (*see* Basics, *above*) has a list of hotels and prices. Holiday houses (rooming houses) pop up July–September; try **Antonianum** (V. Donatello 24, tel. 049/8768711), which has a two-night minimum but offers doubles for L30,000 per person. Most cheap hotels lie southeast of the university.

UNDER L85,000 • Albergo-Locanda La Perla. The friendly guy who runs this place within view of St. Anthony's Basilica has clean doubles for L60,000, but you've gotta deal with sharing a bath, and the stairs can be noisy. *V. Cesarotti 67, 35123, tel. 049/8758939. From P. Santo (basilica), take V. Cesarotti almost to V. San Francesco. 8 rooms without bath. Cash only.*

Albergo Pavia. It's not the most scenic part of town, and the rooms aren't filled with sunshine, but the doubles (L60,000) are large, the staff is casual, and you can *smell* the cleanliness. *V. dei Papafava 11, 35139, tel. 049/661558. From station, take C. del Popolo until it becomes V. VIII Febbraio; turn right on V. Marsala and left on V. dei Papafava. 10 rooms without bath. Cash only.*

Al Santo. You'll get a tiny but scrubbed room here; find the manager in the bar next door. Ask for a room away from the piazza to avoid the noise from nearby Basilica del Santo. Doubles with bath are L80,000. *V. del Santo 147, 35123, ½ block north of P. Santo, tel. and fax 049/8752131. 16 rooms, 11 with bath. Cash only.*

Riviera. The name conjures up something grander, but this hotel has clean doubles (L80,000 with bath, L57,000 without) in a location that straddles the center and Piazza del Santo. *V. Rudena 12, 35123, tel. 049/665413. From Prato della Valle, turn right on V. Belludi, left on Riviera Businello, right on V. Rudena. 10 rooms, 3 with bath. Cash only.*

HOSTEL • Ostello Città di Padova. The staff is friendly and informative; there's always someone around for a chat. The building is well kept and the showers are hot. *Most* of the neighborhood is safe-ish; the "community center" next door is somewhat sketchy. Bed and breakfast costs L22,000, reduced if you make a reservation for three or more nights. *V. Aleardi 30, 35122, tel. 049/8752219. From Prato della Valle, walk toward center on V. Umberto I, left on V. Memmo, right on V. Aleardi. 112 beds. Curfew 11 PM, lockout 9:30 AM–4 PM. Check-in 4 PM–11 PM. Luggage storage. Laundromat L4,000.*

WHERE TO EAT

Whoa—a Veneto town where you can actually afford to eat. Let loose in the daily **market** in twin piazzas Erbe and Frutte, where you'll find deals on everything from peaches to Asiago cheese to horse meat. Old faithful self-service **Brek** (V. Piazzetta Cavour 9, tel. 049/8753788) has consistently cheap fresh salads and pastas, and you get a 10% discount when you show a hostel card.

UNDER L30,000 • Fagiano. Near the Sant'Antonio, Fagiano is a pricey but popular trattoria with locals and tourists. The specialties are hearty standbys: pasta *e fagioli* (and beans) and *fagiano farcito* (stuffed pheasant; L16,000). *V. Locatelli 45, tel. 049/652913. Closed Mon. and last 2 wks in July; no dinner Sun.*

Osteria all'Antica Colonna. A comfortable local place to relax, this *osteria* changes menus daily: Look outside before you come in—there are no menus inside. Primi piatti include pasta with porcini mushrooms, secondi might be a baccalà (cod; L14,000). *V. Altinate 127, tel. 049/8763288. Off V. Zabarella behind P. Eremitani. Closed Sun.*

Primo Piano. The gleaming marble floor leads you into this conveniently sited ristorante/pizzeria with equally convenient prices ranging from L8,000–L15,000. There's a tourist menu at L22,000, and the smoked salmon antipasti are good. *P. del Santo 21, opposite Basilica del Santo, tel. 049/8761919. Closed Wed.*

Trattoria al Pero. Serving typical Veneto food at atypically low prices, this trattoria is usually full of old, emphysemic-looking men. Some of the food may be a little *too* authentic (*trippa* means tripe), but the hungry, adventurous, and omnivorous will have a field day. You can't go wrong with *sedanini al pomodoro* (pasta with tomato sauce; L6,500) or the polenta. *V. Santa Lucia 72, 1 block north of P. dei Signori, tel. 049/8758794. Closed Sun. and Aug.*

WORTH SEEING

If you plan on seeing more than one sight that costs money, the APT's (*see* Basics, *above*) **Biglietto Unico**—a pass that gets you into the Cappella degli Scrovegni, Museo Civico Eremitani, Oratorio San Giorgio, the baptistery, the Orto Botanico, and the Palazzo della Ragione—is worth the L15,000.

BASILICA DEL SANTO • Some critics claim that Catholics are too fervent. Never will you be more tempted to agree than when you see this enormous, incredibly elaborate basilica—all dedicated to Sant'Antonio (St. Anthony, patron saint of lost and found objects). The structure is a strange mix of Gothic, Byzantine, and Renaissance design. Inside you'll find everything from artwork by Donatello—also responsible for the equestrian monument called the *Gattamelata* outside—to the morbid remains of the saint's tongue and jaw in the apse. But the real draw is the people who flood the basilica, praying in tongues that span the globe. Their devotion and their gratitude to "Il Santo" add a touch of spirituality to the circus. *P. del Santo, tel. 049/8242811. Admission free. Open daily 6:30 AM–9:45PM, 6:30 PM in winter.*

CAFFÈ PEDROCCHI • Pedrocchi has more historical significance than your average caffeine pit stop. During the Risorgimento it was a haven for students and intellectuals. On February 8, 1848, it was the seat of a nationalist insurrection—hence the red, white, and green rooms and the commemorative street name outside its door. Pedrocchi is still Padua's most popular spot for an espresso to enhance all that free thinking. The *piano nobile* is worth visiting for rooms decorated in antique styles, including Etruscan, Egyptian, and Moorish. *Piazzetta Pedrocchi, tel. 049/8205007. From station, take C. del Popolo until it becomes V. VIII Febbraio; café is on right. Piano nobile admission L5,000. Open Mon.–Sat. 9:30–12:30 and 3:30–6, Sun. 3:30–6:30.*

In Padua's Cappella degli Scrovegni, look for the "Kiss of Judas" fresco. The torches and weapons in the air create a feeling for the anger and excitement of the crowd; in the center, the quiet figures of Christ and Judas seem to calmly accept their fate.

CAPPELLA DEGLI SCROVEGNI • Hidden inside this tiny chapel is Giotto's New Testament fresco cycle, which is regarded as marking the end of medieval art and the beginning of the Renaissance. Giotto was one of the first painters to conceive of depth existing in pictures—his heady jabs at perspective may seem clumsy today, but this was wild stuff in the 14th century. Luckily Giotto also had a knack for visual storytelling, evident in the lines on Mary's face. The chapel itself is a gift of guilt: Scrovegni commissioned it to atone for the sins of his father, a usurer. *P. Eremitani 8, tel. 049/8204550. From station, walk down C. del Popolo, turn left on P. Eremitani. Admission L10,000. Open daily 9–7 (Nov.–Jan. until 6).*

The ticket to the Cappella degli Scrovegni also admits you to the other museums in the Eremitani complex, including a humdinger of a **Museo Archeologico** (tel. 049/8204550), open Tues.–Sat 9–7, 6 in winter, with some of the best-preserved Roman pieces around. The "modern"—really almost entirely pre-20th century—art museum flounders, but the medieval collection has a few gems, such as Pietro Liberi's *Minerva Armata,* the ultimate woman warrior. The nearby **Chiesa degli Eremitani** (P. Eremitani 10, 049/8756410, open Mon.–Sat. 8:15–12:15 and 4–6, Sun. 9:30–12:15 and 4–6) is unfortunately past its prime; its spectacular Mantegna frescoes were destroyed by bombing in World War II. The **Giardini dell'Arena** (off C. Garibaldi) is generally packed with a mix of visitors fresh from nearby Cappella degli Scrovegni and hippies making, er, transactions.

PALAZZO BO • This palazzo, once part of an ox market, is now the university's main building. *Bò* means ox in local dialect, and the critters were chained by their nose rings to the iron loops where students now lock their bikes. The marble balconies encircling the *teatro anatomico* (anatomy theater) are incredible, and most of the rooms are frescoed or lavishly furnished. Call the **Associazione Guide Turistiche** (tel. 049/8209711) for guided tours (L5,000), Tuesday, Thursday, and Saturday at 9, 10, and 11; Monday, Wednesday, and Friday at 3, 4, and 5. Meet at the university door. *V. VIII Febbraio 2, cater-corner from P. della Ragione.*

PALAZZO DELLA RAGIONE • The Palace of Reason used to hold more of Giotto's masterpieces, but his frescoes were badly damaged by fire in 1420. The restorer wasn't as famous, but they're still good, especially if you pick up the guide that explains the astrological significance. You can't miss the giant horse or the smell of salami wafting in from the nearby markets. Temporary modern art displays transform the building into a postmodern fantasia. *V. VIII Febbraio 3, tel. 049/8205006. Admission L7,000. Open Tues.–Sun. 9–7 (until 6 in winter).*

AFTER DARK

Though you can't exactly party till dawn, you can have beers or froufrou drinks and hang out until 1 or 2 AM. **Indiana Jones** (V. San Francesco 144, tel. 049/650348; closed Wed.) has neon, gem-encrusted walls, and a faux-mine motif without the canned theme-bar atmosphere. **Lucifer Young** (V. Altinate 89, tel. 049/8752251; closed Wed.) is a twisted, imaginative bar based on Dante's *Inferno*. There's a L5,000 minimum, but it's worth it to watch green neon devils from a table suppported by human limbs and surrounded by trees. If you've had enough of the Disney-esque fun, the basic beer joint **Le Clochard** (Riviera Tito Livio 15–17, tel. 049/8761146; closed Sun.) is a refreshing place to pull a pint amid a mixed straight/gay male crowd.

NEAR PADUA

MONSÈLICE

Medieval bricked archways and mom-and-pop places are what you'll find in this unassuming small town consisting of one main street. Even if you're just going to Montagnana (*see below*) for a night, spend some time in Monsèlice on the way. From the train station, if you take a right and continue up the road over the bridge, turn right when the street ends and you're in **Piazza Mazzini,** the heart of town. Behind the piazza the long road winds uphill; turn left to hit **Ca' Marcello** (Castello di Ezzelino, tel. 0429/72931), a hybrid medieval castle and Renaissance villa. Visitors are usually admitted *only* Tuesday–Sunday at 9, 10, 11, 3, 4, and 5 (admission L8,000).

About a 10-minute walk farther up the same street brings you to the arch that marks the beginning of Via Sette Chiese, where six tiny chapels lead to **Chiesa San Giorgio** and the private Villa Duodo next door. The friendly groundskeeper opens the church when he feels like it and all day Sunday. He's more than happy to tell you all about the church, even though he speaks not a lick of English. The inside of the church is full of skeletons of Christian martyrs in Renaissance outfits peering at you from behind glass. They were transferred from the Roman catacombs on the orders of Signore Duodo to add a little spiritual weight to his estate. The most famous corpse is of San Valentino (St. Valentine), who is visited every February 14 by grateful lovers. The **Rocca** (Citadel) on the hill has been closed since 1960 and looks it; but you can hike up to see deer and an incredible view if the groundskeeper opens the iron gate for you.

Near Monsèlice is the sleepy little town of **Arquà Petrarca,** where the poet Petrarch lived in the 14th century. You can only get here if you've got a car or manage to beg a ride off commuters or school buses in the parking lot behind the train station. If you do make it here, **Casa Petrarca** (V. Vallesele, tel. 0429/718294; admission L6000), the poet's house, is open Tuesday–Sunday 9–12:30 and 3–7; afternoon hours October–January are 2:30–5:30.

BASICS • Ask at the **Ufficio Turistico** (V. Roma 1, behind P. Mazzini, tel. 0429/783026; open Wed.–Mon. 10–12:30 and 3–6, 2–5 in winter) for information on buses or bike trail maps.

COMING AND GOING • Trains from Monsèlice's **train station** (tel. 147/888088) run every half hour to Padua (20 min, L3,100) and Venice (1 hr, L5,600); seven daily trains go to Mantova (1 hr 40 min, L7,700); the last train is at 5:31 PM.

MONTAGNANA

Wall-encircled Montagnana blasts you to the medieval past—especially during the Palio on the first Sunday in September, a small but authentic equestrian tournament modeled after the one in Siena. The town is also home to two castles: **Rocca degli Alberi** (a.k.a. the youth hostel) and **San Zeno,** with crenellated battlements and all. Other than that, there isn't much to see here. The information office, **Pro Loco** (P. Trieste, tel. 0429/81320; open Mon. 9:30– 12:30, Wed.–Sun. 9:30–12:30 and 4–7, 3–6 in winter) gives out maps and info on Padua, of all things. From Padua, you have to change trains at Monsèlice to reach Montagnana; take the Legnano or Mantova line (7 trains daily; last at 5:31 PM). The entire trip, not counting the wait at Monsèlice, takes 45 minutes and costs about L6,000.

WHERE TO SLEEP AND EAT • Ostello Rocca degli Alberi (HI; Rocca degli Alberi, 35044, tel. 0429/81076; from station, take V. Spalato past Porta XX Settembre, turn left when it ends—about a 10-min walk; open Apr.–mid-Oct.) is the most impressive-looking lodging in town (with the best view if you climb to the top). The almost spooky brick castle is clean and well-run, and costs a mere L17,000. Generally deserted (except in times of hellish school groups) and architecturally interesting, it's a good place to hang with the owls for a while. Curfew is 11 PM, lockout 9:30–3:30. The **Ezzelino** (V. Prateri 1, tel. 0429/82035; from Piazza Emanuele take Porta Vicenza, turn left and follow walls; hotel is on left, next to hospital—about a 15-min walk) has decent rooms with showers at L90,000, and it's conveniently above a pizzeria.

Big Ben (V. Spalato 2, tel. 0429/81501; closed Tues.), just outside the walls on the road from the station, serves filling pizzas and risotto *agli asparagi* (with asparagus) for around L20,000 in season.

VICENZA

A yuppied-out, tony city whose nouveaux became riches mainly from the textile industry, Vicenza is a dull town full of shops and would be completely uninspiring if it weren't for local boy wonder Andrea di Pietra della Gondola, better known as Palladio. This Renaissance architect spewed out dozens of designs for the city's residents, wealthy mainland relatives of Venice's more powerful families. The buildings range from opulent city palazzi to comfortable villas in the surrounding area, including **La Rotonda,** known to first-year architecture students worldwide. You can get a pretty good idea of the Palladian style just walking down the street without paying a dime. Sleeping and eating are expensive; unless you're really, really into Palladio, stay in Padua or Verona and make Vicenza a day trip.

BASICS

The **APT** (P. Matteotti 12, tel. and fax 0444/320854; open Mon.–Sat. 9–1 and 2:30–6, Sun. 9–1) office has the usual info.

COMING AND GOING

The **Vicenza Station** (P. Stazione, south end of V. Roma, tel. 147/888088) sends hourly trains to Milan (2 hrs 30 min, L16,000). Trains to Venice (1 hr, L6,300), Padua (30 min, L4,500), and Verona (40 min, L5,500) leave every half hour. Air-conditioned **FTV** (Ferrotramvie Vicentine) buses go to Padua (L5,300), Marostica (L4,200), Bassano del Grappa (L5,300), and Asiago (L7,200). They leave from the **bus station** (V. Milano 7, tel. 0444/223115) to the left of the train station; call for schedules. To reach the city center from the train station, follow Viale Roma and take a right on **Corso Palladio.**

WHERE TO SLEEP

Vicenza periodically hosts showy exhibitions of its posh crafts, at which time hotels fill up and travelers are out of luck. The biggies are the goldsmithing displays in January, June, and September and the architecture show in September. The campground **Campeggio Vicenza** (Strada Pelosa 241, tel. 0444/582311; closed Oct.–Mar.) is a 20-minute bus ride from town, but there's almost always space. Sites are L9,800, plus L7,800 per person. To get here, take Bus 1 from the train station to Torre di Quartesolo; ask the driver to stop near the *campeggio*. **Affitacamere di Marchiori Rosina** (Contra Santa Caterina 88, tel. 0444/322580) is really a deal in Vicenza, with doubles at L37,000, or L47,000 with bath. There's no curfew, and reception is open almost 'round the clock. The **Albergo Due Mori** (Contrà Do Rode 26, tel. 0444/321886, fax 0444/326127) is the best of the center's two-star hotels, with doubles from L75,000.

WHERE TO EAT

Vicenza's center has two types of restaurants: pricey and touristy or cheap and repugnant. If you're around on Thursday morning, go to the huge **market,** which winds through half the city (including P. Signori and P. del Duomo). If not, make the first sight you see here the **PAM** supermarket (V. Roma 1, tel. 0444/326015). The **Giardino Salvi** (up V. Roma from the train station) is a shady place to picnic and feed your leftovers to the pigeons. For a huge, cheap pizza, head past the post office to **Al Paradiso** (Contra Pescherie Vecchie 5, tel. 0444/322320; closed Mon.). For a splurge—the outdoor cover alone is L5,000—try **Agli Schioppi** (Contrà P. del Castello 26/28, tel. 0444/543701; closed Sun., no dinner Sat.) for seasonal asparagus ravioli or lasagna.

WORTH SEEING

Vicenza and the surrounding area are strewn with major works by the immensely influential neoclassical architect Andrea Palladio. Many of his palazzi now house ritzy shops, cafés, and restaurants, providing a sumptuous backdrop for Vicentine daily life. The city center is marked by the new(er) and improved basilica, which sits across from the elegant but unfinished pink Palladian shoebox **La Loggia del Capitaniato,** guarded by allegorical statues and decorated with 16th-century frescoes. North on Corso Palladio is **Santa Maria Corona** (tel. 0444/323644; open daily 8:30–noon and 2:30–6:30). This one's not by Palladio, but its imposing, silent chapel does house his tomb and contains a double whammy of Renaissance superstars: paintings by Giovanni Bellini and Paolo Veronese.

The **Basilica Palladiana** made Palladio famous for imposing Renaissance harmony on absolutely anything. The building was originally a monstrous architectural remnant of the unstable medieval style, which had defied prior attempts to make it symmetrical. Palladio's design stylized the facade by placing pilasters of different widths at strategic points so they all looked the same, creating an optical illusion. *P. Signori, tel. 0444/323681. Admission free. Open Tues.–Sat. 9:30–noon and 2:15–5, Sun. 9:30–12:30 (Sun. in summer 9–12:30 and 2–7).*

The **Palazzo Chiericati** was commissioned by local bigwig Girolamo Chiericati, but in 1838 the city acquired the palazzo and made it home to the **Museo Civico,** which contains works by Veronese, Tintoretto, and Van Dyck. *South side of P. Matteotti, tel. 0444/321348. Admission L12,000 combined ticket with Teatro Olimpico, below. Open Tues.–Sat. 9–12:30 and 2:15–5, Sun. 9:30–12:30 (Sun. in summer 9:30–12:30 and 2–7).*

The **Teatro Olimpico's** design was based on Roman indoor theaters. The plan is Palladian, but the stage decoration was done by another artist who went a bit overboard on the perspective thing. The Vicentines also placed so many sculptures around the stage that it would seem to be impossible to pay attention to a plot while watching a play here. The cheapest tickets for performances go for L30,000. Ask for a concert schedule at the APT or call the Assessorato ai Servizi Culturali (tel. 0444/222101) for info. You can buy tickets ahead of time (for a L2,000–L3,000 charge) at Agenzia Viaggi Palladio (Contrà Cavour 16, tel. 0444/546111) or wing it the night of the show. *North side of P. Matteotti, tel. 0444/323781. Admission L12,000 combined ticket with Palazzo Chiericati, above. Open Mon.–Sat. 9–12:30 and 2:15–5, Sun. 9–12:30.*

Palladio's most famous villa, **Villa Rotonda,** has been fussed over and copied around the world by everyone from Christopher Wren to Thomas Jefferson. Technically it's called the Villa Valmarana-Capri, but the perfectly symmetrical villa based on a circle-in-a-square design is nicknamed the Rotonda, which means round. If you can't make its finicky hours, it's worth the 20-minute trek to see the beehive-top villa anyway—it's completely visible from the road. *V. della Rotonda 25, tel. 0444/321793. From Villa Valmarana ai Nani (see below), take tree-lined dirt road Stradella Valamaran and turn right at V. della Rotonda. Admission L10,000 interior, L5,000 grounds. Open Mar. 15–Nov. 4; grounds open Tues.–Thurs. and, if personnel are available, Fri.–Sun. also, 10–noon and 3–6; interior open Wed. 10–noon and 3–6.*

The story goes that **Villa Valmarana ai Nani** is protected by the dwarf servants of a girl who once lived here. The dwarves (*nani*) were turned to stone, and you can see their statues along the gates of the villa. The actual villa isn't as famous (it's non-Palladian), but the angels with threaded wings and Tiepolo frescoes are worth it. To see a chip off the old block, check out the frescoes in the guest house—they're by Gian Domenico, Tiepolo's son. *V. dei Nani 9, tel. 0444/543976. From east side of train station, cross Ponte S. Libera and follow V. Dante; left on V. S. Bastiano, which turns into V. dei Nani (about a 15-min walk). Admission L10,000. Open May–Sept., Mon.–Tues. and Fri. 3–6, Wed.–Thurs. and weekends 10–noon and 3–6; hrs vary slightly mid-Mar.–May and Oct. Visits possible at other times by booking ahead for a fee of L3,000.*

VERONA

A collection of stone-lined streets, stagelike piazzas, and sidewalks paved with characteristic pale marble, Verona is one of the oldest, best-preserved, and most beautiful cities in Italy. The town hit its first peak back in the 1st century BC, when the Romans used it as a stop on the trade route to the rest of Europe, leaving behind some serious monuments (including the Arena in Piazza Brà, where operas are still performed). In the Middle Ages, the slightly bizarre and very rich della Scala built up the city as the prestigious family domain. Later, in the 15th century, Venice came west and sucked the city up into its empire. Instead of challenging Venice's power, Verona decided to turn all its aspirations inward, building up its cultural cachet—Shakespeare placed Romeo, Juliet, and a couple of gentlemen here—and restoring the already-ancient Roman ruins.

BASICS

APT has offices in the train station (tel. 045/8000861; open summer, Mon.–Sat. 8–7:30, Sun. 9–noon; winter, Mon.–Sat. 9–6) and at Cortile dei Tribunale, Scavi Scaligeri, (tel. 045/8068680; open Tues.–Sun. 10–7). The *Passport Verona* brochure comes with a map and a list of inexpensive hotels, plus up-to-date info on concerts and festivals. The **post office** (P. Viviani 7, tel. 045/8003998; open Mon.– Sat. 8:10–7:40) is in a four-story palazzo. The **Fabretto Viaggi e Turismo** branch of **American Express** (C. Porta Nuova 11, 2 blocks south of P. Brà, tel. 045/8060111; open weekdays 8:30–7; Mar.–Sept. and Dec., also Sat. 9–noon) changes traveler's checks for free and has decent rates. Banks here charge outlandish commissions, and "convenient" 24-hour exchange machines are often broken, so plan ahead. There are scores of ATMs all over town; there are several banks on Piazza Brà.

COMING AND GOING

Train superstation **Verona Porta Nuova** (P. XXV Aprile, tel. 147/888088) is a clean, well-lighted stop on the Milan–Venice line. It serves international and regional destinations, including Milan (1¾ hrs, L12,100), Rome (5 hrs, L42,000, plus L17,500 supplement needed for most trains; change at Bologna), Florence (2¾ hrs, L18,800, plus L10,500 supplement needed for most trains; change at Bologna), and Venice (every 30 min, 1½ hrs, L10,100, supplement L6,500). Luggage storage is open 24 hours. Techie types can also while away the hours at **Realtà Virtuale** (upstairs in Track 1, tel. 045/597657; open Mon.– Sat. 7:30 AM–7:40 PM, Sun. 8–1), Porta Nuova's Internet service. A mere L3,000 will send E-mail, L6,000 will buy a half hour of Net time; an hour is L12,000.

Trains are faster and more convenient, but **APT** buses (P. XXV Aprile, opposite the train station, tel. 045/8004129) are often the only way to reach the smaller, less frequently visited towns of the region.

GETTING AROUND

The Adige River runs through Verona, separating the center from outlying neighborhoods. Most sights are in or near the center, which is full of confusing *vicoli* (alleys) and piazzas at every turn. **Corso Porta Nuova** leads north from the train station to **Piazza Brà**, the social heart of the center. From here, **Via Roma** leads west to **Castelvecchio**, where **Corso Cavour** begins; the latter turns into Corso Porta Borsari and finally Corso Sant'Anastasia. From Piazza Brà, **Via Mazzini** stretches northeast to **Piazza delle Erbe** and **Piazza Dante,** also centers of activity. The youth hostel—in addition to the university and most budget restaurants—is east of the Adige in the Veronetta district; cross the Ponte Nuovo to reach this blessedly untouristed neighborhood. Walking is the best way to get around Verona's center, but for the train station and far-flung lodgings in Veronetta and beyond, use public transport: schedules and routes are listed at the station, and half of the buses stop at Piazza Brà. Buy the L1,600 ticket at the machines before you board, valid for one hour after validation.

WHERE TO SLEEP

Floods of wealthy folk, in for a few days of Romeo and Juliet or a night of opera, mean budget hotels are practically nonexistent in the center.

UNDER L90,000 • Albergo Arena. It ain't bright 'n' pretty, and it's not that cheap (doubles without bath, L85,000), but you wanted to sleep central, and it's clean. *Stradone Porta Palio 2, 37122, tel. 045/8032440. From train station, take C. Porta Nuova and go left on V. Roma; at Castelvecchio, turn left onto Stradone Porta Palio. 17 rooms, 11 with bath. Cash only.*

UNDER L110,000 • Armando. This hotel is very central, and it's usually full. Rooms *senza* bath go for L100,000–L110,000. *V. Dietro Pallone 1, tel. 045/8000206. 20 rooms, 10 with bath.*

VERONA

Sights ●

Arche di
Scaligeri, **9**
Arena, **5**
Casa di Giulietta, **7**
Castelvecchio, **3**
Duomo, **13**

Loggia
Fra' Giocondo, **10**
Palazzo della
Ragione, **8**
Sant'Anastasia, **11**
San Zeno
Maggiore, **1**

Teatro Romano/
Museo
Archeologico, **15**

Lodging ○

Albergo Arena, **2**
Armando, **18**
Campeggio Castel
San Pietro, **14**
Cancellata, **17**

Casa delle
Giovane, **12**
Locanda Catullo, **6**
Ostello della
Gioventù Villa
Francescati, **16**
Torcolo, **4**

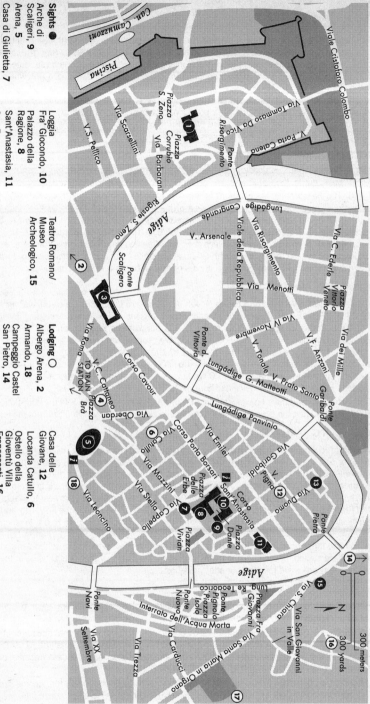

Cancellata. This has functional, unexciting, but clean and quiet rooms without bath for L80,000–L90,000. It's a 10-minute bus ride from the station (five minutes from the center). *V. Colonello Fincato 4, 37131, tel. and fax 045/532820. 11 rooms, 9 with shower. Restaurant.*

SPLURGE • Locanda Catullo. This is the sweetest deal around—you can't get any closer to the center unless you sleep in Piazza Brà. Many of the large, sunny rooms even have balconies. The bathrooms are compulsively clean. Doubles (L90,000) go quickly and the quad (complete with bath and a wee sitting room, L180,000) is a must-reserve, but if you call ahead, there's a three-night minimum. *V. Valerio Catullo 1, 37121, tel. 045/8002786. 21 rooms, some with bath. Cash only.*

Torcolo. The warm welcome extended by the owners, Signoras Diana and Silvia, the pleasany, unfussily decorated rooms, and the central location on a peaceful street close to Piazza Brà and the Arena make the Torcolo an outstanding value in its class. Breakfast is served outside on the terrace in front of the hotel in summer. Doubles go from L100,000. *Vicolo Listone 3, 37122, tel. 045/8007512, fax 045/8004058. 19 rooms with bath.*

HOSTELS • Casa della Giovane. The friendly Catholic management allows women, but there are absolutely no men permitted in this central, immaculately kept hostel. L22,000 gets you a bed in a triple, L25,000 in a double, but no breakfast. For an extra L3,000 you can go to the opera, provided there's a minimum of five going. *V. Pigna 7, 37121, tel. 045/596880. 64 beds. curfew 11 PM. Cash only. Laundry room.*

Ostello della Gioventù Villa Francescati. This tidy hostel is housed in a 16th-century villa adorned with frescoes amid beautiful scenery. It's not as far out of town as you might think, and morning coffee is served in a (completely refillable) bowl. Beds, or mattresses on the floor if they fill up, cost L22,000; camping in the garden is L10,000 with a tent (breakfast included). *Salita Fontana del Ferro 15, 37129, tel. 045/590360. From center, cross Ponte Nuovo, left on Lungadige Re Teodorico, right on Ponte Pignolo, and follow signs; or Bus 73 (take Bus 90 on Sun. or at night) from train station or P. Brà—ask driver where to get off. 170 beds. Curfew 11:30 PM. Luggage storage.*

CAMPING • The cheapest and easiest place to camp is the hostel garden (*see above*), but **Campeggio Castel San Pietro** (V. Castel San Pietro 1, tel. 045/592037; open mid-June–Sept.) is a pleasant alternative. One night, including tent, is L17,000. From the center, cross Ponte Pietra and follow the signs.

WHERE TO EAT

Unless you're willing to hawk all your worldly possessions or craving greasy fries with mayo, stay out of the overpriced center. The one exception is the cafeteria-style **Brek** (P. Brà 20, tel. 045/8004561), where a mere L5,000 gets you grilled vegetables and a view of the piazza. Cross the river into the Veronetta (university) district, and you'll find better food at better prices. Down from the Villa Francescati hostel, family-run **Trattoria dal Ropeton** (V. San Giovanni 46, tel. 045/8030040; closed Tues.) does reasonable primi, like pasta with artichokes, and secondi for less than L25,000. **Gelateria Zac,** on Piazza Brà, dishes out the best gelato in town for L2,000–L4,000. Also on Piazza Brà, **Caffè Motta,** a local gathering spot, has outdoor seating and excellent coffee—at L3,000 for espresso, it better be good. Delectable red Valpolicella wine is a Veronese specialty; L6,000 per liter is a reasonable restaurant price, but you can find it for less in shops.

UNDER L30,000 • Il Grillo Parlante. A cross between a hippie haven and a four-year-old's bedroom, this hidden vegetarian restaurant caters to the "alternative" folk. Enjoy tummy fillers like spinach croquettes or cheese-stuffed peppers with linguine in the company of Jiminy Cricket—the ubiquitous mascot—for under L25,000. *Vicolo Seghe San Tommaso 10, tel. 045/591156. Between Lungadige Re Teodorico and P. Isolo, near Ponte Nuovo. Cash only. No dinner Thurs. Closed Mon.*

Redentore. You can't miss this smart pizzeria—it's housed in a deconsecrated church, right opposite the Teatro Romano on the riverside. The calzones ooze with cheese, and the *vegetariana* is a quartered mother lode of greens. Meals go for about L20,000. Smokers sit downstairs, and you can also sit outside (though this is only fun when the road is closed, during performances at the Teatro). *V. Redentore 15, tel. 045/8005932. No lunch Tues. Closed Mon. in winter, except during theater performances.*

Trattoria Perbacco. This little-known trattoria features stupendous food, nice owners, and a pretty garden. Polenta with Gorgonzola and nuts or one of the many salads (try the arugula, spinach, and mushroom mix) make a refreshing escape from the pasta and pizza rut, but avoid the pricey wines. A meal costs about L35,000. *V. Carducci 48, tel. 045/594193. From Ponte Nuovo, walk on Veronetta side through P. San Tommaso and down V. Carducci almost to V. Muro Padri. Closed Sun.*

Tre Vejete. The name means "three little old women", but you're more likely to find old men here, as well as students and business people, a real mixture in fact. The setting is simple—plain wooden tables—and it fills up quickly. It's good for a lunch time snack (around L25,000), or wine, beer, and excellent tartini (little nibbles on toast) at all times. *Via Pellicciai 32, parallel to V. Mazzini, tel. 045/594681. Closed Sun.*

WORTH SEEING

The center is jammed with Austrian, Venetian, and Roman buildings, all within easy walking distance of each other. You'll find Verona's charm at full throttle if you save some time just to stroll through all of the small alleyways. Roman arches mark the entrances to Piazzas Brà and Dante and the beginning of Corso Porta Borsari. You have to pay L3,000 for a look at the city's churches despite signs outside claiming adamantly that Verona's holy houses are not museums. Luckily, you can buy a pass for all of them in any church for L8,000.

ARCHE DI SCALIGERI • Okay, every family has a wacky rich uncle, but apparently the della Scala had nothing but. Consider the peculiar habit they had of naming themselves after dogs: Mastino (Mastiff) I and II, Cangrande (Big Dog), and Cansignorio (Lord Dog). Their statued Gothic tombs lie next to the Church of Santa Maria Antica, the della Scalas' personal house of worship. The tombs are fully visible from the street if you can see beyond the tourists in front of you. The statue of head honcho Cangrande (he's the constipated-looking fellow on the horse) is a copy of the one in Castelvecchio. *V. Arche Scaligere. Walk through arch at north end of P. Dante.*

ARENA • Ancient and cavernous, this huge Roman amphitheater smack-dab in the middle of Piazza Brà dominates the city with its imposing, crumbly beauty. Built in the 1st century AD, it's Verona's best example of the ingenuity of the Romans and the meticulousness of the Veronese, who have been keeping it shipshape since the Renaissance. Big-name rock stars occasionally play here (although graffiti and damage to the building have discouraged the city from allowing concerts of this sort), but during opera season (*see* After Dark, *below*) is when it truly comes to life. *P. Brà, tel. 045/8003204. Admission L6,000, L2,000 1st Sun. of month. Open Tues.–Sun. 8–6:30, July–Aug. 3:30.*

CASA DI GIULIETTA • The Capuletti (Capulet) and Montecchi (Montague) families did live in Verona, but the protagonists are fictitious, and *nothing* is more hilarious than watching scads of sunburned tourists eat up the totally bunk story of Juliet's house—while staring starry-eyed at a large, sweaty construction worker on Juliet's balcony. Save yourself a trip. *V. Cappello 23, tel. 045/8034303. Admission L6,000, free 1st Sun. of month. Open Tues.–Sun. 9–6:30.*

CASTELVECCHIO • Built by the della Scala in 1354 as a last-ditch attempt to ward off invaders, Castelvecchio is a seriously fortified castle next to a dramatic bridge that crosses the Adige River. The castle was redesigned by local boy Carlo Scarpa and is considered to be one of his best works, if not one of the more interesting modern Italian buildings. The museum inside contains works by Titian, Veronese, Tintoretto, Pisanello, and Rubens, as well as a startling number of breast-feeding Madonnas. *C. Cavour 2, tel. 045/594734. From P. Brà, walk to end of V. Roma. Admission L6,000, free 1st Sun. of month. Open Tues.–Sun. 8–7:15.*

DUOMO • This candy-cane-striped Romanesque-Gothic cathedral was built on an ancient spa site, where early Christian architectural remnants have been found. It houses some vibrant frescoes, including Titian's *The Assumption*. It's not the most riveting of Verona's churches, but if you bought the pass (*see above*) it's worth a look-see. *P. Duomo, tel. 045/595627. From P. delle Erbe, turn right on C. Sant'Anastasia and left on V. Duomo. Admission L3,000. Open Tues.–Sat. 8:30–5:30, Sun. 1–5:30; winter Tues.–Sat. 10–4, Sun. 1–5.*

PIAZZA DELLE ERBE/PIAZZA DANTE • A centuries-old open-air market, nowadays Piazza Erbe is tourist-trap central, complete with Romeo and Juliet snow globes. Don't bother with quaint outdoor fruit shopping—prices are double what you pay at the grocery store. The brilliant, frescoed **Casa dei Mazzanti** on the northwest side is the antidote to all the tackiness, as is the quieter Piazza Dante (a.k.a. Piazza dei Signori). Separated from Erbe by the Arco della Costa, Piazza Dante has the striped **Palazzo della Ragione,** as well as the frescoed **Loggia Fra' Giocondo.** The **Torre dei Lamberti** (tel. 045/8032726; open Tues.–Sun. 9–6; winter 10–1 and 1:30–4) to the right of the piazza has, for a price, a good view of the city. Take the elevator for L4,000 or the stairs for L3,000. *From P. Brà, take V. Mazzini and turn left into P. delle Erbe.*

SANT'ANASTASIA • This beautifully gloomy Gothic church looms large over the Adige at the north end of the town center. As you enter, dark skulls guard the crisscrossed maze of a ceiling while *gobbi* (hunchbacks) support holy-water basins on their humps. In the Giusti Chapel (all the way down to the left) is *St. George and the Princess,* a fresco by Pisanello. *P. Sant'Anastasia, tel. 045/8004235. From P. delle Erbe, turn right on C. Sant'Anastasia. Admission L3,000. Open Tues.–Sat. 8:30–5:30, Sun. 1– 5:30; winter Tues.–Sat. 10–4, Sun. 1–5.*

SAN ZENO MAGGIORE • An imposing Romanesque basilica with a rose window and dragon-slaying frescoes, San Zeno would be perfect if it weren't for all the Viewmaster-like machines explaining its history. The bronze doors were cast in the 12th and 13th centuries, and Mantegna's *Madonna and Saints* triptych, on the high altar, is glorious. The arch-lined 12th-century cloister of the adjoining Benedictine abbey is so thick with atmosphere that if you squint hard, the German tourists become pious medieval monks. *P. San Zeno, tel. 045/8006120. From Castelvecchio, walk northwest along Rigaste San Zeno, turn left on V. Barbarani. Admission L3,000. Open Tues.–Sat. 8:30–5:30, Sun. 1–5:30; winter Tues.–Sat. 10–4, Sun. 1–5.*

TEATRO ROMANO/MUSEO ARCHEOLOGICO • A little bit crumbly and creepy, this flowery open-air theater seems to exude millennia through its cracks. It's been used as a theater since the 1st century BC and is still a venue for cultural events in the city. The summertime jazz concerts (*see* After Dark, *below*) are an appealing way to experience the old magic. The **Museo Archeologico** (take the elevator) offers a great view of the city. It displays fragments of ancient Greek, Etruscan, and Roman sculptures. *Rigaste Redentore 2, tel. 045/8000360. Admission L5,000, free 1st Sun. of month. Open Tues.–Sun. 9–7, 3 during theater season.*

CHEAP THRILLS

The steps of **Castel San Pietro,** near the hostel, are a serene, untrafficked place to watch the setting sun turn the sky pink. Or if you're lucky, you may stumble upon a dress rehearsal at Teatro Romano (*see* Worth Seeing, *above*).

AFTER DARK

The passeggiata down **Via Mazzini** goes on until about 2 AM on weekend evenings, and status consciousness is the password. But there are more edifying ways to spend your time and money in Verona: both the Arena (*see below*) and the Teatro Romano (*see* Worth Seeing, *above*) host **plays, opera,** and **concerts** in summer. The plays, often Shakespeare in Italian, aren't worth it, but if you can catch a jazz concert, pay the L25,000 for the cheapest seat.

OPERA AT THE ARENA • The Arena is famous for its opera, which is definitely worth the cost of the ticket. The season is early July–August, and the company usually stages biggies like *Aïda* and *Carmen* (check out the *Passport Verona* brochure for program schedules). An unreserved seat costs L38,000 Monday to Thursday and L42,000 on Fridays and Saturdays (plus 15% if you buy it more than one day in advance); reserved spots start at L160,000 and go up from there. Shows begin at 9 PM, and the gates open at 7 PM. You are allowed to bring a picnic but no cans or glass. Do bring a candle—everybody lights one up when the show starts. *Box office: V. Dietro Anfiteatro 6/B, tel. 045/8005151. Open July–Aug. daily 10–5:45; performance days 10–9. Telephone service daily 10–noon and 3–6.*

BASSANO DEL GRAPPA

Lying low in the Valsugana Valley and crossed by the green Brenta River, Bassano del Grappa is a wealthy little town. People come to enjoy the scenery; eat fresh porcini mushrooms, white asparagus, and radicchio; buy hand-painted ceramics; and get sloshed on the local grappa. The town was founded around AD 1000 and originally called just Bassano. It didn't take its surname from the alcoholic drink, but adopted it from neighboring Monte Grappa as a testament to the World War I soldiers slain there.

Bassano makes the perfect vacation from your vacation. There's no pressure to see the few but lovely sights, which leaves plenty of time to sample the grappa. When morning numbness wears off, you can commence with day trips to the surrounding villas (*see* Near Bassano del Grappa, *below*). Beware though, this is a wealthy town with local specialties, which means that middle-aged couples and their money jack hotel prices up. If you want to sleep here, call ahead or you'll wind up paying through the nose.

BASICS

The people behind the counter at the **APT** office may be younger than you, but they know their business. *Largo Corona d'Italia 35, off Jacopo del Ponte, tel. 0424/524351. Open weekdays 9–12:30 and 2–5, Sat. 9–12:30.*

COURTLY GESTURES

Marostica, near Bassano del Grappa, is famed for two things: cherries and chess. The latter harkens back to medieval times. Instead of a duel to the death, courtly knights engaged in a gentlemanly match of scacchi (chess) to win the hand of the Most Beautiful Woman in the Kingdom (the poor loser got stuck with her ugly sister). During the second week in September in even-numbered years, the locals re-create this goofy fairy tale with a game of human scacchi in the checkerboard town square, complete with elaborate costumes and ceremonial announcements of each move. Call Associazione Pro Marostica (P. Castello, tel. 0424/72127, fax 0424/72800) for more info.

COMING AND GOING

From the **train station** (tel. 147/888088) you can travel to Trento (8 daily, 1¾ hrs, L8,200), Venice (hourly, 1½ hrs, L6,300), and Padua (12 daily, 1 hr, L5,300; you may need to change at Cittadella). The town is easily covered on foot; everything of interest lies between the station and the Brenta River. To reach the town center from the station, go straight on Via Chilesotti, go right on the wide Viale delle Fosse and left on Via Jacopo del Ponte, which leads to Piazzas Garibaldi and Libertà.

Bus service is more convenient and comprehensive than trains. The main stop is **Piazzale Trento** (from the train station, take V. Chilesotti and go left on V. delle Fosse). The station doesn't have its own ticket counter; **Bar Trevisani** (P. Trento 13, tel. 0424/525025; open Mon.–Sat. 7 AM–8:15 PM) serves as a bar, restaurant, and ticket booth. **FTV** buses (tel. 0424/30850) to Asiago (3–4 weekdays, 1½ hrs, L6,100), Vicenza (hourly, 1 hr, L5,300), and Marostica (hourly, 15 min, L2,200) and **ACTM** buses (tel. 0424/52201) to Asolo (7 daily, 30 min, L3,100), Maser (10 daily, 30 min, L3,100), and Possagno (10 daily, 40 min, L3,900) all leave from in front of Bar Trevisani. To catch **La Marca** buses (tel. 0422/412222) to Treviso (6 daily, 1 hr 20 min, L5,800), go to tabacchi **Ferrara Laura** (Vicolo. J. da Ponte, tel. 0424/521477) across the piazza.

WHERE TO SLEEP

Most of Bassano's hotel prices hover near L100,000 for a double, and the cheapest rooms fill up fast. If you're here in summer, the best deal is the **Istituto Cremona** (V. Chini 6, 36061, tel. 0424/522032, fax 0424/522362; open June 21–Sept. 5), an elementary school/makeshift hostel. If you're arriving on a weekend, you have to call on a weekday 9–noon or 6–8, or they'll take the weekend off. Expect non-functional showers and kid-size sinks; bed-and-breakfast is L25,000–L28,000 (cash only). Next in line price-wise, at L80,000 for a double, is **Conca d'Oro** (Prato S. Caterina 11, 36061, tel. 0424/220364), above the pizzeria of the same name. From Piazzale Trento, go left on Via delle Fosse and left onto Prato S. Caterina; follow the street past Parco Ragazzi del '99. For L90,000–100,000 you can get a double room at the small and slightly faded Alla Favorita (Via S. Giorgio 49, 36061, tel. 0424/502030, cash only); that's provided you can rouse the slumbering owner. The family-run hotel/restaurant **Al Bassanello** (V. P. Fontana 2, 36061, tel. 0424/35347) offers clean, modern doubles for L120,000 with bath and including breakfast. There are only 15 rooms and just a few singles, so reserve.

WHERE TO EAT

Pizza is the cheapest, easiest choice. **Al Saraceno** (V. Museo 60, tel. 0424/522513; closed Mon.), just east of the Museo Civico, is all local and whips up some of the tastiest pies in northern Italy. The pizza *vegetariana* (L10,000) is a work of art, decorated with mozzarella, spinach, radicchio, and, for L1,000 extra in season, Bassano's famous white asparagus. Get tanked at **Nardini** (Ponte Vecchio 2, tel. 0424/527741; open daily 8–8), a distillery that hasn't changed since 1779. Enjoy a glass of juniper, almond, or grape grappa and look out at the Ponte degli Alpini. If you don't know which flavor you fancy, ask and they'll bring out a tray with glasses of each to sample. On Saturday grab some Brie (cheaper than a Coke) from the **outdoor market** in Piazza Garibaldi (open 8–1 or so), and head for a picnic in **Parco Ragazzi del '99.**

WORTH SEEING

Bassano's most famous landmark, the picnic-table brown **Ponte degli Alpini,** is a covered wooden bridge over the Brenta. Also called the Ponte Vecchio, it's been in the same place since 1209, but it keeps getting destroyed (seven times to date) and rebuilt—once by Palladio in 1570. The view of the hills and the river is Arcadian, and the bridge is a strolling spot and a refuge from frequent rain. At the end farthest from town, look for the VEDUTA PANORAMICA sign; from here, Via Marcello leads to the water to a prime spot for viewing the bridge. The sign next to the river is Italian for "no swimming," so if you can't resist stepping into the clean, green water, try to pass as one of the hip-deep anglers. The **Museo Civico,** in the town center, is best known for its works by 16th-century local yokel Jacopo da Ponte, or Bassano. His work shares the gallery with pieces by Tiepolo, Dürer, and Canova as well as other Bassanese artists. *P. Garibaldi, tel. 0424/522235. Admission L7,000. Open Tues.–Sat. 9–12:30 and 3:30–6:30, Sun. 3:30–6:30.*

The Museo Civico ticket will also admit you to the **Museo della Ceramica** housed in the Palazzo Sturm close to the Ponte Vecchio. Frescoes by Giorgio Anselmi (1765) look upon the majolica ware for which the town is renowned, starting with 17th-century Manardi pieces. *V. Schiavonetti, tel. 0424/524933. Admission L4,000. Open Tues.–Sat. 9–12:30 and 3:30–6:30, Sun. 3:30–6:30; winter Fri. 9–12:30, weekends 3:30–6:30.*

NEAR BASSANO DEL GRAPPA

ASOLO

The small streets, crumbling medieval buildings, and stunning views that make up tiny Asolo have prompted writers to coo throughout history. In *Asolando,* Robert Browning gushed pages about this place, where he was one of many pedigreed expatriates. The hilltop city lives up to its description. At sunset pick a horizon, and you'll be sighing wistfully before the stars come out. Asolo's **APT** (P. Gabriele d'Annunzio 2, tel. 0423/529046; open weekdays 10:30–noon and 3–5, hours variable in winter) can be found in the town hall. The **Duomo** (before P. Garibaldi on V. Browning) is a severe three-naved affair containing two *Assumptions,* one by Bassano and one by Lorenzo Lotto. The **Museo Civico** (P. Garibaldi 207, Loggia del Capitano, tel. 0423/952313) has been "temporarily" closed for four years and still is at press time. The museum displays some minor Venetian paintings and the personal effects of Eleonora Duse, a celebrated stage actress who came to Asolo in 1924 to forget love troubles and the hounding press. Only the clock tower of **Castello Cornaro** (up from P. Garibaldi and left at the town hall) is original; the reconstructed building is interesting mostly for being the onetime home of Caterina Cornaro, a Venetian woman who married the king of Cyprus. When the king died, Caterina was placed in the position of having to choose between her homeland and her new subjects. Venice wanted control of Cyprus to boost its naval power. Principled Caterina said no to the hungry Venetians for nearly 10 years, but she was backed into a corner when Venice refused to help Cyprus fend off an attack by the Turks. She gave up control of the island in 1498, and the Venetians gave her Asolo as a consolation prize.

COMING AND GOING • Six buses run daily from Bassano (30 min, L3,100; last bus at 7:35 PM). Buy tickets from the **Bar Commercio** (V. Regina Cornaro 210, tel. 0423/952290). The bus drops you off at the bottom of the hill, where you wait for a minibus to take you up to Piazza Garibaldi; from here Via Roma shoots out from the back.

VILLA BARBARO

Close to Asolo in Maser, Villa Barbaro is the only villa in Italy to feature the dynamic duo of Palladian architecture and Paolo Veronese frescoes. The building was commissioned in 1550 by the Barbaro boys, Daniele and Marcantonio, educated gentlemen who contributed to the work. The middle section of the villa, stern on the exterior but breezy and comfortable inside, is still inhabited. Veronese's frescoes are characteristically colorful and playful and among the most beautiful in Italy. The grounds contain a Palladian temple and a somewhat impressive museum of carriages. From Asolo (pick up the bus at the bottom of the hill), buses go to Maser five times Monday through Saturday, less on Sunday (10 min, L2,200); or take a bus from Bassano (10 daily, 30 min, L4,000). *V. Cornuda 2, tel. 0423/923004. Admission L9,000. Open Tues. and weekends 3–6; winter weekends only 2:30–5.*

TOMBE BRION

The Brion tombs in San Vito, designed by Italy's great postwar architect, Carlo Scarpa, in 1970–73, are diametrically opposed to the Villa Barbaro (*see above*) in style, purpose, and effect. This severe cement construction adjacent to an old graveyard combines right angles, geometric patterns, and obscure symbolism about crossing from one world into the next. Every angle and step of the chapel, pond, and spacecraft-like tombs was precisely planned by Scarpa and is fraught with obscure significance. Try to hunt down Scarpa's remains, which are in the public cemetery and hidden next to the tombs' walls. Admission is free, and the tombs are open daily 8–7 in summer, 9–3:30 in winter. Pick up a bus from Asolo (8 daily, 20 min, L2,400), get off near Via Castellana in San Vito (tell the driver you're going to the Tombe Brion), and walk down the street lined with cypresses—traditional symbols of death—to the tombs.

POSSAGNO

At the foot of Monte Grappa, tiny, shady Possagno is famous in certain circles for being the home of neo-classical pioneer Antonio Canova (1757–1822). The sculptor and architect managed to breathe life into the neoclassical movement with his weighty, expressive interpretations of mythological subjects. Half of **Gypsoteca Canova** (P. Canova 1, tel. 0423/544323) is Canova's childhood home, decorated with his paintings, busy with dancing nymphs. The other half is a stark white showcase designed by Carlo Scarpa, crammed with all of Canova's clay and plaster casts, as well as some marble statues. Everyone sighs over the touchy-feely *Three Graces* and the sleeping lion and angel in *Dolente Genio,* but not to be missed is the violent *Ercole and Lica.* The museum is open Tuesday–Sunday 9–noon and 3–6 (2–5 in winter), and admission is L5,000. On the other side of Stradale del Tempio stands the **Tempio** (open daily 8–6), designed and commissioned by Canova, and now holding his mortal remains. The imposing nouveau Pantheon church, with its mosaic piazza and Monte Grappa hovering in the distance, is enough to make you convert. For food go to one of the small markets on Viale Canova and picnic in the area outside the disintegrating church of **Santa Giustina** (follow signs from V. Cunial, off V. Canova). Possagno is accessible from Bassano by ACTM buses (8 daily, 30 min, L3,800). This is definitely a day trip, but if you have to stay, a rather shrewish woman rents out modern doubles for around L85,000 at **Albergo Stella d'Oro** (V. Canova 46, 31054, tel. 0423/544107), above the café of the same name, where a chatty woman (sister-in-law of the less friendly one) will be happy to serve you filling food.

TREVISO

Treviso has calm, mossy canals, charming frescoes, and some Venetian architecture, but it also has modern glass buildings built after World War II and exhaust-spewing cars that run through the mall-like streets. Hotels tend to be pricey, but you've *got* to eat here. Home to tiramisu—literally, "pick-me-up," the creamy, sinful concoction of ladyfingers, liqueur, espresso, mascarpone cheese, eggs, and cocoa—and famous for its cherries, Treviso is a sweet-lover's paradise. Once you're stuffed, work off those calories with a walk through the town's galleries and churches to catch Tomaso da Modena's charismatic frescoes. Pick up the *Treviso Città Dipinta* brochure from **APT** (P. Monte di Pietà, behind P. Trecento, tel. 0422/547632; open Mon., Tues. 9–1, Wed.–Sat. 9–1 and 3:30–6:30, 3–6 in winter) for maps and descriptions of frescoes that you'll see around town. In summer cheesy but free guided tours leave from Piazza dei Signori every Saturday at 10.

COMING AND GOING

The **train station** (P. Duca d'Aosta, tel. 147/888088), on the south edge of the center, sends trains to Udine (hourly, 1 hr 40 min, L10,300), Venice (3 per hr, 30 min, L3,800), and Vicenza (hourly, 1 hr 10 min, L4,300). Treviso's **bus station** (Lungosile Mattei 29) is used by the **La Marca** bus line (tel. 0422/412222), which serves the province and beyond. La Marca goes to Bassano del Grappa (8 per day, 1¼ hrs, L6,100) and Padua (every 30 min, 1 hr 10 min, L5,400). **ACTV** (tel. 0422/541821) runs from the bus station to Venice (2 per hr, 30 min, L4,200). To reach the bus station from the train depot, take Via Roma and turn left before the bridge.

GETTING AROUND

From the station, Via Roma/Corso del Popolo leads north and forks at Piazza Borsa. To the left is Via XX Settembre, which leads to **Piazza dei Signori,** home of Palazzo di Trecento (the town hall) and the city center. **Via Calmaggiore** is the town's pedestrian area, channeling a slew of well-heeled shoppers under boutique-lined porticoes northeast to Piazza del Duomo. Luckily the city is small enough to walk through, as ACT buses charge L1,200 to drop you off in inconvenient locations. If you must, buy tickets and get info from the booth in the train station.

WHERE TO SLEEP

Treviso specializes in luxury lodgings that start around L125,000 for a double. The only feasible choice in the center is **Albergo Campeol** (P. Ancillotto 10, behind Palazzo di Trecento, tel. 0422/540871), with airy rooms (doubles L110,000) and an excellent restaurant across the piazza, **Le Beccherie,** where the noise might not die down until midnight. Your best option is to join in the din and pay L40,000 or so for a convenient, delicious meal (notify the management beforehand that you plan to eat).

WHERE TO EAT

Treviso specializes in great radicchio, cherries, desserts, and sky-high prices for all of the above. Splurge on tiramisu and espresso at **Nascimben** (V. Calmaggiore 32, tel. 0422/542325; closed Mon.), the best *pasticceria* in town. The price of tiramisu depends on your ambition (about L4,000 for a medium-size piece). For an indulgent dinner, try **Le Beccherie** restaurant (*see* Where to Sleep, *above*). **Al Bersagliere** (V. Barberia 21, tel. 0422/541988; closed Sun., no lunch Sat.) isn't cheap, but the food is unforgettable; try pasta *e fagioli* (a hearty pasta and bean soup; L10,000) or *baccalà* (salt cod) with polenta (L24,000). **Caffè ai Soffioni** (P. dei Signori 26, tel. 0422/52435; closed Sun. in summer, Fri. in winter) has outdoor seating and views of strutting fashion mavens, tasty salads, and *no cover*. The penne *insalata* (pasta salad) with mozzarella, olives, tomatoes, and basil or the grilled vegetables, followed by tiramisu, is heaven in your mouth.

WORTH SEEING

The eclectic works of Tomaso da Modena, 14th-century fresco painter and artistic heir to Giotto, cover Treviso like a rash. Start in the **Capitolo dei Domenicani** (in Seminario Vescovile, on V. San Nicolò next to huge church, tel. 0422/3247). Da Modena painted 40 extraordinary portraits of Dominican monks at their desks, managing to express the personality of each. Some write furiously, some stare sternly, and some look seized with divine beatitude. Admission is free, and the Capitolo is open daily 8–6 in summer, 8–12:30 and 3–5:30 in winter.

The **Museo Civico** (Borgo Cavour 24, tel. 0422/591337; admission L3,000) houses a *Crucifixion* by Bassano, a fresco of *San Antonio Abate* by Pordenone, and the strange *Il Castragatti* (The Cat Fixer), by Sebastiano Florigero. The big yellow **Duomo** (P. del Duomo) is ridiculously ugly, but its Cappella Malchiostro contains Pordenone frescoes and yet another *Annunciation* by Titian, in which an angel breaks the news to a trembling Mary.

The deconsecrated **Chiesa di Santa Caterina** (Piazzetta Mario Botter; call the Museo Civico for info) holds da Modena's other masterpiece, the *Ursula Cycle,* a depiction of one of the more bizarre Christian legends. Eleven thousand virgins make for great subject matter, and da Modena's skill shines through in the unrestored pale frescoes. The frescoes in the restored **Cappella degli Innocenti** (admission L3,000; open Tues.–Sun. 10–12:30 and 3–6; Nov.–Mar., 3–6 only; closed for restoration at press time), to the left as you enter, were thought to have been painted by da Modena as well, but now they're attributed to two unknowns. The frescoes look like an unfinished jigsaw puzzle, but what you can see is expressive and in glowing color. To get here from the station, walk up Via Roma/Corso del Popolo, go straight on Via Martiri di Libertà, and right at Piazza San Leonardo.

3

THE DOLOMITES AND THE NORTHEAST

BY JEANINE GADE

UPDATED BY ROBERT ANDREWS

The provinces of Trentino–Alto Adige, north of the Veneto, and Friuli–Venezia Giulia, northeast of Venice, never belonged to Italy until the 20th century. Trentino–Alto Adige was part of Austria's Tirol region for centuries, and in some areas you'll be hard-pressed to find Italian-speakers. In Friuli you can still find Friuliani who speak their own distinct language, and many of the residents of Trieste, the main city in Venezia Giulia, are Slavic in origin, whether they have a Macedonian great-grandmother or are recent refugees from Zagreb. This is still Italy—but with a twist. You can still drink amazing, unique Friulian wine, visit ancient ruins, or find a school bus to be the most timely way to get around.

Besides sharing a schizophrenic cultural identity and a history of foreign domination, both regions are renowned for their natural beauty and offer an astounding variety of activities, from nude sunbathing on the Adriatic coast to rock-climbing in the jagged limestone peaks of the Dolomites. In Friuli–Venezia Giulia, the white cliffs overlooking the deep blue Adriatic near Trieste inspired poet Rainer Maria Rilke to write his famous *Duino Elegies*. In winter, people come from all over the world to conquer Trentino–Alto Adige's Alpine slopes.

If you want to see the Hollywood definition of Italy, then go rent *Roman Holiday*. But if you want to learn alternative words for "bathroom" and "station" and try different Italian food specialties with heavy Germanic accents, these rugged provinces—of dynamic, hybrid cultures—are for you.

TRENTINO– ALTO ADIGE

Trentino–Alto Adige is often looked upon as a model province—it's cleaner and wealthier than other areas in Italy. But although the two parts of Trentino–Alto Adige may share the same landscape—mountains crisscrossed by a series of lush valleys—their cultural lives are definitely distinct from one another. Alto Adige (or Südtirol) was Austrian for most of its long life; though it was handed over to Italy as a spoil of World War I, Germanic traditions die hard. Locals habitually speak first in German to foreigners to the area, and you're just as likely to see sausage and sauerkraut on restaurant menus as rigatoni and ravioli.

Many Alto Adige natives have been resentful of Italy's hold for decades and are willing to fight for their ethnic rights and outsider status—some say even to secede from Italy. During the fascist period, Mussolini, with his aggressive nationalist campaign, only aggravated the problem by insisting that all German place names in the region be paired with Italian equivalents—a task that busied official linguists for years. This is why Bolzano is also known as Bozen and Brixen as Bressanone, and why you'll encounter German-Italian compounds like Piazza Walther and Castello Runkelstein.

The influence of Alto Adige's German roots on the region of Trentino is apparent: its towns are well kept, manicured, even organized. (Did you ever think you'd hear the word *organized* in relation to Italy?) Even so, Trentino doesn't have the same identity issues as its German-speaking neighbor—the language spoken here is emphatically Italian. One point of agreement, though, is the importance of tourism. You'll probably come here for one feature above most: the Dolomites. These pale, severe mountains rise from the sloping green foothills like giant stalagmites, offering everything from great postcard material and easy strolls to expert climbs over icy rock faces.

BASICS

To make heads or tails of the region's hiking trails, lodging options, and transport system, be sure to visit the **regional APT offices** in Trento and Bolzano (*see below*). You'll also see lots of yellow ι signs denoting smaller offices specializing in *rifugi* (mountain huts) arrangements and more specific trail maps. An invaluable resource is the "Kompass Wanderkarte" series of trail maps available for about L10,000 at bookstores and some tourist offices—don't start your hikes without consulting these godsends.

WHERE TO SLEEP

Many pensions require a minimum stay of two or three nights. When you call ahead, ask if the rate includes full pension, that is, all three meals. Tourist offices can tell you which trails lead to **rifugi** and sometimes help you contact them, which you should *always* do before starting off. Rifugi accommodate hikers in remote, spartan facilities for about L15,000–L25,000 a night. Some have kitchens you can use if you arrange it in advance.

OUTDOOR ACTIVITIES

If you forgot your **hiking, climbing,** and **mountain-biking** gear, don't fret—there's no shortage of supply stores. Trento's **Sportler** (V. Mantova 12, tel. 0461/981290) has a variety of equipment for rent and stores in Bolzano and Merano. In summer you won't need much warm clothing unless you plan on doing some serious climbing. In winter, **skiing** is the region's raison d'être—it's good but not cheap. **CTS** in Trento (V. Cavour 21, tel. 0461/981549) sells a one-week Settimana Bianca student ski package that includes ski passes, accommodations, and some meals. Ski schools in Monte Bondone and Merano offer ski and snowboard lessons.

TRENTO

Breezy and chock-full of frescoes, Trento isn't quite the bustling metropolis one would expect as a province's capital city. The Piazza del Duomo's ornate Baroque birthday cake of a fountain topped with a statue of Neptune is an 18th-century tribute to Trento's history, which dates from Roman times when the town was called Tridentum. Trento's biggest claim to fame is that it hosted the 16th-century Counter-Reformation showdown, the **Council of Trent.** It may not have stopped the spread of Protestantism in Europe, but it did wonders for the aesthetics of the city. The Duomo was spruced up to impress church bigwigs, and most of the palazzi, porticoes, and frescoes date from this era. **Piazza Dante**'s brilliant flowers, swans, and mountain views have derailed many a visitor's best-laid travel plans. Trento is also the bus hub for trips into the surrounding mountains and a good place to relax before tackling the Dolomiti di Brenta (Brenta Dolomites), the Parco Naturale Paneveggio, and nearby Monte Bondone.

BASICS

The **APT** (V. Alfieri 4, tel. 0461/983880; open Mon.–Sat. 9–6, Sun. 9–1) provides helpful info on Trento and Monte Bondone. For glossy brochures or ski and rifugi info in English, head for **APT Trentino** (V. Romagnosi 3, tel. 0461/839000, fax 0461/260245; open Mon.–Sat. 8:30–12:30 and 2:30–5, Sun. morning in high season), which covers the entire region.

Unless you plan to cash large bills, the rates at the train station aren't great; at least the ATM accepts both Cirrus and Plus. Next to APT Trentino is the **Cassa di Risparmio di Trento e Rovereto** (C. III

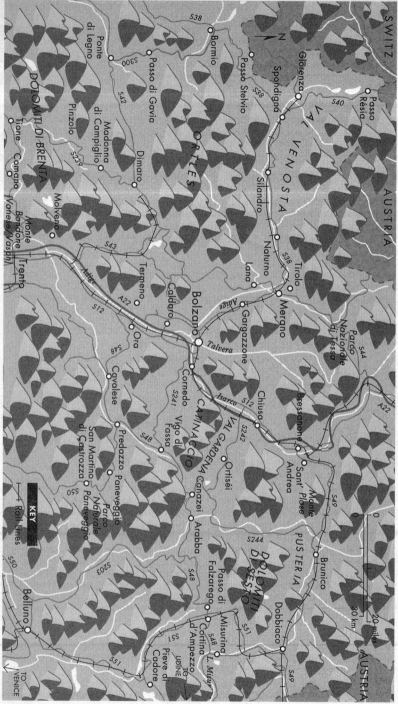

TRENTINO–ALTO ADIGE

Novembre 130, tel. 0461/915700; open weekdays 8:20–1:20 and 2:35–3:35), which has good rates and a 3% commission. The **phone office** (V. Belenzani 30; open daily 8:30 AM–9 PM, customer service closed noon–3:30 and weekends) is housed in a frescoed building across from the Duomo. The **post office** (V. Calepina 16–20, tel. 0461/983106; open Mon.–Sat. 8:10–6:30, Sun. 8:30–noon) is north of Piazza del Duomo.

COMING AND GOING

Stazione di Trento (P. Dante, tel. 1478/88088 toll-free) sends trains to Verona (hourly, 1 hr, L8,200), Bolzano (hourly, 40 min, L5,100), Venice (5 daily, 3 hrs, L14,000), and Bassano del Grappa (11 daily, 2 hrs, L8,200). Luggage storage is L5,000 per piece per 12 hours. To the right of the train station, the **bus station** (V. Pozzo 6, tel. 0461/983627) sends buses to every tiny mountain town. **Atesina** (tel. 0461/821000) runs hourly buses to Riva del Garda (1¼ hrs, L4,800) and with a change at Predazzo, Paneveggio (2 hrs 20 min, L9,400).The ticket booth is inside the train station.

Ferrovia Trento-Malè (V. Secondo da Trento 7, tel. 0461/238350) runs buses and electric trains to strategic mountain destinations. Trains go to Malè (daily, 1 hr 20 mins, L6,500) and buses to Molveno (3–6 daily, 1½ hrs, L5,500). To reach the station from Stazione di Trento, turn left onto Via Dogana, veer left around the curve to Via Segantini, and walk straight ahead; it's at the end of the street to the left.

GETTING AROUND

The muddy Adige River gurgles its way south a few blocks west of Piazza del Duomo, Trento's center. From the train station, turn right onto Via Pozzo; it becomes Via Orfane and then Via Cavour before it reaches the Duomo, an easy 10-minute walk. If you cross through the square diagonally and hang a right on Via Garibaldi, north of the Duomo, you'll find yourself on Via San Vigilio, the busy street that changes its name many times as it heads northeast of the center.

The town is navigable by foot, and the locals take advantage of it; in the evening, head into the shopping district northwest of the Duomo to witness the *passeggiata,* the daily social strut around town. Although you shouldn't need them, local **buses** (L1,500) pass by the train station. If you want a bike, **Sportler** (*see* Basics *in* Trentino–Alto Adige, *above*) rents bikes for L30,000 per day.

WHERE TO SLEEP

Trento is short on budget hotels; those listed below are *it,* and they all cost at least L80,000 for a double. The cheapest deals are Trento's hostels and the campgrounds on Monte Bondone (*see* Near Trento, *below*).

UNDER L100,000 • Al Cavallino Bianco. The nature murals in the lobby of this hotel are straight out of a YMCA circa 1976—complete with horses and rainbows. The large, nondescript doubles (L95,000) come with showers and sinks, but most have no toilet. *V. Cavour 29, 38100, tel. 0461/ 231542. From train station, turn right on V. Pozzo, which becomes V. Cavour. 24 rooms, 6 with shower. Curfew 11:30 PM. Closed June 16–26 and Dec. 16–26.*

Hotel Venezia. All of the dark, cramped rooms here are clean. Doubles in the main building—some with a view of the Duomo—all include bath and go for around L86,000, as does a room in the nicer annex. *P. del Duomo 45, 38100, tel. and fax 0461/234114. From train station, turn right on V. Pozzo and left at P. del Duomo. 48 rooms, 30 with shower.*

HOSTELS • Ostello Città di Rovereto. This spotless hostel is worth the 15-minute train ride south on the Verona line to Rovereto (last train 1:30 AM, L2,800). It's run by a multilingual family that will bend over backward to accommodate you. Rooms have two to six beds and bath, and a few have terraces. Good, nourishing meals are served for dinner (L14,000 each), and they'll whip up a veggie special if you ask. Beds are L25,000, including breakfast. *V. delle Scuole 17, Rovereto, 38068, tel. 0464/433707. From Rovereto station, cross street and go down V. Rosmini, then right onto V. Stoppini until you meet V. delle Scuole. 90 beds. Flexible 11:30 PM curfew, lockout 10–3:30 in winter only.*

Ostello Giovane Europa. It ain't the Ritz, but it's clean, and most rooms come with a special shower/bidet concoction. Best of all, it's in town. For L21,000 you'll get a bed and a surprisingly good cup of coffee with breakfast. *V. Manzoni 17, 38100, tel. 0461/234567. From train station, left on V. Dogana, right on V. Romagnosi, left on V. Manzoni. 68 beds. Reception open 7:15–9 and 3:30–11:30. Curfew 11:30 PM, lockout 9:30–3:30. Elevator.*

RADICAL FILIBUSTER

The Council of Trent (1545–63) marked the beginning of the Counter-Reformation and the reestablishment of the Vatican's control after Martin Luther's reforms. It was by far one of the most important events ever to take place in Trentino–Alto Adige, not to mention Europe, as it helped to prevent Italy's northern regions from adopting the "radical" doctrines of European countries to the north. You can pay homage in person to the two-decades-long deliberations at Trento's Duomo, or better yet, check out the seating plan of the prelates at Palazzo Pretoria.

WHERE TO EAT

Supposedly Trento's specialties stem from traditional peasant fare. Of course, peasants never had to shell out L17,000 for a meal. In general, run from things called "currywurst" and go for the *strangolapreti* (literally, "strangle the priests"), made with spinach gnocchi, eggs, nutmeg, and Gorgonzola or butter. Wash it down with a regional wine, like Teroldego Rotaliano. Grab cheese and fruit on the run at **Supermercati Trentini** (P. Lodron 28, behind P. del Duomo). The busiest lunch spot and home of the best salad bar for miles, **Ristorante Al Giulia** (V. Gazzoletti 15, tel. 0461/984752, closed Sun.) in an alley behind Piazza Dante's Banco di Roma, serves *crauti con polenta e salsiccia* (cabbage with polenta and sausage) for L12,000. On Thursday the **market** gets going in the area behind the Duomo.

Birreria-Pizzeria Pedavena. This place looks like a 1920s hunting lodge (down to the trophy deer heads on the wall) and stays open all day. Pizzas range from a simple tomato and garlic to the grand *Pedavena* (wurst, bacon, mozzarella, tomatoes, and mushrooms). There's a garden as well. *V. Santa Croce 15, tel. 0461/986255. From P. del Duomo, turn right on V. Garibaldi and follow it to V. Santa Croce. Cash only. Closed Tues.*

La Cantinota. You'll get a hearty dose of either taste or tackiness at this restaurant, depending on whether you sit in the garden or the garish red piano bar. Share risotto for two with your honey (L18,000) or try the ultrasinful strangolapreti pasta. *V. San Marco 22, tel. 0461/238561. From train station, go right on V. Pozzo and left on V. Roma, which becomes V. San Marco. Closed Thurs.*

Trattoria Due Mori. The polenta with porcini and cheese (L22,000) is *da morire* (to die for) in this romantic little 600-year-old ristorante. There's also gnocchi and all sorts of tasty risotto. *V. San Marco 11, tel. 0461/984251. Catercorner from La Cantinota (see above). Closed Mon.*

WORTH SEEING

The **Duomo,** site of most of the Council of Trent meetings, is a dark cathedral made gloomier by the ridiculously huge baldachin on the altar. Under the cathedral are the remains of the **Basilica Paleocristiana,** a musty pre-Christian basilica turned into a crypt for bishops. Just next door is the **Palazzo Pretorio** (P. Del Duomo 18, tel. 0461/234419); its Museo Diocesano Tridentino has paintings showing the seating of the prelates during the council, some cool 16th-century tapestries, and more precious stuff. *P. del Duomo. Open daily 6:45–12:15 and 2:30–7:30. Basilica Paleocristiana: admission L5,000; open Mon.–Sat. 9.30–12.30 and 2:30–6.*

Another meeting place for the Council of Trent was the **Castello del Buonconsiglio,** made up of two buildings: the **Castelvecchio,** a 14th-century hunk of stone renovated in the 15th century in the trendy Venetian-Gothic look, and the **Magno Palazzo,** a 16th-century Renaissance palace. The real reason to visit (and pay the L9,000 admission) is to see the **Torre dell'Aquila,** which houses a wonderful Gothic fresco cycle of the months, detailing everyday life for both the plebs and the aristocrats. Not surprisingly, life is all work for the peasants and all play for the lords, who are even having a snowball fight. Access to the tower is limited, but if you ask the friendly staff, they'll be happy to show it off. Off the elaborate courtyard are the cells where Irredentist (*see box* Italia Irredenta, *below*) Cesare Battisti and company were jailed. The small **Museo del Risorgimento,** next to the castle ticket office, is devoted to Battisti. The

Castello now houses the **Museo Provinciale d'Arte,** which exhibits art and archaeological artifacts. *V. Bernardo Clesio 5, tel. 0461/233770. From train station, turn right on V. Pozzo and left on V. Roma; follow it to end and turn left. Admission L9,000. Open Tues.–Sun. 9–noon and 2–5:30 (Oct.–Mar. until 5).*

NEAR TRENTO

Buses run from Trento to practically everywhere; even places closer to Bolzano are more easily reached by a bus from Trento. Monte Bondone is a good day or overnight trip, but you'll need at least two days to see the Parco Naturale Paneveggio and the Brenta Dolomites, accessible from Molveno. Many towns in this area have limited space, so *always* call ahead.

MONTE BONDONE

Trento's very own overgrown pet rock, Monte Bondone, hovers over the Adige River. It rates as the locals' preferred site for picnics, afternoon strolls, and ski trips. The tiny towns of Vaneze and Vason are carved into the side of the mountain. No trails run from Vaneze to Vason, but you can walk the 5 km (3 mi) along the main road, catch the bus, or take the **Telecabina Vaneze–Vason** (tel. 0461/947451) for L4,900 in winter and July–August.

VANEZE • Vaneze offers access to hiking and a **tourist office** (across from bus stop, tel. 0461/947128) that gives out info on trails and ski conditions. The office is open only in July, August, and December–April. The cheapest place to sleep is **Albergo Vaneze** (38040, tel. 0461/947113), with doubles with bath for L70,000. From Vaneze it's an easy two-hour hike on Trail 607 (off the main road) to **Camping Mezavia** (38070, tel. 0461/948178), a year-round campground with all the trappings: showers, restaurant, laundry, and greenery. Sites are L8,000 per person and L9,500 per tent, and they take plastic. To reach Vaneze, hop on the bus (45 min, L4,000) at the station in Trento.

Before hiking in Paneveggio Natural Park, register with the visitor center so that someone knows to look for you if you get hurt, stuck, or attacked by a yak.

VASON • The ski fun starts in Vason; maps of the piste are available from **Sport Nicolussi** (tel. 0461/948163; open mid-June–mid-Sept. and Oct.–Easter), which rents skis and boots (L18,000 per day) and mountain bikes (L35,000 per day). Vason is also home to **Ski School Monte Bondone** (tel. 0461/948211). You can fuel up at **Pizzeria/Pasticceria Alaska** (V. Bondone 15, tel. 0461/948061) and sleep at **Al Caminetto** (V. Bondone 15, 38040, tel. 0461/948122; doubles for L80,000). You can find stellar summer hiking and biking here, but when the snow melts, the town all but shuts down, even the hotel. If you're coming from Trento, buses make the 45-minute, L3,200 trip up to 6 PM.

If you fancy a gentle hour-long hike followed by a luscious meal of local specialties, follow Trail 607 to **Rifugio Tambosi** (at Viote, tel. 0461/948162) for a hearty selection of meat and polenta dishes. Trail 607 continues to the Tre Cime (Three Peaks), a five-hour climb of medium difficulty; the hike is well worth it for the spectacular views atop each peak.

MOLVENO

Okay, so there's a miniature golf course, disco, video arcade, and tourists all over the place, but when the mist settles on top of the Dolomites around Lago di Molveno, this town takes on an undeniable charm. Despite the crowds, Molveno is quite placid and a good base for ventures into the Brenta Dolomites. The **APT** (P. Marconi 7, tel. 0461/586924) offers a map of hiking and mountain bike trails and can help you find a room in one of the atrociously pricey Molveno hotels. Buses make the trip to Molveno from Trento's bus station twice a day, at 11:50 AM and 5:55 PM (1½ hrs, L5,500).

WHERE TO SLEEP AND EAT • Plan ahead, because many of Molveno's hotels shut down off-season. **Garnì Camping** (V. Lungolago, just before campgrounds, tel. 0461/586169), actually a hotel, has large, spartan doubles for L90,000–L100,000. RVs go to **Camping Spiaggia Lago di Molveno** (V. Lungolago 25, tel. 0461/586978) to breed and die. In July, August, and December–March, the cost for campers is a staggering L12,000 per person and L20,000 per tent; prices go down exponentially other times of year. Also on Via Lungolago is **Bar al Caminetto,** where a full meal will run you around L17,000 with the cocktail of your choice (a range so wide that even Hemingway couldn't reckon with it). If you need to stock up for a hike, try **Central Market** (P. Marconi 2, near the APT).

OUTDOOR ACTIVITIES • The **Brenta Dolomites** are jagged, stark peaks that look—and are—forbidding. Hiking on the trails sometimes entails climbing metal ladders hooked onto rock or even gliding over glaciers. These climbing trails, known as *vie ferrate,* require Alpine know-how and skill (as well as

ITALIA IRREDENTA

The Irredentist movement of the early 20th century was Italy's attempt to regain control of areas—especially the cities of Trento and Trieste and their environs—that were inhabited mostly by Italians but ruled by Austria. These regions, called "Italia irredenta" (unredeemed Italy), were, depending on your interpretation, either seized from Austria or returned to Mamma Italia with the 1919 Treaty of Versailles. Irrendentist Cesare Battisti is deified in the small Museo del Risorgimento in Trento.

climbing equipment) to get through. Regardless of your experience, never wander out without a sturdy pair of hiking boots, a map, and some water (a PowerBar or Clif Bar wouldn't hurt either). It's a good idea to scope out the often-steep trails mapped out on the "Kompass Wanderkarte" (*see* Basics *in* Trentino–Alto Adige, *above*). You can rent a bike for L25,000 a day from **Sala Giochi** (V. Lungolago 17, tel. 0461/586977) and ride down Via Lungolago past the campgrounds to the other end of the lake; **Ferdi**'s shoe shop (tel. 0461/586117) also rents bikes, at competitive rates.

To start your hike, take the funicular from Molveno (off V. Nazionale as you come into town) to Pradel, where you catch Trail 12 (mostly marked) and take it to Trail 340 (a steeper trail), which leads to **Rifugio Croz dell'Altissimo** (tel. 0461/585698; L26,000 per person). It's only a one-hour hike, but the rifugio is often full, so call ahead. From the rifugio you have a choice: Trail 319 is more challenging, taking 2½ hours to reach **Rifugio Selvata** (tel. 0464/992364). The easier, less scenic, but still steep Trail 340 to Selvata takes only an hour. From Selvata you can follow the moderately steep Trail 319 for three hours to **Rifugio Tosa** (tel. 0461/948115), which charges L25,000 per person. From here the trails get markedly more difficult and demand special climbing equipment, so nonexpert trekkers are advised to return to Molveno via the trails they arrived on. If you're a hard-core hiking enthusiast, check the "Kompass Wanderkarte" for more advanced trails and farther-flung rifugi.

Skiers pack this area in winter; the best slopes are on **Monte Paganella,** accessible by chairlift from Andalo, a stop on the Trento–Molveno line. Andalo is similar to Molveno but not quite as scenic (something like Lago di Molveno with touristy shops). Still, it's full of hotels and is probably a better base for winter sports action. Rent skis at Molveno's campground or inquire at the **Skipass Paganella- Brenta** office (V. Rindole 3, Andalo, tel. 0461/585869).

PARCO NATURALE PANEVEGGIO—PALE DI SAN MARTINO

The Paneveggio Natural Park, three hours northeast of Trento, gallops over 155 square km (60 square mi) of diverse land, ranging from bushy woods to lakes to flowery meadows—not to mention the steep peaks of the Dolomites. You can stop in at the town of Paneveggio's **visitor center** (S.S. Passo di Rolle, tel. 0462/576283) or head straight to **San Martino di Castrozza,** which is prettier than Paneveggio and has tons of lodgings. The **APT** (tel. 0439/768867) in San Martino all but smacks you in the face as you get off the bus. **Hotel Suisse** (V. Dolomiti 1, 38058, tel. 0439/68087; cash only, closed Oct.–Nov. and Apr.–mid-June) has doubles for L100,000, breakfast included. **Fratazza** (V. Passo Rolle 2, tel. 0439/68170) and **Villa Marina** (V. Fosse 24, tel. 0439/68166) offer the same deal just down the street. From San Martino, take Trail 702–24 up, up, and away; it hits **Rifugio Pedrotti alla Rosetta** (tel. 0439/68308; L25,000 per night) after two to three hours. Unless you're an experienced climber, you'll have to go back the way you came.

COMING AND GOING • Six buses per day run from Trento to Cavalese (1 hr 20 min), where you change to the Paneveggio–San Martino bus (1 hr 10 min). The whole trip is L9,400. Two buses per day run to Paneveggio from Bolzano via Predazzo (2 hrs 40 min, L12,000).

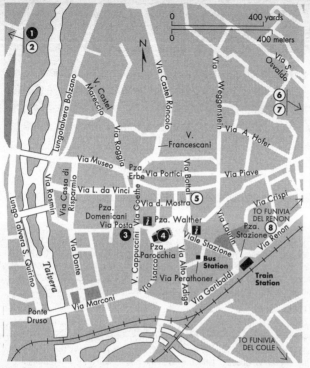

Sights ●

Chiesa dei
Domenicani, 3

Chiesa Parrocchiale
di Gries, 1

Duomo, 4

Lodging ○

Agriturismo
Kandlerhof, 7

Agriturismo
Magdalena
Weinstube, 6

Camping
Moosbauer, 2

Croce Bianca, 5

Hotel Bahnhof
Stazione, 8

BOLZANO

Forty minutes northeast of Trento lies Bolzano (Bozen), the capital of Alto Adige, a laid-back town with
a cosmopolitan flair. Perhaps because it's been tossed back and forth between countries so many times,
this city has learned to roll with the punches and take the best from both of its worlds. Bolzano was part
of Austria for most of its history and is proud of its roots, but don't think that means it lives in the past.
Take a stroll through the centuries-old market in Piazza Erbe (Obstplatz), and you'll hear Italian and German being spoken side by side and—cringe—sometimes even mixed together. The ultimate perk of this
cultural diversity is a trip to the bakery, where rich Bavarian desserts are sold alongside crusty Italian
loaves. German and Austrian tourists, who see Bolzano as a little piece of home, crowd the city in summer and winter, and all sorts of visitors use it as a base for visiting the spectacular mountain ranges in
the **Val d'Isarco** near Bressanone (*see* Near Bolzano, *below*).

BASICS

Bolzano's **APT** (P. Walther 8, tel. 0471/307000; open weekdays 9–6.30, Sat. 9–12.30) has info on
accommodations and local hikes. Walk toward the Duomo on Via Posta from Piazza Walther to reach the
more extensive Alto Adige **APT** (P. Parrocchia 11, tel. 0471/993808; open weekdays 9–noon and 2–5).
The office has an Alpine desk, where English speakers will give you explicit info on hiking, skiing, climbing, and rifugi.

The convenient **Banco Nazionale del Lavoro** (P. Walther 10, tel. 0471/999511; open weekdays 8:20–
1:20 and 3–4:30) has good rates. Cirrus machines are pretty common; Plus cardholders should head
for the ATM at the bus station. The **phone office** (P. Domenicani 19, tel. 0471/314111; open daily 7:30
AM–11 PM) and the **post office** (P. Domenicani 3, tel. 0471/978679; open Mon.–Sat. 8:05–6:30, Sun.
8:05–1:00) sit side by side behind the Duomo.

SAN GIULIANO OSPITALIERE

A fresco in Trento's Duomo tells the legend of San Giuliano Ospitaliere, a sort of tragic cross between Oedipus and Othello: After hearing a prophecy that he would kill his parents, Giuliano left his home for Spain, where he married. His parents searched for him and finally arrived at his house, where his wife let them sleep in her bed while she went to church. Giuliano, returning to see two forms in his bed, assumed his wife was fooling around and stabbed them through the sheets.

COMING AND GOING

The **train station** (P. Stazione, tel. 147/888088) serves Trento (hourly, 40 min, L5,100), Bressanone (hourly, 30 min, L4,300), Verona (hourly, 1 hr 40 mins, L12,100), Merano (hourly, 30 min, L4,300), and Milan (3 per day, 4 hrs, L23,500). From the station, take Viale Stazione and make your first left to reach the **bus station** (V. Perathoner 4; tel. 167/846047 toll-free). **SAD** buses (tel. 167/846047 toll- free) run everywhere, for example to Merano (hourly, 1 hr, L5,500) and Bressanone (hourly, 1 hr, L7,200).

GETTING AROUND

Bolzano's center, **Piazza Walther,** is 300 ft from the train station up Viale Stazione. From Piazza Walther, a left on Via Posta near the Duomo takes you to Via Goethe, where another right will get you to the oh-so-quaint market on **Piazza Erbe.** Much of Bolzano's quotidian life goes on across the Talvera River, which runs southwest of the city. Local **buses** (L1,500) stop at the bus station on Via Perathoner.

There are several *funivie* (funiculars) just outside Bolzano that will take you and your bike up into the mountains for L7,000–L35,000 each way, depending on how far you go. To reach **Funivia del Renon** (V. Renon, tel. 0471/978479), turn right from in front of the train station onto Via Renon. To reach the **Funivia del Colle** (V. Campiglio, tel. 0471/978545), follow Via Renon's curve farther to the end of Via del Macello; you can also take Bus 11 (6 daily) from the station. *See* Outdoor Activities, *below,* for info on hikes from the funivie.

WHERE TO SLEEP

The Bolzano APT has an up-to-date list of places and prices, but it's wise to make reservations in advance, especially in high season. Smack-dab in the center of town, **Croce Bianca** (P. del Grano 3, tel. 0471/977552; cash only), behind Piazza Walther, has doubles, some without bath, for L80,000 including breakfast. If you're hoping for something with, say, a bathroom, you've got a better chance at **Hotel Bahnhof Stazione** (V. Renon 23, tel. 0471/973291, fax 0471/974910), where doubles go for L100,000; singles, L50,000. At **Camping Moosbauer** (V. San Maurizio 83, tel. 0471/918492, fax 0471/204894), camping will cost you L8,500 per person and L8,000 per tent. The place is more like an outdoor hotel than the great outdoors, but even the swarms of Winnebagos can't monopolize the extensive facilities. Take Bus 10A or 10B from the station and tell the driver you're going to the *campeggio* (campground). It's a sweaty uphill hike to **Agriturismo Kandlerhof** (V. Santa Maddalena di Sotto 30, 39100, tel. 0471/973033; cash only), but those who make the trek will be amply rewarded by this cozy, rustic house with an amazing view of the city. The six doubles with bath go for L90,000–L100,000, with breakfast; it's closed November–March. You must also make a reservation at **Agriturismo Magdalena Weinstube** (V. Santa Maddalena di Sotto 22, 39100, tel. 0471/974380; cash only), digs similar in price to Kandlerhof but closer to town and with only three rooms with bath.

WHERE TO EAT

From health freaks to sausage junkies, Bolzano's food satisfies everyone. Stop at any bar for fresh carrot juice or a gelato parfait, then cruise Piazza Erbe's daily market for fresh produce, cheese, honey, and nuts. Sizzling *Würstel* (sausage) carts appear on every corner, and if that's not enough, there's even a

macrobiotic market (P. IV Novembre 2) just across the river. Beer here is blissfully German. Bolzano's specialty is *Knödel,* stick-to-your-ribs dumplings served in a creamy onion sauce.

UNDER L25,000 • Bar-Ristorante Anita. Carnivores gather in Piazza Erbe for the cheapest meaty dishes in town, the likes of *scaloppina milanese* (veal smothered in cheese) or a *bistecca* (steak) with risotto for L12,000. Vegetarians need not cower, though. The English-speaking staff can help you out with some rigatoni *al pomodoro* (pasta in tomato sauce). It closes at 8. *P. Erbe 5, tel. 0471/973760. Closed Sun. No dinner Sat.*

Birreria Forsterbräu. The outdoor patio is a prime people-watching spot, so try not to fumble with your risotto *ai gamberi e asparagi* (with shrimp and asparagus); risottos cost between L9,000 and L12,000. Heady German brews are a favorite. Service can be curt. *V. Goethe 6, tel. 0471/977243. Cash only. Closed Sun.*

Cavallino Bianco. If you speak German, you're in like Flynn at this dark, cavernous beer hall. *Primi piatti* (first courses, L8,000–L9,500) are mostly Italian pasta affairs, but the hearty *secondi* (L8,000–L23,000), such as Wiener schnitzel, tend toward the German. *V. Bottai 6, tel. 0471/973267. Cash only. Closed Sun. No dinner Sat.*

WORTH SEEING

Only the exterior of Bolzano's **Duomo** (P. Parrocchia; open weekdays 9:30–noon, 2–6, Sat. 9:30–noon), built from the 12th to the 14th centuries, is worth a look. Its lacy spire rises above the mosaiclike tiles covering its pitched roof. In the **Chiesa dei Domenicani,** on Piazza Domenicani, the **Cappella di San Giovanni** (Chapel of St. John) has astounding frescoes: *The Martyrdom of St. Matthew* shows the poor guy being maimed by a blue-faced heathen. For more religious art, across the river on Via Martin Knoller is the **Chiesa Parrocchiale di Gries.** Up the stairs through a junkyard of tomb-

One of the best frescoes in Bressanone's Duomo depicts Adam and Eve not yet expelled from Eden, surrounded by monstrous multicolor incubi—each carrying a different garden tool.

stones is a little 9th-century Romanesque church with the painted woodwork of Michael Pacher and the altarpiece *The Coronation of Mary,* so intricately carved it looks like it's moving. It's worth the 20-minute walk, especially if you continue your stroll up the hill behind the church for a picnic.

OUTDOOR ACTIVITIES

A few well-marked, well-touristed *passeggiate* (strolls) start in Bolzano's center. Pick up a brochure, such as "Walks and Hikes" or the more extensive Italian-language "Bolzano a Passaggio" from the APT. The **Passeggiata del Guncina** starts above the Chiesa Parrocchiale di Gries and takes you 2½ km (1½ mi) uphill on a sunny path with an incredible view of the Dolomites. A demanding three-hour hike starts from the end of the **Funivia del Colle** (*see* Getting Around, *above*): take the funicular to the top (L7,000 round-trip) and then Trail 1; at the crucifix on the rock (after Schneiderweisen, about 45 min), walk straight down and hang a left at the fork in the road (where you'll see a rock with a black arrow) to reach a photogenic view of the Dolomites. Head back to Trail 1, which intersects Trail 4 (or E5), for an alternate route back to the funicular.

NEAR BOLZANO

BRESSANONE

Lying north of Bolzano in the greener and more mountainous heart of the Val d'Isarco, Bressanone (Brixen) was relatively isolated and protected from political domination by either Italy or Tyrol. For a thousand years it was ruled by its own set of prince-bishops. Today the town is more peaceful and subdued than Bolzano—a tidy, tiny place loaded with pastel buildings, shady porticoes, and Alpine hotels. Nearby **Monte Plose** isn't as imposing as the mountains near Trento or Merano, but it attracts fewer hikers in summer and has great skiing in winter. Head to the **tourist office** (V. Stazione 9, tel. 0472/836401; open weekdays 8:30–12:30 and 2:30–6, Sat. 9–12:30) for bus schedules and a good selection of maps.

Bressanone's 13th-century **Duomo** (P. del Duomo; open daily 8- -noon and 3–6) was modeled on the one in Bolzano, but better—with a cavernous interior covered in golden Baroque decor. The star of the show is a set of late-Gothic frescoes in the cloisters, with scenes of bodies falling into hell, grave diggers, monsters, and a truckload of bishops. The highlight found in the amber-scented rooms of the **Palazzo**

Vescovile is the Gothic art collection on the first floor, with painted-wood sculptures of stiff and bloody Christs, gnomelike bishops, and smiling Madonnas. To the left of the entrance, take a gander at the *presepi*, an extensive collection of tiny 3-D nativity scenes. *P. Palazzo Vescovile 2, tel. 0472/830505. Admission L8,000. Museum and presepi open mid-Mar.–Oct., Tues.–Sun. 10–5; presepi also open Dec.–Jan., daily. Admission L4,000.*

COMING AND GOING • Bressanone's **train station** (P. Stazione, tel. 147/888088) has service to Bolzano (hourly, 30 min, L6,300). The station is south of the center; walk 15 minutes up Via Stazione to the tourist office. **SAD buses** (tel. 167/846047, toll-free) depart from in front of the train station; you can buy tickets on board. Buses will take you to Bolzano (2 hourly, 1 hr, L7,500) and to Sant'Andrea five times daily, except during ski season, when they run every half hour (20 min, L2,800). A **ski bus** also runs hourly to Sant'Andrea during ski season; pick it up right next to the train station.

WHERE TO SLEEP AND EAT • The **Albergo Cremona** (V. Vittorio Veneto 26, 39042, tel. 0472/835602; closed Jan.; cash only) has large doubles with featherbeds for L90,000, breakfast included; walk up Viale Mozart from the station and turn right on Via Vittorio Veneto. The cheapest deals are *affittacamere* (rooms for rent). **Schmiedhofer Gerlinde** (V. Mercato Vecchio 15, 39042, tel. 0472/836352; cash only) has rooms without bath for around L27,000 per person with breakfast, but call ahead—there are only five rooms—and don't expect luxury. For sleeping in the great outdoors, try **Campeggio Leone** (V. Brennero 60, 39040, tel. 0472/836216; closed Nov.); it's L9,500 low season, L11,000 high per person, and L8,000 low season, L10,000 high per tent. Under the porticoes of Bressanone's center are scores of hotel-restaurants, but unless you dig unremarkable food at high prices, stay away. Instead, try the ricotta-and-veggie tart with arugula sauce or spinach Knödel soup at **Oste Scuro** (Vicolo Duomo 3, tel. 0472/835343).

OUTDOOR ACTIVITIES • **Snow** is Monte Plose's reason for living. Catch the ski bus (*see* Coming and Going, *above*) to the Sant'Andrea **funicular** (tel. 0472/830595, open July–mid- Sept. and in ski season), which takes you to a slew of slopes. Inside the station, you can rent skis and boots for about L20,000 per day or for L80,000 a week or a snowboard for L20,000–L30,000 per day at **Skiservice Erwin Stricker** (tel. 0472/850077). Ski passes (L46,000 per day in high season) can be purchased at **Plose Spa** (tel. 0472/200433).

For a **hike,** try the Alta Via 2, a long footpath that winds up and down Monte Plose. It's not too strenuous and provides great photo opportunities of the valley, but as always, check a map before starting out. Take the bus from Bressanone to Sant'Andrea and catch the funicular to Valcroce (L4,500 each way); Trail 7 runs past the funicular stop. About a three-hour hike uphill is **Rifugio Plose** (tel. 0472/521333 or 0472/521306 for groups; L60,000 per night with breakfast and dinner; open June–Oct. and Dec.– Easter); from here it's a three-hour trek along Trail 6 to **Rifugio Rossalm** (open June–Oct., tel. 0472/521326), where you can catch Trail 17 back to the funicular.

MERANO

A half-hour train ride northwest of Bolzano is Merano (Meran), where the streets are padded with chichi boutiques and German tourists. At the turn of the 20th century, Merano attracted a handful of royals and politicos, come for the mild climate and thermal waters, who left in their wake some stylin' neoclassical and Art Nouveau architecture. The glamour is now gone, but the redolence of money remains. The **centro storico** (historic center) is pleasant, with a 14th- century Gothic **Duomo** in Piazza del Duomo, the octagonal **Cappella di Santa Barbara**, and a swanky shopping district along **Via Portici.** Most visitors still come to Merano for the therapeutic thermal waters; a dip at the **Centro Terme** spa (V. Piave 9, tel. 0473/237724) will run you L12,000. If you've seen even one castle, you've seen one that's more exciting than **Castello Principesco**—the only interesting part is the collection of antique musical instruments. Check posters around town for current cultural exhibits in various locations: past shows have ranged from excellent (the life and times of Austrian writer Stefan Zweig) to hokey (50 years of scouting). The highly original **La Donna nel Tempo** (V. Portici 68, tel. 0473/231216; open weekdays 9:30–12:30 and 2:30–6:30, Sat. 9:30–1) collection takes a look at women's fashion over the past 100 years with a sense of humor you don't find in your average museum.

BASICS

The **tourist office** (C. Libertà 35, tel. 0473/235223; open Mon.–Sat. 9–6:30, Sun. 9:30–12:30; in winter Mon.–Fri. 9–12:30 and 2–6:30) can give you current listings and accommodation suggestions, but the main reason to come to Merano is to use it as a base for excursions into the small Parco Nazionale di Tessa (*see* Near Merano, *below*).

COMING AND GOING

Trains from Merano's **train station** (P. Stazione, tel. 147/888088) head only to Bolzano (hourly, 40 min, L6,300). **Buses,** which leave from the front of the train station, are much more comprehensive. The **SAD** window in the train station (tel. 167/846047) sells bus tickets to Naturno (twice hourly, Sun. hourly, 30 min, L3,250). To the right of the station, Via Europa leads to Piazza Mazzini, where the main drag, Corso Libertà, slices through town. Take **ACT** Bus 1, 2, or 3 (L1,500) to the center or make the 15-minute walk.

WHERE TO SLEEP

Hotels practically outnumber homes in this town. Pensions and *garni* (similar to bed-and-breakfasts) are the best budget bets but usually require a two-night minimum stay. From Corso Libertà, hang a right at Piazza Teatro and cross the river to **Garni Domus Mea** (V. Piave 8, 39012, tel. 0473/236777). The woman who runs the place is ultrasweet, and you may just find a balcony outside your squeaky-clean room (doubles L90,000, breakfast included). All the rooms come "with bath," but be forewarned that some are *senza* toilet. The location isn't as dazzling at **Villa Pax** (V. Leichter 3, 39012, tel. 0473/236290; doubles L72,000 with breakfast), and the mattresses tend toward mushy, but it's a bit cheaper. From Corso Libertà, walk east into Piazza di Rena and cross Ponte Posta, turn left on Via Cavour, right on Via Dante, and left on Via Leichter (about a 15-minute walk).

CAMPING • Surprisingly well located (for a campground) is **Camping Merano** (V. Piave 44, 39012, tel. 0473/231249, fax 0473/235524; closed Oct.–Easter); high-season prices are L11,500 per person and L7,000 per tent. The site is near the racetrack past Garni Domus Mea.

Bolzano locals celebrate the coming of spring and its Alpine flowers with a series of jazz concerts in late April and early May; many are free and most are outdoors. Pick up a "Primavera a Bolzano" brochure from the APT for the current happenings.

WHERE TO EAT

At **Pizzeria Conca d'Oro** (C. Libertà 54, tel. 0473/230308; cash only; closed Thurs.), you can nab spinach- and-ricotta-stuffed ravioli on a shady patio. Yuppie pizza lovers rejoice at **Bayerwald** (V. Portici 242, tel. 0473/210245; closed Mon.), which hides among Via Portici's pricey eateries and offers a fab Brie-and-arugula pizza or hearty Würstel with taters and 'kraut.

OUTDOOR ACTIVITIES

Club Alpino Italiano (C. Libertà 188, tel. 0473/448944; open weekdays 8:30 AM–11 AM, Thurs. 7 PM–8:30 PM) doesn't always have an English speaker on staff, but they'll do their darndest to help you plan hikes and find rifugi. For snow sports check out **Merano 2000**, a ski hill in Merano's backyard; call the tourist office or **Ski School Merano** (V. Carlo Wolff 23, Avelingo, 39012 Merano, tel. 0473/279404) for specific info. **Seggiovia Falzeben** (tel. 0473/279450) rents skis and **Erwin Stricker** (tel. 0473/279607) rents snowboards (L21,000–L31,000 per day) and skis (L13,000 per day) for this nearby slope.

NEAR MERANO

PARCO NAZIONALE DI TESSA

The nearby Tessa range for which this park is named is a series of baby mountains dotted with flowery meadows. The park's visitor center in Naturno (Rathausstr. 1, tel. 0473/666077) sells the invaluable "Kompass Wanderkarte" maps of the area and will supply you with city maps and lodging info. From the bus stop, hang a right onto Via Municipo (Rathausstrasse) and follow the signs to the visitor center. Buses from Merano's station run to Naturno twice hourly (30 min, L3,250).

HIKING • The main trail through the park is the **Meraner Höhenweg** (Trail 24), which has a high road and a low road. The low one runs through Naturno and is speckled with overpriced hotels and restaurants that prey on exhausted hikers. The high road is steeper and less traveled and has a few three- to six-hour stretches between rifugi, most of which are day rifugi, meaning that they offer a rest stop and often a snack bar, but no lodging. Parts of Trail 24 are a lot like hiking through someone's farm, and if you feel like someone is staring at you, it's probably a cow.

From the visitor center, turn right onto Via Principale and follow it to Via Bersaglio. Turn right and take the sketchy-looking but functioning funivia (L4,000, pay at the top) to Unterstell. From here take Trail 10 past Patleid to where it intersects Trail 24 after about 30 minutes. Hang a right onto Trail 24 for a scenic hike. You can grab lunch at one of several rest stops along the way, and after about 1½ hours of walking (just past Gruber), turn right on Trail 6 to head back to Naturno.

If your adrenaline is still going, ignore the Trail 6 turnoff and keep hiking Trail 24. At this point it becomes a bit steeper—yes, stairs—but it's less crowded and meanders through waterfalls. For a complete four-hour trek, continue until Hochforch, hop on the funicular (L4,000), and go right to hit the main road (and the bus stop back to Merano). If at Hochforch you still just can't get enough, stick with Trail 24 to Giggelberg, where you can take a funicular or hike down to the main road that leads back to Naturno, about 3½ km (2 mi) from town.

FRIULI–VENEZIA GIULIA

Friuli–Venezia Giulia is one of those let's-make-a-deal Italian states created when Europe was recarved after World War II, combining relatively poor, agricultural Friuli and beachy, beautiful Venezia Giulia. Until the early 16th century, when Austria began its move into modern-day Friuli, most of the region owed allegiance to Venice, and before that to the former Roman city Aquileia; the area continued to change hands up until 1947. Civil war and unrest in Bosnia have brought a flood of refugees to the region, causing tension and frustration, particularly in Trieste. Friuli–Venezia Giulia's give-and-take has produced a unique and ever-changing society that flaunts its crazy heritage rather than hiding from it. Part of that heritage includes some of the best wines in Italy. Only recently have this province's seven government-certified wine regions begun to garner international acclaim with the rare and sought-after *piccolit* and the dry, fruity pinot *grigio* from Friuli's south-central Grave district. But the tradition has been going strong for hundreds of years and can be sampled by all at *osmizze* (*see box* Simple Supping *in* Near Trieste, *below*), which are backyard celebrations of the best of the harvest.

UDINE

Udine is not the sophisticated big city of the tourist brochure, nor is it the charming farm community one might expect from its location smack in the center of Friuli–Venezia Giulia. What it does have is touches of both: modern shops fill the city center, while hefty meat-and-veggie dinners are finished off with a swig of local grappa. The town is fairly untouristed, and the streets teem with fun-loving students, workers, and old-timers who still speak the Friuliano dialect. You can even find some surprisingly good art museums with paintings by Venetian Baroque master Giovanni Battista Tiepolo.

BASICS

The **APT** (P. I Maggio 7, tel. 0432/295972; open Mon.– Fri. 9–1 and 3–6, 3–5 in winter) will set you up with an informative city map plus info on current local happenings. Agenzia Giovani has two offices (V. Ungheria 41, tel. 0432/292329, open Wed.–Sat. 10–12:30 and 4–7, Mon., Thurs., Fri. 4–7; and Via Asquini 33, tel. 0432/503865, open Mon.–Sat. 3–7:30), where you can get info on current happenings—past offerings included excellent midnight films—and log onto the Internet. It's no Milan, but both sexes may note their gay sensors going off in Udine; contact **ARCI Gay** (V. Manzini 42, tel. 0432/ 523838) for more on the scene.

COMING AND GOING

The **Stazione Ferroviaria** (V. Europa Unita, tel. 147/888088) has trains to Venice (hourly, 2 hrs, L12,100), Cividale del Friuli (hourly, 30 min, L2,800), Pordenone (10 daily, 40 min, L4,800), and Trieste (hourly, 1½ hrs, L8,900). Luggage storage is open 7:45–10, noon–2:30, 4:00–9:15, L5,000. Across from the train station is the **bus station** (tel. 0432/506941), from which **SAITA** (tel. 0432/502463) and **Gradese** (tel. 0432/503004) buses depart for Trieste (L6,900), Cividale del Friuli (L2,800), and Aquileia (L4,600); there's also one early morning departure to Venice (L14,000). The train and bus stations are on the edge of town on Viale Europa Unita. To the right as you exit the train station is Piazzale d'Annunzio, out of which runs Via Aquileia, which turns into Via Vittorio Veneto and terminates in the center at Piazza Libertà. It's doable on foot, but you can take Bus 1 to town center.

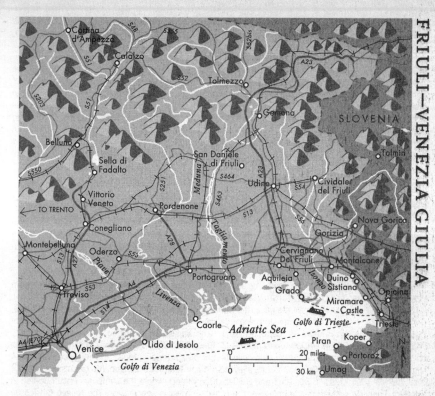

WHERE TO SLEEP

If you can, it's worth ringing ahead to get a room at the family-run **Hotel da Brando** (P. Le Cella 16, 33100, tel. 0432/502837), where a friendly dog or a soccer fan (a club meets here) will greet you, and where doubles without bath go for L50,000. There's a restaurant with a *fogolar* (open fireplace) that has a good-value fixed menu at L15,000. From the station go left along V. Europa Unita, which becomes V. delle Ferriere leading into P. le Cella. An older hotel in the city center, the **Hotel al Vecchio Tram** (V. Brenari 32, 33100, tel. 0432/502516; cash only), offers doubles in scruffy rooms that look as though they've been in a fight, for L55,000 without bath. To reach Vecchio Tram from the train station, turn left on Viale Europa Unita and right on Via de Rubeis, which eventually becomes Via Brenari.

WHERE TO EAT

Local dishes include hearty fare: the words *home style* on Udinese menus tend to indicate a good woodsman's meal replete with game meats. You can join proud locals for a taste of the famed prosciutto *crudo,* thinly sliced from nearby San Daniele, for about L5,000 a plate, with bread, along with a fine glass of grappa at **Enoteca Spezieria Per Şani** (V. Poscolle 13, tel. 0432/226750).

UNDER L25,000 • Trattoria Al Giardino. This is a casual place with a sweetheart owner who's willing to whip up alternative sauces if you ask. Ravioli with nut sauce or omelets with or without prosciutto make a filling lunch for around L10,000. *V. Paolo Sarpi 8, tel. 0432/604253. From P. Libertà, walk up V. Mercatovecchio and turn left onto V. P. Sarpi. Closed Mon.*

La Vecchia Pescheria. This Chinese restaurant/pizzeria can be best described as special. Eating the Chinese gnocchi is like ingesting refuse from the Exxon *Valdez,* but the pizzas and seafood are tasty. Don't miss the *seppie* (squid) in hot sauce for L8,000. *P. XX Settembre, tel. 0432/508888. Closed Mon.*

WORTH SEEING

Piazza Libertà, a Venetian-style square, is flanked by a dull but large rip-off of Venice's grander Palazzo Ducale. Behind the square through the Palladian Arco Bollani and up the stairs is the 16th-century

Castello, where locals go for a killer view of the city. It also houses the **Museo Civico** (Castello, tel. 0432/501824; open Tues.–Sat. 9:30–12:30 and 3–6, Sun. 9:30–12:30). The picture gallery is surprisingly good, with a Carpaccio painting of a Christ whose blood shoots in vector-straight lines into the Holy Grail. The real draw is the Tiepolo painting *Consilium in Arena*, with swirling skies, tumbling cherubs, and voluptuous allegorical babes. It's absolutely worth the L4,000 admission. More of Tiepolo's works line a side of the nave in the **Duomo**; the oratory contains more pieces—ask the sacristan to let you in. The largest collection of Tiepolo's works, however, including frescoes of scenes from the Old Testament, is in the **Palazzo Arcivescovile** (V. Loraria 14, tel. 0432/25003; admission L7,000; open Wed.–Sun. 10–noon and 3:30–6:30). If you're Tiepoloed-out you can get a dose of modernity at the **Museo d'Arte Moderna** (P. Diacono 22, tel. 0432/295891; admission L4,000; open Tues.–Sat. 9:30–12:30 and 3–6, Sun. 9:30–12:30), with token samplings of Picasso and Lichtenstein. Most notable are the lesser-known Italian artists such as Massimo Campigli and Antonio Bauzon, whose *Una Grande Idea* is a Frankensteinian tribute to cinema.

NEAR UDINE

CIVIDALE DEL FRIULI

The town of Cividale is loaded with cool medieval artifacts and can easily be covered in an afternoon from Udine. In the 6th century the Lombards captured Cividale, starting a building frenzy that Aquileia carried on when the Aquileans conquered the town in the 8th century. Despite its history of foreign intrusion, Cividale is proudly Friuli, and Friuliano remains the language of choice. Don't miss the city's age-old *gubana*, the briochelike Easter bread filled with raisins, nuts, and liqueur, perfect for breakfast.

Most of the buildings left from the Lombards and the Aquileians are so diminutive that they would seem cutesy if they weren't so perfectly constructed and preserved. Inside the dark **Duomo** (P. del Duomo, tel. 0432/731144), off to the right of the nave, the **Museo Cristiano** (open Mon.–Sat. 9:30–noon and 3–6, Sun. 3–6) contains two Lombard masterpieces: Callisto's bas-relief baptistery and the cryptlike altar of Duke Ratchis, carved in a wacky, cartoonish style. The **Museo Archeologico** (P. del Duomo 13, tel. 0432/700700; admission L4,000; open Mon. 9–2, Tues.–Sun. 9–7; 8:30–2 daily in winter) elaborates on the Lombard motif with a snazzy little collection of ornate jewelry, tools, and religious artifacts. A signed trail leads from the Duomo through alleys to the tiny **Tempietto Longobardo** (admission L4,000; open daily 9–1 and 3:30–6:30; 10–1 and 3:30–5:30 in winter), where the Lombards once huddled in worship. The view outside this temple over the Natisone River is spectacular. The **Ipogeo Celtico** (V. d'Aquileia; open Tues.–Sun. 7–sunset) is an eerie, possibly pre-Roman catacomb for Celtic military personnel. Admission to the tiny catacomb is limited, and a small donation is requested. Get the key—and the lowdown—from **Bar Ipogeo** (C. P. d'Aquileia 17, tel. 0432/701211; closed Mon.). The **tourist office** (C. P. d'Aquileia 10, tel. 0432/731461; open Mon.–Fri. 9–1 and 3–6, 5 in winter) offers maps and hotel info for anyone enchanted enough to stay.

COMING AND GOING • Trains run to Cividale's station (V. Libertà, tel. 147/888088) from Udine hourly (15 min, L3,500). **Buses** also run between the station next door (V. Libertà, tel. 0432/731046) and Udine (hourly, 30 min, L2,800); buy tickets from the Enoteca (V. Libertà, 50, tel. 0432/701074) opposite the train station. Take Via Marconi from the station, and turn left on Borgo San Pietro through a number of piazzas. Then turn right on Via Tomadini and left on Largo Boiani, which ends at the central Piazza del Duomo (a 10-minute walk).

PORDENONE

Hemingway's Frederick Henry in *A Farewell to Arms* describes Pordenone as "not much" and, well, what more can you expect from a town noted for its domestic appliances? But despite its distinctly suburban feel, film scholars, movie geeks, and celluloid junkies from all over the globe storm the town in October during the world-renowned **International Silent Film Festival**. All films show at **Cinema Teatro Verdi** (V. Martelli 2, tel. 0434/28212); tickets can be purchased through **Cinema Zero** (P. Maestri del Lavoro 3, tel. 0434/520404). For more info, call or write **Le Giornate del Cinema Muto** (c/o La Cineteca del Friuli, V. G. Bini, Palazzo Gurisatti, 33013 Gemona, tel. 0432/980458, fax 0432/970542) or try browsing www.cinetecadelfriuli.org/gcm/. The folks at **APT** (C. Vittorio Emanuele 38, tel. 0434/521218; open weekdays 9–1 and 3–6) will give you a map plus regional brochures and accommodations info.

COMING AND GOING • Trains at Pordenone's **station** (V. Pola, tel. 147/888088) run to and from Udine (twice hourly, 35 min, L4,800), Venice (twice hourly, 1¾ hrs, L7,400), and Trieste (12 per day, 2 hrs, L14,000). From the station, it's a five-minute walk straight up Via Mazzini to Piazza Cavour. To the right is Corso Vittorio Emmanuele, which leads to Piazza San Marco; to the left is Corso Garibaldi. Either way, you've hit the center.

WHERE TO SLEEP AND EAT • Pordenone's already limited lodgings are booked months in advance, making it next to impossible to find a bed during the festival. The people at Cinema Zero (*see above*) will also help you find a place to sleep when you order tickets; name your price range. Be forewarned—even these digs go fast, so chances are you'll still have to take the train into town from Udine. We can't promise anything, but **Al Sole** (P. Bosco 22, 33170, tel. 0434/365240, on V. Montereale to the left; cash only) has large, drab doubles for L55,000–L60,000 and an easygoing atmosphere. If Al Sole is booked, **Hotel Montereale** (V. Montereale 18, 33170, tel. 0434/551011) might have a modern double (L90,000). To reach either hotel from Piazza Cavour, go left onto Corso Garibaldi, which becomes Via Montereale. Behind Piazza San Marco is tavern-style **Al Gallo** (V. S. Marco 10, tel. 0434/520996; closed Sun. and 1 week mid-Aug.), where you can nab bean and barley soup for L10,000 or fried chicken for L19,000.

AQUILEIA

Before Venice was even a twinkle in anyone's eye, Aquileia was *the* Roman outpost in northern Italy (AD 400). Today it's a sparsely populated but well-preserved ghost town with an abundance of impressive ruins. The **Basilica Patriarcale** (P. Capitolo, tel. 0431/91067; open summer, daily 8:30–7, winter, daily 8:30–12:30 and 2:30–5:30) is dotted with incredible mosaic floors that look almost new because their medieval covering wasn't removed until this century. Under the basilica, the Excavation Crypts—currently closed for restoration work—have a mosaic depicting a fight between a rooster and a turtle: it's thought to be an allegory for the battle between good and evil, starring Christ as the rooster and the Antichrist as the peevish-looking turtle. Other mosaics depict Jonah being spit out of the whale like a bad piece of meat and lobsters that swim over peacocks while goats graze nearby; the symbolism stumps scholars. Entrance to the basilica is free (it's still a functioning church), and L1,000 gets you into the **campanile.**

From the back of the basilica, a gravel road (look for the yellow sign) takes you to **Porto Fluviale,** a cypress-lined path studded with ruins. It once ran along a river, but the waterway has been reduced to frog-inhabited streams. The shady walk ends at Via Gemina; a right turn leads to the **Museo Paleocristiano** (Monastero, tel. 0431/91131; open daily 9–1:45), a dumpy but free barnful of worn mosaics and tombstones. The **Museo Archeologico** (V. Roma 1, tel. 0431/91016; open Tues.–Sun. 9–7, Mon. 9–2; winter daily 9–2) is more impressive but costs L8,000, which includes, when they're open, entrance to the excavation crypts. The museum has a huge display of gems and tiny bronzes of Priapus, a Roman god who leaves no doubts about his manhood.

BASICS

Aquileia has an **APT** office (tel. 0431/919491) and a **Pro Loco** (tel. 0431/91087) next to each other on Piazza Capitolo, both open April–October daily 9–6, November–March, Saturday and Sunday 10–12 and Sunday 2–4. Both have maps and accommodation lists, and you can rent bikes at the Pro Loco (from L22,000 per day).

COMING AND GOING

To reach Aquileia, take an **APT** bus from Monfalcone, reachable from Trieste via Grado (L6,200), or a **Gradese** bus from Udine (1 hr, L4,600). In summer, ferries also head to Grado from Trieste (1 hr, L10,000) for a bus connection to Aquileia (2 per hr, 20 min, L2,200). The bus stop in Aquileia is on Via Giulia Augusta near the town center. Sites lie on neighboring Via Roma and Via Gemina.

WHERE TO SLEEP AND EAT

The friendly folks at **Aquila Nera** (P. Garibaldi 5, 33051, tel. 0431/91045) can set you up with clean doubles (L80,000) and a grappa or two in the popular downstairs restaurant, which is noisy at night. **Camping Aquileia** (V. Gemina 10, 33051, tel. 0431/91042 or 0431/91037) is close to town but only open May–September. The cost is L15,000 for a tent and L9,000 per person. If all else fails, try the nearby town of Grado (*see below*), which has more cheap hotels than you can shake a stick at. Buy food at **Despar** (V. Giulia Augusta 17) and have a peaceful picnic at the **sepulchres** at the end of Via XXIV Maggio, which connects Piazza Garibaldi with Via Giulia Augusta.

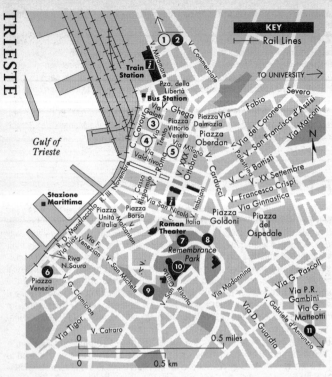

KEY

⊢——⊣ Rail Lines

Sights ●

Castello di
San Giusto, **10**

Castello
Miramare, **2**

Civico Museo
Revoltella e Galleria
d'Arte Moderna, **6**

Colle Capitolino, **7**

Museo Civico di
Storia ed Arte, **9**

Risiera di
San Sabba, **11**

Scala dei Giganti, **8**

Lodging ○

Alabarda-Flora, **4**

Locanda Marina, **3**

Ostello Tergeste, **1**

Pensione Locanda
Centro, **5**

NEAR AQUILEIA

GRADO

A disco full of tans in a bottle; a beach of whining, diapered kids toting plastic buckets; and scads of Flintstone-esque pedal cars—Grado's got more tackiness than a suburban discount store. But there are a few reasons to head to this cheesy peninsular resort on the Bay of Trieste. First, Grado is a good place to find affordable lodging while visiting Aquileia; second, Grado's shallow, warm waters offer great swimming if you can wade through the tourist hell that monopolizes them. Grado's **Duomo** and **Chiesa di Santa Maria** date from the 6th century, when the town was a powerful seaport. Buses run to Grado every half hour from Aquileia (15 min, L2,200) and Udine (45 min, L5,000). In summer you can take a ferry to Trieste (1 hr, L10,000). The **APT** office (V. Dante 72, tel. 0431/8991; open daily 8–noon and 4–7; Thurs.–Tues. 9:30–12:30 and 2:30–5:30 in winter) will give you a list of the area's numerous hotels and literature on the attractions.

WHERE TO SLEEP AND EAT • Despite its resort status, Grado has some affordable one-star hotels. **Hotel Desiree** (V. dei Moreri 83, 34073, tel. 0431/80629; cash only) rents rooms with lagoon views for L47,000 per person, including breakfast. Or try your luck at **Villa ai Fiori** (V. G. Papini 4, tel. 0431/81485), where clean doubles, all with bath, go for L90,000. Hotel prices drop off-season, but almost all close in winter. Via Dante Alighieri is where the budget-conscious dine: at **Onda Blu** (V. Dante Alighieri 3, tel. 0431/81036) try the gnocchi *onda blu,* with mascarpone and salmon. If you're smart, though, you'll skip these tourist traps and hit the **Supercoop** market (V. Europa Unita 35/B; open Mon.–Sat. 8–1 and 5–7:30, Sun. 8–1) for your picnic on the beach.

TRIESTE

Squashed between the Adriatic and Slovenia in the eastern corner of Italy, Friuli–Venezia Giulia's largest city will surprise any traveler curious enough to venture east from Venice. If you meet any locals, they'll probably say they live in a boring city—and then tell you a million fascinating things about it. But that's just the way Trieste is, a puzzle with contradictory pieces that somehow fit. First of all, there's the sea—a bright blue expanse that makes you wonder if it's the same Adriatic that becomes so murky in Venice. The sight of Slovenia's shadowy hills across the water and the sound of Slavic languages in the bustling streets add to the mix. Then there are the menus, which run the gamut from gnocchi to goulash to strudel. The locals are a seemingly impossible combination of urbane and inviting, and the beaches and craggy white cliffs of nearby **Il Carso** (*see* Near Trieste, *below*) are a welcome break from the traffic and noise—could all this be true?

Trieste has been trying to figure out its identity for centuries. It was already an important port in the 2nd century BC, when it came under Roman rule. It remained independent throughout the Middle Ages, rivaling Venice for control of the seas. Venice kept the upper hand, and Trieste eventually fell under the protection of Austria's Habsburg emperor Leopold III. Later, under Maria Theresa, Trieste blossomed as Austria's principal Adriatic port. During the next century, much of Trieste was torn down; the uniform neoclassical buildings that compose most neighborhoods might lead you to think that the whole city sprang up from sea foam in the mid-19th century. After World War I, Trieste became part of Italy, only to be lost during World War II. The battle for the town lasted until 1954, when it was finally given back to Italy, though everything beyond a thin strip of land that surrounds the city limits belongs to Slovenia.

Trieste's chaotic history has led to tension between Italians and the ethnic Slav minority, and relations are becoming increasingly stressful again as more and more people flee the former Yugoslavia, pouring into Trieste in search of a safe haven and work. You may not see evidence of tension in the streets, but any local will tell you it's there, especially if someone is looking for work in an area where employers prefer Slavic-language speakers.

The swastika graffiti in Trieste are a disturbing reminder that this city was the site of Italy's only Nazi death camp. In recent years, though, more and more neofascist sentiments have been countered with anti-fascist responses scribbled next to them.

BASICS

A branch of the **APT** (tel. 040/420182; open Mon.–Sat. 9–7, Sun. 10–1 and 4–7) is in Trieste's train station. If you don't get your fill of brochures there, the **main office** (V. San Nicolò 20, tel. 040/6796111; open Mon.–Fri. 8:30–7, Sat. 8:30–1) will give you the nitty-gritty. Trieste is also home to a **U.K. consulate** (Vicolo delle Ville 16, tel. 040/302884) and has an official **U.S. representative** (V. Roma 15, tel. 040/660177), whose office handles similar matters.

Banca Antoniana (P. Borsa 11/A, tel. 040/68401) offers a decent rate of exchange. The **exchange booth** at the train station (open Mon.–Sat. 7–1:15 and 2–8:30) has hideous rates, but at least there's no commission. The **post office** (P. V. Veneto 1, tel. 040/368224) is open Monday–Saturday 8:15–7:30 and Sunday 8:30–6, and the **phone office** (P. della Libertà) is open daily 9–7. **CTS** (P. Dalmazia 3, tel. 040/361879) can set you up with budget travel arrangements.

COMING AND GOING

Stazione Centrale (P. della Libertà 8, tel. 147/888088) runs trains to Venice (hourly, 2 hrs, L14,000) and Udine (hourly, 1¼ hrs, L8,900). From the adjacent bus station, **SAITA** buses (tel. 040/425001) run to Grado (via Monfalcone, 1½ hrs, L3,400), Udine (1¾ hrs, L6,900), Sistiana (25 min, L2,800), and Duino (30 min, L3,400). If you're bound for Aquileia, you'll need to catch a frequent connection at Grado via Monfalcone. From mid-May–September, **ferries** (45 min, L10,000) will take you from Trieste to Grado, where you can catch a bus to Aquileia. For information and tickets, contact **Agemar** (P. Duca degli Abruzzi, tel. 040/363737).

GETTING AROUND

Trieste is on the large, sprawling side, but most sites are in a nucleus that includes **Piazza Unità d'Italia** and the Colle Capitolino. Via Ghega leads left from the station to **Via Carducci,** the shop-lined main drag. **Corso Cavour** runs from the station down the shoreline, changing names several times as it heads south; Piazza Unità d'Italia is on this street. The café-lined **Borgo Teresiano,** just south of the train station, is a grid of straight 19th-century streets bordered by Via Ghega and Via Carducci to the northeast and Corso Cavour and Corso Italia to the southwest. Colle Capitolino starts at the Scala dei Giganti (Giant's Staircase), off Piazza Goldoni on Corso Italia. **Viale Miramare** runs along the coast north of the train station and hits the hostel (*see below*) and Castello Miramare. Local buses (L1,500) run regularly until mid-

TRIESTE'S LITERATI

Trieste was home to some literary giants in the early part of the 20th century, including James Joyce and native sons Umberto Saba and Ettore Schmitz (a.k.a. Italo Svevo). Joyce taught English at the local Berlitz Institute from 1905 to 1914 and exchanged early drafts of his works with his good pal Schmitz, who penned the novel Confessions of Zeno, *one of the most underrated masterpieces of the modernist period. The poet Rainer Maria Rilke wrote the first of his* Duino Elegies *while staying at the cliffside palace of his patron Princess von Thurn und Taxis in nearby Duino.*

night; call toll-free 167/016675 for bus info or pick up a free bus map at the tourist offices. Bus 36 travels the 7 km (4½ mi) up Viale Miramare to the hostel.

WHERE TO SLEEP

There are a bunch of decently priced rooms in the city center, but unfortunately many may be full if you neglect to reserve in advance. Trieste's hostel and the campgrounds in Opicina and Sistiana (*see* Near Trieste, *below*) are your cheapest options. If all else fails, take Bus 25 from Piazza Goldoni to the remote **Silva** (V. Marchesetti 56, 34100, tel. 040/910749; cash only), which has doubles with bath for around L55,000.

UNDER L75,000 • Alabarda-Flora. The staff is friendly, the rooms huge and fresh. Doubles go for L70,000, and triples are L95,000. *V. Valdirivo 22, 34100, tel. 040/630269. 17 rooms without bath. Cash only.*

Locanda Marina. The pink, neon-lined fish tanks and the funky bookcase in the hall are great, but the actual rooms (doubles L65,000) are much less exciting. They score well on the three C words though—clean, central, and cheap. *V. Galatti 14, 34100, tel. 040/369298. 28 rooms, none with bath. Midnight curfew. Cash only.*

Pensione Locanda Centro. The white walls and institutional beds are a little sterile, but an affable staff invites you to watch TV in the common room and everything is "guaranteed clean." Doubles are L70,000. *V. Roma 13, 34100, tel. 040/634408. 16 rooms without bath. Cash only.*

HOSTEL • Ostello Tergeste. The pros here rate high: seafront location, TV room, plenty of beer, and a bar that's often open until 2 AM in summer, with locals joining the fun. L20,000 gets you a bunk and breakfast, L14,000 a meal. *V. Miramare 331, 34136, tel. 040/224102. Take Bus 36 to just where road heads away from seafront or ask driver (last bus 9 PM). 74 beds. Curfew 11:30, flexible in summer, lockout 9–noon. Cash only. Closed Jan. and Feb.*

WHERE TO EAT

Trieste is known for its buffets—crowded self-serve affairs where you can eat cheap and bump shoulders with locals. One of the most popular is **Buffet Da Pepi** (V. Cassa di Risparmio 3, tel. 040/366858), which charges L15,000. Of course, the cheapest self-service is always at the supermarket: stock up at the gigantic **Eurospar** (Largo A. Roiano 3/3, tel. 040/43394). But what Trieste is really known for is its joe. Not only is it the homeland of the Illy family—of the Illycaffè espresso giant—but it also pays homage to its Austrian heritage with chic Viennese cafés. **Caffè Tergesteo** (Galleria Tergesteo, tel. 040/365812), **Caffè Tommaseo** (Riva III Novembre 5, tel. 040/362665), and **Caffè San Marco** (V. Cesare Battisti 18, tel. 040/363538) are the big three. For about L5,000 you are served a cappuccino on a silver platter or an espresso with cream, just like in Austria. At **Pasticceria Giorgi** (V. Palestrina 4, tel. 040/635978), we dare you to resist a slice of tart topped with *frutti di bosco* (wild berries). But whatever you do, don't miss the phenomenal gelato at **Zampoili** (V. Ghega 10). Locals pack this place in the evenings, and the owners have to make their gelato fresh daily just to keep up with demand.

UNDER L10,000 • Osteria da Libero. Known to literary types as James Joyce's old stomping ground, this place declines to play up its tourist possibilities. At night a few hip intellectuals get drunk on the excellent vat wine alongside salty-dog sailors. Particularly tasty is the Trieste specialty, *polpi alla triestiana* (octopus marinated in paprika and olive oil) for a mere L9,000. *V. Risorta 7, no phone. From Colle Capitolina, take V. San Giusto, to right of Castello San Giusto; it intersects V. Risorta down hill. Cash only. Closed Sun.*

Risoteca. The sign outside looks like something out of *Fat Albert,* but the interior is much less '70s, and the restaurant serves quantities of tasty risotto (hence the name). The *sirtaki* (L10,000), with feta, shrimp, olives, and tomatoes, is a Mediterranean masterpiece. *V. Economo 14, tel. 040/311262. Walk down C. Cavour to waterfront; turn left on V. Campo Marzio and left on V. Economo. Cash only. Closed Mon.*

UNDER L15,000 • Trattoria Istria. The cool interior, friendly owner, and grilled calamari (L15,000) make it easy to see why this restaurant is popular with the sit-down crowd. Vegetarians should ask for the fusilli *con rucola* (corkscrew pasta with arugula), but *senza* prosciutto. *V. Milano 14, tel. 040/634531. From C. Cavour, hang a left on V. Milano. Closed Sun.*

WORTH SEEING

Most of Trieste's older architecture was razed by Austrians in the 19th century, when neoclassic architecture was considered the apex of taste. You'll get a serious dose of this genre walking Trieste's streets, especially in the tidy **Borgo Teresiano** (Theresa's Neighborhood), named after demolition queen Empress Maria Theresa, who jump-started the city's economy in the 18th century. Interesting Art Nouveau designs are also scattered around—look for the clean, delicate lines of architect Max Fabiani in Piazza Borsa and the monumental figures on the columns of the Cinema Eden on Viale XX Settembre.

The Grotta Gigante (V. Machiavelli 17, tel. 040/327312), just outside Trieste, is probably the hugest cave you'll ever spelunk in—as big as a football field. Take Bus 45 (40 min, L1,500).

CASTELLO MIRAMARE • Looming over sunbathers on the shore north of the city is a castle built by Archduke Maximilian, brother of Austrian emperor Franz Josef. The real charms of the castle are its surrounding gardens and Lego-like quality. The inside is stereotypically gaudy, stuffed with red velvet, gold paint, and chandeliers. It's rumored that anyone who sleeps in the castle will die violently, as "proven" by the assassinations of Duke Amadeo of Aosta, who owned the castle from 1931 to 1938, and of Archduke Franz Ferdinand, who stopped here shortly before being offed in Sarajevo, the act that "started" World War I. There's no charge to wander through the gardens and woods (open 8–7) surrounding the castle. *Parco di Miramare, tel. 040/224143. Take Bus 36 (L1,500). Admission L8,000. Open daily 9–6, slightly shorter hrs in winter.*

CIVICO MUSEO REVOLTELLA E GALLERIA D'ARTE MODERNA • This museum's main building, the former palace of 19th-century baron Revoltella, hasn't changed much since he bought the farm; the rooms are still rich and darkly majestic, with bad paintings. The modern annex, designed by the innovative architect Carlo Scarpa, hits you like cold water in the face: Suddenly the lighting becomes starker, and the art becomes much weirder, especially on the top floor. *V. Diaz 27, at left edge of P. Venezia. tel. 040/300938. Admission L5,000. Open Wed.–Mon. 10–1 and 3–8 (3–midnight in summer.*

COLLE CAPITOLINO • Proof that Trieste was a Roman settlement—Capitoline Hill is even crawling with cats—sits in shambles on a huge hill overlooking the city and the sea. The view will captivate you more than the few Roman columns that remain here. Also on the hill, the **Basilica di San Giusto** (P. Cattedrale; open daily 8–noon and 4–8) is an asymmetrical composite of two smaller churches, filled with stiff Byzantine bas-reliefs. The ivy-covered 15th-century **Castello di San Giusto** (P. Cattedrale 3, tel. 040/313636; admission L2,000, L3,000 including museum below; open daily 8–sunset) offers the all-around best view of Trieste, but skip the dull Museo Civico (L2,000; open Tues.–Sun. 9–1) inside. Walk down Via Cattedrale, the small street starting at the basilica, to the **Museo Civico di Storia ed Arte** (V. Cattedrale 15, tel. 040/310500; admission L5,000; open Tues.–Sun. 9–1) for a more profound museum experience. The archaeological museum has medieval and Roman sculptures, but the highlight is a small Egyptian collection, including a female mummy and detailed jewelry. Outside, the **Orto Lapidario** (Lapidary Garden) includes Roman ruins and a temple.

RISIERA DI SAN SABBA • During World War II, this former rice-husking plant was the site of the only concentration camp in Italy, where Nazis massacred 20,000 people. It's now a national monument with a small, chilling museum. *V. Ratto della Pileria 1, San Sabba district, tel. 040/826202. Bus 10 from P. Unità d'Italia. Admission free. Open Tues.–Sat. 9–1 (Apr.–mid-May and early Nov., Tues.–Sat. 9–6, Sun. 9–1).*

AFTER DARK

Trieste's nightlife is fairly mellow—everyone usually hits the numerous pubs. The **Crazy Bull** (V. Milano 5) is an American-theme bar that gets pretty packed around 11 or midnight. **Avant Garde** (V. Matteotti 4, tel. 040/773535) and **Rex** (Galleria Protti, tel. 040/367878) attract students, while the **Birreria Forst** (V. Galatti 11, tel. 040/365276 closed Sun.) puts on live music on Saturdays and karaoke on other nights. In July and August, look for the **Festival Internazionale dell'Operetta** (tel. 040/301716), which sells L12,000 tickets for concerts.

NEAR TRIESTE

IL CARSO

Il Carso refers to the strip of beautiful, jagged limestone cliffs that runs up the shoreline north of Trieste and into Slovenia. Take shaky Tram 2 (L1,500 each way) from Trieste's Piazza Oberdan up the hill to **Opicina,** just before the Slovenian border. In this tiny town, **Camping Obelisco** (V. Nazionale S.S. 58, 34016, tel. 040/211655), a pleasant, woodsy 360-tent site, charges L7,000 per person and L7,000 per tent.

DUINO AND SISTIANA

The small fishing villages of **Duino** and **Sistiana** lie about 15 km (9½ mi) north of Trieste along the sea. They are connected by the **Rilke Trail,** a 2-km (1-mi) cliff-side walk where Rilke began his *Duino Elegies.* The trail starts at the Sistiana Bay and ends in Duino, home to Castello Duino, still owned by the princely Thurn und Taxis family. You can only enter the castle if you're in a group with an appointment, but anyone can climb out to the huge rock known as *La Dama Bianca* (The White Lady). Legend has it that the lord of Duino threw a woman out the castle window when she wore out her welcome; she was turned into stone before she hit the water. **SAITA** buses (tel. 040/425001) run from Trieste's bus station to Sistiana and Duino (25 min).

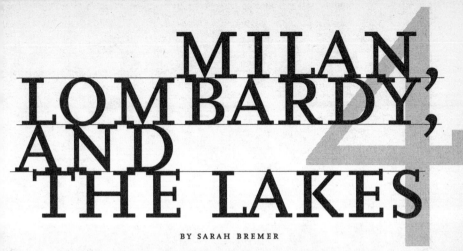

MILAN, LOMBARDY, AND THE LAKES

BY SARAH BREMER

UPDATED BY ROBIN S. GOLDSTEIN

uring the Renaissance, Lombardy's ruling classes erected palaces, churches, and entire cities as monuments to their egos and libidos. Most notable were the Visconti, Sforza, and Gonzaga clans, who ruled Mantua (Mantova), Como, Milan (Milano), and Pavia. Until the Spanish conquered them in 1525, these families spent their time—and other people's money—obsessively building grand memorials to themselves, a boon for 21st-century visitors, especially if you're into art and architecture. In the 20th century, the Lombard tradition of self-aggrandizement continued with writer Gabriele d'Annunzio, who built his kitschy, egomaniacal warehouse Il Vittoriale on the shore of Lake Garda (Lago di Garda).

Although the Risorgimento (the unification of Italy; *see box* Espresso Shot Heard 'Round the World *in* Chapter 5) had its supporters in Lombardy, Lombards retain a deep sense of regional patriotism and a hatred of domination, whether by foreigners, the European Union, or the Italian government. During World War II, the revolt in Lombardy against Mussolini and the Germans was better organized and more effective than anywhere else in Italy. Today, in the Lega Nord (Northern League), an exclusive union between northern Italy's more prosperous regions, some right-wing Lombards are pushing for separation from the southern part of Italy, which they believe saps their region's economy.

And there is much to sap; both economically and geographically, Milan is the most important city in Italy. While it draws fewer tourists than Rome, Florence, or Venice, Milan boasts finance, banking, insurance, and fashion industries that have provided much-needed support to the rest of the country's economy in an era of falling export demand. Malpensa 2000, Milan's new airport, is symbolic of Italy's desperate measures to increase exposure to modern northern Europe by advertising the merits of its only business mecca. And although the Lega Nord continues to draw support (notice the graffiti as you travel through the region), the left-wing L'Ulivo Party has triumphed in recent elections, and many believe that a unified Italy is ultimately necessary, if not desirable.

Lombardy's economic prosperity often translates into high prices and factory towns, not to mention pollution. Still, the metropolis of Milan, with its open-minded populace and fashion and nightlife scene, competes with the lush lakes of the north for your attention. And less-traveled towns such as **Pavia, Bergamo,** and **Cremona** enjoy similar artistic and gastronomic benefits.

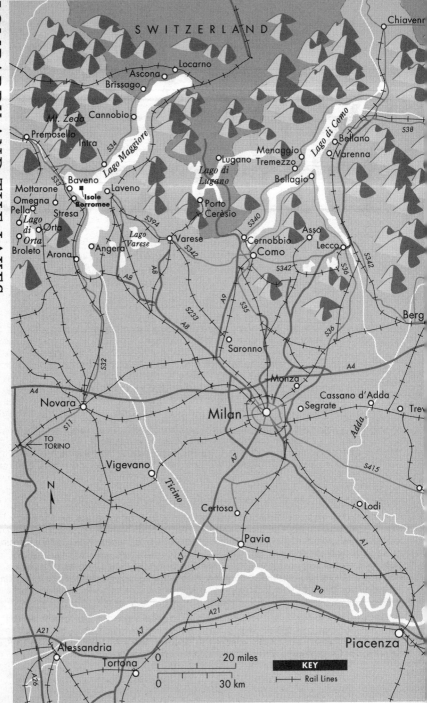

SWITZERLAND

Chiavenn

Locarno

Ascona
Brissago

Cannobio

Mt. Zeda
Premosello
Intra
S34
Lago Maggiore

Lugano
Lago di
Lugano

Menaggio
Tremezzo

Lago di Como
Bellano
Varenna

Bellagio

Mottarone
Omegna
Pella
Lago
di
Orta
Broleto

Baveno
Isole
Borromee
Laveno

Stresa
Orta
Arona
Angera

Lago
Varese
Varese

Porto
Ceresio

S39A

Asso

S340

Cernobbio
Como

Lecco

S342

S36

S342

Berg

S38

Saronno
S233
A8
A8
S35
A9

A4

Monza

Cassano d'Adda
Segrate

Trev

Novara
A4
S11

Milan

Adda

TO
TORINO

Vigevano

Ticino

Certosa

A7

S415

Lodi

N

Pavia

A1

Po

A21

Alessandria
Tortona

A21

A7

A26

0   20 miles
0   30 km

KEY
┼┼ Rail Lines

Piacenza

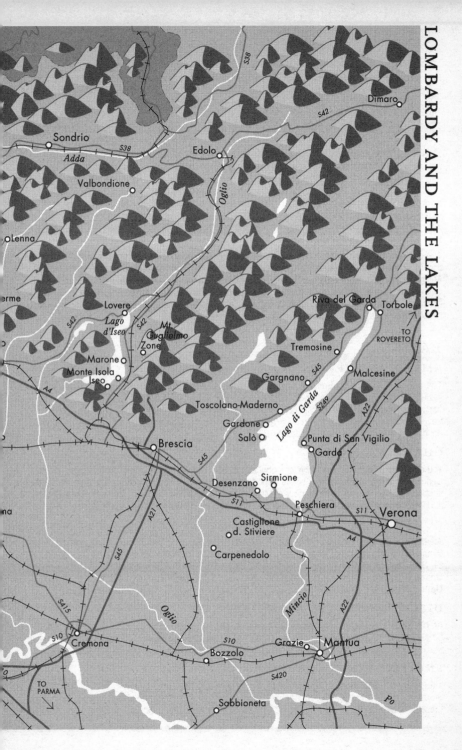

MILAN

In no way will Milan satisfy your yearnings for the laid-back, let-lunch-run-into-dinner Italy; it's faster, more serious, and often prohibitively expensive. Winter is foggy, summer suffocating. Most natives flee the scorching heat by heading to the mountains or the sea, leaving behind a virtual ghost town mid-July–August. Milan also lacks the visual appeal of other Italian cities, thanks to wars in 539, 1157, and 1944. Still, the city has the cultural buzz and amenities of an international metropolis and offers uncompromised shopping, people-watching, nightlife, and one of the few gay scenes in Italy.

Milan's ego-shrinking Gothic Duomo, Pinacoteca di Brera Museum, and da Vinci's *Last Supper* rub elbows with the ready-to-wear modern art by Prada, Armani, and the late Versace. In addition to being Italy's fashion prima donna, Milan produces 25% of Italy's exports and is home to the nation's largest stock exchange, and is inarguably the most important business city and transportation hub in Italy. Even if you don't have a taste for high fashion, the business contingent's tailored-suit, cell-phone culture will make you itch for a nice tie or expensive sunglasses. Yet Milan is as international as it is exclusive; it has long been an immigration center and cultural crossroads, and many Milanese can trace their roots to the Philippines, Africa, Sicily, and Eastern Europe.

The city itself has a history of foreign domination. From 1277 until 1500, Milan was controlled by first the Visconti and then the Sforza clan. These families ruled with iron fists but were largely responsible for Milan's Gothic and Renaissance architecture. Or what's left of it: virtually every invader in European history—Gaul, Roman, Goth, Lombard, and Frank—not to mention rulers from France, Spain, and Austria, has taken a turn here. As a result, stoic churches share Milan's *centro storico* (historic center) with ultra-modern monstrosities and fascist facades.

BASICS

AMERICAN EXPRESS

The only AmEx office (V. Brera 3, on the corner of Via dell'Orso, behind Teatro alla Scala, tel. 02/72003693 or 02/876674, fax 02/86463478; open Mon., Thurs., and Sat. 9–5:30, Fri. 9–5) in Lombardy, Piedmont, and Valle d'Aosta provides the usual services for cardholders. For 24-hour lost/stolen traveler's check service, call toll-free 167/872000; for 24-hour assistance, tel. 167/864046. Cardholders can receive mail free (postal code: 20121).

CHANGING MONEY

You can change currency and traveler's checks for a 1%–2% fee at the information office in Stazione Centrale or at the Malpensa and Linate airports. Otherwise, cash is perilously available to compulsive shoppers: banks all over have 24-hour ATMs, and in touristy areas, 24-hour machines change bills for a 1% fee. **Banca Commerciale** (in front of Stazione Centrale) doesn't charge a commission.

CONSULATES

Australia (V. Borgogna 2, tel. 02/77704217, fax 02/77704242; open Mon.–Thurs. 9–noon and 2–4, Fri. 9–noon). **Canada** (V. Vittor Pisani 19, tel. 02/67581, fax 02/67583900; open weekdays 9–noon and 2–5). **New Zealand** (V. G. d'Arezzo 6, tel. 02/48012544, fax 02/48012577; open Mon.–Thurs. 9–noon). **United Kingdom** (V. San Paolo 7, tel. 02/723001, fax 02/86465081; open weekdays 9–1 and 2–5). **United States** (V. P. Amedeo 2/10, tel. 02/290351, fax 02/76002170; open weekdays 9–11 and 2–4).

DISCOUNT TRAVEL AGENCIES

At **CTS** (Centro Turistico Studentesco; V. Peroni 21, tel. 02/70632059; V. S. Antonio 2, tel. 02/58304121; C. di Porta Ticinese 83, tel. 02/8372674; all open weekdays 9:30–12:45 and 2–6, Sat. 9:30–noon), discount train, plane, and ferry tickets can be purchased by students and those under 25.

ENGLISH-LANGUAGE BOOKS

The American Bookstore (V. Camperio 16, tel. 02/878920), in Largo Cairoli in front of the Castello Sforzesco, has all kinds of English-language reads. Near Stazione Centrale, Milan's first gay bookstore, **Libreria Babele** (V. Sanmartini 23, tel. 02/6692986), sells literature in Italian and English and lists gay

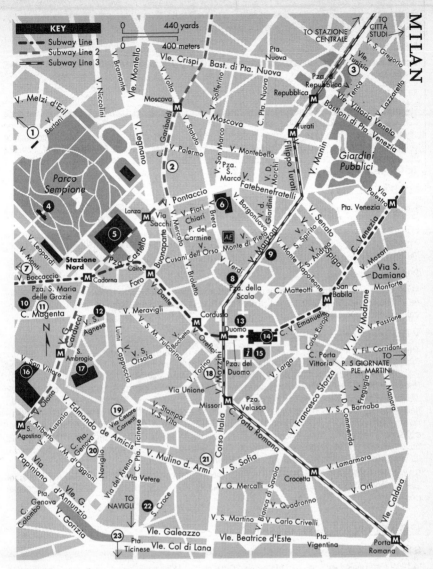

KEY

- ·—·— Subway Line 1
- ––––– Subway Line 2
- ══════ Subway Line 3

0 ⌐————⌐ 440 yards
0 ⌐————⌐ 400 meters

Sights ●

Castello Sforzesco, **5**

Duomo, **14**

Galleria Vittorio Emanuele, **13**

Museo Civico Archeologico, **12**

Museo Civico d'Arte Contemporanea, **15**

Museo Nazionale della Scienza e Tecnica, **16**

Museo Poldi Pezzoli, **9**

Pinacoteca di Brera, **6**

Sant'Ambrogio, **17**

Sant'Eustorgio, **22**

Santa Maria delle Grazie, **10**

Teatro alla Scala, **8**

Triennale di Milano, **4**

Lodging ○

Antica Locanda Leonardo, **11**

Cantore, **20**

Hotel Certosa, **23**

Hotel Cesare Correnti, **19**

Hotel Commercio, **2**

Hotel Fiorella, **7**

Hotel Speronari, **18**

Hotel Ullrich, **21**

Piero Rotta Hostel (HI), **1**

San Tomaso, **3**

community events. For used books and cheap CDs, head to the **Baracchini di Piazza Fontana** (between V. Larga and P. di Porta Lodovica, near Crocetta Metro stop).

LAUNDRY

Vicolo Lavandai (V. Vigevano 20; open daily 8 AM–10 PM), near the Porta Genova Metro stop, charges L5,000 to wash 15 pounds and L5,000 to dry.

MAIL

The **main post office** (V. Cordusio 4, at the Cordusio Metro/M1 stop, tel. 02/8692136) and the **Stazione Centrale branch** (inside the train station, M2 or M3 to Centrale FS) keep later hours than the rest of the city's post offices (both open weekdays 8:30–5:30, Sat. 8:30–noon). Collect *fermo posta* (held mail) at Windows 5 and 6; it should be addressed to: Fermo Posta Cordusio, Milano. **CAI-POST** (in post office), the express-mail service, is open weekdays 8:30–7:30, Saturday 8:30–1. Send telegrams and faxes at the **telegraph office** (tel. 02/8692874; open 24 hrs), also in the post office.

MEDICAL AID

The **Policlinico** hospital (P. Francesco Sforza 35, tel. 02/5510809, emergency tel. 02/5511656) has English-speaking staff members and doctors. Stazione Centrale has a 24-hour **pharmacy** (tel. 02/6690735). Other pharmacies rotate 24-hour service; the "Vivere Milano" section of the newspaper *La Repubblica* and the "Cronaca di Milano" section of *Corriere della Sera* list the schedule under the heading *Farmacie*.

PHONES

Make local as well as long-distance or collect calls from either of **Telecom**'s central offices: in the Galleria Vittorio Emanuele (between P. del Duomo and P. della Scala), open 24 hours, and in Stazione Centrale; open daily 8 AM–9:30 PM.

VISITOR INFORMATION

The two **APT** tourist offices are at Piazza del Duomo (Palazzo del Turismo, V. Marconi 1, tel. 02/72524300; open weekdays 8:30–8 (until 7 in winter), Sat. 9–1 and 2–6 (until 7 in winter), Sun. 9–1 and 2–5), and in Stazione Centrale (tel. 02/72524360; open Mon.–Sat. 8–7, Sun. 9–12:30 and 1:30–6). Both have hotel info and indispensable and free publications on nightlife and cultural events: *Hello Milano* and *Milano Mese*. The free but hefty *Milano: Dove Como Quando* features good in-depth info (in Italian) on sights and shopping spots. Another source for arts info is **Comune di Milano** (Galleria Vittorio Emanuele, tel. 02/8690734; open Mon.–Sat. 8:30–7). Travelers with disabilities can seek info about city services at **Ledha,** Lega Difesa Diritti Handicappati (V. Monte Santo 7, tel. 02/6570425, fax 02/6570426). Far and away the best Web site on Milan, with comprehensive and up-to-date info in English on the metropolis and its surroundings, is at **http://www.milanoin.it.**

GAY AND LESBIAN RESOURCES • ARCI Gay (V. Torricelli 19, tel. 02/89401749) has listings of events happening in the gay and lesbian community. For reading material, *see* English-Language Books, *above*.

COMING AND GOING

BY PLANE

In 1999 the opening took place of **Malpensa 2000,** greater Milan's newly expanded, newly modernized international airport, which has drawn fervent jeers from passengers and airlines alike. Though Malpensa is 45 km (28 mi) from downtown Milan and not yet connected by rail, the Italian government nevertheless relegated the majority of foreign carriers' international flights out to the notoriously delay-plagued airport, thus keeping most of more convenient **Linate Airport,** 10 km (6 mi) southeast of Milan, for its own national airline, Alitalia. Most carriers still have some flights out of Linate, though; be sure to check. Major airlines serving Milan are **Air France** (tel. 02/715155), **Alitalia** (tel. 147/65643 or, in town, 02/733335), **American Airlines** (tel. 02/74866371 at Malpensa), **British Airways** (tel. 147/812266), **Canadian Airlines** (tel. 1678/62216), **Iberia** (tel. 02/74866431 at Malpensa, 02/714648 at Linate), **KLM** (tel. 02/249161), **Lufthansa** (tel. 02/58372237), and **United** (tel. 02/40099392). There are a dozen car-rental agencies with offices at both Malpensa and Linate, including Avis, Hertz, and Maggiore; call ahead to reserve a car, or you'll wind up paying twice the price. Luggage storage is L5,000 per day. If you happen to lose your luggage, try calling 02/70124451.

For **general information** (in English upon request) at both Malpensa and Linate, call 02/74852200. For Malpensa-specific information toll-free, call 167/337337, or check on the web at www.sea-aerportimi-lano.it.

AIRPORT TRANSIT • STAM buses (tel. 02/66984509) ferry passengers between Linate and Stazione Centrale every 20 minutes, 5:40 AM–1 AM. Tickets (L4,500) for the 20- to 30-minute trip to Stazione Centrale can be bought in the airport or on board. Look for signs marked AEROPORTI DI MILANO outside the station to the right. Cheaper city buses (Bus 73) connect the airport with Piazza San Babila, in central Milan, departing every 10–15 minutes (5:30 AM–12:20 AM). Purchase tickets (L1,500) at the airport newsstand.

From Malpensa Airport, **STAM** buses (tel. 02/40099280) leave for Stazione Centrale every 20 minutes, 5:20 AM–10:30 PM, more frequently during the day (1 hr, L13,000). The **Malpensa Express** runs from Stazione Nord every half hour, 5:30 AM–11:30 PM, for the same price. STAM buses connect Malpensa and Linate twice daily, in the morning and the afternoon (L18,000). **Air Pullman** buses connect Malpensa and Linate every hour, 4 AM–11:30 PM (L18,000).

BY TRAIN

Milan's imposing, unofficial monument to fascism, **Stazione Centrale** (tel. 147/888088), a few kilometers northeast of downtown on Metro lines M2 and M3, handles the bulk of Milan's rail traffic. Destinations from here include Venice (14 daily, 4–5 hrs, L34,000), Turin (17 daily, 1½–2 hrs, L22,500), Florence (9 daily, 3 hrs, L37,000), Lake Como (hourly, 40 min), and Rome (10 daily, 5–8 hrs, L68,000), as well as other European cities. The major international connections from Milan are to Paris on the superfast French TGV, to Zurich and Bern via Domodossola, and to Nice via Genoa. U.S.-issued credit cards are no longer accepted here; to charge a ticket with your card, go to a travel agency (there's a CIT office in the station). Luggage storage is open daily 4 AM–1:30 AM (L5,000 for 12 hrs); currency exchange is available, although not at the best rates. **Stazione Nord** (P. Cadorna 14, M1 or M2, tel. 02/8511608) sends twice as many trains to Como (2 per hr, 1 hr). Other Milan train stops with Metro connections include **Stazione Garibaldi** (M2), **Repubblica** (M3), and **Porta Venezia** (M1). Check train schedules to see which stops your train covers.

During the Naviglio Festival in June, look for free open-air jazz and classical concerts throughout Milan. Call 02/89409971 or the APT office for details.

BY BUS

Long-distance buses depart from the **Autostradale** office (P. Castello 1, tel. 166/845010; open daily 6:30 AM–9:30 PM). A call to Autostradale costs L500 per minute, so try to get info in person. Blue buses run to Turin (12 daily, 2¼ hrs, L16,500), Aosta (2–3 daily, 2½–3½ hrs, L21,500), and Rimini (2 daily, 5 hrs, L50,500). At the **Autostradale Viaggi** travel agency (tel. 02/801161 or 02/72001304, fax 02/86460924; open weekdays 9–1 and 2–6:30), next to the Autostradale, book international tickets and buy **Tourbus** tickets to Eastern Europe (they're cheaper and faster than trains, but certainly less comfortable). Buses leave Thursday and Sunday for Prague, also Friday in summer (17½ hrs, L128,000).

GETTING AROUND

If you're in Milan for more than a day, invest in a real map, such as the tourist office's effort on the "Milano è Milano" leaflet. Start with the tourist triangle. Find the central **Piazza del Duomo** (though the plaza itself was under major renovation and virtually inaccessible at press time), on which lie the tourist office and the Museo Civico d'Arte Contemporanea. North of Piazza del Duomo, Galleria Vittorio Emanuele leads to **Piazza della Scala,** site of the famous opera house. From here, the Pinacoteca di Brera is found by taking Via Verdi, at the northwest corner of the piazza, and turning right on Via Brera. Back at the Duomo, look ahead with your back to the church's facade—the big brick building in the distance is the Castello Sforzesco. To reach the castle, take Via Orefici to Piazza Cordusio and continue straight on Via Dante.

For bar hopping, more churches, places to eat, or even to find your hotel, your best bet (lazy types, rejoice!) is to use public transport (*see below*). Milan has several neighborhoods packed with bars and shops. For nightlife, especially student-oriented activity, head to the **Navigli Canals,** near Porta Ticinese, on the south side of town. To get there, take Metro line M2 to Porta Genova and exit at Via Casale (follow signs in the station). Via Casale soon hits Alzaia Naviglio Grande along the canal. This is the thick of things in the Navigli; the street parallel to Alzaia on the other side of the canal is Ripa di Porta Ticinese. For cool shops and restaurants, take Alzaia Naviglio Grande to Piazza XXIV Maggio and go left on Corso di Porta Ticinese. Another nightlife/shopping destination is the **Brera-Garibaldi** area, behind the Brera Museum. Metro stop Moscova (M2) takes you right to Corso Garibaldi, north of Via Brera. This area is brimming with secondhand shops, restaurants, outdoor cafés, and art galleries.

Tickets for the intracity Metro, tram, and bus cost L1,500; buy them at machines and booths in subway stations or at bars and tobacco shops, labeled TABACCHI. Once tickets are punched by inserting them in the box on the bus or tram or at the Metro entrance, they're valid for 75 minutes of travel on all three modes of transport. You can't exit and reenter the Metro with the same ticket, but you can transfer lines. Tickets valid for 24 hours (L6,000) or 48 hours (L9,000) are also available. Buy reduced-fare passes at offices marked ABBONAMENTI in the Cadorna, Romolo, San Donato, and Centrale Metro stations. Generally, ticket windows are open Monday–Saturday 7:45–1 and 1:45–7. The **ATM** transportation offices in the Duomo Metro station (tel. 02/89010797) and Stazione Centrale (train level, tel. 02/6697032) provide maps and info on public transport within the city, including prices and an explanation of the bus and Metro systems in English. Both offices are open Monday–Saturday 8–8.

BY METRO

Milan has only three Metro lines, which means your stop can be a 20-minute walk from your destination. Still, the subway serves most of the city's must-sees, as well as the train and bus stations, and runs 6 AM–midnight. The lines are color coded: M1 (red), M2 (green), and M3 (yellow). The ends of the green and red lines split in two directions, so check the final destination before getting on. Maps are posted throughout the system; transfer points are the Cadorna, Duomo, Stazione Centrale, and Loreto stations.

BY BUS AND TRAM

More comprehensive (thus more confusing) than the Metro, Milan's system of more than 50 bus and tram lines hits almost every corner of the city. Most run every 10–20 minutes 5 AM–1 AM; yellow signs at each stop list destinations. Many people hop on ticketless or don't validate tickets—and risk hefty fines. Buses also circle the city—ideal for an overview of central Milan. From Stazione Centrale, buses marked DESTRA circle to the southeast; buses marked SINISTRA, to the northwest. A 1920s-era **tourist tram,** called "Ciao Milano," circles the city in a 2-hour loop twice per day (11 and 1), leaving from Piazza Castello and providing multilingual narration (L30,000; tickets sold on tram; tel. 02/8055323 or 02/72002584).

BY TAXI

Call **Arco** (02/6767), **Pronto Taxi** (tel. 02/5251), or **Radio Taxidata** (tel. 02/5353), or wait by taxi signs near Metro stops and train stations. Cabs are extremely pricey in Milan, with almost no ride costing less than L15,000; plan accordingly.

WHERE TO SLEEP

Except for Milan's lone hostel, most "cheap" lodgings are reasonably clean and tolerable generic hotels. If you want to stay near the Stazione Centrale, you can find bargain choices near the Giardini Pubblici. But, prices being uniformly high in Milan, you might as well shell out for a hotel either in the center near most sights or, for better nightlife, around Porta Genova and Porta Ticinese. Milan's hotels are at their fullest from March to May and in September, when international trade fairs take over the city, but it's always wise to make reservations in advance.

BETWEEN STAZIONE CENTRALE AND GIARDINI PUBBLICI

UNDER L95,000 • San Tomaso. This clean, popular hotel hosts young'uns from all over. Doubles, all with bath, are*L90,000–120,000, triples around L130,000, and all rooms (apart from some singles) come with telephone and TV and include breakfast. Ask for discounts on longer stays. *V. Tunisia 6, 4th floor, 20124, tel. 02/29514747. M1 to Porta Venezia. 12 rooms, 10 with shower.*

CITY CENTER

UNDER L80,000 • Hotel Cesare Correnti. The modest but tidy Correnti has singles (L45,000–L50,000) and doubles (L70,000–75,000). The manager and the kids who help run the place are accommodating, and the location, between the Duomo and San Lorenzo, is ideal. *V. Cesare Correnti 14, 2nd floor, 20123, tel. 02/8057609, fax 02/72010715. 7 rooms without bath.*

Hotel Ullrich. In terms of location, quality, and price, this hotel is one of the best. Owned by a relative of the man who runs Cesare Correnti (*see above*), the Ullrich is clean and near the Duomo. Doubles are L75,000–L80,000, and singles a mere L40,000. *C. Italia 6, 20122, tel. 02/86450156, fax 02/804355. M1 or M3 to Duomo. 7 rooms without bath. Laundry.*

UNDER L125,000 • Hotel Fiorella. This hardwood- floored hotel costs a bit more (doubles with bath, L120,000), but you get what you pay for. The sparkling rooms come with TV, telephone, and espresso maker stocked with coffee; night owls have no curfew. *V. Marghera 14, 20149, tel. 02/4692302, fax 02/4815938. Between Wagner and De Angeli Metro (M1) stops. 20 rooms with bath. Cash only.*

Hotel Speronari. You're guaranteed a great location—one block from the Duomo. Service is friendly, and the somewhat generic rooms are spotless. There's a café downstairs and a TV lounge. Doubles are a little steep at L110,000 without bath—location is money. *V. Speronari 4, 20123, tel. 02/86461125, fax 02/72003178. M1 or M3 to Duomo. 32 rooms, 22 with bath.*

UNDER L200,000 • Antica Locanda Leonardo. This pension near Santa Maria delle Grazie (*see* Worth Seeing, *below*) has something most budget lodgings here lack: atmosphere. Air-conditioned doubles are pricey (L195,000 and up), but they are clean and have antique wooden furniture and telephones. Even so, the owners are used to putting up grungy vagabondlike travelers. There's a small garden in the back and a cozy TV lounge. *C. Magenta 78, 20123, tel. 02/463317, fax 02/48019012. M2 to Cadorna or M1 or M3 to the Duomo. 14 rooms with shower.*

NEAR PORTA TICINESE

UNDER L70,000 • Cantore. The Cantore's a 15-minute walk from the Duomo (or a quick tram ride) and even closer to the Navigli. And it's cheap: doubles are L65,000, triples L95,000. You won't be snuggling up to fluffy down pillows, but at least it's clean. There's a curfew of 2 AM, but it's 3:30 on weekends. *C. Genova 25, 20123, tel. and fax 02/8357565. M2 to P. Genova; north on C. Colombo, which becomes C. Genova. 11 rooms with bath.*

UNDER L100,000 • Hotel Certosa. You're blocks from the Navigli party action, but there's no bedtime at this unremarkable but decent hotel. Rooms are L95,000 without bath, but try to bargain them down. *C. San Gottardo 7, 20151, tel. 02/58111978. M2 to Porta Genova; east on V. Vigevano to canal, right on V. Gorizia, right on C. San Gottardo at P. XXIV Maggio; or from Stazione Centrale, Tram 9 to P. XXIV Maggio. 26 rooms, 17 with shower.*

Panettone (a cakelike egg bread with raisins and candied fruit) is one bit of Milanese gastronomy that's easy to find, especially at Christmas (and afterward, when prices drop by half). Look for locals with beribboned, colored, hatboxlike packages—inside lurk the golden treasures.

HOSTEL

Piero Rotta Hostel (HI). Milan's hostel is set in a green, peaceful environment on the outskirts of town—an easy commute on the Metro. The midnight curfew makes it difficult to carouse, but the price (L26,000 per person, including breakfast) eases the pain. Other bummers: there's a strict daytime lockout, it smells like sweat, and a HI card is required, though you can buy one here (L30,000). There's luggage storage. *V. Martino Bassi 2, 20148, tel. and fax 02/39267095. 388 beds. Lockout 9:30–3:30. Cash only. Closed Dec. 22–Jan. 13.*

WHERE TO EAT

One look at Milan's food prices and you'll understand why aspiring supermodels stay so skinny. If you want to sink your teeth into some of the city's traditional dishes, keep your eyes peeled for risotto *alla milanese* (the creamy rice concoction flavored with saffron), osso buco, *cotoletta di vitello alla milanese* (breaded veal cutlet), and *cassöeula* (a pork and vegetable stew). However, don't feel obliged to dine only on Lombard fare; Milan is also the biggest gastronomic melting pot in Italy, with a range of Asian and African foods that is unequalled anywhere else in the country. Inquire at the tourist office or consult "Dove Come Quando" if you're in search of a particular cuisine.

Though Milan's haute cuisine does not pander to budget- minded diners, there are self-service chains scattered throughout the city: **Brek** (V. Lepetit 20, tel. 02/6705149; V. del Duca, 5, tel. 02/76023379; P. U. Giordano 1) is a safe bet for pasta and salads. More authentic (and cheaper) are *latterie* (dairy markets); those marked TAVOLA CALDA serve simple local fare. The very cheapest meals are best assembled at a supermarket; try **La Coloniale** (V. Cesare Correnti 6, tel. 02/72000067). For sweets, bread, or pizza by the kilo, try **Il Forno dei Navigli** (Alzaia Naviglio Pavese 2, tel. 02/8323372) or **Pizzeria Mimi** (V. Torino 48, between Duomo and Ticinese, tel. 02/72021075), which doubles as a *rosticceria* (rotisserie). An **outdoor market** on Piazza XXIV Maggio in the Navigli is open weekdays 8:30–1 and 4–7:30.

UNDER L10,000 • Bar Brera. Scrumptious sandwiches (around L7,000–L8,000 each), stuffed with eggplant, peppers, cheese, prosciutto, and more, resemble works of art at this air-conditioned café across from the Pinacoteca di Brera. Don't expect a full meal here, though. At night, future Bellinis unleash their creative juices with a few beers out on the sidewalk. *V. Brera 23, no tel. M2 to Lanza. Cash only. Closed Sun.*

Grand'Italia. This congenial, vaguely pre-packaged family joint serves a rotating menu of very cheap *primi piatti* (L6,000), *secondi* (L12,000), U.S.-style pizza (L10,000), gigantic salads (L10,000), and homemade desserts (L6,000). Recommended are *focacce farcite* (stuffed focaccia) and *tris di primi* (three types of pasta served together). *V. Palermo 5, tel. 02/877759. M2 to Moscova; take C. Garibaldi, left on V. Palermo. Cash only. Closed Tues.*

UNDER L15,000 • Al Gran Galeone. Half the price and twice as nice as other pizzerias in the center, this locals-only place has an outdoor patio in summer. Pizzas run L6,000–L12,000, *piatti secondi* about L10,000. *V. Macedonio Melloni 31, tel. 02/7384898. From Duomo, Tram 60 to P. V Giornate; walk 4 blocks east of piazza. Closed Thurs.*

Calafaria Unione. Though the menu is always different at this latteria near the Duomo, the food is dependably good and the service friendly. Vegetarians can enjoy the large mixed salads. It's pricier than most latterie (L15,000 for pasta, wine, and coffee) but worth it. *V. Unione 8, tel. 02/866013. M3 to Missori; from P. Missori, take V. Unione. Cash only. No dinner. Closed Sun.*

Circolo Combattenti. There's no sign in front of this place hidden in the Arco della Pace, but the eatery—often frequented by war veterans and their pooches—serves simple food, some of the cheapest in town. At lunch a *primo piatto* (first course), *secondo,* and vegetable costs L12,000 (L18,000 at dinner). Call ahead for dinner (by lunchtime of the same day), so they know how much to cook. *P. Sempione 2/A, tel. 02/33101578. M1 or M2 to Cadorna; northwest edge of Parco Sempione, behind Castello Sforzesco (15-min walk from Metro). Cash only. Closed Sun. and late July–Aug.*

Premiata Pizzeria. Pizzas cost a little more (L8,000– L16,000) at this popular pizzeria in the Navigli, but you can order late into the night and dine in the garden. *Alzaia Naviglio Grande 2, tel. 02/8395133. M2 to Porta Genova. Closed Tues. No lunch in Aug.*

UNDER L20,000 • Il Moro. Craving pizza topped with tahini or pineapple? This Egyptian-Italian eatery will have the mummy in your tummy jumping for joy. You'll have to ask a satisfied eater nearby to explain what tagliatelle *alla camicia nera* (in a black shirt) means. Finish with heavily sugared Egyptian coffee and you'll be ready for a night out on the Navigli. Pizzas and pastas run L8,000–L15,000, secondi L10,000–L20,000. *V. Ciceri Visconti 8, corner of P. Martini, tel. 02/55188128. Closed Mon. Other location: V. Salaino, corner of V. Solari, tel. 02/48007652. Closed Tues.*

Il Fondaco dei Mori. One of the showcases of Milan's culinary diversity, this restaurant serves up Islamic food to those in the know (you must ring the bell at the unmarked gate to get in). Enjoy a dinner buffet for under L20,000 either indoors or out. It's hard to find, but worth the trouble, especially if you've had one too many *pasta al pomodoro. V. Solferino 33, tel. 02/653711. M2 to Moscova, then head down V. Statuo toward Piazza S. Marco; Statuo becomes Solferino one block from piazza.*

Quicosì. If you're already full after the antipasti buffet, wait until dessert—with no menu, the waitstaff just keeps bringing plates of food until you burst. You'll get appetizers, two pastas, two secondi, cheese, sweets, liqueur, wine, and coffee for L30,000. Unless you're training for sumo wrestling, there's no way you'll eat it all. At lunch you can stick to one course and coffee for L10,000–L12,000. *V. Poma 6, tel. 02/733849. From Duomo, Tram 60 east; V. Poma on left 7 blocks after P. V Giornate. Closed Mon. No lunch Tues.*

UNDER L30,000 • Al Matarel. This is one of the few places in Milan where you can find authentic Lombard cuisine. Though you pay for it through the nose, it's definitely worth a splurge. It's slightly elegant—no jeans and T-shirts—but you'll welcome the warm trattoria feel. Try the cassöeula (L27,000) or the cotoletta di vitello (L28,000). Primi are about L16,000. *V. Laura Solera Mantegazza 75, off C. Garibaldi, tel. 02/6592196 or 02/654204. M2 to Moscova. Closed Tues. and July. No lunch Wed.*

Arturosa La Latteria. At this cozy neighborhood restaurant the devoted local clientele seems confident of being served the best Lombard food around. Classic Northern Italian dishes abound on the constantly changing menu. *Primi* run L12,000—L14,000, *secondi* a bit higher. *V. San Marco 24, tel. 02/6597653. M2 to Moscova, then head 3 blocks down V. della Moscova to V. San Marco. Closed weekends.*

CAFÉS AND GELATERIE

Expensive cafés line the Galleria Vittorio Emanuele, where you can sip an aperitif or espresso and watch the beautiful people and the not-so-beautiful hordes of tourists strut by. Head south and get pensive at **Portnoy Caffè** (V. de Amicis, at C. di Porta Ticinese, tel. 02/58113429), where art exhibits and poetry readings are occasionally held. When the weather's nice, there's nothing better than **Piazza del Carmine**, in the Brera-Garibaldi area, for seeing and being seen, although you end up paying dearly for the view (L3,000 for an espresso). Try romantic **L'Ecurie** (V. Ponte Vetero 23, tel. 02/804403), with its dim candlelight. Milan's best scoops include **Gelateria Toldo** (V. Sacchi 6, tel. 02/86460863) and **Gelateria Ecologica Artigiana** (C. di Porta Ticinese 40, tel. 02/58101872; closed Wed.), which has flavors for vegans, as well as raspberry gelato so fresh it has seeds.

WORTH SEEING

If your goal is to cover the main attractions, most of which are within the two innermost ring roads, you won't see much of the rest of the city. For a complete tour, tackle one neighborhood at a time. Pick Metro stations central to each district from which to start your exploring. The Duomo Metro (M1 and M3) station is convenient to the city center, the Moscova and Lanza (M2) stations to the Brera area, the Cordusio (M1) and Cadorna (M1 and M2) stations to Castello Sforzesco, and Cadorna to Santa Maria delle Grazie and Leonardo da Vinci's *Last Supper*. The Porta Genova and Romolo (M2) stops will put you in a good position to explore the funky areas beyond the Navigli Canal. Don't forget that buses and trams hit almost every city block, and they can also be good ways to get around. The **tourist tram** (see "Getting Around," above) covers much of the central city with narration. If you want to be held by the hand but prefer to walk, the **APT** (tourist office) runs 2½-hr. guided walking tours covering many of the major sights. The tours (L25,000) leave Mondays at 10 AM or by appointment for groups.

CASTELLO SFORZESCO

In 1450, Francesco Sforza, a wealthy mercenary soldier who married Bianca Maria Visconti, commissioned the rebuilding of this brawny castle. It stands as a monument to the Sforza and Visconti clans and their lasting impact on Milan. Under another Sforza, Lodovico (Il Moro), the castle became an important venue for Renaissance art. Lodovico hired Bramante to design the castle's *rocchetta* (fortress) and da Vinci to decorate the interior. The *castello* now houses a variety of museums. Most memorable is the **Pinacoteca** (tel. 02/62083940), exhibiting Arcimbaldi's *Spring* and works by Bellini, Mantegna, and Foppa. In the dungeon is the **Collezione Egiziano,** a refreshing departure from the usual Italian masterpieces. The **Civici Musei d'Arte** are noteworthy if only for Michelangelo's unfinished *Rondanini Pietà*, which the artist worked on until four days before his death at the age of 89. Even if you've had it with museums, Castello Sforzesco is worth a visit just for a romp about the grounds and courtyard. *P. Castello, tel. 02/62083940. M1 to Cairoli. Admission free. All museums open daily 9–5:40.*

DUOMO

Reigning serenely over city center, Milan's Gothic Duomo is one of the largest—it's said to hold 40,000 people—and most ornate cathedrals in the world. Not surprisingly, the exterior's conglomeration of spires and pinnacles reminiscent of a giant ice castle took centuries to complete. Construction began in 1386 under Galeazzo Visconti III, the first duke of Milan, and wasn't finished until 1897. As late as 1958, workers were still tying up loose ends. The many artists who worked on the mammoth structure created an odd but mesmerizing mix of Gothic and Baroque styles, unified only by the primary building material: marble from quarries near Lake Maggiore. The *Madonnina* (little Madonna), a statue of the Virgin covered in 3,900 gold leaves, stands atop the highest roof pinnacle. The exterior also has beautiful bronze entrance doors and prophets perched on 135 marble spires.

Light filters into the vast interior through stained-glass windows; the first six on the right date from the 15th century. On the right aisle near the south transept is the tomb of Gian Giacomo Medici, sculpted in the 1560s by Leone Leoni. Straight ahead is the Duomo's most famous sculpture—the morbid figure of St. Bartolomeo, who was martyred by being flayed alive. The central crucifix hangs on a suspension device designed by da Vinci. Directly below, under the mosaic floors, the church **treasury** (admission L3,000; open 9–noon and 2:30–6) displays embroidered vestments and bejeweled crowns from the 4th through 12th centuries.

For a view of central Milan and a closer look at the Duomo's prophet-capped spires, walk outside the north transept and take the stairs (L6,000) or the elevator (L8,000) to the roof (open Mar.–Oct., daily 9–

5:45; Nov.–Feb., daily 9–4:15). Depending on major construction projects on the street outside, you may have to walk around to the back of the Duomo and cross a precarious pedestrian walkway to enter. Pollution sometimes detracts from the view, but on a clear day, you can see the Alps. To the right of the church's main entrance, stairs lead down to the original **Roman basilica** (admission free; open Tues.–Sun. 10–noon and 3–5), over which the Duomo was built. The **Museo del Duomo** (P. del Duomo 14, tel. 02/860358; admission L10,000; open Tues.–Sun. 9:30–12:30 and 3–6), next to the Museo Civico d'Arte Contemporanea, presents an account of Il Duomo's construction. *P. del Duomo. M1 or M3 to Duomo. Basilica admission free; see specific admission prices and hrs above. Open daily 7–7.*

GALLERIA VITTORIO EMANUELE

Inside this cross-shaped 19th-century promenade covered by a glass arched ceiling, you'll find expensive cafés, bookstores, and designer boutiques, plus fast food, the Telecom office, and the Comune di Milano info center. The main reason to visit this Italian-style mall, however, is to people-watch: the trendy Milanesi who parade here certainly are a sight. If the crowd becomes too much, switch to gawking at the huge glass dome, or turn your attention to the floor and observe a Milanese tradition that goes back over 100 years—by rudely stepping on the most sensitive part of the inlaid golden bull. *Between P. del Duomo and P. della Scala, no phone. M1 or M3 to Duomo.*

PINACOTECA DI BRERA

Known throughout the world, the Brera's 38 rooms house such masterpieces as Piero della Francesca's *Urbino Altarpiece* (Room XXIV), Raphael's *Marriage of the Virgin* (Room XXIV), Mantegna's *Dead Christ* (Room VI), Giovanni Bellini's *Pietà* (Room VI), and Caravaggio's *Supper at Emmaus* (Room XXIX). Although 14th- to 18th-century art is the museum's strong suit, recent donations have enabled the Brera to acquire numerous contemporary works, including paintings by Picasso and Modigliani, displayed in the first hall as you enter. The building itself was constructed in the 17th century and made into a museum during the Napoleonic era. *V. Brera 28, tel. 02/722631. M3 to Montenapoleone stop or M2 to Lanza. Admission L8,000. Open Tues.–Sat. 9–5, Sun. 9–12:15.*

SANTA MARIA DELLE GRAZIE

To the left of this church is the **Cenacolo Vinciano,** a former Dominican refectory, now basically a shrine to Leonardo da Vinci's **Last Supper,** newly restored and, as of May 27, 1999, completely free from scaffolding for the first time in years. Since Leonardo's death in 1519, the *Last Supper* has suffered an amazingly cruel fate. Leonardo used an experimental primer, which has peeled and crumbled over time. It's said that well-meaning monks in the 19th century actually whitewashed the fresco. Bad idea. Napoleon's troops used the wall for target practice, and in August 1943 an American bombing raid nearly destroyed the work. Worst of all, attempts at restoration over the centuries have mostly hastened the fresco's deterioration, leaving the *Last Supper* in a somewhat sad state. You may have to stand in line for hours to see the newly restored masterpiece (try early weekday mornings), but you're only allowed to gaze for three minutes lest your humid breath ruin everything all over again. Look for Judas, small and dark, calmly reaching for bread as pandemonium strikes the other apostles. Also notice the repetition of threes in the windows and the groupings. The Lombard Gothic church itself was designed by Guiniforte Solari between 1466 and 1490; Bramante added the Renaissance cupola and three apses, as well as the cloister and sacristy. *P. Santa Maria delle Grazie, C. Magenta, tel. 02/4987588. M1 or M2 to Cadorna. Admission L12,000. Open Tues.–Sun. 8–1:45.*

TEATRO ALLA SCALA

La Scala, Shangri-La for opera lovers, opened August 3, 1778, with Antonio Salieri's *Europa Riconosciuta.* Today the bill inevitably includes operas by Puccini and Verdi, as well as classical concerts, ballets, and other usual suspects. The small stalls and horseshoe shape of the auditorium give the interior a feeling of intimate grandeur and incredible acoustics. Best of all, even lowly hostelers can afford to rub programs with the Milanese elite: 200 standing-room tickets (L10,000) go on sale 45 minutes before curtain—but you might have to line up in the morning if the show's really popular. Otherwise try arriving between 6 and 6:30 PM. Gallery seats start at around L30,000. The adjacent **Museo Teatrale** displays strands of hair from Mozart and Puccini; death masks of Puccini, Wagner, and Verdi; and Greek theater props from 4 BC. *P. della Scala. Ticket info: tel. 02/72003744, fax 02/8879297. Open daily 10–6. M1 or M3 to Duomo. Museo Teatrale: tel. 02/8879473. Admission L6,000. Open daily 9–12 and 2–5 (closed Sun., Nov.–May).*

CHURCHES AND CHAPELS

SANT'AMBROGIO • St. Ambrose, the patron saint and 4th-century bishop of Milan, established this basilica and was himself buried here in AD 397. Inside, notice the Byzantine pillar next to the nave, topped with a bronze serpent (symbolizing Aaron's rod), and the pulpit depicting animals in a feeding frenzy. A mosaic of Ambrose, in the church's Cappella di San Vittorio in Ciel d'Oro, is famous for its rendering of his slightly deformed face. *P. Sant'Ambrogio 15, tel. 02/86450895. M2 to Sant'Ambrogio.*

SANT'EUSTORGIO • Near the canal, this beautiful, simple church is named for Bishop Sant'Eustorgio, who according to legend was given the relics of the Magi by Emperor Constantine. Of note in the basilica, rebuilt in the 9th and 14th centuries, is the Portinari chapel, with 15th-century frescoes by Foppa depicting the life of St. Peter. Also look for the fading frescoes on the many columns and the remains of the Roman basilica near the nave. *P. Sant'Eustorgio. M2 to Porta Genova, or Bus 59 from center.*

MUSEUMS

Milan's primary exhibits and collections are in the Castello Sforzesco and the Pinacoteca di Brera (*see above*), but there are smaller museums and galleries throughout the city. Stop by the info office (*see* Visitor Information, *above*) in Piazza del Duomo for exhibit listings—check the free English-language newspaper *Hello Milano.*.

MUSEO CIVICO ARCHEOLOGICO • A vast collection of Greek, Roman, and Etruscan pieces is displayed in Monastero Maggiore, the 16th-century Benedictine convent. One section chronicles the Roman period in Milan. *C. Magenta 15, tel. 02/86450011. M1 or M2 to Cadorna or M1 to Cairoli. Admission free. Open Tues.–Sun. 9:30–5:30.*

The Visconti family ruled medieval Milan with a cruel hand; during your ramblings look for the family crest—a viper with its jaws agape, devouring a child.

MUSEO CIVICO D'ARTE CONTEMPORANEA • Considering it's free and 20 feet from the Duomo, don't skip the opportunity to see works by Mondrian, Modigliani, Matisse, and more. The gallery also traces 19th- to 20th-century Italian art from futurism to the Roman school. The museum was closed for restoration at press time, but it's due to re-open by 2000. *P. del Duomo 12, tel. 02/62083219. M1 or M3 to Duomo. Open Tues.–Sun. 9:30–7:30.*

MUSEO NAZIONALE DELLA SCIENZA E TECNICA • Housed in a former Benedictine monastery, this is one of the world's foremost museums of science and technology. Inside, the **Leonardo Gallery** has a collection of models based on technical designs by the man himself. *V. San Vittore 21, tel. 02/485551. M2 to Sant'Ambrogio. Admission L10,000. Open Tues.–Fri. 9:30–4:50, weekends 9:30–6:20.*

MUSEO POLDI PEZZOLI • Named for the 19th-century art collector who once lived here, the Pezzoli museum displays a private collection of furnishings, ceramics, glassware, and paintings by Mantegna, Piero della Francesca, and Botticelli. Pollaiolo's *Portrait of a Lady* and Guardi's *Gray Lagoon* are highlights. *V. Manzoni 12, tel. 02/794889. From P. della Scala, go northwest on V. Manzoni, or M3 to Montenapoleone. Admission L12,000. Open Tues.–Sun. 9:30–12:30 and 2:30–6, Sat. until 7:30; Apr.–Sept., closed Sun. afternoon.*

TRIENNALE DI MILANO • Not a museum in the traditional sense, the Triennale, housed in Giovanni Muzio's Palazzo dell'Arte, hosts changing shows officially titled the *International Exhibition of Modern Decorative and Industrial Arts and Modern Architecture.* Themes range from fashion to virtual reality. Most exhibits charge admission, but some are free. For info on current shows, inquire at the APT office, check newspapers, or call the Triennale directly. *V. Alemagna 6, inside Parco Sempione, tel. 02/724341. M1 or M2 to Cadorna. Admission L10,000. Open Tues.–Sun. 10–8.*

MUSEO DEL CINEMA–CINETECA ITALIANA • If Italian film's your thing, this museum has a fine collection of pre-cinematic and cinematic apparati. The displays concentrate on the technical aspects of cinema but also include tributes to some of the more notable filmmakers in the rich Italian tradition. *Palazzo Dugnani, V. Manin, 2, on the edge of the Giardini Pubblici di Porta Venezia, tel. 02/6554977. M3 to Turati. Admission L5000. Open Tues.–Fri. 3–6.*

PINACOTECA AMBROSIANA • Founded in the 17th century by Cardinal Federico Borromeo, the musuem combines Borromeo's celebrated trove of ancient manuscripts and his art collection. Here you can contemplate works by artists such as Leonardo, Raphael, Titian, and Pinturicchio. *P. Pio XI 2, tel. 02/8645136. Admission L12,000. Open Tues.–Sun. 10–5:30.*

SHOPPING

Not surprisingly, Italy's fashion capital has more than enough boutiques to plunge you into eternal debt. Stick to window-shopping in the posh Duomo district, nicknamed the Quadrilatero d'Oro (Golden Quadrilateral), where dozens of don't-touch-anything stores line **Via Montenapoleone,** northeast of Piazza della Scala. If your budget screams cubic zirconia instead of diamonds, the bric-a-brac **market,** held the last Sunday of each month along the Navigli canals, is probably more up your alley. For designer seconds, try the Saturday-morning **mercato** on Via Papiniano. Secondhand clothing shops include **Surplus** (C. Garibaldi 7, tel. 02/8693696), **Mercatino Michela** (C. Venezia 8, tel. 02/76003205), and, for groovy 1960s and 1970s styles, **Napoleone** (V. Arcimboldi 5, off V. Unione, tel. 02/875223), near the Duomo. Clothing at warehouse prices lines the shelves at **Il Salvagente** (V. Fratelli Bronzetti 16, M1 to San Babila, tel. 02/76110328). Trip the cobblestones fantastic in cheap but stylish shoes from **Strakam** (C. Colombo 10, M2 to Porta Genova, tel. 02/89402059) or **Alfonso Garlando** (V. Madonnina 1–2, M2 to Lanza, tel. 02/874679). If you crave all things Inter Milan, head out to **Interspazio,** the famed football club's official paraphernalia shop, which also affords a view of their stadium (San Siro stadium, gate 22, under the blue stand; M1 to De Angeli and then tram 24 to Piazza Axum; open Tues.–Sat. 10–12:45 and 2:30–5:30, plus during Inter matches). **Antiques markets** are held the third Saturday of the month (except August) on Via Fiori Chiaria, near Via Brera.

AFTER DARK

Milan's nightlife is hoppin' but costly, especially if you want to have a drink. Watch for deals on tickets and movie festivals, when things can get almost cheap. The newspapers *Il Corriere della Sera* and *La Repubblica* regularly list events and club schedules. On Wednesday check the *Corriere della Sera*'s "Vivi Milano" insert. The info office in the Galleria (*see* Visitor Information, *above*) has flyers on current cultural happenings and can book tickets for most of them. Buy tickets for big-name rock concerts at the **Virgin Megastore** (P. del Duomo 8, at V. Marconi, tel. 02/72003370). If you are a person with a physical disability, you can often attend concerts ticketless (i.e., free), including shows by the megastars who pack Milan's soccer stadium; inquire at the ticket office. For info on Milan's gay scene, call **ARCI Gay** (*see* Visitor Information, *above*).

BARS AND CLUBS

Even if you get into a club wearing sneakers and shorts, you'll wish you hadn't when you inevitably face the disdainful glares of the très elegant Milanese. It's not enough to simply *look* like you're loaded with lire—most dance clubs require a hefty cover of L20,000–L60,000. Hot spots can ice over in a matter of minutes, but if you cruise the **Navigli Canal** near Porta Ticinese, you're sure to stumble on *the* place of the week. The canal and nearby **Piazza Vetra** constitute the clear home base for student nightlife in Milan. Bars are generally coverless, but the average beer starts at L7,000; expect to pay at least L10,000 for a cocktail.

City Square. This huge disco is in the canal district, a few blocks south of Piazza Vetra. Techno music throbs into the wee hours, to the delight of the university students and Beautiful People. *V. Castelbarco 11, tel. 02/58310682; cover L20,000 and up. Closed Mon.–Tues.*

Coquetel. Drawing everyone from dog-toting reggae masters to coat-tie-and-cell-phone types, Coquetel's happy hour overflows onto the sidewalk even in winter. Outside, have your second beer half price; otherwise, invest a small fortune in a cocktail. *V. Vetere 14, tel. 02/8360688. M2 to Sant'Agostino; take V. Vincenzo to V. de Amicis, right on C. di Porta Ticinese, left on V. Vetere. Closed Sun.*

El Tumbun de San Marc. In the bar-happy Brera zone, this English publike joint is never dead on weekend nights, when it overflows with a casual college-age crowd. *V. San Marco 20, tel. 02/6599507. M2 to Moscova; east on V. Moscova, right on V. San Marco. Closed Sun.*

Hollywood. If you can get into the *in* place for the fashion set (cover L30,000 and up), you'll encounter a huge attitude quotient and astronomical drink prices. *V. Como 15/C, tel. 02/6598996.*

Il Bounty. Bartender Lucio and the baseball-capped steer skull on the wall draw in the dreadlocked Milanese "groonge" crowd for L3,500 beers the last Wednesday of every month. A punk panino (sandwich with bacon and anchovies) costs L5,000. *V. Lulli 30, tel. 02/2619277. M1 to Loreto; take V. Costa, right on V. Lulli. Closed Sun.*

Killer Plastic. The second Thursday of the month is Man-to- Man Night at this neon-sign disco, and the lesbian organization Towanda hosts the first and third Thursdays. A snooty supermodelish crowd takes over every Saturday. Cover is L15,000–L20,000. *V. Umbria 120, tel. 02/733996. Metro M3 to Lodi TBB.*

New Parco delle Rose. Want decadence? This place is filled with pools, slides, fountains, and several dance floors on which patrons groove to whatever suits them most—mainstream club scene, Latin, even ballroom dancing (all have separate entrances). Cover runs L25,000 (men) and L20,000 (women). *V. Fabio Massimo 36, tel. 02/5694755. M3 to Porto di Mare. Closed Mon.–Wed.*

Nuova Idea. Polka or tango to a live orchestra at Italy's largest gay disco, or head for the couples' dance floor in the techno room. The cover (L25,000) includes one drink. *V. de Castilla 30, tel. 02/69007859. M2 to Garibaldi. Closed Mon.–Wed.*

Rainbow Club. Spent your last lira but don't feel like dancing in the Metro? Head to the Rainbow on Friday for Karmadrome, the "alternative" night—there's no cover, not even for live shows. Booze beforehand: drinks are far from free. There's no cover Thursday and Friday; Saturday it's L15,000 (varies). *V. Besenzanica, off P. Bettini, tel. 02/4048399. M1 to Bande Nere. Closed Sun.–Wed.*

LIVE MUSIC

If opera is your thing, make an effort to see absolutely *anything* at Teatro alla Scala (*see* Worth Seeing, *above*). Opera season runs from September to July, and even from abroad you can book tickets in advance. Otherwise, check out some of Milan's live music clubs, which mostly feature jazz.

Milan's Teatro alla Scala was the first theater in the world to use electric lights—illuminated December 26, 1883.

Capolinea (V. Lodovico II Moro 119, tel. 02/89122024), in the Navigli district, remains the preeminent jazz club in Milan, featuring big-name Italian and international performers (and a pricey restaurant). **Le Scimmie** (V. Ascanio Sforza 49, south of Piazzale XXIV Maggio, tel. 02/89402874), a small and smoky club, presents a different—usually jazz fusion—band every night except Tuesday. Both clubs charge a cover, depending on the performance. For alternative rock and a crowd to match, try **Tunnel** (V. Sammartini, corner of V. Parravicini, tel. 02/66711370; closed after 10 PM Sun.–Mon.), alongside Stazione Centrale, though you officially need a membership card to get in—try playing the foreigner.

MOVIE THEATERS

A few cinemas show films in English once a week. Hit the **Anteo** (V. Milazzo 9, M2 to Moscova, tel. 02/6597732 or 02/6571093) on Monday, **Arcobaleno** (V. Tunisia 11, M1 to Porta Venezia, tel. 02/29406054 or 02/6571093) on Tuesday, **Mexico** (V. Savona 57, M2 to Porta Genova, tel. 02/48951802 or 02/6571093) on Thursday. Admission is L9,000 for all the above. The **Centrale** (V. Torino 30, M1 or M3 to Duomo, tel. 02/874826), also showing English movies on Thursday, charges L10,000. Pick up listings at the APT or check local papers such as *Corriere della Sera, La Repubblica,* and the free *Hello Milano.*

LOMBARDY

Traveling on a budget in Lombardy will challenge your imagination, your tolerance for bland hotels, and your appetite for pizza, the only consistently affordable food. But your efforts will be rewarded by the medieval and Renaissance glory of Mantua, Bergamo, and Cremona and by the eccentricity of Sabbioneta. Though all of these towns—and the Po Plain on which they sit—are industrialized and heavily touristed, you'll discover intriguing vestiges of many dynasties, from the bullying Longobards and regal Visconti to the ultra-rich, kooky Gonzagas.

The average Lombard is part classic Italian and part stereotypical New Yorker; don't expect everyone to be warm and welcoming. On the other hand, it's not unheard of for a tourist to ask for directions to the nearest sight and get a personal escort. The territory itself is equally diverse, combining fertile plains, rugged mountains, and vacationland lakes. And like the people, the landscape can sometimes be cold and unwelcoming. Other times it will fill you, like a plate of steamy risotto, with comfort and warmth.

FORZA ITALIA

Many Milanese have never visited the Pinacoteca di Brera, but the whole city fixates on the TV when Milan's calcio (soccer) teams, AC Milan and FC Inter (the Chicago Bulls of the Italian soccer league, with marquee superstar Ronaldo and nifty Nike-sponsored jerseys), kick for glory. You can root for one or neither, but definitely not both. The city's G. Meazza Olympic Stadium (V. Piccolomini 5, tel. 02/48707123; M1 to Lotto) was expanded for the 1990 World Cup and can now pack in 85,000 fans. You can be one of them by buying tickets—around L40,000 for cheap seats—at any Banca Popolare di Milano (P. Meda 4, tel. 02/77001) or Banca Cariplo (V. Verdi 8, tel. 02/88661). True fanatics can visit the concrete monstrosity on a guided tour (tel. 02/48700457; admission L5,000), and pick up the requisite Inter memorabilia at Interspazio (see "Shopping," above).

PAVIA

Pavia's redbrick architecture and serene, cobblestone streets belie its bellicose past which started with a 5th-century onslaught by none other than Atilla the Hun. This quiet university town sits on the left bank of the Ticino River, and because of its strategic location, came into being as a Roman outpost. It was later fortified by Goths and Byzantines to ward off the evil Longobards. The Milanese Visconti took over and built Pavia's castle and university in 1360 and 1361, respectively. The Pavesi imprisoned the king of France, François I, after his attempted takeover in 1525. Power passed to Savoy in 1743, then on to the French, the Austrians, and the Spanish. All the while, Pavia continued to develop as an intellectual center, boasting such academics as physicist Alessandro Volta (as in 9-volt batteries), writers Ugo Foscolo and Vincenzo Monti, and such students as poet Petrarch, playwright Goldoni, and explorer Christopher Columbus. Today life still revolves around the university; in summer Pavia takes a siesta. Come during the school year for college-town culture and nightlife, but don't expect prices to cater to student budgets—especially not in Pavia's famous fur shops.

BASICS

The **APT** (V. Fabio Filzi 2, tel. 0382/22156; open Mon.–Sat. 8:30–12:30 and 2–6) is the place for brochures, maps, and hotel info; they aren't supposed to make reservations. From train and bus stations, turn left up Via Trieste and right on Via Fabio Filzi.

COMING AND GOING

Trains run all day between Milan and Pavia (35 min, L3,500). The **train station** (tel. 1478/88088) has luggage storage (L5,000 per 12 hrs). Across the street, buses depart from the **Autocorriere Station** (V. Trieste 21, tel. 0382/302020; open Mon.–Sat. 6:30 AM–8 PM, Sun. 8:45–noon and 5–7); a ticket to Milan costs L4,700. From either station, Bus 3 or 6 goes to the city center; or walk 10 minutes down Via Vittorio Emanuele II (which becomes Corso Cavour) until you hit Strada Nuova, the main drag. Once you're in the small city center, huddled around Piazza della Vittoria, walking is the best way to get around.

WHERE TO SLEEP AND EAT

Stazione (V. B. de Rossi 8, 27100, off C. Manzoni, tel. 0382/35477; cash only) is the best you'll do for budget lodgings. It's not well marked, and noise is a problem due to its location near the train tracks. Doubles without bath are L80,000. Also near the train station, but one step up in luxury, is the **Aurora** (V. Vittorio Emanuele 25, 27100, tel. 0382/23664). Doubles with bath, phones, and TVs are L105,000. Overcome your anti-amphibian bias and try the local fried frog dishes (*rana*), or slurp the Pavese soup of boiling broth, eggs, bread, and cheese at **Osteria della Malora** (V. Milazzo 79, tel. 0382/34302; cash only). **Hosteria del Senatore** (V. Menocchio 21, main entrance on Vicolo del Senatore, off C. Cavour, no phone; cash only) offers an open courtyard in summer and a fireplace in winter; primi are around L8,000, secondi L10,000. Artsy **Caffè Teatro** (C. Strada Nuova 75, across from theater, tel. 0382/23098) transforms from a virtual library of studying students by day to a librarian's noisy nightmare at night. The café often sponsors concerts and readings by musicians, artists, and literati—check out the signed posters on the wall to see who you've missed. A covered **market** is held Monday–Saturday under Piazza della Vittoria; look for staircases leading underground from the piazza.

WORTH SEEING

Part of Pavia's redbrick Renaissance **Duomo** (P. del Duomo off C. Cavour) collapsed on Friday the 17th—Italy's equivalent of Friday the 13th—in 1989. The main structure was closed for restoration at press time. Even if you can't enter, the building remains a must-see. Beginning in 1488, numerous architects, including da Vinci and Bramante, contributed to its design. Its cupola, the third largest in Italy, wasn't completed until 1885, and its facade was finished under Mussolini in 1933.

The church of **San Michele** (at C. Garibaldi and V. Diacono), the last of four Pavese churches dedicated to Michael, patron saint of the Longobards, was the church of choice for crowning medieval kings and emperors such as Charlemagne. It was rebuilt in yellow sandstone and redbrick after a 12th-century earthquake destroyed much of the structure. **San Pietro in Ciel d'Oro** (V. Griziotti) dates from the 12th century and appears in Dante's *Divine Comedy.* **Santa Maria del Carmine** (P. Carmine off V. XX Settembre), begun around 1370, remains a wonderful specimen of Lombard-Gothic architecture. It contains paintings and frescoes by Foppa, da Marzano, Lenzani, Faruffini, and Moncalvo. All of Pavia's churches are open daily 8–noon and 3–6.

Torta paradiso, invented in the 1800s at Pavia's Pasticceria Vignoni (Strada Nuova 110, tel. 0382/22103), is a delicate cream-and-marsala-filled Northern Italian cake made right only by the few. It becomes crunchy, espresso-dipping biscotti after a few weeks.

The imposing **Castello Visconteo** (P. Castello, at north end of Strada Nuova; admission L8,000, L12,000 during exhibitions; open Tues.–Sun. 9–1, also in afternoon during some exhibitions, tel. 0382/304816) houses a museum of Lombard and Romanesque sculptures, as well as a respectable collection of 14th- to 17th-century religious paintings and altarpieces, including works by Bellini and Correggio. The most characteristic landmark in Pavia, the **university** (at Strada Nuova and C. Goldoni), is one of Italy's oldest (founded in 1361). Of its 12 courtyards, you should check out the Sforzesco. Pavia's other defining features are its medieval towers and covered bridge. At the end of Strada Nuova, the **Ponte Coperto** crosses the Ticino River; it's actually a 1951 reconstruction of a bridge originally built on Roman foundations in the 14th century.

NEAR PAVIA

CERTOSA

Even if you'd rather die than tour yet another church, the **Certosa della Madonna delle Grazie,** the Carthusian monastery 8 km (5 mi) north of the Pavia city center, absolutely merits a visit. Founded and financed by Galeazzo Visconti III, the duke of Milan, in 1396, the monastery is an intoxicating swirl of decoration and detail. Only the best marble was transported from the legendary quarries of Carrara, and its sculpted marble facade goes a step beyond ornate—"extravagant grandeur" comes closer to the mark. When he commissioned it, the duke envisioned the "most solemn and remarkable" of buildings. More than half a millennium later, the Certosa certainly remains one of Italy's most remarkable—though hardly solemn—landmarks.

More than 250 artists and architects have had a hand in the design of Certosa. The church's marble facade is covered with friezes and statues—from medallions of Roman emperors and Eastern monarchs to a bas-relief cycle of the life of Christ. Inside stand the incomplete funerary monument to Lodovico II Moro and Beatrice d'Este and the old sacristy, with its triptych made of hippopotamus teeth. Visit one of the monks' cells, each of which has its own garden and a device for passing meals through the wall without speaking. This is still a functioning monastery, as you can tell not only by the wandering robed brothers but also by the ongoing production of their famous Chartreuse liqueur, herbal medicines, and perfumes—all for sale in the adjoining shop. Make your way through alone or take a guided tour, in Italian only, with one of the monks (every 45 min). You might want to pack a picnic; nearby there's a shady area with tables and a bar where you can sample local brews. *V. Certosa, tel. 0382/925613. Admission free. Open Tues.–Sun. 9:30–11:30 and 2:30–6; shorter afternoon hrs in winter.*

COMING AND GOING • From Pavia's Autocorriere Station, take a **SGEA** bus (every ½ hr, 10 min, L2,000) to the Certosa stop along the highway; follow Viale Certosa for 1 km (½ mi) until it ends at the Certosa. Buy your return ticket from the newsstand near the bus stop.

CREMONA

If the little violins placed strategically on everything from postcards to shop windows haven't clued you in by now, Cremona's the home of history's greatest violin-makers. Andrea Amati started it all with the town's first violin crafts shop in the 16th century. His designs are considered prototypes for the modern violin as we know it. Amati's sons followed in his footsteps, and grandson Nicolò continued to refine the art of violin making, taking on Antonio Stradivari as a student. Stradivari's creations remain the Ferraris of the string world, and students from all over carry on the tradition at Cremona's **Scuola Internazionale di Liuteria** (International School of Violin Making). Graduates have opened more than 60 workshops within Cremona itself.

There's more to this little city than stringed contraptions, though. The town was shifted from Roman to Lombard control after a brief period of independence around the 11th century. After 1441 the rulers Bianca Visconti and husband Francesco Sforza commissioned artists such as Boccaccio Boccaccino and the Campi brothers to jazz up Cremona's central piazza, Piazza del Comune, and the surrounding streets. Their handiwork remains impressive five centuries later, but the town center is absolutely dominated by the stupendous Duomo. Blessed also with fine restaurants and famous salami, Cremona makes a good day trip from Milan or a relaxing base from which to explore the Po Plain.

BASICS

APT (P. del Comune 5, opposite Duomo, tel. 0372/23233; open Mon.–Sat. 9:30–12:30 and 3:30–7, Sun. 10–2:30).

COMING AND GOING

Cremona's **train station** (V. Dante 68, tel. 1478/88088; open 7 AM–8 PM) has luggage storage daily 7–7. About 14 trains run daily between Milan and Cremona (1 hr 40 min, L8,300), the last one from Milan leaves around 8:15 PM, from Cremona at 8:30 PM. An early-morning express train to Rome leaves Monday–Saturday (4 hrs, L76,000), and Venice is accessible via Brescia (3 hrs, L21,200).

Buses head from Cremona to Brescia (L7,900), Lodi, Padova, and other spots. Cremona's **Autostazione** (V. Dante, tel. 0372/29212; open weekdays 7:20–1 and 2:15–6:30, Sat. 7:20–1) is on the left of the train station. When the office is closed, buy tickets across the road at Pasticceria Mezzadri (V. Dante 105). From both stations, it's a 10-minute walk down Via Palestro to the city center. City buses also stop in front of the train station (L1,500); get tickets at tobacco shops.

WHERE TO SLEEP

Cremona has reasonably priced *and* clean hotels; just remember to book in advance. As the town is small, none of the hotels is far from the center or the train and bus stations. **Touring** (V. Palestro 3, 26100, at C. Garibaldi, tel. 0372/36976) has large, clean rooms and bathrooms, a TV room, kitchen, dining area, and bar. Doubles fetch L90,000, breakfast is L4,000–5,000, and the negotiable curfew is midnight. A little farther out, try the **Brescia** (V. Brescia 7, 26100, tel. 0372/434615; cash only), where doubles without bath go for L50,000. If these places are booked, the **Bologna** (P. Risorgimento 7, 26100, tel. 0372/24258) is minutes on foot from both stations, and its very basic rooms go for just L55,000. Rooms are often booked up during the week; weekends are the best bet. Otherwise, the APT office (*see* Basics, *above*) books private rooms and *agriturismo* (farm-stay lodgings).

CAMPING • **Camping Parco al Po.** You'll find this shady campground along the Po River, just outside the city. It's a family-oriented place, with little kiddies and lots of RVs, but easing the pain are a restaurant, a boccie ball green, an amusement area with slides and swings, and a bar. Tent sites cost L6,000, plus an extra L8,000 per person and L13,000 more for a car. *V. Lunga Po Europa 12/A, 26100, tel. 0372/21268. Reception closed 2–3:30. Bus 1 from train station, then walk 1500 ft from end of line. Closed Oct.–Mar.*

WHERE TO EAT

The delectable selection of *insaccati* (cured meats) is Cremona's most brilliant culinary achievement. Search for them and the local provolone and *grana padano* Parmesan cheeses at the **open market** (P. Mercato) held every Wednesday and Saturday morning (about 7–1) or save some lire by taking out **Voglia Pizza**'s (C. Garibaldi 38, tel. 0372/413881; cash only) panini or large, portable pies (from L8,000)—you won't mind missing out on the run-of-the-mill dining room. **Nuova Piedigrotta** (P. Risorgimento, tel. 0372/22033; closed Thurs.) is a good bet if you want to enjoy your pizza off your feet. **Ristorante Centrale** (V. Pertusio 4, off V. Solferino, tel. 0372/28701; closed Thurs.) serves first-rate Cremonese cuisine; the local specialty, particularly in winter, is *mostarda* (piquant fruit served in syrup) spooned over *bollito misto* (a mix of boiled meats). It's worth the splurge; but even if you can't afford to eat at the Centrale, check out its bar, filled with old men arguing vehemently about soccer. Check out the violin-shape *torrone* (nougat candy with nuts) at the **Pasticceria Duomo** (V. Boccaccino 6, next to Duomo, tel. 0372/22273), where the owner will gladly recount the legends behind every dessert made in his 19th-century pastry shop.

WORTH SEEING

Cremona's museums are not as thrilling as the town's effusive, goofily translated tourist literature claims, but still consider buying an all-in-one museum ticket (L15,000) from whichever museum you visit first. Not exactly the Louvre, but certainly unusual, the **Museo della Civiltà Contadina** (V. Castelleone 51, tel. 0372/21411; admission L3,000) demonstrates, in Italian only, what life was like for generations of Cremonese peasants. **Museo Civico Ala Ponzone** (V. U. Dati 4, tel. 0372/461885; admission L10,000) displays paintings by minor artists sprinkled with masters like Caravaggio and Boccaccino, as well as various archaeological artifacts. Both are open Tuesday–Saturday 8:30–6 and Sunday 9:15–12:30 and 3–6.

Cremona's **Piazza del Comune** packs several sights into one harmonious square (soccer-playing kids notwithstanding). Started in the 12th century after an earthquake toppled the original, the imposing Duomo has frescoes by Boccaccino and

Antonio Stradivari handcrafted upwards of 1,200 violins, guitars, cellos, harps, and mandolins. More than two centuries later, they remain the world's most coveted string instruments. Cremona's Museo Stradivariano celebrates his 68-year career.

an exterior that successfully blends Gothic, Renaissance, and Baroque styles. Climb to the top of the *torrazzo* (tower) for a L5,000 view of the city. The **Palazzo Comunale** (P. del Comune, tel. 0372/4071319; open Tues.–Sat. 8:30–6, Sun. 9:15–12:15 and 3–6), still used as a town hall, displays 17th- to 19th-century furniture and paintings, as well as violins crafted by the Amatis, Stradivari, and Guarneri. Admission is L6,000 (or use combined museum ticket).

From Piazza del Comune, walk two blocks north along Via Solferino to **Piazza Roma,** a green square that once held the church of San Domenico, where Stradivari was buried in 1737—look for the bronze replica of his tombstone in the piazza's center. For more on the master, head to the **Museo Stradivariano** (V. Palestro 17, tel. 0372/461886; admission L6,000; open Tues.–Sat. 8:30–6, Sun. 9:15–12:15 and 3–6); its designs, wooden models, and finished violins are great if you're a fan of the fiddle.

AFTER DARK

Cremona's after-dark scene is, in a word, bleak. In summer films are sometimes screened outside on **Piazza Roma** (tel. 0372/27501 for movie info). Other nights you'll find local youth carousing on said square. The **Cremona Jazz** festival serenades the town in Mar.–Apr. (tickets L15,000 and up). From July 5 to 31, the Palazzo del Comune hosts a **dance festival** (tickets L15,000), and from May to June classical music performances (tickets L25,000–L30,000) are held at the **Teatro Ponchielli** (C. Vittorio Emanuele at V. Gaetano Cesari, tel. 0372/407273). For more info on events and tickets contact the APT office (*see* Basics, *above*).

BERGAMO

Wedged into the side of a hill, Bergamo is divided like a three-tiered wedding cake. The top two layers (Città Alta, or Upper Bergamo) hoard the icing—castle ruins, winding cobblestone lanes, ornate churches, and jaw-dropping views. Lower Bergamo (Città Bassa) is the plainer though not unappetizing chunk for the masses. At first you might assume Upper Bergamo to be the original walled city-on-a-hill and Lower Bergamo its modern outgrowth, but this geographical stratification dates from Roman times, when the civilized elite lived on high above the peasants below. Later, the city's powers, particularly the Visconti and Venetians, festooned the hill with monuments while merchants downstairs went about their business. A *funivia* (funicular) connects Upper and Lower Bergamo (another runs to the castle above Città Alta), and you can easily rise above your pauper hotel in Città Bassa to partake in the Bergamo good life.

BASICS

Bergamo's two **APT** offices, in Upper Bergamo (Vicolo Aquila Nera 2, off P. Vecchia, tel. 035/232730 or 035/242226; open daily 9–12:30 and 2–5:30) and on Lower Bergamo's main drag (V. Vittorio Emanuele II 20, tel. 035/210204 or 035/213185; open weekdays 9–12:30 and 2–5:30), have lodging and event listings and maps. In Bergamo **exchange houses** uniformly charge L8,000 or 1%, and most close weekdays around 5:30 and on weekends after Saturday morning. Draw lire from the ATM at **Banca Popolare di Milano** (V. P. Giovanni XXIII 104, tel. 035/237642).

COMING AND GOING

There's hourly train service between Milan (1 hr, L6,000) and Bergamo's **train station** (P. Marconi, tel. 1478/88088). One train leaves on Sunday morning from Bergamo to Venice (3 hrs, L24,500); otherwise change trains in Brescia (hourly, 1 hr, L5,200). Luggage storage is available daily 7 AM–9 PM. Bergamo's bus depot, **Stazione Autolinee** (tel. 035/237883 or 035/243789, irregularly), is across the parking lot from the train station. Buses leave every half hour for Milan (1 hr, L7,300) and three times daily for Sárnico (1 hr, L4,300), from which there are frequent connections to Iseo.

GETTING AROUND

West of the stations cluster the cheapest hotels and pizzerias, but the neighborhood is creepy, even during the day. Uphill and to the northwest, in Upper Bergamo, is where you'll find the city's main sites. To reach Upper Bergamo, pick up Bus 1 (L1,500) in front of the train station. The bus stops at the funicular (every 7–10 min, L1,500, or use your bus ticket), the quickest way up. Otherwise stay on the bus, which wends its way up to the back of Upper Bergamo. Buy tickets at newsstands or vending machines at the funicular. For more bus and funicular info, contact the **ATB** office (tel. 035/255255).

WHERE TO SLEEP

Most budget lodgings are in Lower Bergamo, generally in the seedy area northwest of the stations. In summer definitely book ahead. If your pockets are near empty, **Caironi** (V. Torretta 6, 24100, Lower Bergamo, tel. 035/243083; cash only) is the best nonhostel place to crash, with singles for L25,000 and doubles for L45,000. Take Bus 7 or 15 east from the train station to Piazza Sant'Anna, then walk up Via Borgo Palazzo and take right on Via Torretta. **S. Giorgio** (V. S. Giorgio 10, 24100, tel. 035/212043, fax 035/310072), in Lower Bergamo, has doubles with redone bathrooms for L90,000 (L65,000 without bath). It's a 10-minute walk west from the train station, or take Bus 7. **Agnello d'Oro** (V. Gombito 22, 24129, near funicular station, tel. 035/249883, fax 035/235612), in Upper Bergamo, has clean but pricey doubles (L135,000) with satellite TVs and big bathrooms.

HOSTEL • Hostel Bergamo (HI). This hostel in the northeast end of Lower Bergamo has a restaurant, bar, TV, laundry facilities, and bike rental. Beds go for L30,000, including breakfast; other meals cost L14,000. Your HI card is required. *V. Galileo Ferraris 1, 24123, tel. and fax 035/361724. Bus 14 from Porta Nuova. 84 beds. Midnight curfew, lockout 9–3:30.*

WHERE TO EAT

If you crave nothing more than focaccia and pastries, try the *birrerie* (beer halls) along the upper city's Via Gombito. For honestly cheap eats, head to Lower Bergamo. The self-service Chinese joint **Green House** (V. Verdi 31/F, tel. 035/226351; open weekdays noon–3 and 6–midnight) has a fixed menu for L9,500. Also look for pizzerias near the stations on Via Quarenghi, Via Previtali, and Via San Bernardino. For do-it-yourselfers, **Contrabene** (V. Vittorio Emanuele II 17, tel. 035/234767) is on Lower Bergamo's main drag.

Antica Hosteria del Vino Buono (V. Donizetti 25, tel. 035/247993), across from the Mercato delle Scarpe funicular stop in Upper Bergamo, has excellent regional food, including *casonsei* (meat-stuffed pasta) for L12,000 and polenta *del Bergamì* (with wild mushrooms) for L15,000. Skip lunch if you have to, but save enough money to dine at sunset at **I Musicanti** (Albergo San Vigilio, V. San Vigilio 15, tel. 035/253179; closed Tues.), off Via Castello near the upper funicular. Glass walls cover half the restaurant on the edge of Upper Bergamo, so you get an amazing view with exquisite food to match for L14,000–L25,000 per *secondo piatto*. Reserve ahead. **Da Mimmo** (V. B. Colleoni 17, tel. 035/218535;

closed Tues.), in the heart of Upper Bergamo, is busy and has a covered terrace in back and a knight in full armor at the door. The tourist menu is L25,000.

WORTH SEEING

Bergamo contains a few major cultural and visual surprises. According to Bernard Berenson, Le Corbusier, and Frank Lloyd Wright, Upper Bergamo's **Piazza Vecchia** wins the Italian Piazza Beauty Contest. It's the heart of the misty upper city and a favorite gathering spot for locals and tourists alike—particularly during the evening *passeggiata* (stroll), between 5 and 7. Sights farther afield include the simple church of **Sant'Agostino** (P. Sant'Agostino) and the overwhelmingly ornate **Santa Maria Maggiore** (P. del Duomo, tel. 035/219955; open Mon.–Sat. 8:30–noon and 3–6, Sun. 10–noon and 3–6), begun in 1137 and finished several centuries later. The latter's marble facade, frescoed interior, and divine choir stalls designed by Lotto leave you a bit bleary-eyed.

ACCADEMIA CARRARA • You'd hardly expect a town like Bergamo to have such an exceptional art museum, but it does, with mostly Italian art from the 12th through 18th centuries. Highlights include works by Raphael, Mantegna, Bellini, Tiepolo, Titian, Canaletto, and Guardi, as well as by major Bergamo artists. Across the piazza, the **Museo dell'Arte Contemporanea** (V. San Tommaso 53, tel. 035/399529) has temporary exhibitions with an emphasis on modern Lombard artists. *P. dell'Accademia, tel. 035/399527. From station, take V. P. Giovanni, which becomes V. Vittorio Emanuele, right on V. Verdi. Admission to museum L10,000, Accademia entrance free. Open Wed.–Mon. 9:30–6:30, Thurs. until 10:30 PM.*

CAPPELLA COLLEONI • Considered the most notable edifice on Piazza Vecchia, this small but impressive chapel was commissioned in the late 13th century by Bartolomeo Colleoni as a mausoleum for himself and his daughter. Designed by Giovanni Antonio Amadeo, the pink-and-white marble facade encases an equally elaborate interior, with an equestrian statue of Colleoni that looks slightly awkward perched atop his sarcophagus. Dress conservatively (show no shoulders lest you face the wrath of the strict fashion police) to peek inside Bergamo's **Duomo** (P. Vecchia), dedicated to St. Alexander, the city's patron saint. Be forewarned that the interior's swirls of gold, pale green, and pink might make you queasy. *P. Vecchia. Open Apr.–Oct., Tues.–Sun. 9–noon and 2:30–5:30; Nov.–Mar., Tues.–Sun. 9–noon and 2:30–4:30.*

CASTELLO • Though there's not much left of Bergamo's ancient castle, the ruins atop Calle di San Vigilio provide free breathtaking views of the city. You can arrange a free tour of the *castello's* underground passageways with the **Gruppo Speleologico le Nottole** (Bergo 5, Caterina 11/B, tel. 035/241020 or 035/211233). *V. San Vigilio. Take funicular (L2,500) at bottom of V. San Vigilio. Admission free. Open Apr.–Sept., daily 10–8; Mar. and Oct., daily 10–6; Nov.–Feb., daily 10–4.*

MUSEO DONIZETTIANO • Dedicated to native Gaetano Donizetti, this museum assembles a collection of the composer's scores, manuscripts, piano, and other instruments, plus portraits and even his deathbed. *V. Arena 9, tel. 035/399269. Admission free. Open Tues.–Sun. 10–1 and 2:30–5.*

If you're a fan of Donizetti and his operas, visit the house where he grew up, **Casa Natale di Gaetano Donizetti** (Borgo Canale 14, tel. 035/231872; open Sat. 2:30–5, Sun. 2:30–5:30); admission is free. A local theater has also been dedicated to him, the **Teatro Donizetti** (P. Cavour 14, tel. 035/249631).

BRESCIA

The town, called the "iron cave on the hill" in the 16th century, has stocked Italy's arsenals for years, and its factories still produce a large portion of the world's landmines. One of the world's oldest arms industries has brought the city enviable wealth, and its attractions carry on the theme—an arms museum, a securely defended castle on a hill, and the fascist eyesore Piazza Vittoria, arguably the ugliest piazza in all of Italy.

Oddly enough, this Rambo paradise hasn't defended its independence too well throughout history. After the Romans left, the city had a dukedom for a while, but the Lombards soon took over, followed by various clans: the Roman Ezzelino, the Veronese Scaligeri, the Milanese Visconti, and the Venetians, plus a French chapter around 1510. Amid all this, Brescian artists drew pretty pictures—Vicenzo Foppa (1400s) and the 16th-century Brescian School of Salvado, Romanino, and Moretto are the names to know. Today factories draw a large immigrant population. And the university whips up some decent nightlife. Brescia is also a convenient transport hub to lakes Garda and Iseo, so you might pass through even if this weapons center doesn't fit into your dream of an Italian vacation.

BASICS

The **APT** (C. Zanardelli 34, tel. 030/43418; http://www.gardanet.it/aptbs; open weekdays 9–12:30 and 3–6, Sat. 9–12:30) provides info on hotels and sights. From the station, take Via Stazione to Corso Martiri della Libertà, right on Corso Palestro, which becomes Via Zanardelli.

COMING AND GOING

From Brescia's **train station** (P. Stazione, tel. 1478/88088) there are roughly 35 trains daily to Venice (2¼ hrs, L16,000), the same number to Milan (1 hr 10 min, L8,300), and one morning *pendolino* (super-express train) to Rome (4¾ hrs, L76,000). A private company runs trains to Iseo (7 daily except Sun., 40 min, L3,500), with stops at Sulzano and Marone (to reach Zone). The **bus station** (tel. 030/3774237), to the left of the train station, runs three daily buses (two on Sun.) to Milan (2 hrs, L12,100). The *centro storico* is a short walk from the station along Corso Martiri della Libertà or Via Gramsci.

WHERE TO SLEEP AND EAT

A bunch of scummy hotels, none of which is recommended, surrounds the station. One exception is **Albergo San Marco** (V. Spalto S. Marco 15, 25121 tel. 030/45541; cash only), which is a spotless deal at L60,000 for a bathless double (L101,000 with meals). The **Regina e Due Leoni** (C. Magenta 14, 25121, tel. 030/3757881; cash only), also central and clean, has doubles for L100,000.

Typical Brescian dishes include polenta *pasticciata* (with cheese, meat, or vegetables) and *casonsei* (meat-stuffed pasta) and the area produces enough good wine to make a Frenchman tipsy; try a red Botticino or a white Franciacorta. Corso Mameli and the surrounding streets have budget-friendly eateries, such as **Caffè Osteria dei Mercantini** (V. delle Battaglie 2, tel. 030/40258; cash only), where a two-course lunch with wine is just L15,000. Another cheap spot for lunch, dinner, or just a drink is **Osteria delle Dame** (V. San Francesco d'Assisi 1/B, tel. 030/3771868; closed Sun.), which serves sandwiches and salads. Brescian students crowd **Gelateria Piccinelli** (C. Palestro 27, tel. 030/49343; closed Sun.). There are **markets** on Piazza Rovetta and Piazza del Mercato Monday–Saturday mornings.

WORTH SEEING

If you stand at the corner of Piazza del Duomo, it's hard to miss the **Broletto** (Vicolo Sant'Agostino 29), a medieval town hall and the seat of Brescia's local government. The rooms are closed to the public, but you can see the inner courtyard. The Broletto incorporates the city's oldest tower, the **Torre del Popolo**, which dates from the 11th century, and the church of **Sant'Agostino**, a 15th- century structure with a colorful terra-cotta facade. On Piazza del Duomo itself, the late Renaissance **Duomo Nuovo** (open daily 8–noon and 4–7:30), much too large for its square, overshadows (but does not outdo) its simpler and more elegant tile-roofed grandpa, **Duomo Vecchio** (a.k.a. the Rotonda), begun in the 11th century. Visit the Rotonda's treasured mosaics, estimated to date from 1 BC, in front of the presbytery.

The **Capitolino** (V. Musei 57), a temple built by Emperor Vespasian in AD 73, has eroded to just a stairway, columns, and lintel, but it's still an impressive testament to Brescia's Roman origins. The adjoining **Museo Romano** displays artifacts from Rome to Greece to Egypt, including *Winged Victory,* the famed 1st-century bronze sculpture. *V. Musei, tel. 030/44327. Admission L5,000. Open Oct.–May Tues.–Sun. 9:30–1 and 2:30–5; June–Sept. Tues.–Sun. 10–5. Last admission 1 hr before closing.*

The churches of **Santa Giulia, Santa Maria in Solario,** and **San Salvatore** join together to form a single museum. Respectively dating from the 16th, 7th–9th, and 12th centuries, the churches form part of the monastery of San Salvatore, where Charlemagne's wife, Ermengarde, spent her last days. On Saturday and Sunday, free museum tours with varying topics are available; call for reservations. *V. Musei 81, entrance around corner at V. Piamarta 4, tel. 030/44327. Combined admission to all three L5,000. Open Oct.–May, Tues.–Sun. 9:30–1 and 2:30–5; June–Sept., Tues.–Sun. 10–5. Last admission 1 hr before closing.*

Brescia's central network of squares and lanes is great for aimless strolls. You'll inevitably stumble on the once stately, now filthy Renaissance **Loggia** (P. Loggia 1, tel. 030/29831), completed in 1574 after being fiddled with by Palladio, Sansovino, and Titian. Facing the Loggia is the **Torre dell'Orologio,** modeled on the campanile in Venice's Piazza San Marco. The town's **Castello** (P. Castello, end of V. del Castello), atop Cydean Hill, has ancient origins but largely owes its present structure, including the Mirabella Tower, to the 13th-century designs of the Visconti. Today the castle houses armor and weaponry from a variety of eras in its **Museo di Armi** (Arms Museum; V. Castello 9, tel. 030/293292; admission L5,000; *see* hours of Museo Romano, *above*).

AFTER DARK

Listen to live music at **Babida** (V. Rua Sovera 19, tel. 030/2400961; closed Thurs.) and the **Fahrenheit Club** (V. Inganni 6/C, no phone), open until 6 AM. In July and August, don't miss **open-air concerts** or **films** on the Castello grounds. Check with the APT (*see* Basics, *above*) for details.

MANTUA

A city rich in art, history, political intrigue, and that elusive quality atmosphere, lakeside Mantua (Mantova) alternates between solemn and decadent. Even its origins are dark and exotic: some say the town was settled by a witch named Manto, who after years of wandering, settled where the river Mincio becomes a swampy lowland. She practiced magic until her death, when loyal followers built this city over her grave and named it Mantua in her honor.

Although Mantua's origins go back to the Etruscan period and its fame is due partly to the 1st-century BC poet Virgil's birthplace nearby, the conspicuously wealthy city you see today was essentially created by the Gonzaga family and their preferred artists: Leon Battista Alberti, Andrea Mantegna, and Giulio Romano. The Gonzagas—the Addams family of the Renaissance—ruled the city for 3½ centuries with great skill, seeing to the creation and decoration of everything from Palazzo Ducale, Palazzo Te, and the Duomo to the churches of Sant'Andrea and San Sebastiano. With each generation the clan grew more ostentatious, leaving a legacy of flamboyance that makes Mantua one of the most fascinating towns in the region despite its small size, factories, and swarms of mosquitoes (bring repellent).

Peace-loving hippies and politically correct folks stand back: Brescia doesn't produce cars, cheese, or opera composers; it makes bombs and bullets.

BASICS

The **APT** office (P. Mantegna 6, next to P. delle Erbe, tel. 0376/328253; open Mon.–Sat. 8:30–12:30 and 3–6, in summer also Sun. 9:30–12:30) has bus schedules, maps, and pamphlets along with info (mostly in Italian) on nature walks, bike paths, boat trips, and festivals in the area. From the station, take Via Bonomi, go left on Corso Vittorio Emanuele II (it becomes Corso Umberto I) to Piazza Mantegna. If you're arriving after 6 PM or on Sunday, change money beforehand—exchange places will be closed. Banks scattered around the city generally change money for a 1% fee. The main **post office** (P. Martiri di Belfiore 15, tel. 0376/326403) also changes money and AmEx traveler's checks for L2,000–L5,000.

COMING AND GOING

Mantua's small **train station** (P. Don Leoni, tel. 1478/88088) has luggage storage 6:15 AM–8:15 PM (L5,000 per 12 hrs). Trains leave for Milan (6 daily, 2 hrs, L15,000), Cremona (every hr, 1 hr, L6,800), and Verona (17 daily, 40 min, L3,900), where you can change for Venice (2 hrs, L14,000). For trains to southern Italy and Emilia-Romagna, transfer at Modena (14 daily, 1 hr, L6,400); weekdays there's one direct Mantua–Bologna train in the morning.

Buses are useful for reaching nearby small towns such as Sabbioneta (L5,800), and they also run to Brescia (L9,500) and Peschiera (L7,000) on Lake Garda; all buses depart from the **Autostazione** (P. Mondadori, tel. 167/821194 toll-free, 0376/327237 for schedules; open Mon.–Sat. 8:30–12:30; otherwise get tickets on bus). From the train station, turn right, and go left onto Via San Bettinelli (which becomes Via Mutilati e Caduti del Lavoro) to the piazza.

GETTING AROUND

To get to the city center from the train station (a 10-minute walk), turn right on Via A. Pitentino, go left on Corso Vittorio Emanuele to Piazza Cavalotti, and pick up Corso Umberto to reach piazzas Mantegna, delle Erbe, and Sordello, making up the heart of the city. To reach Palazzo Te from the center, take Via Roma to Via Amadeo and continue straight (the street changes names). Rent a bike at **La Rigola** (Lungolago dei Gonzaga, at P. Arche, tel. 0335/6054958) either by the hour (Mon.–Sat. L4,000, Sun. L5,000) or the day (Mon.–Sat. L11,000, Sun. L16,000). You can also rent boats and *pedalos* here in summer (L15,000 per hour).

BY BUS • Apam bus tickets (L1,300) are available in bars and newsstands. Bus 2M makes the trip along Corso Vittorio Emanuele II to the center, and Bus 4 goes to Palazzo Te (get off at the Risorgimento

SABBIONETA: A UTOPIA FORGOTTEN

Ambitiously nicknamed "little Athens" for the hoity-toity nobility who once cavorted here, Sabbioneta is the physical manifestation of Vespasiano Gonzaga's ego. Upon retiring from military life at 47, he resolved to turn an old castle and a few squalid cottages into the perfect city. From 1577 until 1591, the duke built incessantly, transforming this once-rural hamlet into a bejeweled minimetropolis. It's extraordinary how much Gonzaga was able to build in 15 years, and stunning how quickly his dream crumbled. Following his death the town was forgotten by the outside world, and Vespasiano's son died before he did, leaving no heir. Sabbioneta still feels like a Renaissance ghost town, but Gonzaga's "monuments"—Palazzo Ducale, Teatro, Palazzo Del Giardino, Galleria, and Chiesa dell'Incoronata—are interesting enough for a brief visit. You can see the interiors on guided tours only (in English on request; admission L10,000 for all five sites, L5,000 for one), which leave from the tourist office (V. Vespasiano Gonzaga 31, tel. 0375/52039; closed Mon.). To reach Sabbioneta from Mantua, hop on a bus (7 daily, 45 min, L6,000); on Sunday only, one noontime bus will get you to Sabbioneta in time to see the sights.

or Repubblica stop). Maps and timetables are available at the APT (*see* Visitor Information, *above*) or at the Apam office (Dosso del Corso 4, tel. 0376/2301).

WHERE TO SLEEP

To save money, consider making Mantua a day trip from Verona (*see* Chapter 2), a half hour away by train. You can also inquire at the APT office for agriturismo options.

If a cheap bed is all you're after, try **Maragò** (V. Villanova de Bellis 2, 46030, tel. 0376/370313) in nearby Virgiliana. Accommodations are rudimentary, and it's inconvenient, but you might not care with L48,000 doubles (L70,000 with bath). There's a decent restaurant too. In Mantua, from Piazza Cavalotti, take Bus 2M (15 min; last bus 8 PM) to the last stop. **Hotel ABC** (P. Don Leoni 25, 46100, across from train station, tel. 0376/323347) is in better condition than many of the city's three-star spots and is the cheapest place in town aside from the Maragò. Doubles cost L60,000 without bath, L100,000 with bath, including breakfast, and guests can rent bikes (L10,000 per day). Once-budget, fluent-in-English **Albergo Bianchi Stazione** (P. Don Leoni 24, 46100, next door to ABC, tel. 0376/326465, fax 0376/321504) has undergone extensive renovations, and every room has air-conditioning, bath, and a TV. Doubles are a steep but negotiable L130,000–L160,000.

WHERE TO EAT

Many Mantuan delicacies—like *stracotto d'asino* (braised donkey meat and vegetables)—may sound bizarre to newcomers, but try them and you may never look at spaghetti again. When made right, *tortelli di zucca* (large, pumpkin-stuffed pasta sweetened with amaretto cookies) are exquisite. Satisfy your sweet tooth with *torta di tagliatelle* (pie topped with sugared pasta) or the shortbreadlike *sbrisolona* (named for the crumbs or *briciole* it makes when broken), and wash it down with red, fizzy Lambrusco wine. Pizza *alla Mantovana* is a huge, flat, two- to-three-person pie, more like its U.S. counterpart in size (but not taste). For scooter-delivered pies, try **Speedy's Spizza** (V. Grazioli 12, off V. Roma, tel. 0376/224540) or stop by any day but Tuesday for a quick slice to go. For groceries, head to **Colmark** (V. Giustiziati 11, behind Palazzo della Ragione, tel. 0376/321244). Mantua's **open market** operates Thursday morning and Saturday afternoon in Piazza delle Erbe and Piazza Sordello.

UNDER L15,000 • **Antica Osteria Taverna S. Barbara.** Surprisingly affordable considering its terrace bordering the Palazzo Ducale, the Barbara draws tourists during the day but teems with local youth on weekends until 2 AM (though the kitchen's only open 'till 11). Regional dishes include *stracotto alla mantovana* (braised beef), *lumache della casa* (home-cooked snails; L14,000), and tripe soup, as well as pasta. *P. S. Barbara 19, tel. 0376/329496. From P. Sordello, take V. Tazzoli, left on V. Rubens, and follow signs. No dinner Tues. Closed Mon.*

Antico Osteria ai Ranari. Mantovan pasta dishes (L10,000–L13,000) are at their best here, but enjoy an all-out multi-course feast to truly fit in with the locals. It's all served up in a cozy environment—you'll feel right at home. *V. Trieste 11, tel. 0376/328431. Head up V. Pomponazzo, which turns into V. Trieste. Closed Mon.*

Leoncino Rosso. This truly antique *osteria* opened in 1750 and still serves up local goodies like *luccio in salsa* (pike in green sauce) and tortellini with nuts or pumpkin. At night it's a spot for low-key carousing. *V. Giustiziati 33, off P. Broletto, tel. 0376/323277. Open Mon.–Sat. noon–3 and 7–10. Closed Aug. and 3 wks in Jan.*

Trattoria Due Cavallini. Run by the same family for more than 50 years, this slightly out-of-the-way place is *the* spot for Mantuan specialties. The menu's short, but you can't go wrong with primi for L8,000, meats for L12,000–L14,000, a shady courtyard, and an aproned *signora* who'll make you drool over her pumpkin pasta. Eat here and your stomach will say *grazie* (thank you). *V. Salnitro 5, tel. 0376/322084. From P. Broletto, take V. Broletto, right on V. Accademia, right on V. Pomponazzo (which becomes V. Trieste and C. Garibaldi), left on V. Salnitro. Closed Tues., mid-July–mid-Aug., and 1st wk in Jan.*

Mantuans still brag about local boy Virgil, the celebrated Latin poet who penned the epic "Aeneid." Virgil was born in 70 BC in Andes (now called Pietole), 5 km (3 mi) outside Mantua.

WORTH SEEING

Mantua is not a place to bury your nose in a guidebook. Look around and gape at architecture ranging from severe and heavy-handed to frothy, eccentric, and over-the-top. Whether you're a fan of Renaissance grace or mannerist kitsch, Mantua won't disappoint.

CASA DEL MANTEGNA • Commissioned by Mantegna in the late 15th century, the upper floors of this house now hold offices, but downstairs, free art exhibitions rotate almost year-round. Although it's unclear whether Mantegna himself designed the place, its structure resembles the ceiling oculus in the Ducal Palace's Camera degli Sposi (*see below*), which the artist frescoed between 1465 and 1474. *V. Acerbi 47, tel. 0376/360506. From Palazzo Te, walk northeast on V. Acerbi. Open Tues.–Sun. 10–12:30 and 3–6 during exhibits, otherwise Mon.–Fri. 10–12:30 only.*

PALAZZO D'ARCO • In 1872 Antonio d'Arco bought a plot of land next to a small Renaissance palace. He built a lovely garden, being careful not to interfere with or diminish the beauty of the adjoining Renaissance buildings that still form the garden's boundary. Giovanna d'Arco, the last member of the family, willed the palace to the city, and today you can visit a number of its rooms, the most stellar of which is the **Sala dello Zodiaco,** frescoed by Giovanni Falconetto in 1520, to get a feel for life as it was lived by 16th-century aristocrats. *P. d'Arco 1, tel. 0376/322242. From P. Mantegna, west on V. Verdi, which becomes V. Fernelli and ends at palazzo. Admission L5,000. Open Mar.–Nov. 5, Tues.–Sun. 10–12:30 and 2:30–6; Nov. 5–Feb., Sat. 10–12:30 and 2–5, Sun. 10–5.*

PALAZZO DUCALE • The "simple" 500-room, 15-courtyard abode of the Gonzaga family, originally built around seven large gardens and eight courtyards, was practically a city within a city. Between the 14th and 17th centuries, the Gonzagas continued to add and renovate, creating a sprawling complex of living quarters, courts, meeting halls, and much more. In the 18th century all structures were joined by a web of halls and covered passageways. Today it bears the mark of such luminaries as Mantegna, Romano, Titian, Rubens, and Correggio. Many rooms are closed for restoration—your tired feet will be thankful.

Among the Palazzo's rooms are the **Sala del Pisanello,** where Pisanello frescoes were discovered in 1969, and the dining room, a.k.a. the **Salone dei Fiumi,** which has gnarled miniature grottoes through which water once flowed. The **Galleria delle Metamorfosi,** frescoed with Ovidian scenes, once housed a mummy, which the Gonzagas believed was a good-luck charm. Many blamed the fall of the dynasty on the destruction of the mummy by the last Gonzaga duchess. The world's first modern opera, *L'Orfeo,* was conducted by Monteverdi in the palace's music hall and ballroom, the **Galleria degli Specchi** (Hall of Mirrors).

The first floor of **Castello di San Giorgio,** also part of the Palazzo Ducale, contains Isabella d'Este's apartments, which once housed a troupe of court dwarves. (Renaissance nobility had a peculiar affection for dwarves, who acted as servants and entertainers.) The most famous room is the **Camera degli Sposi,** lavishly painted by Mantegna between 1465 and 1474. Look closely to see Mantegna himself sternly watching the room from a column just to the right of the door, near the painting *The Meeting. P. Sordello, tel. 0376/320283. Admission L12,000. Open Tues.–Sat. 9–6, Sun. 9–1. Last tickets sold 1 hr before closing.*

Outside the palazzo, on **Piazza Sordello,** look for the **Torre della Gabbia** (Tower of the Cage), named for the 16th-century cage that Guglielmo Gonzaga had built for his prisoners so they could be gawked at publicly. Piazza Sordello is notable as the site of many Gonzaga family events, from executions to jousts to weddings. To the right of the **Palazzo Ducale** as you exit stands the town's modest redbrick Renaissance **Duomo,** with interior paintings attributed to Giulio Romano (1545). Call the tourist office for opening hours, as they change constantly.

PALAZZO TE • Between 1525 and 1535, Federico II Gonzaga had Palazzo Te built on the island of Tejeto (later called Te) to be the pleasure palace for his amorous exploits with his mistress Isabella Boschetto. Giulio Romano was commissioned to design and decorate the place, and he let the fantastic and rhetorical run wild, hence the mythological trompe l'oeil frescoes, puffy moldings, gilded fixtures, lizard motif (whose cold blood symbolically contrasts Federico's hot-blooded passions), and Federico's motto, QUOD HUIC DEEST ME TORQUET (what the lizard lacks, i.e. warm blood, is what tortures me).

The **Sala dei Cavalli,** a reception area and ballroom, immortalizes Federico's favorite stallions and recalls the island's former use as Lodovico II's stud farm. The **Sala di Psiche** banquet hall is dedicated to Federico and Isabella's love affair. The **Sala dei Giganti** explores Jove's revenge on the giants who conspired against him; the room is covered with frescoes, immersing you in the scene of destruction. *V. Te, tel. 0376/323266. Admission L12,000. Open Mon. 1–6, Tues.–Sun. 9–6; last tickets sold at 5:15.*

PIAZZA BROLETTO AND PIAZZA DELLE ERBE • The **Palazzo del Podestà,** built in 1227 and rebuilt in 1462, divides two of Mantua's better-known piazzas—Broletto and delle Erbe, around which there's a gaggle of palaces and lesser piazzas. In a niche shooting off from Piazza Broletto stands the *Statue of Virgil.* Sculpted by an unknown artist at the time of the palace's construction, it pays homage to Mantua's greatest writer. Nearby Palazzo del Massaro and Palazzo Comunale are connected by a dark, vaulted *arcone* (arch). Check out the ceiling and its rings once used to hang prisoners by their wrists after their hands had been bound behind their backs.

SANT'ANDREA • In 1470, after Ludovico Gonzaga obtained permission from Pope Sixtus IV to raze this site, Ludovico commissioned Leon Battista Alberti to design Sant'Andrea, his much-imitated landmark. Even though work on the church wasn't completed until the 18th century, Sant'Andrea was widely emulated by lesser architectural talents in the Renaissance, which may explain its familiar profile. In the church's cavernous interior lie Mantegna's tomb, a burial chapel, and in the crypt, a reliquary containing the supposed blood of Christ. Legend has it that Longinus brought the blood to Mantua after thrusting his very own spear into Jesus—earning him some seriously bad karma. Golden vases that hold the blood are displayed on March 18, the feast day of Sant'Anselmo (Mantua's patron saint), then carried in a procession to the Duomo for a special mass. *P. Mantegna. Admission free. Open daily 8–noon and 3:30–7.*

AFTER DARK

Mantua isn't exactly throbbing after dark, but two good places to have a drink are **Leoncino Rosso** (*see* Where to Eat, *above*), also a bar between 10 PM and 2 AM, and **Oblo** (V. Arrivabene 50, tel. 0376/ 360676), which serves light meals and has a big selection of beer and wine. A **jazz festival** rocks Mantua during the last week of July; concerts are held indoors and out.

THE LAKES

When the sun beats through the smog in Milan, an exodus begins to the lakes of melted Alpine glaciers spreading over Lombardy, Piedmont, Veneto, and even Switzerland. In high season (July–August), the major port towns of lakes **Maggiore, Como,** and **Garda** resemble showrooms of Mercedes and tourbuses, but even the big-name lakes have some less-traveled nooks, and the smaller lakes, like **Iseo** and **Orta,** are always tranquil. The entire area is watched over by the snow-capped Alps and blanketed with forested hills for bikers, hikers, and climbers. This is also prime windsurfing territory. Windsurfers should point their sails to the north end of Garda, which attracts the most lively and youngest crowd, and trekkers should consult Richard Sale's *The Pathmaster Guide of the Italian Lakes* for 30 detailed hiking routes.

Besides the crowds, the only downside to the lakes is that they can be tricky to get around without a car. If you're using public transit, Brescia is a transport hub to Iseo and Garda. Verona and Rovereto (near the Dolomites) also give easy Garda access. Milan is the best base for Maggiore, Como, and Orta.

LAKE GARDA

Shared by Lombardy, the Veneto, and Trentino–Alto Adige, Italy's largest lake (Lago di Garda) combines grand-hotel ritziness with RV camper culture. Hordes of young and old travelers alike show up each summer to take in the lake's quiet waters and, most distinctively, the surrounding majestic mountain ranges. Luckily, the lake's large size means finding a little peace and quiet is not that hard. But if masses of well-heeled tourists tend to fray your nerves, you'd be happier at calmer Iseo or Orta.

Among the thousands of visitors to this lake, Garda has hosted its share of famous people. The Roman poet Catullus is said to have owned a villa here in the 1st century BC. Irish writer James Joyce and the American poet Ezra Pound met more than once along this lakefront. And Gabriele d'Annunzio, the ultra-nationalist Italian poet and chum of Mussolini, built his extravagant home, *Il Vittoriale,* in Gardone. Mussolini even set up his short-lived puppet government, the Republic of Salò, here.

Garda's topography holds noticeable contrasts. The south is smooth and shrubby, the north mountainous and leafy. The weather is more constant: mild to warm and breezy, except in winter, when rain and cooler temperatures may dampen your spirit. Throughout the year you can enjoy water sports—from sailing to diving to windsurfing—in towns like Riva del Garda, and excellent mountain hikes start from Riva del Garda, Malcesine, and Gardone. Finally, at the end of a long day, indulge in fine local wines and prepare yourself for meals flavored with two local specialties: olive oil and juicy lemons.

COMING AND GOING

Lake Garda is triangle-shaped, with Desenzano (the main transportation hub) on the bottom west corner, Peschiera on the bottom east. Desenzano's **train station** (V. Cavour 48, tel. 1478/88088), on a hill behind the city, serves Milan (32 trains daily, 1½ hrs, L10,800) and Venice (19 daily, 2 hrs, L14,000). **SAIA** buses in Brescia (V. S. Zeno 101, tel. 030/223761) run 18 buses daily each way along the south coast, connecting Brescia, Desenzano, Sirmione, and Verona. Buses also run up each coast toward Riva del Garda at the northern tip; the closest train station to Riva del Garda is in Rovereto (*see* Coming and Going *in* Riva del Garda, *below*). **Navigarda** (P. Matteotti, Desenzano, tel. 030/9149511) runs **boats** and **hydrofoils** connecting lakeside towns Easter–September.

VISITOR INFORMATION

An invaluable resource to the Web-savvy traveler, **www.gardanet.it** provides a network of Web pages detailing accommodations, restaurants, tourist resources, and other info about virtually every town in the Lake Garda region.

SIRMIONE

Sitting on a strip of land on Lake Garda's southwestern shore, the village of Sirmione ought to be an idyllic place to ponder the rhythms of nature. But its beauty has been tainted by the tourist trade—expect steep prices, gaudy souvenir shops, and snack bars galore. There's little to do here, but the beaches are nice. Encased by a 13th-century castle, the old part of town sits in the shadow of the fortress **Rocca Scaligera** (tel. 030/916468; admission L8,000; open May–Sept., daily 8:30–6; Oct.–Apr., Tues.–Sun. 8:30–1). The fortress, built by the della Scala family in the 14th century, isn't too interesting inside but provides sweeping views from its tower.

Around 1 BC the piles of rocks and lonely pillars at the tip of Sirmione formed a grand Augustan villa and may have belonged to the Roman poet Catullus. Visit the excavated ruins of the **Villa of Catullus** and sit atop its grotto and ancient hot springs. *P. Orti Manara, tel. 030/916157. From Scaligera castle, take V. Vittorio Emanuele, right on V. Catullo. Admission L8,000. Open Apr.–Sept., Tues.–Sat. 8:30–7, Sun. 9– 6; Oct.–Mar., Tues.–Sun. 9–4.*

BASICS

The **APT** tourist office (V. Marconi 2, tel. 030/916114; open Easter–Oct., daily 9–12:30 and 3–6; Nov.–Easter, weekdays 9–12:30 and 3–6, Sat. 9–12:30) has plenty of info on lodging, sights, and water sports. The number is also staffed by an accommodations info/booking service after hours until 9 PM.

COMING AND GOING

Buses run by SAIA and ATP connect Verona, Sirmione, Desenzano, and Brescia hourly from 6 AM to 8 PM. It's about an hour to Verona or Brescia and 25 minutes to Desenzano, where you can change buses to go up the coast toward Riva del Garda. **Navigarda** boats (tel. 030/9149511) also dock at Sirmione (10 daily).

WHERE TO SLEEP

Avoid Sirmione in July and August, when it's crowded and a place to stay is impossible to find without a reservation. If you're looking for a crash pad in the historic center, a cheap option is **La Magnolia** (V. Vittorio Emanuele 43, 25019, tel. 030/916135; cash only; closed Oct.–May), where doubles with bath are L60,000. Outside the center, **Lo Zodiaco** (V. XXV Aprile 18, 25019, tel. 030/916095; cash only; closed Dec.–Feb.) has doubles without bath for around L55,000; you'll miss out on the castle theme but will have easier access to beaches and cheapo restaurants.

CAMPING • Camping Sirmione (V. Sirmioncino 9, 25019, tel. 030/919045 or 030/9904665) fills up with RVs and teens on mopeds, but it's cheap compared to a hotel (L15,000–L24,000 per tent site, plus L8,000–L13,000 per person) and has a beach. Beds in bungalows are also rented out for L90,000–L160,000. To get here from the historic center, follow Via XXV Aprile east to Via Lucchino; the campground is a few blocks farther on the right.

WHERE TO EAT

Sirmione's castle-encircled center has an army of *gelaterie* and pizza/sandwich stands (just pick one, you can't go wrong) and mediocre restaurants, especially along V. Emanuele. Sit-down restaurants cost more closer to the water, but you can eat well for about L8,000–L12,000 at **La Botte** (V. Antiche Mura 25, tel. 030/916273), which serves simple food like homemade cheese tortellini. Half-pension deals (breakfast and dinner) at some of the lodging spots in town can offer you full, multi-course evening meals for far less than you'd pay elsewhere.

OUTDOOR ACTIVITIES

Although some stretches stink of sulfur, Sirmione has several nice beaches that fill up with day-trippers on weekends. At **Lido delle Bionde** (access near the castle off V. Dante), bake on a chaise with an umbrella for L7,000–L10,000 per day or strain yourself kayaking (L7,000–L10,000 per hour) or pedal boating (L12,000 per hour). Hordes of boat and water-ski renters will greet you when you get off the bus—never accept the first price they offer.

GARDONE

Gardone, Garda's western shore, is a turn-of-the-century resort turned sleepy and faded. Crowds are a problem, but what else is new? Cynics may say that Gardone has little to offer aside from "resorting," but that's not entirely true: Il Vittoriale is definitely worth a day of checking out. Plant lovers should stop on the way at the **Hruska Botanical Gardens** (V. Roma, tel. 0336/410877; admission L7,000; open mid-Mar.–mid-Oct., daily 9–6:30), which nurtures 2,000 species assembled by naturalist Arturo Hruska between 1940 and 1971.

When poets become interior designers, you get **Il Vittoriale**, a 22-acre noble-estate-turned-eccentric-haven that was the home of Gabriele d'Annunzio (1863–1938), one of Italy's great modern poets. It is probably the most important—and unusual—tourist attraction in the Lakes region, so if you're in the area, don't miss it. The official line is that d'Annunzio bought the villa himself in 1921, but some suspect that Mussolini gave it to him to shut his poetic but prolific mouth. Residing there until his death, d'Annunzio and architect Gian Carlo Maroni added porticoes, a mausoleum that would become d'Annunzio's grave, and myriad bizarre theme rooms, including an auditorium displaying the biplane from which d'Annunzio dropped leaflets during a wartime protest. D'Annunzio even dry-docked the warship *Puglia* in the garden. Operas and ballets are still staged in the outdoor theater—tickets start at L20,000. Contact **Agenzia Molina** (P. Wimmer 2, tel. 0365/21551, fax 0365/290216; open Mon. and Wed.–Sat.

9–12:30 and 3–6, Tues. 9–12:30) or the **tourist office** (V. Repubblica 35, tel. 0365/20347) for info. You can roam the grounds and small museum unaccompanied, but the house is only accessible via guided tour (in Italian only except for groups, with prior notice). *P. Vittoriale, tel. 0365/20130. Grounds admission L8,000; grounds and villa L16,000. Grounds open Tues.–Sun. 8:30–8, house open Tues.–Sun. 10–12:30 and 2:30–6. Both open only until 4:30 in winter.*

COMING AND GOING

Gardone lies on the Desenzano (40 min, L3,900) and Riva del Garda (1 hr 15 min, L5,600) bus route; from three to six buses pass daily between 6 AM and 8 PM. Two buses per day go all the way to Milan (3 hr, L15,100). In Gardone, buy bus tickets at **Agenzia Molina** (*see above*). Molina also sells boat tickets, or you can buy them directly from **Navigazione Lago di Garda** (tel. 030/949511), which runs five daily ferries March–September from Desenzano (1 hr 10 min, L9,500) via Sirmione (1 hr, L9,500) and three from Riva del Garda (2 hrs, L11,600) to Gardone's pier on Piazza Wimmer. From the port or bus stop, follow the yellow signs up the hills.

RIVA DEL GARDA

Riva del Garda is a mosaic of neon windsurfing sails, a 12th-century fortress, and palm-tree-lined piazzas. Coveted both for its beauty and its strategic position on the northern tip of the lake, the town has bounced from ruler to ruler over the past centuries. After the 19th-century Napoleonic occupation, it joined Bavaria, then a unified Italy, and finally Austria. Although back in Italian hands since 1918, you're still as likely to hear "Wie geht's" as "ciao," because hundreds of German and Austrian tourists come for the town's sport-filled beaches, mild climate, and nightlife; and the cheap accommodations are a budget traveler's dream. The **La Rocca** castle also houses a civic museum with a collection of primarily local artworks. *Tel. 0464/573869. Admission L8,000. Open Sept.–Feb., Tues.–Sun. 9:30–12:30 and 2–5:30; Mar.–June, Tues.–Sun. 9:30–12:30 and 2–6; July–Aug., Tues.–Sun. 9:30–12:30 and 5–10.*

Smell that? Octogenarians from all over make the exodus to Sirmione to soak in its supposedly rejuvenating sulfur springs.

BASICS

Someone at the **tourist office** (Giardini di Porta Orientale 8, tel. 0464/554444; open Apr.–mid-Sept., Mon.–Sat. 9–noon and 3–6:15; mid-Sept.–Oct., Mon.–Sat. 9–noon and 3–4:30; Oct.–Mar., Mon.–Fri. 9–12 and 2:30–5:15) went bonkers with their PC to offer you tons of graphics-covered leaflets on sports, hotels, restaurants, and clubs. They also have info on climbing and mountaineering, as does nearby Arco's **Alpine Club** (V. Segantini 64, tel. and fax 0464/519805).

COMING AND GOING

Buses go to Riva's **Autostazione** (V. Trento, tel. 0365/552323), but you're better off using the bus stop on Via Roma next to the city center. From here, walk through Porta San Michele; the hotels Montanara and Vittoria (*see below*) are to your right, and the lake's a few blocks down the hill. The nearest **train station** is in Rovereto—15–18 buses run there daily (30 min, L3,700), and train schedules are posted in the Autostazione and travel agencies so that you can figure out your (inevitably long) transfer plans. Fifteen buses run daily down the lake's east coast; stops include Malcesine (25 min, L3,500 or L4,500), Peschiera (a transfer point to Sirmione, 1¾ hrs, L8,300), and Verona (2¼ hrs, L9,300). Six buses go down the west coast daily, stopping everywhere including Gardone (1¼ hrs, L5,600) and ending in Desenzano (2 hrs). Three daily buses bypass Desenzano and go to Milan (4 hrs) via Brescia (2 hrs). **Navigarda** (tel. 030/9149511) runs boats connecting Riva's Piazza Cattena with many lake towns, including Gardone (2¾ hrs, L11,600), Sirmione (4 hrs, L13,200), and Desenzano (4 hrs, L15,800). Hydrofoils are faster but charge a supplement of L2,000–6,000.

WHERE TO SLEEP

Riva has decent, central budget accommodations, but you must reserve ahead, especially in summer. Try to get a room at **Montanara** (V. Montanara 18–20, 38066, tel./fax 0464/554857; cash only), which charges L54,000 for a double without bath (L58,000 with), or the **Vittoria** (V. Dante 39, 38066, tel. 0464/554398), where doubles are L85,000 with bath. Both are clean, central, and have no curfew. Montanara's casual trattoria also serves some of the best eats in town—you can only get what the chef makes, but it's sure to be good and reasonable (primi run L9,000).

HOSTEL • The Benacus Youth Hostel (P. Cavour 10, 38066, tel. 0464/554911; closed Nov.–Feb.) has clean rooms (L22,000 with breakfast) with hot showers and laundry (L5,000); it's in the center of town, two blocks from the lake. Reception is only open 10–noon and 4–midnight, when they lock up the place for the night. An HI card is required, and reservations are highly advised.

CAMPING • Camping Monte Brione (V. Brione 30, 38066, tel. 0464/520885), amid olive trees and within a stone's throw of the beach, has 100 tent sites (L18,000 plus L12,000 per person). They offer excellent facilities: a pool, showers, bike rental (L7,000 per hr), discounts to the nearby dance club, pizzerias, and a windsurfing school (*see* Outdoor Activities, *below*).

WHERE TO EAT

For late-night cravings, head to **Pizzeria Da Pino** (V. Monte D'Oro 10, no phone; cash only; closed Mon.), which, along with pizza (L8,000–L13,000), has *farfalle* (butterfly-shape pasta) with vodka sauce. The best deals are at the bakery **Vivaldelli** (V. Roma 23, tel. 0464/552310), where a slice of pizza or a croissant will set you back only L1,200.

OUTDOOR ACTIVITIES

Riva del Garda packs in enough activity to tire Schwarzenegger, so don't just lie on the pebbles perfecting your sunburn. There are three schools of bronzed experts ready to share their wisdom—for a fee. Try the **Professional Windsurfing School** (V. Rovereto 100, tel. 0464/556077; closed Nov.–Easter), where full rentals (boards, wet suits, and life jackets) cost about L22,000 per hour or L75,000 per day and up, depending on level of equipment. Meanwhile, Paolos have a monopoly on beach rental stations: on the shore left of the castle, **Paolo Furletti** (tel. 0464/506301 or 0368/930348 for cellular) rents paddleboats and rowboats for L11,000–L14,000 per hour. He's usually there March–October, daily 8–8. Rent a canoe or kayak from **Paolo Fazi** (tel. 0337/459785) at the Sabbioni Beach for L10,000 per hour (L15,000 for a double) or L30,000 per day (L40,000 for a double). Landlubbers can pedal mountain bikes (L7,000 per hour, L20,000 per day) from **Girelli** (V. D. Chiesa 15/17, tel. 0464/556602).

AFTER DARK

Many nightspots near the lake are difficult to access without a car, but in Riva there are good clubs right in town. Shake your booty at **Après Club** (V. Monte d'Oro 14, tel. 0464/552187) or **Discoteca Tiffany** (Giardini di Porta Orientale, tel. 0464/552512; disco open Thurs.–Sun., otherwise it's a bar). Covers range from L10,000 to L20,000. Among the watering holes, **Pub al Gallo** (V. S. Rocca 11, tel. 0464/551177) stays open the latest, until 3 AM. Otherwise, rock all night on a **disco boat** cruising around Lake Garda (cover L20,000 and up, including a drink; open Aug.; tel. 0464/9149511).

LAKE ISEO

Sandwiched between Garda and Como, little Lake Iseo (Lago d'Iseo) is easy to overlook. But if you visit its central island of Monte Isola or hike to the geological pyramids of Zone, it's equally hard to forget. This is a place for swimming or sailing in relatively clean water, trekking through olive groves, or just plain snoozing. Iseo's towns exist without the glitz, tourism, and pretensions that burden many lakeside resorts, so even in summer you shouldn't have to battle crowds. However, there are also fewer hotels here, so still plan on booking ahead. Great fishing on the lake translates into affordable fresh fish, best accompanied by local Franciacorta wines. Como may be tonier and Garda livelier, but Iseo is the true place for getting away.

ISEO

Aside from the evening "traffic" of bike bells, screaming kids, and neighbors chattering from the windows, Iseo sits quietly on the lake's southern shore. The pretty town has a few sights, namely the **Santa Maria del Mercato** church (V. Mirolte at Vicolo Borni), with its recently discovered and restored 14th-century frescoes. The moss-covered statue of Giuseppe Garibaldi in the adjacent piazza is worth a gander. And **Oldofredi Castle** (V. Mirotte 74, tel. 030/980035) now houses a public library and cultural center. A **market** takes over the town's medieval center on Friday morning. Stop by the **tourist office** (Lungolago Marconi 2, tel. 030/980209) for maps and info on **Torbiere Sebine,** a protected marshland just outside Iseo. Prehistoric carvings sound interesting? Ask about the **Naquane National Park,** in nearby Valle Camonica. The office also has info on bike rentals, available at the train station in Piovaglio d'Iseo (about L8,000 per hr, L30,000 per day).

COMING AND GOING

Privately run trains to the lake start in Brescia. At the Brescia train station, look for the small platforms at the west end of the station, adjacent to the main Platform 1. Trains to Iseo depart throughout the day, the last leaving at about 8:20 PM (40 min, L3,700). Iseo's **train station** (tel. 1478/88088) is on Via XX Settembre. There's no official bus station, only a long-distance bus stop at the end of Viale Repubblica at Via XX Settembre. Buy tickets at newsstands in town. **Buses** primarily go to other lake towns and Brescia, but there are a few to Bergamo and Milan—call 030/980060 or ask at the tourist office for up-to-date schedules. On Sunday, train and bus service is limited. **Gestione Navigazione Lago d'Iseo** (tel. 035/971483; open daily 9–noon) runs ferry service between Iseo, Monte Isola, and other lake towns. Check the schedule posted at Porto G. Rosa, Iseo's landing dock, or ask for one at the tourist office. Buy tickets on board if the port's ticket booth is closed (it usually is).

WHERE TO SLEEP

The best choice in town is probably **Milano** (Lungolago Marconi 4, 25049, tel. 030/980449, fax 030/9821903), which ain't cheap (doubles with bath, phones, and TVs L90,000–98,000), but then neither is the **Rosa** (Via Roma 47, 25049, tel. 030/980053, fax 030/9821445), and it's not as nice (doubles with bath L80,000–L90,000).

CAMPING • Campers will have better luck: **Campeggio del Sole** (V. Per Rovato 26, 25049, tel. 030/980288; cash only) is equipped with everything you could possibly need. We're talking restaurant, bar, and bike and paddleboat rental. A space costs*L14,300–L27,000, plus L7,600–L12,600 per person. Cheaper and more informal is **Quai** (V. Antonioli 73, 25049, tel. 030/9821610 or 030/981161; cash only; closed Oct.–Mar.). It's on the lake and charges L13,000–L19,000 for campsites, plus L7,200–L8,000 per person. It also has bungalows (L45,000 for two, L62,000 for four). Buses stop at Quai on request.

WHERE TO EAT

Follow the blasting music to **All'Incontrario** (V. Campo 25, tel. 030/9821464; cash only; closed Mon.), a real diner joint that's got everything from panini (L5,000) and salads (L6,500) to pizza—as if you haven't had enough by now. If the fishy aroma in the air stimulates your appetite, try spaghetti with clams or seafood pizza (L12,000) at an outdoor table at **Promessi Sposi** (Largo Zanardelli 15, tel. 030/980306; closed Mon.).

MONTE ISOLA

Hills peppered with with olive groves, vineyards, and chestnut trees rise above fishing ports and beaches on Europe's largest lake island. Monte Isola seems caught in a medieval time warp—until a gang of mopeds buzzes by. Don't come here if you're into nightlife: besides being the primary mode of transport, the aforementioned scooters are also the major entertainment, and Friday nights sound like a beehive. Pass your days lounging on the beach (try those near Carzano and east of Siviano), rambling between waterfront villages, and hiking up the so-called mountain. Rent a **bike** at the Carzano, Sensole, and Peschiera Maraglio ports—L5,000 for the first hour, L4,500 for each additional hour; tandems cost L10,000 per hour. The island's major sight is the **Madonna della Ceriola,** where the view from the 2,000-ft peak makes yet another 15th-century church a lot more appealing. Walk here from Peschiera Maraglio or Siviano (about 3½ km/2 mi), yellow SANTUARIO signs mark the way), or take a bus to Cure and hike only the final 20-minute stretch. You can walk around the island in about three hours and hit all of the waterfront towns by sticking to the main road. Or hop on one of the buses that crisscross the island from 5 AM to 2 AM (L1,500); buy your ticket on board.

BASICS

The **tourist office** (tel. and fax 030/9825088; open Mar.–Oct., Mon. 3–6, Wed.–Sun. 10–1 and 3–6), near the dock at Peschiera Maraglio, has bus and ferry schedules and hotel info—but you have to pay for some of the brochures.

COMING AND GOING

To get to Monte Isola, take a ferry (round-trip L7,000) from Iseo (*see above*), which runs about every half hour 8 AM–11 PM (less frequently in winter and on weekends); a few ferries stop at other ports like Marone (for Zone). Monte Isola has five ports; make sure the ferry stops where you want, and don't just jump off when you hit the island. You can bring a bike on for L1,500.

WHERE TO SLEEP AND EAT

Stupendous views, welcoming owners, loaner mountain bikes, and a roof terrace up the value of the basic L80,000 doubles at **Bella Vista** (Siriano di Montesola, Via Roma 88 (the only road), 25050, tel. 030/9886106). It's on the north, less touristy side of the island, which has the best beaches. Get off the ferry at Siriano, hike up the path, and turn right. **Sensole** (V. Sensole 10, Loc. Monteisola, 25050, tel. 030/9886203; cash only) has the cheapest doubles, for L70,000—get off at the Sensole ferry stop. In Corzano, **Campeggio Monte Isola** (V. Croce 144/143, 25050, tel. 030/9825221; cash only), on the beach, has 86 sites (L8,000 plus L10,000 per person and L8,000 per car) and bungalows for L50,000 for two, L75,000 for three, and L90,000 for four. Most trattorias on the island serve the same kind of food at the same price, so just pick a pretty spot and park yourself. In Sensole, the **Vittoria** (tel. 030/9886222; closed Thurs.) is a nice, quiet choice—sample the bounty of clean waters by trying the fish (L14,000–L16,000). The shops in front of the Peschera Maraglio port will make you a really cheap sandwich (L2,000), or you can sit down and munch in **Caffè dei Porti** (tel. 030/9886331).

ZONE

This village at the northeast end of the lake is largely undiscovered by tourists. The only folks who seem to know of green and hilly Zone are ambitious hikers who crave an escape from civilization. It's a beautiful place, with cobblestone streets and stunning views. Yet the real highlights are the **Piramidi d'Erosione,** a large rock formation that dates to when the Camonica Valley was first eroded by glaciers. Below town in a river basin, these "pyramids" look like a Gaudi-inspired Stonehenge and alone are worth the trip.

Apart from its rugged scenery, Zone is a good base for an ascent of **Monte Guglielmo,** which rises majestically behind the town. Stop by the **Pro Loco** (V. Monte Guglielmo 42, tel. 030/9880116) for hiking maps; the staff will also call the **Almici** (tel. 030/9870919 or 030/9870990), a lodge on the mountain, to check the availability of its 19 beds (L30,000 per person including breakfast). Try to reserve in advance though—it books up months ahead. The hike to the lower elevations of Monte Guglielmo takes about 2½ hours and is fairly easy. Budget a few more hours to reach the peak (elevation 6,430 ft).

COMING AND GOING

To reach Zone, you must first get to Marone. There are 15 daily trains (20 min, L3,000) between Iseo and Marone's **train station** (V. Metelli, tel. 1478/88088). Buses connect Iseo and Marone 12 times daily (20 min, L2,500). On Sunday the number of buses and trains drops dramatically. If you take the train, rush to the left of Via Zanardelli and hop on the bus for Zone, or you might—heaven forbid—get stuck in Marone. Tickets can be bought on board. You can walk to Zone from Marone, but it's a steep—albeit scenic—6-km (4-mi) hike; take the road toward the mountains near the train station. Boats for Iseo depart from Marone once a day (1 hr, L45,000).

WHERE TO SLEEP AND EAT

If you want to stay overnight, one-star **Piramidi** (V. Sebino 28, 25050, tel. 030/9870932; cash only) has L65,000 doubles, all without bath. It's also a good place to grab a bite—the restaurant downstairs serves good food with a view of the Piramidi. A cheaper option, but not as nice, is **Reduce** (Via Loden 4, Loc. Cusato, 25050, tel. 030/9870935; cash only), which rents doubles with bath for only L45,000–L50,000. **Camping Corni Stretti** (V. Valle di Gasso, 25050, tel. 030/9870910; cash only), on a lush hillside, has 35 sites (L10,000, plus L8,000 per person) and five bungalows (from L40,000). It's closed in winter.

LAKE COMO

In his 19th-century novel, *I Promessi Sposi,* Alessandro Manzoni described Lake Como (Lago di Como) as a set of ram's horns pointed south toward the town of Erba and its love sagas. The forked lake does indeed resemble an upside-down pair of horns, with the town of Como on its southwest tip. More than 100 years after Manzoni, the lake region's silk, furniture, and iron manufacturers, as well as tourism, have contributed to some urban sprawl. Como, in particular, has been responsible for the pollution that has killed off most of the lake's underwater inhabitants, but while Como still attracts the package tours, many of the smaller lakefront towns have borne the brunt of Lake Como's economic slowdown. These lakefront spots remain peaceful and unpolluted, and while sometimes haunting, they offer beautiful views of water, mountains, and the still-grand resort hotels of the region's opulent past. On the Milan–

Switzerland train line, the lake draws Milanese on the weekends, but water sports and challenging mountain hikes attract enough younger types to help offset some of the stuffiness that comes with the summer crowds of luxury-package tourists.

COMO

The Romans took Como from the Celts around 2 BC; in the late 1800s, the ritzy set occupied the lake's namesake city. Unfortunately, Como has decayed visibly since those glory days; the built-up and carnivalized city is largely responsible for the pollution of Lake Como and even for the resulting decline of some of its more peaceful destinations. Still, Como has good tourist facilities and a pleasant view of the lake and its surroundings. Its historic core centers around lakefront Piazza Cavour, a pink-and-yellow palazzoed square bordered by the tourist office, boat port, pricey cafés, and souvenir shops. Behind the piazza on Via Vittorio Emanuele II stands the impressive **Duomo**, a Gothic-Roman facade from the 15th century paired with a dome designed by Juvarra in 1740. Farther along Via Vittorio Emanuele II, the **Basilica di San Fedele** has drawn the devout since the 6th century and typifies Lombard architecture. Once the private party grounds of the nobility of the 18th–19th centuries, the **Villa Olmo** (V. Cantoni, tel. 031/572910; open weekdays 8–6) has been public property since 1927. Concerts and special events are sometimes hosted in its big, beautiful, and free gardens, a 15-minute walk west of Piazza Cavour along the lake. On the more macabre side, the ruins of **Castello di Baradello** were a prison to Napo Torriani, a noble who dangled from the wall in a cage for 19 months before finally croaking in 1278. The castle, erected in the 12th century by Barbarossa and destroyed by

The landscape around Zone is so evocative that da Vinci used it as the backdrop for his painting "Madonna of the Rocks."

the Spanish about 300 years later, lies on the southeast edge of town on Via Castel (take Bus 1 or 12 to Piazza Camerlata, L1,300, then walk). Finally, if the boutiques with reams of Como's renowned silk get you tempted to blow big bucks on some silk PJs, decompress at the **Silk Museum** (V. Valleggio 3, tel. 031/303180; open Tues.–Fri. 9–12 and 3–6, Sat. by reservation only), L15,000 to enter.

BASICS

Como is not a good place to change money—rates are poor and commissions high. Stick to the **ATMs** in the center of town. If you're desperate, the **main post office** (V. Gallio 6, tel. 031/262026) offers half-decent exchange rates; it's open weekdays 8:15–6, Saturday 8:15–noon. The **APT** (P. Cavour 16, tel. 031/269712; open Mon.–Sat. 9–1 and 2:30–6; summer, also Sun. 9–12:30) offers the usual info and an after-hours and Sat. exchange booth with exorbitant rates and a 3% commission.

COMING AND GOING

Como has two **train stations.** The smaller **Stazione F.N.M.** (Largo Leopardi, tel. 1478/88088), next to the bus station, serves Milan, Varese, and smaller towns along the way. The main **Stazione San Giovanni** (P. San Gottardo, tel. 1478/88088), on the Milan–Switzerland–central Europe rail line, is at the end of Via Gallio, a 15-minute walk from central Piazza Cavour (frequent buses, L1,400). From the main station, more than 40 trains run daily to Milan (35–40 min, L4,400–L9,200), with connections to Rome, Naples, Genoa, and Venice. Como's **bus station, Stazione Autovie** (P. Matteotti, tel. 031/247247) services principal lake villages and Bergamo (5 daily, 2 hrs, L8,500). **Navigazione Lago Como** (tel. 031/304060) runs ferries between all lakeside villages. In Como boats dock at Piazza Cavour.

WHERE TO SLEEP

A handful of budget hotels lie on Via Borgo Vico, which intersects the stairs leading to the main station. **Dinner**—yes, Dinner—(V. Borgo Vico 45, 22100, tel. 031/570108; cash only) has doubles for L70,000. Near Piazza Cavour, **Sociale** (V. Maestri Comacini 8, 22100, tel. 031/264042) has doubles for L60,000 or L80,000 with bath. As always, reserve during summer.

HOSTELS • The convent **Protezione della Giovane** (V. Borgo Vico 182, 22100, tel. 031/574390; cash only) is a good deal, with beds for L25,000. The **Villa Olmo Youth Hostel** (V. Bellinzona 2, 22100, tel. and fax 031/573800; cash only; closed Dec.–Feb.), in an ancient building close to the lake, charges L15,000 for a bed and breakfast and offers tons of services and discounts for guests, including bike rental (L15,000 per day) and laundry (L5,000). From the main station, follow signs or Bus 1, 6, or 11. Curfew is 11:30, lockout 10–4.

WHERE TO EAT

Eating cheaply in Como is not easy. Cruise Via Borgo Vico for the handful of pizzerias and *birrerie* where sandwiches and slices won't deplete your life's savings. Como's cuisine logically centers around fresh-water seafood such as *missoltini* (sun-dried fish). **Carrettiere** (V. Coloniola 18, tel. 031/303478) has a L25,000 menu that'll let you sample local cuisine without drowning in debt. **Free Break Self Service** (V. Innocenzo XI 19, tel. 031/261449), near the train station, and **Golosone Self Service** (V. B. Luini 42, tel. 031/264144; cash only) also have quick deals. For centuries Como's residents have devoured *la miascia* or *torta da paisan,* a warm, sweet bread filled with apples, pears, raisins, and at the chef's discretion, chocolate, grated lemon, rosemary, and almonds; sink your teeth into it at most *pasticcerie* (bakeries) in town.

OUTDOOR ACTIVITIES

For swimming or sunbathing, you'll find public beaches on Viale Geno and in front of the Villa Olmo on Via Cantoni. The ambitious can tackle the 50-km (31-mi) hike mapped out by the tourist office (shorter treks are available), along which lie several *rifugi* (mountain huts) and campsites. If you want stunning views without physical exertion, take the **funicular** (tel. 031/303608; L8,000 round-trip) from Piazza Funicolare (several blocks east of P. Cavour along the lake) to Brunate. Taking just seven minutes, this funicular is claimed to be Europe's fastest. The sedate will enjoy the hour-long boat loop (L9,000) departing regularly from the port at Piazza Cavour, or better yet, a 7-hour trip around the whole lake (L27,000). For more info on the boats, call **Navigazione Lago Como** at 031/304060.

BELLAGIO

This flowery, hilly village nestled in the fork of Lake Como has made cameos in works by Flaubert, Stendhal, Twain, and Shelley. Iron-balconied homes looking out onto narrow streets make the town center a sight in and of itself, but Bellagio offers many ways to enjoy the local nature as well. While package tours and urban decay center around Como to the south, Bellagio remains a picturesque and more relaxing throwback to the lakeside's lost youth. Relax by the clear waters at its *lido* or water-ski with the **Bilacus ski school** (Lido di Bellagio, tel. 031/950597). Rock climbers should contact the **Alpine Club** (V. Roma 41, tel. 0341/363588) in nearby Lecco for the skinny on surrounding mounts. **Arco Sport** (Salita Monastero 6, tel. 031/950959) rents mountain bikes. The **APT** (P. della Chiesa 14, tel. 031/950204; open daily 9–noon and 3–6, shorter hrs in winter) hands out brochures, maps, and town info.

The most worthwhile sight in Bellagio is **Villa Serbelloni** (entrance visible from P. della Chiesa, tel. 031/950204), now part of the Rockefeller Foundation. This strategically-located building, at the tip of the lake's little peninsula, is closed to the public, but its lush gardens overlooking the picture-perfect town and across the crux of the lake to the surrounding mountains are definitely worthwhile. The gardens can be visited by guided tour (L5,000) at 11 AM or 4 PM. Continue your tour at the free **Villa Melzi** (tel. 031/950318; admission L7,000; open late Mar.–Oct., daily 9–6:30), built in 1808 for Napoléon's lieutenant. The villa, 3 km (2 mi) east of town along Via P. Carcano, has a garden that alternates blooming azaleas and rhododendrons, as well as a tiny archaeological museum and chapel.

COMING AND GOING

Buses run from Como to Bellagio and let you off at Lungo Cago Marconi; pick up tickets at the tobacco shops on Salita Serbelloni, which crosses Lungo Cago Marconi. **Navigazione Lago di Como** (tel. 031/304060) also serves Bellagio by boat (2 hrs, L10,500) and hydrofoil (35 min, L15,500).

WHERE TO SLEEP AND EAT

Cheap rooms abound at **Giardinetto** (V. Roncati 12, 22021, tel. 031/950168; cash only; closed Oct.–Easter), which has doubles with bath for L90,000 (L70,000 without). Hostel **La Primula** (V. IV Novembre 86, 22017, tel. 0344/32356; open Mar.–Oct.; cash only), in nearby Menaggio, serves up beds and breakfasts for L17,000. Their acclaimed meals (L16,000) are worth the trek even if you aren't staying there. At all hotels in town, beware *letti matrimoniali* which are actually two single beds pushed together. Boats leave Bellagio every hour for Menaggio (L5,000), on the central west shore.

LAKE MAGGIORE

Bordered by Piedmont to the west, Lombardy to the east, and Switzerland to the north, the idyllic beauty of Lake Maggiore (Lago Maggiore) has inspired musicians Wagner and Toscanini, writers Flaubert, Mann, Hemingway, and Goethe, and the Borromeo family, who built palaces on the lake's islands. For whatever reasons, though, it's lost considerable tourist esteem in comparison with the lakes to the east. On today's Lake Maggiore you're more likely to bump into Grandma than a prince or a poet. Crowded with lavish resorts dating to the turn of the century, Maggiore is now an overpriced stomping ground for retired travelers with expendable cash. Whether it's described as a "characteristic fishing village" or "art nouveau," each town feels contrived and decidedly well established. However, the advantage is that it's considerably calmer than the frenzied Lago di Garda or overbuilt Lago di Como. Stresa, on the western Piedmont shore, has a whole waterfront full of luxury hotels, so you may prefer to stay in a less-touristed town like Connobio or to camp and hike in the hills bordering the lake.

STRESA

Stresa's spotless streets—lined with resorts, smiling locals, and restaurants with menus in three languages—cater to spendthrifty visitors. Some guidebooks describe Stresa as genteel and pleasantly languorous, but swank and overdeveloped come closer to the mark. Still, as a transport hub, it's convenient for coming and going and for exploring the mountains and the nearby Isole Borromee.

When crossing the street in Como, look both ways and cross your fingers: Locals have a reputation for reckless driving, even among Italians.

BASICS

The **post office** (V. Roma 5/7, tel. 0323/30065; open weekdays 8:15–6, Sat. 8:15–11:40) and the banks along the waterfront change money and AmEx traveler's checks. Stresa's **APT** (V. Principe Tomaso 70/72, tel. 0323/30150, fax 0323/32561; open weekdays 10:30–12:30 and 3–6:15, Sat. 8:30–12:30, Sun. 9–noon; closed Sat.–Sun. in winter) offers the standard info, but they don't make reservations. From the train station, take a right on Via Carducci, which becomes Via Gignous, and a left on Via Principe Tomaso.

COMING AND GOING

The **train station** (P. Stazione, tel. 1478/88088) has trains to Milan (19 daily, 1–1½ hrs, L7,400–L12,200), Genoa (1 daily, 2½ hrs, L18,600), and towns in Switzerland. Boats and buses both depart from the *imbarcadero* (loading dock) at Piazza Marconi, along Corso Umberto I, where you'll find ticket booths. For more information contact **Navigazione Sul Lago Maggiore** (V. F. Baracca 1, tel. 0322/242352), whose boats dock at the imbarcadero.

WHERE TO SLEEP

Stresa's budget lodging is a joke, with only a meager selection of generic one-star hotels. If you can weather the bad-tempered owner, the best deal is at **Chez Osvaldo** (V. A. M. Bolongaro 57, 28049, tel. and fax 0323/31948), with nine rooms above its restaurant (*see* Where to Eat and Be Merry, *below*); it's L70,000 per double with bath, the latter ranging from full-tub affairs to shower-above-your-toilet numbers. You'll get a sweeter reception at **Orsola** (V. Duchessa di Genova 45, 28049, tel. 0323/31087), a short walk from the station. Noise is a drawback, but with closed shutters you should be able to sleep. If not, watch TV amid porcelain kitties and fake flowers in the common room. Doubles run L100,000 with bath, L80,000 without.

CAMPING • Discover the side of Lake Maggiore untouched by the air-conditioned-bus crowd by staying at one of 11 campsites around nearby Baveno, which has a train station on the same line as Stresa's. Stresa's APT (*see above*) has a full campsite listing. The only site open year-round is **Cala Speranza (S. S. Sempione 24, 28042 Baveno, tel. 0323/924178; cash only); it's about L9,000 per person.

WHERE TO EAT AND BE MERRY

For cheap takeout, try **Gastronomia de Piero** (V. A. M. Bolongaro 36, tel. 0323/31934). Stop by the **Pasticceria Marcolini** (V. P. Margherita 24, tel. 0323/30364) and sample the *Margheritine di Stresa*—Stresa's shortbreadlike cookies named for Savoy's Queen Margaret. If you want to eat sitting down, be careful—Stresa is prone to culinary disasters. One exception is **Chez Osvaldo** (*see* Where to Sleep, *above*). Despite his surly demeanor, Osvaldo concocts meals with a Lake Maggiore flair—try the *cotoletta alla novarese* (baked pork chop with basil and tomato) or the *coregone al timo* (whitefish with thyme, L10,000). Sip beer on tap (L3,000) and play cards with the folks at the **Irish Bar** (V. P. Margherita 11).

OUTDOOR ACTIVITIES

The major lake sport is basking on the beach on the east side of town. Equally unstrenuous is a visit to the **Parco di Villa Pallavicino** (tel. 0323/31533; open daily 9–6), a zoo with picnic grounds, monkeys, and zebras. To get here, follow Corso Italia to the western edge of town. **Hiking** is big—done either in the surrounding forested hills or on Monttarone, the small mountain that doesn't quite loom over town. For info and maps on hiking, visit the APT (*see* Basics, *above*) and ask for the *Lago Maggiore Trekking Per Tutti* brochure with English translation. To reach the trailheads, take the **funivia** from Piazzale Lido 8 (tel. 0323/30295). It leaves every 20 minutes 9:15–noon and 1:40–5. Tickets are L10,000, or L15,000 with your own mountain bike. You may also rent a bike in the funivia station (L30,000 per day) and pay L9,000 for the funivia.

NEAR STRESA

ISOLE BORROMEE • The crown jewels of Lake Maggiore are the Isole Borromee (Borromeo Islands), which form a triangle between Stresa, Baveno, and Pallanza and make a nice day trip from Stresa. Although a bit tarnished by the nascent tourist trade, the islands shine through the videotaping hordes and chintzy souvenirs. They take their name from the Borromeo family, which has owned them since the 12th century. These days you don't need an engraved invitation to reach them—only a few thousand lire and a water-worthy stomach. Boats for the islands leave every half hour from the dock on Stresa's Piazza Marconi (tel. 0323/30393; open daily 8:30–7) and stop at the lakeside towns of Isola Bella (5 min, L4,400), Isola Superiore (10 min, L5,000), and Isola Madre (30 min, L6,000). If you want to visit all three, buy a day pass for L14,000. The islands are covered with stairs except for a few makeshift ramps on Isola Bella, so wear good walking shoes. Everything edible here is overpriced—shop for groceries before you come.

Isola Bella (Beautiful Island) is just off Stresa's shore. It takes its name not only from its beauty but also as a play on words with the name of Count Borromeo III's wife, Isabella. The count also commissioned the island's Baroque **palazzo** (tel. 0323/30556; admission L14,000) and its 10 terraced gardens in 1670. Tiny **Isola Superiore** (a.k.a. **Isola dei Pescatori**), less than 330 ft wide, supposedly retains the look of an old fishing village. In reality, the island is little more than a patch of sand with tacky restaurants and souvenir stands. Most of the **Isola Madre** is covered by a 16th-century **palazzo** and its pleasant **Orto Botanico** (tel. 0323/31261; admission L14,000; open late Mar.–Sept., daily 9–12:30 and 1:30–5:30, until 5 Oct. 1–midnight). If you splurge on the gardens' entrance fee, don't miss the Palazzo's vinyl-covered furniture and bizarre mannequins in period dress, where you'll encounter oddities such as 17th-century skeleton marionettes and a stuffed peacock.

CANNOBIO

Cannobio, the last Italian town before the Swiss border, has narrow streets bordered by houses with tall wooden shutters—a Kodak moment indeed, although in high season crowds of vacationers might block your view. The area offers more outdoor activities than Stresa; its breezes attract windsurfers and sailors in summer. For hikers, an old network of footpaths and mule tracks around the lake has been developed into a trail system. The **tourist office** (V. Vittorio Veneto 4, tel. 0323/712121; open daily 9–noon and 4:30–5, closed Sun. afternoon, and Thurs. afternoon in winter) provides lodging listings as well as hiking maps for every experience level, from he-man to heavy smoker. Ask for *Lago Maggiore Trekking Per Tutti*, which outlines routes around the lake—try Trail 17 to Monte Giove, above Cannobio.

Giardino (V. V. Veneto 24, 28052, tel. 0323/71482) is the town's only budget hotel, charges L100,000 for doubles with bath and breakfast. The area has about 10 campgrounds; **Del Fiume** (V. C. Darbedo 24, 28052, tel. 0323/70192; closed Nov.–Dec.) charges L10,000 (L14,000 with a car) plus L9,000 per head. If you want to swim and sunbathe, Cannobio has Maggiore's largest public beach, which means it gets crowded in July and August. For water sports, rent equipment at **Tomaso Sail and Surf** (Lido Cannobio, tel. 0323/72214).

COMING AND GOING

From April to the third week of September, two boats daily ply the waters between Stresa and Cannobio (1 hr 50 min, L12,100); two hydrofoils (55 min, L15,000) also make the trip. Otherwise, take a boat from Stresa to Intra (15 daily, 1 hr, L6,800) and catch an **ASPAN** bus to Cannobio (16 daily, 30 min, L3,000).

LAKE ORTA

Hiking from the station on a road where nightingales make more noise than cars, you'll actually believe the brochures waxing eloquent about sapphire lakes nestled in emerald valleys. Lake Orta (Lago d'Orta), the smallest of the lakes, doesn't attract the hordes like Lago Maggiore does, and that's all the more reason to come. It's a nature lover's paraadise, but one that (ironically) can't really be explored without a car. **Orta,** the lake's most visited town, is a good base for exploring the region. Its medieval squeeze-to-the-side-when-a-truck-passes-by streets and central Piazza Motta have a few touristy shops, but they sell locally produced honey, *amaro* (bitter) liqueur, and woodcrafts rather than cheesy trinkets. Orta's **tourist office** (V. Olina 9/11, tel. 0322/911937, fax 0322/905678; open Tues.–Sat. 9–noon and 3–5:30, Sun. 10–noon and 3–5) supplies info in four languages.

COMING AND GOING

Orta's **train station** (Via Lunati; 1478/88088) is so small that no one save the bartender works here; schedules are posted, and you buy tickets on board. From Orta there are about 14 trains to Novara (L4,200), where you can change for Milan (1 hr 30 min, L8,600) and Turin (2 hrs, L10,500). There are four trains daily from Stresa on Lago Maggiore to Orta, but stopover time to change trains in Premosello varies widely (1½–3 hrs, L5,400). No bus service connects the station to Orta, 2 km (1 mi) away, but a local entrepreneur has a makeshift taxi service with flexible rates—call 0336/845311 or case the front of the station for a taxi. Otherwise, take a left after the station, a left when the road ends, and a left after the only stoplight for miles.

> *If romantic Orta was enough of an aphrodisiac to distract Friedrich Nietzsche—who went gaga here over Russian poetess Lou Salomé in 1882—just think what it may do for you.*

WHERE TO SLEEP

At **Olina** (V. Olina 40, 28016, tel. 0322/905656), doubles with bath run L95,000 and up, and there are also apartments with kitchens for groups of four or five for a week minimum. Rates vary according to season and location, from L600,000 to L2,000,000. **Taverna Antico Agnello** (V. Olina 18, tel. 0322/90259; cash only) serves up outstanding local food, but it's not cheap (pasta around L12,000–14,000).

CAMPING • You'll hardly be roughing it at **Cusio** (V. S. G. Bosco 5, 28016, tel. 0322/90290 or 0322/90160 in winter, fax 0322/911892), a campground with pool and tennis (L10,000 per hour). Rates are L8,000 plus L7,000 per person; reception is open 8:15–noon and 2–9. From the station, go right on Via S. G. Bosco on the road to Orta. Or try **Camping Orta** (V. Domodossola 28, tel. 0322/90267), which costs L8,000 per person plus L14,000 per campsite.

WHERE TO EAT

One of Orta's only pizzerias, **L'Oasi** (V. Domodossola 7, 0322/90193) has everything from sandwiches to grilled fish. Behind the central piazza, **L'Edera** (V. Bersani 11, tel. 0322/905534; cash only) serves sandwiches and crepes until 1 AM.

WORTH SEEING

An easy 1½-km (1-mi) hike from central Orta, the **Sacro Monte** (tel. 0322/905642; open summer, daily 8–6; free) is a national reserve with 20 chapels setting the stage for 376 scenes from the life of St. Francis of Assisi. If this 16th- to 17th-century version of televangelism isn't enough, there are magnificent views and boccie ball courts. The altitude might make you delirious enough to forget the prices at **Ristorante Sacro Monte;** if not, grab a sandwich at the adjacent bar or picnic on the tables near the entrance. To get here, take the path to the right of the church behind Orta's Piazza Motta.

PIEDMONT AND VALLE D'AOSTA

BY SARAH BREMER

UPDATED BY ROBIN S. GOLDSTEIN

Sequestered in Italy's northwest corner, the provinces of Piedmont (Piemonte) and Valle d'Aosta share the lush Parco Nazionale del Gran Paradiso and border the Alps; their stunning landscapes mix dramatic snow-capped mountains with peaceful valleys, with the exception of Piedmont's vital metropolis, Turin. Napoléon's regime controlled both regions in the 19th century, and French influence remains evident in everything from traditional recipes redolent of mountain cheeses, truffles, and cream to Versailles-style gardens and wide, tree-lined boulevards. Despite its cultural and geographical ties, tiny Valle d'Aosta—Italy's smallest region—certainly doesn't consider itself part of its larger neighbor Piedmont and has even maintained semiautonomy within the Italian nation since 1945.

Both regions' general lack of tourism means you will encounter the warm, unjaded spirit of the locals. In winter, though, Alpine resorts jack up costs for the glitzy set. Planning ahead will improve your trip, as transportation, especially in Valle d'Aosta, can be tricky. All things considered, if you veer off the Rome–Florence–Milan–Venice line, you'll be rewarded.

PIEDMONT

Piedmont, or Pedemontium as originally named by the Romans, means "foot of the mountains," and more than 500 km (310 mi) of mountain ranges wind around its borders, peaking at the slopes of Mon Viso, Gran Paradiso, and Monte Rosa. Lucrative industries radiating from the region's business capital, Turin, have filled Piemontese pockets. The computer/mobile phone megafirm Olivetti and acres of Fiat factories combine to make Piedmont one of the wealthiest regions in Italy. Perhaps as a result of this prosperity, Piedmont has become a stronghold of the Lega Nord, a controversial organization pushing for northern secession from the poorer southern regions. Ironically, Piedmont—Turin in particular—is also known for its left-wing politics.

Some fragments of the Roman era linger in Turin; but more notably, the region is peppered with well-preserved medieval castles and sacred mounts dating from the kingdoms of the Franks, the Lombards, and the marquises of Saluzzo, who reigned during the 10th–14th centuries AD. The Savoy dynasty subsequently usurped most of the power over the region, sanctioning an extravaganza of Baroque palaces, hunting lodges, and vineyards. After Napoléon interrupted Savoy rule in the 1800s, Piedmont nobles propelled the unification of Italy, and Turin became the capital of the new nation.

But you don't have to spend your entire Piedmont sojourn in Gothic monasteries and museums. Sip sumptuous local wines and savor the seasonal cuisine characterized by local *tartufi* (truffles), often paired with baked hare and asparagus, Alpine trout, and regional pastas like *taglioni* (long flat noodles) and *agnolotti* (stuffed pasta). Typical cheeses include *Tome di Cocconato* and soft *robiola di Roccovereno*. In winter wash your tummy with *bagna cauda* (literally "hot bath," a dish in which you dip veggies in a sauce of garlic, anchovies, and oil). If you can hoist yourself from the table, take the time to go rafting on the Po River, hike the "hills," and chat (or play charades) a bit with the friendly locals.

TURIN

Though it holds the dubious title Car Capital of Italy, Turin (Torino) is much more than just a factory town. Years of planning have made the city an urban designer's dream; it possesses a grace that defies its size and modernity. The bordering suburbs consist of bleak housing projects built in the '50s and '60s for migrant Fiat workers. Chic shops, elegant *fin-de-siècle caffès,* and museums populate the city center's spacious piazzas, which are connected by wide arches and graceful colonnades. The Crocietta district is home to Turin's amazing aristocratic residences.

Turin's position at the confluence of two rivers has long made it desirable as a military stronghold. In the 1st century BC it came under the rule of Augustus Caesar, who commissioned the easy-to-navigate grid of streets. In the 11th century AD, the city became part of the Savoy domain. The counts and later dukes of Savoy transformed Turin into a sophisticated European capital, bringing in artists and thinkers to enrich the city's culture and skyline. The city's polished, educated, and liberal atmosphere has drawn such intellectuals as Nietzsche, leftish Italians like novelist Natalia Ginzburg and poet Cesare Pavese, and the writer Primo Levi. Turin's distinguished university has a large, politically active student population that carries on the literary and artistic traditions.

Turin was crucial to the Risorgimento (*see box* Espresso Shot Heard 'Round the World, *below*), and it served as the capital of a newly unified Italy in 1861. Expansion slowed when Florence replaced Turin as the capital in 1864, but the beginning of the 20th century saw a surge in both industrialization and worker activism. The powerful industrialist Gianni Agnelli and his clan began an empire that now holds a monopoly on Italian car manufacturing—not just Fiat but also Ferrari, Alfa Romeo, and Lancia—in addition to controlling Olivetti, La Stampa, and the Juventus soccer team. Meanwhile, the leftist Antonio Gramsci became a folk hero in the 1920s and '30s for organizing occupations of the Fiat factory and later helping to found the Italian Communist Party. Along with a large working-class population, Turin boasts a nobility that is still intact, if a little worse for wear, in all its snobby glory.

BASICS

CHANGING MONEY • Both train stations have 24-hour ATMs and exchange booths (open daily 8 AM– 9:30 PM) with decent rates (though those at the ATMs are usually better) and no commission. Almost every piazza or *corso* has a bank; they are generally open weekdays 8:30–1:30 and 2:30–4:30, and most have 24-hour ATMs. The one at **Banca Popolare di Milano** (C. Matteotti 8) makes AmEx transactions.

DISCOUNT TRAVEL AGENCIES • **CTS** (V. Montebello 2a, tel. 011/8124534 or 011/8125149; open weekdays 9:30–6, Sat. 9:30–1) offers discounted plane tickets to students under 26 with ID.

MAIL • Along with normal postal services, the main **post office** (V. Alfieri 10, off P. San Carlo, tel. 011/ 535894 or 5628100; open weekdays 8:15–7:20, Sat. 8:15–1) offers 24-hour telegram and international fax services in an office to the left of the front door—ring the bell outside after hours.

VISITOR INFORMATION • Turin has two **IAT** offices: at Stazione Porta Nuova in the Trasporti Torinesi office (tel. 011/531327) and at Via Roma 226 (near P. San Carlo, tel. 011/535181). Both are open Monday–Saturday 9–7:30 and offer the weekly magazine *News Spettacolo*, a treasure trove of cultural events. The **Centro Informa Giovani** (V. Assarotti 2, tel. 011/4424976 [2–6:30]; open Mon. and Wed.– Sat. 10:30–6:30) has everything from job listings to sports info. Check them out at www.comune.torino.it/infogio/i_n.html, or pick up their pamphlet *Torino Giovani* for info on art happenings and nightlife. **La Vetrina per Torino** (P. San Carlo 159, tel. 011/4424740) has the scoop on entertainment and cultural events and sells tickets for museums and shows. **Club Alpinisti Italiani** (V. Barbaroux 1, tel. 011/546031) can tell you all about mountain sports.

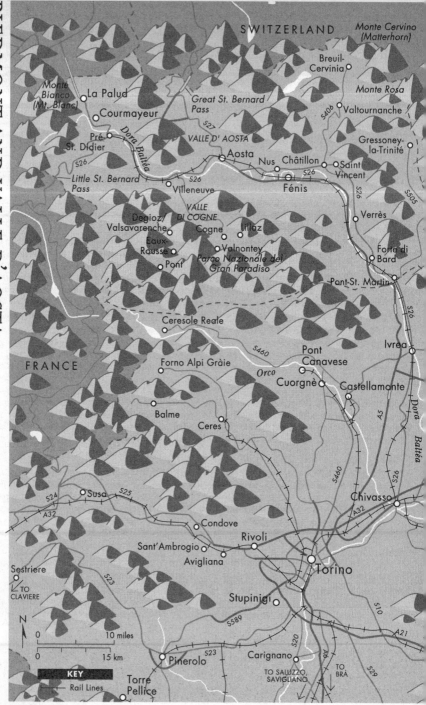

SWITZERLAND

Monte Cervino
(Matterhorn)

Breuil-
Cervinia

Monte Bianco
(Mt. Blanc)

La Palud

Courmayeur

Great St. Bernard
Pass

Monte Rosa

Valtournanche

Pré-
St. Didier

Dora Baltea

S27

VALLE D' AOSTA

Gressoney-
la-Trinité

Little St. Bernard
Pass

S26

Aosta

Nus

Châtillon

Saint
Vincent

Villeneuve

S26

Fénis

S26

VALLE
DI COGNE

Degioz/
Valsavarenche

Cogne

Lillaz

Verrès

Eaux-
Rousse

Valnontey

Forte di
Bard

Pont

Parco Nazionale del
Gran Paradiso

Pont-St. Martin

FRANCE

Ceresole Reale

S460

Pont
Canavese

Ivrea

Forno Alpi Gràie

Orco

Cuorgnè

Castellamonte

A5

Dora Baltea

Balme

Ceres

S460

S26

S2A

Susa

S25

Chivasso

A32

Condove

Rivoli

A32

Sant'Ambrogio

Avigliana

Torino

Sestriere

TO
CLAVIERE

S23

Stupinigi

S10

N

0   10 miles

0   15 km

S589

Carignano

TO
BRÀ

A6

S29

KEY

Pinerolo

S23

TO SALUZZO,
SAVIGLIANO

S20

Torre
Pellice

Rail Lines

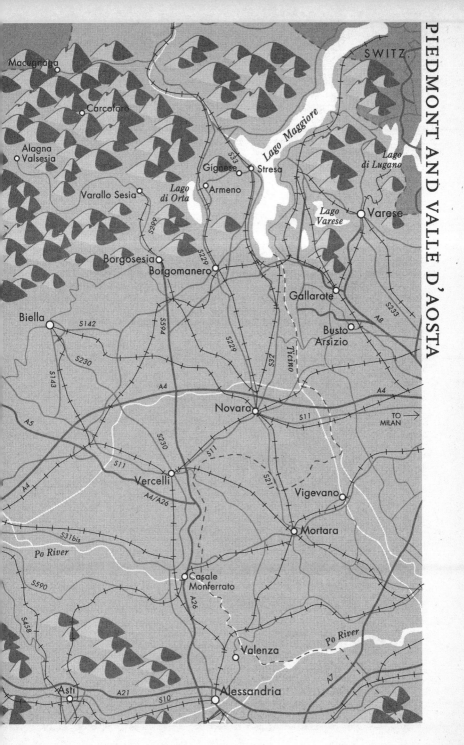

Macugnaga

Carcoforo

Alagna
Valsesia

Varallo Sesia

Lago
di Orta

Gignese

Stresa

Armeno

Lago Maggiore

SWITZ.

Lago
di Lugano

Lago
Varese

Varese

Borgosesia

Borgomanero

Gallarate

Busto
Arsizio

Biella

S142

S594

S229

S3

S229

S65

S33

Ticino

S33

S253

A8

S230

S143

A4

S230

S230

A5

Novara

S11

A4

TO
MILAN

S11

Vercelli

A4/A26

S11

S211

S211

Vigevano

Mortara

S316bis

Po River

Casale
Monferrato

A26

S590

S458

Valenza

Po River

A7

Asti

A21

S10

Alessandria

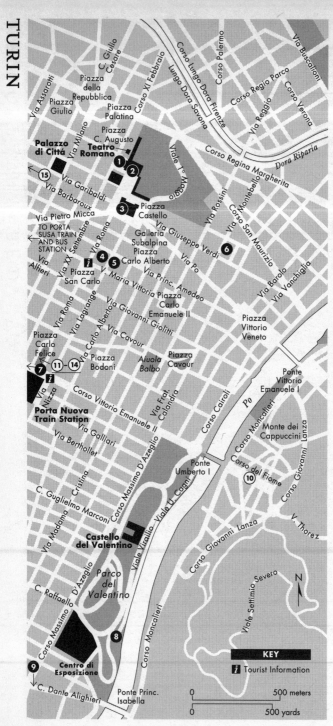

TURIN

Sights ●

Duomo di San Giovanni, **1**

Galleria Civica d'Arte Moderna e Contemporanea, **7**

Mole Antonelliana, **6**

Museo dell' Automobile, **9**

Museo del Risorgimento, **5**

Palazzo dell' Accademia delle Scienze, **4**

Palazzo Madama, **3**

Palazzo Reale, **2**

Rocca e Borgo Medioevale, **8**

Lodging ○

Astoria, **11**

Canelli, **15**

Hotel Bologna, **12**

Hotel Campo di Marte, **13**

Magenta, **14**

Ostello Torino, **10**

KEY

i Tourist Information

Palazzo di Città

Teatro Romano

Piazza della Repubblica

Piazza Giulio

Piazza Palatina

Piazza C. Augusto

Piazza Castello

Galleria Subalpina

Piazza Carlo Alberto

Piazza San Carlo

Piazza Maria Vittoria

Piazza Carlo Emanuele II

Piazza Vittorio Veneto

Piazza Carlo Felice

Piazza Bodoni

Aiuola Balbo

Piazza Cavour

Porta Nuova Train Station

Ponte Vittorio Emanuele I

Monte dei Cappuccini

Ponte Umberto I

Castello del Valentino

Parco del Valentino

Centro di Esposizione

Ponte Princ. Isabella

Via Assarotti

C. Giulio Cesare

Corso XI Febbraio

Lungo Dora Firenze

Corso Lungo Dora Savona

Corso Palermo

Corso Regio Parco

Via Buscalioni

Corso Verona

Via Reggio

Corso Regina Margherita

Dora Riparia

Viale T. Michel

Via Rossini

Corso San Maurizio

Corso Montebello

Via Giuseppe Verdi

Via Po

Via Barolo

Via Vanchiglia

Via Giovanni Giolitti

Via Cavour

Via Princ. Amedeo

Via Carlo Alberto

Via Lagrange

Via Roma

Via Maria Vittoria

Via Pietro Micca

Via XX Settembre

Via Roma

Via Milano

Via Garibaldi

Via Barbaroux

Via Alfieri

Corso Vittorio Emanuele II

Via Frat. Calandra

Corso Cairoli

Po

Corso Moncalieri

Corso del Fiome

Corso Giovanni Lanza

V. Thorez

Via Galliari

Via Berthollet

C. Guglielmo Marconi

Via Madama Cristina

Corso Massimo D'Azeglio

Viale Virgilio

Viale U. Cagni

Viale Settimio Severo

Corso Moncalieri

Corso Giovanni Lanza

C. Raffaello

C. Massimo D'Azeglio

C. Dante Alighieri

Via Nizza

TO PORTA SUSA TRAIN AND BUS STATION

N

0   500 meters

0   500 yards

128

COMING AND GOING

BY TRAIN • Near the center, **Stazione Porta Nuova** (P. Carlo Felice, tel. 1478/88088 toll-free) handles most of Turin's rail traffic. Every day about 24 trains run to Milan (2 hrs, L14,000; InterCity 1½ hrs, L22,500), three to Venice (4½ hrs, L41,000), and 10 to Rome (8 hrs, L56,000). To reach the town center, walk 1½ km (1 mi) up Via Roma to Piazza Castello, or take Bus 61 or 63 or Tram 4 or 15 from in front of the station.

Turin's second station, **Stazione Porta Susa** (P. XVIII Dicembre, tel. 1478/88088 toll- free) serves the same destinations with similar prices. Tram 1 and Bus 52 connect this station to Porta Nuova; Tram 13 and Bus 55 go to Piazza Castello.

BY BUS • Turin's **bus station** (C. Inghilterra 3, tel. 011/4332525) has one long line for tickets, but you can also buy them at **Bar Milleluci** (P. XVIII Dicembre 5) and catch the buses in the piazza. Buses serve Milan (every hr. except 8:30PM–6AM, 2 hrs, L16,700) and, leaving from Corso Marconi, Saluzzo (30 min, L5,000). Tram 15 runs from the bus station to Porta Nuova and Piazza Castello.

BY PLANE • Turin's **Caselle Airport** (about 15 km/9 mi north of city center, tel. 011/5676361), with flights to most major European and Italian cities, is served by **Alitalia** (1478/65641), **British Airways** (tel. 167/287287), and many other major airlines. **Sadem** (V. della Repubblica 14, tel. 011/3111616) buses connect the airport to the bus station (40 min, L6,000) and run every 30–45 minutes.

GETTING AROUND

The Po River snakes around the eastern edge of Turin and divides the larger left bank, where streets follow a grid pattern of interlocking piazzas, from the monied right bank, where roads wind up the hills. Most sights lie in the left bank, north of Stazione Porta Nuova and **Piazza Castello,** which marks the heart of the city. **Via Roma,** Turin's snooty shopping street, runs out of the piazza to the southwest, passes through the stately **Piazza San Carlo,** and ends at the junkie-infested **Piazza Carlo Felice** in front of the Porta Nuova station. **Via Po,** a caffè-lined avenue, also stretches from Piazza Castello to **Piazza Vittorio Veneto** before opening onto the Po River. The **Murazzi** is the path along the left bank of the Po between Ponte Umberto I and Ponte Vittorio Emanuele I. Funky stores and cool caffè line **Via Garibaldi,** which heads northwest out of Piazza Castello.

BY BUS OR TRAM • In the lobby of the Porta Nuova station, the **Trasporti Torinesi** office (tel. toll-free 167/019152) has info on Turin's comprehensive system of buses and trains. Buy tickets anywhere the CONSORZIO TRASPORTI TORINESE sign is displayed, including at automatic ticket machines and the Porta Nuova IAT office (*see* Visitor Information, *above*). Tickets cost L1,400 and are good for 70 minutes after validation, or you can buy a ticket for unlimited travel for a day for L4,200.

WHERE TO SLEEP

Turin is an outlandishly costly place to sleep. The cheapest hotels are clustered in the seedy red-light district around Via Nizza, just east of Stazione Porta Nuova. For nicer hotels, try those along Corso Vittorio Emanuele II and off Corso Re Umberto I, a block west of Stazione Porta Nuova.

DIRT CHEAP • **Canelli.** The cheapest hotel in the town has a *centralissimo* location, off the pedestrian Via Garibaldi—that's the highlight of this dive with rather grungy doubles (L55,000, or L35,000 without bath). But if you're not planning to spend too much time here, this is a great deal. *V. San Dalmazzo 7, 10122, tel. 011/546078. From Stazione Porta Nuova, take Bus 67 (from other side of Corso Vittorio Emanuele) and get off at P. Alberello, walk along V. Garibaldi, right into V. S. Dalmazzo. 36 rooms, 30 with bath. Cash only.*

UNDER L100,000 • **Hotel Campo di Marte.** The management admits that the listed L90,000 price for a double with bath drops on command, so bargain away. In a central, relatively safe zone, the hotel's clean, spacious rooms with TV and phone are split among singles, doubles, triples, and even quads with extra rollaway beds. Quads can cost as little as L30,000 a head. Reception is open 24 hours. *V. XX Settembre 7, northeast of C. Vittorio Emanuele II, 10123, tel. 011/545361 or 011/530650. 12 rooms with bath.*

Magenta. The rooms here are large and airy, with high ceilings and huge windows. The turtle-print curtains prove that taste is subjective. Doubles cost L100,000 with bath, L70,000 without. *C. Vittorio Emanuele II 67, west of Stazione Porta Nuova, 10123, tel. 011/542649, fax 011/544755. 18 rooms, 10 with bath.*

UNDER L130,000 • **Hotel Bologna.** This clean hotel across from Porta Nuova has luxurious triples complete with Jacuzzi bath and ornate ceilings for L120,000. Doubles, most with bath, TV, and phone, start at L100,000 with breakfast; those on the second floor cost a bit more. *C. Vittorio Emanuele II 60,*

10123, tel. 011/5620191, fax 011/5620193. Near northwest corner of Stazione Porta Nuova. 46 rooms, 44 with bath.

UNDER L140,000 • Astoria. Pleasant management and a convenient position within walking distance of Stazione Porta Nuova make this a good choice. The rooms (L130,000 for a double, including breakfast) all have cable TV, telephone, and air-conditioning. Ask for discounts for longer stays. *Via XX Settembre 4, 10121, tel. 011/5620653, fax 011/5625866. From Stazione Porta Nuova, walk left out of station along C. Vittorio Emanuele, turn right into V. XX Settembre. 60 rooms with bath.*

HOSTELS • Ostello Torino. In Turin's ritzy right bank, this clean hostel is a bargain. It has a restaurant, balconies, and a TV room. Beds go for L19,000 with breakfast; dinner costs L14,000. The reception closes at 11:30 PM, but you can borrow a key. Only HI members can stay here (but you can buy a membership), and only large groups are admitted December 22–February 15. Lockers are available for a L20,000 deposit. *V. Alby 1, 10131, at V. Gatti, tel. 011/6602939, fax 011/6604445. Take Bus 52 (64 on Sun.) from Stazione Porta Nuova. 76 beds. Reception open 7 AM–10 AM and 3:30 PM–11:30 PM, lockout 10–3:30. Laundry. Cash only. Closed last wk of Dec.–end of Jan.*

CAMPING • Villa Rey. This site nestled in the hills is within the city limits and charges L4,000–L7,000 per tent according to number of people, plus L7,000 per person. Electricity (L2,000) is available. *Strada Superiore Val San Martino 27, 10131, tel. 011/8190117. From Stazione Porta Nuova, Bus 61 east to P. Vittorio, transfer to Bus 56 as far as V. Gabetti, then follow signs. Showers. Cash only. Closed Nov.–Feb.*

WHERE TO EAT

The rich Torinese cuisine oozes with butter, cream, and cheese. Local specialties include *agnolotti* (ravioli stuffed with meat or spinach), *bollito misto* (a concoction of boiled meats), and *corne all'albese* (slivers of raw veal with oil, lemon, Parmesan, and white truffles). The decadence continues with dessert—pastries with Chantilly cream and liqueurs, glazed chestnuts, baked peaches stuffed with crushed *amarettini* (almond cookies), and treats from local chocolatier **Cafarel**, made outside of Turin. If you're craving Chinese food, try **Du Cheng** (V. XX Settembre 62, tel. 011/546159); they refer to chow mein as spaghetti and have lunch menus starting at L10,500. Pick up picnic loot, like meats and and cheeses for L20,000–L30,000 per kilo, at the morning **market** in Piazza della Repubblica (Mon.–Fri. 8–1, Sat. 8–6), or check out self-service restaurants (L3,000–L8,000 per meal) such as **Brek** (two locations: P. Carlo Felice 22, tel. 011/534556; P. Solferino at V. S. Teresa, tel. 011/545424; both closed Sun.).

UNDER L10,000 • Lossolo. With a patio and mirrored dining rooms, it's no wonder this self-service restaurant gets packed at lunch. There are slices of cheap pizza, sandwiches, and pastries galore. *V. Garibaldi 9, tel. 011/540817. 1½ blocks southwest of P. Castello. Sometimes closed Mon.*

UNDER L15,000 • Da Mauro. If you look up from the scrumptious Piemontese and Tuscan delicacies piled before you, you might spot one of Italy's top *calcio* (soccer) players digging into a plate of *fagottini alla crema di tartufo* (pasta with truffle cream sauce). At the very least you can see signed pictures of Roberto Baggio and others who've frequented this three-room taste-bud heaven. *V. Maria Vittoria 21, west of P. Carlo Emanuele II, tel. 011/8170604. Cash only. Closed Mon. and July.*

La Pergola Rosa. At this cozy, Spanish and Italian restaurant, stick to the so- called *monopiatti* (one-course) meals—one price includes coffee, water, or vino; dessert; and unusual entrées like tagliatelle *al limone* (with lemon). *V. XX Settembre 18, just northwest of P. Carlo Felice, tel. 011/537562.*

UNDER L40,000 • Arcardia. When a Japanese restaurant came from Milan in 1994 to host four sushi nights, the waiting lists inspired Arcardia's owners to offer these goodies on a regular basis. This is now one of the few spots in all of Italy with sushi and sashimi (from L30,000), *unagi* (eel), and sake. The L25,000 lunch menu is a good deal. *Galleria Subalpina 16, tel. 011/5613898. Closed Sun.*

CAFFE • Turin's caffè culture peaked in the 19th century, when plans for the Risorgimento were hatched over coffee and pastries (*see box* Espresso Shot Heard 'Round the World, *above*). Cruise Via Roma between the train station and Piazza Castello for *gelaterie* and caffè with interiors as elegant as their customers. Sip an espresso (L1,500, or L4,000 sitting) at **Baratti e Milano** (P. Castello 27, tel. 011/5613060), a crystal-chandeliered caffè older than the Italian nation itself. Or follow in the steps of Count Camillo Cavour to **Caffè Fiorio** (V. Po 8, tel. 011/9676654), whipping up Turin's most celebrated concoctions a few blocks from Turin's original university (V. Po 17). Those feeling less than svelte can run to **Columbo** (V. Po 35/F, tel. 011/835430) for nonfat frozen yogurt.

WORTH SEEING

If you think the only things to see in Turin are car factories and the Holy Shroud (*see below*), you're in for a surprise. Besides these claims to fame, architectural jewels and museums housing everything from

Egyptian artifacts to contemporary art are here for the taking (er, not the museum pieces). The civic museums are free the first Friday of every month.

BASILICA DI SUPERGA • The Savoy kings from Vittorio Amadeo II to Carlo Alberto rest in the crypt of this apricot-hued basilica, designed by Filippo Juvarra and completed in 1731. It stands atop a hill northeast of the city; in the adjacent park, you can get a great view of all of Turin. *Piazzale di Superga, tel. 011/8980083. From P. Vittorio Veneto, take Tram 15 to Sassi, catch funicular (hourly, L5,000 round-trip). Admission free. Crypt open Apr.–Sept., daily 9:30–noon and 3–6; Oct.–Mar., daily 10–noon and 3–5.*

DUOMO DI SAN GIOVANNI AND THE SACRA SINDONE • Although it was swept by a disastrous fire in April 1997, Turin's Renaissance cathedral is now re-opened. The cathedral's crowning attraction, the black marble **Cappella della Sacra Sindone** (Chapel of the Holy Shroud), was ruined in the fire and is expected to remain closed for at least the next few years. Thanks to the firefighters, though, the much-venerated Sacra Sindone—in which Jesus was supposedly wrapped after the crucifixion—was saved, and it will be displayed in the Duomo from August 26 to October 22, 2000, to celebrate the new millennium. If you want to see the relic, you must call ahead for reservations. Contact either of the IAT offices (*see* visitor information, *above*) for an update. *Piazza S. Giovanni, tel. 011/4361540. Admission free. Open Mon.–Sat. 7–12 and 3–7, Sun. 8–12 and 3–7.*

MOLE ANTONELLIANA • This landmark (V. Montebello 20, tel. 011/8170496), designed as a synagogue in 1863 by architect Alessandro Antonelli, is one of Europe's highest brick buildings and Turin's unofficial logo. The elevator to the top of the 550 ft needle-like spire—which gives a mole's-eye view of the city—will unfortunately be closed for restoration until at least 2000.

Martini lovers everywhere are forever indebted to Vittorio Emanuele II's personal chef, Vialardi, who concocted the essential vermouth by spicing up white wine with 13 special ingredients.

MUSEO DELL'AUTOMOBILE • Turin's car museum naturally stars the Fiat, but Bugattis, Bentleys, Mercedes Benzes, and Fords round out the collection. You can also see the beautiful blue Isotta Franchini that bears the golden initials *ND* for its onscreen owner Norma Desmond, Gloria Swanson's character in *Sunset Boulevard. C. Unità d'Italia 40, tel. 011/677666. From Stazione Porta Nuova, take Bus 34. Admission L10,000. Open Tues.–Sun. 10–6:20.*

PALAZZO DELL'ACCADEMIA DELLE SCIENZE • The Palace of the Academy of Sciences houses two noteworthy collections. The **Museo Egizio** displays one of the world's best Egyptian artifact collections, with about 30,000 pieces dating from the 6th century BC to the 7th century AD. Of particular note are findings from the 1400 BC tomb of the royal architect Kha, including pages from the Book of the Dead. *V. Accademia delle Scienze 6, tel. 011/5617776. Admission L12,000. Open Tues.–Sat. 9–10, Sun. 9–2.*

Above the Museo Egizio, the large **Galleria Sabauda** emphasizes religious subjects and portraiture, including pieces from the Savoy princes' personal collections. *V. Accademia delle Scienze 6, above Museo Egizio, tel. 011/547440. Admission L8,000. Open Fri.–Wed. 9–2, Thu. 10–7.*

PALAZZO MADAMA • A 13th-century castle complete with a moat, 15th-century Savoy additions, and a Baroque front designed by Juvarra in the 18th century somehow join together in the center of Piazza Castello. The Palazzo had been serving as a civic museum containing regional art from the Middle Ages through the 1900s; at press time it was closed for restoration.

PALAZZO REALE • Home to the Savoy princes from the mid-1600s until 1865, this labyrinth of rooms in period decor, on the site of the ancient Roman city gates, can be viewed only on guided tours every 40 minutes; the last tour leaves at 5:30. *Piazza Castello at Via dei Partigiani, tel. 011/4361455; open Tues.–Sun., 9– 6:15.*

Behind the palazzo, the **Giardini Reali** have pebbled pathways, a rose garden, and soccer-playing youngsters. The gardens were designed in the 1600s by André le Nôtre, of Versailles fame. At the gardens' northern edge, a tunnel leads to the **Antiquities Museum** (C. Regina Margherita 105, tel. 011/5212251; open Tues.–Sat. 9– 7, Sun. 2–7), where you can get a gander at prehistoric artifacts for L8,000.

PARCO DEL VALENTINO • At the center of this park, designed in 1830, lies the 17th-century **Castle of Carlo di Castellamonte** (also known as the Castello di Valentino); it houses the university's architecture faculty and is closed to the public. Nearby, at the University's **Orto Botanico** (Botanic Gardens), smoochers uphold the Valentino name amid well-tended hills of roses and trees. At the park's south end, explore the **Borgo Medioevale**, a Disney-style medieval theme park, and its faux but fun **Rocca Medioevale**, a medieval castle created for the 1884 world's fair. *Along Po's left bank below P. Umberto.*

ESPRESSO SHOT HEARD 'ROUND THE WORLD

In the 1830s, café philosophers and radical thinkers decided it was time to oust Italy's foreign rulers and forge an Italian state. Almost 30 years later, King Vittorio Emanuele II of Piedmont and his prime minister, Count Camillo Cavour, whipped up a nationalist, anti-Austrian frenzy in the north. To get rid of a pesky Bourbon king in Sicily who menaced the country's unification, the two conspired with trigger-happy Giuseppe Garibaldi. With 1,000 volunteer soldiers, the Red Shirts, Garibaldi made a famous voyage from Genoa to Sicily, where he helped the Sicilians oust King Francis II and turned the territory over to Vittorio Emanuele. In 1861, after war with Austria and much political backstabbing and wheedling, the kingdom of Italy was established with Turin as its capital and Vittorio Emanuele as its monarch.

Though the capital moved to Florence three years later, many street signs in Piedmont are reminiscent of the Risorgimento, and in Turin's Palazzo Carignano, the Museo del Risorgimento (off V. Accademia delle Scienze, tel. 011/5621147; free; open Tues.–Sat. 9–7, Sun. 9–1) displays the country's largest collection of artifacts from both the Risorgimento and the antifascist movement of the early 20th century.

Orto Botanico: tel. 011/6707446. Admission free; must book in advance. Borgo Medioevale: free, open daily 9–8. Rocca Medioevale: tel. 011/6692545; admission L5,000; open Tues.–Sun. 9–7.

CHEAP THRILLS

Every Saturday from 5 to 2, the streets around Piazza della Repubblica come alive with the **Balôn Market,** where you can get used (and stolen) goods and even have your fortune told. *Tarocchi* (tarot cards) are a big deal; if you've ever wanted to try your hand, here's the place. Also here an antique- and curio-hawking Gran Balôn—a mega flea market—gets underway on the second Sunday of each month. Crash a game of bocce at the Parco del Valentino (*see above*), or watch a Teatro Regio opera (*see* After Dark, *below*) for free, live on the TV of the Piccolo Regio, a neighboring bar.

FESTIVALS • The two-day **Feast of San Giovanni** (June 23–24) honors Turin's patron saint with parades and a canoe race on the Po, ending with impressive fireworks. If you're here at this time, be sure to book hotels ahead. The **International Festival of Young Cinema** in November showcases young filmmakers from all over the globe. The films show at the cinemas Massimo, Romano, and Centrale; call the festival directly at 011/5623309 for more info, or check out their English-language Web site at web-com.com/~ficg. Several other annual **film festivals** celebrate movies in their original language throughout the year; ask La Vetrina per Torino (*see* Visitor Information, *above*) for details.

AFTER DARK

Couldn't get seats at La Scala? Check out operas by Verdi, Puccini, and the like at **Teatro Regio** (P. Castello 215, tel. 011/88151, fax 011/8815214), where discount tickets sell for L25,000 one hour before the show. The city also sponsors the **Sere d'Estate** (Summer Nights) series, with concerts, dance performances, and films for cheap or free (tel. 011/4424736). **Cinema Cuore** (V. Nizza 56, tel. 011/

6687668) shows films in English Thursdays October–April. Other movie theaters cluster in the piazzas and streets near the train station.

Via Garibaldi hops in the evening hours. Devils imbibe brews at **Divina Commedia** (V. San Donato 47, tel. 011/488356), with a *birreria* (beer hall) on the ground floor (Purgatory), a steaming dance floor in the basement (Hell), and a tearoom upstairs (Paradise). From the Stazione Porta Susa, take Bus 13 to Piazza Statuto and follow Via San Donato. At **Café Elena** (P. Vittorio Veneto 5, tel. 011/8177332), near the university, you can cogitate over a glass of Turin's sweet-spicy brainchild, vermouth.

DISCOS • Between sunset and sunrise, a crowded line of clubs overwhelms the left bank's **Murazzi.** If you avoid the aggressive junkies and leave your valuables at home, you can have a great time. Circulate between **Alcatraz** (tel. 011/836900), which plays mostly world music Thursday–Saturday; the **Centro Sociale** (Lungo Po A. Diaz, tel. 011/835478) for live bands; and the disco next door, serving the Polo-and-Lacoste set. From the Murazzi, you can take a round-trip **boat ride** down the Po for L3,000 (Navigazione Sulpo, tel. 011/888010). Get off at the Parco Valentino and salsa to live Latin-American music at the **Green River Bar** (V. Umberto Cagni 7, tel. 011/6687953), which has terraces stretching out over the river.

NEAR TURIN

PALAZZINA DI CACCIA DI STUPINIGI

Not your average hunting lodge (a large bronze deer caps the cupola), the palazzina is a rococo pleasure palace built for Vittorio Amadeo II by master architect Filippo Juvarra. The gilded interior now holds a **Museo d'Arte e dell'Ammobiliamento** (Museum of Art and Furnishings) that gives you a glimpse of the highbrow life Piedmont nobles enjoyed. In the round central room once used for balls, a massive crystal chandelier hangs from the frescoed ceiling, and gold-leaf sconces—complete with carved deer heads—hang from columns ringing the room. Required guided tours begin every half hour (10–11:50 and 2:30–4:20), last 40 minutes, and are available in English. The ride to the palace from Turin takes about an hour. *8 km (5 mi) west of Turin, beyond Mirafiori suburb, tel. 011/3581220. From Stazione Porta Nuova, Bus 63 or Tram 4 to P. Caio Mario, then Bus 41 to palace. Admission L10,000. Open daily 10–4:20.*

If you liked Antonelli's Mole, head to the corner of Turin's Corso San Maurizio and Via Barolo to see his etta di Polenta (Slice of Polenta): a 90-ft-high, 90-ft-long building that's less than 3 ft wide at some points.

SACRA DI SAN MICHELE

The hallucinations caused by thin air and overexertion during the uphill hike will bring you closer to the deity long before you even arrive at this vast, creepy abbey. Begun in AD 998, the Sacra protected the mouth of the Susa Valley from passing marauders; more recently, it served as the setting for Umberto Eco's chronicle *The Name of the Rose*. The steep **Scalone dei Morti** (Stairs of the Dead), where corpses were once laid out for last respects, now simply provide access to the Gothic-Romanesque complex, but the air of solitude and death somehow lingers. Whimsical frescoes inside the church are overshadowed by views of the valley past the flying buttresses. From Turin's Porta Nuova station, take a regional train in the direction of Modane or Bussoleno, and get off at Sant'Ambrogio (30 min, L2,800). Behind the village church, take the right-hand path leading to another small church, and follow the trail up to the top (about 1½ hrs). If you're lucky, you might be able to score a ride down with a car-owning visitor. *Tel. 011/ 939130. Admission L4,000. Open Tues.–Sun. 9:30–12:30 and 3–6.*

SALUZZO

The medieval center of Saluzzo has steep, winding paths bordered by facades of crumbling frescoes and bricks that date back four centuries to when the town was capital of the Alermo kingdom. Down below, the modern section has Renaissance porticoes and piazzas from the Savoy era that today house caffès, shops, and locals who are happy to chat the day away. The people here claim to be able to cure any Turinese of his or her industrial weariness, and judging by the food, mountain views, and fresh air, they might be right. Saluzzo has zero budget hotels, though, so it's best explored on a day trip for a picnic and stroll. Head to the **APT** office (V. Griselda 6, tel. 0175/46710; open Tues.–Fri. 8–12:30 and 2–5:30, Sat. 8–noon) to get started.

COMING AND GOING • From Turin take the train to Savigliano (20 daily, 35 min, L5,000) and change trains (hourly, 15 min, L2,500) to reach Saluzzo's station at Piazza Vittorio Veneto. It's easier to catch a bus directly from Turin's Corso Marconi station (6 daily, 30 min, L6,000) or Savigliano (15 daily, 15 min, L1,500), but the last bus back to both leaves around 8:30 PM.

WHERE TO SLEEP • If you have to stay, try **Il Persico** (Vicolo Mercati 10, 12037, tel. 0175/41213; closed July), which has doubles with bath, TV, and phone for L85,000. About a km (½ mi) from the Castello della Manta (*see below*), the *agriturismo* (a rural home that rents rooms) **Le Camelie** (V. Collina 4, 12037, Manta, tel. 0175/85422; cash only; closed Jan.–Mar.) has three rooms available in a honeymoon setting with a pool and surrounding woods. A double room costs L90,000 a night, and the chef concocts fixed-price multicourse feasts for about L50,000 (wine included).

WORTH SEEING • You can hit all the big sites in one loop starting at Piazza Garibaldi, where the **Duomo** has a 4th-century wooden crucifix on display. Turn left on Corso Italia and enter the old city through Porta Santa Maria. Head up Via A. Volta, then follow the **Salita al Castello** just past the clock tower, then continue on to the **Castello,** or Castiglia, but don't get too close: far from its 13th-century glory as home of Saluzzo royalty, the castle was a prison for antifascists under the dictator Morandi and is now overrun with rats.

The **Castello di Manta,** a haunted old fortress converted into a noble pad in the 15th century, is decorated with fresco cycles on *The Fountain of Youth* and *The Nine Heroes and Nine Heroines*. Tel. 0175/ 87822. From Saluzzo bus station, take AT bus 4 km (2½ mi) south and ask driver to stop. Admission L6,000. Open Tues.–Sun. 10–1. Closed mid-Dec.–end of Jan.

ASTI

With its amazingly well-preserved medieval towers and Baroque palaces, the town of Asti sparkles like a glass of its famous spumante wine. From its beginnings as a Ligurian village, Asti became the Roman colony of Hasta in 1 BC, then a Lombard dukedom, a Frankish countship, and, around the 12th century, a powerful Church-governed commune. A chain of nobles took the reigns soon afterward: the D'Anjiò, the marquises of Monferrato, the Visconti, the dukes of Orléans, the Sforza, Charles V, and the dukes of Savoy, whose rule was interrupted by the Napoleonic occupation. The cornucopia of architecture left from these eras lends remarkable beauty to Asti's quiet and friendly streets.

BASICS

The **APT** (P. Alfieri 34, tel. 0141/530357; open weekdays 9–12:30 and 2:30–5, Sat. 9–12:30, Sun. 10–12) has lists of lodging and restaurants, as well as transport schedules and info on wine-tasting excursions. From train station, cross Campo del Palio (usually a parking lot) and go up the steps on the far east side.

COMING AND GOING

The **train station** (P. Marconi 7, tel. 1478/88088) has 50 daily trains from Turin (45 min, L5,100). The **bus terminal** (V. N. Costa 6, tel. 0141/433209), serving outlying areas, is to the right of the station; the office (tel. 0141/352678) for city buses is at Piazza G. Saragat 2.

WHERE TO SLEEP

Asti lacks decent, central budget hotels; what exists fills up only in September. The APT office (*see* Basics, *above*) has a list of rooms for rent in private homes and a list of nearby agriturismo sites. **Campground Umberto Cagni** (Strada Valmanera 152, 14100, tel. 0141/271238; closed Oct.–Mar.) is 2 km (1½ mi) from town and costs L6,000 per tent plus L6,000 per person, or L40,000 for a bungalow with kitchen. There are free showers, but electricity costs an extra L3,000. From the train station, take Bus 1 to Corso Volta and walk 1½ km (1 mi) north on Strada Valmanera.

A half-hour walk from the center, **Antico Paradiso** (C. Torino 329, 14100, tel. 0141/214385; cash only) has clean, quiet doubles with bath for L85,000. From the station, take Bus 3 or 4 toward Corso Torino and get off at the Via Corridoni stop. The **Cavour** (P. Marconi 3, 14100, tel. 0141/530222), across from the train station, has small, decent doubles for L75,000, or L97,000 with bath, TV, and phone—though you'll have to put up with pea-green decor.

WHERE TO EAT

Asti's wines were designed to go with the specifics of regional cuisine: Pair bitter Grignolino with salami, sweet Malvasia di Casorzo with dessert, and fruity, white Moscato Naturale d'Asti with anything, anytime. You might appreciate how locals add another meal to the day: the *merenda' snoira,* a late-afternoon snack of wine and sweets.

Asti has more than its share of pricey places. However, the town is famous for its classic Piedmonte food and cheeses, so it might be worth the extra lire. **Ristorante Reale** (P. Alfieri 5, tel. 0141/532279; closed Tues.) has multicourse meals with classic Piedmontese dishes, like *agnolotti* (a piedmontese pasta) and *funghi ai tartufi* (mushrooms with truffles), for L25,000–L30,000. **Ristorante Porta Torino** (V. Partigiani 114, tel. 0141/216883; closed Fri.–Sat.) serves very cheap primi (L6,000–L10,000) and secondi (L9,000–L15,000) to a local crowd. Otherwise, you're limited to pizzerias, most of which serve local pastas as well: **Leon d'Oro** (V. Cavour 95, tel. 0141/592030) and **Pizzeria Tre Re** (V. Alfieri 378, tel. 0141/592753; closed Tues.) are two of the best; pizzas here cost L7,000–L12,000.

WORTH SEEING

The **Collegiata di San Secondo** (P. San Secondo, south of Corso Alfieri, tel. 0141/50066; open daily 8–noon and 3–7) commemorates Asti's patron saint, who got his head lopped off here. His decapitated remains are kept in the church's crypt. Asti's **Duomo** (P. Cattedrale, tel. 0141/592924; open 8:30–noon and 3:30–6:30) is a mammoth structure with frescoes covering its ceiling and walls, two altarpieces by Gandolfino d'Asti in the left-hand chapels, and San Giovanni's remains in the crypt downstairs. The brick exterior's stunning 15th-century portal is on its south side. The ruins of the 9th-century **Cripta di Sant'Anastasio** (V. Goltieri 3/A, tel. 0141/399111) were discovered when the Baroque church built over it was demolished in 1907. A collection of the recovered capitals and architectural fragments is now housed in the **Museo Lapidario** (closed for restoration at press time) on the site. Contact the **Pinacoteca Civica** (C. Alfieri 357, tel. 0141/54791) for current details. **Torre Rossa** (Corso Alfieri; admission free; open daily 9–12 and 3–7), which has stood in various forms for about two thousand years, also served as San Secondo's prison; the oldest building in Asti, the tower has an interesting 16-sided form. Other notable medieval towers in the city center include the **Torre Troyana** (currently closed for restoration), attached to the **Palazzo Troya,** in Piazza Medici.

Since 1275 Asti has pumped up for Il Palio, a crazed bareback horse race on the third Sunday in September, accompanied by folk festivities. Fuel up for the race with the Douja d'Or Wine Festival and the Festival of Village Feasts, both held the week before.

NORTHERN PIEDMONT

Stretching from the Vercelli Plains to the Alps, the vast valleys and hills of northern Piedmont stand in dramatic contrast to overdeveloped Lombardy, which lies to the east. The Alpine sports here will help you muster up enough of an appetite for the region's very rich foods and full-bodied wines. This part of Piedmont is quite remote, and it's really easier to reach from the lake region of Lombardy (*see* Chapter 4) unless you have your own wheels. Mountain traditions and nature are well preserved, giving outdoorsy types two good reasons to make the trek.

VARALLO SESIA

Varallo Sesia is the principal town of the greenest valley in Italy, the Valsesia, once an area of fabric, butter, and wine production. The valley is dotted with villages where residents' lifestyles have hardly changed in 100 years; villagers still wear traditional garb for festivals and practice the crafts of lace making and wood carving. Varallo serves mainly as a hub for sports enthusiasts who come to hike, ski, climb, mountain bike, and raft.

High on a mountain above Varallo, in a forested natural reserve, the massive complex of **Sacro Monte** (tel. 0163/53938), almost a city in itself, comprises a basilica and 45 chapels. It was founded in 1486 by the Franciscan monk Bernardino Caimi in an attempt to evoke the holy sites of Palestine. In the late 16th century, St. Carlo Borromeo added lifelike mannequins reenacting scenes from the life of Christ to the chapels. In many chapels, popular Valsesian artist Gaudenzio Ferrari painted frescoes that create an overwrought—at times eerie—atmosphere that continues to draw hordes of pilgrims. The serene reserve is free and always open. To reach Sacro Monte, either walk about a half hour up the steep grade called Salita Sacro Monte from Piazza Ferrari or catch the bus (7 daily, 15 min, L1,500) in front of the train station's café.

BASICS

The **APT** (C. Roma 38, tel. 0163/51280; open daily 9–1 and 3–7; closed Mon. and Wed. Oct.–May) has info on hotels, outdoor activities, and nearby towns. From the station, take Via Alberato, and go left at the stop sign. For maps of the area's mountains and rivers, go to the **Club Alpinista Italiano** headquarters (V. C. Durio 14, tel. 0163/51530). **Scuola Trial** (tel. 0163/53760) rents mountan bikes for L30,000 per day, L20,000 on their organized excursions.

COMING AND GOING

Varallo's **bus depot** is in front of the **train station** (P. Marconi, tel. 1478/88088). To reach Varallo, take a bus from Turin (2–4 daily, 2¼ hrs, L12,000) or one of the nine daily trains from Novara (1¼ hrs, L5,600). One evening bus (2½ hrs, L10,200) arrives from Milan's Piazza Castello daily (another is added in the morning July–Sept.). **Autoservizi Novaresi** (tel. 011/9031003) sends a bus from Turin's Porta Susa daily on weekdays and twice daily weekends. You can also reach Alagna Valsesia (*see below*) by bus (1–3 per day, 1 hr, L4,000).

WHERE TO SLEEP AND EAT

The cheapest lodgings are *affitacamere* (private rooms); spacious **Monte Rosa** (V. Regaldi 4, 13019, tel. 0163/51100; cash only, but USD accepted) is a good choice, with views from the balconies and a friendly staff. A double with bath is L90,000. The closest campsite, **Valsesia** (13019, tel. 0163/52307), is 3 km (2 mi) away in Balangera; sites cost L8,500 plus L8,000 per person. On your way up to the Sacro Monte, grab some regional *tome* cheese for a picnic at **La Casera** (V. Camaschella 6, tel. 0163/54181); next door is a market and a bakery.

ALAGNA VALSESIA

At the foot of Monte Rosa, tiny Alagna Valsesia hosts Alpine sports. Mountain biking has gained prominence, but skiing and hiking remain tremendously popular. For a dose of culture amid all this outdoor fun, visit the small **Walser Museum,** whose wood and stone buildings are remnants of the town's Walser origins. The Walsers were Germanic nomads who wound up in northern Piedmont in the 9th century. A 1628 wooden cabin has rooms full of their clothing and furniture, as well as the tools they used for cooking, farming, and weaving. *Pedemonte, tel. 0163/91180 or 0163/922935. Follow V. Centro out of town for 10 min, then follow signs up road to right. Admission free. Open July–Aug., Tues.–Sun. 2–6; Sept.–June, weekends 2–6.*

BASICS

IAT (P. Grober, tel. 0163/922988) gives out listings for hotels and *rifugi* (mountain shelters); it's also home to the **Guide Alpine di Alagna,** which leads guided trips across and around the Alps and provides maps and general info on free climbing and skiing.

COMING AND GOING

Getting to Alagna Valsesia is no piece of cake. Two buses arrive here daily from Varallo (1 hr, L4,000), with an additional bus on Monday and Tuesday (but there's only one bus on Sunday). Buses from Milan run twice daily July–September and once daily in winter (3¼ hrs, L14,000).

WHERE TO SLEEP AND EAT

Ask the APT for the rifugio best suited to your hiking plans. The **Alagna** campsite (V. Miniere 3, 13020, tel. and fax 0163/922947; cash only) is 3 km (2 mi) away in Miniere and charges L6,000 per site plus L6,500 per person. Amenities include Ping-Pong; it closes for the first three weeks of September. The rifugio **F. Pastore** (Alpe Pile, 13020, tel. 0163/91220; closed weekdays in Oct. and Nov.–mid-April) is near the entrance to Valsesia's natural reserve and is surrounded by waterfalls. Beds cost L26,000 (L60,000 with half-pension, or 2 meals), and a tent site is L10,000 per person. The **Mirella** hotel (Bonda 10, 13021, tel. and fax 0163/922965; closed mid-May–late June) has woodsy doubles for L110,000 and small apartments ranging from L700,000–L800,000 per week for two. In Via Centro, the **Stalinberg** restaurant serves primi such as *crespelle* (crepes filled with ham and cheese; L12,000) and secondi such as venison with polenta for around L25,000 (tel. 0163/91125; closed Tues.). For cheaper eats, get mountain grub at rifugi along the various trails.

OUTDOOR ACTIVITIES

You can ski year-round at Monte Rosa (winter costs more). Buy ski passes (L43,000–L50,000 a day) at the *funivia* (funicular) station on Piazza Funivia (tel. 0163/922932; generally open 6:30–4; call ahead). **Monterosa Sport** (P. degli Alberi, tel. 0163/922970) rents skis (L23,000 a day) and snowboards (L20,000) and hiking and climbing equipment. You can rent a mountain bike for L35,000 per day from **Maurizio Restelli** at the gas station along the *autostradale* (highway), at the border of Alagna and Riva Valdobbia.

VALLE D'AOSTA

Only Mother Nature could have carved this masterpiece of aquamarine cascades and snow-capped, sky-scraping peaks. The valley stretches from **Mont Blanc** (Monte Bianco) and the **Matterhorn** (Monte Cervino) in the north—where the two most important ski resorts in Italy, Courmayeur and Breuil-Cervinia, respectively, are to be found—to the southern valleys of the **Parco Nazionale del Gran Paradiso**. It is a natural playground that beckons Italian skiers (many of whom keep winter houses in the ski resorts), bikers, hikers, and even bungee-jumpers, as well as a smattering of revelers from France, Great Britain, and the U.S. Not only natural wonders but also the warmth and hospitality of the innkeepers and residents and the rich, hearty, French-inspired Valdostan food are the attractions here. The architcture, like the food, is hardly traditional Italian—the tiny alpine villages with A-frame mountain lodges seem almost Swiss or Austrian.

Near France, Valle d'Aosta was once controlled by Napoléon, and French influence here remains strong: bilingual street signs and eateries with crepes and pasta abound. French is the second official language, but most locals' mother tongue is Italian.

The Gallic Salassi were long thought to be the valley's first settlers, but recent digs have uncovered civilizations dating to 3000 BC. The Romans overthrew the Salassi around 25 BC, and evidence of their 500-year stay can be found in Aosta's well-preserved ruins. More than 100 medieval castles from the periods of Savoy (11th century) and Challant (13th century) domination mark the valley's horizon. Each perched high enough to signal one another in case of attack, the castles today acquire a luminous, other-worldly quality after sundown, thanks to electric lighting. The valley obtained independence in 1416 and has fought to defend its freedom ever since. After World War II, the region was granted semi-autonomy under the Italian constitution.

High season in Valle d'Aosta coincides with school vacations (winter break, Carnevale in February, around Easter, and in summer), when resort cities like Courmayeur and Breuil-Cervinia get crowded; the entire month of February is also high season at ski resorts, and hotels jack up prices accordingly—it's smart to book ahead. Summers tend to warm up, but if you're planning to mount the mounts, bring a jacket, even in August.

AOSTA

Some of the country's best-preserved Roman ruins help to form the city's distinctive skyline, backed by the surreal peaks of Mont Blanc and San Bernardo. Aostans—about 40,000 in number—are proud of their unique heritage, a story of alternating periods of invasion and independence. Valle d'Aosta's compact capital became a Roman military camp led by Augustus in 25 BC, when the local Salassi were sold into slavery and forced to construct the Roman fort; pieces of the old encampment's walls, theater, and arches still stand today. In the Middle Ages, St. Anselm, an archbishop of Canterbury, and St. Bernard (hospice founder and dog namesake) steeped Aosta in Christianity and left behind scads of churches and crucifixes. Napoléon also controlled the area for a while in the early 19th century, and the Aostan dialect sounds like an Italianized Provençal.

Tourists stage an invasion of their own around ski season, flocking to the nearby slopes and laying siege on the stores filled with Alpine merchandise: carved wood and wrought-iron utensils, traditional garb, local wines and liqueurs, and fontina cheese, with which the local fondue is made. The town has no university of its own, but the pubs and pizzerias swell with students returning home from their studies in

Turin or Milan during vacation. Despite the activity, the town never becomes a bottomless tourist pit but remains a good base for exploring the nearby castles and mountains. And for most of the year, Aosta retains a soothing Alpine tranquillity.

BASICS

CHANGING MONEY • Banca CRT (Av. Conseil-des-Commis 19, tel. 0165/23721) charges no commission for currency exchange but levies a L4,000 fee for cashing traveler's checks. ATMs abound in P. Chanoux. If you need to exchange on a Sunday, you'll have to suffer the rates at the travel agency **Club Soleil** (P. Chanoux 12, tel. 0165/361943; open daily 9 AM–12:30 PM).

MAIL AND PHONES • The phone office (V. della Pace 9, tel. 0165/43997) is open weekdays 8:15–12:15 and 2:30–6:30, Sunday 8–3. Aosta's **main post office** (P. Narbonne 1/A, tel. 0165/44138) is open Monday–Saturday 8:15–7.

VISITOR INFORMATION • The tourist office (P. Chanoux 8, tel. 0165/236627; open Mon.–Sat. 9–1 and 3–8, Sun. 9–1), up Avenue Conseil-des-Commis from the train station, doles out maps, accommodation lists, and info on all of Valle d'Aosta. The **Club Alpinisti Italiani** (P. Chanoux 15, tel. 0165/40194; open Mon. and Wed.–Thurs. 5 PM–7 PM, Tues. and Fri. 8 PM–10 PM) runs a network of rifugi and is an invaluable source of climbing info. The **Società Guide,** V. Monte Emilius 13 (tel. 015/44448), provides good info on mountain climbing and off-piste skiing. For news on the Parco Nazionale del Gran Paradiso, visit Aosta's **park headquarters** (V. Losanna 5, off V. Gramsci, tel. 0165/44126).

COMING AND GOING

Aosta's **train station** (P. Manzetti 1, tel. 1478/88088) sends 11 trains daily to Turin (2 hrs, L12,200). Luggage storage costs L5,000 for 12 hours (open weekdays 8–noon and 2:30–5). The SAVDA **bus station** (V. Carrel, tel. 0165/262027) is across from the train station. Buses run to Turin (1 daily, 2 hrs, L12,500), Milan (3 daily, 2½ hrs direct or 3½ hrs with local stops, L20,500), Cogne (50 min, L4,000), Courmayeur (1 hr, L4,800), Brueil-Cervinia (1½ hrs, L5,800), and other key valley spots. Check the schedule in front of the station.

GETTING AROUND

The city centers around **Piazza Chanoux,** a five-minute stroll from the station up Avenue Conseil-des-Commis. Out of this piazza run the two major shopping drags, **Via Porta Pretoria,** which heads toward the Roman theater, and **Via de Tillier,** which becomes Via E. Aubert after Piazza des Franchises.

WHERE TO SLEEP

In the center, **La Belle Epoque** (V. d'Avise 18, 11100, tel. 0165/262276) has immaculate doubles with bath for L80,000 and a restaurant, but you'll turn into a pumpkin at midnight unless you can finagle a key from the moody signora in charge. From the train station, take Avenue Conseil-des-Commis and hang a left on Via de Tillier and a right on Via d'Avise. In the industrial part of town, **Mancuso** (Strada Voison 32, 11100, tel. 0165/34526) has doubles for L55,000. Take the *sottopassaggio* (underpass) from the train station to Via Paravera, turn right, then go left on Strada Voison. West of the Piazza della Repubblica on a bustling street, the **Sweet Rock Hotel** (V. Piccolo S. Bernardo 18, 11100, tel. 0165/553251) has semideluxe doubles with bath, TV, and phone for L90,000. The hotel's adjoining pub hops until the wee hours, assuring you no curfew, a young clientele, and music vibrating through your walls while you try to sleep.

CAMPING • The hills just outside Aosta are home to **Milleluci** (Località Roppoz, tel. 0165/235278, fax 0165/235284), a campground that offers hot showers, laundry, a bar, tennis courts, bathrooms, and electricity. You pay L7,000 per person plus L15,000–L18,000 for the site. Take Bus 6 from the train station or Piazza Chanoux, and ask the driver where to get off.

WHERE TO EAT

Finding good grub is surprisingly easy in Aosta. Restaurants and pizzerias line Via E. Aubert and Via Porta Pretoria, and Piazza Chanoux has several cheery cafés. **Ulisse** (V. E. Aubert 58, tel. 0165/41180; closed Tues. in winter) offers tagliatelle *alla Ciociara* (with mushrooms, tomatoes, peas, and bacon; L10,000) and other Valdaostan goodies in a sedate setting. **Piemonte** (V. Porta Pretoria 13, tel. 0165/40111; closed Fri.) offers somewhat expensive specialties like fondue, *padellina di funghi trifolati* (porcini and vegetables in a savory broth; L16,000), and *camoscio* (chamois) dishes (L12,000–L15,000), as well as a platter of mixed grilled vegetables. For savory Spanish paella (L10,000–L15,000) and tortillas, head to **La Paella** (V. dell'Archibugio 19, tel. 0165/31664; closed Mon.). **La Brasserie du Commerce** (Via de Tillier 10, tel. 0165/35613; closed Sun.), in a very central location near P. Chanoux, serves up delicious local food indoors and outdoors to a local crowd. Prices here are a bit higher; expect to pay L9,000–L15,000 for primi and L15,000 for secondi.

WORTH SEEING

Aosta's ancient ruins jut out amid its more modern buildings and piazzas. Dating to 25 BC, the **Arco d'Augusto** looms over Aosta's eastern entrance on Via S. Anselmo as a monument to the Roman victory over the local Salassi. West down Via S. Anselmo stands the **Porta Pretoria,** built around 1 BC as the original door to the city. The neighboring **Teatro Romano** (V. de Baillage, tel. 0165/362149; open daily 9:30–noon and 2–5:30, Sat. 9–7), is free but can be seen by appointment only—call first; the amphitheater retains about half its original stony, gray structure, built between 1 BC and AD 1. Between Porta Pretoria and the Arco d'Augusto, the **Sant'Orso complex** (tel. 0165/362026; same hrs as Teatro Romano) assembles a group of 11th-century buildings dominated by a Roman campanile (bell tower) built in 1131. When the complex was renovated in the 15th century, artisans spruced up its interiors with frescoes, carved wooden choir stalls, and stained-glass windows. The church also has a series of Ottoman frescoes in the attic upstairs. The impressive 12th-century **cloister** at Sant'Orso is the most beautiful courtyard in Aosta, with a series of delicately carved columns and views of the campanile and mountains above. In the 4th century, the **Duomo complex** (P. Giovanni XXIII, tel. 0165/40251) housed sepulchres, churches, and baptismals decorated with beautiful mosaics that are still visible today. The Gothic cathedral stairs lead down to the original underground church. The cathedral also holds the **Museo del Tesoro** (open Mon.–Sat. 10–noon and 3–6, also Apr.–Sept., Sun. 3–5:45), featuring ancient wooden and stone sculptures. Behind the complex is an old palace of the Challant family, now the **Museo Archeologico Regionale** (P. Roncas, tel. 0165/238680; open daily 9–7), displaying artifacts

With Rafting Adventure (tel. 0165/95082; closed Nov.–Mar.), at the park's entrance in Villeneuve, you can raft, hydrospeed, and bungee-jump.

dating from the Neolithic Age. Behind the *teatro*, the **Tour Fromage** often holds art exhibits (tel. 0165/42338; open summer, daily 9–7; winter, daily 9:30–noon and 2–6:30).

AFTER DARK

The **Service Activités Culturelles** (P. Deffeyes 1, tel. 0165/273413) sponsors an extensive program of theater, music, and movies (some in English); tickets for events cost L8,000–L30,000. The events take place all over Valle d'Aosta, and free transportation is available. Tickets go on sale about 10 days before an event at **Madaschi** (Biblioteca Regionale, Via Torre Libbrosi, tel. 0165/274831); for complete listings, pick up the *Saison Culturelle* booklet from the APT.

Aosta's nightlife begins with the usual *passeggiata* (promenade) through Piazza Chanoux and adjacent avenues, where you're likely to recognize faces after a day or two. During yuletide and summer vacations, university students descend upon the town's collection of pubs and dance clubs. Several pubs sponsor live music—keep your eyes peeled for posters. Boogie at the **Sweet Rock Café** (V. Piccolo S. Bernardo 18/20, west of P. della Repubblica, tel. 0165/553251), which books live bands every Monday. The oak paneling and waitresses in the Brit-style **Old Distillery Pub** (V. Prés Fossés 7, tel. 0165/230511) are imported from the United Kingdom; it's the local haunt for university types. Meanwhile, the **Duit Club** (P. Wuillermin 12, tel. 0165/363484; closed Mon.) is frequented by an older gay and straight crowd.

PARCO NAZIONALE DEL GRAN PARADISO

Five heavenly, lake-filled valleys render this huge National Park worthy of its title. In 1865 Vittorio Emanuele II launched preservation efforts (ironically) by establishing a royal hunting ground in the valleys and awarding official endangered-species status to the ibex, a nearly extinct type of mountain goat. Immediately after World War I, Vittorio Emanuele III offered the property and his shooting rights to the Italian state, and Gran Paradiso became a national park in 1922.

You can play among the spectacular mountains and waterfalls in organized excursions, semiplanned adventures, or day-trip wanderings. Except for a few horseback-riding clubs and kayaking gangs, the park has avoided overdevelopment. Of its five valleys, the Cogne, Valsavarenche, and Rhêmes are the best known and the easiest to reach from Aosta. Farther south, the relatively untouched Orco Valley slopes down from the Nivolet Pass where it borders the equally obscure Soana Valley.

BASICS

For maps, brochures, and insight, stop by the tourist offices in Turin or the park headquarters in Aosta (*see above*). There's another office in **Villeneuve** (Località Champagne 18, tel. 0165/236627).

WHEN TO GO

Gran Paradiso is marked by freezing winters and mild summers. Summer is the most popular season, with great hiking, beautiful vegetation, and—particularly if it snows at higher elevations—the chance of seeing ibex and chamois. Even though it's usually warm in the summer months, don't get caught without a light jacket. Winter is actually a better time to see wildlife at lower altitudes (3,000–5,000 ft), when there's also good skiing. In spring the animals move down to the valleys, hungry for new grass, and the waterfalls and rivers swell with snowmelt, making for great rafting. Fall's striking colors and cool air promise nicer hiking and horseback riding.

VALLE DI COGNE

The Valle di Cogne is the most developed of the park's valleys and the most popular with travelers, though even here the visitors aren't too intrusive. Lodged in the widest part of the valley, Cogne offers modern conveniences without being overdeveloped. Cogne's **tourist office** (P. Chanoux 34–36, tel. 0165/74040; open weekdays 9–12:30 and 3–6, weekends 9–12:30) offers accommodation lists as well as hiking maps. Five daily **buses** run from the northwest side of Aosta's Piazza Chanoux to Cogne (50 min, L4,000); buy tickets on board. Between July and September, a network of buses connects the valley's villages; at other times you'll have to use your own locomotive power or try to find a ride. Most towns are within a few kilometers of one another, but walking may be inconvenient when you're carrying tons of gear.

WHERE TO SLEEP

Finding a place to sleep here is easy, though it's smart to call ahead during July and August and from October to April. At the tourist office, grab the lodging pamphlet, which has listings of rooms in private homes, hotels, and campsites. In Cogne itself, **Hotel Au Vieux Grenier** (V. Linea Boreale 28, 11012, tel. 0165/74002; closed Easter–mid-June) has doubles with bath and breakfast for L80,000–L105,000 (depending on season and meal plan) and was the resort of choice for the Yugoslavian ski team in 1986.

In **Valnontey**, 3 km (2 mi) away on Trail 55 (buses run there only in July and August), **Paradisia** (11012, tel. 0165/74158) has doubles with bath, breakfast, and phone for L73,000–L94,000. Guests get free guided tours from the owner of the alpine-scented **Petit Dahu** (11012, tel. and fax 0165/74146; open Dec.–Easter and May–Sept.), and doubles with bath and breakfast go for L127,000.

CAMPING AND RIFUGI • One of several campgrounds in the valley is **Lo Stambecco** (11012, tel. 0165/74152; cash only; closed Oct.–May), on the road from Cogne to Valnontey (it's marked by signs). You'll find a spacious spread of wooded grounds and riverbanks, with plumbing and a telephone. The sites cost L9,500–L14,000 plus L8,000 per person. For winter camping, the small **Al Sole** (11012, tel. 0165/74237; cash only) in Lillaz, 1½ km (1 mi) from Cogne, has sites open year-round for L10,000–L13,200 plus L8,000 per person and L5,000 per car. Farther into the park, the nearest rifugio is hotel-like **Vittorio Sella** (tel. 0165/74310; closed Oct.–Easter), a three-hour walk on a marked trail from Valnontey. It's L26,000 per person, and you should call ahead to reserve a bed. In Valnontey, **Camping Gran Paradiso** (tel. 0165/749204) charges L6,500 per person, L6,000 per shower, and L10,000 per car and per tent. Other rifugi lie three to six hours on foot from Cogne; a full list is available at the tourist office.

WHERE TO EAT

Unless you scrounge for nuts and berries, eating in the park is hell on the budget. Even picnic supplies cost almost twice as much as usual, but get them anyway at **Végé** (Rue Mines de Cogne 9), which has *mecülin*, a sweet Cognese bread with raisins (L4,000 a piece). You'll find sandwiches (L5,000–L7,000) and beer (L7,000) at **Le Bistrot** (Rue Mines de Cogne 5, tel. 0165/749310). Splurge on Frenchified local dishes like potato and corn crepes (L12,000) at **La Brasserie du Bon Bec** (Rue Bourgeois 72, tel. 0165/749288; cash only). In Valnontey fill up on sandwiches and crepes for L3,000–L6,000 while relaxing in the lawn chairs of the **Bar du Village** (tel. 0165/749208; cash only), one of the few eateries in the tiny village.

OUTDOOR ACTIVITIES

The tourist office (*see above*) has details on local sports with lists of useful addresses and phone numbers. You'll find many sporting goods stores that also rent equipment in the tiny towns flanking Cogne, all within easy walking distance. The park has a well-marked system of numbered trails, and the **Associazione Guide della Natura** (P. Chanoux, tel. 0165/74282; open daily 9–noon) in Cogne arranges hiking excursions. You can rent mountain bikes at the **Hotel La Barme** (tel. 0165/749177) in Valnontey for L35,000 per day. If you want to fish, you'll need a license and your own gear; for details contact the **Pesce Sportiva** offices (tel. 0165/749172) in Lillaz.

The focus here is on cross-country, but depending on snow conditions, downhill skiing can be okay (easy terrain, though). Ski passes are available at the funivia station (tel. 0165/74008; costs L10,000 round-trip) and cost L24,000–L29,000 for a full day, L54,000 per week, or L450,000 for the season; White Weeks packages (*see box, below*) are offered at many hotels. **Noleggio Ski** (Rue Grand Paradis 20, tel. 0165/74211) rents equipment, and the ski school (tel. 0165/74300) offers lessons. You can tear around the rink at the **Stadio Comunale** (tel. 0165/74676; open daily 10–12:30, 2:30–6:30, and 8:30–11) on either inline, roller, or ice skates, depending on the season. The **Centro di Turismo Equestre** (tel. 0165/907667) arranges excursions on horseback out of a school in Rhêmes-Saint-Georges for L60,000 for three hours.

VALSAVARENCHE

The largest community in the rugged central valley of Valsavarenche is **Degioz** (sometimes called Valsavarenche). Nearby **Pont** has great camping and is the best base for hikes into the heart of the park and up the mountain of Gran Paradiso. Valsavarenche is farther into the mountains and therefore more rugged than Cogne, though the flora and fauna here are much like those in the rest of the park: larch, pine, and spruce trees; alpine wildflowers; and the rare ibex, chamois, marmots, and eagles.

If you are in Aosta during the biannual summer and autumn Bataille des Reines (Battle of the Queens), you can watch cows fiercely duke it out for the honor of being crowned queen of the pasture. The mad bovines lock horns, and the one to retreat first loses.

BASICS

Come to Degioz to get mapped and brochured by the folks at the **Pro Loco** visitor information office (Degioz, tel. 0165/905816; open July–Aug. only), the **Municipo office** (Degioz 70, tel. 0165/905703; open weekdays 8:30–noon, Wed.–Thurs. also 1:30–3:30), or the **Gran Paradiso visitor center** (Degioz 76, 2nd floor, tel. 0165/74147). From Aosta, three daily buses stop in Degioz (1 hr, L3,500) before continuing 9 km (5½ mi) down the road to Pont.

WHERE TO SLEEP

Fior di Roccia (Località Pont 6, 11010, tel. 0165/95478) is only open July–September and charges L70,000 per double.

CAMPING AND RIFUGI • Luckily, the camping in Pont is good, and there are four rifugi within a three-hour hike. At the gateway to the heart of the park, **Campground Pont-Breuil** (Località Pont-Breuil 24, 11012, tel. and fax 0165/95458) comes with hot showers, laundry facilities, electricity, pay phone, bar, restaurant, and market. Prices run L8,000 per person plus L13,000 for the site, plus L3,000 for electricity. One kilometer (½ mi) away (closer to Degioz) is **Campground Gran Paradiso** (Località Plan de la Presse, tel. 0165/95433). Smaller and a bit more secluded, it has the same facilities as Pont-Breuil and costs L6,000 per person plus L9,000–L10,000 per site. Both sites are open June–September, and it's wise to call ahead—especially at the latter, since it's smaller and less likely to have vacancies. The nearest rifugio is **Vittorio Emanuele** (Località Moncorvé, tel. 0165/95920; closed late Sept.–early Apr.), a two-hour hike into the park. Call ahead to reserve a bed. Another option is agriturismo—contact Emilia Vittoria Dupont (tel. 0165/905735), who rents out rooms in her quiet house in Bien, a 30-minute walk from Pont; she imposes a minimum stay of two nights (negotiable).

For a challenging—but not heart-attacking—alpine hike complete with a night in a rifugio, contact **Savoia Nivolet** (tel. 0165/94141) or **Città di Chivasso al Nivolet** (tel. 0165/953150); all rifugi are within a three-hour hike from Degioz. Food options in Valsavarenche are basically limited to campground markets, a few cafés, and restaurants in hotels, so stock up before arriving.

OUTDOOR ACTIVITIES

Untouched Valsavarenche is an ideal refuge from ski resorts and crowded slopes, but it also limits options for organized outdoor adventures. The high season is in July and August, when families come to relax and hike in the tranquil valley. Tickets cost L24,000 per day for downhill skiing during the cold,

WHITE WEEKS: SKI-LODGING PACKAGES

Skiing on Mont Blanc will never come cheap, but you can save a little green with White Weeks—promotional deals offered in conjunction with hotels and agriturismo sites throughout the valley. Prices depend on location and the number of mints you want on your pillow: a week in Courmayeur starts around L500,000 for six nights with breakfast plus a six-day ski pass, while a similar package in Cogne costs L380,000. Prices also vary wildly depending on season; contact the Valle d'Aosta tourist offices or individual hotels for more info.

isolated winters; most people, however, stick to cross-country; contact one of the visitor offices (*see* Basics, *above*) for more details, or call **Degioz Daniela** (tel. 0165/905708) for rental and lessons. The **Società Guide Gran Paradiso** (tel. 0165/95574 or 0165/905734) leads guided excursions and nature walks. In summer only due to lofty cold temperatures, you can ascend 10,000 ft plus from Degioz to **Punta Bioula** for a magnificent view of the central valley. Rent mountain bikes at the **Hostellerie du Paradis** (3½ km/2 mi from Degioz in Eaux-Rousse, tel. 0165/905972).

MONT BLANC AND THE MATTERHORN

MONT BLANC

In a valley just below this Alpine giant, lies the tiny town of **Courmayeur.** Because of its prime position on a passage through the Alps, the town once attracted the ancient Romans and the Savoys, who set up shop here in 1032. Now littered with hotels and chintzy souvenirs, it is the stomping ground for exploring the mountain towering above. Courmayeur hibernates April–July, when many restaurants and hotels close in preparation for flocks of wealthy tourists. Mont Blanc is covered with slopes, trails, and glaciers just waiting to be climbed, cycled, skied, or photographed. The **tourist office** (P. Monte Bianco 13, tel. 0165/842060) where you get off the bus has info on everything from hotels to white-water rafting.

COMING AND GOING

SAVDA (tel. 0165/842031; bus station 0165/841397) runs 12 buses daily (fewer on Sunday) between Courmayeur (1 hr, L4,000) and Aosta. In Courmayeur you'll be dropped off in Piazzale Monte Bianco, the bus depot. Two main **funivie** (funiculars) climb Mont Blanc's surrounding slopes. In Courmayeur, buses run every half hour from Piazzale Monte Bianco (L2,500) for a three-minute ride to the scenic **Funivia Monte Bianco** (tel. 0165/89925), which leaves from **La Palud** (5 km/3 mi from Courmayeur), peaks at Punta Helbronner (11,000 ft) on the French-Italian border, and descends to Chamonix in France. A La Palud–Punta Helbronner round-trip costs L46,000 (30 min each way). You can catch frequent buses to the **Courmayeur Mont Blanc Funivia** (tel. 0165/846658), which starts in Entrèves (3 km/2 mi north of Courmayeur) and goes to Val Veny, Dolonne, and Checrouit for L14,000 round-trip. All the above are covered by ski passes (*see* Outdoor Activities, *below*).

WHERE TO SLEEP AND EAT

Courmayeur has enough four-star hotels to make a galaxy, but there are also a few one-star joints. **Serena** (V. Villair 3, 11013, tel. 0165/842263; closed May–June) and **La Quercia** (Strada La Palud 6, at base of La Palud funivia, 11013, tel. 0165/89931) offer half-board only for about L75,000 per person, and **Villa Bron** (Località Villair Inferiore, 11013, tel. 0165/842390) and **Venezia** (V. delle Villette 2, 11013, tel. 0165/842461) charge between L70,000 and L75,000. Venezia has pleasant rooms with shared baths and balconies with great views of the mountain range. Sleep on the slopes at the rifugi

Pavillon (tel. 0165/844090) and **Torino** (tel. 0165/846484), which have doubles for L70,000; they're on the first and second stops of the La Palud funivia and come complete with restaurants. In summer you can take the Courmayeur Mont Blanc Funivia and stay at **Rifugio Monte Bianco Cai-Uget** (11013 Val Veny, tel. 0165/869097; call ahead to make sure it's open), overlooking a sweeping moutain vista from 5,464 ft. Basic rooms with shared baths cost L60,000–L70,000 per night, and fantastic Valdostan food (like polenta with fontina, sausage, and wild mushrooms, L21,000) is served amid stunning views at the ski-in, ski-out restaurant below. Eating out in Courmayeur is not cheap; however, the pizza (L12,000) at the eternally packed **Snack Bar du Tunnel** (V. Circonvallazione 80, tel. 0165/841705) is priceless– -it's literally some of the best in all northern Italy. Crepes *alla valdostana* (with fontina and prosciutto), along with other valley specialties, are in the L10,000–L15,000 range. Reservations are essential. Another choice is the pizza at **K2** (Villair Inferiore 8, tel. 0165/842475), which has the usual favorites for L10,000–L13,000. For L4,000–L6,000 sandwiches, hit **Cadran Solaire** (V. Roma 122, tel. 0165/844609; closed May and Oct.), where full meals are good but very expensive (L50,000–L60,000).

OUTDOOR ACTIVITIES

True to its name, Mont Blanc stays white all year: even in summer you can ski down Colle del Gigante and Colle del Flambeau. A blizzard of package deals allow non-Rockefellers to enjoy the area's 100 km (62 mi) or more of slopes (*see box,* White Weeks: Ski-Lodging Packages, *above*). Otherwise, lift tickets at Courmayeur cost L45,000 per day, and ski, boot, and pole rentals go for around L30,000. You can learn from the experts at the **Mont Blanc Ski School** (Strada Regionale 51, Courmayeur, tel. 0165/842477), where a private lesson runs about L60,000. **Noleggio Ulisse** (tel. 0165/842255), in front of the La Palud funivia, rents skiing equipment. For more specific info on slopes and prices, contact the tourist office and the **Società delle Guide** (P. Abbé Henry 2, tel. 0165/842064), which also has programs for climbers, hikers, and bikers. As the snow melts, go rafting with **4810 Per Lo Sport** (V. Roma 106, tel. 0165/844631).

THE MATTERHORN

In the shadow of the crooked Matterhorn, Europe's highest peak and the best-known emblem of the Alps, **Breuil-Cervinia** (known to most Italians as simply Cervinia) is perhaps the most popular place in all Italy to ski (rivaled only by Courmayeur); many slopes are open year-round. Long, graceful (but not particularly steep) trails affording spectacular views of the Alps guide skiers from village to village. The town itself is fairly built up and hardly picturesque, though, so come only for the skiing.

BASICS

For info on accommodations, food, climbing, and ski conditions, rentals, and lessons, contact the Breuil-Cervinia **tourist office** (Via Carrel 29, tel. 0166/949136). The tourist office is also where serious climbers should head to register for the difficult ascent to the Matterhorn's peak. The Matterhorn itself lies on the Swiss-Italian border, and is jointly owned; ski passes are available just for Cervinia (L42,000 per day) or in combination with Zermatt (66 SFr per day), the Swiss resort on the other side.

COMING AND GOING

SAVDA (tel. 0165/361244; ticket office and schedules 0165/262027) runs 5 buses a day between Aosta and Breuil-Cervinia (L7,500; 1¾ hrs including one changeover). You can also reach Plateau Rosa and the Cresta del Furggen—great places to view the Matterhorn in all its glory—aboard the Cervina cable car the **Funivia Cervino** (tel. 0166/944411; early Dec.–mid-April open daily 8:30–5, late June– mid-Sept. 8:30–2). Lift tickets run around L45,000 per person.

THE
ITALIAN
RIVIERA

BY SARAH ATTIA

UPDATED BY ROBIN S. GOLDSTEIN

The Italian Riviera of the flashy '60s postcard—absurdly long yachts and beach goddesses in gold-plated bikinis—is a hazy delusion for most. The reality is more quaint than grandiose: piles of faded pastel houses cling to cliffs and cluster around quiet sun-soaked beaches; painted facades and palm-lined seaside promenades exert a calming influence on visitors. While mansions bearing traces of the jet-set Riviera of legend still exist in places like Portofino and San Remo—behind spiked castle walls and guard dogs—the rest of us will have to settle for warming rays, honeysuckle blossoms, balmy air, and fresh focaccia. In the center of the Ligurian coast lies the port town of **Genoa,** challenged historically by conquering nations and currently by its grim economic status. It seems like an inappropriate hub for the palm-covered landscape of the **Riviera di Ponente** region to the west and the rugged and breathtaking **Riviera di Levante** to the east. Ponente beach towns have catered to tourists for the past 100 years or so. As their grandeur has faded, the towns have become sleepy getaways for the over-40 set, but some are still worth a visit. Hike to the modest yet impressive castles in the hills behind Finale Ligure or bargain for a snazzy belt in the outdoor markets of San Remo, and you will succumb to the unique Ligurian spirit. Unsung mountain villages a few kilometers inland are respites from coastal vacationers and the heat. Finally, the Levante coastal towns, particularly **Santa Margherita Ligure** and **Cinque Terre,** draw younger crowds of hikers and campers and are more lively than Ponente towns. The Riviera is an exceptionally seasonal place. In July and August, outdoor promenades teem with activity day and night, seaside bars and discos hop, and accommodations and beaches fill up fast. There is generally good beach weather—and thus reasonable vitality—from April or May to September; the mild months of spring and early fall are very pleasant in Liguria. In winter, however, temperatures drop to near freezing, tourists clear out, hotels, restaurants, and beaches close for the season, and the towns become spookily empty.

Blessed with a mild climate and a profusion of fruit trees, olive groves, and vineyards, Liguria produces magical and surprisingly affordable cuisine. Fresh seafood abounds (although it can be expensive), mushrooms foraged from the mountains are delectable over pasta or baked into focaccia, and each *trofie al pesto* (potato-based pasta twists with pesto sauce) seems better than the next. Wash it all down with the region's wines, including Rossesse, Pigato, Sciacchetrà, and Moscadello de Taggia. The cheapest sit-down meals are in the *casalinga* (homestyle) joints, where proprietors give you sound, if unsolicited, nutritional advice, banging both fists on the table for emphasis.

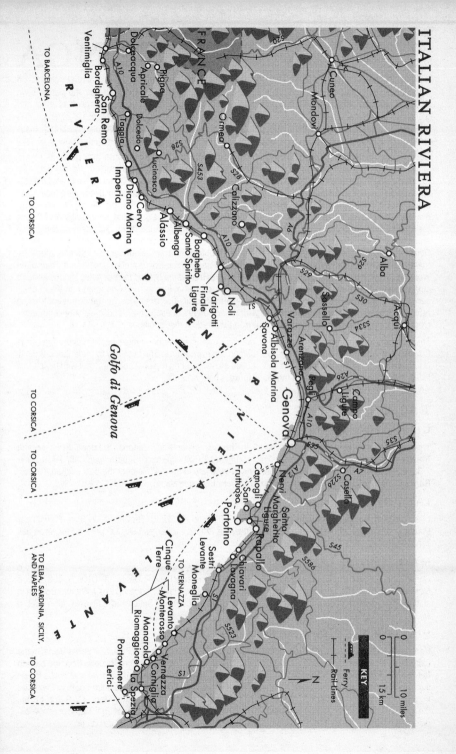

ITALIAN RIVIERA

TO BARCELONA

TO CORSICA

Ventimiglia
Bordighera
San Remo
Taggia
Imperia
Diano Marina
Cervo

FRANCE

Dolceacqua
Apricale
Pigna
Dolcedo
Lucinasco

Ormea

S28
S453
S28

Cuneo
Mondovi

A10

RIVIERA DI PONENTE

Aléssio
Albenga
Borghetto
Santo Spirito
Finale Ligure
Varigotti

A10

Calizzano

A6

S29

Alba

Noli
Savona

Varazze
Arenzano

Sassello

S30

Acqui

S334

S29

Golfo di Genova

Albisola Marina
Pegli

S1

Genova

A10

Campo
Ligure

S35

A26

TO CORSICA

TO CORSICA

RIVIERA DI LEVANTE

Camogli
San
Fruttuoso
Portofino

Nervi
Santa
Margherita
Ligure
Rapallo

A7

S225

Casella

A7

S35

TO CORSICA

TO ELBA, SARDINIA, SICILY,
AND NAPLES

Cinque
Terre

TO VERNAZZA

Sestri
Levante
Lavagna
Chiavari
Moneglia

S586

S45

Levanto
Monterosso
Vernazza
Corniglia
Manarola
Riomaggiore
Portovenere
Lerici
La Spezia

S523

S1

KEY

Ferry
Rail lines

0   10 miles
0   15 km

N

145

GENOA

Imagine a wrinkled old lady across from you on the bus who you really don't pay much attention to; on closer inspection, she reveals a fascinating history and hidden beauty. Like that old lady, the historic town of Genoa (Genova), Liguria's main port and Italy's largest gateway, challenges you to peel off its layers and grasp its multiple personalities. Inside Genoa's medieval walls—testimonies to centuries of defense—lies a typically rough port town. But while at one turn you might chance upon a prostitute in 5-inch heels strutting over filthy cobblestones, at another you'll glimpse a stunning fountain through a palace portal.

Genoa would like to play up the "home of Christopher Columbus" schtick and play down its mean-streets reputation. The local government tried to spruce up the city—particularly the old port—for tourists in 1992, to celebrate the 500th anniversary of the voyage of the Genoese explorer. Unfortunately, not many people showed up, and the port and historic center are still ghostly at night; they'll give it another go in 2004, when Genoa will be Europe's Cultural Capital. For now, the streets *are* still mean: the city's serious crime, drug, pollution, and traffic problems are aggravated by inklings of a fascist resurgence; visibly, Genoa has come down in the world since its Renaissance glory days of commerce and conquest. Nicknamed *La Superba* (The Proud), it was once the province of noble rulers like Andrea Doria, who drafted Genoa's independent constitution before the town fell under Spanish and later Austrian rule. It was also the launching point of the Risorgimento (*see box* Espresso Shot Heard 'Round the World *in* Chapter 5) and the home of Giuseppe Mazzini, the brains behind the operation. Sadly, Genoa's struggle with industrialization and urbanity has been somewhat less heroic. Crammed into a thin crescent of land sandwiched between sea and mountains, the city has expanded up rather than out, piling buildings, streets, highways, and entire neighborhoods on top of each other; public elevators and funiculars are now as common as buses and trains in this vertical metropolis.

Still, you don't have to look hard to see *La Superba*'s former splendor—artistic spoils procured from the Crusades, the colonial era, and foreign occupation are everywhere. The best way to understand the city is to surrender to its mood swings: get lost in back alleys, feast on regional cooking, chat with hospitable locals, and take in the view from a medieval fortress high on a hill.

BASICS

CHANGING MONEY

The *casse di cambio* (exchange bureaus) in the two major train stations, **Stazione Principe** and **Stazione Brignole,** offer mediocre rates and charge a L1,000 commission (both open daily 7:15–1 and 2:30–7:30. Banks in town offer better rates. As everywhere in Italy, ATMs offer the best exchange rates. **Banca Carige** and **Banca di Chiavari e della Riviera Ligure** branches with ATMs dot the city.

LAUNDRY

Lavanderia di Boccia Armando (V. Gramsci 187–203R, tel. 010/256735; open daily 9 AM–7 PM), near Piazza Commenda, on the seafront south of Stazione Principe, charges L20,000 per load for same-day service (a rarity), less for self-service.

MAIL AND PHONES

Genoa's main **post office** is at V. Dante 4/R, between P. de Ferrari and P. Dante (tel. 010/2594687; open Mon.–Sat. 8:10–7:40). Buy *francobolli* (stamps) at any Tabacchaio (tobacco store) in Genoa. Both train stations have banks of pay phones, but the main **phone office** (V. XX Settembre 139; open Mon.–Sat. 8 AM–10 PM) also offers operator-assisted phone calls.

VISITOR INFORMATION

Genoa's most convenient **Ente Provinciale Turismo (EPT)** tourist office is at Palazzina Santa Maria, in the old port to the left of the aquarium (tel. 010/24871; open daily 9–6:30). At the **Stazione Principe branch** (tel. 010/2462633; open Mon.–Sat. 8–8, Sun. 9–noon), the English-speaking staff will call hotels to see if rooms are available, although they cannot make reservations. There is also a branch **booth** in Piazza de Ferrari (open daily 9–12:30 and 2–6:30), and a bigger but more remote **headquarters** at V. Roma 11 (tel. 010/576791; from either station, take Bus 39 to P. Corvetto, and head southwest on V. Roma; open weekdays 8–1:15 and 2–6:30, Sat. 8–1:30) is likely to simply foist a bunch of brochures off on you.

In case you want to see the world.

At American Express, we're here to make your journey a smooth one. So we have over 1,700 travel service locations in over 130 countries ready to help. What else would you expect from the world's largest travel agency?

do more   AMERICAN EXPRESS

Travel

Call 1 800 AXP-3429 or visit
www.americanexpress.com/travel

In case you want to be welcomed there.

We're here to see that you're always welcomed at establishments everywhere. That's why millions of people carry the American Express® Card – for peace of mind, confidence, and security, around the world or just around the corner.

do more **AMERICAN EXPRESS**

Cards

And in case you'd rather be safe than sorry.

We're here with American Express® Travelers Cheques. They're the safe way to carry money on your vacation, because if they're ever lost or stolen you can get a refund, practically anywhere or anytime. To find the nearest place to buy Travelers Cheques, call 1 800 495-1153. Another way we help you do more.

do more AMERICAN EXPRESS

Travelers
Cheques

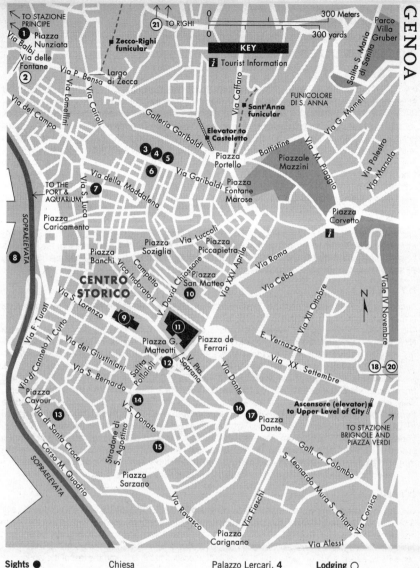

TO STAZIONE PRINCIPE

1 Piazza Nunziata

Via Balbi

Via delle Fontane

2

Via del Campo

Via P. Bensa

Via Caroli

Via tomellini

Largo di Zecca

Zecco-Righi funicular

21 TO RIGHI

Galleria Garibaldi

Via Caffaro

Sant'Anna funicular

KEY

i Tourist Information

0 ___ 300 Meters
0 ___ 300 yards

Parco Villa Gruber

Salita S. Maria di Sanità

FUNICOLORE DI S. ANNA

Elevator to Casteletto

Piazza Portello

Piazzale Mazzini

Battistine

Via G. Mameli

Via M. Piaggio

Via Palestro

Via Marsala

3 **4** **5**

6

Via della Maddalena

Via Garibaldi

TO THE PORT & AQUARIUM

7

Via S. Luca

Piazza Caricamento

Piazza Fontane Marose

Piazza Corvetto

i

8

SOPRAELEVATA

Piazza Banchi

Piazza Soziglia

Vico Indoratori

Campetto

Via Luccoli

Piazza Piccapietra

Piazza San Matteo

V. David Chiossone

Via XXV Aprile

Via Roma

Via Ceba

Via XII Ottobre

Viale IV Novembre

CENTRO STORICO

Via S. Lorenzo

Via F. Turati

10

9

11

Piazza G. Matteotti

Piazza de Ferrari

E. Vernazza

N

Via di Canheto Il Curto

Via dei Giustiniani

Via S. Bernardo

Salita Pollaioli

12

V. Pta. Soprana

Via Dante

Via XX Settembre

18—**20**

Piazza Cavour

Via di Santa Croce

13

14

V. S. Donato

Stradone di S. Agostino

15

16 **17**

Piazza Dante

Ascensore (elevator) to Upper Level of City

TO STAZIONE BRIGNOLE AND PIAZZA VERDI

Corso M. Quadrio

SOPRAELEVATA

Piazza Sarzano

Via Ravasco

Gall. C. Colombo

S. Leonardo Mura S. Chiara

Via Fieschi

Via Corsica

Piazza Carignano

Via Alessi

Sights ●

Acquario di Genova, **8**

Casa di Colombo, **17**

Cattedrale San Lorenzo, **9**

Chiesa San Matteo, **10**

Chiesa Sant'Ambrogio (Gesù), **12**

Galleria Nazionale di Palazzo Spinola, **7**

Museo di Sant'Agostino, **15**

Palazzo Bianco, **3**

Palazzo Ducale, **11**

Palazzo Lercari, **4**

Palazzo Podestà, **5**

Palazzo Reale, **1**

Palazzo Rosso, **6**

Porta Soprana, **16**

San Donato, **14**

Santa Maria di Castello, **13**

Lodging ○

Albergo Carletto, **18**

Albergo Fiume, **20**

Mini Hotel, **2**

Ostello per La Gioventù (HI), **21**

Pension Ricci, **19**

GAY AND LESBIAN RESOURCES • ARCI Gay (V. San Luca 11, tel. 010/2470945) provides information on the gay and lesbian scene.

COMING AND GOING

BY TRAIN

Genoa has two main train stations: **Stazione Principe** (P. Acquaverde, tel. 1478/88088 toll-free) and **Stazione Brignole** (P. Verdi). More trains stop in Stazione Principe, but Stazione Brignole is more convenient to the safer lodging area and the hostel. Both stations are on the same line, but sometimes trains scheduled to pass through both will only stop at one, so ask the conductor when you board. The trains to Milan (hourly, 1½–2 hrs, L12,100) and Torino (hourly, 2–2½ hrs, L11,500) run through both stations unless otherwise noted. The train to Rome (every 2–2½ hrs, 6 hrs, L59,500) leaves from both stations. Trains head west to Ventimiglia (every 30 min, 3 hrs, L14,000) from Stazione Principe and east to Cinque Terre (28 daily, 1¼–1¾ hrs, L7,400) and Pisa (2–2¾ hrs, L22,500) from Brignole. There is also service from Principe to Venice (4–5 hrs, L50,000). Both stations have post offices, money exchanges, and 24-hour luggage storage (L5,000 for 12 hrs).

BY BUS

The **AMT** bus (Via dell'Annunzio 8/R, tel. 010/5997414, and Piazza della Vittoria, tel. 010/5582414) runs every half hour from Piazza della Vittoria (near Stazione Brignole), linking Genoa with the Riviera di Levante (take bus toward Recco). Bus tickets, reservations, and information in Genoa are handled by **PESCI** (P. della Vittoria 94/R, tel. 010/564936), another coastal line.

BY FERRY

Genoa is a good jumping-off point for Corsica and Sardinia, but Sicily and Tunisia are better reached via Naples (*see* Chapter 12). **Vintiadis Shipping & Travel** (V. Ponte Reale 27, tel. 010/205651; open Mon.–Sat. 9–4) has information and makes reservations, as does any other travel agency in town. **Tirrenia Navigazione** (Stazione Marittima, Ponte Colombo, tel. 010/2758041) has ferries to Sardinia's Porto Torres (daily, 13 hrs, L58,000) and Olbia (daily, 10 hrs, L60,000–L80,000). **Grimaldi Lines** (Stazione Marittima, tel. 010/589331) sends posh Grande Navi Veloci ships to Barcelona (a new service in 1999, re-initiated after 30 years; 3–7 per week, L90,000–150,000), Sicily (Palermo), and Sardinia (Olbia and Porto Torres). **Moby Lines** (tel. 010/252755) has ferry service to Bastia, Corsica (mid-June–mid-Sept., daily; last 2 wks of Sept. and end of Mar.–mid-June, 2 per wk; 6½–8 hrs, L43,000–L58,000); **Corsica Ferries** (Ponte Andrea Doria, tel. 010/593301) also heads there (2 per day, L50,000). **Grandi Traghetti** (010/5761363) sends ferries to Palermo. There is also a boat service run by **Golfo Paradiso** (V. Scalo 3, Camogli, tel. 0185/772091) from Genoa's Porto Antico along the Ligurian coast, stopping at Camogli (1¼ hrs; L10,000), San Fruttuoso (1½ hrs, L13,000), and Portofino (1¾ hrs, L15,000, or L22,000 round-trip). Departures are at 2 on Saturday mid-June–mid-September and 2 on Sunday mid-September–mid-June. Ferry schedules are available at any travel agency or tourist office.

BY PLANE

Genoa's international airport, **Aeroporto Cristoforo Colombo** (tel. 010/6015410), is 9 km outside the city. A cab ride will run you L40,000–L50,000, but the Aerobus runs a regular schedule from Piazza De Ferrari and Stazione Brignole. Alitalia (tel. 147/865641) serves Rome, Milan, Reggio di Calabria and other cities, while Air France (tel. 167/824041), Swissair (tel. 010/6505335), and British Airways (tel. 167/287287) serve Paris, Zurich, and London, respectively, with connections to the U.S. and the rest of the world.

GETTING AROUND

You'll inevitably get lost on foot, but you'll get even more lost in a car, and walking is the best way to see this city. Stazione Principe is in the west end of the city center, Stazione Brignole in the east. From Stazione Principe, walking 1,000 ft down Via Balbi or taking Bus 18, 19, 20, 30, 37, or 41 to Piazza de Ferrari will land you in the **centro storico** (historic center), home to most of the interesting sights. Major landmarks include **San Lorenzo** (the main cathedral) and **Piazza de Ferrari,** an important transportation hub and the dividing point between the old and new towns. **Taxis** cluster in front of the two train stations and Piazza de Ferrari. Rumor has it that they jack up their prices for naive tourists, so ask around for a fair price (about L10,000 in the city center). Also, prohibitively narrow streets prevent taxis or other cars from entering the centro storico.

BY BUS

Bus tickets are available at tobacco shops, marked TABACCHI, and at train stations. One ticket (L1,500) is good for 90 minutes on any city bus. Buses 18, 19, 20, 30, 33, 37, and 41 travel between the train stations, and from Stazione Principe all but 33 go through the city center. For buses to the waterfront, turn right out of the station to Via Andrea Doria. Alternatively, catch the distinctively painted Artbus, which hits the main sites, the waterfront, and the two stations. The bus runs every 20–30 minutes; tickets cost L1,500 (L5,000 for a day of travel) at tobacco shops or at the station.

BY FUNIVIO AND ASCENSORE

A series of *funivie* (funiculars) and *ascensori* (elevators), traveling at a very steep incline, help truck you up and down the hills. One-day bus passes (L5,000; see above) and 90-minute bus tickets (L1,500; see above) are valid on the elevators and funiculars. However, automated ticket machines at the bottom and top of the elevators allow you to buy one-way elevator tickets for only L600. Funiculars also have ticket machines but cost the standard L1,500.

WHERE TO SLEEP

The area around Stazione Principe is cheap but uninviting; a better choice for affordable lodging is near Stazione Brignole. Way up high, like a beacon on the hillside, lies the glorious youth hostel.

For a great escape from Genoa, take the funicular from Largo della Zecca, near Piazza Nunziata, to Righi, which overlooks the city. You can also ride the ascensore from Piazza Nunziata up to Spianata di Castelletto and take in the panoramic view.

UNDER L85,000 • Albergo Carletto. If you can't stand the noise of Vespas whizzing by, come to this hotel in a pedestrian zone. Clean, spacious doubles (L80,000) have high ceilings and mosaic floors, with TV and telephone. Call a day in advance to reserve. *V. Colombo 16/4, 16122, off P. Verdi in front of Stazione Brignole, tel. 010/561229. 24 rooms, most with shower.*

Albergo Fiume. Rooms, starting at L80,000 for a double, are clean and charming, and the original mosaic floors are perfectly intact. Reception stays open all night. *V. Fiume 9/R, 16121, tel. 010/591691, fax 010/5702833. From west end of P. Verdi, take V. Fiume. 23 rooms, most with shower.*

Pension Ricci. This neat, efficient place is a mere five minutes from Stazione Brignole. The two rooms facing the street have bigger windows but more noise than those on the inside. Prices vary depending on the season; doubles run L75,000 in summer. *P. Colombo 4–5, 16122, tel. and fax 010/592746. From Stazione Brignole, take V. Fiume to V. Colombo to P. Colombo. 8 rooms, 6 with shower.*

UNDER L110,000 • Mini Hotel. The owners at this small hotel a few minutes from Stazione Principe will be your Italian *nonni* (grandparents), though they do speak some English. Their pad is nondescript, but the doubles (L90,000–L110,000) are immaculate. *V. Lomellini 6/1, 16126, tel. 010/2465876, fax 010/2465803. 15 rooms, 12 with shower.*

HOSTEL • Ostello per La Gioventù (HI). This hostel, high on a hill overlooking the town and the sea, has to be the most efficient establishment in the country aside from the Mafia. Although it's about a 25-minute bus ride, in Genoa-Oregina, the hostel (and its curiously helpful, multilingual staff) is such a relief at the end of the day that it's worth the trip. HI members pay L22,000 (nonmembers, L27,000) for a bunk bed in a dorm-style room with six others, or L23,000 per person for a four-person "family room" with bath. Rooms are immaculate and spacious, and breakfast is included. Dinners start at only L7,000. There's E-mail access (L2,200) and a laundry (L12,000 for 5kg). *V. Costanzi 120, 16136, tel. and fax 010/2422457. From Stazione Brignole, Bus 40 to top of hill; from Stazione Principe, take Bus 35, switch to Bus 40 at V. Spinola, and get off at V. Costanzi (both buses run until midnight). 210 beds. Midnight curfew, lockout 9–3:30. Laundry.*

CAMPING • The best place to camp is **Villa Doria** in Genoa-Pegli, in a wonderfully scenic spot. At night the guy who runs the place brings out his guitar and everyone sings. Sites go for L8,000 per person, plus L4,000 per car and L9,000–L15,000 per tent. You can also stay in two- to six-person bungalows for L50,000–L100,000. A food store and a snack bar are on site. *V. al Campeggio Villa Doria 15, tel. 010/6969600. From either station, take local train to Pegli, then transfer to Bus 93. Kitchen, showers.*

WHERE TO EAT

Genoa is the home of pesto, so don't leave town without indulging in some of it over *trofie* (a potato-based pasta) or smothered with delicious Stracchino (a soft, mild cheese) on pizza. Genoa's food is among the cheapest in any big Italian city; the centro storico, Corso Italia toward the east along the water, and the hills overlooking the sea all overflow with trattorias and pizzerias. Via San Vicenzo (near Stazione Brignole) and Via San Luca (near the old port) are flooded with bakeries and shops that sell big, unctuous slabs of *focaccia*, the regional specialty, similar to salted and oiled pizza bread served plain or with a range of toppings. The little flaky snack that residents eat at lunchtime is *torta pasqualina,* a pastry filled with spinach (sometimes artichoke) and egg. **Mercato Orientale,** near Piazza Colombo, is bursting with stands that sell delicious bread, cheese, and fruit. From Stazione Brignole, cross the piazza and look for signs on the left side.

CENTRO STORICO

UNDER L10,000 • Trattoria da Maria. This place may seem a bit intimidating when you hear the roar of heated Italian "discussions" from half a block away, but come on in and squeeze yourself between toothless sea dogs and respectable townfolk at the communal tables; Maria will welcome you whoever you are. Pasta courses, including good linguine with pesto (L5,000), are her strong point. A full meal, including first and second courses and wine, costs L14,000. *Vico Testa d'Oro 14/R, tel. 010/ 581080. From P. Fontane Marose, take V. XXV Aprile toward Piazza de Ferrari, and make 2nd left on Vico Testadoro. Cash only. Closed Mon. evening and Sat.*

UNDER L15,000 • Caffè degli Specchi. This restaurant-tearoom-bar for lunch only is filled with harried businesspeople grabbing cappuccino on their coffee breaks and refined locals enjoying their teatime rituals. The building dates from the 17th century, and the original decor of tile and lead-glass *specchi* (mirrors) has been maintained. A plate of cold house specialties includes a *torta* (pie) made with artichoke and squash. *Salita Pollaioli 43/R, off P. Matteotti, tel. 010/2468193. Cash only. No dinner. Closed Sun.*

Pizzeria Funicolare. This unpretentious and relatively unkown spot in scenic Castelletto fills its second floor each night with locals who come to enjoy the best pizza in Genoa, some say in all of northern Italy. Individual pies run L10,000–L12,000; or try the local specialty, delicious focaccia pizzata (with tomato, cheese, ham, mushrooms, and anchovies, L13,000 per person). From Piazza Portello, take the Santa Anna funicular, and climb up a few stairs; it's across the street and facing you. *Corso Magenta, tel. 010/ 2513286. Closed Sun.*

UNDER L25,000 • Trattoria Ugo. Enter old Italy through a door made of ropes at this authentic locals' place. The proprietor gives you the daily menu orally and proceeds to order for you. If you're lucky, you'll end up with the delicious *pansoti alla salsa di noci* (spinach and ricotta ravioli with a creamy walnut sauce). Lunch runs L15,000–L20,000, dinner L20,000–L35,000. *V. Giustiniani 86/R, tel. 010/2469302. From P. Matteotti, take Salita Pollaioli, and turn right onto V. Giustiniani. Cash only. Closed Sun.–Mon.*

DINING WITH A VIEW

UNDER L15,000 • Bagni Italia. Overlooking the beach, this is the happening summertime dining joint for Italian families and yuppies, with amazing calzone and fresh seafood (L12,000 and up). *C. Italia 9, on water south of Stazione Brignole, tel. 010/3620685. From Stazione Brignole, Bus 31 to C. Italia.*

UNDER L20,000 • La Bolognese. Locals drive up Genoa's hills to reach this oasis, which serves some of the best pesto in Genoa. Dine outside under a shady ivy canopy and observe the entire port, complete with steamboats competing for the loudest toot. Specialty pizzas are cooked in stone ovens. *Passa Porto Chiappa 1, tel. 010/8318007. From hostel (see above), wind upward on road for about 15,000 ft. Open Fri.–Tues. 9 AM–midnight.*

WORTH SEEING

Genoa's allure isn't instantly apparent, but it's not hard to imagine the city's former Baroque majesty as you walk down palace-packed **Via Garibaldi** to the west of Piazza delle Fontane Marose. Now an office building, **Palazzo Podestà** (V. Garibaldi 7) is worth a peek for its rococo fountain in which male sea creatures of Herculean stature emerge from a mossy, vine-covered grotto. The fountain is hidden behind a sometimes-open portal—typical of Genoa's tendency to shield its beauty under a layer of grime. Glance at the statues adorning **Palazzo Lercari** (V. Garibaldi 3), with the unfortunate traits of being noseless and earless. Also on Via Garibaldi, **Palazzo Rosso** houses outstanding 15th- to 18th-century paintings by Italian and Flemish masters. *V. Garibaldi 18, tel. 010/5574741. Admission L6,000 (L10,000 in combination with Palazzo Bianco). Open Tues., Thurs., and Fri. 9–1, Wed. and Sat. 9–7, Sun. 10–6.*

The **centro storico** is a perfectly preserved medieval web of alleys, down to the authentic squalor. But limit your exploration of the centro to daylight and business hours—it even gets eerie when things close down during the afternoon siesta. **Palazzo Ducale** (P. de Ferrari/P. Matteotti 5, tel. 010/562440) now contains offices, a *gelateria,* and the music academy, but back in the 14th century it was the palace of the doges. In summer, you can pick up maps of the historic center from tables lining the palazzo. Next door, the **Chiesa Sant'Ambrogio,** or **Gesù,** is decorated in blinding Baroque gold and silver—appropriate splendor for Rubens's *Circumcision* inside. Farther south, off Stradone di Sant'Agostino near Piazza Sarzano, the simple, early-12th-century basilica **San Donato** (Vico San Donato) holds an 18th-century tabernacle. The stunning **Porta Soprana,** an entrance to the medieval district off Piazza Dante, is one of the few remaining sections of Genoa's 12th-century city wall. The portal leads to a maze of convents and monasteries and to Piazza Sarzano. It stands next to the **Casa di Colombo** (in fact, Christopher Columbus's father was the gatekeeper of the Porta Soprana), a curiously lonely, ivy-shrouded stone house that you can only view from the outside.

The **Università di Genova,** centered on Via Balbi, is housed mostly in a series of grand but faded palazzi, where historic grandeur meets frenzied student energy. The 17th-century **Palazzo Reale** was originally built by the prestigious Balbi family but was taken over by Savoy royalty in the 1800s. The most noteworthy paintings in the upstairs art gallery are by Van Dyck. Good free guided tours are given by conscientious objectors choosing military-service alternatives. *V. Balbi 10, tel. 010/27101. Admission L8,000. Open Sun.–Tues. 9–1:30, Wed.–Sat. 9–7; free guided tour Thurs. at 10.*

In the 17th–19th centuries, about 900 marble statues, shrines, and paintings of the Madonna were placed on street corners throughout Genoa, probably to ask for protection from the problems plaguing the city. About half remain in place today.

At the **Old Port** (Piazza Caricamento), focaccia and fresh seafood vendors line the streets, and luxury yachts anchor side-by-side with battleships and Greek and African ferries. The city's seamy port flavor increases as you head west through the narrow streets toward Stazione Principe; **Via San Luca,** in the heart of it all, is the historic center's most vital shopping street. Off that street, the dark and brooding church of **San Siro,** which has existed in various incarnations since the 4th century AD, is Genoa's oldest and spookiest place of worship, complete with crooked chandeliers and hunchbacked organists playing fugues. Continuing deeper into the *vicoli,* **Via della Maddalena** and environs form a fascinating cultural melting pot that should only be visited by day.

ACQUARIO DI GENOVA

This four-story aquarium is the biggest and best little fish tank in all of Europe. Among more than 1,000 species and 50 tanks, you'll see sharks, dolphins, harbor seal pups, and penguins. *Porto Antico, tel. 010/2481205. From Stazione Principe, take V. Andrea Doria to Stazione Marittima; take Bus 1, 2, 7, or 8. From Brignole, Bus 4, 12, or 15 (but not the 15/). Admission L19,000. Open weekdays 9:30–7, weekends 9:30–8 (closed Mon. Oct.–Mar.). Ticket office closes 6:30.*

CATTEDRALE SAN LORENZO

The exterior of this cathedral, built in 1118, is made of the signature Genovese black-and-white-striped marble—which is supposed to symbolize Genoan austerity—and has an elaborately carved French-Gothic portal. Inside, a 16th-century Renaissance ceiling shelters 14th-century frescoes and a huge World War II bomb that hit the church in 1941 but never exploded. The stunning **Cappella di San Giovanni** (Chapel of St. John the Baptist), containing his 13th-century sarcophagus, is on the north side of the cathedral. Visitors should dress conservatively. *V. San Lorenzo off P. Matteotti, tel. 010/311269. Admission free, museum L10,000. Open daily 9–noon and 3–6; guided tours every 1/2 hr. until 11:30 AM and 5:30 PM.*

GALLERIA NAZIONALE DI PALAZZO SPINOLA

As you move through remarkably well-preserved 17th- and 18th-century rooms in the Ligurian National Gallery, notice the detailed old maps lining the stairway walls. Look for Van Dyck's *Madonna in Prayer, Portrait of a Young Boy,* and *The Four Evangelists,* all of which master the use of light and luminescent color. *P. Pellicceria 1, tel. 010/2477061. From V. Garibaldi, walk south on V. Angeli, turn right onto V. della Maddalena and left onto P. Pellicceria. Admission L8,000. Open Tues.–Sat. 9–7, Sun. 2–7.*

PALAZZO BIANCO

Though it's not so *bianco* (white) anymore, this palace is one of the few that's open to the public. It houses a collection of Ligurian, Dutch, and Flemish masters, with pieces dating from the 13th century (Byzantine School) to the 18th century. Among the works are *San Sebastiano* and *Madonna and Child with Saints* by Filippino Lippi, *Christ and the Tribute Money* by Van Dyck, and *Venus and Mars* by Rubens. *V. Garibaldi 11, tel. 010/2476377. From P. de Ferrari, walk north on V. XXV Aprile to P. Fontane Marose and turn left onto V. Garibaldi. Admission L6,000 (or L10,000 in combination with Palazzo Rosso). Open Tues., Thurs., and Fri. 9–1, Wed. and Sat. 9–7., Sun. 10–6.*

The richly adorned **Doria Apartments**—mansions, really—and the **Chiesa San Matteo** ring Piazza San Matteo, home of the powerful Doria family during the Renaissance. The church was built before the rest of the piazza and bears the traditional Genovese black-and-white stripes. Summaries of glorious Dorian achievements are ever so modestly inscribed on the outside of the church. Though most of the interior dates from the 16th century, the cloister and frescoes by Luca Cambiaso and Bergamasco are from the 14th century. *P. San Matteo, tel. 010/2474361. Admission free. Open Mon.–Sat. 8–noon and 4–7, Sun. 9:30–10:30 and 4–5.*

SANTA MARIA DI CASTELLO

Once a way station for the Crusaders, this 12th-century Gothic and Romanesque basilica still has Roman columns and capitals. Attached is a 15th-century Dominican convent and library. The museum houses works by Barnaba da Modena and Ludovico Brea. *Salita Santa Maria di Castello 15, tel. 010/ 292986. From P. Sarzano, head northwest to Salita Santa Maria di Castello. Admission free. Open daily 9–noon and 2:30–6.*

CHEAP THRILLS

Tired of its less-than-hospitable reputation, Genoa has started a program called **Genova Si Apre** (Genoa Is Open). During the high seasons in summer and winter, information tents pop up around the city with multilingual workers who will shower you with information on free concerts, guided tours, and other events. Mid-July's **Genova Jazz** attracts big names like the Joshua Redman Quartet but maintains modest prices; tickets are around L20,000. A sweeping view of Genoa and its environs can be had from one of the network of medieval fortresses—Genoa's ancient defense structure—high above the city, one of which lies at the top of the **Zecca-Righi Funicular.** The seven-stop funicular leaves from Piazza dell'Annunziata, at the end of Via Balbi from Stazione Principe (take any of the buses running between Principe and Brignole; L1,500; runs daily, every 15 min., 7 AM–midnight). A more modest path to a view is on the **Castelletto Elevator,** which whisks you up to a port panorama from Piazza Portello, near Piazza Fontane Marose (L600). To cruise around Genoa's port, hop on a 45-minute **boat ride** (L10,000); boats depart hourly (in summer only; call 010/256775 for info) from the port in front of the Acquario di Genova (*see* Worth Seeing, *above*).

AFTER DARK

Stay away from the centro storico after dark unless you know exactly where you're going or have local friends who do. Especially avoid Via della Maddalena, Piazza Matteotti, and the bus station near Stazione Brignole, frequented by nocturnal prostitutes and drug peddlers. Check posters around town for theater and club listings, and look for the publications *Succedere a Genova, La Rosa Purpurea del Cairo,* and *Il Secolo XIX.* Big concerts featuring international artists take place at **Teatro Verdi** (P. Oriani 1, Genoa-Sampierdarena, tel. 010/671263). The **Palazzo Ducale** (P. de Ferrari) hosts concerts in its courtyard.

South of Stazione Brignole, get your karaoke fix at **Bla** (V. Casaregis 64/R, at V. Cecchi, no phone), a good *panificio* (bakery) and sandwich shop in a converted train car. **Antica Vetreria del Molo** (Vico Chinso Gelsa 8/R, tel. 010/293451), on the *sopraelevata* (levee) at Piazza Cavour, is a great place to relax, have a beer, and listen to music. No one sleeps through the live music and dancing at **Nessundorma** (Via Porta d'Archi 74/R; tel. 010/561773), off Via XX Settembre near the big arch. In the hot summer months when the university is closed, most of the action relocates to the beachfront. Discotheques like **Makò** (Corso Italia 28/R, tel. 010/367652) line Corso Italia, but covers are high (about L20,000). **Senhor do Bonfim** (Passeggiata Garibaldi, Nervi, tel. 010/3726312; take bus 15, 15/, or night bus 607 to Nervi train station, then exit through tunnel to Passeggiata), along the water, hops on weekends with live music and dancing but less pretension than the discos. The various *bagni* (beach clubs) also become outdoor bars and hangouts. Take Bus 31 or 32 (L1500) from Brignole to the beach promenade.

RIVIERA DI PONENTE

Along the Riviera di Ponente, which extends west from Genoa as far as Ventimiglia, water, mountains, and tourists peacefully coexist. There is no untouched sand in these parts, nor is there the quaintness of pastel-washed Riviera di Levante towns clinging to the rocks, but the palm-lined coast and tranquil waters are so exquisite that it takes little coaxing to resign yourself to a herd mentality. With the exception of **Finale Ligure** and **San Remo,** the pace is pretty slow. You're more likely to see wanna-be Bain de Soleil models—middle-aged folks from France, Germany, and Italy—than backpackers. If you're looking for the "real" Ponente, locals insist you'll have to go at least a kilometer (½ mi) inland from the coast. Excursions into the mountains from coastal Finale Ligure and San Remo uncover dramatic transformations as the Mediterranean meets the Apennines and casinos are replaced by castles. The coastal towns are easily accessible by train along the Genoa–Ventimiglia line, but sporadic buses are the only means of transportation inland. A good source of Riviera di Ponente information on the internet is a web site run by the tourist board, at **www.italianriviera.com.** The site has transportation info, tourist office contacts, and listings of accommodations and food running the whole price gamut; it covers virtually every town in the region, no matter how small.

FINALE LIGURE

Finale Ligure is the choice vacation spot for many a Birkenstock-wearing German tourist. Probably the most happening town on the Riviera di Ponente, Finale Ligure has a lively local street life, numerous young travelers, and beautiful hiking and biking terrain. The city is divided into three districts, all of which are easily accessible on foot or by bus. Social life revolves around the beach, and the two nearby districts **Finalmarina** and **Finalpia** are filled with shady benches, sprays of flowers, and people of all ages. At night Finale Ligure's overpriced beach restaurants turn up their music, and the entire town shows up to mingle and compare sunburns.

When sunstroke threatens, check out the most attractive of the three villages, the historic and walled-in **Finalborgo,** a 20-minute walk from the beach. The Baroque **Basilica di San Biagio** (P. San Biagio; open daily 9–noon and 4–7), constructed during the Spanish occupation, crouches between an octagonal Gothic belfry and a medieval tower. The plain facade doesn't prepare you for the ornate interior filled with amazing trompe-l'oeil frescoes. The Dominican convent **Chiostro Santa Caterina** (P. Santa Caterina, tel. 019/690020; open July–Oct. Tues.–Sat. 10–noon and 3–6, Sun. 9–noon; Sept.–June Tues.–Sat. 9–noon and 2:30–4:30, Sun. 9–noon; L5,000) houses the **Museo Archeologico,** with a fascinating display of relics from Finale Ligure's grottoes, once the homes of Paleolithic peoples. Higher up in Finalborgo on a tortuous cobblestone path (reminding you how modern security systems are *so* much more convenient than the old citadel approach) is the **Castel San Giovanni.** The castle's architectural identity crisis reflects its varied incarnations: It was built by the Spanish in the 1600s, partially destroyed by the Genovese in 1715, then later converted to a women's prison. The castle interior is now closed to the public.

BASICS

Informazione Accoglienza Turistica (IAT; V. San Pietro 14, tel. 019/681019; open Tue.–Sat. 9–12:30 and 3–6:30, Apr.–Sept. Mon. 3–7, Tues.–Sat. 9–12:30 and 3–7, Sun. 9–12:30) will try to get you oriented with maps, hiking information, and promotional brochures for Finale Ligure and other Riviera di Ponente towns. They can also reserve rooms for you. From the station, cross Piazza Vittorio Veneto to Via Saccone, and turn left on Via della Concezione, which becomes Via San Pietro.

COMING AND GOING

Finale Ligure is more or less dead center on the Genoa–Ventimiglia train line. From the **train station** Finalmarina (P. Vittorio Veneto, tel. 1478/88088), about 18 trains depart daily in both directions (to Ventimiglia, 2 hrs, L7,400; to Genoa, 1 hr, L9,900). Twelve trains daily go to Milan via Genoa (3 hrs; L18,000). For Torino, change at Savona (2 hrs), from which there are hourly connections (total 2 hrs 20 min; L18,100).

Two bus lines depart from the piazza in front of the train station. **SAR** (V. Mazzini 28, tel. 019/692275; open weekdays 8–12:30 and 3–7, weekends 10–1 and 3–6, shorter hrs in winter), a coastal service,

THE SKINNY ON THE BEACHES

Unlike many other resorts in Italy, most of the Riviera's beaches have not been totally monopolized by private clubs. You may not always find smooth-as-silk white sand, but in most towns you can just head toward the blue horizon and pick your spot in the sun. If you simply cannot find a free beach, don't stake out a renegade spot—security at private beaches is stringent. Private beaches are broken up into blocks of color representing the businesses that own them, and the basic fee for a patch of sand is L5,000–L8,000. This sometimes includes an umbrella and two chairs, and most establishments don't care how many bodies you pack into a spot.

runs from Savona through Finale Ligure to Andora, its westernmost stop. **ACTS** (office in Savona, tel. 019/220123) offers the same service, but its buses also go up into the hills and all around Finale Ligure. Buy tickets for ACTS buses at the *giornalaio* (newsstand) outside the train station. SAR tickets are sold at the SAR office. Buses to nearby Noli (15 min) cost L2,000.

WHERE TO SLEEP

Finale Ligure has yet to achieve the snootiness and inflated prices of San Remo or Portofino, and it's generally safe. The only problem is availability of cheap stays during the summer, when you may have to settle for a campsite or an *affittacamere,* a bed in someone's home. Just across the piazza from the train station, the **Associazione Alberghi e Turismo** (P. Vittorio Veneto 10, tel. 019/694252; open Mon.-Fri. 2:30–6:30) will help you find a place in high season, but they'll only recommend hotels affiliated with the bureau. SAR and the tourist offices (*see* Basics, *above*) can also help locate affittacamere (about L80,000 per double).

UNDER L90,000 • Albergo San Marco. This place lacks character, but its singles (L45,000) and doubles (L85,000–90,000 with bath) are some of the cheapest you'll find in summer. It has a decent trattoria downstairs, but its real advantage is that it's right across from the beach. *Via Concezione 22, 17024, tel. 019/692533. From station, cross street and turn left on V. Unità d'Italia, left onto main boardwalk, and walk up 300 ft. 14 rooms with bath.*

Hotel Marina. Only two blocks from the beach, this hotel has fresh, pleasant doubles with bath for L85,000–L90,000 with a distinctly nautical air. The small eatery downstairs serves up good home cooking. *V. Barilli 22, 17024, tel. 019/692561. From station, take V. de Raymondi, which becomes V. Barrili. 16 rooms, 12 with bath.*

HOSTEL • Castello Wuillermin (HI). Inconveniently perched atop a virtual Mt. Everest, this hostel in a turreted pseudo-castle is more than worth the 20-minute, 312-step hike; HI members pay L19,000 a head, nonmembers L24,000. It's got a great view and serves a delicious three-course dinner with vegetarian options for L14,000. The facilities are new and the staff helpful—but watch out for the ferocious dog. They don't accept reservations, but call before you make the trek. *V. Caviglia 46, 17024, tel. 019/ 690515. From train station, turn left at V. Mazzini, which becomes V. Torino, turn left at Esso gas station, go up Gradinata delle Rose, and follow signs. 80 beds. Reception open 5 PM–10 PM. Curfew 11:30 PM, lockout 10–5. Closed mid-Oct.–mid-Mar. Laundry (L8,000 per load).*

CAMPING • At Camping del Mulino (tel. 019/601669) you'll pay L8,000–L14,000 per tent to plop down.

WHERE TO EAT

Despite the proliferation of touristy trattorias and restaurants with dull fixed-price menus, you can eat cheaply and well in Finale Ligure. **Asterix Pub** (V. Roma 45, no phone) is done out like its namesake cartoon strip but serves savory, original pasta dishes; both the gnocchi and tortellini are exceptional. **II**

Posto (V. Porro 21, Finalpia, tel. 019/601677) has a unique approach: they dole out fabulous pastas for two from huge pots. Bring a date and enjoy the pasta *all'arrabbiata* (with hot-pepper tomato sauce) for L8,000 per person. **La Grotta** (Via Massaferro, 17) is near the tourist office on the waterfront; it's not exactly traditional Italian fare, but it offers cheap pizza and draws a crowd.

AFTER DARK

A long stroll along the beach, with all its *caffè* and gelaterias, is a party in Finale Ligure. After a five-minute bus ride or a leisurely 20-minute stroll to Varigotti, you'll find **Il Covo** (Capo San Donato, tel. 019/601284), an indoor/outdoor bar and disco right on the water. Players can head to the **Scotch Club** (V. San Pietro, tel. 019/692481), pretty much a pickup joint.

OUTDOOR ACTIVITIES

For info on hiking and rock climbing, inquire at the **IAT** office (*see* Basics, *above*). **The Rock Store** (P. Garibaldi 14, Finalborgo, tel. 019/690208; open Tues.–Sun. 9–12:30 and 4–7:30) will help you out with equipment and maps. Biking is great around Finale Ligure; you can rent bikes (L15,000 per hr) or scooters (L30,000 per hour) at **RC Bike** (Via Brunengi 65, Finalborgo; tel. 019/681058). Also, rent paddle boats (L12,000 per hr) on the free beach past the umbrella owners on the boardwalk. You can check out the Roman arches in the **Val Ponci,** behind Finale Ligure, by bike or on foot. The IAT office has maps and details about this day trip.

NEAR FINALE LIGURE

SASSELLO

Tiny, mountainous Sassello north of Savona and northeast of Finale Ligure is punctuated by three small rivers and the Savonese Apennines. A ski resort in winter and a cool retreat in summer, it becomes a wall-to-wall carpet of mushrooms come fall. Because it's cool and high in the hills, Sassello has a northern feel—a nice contrast to the sun and crowds of coastal towns. Precious few tourists come to this tiny escape in the mountains, so the locals aren't yet jaded.

Despite its present-day placidity, Sassello had a turbulent past. It fortified the Genovese Republic against rebellious subjects in the 13th century and then rebelled itself in the 16th century. The **Torre Saraceno** is all that remains of a former castle in the middle of town. Go to the **AAST** information office (V. Marconi 3, tel. 019/724020; open sporadically in summer) to pick up a brochure that discusses sights and walks in endearingly bad English. The tourist office in neighboring Savona (V. Paleoccupa 24, tel. 019/930099; open Mon.–Sat. 9–noon and 3–5) might prove more reliable.

COMING AND GOING • Sassello is accessible only by **car** or **bus** from Savona, which you can reach by train from Finale Ligure (20 min, L3,500). Near Savona's train station on Piazza Popolo, catch the ACTS bus (9 daily) toward Martina or Urbe and get off at Sassello (1 hr, L3,100). You can buy your ticket on board. Ask the driver if he goes to Sassello before you get on—service is inconsistent, and (surprise, surprise) stops are poorly marked. Six buses a day return to Savona, fewer on Sunday.

WHERE TO SLEEP AND EAT • San Giovanni (V. A. Villa 4 17014, tel. 019/724025; closed Jan.), one of only three hotels in the whole village, is a family-run albergo/trattoria that has clean doubles with shared baths (L60,000) overlooking rolling, green farm country and the mountains. The kitchen turns out a mean penne all'arrabbiata, and literally half the town eats here for dinner.

NOLI

About 8 km (5 mi) north of Finale Ligure on the coast, Noli is one of the few preserved medieval centers in Liguria. Although it's touristy, the town has nice beaches and plenty of lodging. The ancient buildings hardly betray the town's impressive autonomous past: Noli was a naval republic with its own statutes from 1196 to 1797. The Romanesque **Chiesa di San Paragorio** (off V. Collegio Cesari, just east of V. Turin) dates from the 11th century and is jammed full of goodies, including a baptismal font and a painting of a bloody St. Sebastian. For outdoor buffs, the **Paleolithic grottoes** (whose spoils are now in the Museo Archeologico in Finale Ligure) are easily accessible, and free-climbing has become popular in the area; head to the **tourist office** (C. Italia 39, tel. 019/7490101) by the beach for more information. Dante's *Divine Comedy* speaks of Noli's inaccessibility, but these days the town can be reached by an ACTS or SAR bus (every 15 min, 10 min, L2,200) on the Finale Ligure–Savona line. Accessible by the same bus line is **Varigotti,** an even tinier inviting beach town 2 km (1½ mi) south of Noli.

WHERE TO SLEEP AND EAT • Albergo-Ristorante Romeo (V. C. Colombo 81–83, 17026, tel. 019/748973; cash only; closed mid-Oct.–mid-Mar.) is a family-run pension with small, cheerful rooms (doubles L75,000–L90,000 with bath). For great food and an Old World feel, try **Da Gigi** (V. Sartono 4, tel. 019/7485109; cash only).

SAN REMO

San Remo cannot hide the wear and tear of 100-odd years of international carousing. In the early part of the century, this was the Riviera's high-class vacation spot. Though its jet-set culture has since faded, its casino has remained open, and the town has more to offer in terms of street life and nightlife than other Ponente towns. It's great for people-watching—full of the young and the old, the chic, the tacky. Leathery elderly men who've been roasting in the sun for millennia drive underage girlfriends around in brand-new Ferrari Testarossas. And look out for the young gangs of jaw-clenching idlers on Vespas (Testarossa testosterone in training). Miles upon miles of groomed, sandy beaches are mostly private, but if you head east, you'll find some free rocky areas. On Tuesday and Saturday mornings, the best from belts to olives are pawned at the flea market near **San Siro Cathedral.**

The hilltop medieval town in San Remo, **La Pigna** (the fir cone)—an appropriate description of its bunched contours—is worth a gander for its churches and tiny artisan shops. In the newer part of town, you'll find all the stuff that makes San Remo party central: palm-lined **Corso Matteotti** features chichi shops and is a locus for the town's clubs, casinos, live music, drinking, and general hedonism. The grandiose **Casino Municipale** (C. Inglese 18, tel. 0184/5951; open daily 2:30pm–3am) keeps the spirit of Monte Carlo alive, although it looks more like a courthouse or town hall than a blackjack palace. If you're 18 or older, you can play the slot machines downstairs without being subjected to a snooty dress code. But to play the tables in the main casino, don't even think about sporting your FIRENZE T-shirt. The dress code (jackets and ties for men) is stringent, and it costs L15,000 (L5,000 weekdays) just to enter.

BASICS

At the no-nonsense, friendly **Azienda di Promozione Turistica** (Largo Nuvoloni 1, across from train station, tel. 0184/571571; open Mon.–Sat. 8–7, Sun. 9–1), you can state your price range, and they'll call hotels for you. They also provide hiking information.

COMING AND GOING

San Remo's **train station** (tel. 1478/88088) is on the Ventimiglia–Genoa line, and hourly trains to Bordighera (10 min, L2,200), Ventimiglia (25 min, L2,200), Finale Ligure (1½ hrs, L9,900), and Genoa (2 hrs, L12,100) are the most convenient. The luggage deposit in the station (6 AM–10 PM) charges L5,000 for 12 hours. From San Remo, **RT buses** (tel. 0184/592706) make a run to the French Riviera, hitting Ventimiglia and Monaco (6 buses daily). RT buses also run from San Remo to Bordighera (20 min, L2,200) and Finale Ligure (2 hrs, L5,000).

WHERE TO SLEEP AND EAT

Don't plan on finding a room without a bit of digging, though the sheer number of pensions on the tourist office list should unearth something. Picturesque, with rooms opening onto a balcony above a pizzeria, the **San Remo** (V. Astraldi 3, 18038, tel. 0184/506924; cash only) has bathless doubles at L50,000–L70,000, but it gets noisy at night. **Albergo Vittoria** (V. San Francesco 1, 18038, tel. 0184/507294; cash only) offers doubles (L80,000) that would appeal to your grandmother's decorating sensibilities. Along Corso Matteotti, you'll find shops that specialize in ready-made food like *peperoni ripieni* (stuffed peppers). For scrumptious fettuccine *con carciofi* (with artichokes) in a charming atmosphere, try **Antica Trattoria Piccolo Mondo** (V. Piave 7, tel. 0184/509012; cash only; no dinner Wed., closed Sun.).

AFTER DARK

When San Remo's churches lock their doors and the sun sets, Vespas congregate along the boardwalk, where you'll also find plenty of bars and restaurants. They're all kooky and fun, but the **Dick Turpin Pub** (C. Nazario Sauro 15, tel. 0184/503499; closed Mon.) rules, with cactus plants and outdoor tables to get you in that beachy mood.

NEAR SAN REMO

BORDIGHERA

Dominated by the sea and some manicured palm gardens—the official source for the Vatican's Holy Week—hospitable Bordighera may not be the gem of the Riviera, but it's a mellow and welcome change from its glitzy neighbors. A British colony turned resort, Bordighera still retains a certain elegance, with winding streets, small stores, and the requisite views in **Bordighera Alta,** the walkable centro storico. You can see proof of its former glory days in the once-grand **Hotel Angst** (V. Manzoni); now boarded up, it resembles a haunted house with its Gothic spiked fence and cobwebs.

For some fresh air, take the steep walk to **Sant'Ampelio** (V. S. Ampelio, in Bordighera Alta), a church with Romanesque foundations. Sloping down the hill toward the ocean is the **Giardino Esotico Pallanca** (V. Madonna della Ruota 1, tel. 0184/266347), an exotic garden specializing in transplanted flora from South America. Bordighera's sandy beaches are right in front of the train station, but if you head a bit east, you'll find less crowded but rocky promontories. Bordighera is a good place to hole up and hibernate for a while. Pensions become like home—you sleep and take all your meals in them. Head to the **IAT information office** (V. Roberto 1, tel. 0184/262322; open Mon.–Sat. 8– 7) for a list of hotels and more info about the town.

COMING AND GOING • Bordighera's **train station** (P. Eroi della Libertà, tel. 1478/88088) lies on the Ventimiglia–Genoa train line, with service to Genoa (2¼–3½ hrs, L12,100), San Remo (15 min, L2,200), and Ventimiglia (10 min, L1,700). The bus company **Riviera Trasporti** (in San Remo, tel. 0184/ 502030 or 592706) serves the surrounding area.

WHERE TO SLEEP AND EAT • In the high season (July– August), most places require full pension, which includes a room and three full meals; ask if you're really required, as sometimes it depends more on the proprietor's mood than the time of year. At **Albergo Centrale** (V. Libertà 48, 18012, tel. 0184/ 262630), some of the spotless rooms have delicately hand-painted walls, and excellent meals are served in a charming dining room with a view. Doubles go for L70,000 per person with pension in high season (min. 3 nights; L30,000 per person without). From the station, cross the piazza to Via Vittorio Emanuele and go right; the street becomes Via Libertà. You can relax on the flower-covered terrace overlooking the sea at **Albergo Nagos** (P. Eroi Libertà 7, 18012, tel. 0184/ 260457), just in front of the train station. You're guaranteed decent food and a group of loud regulars chugging their weekly supply of red table wine. Doubles with pension cost L130,000 (L65,000 without).

Much of Italian socializing occurs outdoors, and the beach is no exception. On summer weekends and during ferragosto (the mid-August holiday), the beach is filled with families, packs of teenagers, and persistent towel-to-towel merchants.

VENTIMIGLIA

Primarily a transport hub near the Italian-French border, Ventimiglia has an 11th-century church, **San Michele** (P. Colleta, tel. 0184/351813; open daily 10– 12 and 4:30–7:30), and a terrific **open-air market** every Friday until 7 PM on Via della Repubblica. RT Bus 1 leaves the Ventimiglia train station hourly for the **Giardino Hanbury** (Hanbury of Mortola Botanical Gardens; on way to Ponte San Luigi, tel. 0184/ 229507; open Mar.–mid-June daily 10–6, mid-June–Sept. daily 9–7, and Oct.–Mar. Thu.–Tue. 10–5; admission L8,500). Less than a half hour out of town, the enormous gardens display both wild Mediterranean vegetation and exotic flora from all over the world amid panoramic sea views. The **IAT** tourist office (V. Cavour 61, tel. 0184/351183) is open Monday–Saturday 8–7, also Sunday 9–1 in summer.

COMING AND GOING • Trains travel from Ventimiglia's **train station** (P. Cesere Battisti, tel. 1478/ 88088) to Genoa (12–24 daily, 2–3 hrs, L14,000), Milan (12 daily, 4½–5 hrs, L25,500), and Turin (6 daily, 3–3½ hrs, L16,000). Trains from Ventimiglia to Nice, France (6 daily, 45 min, L12,000–L15,500) run until 10 PM. The **RT** bus service (tel. 0184/351251) operates out of Ventimiglia, with Bus 7 heading to the Nervia Valley and its mountain villages. For bus info, also try **Agenzia Viaggi & Turismo Monte Carlo** (Via Cavour 57, tel. 0184/357577; open Mon.–Sat. 9–12:30 and 2:30–7).

WHERE TO SLEEP AND EAT • Accommodations in Ventimiglia are generally expensive, but budget options do exist. **Hotel Vittoria** (V. Hanbury 5, 18039, tel. 0184/351231) has tacky but clean doubles (L60,000), and it's right across from the train station. **Albergo Calypso** (V. Matteotti 8, 18039, tel. 0184/352742, fax 0184/351588) has doubles from L70,000 and singles from around L45,000. **Ristorante Bolognese** (V. Apriosio 21A, tel. 0184/351779) cooks up a divine ravioli *al sugo* (L10,000).

DOLCEACQUA: WINE, PAINTERS, AND SONG

The temperature drops dramatically as you enter the labyrinthine stone alleyways of Dolceacqua's old hilltop town, on the banks of the Nervia River. The medieval quarter, or terra, is connected to the main piazza (in the new part, or borgo) by the frequently photographed medieval Ponte Vecchio. Though 19th-century Impressionist painter Claude Monet no longer hangs out here (the bridge was one of his haunts), Dolceacqua's woodworkers and ceramic artists operate as they have for centuries—except that some now accept credit cards.

Like many Ligurian towns, Dolceacqua has seen its share of foreign rulers, from the days of the Guelphs and Ghibellines up to the 18th century, when the Austrian wars of succession against France and Spain resulted in the destruction of the Castello Doria. The remains of the castle now perch precariously atop terra's Monte Rebuffao, and every July and August a theater and music festival is held on the castle steps. Try the Rossesse wine while you're here—locals brag that theirs is Liguria's finest. The local olive oil ain't bad either. RT Bus 7 makes the trip from Ventimiglia's train station to Dolceacqua (10 daily, 30 min, L2,800).

RIVIERA DI LEVANTE

Although the Ponente's gentrified coastal resorts have gone into decline, the towns in the Riviera di Levante—filled with rich vacationers and young turks alike—are still going strong. Pleasant walking and hiking paths through the hills and along the cliffs lure travelers to the painfully picturesque former fishing villages of **Camogli** and **Portofino** (the Levante's most polished tourist town, with a stunning semicircular port, immaculate streets, and an old castle with a commanding view). **Santa Margherita Ligure** and **Rapallo** have nice beaches and a lively nightlife, and the **Cinque Terre,** on the east end of the Levante, welcome ever-increasing hordes of hungry backpackers with postcard-ready fishing harbors and cliff-clinging pastel neighborhoods, fantastic hiking paths, terraced vineyards, homey accommodations, and the deep blue sea. **La Spezia,** an industrial but attractive port town in a stunning location in the bay, marks the end of the Riviera di Levante.

CAMOGLI

The name Camogli, an adaptation of *casa delle mogli* (house of wives), refers to a past when toothless, tough women stood in for their seafaring husbands. No longer famous for its merchant ships or its matriarchal culture, this small fishing port has resigned itself to a tranquil resort-town status. Camogli retains a classic watercolor Mediterranean look, intermittently pockmarked by graffiti and disrepair. The town boasts a beautiful seaside promenade with one of the better stretches of pebble beaches in the area, a separate harbor overlooked by a castle, and an ancient old town with single-file streets. Picturesque hiking trails take you along the cliffs to gorgeous views of the sea and the monastery of **San Fruttuoso.**

Camogli's already expensive rooms can be difficult to find in summer, but luckily you can see the town and beach on a day trip from Santa Margherita or Genoa.

The Baroque **Chiesa Santa Maria Assunta** (V. Isola, tel. 0185/770130), just off Piazza Colombo in the Old Town (by the castle), is a hodgepodge of swirling columns and simple Doric capitals. The first altar on the left after you enter looks like the tomb of a pirate: it's done entirely with inlaid black-and-white marble and uses skulls and crossbones as capitals. The church invites you to donate money to "souls burning in hell"—a kind of Western Union cable to the damned. Right around the corner, a fee of L4,000 will get you into the **Acquario Tirrenico** (Castel Dragone, tel. 0185/773375; open daily 10–noon and 3–7, in winter Tues.–Thurs. 10–noon, Fri.–Sun. 10–noon and 2:30–6; L4,000), a modern aquarium housed in the crumbling remains of an old castle.

BASICS

Camogli's **train station** (V. XX Settembre, tel. 1478/88088) is on the Genoa–La Spezia line. Trains run to Santa Margherita (3 per hour, 6 min, L1,700), Genoa (3 per hour, 35 min, L2,500), and Milan (3 daily, 2½ hrs, L14,000). The **Tigullio** bus from Camogli's train station to Santa Margherita (17 daily, 30 min, L2200) isn't as quick as the train, but it offers excellent views of the sea. **Boat service** to the tiny cliffside monastery of San Fruttuoso (L13,000 round trip; more frequent service in summer) is offered by **Golfo Paradiso** (Via Scalo 2, tel. 0185/772091). In summer, try **Tigullio** (tel. 0185/284670) for service to Portofino. Across the street and to the right of the train station you'll find the **IAT tourist office** (V. XX Settembre 33/R, tel. 0185/771066; open Mon.–Sat. 8:15–12:15 and 3:30–6, Sun. 9:30–12:30).

If you're traveling through Camogli on the second Sunday in May, you'll witness the Sagra del Pesce (Blessing of the Fish), a blessing for you if you're hungry: fried sardines cooked in huge kettles of oil (weighing more than 200 pounds) are on the house.

WHERE TO SLEEP AND EAT

Check hotel availability at the tourist office if you happen to fall in love with the town and decide to stay. **Aurelia** (V. Aurelia 249, 16032, tel. 0185/770281; cash only) is a classic small-town inn perched above Camogli. Doubles with bath run L100,000 year-round. To reach Aurelia from the train station, take the bus to Ruta, and head southeast on Via Aurelia just beyond the arch. **La Camogliese** (V. Garibaldi 55, 16032, tel. 0185/771402), in front of the train station, has big, spotless rooms with private bath and TV for L90,000–L110,000, and the affable management will give you advice on everything from restaurants to hiking trails. The restaurants in the town center take advantage of the few dining choices, but you can find down-home cooking and typical Ligurian fare at the modestly priced **Trattoria del Boschetto** (V. P. Risso 33, tel. 0185/771068). Other than that, focaccerias line the seaside promenade.

If the gourmet in you is feeling neglected, the effort to get to **Trattoria Barache** (Località San Nicolò 6/R, tel. 0185/770184; closed Tues.) is well worth it. Sisters Martola and Luigia produce edible ecstasy for any unsuspecting non-Italian. Don't leave without trying the lasagna al pesto, *tortelloni di ortiche* (melt-in-your-mouth spinach-stuffed homemade pasta), and oven-fresh focaccia *al formaggio* (with cheese). Good luck waddling back up to the bus stop after your meal. Take the bus to San Rocco (hourly, L2,200; change at Ruta) and then the footpath behind the church toward Punta Chiappa/San Nicolò.

SANTA MARGHERITA LIGURE

In a setting worthy of Captain Steubing, the town epitomizes the Riviera, with brightly colored flower stands, expanses of palm fronds, pastel houses, and one too many lapdogs on semiprecious leashes walking their bronzed owners. Easily accessible trains, buses, and bikes make comfortable day trips out of neighboring Portofino, Camogli, and Rapallo, or you can just while the day away on Santa Margherita's small but pleasant beach. Between seaside snoozes, investigate the **Basilica di Santa Margherita** (P. Caprera), a testament to Baroque ornateness with its crystal chandeliers and abundant gold leaf.

BASICS

The **IAT** office (V. XXV Aprile 2/B, tel. 0185/287485; open Mon.–Sat. 9:30–12:30 and 3:30–6:30, in winter Mon.–Sat. 9:30–12:30 and 2:30–5:30, Sun. 9:30–12:30) has an eager staff and detailed information on the Riviera di Levante.

SAN FRUTTUOSO

Legend says the village of San Fruttuoso, tucked away in a secluded bay, was first populated when St. Prospero, a Spanish bishop, fled Arab occupation and took refuge in this inlet in 711. Today the port is overshadowed by the Abbazia di San Fruttuoso di Capodimonte, a 10th-century monastery and restored 13th-century abbey, now the property of a national conservation fund. A simple structure with a wooden interior, the abbey houses a replica of a bronze statue of Christ with his hands raised to the sky. The original "Christ of the Abyss"— weighing in at 3 tons—was immersed under water by locals to honor San Fruttuoso's divers lost at sea.

For a breathtaking view of the entire bay, climb to the top of the medieval Torre Andrea Doria. Admission to the tower and abbey is L8,000, and it's open Tuesday–Sunday 10–6 (sporadically 10–4 in winter). The town is accessible by boats (hourly in summer, 1–2 per day in winter) from Portofino (L10,000 round trip), Santa Margherita Ligure (L19,000 round trip), and Rapallo (L25,000 round trip), operated by Servizio Marittimo del Tigullio (in Portofino, tel. 0185/284670), and from Camogli (operated by Golfo Paradiso, 0185/772091), but it's best to hike to it. From Portofino's main piazza, continue up the main street to the dirt trail on your left. The hike (1½ hrs, 6 km or 3½ mi) leads you along cobblestone paths and through olive groves; follow the red dots marking the path. A more arduous trail (3 hrs) leads all the way to Camogli, and ambitious hikers can hike Camogli–Portofino through San Fruttuoso in a day. If you decide to stay or want a great dinner, head to Albergo da Giovanni (Casa Portale 23, tel. 0185/770047 or 0185/774002).

COMING AND GOING

Santa Margherita is on the Genoa–La Spezia train line. The ticket window and luggage deposit at the train station (P. Nobili, tel. 1478/88088) are open daily 7 AM–9 PM. Trains to Genoa (40 min, L2,500) run every 40 minutes. Trains also run to Milan (3 daily, 2½ hrs, L16,500) and Rapallo (every 20 min, 5 min, L1,700). Local **buses** leave from Piazza Vittorio Veneto (along the Lungomare). Buy bus tickets at the **Tigullio** bus information office (P. Vittorio Veneto, tel. 0185/288834; open daily 7:10 AM–7:40 PM, winter until 5:40) or from the vending machine just outside the office. Buses leave every 40 minutes for Camogli (35 min, L2,000), Portofino (25 min, L1,700), and Rapallo (30 min, L1,400).

WHERE TO SLEEP

The nearest camping is in Rapallo, just a six-minute train ride or a 30-minute bus ride away.

UNDER L90,000 • Albergo Annabella. This is a comfortable, quiet hotel with dark green walls and antique furniture. The food, if you decide to take pension, is good. Doubles without pension run L90,000. *V. Costasecca 10, 16038, tel. 0185/286531. From P. Vittorio Veneto, walk north on V. Cavour to P. Mazzini, and follow signs to V. Costasecca. 11 rooms without bath. Cash only.*

UNDER L100,000 • Pensione Azalea. If you're exhausted after your journey, this is the place to crash—it's practically across the street from the train station. The comfortable rooms all have views of the bay. Doubles start at L95,000 with breakfast. *V. Roma 60, 16038, tel. 0185/288160. 10 rooms with bath. Cash only.*

WHERE TO EAT

All the restaurants by the water are attractive, but head slightly inland if you want to save money. For good takeout, try **Da Renato** (Largo Amendola 1, tel. 0185/287038); a great hunk of lasagna is L4,000, and fresh seafood salads will run you only L6,000. At **La Paninoteca** (Vico Chiuso Masaniello 5, no phone), communal wooden picnic tables make it easy to meet locals, and you can carve your initials into them (the tables, not the people). Delicious sandwiches and frosty beers make for a perfect midday escape. At **Trattoria da Pezzi** (V. Cavour 21, tel. 0185/285303; closed Sat.), a hearty Ligurian meal including drinks can cost as little as L14,000.

AFTER DARK

The decor is reminiscent of Disneyland's Pirates of the Caribbean ride, but **Cutty Sark** (V. Roma 35, tel. 0185/287009) is a good place to hang. It stays open until 2 AM and tap beers start at L4,000.

OUTDOOR ACTIVITIES

Hiking trails connect Santa Margherita with neighboring coastal and mountain villages; get a map from the tourist office. **Bici a Noleggio** (V. Roma 1, no phone) rents bikes for L7,000 per hour (L3,500 after 3 PM) and L35,000 per day. They also rent mopeds hourly (L15,000) and daily (L70,000). Bike between Santa Margherita Ligure and Portofino (20 min) for a breezy view of the coast, but only if you're willing to dodge cars whipping around blind cliffside turns.

NEAR SANTA MARGHERITA LIGURE

PORTOFINO

In the '70s and '80s, Portofino was a prime "champagne wishes and caviar dreams" hot spot. But the town was hardly a new discovery; British tourists have been flocking to Portofino since the mid-1800s, and pirates had been stopping by for hundreds of years before that. Nowadays, the flood of yachts and yacht owners has slowed to a stream of curious, deep-pocketed older Americans, Brits, and Germans with braided belts and rose-tinted sunglasses. But a look at the cozy port carved out of the Ligurian hills, with tiny pastel houses lining its famous curve in the coast, will help explain why Portofino is one of the oldest pure-bred tourist towns on Earth.

Despite its late decline in popularity, Portofino's minuscule seafront is still taken up entirely by boats, so unless you happen to have a yacht handy or have somehow managed to charm the owner of one, swimming is not an option. Instead, get a hiking trail map from the **IAT** tourist information office (V. Roma 35, tel. 0185/269024). The half-hour hike up the well-marked hilly path past Chiesa di San Giorgio to **Hotel Splendido** (V. Baratta 13) affords an awe-inspiring view of the sea and a glimpse of the lifestyles of the rich and catatonic, who cook themselves by a swimming pool for nearly a million lire a night. A slightly more rugged hike up to the ruins of **Castello di San Giorgio** (Castello Brown) (V. La Peninsula, tel. 0185/26933) also takes around 45 minutes and affords views approaching perfection. A longer outing is to the **Abbey of San Fruttuoso** (*see box* San Fruttuoso, *above*), a two-hour hike or 15-minute boat ride. If you come to wallet-shrinking Portofino, don't plan on sleeping here; take the boat from Santa Margherita (10 min; L6,000 one-way, L10,000 round-trip). Buses also run from Santa Margherita every 20 minutes (25 min, L1,700).

RAPALLO

At first glance, Rapallo seems like just another high-priced, tourist-filled Levante town, but it's actually an appealing place to stay, with several affordable hotels and campgrounds. You'll spot honest-to-goodness Italian residents here, not just foreign visitors. Hike up to Montallegro, in the hills above Rapallo, to see the striking 16th-century **Sanctuary of Montallegro**, which enshrines a Byzantine icon called the Madonna di Montallegro. An expansive daily **market** is held every morning in the main piazza, where you can buy fruit, flowers, fish, bread, and cheese, among other things. During the first three days of July, Rapallo celebrates the Virgin with incredible fireworks and general partying in the streets. Contact Rapallo's **tourist office** (Via A. Diaz 9, tel. 0185/230346) for info on sights or festivals.

WHERE TO SLEEP, EAT, AND BE MERRY • Albergo Bandoni (V. Marsala 24, 16035, tel. 0185/ 50423) is top-notch, with terraces overlooking the water and stuccoed rooms for L70,000–L80,000 (more in summer). You'll also find one of the area's only two campgrounds here: **Campeggio Miraflores** (V. Savagna 10, 16035, tel. 0185/263000; cash only; closed mid-Oct.–Easter), where camping costs L8,000 per person, and a campsite is L14,000; bring your own tent. From the train station, take the bus (every 20 min, L1,500) toward San Pietro or Santa Maria, getting off near the autostrada, or walk the 1½ km (1 mi). Vittles at **Da Ardito** (V. Canale 9, San Pietro di Novella, tel. 0185/51551; closed Mon. and Feb.) are on the expensive side, and you need a reservation (at least they take plastic), but it has a primo wine list; for a change from seafood, try the *pansoti alla salsa di noci*. The young and old in Rapallo stay out until all hours on the weekends at dance clubs, gelaterias, and piano bars (on Saturday) that double as pizzerias. **Lungomare Vittorio Veneto,** along the water, is dotted with piano bars, some with open mikes so you can croon along to Stevie Wonder and Neil Diamond. The simpler and perhaps more appealing option is to take a *passeggiata* (stroll) at dusk along the beach with a *gelato* in hand. From Santa Margherita, trains (5 min, L1,700) and Tigullio buses (10 min, L1,700) run every 20 minutes to Rapallo.

CINQUE TERRE

The cluster of five tiny villages—Monterosso al Mare, Vernazza, Corniglia, Manarola, and Riomaggiore running west to east—called Cinque Terre (Five Coasts) is the Cinderella of the Italian Riviera. In their rugged simplicity, these old fishing towns seem to mock the caked-on artifice of glitzy neighboring resorts. With a clear blue sea in the foreground, multicolored buildings emerge almost seamlessly from cliffs, and rocky mountains rise precipitously to gravity-defying vineyards and dusty olive groves. Both the natural geography and the government's protection of the region have prevented major expansion, so the small towns can't help but retain their enchanting intimacy. One word of warning: Cinque Terre has been long discovered and, like all hot spots, is slightly overrun by hikers and desperados looking for bed and beach space. You can hike along the Cinque Terre in about five hours taking in the endless views, which makes for a great day excursion from one of the villages or from Santa Margherita, Rapallo, or Genoa (*see* Outdoor Activities, *below*). Be sure to call ahead if you plan to stay here in summer, and remember that the towns merit both their popularity and their visitors' respect.

Farthest west is **Monterosso al Mare,** the largest, most touristed, and most expensive of the towns—a good place to take care of business (sending mail and changing money) but a lousy place to find a hotel. It does have the sandiest beaches, however, and offers the 14th-century hillside Castello Cappuccini and the Chiesa Cappuccini (up V. Bastione from the station; open daily 9–noon and 4–7). The latter, built in 1619, houses a *Crucifixion* by Van Dyck. Vernazza, Manarola, and Riomaggiore are more appealing. **Vernazza**'s irresistible allure lies in its cozy natural harbor framed by pastel buildings and a compact piazza. You can climb the octagonal bell tower of the 14th-century church dedicated to Santa Margherita, on a hill overlooking Vernazza's piazza and the water. From its tiny windows, you can see the port and the entire area. Next along the line is isolated **Corniglia,** offering the best swimming off of its rocks, then **Manarola,** a beautiful and delicate village perched implausibly on a steep bluff dropping straight down to the sea and a tiny harbor. Manarola is the center of the region's formidable winemaking, and home to a wonderful new youth hostel. The tight-knit community of **Riomaggiore** shares one common alarm clock: church bells attempt to wake even the dead every morning at 7. The most locally inhabited of the five (and best connected to La Spezia by highway), Riomaggiore has also attracted many artists.

BASICS

The **Associazione Turistica Pro Loco** (V. Fegina 38, tel. and fax 0187/817506; open Mon.–Sat. 10–noon and 5–7:30, Sun. 10–noon; shorter hrs in winter), just outside the Monterosso train station, has helpful employees and lots of info about hotels, boat rides, and hiking trails. The **Cassa di Risparmio della Spezia** (V. Roma 49, tel. 0187/817509; open weekdays 8:10–1:10 and 2:45–5:45), in Monterosso, has good rates and only charges a L3,000 commission. Monterosso also has a **post office** (V. Roma 73, tel. 0187/818394; open weekdays 8–1:30, Sat. 8–noon).

COMING AND GOING

Train service to Cinque Terre is good: Take the hourly local (slow) train from either Genoa or La Spezia, which stops at each town. Many faster trains stop only at Monterosso and Riomaggiore. The towns are only a few minutes apart by train; trips cost L1,700 Between Easter and October, various boats connect the towns (but not Corniglia, which has no port); a boat from Monterosso al Mare to Vernazza departs hourly (L4,000 one-way or L6,000 round-trip). Trips between towns take about 15 minutes. There is also a boat from Nervi's *portocciolo* (in Genoa) that runs in summer. Most towns have only one narrow road, so buses and taxis are not a viable option, but you can navigate the towns with your own car.

WHERE TO SLEEP

Because this area is so trendy, places to sleep fill up early, especially in the high season, and reservations are necessary. If you get stuck, talk to Ivo at the gelateria in Riomaggiore (sounds like finding a rave, doesn't it?), and he'll do his best to set you up. Riomaggiore, Vernazza, and Corniglia have the best lodging in terms of both price and atmosphere; hotels in Monterosso al Mare are ridiculously overpriced and often insist that you take full pension in the high season. Affitacamere abound, especially in tiny Riomaggiore; look for signs posted on houses or ask the first matronly person you encounter. Often these are not just rooms in people's homes but whole separate apartments, fully equipped with a bathroom, kitchen, terrace, and a spectacular view. In the low season, prices are generally negotiable. If you call ahead, reservations are possible at all places listed below, except the hostel.

UNDER L75,000 • Luciano and Roberto Fazioli. The Fazioli brothers rent out an assortment of rooms and apartments around Riomaggiore that range from tiny and immaculate to grandiose and slightly rank—ask to see the place before agreeing to pay the average fee of L30,000 per person. The cost is the same regardless of whether you get a bath or kitchen, so you might as well go whole hog. Call ahead, and someone will meet you at the train station to escort you to your place. *Via Colombo 94 and Via Tracastello 132; tel. 0187/920587 or 0187/920904, mobile 0368/442051.*

UNDER L90,000 • Pensione Barbara. In Vernazza's main piazza, this pension has pleasant rooms, some overlooking the port, for L90,000 per double. From the nine rooms that share two bathrooms and one shower, you just might hear a sax playing "The Pink Panther" or "Feelings." The family-run restaurant downstairs serves tasty food. *P. Marconi 23, 19018, tel. 0187/812201. 9 rooms without bath. Closed Dec.–Jan.*

Rumor has it that halfway through the main trail between Corniglia and Vernazza is a bridge that leads to a nudist beach.

UNDER L115,000 • Hotel Ca' d'Adrean. This hotel is a bit pricey but well worth it. The 10 rooms are absolutely immaculate, and there's a TV lounge downstairs where you can chat with the sweet couple who own the place. Doubles with full bath are L110,000. *V. A. Discovolo 101, Manarola 19010, tel. 0187/920040, fax 0187/920452. From train station, turn right after tunnel and walk 300 ft uphill. 10 rooms with bath. Cash only. Closed Nov.*

HOSTELS • Ostello Cinque Terre. New in '98, this Manarola hostel has taken on Mamma Rosa's (*see below*) in an epic battle for backpacker dollars and, by most accounts, won easily. It's not hard to see why, with very clean rooms, facilities like a solarium, outdoor terrace, e-mail access, and telephones, and good, cheap meals (L7,000 per course) served nightly. Beds cost L25,000 per person. The hostel is across from Manarola's church. *V. Riccobaldi 21, Manarola 19010, tel. 0187/920215, e-mail ostello£cdh.it, www.cinqueterre.net/ostello. Closed most of Nov. Reserve ahead in summer.*

Rifugio Mamma Rosa. Mamma Rosa's is the best specimen of the peculiar budget-traveler subculture that has sprung up in the Cinque Terre (and all over Europe); in the past few years, Mamma Rosa has earned almost a cult following among a certain set, cheerfully ignoring such trivialities as lockouts and curfews and calling around to find you a place if her hostel's full. In spite of the opening of the Cinque Terre Hostel (*see above*), hers is clearly still a hot spot for backpackers' evening social gatherings. However, the hostel is also redolent of cats—and cat hair. Regardless of Mamma Rosa's popularity, her bathrooms are subpar and budget travelers are packed into rooms like sardines (L25,000 per person). Of course, that may or may not be a good thing, depending on your goals. *P. Unità 2, Riomaggiore 19017, tel. 0187/920050. Head straight out of train station and turn right immediately at weathered sign. 60 beds. Cash only. Reserve ahead in summer.*

CAMPING • The closest campground is in neighboring Levanto. **Acquadolce** (V. Guido Semenza 5, 19010, tel. 0187/808465; sometimes closed Dec.–Jan.) charges L9,000 per person (L11,000 in high season), plus L9,000 for a small tent and L14,000–L15,000 for a large one. Take the five-minute ride on the Genoa–La Spezia train from Cinque Terre to Levanto (twice hourly, L1,700).

WHERE TO EAT

For snacks or bag lunches, locals go to the popular **Focacceria Il Frantoio** (V. Gioberti 1, off V. Roma, tel. 0187/818333), in Monterosso. Crammed between clothing stalls along Monterosso's waterfront every morning is an **open-air market** with fresh cheeses, fruits, veggies, roasted chickens, and deep-fried seafood. There are also a couple basic supermarkets in Vernazza and Riomaggiore. **Vecchio Rio** (V. T. Signori 30, Riomaggiore, tel. 0187/920173) serves nice, heaping portions. Try spaghetti Vecchio Rio (L13,000), a seafood pasta spiced with curry. There's a terrace for outside dining. **Controvelaccio**

(V. Columbo 237, Riomaggiore, tel. 0187/920820; closed Thurs.) produces some of the best pasta sauces in Liguria. The penne al pesto is amazing, and the unusual spaghetti *all'oliva* (with olives) is a rich creamy dish made with black olives. The tourist menu (L22,000; cash only), with pasta, fresh seafood, and a salad, is a bargain. The absolutely best food at a bargain can be found at **Ristorante Bar da Cecio** (Corniglia, on the main piazza, tel. 0187/812043; closed Wed.). Try the house specialty, *risotto alla Cecio,* a huge clay pot of rice and fresh seafood in a tasty tomato-cream base, or sample delicious gnocchi al pesto. Nice rooms are also rented upstairs for L90,000 per double. Enjoy your view of the sea with a bottle of Cinque Terre's sweet white wine (try scacchetra). For info about visits to winemaking centers and wine-tasting events, contact the **Cooperativa Agricoltura di Riomaggiore, Manarola, Corniglia, Vernazza e Monterosso** (tel. 0187/920435) at Groppo, just outside Manarola.

AFTER DARK

There are a few cheesy discos in Monterosso, where tanned *ragazzi* (kids) peacock around. Some cafés stay open until 2 AM, so you can get coffee, alcohol, and food until late. **Caffè Cagliari** (V. Roma 13, tel. 0187/817164) is a trendy coffeehouse replete with posters of Quentin Tarantino movies and the Smiths plastered on the walls. It gets packed around midnight.

OUTDOOR ACTIVITIES

A visit to Cinque Terre should revolve around the great outdoors. The best places to go **swimming** are at Monterosso's "sandy" beaches or off the rocks between Corniglia and Vernazza. You can even sunbathe while floating on a paddle boat (L13,000 per hr) off Monterosso's beach. In addition to unbelievably clear blue waters, Cinque Terre is famous for its **hiking,** which is the best way to see the vineyards, olive groves, and the sea. Following a series of well-marked trails will get you from one town to the next; some of the 7-km (4½-mi) hike is steep and narrow. It's a good idea to check with the tourist office about trail conditions, as some trails are periodically closed either for improvement or due to torrential rains that sometimes submerge them in mud and water.

It is easier to walk in the Monterosso-to-Riomaggiore direction (west to east) than vice versa because of relative elevations. Taken this way, the hardest and longest trail is from Monterosso to Vernazza (1½ hrs), most of which is uphill. The hike from Vernazza to Corniglia (1½ hrs) is less strenuous, but you'll still think Corniglia looks like the Emerald City of Oz after all the hilly terrain. Along the way, amid cacti and olive groves, you'll find **Bar Il Gabbiano** (tel. 0187/812192), a pit stop with a view. It specializes in pastries like *crostate* (tarts) baked in a wood-burning oven and sciacchetrà wine. The next leg between Corniglia and Manarola (1 hr) is down by the cliff line, and the last easy stroll from Manarola to Riomaggiore (30 min) is so famous that it has its own name—**Via dell'Amore.** At night courting couples (and graffiti artists) make it live up to its appellation. **Trail 6,** one of the area's most difficult hikes, is a terrific alternate route if you want to do the Manarola–Corniglia segment with fewer tourists. The untrodden trail starts immediately to the right of the tunnel outside Manarola's train station and takes about three hours, winding through endless terraced vineyards and flowers sprouting out of stone steps on the way to Corniglia.

BOLOGNA AND EMILIA-ROMAGNA

7

BY SARAH BREMER WITH JEANINE GADE

UPDATED BY ROBIN GOLDSTEIN

Take a look at the map, and you'll see that most of the towns in Emilia-Romagna line up in a row. This is because each was once an outpost that straddled the Via Emilia, a road the Romans built in 187 BC. Through the Middle Ages the towns were built up, reinforced, and fought over, and they later flourished under the control of ruthless families that—although not doing much for their subjects—cultivated the arts and hosted some of the greatest artists and intellects of their age. The world's first university was founded in Bologna in 1088; Dante hung out in Ravenna after being booted out of his native Florence; rulers financed painters, sculptors, and writers; and the world's first cookbook and opera were written here. More recently, the province gave birth to film director Federico Fellini, tenor Luciano Pavarotti, and Vasco Rossi, Italy's cult daddy of rock and roll.

After their Renaissance heyday, the towns were taken over by the Papacy until the two regions—Emilia to the west, Romagna to the east—were brought together under Italian unification. You might not notice much difference between the two regions, but the towns themselves are unique in their size and feel and are easily explored thanks to frequent train service. The main hub is Bologna, the regional capital and a beautiful and lively city in its own right. And though Emilia-Romagna has become one of Italy's most prosperous regions, travelers drained by northern Italy's high prices can take heart that the progressive local governments, supported by citizens who know how to prosper without forgetting to stop and smell the roses, often subsidize concerts and cultural events. Aside from the Adriatic resorts, which become infested with sun worshipers in August, Emilia-Romagna hosts surprisingly few tourists. Those who do come might be tempted to turn a pit stop into a lifelong visit.

Don't be put off because the cuisine of the region is known throughout Italy as *la grassa* (the fat)—they also say that *"si mangia bene"* ("one eats well") in Emilia-Romagna. This is no trivial statement. A few minutes in any of these towns and you'll see why many of the best things gracing the Italian table come from the region, like Parma's sublime *prosciutto crudo* (cured pork leg sliced paper thin) and the famous *parmigiano reggiano* (Parmesan cheese), the intensely flavored, crumbly cheese savored in pieces as well as grated over pasta—not remotely familiar to the American imitation in the green can—and real heady balsamic vinegar from Modena. This is also the land of fresh pasta rolled into dozens of different shapes. Typical Emilian pastas include *tagliatelle* (a flat, wide pasta generally served with a rich meat sauce known everywhere else as *bolognese,* but here as *ragu*), tortellini (pasta shaped like a belly button, filled with meat), and *tortelloni* and *tortelli* (pasta filled with ricotta and spinach). In Romagna you'll find the Roman-derived *piadina* (unleavened bread filled with cold cuts, cheeses, veggies, or even Nutella) and the affordable and ever-present *crescioni* (cheese- and veggie-filled pastry pockets).

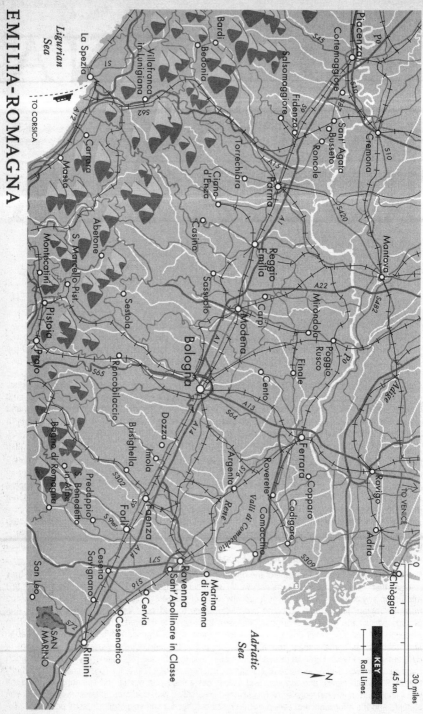

EMILIA-ROMAGNA

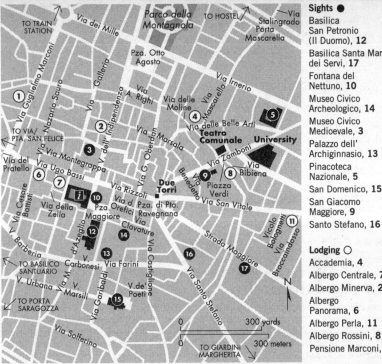

Sights ●

Basilica
San Petronio
(Il Duomo), **12**

Basilica Santa Maria
dei Servi, **17**

Fontana del
Nettuno, **10**

Museo Civico
Archeologico, **14**

Museo Civico
Medioevale, **3**

Palazzo dell'
Archiginnasio, **13**

Pinacoteca
Nazionale, **5**

San Domenico, **15**

San Giacomo
Maggiore, **9**

Santo Stefano, **16**

Lodging ○

Accademia, **4**

Albergo Centrale, **7**

Albergo Minerva, **2**

Albergo
Panorama, **6**

Albergo Perla, **11**

Albergo Rossini, **8**

Pensione Marconi, **1**

BOLOGNA

Bologna is sure to bedazzle. Renaissance architects went to great lengths to distinguish Bologna from Florence, and the result is one of the most spectacular skylines in Italy, with a sea of red rooftops and gracefully arched porticoes interrupted only by towers and domes rising skyward. But appearances aside, Bologna truly has spirit: it's crowded, it's cosmopolitan, and with 80,000 students attending the world's oldest university—founded in 1088—it's a great place for cultural events. Bologna is also known as one of the few greatest food towns in Italy, with outstanding *osterie,* restaurants, and *salumerie.* The town is also thought to be more than a little left-leaning. Priests, pundits, poets, professors, communists, gluttons, and musicians pass each other nonchalantly on the street, earning the city its well-known moniker: *la Dotta, la Grassa, e la Rossa* (the Learned, the Fat, and the Red). More or less untouched, and certainly unmarred, by foreign tourists, Bologna is one of the best-hidden gems on the boot, encapsulating the lushness of Italy's culture, heritage, and food.

BASICS

CHANGING MONEY

You'll find banks with ATMs along Via Rizzoli and Via Marconi. You can also change money at the train station.

DISCOUNT TRAVEL AGENCIES

Centro Turistico Studentesco (CTS; Largo Respighi 2/F, tel. 051/261802 or 051/234862; open weekdays 9–12:30 and 2:30–6) offers travel discounts, particularly on plane tickets, to students under 26 with ID. ISIC card equivalents are also sold. From Due Torri, take Via Zamboni, and at Piazza Verdi go left on Largo Respighi.

ENGLISH-LANGUAGE BOOKS AND NEWSPAPERS

Feltrinelli International (V. Zamboni 7/B, tel. 051/268070 or 051/268210; open Mon.–Sat. 9–7:30) has a decent English-language section, including books and tapes for those learning Italian, and a TV upstairs exclusively showing CNN (don't confuse this with the non-English-language Feltrinelli on V. dei Giudei). For English newspapers, check the newsstands on Via Ugo Bassi and Via Rizzoli.

LAUNDRY

Wash and Dry (Via Petroni 38, near the University zone and Via Zamboni, tel. 051/237174), is open daily 9–9. Big washing machines (made in the USA) with English instructions will wash and dry in an hour, but in the meantime you can entertain yourself with music, drinks, and TV.

MAIL, PHONES, AND E-MAIL

The **phone office** (P. VIII Agosto 24) is open daily 7 AM–10:30 PM. The **post office** at Piazza Minghetti (tel. 051/237239) is open weekdays 8:15–6:30 and Saturday 8:15–12:20. Free **E-mail access** can be found at **Ufficio per le Relazioni con il Pubblico** (P. Maggiore 6 (tel. 051/203184; open Mon.–Sat. 8:30–7), but you have to book ahead.

PHARMACIES

Most pharmacies in Bologna alternate staying open all night, but **Farmacia Comunale Centrale** (P. Maggiore 6, tel. 051/238509) is open 24 hours. For emergency medical service, call 113.

VISITOR INFORMATION

APT tourist offices can be found at the train station (tel. 051/246541; open Mon.–Sat. 9–1 and 2:30–7), airport (tel. 051/6472036; open 8:30–3 and 4–8), and in the town center (P. Maggiore 6, Palazzo Comunale, tel. 051/239660; open Mon.–Sat. 9–7 and Sun. 9–2). In addition to the usual info, they can help with accommodations. For on-line information and events listings, try www.comune.bologna.it. **Bologna Online** (V. Tordaro 6, tel. 051/247536) has another guide at www.bolognaonline.it which even includes movie listings in English.

GAY AND LESBIAN RESOURCES • ARCI Gay (P. di Porta, Saragozza 2, 40123, tel. 051/6447054).

COMING AND GOING

Bologna's **train station** (P. Medaglie d'Oro, tel. 1478/88088 toll-free) is a major rail hub. More than 20 trains depart daily to Milan (2 hrs 20 min, L22,300) and to Rome (3½ hrs, L35,000) via Florence (50 min, L13,200). Trains also run frequently to Genoa (4 hrs, L29,000), Venice (2 hrs, L18,800), and Ancona (2 hrs, L21,400). The station's info desk is open daily 7–9. A supplement of L5,000–L8,500 is charged on many of these routes for the InterCity trains. There's also 24-hour luggage storage (L5,000 per 12 hrs).

Regional **buses**, though generally less efficient than trains, leave from the **Autostazione,** P. XX Settembre at V. dell'Indipendenza (tel. 051 290 290).

Bologna's **Guglielmo Marconi Airport** (Borgo Panigale, tel. 051/6479615; open 6 AM–midnight), named after the inventor of the radio, born just outside town, has flights to several other cities in Italy and Europe, including seven daily to Rome and three to Milan. The **ATC** runs Aerobuses to and from the airport, city center (from V. Ugo Bassi at the Mercato delle Erbe), and the train station (20 min). Buses run every half hour 6:30 AM–11 PM, and you buy tickets (L7,000) on board.

GETTING AROUND

Though Bologna is a major Italian city, it has the look and feel of a small town, and all of the major attractions are concentrated in the *centro storico* (historic center). Piazza Maggiore—with one of the finest groupings of public buildings in all of Italy—and most of the hotels are less than a 15-minute walk from the train station, so you'll probably only need the bus when you're lugging your luggage. From the station go through Piazza XX Settembre to Via dell'Indipendenza/Via Massimo d'Azeglio, which runs north–south and will take you (past a long string of outdoor vendors) to the town center, toward **Via Ugo Bassi/Via Rizzoli** (which runs east–west). The city walls are punctuated by 12 city *porte* (gates), usually connected to streets that one way or another lead to Piazza Maggiore. It's easiest to orient yourself using the **Due Torri,** the leaning medieval towers in Piazza di Porta Ravegnana at the end of Via Rizzoli that are visible from about anywhere. Rent a **bike** at the train station (tel. 051/6302015; open weekdays 6:30 AM–10 PM, Sat. 7–3) for L3,000 per hour, L15,000 per day, or L45,000 per week.

BY BUS

Getting around Bologna is made easy by an efficient system of shiny orange **ATC** buses that crisscross the city. Buses 32 and 33 run around the perimeter of the city walls, starting at the train station and stopping at the city gates along the way. From the station, Buses 11, 17, 25, and 37 head to the center and Piazza Maggiore. Offices at the train station and bus station (P. Galvani 4, tel. 051/350172) have maps and info daily 7–7. Purchase tickets (L1,500), good for one hour, at tobacco shops (marked TABAC-CHI) or newspaper stands. Buses run 5:30 AM–12:30 AM. To call a **taxi,** dial 051/372727.

WHERE TO SLEEP

Unless you stay at the youth hostel or the brand-new campground, accommodations in Bologna are expensive. As for hotels, you won't find a double for less than L70,000, but prices often drop in July and August. Call ahead, especially in summer, when many places shut down for a few weeks. The tourist office at the train station has a list of hotels, and they'll check availability for you.

While wandering through Bologna, be sure to check out the portico at Strada Maggiore 19. Wooden arrows lodged in the ceiling during medieval warfare are still visible today.

UNDER L95,000 • Albergo Minerva. You'll find this a tad institutional, but it's relatively cheap (L90,000 and up for a double), clean, and central. They prefer that you pay cash when you arrive. *V. de Monari 3, 40121, tel. 051/239652. From station, walk south on V. dell'Indipendenza, right on V. de Monari; take Bus 11 or 27. 15 rooms without bath. Cash only.*

Albergo Panorama. The Panorama is one of Bologna's best deals. For L95,000 you get immaculate rooms with TVs, views of Bologna's red rooftops, firm beds, and a pleasant staff that will give you the key and let you come and go as you please. Doubles with bath L120,000, without L95,000; rooms for five L170,000. *V. Livraghi 1, off V. Ugo Bassi between V. Cesare Battisti and V. della Zecca, 40121, tel. 051/221802, fax 051/266360. From train station, take Bus 25 to V. Ugo Bassi. 10 rooms, 2 with bath. Laundry.*

UNDER L100,000 • Pensione Marconi. This hotel is centrally located and not too dingy, but you'll have to put up with a lot of street noise. Plain doubles (L100,000 with bath, L82,000 without) come with high ceilings and a sink. *V. Marconi 22, 40121, tel. 051/262832. From train station, take Bus 21, 30, or 38 for 3 or 4 stops; get off on V. Marconi a block after PAM supermarket. 46 rooms, 20 with bath. Cash only.*

Albergo Perla. Under new management, this simple hotel is slowly shaping up after years of neglect. Plain but reasonably tidy doubles with sink and phone cost L100,000, and the owner likes to practice his English. *V. San Vitale 77/2, 40125, tel. 051/224579, fax 051/391003. From train station, take Bus 32 to V. San Vitale. 10 rooms without bath.*

UNDER L150,000 • Accademia. This spacious hotel is near Piazza Verdi and the university district. Its tidy doubles run L140,000 with bath. Prices drop in July and August. *V. Belle Arti 6, 40126, tel. 051/ 232318, fax 051/263590. 28 rooms, 24 with bath. Cash only.*

Albergo Centrale. As the name says, it is central (a block from the Duomo), and one of the oldest hotels in town. Top-floor rooms have great views, and all rooms are well kept, with TV, soundproof windows, and phones. There's also a lounge with a coffee bar. Doubles run L140,000 with bath, L110,000 without. *V. della Zecca 2, 40121, tel. 051/225114, fax 051/235162. From train station, take Bus 25 to V. Ugo Bassi, get off 1 block before P. Maggiore (look for the big yellow-and-blue sign on your right). 22 rooms, 12 with bath.*

Albergo Rossini. Near Piazza Verdi, the university's main piazza, the Rossini has decent doubles without bath for L100,000, with bath L140,000. The friendly proprietor prides himself on his relaxed establishment, open 24 hours a day, 365 days a year. Though the striped red-and-white curtains and rickety desks scream college dorm room, this hotel is clean and has a lively bar. *V. Bibiena 11, 40126, tel. 051/ 237716, fax 051/268035. From train station, take Bus 50 to P. Verdi/Teatro Comunale and turn right down V. dei Bibiena. 23 rooms, 12 with bath.*

HOSTEL

Ostello per La Gioventù San Sisto (HI). This hostel is far from the center but is housed inside a former villa with peaceful grounds and a comfortable bar, and it's curfew isn't as bad as some. Beds cost L21,000 per night, breakfast included. **Due Torri** (V. Viadagola 5, tel. 051/501810), a satellite hostel down the street, is run by the same management. *V. Viadagola 14, 40121 San Sisto, tel. 051/519202. From train station, walk 2 blocks south to V. dei Mille/V. Irnerio and take Bus 93 or 21B to Località San Sisto. 80 beds. Reception open 7 AM–midnight. Curfew midnight, lockout 10–3:30. Cash only. Closed Dec. 20–Jan. 19.*

WHERE TO EAT

Where to begin? In a country so rich with food traditions and irresistible offerings at table, Bologna just might deserve a special prize. You'd be crazy not to indulge and enjoy, and there is no shortage of places to do so in a city that is known even among Italians as a culinary mecca. A morning walk through the **Mercato delle Erbe** (V. Ugo Bassi 2; open Mon.–Wed. and Fri. 7:15–1 and 5–7, Sat. 7:15–1) and the food shops on the streets around Piazza Maggiore and Via Pescherie Vecchie can be as enriching as a visit to any museum. If you find enough to make a picnic, you can have a seat at **Osteria del Sole** (*see* Bars and Osterie, *below*), where Bolognesi have gone to schmooze over a glass of wine for the last 500 years—though the current owner has only been around for about 50.

Even if there are more important things on your mind than where you will eat your next meal, don't miss the famous **Salsamenteria Tamburini** (V. Vaprarie 1, tel. 051/234726; closed Tues. and Wed. afternoon in winter, Thurs. and Sat. afternoon in summer), a food shop and *antica salumeria* with an aroma as alluring as its deli case. This is the place to sample local cheeses, meats, breads, salads, and vinegars, and take something to go (or sit down to the buffet if you're there at lunchtime). For something sweet, try the pastry shop a few doors down. For those who prefer their Italian food meatless and organically grown, head to **Piccolo Primo Bar Naturale** (V. Riva Reno 114, tel. 051/236389; closed Sun.) for a dose of whole foods. With these (and dozens more) options for a quick bite, plan on at least a few trattoria meals, or at the very least, hit the Mensa (see below) or the **Minestroteca** on Via San Vitale, which serves L5,000–6,000 pasta dishes. (Just say no to the supermarket!)

UNDER L10,000 • Mensa Universitaria. The food at the bright, bustling student dining hall of the legendary University of Bologna will put your *alma mater's* cafeteria to shame—this is Bologna, after all. Most dishes are under L6,000. There's also good conversation to be had with local students, most of whom speak English. *V. Zamboni 47. Open daily for lunch noon–2:30, Mon.–Fri. for dinner 7–9.*

UNDER L15,000 • Trattoria Amedeo. At this simple trattoria you can dig into homemade Bolognese pasta standards like tortellini and tagliatelle; but save room for the wonderful *bollito misto* (assortment of boiled meats and sausages, served with the piquant green sauce *salsa verde*). Fish served on Fridays. *V. Saragozza 88A, in the southwest area, tel. 051/585060. Closed Sun. and Aug.*

Ustaria da Matusel. This restaurant's lurid past as a brothel is immortalized on the walls decorated with murals and an official letter of condemnation. It's particularly busy at lunchtime, and very popular with students. *Primi piatti* (first courses) run L9,000–L11,000. *V. Bertoloni 2, off V. delle Belle Arti, near the Pinacoteca Nazionale. tel. 051/231718. Closed Sun.*

Trattoria & Pizzeria Belle Arti. The pizza and traditional Bolognese pasta dishes are great, the staff is friendly, the ambience puts you at ease, and it's in a cool part of town. What more could you want? *14 Via Belle Arti, tel. 051/225581.*

Clorofilla. This is a safe, meat-free haven in a country always striving to put a little meat on your bones—literally. Veggie burgers, diet and soy desserts, monster salads, American coffee, and organic beer alongside pasta and sandwiches abound; most dishes are L12,000–20,000. *Strada Maggiore 64/C, tel. 051/235343. From Due Torri, take Strada Maggiore east. Closed Sun.*

Serghei. Mamma's in the kitchen makin' sauce and rollin' pasta, and you are lucky to be there to taste the results. Rabbit, chicken, and *osso buco* frequently appear on the menu as *piatti secondi* (second courses), as well as memorable stuffed zucchini. Take a break, then try the *torta di ricotta* (ricotta cake) for dessert. *V. Piella 12, off of V. dell'Indipendenza, 4 blocks north of P. Nettuno, tel.051/233533. No dinner Sat. Closed Sun.*

Trattoria Anna Maria. From the framed black-and-white pictures of actors and singers on the wall—the Teatro Comunale is around the corner—you can tell this place has been a local favorite for years. You'll find all the usual trattoria fare, all *alla Bolognese. V. Belle Arti 17/A, tel. 051/266894. Closed Mon.*

UNDER L20,000 • Da Pietro. Score one for you budget gourmands. You wouldn't necessarily know by the looks of the place, but the food here is just a cut above the already high standards of local eateries, and the prices are just about the same. There's outside dining. *V. dei Falegnami 18/A, off V. dell'Indipendenza, 6 blocks north of P. Nettuno, tel. 051/230644. Closed Sun.*

Teresina. If you can't stand the thought of another bowl of tortellini *in brodo* (in broth) or anything else *alla bolognese,* head over to Terasina for the best Sicilian food north of Rome. *V. Oberdan 4, tel. 051/228985. Closed Sun. and Aug. Cash only.*

Da Cesari. Treat yourself to a semisplurge: traditional food with a modern touch and a light hand. Delicate touches like *tartufi* (truffles) make the *antipasti* heavenly, and the chef has creative takes on dishes like *gramigna alla salsiccia* and braised rabbit. Wash it down with local wine, like Lambrusco and Sangiovese, from Da Cesari's own vineyards (wine also for sale). Across the street is one of Bologna's best-known chocolatiers, Casa Dolciaria Giuseppe Majani. *V. Carbonesi 8, tel. 051/237710. Closed Sun. and Aug.*

CAFFE AND GELATERIE

There are about a hundred *caffè* in the university quarter alone, so don't fear missing your caffeine fix. The hippest (and cheapest—L800 for a coffee) place to sip is the **Bar dello Studente,** with windows overlooking Piazza Verdi. To get there, enter the university building (V. Zamboni 25) on the east corner of Piazza Verdi and go up one flight of stairs. It's open weekdays 9:30–7:30 and closes in August. Near the Duomo, watch the bartender's hands whiz at about 30 cups per minute as the morning crowd packs into **Mocambo** (V. d'Azeglio 1/E, tel. 051/229516) for their creamed coffee. You could, meanwhile, shell out L4,000 to do the espresso thing at **Bar Giuseppe** (P. Maggiore 1, tel. 051/264444) facing the Duomo, but you're better off grabbing a cone of their coveted Pino brand of gelato and eating it on the Duomo steps. Perhaps Bologna's most famous *gelateria,* though, is **La Sorbetteria Castiglione,** worth the long walk up Via Castiglione (44 Via Castiglione, tel. 051/233257); if you continue up V. Castiglione, you can walk around **Giardini Margherita** (see below) with your delectable ice cream. **Gelateria delle Moline** (V. delle Moline 13, tel. 051/248470; closed Tues.), off the east end of Via delle Belle Arti, makes not only gelato, but also a *granita al caffè con panna* (coffee slushy with whipped cream; L4,500). At **Gelateria Ugo** (V. San Felice 24, off V. Ugo Bassi, tel. 051/263849; closed Nov.–Feb., and Mon.–Tues.), indulge in a delicious twist on the ice-cream sandwich: gelato stuffed inside warm raisin focaccia and topped with whipped cream (L4,000).

WORTH SEEING

You might be content strolling under Bologna's shady porticoes (come rain or shine, you'll be dry wherever you go) or people-watching in the shadow of the Duomo and the naughty Neptune Fountain in Piazza Maggiore, but don't get so swept away that you miss visiting Bologna's architectural and artistic treasures. Even if you've seen enough churches to merit sainthood, explore the ancient labyrinth of Santo Stefano, see the Duomo, and make the pilgrimage to San Luca. The medieval museum has an exceptional collection of artifacts, and the National Gallery houses a few must-sees as well. Although the venerable **Università di Bologna,** the world's oldest, doesn't have a distinct campus, students congregate in the streets northeast of the Due Torri and around Via Zamboni. In late July and August, Bologna can be hellishly hot: beware of scalding afternoons and plan on a siesta as the locals do.

BASILICA SAN PETRONIO (IL DUOMO) AND PIAZZA MAGGIORE

The plans for this 14th-century basilica were so ambitious that, according to one account, its construction was curtailed by a papal decree to prevent it from surpassing St. Peter's in size. On either side of the triangular brick facade, the transepts abruptly cut through the windows, allowing you to see the exact point at which the Duomo grew too large. From the piazza, the basilica's unassuming red façade is refreshing in its starkness. Also notice that the marble runs out before reaching the top—a good indication that the money ran out as well. Other noteworthy features include the Gothic arches, Parmigianino's *San Rocco,* the frescoes by Giovanni da Modena, and the interestingly complex sundial on the floor (the sun shines through a slit in the wall and marks the time). Take a moment to check out the rest of this much-admired piazza, with Palazzo Comunale (town hall), Palazzo del Podestà (once next to the Torre dell'Arengo, whose bells were rung when the city celebrated, mourned, or called its citizens to arms), Palazzo di Re Enzo (named after a Sardinian king who was imprisoned there in the 13th century), and the Fountain of Neptune at the middle. *P. Maggiore, tel. 051/225442. Open Apr.–Sept. 7:30–1:30 and 2:30–7:30, Oct.–Mar. 7–1 and 2–7. Museum open Mon. and Wed.–Sun. 10–10:20.*

FONTANA DEL NETTUNO

The original version of this fountain in Bologna's Piazza Maggiore—with Neptune's monumental endowment, highly erotic cherubim, and breast-clenching sirens—was vetoed by the Catholic Church as indecent, so sculptor Giambologna had to manipulate Neptune's left arm in the interest of modesty. Any doubt why it was nicknamed Il Gigante? If you enter Piazza Maggiore from Via Rizzoli at Via dell'Indipendenza, veer right up the slope that leads to the memorial wall; look at Neptune's left thumb from this angle and decide for yourself if Giambologna suffered any artistic castration.

BASILICA SANTA MARIA DEI SERVI

If you're sweltering in the heat of summer, the interior of this well-preserved Gothic church provides a cool, relaxing respite. Cross through the porticoed courtyard and enter the basilica to see Cimabue's *Blessed Virgin* and Vitale da Bologna's fading 14th-century frescoes. *Strada Maggiore 43, tel. 051/226807. Open daily 7–11:45 and 3:30–7:45.*

BASILICA SANTUARIO DELLA MADONNA DI SAN LUCA

This 19th-century tribute to the Virgin Mary is perched high above Bologna, 3 km (2 mi) from the city center. The church can be reached on foot from Via Saragozza by following the city's longest portico, supported by 666 arches. Thousands of pilgrims make the arduous climb each year during Easter. The basilica's interior is nothing special, but the view is well worth the trek. It's also an ideal spot for a picnic. *V. di San Luca 36, tel. 051/6142339. From train station, take Bus 20 or 94 to steps on V. Saragozza: From Due Torri, head south on V. Castiglione, turn right on V. L. Farini, veer left on V. Collegio di Spagna (which becomes V. Saragozza), follow signs to basilica. Open 7–12:30 and 2:30–7 (until 5:30 in winter and on Sun.).*

MUSEO CIVICO ARCHEOLOGICO

This museum is known for its art and artifacts from prehistoric times through the Greek, Etruscan, and Roman eras. The impressive Egyptian collection includes some great mummies and a text from the *Book of the Dead.* Don't miss the courtyard medley of inscribed stone slabs from various periods. *V. dell'Archiginnasio 2, off V. Rizzoli, tel. 051/233849. Admission L8,000. Open Tues.–Fri. 9–2, weekends 9–1 and 3:30–7.*

MUSEO CIVICO MEDIOEVALE

This stellar collection of 13th- to 14th-century sepulchres, depicting scholarly professors with their sleeping or otherwise distracted students, is displayed in **Palazzo Ghilisardi-Fava**, along with medieval and Renaissance ceramics, glass, and bronze instruments. The palace, although typical Bolognese Renaissance, incorporates the remains of a Roman wall, still visible from the courtyard. *V. Manzoni 4, off V. dell'Indipendenza, tel. 051/228912. Admission L8,000. Open weekdays 9–2, weekends 9–1 and 3:30–7.*

PALAZZO DELL'ARCHIGINNASIO

Festooned with intricate family shields and tributes to Renaissance intellectuals, this palace became the first permanent seat of Bologna's university in 1563, five centuries after its founding. Thomas Becket, Dante, Petrarch, Copernicus, and Marconi are all alumni of the **Università di Bologna,** an institution made avant-garde by its early acceptance of female professors. (Not *too* progressive though: Legend has it the first women professors had to cover their faces to keep from distracting male students.) You'll pass beautifully carved sarcophagi to reach the **Anatomical Theater** and its impressive interior of inlaid-wood designs by Antonio Levanti. The famous "skinless" caryatids (human-shape pillars) by Erobe Lelli hold up the canopy that covers the lecturer's chair. *P. Galvani 1, west of Duomo, tel. 051/236488. Admission free. Open Mon.–Sat. 9–1.*

PINACOTECA NAZIONALE

Well worth a stop, this great collection ranges from Byzantine to Baroque. A highlight is Raphael's *Ecstasy of St. Cecilia* (for her story, *see* Exploring Rome *in* Chapter 10). Huge canvases by Guido Reni include the impressive *Pietà dei Santi Petronio, Domenico, Carlo Borromeo, Francesco d'Assisi e Procolo,* and a dramatic *Crocifissione.* There are more paintings of the martyrdom of St. Sebastian than you can shoot an arrow at. Carracci's *Madonna and Child* (1590) combines a rich Venetian palette with an attention to anatomy (notice Mary's bare feet) that evokes the work of his contemporary Caravaggio. Also interesting are some small canvases by Bolognese Giuseppe Crespi, who painted scenes of daily life in the 18th century. *V. delle Belle Arti 56, tel. 051/243222. Admission L8,000. Open Tues.–Sat. 9–2, Sun. 9–1.*

SAN DOMENICO

This church houses one of Bologna's greatest treasures, the *Arca di San Domenico* (St. Domenico's Tomb), an intricately carved effort by Nicola Pisano, Michelangelo, and others. The stance and gaze of Michelangelo's *San Procolo* resembles his famous *David,* which he sculpted in Florence nine years later. *P. San Domenico 13, off Via Garibaldi, tel. 051/6400411. Open daily 7:30–1 and 2–8 PM.*

The meridian line on the floor of Bologna's Duomo is actually a giant sundial; the sunlight streaming in from the hole in the ceiling indicates the time and date.

SAN GIACOMO MAGGIORE

San Giacomo is a 13th-century Romanesque church gone Gothic. Don't miss the **Bentivoglio Chapel,** with fresco cycles by Lorenzo Costa depicting the *Madonna Enthroned* and the Bentivoglio clan, which ruled Bologna through the 15th century. The crypt is connected by an underground passage to what was once the family palazzo across the street (now the Teatro Comunale). You can find more Costa frescoes in the **Oratorio di Santa Cecilia** (ask the sacristan to let you in). *P. Rossini, tel. 051/6493594. From Due Torri, take V. Zamboni to P. Rossini. Open daily 6–noon and 3:30–6.*

SANTO STEFANO

While the sheer mass of the Duomo may bowl you over, this complex of four adjoining churches (there were originally seven) appears rather ordinary at first glance. The oldest in the group is the **Chiesa dei Santi Vitale e Agricola,** built from bits and pieces of Roman artifacts in the 5th century. The **Chiesa di San Sepolcro,** containing St. Petronio's remains, however, is thought to have been a pagan temple in the 1st century AD before its conversion to a baptistry. Legend has it that St. Agricola was nailed to the metal cross now hanging on the wall. The Romanesque **Chiesa del Santo Crocifisso** has been restored to its medieval Lombard style after a series of alterations. Don't overlook **Pilate's Courtyard,** with the fountain where Pontius Pilate is said to have washed himself after the blunder of his career—ordering Christ's cruxifiction. The courtyard features sepulchres and *St. Peter's Cock,* a stone rooster whose presence is a reminder of St. Peter's denial of Christ. Inside the fourth church, called **Trinità,** is an underwhelming but free museum containing a 13th-century fresco and later paintings and a shop where you can buy jams, shampoo, honey, chocolate, and more products made by monks. *V. Santo Stefano 24, P. Santo Stefano, tel. 051/223256. From Due Torri, follow V. Santo Stefano southeast to P. Santo Stefano. Admission free. Open daily 9–noon and 3:30–6.*

CHEAP THRILLS

The last relics of the macho my-tower-is-taller-than-your-tower contest that once put 200 towers on the Bolognese skyline are the **Due Torri,** built in 1488, which lean precariously in Piazza di Porta Ravegnana. Don't worry if the 265-foot **Torre Garisenda** looks about ready to topple: it was shortened in the 1500s to prevent a disaster (to the delight, no doubt, of the Asinelli). You can climb the 320-foot, 500-step **Torre degli Asinelli** (open daily 9–6, until 5 in winter; admission L3,000). The trek is long, but a great view of Bologna in her red-roofed splendor awaits you at the top. For a completely different perspective on the city, peek through the little window on Via Piella off Via Righi. You'll see what remains of the 14th-century canals that once ran beneath Bologna. If you're tired of sightseeing, the sprawling **Giardini Margherita,** off Viale Gozzadini, has a merry-go-round and basketball courts, as well as outdoor concerts and plays (*see* After Dark, *below*). On Friday and Saturday from 7 to 6, you'll find everything from L30,000 leather jackets to antique lamps at the amazing **outdoor market** in La Montagnola Park and the adjacent Piazza VII Agosto, off Via dell'Indipendenza.

AFTER DARK

Unless you're here in August, you can count on one of the best scenes for miles around. For bar hopping galore, check out **Via del Pratello** or the university quarter near **Via Marsala** and **Via delle Belle Arti** after 10 PM. Pick up the indispensible *Zero in Condotta* (L4,000) at any newsstand for an extensive listing of nightlife options. For info on the gay and lesbian scene, call **ARCI Gay** (*see* Visitor Information, *above*).

From July to September the city hosts **Bologna Sogna** (Bologna Dreams), a series of free events ranging from classical concerts and live jazz in palace courtyards to DJs spinning dance grooves in parks and on hillsides. Ask at the tourist office for a list of events or access it on-line at www.comune.bologna.it. **Teatro Comunale** (Largo Respighi 1, tel. 051/529999) hosts seasonal opera, ballet, and music festivals, some of which are free. **Circolo della Musica di Bologna** (V. Galliera 11, tel. 051/227032) has free classical music concerts throughout the summer. From mid-May to September 10, a variety of concerts—often free—are held in **Giardini Margherita** from 9:30 PM to 3 AM, and the park turns into a makeshift public disco as the hours go by. Just off Via San Vitale, the bar **Vicolo Bolognetti,** in the eponymous alleyway, serves up watermelon, beer, and free outdoor concerts every night from mid-May to September. Performances vary from reggae to punk to (gasp) country.

BARS AND OSTERIE

A bunch of great bars and osterie line **Via del Pratello,** where Via Ugo Bassi meets Via Marconi, but places for drinking and snacking are scattered all over the city. Search for the ancient and charmingly squalid **Osteria del Sole** (Vicolo Ranocchio 1, near V. Clavature, no phone; cash only; closed Sun. and Aug.). There's no sign, and it's only open from 8–2 and 7–8:45, but it's worth finding this hovel for its authentic old-world atmosphere and an incredibly cheap glass of wine (L2,500). Another centuries-old Bolognese classic is the classier **Osteria de' Poeti** (V. de' Poeti 1/B, tel. 051/236166), between Via Farini and Porta San Domenico. If you're spouting free verse after these two, put some treats in your tummy at **Osteria Broccaindosso** (V. Broccaindosso 7/A, off Strada Maggiore, tel. 051/234153; closed Sun.), which serves a mean *strozzapreti con funghi porcini* (rolled dumplings with porcini mushrooms); it's where the "cool" people go. A rowdier crowd fills the **Buca delle Campane** (V. Benedetto 14, off V. San Vitale, tel. 051/220918), two blocks from Due Torri. Listen to sweaty bands covering American and Italian hits from the '70s and '80s. Dance, sing along, or just laugh over a pricey beer (L8,000). Have a hankering for a margarita or sangria? Head to **Piedra del Sol** (V. Goito 20, tel. 051/227229) and shake it on the dance floor.

The **Irish Times Pub** (V. Paradiso 1, off V. del Pratello, tel. 051/261648) pours Guinness and Harp on tap (L7,000) until 2 AM. Stop by for happy hour 7:30–9 and mingle with the throngs of English and Italian students. **Proloco** (V. dell'Unione 2/B, tel. 051/227320; closed Mon.) has almost as many board games as FAO Schwarz; luckily most of them don't require a knowledge of Italian (Connect Four anyone?). A wide assortment of beer and cocktails make it worth a stop.

DISCOS

Unfortunately, many of the best discos are either outside the city in the hills or closed in summer, but do your best to get to Made in Bo (*see below*) in summer, and check out the bars and osterias for dancing as well as munching.

Cassero. This dance place caters to a gay crowd and is always happening, even in summer, when most of the action moves to the hills. Though a *tessera* (prepaid membership) is usually required, bouncers will often make exceptions for tourists. It also hosts theme events and films—see *Zero in Condotta. P. di Porta Saragozza 2, tel. 051/6446902. From V. Ugo Bassi, take V. d'Azeglio south to V. Barberia and veer left on V. Saragozza.*

Link. This is just about the hippest club in town—this year, that is—featuring live music by cool bands running the whole musical gamut. It's worth the healthy walk from the center of town (find friends and split a cab). Officially, you need a *tessera* (L10,000) to get in, but if you're from out of town, that's negotiable. *Behind the train station, tel. 051/370971, www.commune.bologna.it/iperbole/link.*

Made in Bo. This summertime (June–August) extravaganza pushes night fun to the limit. In a huge grassy park, dance on two outside floors, drink in the café-like bars, or shop at the hippie-style vending stands. Get a full schedule of concerts and events from the tourist office or newsstands; bigger names may have a cover charge (up to L32,000) but any night of the week Bo is never boring. It's a bit out of town (about a 15-minute bike ride), but if you taxi there, it's easy to hitch back. *Arena Parco Nord, tel. 051/532272. Free admission to the complex unless there's a major concert. From Porta Mascarella, follow V. Stalingrado north on foot 30 min; or from station, take Bus 25 (last bus 8:30 PM).*

MOVIE THEATERS

Movies in English play Monday at **Adriano d'Essai** (V. San Felice 52, tel. 051/555127) for L7,000–L10,000. **Tiffany** (P. di Porta Saragozza 5, tel. 051/585253) shows English-language films on Thursday. Both close in July and August. Check the **www.bolognaonline.com** web page for details and schedules for current screenings in English.

EMILIA-ROMAGNA

In true Italian style, the union of Emilia and Romagna more than 130 years ago has remained merely a political hyphenation, and any local will proudly point out the differences between those from Emilia and those from Romagna—and for that matter, between Reggio-Emilia and Modena. The distinction probably won't be obvious to you. In general the architecture and artistic jewels of Emilia date from the ducal Renaissance era, and Romagna is stocked with Roman artifacts. With many towns bordering on the beach, Romagna also upholds the Roman tradition of carpe diem—especially in Rimini's decadent discotheques. But a painstaking attention to good food and good wine unites the region; a star-studded culinary landscape spreads out in every direction from Bologna.

> *Those still pursuing their diplomas should stay away from Bologna's Torre degli Asinelli. Urban lore has it that university students who climb the tower won't graduate.*

FAENZA

A worthwhile day trip from Bologna, situated right on the ancient Via Emilia 49 km toward the coast, Faenza is the birthplace of *faience* pottery, which it has produced since the 12th century. **Piazza del Popolo,** smack in the middle of town, hosts hosts of shops selling Faenzan pottery creations. The giant **Museo delle Ceramiche** (Viale Baccarini 19, tel. 0546/21240; L10,000; open Apr.–Oct., Tues.–Sat. 9–7, Sun. 9:30–1; Nov.–Mar., Tues.–Fri. 9–1:30, Sat. 9–1:30 and 3–6, Sun. 9:30–1) details the history and current state of the craft. Faenza is conveniently situated train-wise, connected to Bologna (1 hr 15 min, L7,400) and Rimini (1 ½ hrs, L8,800) on the Bologna-Rimini line, and Ravenna (45 min, L5,100).

MODENA

In Modena, the motherland of Vignola cherries, Lambrusco wine, and the Ferrari, life is sweet, subtly snooty, and bright red. The city began as a Roman colony in 183 BC and was revived in the Middle Ages after years of war and neglect. If you come to do the sights in the tiny centro storico, which include frescoed and porticoed relics of the 17th-century d'Este dukedom, you can zip in and out in about a day. But take the time to live life *alla* Modenese and you might just miss your train to Florence. Some claim that Modenese cuisine, with its trademark balsamic vinegar, excellent *grana* cheese, and multi-course extravaganzas, surpasses even that of Bologna. With surrounding factories and fields producing everything from Maseratis to biomedical technology, Modena's got money in the coffers—along with a leftist government to spread it around. Despite the roar of mopeds and Fiats barreling down central Via Emilia, Modena's a place for extended outdoor feasts, concerts in the piazza, and gelato-licking strolls in the park.

BASICS

The **phone office** (V. Luigi Farini 26) is open 24 hours, the central **post office** (V. Emilia 86, tel. 059/242137) is open Monday–Saturday 8–5, Sunday until 2. Change money at any of the banks along Via Emilia. The central **tourist office** (P. Grande 17, tel. 059/206660; open weekdays 8:30–1 and 3–7, Sat. 9:30–12:30) is stocked with the usual info; it shares its space with the **Informa Giovani** (tel. 059/206580) office, which has the skinny on nightlife, as well as computers hooked up to the **Internet** free for public use. Get general info and events listings at www.comune.modena.it. From the train station, take Bus 7 to Piazza Grande.

COMING AND GOING

Trains shuttle back and forth to Milan (1 hr 30 min, L16,000) and Bologna (20 min, L3,900) day and night. Modena's **train station** (P. Dante Alighieri, tel. 1478/88088) lies on the northern edge of the historical center. Luggage storage is open daily 6:35 AM–8:10 PM (L5,000). From the train station, Bus 7 runs to the **bus station** (V. Bacchini 27, tel. 059/308833), where you can catch a bus to one of the smaller towns around Modena. Pick up a schedule here or at the tourist office (*see* Basics, *above*). Buses to mountain towns run about every two hours.

GETTING AROUND

Modena is easily traversed on foot. Via Emilia bisects the town into northern and southern halves. At the center, **Piazza Mazzini,** better known as the **Via Emilia Centro,** is a transportation hub and gathering place. To reach Via Emilia Centro from the train or bus station, take Bus 7. If you're walking, take Viale Crispi out of Piazza Dante, and turn right onto Via Vittorio Emanuele, which runs smack into the back of the **Palazzo Ducale.** Walk around the palace to Piazza Roma; from here Via Cesare Battisti heads south to Piazza Grande and Via Emilia; Piazza Mazzini is two blocks east on Via Emilia.

WHERE TO SLEEP

Modena doesn't have a hostel, and its campground is outside town, but with several bargain hotels off Piazza Grande, the city is well equipped for budget travelers. The tourist office also has a list of *affitacamere* (rooms in private homes) for rent. The central **Albergo Sole** (V. Malatesta 45, tel. 059/214245; cash only) has basic bathless doubles for L80,000. **International Camping Modena** (V. Cave Ramo III, Località Bruciata, tel. 059/332252; cash only) costs L17,000 for a tent plus L9,000 per person. To get here, take Bus 19 from the bus station.

WHERE TO EAT

The Modenese have found 101 ways to prepare the meat of the pig, from traditional cured hams to the more unusual *cotechino* (a boiled sausage of minced pork shank and skin) and *tigella* (a sort of piadina filled with herbed lard and Parmesan). Vegetarians and the gastronomically meek will find refuge in the tortelloni *di ricotta e spinaci* (stuffed with ricotta and spinach). Accompany any meal with Lambrusco, a fizzy, dark violet wine. But even more than pork and wine, the town is famous for *aceto balsamico tradizionale di Modena*—traditional balsamic vinegar. Totally different from the sweet caramelly stuff splashed around in Italian restaurants back home, the thick, syrupy, lightly acidic real thing is only produced in a small area around Modena according to strict guidelines that stipulate no less than 12 years of aging in casks of different kinds of wood. It must pass a strict tasting panel in order to get the seal of authenticity. For that seal you'll pay upwards of L120,000 for a bottle (but a small bottle goes a long way—the *aceto balsamico tradizionale* is never cooked with). Look for the small, round bottle and the label identifying it as Aceto Balsamico Tradizionale di Modena.

The bustling **covered market** (entrances at V. Albinelli 15 and V. Mondatora 18; open weekdays 7:15–1:30) overflows with fruits, vegetables, meats, and cheeses. **Caffè Molinari** (V. Emilia 153, tel. 059/222357) has gelato so scrumptious you'll be tempted to eat it for breakfast, but don't—they have good coffee, too. If an outside table's free, grab it fast. You can buy sausages and cured meats on every corner, but for the great Modenese pork experience, there is only one address: **Salumeria Giusti** (Vicolo Squallore 46, tel. 059/222533).

The area around **Piazza Mazzini** is thick with excellent eateries that whip out tables alfresco in summer. For the financially challenged, there's self-service **Ghirlandina** (V. Leodino 9, off V. Sant'Eufemia, tel. 059/237255). But economize somewhere else—none of the following eateries will empty your wallet before filling your stomach and heart with sweet memories of Modena. A favorite is **Trattoria Bianca** (V. Spaccini 24, 059/311524; no lunch Sat.; closed Sun.), which serves lunch and dinner; try the dishes with balsamic vinegar. **Osteria Ermes** (V. Ganaceto 89–91, no phone; cash only; closed Sun. and Aug.) is a cheap neighborhood place stuffed with locals and open only for lunch. There is no menu, but Ermes knows what you want, be it *quadrucci in brodo* (pasta with chicken livers in broth) or braised pork jowl. In an apartment building across from the covered market (see above) hides the **Trattoria Aldina** (V. Albinelli 40, tel. 059/236106; cash only; closed Sun.), also crammed with Modenese diners and open only for lunch, serving classic Emilia-Romagnan dishes (*primi around L10,000*). **Antica Masone** (V. Masone 16, tel. 059/238036; no lunch; closed Tues. and Aug.).

WORTH SEEING

DUOMO DI SAN GIMIGNANO • Whether due to miscalculated engineering or the earth shifting over time, Modena's pink-and-white Duomo has a few crooked angles that give it a surreal, Silly-Putty effect. Begun in 1099, the original design was altered by Lanfranco and Wiligelmo and finally finished two centuries later. The facade features reproductions of sculptures by Wiligelmo recounting the story of Genesis (the originals are now in the **Lapidary Museum,** closed for long-term restoration). Inside, a long, sculpted panel of the *Last Supper* divides the crypt of San Gimignano from the sanctuary. The **Torre Ghirlandina** ("the little garland"), the white tower leaning a bit lopsided next to the Duomo, once kept time and warned of danger with banging bells. On Sunday you can climb to the top for an amazing view (admission L2,000; open Sun. 10–1 and 3–7; closed Aug.).

GALLERIA FERRARI • For all you speed demons dreaming of slick, shiny automobiles, this place will make your heart race. The Ferrari factory, a vast complex employing thousands, is in Maranello, a suburb of Modena. You can't wheedle your way into the factory itself, but there is a museum with trophies, engines, and new and vintage Ferraris. *V. Dino Ferrari 43, Maranello, tel. 0536/943204. From the bus station on V. Bacchini, buses leave hourly for Maranello (L2,300). Admission L12,000. Open Tues.– Sun. 9:30–12:30 and 3–6.*

PALAZZO DEI MUSEI • This museum complex extraordinaire houses the city's most famous works of art, a research library, and an enormous collection of relics. The **Galleria Estense** (4th floor, tel. 059/222145; admission L8,000; open Tues., Fri., and Sat. 9–7, Wed.–Thu. 9–2, Sun. 9–1) was established in 1598 in an attempt to save family treasures when the papacy snatched Ferrara from the d'Este dukes. Among the treasures are Bernini's bust of Francesco d'Este, Correggio's *Madonna dei Limoni,* Veronese's organ doors from the Church of San Geminiano in Venice, along with other works by Tintoretto and Velasquez. Below the gallery, the **Museo Civico Archeologico** (tel. 059/223892) displays Roman artifacts from the region as well as instruments and ceramics from Asia, Africa, and the Pacific. The **Museo Civico d'Arte Medioevale e Moderna** traces Modenese history from the Middle Ages to the present with an assortment of medieval objects and antiques. Both museums are open Wednesday–Friday 9–noon, Tuesday and Saturday 9–noon and 4–7, and Sunday 10–1 and 4–7; combined admission is L5,500. On the first floor, the **Biblioteca Estense** (tel. 059/222248; open Mon.–Sat. 9–1; admission free) hosts a permanent exhibit of rare books, manuscripts, and maps. Most notable among them is the world's most decorated book—the 15th-century Bible that belonged to Borso d'Este—with more than 2,000 miniature paintings. *P. Sant'Agostino. Go west on V. Emilia Centro to V. Veneto.*

CHEAP THRILLS

Getting low on lire? Check out the **Biblioteca Delfini** (C. Canalgrande 103, tel. 059/206940), a popular library and student hangout where you can listen to CDs, watch movies, read magazines from all over, play on the Internet (L3000—but it's pretty slow), or have a drink in the ignore-your-studies bar. The library also sponsors free plays and concerts in its leafy courtyard (open Mon. 2–8, Tues.–Fri. 9–8, until 11 in summer, and Sat. 9–8). Upstairs is a modern art gallery that occasionally hosts big-name exhibits (admission L8,000; open Tues.–Sun. 10–1 and 4–7).

AFTER DARK

For a mellow evening out, head to the bars and gelaterie complete with swinging seats in Parco Amendola, which borders the south end of the centro storico. **Compagnia del Taglio** is an excellent *enoteca* (wine bar), which will serve you some fine local *Parmigiano Reggiano* cheese and flatbread with your glass of wine. Or ask around for the nearly hidden **Irish Pub** on Via Gallucci. If it's a raucous time you crave, though, Modena is sure to disappoint. In late July and August the city hosts the **Sipario in Piazza,** a series of concerts and ballets in Piazza Grande, sometimes featuring star performers (tickets L15,000–30,000). Check the tourist office for details.

NEAR MODENA

REGGIO-EMILIA

You can kind of get the feeling that Reggio-Emilia got lost somewhere between the better-known Via Emilia outposts Modena and Parma. Everybody seems to forget that the region's most famous cheese— Parmigiano Reggiano—is made here, too. Italians know Reggio as the birthplace of the *tricolore* (national flag). Today the sleepy town very much typifies Emilia, combining a high standard of living with a decidedly left-wing political climate. There's not a tremendous amount to see, but you'll find Reggio a relaxing town, and the restaurants and food shops overflow with the region's bounty.

Reggio is just the right size for a day of wandering, and the best place to start is the town's central pair of piazzas, each with its own basilica. Piazza Prampolini boasts Reggio's sprawling medieval **Duomo;** the Baroque **Basilica di San Prospero,** in neighboring Piazza San Prospero, has six roaring lions of pink Veronese marble and an incomplete octagonal tower from the 16th century. Every Tuesday and Friday, Piazza San Prospero overflows with an **outdoor market,** where booths selling everything from flowers to fish heads line the covered passage leading to Piazza Prampolini. Nearby is **Palazzo del Capitano del Popolo,** which dates to the 13th century and has the town's best facade. It's now a part of Reggio's old-est hotel. Also of architectural merit is the 17th-century Baroque church of the **Madonna della Ghiara** (C. Garibaldi), containing frescoes by the school of Carracci and a painting by Guercino. As small and peaceful as it is, Reggio draws an astonishing number of performances and exhibits to its six theaters. The palatial **Teatro Municipale Valli** (P. Teatro, tel. 0522/458811) often has good art exhibitions, as well as music and ballet performances.

BASICS • The **tourist office** (P. Prampolini 5, tel. 0522/451152; open Mon.–Sat. 8:30–1 and 2:30–6, Sun. 9–12) has info on Reggio and surrounding areas. **Bicittà** (Parcheggio di V. Cecati, no phone) will rent you a bike for L1,000 per hour or L5,000 per day, Monday–Saturday 7:30–7.

COMING AND GOING • Trains come and go about hourly to Bologna (40 min, L6,000) via Modena (15 min, L3,100). From the **train station** (P. Marconi 8, tel. 1478/88088), take Bus 1, 4, or 9 to the town center. Or you can walk down Viale IV Novembre to Piazza del Tricolore, turn right on Via Emilia and con-tinue until you hit Piazza del Monte. Turn left on Via Corridoni to find Piazza Prampolini. In summer, air-conditioned **buses** pass through Reggio on their way to Rimini (4 hrs, L25,000) and other towns on the Adriatic coast. Contact the bus station (V. Trento Trieste 11, tel. 0522/431667) for info; it's open daily 8–1 and 4–7.

WHERE TO SLEEP AND EAT • Reggio has plenty of hotels to choose from. The following two are in the centro storico and offer clean double rooms with bath for L90,000–L100,000: **Hotel Cairoli** (P. XXV Aprile 2, tel. 0522/453596, fax 0522/453148) and **Hotel Royal** (V. Roma 45, tel. 0522/541400, fax 0522/451209). The **Ostello Tricolore** (V. dell'Abbadessa 8, tel. 0522/454795), off Via Emilia, charges L17,000 per night, and curfew is midnight (later when there are concerts).

In addition to the food shops that line Piazza San Prospero (where the market is held two days a week), try **Pasticceria Boni** (V. Roma 28/A), the oldest pastry shop in town, and the **Antica Salumeria Giorgio Pancaldi** (V. Finlandia 1, 0522/304738). **La Brenta** (P. XXIV Maggio 1/A, tel. 0522/451293; cash only; no lunch Thu.–Sat.; closed Sun. and 2 wks in Aug.) is the bar-*enoteca* (wine bar) of choice, with plenty to eat as well as to drink. **Cantina del Carbone** (V. del Carbone 4/D, tel. 0522/452287; closed Sun. and Aug.) also deserves high marks for great local food at reasonable prices, just a few steps from the Duomo. The cafeteria-style **Job's Bar** (P. Gioberto 2/E, tel. 0522/452999; open Mon.–Sat. noon–2:30) serves cheap and tasty lunches for around L12,000. After a night at the theater or out on the town, choose from one of the many beers at **Vecchia Reggio** (Vicolo del Clemente 1/C, off V. Angelo Secchi).

PARMA

In Parma, a town of parks, piazzas, and Parmigiano cheese, flawlessly dressed locals leisurely pedal their bicycles over the cobbled streets, giving you a sense of what Italian life is supposed to be about. An hour west of Bologna, life in Parma ambles along at the unhurried pace of the well fed, and visitors have to drag themselves out of the city's excellent restaurants to get any sightseeing done. It's worth the effort, though: Parma is home to the internationally renowned opera house, Teatro Regio, and a vast col-lection of artwork by homeboys Correggio and the appropriately-named Parmigianino.

Much of Parma's beautiful architecture and artwork dates from the reign of the outlandishly decadent Renaissance court of the Farnese dukes (in control of the city from 1545 to 1731), who, like their coun-terparts in other cities in the region, drew heavily on the riches of the town while mercilessly oppressing the locals. Following the Farnese, the city flourished under the 30-year rule of Napoléon's widow, Marie-Louise of Austria. The resulting wealth and prosperity would seem to put Parma beyond the reach of budget travelers, but the youth hostel and campground, plus free summer concerts in the churches and piazzas, make a piece of Parma's opulence accessible.

BASICS

The main **post office** (V. Melloni 4, off P. Pilotta, tel. 0521/237554; open Mon.–Sat. 8:15–1) has an exchange and does normal mail stuff. The helpful, centrally located **tourist office** (V. Melloni 1/B, tel. 0521/234735; open Mon.–Sat. 9–7, Sun. 9–1) hands out maps and festival info in six languages.

COMING AND GOING

Hourly trains pass through Parma's **train station** (P. A. dalla Chiesa, tel. 1478/88088) on their way to Milan (1½ hrs, L12,100), Bologna (50 min, L7,400), Ancona (2 hrs 50 min, L23,800), and Rome (4 hrs, L42,500). Luggage storage (L5,000 per 12 hrs) is open 6:30 AM–8 PM. The main **TEP bus station** is near the train station. For bus info 24 hours a day, call 0521/2141.

GETTING AROUND

The Po River bisects the city into east and west halves. Via della Repubblica (the local section of Via Emilia) runs north–south, and most tourist destinations, sights, and lodgings lie in the northeastern part. From the train station, take Bus 9 to **Piazza Garibaldi** or Bus 1 to **Via Mazzini.** If you'd rather make the 10-minute walk, follow Via Verdi from the train station until you cross under the arches of the **Palazzo della Pilotta** and find yourself in the shadow of the hulking fortress. To get to Piazza Garibaldi, turn left down Via Melloni; at Piazza del Duomo turn right on Strada Cavour; four blocks south is Piazza Garibaldi.

Need a dose of nature in Parma? Directly across the river from the Palazzo della Pilotta, the Parco Ducale is a great spot for a run or a picnic among flowers and Farnese grandeur.

WHERE TO SLEEP

Most of Parma's hotels are geared toward people with fat wallets; even the cheaper places reflect the city's high standard of living. One block south of the Duomo, **Lazzaro** (V. XX Marzo 14, tel. 0521/208944) has eight highly coveted rooms (doubles with bath L82,000). Reserve early—the rooms fill up fast, and the limited open hours of the reception don't help (Mon.–Thurs. noon–4, Fri.–Sat. noon–3 and 7–midnight). The expensive **Hotel Astoria** (V. Trento 9) will help you find their hidden satellite operation, **Hotel Brozzi** (V. Trento 11, off V. Altissimo, tel. and fax 0521/272724). The furniture looks like it came from a flea market and some of the beds aren't much better than cots, but you'll pay only L66,000 for a double without bath. Up from there is the tidy **Hotel Button** (V. Saline 7, near Pallazzo Municipio, tel. 0521/208039, fax 0521/238783), where doubles with bath cost L135,000–145,000.

WHERE TO EAT

As a capital of Parmigiano cheese (only the American imitation is called "Parmesan"), prosciutto, and the even more coveted *culatello* (best cut of pig's thigh, lightly salted, spiced, and cured), this city screams *mangia!* (eat!). The highest concentration of eateries is found in the Piazza Garibaldi/Piazza del Duomo area. For lunch fixings at a third the price and three times the fun of a ready-made *panino* (sandwich), head to the **covered market** (P. Ghiaia, south of P. Pilotta; open summer Mon.–Sat. 7–1 and 4–7:30; winter, Mon.–Sat. 7–1 and 3:30–7). The surrounding shops in the piazza also tempt you with a storehouse of treats to fatten your suitcase. Or stop by Parma's oldest food shop, **Salumeria Specialità di Parma** (Strada Farini 9/C, tel. 0521/233591) and pick up some of the city's finest food items.

Is there more to eating in Parma than prosciutto and Parmesan? You bet. There's great food all around you, but two good places to try *la cucina Parmigiana* are: **Trattoria Fratelli Monica** (V. F. Santi 2/A, tel. 0521/601757; cash only; no lunch Tues.–Wed.; closed Sun.–Mon.) and **Antica Osteria Fontana** (Strada Farini 24/A, tel. 0521/286037; from P. Garibaldi, walk 2 blocks down Strada Farini; closed Sun.–Mon.). If you're gonna splurge, try **Parizzi** (V. della Repubblica 71, tel. 0521/285952; closed Mon.), or go all out at **Gallo d'Oro**, V. Borgo della Salina 3 (tel. 0521/208846; closed Sun.), in a beautiful old yellowish bodega, where you can try Parma specialties like *tortelli alla zucca* (pockets of pasta stuffed with pumpkin, L16,000).

WORTH SEEING

Enough eating—Parma's art and architecture are as rich as its cheese.

BATTISTERO • Romanesque on the outside, Gothic on the inside, Parma's pink four-story medieval baptistery is worth the price of admission. Benedetto Antelami decorated the outside of the 12th-century octagonal structure with a band of mythical beasts and animals and the inside with statues that symbolize the months and the seasons. *P. del Duomo, tel. 0521/235592. Admission L4,000. Open daily 9–12:30 and 3–6.*

CHEAP THRILLS

Just about everywhere in Italy there is a festival (sagra) for local food products at some time during the year, but Parma and the surrounding hill towns produce enough great foodstuffs to find an excuse to party just about every weekend. If you're really a cheese fanatic, call the Consorzio del Parmigiano (V. Gramsci 26/A, tel. 0521/292700) a week in advance to reserve a free guided tour of a Parmesan-making facility, samples included. In summer the city hosts classical and jazz concerts (most free) almost every evening, in the Parma Estate series. Contact the tourist offices for more details.

CAMERA DI SAN PAOLO • The highly decorative frescoes found here were painted in 1518 as a protest against the ever-growing papal power that threatened this convent's independence. Correggio and Araldi were commissioned for the job by the avant-garde humanist abbess Giovanna Piacenza. *V. Melloni 3, tel. 0521/233309. From P. Pilotta, follow V. Melloni; it's on the left in a recessed courtyard. Admission L4,000. Open daily 9–1:45.*

CHIESA DI SAN GIOVANNI EVANGELISTA • Once part of a simple 10th-century cloister, the church of San Giovanni has undergone several face-lifts—with Renaissance reconstruction around 1490–1519, frescoes by Correggio and Parmigianino in the 16th century, a Baroque facade, and finally a campanile in 1613. Visit the adjacent monastery with serene courtyards and a gift shop of herbs and lotions. Around the corner is the **Spezieria di S. Giovanni** (ancient pharmacy; Borgo Pipa 1, tel. 0521/233309; admission L4,000; open daily 9–1:45) that produced herbal medicines and cures as early as the 13th century; recipes and weighing devices are still on display. *P. San Giovanni, tel. 0521/235592. From P. Pilotta, head toward Duomo along Strada Pisacane and continue right of Duomo. Open daily 6:30–noon and 3:30–8.*

CHIESA DI SANTA MARIA DELLA STECCATA • Built in the shape of a Greek cross, this church's design follows the 16th-century Renaissance notion that a temple of worship should embody the universe itself: the four branches of the cross represent the four corners of the world, while the cupola, frescoed by Bernardo Gatti, mimics the heavens. Gatti modeled his swirling clouds, men, and angels after Correggio's paintings in Parma's Duomo, completed 10 years earlier. In the crypt rest the bones of the Farnese dukes, and the entrance features a pair of organ doors by Parmigianino, who was actually imprisoned at one point for his slow pace of work on the incredible fresco cycle that is also in the church. *V. Garibaldi between V. Dante and P. della Steccata, tel. 0521/234937. From P. Pilotta, follow V. Garibaldi south. Open daily 10:30–noon and 3–6.*

DUOMO • Built in the mid-11th century, the Duomo is noteworthy for its Romanesque triangular facade and the striking frescoes that cover nearly every inch of the interior walls. Above the pulpit, Correggio's *Ascent of the Virgin,* famous for its innovative perspective, shows the Virgin suspended in space, providing some pretty risqué views up her billowing skirt. The Duomo also contains the *Deposition,* Benedetto Antelami's first sculpture. *P. del Duomo, tel. 0521/235886. From P. Pilotta, follow Strada Pisacane, which turns into Strada al Duomo and leads into P. del Duomo. Open daily 7–12:30 and 3–7.*

PALAZZO DELLA PILOTTA • Built by Pope Paul III (Alessandro Farnese) for his son in 1600, the Palazzo della Pilotta has long been the biggest building in Parma. So big in fact that it was an easy target for Allied bombing and was reduced to a shell of a building in 1944. Much of the building has been restored—note the jagged remnants of the walls as you pass under the archways—and it is now home to the **Museo Archeologico Nazionale** (tel. 0521/233718; admission L4,000; open Tues.–Sun. 9–6:30), which features artifacts from Egypt and Rome, as well as prehistory. Don't miss the Roman bronze inscription *Tabula Alimentaria* (AD 2). Upstairs is the **Teatro Farnese** (admission L4,000; open daily 9–1:30), a lavishly sculpted and frescoed court theater that opened in 1628 with the performance of *Mercury and Martha,* by Claudio Achillini (music by Monteverdi), to celebrate the marriage of Odoardo Farnese with Margherita de' Medici. Next to the theater, you can visit the **Galleria Nazionale** (open daily 9–1:30), a multistory showcase for Correggio, Parmigianino, and other big names. Toward the back of the museum, look for Leonardo da Vinci's drawing, *Head of a Young Girl,* unobtrusively facing a wall. The gallery's L12,000 admission price includes a look at the Teatro Farnese. *Palazzo della Pilotta, tel. 0521/233309. From train station, follow V. Verdi 6 blocks.*

AFTER DARK

I parmagiani pack into **Enoteca Antica Osteria Fontana** (Via Farini 24/A, tel. 0521/286037) for a drink and a snack before dinner; it's a fantastic wine bar that serves up the spoils of Emilian vineyards to a gregarious half-standing, half-sitting crowd. Opera fanatics might be able to find last-minute tickets to the famous **Teatro Regio** (V. Garibaldi, tel. 0521/21890) for under L15,000 (otherwise, sign up days in advance for the real tickets, L30,000 and up).

PIACENZA

Piacenza may not be as popular a destination as it was 900 years ago, when it was the economic center of the Carolingian Empire, but it's still well worth a visit. The Farnese family, which took control of the town in 1545, built much of the tiny city center and commissioned embellishments by the region's most important artists, among them Guercino and Alberti. Piacenza can be explored in a day, but bear in mind that on Thursday afternoon everything closes and the city moves at a snail's pace and that on Wednesday and Saturday the streets teem with market-day merchants. In summer most shops stay open until midnight on Friday.

When in Piacenza, don't miss the city's weirdest museum piece, a bronze sheep's liver purported to have magical properties.

BASICS

Piacenza's **tourist information** office (Palazzo Farnese, Piazza Citadella, tel. 0523/329324; open Tues.–Sat. 9:30–12:30 and 3:30–6:30) is built into the side of Il Gotico, Piazza dei Cavalli's double-decker brick-and-stone palace. Get the lowdown on nightlife from the **Informagiovani** office (V. Taverna 37, tel. 0523/334013; open Mon.–Wed. and Fri. 9:30–12:30 and 3–6, Sat. 9:30–12:30).

COMING AND GOING

From Piacenza hourly trains run to Milan (50 min, L7,600) and Parma (35 min, L5,900). The **train station** (P. Marconi, tel. 1478/88088), on the eastern edge of town, has an ATM and luggage storage (open daily 8–5, L5,000). The walk to the town center takes about 15 minutes. To reach Piazza dei Cavalli and Piazzetta dei Mercanti, the two conjoined piazzas at the heart of the city, cross diagonally through the park opposite Piazzale Marconi (in front of the train station); on the opposite side of the park, follow Via Alberoni to the right and turn left on Via Legnano, which leads into Piazza del Duomo; from here Via XX Settembre leads straight to Piazza dei Cavalli.

WHERE TO SLEEP

The nearest hostel is a long bus ride away, but at least the budget hotels are central. **Albergo Moderno** (V. Tibini 29, tel. 0523/329296, fax 0523/384438; cash only) has clean, modern doubles with bath for L85,000. The furniture at **Hotel Corona** (V. Roma 141, tel. 0523/320948, fax 0523/337863) is a bit shaky, but the rooms are well kept and newly restored. Doubles, all with bath, cost L80,000; call ahead if you plan to check in on a Wednesday. Women under 25 can stay with the ever-present and cheerful nuns at **Casa della Giovane** (Cantone San Nazaro 2/A, tel. 0523/337989, fax 0523/337089; Bus 2 or 31 from station; cash only). Curfew is 10:30 PM; full pension (a bed plus three meals) costs L40,000 (L30,000 for just a bed and breakfast). Reservations are required—it fills up fast.

WHERE TO EAT

The streets south of Piazza dei Cavalli are filled with great restaurants, and if you've ever felt hungry enough to eat a horse, here's your chance: *picula ad caval* (minced horse meat stewed in tomato sauce) is a tasty local favorite. You'll also find Piacenza's signature dish, *pisarei e fasò* (minidumplings served in a bean and tomato sauce). Eat outside in a pretty little garden if it's warm at **Osteria del Trentino** (V. Castello 71, tel. 0523/24260; closed Sun. and Aug.). Or try **La Pireina** (V. Borghetto 137, tel. 0523/324260; no dinner Mon.; closed Sun.). Cool off at Gelateria **Stradone** (V. Stradone Farnese) or **Gallery** (C. Vittorio Emanuele).

WORTH SEEING

Most of Piacenza's sights cluster around **Piazza dei Cavalli,** named after Francesco Mochi's 17th-century equestrian statues of Ranuccio and Alessandro Farnese that stand in the middle of the square. Behind them towers **Il Gotico,** a 13th-century turreted and crenellated Gothic palace used as a town hall. Although you can't go inside, the elaborate mesh of archways and battlements out front attracts all kinds of loitering. The medieval **Chiesa di San Francesco** (P. dei Cavalli 70) is to the left of Il Gotico; intricate stained-glass windows illuminate its arching Gothic interior. The Lombard Romanesque **Duomo** (down V. XX Settembre), with three large doors, a rose window, and a *gabbia* (cage) in which wrongdoers were put on display and pelted by those who passed by, contains a cupola frescoed by Guercino and a painting of St. Jerome by Guido Reni.

The 16th-century **Palazzo Farnese** houses the **Museo Civico,** with an inordinate number of works glorifying (surprise?) Alessandro Farnese, mercenary turned pope. The museum also houses Botticelli's *Madonna with St. John the Baptist,* but the main attraction is the bizarre *Fegato Etrusco,* an ancient bronze sheep liver engraved with the symbols of the Etruscan gods of good and ill fortune. By comparing this "master" liver with one taken from a freshly sacrificed sheep, the priests would predict the future. *P. Cittadella, tel. 0523/330567. Admission L10,000 for all, L4,000–L8,000 for individual exhibits. Open Tues.–Sat. 9–12:30 (Thurs. also 3-6), Sun. 9:30–12:30 and 3:30–6:30.*

One of Italy's finest collections of 19th- to 20th-century art is hidden away in Piacenza's **Galleria Ricci Oddi** (V. San Siro 13, off C. Vittorio Emanuele II, tel. 0523/320742), including two paintings by Klimt. The gallery is unfortunately closed for restoration until at least mid-2000; call the gallery or the tourist office for an update. Not an inch of the interior of the **Chiesa di Santa Maria di Campagna** (P. Crociate 5, off V. Campagna) remains unfrescoed, and the effect is dizzying. The cupola by Pordenone is particularly spectacular.

AFTER DARK

The Informagiovani office (*see* Basics, *above*) has a full listing of current clubs. **Teatro Gioco Vita** (Vicolo San Matteo 6, tel. 0532/332613) sponsors a film festival in June and July with some films (L8,000) in English.

FERRARA

It was the rapacious Renaissance dukes of the d'Este family who shaped Ferrara into a one-of-a-kind little city. Just a block from their towering castle and cathedral, a dark knot of arch-covered alleys winds through the medieval quarter, evoking a vivid sense of how most of Ferrara's citizens were living while the d'Este built themselves pleasure palaces, threw lavish parties, and patronized great artists and intellects of the age, Ariosto, Tasso, Cellini, and Copernicus among them. After three and a half centuries of rule, they found themselves without a legitimate heir in 1598—the pope stepped up, and the d'Este fled to Modena, carrying many of their court's treasures with them. These days the castle that once symbolized domination is now a caffè and concert venue, and the peaceful town is notably bustling, completely dominated by ubiquitous bicycles and outdoor vendors.

BASICS

Change money at **Credito Italiano** (C. Martiri della Libertà 51, tel. 0532/207440) or **Banca Nazionale del Lavoro** (C. Porta Reno 19, tel. 0532/781674). Both are open 8:30–1:30 and 3:15–4 and charge a L3,000 commission. Stop at the helpful **tourist office** (C. Giovecca 21, tel. 0532/249751, across from the castle; open Mon.–Sat. 9–1 and 3–6, Sun. 9–1) for maps and info on museums and hotels. From the station veer left on Viale Costituzione until it turns into Via Cavour (it becomes Corso Giovecca).

COMING AND GOING

Ferrara's **train station** (P. Stazione 20–26, tel. 1478/88088) is a 15-minute walk from the town center and the Castello Estense. Luggage storage (L5,000 per 12 hrs) is available. Ferrara lies on the Bologna–Venice train line, which runs about every half hour in each direction until 11 PM. From Ferrara it's a half hour to Bologna (L4,700) and 1½ hours to Venice (L10,100). Another line connects Ferrara with Ravenna (1 hr 10 min, L7,500) and Rimini (2 hrs, L9,700); trains pass through about once every two hours.

GETTING AROUND

Ferrara is divided in half by **Viale Cavour,** which becomes **Corso Giovecca** as it passes Castello Estense, the moated fortress. To the south of Viale Cavour, with the castle and cathedral, is the medieval part of the city; the north side filled with stately palazzi along wide avenues would be the Renaissance 'hood. The Ferraresi are bike-aholics—cars even slow down for cyclists!—so if you prefer to roll rather than stroll, rent a **bike** by the hour (L4,000–L5,000) or by the day (L20,000) at **Itinerando** (tel. 0532/765123, daily 9–1 and 2–6), adjacent to the tourist office. Hours are sporadic, so call ahead or ask at the tourist office, and someone should come running within 15 minutes. Ferrara's **train station** is on the western edge of town: To reach Castello Estense on foot, take Viale Costituzione to Viale Cavour; Bus 1, 2, or 9 will also get you there. Bus 9 continues down Corso Giovecca to the medieval quarter. To reach the Renaissance area, take Bus 3 from Corso Porta Reno (just south of P. Cattedrale). Most **buses** run 6 AM–11 PM, and bus tickets (L1,300) can be found in any tobacco shop.

WHERE TO SLEEP

The tourist office has a list of rooms for rent in Ferrara and in nearby beach towns. All doubles (L80,000) in the newly renovated **Albergo Alfonsa** (V. Padiglioni 5, behind the tourist office, tel. 0532/205726; cash only) have private baths and TVs, but you'll have to be careful not to bump your knee on the toilet when taking a shower. Central **Albergo San Paolo** (V. Baulardi 9, tel. and fax 0532/7620400; cash only) is a step up in both price and quality, with a lobby, spacious rooms with matching, comfy furniture, TVs, and phones. Doubles with bath are L120,000 (the one without is L80,000), and the talkative reception-ist might hook you up with a jalopy bike for L5,000 per day. A definite step down is **Albergo Centro Storico** (V. Vegri 15, tel. 0532/209748). Luckily, it's also cheap (L60,000 for a nondescript but spacious double) and, as the name indicates, central. Light streams through enormous windows into the impec-cably clean rooms (L56,000 without bath, L80,000 with) at the **Casa degli Artisti** (V. Vittoria 66, tel. 0532/761038). Each floor has a kitchenette with a fridge and stove, the showers are large, and you can see all of Ferrara's tiled roofs from the rooftop patio. Call *now* because it books up fast.

CAMPING • Camping Estense. This campground on the outskirts of town charges L12,000 per tent, plus L7,000 per person. It's a shadeless lot at the edge of farmland, and the hike from the nearest bus stop is 20 minutes of hard walking. They rent bikes for L4,000 per hour, L15,000 per 12 hrs, available daily 9–9. *V. Gramicia 76, 44100, tel. 0532/752396. From station or C. Giovecca (a little east of castle), take Bus 1 to Borgo Punta and ask driver when to get off (last bus 8:20 PM); from here, walk along V. Calzolai to V. Pannonio, turn left, and follow signs. Turn right on V. Gramicia; the campground is about 800 m ahead on right. Reception open 8–1 and 2–10. Curfew 10 PM (but an after-hours key is avail-able). Cash only. Closed Nov.–Apr.*

WHERE TO EAT

The medieval neighborhood abounds with restaurants, markets, and shops for doing it yourself. The area with the *pasticcerie* and *forni* (bakeries), *salumerie* (delis), cheese shops, and produce stands is **Via Cortevecchia,** off Piazza Cattedrale. Just down the road, the **Mercato Coperto** (V. Santo Stefano 14/ E) is open Monday–Saturday 7–1:30, Friday also 4:30–7.

Ferrara's castle-dwellers funded chefs to concoct decadent delicacies that remain popular today. Sub-mit your taste buds to *cappellacci,* thick pasta shells stuffed with pumpkin, nutmeg, and Parmesan (vegetarians should choose those served with butter rather than pork sauce); or *salama da sugo,* pork and liver mixed with wine and spices, dangled in the dark for at least a year, then boiled for hours before arriving on your plate. For dessert try *pampepato,* a spicy chocolate bread.

If you only eat one place in Ferrara, make it **Antica Trattoria Volano** (V. Volano 20, tel. 0532/761421; closed Fri.), where you'll find classic dishes at fair, if not budget, prices—about L35,000 for a full meal. For something a little more creative, try **Quel Fantastico Giovedì** (V. Castelnuovo 9, tel. 0532/760570; closed Wed.). **Osteria al Brindisi** (V. degli Adelardi 11, next to cathedral, tel. 0532/209142; closed Mon.) is the joint where the Ferraresi have gone to get tipsy since 1435. It's earned itself a place in the *Guinness Book of World Records* as the world's oldest wine bar, proffering wine, grappa, whiskey, and port. They also make panini (L5,000–L7,000) to give your stomach a fighting chance. **Pizzeria Orsucci** (V. Garibaldi 76, tel. 0532/205391; closed Wed.) serves terrific pizzas and typical Ferrarese pastas like tagliatelle *alla boscaiola* (with mushrooms, ham, and peas) for only L7,000.

FERRARA'S STAR OF DAVID

Ferrara became a refuge for persecuted Jews from Rome, Spain, and Germany as early as 1100. The largest immigration occurred in 1492, when Ercole I welcomed Sephardic Jews exiled from Spain. In the following century, the Jewish community flourished as Jews became scientists, doctors, and merchants. But by 1624, Ferrara was under papal control, and Jews were ordered into a ghetto. Five massive, locked gates confined up to 1,800 people into a triangular zone bordered by Vie Mazzini, Vignatagliata, and Vittoria. For more than 200 years, most ghetto residents suffered extreme poverty, but a self-sufficient city within a city developed, with schools, government, synagogues, and a welfare system. Today, behind the stark exteriors lies an intricate web of secret passageways and courtyard gardens.

The Museo Ebraico di Ferrara (V. Mazzini 95, tel. and fax 0532/210228; open Sun.–Thurs. 10–1 for prearranged tours, closed Aug.) houses three hidden synagogues and has a plaque commemorating 95 Ferrarese Holocaust victims. At the Cimitero Ebraico (on V. Vigne, behind the Cimitero Certosa; open Apr.–Sept., daily 9–12 and 3–6:30; Oct.–Mar., daily 9–12 and 3–4:30), haphazard grave sites provide a memorial to loved ones whose bodies had to be transported by night from the ghetto.

WORTH SEEING

Ferrara's sights are clustered in three main areas: the medieval quarter south of Corso Giovecca, the southeast additions that date to the 14th and 15th centuries, and the stately Renaissance district commissioned by Duke Ercole I d'Este, which stretched the city northward in the late 15th century.

THE MEDIEVAL QUARTER • The medieval quarter's twisted web of narrow alleys and crumbling buildings stands in stark contrast to the mint-condition castle and cathedral. Southeast of the Duomo are the three thin streets of Ferrara's Jewish ghetto, and arches topped with apartments traverse the 2-km-long (1-mi-long) **Via delle Volte,** a rare surviving example of medieval architecture.

Castello Estense. A testament to the policies of the Renaissance rulers, one of the country's most magnificent fortified castles was never meant to protect the city from outside invasion but rather the dukes from their subjects. Niccolò II d'Este ordered the castle built in 1385 after his treasurer was killed during a citizens' revolt over unjust taxation. The drawbridges and the murky moat guard a massive fortress, symbolic of the Este family: cold and menacing on the outside, lavishly decorated within. Inside, the 16th-century ceiling frescoes in the **Sala dell'Aurora** depict Time in the center, surrounded by Aurora (Dawn), Sunset, and Night. The frescoes in the **Sala dei Giochi** (Game Room) portray buff nude men and chubby cupids playing various games. There's a small Protestant chapel (built for Duke Ercole II's wife) and a throne room to admire, but the most intriguing part of the castle's interior is its dark **dungeon,** reached via a rickety staircase that runs through a trapdoor. Descend into the creepy low-ceilinged corridor and crouch through half-size doorways into the cells where the denizens languished: Niccolò III had his young wife, Parisina Malatesta, and her lover, Ugo d'Este (Niccolò's son), incarcerated here before having them beheaded. *Tel. 0532/299233. Admission L10,000. Open Tues.–Sat. 9:30–5.*

The 12th-century **Cattedrale di San Giorgio** has a remarkably unusual facade divided into three symmetrical sections and laced with carved illustrations of the *Last Judgment*. The campanile, designed by Leon Battista Alberti, was added in 1412 and remains unfinished. Check out the **Loggia of the Merchants** along the length of the Piazza Trento Trieste side, added in the 18th century. To see the sculptures that were removed to make way for this addition, climb the steps at the cathedral entrance to the **Museo del Duomo**. *P. Cattedrale, tel. 0532/207449. Admission free. Cathedral open daily 8–noon and 3–6:30. Museo del Duomo open Tues.–Sat. 10–noon and 3–5, Sun. 10–noon and 3:30–6.*

EAST OF THE MEDIEVAL QUARTER • The cluster of palazzi in this area can be squeezed into a morning or afternoon of sightseeing. Bus 1 or 9 will take you from the train station or the castle down Corso Giovecca, a good starting point for seeing this section of the city.

The **Casa Romei** belonged to Giovanni Romei, a wealthy banker who married into the d'Este family, and it still looks much like it did when it was built in 1445. Inside the villa, you'll find two peaceful courtyards, a lovely loggia, and walls covered with 15th-century frescoes. It's now an orphanage for statues and frescoes rescued from decaying churches. *V. Savonarola 30, tel. 0532/240341. From Castello Estense, take C. Giovecca, right on V. Coramari, and left on V. Savonarola. Admission L4,000. Open Tues.–Sun. 8:30–2, depending on the schedule of exhibitions.*

Palazzina di Marfisa d'Este. Large rooms, vaulted and frescoed ceilings, and beautiful wooden furniture make this *palazzina* seem a bit more lived in than the rest of the d'Este palaces. Don't miss the **Loggia degli Aranci**, with a vaulted ceiling painted with an arbor of twisting grapevines. *C. Giovecca 170, tel. 0532/207450. Admission L3,000, free 2nd Mon. of month; combined ticket with Palazzo Schifanoia L10,000. Open daily 9:30–1 and 3–6.*

Palazzo Paradiso. Fans of Ariosto won't want to miss the writer's tomb and the **Biblioteca Ariostea** housed in this 14th-century palazzo. The library holds more than 150,000 volumes, 3,400 prints, and 2,500 manuscripts written at the d'Este court. Highlights include a manuscript of *Orlando Furioso* and the illuminated astrological tables of Blanchinius. There are usually a number of highly decorative manuscripts on display. *V. Scienze 17, tel. 0532/206977. From Castello Estense, take C. Giovecca, turn right on V. Terranuova, which becomes V. Scienze. Admission free. Open weekdays 9–7, Sat. 9 AM–10:30 PM.*

Run or bike the flat, shady path that winds alongside Ferrara's city walls, about a 9-km/5½-mi loop. On the way, study the various 15th- to 16th-century wall styles and witness an even rarer sight—Italians perspiring in their elegant sweat suits.

Palazzo Schifanoia. The palace's name, related to Latin for "fleeing boredom," reveals the palace's function as a house of folly, so to speak—one of many inhabited by the pleasure-loving d'Este family. Construction began in 1385, but the upper story was added by Borso d'Este in the 1460s, making it the first Renaissance palazzo in town. The famous **Salone dei Mesi** is frescoed in 12 sections, representing the months of the year. Within each, the upper section depicts mythical rebellion and revelry, the middle is filled with the zodiac sign corresponding to the month, and the large lower section contains scenes with Borso d'Este and his cronies. The **Museo Civico** downstairs contains various medieval and Renaissance paintings and artifacts. *V. Scandiana 23, tel. 0532/64178. From Castello Estense, follow C. Giovecca, turn right on V. Ugo Bassi, left on V. Scandiana. Admission L8,000, free 2nd Mon. of month. Open daily 9–7.*

RENAISSANCE QUARTER • On orders from Duke Ercole I, master planner Biagio Rossetti laid out a major civic expansion project to be built over the following century. The result is the orderly Renaissance quarter, with Piazza Ariostea (off C. Porta Mare) as its centerpiece.

Church of San Cristoforo. A Biagio Rossetti masterpiece, this church has long, porticoed wings that sweep out like a pair of welcoming arms encircling the green lawns. The adjoining **Certosa Cemetery**, added in 1813, contains rows of manicured grave sites topped with flowers and enclosed by porticoes. Try not to miss this quiet corner of the city. *V. Borso 1. From Castello Estense, take C. Ercole I d'Este, turn right on C. Porta Mare, and left on V. Borso. Open daily 8–8.*

Palazzo dei Diamanti. One look at this palace, covered in thousands of diamond-shape marble stones, and you'll see why it's considered Biagio Rossetti's most brilliant work. Then try to make out the facade's optical tricks: Although all of the 8,500 or so diamonds appear identical, the ones on top point skyward; the ones below have their noses to the ground. Inside, the **Pinacoteca Nazionale** exhibits 14th- to 18th-century works by local painters. Downstairs, the **Galleria dell'Arte Moderna** sometimes sponsors temporary exhibitions. *C. Ercole I d'Este 21, tel. 0532/205844. Admission L10,000. Open Tues.–Sat. 9–2, Sun. 9–1.*

Palazzo Massari. In the corner of fountain-drenched Parco Massari, this 16th-century palace show-cases the work of 19th-century Ferrarese figurative painter Giovanni Boldini, who fancied painting pretty Parisian socialites. The **Museo Boldini** is attached to the **Museo dell '800,** which features 19th-century sculptures and paintings by local artists. Adjacent is a pavilion with free temporary modern art exhibits. *C. Porta Mare 9, tel. 0532/206914. From Castello Estense, follow C. Ercole I d'Este to C. Porta Mare and turn right. Admission L6,000. Open daily 9–1 and 3–6.*

AFTER DARK

As usual, the night scene changes from year to year, so check with the tourist office for a listing of hot spots. Discoers usually commute to the surrounding countryside or to Rimini, and the all-night **Discobus** (July–Aug., tel. 0532/599411) can take you there. In town, though, you can still have a drink on the river at **Birreria Sebastian** (V. Darsena 53/A, tel. 0532/768233; closed Tues.), a floating pub. If solid ground is more your scene, **Bar Ariosto** (P. Ariosto 13–15, tel. 0532/207600) overflows any day of the week except Wednesday, while next door **Gelateria Ariosto** (P. Ariosto 1–3) scoops up Ferrara's best frozen fantasia. The **Buskers' Festival** brings outdoor performances to a piazza near you during the last week in August (tel. 0532/249337). In June and July, the **Ferrara Jazz Club** (tel. 0532/202135 ARCI Ferrara) produces various concerts; check with the tourist office for info. Finally, the **Palio di S. Giorgio** is a joust, with all the flying colors, which takes place each year the last Sunday of May.

RAVENNA

Not your garden-variety central Italian town, Ravenna shows the influence of several centuries of Byzan-tine rule, most noticeably in some of the finest mosaics in the Western world. Once just an ordinary Roman town, Ravenna became the capital of the Roman Empire 1,500 years ago, but by then the empire was already in steep decline. Eventually it was conquered by the Byzantines and ruled from Con-stantinople. It was Byzantine emperor Justinian and his scandalous wife, Theodora, who brought the city to its artistic and cultural zenith, creating the blend of East and West that gives Ravenna its unique appeal and the city's art treasures you see today. Today's visitors form a colorful mosaic of their own, and the friendly Ravennati try their darnedest to keep them—and their money—coming back.

BASICS

Coming out of the train station, Viale Farini becomes Via Diaz, where the banks are, and then leads to the central Piazza del Popolo, with the **post office** (and good currency exchange) on nearby Piazza Garibaldi (tel. 0544/213593). The main **tourist office** (V. Salara 8, tel. 0544/35404; open Mon.–Sat. 8:30–6, Sun. 10–4) is not far from there. Bike rental at the office costs L3,000 per hour, L15,000 per day. From Piazza del Popolo, head right on Via Cavour, veer left at Piazza Costa, right at Via Salara.

Stop by the **Informa Giovane** (V. Guido da Polenta 4, tel. 0544/36494; open Tues.–Sat. 9–1, Tues. and Thurs. also 3–7) office for computer printouts of pubs and info on seaside discos (say, "*informazioni sulle discoteche/sui pub*"). Chances of finding an English-speaking staff member are slim, but you can always pantomime with those slick dance moves you've been saving for a special occasion. Take a look at the monthly *Fred* (in Italian) for listings of current happenings or buy one from a newsstand. From Piazza del Popolo, cut south through Piazza Garibaldi to Via Dante Alighieri, right on Via Guido da Polenta.

COMING AND GOING

Trains are faster, cheaper, and more frequent than buses; they shuttle in and out of Ravenna from Brisighella (10 daily, 45 min, L5,100; change at Faenza), Bologna (1 hr 20 min, L7,400), Ferrara (15 daily, 1 hr 10 min, L7,400), and Rimini (hourly, 1 hr, L6,300). The **train station** (P. Farini 13, tel. 1478/88088) has luggage storage (open daily 7:20–1 and 1:30–10; L5,000 per 12 hrs). Most local and some long-distance buses leave from Piazza Farini, next to the train station. The **ATM** office (P. Farini, tel. 0544/35288; open daily 6:30 AM–7:30 PM, until 8:30 PM in summer) sells bus tickets to Ravenna's beaches (hourly, 20 min, L1,700) and the Basilica of Sant'Apollinare in Classe (*see* Worth Seeing, *below;* hourly, 15 min, L1,200). For cities outside Ravenna's provinces, buses leave from **Piazza Aldo Moro,** behind the station. The ticket window (V. Magazzini Anteriori 55, tel. 0544/420428; open Mon.–Sat. 6:15 AM–9 PM) is in the white building across the piazza. Buy tickets in advance; they cost more if you buy them on the bus.

GETTING AROUND

Ravenna's small centro storico spirals out from the main square, Piazza del Popolo; the train and bus stations are a 10-minute walk eastward. Ravenna's sights are spread out—the city *is* attackable on foot (even if you're staying at the hostel) but you will be working those glutei a bit. The breeziest way to cover the city is by bike. Rent one to the left of the station from **Coop San Vitale** (P. Farini, tel. 0544/37031; open Mon.–Sat. 6:15 AM–8 PM). Bikes cost L2,000 per hour, L15,000 per day. Otherwise, rent one at the tourist office (see above). If you're getting around town by bus, Line **MB** (minibus) squeezes through the alleys of the city center, stopping near most of Ravenna's attractions. Buses leave every 10 minutes and stop in piazzas Caduti and del Popolo and near the Duomo. Tickets cost L1,200 and are good for one trip.

WHERE TO SLEEP

Ravenna's budget hotels are a two-minute walk from the train station and a 10-minute walk from the town center. The youth hostel is a little farther, about a kilometer (half mile) from the train station. If beaches and discotheques are your thing, the campgrounds and cheap hotels at Ravenna's beaches (*see* Near Ravenna, *below*) are your best option; they're only a 20-minute ride via hourly bus.

UNDER L65,000 • Albergo al Giaciglio. The sink showers with you in the teeny hall bathrooms, but a well-maintained double without bath is a wee L50,000 (L65,000 with bath). For L25,000 you can enjoy a meal in the restaurant downstairs. *V. Brancaleone 42, 48100, tel. 0544/39403. Follow V. Farini out of P. Farini, right into P. Mameli; V. Brancaleone is to the right. 16 rooms, 11 with bath.*

UNDER L100,000 • Albergo Ravenna. Somebody here is hard at work making sure you're comfy— from the housekeepers who keep the white marble stairs (and your bathroom) immaculate to the management, which remodeled the hotel. Noisy traffic in nearby Piazza Farini is the only drawback, but all hotels around here have the same problem. Doubles with bath are L80,000, without L60,000–L70,000. *V. Maroncelli 12, 48100, tel. 0544/212204, fax 0544/212077. From P. Farini, turn right down V. Maroncelli. 25 rooms, 23 with bath.*

Albergo Roma. You're stylin' in this hotel—comfy, decked-out doubles (L100,000–115,000) are pricey but come with phone, TV, bath, hair dryer (doubling as an underwear dryer), luxurious towels, and an English-speaking staff. *V. Candiano 26, 48100, tel. 0544/421515, fax 0544/421191. From station, turn left and walk 300 ft to underpass to V. Darsena, right on V. Darsena, quick left on V. Candiano. The underpass is closed by night, but you can just continue aboveground on the same road. 49 rooms with bath.*

HOSTEL • Ostello Dante (HI). This hostel is big, noisy, friendly, and between a supermarket and a park that sporadically hosts local bands (Foo Fighters *in Italiano*). It's clean and run like a tight ship by a strict but kind woman who minces no words. The price of L22,000 includes a morning roll and coffee. *V. Aurelio Nicolodi 12, 48100, tel. and fax 0544/421164. From train station, take Bus 1 to V. Molinetto at V. Aurelio Nicolodi. 140 beds. Curfew 11:30 PM, lockout 9–5. Cash only.*

WHERE TO EAT

Even if you've seen every last mosaic, you might want to think about hanging around Ravenna for the food. The **Mercato Coperto** (P. Costa, off P. del Popolo) is one of the prettiest in the region and overflows with fresh bread and hot *piadine,* fresh pasta in all the local shapes and sizes, cheeses, fruits, and vegetables Monday–Saturday 7–2 (Friday also 4:30–7:30). Round out your food tour with a stop at **La Butega di Giorgioni** (V. IV Novembre 43, tel. 0544/212638), a great herb shop where you can get a potion for bad kidneys or a broken heart.

There's no place more hip than the beautiful osteria **Ca' de Ven** (V. C. Ricci 24, tel. 0544/30163; open Tues.–Sun. 11–2 and 6:30–10), just steps from Dante's Tomb, where you can sip wine, read bilingual art and poetry books, and munch on cheap *piadine* (L6,000) or *crescioni* (L4,000–L5,000). Excellent wine by the glass costs L2,700. You can also get pasta for L9,000. You may have to wrestle a local for a table at **Giamba e Coco'** (V. Pasolini 36, tel. 0544/39772; cash only; closed Sun. afternoon and Mon.), a good little trattoria in the town center that stays open late for dinner. You can eat a solid meal of grilled meat and local specialties at **Ristorante La Gardela** (V. Ponte Marino 3, tel. 0544/217147; closed Thurs., 10 days in Aug., and 10 days in Feb.) for around L35,000, excluding wine. For just a bit more, treat yourself to the best meal in town at **Capannetti** (Vicolo Capannetti 21, just off of V. Ravegnana, tel. 0544/66681; no dinner Sun., no lunch in Aug.; closed Mon.).

WORTH SEEING

Ravenna's sights are a bit spread out, so if you're gonna cover a lot of ground, consider renting a bike (*see* Getting Around, *above*). If you plan on seeing more than a couple of mosaics, it's worth buying a

RAVENNA'S MOSAICS

The mosaics that make Ravenna's churches sparkle like no others in the Western world are the product of highly technical skills that reached their peak in the 4th and 5th centuries. The glittering effect is achieved by carefully placing tesserae (bits of glass or calcareous rock) at uneven levels in the plaster base so different colors catch the light at different angles. Most modern mosaic artists have abandoned this older, more difficult technique, and their works lack the shimmer of the ancient mosaics.

Ravenna's mosaic workshops continue to use the old techniques, and you can watch the artists at work inside the courtyard of Basilica di San Vitale. Coop Mosaicisti Ravenna (V. F. Andrini, opposite the entrance to San Vitale, tel. 0544/34799; open 8–noon and 1–7) does mostly restoration work.

special L10,000 ticket (L8,000 students) at any of the sites, which will get you into all of the places described below.

BASILICA DI SAN VITALE AND TOMBA DI GALLA PLACIDIA • This great church and nearby tomb are illuminated by mind-boggling, stunning mosaics—some of the most glorious examples of Byzantine art in the West. The church of San Vitale was built in AD 547, after the Byzantines had taken control of Ravenna, and the Eastern influence is present in the very shape of the building—octagonal instead of a more standard cross shape—as well as the mosaics. In the apse, Christ is portrayed young and uncharacteristically beardless, though the somber Christ overhead sports the usual facial hair. To the left, the Byzantine emperor Justinian is flanked by Bishop Maximian, who consecrated the church, and the empress Theodora, dripping with jewels. Note how irregularly shaped tesserae give them a more lifelike look than the surrounding figures.

Behind the basilica, a small, unremarkable brick building hides still more splendid mosaics. The **Tomba di Galla Placidia** (V. Fiandrini) was built for the sister of Emperor Honorius, who had made Ravenna the capital of the Roman Empire in AD 402, although she was never buried here. She is said to have been beautiful and strong-willed and a very active Christian, endowing churches and supporting priests throughout the realm. Compared to the church, the decoration shows an earlier, more Roman style. The central dome reveals symbols of Christ and the Evangelists, and over the door is a depiction of the Good Shepherd. Eight apostles line the inside of the dome. Notice the small doves at their feet, drinking from the water of the faith. Between the scenes are ribbons, leaves, geometrical designs, flowers, and circular patterns that make the walls and ceilings vibrant with color; the vault is a sublime night sky decked with stars, with the symbols of the four evangelists decorating the corners. Although there are three sarcophagi in the tomb, it is thought that Galla Placidia was interred in Rome. The Tomba is unfortunately under restoration until at least mid-2000; call the number below or the tourist office for an update. *V. San Vitale, tel. 0544/34266. Admission to basilica and mausoleum L6,000. Basilica open Apr.–Sept., daily 9–7; Oct.–Mar., daily 9–4:30.*

BASILICA DI SANT'APOLLINARE NUOVO • Women and men sat on separate sides of this 6th-century church, so the corresponding mosaics depict on one side a procession of 22 virgin saints offering gifts to the Virgin Mary, enthroned with the Christ child on her lap, and on the other a group of male saints offering crowns of martyrdom to the enthroned Christ on the other. All the figures in the processions represent contemporary Christian martyrs. *V. Roma, tel. 0544/497629. From P. del Popolo, take V. Diaz to V. Roma, turn right and continue to corner of V. Carducci. Admission L5,000. Open Apr.–Sept., daily 9–6; Oct.–Mar., daily 9–4:30.*

BATTISTERO DEGLI ARIANI • The Arian Baptistery was built under Theodoric in the late 5th century, when Arianism was Ravenna's official religion (it was declared heretical 100 years later). The Catholics took over the bapistery in the 6th century, along with the neighboring Chiesa di Santo Spirito.

The remaining ceiling mosaic depicts the baptism of Christ. *Piazzetta degli Ariani, tel. 0544/34424. From P. Farini, walk up V. Farini past V. Roma, right on V. Ariani. Admission free. Open daily 9–7, shorter hrs in winter.*

BATTISTERO NEONIANO • Next door to the 18th-century Duomo (rebuilt after an earthquake in 1733), the Neonian Baptistery is another mosaic treasure house. Begun in the 4th century—appropriately enough atop the foundations of an ancient Roman bathhouse—the baptistry was decorated in the 5th century under Bishop Neone. Behind the baptistery and the unimpressive Duomo lies the **Museo Arcivescovile,** containing the Oratorio di Sant'Andrea, the marvelously ornate private chapel of the bishops. In the vault, four angels uphold the heavens; above the door, Christ is shown as a warrior. The museum also houses Bishop Massimiano's carved ivory throne and fragments from the original Duomo. *V. Battistero, tel. 0544/33696. From P. del Popolo, walk through archway of Palazzo del Comune into P. XX Settembre and go left on V. Rasponi; it ends in P. del Duomo. Admission to baptistery and museum L5,000. Open Apr.–Sept., daily 9:30–7; Oct.–Mar., daily 9:30–4:30.*

MAUSOLEO DI DANTE • The humble proportions of this monument belie the scope of the battle that was waged between the Ravennati and Florentines for the remains of Italy's greatest poet. Dante made Ravenna his home several years after he was exiled from Florence in 1302; he died here in 1321. In the 16th century, the Florentines were given papal permission to take his body home. The monks of the attached **Basilica di San Francesco** spooked it away in the night, and the Florentines never got their hands on it. Three hundred years later the poet was finally given a tranquil resting place, and now an oil lamp burns perpetually with oil given ceremoniously by the resigned Florentines, a rite that is repeated yearly in the basilica on September 10. Inside, don't miss the sunken crypt. Through the gate, the **Museo Dantesco** (V. Dante Alighieri 4, tel. 0544/30252; open Apr.–Sept., Tues.–Sun. 9–noon and 3:30–6; Oct.–Mar., Tues.–Sun. 9–noon) contains a manuscript of the *Divine Comedy,* Dante memorabilia, and some minor works of art. Admission to the museum is L5,000, free Sunday. *V. Dante Alighieri. From P. del Popolo, walk straight through P. Garibaldi and along V. Alighieri. Basilica and tomb free. Open Apr.–Sept., daily 9–7; Oct.–Mar., daily 9–noon and 2–5.*

CHEAP THRILLS

The antiques and handicrafts fair (third weekend of each month) in the center will please the antiquarian in you. Free classical music concerts and theatrical performances take place outdoors in the central piazzas from early June to late August. Pick up *Bella di Sera* from the tourist office for schedules and info.

FESTIVALS

In June and July, **Ravenna in Festival** hosts the likes of Pavarotti, Teatro della Scala's orchestra, and the Emilia-Romagna Symphony, as well as ballet and dramatic performances. Tickets can get outrageously expensive, but most shows also sell balcony seats at student prices (L10,000–L30,000). For info call **Teatro Alighieri** (V. Mariani 2, just off P. Garibaldi, tel. 0544/32577; Mon.–Sat. 10–1 and 4–6) or check the useful web page at **www.netgate.it/ra.festival.** There are two **Ravenna Jazz festivals:** one during Easter week, the other in late July. Both bill big-name American artists. Tickets run L25,000–L40,000, and can be bought at **Ravenna Jazz** (V. San Mama 75, tel. 0544/408030 or 0544/405666), or check out their Web site at www.ejn.it/ejn/ for the whos, whats, and wheres.

NEAR RAVENNA

RAVENNA'S BEACHES

Ravenna's beaches are close enough (20 min by bus) to serve as a base for exploring Ravenna while you take advantage of the budget seaside accommodations and raging nightlife. **Marina di Ravenna** has a little bit of everything: the best campground, some hopping discotheques and pubs, and a beach full of young surfer yahoos fighting over waves. **Lido Adriano** has a few discos but is the least attractive of the three areas, and **Punta Marina** has campgrounds and spectacular beaches abutting a pine forest, but a quieter nightlife. **Visitor information** for the beaches is available at the main tourist office in Ravenna (*see* Basics, *above*) or at Marina di Ravenna's **Pro Loco** (V. delle Nazioni 159, tel. 0544/530117, daily 9:30–12:30 and 3–6) in summer only.

COMING AND GOING • Bus 70 from Ravenna's Piazza Farini hits Punta Marina and Marina di Ravenna twice hourly until 10:20 PM. Bus 71 leaves hourly from Piazza Farini for Punta Marina and Lido Adriano until 7:30 PM. Tickets cost L1,700 each way and can be bought in tobacco shops in Piazza Farini and newsstands at the bus station. Buses drop off and pick up passengers from nearly every

MOSAICMANIA

Among the precious few dusty remains of the old port town of Classis, a mile or so outside Ravenna and now landlocked, is the Basilica di Sant'Apollinare in Classe. The church is not much on the outside, but inside this 6th-century plain redbrick structure are exceptional Byzantine mosaics still retaining their original glitter after more than a millennium.

The lower portion in the central mosaic depicts Ravenna's patron saint, Sant'Apollinare, in a pastoral setting—a symbol of the faithful being shepherded toward Christ. The upper part, in lustrous gold—achieved by applying real gold leaf to glass tesserae—portrays the transfiguration of Christ on Mt. Tabor. The four mythical creatures flying toward Christ in the apse represent the evangelists: John, the eagle; Matthew, the angel; Mark, the lion; and Luke, the bull. Precious marble columns and surfaces and vibrant colors add to the richness. The bus ride, 5 km (3 mi) southeast from Ravenna, is well worth it. V. Romea Sud, Classe, tel. 0544/527004. Bus 4 or 44 from P. Farini or P. Caduti. Admission free. Open daily 8:30–noon and 2–5:30.

bagno (beach club) on the *lungomare* (boardwalk). The beaches are separated by only a few kilometers, and a good way to get around is to rent a **bike** for about L15,000 per day (in Marina di Ravenna, V. dei Mille 27, no phone; in Punta Marina, P. Saffi 19, tel. 0544/437226; and in Lido Adriano, V. Marziale 19 and V. Virgilio 6, no phone).

WHERE TO SLEEP AND EAT • The tourist office in Ravenna can give you an ample list of hotels in all three towns. **Regina** in Punta Marina (V. Fontana 73, tel. and fax 0544/437148) is the queen of budget hotels, with its great location behind the pine grove and low prices (L95,000 for a double with bath), but if you show up in July and August, rooms with meals (3-day minimum; officially no other option, but negotiable) run L75,000 per person (L55,000 in low season). In Marina di Ravenna, **Oasis** (V. Bernardini 52, off V. delle Nazioni, tel. 0544/530404, fax 0544/531636) does friendly doubles with bath for L90,000 including breakfast. For camping, the huge **Rivaverde** (V. delle Nazioni 301, tel. 0544/530491; reception only open until 8 PM; closed Sept.–late Apr.), in Marina di Ravenna, is staked out just across from the beach in a quiet forest, only a 10-minute walk from pubs, discos, and restaurants. In July and August you'll pay L16,500 for a spot and L9,500 per person, less in low season. If desperate, take Bus 71 from Ravenna to **Camping Adriano** (V. dei Campeggi 7, tel. 0544/437230) and **Coop 3** (V. dei Campeggi 8, tel. 0544/437353), both noisy, crowded, and very close to the road. Both campgrounds charge L8,000 per spot and L8,000–L14,000 per person. Fortunately for travelers, Italians aren't into roughing it—all three sites have showers and electricity.

Most of the beach restaurants are glorified (or not-so-glorified) fast-food joints, dishing up greasy pizza and foul fried fish to sun-warped crowds. Hit one of the rolling carts along the *lungomare*, which sell fortifying *piadine* (L3,000–L6,000). If you aren't up to the astronomically priced pastas, you can get pizza by the slice (L3,500). Or simply grab picnic vittles from **Euro Mix Market** (V. delle Nazioni 138, tel. 0544/530508); they're open daily 8–1 and 4:30–8 (limited hrs in winter).

AFTER DARK • Marina di Ravenna is where the action is. The evening generally begins at one of the numerous pubs. When you're ready to hit the dance floor, **Sud** (alias **Balla coi Lupi**; V. delle Nazioni 159, tel. 0544/530514) is the starting point. Another disco is **B. B. King** (Lungomare Colombo 171B, tel. 0544/438494). Both discos go on until 3 or 4 on weekends in high season—and both are cover-free. The weekly *Fred*, available from newsstands, has up-to-date listings.

BRISIGHELLA

Brisighella's trio of craggy peaks lift a castle, a clock tower, and a church up against the sky while the town stretches through the valleys and vineyards between them, making all your Disney-inspired medieval dreams come true. In the Apennine foothills, where the green foliage is brilliant and the brick of ancient buildings glows russet and orange, this medieval village has a beauty like no other in Romagna. Brisighella dates to the days of Galla Placidia, and its outrageous Medieval Festival (*see below*) affords a taste of Italy's bygone days. Although the incredible scenery is the real reason to come, Brisighella has a fair number of sights for so small a town. Poke your nose into the **Antica Via degli Asini,** the oldest street in town, a raised and covered mule-train path with low beamed ceilings and crescent windows. To find the hidden path, head uphill from Piazza Carducci, the town's main square, go right on Via Naldi, and follow the signs. The **clock tower** has been bonging off the hours since 1290. Inside, the **Museo del Tempo** (Museum of Time) is an overdone but funky tourist trap with clocks, tarot cards, alchemical vials, and arcane devices, including a copy of Foucault's pendulum. Included in the L1,000 admission is an astrological reading by the tower's keeper. The museum and clock tower (tel. 0546/80267) are open April 15–October 15, weekdays 3–7, weekends 10–noon and 3–7; in winter only 2–6 on Sunday.

On the town's central peak sits the 14th-century **rocca** (fortress), which now holds the **Museo del Lavoro Contadino** (Museum of Country Life; tel. 0546/83129; admission L3,500). Re-creations of country kitchens, bedrooms, and workrooms of the Middle Ages fill the castle's towers, and the view from the battlements and catwalks is stunning. It's open April 15–October 15, daily 10–noon and 3:30–7, weekends 10–12:15 and 3:30–7:30; October 16–April 14, Sat. 2:30–4:30 and Sun. 10–noon and 2:30–4:30. The town's third and most distant peak, topped by **Il Santuario del Monticino,** isn't really worth the arduous journey to get to. On Friday, Brisighella abounds with open markets and free small concerts in its piazzas. Brisighella's **Pro Loco** (V. Metelli/Piazzetta Gabolo 5, tel. 0546/81166; open Mon.–Sat. 9:30–12:30 and 3:30–5:30, Sun. 10–noon and 4–7:30, shorter hrs in winter) hands out maps and festival information.

The inscription on Dante's tomb in Ravenna reads "Here in this corner lies Dante, exiled from his native land, born to Florence, an unloving mother," which pretty much sums up the locals' attitude about their rightful claim to Dante's body.

COMING AND GOING • Brisighella's **train station** (V. de Gasperi 12, tel. 1478/88088) lies on the Florence–Faenza and Bologna–Rimini train routes, and getting here is a bit of a pain. First, you have to go to Faenza. Ten trains daily run to Faenza from Ravenna (L5,100, 45 min), and hourly trains run to Rimini (1 hr, L5,700). Once in Faenza, you must hunt down one of 10 daily trains to Brisighella (10 min, L2,200)—these aren't always posted, so you may want to ask when the next one leaves.

Getting around Brisighella's hilltop sights takes some climbing; you'll find the staircases up to the fortress and the clock tower uphill from Piazza Carducci—follow the signs. You can also take Viale Pascoli from the train station to the fortress; a dirt path loops around the local vineyards joining the fortress and the clock tower, providing a splendid view of both.

WHERE TO SLEEP AND EAT • Charming and scenic as it may be, staying in Brisighella can be predictably expensive. **Tre Colli** (V. Gramsci 9, tel. 0546/81147, fax 0546/81203) has three-star doubles for L100,000 including breakfast. To reach it from the station, go right on Via Gaspari and right on Via Gramsci. In the medieval middle, **Albergo La Rocca** (V. delle Volte 10, tel. 0546/81180, fax 0546/80289) commands L110,000 for smart doubles. Wherever you end up, don't miss one of the best restaurants in the area: **La Grotta** (V. Metelli 2, tel. 0546/81829; closed Tues.) offers a set vegetarian menu (L55,000) in addition to an excellent à la carte menu based on seasonal ingredients.

FESTIVALS • Brisighella's **Medieval Festival** is a pagan pleasure fair that transforms the village, taking it back to rowdier and more colorful days. Banquet halls serve plebeian meals in the "garden of delights" (off Piazza Carducci), and restaurants serve medieval feasts. The annual festival goes on for roughly two weeks between mid-June and mid-July (weekends are liveliest). Admission to the city center (unless you're staying in a local hotel) and performances is L15,000. For details, call the tourist office. The **Sagra della Polenta,** in October, celebrates—guess what—polenta; in November, the truffle is hallowed, and the olive gets the limelight in December.

FELLINIVILLE

Federico Fellini, Italy's most famous film director, was from Rimini. Best known for classics like "8½" and "La Dolce Vita," he waxed nostalgic about his formative years in Amarcord—dialect for Mi Ricordo (I Remember)—and in Rimini, Il Mio Paese (Rimini, My Hometown), an essay and photographic series. In return, the town honored its favorite son with a park that bears his name. An international film festival focusing on independent and student films is held around the last week of September. For more info contact Riminicinema (V. Gambalunga 27, 47037 Rimini, tel. 0541/26399, fax 0541/24227).

RIMINI

If you have never been to Rimini in summer, you probably wouldn't guess that it is the fourth most visited city in Italy. Although the top three cities—Venice, Rome, and Florence—are known for art and culture, the 4 million tourists who come to Rimini every year are looking for sun and sand. There are really two Riminis: one is the family-oriented beach playground on the warm and murky Adriatic; the other, a hot international beach scene, thong bathing suits by day, sweaty discos by night. You wouldn't know by the look of things these days, but Rimini was born as a Roman town at the junction of two great consular roads and remained a sleepy fishing village until it was almost entirely destroyed in World War II. If you're out for a little sleazy, cheesy fun *alla* Seaside Heights, Rimini is great. But if overpriced strips of touristy shops and polluted waters don't float your boat, bypass this resort or head straight from the train station to the centro storico—never seen by most sun worshipers and nightclub habitués—for a look at the phenomenal Tempio Malatestiano and some Roman ruins (*see* Worth Seeing, *below*)—then continue on your way.

BASICS

Rimini has two **tourist offices** (train station, Via Dante 86, tel. 0541/51331; open June–Sept., daily 8–8; Oct.–May, Mon.–Sat. 8–7, Sun. 9:30–12:30; also at the waterfront, P. Fellini 3 (tel. 0541/56902 or 0541/54019; open daily 8–8, in winter daily 8–2) in key locations. Both have exhaustive info on activities, excursions, and lodgings but won't make reservations. While you're there, ask for a copy of *Chiamami Città* for the nitty-gritty on nightlife. You can change money just about anywhere along the waterfront. For recorded general info on events and hotels, call toll-free 167/273570.

COMING AND GOING

Frequent trains run between Rimini and Ancona (1 hr, L8,800), Ravenna (1 hr 20 min, L4,700), and Bologna (1 hr, L10,100). Rimini's **train station** (P. Cesare Battisti, tel. 1478/88088) forms the boundary between Rimini-Città and Rimini-Marina, the Jekyll-and-Hyde city zones. In high season it's an absolute zoo, but helpful hotel-locating services abound at the station. Luggage storage is open 24 hours a day. If the excitement incites a sudden desire to get the hell out, take in some sun for an hour and then head straight for **Centro Turistico Studentesco** (V. Matteucci 4, off V. Principe Amedeo, tel. 0541/55525), which can take you far, far from Rimini at student-youth prices.

You need never lay eyes on the **bus station** (V. Clementini 33, tel. 0541/24547), because almost all buses pass through the more convenient Piazza Battisti, in front of the train station. The ticket window in Piazza Battisti, open 6 AM–2 AM, sells city bus and tram tickets as well as tickets to nearby towns (consult **TRAM,** tel. 0541/396444). In Rimini-Marina, buses also depart from Piazza Tripoli (Tram 11, Stop 14), on the waterfront. The ticket window (P. Tripoli 8/B, tel. 0541/390444) is open daily 5 AM–2 AM. Tickets are also sold in tobacco shops; schedules and prices are posted at the train station and on nearby windows at Piazza Tripoli. Buses to San Marino (every hr, 1 hr, L4,000) are run by **Borelli** (tel. 0541/372432) and **Benedettini** (tel. 0541/903854).

GETTING AROUND

For the crowded, dizzying array of minuscule bikinis and bare chests, head for **Rimini-Marina**. The stretch of beaches extends south of Marina Centro—Rimini's central beach area—to Miramare, Riccione, Cattolica, and Gabicce, and north to Rivabella and Viserba. **Tram-buses** tote people up and down the coast. Two lines begin in Piazza Tre Martiri (5:30 AM–2:35 AM in high season) in the centro storico, stopping at the train station and heading to beaches north and south, with connecting lines farther down. One-hour tickets cost L1,500, a day pass costs L5,000, and a L20,000 ticket is good for eight days; tickets are sold at tobacco shops and ticket windows (*see* Coming and Going, *above*). A special bus service called **BlueLine** has several lines that run all night, passing most of the discos in the hills around town. All lines depart from the train station; tickets cost L4,000, and you buy them on the bus.

Via Vespucci is the main strip in Marina Centro, but it changes names every few blocks. You don't have to pay much attention to addresses, though, because hotels and discos print the number of their tram stop on all business cards and flyers, and you'll soon find yourself speaking in *fermate* (stops). The centro storico, full of beautiful piazzas and ancient monuments, is only slightly more complicated: the main street, Corso d'Augusto, cuts across town from the Bridge of Tiberius to the Arch of Augustus, passing through the two main piazzas on the way. To reach Piazza Tre Martiri from the train station, take Minibus 1 or 2, Tram 11, or walk 10 minutes up Via Dante, which changes name to Via IV Novembre. If you're just doing things in town, most of it is fairly walkable, but many of the discos are a ways out. Get your mopeds (L25,000 per hr, L80,000 per day) at **Noleggio Ambra** (P. Kennedy 6, Stop 12, tel. 0541/27016) from May to September, 8 AM–midnight.

WHERE TO SLEEP

With 1,400 registered hotels, cheap sleeps are not a problem unless you show up in August, when prices go sky high and "reservation" is the magic word. For reservations, call **hotel reservation service** (tel. 0541/51194) or visit their desk at the train station, open June–August, daily 8–8. Representatives from local hotels will undoubtedly accost you—take advantage, because they'll usually arrange transportation to the hotel. But beware hidden charges and distant locales; always establish cost and location ahead of time. Prices are generally negotiable, so play hardball. Most hotels in Rimini are full-pension establishments; unless you plan to live at your hotel, look for a half-pension or *meublé* (room only) establishment, which often serves optional breakfast for around L5,000. Note that many hotels in Rimini are closed October–Easter.

Hotel Meublé Lucciola (V. Derna 25, Tram 11 to Stop 13, tel. and fax 0541/390852; cash only), in Marina Centro, is packed with young people during the summer. The beach is only two blocks away, and doubles (L70,000–L100,000, all with bath) are decent and generally clean. **Hotel R. Lily** (V. Regina Elena 175, Tram 11 to Stop 20, tel.and fax 0541/392800; closed Oct.–1 wk before Easter) offers slightly upscale doubles with bath for L76,000 per person with full pension, or L30,000 per person without meals (not available in August). **Hotel Amsterdam** (V. Regina Elena 9, near Tram 11 Stop 14, tel. and fax 0541/391132; closed Oct.–Easter) is also right on the strip. This full-pension hotel offers a breakfast-only option, charging L70,000 for a double. **Hotel Meublé Tergeste** (V. Trieste 4, tel. and fax 0541/53015) charges L70,000–L110,000 for a clean but somewhat cramped double with bath.

APARTMENTS • If for some reason you'd like to stay a whole week in Rimini and have some friends with you, it's best to rent an apartment. Check at the tourist office for listings. One to try is **Residence Internazionale** (V. Regina Elena 37, Tram 11 to Stop 15, tel. and fax 0541/390160; cash only), just one block from the beach and open all year. As everywhere else, the rates basically double in July and August (from around L720,000 per week for 4 people to upwards of L1,500,000).

CAMPING • Trams will take you to campgrounds, which fill up in the summer with Italian families and their RVs. Prices range from L8,000 to L12,500 per person and L12,000 to L15,000 per tent—making a hotel a very attractive option. Well-equipped but unsightly **Camping Maximum** (V. Principe di Piemonte, Tram 11 to Stop 33, tel. 0541/372602, fax 0541/370271; open only Aug.; cash only) is across from the beach in Miramare. There's a bar, showers, and plenty of electricity. Bathroomless bungalows run about L90,000–L140,000 (four people) and L120,000–L240,000 (six people), depending on the season. Shady lawns and proximity to Rimini (10 min north on Tram 4) make **Camping Italia** (V. Toscanelli 112, Tram 4 to Stop 14, tel. 0541/732882; cash only) slightly more pleasant than Maximum. For even more comfort try the bungalows, which cost from L70,000 to L110,000, depending on the season.

WHERE TO EAT

The main strip is lined with tourist traps with sidewalk menus in six languages—always a bad sign—and dozens of overpriced snack bars. But there are a few places that are a good value for your lire. First and foremost, some claim that the best seafood in all of Italy can be found at **La Locanda di San Martino** (V. Emilia, 226, tel. 0541/680127; closed Mon.; reserve well ahead). The *spaghettoni al frutti di mare*, *grigliata di pesce mista*, or just about anything else you order will send you spinning toward gustatory euphoria. Meals run around L50,000 per person for multiple courses and wine. It's off the road out of Rimini heading toward Bologna (Bus 9 toward Sant'Arcangelo will take you there; keep your eyes peeled for the green sign). Otherwise, treat yourself to a meal at **4 Colonne** (V. Ortrigara 65, tel. 054151252; closed Mon. and Nov.), right on the wharf, or **Ristorante Europa** (V. Roma 51, tel. and fax 0541/28761; closed Sun.), near the train station, both good places to try local fish dishes; expect to pay about L60,000 for a complete meal, excluding wine. Another good bet is **Osteria de Borg** (V. Forzieri 12, tel. 0541/56074; no lunch; closed Mon.), where a tasting menu with wine costs a reasonable (for Rimini) L40,000. For lighter (and cheaper) fare, get a pizza from **Cavalieri della Rosa** (P. Cavour 15, tel. 0541/781400; open Thurs.–Sun. noon–3 and 7–11), or pick up a pair of crepes at **La Crêperia** (P. Gregorio da Rimini 9, off Vecchia Pescheria, tel. 0541/52477; cash only). Top it off with good gelato from **Marselli** (V. Tripoli 110). For groceries, the **Standa** supermarket on the strip (V. Vespucci 133, tel. 0541/391494) is open Monday–Saturday 8:30 AM–11 PM, Sunday 9 AM–11 PM.

WORTH SEEING

As is only appropriate for the city that lies at the finish line of the legendary Via Emilia, Rimini maintains vestiges of ancient Rome: on central Piazza Cavour you'll find the **pescheria,** a Roman open-air fish market with a triple-arched entrance (now the territory of junk vendors), a long marble arcade, and four dolphin fountains in its corners. Straight down Corso d'Augusto is the **Arco d'Augusto** (where C. d'Augusto meets Largo G. Cesare, south of P. Tre Martiri) at the southern edge of the centro storico. It's the oldest Roman triumphal arch still standing in Italy (27 BC); it marks the meeting point of the Via Flaminia (which runs to Rome) and the Via Emilia. At the other end of Corso d'Augusto is **Ponte di Tiberio.** The stone bridge, constructed between AD 14 and 21, still supports heavy traffic after nearly 2,000 years of wear and five years of heavy World War II bombing. Beyond the bridge on the right lies the cute neighborhood of small, brightly painted houses called **Borgo San Giuliano,** where Fellini filmed most of the movie *Amarcord.*

The imposing brick **Chiesa di Sant'Agostino** (V. Cairoli, near Castello Malatestiano; open daily 8–noon and 3:30–6), built in 1247, contains an amazing fresco cycle painted by three Riminese artists. On the right wall of the apse, a scene of particular interest depicts Dante (in profile in the long gown) and Petrarch in a crowd welcoming St. John home from exile. The **Castel Sismondo** (P. Malatesta, up V. Poletti from P. Cavour) was once a massive moated fortress complete with six towers, four bridges, and several dungeons. Built in 1437 and dismantled in the 19th century, this shell of a castle is now home to the **Museo Dinz Rialto** (tel. 0541/785780; admission L4,000; open weekdays 8–1:30, Tues. and Thurs. also 3:30–6), with anthropological relics collected by Italian adventurer Delfino Dinz Rialto. The castle's **Corte degli Agostiniani** (V. Cairoli 42) hosts a smashing retrospective selection of **summer films** every July, with past choices ranging from Hal Hartley to Bernardo Bertolucci. Admission is L8,000. Pick up a schedule at the tourist office. The **Museo della Città** (V. Tonini 1, tel. 0541/21482; admission L6,000; open Tues.–Fri. 8:30–12:30 and 5–7, Sat. 5–7, Sun. 4–7) is a showplace for centuries of Rimini's painters; Bellini's *Pietà* is the high point.

It's worth making the trip into the centro storico just to see the **Tempio Malatestiano** (V. IV Novembre, a block west of Piazza Tre Martiri, tel. 0541/51130; admission free; open daily 9–1 and 3:30–6). Notoriously witty, learned, and unscrupulous even among his 15th-century peers, Sigismondo Malatesta banished his first wife, strangled his second, and poisoned his third. He finally settled down with his mistress Isotta degli Atti, and when she died he was so grief-stricken that he had the humble Romanesque-Gothic Basilica di San Francesco transformed into a monument in her honor. Leon Battista Alberti's facade, Agostino di Duccio's sculptures, Giotto's crucifix, and a fresco by Piero della Francesca turned this once-ordinary church into a Renaissance treasure house. Don't miss the rest of the interior, decorated with pagan images of nymphs, grape clusters, and elephants (the family symbol) and marked with the intertwined lovers' initials (which look like dollar signs). How romantic. Though the church retained its dedication to St. Francis, Pope Pius II was not fooled—he called Sigi an incestuous, adulterous, homosexual tyrant and had him not only excommunicated but also burned in effigy on the steps of three churches in Rome.

AFTER DARK

Like a vampire, Rimini lives for the night, packing its strip with partyers and sucking the money straight from their veins. The *passeggiata* (social stroll) begins early in the evening and keeps going until well after midnight, with a few pit stops at pubs along the way. The discos pick up where the *passeggiata* drops off and boom until around 3:30 or 4 AM. For info on nightspots, pick up the free *Chiamami Città* at the tourist office.

DISCOS • The most extensive collection of discos in Italy lights up the Adriatic around Rimini every summer. Glitter and glamour has its price—expect to pay as much as a L50,000 cover to get dancin', so keep your eyes open for passes distributed around town. Sort of a rave-meets-pretentious-fashion-show, **Barcelona** (V. Vespucci 119, Tram 11 to Stop 10, tel. 0541/390820) is central and kickin', and **Chic** (V. Regina Margherita 83, Marebello, Tram 11 to Stop 24, tel. 0541/374304), which is loud and crowded, has a slightly Xanadu-esque quality (its theme is "Get into Magic"). Some of the best discos are in the hills outside of town. Getting to them can be difficult without a car or *motorino*, but if you are visiting between mid-July and the end of August, take the special BlueLine buses (*see* Getting Around, *above*); expect to pay as much as L35,000 cover charge. One such out-of-town spot is **Bandiera Gialla** (V. Antiche Fonti Romane 95, Covignano, tel. 0541/752053), known throughout Italy as the location for a cheesy but popular TV program is filmed. Or try **Coco Rico** (Via Chietti 44, Riccione; take BlueLine Bus 10 or 11; cover L50,000).

PUBS • Three pubs with live music and locals are the **Bounty Adventure Club** (V. Weber 4, tel. 0541/391900), **The Barge** (Lungomare Tintori 13, tel. 0541/22685), and **Rock Island** (end of Rimini Pier, tel. 0541/50178, cover on weekends, nightly in summer L15,000 with 1 free drink).

OUTDOOR ACTIVITIES

Hit the beach and pay. Rimini's 29 km (18 mi) of brown-watered coastline are divided into sections, each consisting of a bagno governed by a *bagnino* (the guy with the cash register), who rents umbrellas (L10,000) and deck chairs (L7,000). Bagni 1–50 are the hippest, as they're closest to central Rimini; some even have waterslides. Bagno 12 has free volleyball and basketball courts. Actually venturing into the water has the vague feeling of dipping your body into a stagnant pool of warm sewage; hold your nose and try to keep your head above the surface. If waterslides and wave machines are your thing, you'll be happy as a clam at **Aquafan,** a water park that magically transforms into a pretty happening disco on summer nights. *V. Pistoia, off Autostrada 14, Riccione, tel. 0541/603050. From Marina Centro, Tram 11 to end of Riccione, transfer to Bus 41, 42, or 45. Admission L32,000, L20,000 after 3 PM. Open 10 AM–12:30 PM and 3–6:30 PM (water park); 10 PM–4 AM (disco).*

NEAR RIMINI

REPUBLIC OF SAN MARINO

An excursion into "the world's smallest and oldest republic" is about as culturally enriching as a trip to the video arcade. According to legend, San Marino was founded by a stonecutter named Marino who settled here with a small community of Christians, escaping persecution by pagan emperor Diocletian. Today it's impossible to tell whether San Marino has been around that long or sprang up yesterday as a tourist trap, with fairy-tale castles and a shameless tourist economy. Other than the novelty of getting a passport stamp and seeing different phones, stamps, and coins, the only reason to make the trek from Rimini (14 buses daily from the train station, 50 min, L4,000) is the castle-top view of the stunning green countryside around the tiny country. Still, this view is nothing to scoff at; the sheer drops will make jaws drop and acrophobes quiver. For more info, call the San Marino **tourist office** (Contra Omagnano 20, tel. 0549/882400; open Mon. and Thurs. 8:15–2:15 and 3–6, Tues., Wed., and Fri. 8:15–2:15), which will also stamp your passport—get this—for L2,000.

However, if you travel here, you should follow the yellow brick road to **Castello della Guaita** (tel. 0549/991369; admission L4,000; open 8–8, shorter hrs in winter) and **Castello della Cesta** (tel. 0549/991295; admission L4,000; same hrs); both have ramparts for wandering and towers for exploring, as well as fabulous views and sheer drop-offs. Other must-sees are the **Piazza della Libertà,** whose battlemented and clock-topped Palazzo Pubblico is guarded by San Marino's real-life soldiers in their green uniforms, and the **Ferrari Museum** (Maranello Rosso; V. III Settembre 3, get off the bus at the border crossing, tel. 0549/900824; admission L10,000; open Mon.–Sat. 10–6, Sun. 10–1 and 2–6), with an example of every Ferrari made since the 1950s.

FLORENCE AND TUSCANY

BY REBECCA LIM

REVISED BY PATRICIA RUCIDLO

For many, Tuscany is quintessential Italy: idyllic landscapes, dramatic hill towns with stunning views, great food and wine, and, of course, superlative art. No surprise, then, that the region has long been a favorite of foreign visitors. Towns are relatively close together, easy to get to with public transportation, and particularly well preserved. First on most lists is a visit to Florence followed by Siena and Pisa—all three justly famous for art and architecture. But the bounty of Tuscany does not stop there, and just about everywhere you go you will be rewarded with similar joys—and often smaller crowds.

The name Tuscany evokes the Etruscan origins of many of the towns on the map today. In almost every case, the Romans built on the foundations of their Etruscan predecessors. Later the towns were walled in order to keep out invaders, usually neighboring rivals. Sometimes several towns banded together for security. By the 14th century, Florence, Siena, and Pisa had emerged as principal powers. Ultimately the rise of a solid banking industry and a rapidly growing merchant class guaranteed Florence's political and economic dominance. In this monied climate, humanism and the arts flourished, giving birth to what we now call the Renaissance.

Industry thrives in Pistoia, Prato, and the exurbs of Florence. Vine-laden Chianti, farm-flanked Arezzo, and the resort island of Elba mostly rely on either agriculture or tourism to bolster their economies. Hill towns like San Gimignano, Volterra, and Cortona remain behind their original walls, with populations smaller than in medieval and Renaissance times.

As you might expect of the home of Michelangelo's *David* and the Leaning Tower of Pisa, Tuscany is subject to a year-round tourist invasion that peaks in summer. But a refuge from the crowds is never far. Short bus rides to small towns, abandoned abbeys, family-run vineyards, and crumbling fortresses with staggering views are almost always escape possibilities. When you decide to visit Florence's Uffizi Gallery, remember that you can now book it in advance and skip the mind-numbingly long lines. It's a real treat to see the extraordinary and unparalleled masterpieces that await you.

Tuscans know a thing or two about good eating. Meals often begin with *crostini di fegatini,* an aromatic chicken liver spread usually served warm on garlic toast, and tasty *finocchiona,* a pork salami spiked with fennel seeds. Day-old saltless Tuscan bread is toasted, rubbed with garlic, and drizzled with olive oil (*fettunta*) or topped with various ingredients (*bruschetta*). Bread is also used to thicken wonderful soups—*ribollita* (minestrone thickened with bread and beans) and *acquacotta* (vegetable soup with eggs)—and for summer concoctions like *panzanella* (a salad composed of moistened bread, olive oil,

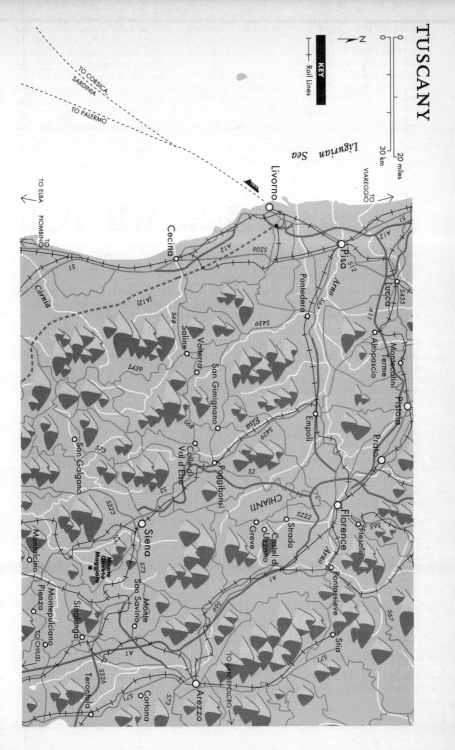

TUSCANY

KEY

Rail Lines

N

0   20 miles
0   30 km

Ligurian Sea

TO CORSICA,
SARDINIA

TO PALERMO

TO ELBA

TO PIOMBINO

TO VIAREGGIO

Livorno

Cecina

Pisa

Lucca

Pistoia

Prato

Altopascio

Montecatini Terme

Pontedera

Arno

Empoli

Fiesole

Florence

Pontassieve

Arno

Stia

Greve

Castel di Uzzano

Strada

CHIANTI

Poggibonsi

Colle di Val d'Elsa

San Gimignano

Volterra

Saline

Elsa

San Galgano

Siena

Monte Oliveto Maggiore

Monte San Savino

Sinalunga

Pienza

Montepulciano

Montalcino

Cortona

Terontola

Arezzo

TO SANSEPOLCRO

TO CHIUSI

Cornia

TO CORSICA, SARDINIA

S1

S12

A12

S206

S435

A11

S439

S67

S68

S2

S222

S595

S326

S73

S223

A1

S71

S5

S429

197

tomatoes, and basil). Typical Italian first courses like pasta, gnocchi, and risotto, while good, are usually not the strong suit in Tuscan cuisine. Start with *crespelle alla fiorentina* (crepes stuffed with ricotta and spinach and served with a bechamel sauce) or pappa al pomodoro (tomato and bread soup). Move on to any of the grilled meat selections such as the enormous slabs of prime Chianina beef that make the *bistecca alla fiorentina* or the *lombatina* (a veal chop) eaten in a bite or two. A serious passion for meat is balanced with some of the best vegetables in the country, often homegrown. Tuscans can seriously deep fry their vegetables—you'll be blessed if you're visiting during artichoke season. Along the coast and on the islands, fish replaces meat: cuttlefish with peas, fried calamari, salt cod fillets fried and baked with olives in a tomato sauce, to name a only few. White beans called *cannellini*, a rich source of protein for those who in the past couldn't afford meat, often round off many a dish. Spinach is so beloved by Tuscans that they created a special expression for it: *inzimino*, meaning "stewed with spinach." Wash it all down with Chianti, Brunello, or Vino Nobile.

FLORENCE

Though it's true that stirrings of the Renaissance were appearing all over Italy from the mid-13th century, Florence is the city that really gave it a push. Imitation of Roman antiquity gave birth to something completely new and different: a new respect for learning and a new creativity in art and architecture. Interest in things classical spread quickly among painters, sculptors, architects, poets, and writers. Because Florence enjoyed an expanding and rapidly growing economy, thanks in large part to its prowess in banking and the cloth industry, many merchants became wealthy. With such wealth came building projects, including ornate palazzi and grandiose refurbishment of churches, and a boom in art patronage.

First a Roman town of relatively little importance, Florence grew in size and prominence as it conquered and took control of most of the small towns around it, as well as important neighbors such as Pisa and Siena. Meanwhile, the banking families became more and more powerful, and by the 1430s one of them—the Medici—dominated the rest. The most famous of the clan was Lorenzo de' Medici—called il Magnifico—a brilliant politician and a highly educated patron of the arts. He gathered at his court a circle of poets, artists, philosophers, architects, and musicians and organized workshops for young talents to learn from the masters.

The Renaissance was Florence's golden period of creativity. Art made great leaps toward a new naturalism through the study of perspective and anatomy. Architects rediscovered the techniques used by the great builders of the past, the ancient Romans. Sculptors sought to render flesh from stone. Above all, the human mind and body were placed at the center of their universe, and for the first time since the fall of Rome an educated mind was esteemed as much as a pious soul. The Renaissance man was born: someone who, like Leonardo da Vinci, could design a canal, paint a portrait, or solve a mathematical problem with equal ease. Not everyone took part in the Renaissance; it was somthing largely enjoyed by upper-class men, and sometimes, if they were lucky enough, the women in their families.

What's left of the Florentine Renaissance is visible all over the *centro storico* (historic center) of the town. You can walk through narrow streets that haven't changed much since the 15th century, duck into churches with their Renaissance fresco cycles still intact on the walls of private chapels, and listen to the bells of the Duomo chime—much as they would have 500 years ago.

BASICS

AMERICAN EXPRESS

Florence's AmEx office (V. Dante Alighieri 22r, tel. 055/50981; open weekdays 9–5:30, Sat. 9–12:30) offers the whole range of services.

CHANGING MONEY

If you arrive without a lira in hand, you can change money at the train station (no commission), although better rates await you at the many banks and ATMs in the town center.

CONSULATES

For emergencies ranging from lost documents to arrests, births, deaths, or military invasions, head to your consulate. Both the **U.S. Consulate** (Lungarno Vespucci 38, tel. 055/2398276; open weekdays 9:30–12:30 and 2–3:300) and the **U.K. Consulate** (Lungarno Corsini 2, tel. 055/284133; open weekdays 9:30–12:30 and 2:30–4:30) are on the north bank of the Arno, west of the Ponte Vecchio. Canadian, New Zealand, Irish, South African, and Australian visitors need to contact their consulates in either Rome or Milan.

DISCOUNT TRAVEL AGENCIES

Centro Turistico Studentesco (CTS; V. dè Ginori 25r, tel. 055/289570; open weekdays 9:30–1:30 and 2:30–6 and Sat. 9:30–12:30) is the place for cheap fares. To be eligible for discounts, you need to have a CTS membership card (L45,000) or if you're a student, an ISIC card (L15,000). From the Duomo, walk north on Borgo San Lorenzo until it becomes Via de' Ginori.

EMERGENCIES

The main **police** station is near Piazza della Libertà (V. Zara 2, tel. 113). For **ambulance** service, call 118. If you need hospital treatment—and an interpreter—you can call **AVO** (tel. 055/2344567; Mon., Wed., Fri. 4–6, Tues. and Thurs. 10–12), a group of volunteer interpreters who offer their services free.

Each region in Italy has its own specialties, usually based on simple ingredients. Tuscans are disparagingly called "mangiafagioli," or bean eaters, by other Italians.

ENGLISH-LANGUAGE BOOKS AND NEWSPAPERS

There's no problem getting books in English, but you'll pay for the pleasure of having them here. The **Paperback Exchange** (V. Fiesolana 31r, tel. 055/2478154) has the best deals on new and used books and will let you trade in your paperbacks for used ones. **BM Bookstore** (Borgo Ognissanti 4/r, tel. 055/294575) has a small but comprehensive selection of Italian cooking, history, and travel books, as well as the latest in American and English fiction. Go to **After Dark** (V. de' Ginori 47r, tel. 055/294203) for the town's best selection of English-language newspapers and magazines, from the *L.A. Weekly* to the latest biker tattoo 'zine.

LAUNDRY

Wash & Dry Lavarapido (V. de' Servi 105r, just south of P. Santissima Annunziata) is a coin-op chain with other locations around town. Ask your pension or hostel proprietor for the closest branch. It costs about L12,000 to wash and dry one load. There's also the **Lavanderia Guelfa** (V. Guelfa 55r, tel. 055/490628; open weekdays 7–7, Sat. 7–2).

MAIL

If you're an American Express card holder, have your mail sent there (*see above*). Otherwise, mail marked *fermo posta* (held mail; postal code: 50100) will be held at the main post office (Palazzo delle Poste, V. Pellicceria 3, off P. della Repubblica, tel. 055/2774266; open weekdays 8:15–6:15, Sat. 8:15–6:15) for up to a month; it also offers money exchange weekdays 8:15–5, but the rates aren't the greatest. Other branch offices around town close at 1:40 on weekdays and at noon on Saturday.

MEDICAL AID

For 24-hour medical service with multilingual doctors, call 055/475411. For emergencies call 113. In addition to the Farmacia Comunale (tel. 055/289435) in the train station, **Molteni** (V. Calzaiuoli 7r, tel. 055/215472, near P. della Signoria) is always open and posts a schedule of rotating pharmacies that also do 24-hour duty.

ON-LINE RESOURCES

Set up an E-mail account at the **Internet Train** (V. dell'Oriuolo 25/Ar, tel. 055/2345322), which charges L12,000 per hour for non-members and L10,000 per hour if you're a student; rates are slightly lower for members. It's open Monday–Thursday 10 AM–10:30 PM, Friday–Saturday 10 AM–8 PM, and Sunday 3–7.

Sights ●

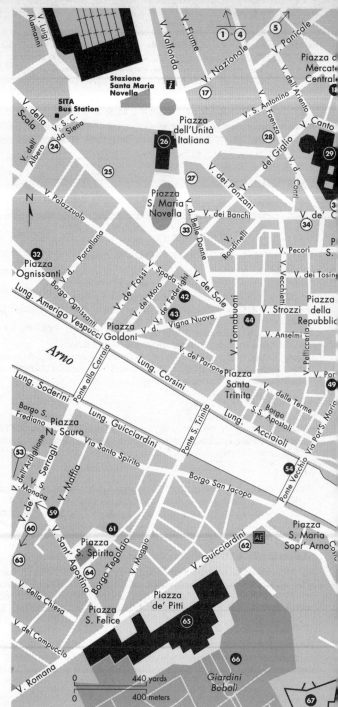

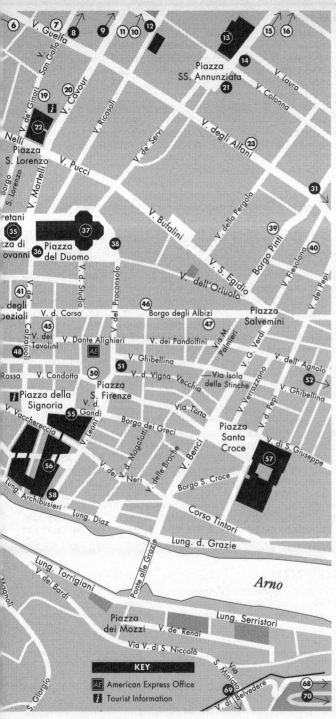

FLORENCE

VISITOR INFORMATION

Three offices with helpful, harried English-speaking staffs dispense maps, historical info, and special-events listings. The best visitor center (V. Cavour 1r, tel. 055/290832; open Mar.–Oct., Mon.–Sat. 8:15–7:15, Sun. 8:15–1:45, off-season Mon.–Sat. 8:15–1:45) is right beside the Palazzo Medici-Riccardi, two blocks north of the Duomo. Other offices are just around the corner from the church of Santa Croce (Borgo Santa Croce 29/r, tel. 055/23404444, open weekdays mid-Mar.–Oct. 8:30–7:15, Sat. 8:30–1:45; shorter hours in winter), and next to the train station, across from Track 16 (P. della Stazione, tel. 055/212245; open Apr. and Oct.–Mar. Mon.–Sat. 8:30–1:45, May–Sept. Mon.–Sat. 8:30–7:15). Pick up a free copy of *Florence Concierge Information* in hotels for a listing of events and other useful tourist info.

GAY AND LESBIAN RESOURCES • ARCI Gay/ARCI Lesbica (V. del Leone 5r–11r, tel. 055/476557) is the local gay resource center, where you can pick up a copy of *Quir* magazine, a monthly Italian/English publication with listings of gay and lesbian clubs and cultural events. You can also find *Quir* at tourist offices or the Paperback Exchange (*see above*).

COMING AND GOING

BY TRAIN

Don't get off the train at one of Florence's satellite stations; you'll know you're in the right place when you see the FIRENZE SMN signs and enter the huge Stazione Santa Maria Novella (tel. 1478/88088 toll-free). The station, open 24 hours, has luggage storage (Track 16: L5,000 for 12 hrs; open 4:15 AM–1:30 AM), info counters (open daily 7 AM–8 PM), a reservation counter, the Consorzio ITA hotel booking service (*see* Where to Sleep, *below*), and a 24-hour pharmacy.

Intercity trains to Rome (3 hrs, L38,500) and Milan (about 3 ½ hrs., L38,500) leave about every hour. There's a morning train to Venice (3 hrs, L34,000). A few trains from Rome stop just outside the city at the Campo di Marte station. Bus 12 connects the two stations. Many visitors to Florence fly in and out of Pisa and catch one of the express trains that run hourly between Pisa's airport and Florence's station (1 hr, L7,400). Some airlines even allow you to check bags through to your Pisa flight at an air terminal in the Florence train station, near Track 5. If you want to splurge (L10,000 extra), take the Eurostar, the high-speed train (a half-hour faster), from Rome, Milan, or Venice.

BY BUS

Siena, San Gimignano, and most other hill towns are best reached by bus, whereas Pistoia, Lucca, and Pisa are easier to get to by train. The most comprehensive service is **SITA** (V. Santa Caterina da Siena 15r, tel. 055/214721 weekdays; open daily 6:40 AM–7 PM), with hourly trips to Siena (1¼ hrs, L11,000) and San Gimignano (1½ hrs, L10,000; change at Poggibonsi) and buses to Arezzo (2 hrs, L8,000) and Greve-in-Chianti (1 hr, L5,000) a few times a day. To reach the SITA office from the train station, walk out the doors by Track 5, cross Via Luigi Alamanni and go left, and make a right on Via Santa Caterina da Siena.

BY CAR

If you're planning on exploring the Tuscan countryside, think about renting a car. Rates vary considerably, so look out for special offers. It's usually cheapest to rent in advance from your own country rather than in Italy. Agencies include **Europcar** (Borgo Ognissanti 53/59r, tel. 055/290438), **Italy By Car** (Borgo Ognissanti 134r, tel. 055/2654301), and **Avis Autonoleggio** (Borgo Ognissanti 128/r, tel. 055/2398826).

GETTING AROUND

It's usually faster to walk in Florence—even to the Oltrarno—than to wait for the bus and inch slowly through traffic. If you're covering a lot of ground or want to head out of town, you can rent a bike (L20,000 per day) or a moped (L45,000 per day) at **Alinari** (V. Guelfa 85r, tel. 055/280500).

BY BUS

If you're going to Fiesole (a 20-min ride), the HI hostel, or the campgrounds, you'll need to get to know the municipal bus line, **ATAF** (tel. 055/56501). Pick up free route maps and schedules from a booth just outside the train station, where most major bus lines stop. A ticket good for an hour costs L1,500 and can be purchased at tobacco shops (marked TABACCHI) or ticket machines. Three-hour (L2,500) and 24-hour (L6,000) tickets are also available. Most buses stop running at midnight or 1 AM. When you climb aboard, punch your ticket—otherwise you could pay a L100,000 fine. As always, keep an eye on your belongings.

WHERE TO SLEEP

It's hardly surprising that the areas right around the station are less desirable than more central addresses, but wherever you stay, you will be either within walking distance of the *centro storico* (historic center) or a short bus ride away.

Florence's budget hotels fill up fast, so get yourself squared away early. It can be as easy as a phone call if you take advantage of one of the free reservation services: **Florence PromHotel** (tel.055/570481 or 1678/66022 toll-free) or **Family Hotel** (tel. 055/4620080). Expect to pay around L100,000 for a double and upwards of L80,000 for a single. If you want to speak to someone in person, the **Consorzio ITA** office at the train station (tel. 055/282893; open daily 8:45–8; in winter Mon.–Sat. 9–8, Sun. 10–2) books rooms for a small service fee (L4,500 minimum). To reserve a room in an *affittacamere* (a room in a private home), call **A.G.A.P.** (tel. 055/284100); doubles without bath start at L80,000, but if you're staying for more than a few days, you can often get a discount.

WEST OF STAZIONE SANTA MARIA NOVELLA

On the map, the area west of the station seems far from the major sites, but the hotels here are generally within a 10-minute walk of the Duomo and a hop, skip, and jump from the train station. The area is filled with budget inns tucked into the top floors of old apartment buildings. Note that you should check these places out before you pay. A word of warning: Piazza Santa Maria Novella gets rather seedy at night.

In Florence, each street has two numbering systems: blue numbers for hotels and residences; red numbers (denoted by an "r") for businesses. The blue and red numbers—not to mention the numbers on either side of the street—can be wildly out of sync.

UNDER L100,000 • Albergo Montreal. Roberto, the young, mellow manager here, charges fair prices, and the rooms have much more light than others in the area. Doubles begin at L85,000. Curfew is 1:30 AM. *V. della Scala 43, 50123, tel. 055/ 2382331, fax. 055/287491. 14 rooms, 6 with bath. Cash only.*

Hotel Elite. The pleasant, English-speaking staff in this little place is enthusiastic and helpful. The rooms have high ceilings and comfortable beds and are surprisingly tranquil considering the hotel is on a busy street. *V. della Scala 12, 50123, tel. 055/215395. 8 rooms, 5 with bath. Cash only.*

UNDER L120,000 • Pensione Ferretti. Because of the odd shape of the building, each room in this simple inn run by the genial English-speaking Luciano Michel and his South African-born wife Sue has a distinct character. Ferretti lies just beyond the Piazza Santa Maria Novella, so it stays peaceful. Doubles cost L105,000 (breakfast included), L125,000 with bath. *V. delle Belle Donne 17, 50123, tel. 055/ 2381328, fax 055/219288. 16 rooms, 6 with bath.*

EAST OF STAZIONE SANTA MARIA NOVELLA

Begin your search east of the station on Via Faenza, which has 20 or so small *alberghi* (hotels); most one-star places have doubles in the L75,000–L85,000 range. Hotels on Via Fiume (2 blocks east of the station) are generally very quiet, while the places on crowded Via Nazionale (heading northeast from Piazza Stazione) are often dingier and noisier.

UNDER L100,000 • Albergo Merlini. Great top-floor views of the hills surrounding Florence and rooms with tasteful decor and comfy beds are the draw at the Merlini, one of the more tranquil hotels near the train station. Curfew is 1 AM. Doubles without bath cost L80,000. *V. Faenza 56, 50129, tel. 055/ 212848, fax 055/283939. 10 rooms, 1 with bath.*

Hotel Il Bargellino. This well-kept hotel has Mediterranean tile, antique bed frames, and a gorgeous garden terrace where you can kick back. Some rooms open onto the terrace. Doubles start at L100,000. *V. Guelfa 87, 50129, tel. 055/2382658, fax 055/2382698. Exit train station at Track 16 and turn left, then right on V. Cennini, left on V. Faenza, right on V. Guelfa. 10 rooms, 5 with bath. Cash only.*

Pensione Indipendenza. This tiny *pensione* next to Piazza Indipendenza offers typical one-star amenities. Double rooms without baths cost L90,000. *P. Indipendenza 8, off V. Nazionale, 50129, tel. 055/ 496630. 10 rooms without bath. Cash only.*

UNDER L115,000 • Albergo Azzi. This affordable, somewhat ramshackle hotel is worth checking out as there are several others just like it in the same building. Good double rooms start at L120,000. Rates drop by almost 50% in the low season. There's a 2 AM curfew. *V. Faenza 56, 50123, tel. 055/ 213806, fax 055/213806. 12 rooms, 3 with bath.*

UNDER L150,000 • Le Vigne. At this small hotel in one of Florence's most beautiful squares, the new owners have created the warm atmosphere of a private home. The spacious, air-conditioned rooms are decorated in 19th-century Florentine style. Doubles go for L150,000. *Piazza Santa Maria Novella 24, 50123, tel. 055/294449, fax 055/2302263. 25 rooms.*

UNDER L200,000 • Pensione Accademia. A few minutes from the station and town center, this hotel in a building dating from the 13th century has spacious rooms, immaculate baths, and peaceful common areas. It may be a splurge (doubles cost L200,000 with breakfast), but it's one you'll enjoy. *V. Faenza 7, 50123, tel. 055/293451, fax 055/219771. 16 rooms with bath.*

NVI

Hotel Monica. A small oasis in a very busy part of town, the Monica has well-appointed rooms and a tremendous terrace, perfect for breakfast in the summer or for just lolling about. Clean, bright doubles without bath run L130,000, L190,000 with bath. *V. Faenza 66, 50123, tel. 055/283804, fax 055/281706. 15 rooms, 10 with bath.*

CENTRO

The *centro storico* is right where the action is (and the noise), and you'll find that in general standards are slightly higher than in other areas. Just watch the prices.

UNDER L100,000 • Albergo San Giovanni. A high standard of cleanliness and a central location make the San Giovanni a good deal. Most rooms (doubles run L90,000–L100,000) with large windows and hardwood floors overlook the Duomo and the Battistero. *V. de' Cerretani 2, 50123, tel. 055/288385, fax 055/213580. 9 rooms, some with bath.*

Hotel Cristina. A block from the Uffizi and the Bargello, this hotel is in a fantastic location. Large and clean rooms are fresh and well furnished, but the prices are still low. Doubles start at L90,000, and rooms for four to five people go for L170,000. *V. della Condotta 4, 50122, off V. Calzaiuoli before P. della Signoria, tel. 055/214484, fax 055/215518. 9 rooms, 4 with bath.*

Locanda Orchidea. The rooms are small but comfortable, with enormous windows that open onto pleasantly neglected gardens or the bustling street life below. Doubles without bath run L90,000. *Borgo degli Albizi 11, 50122, tel. and fax 055/2480346. 7 rooms without bath. Closed 1 wk in Aug. Cash only.*

UNDER L150,000 • Albergo Firenze. If you want the security and comfort of an American-style hotel in the heart of Florence, this is the place for you. The rooms vary markedly between the Best Westernesque wing and the shabbier though pleasant old wing. Doubles with bath, including breakfast, go for L130,000. *P. dei Donati 4, 50122, off V. del Corso, tel. 055/214203, fax 055/212370. 57 rooms with bath. Cash only.*

Hotel Pensione Maxim. Students and young wayfarers flow in and out of this hotel, one block south of the Duomo. The walls are thin, but the rooms and baths are more than adequate. Doubles cost L140,000 (breakfast included). *V. dei Calzaiuoli 11/r, 50123, tel. 055/217474, fax 055/283729. 22 rooms, 14 with bath.*

Pensione Il Perseo. Almost every room in this hotel has a stunning view of Florence—plus ceiling fans. Try to snag Room 30—it's got its own tiny terrace. The church bells that ring at 7 AM, however, could wake the dead. Doubles go for L120,000, breakfast included, L145,000 with bath. *V. de' Cerretani 1, 50123, tel. 055/212504, fax 055/288377. 19 rooms, some with bath.*

Soggiorno Bavaria. This renovated inn atop an old palazzo has top-floor rooms verging on the enormous; most are very sunny and have great views. Try to avoid the smaller, darker downstairs rooms. Prices vary dramatically, but the cheapest double is L100,000. *Borgo degli Albizi 26, 50122, tel. and fax 055/2340313. 17 rooms, 3 with bath.*

UNDER L170,000 • Hotel Ariston. This hotel has a small, intimate feel to it; set on a side street, it's only minutes away from the Duomo. It's got a small bar and sitting room where you can enjoy an *aperitivo*. Doubles are L170,000, but slightly less in low season. *V. Fiesolana 40, just down the street from Piazza Salvemini, tel. and fax 055/2476980. 29 rooms with bath.*

PIAZZA SAN MARCO AND THE UNIVERSITY QUARTER

If you don't relish a good 15-minute walk from the train station, take Bus 7 to Piazza San Marco and the University Quarter. Busy Via Cavour, which runs north–south through the piazza, has some good upper-floor inns, and one block west on Via de' Ginori and Via San Gallo are a few quieter options. As you walk farther down Via degli Alfani, which runs east from Via Cavour one block south of Piazza San Marco from the station, more student bars and restaurants pop up.

UNDER L110,000 • Albergo Mirella. Enormous, squeaky-clean doubles without bath cost L100,000 here. All look onto a quiet courtyard. A 25-minute walk from the train station, the Mirella also tends to fill more slowly than other budget hotels. *V. degli Alfani 36, 50121, tel. and fax 055/2478170. 10 rooms, 8 with bath. Cash only.*

Hotel San Marco. The rooms in this hotel just off Piazza San Marco are a cut above the norm and justify the initial schlep up the stairs. The heavenly smell of pastries from the shop downstairs might just inspire you to get up early. Doubles without bath begin at L110,000, including breakfast. *V. Cavour 50, 50129, tel. 055/281851, fax 055/284235. 14 rooms, 12 with bath.*

Hotel Tina. If you're not charmed by the tidy, perfectly maintained rooms, you will be by Piero and Lorenzo, the happy-go-lucky managers. They dispense friendly advice and keep a bunch of magazines for guests to peruse in the sitting rooms of this welcoming inn. Some rooms have showers in the corner. Doubles start at L90,000. *V. San Gallo 31, 50129, tel. 055/483519, fax 055/483593. 16 rooms, 2 with bath. Cash only.*

UNDER L180,000 • Hotel Casci. Splurge and treat yourself to a stay in a refurbished palace lived in by Giaocchino Rossini in the mid-19th century. In the renovated 14th-century building, the Lombardi family offers spotless rooms, all with modern bathrooms and TVs. The atmosphere is so peaceful that you don't realize how close to the bustling centro you are. Doubles run about L180,000, including a large buffet breakfast. *V. Cavour 13, 50129, tel. 055/211686, fax 055/2396461. 25 rooms with bath.*

Hotel Ginori. The modern, streamlined rooms in this hotel are much more inviting than those in the cheap hotels that surround it. Immaculate and comfortable, it's deservedly popular with students. Bright doubles with TVs and semidisposable Swedish furniture cost L160,000, breakfast included. *V. de' Ginori 24, 50123, tel. 055/218615, fax 055/211392. 7 rooms with bath.*

THE OLTRARNO

Although the Oltrarno, across the river, is a good area for eating and hanging out, budget options are pretty scarce.

UNDER L165,000 • Pensione Sorelle Bandini. The Bandini has spacious sunny rooms, antique furniture, and a peaceful loggia. It's worth the splurge if you enjoy Old World atmosphere and being right on lively Piazza Santo Spirito. Doubles run about L162,000. *P. Santo Spirito 9, 2nd floor, 50125, tel. 055/215308, fax 055/282761. 13 rooms, 5 with bath. Cash only.*

UNDER L190,000 • Pensione La Scaletta. Quiet rooms and two sunny rooftop terraces, one facing the Boboli Gardens, the other looking out onto the town, make staying here pleasant and relaxing. Breakfast, included, is served on white linen. Doubles with bath start at L180,000. *V. Guicciardini 13, 50125, tel. 055/283028, fax 055/289562. 11 rooms, 10 with bath.*

HOSTELS

Florence's hostels are a great bargain, but they can fill up with dizzying speed in the high season. If you haven't reserved ahead, try to be at the door when the office opens. You'll have to arrive early and get to know your fellow desperados while waiting in line.

Istituto Gould. Imagine spotless rooms with big windows that resemble nice university dorms, where you'll find a towel and complimentary bar of soap and a key so you can come in whenever you want. Now you know why the Gould is one of the first places in town to fill up. The office opens at 9 AM. Per person, doubles cost L39,000, triples L35,000, and quads L33,000. *V. de' Serragli 49, 50124, tel. 055/212576, fax 055/280274. Office open weekdays 9–1 and 3–7, Sat. 9–1. 89 beds. Cash only.*

Ostello Archi Rossi. It's worth showing up at the crack of dawn to get a spot in this clean and well-located hostel. A snack shop, patio, and free movies in English are added bonuses. Beds cost L24,000; in a room with bath they run from L27,000 to L35,000. You can make reservations provided you plan on arriving in the morning. The maximum stay is one week. *V. Faenza 94r, 50123, tel. 055/290804, fax 055/2302601. 86 beds. Curfew 12:30 AM, lockout 11–2:30. Cash only.*

Ostello Santa Monaca. The bathrooms and dorms (8–10 beds) are standard hostel fare at best—the sexes are strictly segregated—but at least they have a deal with a local trattoria that provides slightly reduced-price meals. Beds go for L23,000 per person. *V. Santa Monaca 6, 50124, off V. de' Serragli, tel. 055/268338, fax 055/280185. 16 beds. Curfew 1 AM. Reception open 9:30–midnight. Cash only.*

Ostello Villa Camerata (HI). Florence's megahostel isn't convenient to the city center, but if you make it out here, you'll be glad you did. It really is a villa, and it's on a mountainside surrounded by green acres; a campground (*see below*) adjoins the hostel. You won't bask in luxury, but the rooms are fine. You can reserve by writing months ahead and making a credit-card deposit or by faxing several weeks in advance. Check-in begins at 7 AM. Beds cost L25,000 (hostel card mandatory), and breakfast is included, though dinner costs L14,000. The maximum stay is three nights. *V. Agosto Righi 2, 50127, tel. 055/601451, fax 055/610300. Exit train station at Track 5 and take Bus 17 for 15 min to hostel gates; it's a 10-min walk from here. 320 beds. Curfew midnight, lockout 9–2 (until 3 in winter). Cash only.*

Pensionato Pio X. You're likely to share a room with three or four others, and there's a midnight curfew, but the rooms are large and clean, and the management is friendly. Beds cost L22,000 per person. They don't take reservations, but if you show up between 8 AM and 10 AM or call ahead from the train station, you'll probably get in. The maximum stay is five days. *V. de' Serragli 104–106, 50124, tel. and fax 055/225044. 54 beds. No lockout. Cash only.*

Suore Oblate dell'Assunzione. If you can deal with an 11 PM curfew, the sisters will warmly welcome you into their restored, refreshingly clean, and elegantly furnished pension just five minutes from the Duomo. Ask for a room with a frescoed ceiling or one that overlooks the gorgeous garden. Per person, you'll pay about L45,000 (without bath) or L54,000 (with bath) a night, whether you share a room or not. Half or full board is available. Reservations are accepted. *Borgo Pinti 15, 50123, tel. 055/2480582, fax 055/2346291. 45 beds. Curfew 11 PM, no lockout. Cash only. Closed Nov.–late June.*

Suore Oblate dello Spirito Santo. A short jaunt from the station, this nun-run pensione opens its arms to women and married couples. Reserve a room and enjoy extreme quiet, cleanliness, and convenience. Doubles are L80,,000, triples L90,000. If you have the patience to endure the language barrier, this is a convenient spot. The minimum stay is two nights. *V. Nazionale 8, 50123, tel. and fax 055/2398202. 27 beds, all rooms with bath. Curfew 11 PM. Cash only.*

CAMPING

Campgrounds may be cheap, but they're also hot and crowded in summer. The sites themselves are nice, but wall-to-wall people distract from the great outdoors. From July 1 through mid-September, the city opens a free campsite to accommodate the hordes of tourists: **Camping Panoramico Fiesole** (V. Peramonda 1, tel. 055/599069; cash only) is great if you don't mind staying a 20-minute bus ride outside the city. It's about 2 km (1 mi) from Fiesole, with its own market, a restaurant (summer only), and better facilities than many hotels. The price (L13,000 per person, L39,000 per tent) is unbelievably low for this area. Take Bus 7 to Fiesole, then take STAM Bus A from Piazza Mino da Fiesole to the campground stop and follow the signs.

Camping Italiani e Stranieri. Tremendous views of the city redeem this scorching-hot campground just below Piazzale Michelangelo, where you've got to arrive super early to rumble with 1,000 other campers for a minimally shady site. Still, it's hard to argue with a price of L10,000 per person (and L8,000 per tent). *V. Michelangelo 80, tel. 055/6811977. Exit train station at Track 5, Bus 13 to stop after P. Michelangelo. Reception and check-in 10 AM–11 PM. Cash only. Closed Nov.–Easter.*

Camping Villa Camerata. Just beside the Ostello Villa Camerata (*see above*), in a wooded area northeast of town, this year-round site is cool and calm. Facilities are basic; some campers have been known to sneak into the hostel in pursuit of nicer bathrooms. It's L9,000 per person, L8,000 per small tent, L16,000 for a larger one. Check in at the hostel if the campsite kiosk is closed. *V. Augusto Righi 2, tel. 055/601451. Cash only.*

WHERE TO EAT

Good food town that Florence is, don't plan on skipping too many meals for sightseeing. If you are gathering food piece by piece, don't miss the **Mercato Centrale** (open Mon.–Sat. 7–2), right near the Church of San Lorenzo. Produce is upstairs; bread, cheese, and meat downstairs. If you're feeling brave and really want to eat like a Florentine, try a tripe sandwich from one of a half-dozen tripe stands that set up around town. Ask for it either dipped in sauce or dry, with or without *salsa verde*.

PIAZZA SANTA MARIA NOVELLA

UNDER L10,000 • Amon. If you're momentarily tired of Italian food, drop into this standing-only little spot that serves terrific Egyptian and other Middle Eastern treats at rock-bottom prices. *Via Palazzuolo 26/28r, tel. 055/293146.*

La Lampara. With a sports bar in the back and a pizzeria in the front, the busy Lampara cooks up top-quality, creative pizzas just a stone's throw from the train station. Enormous pies (starting at L8,000) are topped with regional specialties like *fagioli* (white beans) and *salsiccia* (sausage) or just the traditional fresh tomato sauce and cheese. *V. Nazionale 36r, tel. 055/215164.*

UNDER L20,000 • Trattoria da Giorgio and **Trattoria Il Contadino.** Just across the street from each other, these places have different names but they serve similar food at the exact same price in the same, non-inviting atmosphere. Here's the place to come to fill up for little—if filling up is the main objective. You get pasta, meat, a vegetable, bread, water, and wine for L15,000 at lunchtime and L16,000 at dinnertime. *Da Giorgio: V. Palazzuolo 100r, no phone. From P. Santa Maria Novella, walk down V. de' Fossi, turn right on V. Palazzuolo. Open Mon.–Sat. 11–3 and 6–10. Il Contadino: V. Palazzuolo 69r–71r, tel. 055/2382673. Closed Sun.*

UNDER L25,000 • Rosticceria La Spada. Walk into this place and inhale the lovely aroma of grilled meats emanating from the huge wood-burning oven. They do a roasted or grilled chicken (enough to feed two) to go for L11,000. There's also an inexpensive trattoria. *Via del Moro 66/r, tel. 055/218757.*

UNDER L40,000 • Il Latini. As soon as you spy the primary decoration pieces—whole legs of cured ham better known as prosciutto—you'll realize that you're in hog-lover's heaven. This place packs in tourists and locals alike, with good reason: big portions of meat dishes that don't get much better than this. *V. dei Palchetti 6r, tel. 055/210916. From P. Santa Maria Novella, walk down V. de' Fossi, turn left on V. della Spada, right on V. de' Federighi, and left on V. dei Palchetti. Cash only. Closed Mon.*

Not all olive oils are created equal. Extra virgin oils—those with relatively low acidity—are best, but like wine there is great variation according to region and producer. Olive oil can be deep green or pale yellow, fruity, spicy, mellow, or sharp.

CENTRO

UNDER L10,000 • Angie's Pub. Don't let the word "pub" fool you—this place serves panini any which way you want them (starting at L4,000), as well as, scarily enough, hot dogs and hamburgers. *V. de' Neri 35/r, tel. 055/2398245.*

Antico Noè. One of the best *panino* (sandwich) counters in Florence is little more than a hole in the wall, but it's got the freshest turkey and roast beef sandwiches (around L5,000 each) in town—and tripe, too. Mouthwatering additions (L500 extra) like spinach or sautéed bell peppers liven things up. You can either enjoy the local color—consisting largely of drunks and heroin addicts—or take your sandwich and run. *Volta di San Piero 6r, tel. 055/2340838. From Duomo, walk east on V. dell'Oriuolo; look for covered passageway—Volta di San Piero—on right just before P. Salvemini. Closed weekends June–July.*

I Fratellini. Just a hop, skip, and jump from Orsanmichele, this little *enoteca* (wine bar) has been around since 1875. It sells wines by the glass and has a list of 27 sandwiches—try the pecorino with sun-dried tomatoes (L4,000) or the spicy wild-boar salami with goat cheese if you're feeling brave. Pull up a piece of the sidewalk and enjoy—there are no tables to be had. *V. dei Cimatori 38/r, tel. 055/2396096. Closed Sun.*

UNDER L15,000 • Mario. Florentines flock to this narrow, dinerlike restaurant 30 at a time to feast on Tuscan favorites such as *taglierini al ragú* (L10,000). It's open only at lunch; arrive early to beat the crowds —otherwise, plan on an agonizing wait. *V. Rosina 2/r, Piazza Mercato Centrale, tel. 055/218550.*

UNDER L30,000 • Gauguin. The orange interior casts a warm glow in this little vegetarian place that serves Italian and ethnic dishes at L10,000 a pop. Don't come expecting pasta—there's none on the menu. They serve some other Italian meatless dishes, but try the couscous with vegetables (L10,000) if you need a break from Tuscan cooking. *V. degli Alfani 24/r, tel. 055/2340616. Closed Sun.*

UNDER L40,000 • Acqua al Due. Come here for a good meal with half the Americans in Florence. Original, velvety sauces top the pastas (about L9,000 each); try out five of them with the pasta sampler (L13,000). Save room for the homemade tiramisu, a creamy espresso-and-liqueur-soaked dessert. *V. della Vigna Vecchia 40r, near Bargello, tel. 055/284170. No lunch.*

Trattoria Pallottino. With its tiled floor, photograph-filled walls, and wooden tables, Pallottino is the quintessential Tuscan trattoria with hearty, heart-warming classics like *pappa al pomodoro* (thick soup of bread and tomatoes anointed with a swirl of extra-virgin olive oil) and *peposo alla toscana* (beef stew laced with black pepper). The lunch special, at L10,000 for a primo and secondo, might be the best bargain in town. *V. Isola delle Stinche 1r, tel. 055/289573. From P. Salvemini, take V. M. Palmieri south, which becomes V. Isola delle Stinche. No credit cards at lunch. Closed Mon.*

FLORENTINE RENAISSANCE

Inspired by the Greeks and Romans, whose achievements had been ignored during the Dark Ages, artists flocked to Florence in the 14th century, embarking on a new era of humanism and individual expression—the Renaissance.

GIOTTO DI BONDONE (c. 1267–1337) worked all over Italy, so his most famous creations in Florence are limited to design work on the Duomo, altarpieces now housed in the Uffizi, and the Bardi and Peruzzi Chapels at Santa Croce. In some ways, Giotto started the Renaissance rolling. He broke new ground with the naturalism of his figures and his dramatic sense of narrative.

FILIPPO BRUNELLESCHI (1377–1446) went to Rome in a pique, studied the ancients, and eventually became one of the greatest architects ever. Most famous for his ingenious design proposal for the Duomo's cupola, he was also responsible for the Ospedale degli Innocenti and the churches of San Lorenzo and Santo Spirito, among other major Florentine buildings. His work is famous for its scientific display of measure and proportion.

DONATELLO (1386?–1466) sculpted figures that move with intense yet subtly drawn expressions suggestive of their inner lives, as in his bronze David. His major works are in the Bargello and the Museo del Duomo.

MICHELANGELO BUONARROTI (1475–1564) was equally gifted as a sculptor, painter, and architect. In Florence his greatest achievements can be seen in his monumental David, the imprisoned slaves, and the majestic figures of Dawn and Dusk and Night and Day in the Medici Chapel.

Trattoria Che C'è C'è. The best trattoria in the shadow of the Palazzo Vecchio serves everything from staggeringly large bowls of ribollita (L7,000) to the costly local specialty, *bistecca alla fiorentina,* a grilled T-bone steak big enough for two. Reservations for dinner are a must. *V. de' Magalotti 11r, tel. 055/216589. From P. Santa Croce, walk west down Borgo dei Greci and turn left on V. de' Magalotti. Closed Mon.*

PIAZZA SAN MARCO AND THE UNIVERSITY QUARTER

In the small area around Piazza San Marco and Piazza Santissima Annunziata, neighborhood joints cater to the thin wallets of the university population. Students ands tourists gather at bars on Via degli Alfani. You'll find solid, reasonably priced restaurants along Via Guelfa and Via XXVII Aprile.

UNDER L10,000 • Caffellatte. This dreamy organic-food haven is just a caffè, but it's a caffè in the best sense, with six uneven wooden tables that seem to invite a long-winded conversation or a slow, solitary perusal of a newspaper. Students drop in for a quick cappuccino or one of dozens of fresh teas and a piece of homemade cake. It's probably the only place in town where you can get a bowl of yogurt topped with fresh fruit or muesli (L7,000). *V. degli Alfani 39r, just west of V. della Pergola, tel. 055/2478878. Closed Sun.*

Gran Caffè. If you want to grab a delectable panino or treat yourself to a sweet after visiting the Museo San Marco, drop in here. Stand at the bar, though, or the cost of that panino (L2,500–L5,000) will more than double. *Piazza San Marco 11/r, tel. 055/215833.*

Rosticceria. Labeled only with an unassuming ROSTICCERIA sign, this tiny eatery has delicious Arab sandwiches and salads (all around L4,000), including a wide range of vegetarian choices. It's a nice change from pizza. *V. Guelfa 40r, no phone. Closed Sun.*

Rosticceria Alfio e Beppo. Walking by, you might think this *tavola calda* (cafeteria) is like all the rest, but try the lasagna, ravioli, and tortellini, fresh vegetables, rice salads, or roasted chicken. You might just turn into a regular. *V. Cavour 118–120r, near P. San Marco, tel. 055/214108. Closed Sat.*

UNDER L15,000 • Trattoria San Zanobi. Off the beaten tourist track, this trattoria offers rich and filling pastas (around L8,000) amid gleaming brass and linen. Homemade desserts, ranging from cakes to *macedonia* (fresh fruit salad), are a must. *V. San Zanobi 33r, tel. 055/475286. V. Panicale becomes V. San Zanobi. Closed Sun.*

AROUND SANTA CROCE

Near the church, follow Via dell'Agnolo east to Piazza Ghiberti, and you'll hit the Mercato Sant'Ambrogio (*see* Shopping, *below*), the town's oldest food market. In addition to meat and cheese (sold inside) and produce (sold outside), vendors peddle inexpensive clothes and knickknacks.

UNDER L15,000 • Baldovino. You can just squeak by on L15,000 if you stick to one of their fine pizzas (L12,000) or *insalatone* (big salads; L12,000–L15,000), but you might want to order other stuff, too: it's good. For equal taste at reduced prices, check out their enoteca right next door. *V. San Giuseppe 22/r, tel. 055/241 773. Closed Mon.*

Caffètteria Piansa. All bars in Italy ought to be like this one: Brick vaulted arches, sponged yellow walls, and wood paneling provide the setting for great breakfasts, lunches (lovely salads at L10,000, panini from L2,500 to L3,500, and pasta specials of the day at L10,000), and drinks. *Borgo Pinti 18/r, 055/2342362. Cash only. Closed Sun.*

da Rocco. Not quite a *tavola calda* and not quite a cafeteria, this place is open only for lunch and fills up quickly with Florentines on their breaks. Small wonder—it's good, it's cheap, and it's fast. *Inside Mercato Sant'Ambrogio, no tel. Cash only. Closed Sun.*

To gain the commission for Duomo's cupola, Brunelleschi—practically blacklisted—proposed that whoever could stand an egg on a flat surface would win. The challenge was accepted, and of course only Brunelleschi succeeded—he simply cracked the egg on its base.

il Pizzaiuolo. Some aficionados claim that this is the best place in town for a pizza, Neapolitan style. Get here early, or be prepared to wait in the street. You can also reserve a table to skip the wait. *V. dei Macci 113/r, tel 055/241171. Closed Sun.*

UNDER L25,000 • Danny Rock. If you should inexplicably find yourself tired of Italian food, pop in to this lively spot teeming with Italians, order their divine cheeseburger, and enjoy Looney Tunes on the big screen. *V. Pandolfini 13/r, 055/2340307. No lunch.*

UNDER L40,000 • La Maremmana. This place has been around for 19 years, and it shows—service and food are down to a fine art. Fish is good here, and so is the buffet antipasto misto, where with careful cramming you can sample a whole lot of goodies for very little. *V. de' Macci 77r, tel. 055/241226. From Santa Croce, take V. dei Pepi, turn right on V. Ghibellina, left on V. de' Macci. Closed Sun.*

Trattoria Cibreo. Have a look at the menu in the window of one of Florence's most famous restaurants. Then go around the corner to the back door and have a seat in the room off the kitchen, where many of the same dishes are offered in smallish portions at much lower prices. *P. Ghiberti 35, tel. 055/2341100. Closed Sun.–Mon. and Aug. Cash only.*

THE OLTRARNO

Some of the best food in Florence is south of the Arno. Just one block from the river, Borgo San Jacopo–Via Santo Spirito–Borgo San Frediano (one long street that changes names) is packed with restaurants. Farther south, bars line Piazza Santo Spirito, a pleasant place to sit outside in the warm months. You can pick up organic food at **Sugar Blues** (V. de' Serragli 57r, tel. 055/268378), right beside the Istituto Gould (*see* Where to Sleep, *above*).

UNDER L15,000 • Fuori Porta. This cool little *enoteca* (wine shop) is on the other side of the river, not far from the Forte Belvedere, and is worth the walk. You can sit down (inside or out), have wine by the glass, and choose from dozens of bruschette and crostoni. *V. Monte alle Croci 10/r, tel. 055/ 2342483. Closed Sun.*

I Tarocchi. What tarot cards have to do with pizza is open to speculation; what's abundantly clear, however, is that they do pizza well here. The menu also includes pastas and daily specials, but it's the thin-crust pizzas, including the *margherita* (fresh tomato and mozzarella) and the *quattro stagioni* (prosciutto, mushrooms, artichokes, and olives), that make the trek worthwhile. *V. de' Renai 12r–14r, tel. 055/2343912. Cross Arno at Ponte alle Grazie and make 2nd left on V. de' Renai. No lunch weekends. Closed Mon.*

Trattoria La Casalinga. There's plenty to choose from at this typical trattoria packed with locals. The decor is simple, and the food is good. Order course by course or all at once. The harried waiter will come by at the end and total up the bill for you right on the paper tablecloth. *V. dei Michelozzi 9r, to left of Santo Spirito, tel. 055/218624. Closed Sun., and weekends in July.*

UNDER L20,000 • Il Cantinone del Gallo Nero. Though too pricey at dinnertime, this dark medieval cellar is perfect for a Tuscan lunch by candlelight. For your *primi* and *secondi piatti* (first and second courses), choose two dishes from the list of daily lunch specials for l15,000 (set price) and chow down immersed in rustic ambience. Crostoni topped with tomatoes, mushrooms, and mozzarella are an excellent part of the experience. *V. Santo Spirito 6r, tel. 055/218898. Cross Ponte Santa Trinità and turn right on V. Santo Spirito. Closed Mon.*

UNDER L25,000 • Borgo Antico. Teeming with locals and visitors alike, this is the place to come for a fine pizza (L10,000) or creative plate of spaghetti (L12,000–L15,000). There's outdoor seating in one of Florence's most beautiful Renaissance piazze during the warmer months. *P. Santo Spirito 6/r, tel. 055/210437.*

Osteria Antica Mescita San Niccolo. This bustling osteria is directly next to the church of San Niccolo, and if you sit in the lower part, you will find yourself in what was once a chapel dating from the 11th century. The dramatic background makes a nice complement to the food, which is simple Tuscan at its very best. The *pollo con limone* is tasty little pieces of chicken in a fragrant lemon-scented broth. In winter, try the *spezzatino di cinghiale con aromi* (wild boar stew with herbs). *Via San Niccolo, 60/r, tel. 055/ 2342836. Closed Sun.*

GELATERIE AND PASTICCERIE

Maybe you've heard about **Vivoli** (V. Isola delle Stinche 7, tel. 055/292334), the most famous gelateria in Florence. But the new kid in town, **Carabè** (V. Ricasoli 60r, tel. 055/289476), is run by a Sicilian couple who know gelato and bring essential ingredients (pistacchios, hazelnuts, and lemons) from Sicily. Taste the difference. Florence's only whole-food *pasticceria,* **Troponais** (V. San Gallo 92r, tel. 055/ 483017) sells sugarless sesame or sunflower brittle as well as more traditional sweets. From San Lorenzo, walk north 10 minutes on V. San Gallo.

MAJOR SIGHTS

In Florence in the first half of the 15th century, while Ghiberti was working on the panels for the doors of the Baptistery (*see below*), three of his contemporaries were bringing the same new focus to their own work in different media. Donatello was creating statuary for churches and private patrons such as the Medici; Masaccio was painting frescoes in the churches of Santa Maria Novella and Santa Maria del Carmine; Filippo Brunelleschi was designing the cupola for the Duomo and other churches and buildings. These four were the artistic fathers of the Renaissance—geniuses who created a new artistic vision—and they began a revolution that made Florence the artistic capital of Italy for a hundred years.

With Renaissance masterpieces everywhere, where to begin? Florence is small but densely packed with things to see. Your best bet is to hit the main museums—the Galleria degli Uffizi and the Accademia—at least 30 minutes before they open, as the lines to get in grow quickly. Or you can go in the late afternoon, when the crowds usually thin out. If you're watching your lire, admission fees can really add up. Churches are still free, but you may have to pay to enter their cloisters, chapels, towers, or domes. Also keep in mind that many museums are closed Monday and that hours can change drastically from season to season—it's worth getting an updated schedule of opening times and prices (including special cumulative tickets) from the tourist office.

Money From Home In Minutes.

If you're stuck for cash on your travels, don't panic. Millions of people trust Western Union to transfer money in minutes to 165 countries and over 50,000 locations worldwide. Our record of safety and reliability is second to none. For more information, call Western Union: USA 1-800-325-6000, Canada 1-800-235-0000. Wherever you are, you're never far from home.

www.westernunion.com

The fastest way to send money worldwide.

PIAZZA DEL DUOMO

DUOMO • Even the thousandth glimpse of the Duomo—officially called **Santa Maria del Fiore**—is bound to astound you. Brunelleschi's huge dome is offset by the intricacy of the heavily patterned green, white, and pink marble on the exterior. Construction of the cathedral was fitful in the 14th century because the cupola that had been projected could not be constructed by contemporary building methods. Finally, in 1418, after a steady stream of boasts, challenges, and insults, Filippo Brunelleschi persuaded the cathedral committee to allow him to give it a try. His dome, slightly taller than it is wide, is an adaptation of the perfectly hemispherical dome of the Pantheon in Rome, built 12 centuries earlier. The structure consists of an interior and exterior shell linked by an elaborate system of hidden ribs, and the interlaced brickwork creates a self-supporting structure. Brunelleschi even designed special types of tools to be used in the construction. The facade wasn't completed until the 19th century. For L10,000 you can climb the **cupola** (open summer, Mon.–Fri. 8:30–6:20, Sat. 9:30–5; 1st Sat. of month 9:30–3:20) for a superlative view of Florence. Or huff and puff up the stairs of Giotto's **campanile** (admission L10,000; open Apr.–Sept., daily 9–6:50; Oct.–Mar. 9–4:20), which offers multiple look-out points along the way.

In contrast to the dazzling exterior, the Duomo's enormous interior space is rather spare, especially because its best artistic works have been moved to the cathedral museum (*see* Museo dell'Opera del Duomo, *below*). Two monumental frescoes of equestrian figures (to the left as you enter) represent foreign mercenaries hired to protect Florence. In Paolo Uccello's portrait of John Hawkwood (1436), on the right, the horse and rider appear at eye level, yet your perspective is from the pedestal below them. It is said that Uccello changed his mind about how to portray Hawkwood while painting the fresco and never got around to unifying the two halves. Uccello also created the clock above the entrance, an intriguing device that moves counterclockwise and counts down the hours from the last sunset until the next one. Downstairs, the **crypt** (open Mon.–Sat. 10– 5) holds the remains of several churches dating to the late Roman period—hardly worth the L5,000 admission fee, but if you head down the stairs and turn left, you'll get a free look at Brunelleschi's tomb, discovered during an excavation in the early 1970s. *P. del Duomo, tel. 055/2302885. Open Mon.–Sat. 10–5, Sun. 1–5, 1st Sat. of month 10–3:30.*

BATTISTERO • Just opposite the Duomo's facade, the octagonal baptistery is the city's oldest standing building, originally built in the 6th or 7th century and adorned with distinctive marble patterning in the 11th century. Inside, brilliant gold mosaics cover the ceiling and a massive portrait of Jesus looms above the altar. Marching around the rest of the dome are five levels of biblical allegories; the most arresting one, over the west door, is a lively, macabre depiction of the Apocalypse. But the real story here is the doors, the most famous sculptured panels in Renaissance art. In 1401 Lorenzo Ghiberti beat out Jacopo della Quercia and Brunelleschi for the chance to redesign the doors to the baptistery and spent the next 48 years of his life on the project. The originals were removed after the great flood of 1966 to the Museo dell'Opera del Duomo (*see below*) to protect them from erosion caused by pollution, and copies have been put in their place.

Ghiberti started with the north doors, on which he depicted scenes from the life of Christ. On his later east doors, facing the Duomo facade, he recounted scenes from the Old Testament. They are worth close examination, for they are very different in style and illustrate with great clarity the artistic changes that marked the beginning of the Renaissance. Look, for instance, at the far right panel of the middle row of the earlier north doors (*Jesus Calming the Waters*), in which Ghiberti captured with great skill and economy the chaos of the storm at sea. Note his archaic use of pre-Renaissance technique: Jesus is the most important figure and thus the largest, the disciples next in size, the ship merely a toy. The whole story is contained in the decorative borders.

On the east doors, the decorative borders are gone and the panels are larger, more expansive, more sweeping, and more convincing. The middle panel of the left-hand door tells the story of Jacob and Esau, and the various elements of the story have all been brought together into a street scene. A perspective grid suggests depth, the architecture looks more realistic, the figures more natural. Although the religious content remains, the natural world is given new prominence and is portrayed with a realism not seen in art since the fall of the Roman Empire in AD 476. Michelangelo declared that the doors were so beautiful they could serve as the "gates of paradise." *P. del Duomo, tel. 055/2302885. Admission L5,000. Open Mon.–Sat. 12—6:30, Sun. 8:30-1:30.*

MUSEO DELL'OPERA DEL DUOMO • It's worth stopping at this superb, uncrowded museum just opposite the dome end of the cathedral to have a look at several of Ghiberti's original panels, restored and on display. You'll also find interesting works taken from the interior chapels and sculpture from the facade and campanile. There are free guided tours in English during the summer (Wed. and Thurs. at 4), which meet inside the courtyard.

Dominating the landing between the ground level and second floor is Michelangelo's *Pietà* (no relation of his early, more famous *Pietà* in St. Peter's in Rome). Constantly frustrated with the sculpture, the 80-year-old genius once hacked off Christ's left arm and leg in a fit of anger over his failure to achieve perfection. A servant stopped him, and a student reattached the arm, but the back leg is still missing. Upstairs, the most impressive room holds Donatello's harrowing and haggard *Mary Magdalene* sculpture and several of his sculptures of prophets, most notably the prophet Habakkuk, also known as Zuccone (which means big pumpkin) because of his very bald head. The room also contains a wonderful celebration of youth, Luca della Robbia's *Choir Stall*. The 10 sculpted panels offer an affectionate depiction of riotous young boys and girls clashing cymbals, banging drums, and dancing in circles. *P. del Duomo 9, tel. 055/2302885. Admission L10,000. Closed for renovation at press time; expected to reopen in time for Jubilee.*

PIAZZA DELLA SIGNORIA

Long a major tourist spot and now recognizable from Merchant-Ivory's *A Room with a View,* Florence's principal piazza has been the center of Florentine political life since the 13th century. The Medici family lived in the Palazzo Vecchio and financed the Palazzo degli Uffizi (now the Uffizi Gallery) and the Loggia della Signoria. The last, a gallery with a roof on the square's south side, was originally a platform for political uses but since the late 1700s has contained Cellini's bronze *Perseus* (carrying Medusa's head) and Giambologna's spiraling *Rape of the Sabines,* both masterpieces of the 16th century. It offers a relatively cool and shaded spot to sit and take a break in the middle of the summer heat.

In front of **Palazzo Vecchio** are copies of Michelangelo's *David* (the original stood here until 100 years ago), Donatello's *Judith and Holofernes* (the original is inside the palace), and *Marzocco* (in the Bargello), as well as the original ornate *Neptune Fountain.* The piazza itself was overhauled in the late 1980s. During the renovation, archaeologists discovered extensive remains of a Roman bath and a 5th-century church, as well as Bronze Age relics, which suggested that the entire city center was built over a Roman settlement. What could they do? Rip out magnificent Renaissance buildings so that a pile of ancient rubble could be unearthed? Three years into the dig, the city chose to sew it up and complete the piazza's face-lift in the interest of tourism and staying with the times.

GALLERIA DEGLI UFFIZI • Artist, architect, and art historian Giorgio Vasari was commissioned by the Medici family in 1560 to design offices for the local government, with a top floor reserved for the family's art collection. The last of the Medici, Anna Maria Ludovica, donated the entire collection to the city of Florence in 1737. The amazing trove of Renaissance artworks represents nearly every breakthrough of the period. A thorough visit merits several hours or lifetimes, but the museum can be covered in less. Some rooms remain closed for repairs in the aftermath of a devastating terrorist bombing in May 1993 and because of a plan to extend the museum (now on the third floor) to the lower floors of the palace. Before heading up the stairs to the main gallery, have a look at the remains of **San Piero Scheraggio,** off the entrance hall. The walls of the 11th-century church are lined with fabulous frescoes, including an *Annunciation* by Botticelli and portraits by Andrea del Castagno.

The museum is arranged chronologically through the galleries lining the long corridors on the palazzo's third floor. **Room 2** contains three masterly Madonna altarpieces by Cimabue, Duccio, and Giotto, the earliest artists represented in the museum. Giotto's altarpiece, in the center of the room, reflects the artist's dramatic departure from Byzantine stylization and his interest in capturing the mass and weight of human figures. In **Room 3,** Simone Martini's *Annunciation* (c. 1333) is an important Sienese altarpiece rich with gold punch work, while Gentile da Fabriano's *Adoration of the Magi* (**Rooms 5–6**), in which gold leaf is used to great effect, exemplifies the Florentine contribution to International Gothic. Tiny **Room 7** shows off the most talented artists of the mid-15th century. Do not miss Piero della Francesca's superb profile portraits of Federico da Montefeltro and his wife, Battista Sforza. She's deathly pale, perhaps because the portrait was done from her death mask, and he's missing a chunk of his nose due to a battle injury. Paolo Uccello's *Battle of San Romano* (from the 1430s) is one of three paintings commissioned by Lorenzo il Magnifico to adorn his private chambers; the others are now in the Louvre and London's National Gallery. The perspective is fascinating: check out the enormously foreshortened legs of the rearing orange horse on the right side. Room 7 also contains two Fra Angelicos, a *Madonna and Child* by Masolino and Masaccio, and one of Veneziano's paintings, *Madonna and Child Enthroned.*

Room 8 is full of fine works by Filippo Lippi and his illegitimate son, Filippino, but most first-time visitors rush anxiously through it to reach Botticelli's showcase (in **Rooms 10–14**), which contains just about every major panel painting by the artist, including *The Birth of Venus* (concealed behind thick glass), *Primavera, Adoration of the Magi, Pallas and the Centaur,* and the circular *Madonna of the Pomegranate.* **Room 15** contains some of Leonardo da Vinci's work, a *Baptism* by his teacher Verrocchio that includes an angel (far left), and Leonardo's mysterious, unfinished *Adoration of the Magi* (1482). The

Annunciation, for which the young Leonardo painted the angel (and perhaps more), shows the angel Gabriel revealing to the Virgin Mary that she will give birth to the son of God.

After being funneled back into the main corridor, traffic flows into the octagonal Tribuna, containing sculptures of the Medici, Rosso Fiorentino's endearing *Angel Playing a Lute,* and several impressive portraits by Bronzino. **Room 19** holds works by Umbrian artists Perugino and Signorelli. **Room 20** contains works from northern Europe, including Dürer's *Adam and Eve,* hung directly across from Cranach's similar (but more subtle) portraits of the two. Important to note in these northern Renaissance paintings is the attention to minute detail and surface texture. **Room 23** has works by Mantegna and Correggio, most notably the latter's accomplished *Rest on the Flight into Egypt.*

You're only about halfway through when you reach **Room 25,** which contains Michelangelo's *Doni Tondo,* known for its richly colored Holy Family, set masterfully in a round frame. Michelangelo's sculptural approach to painting is demonstrated, as is his dazzling use of color. **Room 26** contains treasures by Raphael, including a stunning *Self-Portrait* from 1508, his celebrated *Madonna of the Goldfinch,* and *Leo X with Cardinals.* **Room 28** houses the sensuous *Venus of Urbino,* a major work by Titian. **Room 41** contains various works by Rubens and van Dyck. Caravaggio has several major works in **Room 43,** including a very sick-looking *Young Bacchus,* the unnerving *Medusa,* and *The Sacrifice of Isaac.* Rembrandt's masterly self-portraits, as both a young and an old man, hang in **Room 44.** Finally, the Corridoio Vasariano, an extraordinary covered passage designed by Vasari in 1565, offers astonishing views of the city—when it's open. The passageway usually displays scores of self-portraits by Renaissance artists but is currently closed for repairs. *Uffizi Gallery: Loggiato degli Uffizi 6, tel. 055/23885; reservations, 055/ 2347941. Admission L12,000. Open Tues.–Sat. 8:30–10, Sun. 8:30–8; shorter hours in winter.*

> *Don't expect to see Florence's Duomo without scaffolding on at least one portion of the exterior: the building undergoes constant restoration and cleaning. It takes about a year for the crew to work their way around, at which point they begin again!*

PALAZZO VECCHIO • The Palazzo Vecchio, a fortresslike brick structure at Piazza della Signoria's southeast corner, was the city hall in medieval times and is so again today. The off-center, top-heavy bell tower atop an intimidatingly tall (by medieval standards) building is, along with the Duomo, a recognizable symbol of the city. The original design by Arnolfo di Cambio, who also designed the Duomo, was flawed, and a fair share of Renaissance talents took a swing at fixing it, including Michelozzo—who designed the harmonious courtyard—and Vasari, who redesigned much of the interior for the Medici when they moved in briefly in the 1540s.

The first room at the top of the stairs is the **Salone dei Cinquecento,** the meeting room for Italy's Grand Council during Florence's brief re-attempt at republican government in 1494. Vasari and his assistants painted the frescoes of glorious battle scenes, and Michelangelo's *Victory* sculpture is along the wall facing the entrance. Off to the side is the interesting **Studiolo di Francesco I,** devoid of windows but covered with Mannerist paintings and frescoes by Bronzino and Vasari, among others, as well as statues by Giambologna. Beyond that, some 20 rooms celebrate the humanist republic with never-ending gold glitz. *P. della Signoria, tel. 055/2768965. Admission L10,000. Open Mon.–Wed. and Fri.–Sat. 9–7, Sun. 8–1.*

BARGELLO

Florence's police headquarters and jail during the Renaissance, the Bargello is now Italy's foremost museum of Renaissance sculpture. Downstairs are a few of Michelangelo's early works: A grape-strewn *Bacchus* (the Roman god of wine), a somber bust of *Brutus,* and a *Madonna and Child* tondo. Several small bronze statues of Perseus by Cellini (studies for the Loggia della Signoria) and a few of Giambologna's major works, including the spiral *Florence Defeating Pisa* and the harmonious bronze *Mercury,* also reside here. These artists were heavily influenced by the early Renaissance master Donatello. You can get up close and personal with several of his works on display upstairs. His bronze *David* is the most famous piece in the museum, the first freestanding male nude in Christian sculpture since ancient times. He's naked save for a strangely decorated hat and his booted feet; check out the oddly positioned feather. Donatello's earlier and more classical marble *David* (1408) is also here, as is his *Marzocco,* the heraldic lion symbol of Florence; his guarded, watchful *St. George;* and his colored bust of *Niccolò da Uzzano.* Don't miss the bronze relief panels of the *Sacrifice of Isaac,* made in 1401 by Brunelleschi and Ghiberti in competition for the commission for the baptistery doors (*see* Battistero, *above*). The second-floor loggia is home to a series of bronze birds by Giambologna. The top floor houses della Robbia terracottas and Verrocchio's small, youthful *David. V. del Proconsolo 4, tel. 055/ 2388606. Admission L8,000. Open Mon., Wed.–Fri. daily 8:30–1:50; Tues. and Sat. 8:30–4, closed 2nd and 4th Mon. of month and 1st, 3rd, and 5th Sun. of month.*

ORSANMICHELE

A solitary Gothic presence, Orsanmichele dwarfs the other buildings on Florence's premier *passeggiata* (social stroll) street, Via de' Calzaiuoli. Some of the earliest and best examples of Renaissance sculpture decorate the facade, including copies of Verrocchio's *Christ and St. Thomas* and Ghiberti's *John the Baptist,* on the Via de' Calzaiuoli side of the building, and a copy of Donatello's alert *St. George,* on the north side (the original is in the Bargello). Copies have been put in place of some of the original sculptures in order to preserve them. Inside, an ornate tabernacle by Andrea Orcagna, complete with pinnacles and colored stone, dominates the altar. *V. Arte della Lana off V. de' Calzaiuoli, tel. 055/284944. Admission free. Open daily 9–noon and 4–6. Closed 1st and last Mon. of month.*

SANTA MARIA NOVELLA

Much of the black-and-white-marble facade of the church is textbook classical, but Renaissance architect Leon Battista Alberti's use of S-curve scrolls to soften the transition between the older ground floor and narrow upper story was such a useful innovation that it was copied all over Italy. Like other churches in town, the interior—dotted with remarkable art treasures—feels like a huge Gothic-style warehouse space. Halfway up on the left is Masaccio's *Holy Trinity* (c. 1427), revolutionary for his use of single-point perspective. Check out Ghirlandaio's realistically rendered *Scenes from the Life of St. John the Baptist* and *Life of the Virgin* in the *cappella maggiore* (high altar). To the right, the **Strozzi Chapel** holds Filippino Lippi's melodramatic frescoes and stained glass. Don't miss Paolo Uccello's faded but excellent frescoes of scenes from Genesis in the adjoining cloister **museum** (tel. 055/282187; admission L5,000; open Mon.–Thurs., Sat. 9–2, Sun. 8–1). Closed for restoration at press time (summer 1999), the church is scheduled to reopen in 2000. The piazza may get seedy at night, but by day it's the best open grassy space in the center of Florence. *P. Santa Maria Novella. Open daily 7–noon and 3–6, Sat. until 5.*

The Loggia della Signoria, a covered gallery built between 1376 and 1382, recently reopened after a lengthy restoration. It's filled with priceless sculptures (including Giambologna's 1583 Rape of the Sabine) as well as copies of priceless sculptures. It also affords an excellent opportunity to sit and relax in a shaded spot—a rare commodity in Florence, particularly in summer. Perhaps it was the "no loitering" admonition posted at the steps of the Palazzo Vecchio (the town hall at right angles to the loggia) that prompted one tired tourist to sit on one of the sculptures, a marzocco (lion) that has, for centuries, been regarded as a symbol of the city. The lion crumbled, and the work is once again scaffolded. The moral of the story: sculpture is to be looked at, not sat upon.

SAN LORENZO

The power of the Medici went beyond politics and culture—they even forked out most of the money to build, in their own back yard, a church on the site of an early Christian basilica. The family rounded up the usual suspects—Brunelleschi, Donatello, Michelangelo—to create a church that would match the beauty and prestige of the Duomo. Although they filled the interior with great works by great artists, the overall goal was never realized: The Medici fell from power before Michelangelo's designs for the facade and exterior could be carried out. From the outside, San Lorenzo is a most unimpressive building.

Brunelleschi's gray-and-white interior is one of the earliest examples of pure Renaissance design, with monumental pillars and arches forming a strictly measured Latin cross. Bronze pulpits by Donatello are suspended on columns on either side of the nave. The sculptor's body rests in a chapel in the left transept, to the right of Filippo Lippi's *Annunciation.* On the other side of the transept is the **Sagrestia Vecchia** (Old Sacristy), designed by Brunelleschi, which has more sculpture by Donatello, including bronze doors and the polychrome tondi of *St. John the Evangelist. P. San Lorenzo, tel. 055/216634. Open daily 7–noon and 3:30–5:30.*

In the cloisters to the left of the church is the **Biblioteca Medicea Laurenziana** (tel. 055/210760; open Mon.–Sat. 9–1). The library itself, full of stiff-backed, uncomfortable-looking wooden carrels, usually has several manuscripts on display from the collection of more than 10,000. But the real attraction here is the vestibule and convex staircase, both designed by Michelangelo, which emerge with the visual force of an unstoppable lava flow.

Nowhere is Medici ostentation more apparent than in the **Cappelle Medicee** (admission L10,000; open daily 8:30–1:50; closed 1st, 3rd, and 5th Mon. of month). Although the chapels were originally integral parts of the church, visitors today must enter from the back side of the building. One of the most unbe-lievably opulent chapels ever made for a single family, the **Cappella dei Principi** (Princes' Chapel) will either move you to tears or make you think it's the gaudiest thing this side of Vegas. A dome of deep green, maroon, and black marble soars dizzyingly above. Off to the side is Michelangelo's much more subtle **Sagrestia Nuova** (New Sacristy), containing the sculpted tombs of two members of the Medici clan. The tomb of Lorenzo, Duke of Urbino (to the left of the entrance), shows him in a thoughtful pose above the recumbent figures of *Dusk* and *Dawn;* the tomb of Giuliano (opposite) shows him in sculpted form towering over *Night and Day.*

PALAZZO MEDICI-RICCARDI

Michelozzo's original design for the home and headquarters of the Medici helped establish a new stan-dard for Florentine civic architecture, effectively combining fortresslike authority with classical refine-ments like arched windows and carved pilasters. The building was redone over the years by subsequent owners (the Riccardi came into the picture 200 years later), and part of it is still used for government offices, but its most famous feature, the second-floor chapel, hasn't been touched. Inside is the exquis-ite *Procession of the Magi* by Benozzo Gozzoli (1460), which flies in the face of realism and conjures up fanciful landscapes and portraits of various Medici. Unfortunately, the cost to enter the small chapel is L6,000, and the frescoes, though delightful, are all there is. *V. Cavour 1, tel. 055/2760340. Open Mon.–Tues. and Thurs.– Sat. 9–1 and 3–6, Sun. 9–1.*

If you stand in the right spot, you can make eye contact with Ghiberti's tiny self-portrait bust in the lower left corner of the Jacob and Esau panel on his glorious baptistery doors.

MUSEO DI SAN MARCO

This serene museum is one of Florence's best. San Marco was once a Dominican convent and the home of Girolamo Savonarola, the hot-headed friar who conducted the Bonfire of the Vanities (*see box* Fanatic Flambé, *below*) in 1497. Fra Angelico, the friar- artist, lived and painted here. To the right of the entrance, a gallery contains his oil paintings and altar-pieces, including two *Depositions* and a *Last Judgment* with a graphic vision of hell on the right side. In the Sala Capitolare is his wall-size *Crucifixion,* and at the top of the stairs near the dormitory cells, you'll find his most famous work, the *Annunciation,* with wonderfully fresh colors in a geometrically balanced space. Also on the second floor are 44 monks' cells, each with its own small fresco by Fra Angelico and his students. The museum further displays works by Ghirlandaio, among others. *P. San Marco 1, tel. 055/2388608. Admission L8,000. Open Tues.–Sun. 8:30–1:50, closed 1st, 3rd, and 5th Sun. and 2nd and 4th Mon. of month.*

GALLERIA DELL'ACCADEMIA

There's more to this place than Michelangelo's *David,* and once you're through battling the camera-tot-ing swarms, do check out the rest of the museum, which offers a superb collection of Renaissance art. Michelangelo began with a single block of discarded marble in 1501. He finished three years later, at age 29, and the monumental work was placed in the Piazza della Signoria. The left wrist was broken in a riot in 1527 and was only reattached in 1543. The statue was moved inside (and a copy put in its place) in 1873. When viewed this close, David's proportions (big hands, big head) look more skewed; they are meant to suggest his youthful strength and power. It's not for nothing that he was a symbol of Florentine civic pride.

The gallery that leads to David is lined with Michelangelo's series of *Slaves* from the 1520s. Believing that every slab of marble inherently possessed a figure struggling to emerge, Michelangelo partially "freed" them. The museum also contains a distinguished collection of Renaissance paintings and a room full of altarpieces. *V. Ricasoli 60, tel. 055/2388609. Admission L12,000. Open summer, Tues.– Sat. 8:30–10, Sun. 8:30–8. Shorter hours in winter.*

PIAZZA SANTISSIMA ANNUNZIATA

This square north of the Duomo is a lunchtime hangout for local students and some of the city's poor-est, as there's a soup kitchen in the square. This is nevertheless one of Italy's most architecturally sig-nificant piazzas. It is also one of Florence's most artistically important squares. The colonnade along the east side of the piazza is harmonious, balanced, and symmetrical. Brunelleschi designed the **Ospedale degli Innocenti** (Foundling Hospital) in 1419, and it's one of the first examples of true Renaissance style in architecture, copied all over Florence and the Western world. The hospital's simple columns, topped by perfect half-circle arches, mark the beginning of Brunelleschi's infatuation with perfect mathemati-

FANATIC FLAMBÉ

"Bonfire of the Vanities" wasn't was just a Tom Wolfe novel. In Florence's Piazza della Signoria during Carnevale in 1497, the radical Dominican monk Girolamo Savonarola, briefly ruling during the Medici exile, thought the city was going to hell in a handbasket. In carnival dress, Savonarola and devoted henchmen—or, in this case, henchboys—torched sinful loot that had been ransacked from homes: Latin manuscripts, women's ornaments, even Botticelli paintings. Florentines soon tired of his puritanical rule; a plaque on the square notes the spot where Savonarola himself was hanged and burned.

cal equilibrium: The distance between the centers of two columns equals the distance between the center of a column and the wall of the building, which also equals the height of a vertical support from the floor to the point where two arches meet.

The 10 medallions mounted on the facade were crafted by Andrea della Robbia in 1487. About 150 years later, a symmetrical loggia was built across the piazza to complement Brunelleschi's porch. Inside the old hospital is the **Galleria dell' Opedale degli Innocenti** (P. Santissima Annunziata 12, tel. 055/2491708; open Mon.–Tues. and Thurs.–Sun. 8:30–2). These lesser- known paintings may be an acquired taste, but if you go, don't miss Ghirlandaio's *Adoration of the Magi*.

On the north side of the square is **Santissima Annunziata,** one of the city's most beautiful churches. You don't have to interrupt Mass to see the lively frescoes by Andrea del Sarto, Jacopo Pontormo, and Rosso Fiorentino; they're in the atrium outside the church. If you do make it into the incredibly ornamented, overdone interior, check out Andrea del Castagno's intense *Vision of St. Jerome* in the second chapel to the left.

SANTA CROCE

Santa Croce serves as Florence's equivalent of Westminster Abbey, providing an eternal resting place for many of its illustrious citizens. The city's Franciscan basilica, begun in the late 13th century, holds the tombs of an all-star lineup including Michelangelo, Galileo, Ghiberti, and Machiavelli, as well as monuments to Dante, Leonardo da Vinci, and Raphael (the last three are buried elsewhere). To the right as you enter is Michelangelo's sculpted tomb, designed by Vasari, although the artist's body is actually under the Buonarroti family medallions carved into the floor to the left of the tomb. Also on the right (just below the organ) is Donatello's beautifully rendered *Annunciation,* one of the better Florentine sculptures of the familiar scene. Galileo's tomb lies opposite Michelangelo's. Because the astronomer advanced the theory that the sun, not the earth, was the center of the solar system, his corpse wasn't allowed in until 100 years after his death, when the Vatican formally conceded that the universe wasn't geocentric after all.

Giotto's impressive fresco cycles of the lives of St. Francis (in the **Cappella Bardi,** close to the altar) and St. John the Baptist (in the adjacent **Cappella Peruzzi**) helped prod painting out of stiff medieval conventions and into explorations of spatial depth and psychologically complex compositions. The color has faded and huge chunks are missing, but the frescoes remain impressive. The chapel at the far end of the left transept contains Donatello's *Crucifix,* sharply criticized by Brunelleschi, who sculpted his cross in Santa Maria Novella in a show of one-upmanship. P. Santa Croce. Open summer, Mon.– Sat. 8–6:30, Sun. 3–6; winter, Mon.–Sat. 8–12:30 and 3–6:30, Sun. 3–6.

On the right-hand side of the facade is the entrance to the cloisters, which contain the church **museum** and the exquisite **Cappella dei Pazzi** (combined admission L5,000; open Tues. and Thurs–Sun. 10–12:30 and 2:30–6:30, shorter hrs in winter). Go in and take the measure of Brunelleschi's mathematically calibrated and geometrically planned chapel. The tondi of the apostles and evangelists above the door are the work of the della Robbia family. The adjacent museum has Donatello's massive bronze *San Ludovico d'Angio* (1423) and Cimabue's *Crucifixion,* heavily damaged by Florence's disastrous flood in 1966.

THE OLTRARNO

Although Florentines once perceived the other side of the Arno as a world away, most sights, except those up the hill, are really quite close to the centro. On the way over, cross the **Ponte Vecchio,** the oldest bridge in Florence. Rebuilt in the 14th century on the site of a Roman bridge, it was originally lined with butchers' and produce merchants' shops. In the late 16th century, Ferdinando I—who decided that all this plebeian commerce was unseemly—sent them packing and installed jewelry merchants on the bridge, and the tradition continues today. The Oltrarno is a pleasant area to explore, especially once you clear crowded Via Guicciardini between the Ponte Vecchio and the Pitti Palace.

PALAZZO PITTI • Designed as a home for Luca Pitti, a prosperous local businessman, the original building of the palace—the middle section, minus the wings—was begun in the 15th century. Then the Medici got their hands on the place and made enormous additions. In its expanded state, it is by far the largest building in Florence, nearly twice the size of the Duomo. The palace is still considered extravagant today, especially for budget travelers: If you're not careful, you could spend more than L20,000 visiting all of its museums and gardens.

The most substantial of the palace's museums is the **Galleria Palatina** (tel. 055/2388611; admission L12,000; open Tues.–Sat. 8:30–10, Sun. 8:30–8; shorter hours in winter), with works by Rubens, Caravaggio (look for his tooth-pulling scene in the first room), Tintoretto, and van Dyck. Titian and Raphael are well represented, the former by *La Concerta* and some moving portraits, the latter by a number of stirring *Madonna and Child* scenes. The **Galleria d'Arte Moderna** (tel. 055/2388616; closed indefinitely for restoration) offers a host of Tuscan Impressionist paintings, though its views onto the gardens (*see* Giardini Boboli, *below*) and the city are almost more memorable.

The other major museum in the palace, the **Museo degli Argenti** (tel. 055/2388710; admission L8,000; open Mon., Wed., Fri.–Sun. 8:30–1:50; Tues., Thurs. 8:30–5, closed 1st, 3rd, 5th Mon. and 2nd and 4th Sun. of month), holds Medici capes, urns, chalices, and other such loot. As with the palace's art galleries, it's hard to take in everything in just one visit. The **Galleria del Costume** (closed indefinitely for restoration) has attractive displays. The admission fee for the Museo degli Argenti also gets you into the cloying, unimpressive **Museo delle Porcellane** (tel. 055/2388710; open daily 9–1:50, closed 2nd and 4th Sun. and 1st, 3rd, and 5th Mon. of month). *P. Pitti, tel. 055/210323.*

Though its origins are slightly obscure (an earlier bridge may date from Roman times), the Ponte Vecchio as we know it today was in place by the early 12th century. Rebuilt in 1345, it's the only bridge in Florence that survived destruction by fleeing Nazis in 1944. In the middle of the bridge, there's a tiny piazza where you can take in the view.

GIARDINI BOBOLI • These luxurious, spacious gardens, opened to the public in the 17th century, were built by the Medici as an idyllic and private outdoor retreat. A succession of landscapers groomed the grounds, creating an odd blend of formal, classical gardens and twisting, shaded bowers. Look for the **Grotta del Buontalenti,** next to the park exit on the palace's north side. Inside the dazzlingly ornamented artificial cave are copies of Michelangelo's *Slaves*—the originals are now in the Accademia. Near the grotto, don't miss the bizarre statue of a nude Morgante, Cosimo I's obese court dwarf, riding a turtle. The rest of the garden offers fantastic views of the city—especially at the highest point, near Forte Belvedere—and breezy walks. The most spectacular of the fountains, the **Isolotto,** features a huge pond with a garden island in the center. *P. Pitti, tel. 055/2651816. Admission L4,000. Open Nov.–Feb. daily 9–4:30; Mar. and Oct. daily 9–5:30; Apr., May, Sept. daily 9–6:30; June—Aug. daily 9–7:30; closed 1st and last Mon. of month.*

SANTA MARIA DEL CARMINE • Perhaps the most important and moving fresco cycle in Florence is the one in the tiny **Cappella Brancacci,** in the church of Santa Maria del Carmine, a few blocks west of Santo Spirito (*see* Not-So-Major Sights, *below*). Visitors are grouped together and brought in for a brief look. The chapel is known for Masaccio's brilliant, legendary frescoes *Expulsion from Eden* and *The Tribute Money.* The latter is a dramatic three-part painting taken from the New Testament: in the center, the tax man comes to collect from Jesus and the apostles; to the left, St. Peter reaches into the river and takes a gold coin from a fish's mouth; and on the right, St. Peter pays the tax man. Masaccio, who died at age 27, painted it in less than a month. Later Renaissance painters like Paolo Uccello and Michelangelo came here to study Masaccio's revolutionary technique. The Adam and Eve expulsion scene—the first painting to have only one source of light on its figures—is probably the most wrenching artistic image of the Renaissance. A recent but somewhat controversial restoration brought to light the brilliant color and revealed that the fig leaf covering Adam's privates was added by prudish clerics soon after Masaccio's death. *P. del Carmine, tel. 055/2382195. Admission L5,000. Open Mon. and Wed.–Sat. 10–5, Sun. 1–5.*

NOT-SO-MAJOR SIGHTS

CASA BUONARROTI

Owned but never inhabited by Michelangelo, Casa Buonarroti houses the largest collection of his drawings in the world. Upstairs are several impressive sculptures by the young Michelangelo, including *Madonna of the Steps* and *Battle of the Centaurs,* both unfinished. A wooden crucifix from Santo Spirito dates from 1492, when the artist was only 17 years old. Downstairs are rotating displays of his sketches. *V. Ghibellina 70, tel. 055/241752. Admission L10,000. Open Wed.–Mon. 9:30–1:30.*

MUSEO ARCHEOLOGICO

An extensive collection of ancient finds begun by the Medici contains—surprise, surprise—mostly local Etruscan and Roman urns and tiny bronze figurines, but also Egyptian mummies and masks. The most notable pieces are several spectacularly preserved life-size male bronzes from the Roman period; the 5th-century BC *Chimera,* a mythical beast; and an astonishing Roman sculpture of a horse's head. The museum provides a nice break from endless collections of Renaissance art. *V. della Colonna 36, off P. Santissima Annunziata, tel. 055/23575. Admission L8,000. Open daily 9–2, Sun. 9–1, closed 1st, 3rd, and 5th Sun. and 2nd and 4th Mon. of month.*

MUSEO DI STORIA DELLA SCIENZA

The Museum of the History of Science displays the Medici's collection of astrolabes, quadrants, globes, compasses, telescopes, sextants, and barometers, and, as an added bonus, Galileo's middle finger. The first floor contains most of the good stuff, but upstairs is a fascinating room of wax and terracotta models of the uterus that illustrate the stages of pregnancy. *P. dei Giudici 1, right on the Lungarno, tel. 055/2398876. Admission L10,000. Open Mon., Wed., Fri. 9:30—1 and 2—5, Thurs. and Sat. 9:30—1.*

MUSEO MARINO MARINI

Florence's only full-time modern art museum contains the work of just one artist, the marvelous Marino Marini (1901–80). The artist was a native of nearby Pistoia, where the Centro di Documentazione Fondazione Marino Marini (*see* Pistoia *in* Near Florence, *below*) is also devoted to his work. The roomy gallery, a former church with fading frescoes on the ceiling, has been converted into a sleek, multilevel exhibition space containing mostly sculpture. Marini's favorite subjects—clowns, acrobats, and horses—are well represented, and his work has a childlike, playful quality. *P. San Pancrazio, corner of V. della Spada and V. de' Federighi, tel. 055/219432. Admission L8,000. Open Sept.–July, Mon., Wed.–Sat. 10–5, Sun., 10–1.*

OGNISSANTI

Originally a 13th-century Romanesque structure, this church got a Baroque overhaul in the 17th century when the Franciscans redid the exterior. Inside you'll find a matching pair of portraits facing each other across the nave: Botticelli's *St. Augustine* (to the right of the entrance) and Ghirlandaio's *St. Jerome* (to the left). Continue to the refectory off the church cloisters; Ghirlandaio's massive *Last Supper* hangs brightly along the far wall. *Borgo Ognissanti 42, tel. 055/2398700. Church: Open Mon.–Sat. 9–noon and 3:30–7, Sun. 3:30–5:30. Refectory: tel. 055/2396802; open Mon., Tues., Sat. 9–12.*

OLTRARNO

Buses 12 and 13 head from the train station up to **Piazzale Michelangelo,** with a terrific view of Florence. Nearby sits the church of **San Miniato al Monte,** surveying the city from a cozy perch. The church dates from the early 11th century; only the Duomo's baptistery is older. The patterned green-and-white-marble facade is particularly Florentine, different from the many Tuscan churches with the striped Pisan Romanesque look. Intricately detailed and exquisitely crafted marble work inside makes this well worth the trip. Look for the terracotta angels by Luca della Robbia on the ceiling of the chapel, off the left aisle. Throughout the year, monks perform chants at special twilight services. *V. Monte alle Croci, tel. 055/2332731. Open daily 8–12 and 2–7 (in winter until 6).*

Just beyond the valley west of San Miniato is a peak crowned by **Forte Belvedere,** yet another Medici project, largely designed by Ammanati and Buontalenti. The views, which rival those from San Miniato, are more impressive than the building itself, but the fort is an excellent place to spend several peaceful hours lolling about. It's usually free, except when special exhibitions are on. *V. San Leonardo, tel. 055/244577. Open Wed.–Mon. 9–8 (in winter until 5).*

PALAZZO STROZZI AND PALAZZO RUCELLAI

Though Palazzo Medici-Riccardi (*see* Major Sights, *above*) is one of the most important examples of Florentine architecture, Palazzo Rucellai (V. della Vigna Nuova 16r) was the prototype, designed by Leon Battista Alberti in the mid-15th century. The street that houses Palazzo Rucellai, Via della Vigna Nuova, is lined with Florence's swankiest shops. The nearby Via Tornabuoni also reeks of money, thanks to its designer stores and the Renaissance Palazzo Strozzi (P. Strozzi), which also follows Alberti's lead.

SANT'APOLLONIA

Andrea del Castagno's brilliantly colored *Last Supper* covers a wall of the refectory in this old Benedictine monastery. Around the corner is the 15th-century cloister (V. San Gallo 25) that once belonged to the monastery, now a part of the University of Florence. *V. XXVII Aprile 1, tel. 055/2388607. Admission free. Open daily 8:30–1:50. Closed 1st, 3rd, 5th Sun. and 2nd and 4th Mon. of month.*

SANTO SPIRITO

You wouldn't guess it from the simple, unadorned yellow exterior, but the church of Santo Spirito is one of the most ambitious creations to come out of the Renaissance—another one of Brunelleschi's mathematically precise projects. The church was intended to be perfectly symmetrical (in the shape of a Greek cross), but after Brunelleschi's death the plans were modified and the church extended into a Latin cross. In the right transept is Filippino Lippi's *Madonna and Child with Saints* (also known as the Nerli Altarpiece), and off the left aisle of the nave sits a harmonious sacristy designed by Giuliano da Sangallo. In 1985 a competition was held to decorate the bare facade of Santo Spirito, and entries were made into slides and projected onto the facade for all to see. You can check out many of the designs on permanent display in the Caffè Ricci on the piazza. *P. Santo Spirito, tel. 055/210030. Open Thurs.–Tues. 8–12 and 4–6; Wed. 8–12.*

SINAGOGA AND MUSEO EBRAICO

In the mid-19th century, as most of Florence's old synagogues were being demolished to facilitate modernization, the leader of the local Jewish community, David Levi, bequeathed his estate for the founding of a new synagogue. Built in the 1870s in Moorish-Byzantine style, the enormous synagogue is both wonderful and garish, with ornate hand-painted arabesques covering the walls and Turkish-style domes on the exterior. Upstairs, the small but worthwhile Jewish Museum depicts the history of Florence's Jews. Orthodox services are held weekly. Next door, **Ruth's** (V. Farini 2, tel. 055/241890) serves tasty, mostly vegetarian lunches and dinners (around L25,000). *V. Farini 4, tel. 055/245252. Admission for both L6,000. Open Sun.–Thurs. 10–1 and 2–5, Fri. 10–1; shorter hours in winter.*

CHEAP THRILLS

If you want to spend some time outdoors, the gorgeous public park adjacent to the Fortezza da Basso offers grass, flowers, and a small lake. Head north on Via Faenza to Viale Filippo Strozzi and make a right to reach the park. A hike up to Piazzale Michelangelo or Forte Belvedere may be the perfect way to escape the confining streets and tourist congestion of the city. Arm yourself with a bottle of water and expect to sweat. Your efforts will be rewarded by the thrill of the views and the freedom of wide open space. Don't forget that you can also rent a bicycle or moped (*see* Getting Around, *above*) and explore the fringes of Florence or the outlying countryside. Take a picnic and you're set.

In the evening, head out to the larger piazzas, where bands and street performers often favor crowds with heartfelt song. For a night of art and culture between July and September, ask at the tourist office about **Le Notti dei Tesori** (Summer Night Treasures), when certain museums remain open until 11 PM, often with music. Small churches often hold free or inexpensive community classical concerts—peek inside the churches for posted info.

FESTIVALS

Florence's patron saint celebration, the **Festa di San Giovanni,** is a massive festival that is held June 24 but has the entire city talking year-round. Colorful medieval-dress parades, ornate flower arrangements that blanket Piazza della Signoria, and a fireworks show over the Arno make the festival unforgettable. In the weeks leading up to it, teams representing Florentine neighborhoods square off in medieval soc-

CALCIO-CRAZY

Italians are passionate about calcio (soccer), and Florentines are no exception. Tifosi (fans) of the team Fiorentina are fervent and as entertaining as the play. Taking in a match will give you an eyeful of an Italian tradition. Tickets to the local games at the Stadio Comunale can cost as little as L30,000, but the cheap seats always go very fast—head to the Chiosco degli Sportivi (V. Anselmi, off P. della Repubblica, tel. 055/292363). Tickets for most matches are difficult but not impossible to come by. Don't even bother for those against their biggest rivals—Juventus of Turin and A. C. Milan.

cer matches in the **Calcio Storico Fiorentino** competition. The finals are played on June 24. Purchase tickets (cheap seats go for about L21,000) at the box office (V. Faenza 139r, tel. 055/210804).

From May through June, the city also hosts a music festival called **Maggio Musicale,** packed with concerts, opera, ballet, and movies (some free) at various venues throughout the city. Publicity posters are plastered everywhere, but you can get details at the **tourist office** or by calling the box office of the Teatro Comunale (V. C. d'Italia 16, tel. 055/2779236).

SHOPPING

No matter what your tastes are, Florence's shopping scene will grab your attention and seize your wallet. Here you can bargain for quality leather goods at an open-air market, drool over an elegant Italian suit in a window, or visit an artisan's workshop in the Oltrarno. Walk down Via Tornabuoni and the other streets west of Piazza della Repubblica to get a glimpse of the latest by Ferragamo, Gucci, and other hot Italian designers. Florence is also known for its jewelry—a good place to browse is Ponte Vecchio, which has overpriced but beautiful stuff—and its distinctive peacock-patterned, marbleized hand-printed paper.

MARKETS

Leave Florence in shame if you don't check out the fabulous open-air markets held throughout the city. Most open early in the morning and close down at sunset. The main market is the **Mercato di San Lorenzo** (near the church of San Lorenzo), known for its leather goods ranging from handbags and gloves to jackets and boots. Booths also sell belts, T-shirts, candy—you name it. To pick up religious paraphernalia and time-honored souvenirs like piggy banks modeled after Michelangelo's *David,* head over to the **Mercato Nuovo** (off P. della Signoria). Fruit, vegetables, household goods, and flowers are the attractions at **Sant'Ambrogio** (P. Ghiberti; open weekday mornings)**,** Florence's oldest market. You may even get some assertiveness training while standing in line with the local grandmas: don't let them butt in line even if they are older than you. Visit the **Mercato delle Pulci** (P. dei Ciompi) on the last Sunday of the month if antiques, prints, and trinkets from the past are your passion. When you're thinking about buying, remember that prices in a market are never set in stone. Bargain when there's no price tag (especially on leather); when a vendor names a figure, counter with half and go from there.

SPECIALTY STORES

If retail therapy is simply out of the question, take refuge in some serious window-shopping.

YARNS • Filpucci (V. della Vigna Nuova 14/r) is Italy's largest manufacturer of yarns. Nearby factories produce miles of the stuff for Italy's top designers.

GIFT IDEAS • Officina Profumo Farmaceutica di Santa Maria Novella (V. della Scala 16/r) is blissfully redolent of the thousand perfumes in this Art Nouveau emporium of herbal cosmetics, soaps, and sachets based on centuries-old recipes devised by monks. For housewares nothing beats **Bartolini** (V. dei Servi 30/r), with a wide selection of well-designed, practical items. **Sbigoli Terrecotte** (V. Sant'Egidio 4/r) carries a wide selection of terracotta and ceramic vases, pots, cups, and saucers.

LEATHER • Leather Guild (P. Santa Croce 20/r) is one of many shops in the Santa Croce neighborhood that produce inexpensive, antique-looking leather goods of mass appeal, but here you can see the craftspersons at work, a reassuring experience. **Il Bisonte** (V. del Parione 31/r, just off V. della Vigna Nuova) is known for its natural-looking leather goods, branded with the store's bison symbol.

PAPER AND BOOKS • Stationery shops here don't just carry greeting cards—leather-bound journals and parchment-lined albums from **Il Papiro** (V. Cavour 55r and other locations) or **Il Torchino** (V. de'Bardi 17) make great gifts. One of Florence's oldest paper-goods stores, **Giannini** (P. Pitti 37/r, Oltrarno) is the place to buy the marbleized stuff, which comes in a variety of forms, from flat sheets to boxes and even pencils. Long one of Florence's best art-book stores, **Libreria Salimbeni** (V. Matteo Palmieri 14/r) specializes in publications on Tuscany and publishes many itself. **Alinari** (V. della Vigna Nuova 46/r) is one of Florence's oldest and most prestigious photographers, and in this store, next to its museum, prints of its historic photographs are sold along with books and posters.

AFTER DARK

The main evening socializing occurs during the passeggiata. Hordes of people, young and old alike, grab a gelato and stroll from the Duomo to the Piazza della Signoria and back again. Street performers set up in the piazzas and pickup artists line the streets. Other hot spots to check out are the Ponte Vecchio and Piazzale Michelangelo.

BARS AND CAFFE

Florence is full of pubs. **Robin Hood's Tavern** (V. Oriuolo 58/r, tel. 055/244579) is in the Duomo's backyard and oddly serves terrific Buffalo chicken wings along with fine pints. The **Fiddler's Elbow** (P. Santa Maria Novella 7r, no phone) has seats out on the piazza and attracts hordes of students, foreign and native alike.

On the west side of Mercato Nuovo, look for the Porcellino fountain—it's a wild boar with a shiny snout that has become a Florentine talisman. Rubbing it supposedly brings good luck.

Piazza Santo Spirito draws a good night-time crowd. Most locals buy beer at the bar and take it outside. **Cabiria Café** (P. Santo Spirito, tel. 055/215732; closed Tues.) is one of the more popular hangouts in town. In the student area on the other side of town, try the happening **Cardillac Caffè** (V. degli Alfani 57r, tel. 055/2344455; closed Sun.), which hosts gay and lesbian night every Friday beginning at 10. **Rex** (V. Fiesolana 23–25r, tel. 055/2480331) has a hip, trendy atmosphere and an arty clientele. June to September, Rex moves its operations to the courtyard of Le Murate, a convent in the Renaissance and a prison in the 19th century. There's live music, movies, and performance art. **Be Bop** (V. dei Servi 76r, no phone) hosts jazz bands every night of the week, with special prices for students. **Bar Sant'Ambrogio** (P. Sant'Ambrogio 7– 8/r, tel. 055/241035) has outdoor summer seating with a view of an 11th-century church as well as a happy hour that goes until 9 pm.

DISCOS

Admission to discos is around L15,000–L20,000, but women often get in free. Also look for discount passes handed out on Piazza del Duomo, Piazza della Repubblica, and Via de' Calzaiuoli. Few places in the center get much business from the locals. The cavernous **Yab** (V. Sassetti 5r, tel. 055/282018; closed Mon. and summer) is as full of Americans as Italians, but the techno/house music brings natives and foreigners together, at least rhythmically. **Maramao** (V. dei Macci 79, tel. 055/244341) plays better-than-average music and draws a good-looking crowd. For a slightly more sophisticated evening, stroll into **Full-Up** (V. della Vigna Vecchia 21r, tel. 055/293006; closed Tues.) and catch some action at the piano bar. **Andromeda** (V. Cimatori 13, tel. 055/292002; closed Sun.) is the place to be if you're more in the mood for a night of neon and '90s funk.

Most locals are much more keen on places outside the center, where there's space to dance outdoors. In summer the wildest dancing takes place at **Meccanò** (V. degli Olmi 1, on southern edge of Cascine Park, tel. 055/331371), which has live music, women dancing in go-go cages, and a general air of debauchery. Covers run L25,000–L30,000. You can get here on Bus 17, but the area is iffy and the bus stops running around midnight. Also on the outskirts is **Tenax** (V. Pratese 47, tel. 055/308160). Take Bus 29 or 30 out here, and you may hear big-name bands from around the world for free.

GAY AND LESBIAN CLUBS • Gay discos come and go in Florence, and the scene here is much more accommodating for gay men than for lesbians. **Tabasco** (P. Santa Cecilia 3, just off P. della Signoria, tel. 055/213000; closed Mon.), traditionally for men only, has become a popular disco bar for both gay men and lesbians. **Piccolo Café** (Borgo Santa Croce 23, tel. 055/241704) offers a casual meeting ground, where late-night coffee and art exhibits are all part of the scene. Hot spot **Satanassa** (V. de' Pandolfini 26r, near P. Salvemini, tel. 055/243356; closed July–Aug.) is for men only. Call **ARCI Gay/ARCI Lesbica** (tel. 055/476557) for more info or look for *Quir,* an Italian/English bilingual gay magazine listing local events (*see* Basics, *above*).

MOVIE THEATERS

Florence has plenty of cinemas, although nearly all of them close in summer because they lack air-conditioning. The obvious remedy is outdoor screens, and many have popped up in and around Florence. The closest is just outside the walls of Forte Belvedere (*see* Not-so-Major Sights, *above;* tel. 055/244577). From late June to early September, recent films are shown nightly at 9:30 (admission L10,000). All English films are dubbed into Italian. To get here, catch Bus 13 or cross the river at Ponte alle Grazia and follow the signs. The only screen in town that shows English-language films full-time is the indoor **Cinema Astro** (P. San Simone, no phone; closed mid-July–early Sept.). For L8,000 you can sit in uncomfortable wooden seats and watch American hits from one year ago alternating with the inevitable showings of anything with Bruce Willis in it. The **Odeon** (v. Sassetti 1, tel. 055/214068) shows first-run movies in English on Mondays. On Wednesday nights in the Oltrarno, you can also see recent releases in English at **Cinema Goldoni** (V. dei Serragli 109, tel. 055/222437). For both theaters' schedules, check the tourist office and English-language bulletin boards.

NEAR FLORENCE

FIESOLE

Just a 20-minute bus ride (8 km/5 mi, L1,500) from downtown Florence, Fiesole has all the characteristics of the tiny hill towns that dot the Tuscan countryside and a history predating that of Florence. Etruscans founded the city around 600 BC on the site of a long-defunct Bronze Age town, and the Romans constructed one of the region's most sophisticated amphitheaters here around 80 BC. Its ruins and the remnants of Roman bathhouses stand before an unspoiled series of hills north of the city. Today many visitors explore the hillside on mountain bikes; the steep, uncrowded roads around town afford stunning views. During summer the city is home to the spectacular **Estate Fiesolana** festival, a music, dance, theater, and film series that many consider the region's richest cultural event.

Even if you have only two hours to spare, make the simple journey up the hill to get a different angle on the local scene. Monday is a good day for a visit; Fiesole's main attractions are open while Florence's are closed. Unless you plan to camp at Camping Panoramico Fiesole (*see* Where to Sleep, *above*), you'll probably want to head back down to Florence for the night as there are no budget hotels in Fiesole. Restaurants are pricey—think picnic and head up the main drag, Via Gramsci, which has a Coop supermarket, a bakery, and places to buy fruit and other picnic loot.

BASICS

Pick up Bus 7 at the station or Piazza San Marco. It drops you in Piazza Mino da Fiesole, in the middle of Fiesole one block south of the entrance to the Roman ruins. The last bus returns to the city around 12:30 AM. The **tourist office** (P. Mino da Fiesole 37, tel. 055/598720) is right next to the stop.

WORTH SEEING

There's a lot to see in Fiesole. A combination ticket for L10,000 admits you to the Museo Bandini, the amphitheater, the Museo Civico, and the Antiquarium Costantini, all of which are open daily 9–7 (until 5 in winter) except the first Tuesday of the month. All of the churches mentioned below are open Monday–Saturday 10–noon and 3–5 (until 6 in summer), but be careful about early morning services, when nonworshiping visitors are not very welcome.

The town's well-preserved Roman ruins merit more attention than they get from most visitors. The partially restored **Teatro Romano** still holds performances and offers an impressive view of the hills beyond the theater. Below the theater are remains of the baths; only one arch still stands to give you a sense of the original architecture. The **Museo Civico** (V. Portigiani 1, tel. 055/59477) contains Etruscan and Roman finds from the area. The most prized piece is a barely recognizable bronze copy of Rome's symbol, the she-wolf suckling Romulus and Remus. The **Antiquarium Costantini** (V. Portigiani 1, tel. 055/59477) houses the well- maintained private collection of mostly Greek and Etruscan urns and vases from Sicily and southern Italy that was donated to the city of Fiesole in 1985 by Alfiero Costantini. The air-conditioned **Museo Bandini** (V. Duprè 1, tel. 055/59477) has a collection of early Renaissance art, including works by the della Robbia family.

The **Chiesa di San Romolo** (P. della Cattedrale, tel. 055/59400) has a flattened sandstone facade thanks to messy restoration work, but inside it's a somber take on the Pisan Romanesque style with several sculptures by local artist Mino da Fiesole. Head up the hill outside the church (on V. di San Francesco) and you'll reach the town's main lookout point, just below the two highest churches. The **Chiesa di San Francesco** (V. di San Francesco, tel. 055/59175; admission free), at Fiesole's highest point, has probably the best museum in town in its basement. It's filled with both Egyptian finds and dozens of fabulously detailed ivory and alabaster carvings brought from China by missionaries, many of which date from the 1st century BC and are much more sophisticated than Roman sculpture of the period.

FESTIVALS

One of Italy's most prestigious cultural festivals, the **Estate Fiesolana,** runs nightly from late June to late August, with most events taking place in the **Teatro Romano.** Events change nearly every night, and the variety is incredible. Plays are performed in Italian, and films are shown in their original language with subtitles. The dance and music performances attract an eclectic group of performers—primarily Italian, but international acts do appear. Purchase tickets for theater and dance, musical events, or films. Prices vary from L20,000 to L40,000 depending upon the event. You can pick up pamphlets for the festival all over Fiesole and Florence, or call the box office at the Teatro Romano (tel. 055/59477). Events rarely sell out, so just arrive early enough to find a good seat.

PRATO

Minutes away from Florence, Prato offers a restful break from crowds, mopeds, and outrageous prices—but stay away on Tuesday, when all the museums are closed. Florence's neighboring industrial center, Prato has been one of the major cities in Europe for cloth and textile production since the 14th century, and it's still the place to go to shop for clothing and shoes. Even though it's Tuscany's third-largest city, most of the factories have been built outside the city walls, and attractive piazzas lend a relaxed tranquility to the centro storico. If you're bedazzled by the barrage of Renaissance relics in Tuscany, the town's major contemporary art museum will be a welcome change.

BASICS

To reach the **tourist office** (P. Santa Maria delle Carceri 15, tel. 0574/24112; open Mon.–Sat. 9–6:30, shorter hours in winter) from the central train station, cross the piazza and the bridge, take Viale Vittorio Veneto across Piazza San Marco onto Viale Piave, and turn right just beyond the fortress on Piazza Santa Maria delle Carceri. Opposite the church is the back entrance to the office, marked with a yellow "ı." If you're coming from the Porta al Serraglio station, take Via Magnolfi through Piazza del Duomo to Via G. Mazzini and go left at Piazza del Comune onto Via Cairoli.

COMING AND GOING

Trains make the 15-minute trip to Prato from Florence (L2,200) about three times an hour. They stop first at Prato's Stazione Centrale, but westbound trains—to Pistoia, Lucca, and Pisa—also stop at a far more convenient second station, Porta al Serraglio, two blocks north of the Duomo. Prato's two busiest spots are Piazza del Duomo and Piazza Santa Maria delle Carceri. To the east is the enormous Piazza Mercatale, with a park and a number of bars and restaurants.

WHERE TO SLEEP AND EAT

The name Prato means "grassy field" in English, but there is neither a campground here nor a youth hostel, so for budget accommodations head back to Florence or somewhere else. If you are staying, two good options are the **Hotel Stella d'Italia** (P. del Duomo 8, tel. 0574/27910, fax 0574/40289), with bright rooms L115,000 with bath, L90,000 without) that overlook the cathedral, and **Albergo Il Giglio** (P. San Marco 14, tel. 0574/37049, fax 0574/604351; cash only; L112,000 with bath, L90,000 without), closer to Stazione Centrale.

Prato has a few dishes of its own that the Florentines don't do, and you can get them at **La Vecchia Cucina di Soldano** (V. Pomeria 23, near P. San Marco, tel. 0574/34665; cash only; closed Sun.). For solid food to go, stop by **Rosticceria Gigi** (V. del Sirena 11, off P. del Duomo, tel. 0574/25227) for servings of lasagna and roast chicken. As Prato has a dearth of good picnic spots, you'll probably have to dine on the steps of the Duomo.

WORTH SEEING

The Duomo, at the center of town, has a green-and-white-striped marble facade crowned by a lunette by Andrea della Robbia. Michelozzo's unusual *Pulpit of the Sacred Girdle* hangs off the upper corner, decorated with casts of friezes by Donatello (the originals are in the museum next door), and positioned so that the priest could address both the crowd inside the small church and the spillover outside on the piazza. The girdle itself, given by the Virgin Mary to the perpetually doubting Thomas—who wondered if Mary really ascended full body into heaven—is carried out onto the pulpit and displayed to a cheering crowd about five times a year. Inside the Duomo are several fresco cycles: to the left as you enter is Agnolo Gaddi's illustrative *Legend of the Holy Girdle* fresco cycle; behind the altar is Filippo Lippi's *St. John the Baptist and St. Stephen,* and to the right is the *Lives of the Virgin and St. Stephen,* partly attributed to Paolo Uccello. Bring a flashlight: the frescoes are gorgeous and there's no illumination.

Next door, the **Museo dell'Opera del Duomo** (P. del Duomo 49, tel. 0574/29339) holds Filippino Lippi's *Santa Lucia,* Uccello's *Jacopone da Todi,* and the original panels from Donatello's pulpit. Your L8,000 ticket includes admission to the **Museo Civico** (Palazzo Pretorio, P. del Comune, tel. 0574/616302), which has several impressive altarpieces by both Lippis. The museums are both open daily 9:30–12:30 and 3–6:30 (except Tues. and Sun. afternoon). Save the ticket, which will also get you into the **Museo di Pittura Murale** (P. San Domenico 8, tel. 0574/29339; open Wed.–Mon. 9—noon and 3:30–7:30, Sun. 10–1), which displays frescoes in various stages—from *sinopie* (preparatory drawings) to completed works. Also on hand is a fine collection of paintings by Filippo Lippi and other works from the 13th through 15th centuries on view through 2000.

The church of **Santa Maria delle Carceri** (P. Santa Maria delle Carceri) is the local Renaissance gem, designed by Giuliano da Sangallo and decorated with della Robbia terracottas. Next door to the church is the **Castello dell'Imperatore** (admission free; open Mon., Wed.–Sat. 10–1:30 and 3:30–7, Sun. 10–2; slightly different hours in winter), a 13th-century fortress that now hosts an occasional classical music concert or recent Italian and dubbed American movies, shown nightly in the courtyard from late June to September (L8,000). The tourist office can fill you in on the schedule.

The **Centro per L'Arte Contemporanea Luigi Pecci** (V. della Repubblica 277, tel. 0574/570620; admission L12,000; open Wed.–Mon. 10–7), an enormous gallery and art center complete with a library, presents temporary exhibits by today's most experimental Italian and foreign artists. There's no permanent collection; look for posters or call the museum to make sure the exhibit is of interest. Downstairs you'll find Prato's hippest caffè-bar, where you can get a salad or a plate of pasta. Next to the caffè is an outdoor amphitheater, which books excellent concerts in the summer. Call the tourist office for a complete schedule. The museum is a couple of miles to the east of the centro storico and is served by Buses 7 and 8 (L1,200), which you can catch across from Castello dell'Imperatore.

PISTOIA

Nestled in the foothills of the Apennines, in the Tuscan industrial belt west of Florence, Pistoia intriguingly combines art and industry. An independent city in medieval times, it was annexed by Florence in 1538, just about the time Pistoians perfected the pistol, which took its name from the city. Although it is not nearly as popular with tourists as neighboring Lucca, Pistoia's many Romanesque churches and varied cultural activities, including a famous blues festival in mid-July, make it a worthwhile day trip from Florence. You'll find the **tourist office** (Palazzo dei Vescovi, tel. 0573/21622; open daily 9–1 and 3–6; closed Sun. in winter) between the Duomo and the baptistery.

COMING AND GOING

Reaching Pistoia is a breeze. The **train station** (P. Dante Alighieri, tel. 1478/88088), a 10-minute walk from the town center, has frequent trains from Prato (20 min, L2,200), Lucca (30 min, L4,700), and Florence (50 min, L3,900). Buses take longer than the train and are more expensive, but the CO.PI.T. office (P. Mazzini, tel. 0573/21170) sends hourly buses to Florence (50 min, L5,000) and will store your bags (L3,000 per day).

Pistoia is basically square and pretty compact. To reach the central Piazza del Duomo, walk straight out of the train station onto Via XX Settembre, which becomes Via Atto Vannucci and later Via Cino; turn right on Via Cavour and left on Via Roma. This main piazza is lined by the cathedral and its baptistery, as well as by Pistoia's most important medieval buildings.

WHERE TO SLEEP AND EAT

Budget options are few. The **Firenze** (V. Curtatone e Montanara 42, tel. and fax 0573/23141) is the best budget option in town, with doubles with bath at L115,000, breakfast included; without bath L100,000. Cheap food is less of a problem. Take a number at popular **Rosticceria Francesco** (C. Gramsci 10, just west of V. Atto Vannucci, tel. 0573/22216; open 7 AM–8 PM), where you can get delicious baked pastas or roasted meats. You need not spend more than about L25,000 to eat at Pistoia's oldest *osteria*, **Lo Storno** (V. del lastrone 8, tel. 0573/26193; cash only), but you will have to work around their schedule. They are open Monday–Saturday for lunch and Thursday–Saturday for dinner.

WORTH SEEING

Pistoia's **Duomo** has that familiar horizontal black-and-white striping you find in this part of Tuscany, but how many other churches sport such a stylistically confused **campanile**? Plain sandstone blocks give way to busy marble stripes and then to ornate red brickwork, topped off with a copper cupola. Inside the church, the highlight is, appropriately enough, the metalwork of the silver altar in the Cappella di San Jacopo. Portraits of saints fill the upper niches, and biblical scenes are depicted below. Just opposite the facade is the octagonal **Battistero,** built by Cellino di Nese in 1337.

Three 12th-century churches in town are known for their beautifully carved 13th-century pulpits. The most impressive is by Giovanni Pisano, in **Sant'Andrea** (V. Sant'Andrea 21); a pupil of his father did the one in **San Giovanni Fuorcivitas** (V. Cavour between V. Carducci and V. Crispi), though Giovanni did do the holy water stoup. There is also a *Visitation* in terracotta by Luca della Robbia. A third pulpit, in **San Bartolomeo in Panatano** (east of Duomo), is by Guido da Como.

Filippo Lippi's model for the biblical prostitute Salomè was a novice who posed for a figure of the Virgin commissioned by an order of nuns. Like something scripted from Boccaccio at his bawdiest, this young woman and the artist-monk produced a child, Filippino Lippi, who also became a painter. Works by both father and son are in Prato's Cathedral Museum and temporarily on display in the Museo di Pittura Murale.

Pistoia has almost as much modern art as Renaissance art, thanks to dozens of works by native son Marino Marini (1901–80). You can see an excellent display of his graphic works and a few sculptures, including a bronze head of Igor Stravinsky, at the **Centro di Documentazione Fondazione Marino Marini** (Palazzo del Tau, C. San Fredi 72, tel. 0573/30285; admission L6.000; open Tues.–Sat. 9–1 and 3–7, Sun. 9–1:30), one block south of San Giovanni Fuorcivitas. Marini returned again and again to renderings of acrobats and riders on horseback, often portraying them as stick figures.

FESTIVALS

Screaming hordes descend on Pistoia in the middle of July for the three-day festival known as **Pistoia Blues** (tel. 0573/21622), which hosts big names in jazz and rock at Piazza del Duomo. Tickets cost about L38,000.

TUSCANY

Teeming with small vineyards, silver-green olive groves, and fields of sunflowers stretching out to the horizon, Tuscany's countryside radiates an allure that has attracted artists for centuries. If in the past this vibrant and verdant area inspired poets like Keats and Shelley, today rural Tuscany is more the territory of nature enthusiasts and wine lovers, who come to enjoy the beauty of a relatively untainted landscape and to visit some of the world's best vineyards. With the exception of towns like Livorno—the second-biggest port in Italy—and those on the mercantile belt northwest of Florence, most of of the region is still agricultural. Hop a train or bus out of Florence, and you'll see just how much of the region is given over to wine, olive oil production, and tourism.

The best way to explore the rural areas of Tuscany is by bus or car (for rental information, *see* Coming and Going *in* Florence, *above*). Once you get inside a town's walls, you'll find hidden- away art collections, fantastic views of the countryside, medieval ambience, and friendly locals, especially in the less-trafficked parts.

LUCCA

Lucca feels so particularly low-key that it's as if the 4 km (2½ mi) of impressive and perfectly preserved walls encircling the town still protect it from the outside world. At the same time, the town is large enough that you don't feel walled in at every turn. Bicycles are the preferred mode of getting around, and the sites are undemanding and uncrowded.

It wasn't always this peaceful. The remarkably fertile land surrounding Lucca has been hotly contested since Roman times. The first city in Tuscany to accept Christianity, Lucca was actually a political powerhouse through the 14th century. It quickly shook off conquering Pisa and even kept its voracious neighbor Florence at bay, remaining autonomous until Napoléon moved in. Thanks to Napoléon's sister, an art fanatic who took up residence here, Lucca flourished in the 19th century and is still one of the most affluent Tuscan cities, as you'll see from the abundance of luxury stores that line its streets.

BASICS

Lucca's only **tourist office** (P. Verdi, tel. 0583/419689; open March–Nov. daily 9–7, Nov.–Feb. daily 9:30–4:30) is in a park near the bus station. Nearby **Centro Prenotazione** (tel. 0583/312262) will help out with hotel reservations. The local **post office** (V. Antonio Vallisneri 2, tel. 0583/496669; open Mon.–Sat. 8–2) is next to the cathedral.

COMING AND GOING

Frequent trains run to Florence (1¼ hrs, L7,400) and Pisa (20 min, L3,100) from Lucca's **train station** (P. Ricasoli, just south of the city walls, tel. 1478/88088). Luggage storage is open 8–8 (L5,000 for 12 hrs). Lazzi buses leave from the **bus station** (P. Verdi 2, tel. 0583/584877; open daily 6 AM–8 PM), in a wide-open park just west of the city center. Buses head to Pisa (40 min, L3,600) every 30 minutes and to Florence (1 hr, L9,700) hourly.

GETTING AROUND

If you plan to stay at the hostel or outside Lucca, you can catch the orange CLAP buses (P. Verdi, tel. 0583/541214, buy tickets in bars or tobacco shops) that pass by the train station or stop in Piazza del Giglio, just east of Piazza Napoleone. Otherwise your best bet is to do as the locals do and get yourself some wheels: **Cicli Barbetti** (V. Anfiteatro 23, just off P. Anfiteatro, tel. 0583/954444) charges L4,000 per hour or L20,000 per day.

To reach the town center from the train station, turn left and then right through the city gates at Piazza Risorgimento, drift to the left one block, and walk up Via Vittorio Veneto, which passes the main squares, Piazza Napoleone and Piazza San Michele. The bus station and the tourist office are west of these squares.

WHERE TO SLEEP

Cheap sleeps are pretty limited in Lucca, and reservations are advisable. A small splurge can be had just down the street from the Piazza del San Michele at the **Piccolo Hotel Puccini** (V. di Poggio 9, tel. 0583/55421, fax 0583/53487). Doubles with bath go for L125,000.

HOSTEL • Ostello Il Serchio (HI). Lucca's hostel offers blocky, functional architecture, six beds per room, and tolerable bathrooms. A bed and breakfast will cost you L19,000 a night. The staff cooks lunch and dinner every day (L14,000 a meal). Call ahead before you trek out here, and remember that buses stop running at 8 PM. V. del Brennero 673, 55050, tel. and fax 0583/341811. From train station, take Bus 6. 90 beds. Curfew 11:30, lockout 10–3:30. Cash only. Closed Nov.–Feb.

WHERE TO EAT

Lucca won't let you down on the food front. A local specialty is *buccellati,* slightly sweet anise-flavored raisin rings. The famous place to try them is **Pasticceria Taddeucci** (P. San Michele 34, tel. 0583/44933; closed Wed. and Aug.). The indoor **produce market** just off Piazza del Carmine is a good place to get supplies together, but you'll have to get creative because Lucca lacks good picnic sites. **Antica Bottega di Prospero** (V. Santa Lucia 13, tel. 0583/343747; closed Wed. afternoon), off Piazza San Michele, sells organic produce and bulk foods.

Check out **Lì per Lì** (V. Fillungo 150, tel. 0583/46479; closed Tues.) for a great selection of crepes, either savory (tomato, basil, and mozzarella) or sweet (Grand Marnier and coconut). You'll also find fresh vegetable and fruit juices (L3,500–L6,000) made right before your eyes. **Giulio in Pelleria** (V. delle Conce

47, northwest corner of town, tel. 0583/55948; closed Sun.–Mon.) is well known for solid Lucchese cooking at low prices. Another reliable place is **Buatino** (V. Borgo Giannoti 508, just outside city walls, exit Porta Santa Maria, tel. 0583/343207; cash only; closed Sun.). The huge **Trattoria da Leo** (V. Tegrimi 1, tel. 0583/492236; cash only; closed Sun.) rarely has an empty table; you can savor pastas with very rich sauces for about L8,000 and large main dishes, including terrific fried calamari, for around L12,000. From Piazza San Michele, walk north one block on Via Calderia and look for the restaurant on the left.

WORTH SEEING

One of the best ways to see Lucca is to rent a bike and cruise through the city's colorful streets and the rich green fields that surround its walls. Even without a bike, meandering around and stumbling upon the various churches and piazzas allows you to slip into the city's easy-does-it attitude. Stroll up **Via Fililungo,** the town's best-preserved street, and check out the marvelous array of Art Nouveau buildings. Nearby is **Piazza Anfiteatro,** an oval piazza built on the site of an ancient Roman amphitheater.

The **Duomo** (P. San Martino; open summer, daily 7–7; winter, daily 7–5) sits off the main street at the south end of the town. Its fanciful facade is a good example of the Pisan Romanesque style, in this case lightened up by differently carved colonnettes. The Gothic interior contains a moving wood crucifix called the *Volto Santo* (Holy Face), brought here, as legend has it, in the 8th century, though it probably dates from between the 11th and early 13th centuries. Jacopo della Quercia's masterpiece, the marble tomb of Ilaria Carretto (1408), is well worth the L3,000 admission. Check out another great facade at **San Michele in Foro** (P. San Michele, tel. 0583/48459), an unusual variation on the Pisan Romanesque style, with some updated imagery in the form of busts of Italian patriots Garibaldi and Cavour.

The Gothic interior of Civitali's Tempietto in Lucca contains a moving Byzantine crucifix (called the Volto Santo, or Holy Face) brought here in the 8th century, as legend has it (though it probably dates from between the 11th and early 13th centuries), and the masterpiece of the Sienese sculptor Jacopo della Quercia (1374–1438), the marble tomb of Ilaria del Caretto.

For the best view of Lucca, head to the **Torre Guinigi** (V. Sant'Andrea, tel. 0583/47261; admission L4,500; open daily 9–7:30, in winter, daily 10–4:30), once the home of the Guinigi clan, Lucca's most powerful family. Trees now grow from the tower's top. Another palace, the Villa Guinigi, has become the home of the **Museo Nazionale** (V. della Quarquonia, tel. 0583/496033; admission L4,000; open Tues.–Sun. 9–7, 9–2 in winter), with a collection of local Romanesque and Renaissance art. The **House of Giacomo Puccini** (Corte San Lorenzo 9, tel. 0583/584028; open daily 10–1 and 3–8, in winter, daily 10–1) is where Lucca's most famous native son (1858–1924) lived. For L5,000 you'll see the Steinway, furniture, and mementos of the composer of the operas *Madame Butterfly, Tosca,* and *La Bohème.*

FESTIVALS

Several festivals keep things alive in Lucca during the heat of summer. In July and August, an open-air cinema on Piazza Guidiccioni, a short walk from Piazza Anfiteatro, screens the latest American (dubbed into Italian) and Italian hits. Tickets cost around L10,000. Also in July and August, classical music venues spring up everywhere for the **Estate Musicale Lucchese.** Every July 12 locals dress up in period costume for the **Palio di San Paolino,** a centuries-old crossbow competition. And on September 13, the *Volto Santo* is paraded through the town in commemoration of its miraculous journey to Lucca.

PISA

Thanks to an engineering mistake, Pisa's name is instantly recognized worldwide. A nonstop flood of tourists pours through town long enough to pass the Campo dei Miracoli (is that why it's called Field of Miracles?) to catch a glimpse of the famous Leaning Tower and maybe to peek into the remarkable Duomo and Battistero. There's more to see in Pisa than that, but visitors hardly ever bother. The highly regarded university here gives the town a youthful character, and a few good *trattorie* make up for any touristic shortcomings. If possible, arrive in the late afternoon when the Campo dei Miracoli quiets down, see the sights, and move on.

Pisa's location near the mouth of the Arno made it an essential port for the Romans. After the empire crumbled, the port remained strong enough to form its own republic. The city's power peaked in the 11th and 12th centuries, earlier than that of rivals Siena and Florence. Work began on the baptistery, cathedral, and campanile (today's Leaning Tower) in the late 12th century. The simultaneous construction gave the three buildings a unique architectural unity that helped establish the distinctiveness of the Pisan Romanesque style, with its trademark black-and-white-striped marble; tall, sculpted columns supporting miniature arches; and long loggias, which became popular in the region.

By the early 15th century, however, the city had been defeated at sea by Genoa and on land by Florence. Its glory days long gone, Pisa became just another Florentine colony. Since then, the most famous local to emerge has been Galileo Galilei.

BASICS

The **Informagiovani** office (tel. 050/42291; open daily 8:30– 6) at the train station will gladly point you in the right direction. A second office (tel. 050/560464; open daily 8:30–7:30, daily 8:30–6 in winter) on via Cammeo has more resources and a multilingual staff.

Currency exchanges on Campo dei Miracoli have awful rates; instead try a bank on the Corso. **CTS** (V. Santa Maria 12, tel. 050/48300, fax 050/45431; open Mon.–Sat. 9:30–12:30 and 4–7, closed Sat. afternoon), a discount travel agency, will help with your local and international travel plans. The central **post office** (tel. 050/501869; open weekdays 8–7, Sat. 8–noon) is one block north of the station on the left side of Piazza Vittorio Emanuele II.

COMING AND GOING

Busy **Pisa Centrale** (P. Stazione, tel. 1478/88088) is a major stop for trains on the Rome–Genoa line and a transfer point for those heading to Florence. Trains to Florence (1 hr, L7,400) and Lucca (30 min, L3,100) leave hourly, as do trains to Siena (1 hr, L10,100; change at Empoli). The station has 24-hour luggage storage (L5,000 for 12 hrs).

Buses to and from Pisa aren't nearly as efficient as trains, but if you insist, **Lazzi** (P. Vittorio Emanuele II, tel. 050/46288) sends buses to Lucca hourly (L3,600). **Galileo Galilei International Airport** (P. d'Ascanio, tel. 050/500707) is 1 km (½ mi) south of the train station. Bus 7 leaves for the airport (L1,500) from the central station every 20 minutes.

GETTING AROUND

The Arno River splits Pisa in two. The area south of the river is dominated by the train station, wide streets, and a luxurious pedestrians-only thoroughfare called **Corso Italia**, lined with banks, chic caffè, and boutiques. North of the Arno lie the **Scuola Normale Superiore**, a prestigious university centered around **Piazza dei Cavalieri**, and the **Campo dei Miracoli.** If you want to see the Leaning Tower, walk through town (30 min) or jump on one of the city's frequent and efficient buses (L1,500). Most buses stop in front of the train station: Bus 1 runs to the Campo dei Miracoli, Bus 3 to the youth hostel.

WHERE TO SLEEP

Hotel prices in Pisa are much more reasonable than in most of Tuscany, and it's usually easy to find a room. Pick up the accommodations booklet from the tourist office for suggestions on cheap digs.

UNDER L60,000 • Albergo Gronchi. Rooms in this ideally located hotel beside the Campo dei Miracoli are big and comfortable, marred ever so slightly by bathrooms that show their age. The tiny hotel emanates an air of fading elegance. Doubles cost L56,000. Reservations are advisable. *P. Arcivescovado 1, 56100, tel. 050/561823. From P. del Duomo, walk east past tower to P. Arcivescovado. 23 rooms without bath. Cash only.*

UNDER L100,000 • Albergo di Stefano. This hotel has some of the best cheap rooms in the area, and it's only about three blocks from Piazza dei Cavalieri. Rooms (doubles L115,000 with bath, L80,000 without) are large, clean, and well lighted; some even open onto a terrace. The nice family that runs the inn also has a small bar downstairs. *V. Sant'Apollonia 35, 56100, tel. 050/553559, fax 050/556038. From P. del Duomo, walk east past tower, veer left on V. San Giuseppe, right on V. Sant'Apollonia. 25 rooms, 13 with bath.*

Hotel Milano. Its spotless rooms just a stone's throw from the station are large, sunny, and equipped with TVs and telephones. Remodeled bathrooms are a plus. Doubles run L77,000–L105,000. *V. Mascagni 14, 56100, tel. 050/23162, fax 050/44237. From train station, turn left, then right on V. Mascagni. 10 rooms, 6 with bath.*

HOSTEL • Ostello Madonna dell'Acqua. Adequate rooms (for two to four people), a pretty setting, and the friendly managers at this church-run hostel can't hide the questionable odor emanating from the nearby canal, actually called the Dead River. The family rooms cost L60,000 for double occupancy, and they really mean it when they say "family"—no unmarried couples allowed. The signs at the train station promising a mere 1-km (½-mi) walk are cruel lies; wait for Bus 3 across the street from the station. *V. Pietrasantina 15, 56100, tel. 050/890622. 40 beds. Curfew 11 PM, lockout 9–6. Reception open July–Aug., daily 6 PM–midnight; Sept.–June, daily 6 PM–9 PM.*

WHERE TO EAT

Wander a few blocks from the RISTORANTE SELF-SERVICE tourist traps that surround the Campo dei Miracoli. Across the river, **Il Cristallo** (C. Italia 34, tel. 050/20031; closed Sun.) is great for snacks like homemade ricotta pastries, panini, gelato, and espresso, all served on the back patio. Taste the local snack, *torta di ceci* (a cake made from chickpea flour), but save room for real meals at one of the following places: **La Grotta** (V. San Francesco 103, near P. San Paolo all'Orto, tel. 050/578105; cash only; closed Sun.) is the old eatery in town, with excellent food and late hours. Piazza dei Cavalieri is home to starving students, and numerous *tavole calde* and reasonably priced trattorias line the nearby streets, such as **Numero Undici** (V. Cavalca 11, tel. 050/544294; cash only; no lunch weekends), where you can eat well for around L15,000, and **La Mescita** (V. Cavalca 2, tel. 050/544 294), a few doors down and a bit of a splurge. The food at the **Mensa Universitaria** (V. Martiri, tel. 050/567111; open mid-Sept.–mid-July, weekdays noon–2 and 7–9, weekends noon–2), is passable, but swing by just to check out its bulletin boards, which list local concerts, films, and theater events. For fresh fruits and vegetables, head to the **outdoor market** (open Mon.–Sat. mornings) on Piazza Sant'Omobono.

The biscotti you might know from back home are called cantucci in parts of Tuscany, and they are a local specialty. Pay homage to the original and sample some biscotti di Prato at Antonio Mattei (V. Ricasoli 20/22, tel. 0574/25756).

WORTH SEEING

Contrary to popular belief, Pisa isn't a provincial town with just one major sight—it's a town teeming with Romanesque and Gothic gems. You can buy an inclusive ticket for five sights (the Duomo, Battistero, Camposanto, Museo del Duomo, and Museo delle Sinopie) for L17,000, four sights (excluding the Duomo) for L15,000, two for L10,000, or pay L2,000 to see only the Duomo.

If you take the time to stroll along the river, you'll stumble upon the ornately Gothic **Santa Maria della Spina** (Lungarno Gambacorti, no phone), with its pinnacles and spires jutting from every surface. After 500 years, in 1871, the church, originally built to showcase a thorn allegedly from Christ's crown, had to be completely dismantled and rebuilt farther away from the river, which was causing water damage. Head farther east along the river to the **Museo Nazionale di San Matteo** (tel. 050/541865; admission L8,000; open Tues.–Sat. 9–7, Sun. 9–1), which houses works by Masaccio, Ghirlandaio, Donatello, and Simone Martini. When you tire of tramping through the city, you can collapse on a bench in the peaceful (and free) **Botanical Gardens** (V. L. Ghini, tel. 050/561795; open weekdays 8–5:30, Sat. 8–1, closed Sun.), two blocks south of the Leaning Tower.

CAMPO DEI MIRACOLI AND THE TORRE PENDENTE • The **leaning tower** on Campo dei Miracoli is one of the world's most famous buildings because of its amazing tilt (about a 16-ft discrepancy between top and bottom). Originally intended as the Duomo's bell tower, it's majestic in spite of, or perhaps because of, its tilt: at 179 ft, its highest point barely clears the top of the Duomo and baptistery. Work began on the tower in 1174, but the soil under the site began to shift by the time the third tier had been built. A slew of architects attempted to correct the tilting over the next two centuries, with little success. Galileo made use of the tilt for his famous gravitation experiments and used the tower as an observatory, too. The tower's six floors are decorated with blind arcades that match the cathedral's facade. On top is a wonderful belfry by Tommaso di Andrea da Pontedera. The tower has been closed to visitors since 1990, and it is not likely to reopen.

The glorious **Duomo,** however, is very much open and deserves a long visit. Each column on the facade's three-tiered arcades is slightly different. The charcoal-gray and white striping is perhaps the cathedral's most famous and most imitated characteristic. The richly decorated arcade stretches on into a deep apse, where Cimabue's enormous golden mosaic of an enthroned Christ looks down upon the crowd. Have a look at Giovanni Pisano's eight-sided pulpit, more complex and grandiose than his father's in the baptistery. Its 11 columnar supports depict all sorts of figures, including Hercules and the four cardinal virtues. Sculpted in the supports' capitals are sibyls; above them rest nine panels that dramatically illustrate events in Christ's life. Also in the Duomo are several paintings by Ghirlandaio that survived a destructive fire in 1596. *P. del Duomo, tel. 050/560547. Open summer, Mon.–Sat. 10–7:40, Sun. 1–7:40; winter, Mon.–Sat. 10–12:45, Sun. 3–4:45.*

The remarkable circular **Battistero,** designed by architect Diotisalvi, is externally as elaborate as the Duomo, with Gothic fluted spires and detailed scrollwork on the upper levels that contrasts sharply with its Romanesque base. It's probably the most famous baptistery in the world, thanks to its perfect acoustics and an irregularly shaped dome that looks as if some big hand had squeezed the top. Free guided tours move regularly through the building, with tour guides singing a few notes to demonstrate the amazing acoustics. Another highlight is the carved pulpit by Nicola Pisano. *P. del Duomo, tel. 050/560547. Open summer, daily 8–8; winter, 9–4:40.*

The least known of the major buildings on the Campo dei Miracoli is the **Camposanto,** the long, white edifice on the north side of the field. According to legend, the soil in this cemetery was brought to Pisa during the Crusades from the hill where Jesus was crucified. The tombs inside have been in sad shape since a large fire swept the interior during an Allied bombing raid in 1944, but you can still get a look at several Roman and Greek sarcophagi. Most of the frescoes were destroyed, but the twisted 14th-century frescoes depicting *The Triumph of Death,* by an unknown artist, remain visible. Unless you're a fanatic for 14th-century fresco painting, or have a deep love of sarcophagi, you might want to consider skipping it. *P. del Duomo, tel. 050/560547. Open summer, daily 8–7:30; winter, daily 9–5:30.*

If you want to see the two museums on the perimeter of the *campo*— –the **Museo dell'Opera del Duomo** (tel. 050/560547; admission L10,000 with admission to one other site, open daily summer 9–7:30, winter 9–5:30) and the **Museo delle Sinopie** (tel. 050/560547; admission L10,000 with admission to one other site; open daily 8–7:40, and 9–5:40 in winter)—it's really worth it to get the combined ticket (*see above*). The first displays a hodgepodge of works stripped from the Battistero and Duomo, including Giovanni Pisano's ivory *Madonna and Child;* the second shows the *sinopie* (preliminary drawings for frescoes) found in the Camposanto.

PIAZZA DEI CAVALIERI • Currently the home of both the University of Pisa and a flock of obese pigeons, the elaborately decorated **Palazzo dei Cavalieri** and the adjacent church of **Santo Stefano** were originally Giorgio Vasari's answer to the Medici's request for headquarters for the Cavalieri di Santo Stefano, a group of crusading knights. The strange building in the corner with peeling frescoes is the **Palazzo Gherardesca,** adapted by Vasari from several medieval buildings. Here, in 1208, it was rumored that Count Ugolino della Gherardesca ate his children in a futile attempt to ward off starvation after his imprisonment in the wake of a humiliating naval defeat. Dante condemned the count to eternal hunger in one of the lower rings of hell.

CHEAP THRILLS

On summer evenings, free **classical music concerts** are held on the steps of the Duomo for music lovers sprawled out on the lawn. Concerts are also regularly held on Piazza dei Cavalieri; performances range from classical to tribal rhythm. If you're in Pisa on June 16, don't miss the **Iluminaria,** a feast day devoted to honoring St. Ranieri, the city's patron saint. Palaces along the Arno are lit with white lights, as are boats that make their way along the river. There's a fireworks show that does the city proud. On the last Sunday in June, the city breaks out in medieval pageantry for the **Gioco del Ponte.** Each quadrant of the city presents richly costumed parades, then meets for a showdown in the middle of Ponte di Mezzo.

LIVORNO

The ferry hub of Livorno is a gritty city with a long history: In the early middle ages, it belonged alternately to Pisa and to Genova. In 1421, Florence, seeking access to the sea, bought it. Cosimo I (1519–1574) started construction of the harbor in 1571, putting Livorno on the map. Ferdinando I Medici (1549–1609) proclaimed Livorno a free city, which meant that it became a haven for people suffering from religious persecution—Roman Catholics from England and Jews and Moors from Spain and Portugal, among others, settled here. If you have time to explore the city, investigate the moated **Fortezza Nuova,** a crumbling fort surrounded by canals on three sides. Also interesting is the **Acquario Comunale** (P. Mascagni, tel. 0586/805504; closed at press time; due to reopen in 2000). The postmodern **Sinagoga** (P. Benamozegh 1, tel. 0586/896290; tours by appointment only) was built in 1962 to replace a beautiful structure destroyed in World War II that held 5,000 congregants in Napoléon's time.

BASICS

If you come in to Livorno via ferry, there's a tourist info desk (tel. 0586/895320; open June–Sept. Mon.–Thurs. 8–1 and 4–9, Fri.–Sun. 8–1 and 3–10) within the **Porto Mediceo** (v. del molo Mediceo). The **main office** (P.za Cavour 6, tel 0586/898 111; open Mon.–Sat. 9–1, Tues. and Thurs. also 3–5) is centrally located uptown but very hard to find. Take Bus 2 to Piazza Cavour; it's up two flights of stairs. The best place to change money is at one of the many banks (usually open weekdays 8:30–1:30 and 2:30–4) that line Via Cairoli, which links Piazza Grande and Piazza Cavour.

COMING AND GOING

BY TRAIN • **Livorno Centrale** (P. Dante, tel. 1478/88088) is on the coastal train line. Trains run twice every hour to Pisa (15 min, L2,200) and Florence (1½ hrs, L10,000). You don't want to be caught in the huge complex after dark unless you've got a strong interest in transvestite and transsexual sex-for-hire; it's also well out of walking distance from the port and the rest of the town, so plan your travels accordingly.

BY BUS • The **ATL** (V. Lungo Duomo 2, tel. 0586/899562) are well marked, their routes clearly posted on most bus stops. Buses leave regularly for Pisa (30 min, L5,000). From there you can transfer to Lazzi buses for other destinations. To reach the bus station from Piazza Cavour, walk straight down Via Cairoli about five blocks.

BY BOAT • Chances are you're here to catch a ferry–Livorno is Tuscany's gateway to Corsica and Sardinia. Ferries leave from the **Porto Mediceo** (V. del molo Mediceo) or the **Stazione Marittima Calata Carrara**. Prices for Corsica generally run about L38,000–L50,000 for daytime ferries, L65,000 for night voyages. **Corsica Marittima** (tel. 0586/210507) sends ferries to Bastia, Corsica, Monday, Wednesday, Friday, and Saturday at 3:40 from late June through mid-September, and on Saturday only in April and May. **Moby Lines** (tel. 0586/826823) offers more frequent and cheaper (about L10,000 less) service to Bastia; they send at least one ferry daily from mid-June through early September. Moby also runs to Olbia, Sardinia (L42,000 low season, L85,000 high season), daily at either 10 AM or 10 PM, at both times from June to late September. **Toremar** (tel. 0586/896113) does send one ferry a week to Elba from September to May, but it's much easier to leave from Piombino (see Elba, below).

It's estimated that Pisa's Leaning Tower, supported by a foundation that's some 52 ft in diameter, sinks about 1 millimeter every year.

GETTING AROUND

A branch of **ATL** (tel. 0586/896111) manages the city bus system, which is easy to use; tickets cost L1,500. The buses are well marked, and their routes are clearly posted on most bus stops. From the train station, Bus 1 goes to central **Piazza Grande** and **Piazza della Repubblica**, just south of an area full of good cheap restaurants; Bus 2 gets you to **Piazza Cavour**, a good base for lodging, buses, and tourist info; and Bus 18 heads for the docks. Buses 1 and 7 go back to the station.

WHERE TO SLEEP AND EAT

Two hotels offer fair deals and have big, clean rooms behind dilapidated exteriors. The best option near Piazza Cavour is **Albergo Cavour** (V. Adua 10, tel. 0586/899604), with doubles at L70,000 (L80,000 with bath). **Hotel Ariston** (P. della Repubblica 11, tel. and fax 0586/880149; cash only) is out of the transit hubbub and charges L90,000 for a double with bath. If convenience is paramount, **Albergo Giardino** (P. Mazzini 85, tel. and fax 0586/806330; cash only) is only a 10-minute walk from the port. Doubles with bath cost L100,000 in high season, half that the rest of the year.

A visit to Livorno is at least partially redeemed by the utterly delicious and surprisingly affordable seafood calling to you from nearly every corner restaurant. The local specialty is a seafood stew called *cacciucco,* but beware: "bargain" fish stews are generally pretty short on fish. If it's lunchtime, head for **Cantina Nardi** (V. Cambini 6, tel. 0586/808006; no dinner; closed Sun.). Otherwise, **L'Antica Venezia** (V. dei Bagnetti 1, tel. 0586/887353; closed Sun. and Mon.) and **Il Sottomarino** (V. Terrazzini 48, tel. 0586/887025; cash only; no dinner Sun.; closed Thurs.) are also good bets but pricier. Another local specialty is *farinata,* which in the Livornese version is a baked pancake made from chickpea flour, thinner than *torte di ceci.* **Da Cecco** (V. Cavaletti 2, tel. 0586/881074; closed Sun. and July) and **Torteria Gagarin** (V. del Cardinale 24, no phone) are good places to try it.

SAN GIMIGNANO

When you're high on a hill surrounded by crumbling towers in silhouette against the blue sky, it's difficult not to fall under the medieval spell of San Gimignano. Fifteen towers dominate the skyline, what's left of the 70-something that were built in the 12th and 13th centuries by the feuding Ardinghelli and Salvucci families. Used as tools in their struggle for status (and more practically as warehouses), the towers so filled the compact city that it became possible to cross the town by rooftop rather than on the street. The pandemonium of the feud must have weakened San Gimignano's immune system, for when the Black Plague devastated the population in 1348, power and independence faded fast. In a last-ditch effort to salvage the economy, the Ardinghelli family surrendered civic autonomy and struck an alliance with Florence.

Today San Gimignano isn't much more than a gentrified walled hamlet, amply prepared for its booming tourist trade but still worth exploring. Unfortunately, tour groups arrive early and clog the wine-tasting rooms—San Gimignano is famous for its light white Vernaccia—and art galleries for the greater part of the day, but most sights are open through late afternoon in summer. Escape midday to the uninhabited areas outside the city walls for a hike and a picnic and return to explore town in the afternoon and evening, when things quiet down and the long shadows cast by the imposing towers take on fascinating shapes.

BASICS

Get the low-down on what to see and where to stay at the local **Pro Loco** (P. del Duomo 1, tel. 0577/ 940008; open daily 9–1 and 3–7, 2–6 in winter); they change money, too.

COMING AND GOING

Whether you take a bus or train, you'll have to get to Poggibonsi, then catch a TRA-IN bus for the 20-minute ride to San Gimignano (hourly, L2,600). Poggibonsi's **train station** (tel. 1478/88088) is on the line between Florence (1 hr 20 min, L6,500) and Siena (30 min, L2,000). The station's luggage storage (open daily 5 AM–8:30 PM) helps if you plan to make San Gimignano a day trip. TRA-IN buses leave Florence and Siena about every 1½ hours for Poggibonsi's **bus station** (V. Trento 33, tel. 0577/937207), where you switch to the San Gimignano line. The entire trip costs L9,400 from Florence, L8,600 from Siena. Buses leave Volterra for San Gimignano four times a day (1¾ hrs, L6,500) and involve two changes (at Colle di Val d'Elsa and Poggibonsi).

The city is so small that buses don't travel within the walls, and few cars are allowed. Buses to and from other cities stop outside the town's southern gate. Schedules to Poggibonsi and the campground in nearby Santa Lucia are posted at the stop, but there's no station; buy your tickets at bars and tobacco shops. Most streets within the city walls point toward the town's central Piazza Cisterna and Piazza del Duomo.

WHERE TO SLEEP

The hostel is comfortable and convenient, and the tourist office has a list of rooms you can rent in private homes (affittacamere), as do the private agencies around town with the I signs out front. Reservations in summer are a good idea, and it's wise to arrive early in the day to look for a place. Other options include: **Conforti Totti Dina** (V. Mainardi 6, off V. San Matteo, tel. 0577/940478), which charges L55,000 for a double with use of the kitchen; the place rents only two rooms—you'll be staying in a separate wing of a private family apartment. At **Le Vecchie Mura** (V. Piandornella 13, tel. 0577/940270) you can get a double (L80,000) with a view (with bath is extra), right above the property's restaurant (see Where to Eat, below). If you want to sleep in the great outdoors, head to **Campeggio Il Boschetto di Piemma** (Santa Lucia, tel. 0577/940352; cash only; closed mid-Oct.–Mar.). Great facilities, a fabulous setting, and an easy bus ride from Piazzale Montemaggio make this an excellent option. Take the bus marked SANTA LUCIA; the last one departs at 7 PM. Sites cost L8,500 per adult, L8,000 per tent, and L3,500 per car.

HOSTEL • San Gimignano Youth Hostel. The conscientious managers of this central and very clean hostel recycle—a rarity in Italy—and ask guests not to waste water (the town has long drought periods). Beds are L21,000 (in dormitories) and L24,000 (in small rooms) per person, including breakfast. No HI card is required. V. delle Fonti 1, 53037, tel. 0577/941991. From bus station, walk through Porta San Giovanni along V. San Giovanni, cross both piazzas to V. San Matteo, turn right on V. XX Settembre (which becomes V. Folgore), right on V. delle Fonti. 75 beds. Curfew 11:30 PM, lockout 9–5. Cash only. Closed Nov.–Feb.

WHERE TO EAT

Try the **open-air market** held in Piazza del Duomo every Thursday morning; it's the place to pick up fresh fruits and veggies for picnics. Within the city walls are numerous trattorie and gelaterie, especially around the gathering point, Piazza Cisterna. If you want to taste the local Vernaccia or Chianti, wine stores line every street. They have signs saying FREE ENTRY, but that usually doesn't extend to tasting. It's best to bypass the ultratouristy stores on Via San Giovanni and go for the ones on Via San Matteo.

A delicious gourmet deli counter, **Antica Latteria di Maurizio e Tiziana** (V. San Matteo 19, off P. del Duomo, tel. 0577/941952), serves up salads and panini any way you want them, priced by weight. Get a bottle of wine a few steps away at **Enoteca Gustavo** (V. San Matteo 29, tel. 0577/940057; closed Fri.), or sit down and nibble on cheese and salami. Then trot on down to **Bar-Pasticceria Maria e Lucia** (No. 55, tel. 0577/940379) for some homemade gelato or other desserts. For a sit-down meal, **Osteria delle Catene** (V. Mainardi 18, tel. 0577/941966; closed Wed.) is the place to go for regional specialties that change with the season. Tourists keep **Le Vecchie Mura** (*see* Where to Sleep, *above*) busy year-round, but they haven't lowered the cooks' standards or ruined the atmosphere.

WORTH SEEING

San Gimignano's most impressive sight is the city itself. Its truncated towers compete with one another for prominence while providing shade on nearly every street. For the best free view of the city, head up the hill to La Rocca, the town's medieval fortress. There you'll find a small public garden and exhilarating views from the fortress's wide-open courtyards. If you plan on covering the in-town sites, consider the L18,000 inclusive ticket, which gives you access to the Museo Civico, the Torre Grossa, the Museo d'Arte Sacra ed Etrusco, the Museo Ornitologico, and the Cappella.

Romantic poet Percy Bysshe Shelley drowned off the Livorno coast. Ironically, when his body was recovered, a copy of his poem "The Triumph of Life" was found in his pocket.

The principal civic building, the Palazzo del Popolo, was built in the late 13th and early 14th centuries, when the city reached its economic peak. Today the palazzo houses the **Museo Civico,** where Taddeo di Bartolo's celebratory dossal depicts scenes from the life of San Gimignano. Gimignano, a bishop of Modena, was sainted because he drove hordes of barbarians out of the city in the 10th century. Head to the Sala di Dante to check out the *Maestà*, by Lippo Memmi. (Dante visited San Gimignano for only one day in 1300 as a Florentine ambassador, but it was long enough to get a room named after him.) Across the stairwell, a small room contains Memmo di Filippuccio's frescoes depicting the courtship, shared bath, and wedding of a young, androgynous-looking couple. The highly charged eroticism of the frescoes may be explained, in part, by the fact that they were located in what were probably the private rooms of the commune's chief magistrate. The nearby **Torre Grossa** is the only tower you can climb, but at least it's the biggest in town. *P. del Duomo, tel. 0577/940340. Admission to museum L7,000, to tower L8,000. Open Mar.–Oct., daily 9:30–7:30; shorter hrs off-season.*

The **Museo d'Arte Sacra ed Etrusco** (P. Luigi Pecori, beside Museo Civico, tel. 0577/942226; open daily 9:30–7:300, shorter hrs in winter) contains mildly interesting relics dating from the 7th century BC to the 2nd century AD, all discovered in excavations. Admission is L6,000. Around the corner is the **Museo Ornitologico** (V. di Quercecchio, tel. 0577/941388; admission L4,000; open 9:30–12:30 and 3–6, shorter hrs in winter), which is not terribly exciting unless you have a deep passion for birds.

The Romanesque **Collegiata,** San Gimignano's cathedral, isn't much to look at from the outside, but inside you'll find a treasure trove of well-preserved frescoes. To the left of the entrance, Bartolo di Fredi's Old Testament scenes (14th century) have a medieval feel, with misshapen bodies, skewed perspectives, and buckets of spurting blood. The New Testament scenes on the opposite wall, probably done by Lippo and Federico Memmi in the 1330s, suggest a more reserved, balanced Renaissance style. Taddeo di Bartolo's otherworldly *Last Judgment,* on the arch just inside the facade, depicts distorted and suffering nudes—avant-garde for such an early work. The biggest name on display is Domenico Ghirlandaio, whose work (under restoration at press time) in the Cappella di Santa Fina tells the story of a local saint. *P. del Duomo, tel. 0577/940316. Admission to Collegiata free, to chapel L3,000. Both open 9:30–12:30 and 3–5:30.*

The **Museo di Criminologica Medievale** displays what was the cutting edge in medieval torture technology. Almost all the devices are originals, and each display includes operating instructions and a clear description in both Italian and English of the intended effect. It's been suggested that the museum was created simply to lure tourist dollars—you've been warned. *V. del Castello, off P. della Cisterna, tel. 0577/942243. Admission L15,000. Open Weekdays 10–6, weekends 10–7.*

VOLTERRA

If you think that all Tuscan hill towns rise above sprawling vineyards and rolling fields of green, think again. Some towns, like Volterra, look out onto a terrain that is more harsh and rocky than soft and green. The Etruscans made use of the rich mineral deposits in the area, particularily alabaster, as did the Romans and later the warring cities of Florence, Siena, and Pisa. Today the population stands at a fraction of what it once was, and the town is known for Etruscan relics and alabaster. The fortress, walls, and gates still stand mightily over Le Balze, a stunning series of gullied hills and valleys formed by irregular erosion. Man-made structures bow before this unrelenting natural process: as the ground has crumbled over the years, some of the town's medieval and Renaissance buildings collapsed, and an Etruscan burial site was literally unearthed.

Volterra is at its best in the late afternoon and evening, when the locals take over and the pizzerie start swinging. The exceptional small-town museums, the crumbling historical remnants, incredible views of the rolling countryside, and a decent youth hostel also add to Volterra's appeal. Stop by the **tourist office** (P. dei Priori 19/20, tel. 0588/86099; open daily 10–1 and 2–7, until 6 in winter) for info.

COMING AND GOING

Train service to Volterra is almost nonexistent. Buses make the journey from Siena (5 daily, 1½ hrs, L8,000; change at Colle di Val d'Elsa), Pisa (6 daily, 1¾ hrs, L9,500; change at Pontedera), dropping you off at Piazza Martiti della Libertà, just inside the city gates. Tickets are sold at the tourist office, tobacco shops, and bars, and schedules are posted in the piazza, the tourist office, and the youth hostel. Call **APT** in Volterra (tel. 0588/67370) or TRA-IN in Siena (tel. 0577/204111) for info.

WHERE TO SLEEP

The best deals in Volterra are the hostel, the convent, and the campground, but you can also ask about affittacamere at the tourist office, or call the **Centro Prenotazione** (tel. 0588/87257) fpr commission-free reservations. The least expensive of the hotels is **Albergo Etrusca** (V. Porta all'Arco 37, tel. and fax 0588/84073), with doubles (including bath) at L100,000. **Camping Le Balze** (tel. 0588/87880; closed Oct.–Mar.) has a ton of grassy sites with views for L9,000 per person, L7,000 per tent. You get free use of a swimming pool, hot water, and electricity. Follow signs from the city toward **Le Balze** (about 2 km/1 mi), and you'll reach the campground and a great spot from which to view the town's crumbling hills. The large convent, **Seminario Sant'Andrea** (Vittorio Veneto 2, tel. 0588/86028; cash only), is a five-minute walk from Porta Marcoli and offers a peaceful, friendly atmosphere. Doubles with bath go for L32,000; without, L25,000. Its three- and four-person rooms have stunning views.

HOSTEL • Ostello della Gioventù. True to the abandoned look of its exterior, the town's youth hostel is largely empty, even in July and August. Rooms have good views, the manager isn't too strict with the 11:30 curfew, and it's plenty quiet. Beds cost L20,000, and no HI membership is required. *V. del Poggetto 3, across from fortress, 56048, tel. and fax 0588/85577. 90 beds. Lockout 10–6. Cash only.*

WHERE TO EAT

Streets branching off Piazza dei Priori have restaurants with four-language menus and flashy signs; steer clear and head for a solid lunch at **Trattoria Da Badò** (Borgo San Lazzarro 9, tel. 0588/86477; cash only; no dinner; closed Wed.), well worth the 10-minute walk outside the western edge of town. If you'd rather stay inside the walls, try **Trattoria del Sacco Fiorentino** (P. XX Settembre, tel. 0588/88537; closed Wed.); they're open for dinner as well as lunch.

Grab a pizza at the local hangout, **Pizzeria da Nanni** (V. delle Prigioni 40, tel. 0588/84087). **Gastronomia Scali** (V. Guarnicci 3, tel. 0588/86939) has a great selection of picnic goodies. Buy groceries at **Coop** (P. Colombaie, tel. 0588/88157; closed Sun.), a 15-minute walk from Porta San Felice.

WORTH SEEING

Besides a medieval atmosphere and fabulous views, Volterra can also claim two of Italy's best small-town museums, which share the same ticket (L12,000). The first is the **Museo Etrusco Guarnacci** (V. Don Minzoni 15, tel. 0588/86347), which displays hundreds of Etruscan funeral urns found in nearby excavations. On the second floor, check out the *Ombra della Sera* from the 3rd century BC, a 2-foot-high, 1-inch-wide male figurine so elongated that it resembles a shadow cast by a setting sun—thus the poetic name. The **Pinacoteca e Museo Civico** (V. dei Sarti 1, tel. 0588/87580) houses a highly acclaimed collection of religious art in a very quiet palazzo just off Piazza dei Priori. Luca Signorelli's

Madonna and Child with Saints is the best-known painting in the museum, but look directly across from it at Rosso Fiorentino's amazing *Deposizione,* with its writhing figures and startlingly brilliant colors. Both museums are open 9–7 (until 2 in winter).

Medieval **Palazzo dei Priori** (P. dei Priori) has an impressive facade adorned with Florentine medallions and a large five-sided tower that you can't climb. The town's unfinished **Duomo** (P. San Giovanni, tel. 0588/86192) has Pisan marble striping on the back side and a detailed gold ceiling inside. To the right of the altar is a painted *Deposizione* from the 13th century, now restored in disturbingly bright colors. Check out the Capella dell'Addorolato, which has an Andrea della Robbia terracotta and a fresco by Benozzo Gozzoli. The church faces the recently restored **Battistero** (open during church hours). Original works from the Duomo and baptistery are in the **Museo Diocesano d'Arte Sacra** (V. Roma 7, tel. 0588/86290); admission is part of the L12,000 inclusive ticket.

Volterra was confident enough in the strength of its medieval **Fortezza Medicea** to turn it into a prison during the 19th century. Right beside this still-functioning facility is the **Parco Archeologico,** with grassy hills, couples making out, and brigades of insects. In summer the archaeological excavations are open from 11–7 (closed in winter), and it's a wonderful refuge from the phalanxes of tourists elsewhere in town. A few excavated remains are scattered about the park, but they're nowhere near as exciting as those in the extensive **Teatro Romano** (open daily 11—4, closed in winter)—definitely one of the best-preserved Roman remains in Tuscany—just north of the city gates. About half of the theater stands, but the adjoining bath complex is skeletal. Even more ancient is the Etruscan **Porta all'Arco** (V. Porta all'Arco), a 3rd-century arch built without the aid of cement but now supported by bricks and concrete.

CHIANTI

The wine-making region between Florence and Siena is a long stretch of vineyards and picturesque hill towns, perfect for long walks in secluded fields and picnics in the shade of abandoned stone villas. You'll need a car to explore the entire Chianti region because buses miss most of the out-of-the-way towns. Greve, Radda, and Castellina di Chianti give the best sense of the region. To do Chianti right, you'll need to taste plenty of wine and spend a little extra on a meal—in short, an enjoyable visit to the region might be a budget buster, but one you'll relish.

GREVE

If you're short on time, the town of Greve is relatively easy to reach by bus, and it's only a quick scooter ride away from many vineyards, country villas, and castles. Plus, Greve's tourist office is loaded with great information.

BASICS • The staff at the greve **tourist office** (viale giovanni da verrazzano 33, tel. 055/8545243; open June–Sept. Mon.–Sat. 9–1, 2:30–5, winter Mon., Wed., Thurs, Sat., Sun. 9:30–3:30) has maps of the region, lists of wineries, and lodging information.

COMING AND GOING • Sita **buses** from Florence's main station go to Greve (every 1½ hrs, 1 hr, L5,000) and drop you off on Via Vittorio Veneto, one block from the central Piazza Matteotti. If you rent a **car** in Florence (for car-rental information, *see* Coming and Going *in* Florence, *above*) and drive to Greve, you can stop at vineyards along the way. Considering the challenges of driving on Chianti's winding roads, however, you'll need a designated driver if you plan on doing some tasting.

GETTING AROUND • A good way to get around is by mountain bike or moped. In Greve try **Marco Ramuzzi** (V. Italo Stecchi 23, tel. 055/853037; closed Sun.), where mountain bikes go for L25,000 per day and mopeds start at L50,000. Helmets are included in the price—a help since you'll have to contend with speeding Fiats and buses that drive down the center of terrifyingly narrow and winding roads. Be warned that bike trails are still an alien concept, and even though some tremendous vineyards are less than 10 km (6 mi) away, you're in for a pretty good workout.

WHERE TO SLEEP AND EAT • As this is the domain of upscale tourists, luxurious accommodations are the norm, with no camping allowed. The best bet is to stay in an *affitacamera* (room in a private home). The tourist office (*see* Basics, *above*) can provide a list of private rooms and will even help make phone calls for you. The best hotel price you're likely to find in Greve is about L100,000 for a double. Ask at the tourist office about cheaper lodging options a 10-minute bus ride away in **Panzano.**

Dining out can be rather expensive; if you want to pick up your own supplies, you won't have any problems finding a butcher, baker, or market around Piazza Matteotti in Greve. The piazza holds a great market on

WHAT'S UP DOC?

Grapes have been cultivated in Tuscany since Etruscan times, and Chianti is still the best-known Italian wine throughout the world. For most people, until the 1970s Chianti meant strong red wine in a straw-wrapped flask. Problem was, to meet that great demand for Chianti, a lot of clever Italians started labeling red wine made just about anywhere in Italy as "Chianti" to take advantage of its popularity. Folks in the region between Florence and Siena—where the wine originated—were not amused. They banded together and got the government to establish a zone of production for Chianti (thus preventing wines made outside the region from being called Chianti) and created a set of guidelines for the production of the wine (type of grape, harvest, aging). Wines that meet these requirements can carry the DENOMINAZIONE DI ORIGINE CONTROLLATA or DOC label around the neck of the bottle, or the even more stringent DOCG (Garantita). Look for the DOC label around the bottle's neck and for GALLO NERO BLACK ROOSTER, denoting one of the region's most powerful wine-growing consortiums, or the putto on the label. Similar production zones have been set up to protect wine, cheese, and other food products all over the country.

Saturday (morning to early afternoon), with produce and fish, music and leather goods. In addition, the **Coop Supermarket** (V. Vittorio Veneto 76, tel. 055/853053) has a deli counter with regional favorites.

WORTH SEEING • The helpful staff at the visitor center will happily trace out the easiest routes from Greve to the region's various vineyards on a well-detailed map. For two weeks in early July, St. Anne's park hosts the Festa dell'Unità, a local festival with live music, films, and lots of different food stands.

For a great excursion, head for beautiful **Castello di Uzzano** (V. Uzzano 5, about 3 km/2 mi north of Greve, tel. 055/854032), the onetime home of Niccolò da Uzzano—15th-century humanist, philanthropist, and patron of the arts. You can taste the wines produced on the premises (L5,000), or visit the garden of the austere, ivy-covered castle for L10,000, but one look at the place, and chances are you'll opt for the picnic lunch in the garden, with bread, prosciutto, salami, tomatoes, eggs, and coffee for about L40,000 (excluding wine) per person (including admission to the gardens). To reach the castle from Greve, head north from the town center, go right at the Uzzano turnoff, and follow the signs up the dirt road. Visitors are welcome Monday–Saturday 8–noon and 1–6. You can even get to this one on foot; it's a 45-minute walk from Greve's bus station.

CASTELLINA IN CHIANTI

Castellina in Chianti is a pretty little town with wonderful wines and clean air. It's perched on a hillside overlooking views of three valleys (the Arbia, Elsa, and Pesa). If you're looking for a break from relentless sightseeing but still want to feel very much in Tuscany, Castellina is well worth a visit.

BASICS • The **tourist information office** stands in the center of town (P. del Comune 1, tel. 0577/740201, fax 0577/740 625).

Colline Verdi (V. della Rocca 12, 53011, tel. and fax 0577/740620-741297) can find affitacamere or beds at an agriturismo, change money, arrange car rentals, and sell tickets for planes, trains, and ferries.

COMING AND GOING • Getting to Castellina from Florence by **bus** is tricky, as there's only one bus that leaves in the late afternoon (1 1/2 hours, L6200); the only return bus to Florence is first thing in the morning. It's much easier to get there by bus from Siena, which has frequent daily service both going and returning (30 minutes, L3300). Call TRA-IN (0577/204 245) in Siena for more info. The **train** station is at Castellina Scalo, 10 km (6 mi) from the center. Trains run from Siena 10 times daily (1 hour, 10 min., L2400).

GETTING AROUND • Castellina is a very small town with a main drag that can easily be traversed in about a half hour—that is, if you don't stop in any of the fine wine bars that line the street.

WHERE TO SLEEP AND EAT • Budget options are slim to non-existent in Castellina. A double room with bath, breakfast included, can be had for L170,000 at the recently restored 14th-century **Palazzo Squarcialupi** (V. Ferruccio 26, 53011, tel. 0577/740454, fax 0577/741 238). Campers can set up tents outside the town at **Luxor** (Loc. Trasqua, 53011, tel. 0577/743047). Tariff is L11,000 per adult per night and L12,000 for the spot.

Seems like everyone in town can be found chowing down on the hearty food offered at **La Torre** (P. del Comune 15, tel. 0577/740236, closed Fri.) which has an extensive but well-priced list of superlative local wines that pair very nicely with typical Tuscan specialties. **Pizzeria il Fondaccio** (V. Ferruccio 27, tel. 0577/741084) turns out terrific pizze to accompany the local wine. To grab a primo, panino, or simply to enjoy a glass of wine, pop into **Le Volte Enoteca** (V. Ferruccio 12, tel. 0577/741314, closed Tues.).

WORTH SEEING • **Piazza del Comune** probably looks now as it did 500 years ago, but there's not much to see in any of the buildings that line it. Absorb the medieval ambience and try the local wines.

RADDA IN CHIANTI

Radda in Chianti stands between two valleys (the Pesa and the Arbia). The Etruscans settled here, and then the Romans. In 1176, Radda became a satellite in the Sienese orbit and then, like practically every other town in Tuscany, fell into Florence's hands. Now it's a quiet little town with narrow streets and a pleasingly small Renaissance piazza; the best thing to do if you decide to visit is to stroll and sample the local wine, which happens to be among Italy's best.

BASICS • You'll have a smile on your face as you walk into the **tourist information office** (Palazzo del Podestà, P. Ferrucci 1, tel. and fax 0577/738 696) in Radda: "Life's too short to drink bad wine" is posted on the door. The office, in a Renaissance palazzo, is staffed by friendly English-speakers who will point out the sights and help you find a place to stay as well.

COMING AND GOING • From Florence, Radda is not an easy trip by **bus**. Though there's twice daily service (about 1 1/2 hrs., L6200), the only return bus is very early in the morning, which makes a simple day trip quite difficult. It's far easier from Siena, which is linked by five buses daily (40 minutes, L4700) each way. Call TRA-IN in Siena (0577/204 245) for more info.

GETTING AROUND • Radda, like Castellina, is basically a one-horse town. It's easy to get around by foot, and it's flat enough that you won't break a sweat.

WHERE TO SLEEP AND EAT • You can rent a room in the absolutely charming affitacamera called **La Bottega di Giovannino** (V. Roma 6–8, 53017, tel. and fax 0577/738056), which also has an apartment for two and one for four. Another option is a stay at **Carparsa** (Loc. Caprarsa, 53017, tel. 0577/738174, fax 0577/738651), a small agriturismo just outside town where the owners make their own organic olive oil and a variety of fine wines.

Il Girarrosto (V. Roma 41, tel. 0577/738010, closed Wed.) offers a *menu turistico* for L25,000 that draws both locals and tourists. If you'd like to assemble your own meal, the affable **Giovannino** (*see above*) also runs an alimentari right next door to his affitacamere where you can pick up cheese, bread, and wine. Another good bet is **Porciatti** (P. IV Novembre 1, tel. 0577/738055, fax 0577/738234) which is also stocked with homemade products, local wine, and has the indubitable honor of being open Sunday mornings during high season.

WORTH SEEING • Radda's charming renaissance palace, the **palazzo del podestà** is decorated with coats of arms dating from the 15th through the 18th centuries. There's nothing much to see inside (except the tourist information office)—it's the façade that's fun to look at. The church of **san niccolò** (p. della Chiesa) has a 15th-century crucifix, thought by many to be miracle-working, which was paid for by the campagnia di penitenza. If you'd like to see a 14th-century polyptych attributed to bernardo daddi and other local works of art, make a special appointment (as they are temporarily being housed in the pietro fedi) through the director of the **casa di riposo** (v. Santa maria, tel. 0577/738350) or the tourist information office. Check out the franciscan convent of **santa maria al prato** (via santa maria), parts of which probably date from the 12th century.

WINE-SNOB ETIQUETTE

As you tour Chianti's many wineries, you may need a few tips on how to pick up the subtle aromas and proper balance of flavors in a great vino. Hold your glass by its stem and have a look at the wine's tint (hue) and depth of color (lightness or luminance). Swirl it around and inhale. Is it floral, fruity, spicy, or woody? Sip the wine and swish it around your mouth, then swallow and savor the aftertaste. Is the amount of sweetness, sourness, bitterness, and astringency to your liking? To sound like a real connoisseur, use words like dolce (sweet), abboccato (slightly sweet), secco (dry), and amaro (bitter).

SIENA

If you had only visited seven centuries ago, you would have found Siena a powerful city-state and flourishing center of finance and culture, with Italy's first bank and some of Europe's greatest artists. But alas, the city-state lost out in its bitter rivalry against Florence; Siena was besieged and brought to its knees, and by the mid 1500s it had been absorbed by the Grand Duchy of Tuscany, under Florentine control. Unlike Renaissance Florence, Siena is a medieval city, laid out over the slopes of three hills and practically unchanged since medieval times. Narrow streets—patterned by brickwork, wrought iron, and sun-bleached stone—slope down and twist around toward the town's glorious main square. Sienese identity is still very much defined by the 17 medieval *contrade* (neighborhoods), which uphold ancestral rivalry during the centuries-old Palio, a biannual free-for-all in which civic pride rests on the outcome of a horse race (*see box* This Ain't No Rodeo, *below*).

Once a leading force in art, banking, and commerce, Siena prospered during the Middle Ages, retaining autonomy as a city-state when the rest of central Italy was in shambles. Siena began vying for power with Florence, and the resulting battles claimed over half its population in the 13th century alone. The black plague struck a century later, decimating the population once again. Siena still hasn't completely recovered from these demographic misfortunes: its current population is around 65,000, while the pre-plague total was closer to 100,000. Siena and its cosmopolitan neighbor have battled on the cultural as well as the political front. Some say that the Renaissance started here—not in Florence—with Sienese masters Duccio, Simone Martini, and the Lorenzetti brothers.

Siena's geographic and social center is the town square, **Il Campo,** a fan-shape redbrick piazza beloved by locals and visitors alike. The piazza was built on the site of the Roman forum that had been used through the Middle Ages as a marketplace and did not belong to any of the town's 17 contrade. The brick pavement is divided into nine sections representing the Council of Nine, which governed Siena.

BASICS

Siena's **tourist office** (P. del Campo 56, tel. 0577/280551; open June-Aug. Mon.–Sat. 8:30–7:30, mid-Mar.–May and Sept.–mid-Nov. Mon.–Sat. 8:30–7:30, Sun. 8:30–2, Nov.–Mar. 8:30–1 and 3:30–6, Sat. 8:30–1) is right on Il Campo. The office has an exchange bureau with absurd rates, pamphlets that list hotels and places to eat, and a **travel agency** (tel. 0577/228044) that books train tickets for long-distance trips.

The crowded main branch of the **post office** (P. Matteotti 36–37, between bus station and P. Gramsci, tel. 0577/280748; open weekdays 8:15–7) may well be the best place to change money, offering decent exchange rates without commission. You can do laundry at **Ondablu** (V. del Casato di Sotto 17).

COMING AND GOING

Siena's **train station** (P. Fratelli Rosselli, tel. 1478/88088; ticket office open daily 6 AM–9:30 PM; info and currency exchange daily 7–2:30) has a tourist info counter, a currency exchange with adequate rates,

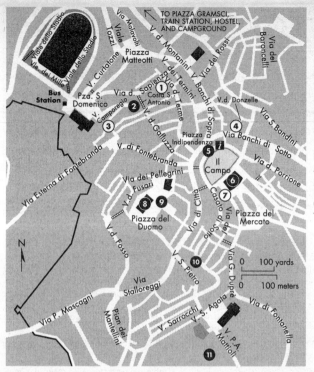

Sights ●

Duomo, **8**

Fonte Gaia, **5**

Museo dell'Opera
del Duomo, **9**

Orto Botanico, **11**

Palazzo Pubblico, **6**

Pinacoteca
Nazionale, **10**

Santuario e Casa di
Santa Caterina, **2**

Lodging ○

Alma Domus, **3**

Bernini, **1**

Locanda
Garibaldi, **7**

Tre Donzelle, **4**

and 24-hour luggage storage (L5,000 for 12 hrs). Trains from Florence aren't as frequent as buses, but they're cheaper (12 daily, 1½ hrs, L7,400). You may have to transfer at Empoli. Trains to Rome (every 2 hrs, 2½ hrs, L29,900) require a switch at Chiusi. From the station, it's a 30-minute uphill climb to town, so save your breath and catch Bus 2, 4, or 10 to Piazza Gramsci. Buses 3, 10, and 15 go to the hostel. Bus 8 gets you to the campground.

Smooth, efficient, blue **TRA-IN/SITA** buses run hourly to Florence (1½ hrs, L11,000) and San Gimignano (1 hr, L8,600; change at Poggibonsi) and a few times daily to Montepulciano (1:1//2::hrs, L8,000). There are also six daily buses to Arezzo (1½ hrs, L8000). **SENA** buses run regularly to Rome (2½ hrs, L25,000). The *extraurbano* (intercity) **bus station** (tel. 0577/204245; office open daily 5:50 AM–8:15 PM) is about a 10-minute walk uphill from Il Campo; it's easy to find because the behemoth church of San Domenico looms next door.

GETTING AROUND

It seems as if no matter which direction you choose in Siena, it's always uphill. Orange city buses go from the outskirts of town (train station and hostel) to the city center, but beware—Siena's bus system is loopy (literally), because some buses take surprisingly roundabout routes. To avoid this headache, ask the driver if the bus is going to your destination *diretto* or *in giro* (direct or circuitous routes; you want the former). Whichever orange bus you hop on, though, will take you nearer to the center or to the train station eventually. Tickets are sold at tobacco shops and at automated machines in major piazzas. A ticket rated "A" (L1,400) is good for one hour. Buses that make their last stop in the center drop you off on **Piazza Gramsci,** about one block from the bus station. To get to Il Campo from here, take Via Malavolti through Piazza Matteotti to Via delle Terme.

WHERE TO SLEEP

Masquerading under a yellow INFORMATION sign, the **Siena Hotels Promotion** (P. San Domenico, tel. 0577/288084; open Mon.–Sat. 9–8) will do the looking for you and book a room for a L3,000 fee. Within the city walls, lodging is just as cheap near Il Campo as it is on the outskirts, so you might as well be close to the action. For a list of affittacamere, go to the tourist office. Prices skyrocket during the Palio (July 2 and August 16), so make reservations well in advance if you want to stay here then.

UNDER L100,000 • Alma Domus. Enjoy monastic calm in this Dominican convent. The 11:30 PM curfew is outweighed by the clean and spacious rooms (doubles L95,000) overlooking the city. *V. Camporegio 37, 53100, tel. 0577/44177, fax 0577/47601. From bus station, turn right down V. Camporegio and right down alley (follow signs). 27 rooms with bath. Cash only.*

Locanda Garibaldi. Right behind the Palazzo Pubblico, this comfortable hotel embraces you like one of the family. Small doubles (L100,000 without bath) fill with tantalizing aromas from the restaurant below. A midnight curfew is part of the deal. *V. Giovanni Duprè 18, 53100, tel. 0577/284204. V. Giovanni Duprè begins on right-hand side of Palazzo Pubblico. 7 rooms with bath.*

Tre Donzelle. A never-ending series of staircases leads to sizable rooms overlooking steep medieval alleys. The hotel is rough around the edges, but it's still the best deal in town, with doubles at L75,000 (with bath, L95,000). With the wind at your back, you can walk to Il Campo in about 10 seconds—which could help you obey the 1 am curfew. *V. delle Donzelle 5, 53100, tel. 0577/280358; fax 0577/223933. From Il Campo, climb stairs next to tourist office, turn right on Banchi di Sotto, left on V. delle Donzelle. 27 rooms, 11 with bath.*

UNDER L125,000 • Bernini. If you have always dreamed of throwing open your bedroom shutters to a postcard panorama of a medieval hillside village, try the Bernini, a bit removed from Il Campo but only one block from the bus station. Sunbathing chairs and a spectacular view await you on the rooftop terrace. Doubles are L110,000 (L150,000 with bath), though prices drop considerably in low season. Request a room with a view and make sure you make it back to the castle before midnight. *V. della Sapienza 15, 53100, tel. 0577/289047. From bus station, take V. della Sapienza. 9 rooms, 5 with bath.*

HOSTEL • Ostello Guidoriccio. L23,000 buys you a bed and breakfast in this superclean hostel. Getting here is a bit complicated: take Bus 15 (Bus 10 on evenings and weekends); the last bus is at 11:10 PM. You can also ask the driver on the Florence bus to let you off at the hostel. *V. Fiorentina 89, 53100, tel. 0577/52212, fax 0577/56172. 111 beds. Curfew I AM, lockout 9–3. Cash only.*

WHERE TO EAT

With great wines—Brunello, Vino Nobile, and Chianti Classico—produced in these parts, as well as great salami and sheep's-milk cheese, you can easily create your own meals. But then again, Siena has a neighborhood pasticceria and rosticceria on every corner, so you'll never be hurting for inexpensive, homemade take-out food. For good vegetarian pizza and spectacular focaccia (sold by weight), come to **Forno Indipendenza** (P. Indipendenza 27, tel. 0577/280295; closed Sun.), Siena's premier bakery. Have your picnic in the sun on Il Campo's slanted brick surface, two blocks away. Enjoy a passeggiata with a fruit sorbet or homemade granita from **Gelateria Brivido** (V. dei Pellegrini 1, tel. 0577/280058), or look in specialty shops for delicious *ricciarelli*, airy almond cookies. Of Siena's many great pasticcerie, the oldest and most famous is **Nannini** (V. Banchi di Sopra 22–24). It offers an assortment of temptations in the form of homemade candies and cookies, but the *panforte* is what has made the place famous. There's no supermarket in the center; if you want to pick up some basics, **CRAI** (V. di Città 152–156; closed Sun.) carries a good selection.

UNDER L10,000 • Antica Pizzicheria al Palazzo del Chigiana. A great place to pick up food to go, this salumeria has hanging salami and a bespectacled wild boar's head peering down from the entry-way. This is a perfect place to assemble a tasty sandwich with fine local ingredients, stock up on cheese, and grab some olives. Panini start at L4,000. *V. di Città 93–95, tel. 0577/289164.*

UNDER L15,000 • Osteria La Chiacchiera. Possibly the only good restaurant in Siena's center that doesn't charge a cover, Osteria La Chiacchiera is also quite intimate. Dine at a leisurely pace on pici, a twirled pasta that's famous in these parts. If you're after lighter fare, the restaurant's little enoteca just around the corner serves bruschetta, salumi misti, and that fine local red wine. *Costa di Sant'Antonio 4, tel. 0577/280631.*

Osteria del Ficomezzo. A L25,000 lunch menu is one of the best deals in town in this little trattoria popular among students and locals. You'll find it just off Piazza del Campo, *V. dei Termini 71, tel. 0577/222384. Closed Sun.*

WORTH SEEING

No motorized form of transportation can handle Siena's streets or hills, so you have to explore the town in all its hilly glory on foot, with amazing views of the Duomo and the city's many towers as a reward. If you have only one day in Siena, see the Duomo, its museum, and the Palazzo Pubblico; if you have more time and want to save money, purchase a **cumulative ticket** (valid for three days; L8,500), good for entrance to the Duomo's Biblioteca Piccolomini, Battistero, and Museo dell'-Opera del Duomo. Meander a bit, and you'll discover the free **Orto Botanico** (V. Pier Andrea Mattioli 4, tel. 0577/298874; open weekdays 8–5, Sat. 8–noon), a lush expanse overlooking the countryside.

Every caffè and market in Siena sells the legendary local specialty, panforte. Dense enough to double as a lethal weapon, it's a spicy-sweet treat thickened with honey, almonds, and candied fruit.

IL CAMPO • Piazza del Campo, known as Il Campo (the Field), is one of civic architecture's crowning achievements and is the city's heart. At the top of Il Campo is the **Fonte Gaia,** decorated in the early 15th century by Siena's greatest sculptor, Jacopo della Quercia, with 13 reliefs of biblical events and the virtues. Those now lining the rectangular fountain are 19th-century copies; the originals are in the Museo Civico (*see below*). The fountain is the only body of water in the entire town, and it starts to look enticing around high noon in summer.

PALAZZO PUBBLICO • Built as the town hall at the height of the city's power, in the late 13th and early 14th centuries, the building has the crenellations and three-light windows that define Sienese architecture. Inside, the **Museo Civico** contains frescoes and paintings by Siena's greatest artists. The best room is the **Sala del Mappamondo,** with Simone Martini's great *Maestà,* or Virgin and Child (1315), rendered with tremendous delicacy and balance. On the opposite wall is a famous portrait of Sienese general Guidoriccio da Fogliano on horseback, previously attributed to Simone Martini but which might, in fact, have been painted several centuries later.

The nine governors of Siena once met in the **Sala della Pace,** famous for having the most important medieval frescoes in Italy: Ambrogio Lorenzetti's *Allegories of Good and Bad Government.* The Good Government side depicts a utopia, showing first the virtuous ruling council surrounded by angels and then perfectly harmonious scenes representing the city and countryside. Conversely, the Bad Government fresco tells a tale straight out of Dante. The evil ruler and his advisers have horns and fondle strange animals, while the town scene depicts the seven mortal sins in action. Why is it that the Bad Government fresco is so much more visually interesting than its counterpart? *P. del Campo, tel. 0577/292263. Admission L6,000. Open Mar.–Oct., Mon.–Sat. 9:30–6:30, Sun. 9–12:45; shorter hours in winter.*

The Palazzo Pubblico's most distinctive feature is the **Torre del Mangia,** named after one of the tower's first bell ringers, Giovanni di Duccio (whose nickname was Mangiaguadagni, or earnings eater). It's a 335-ft structure built by Muccio and Francesco di Rinaldo between 1338 and 1348, and it offers the greatest possible view of Siena—only fair, as you'll climb more than 400 stairs to get to the top. *Tel. 0577/292263. Admission L6,000. Open daily 10–1 hr. before sunset.*

DUOMO • When the city council approved the cathedral's color scheme in the late 13th century, they touched off the construction of one of Italy's finest churches. A bizarre combination of Gothic

MEDIEVAL RIVALRY
MEN IN TIGHTS

Each of Siena's contrade has its own church, museum, and symbol. Look for streetlights painted in the 17 contrades' colors, plaques displaying each symbol, and statues embodying the spirit of each neighborhood. Should you hear beating drums early Sunday morning, don't be surprised to see a throng of men in tights twirling flags and singing the praises of their contrada as if heading off to war. Twice a year, the main square, Il Campo, explodes in a frenzy of rival contrade as the site of the Palio, a horse race to win possession of the cloth banner that gives the contest its name. See box This Ain't No Rodeo, below.

and Romanesque architecture, Siena's cathedral makes all other Tuscan cathedrals appear underdecorated. Major artists of the era, like the Pisano family, came to town to leave their mark on the church. Both outside and in, the vivid black-and-white color scheme prevails. In the nooks and crannies of the facade's bottom half are Giovanni Pisano's statues of great figures from philosophy and religion, whose kinetic poses were a major sculptural innovation (the originals are housed in the Museo dell'Opera del Duomo). When you enter the Duomo, look up: the enormous vaulted ceilings are painted a rich midnight blue with scattered golden stars to symbolize the cathedral's proximity to the heavens. When your neck starts to cramp, look down: more than 40 artists created inlaid marble floorings that tell assorted biblical stories. About two-thirds of the different works are covered at any given time for protection. Don't miss Nicola Pisano's beautifully carved pulpit, which depicts the life of Christ. Sadly, the distinctive **campanile** is closed to the public. Also in the cathedral is the **Biblioteca Piccolomini,** which contains frescoes by Pinturicchio depicting scenes from the life of Aeneas Sylvius Piccolomini, who later became Pope Pius II. *P. del Duomo, tel. 0577/47321. Admission to Duomo free; Biblioteca Piccolomini L2,000. Open mid-Mar.–Oct., daily 9–7:30; Oct.–mid-Mar., daily 10–1 and 2:30–5. Organ recitals Sun. at noon.*

MUSEO DELL'OPERA DEL DUOMO • Right next door to the Duomo is the Museo dell'Opera del Duomo, an enchanting collection of paintings, sculptures, and religious articles from Siena's golden age. The first floor displays numerous unlabeled sculptures, mostly prophet figures by Giovanni Pisano. At the top of the first flight of stairs is the museum's best room, the dimly lighted **Sala di Duccio,** which houses Duccio's *Maestà* (1310). Brave the slippery, worn steps of the museum's **tower** (Number 4 on the museum map) for an amazing view of the surrounding hills and farms. *P. del Duomo, tel. 0577/283048. Admission L6,000. Open daily 9–7:30, shorter hrs in winter.*

BATTISTERO • The baptistery was built underneath the Duomo—it provides structural support for the portion of the huge cathedral that sprawls off the hilltop site. The baptistery's highlight is a carved baptismal font, sculpted by four top-notch artists: Donatello, Ghiberti, Jacopo della Quercia, and Giovanni di Turino. *Admission L3,000. Open Mar.–Sept., daily 9–7:30, shorter hours in winter.*

PINACOTECA NAZIONALE • On the south side of town, the National Picture Gallery houses a memorable collection of Madonna-and-child paintings by Sienese artists, arranged in chronological order. *V. San Pietro 29, tel. 0577/281161. Admission L8,000. Open Tues.–Sun. 8:30–1:30.*

SANTUARIO E CASA DI SANTA CATERINA • The cell of Catholicism's first beatified woman isn't much more than a small brick altar that's chained shut with a bicycle lock. Through a small window, you get to peer at St. Catherine's disintegrating bones. It's worth a brief stop to pay homage to Italy's patron saint (along with St. Francis) and one of Christianity's true heroines. Catherine was a much-respected diplomat, noted for ending the Great Schism by convincing the pope to return to Rome from Avignon. Above her cell are two unspectacular churches. *Costa di Sant'Antonio, tel. 0577/280330. Admission free. Open daily 9–12:30 and 2:30–6, 3:30–6 in winter.*

FESTIVALS

Free entertainment doesn't end with the Palio, because Siena also becomes an open-air concert hall in summer. Around the third week in July is the **Settimana Musicale Senese,** a week of classical music concerts, with tickets for various performances starting at L25,000. Overlapping this is **Siena Jazz,** a five-day event that draws jazz greats.

AFTER DARK

Siena's nightlife revolves around the passeggiata and hanging out in Il Campo. It will cost you about L10,000 just to sit and have a beer in a caffè along the fashionable piazza, but where else are you going to hang out? Siena has several nightclubs, but whether they're open or not is a crapshoot.

A place that attracts a young, relaxed crowd is the **Blue Eyes Pub** (V. Giovanni Duprè 64, tel. 0577/42650), serving up local and imported beer until the wee hours. You can grab an espresso and enjoy a fabulous view of redbrick Siena at **Caffè Nova** (V. Camporegio 13; closed Mon.) until 1 AM.

NEAR SIENA

SAN GALGANO

Standing alone in an open field, roofless and overgrown with grass, the **Abbazia di San Galgano** is one of Italy's most compelling and memorable sights. The simple Gothic structure was built by Cistercian monks in the late 12th century to commemorate Galgano, the local saint who, in a renunciation of violence, thrust his sword into a stone and prayed to it as if to a cross. Relations between Siena and the abbey were good, and the Cistercians quickly flourished. But war with Florence and the plague wiped out much of the population, and soon both order and church were reduced to ruin. It's remarkably peaceful to stand among the pointed arches or gaze through the missing rose window out to the open sky.

Up the hill from the abbey, the circular **Chiesa di Monte Siepi** (open daily 7 AM–sunset) marks the spot where Galgano lived and was buried. Inside, look for the sword in the stone, the spiral designs on the interior of the cupola, and the crumbling frescoes by Ambrogio Lorenzetti in the side chapel.

COMING AND GOING • The only public transportation to San Galgano is a single bus that leaves Siena at 3:50 PM (40 min, L4,200, marked MASSA MARITTIMA) and returns to Siena at 6 PM. Make sure you tell the driver that you're going to San Galgano. If you have a car, drive south from Siena toward Massa Marittima on Route 73.

MONTALCINO

Vineyards blanket the hillsides on the way up to this walled town, once a stronghold of Siena's union of towns in the region. But these are not just ordinary vines—some of the grapes are used to make Brunello di Montalcino, arguably Italy's finest red wine and undoubtedly the town's lifeblood.

Just about every shop sells Brunello and Rosso di Montalcino, Brunello's fruity, less expensive cousin. Other regional specialties are honey and the crunchy *ossi morti* (dead bones), dry biscuits you can find neatly packaged in any bakery. Action in the town—if it can be called that—gathers around the central Piazza del Popolo, where the **Fiaschetteria Italiana** (P. del Popolo, tel. 0577/849043; closed Thurs.) is one of the coolest bars this side of Siena. If you are in town at mealtime, **Sciame** (V. Ricasoli 9, tel. 0577/848017; cash only; closed Tues.) is a good stop. The **tourist office** (tel. 0577/849331; open Tues.–Sun. 10—1 and 2—6) is right on the piazza. Accommodations aren't cheap, so it may be best to make Montalcino a day (or afternoon) trip from Siena.

COMING AND GOING • From Siena, avoid the 10:45 AM bus that stops in every town along the way and arrives when everything closes down at midday; instead, catch a **TRA-IN** bus (1¾ hrs, L5,500) in the afternoon. In Montalcino the bus drops you at Piazza Cavour, a 10-minute walk from the fortress on the opposite end of town. Buy tickets for the bus from one of the bars nearby.

WORTH SEEING • You can get a double dose of culture by sampling local wine and exploring the town's **fortezza.** Built in the mid-14th century and still standing proudly after repeated assaults, the fortress now hosts occasional exhibitions of contemporary paintings. From the fortress walls you get one picture-perfect view after another: whereas land surrounding other hill towns has been developed commercially, land around Montalcino is still most profitable as vineyards. Climb one of the towers and check out the endless hills, covered with patches of rich earth tones. On the main floor of the fortress is Montalcino's most elegant enoteca. Sample Brunello (L6,000 a glass) as you sit in the shadow of the fortress and munch on bread and prosciutto. If you want to walk off the heady wine, continue straight

THIS AIN'T NO RODEO

Siena's Palio, a centuries-old horse race, takes place twice a year, on July 2 and August 16, but its spirit infects the city all year long. Three laps around a makeshift track in Il Campo earn Palio participants either the respect or scorn of the other 16 contrade. The event is so important to the Sienese that bribery, brutality, and kidnapping of the jockeys are commonplace—sabotaging a horse's reins is the only thing that remains taboo.

Festivities kick off three days prior to the main event, with trial races, street parties, and late-night carousing. As the Palio approaches, residents don scarves with their contrada's colors and march through city streets in medieval costumes. This race, however, has a dark side: horses are often injured as they turn the brutal corners, and frequently they must be put down as a result of their injuries. Television hasn't helped: super-slow-motion replays of horses falling and twisting in pain just make the event gorier. The Palio, however, is too ingrained in the hearts of the Sienese to be stopped; it's also a huge money-maker, as it draws tens of thousands of people.

from the fortress steps down (and then up) Via Ricasoli, which becomes Via Cialdini. This narrow, steep residential street of well-worn brick is one of Tuscany's loveliest. It will eventually bring you back to Via Mazzini. *Piazzale Fortezza, tel. 0577/849211. Admission L4,000 to fortress and walls. Open Apr.–Sept., Tues.–Sun. 9–8; Oct.–Mar., Tues.–Sun. 9–1 and 2–6.*

AREZZO

Arezzo has a lot in common with other Tuscan hill towns: It was founded by the Etruscans, taken over by the Romans, fortified in the late Middle Ages, and fought over and eventually conquered by Florence. It was also the birthplace of a number of famous names: Petrarch, the humanist; Giorgio Vasari, the artist and art historian; and Guido d'Arezzo, the inventor of musical notation. The town also has its own Renaissance masterpiece, Piero della Francesca's fresco cycle in the Basilica di San Francesco. Though part of Piero's work has been scaffolded for years, it's possible to climb up on the scaffolding to view the partly restored sublime frescoes (scaffold visits cost L10,000 and must be reserved in advance). Although Arezzo is not likely to captivate you at first glance—its streets and general atmosphere aren't particularly charming or memorable—it does offer an interesting mix of modernity and history against a rural backdrop. Good bus and rail connections make Arezzo an easy trip from Florence or Siena, and amenities like the top-notch youth hostel make it a convenient base for day trips to Cortona and Sansepolcro.

BASICS

The town has two well-stocked **tourist offices.** The most convenient one is directly in front of the train station entrance on Piazza della Repubblica (tel. 0575/377678; open Mon.–Sat. 9–1 and 3–7, summer also Sun. 9–1). The other office (P. Risorgimento 116, tel. 0575/23952; open weekdays 9–1 and 4–7:30) is two blocks away; use it only if your Italian is up to snuff.

COMING AND GOING

Frequent trains from Florence (1 hr, L7,400) and from Rome (2 hrs, L20,000) stop at Arezzo's **station** (P. della Repubblica, tel. 1478/88088). Buses are much less frequent. The **bus station** (P. della Repubblica, tel. 0575/483651) is just outside the train station. Look for the sign that says ATAM POINT. Buses leave only a few times a day for Florence (1½ hrs, L8,000) and Siena (1¼ hrs, L8,000), hourly for Cortona (1 hr, L4,500) and Sansepolcro (45 min, L5,500). Local ATAM buses (tel. 0575/382651, L1,300 from any bar) make a circuit through Piazza Guido Monaco, one block from the train station. Bus 4 takes you to the hostel.

WHERE TO SLEEP

Arezzo's youth hostel is nicer than many *alberghi,* but if you prefer your own room, the tourist office has a complete list of accommodations. Book ahead in June and July and on weekends when the antiques fair is held (*see* Festivals, *below*). Just outside the city walls, **La Toscana** (V. M. Perenio 56, tel. 0575/21692) is a 10-minute walk from the town center, but it contains some of the best cheap rooms around, with bright white walls and garden views. Doubles with bath cost L80,000. A double with bath at the **Hotel Cecco** (C. Italia 215, tel. 0575/20986, fax 0575/356730) goes for L95,000. You're looking at about L105,000 for a double with bath at the **Astoria** (V. Guido Monaco 54, tel. 0575/24361, fax 0575/24362).

HOSTEL • Ostello Villa Severi. It's practically worth the trip to Arezzo just to stay in this magnificent hostel, ensconced in the Tuscan countryside in a beautiful restored 16th-century villa. The bathrooms are works of art, with spotless floors and those cool metal-trough sinks that you never see anymore, which make up for the single shower per sex per floor. Beds go for L20,000 per person; breakfast is L3,000. HI cards are not required. *V. F. Redi 13, 52100, tel. and fax 0575/299047. 15-min walk from train station: take V. Guido Monaco, then right on V. Cavour (which eventually becomes V. F. Redi). Bus 4 stops nearby. 70 beds. Curfew 11:30 PM (sometimes flexible), lockout 2–6. Cash only.*

There's no lack of places to try local wines in Tuscany. If you want it right from the source, many local vineyards are open to the public, and some have restaurants. Tourist offices can help; see also Chianti, above.

WHERE TO EAT

For great food and the true Tuscan trattoria experience, choose between **Il Saraceno** (V. Mazzini 6/B, tel. 0575/27644; closed Wed. and two weeks in July), **Antica Osteria L'Agania** (V. Mazzini 10, tel. 0575/25381; closed Mon.), and **Il Cantuccio** (V. Madonna del Prato 76, tel. 0575/26830; closed Wed.). On Tuesday, Thursday, and Saturday mornings, the outdoor market in Piazza Sant'Agostino can help you out with fresh groceries. The best bakery, right in the center, is **Forno Pane e Salute** (C. Italia 11, tel. 0575/20657; closed Sun.). The large, aromatic **Rosticceria Polleria Corrado** (V. della Madonna del Prato 54, tel. 0575/27376; closed Mon.) sells whole roast chickens (L13,000) that will feed three comfortably; a sizable chunk of homemade lasagna costs about L5,500. Along the same street are other food shops and a good gelateria, **Il Gelato** (V. Madonna del Prato 45, tel. 0575/23240; closed Wed.).

WORTH SEEING

The ravages of time and circumstance have not been kind to Piero della Francesca's frescoes in the **Basilica di San Francesco** (P. San Francesco, tel. 0575/20630, reservations for visits on scaffolding 0575/35568); the hope is that the complicated restoration project will be finished before the end of the century. The Renaissance master painted 12 scenes behind the altar during the 1450s and '60s. The cycle illustrates the legend of the true cross, according to which a tree planted over the body of Adam later served as the cross of Christ's crucifixion, which was discovered in Jerusalem by St. Helena, the mother of Constantine, sometime in the 4th century.

Arezzo's only other work by Piero, a small fresco of *Mary Magdalene,* is next to the gold coffin of St. Donatus in the cream-color **Duomo** (P. del Duomo). Nearby, the church of **San Domenico** (P. San Domenico) contains Cimabue's bloated, contorted 13th-century *Crucifix,* in which Christ's chest is twice the size of his belly and his feet look like toothpicks. In the other direction is the steep **Piazza Grande,** a virtual museum of architectural styles. One one side, the piazza is lined by Vasari's Renaissance **loggia.** At the center is the church of **Santa Maria della Pieve** (C. Italia), a 12th-century Romanesque masterpiece, and its **campanile,** dubbed "the tower of 100 holes" for its many double-arched windows. Next to the church are the 17th-century **Palazzo del Tribunale** and the **Palazzo della Fraternita' dei Laici,** with a combined Gothic and early Renaissance facade. The piazza hosts the **Joust of the Saracen** (*see below*) every September.

From Piazza Grande it's a short walk to the **Passeggio del Prato,** a park with a Renaissance fortress, sunbathers, and ranks of shady benches. Down the hill at the bottom of town you can explore the ruins of the 2,000-year-old **Roman amphitheater** and the adjoining **Museo Archeologico Mecenate** (V. Margaritone 10, tel. 0575/20882; admission L8,000; open Mon.–Sat. 9–2, Sun. 9–1), which has collections of Etruscan and Roman bronzes, coins, and artifacts.

To get to know one of Arezzo's favorite sons a little better, check out **Casa Vasari** (V. XX Settembre 55, tel. 0575/300301; admission free; open daily 9–7, Sun. 9–1), the house Vasari designed for himself.

FESTIVALS

Medieval Arezzo is remembered the first Sunday of every September in the **Giostra del Saracino** (Joust of the Saracen), in Piazza Grande. Costumed knights from different quarters of the city charge on horseback to tilt at an effigy of a Turk and commemorate the glory days. The medieval buildings in the piazza are decked out with colorful flags, and musicians and jugglers keep the atmosphere festive. The first weekend of every month, the city hosts the **Fiera Antiquaria,** an enormous antiques fair that spills out from Piazza Grande onto just about every street of the upper town. Arezzo is also the home of **Arezzo Wave,** the self-proclaimed biggest free rock concert in all of Europe. Acts from around the world come to play for the three-day event, which is usually held on the last weekend of June.

NEAR AREZZO

SANSEPOLCRO

Birthplace of 15th-century painter Piero della Francesca and home to one of his greatest works, Sansepolcro is a quiet little town set in a valley (for a change), easily reachable from Arezzo. The second weekend in September the town holds its Palio della Balestra, a crossbow competition and medieval festival similar to the one held in Lucca. The **tourist office** (P. Garibaldi 2, off V. N. Aggiunti, tel. 0575/740536) is open daily 10–noon and 3:30–5:30.

There are several fine churches to see and plenty of cobblestones to walk, but the town's highlight is Piero della Francesca's magnificent *Resurrection* (painted 1458–74), on display in the **Museo Civico** (V. Aggiunti 65, tel. 0575/732218; admission L10,000; open Tues.–Sun. 9–1:30 and 2:30–7:30). The fresco, moved from its original location across town, shows Piero's pioneering use of single-point perspective and unified, symmetrical groupings. The resurrected Christ stands triumphant above four guards who sleep, oblivious to His triumph. According to Vasari, the second sleeping soldier on the left is the artist's self-portrait. The room contains several other terrific works by Piero, including the massive Misericordia polyptych showing a serene Virgin Mary protecting the faithful gathered under her mantle. You'll also find a collection of crucifixes, papal capes, and della Robbia terracottas in the museum.

COMING AND GOING • Frequent buses from Arezzo (1 hr, L5,500) make the memorable descent into Sansepolcro's valley. The bus stops right outside the city walls, and you can buy tickets for the return trip next to the stop at **Bar Autostazione.** The last bus back to Arezzo leaves around 7:30 PM. For more bus information, check the schedules posted outside the bar or call the local bus company, **SITA** (tel. 0575/742999).

WHERE TO SLEEP AND EAT • Reasonably priced lodging is available if you miss the bus back to Arezzo or decide to hang around a while. Three hotel-restaurants in town make sleeping and eating arrangements easy. **Albergo Fiorentino** (V. Luca Pacioli 60, tel. 0575/740350, fax 0575/740370, restaurant closed Fri.) has small, tastefully decorated rooms (doubles with bath, L100,000). The restaurant, Sansepolcro's most romantic spot, serves superb homemade pastas and desserts. **Da Ventura** (V. Aggiunti 30, tel. 0575/742560, restaurant closed Sat.) has doubles with bath for L70,000 and a good restaurant specializing in truffles and wild mushrooms in season (watch it: tartufo and porcini can double the price of your meal). A third choice is the **Orfeo** (V. A. Diaz 12, tel. 0575/742061, restaurant closed Mon.), just outside the city gates and half a block from the bus stop. Doubles, all with bath, cost L80,000; their pizzeria, **Da Beppino,** is downstairs. End your wanderings with a drink at the popular pub-pizzeria **Don Chisciotte** (V. Marconi 40–42, tel. 0575/741134; closed Mon.).

CORTONA

From the peaceful hilltop town of Cortona, the plains of the perfectly flat Valdichiana valley stretch out into the distance, making the few towns below seem minute and insignificant. Cortona holds the distinction of being the oldest Tuscan hill town; archaeological finds date the city to well before the Etruscans arrived, in the 8th century BC; Virgil claimed that it was founded by the mythological warrior Dardanus. This hard-to-conquer town passed from Roman to Gothic to Arezzian to Florentine hands over the ages. The Museo Diocesano contains a Fra Angelico Annunciation as well as some large works by local boy Luca Signorelli.

BASICS

In addition to handing out the usual info, Cortona's handy **tourist office** (V. Nazionale 42, tel. 0575/630353; open Mon.–Sat. 8–1 and 3–6, Sun. 9–1, in winter closed Sat. afternoon and Sun.) sells rail and bus tickets.

COMING AND GOING

Buses are the best way to reach Cortona. Frequent trips from Arezzo (1 hr, L4,500) go up the hill to Piazza Garibaldi, just outside the city walls. The **bus station** (P. Garibaldi, tel. 0575/630353) sells tickets for LFI buses to major cities. There are two **train stations** in the Cortona area, but at each you'll wait forever for a bus in which to scale the hill into town. The station in Camucia (P. della Libertà, tel. 1478/88088) is closer than the one in Terontola (P. Nazioni Unite, tel. 1478/88088). Trains to Florence (1 hr, L10,500), Siena (1 hr, L9,800; change at Chiusi), and Arezzo (20 min, L3,100) come about every 1½ hours.

GETTING AROUND

Get ready to work those calves, Cortona is one steep hill town, and there's no bus. From Piazza Garibaldi, Via Nazionale (with both the tourist and the bus offices) heads north into Piazza della Repubblica, the town center.

WHERE TO SLEEP

The cheapest option in town is the clean and central **Ostello San Marco** (V. Maffei 57, tel. and fax 0575/601392; cash only), where a bed and breakfast cost L19,000 per person (HI card required). Lockout is 9:30–3:30, but there's no curfew. The hostel is open mid-March to mid-October; call ahead for reservations in summer. To get here from the bus stop, take Via Margherita up the hill and look for the hostel sign.

You might be a bit more comfortable at one of the town's two convents, which offer immaculate rooms at low prices. A double with bath will cost you L55,000 at **Convento Betania** (V. G. Severini 50, tel. 0575/62829; cash only) or L58,000 at **Istituto Santa Margherita** (V. C. Battisti 15, tel. 0575/630336; cash only). Men are welcome as long as they don't want to share rooms with women to whom they're not married. **Albergo Italia** (V. Ghibellina 7, tel. 0575/630254, fax 0575/630564) has nice doubles with bath (L130,000) that make for a relaxing retreat.

WHERE TO EAT

For a cheap picnic, wander through the town's food shops, lining Via Nazionale, Piazza della Repubblica, and Via Dardano. A food, fruit, veggie, you-name-it market comes to Piazza Signorelli every Saturday. Two decent local trattorias are **Trattoria Etrusca** (V. Dardano 37–39, tel. 0575/604088; closed Thurs.), which has an outdoor patio, and **Trattoria Dardano** (V. Dardano 24, tel. 0575/601944; closed Wed.). Next to the bus stop on Piazza Garibaldi is the large **Ristorante Tonino** (P. Garibaldi 1, tel. 0575/630333), with amazing views of the valley below. A full meal with drinks will run you about L30,000, but do note that the menu requires all patrons to order at least a primo and a secondo, a practice that mercifully has died out in most other places in Italy.

WORTH SEEING

Cortona's most impressive church, **Santa Maria delle Grazie al Calcinaio** (tel. 0575/62537), lies a couple of kilometers (1 mi) outside the city. If you're riding the bus up to Cortona, you can hop off and check out the church; another bus will come in 30 minutes (except Sun.), and your ticket should still be good. The building was designed in the late 15th century by Francesco di Giorgio Martini, who adapted Brunelleschi's geometric style (elongated dome, interior colonnades and arches) with wonderfully harmonious results inside and out. Next door is an ornate cemetery, with many decorated graves.

In town, start your exploration at **Piazza della Repubblica.** Just behind the Palazzo Comunale (the very medieval-looking building with the tower) is Palazzo Casali, a 13th-century Gothic building housing the **Museo dell'Accademia Etrusca** (P. Signorelli, tel. 0575/630415; admission L8,000). The museum gives a rich picture of local life, with surprisingly deep coverage of various periods (it even includes modern art), but the best rooms display finds from the Roman and Etruscan eras. Nearby, the **Museo Diocesano** (P. del Duomo, tel. 0575/62830; admission L8,000) houses a small but wonderful collection of Renaissance paintings by Fra Angelico, Luca Signorelli, and Sassetta; Fra Angelico's *Annunciation,* with its vibrant colors and gold punch work, is a gem. The museums have the same hours: summer, Tuesday–Sunday 9:30–1, and 3:30–7; winter, Tuesday–Sunday 10–1 and 3–5.

Up the hill, the church of **San Niccolò** (V. San Niccolò) contains an interesting standard by Luca Signorelli, with a *Madonna and Child with Saints* on one side and a *Deposizione* on the other. If you've got the stamina, hike up to the Venetian church of **Santa Margherita,** remodeled in the 19th century. Inside are the saint's mummified remains, peacefully residing in a glass coffin. The dirt road on the right-hand side as you exit leads up to the town's **Fortezza Medicea** (admission L5,000; open summer, Mon.–Sat. 10–1 and 4–7, closed winter). The **Giardino Pubblico,** just outside the city walls beyond Piazza Garibaldi, offers shady lanes and benches.

AFTER DARK

Holed up in a hill town at night? Go for a walk like everybody else. Piazza della Repubblica, the Giardino Pubblico, and Palazzo Comunale are where the crowds go. The local disco, **Route 66** (P. Garibaldi 8, tel. 0575/62727), rocks into the wee hours most nights, and many restaurants keep their bars open until 1 AM or later. For a late-night beer or Campari, try **Trattoria Etrusca** (*see* Where to Eat, *above*) or **Fufluns** (V. Ghibellina 3, tel. 0575/604140; no lunch; closed Tues.).

SOUTHERN TUSCANY

Italy's most potent red wines are produced in a region so topographically demanding that towns have been unable to expand outside their medieval city walls. The original planners of southern Tuscany sought dramatic cliffs that provided great defense during the nonstop wars between Florence and Siena. Like the rest of Tuscany, the southern region is incredibly beautiful, and the towns' lingering rural character—the result of an economy based on wine-making and tourism—makes them even more appealing. It's easiest to tour the region by car, but you can do it by bus with a bit of patience.

MONTEPULCIANO

Longer, narrower, and higher than any other Tuscan town, Montepulciano is made up of a pyramid of red-brick buildings set within a circle of cypress trees. Founded by the Etruscans, the town owes its harmonious look to a 15th-century alliance with Florence that brought three Renaissance masters to town—Antonio da Sangallo il Vecchio, Michelozzo, and Vignola—who built city walls, palaces, and churches complemented by gracefully aging streets and stunning views of the surrounding plains. If that isn't enough to make Montepulciano a fine day trip from Florence or Siena, there's good local wine, too.

BASICS

The **tourist office** (V. Ricci 9, tel. 0578/758687; open Mon.–Sat. 9–1 and 3–8, Sun. 9–1) is just below Piazza Grande and across from the Museo Civico, in Palazzo Ricci.

COMING AND GOING

Local trains from Siena (1 hr, L6,700) and Chiusi (12 min, L2,200) stop at Montepulciano Stazione, but infrequent bus service up to the town center (10 km/6 mi, 30 min, L1,600) makes the direct bus from Siena or Chiusi the best option (from Siena, 3 times daily, 2 hrs, L8,000; no service Sun.; for Chiusi, several times daily, 45 minutes, L3,300). Call **TRA-IN** (tel. 0577/204111 in Siena or 0578/31174 in Chiusi) for more info.

GETTING AROUND

The town is long and narrow, and for the weary there is frequent minibus service (L1,200) from the bus station to Piazza Grande and out to the church of San Biagio. Buy tickets at tobacco shops. Outside the walls, there is great biking (if you don't mind a few hills). **Cicloposse** (V. Matteotti 45, tel. 0578/716392) rents bikes for L30,000 per day and less for longer rentals.

WHERE TO SLEEP

There are four choices for renting a private room in Montepulciano: **Il Cittino** (Vicolo della V. Nuova 2, tel. 0578/757335; cash only), an inn and restaurant run almost single-handedly by one supermom, offers pleasantly decorated rooms for L55,000 per bathless double. The **Bellavista** (V. Ricci 25, across from tourist office, tel. 0578/757348; cash only), on a quiet corner in the town center, has basic doubles (some with views) that cost L70,000 (with bath). **La Terrazza** (V. del Pie al Sasso 16, tel. and fax 0578/757440) has doubles with bath for L95,000. **Meublé Il Riccio** (V. Talosa 21, tel. and fax 0578/757713) is more expensive (doubles with bath L100,000), but the comfort level and views of the countryside justify the price.

WHERE TO EAT

The breezy, comfortable **Antico Caffè Poliziano** (V. di Voltaia nel Corso 27–29, tel. 0578/758615; no dinner Wed.), open since 1868, has an oak bar, chess sets, and a balcony overlooking the valley with a view you need to see to believe. The menu offers coffee, drinks, and, amazingly, a good selection of entrée-size fresh salads. Montepulciano's best pizzas are served on an outdoor patio at **Evoè** (V. dell'Opio nel Corso 30, tel. 0578/758757). Two places that stay open late at night are **La Briciola** (V. delle Cantine 23, tel. 0578/716903), where you can choose from an assortment of German beers (L4,000–L7,000), and **Osteria dell'Acquacheta** (V. del Teatro 22, tel. 0578/758443; closed Tues. in winter), where you can sip vino and sample local cheeses on the cheap.

In Montepulciano on the last Sunday in August, you can catch Il Bravìo delle Botti, a 500-year-old contest. Strapping young lads in Renaissance garb representing the town's eight contrade roll barrels up the steep hill of the centro storico.

If you're looking for something to eat in order to wash it down with some Vino Nobile, find **Il Cantuccio** (V. della Cantine 1, off the Corso; closed Mon.), a brick basement tucked away on a dark, cavelike street. For a meal at ground level, **Trattoria Diva** (V. di Gracciano del Corso 92, tel. 0578/716951; closed Tues.) is a stone's throw away. Come to **Il Cittino** (Vicolo della V. Nuova 2, tel. 0578/757335; closed Wed.) and its adjoining inn (*see* Where to Sleep, *above*) if you aren't sure what you're hungry for. A menu is posted by the door, but Marcella usually serves whatever she feels like making, and it's sure to be good.

WORTH SEEING

Beautiful **Piazza Grande** sits on the highest point in the town, with the unfinished **Duomo** at one end. A well-regarded tryptich of the Assumption of the Virgin by Taddeo di Bartolo adorns the high altar. Across the piazza is handsome **Palazzo Comunale** (city hall), complete with tower and redecorated by Michelozzo to look like the Palazzo Vecchio in Florence. You can go inside the courtyard and climb the tower for great views. Sangallo designed most of the remaining palazzi along the piazza, including the Palazzo Tarugi, which faces the cathedral.

The Corso, Montepulciano's major thoroughfare, is dominated by foot traffic and imposing Renaissance buildings. Coming from Porta Il Prato, you'll encounter two of da Sangallo's creations, the **Palazzo Cucconi** (V. di Gracciano nel Corso 70) and the **Palazzo Bucelli** (V. di Gracciano nel Corso 73), which face one another in imitation of the Florentine civic architecture pioneered by Alberti. A bit farther along is Michelozzo's Church of **Sant'Agostino** (P. Michelozzo), a white-stone building with fake spires carved into the second tier of the facade.

Montepulciano's most important sight is da Sangallo's **La Chiesa di San Biagio,** just outside the city walls down a very steep street. Built on a Greek-cross plan with a dome and a serene, perfectly balanced facade, it is widely considered one of the great Renaissance buildings in the region. A bus runs to the church from the Corso and Piazza Grande. *V. di San Biagio, tel. 0578/758304. Open daily 9–7, until 6 in winter.*

CHEAP THRILLS

Forget the late-night pub crawl; Montepulciano is the place for an afternoon cantina-gastronomia stroll, where you can nibble fresh salami and local pecorino in between glasses of the highly regarded local wine, Vino Nobile di Montepulciano. Don't miss the **Cantina del Redi** (V. di Collazzi 5, tel. 0578/757166; open weekdays 10–1 and 3–7, weekends 10–7), established in the 14th century. Beyond its automatic glass doors lie the cool vaults of one of the town's oldest cellars, carved right out of the rock.

FESTIVALS

Montepulciano comes alive in late July and early August with the **Cantiere Internazionale d'Arte,** a series of musical performances by artists from around the world. Also worthwhile is the **Bruscello** in mid-August, when locals put on lavish amateur productions in front of the Duomo. Get info from the tourist office.

PIENZA

When poet and politician Enea Silvio de' Piccolomini became Pope Pius II in 1458, he had his tiny hometown of Corsignano redesigned as a model Renaissance city by Bernardo Rossellino, a student of Alberti. Rossellino's harmonious plan, with a central piazza, cathedral, city hall, and a palace for the ruler, was realized in just three years, and Pius II was so pleased he renamed the town after himself.

The town hasn't lost its model quality—the scaled-down buildings and streets are perfectly maintained and manicured, the views postcard-stunning. You won't need a map to find your way around, but the **tourist office** (tel. 0578/749071; open daily 9:30–1 and 3–6) is in Palazzo del Comune on the central (surprise!) Piazza Pio II. Despite all the great design, the **Cattedrale dell'Assunta** was built on shifting ground and has been shored up several times over the centuries. The interior is bathed in light from high windows, and the five 15th-century altarpieces are worth a visit. The highlight of the main square is **Palazzo Piccolomini** (tel. 0578/748072; open Tues.–Sun. 10–12:30 and 3–6), where Pius II and his descendants lived up until 1962, when the last Piccolomini died. If you've been to Florence, the facade might look familiar, as Rossellino modeled it after Alberti's Palazzo Rucellai. Several rooms are open to the public. Pienza is known for pecorino *di Pienza,* the sheep's-milk cheese produced in the surrounding countryside and sold in a slew of shops in town, several along the Corso Rossellino. If you're around for a meal, **La Buca delle Fate** (C. Rossellino 38/a, tel. 0578/748272; closed Mon.) serves up local specialties at affordable prices. If not, the least you could do is try the best gelato around at **Dolce Sosta** (C. Rossellino 87), down the street.

COMING AND GOING

Pienza is on the Siena–Montepulciano bus line; because it's much closer to the latter, it makes a good detour for a couple of hours of sightseeing before your arrival in Montepulciano. **TRA-IN** buses leave from Siena (1½ hrs, L5,900) or Montepulciano (½ hr, L8,000) about four times per day. Buy bus tickets at the nearby bar.

ELBA

The Greeks, Etruscans, and Romans once came to Elba for its iron ore, and Napoléon was confined here after his disastrous Russian campaign. Today European tourists come in droves for the 147 km (91 mi) of coastline, crystal-clear water, green interior, and all-night discos, making the island one of Italy's most popular—and expensive—destinations in July and August. If you've seen all the Tuscan hill towns, churches, and art treasures you care to see for awhile, Elba is the answer. The island's main ferry landing, Portoferraio, is only an hour from the mainland. If timed correctly, a trip from Florence or Pisa could take as little as three hours. Finding accommodations in July and August can be a nightmare: plan ahead. The rest of the year, tourists clear out and the island becomes more affordable.

COMING AND GOING

To reach Portoferraio, the island's transit hub, take the ferry from the mainland town of **Piombino.** Trains heading south on the coastal route from Pisa to Rome stop at Campiglia Marittima; from here take a train to **Piombino Marittima** (tel. 0565/226017), right next to the docks. At the port, you can choose from two ferry lines: **Navarma/Moby Lines** (Piombino, P. Premuda 13, tel. 0565/221212; Portoferraio, V. Elba 4, tel. 0565/914133) and **Toremar** (Piombino, P. Premuda 13–14, tel. 0565/31100; Portoferraio, Calata Italia 22, tel. 0565/918080). The standard cost is L10,000–L14,000 per person for the pleasant hour-long trip.

GETTING AROUND

Mopeds and mountain bikes give you the freedom to scout beaches off the bus routes without wasting too much time or energy. You can rent them almost anywhere and can often return them somewhere else; prices peak from mid-June to late August. One of the best rental shops is **Two Wheels Network Motonoleggio** (in Portoferraio next to bus station, tel. 0565/914666), with branches in Marina di Campo, Lacona, Porto Azzurro, and Marciana Marina, among others. Bring your rail pass or HI card for a 20% discount.

During July and August the shop rents mopeds for L42,000 per day or L189,000 per week if you reserve in advance (if you don't, it's L294,000) and mountain bikes for L30,000 a day or L210,000 per week. If you want to circumnavigate Elba by sea, you can rent a kayak (L28,000 per day). If you don't kayak, they'll teach you, but you must be over 18 and leave a L100,000 credit-card deposit. Prices drop in low season.

BY BUS • Buses run from Portoferraio's **bus station** (V. Elba 20, ½ block from port, tel. 0565/914392) all over the island. Frequent buses go to Marina di Campo, Marciana Marina, and Porto Azzurro; a ticket to any of the three costs L3,500, and the trips from town to town average about half an hour. The station offers the island's only luggage storage (L2,500 per bag), open daily 8–1:30 and 4–6:30. Buy bus tickets at any of the many bars around the island.

AFTER DARK

The discos in the hills are the places to be after midnight, but they are not easily reached on foot. The two places to aim for are side by side on the Portoferraio–Procchio road, in the town of Capannone. **Club 64** (tel. 0565/969988) looks like a palace and has an outdoor dance floor; **Norman's Club** (tel. 0565/969896) has the same crowd in slightly less swanky surroundings. Both charge a L20,000 cover. In the off-season, call ahead to find out what nights they will be closed. If you just want to hang out and have a drink or two, finding bars along the water's edge isn't difficult.

OUTDOOR ACTIVITIES

Tourist offices have info and maps of the island's main roads and walking paths. The best hike leads up to Monte Capanne from Marciana Marina (*see below*). Major resort beaches, particularly Marina di Campo and Porto Azzurro, are centers for water sports, but only during peak months. For windsurfing, snorkeling, or boat rentals, look for signs along any beachfront or for brochures at the tourist office. If you want to try scuba diving, a good place is in Marina di Campo, called **OndaSub** (V. Roma 93, tel. 0565/977058; open daily 9–1 and 3–7:30). A dive with instructor and equipment goes for L50,000.

PORTOFERRAIO

From a distance, Portoferraio looks like a lovely seaside town, with stone houses angling to the sea and dramatic hills rising in all directions. A closer look reveals an overcommercialized strip of pricey bars and tourist traps. In any case, Portoferraio will be your jumping-off point, as all ferries from Piombino pull in here. The picturesque centro storico and the two forts overlooking the town are worth a twilight stroll, and the **Museo Civico Archeologico** (Fortezza della Linguella, tel. 0565/937370; admission L4,000) is good for a peek into the area's ancient culture, with Etruscan and Roman archaeological finds from land and sea.

The **tourist information office** (tel. 0565/914671; open daily in summer 8–8, shorter hrs off-season) is near the port, as is the **Associazione Albergatori** (tel. 0565/914754, Mon.–Sat. 9–1 and 3–7), which offers commission-free hotel reservations.

Elba is definitely the place to suffer exile in style. Poor Napoléon, sequestered in 1814 after becoming a bit too ambitious, suffered immensely while here: he had two villas in Elba and ruled over the entire island during his exile. One of his houses, **Villa dei Mulini** (V. Villa Mulini, tel. 0565/915846), lies right above Portoferraio in the old part of town. His "country" estate, the **Villa Napoleonica** (tel. 0565/914688; open weekdays 9–7:30, Mon.–Sat. 9–7, Sun. 9–1, shorter hours in winter), in San Martino, is only about 5 km (3 mi) away. The location in the foothills is exquisite: the break in the surrounding mountains provides a breathtaking view of Portoferraio and the bay from the house's upper level. The interior is not much to write home about, although the very short bed is a convincing sign that he actually did live here. From Portoferraio take Bus 1 (L1,500 one-way) to San Martino; by moped, follow the road to Procchio and turn left at the sign to San Martino. An L8,000 ticket includes same-day admission to both villas.

WHERE TO SLEEP AND EAT

The two best budget hotels in town are the **Elbana** (Salita Cosimo de' Medici 2, tel. and fax 0565/914245), in the heart of the centro storico, where doubles with bath start at L80,000 (low season) and move on up to L105,000 (high season), and **Nobel** (V. Manganaro 72, tel. 0565/915217, fax 0565/915415), which has doubles with bath for around L120,000 in the high season, L80,000 in low season. A good spot for fish is **Osteria Libertaria** (Portoferraio calata Matteotti 12, no phone; closed Mon. off-season).

MARINA DI CAMPO

The nearly perfect sandy beach at Marina di Campo is obviously the town's major draw—the other island cities generally have less comfortable, rocky shores. Mountains plunge into the sea on all sides of the gorgeous bay, but despite the long stretch of coast, you can expect major crowds in high season. The **tourist office** (tel. 0565/977969) is open June through September, Monday and Wednesday through Saturday 8–8, and Tuesday and Sunday 8–2.

WHERE TO SLEEP AND EAT

Good budget options by the beach are **Hotel Lido** (V. Mascagni 29, tel. 0565/976040), where doubles with bath, breakfast included, cost L110,000 during high season, and **Hotel Elba** (V. Mascagni 51, tel. 0565/976224, fax 0565/977280; cash only), where a double with bath goes for about L122,000 in high season, half pensione included; prices are considerably lower off season. Three side-by-side camp-grounds are a 20-minute trek from the bus station (follow the yellow signs), but once there, you'll want to stay for a while. **La Foce** (tel. 0565/976456; open year-round) is on hard dirt above the beach rather than right on the water. **Del Mare** (tel. 0565/976237; closed Nov.–Dec.) is crowded with motor homes but has shade and charges various prices depending on the season: expect to pay L11,000 for a small tent, and anywhere between L11,000 and L19,000 per person. Both sites have showers. From early June through September, reserve well ahead of time.

Food is easy to find along Via Roma, one block up from the beach, and on its extension, Via Marconi. In addition to the numerous markets, several fruit trucks line the street in summer, selling incredibly fresh produce. The best place to pick up prepared pasta dishes is the **Rosticceria e Gastronomia** (V. Roma 19, tel. 0565/977304), which also sells large roast chickens stuffed with rosemary (L12,000). The only other relatively affordable joint is **Canabis** (V. Roma 41–43, tel. 0565/977555; closed winter). Aside from the atmosphere, which is reminiscent of Cabo San Lucas, this place is pretty good—beer on tap is L3,500, and tasty crepes are L7,000. They also host regular tequila blowout shindigs during the summer.

AFTER DARK

Have a cocktail with a view at one of the swinging "American bars" that line Via Marconi and the western edge of the waterfront. They stay open late, but most will gouge you for a drink. A small beer at **La Ruota** (P. della Vittoria 2, tel. 0565/978011), however, is only L4,000, and you'll get to relax on comfy bamboo chairs beneath large canvas umbrellas. If you aren't ready to go to bed yet, **Tinello** (Località La Casina, tel. 0565/976645) stays open until dawn.

MARCIANA MARINA

Much of the activity on Elba hovers around Marciana Marina, a lively and accommodating town. It has a dandy waterfront area and is conveniently near the region's main attraction, Monte Capanne (*see below*). Right in the center of town is the **Soggiorno Tagliaferro** (V. Principe Amedeo 10, tel. 0565/99029; cash only), a little villa a block from the beach with doubles at L75,000 in high season, L50,000 in low. From the bus stop, make the first right. You can get a good crepe at **Creperie L'Onda** (V. Principe Amedeo 4, no phone), which has both sweet and savory varieties. Or treat yourself to some fine fish at **Osteria del Noce** (V. Madonna 27, tel. 0565/901284). *Primi* loaded with fish hover at around L15,000, and *secondi* around L20,000.

OUTDOOR ACTIVITIES

Monte Capanne, the island's highest point (3,342 ft), is prime hiking territory. From the top, you can look out over the entire island, west to Sardinia, and east to the mainland. To walk it, catch a bus from Marciana Marina toward Poggio, a town with an abundance of cultural happenings, and ask the driver to let you off near the hiking trail; or take the bus to Marciana, which is at the base of one of the hiking trails. The walk up takes about two hours. The alternative is a steep (in many aspects) cable car (tel. 0565/901020, L12,000 one-way, L20,000 round-trip) that runs several times a day to the mountaintop from just above Marciana, the hillside sister town of Marciana Marina. Take the bus to Marciana and ask the driver to drop you off outside town by the cable car. At the summit of the Monte is a little church next to a font of blessedly cool spring water.

UMBRIA
AND
LE MARCHE

BY REBECCA LIM

UPDATED BY JEFFREY KENNEDY

entral Italy does not begin and end with Tuscany—the pastoral, hilly provinces of Umbria and Le Marche (The Marches) pick up where the well-traveled route between Florence and Rome leaves off. Extending from the middle of the peninsula all the way to the Adriatic, the area's remarkable landscape is rich with velvety plains, sparkling lakes, and dramatic crags. Relatively untainted by industry, its medieval towns and ancient remains lie amid stretches of thriving fields and vineyards. Aside from visual allure, these regions have more than their fair share of cultural appeal, too. Many towns sponsor acclaimed festivals and are graced with world-renowned architecture. Though growing in popularity, Umbria's bounty still goes unappreciated by most visitors to Italy, and the off-the-beaten-path treasures of Le Marche are even less known. Steep and twisting roads lead to well-preserved medieval towns like Urbino and Ascoli Piceno before settling down to the sandy beaches on the Adriatic coast. Despite a few crowded seaside resorts, the region as a whole rewards those who venture in, proffering sunset-dappled villages, brilliant skies, and wind-churned fields peppered with golden sunflowers and red poppies.

Touring Italy during the year 2000 will involve numerous unknowables. The availability of lodging, for example, will be anybody's guess, as will the price charged for just about everything. This will hold particularly true in areas associated with Church spiritual history, such as Umbria and Le Marche. Unprecedented crowds are expected in such pilgrimage sites, and almost every spare room will be let, possibly at greatly inflated rates in many cases. In any event, prices from year to year normally rise 5%–20% for restaurants, hotels, and trains. Bus tickets and entrance fees to monuments tend to remain more stable.

UMBRIA

Tuscany's quiet sister Umbria has a wealth of extraordinary hill towns connected by sinuous roads lined with olive groves and vineyards. Looking out the train, car, or bus window at the passing densely wooded valleys and verdant crops, you can easily see why the region is often called Italy's green heart. Three thousand years of history are rooted in Umbria's fertile soil. The region takes its name from the Umbrii, a tribe that settled in central Italy around 1000 BC, though there is much more evidence of the Etruscans, in the form of necropolises and wells. The Romans made their mark later, fighting barbarian

KEY
—|— Rail Lines

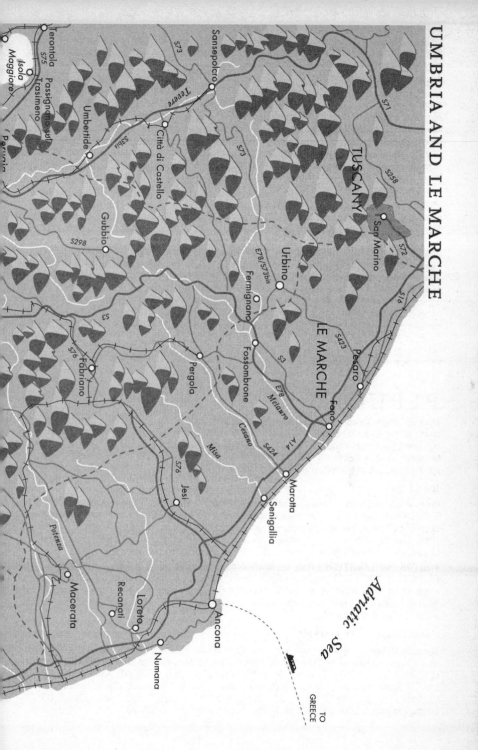

UMBRIA AND LE MARCHE

TUSCANY

LE MARCHE

Adriatic Sea

TO GREECE

Isola Maggiore

Terontola
Passignano sul Trasimeno
S75
(Perugia

Sansepolcro
S73
Tevere

Umbertide
Città di Castello
S3bis
S73

Gubbio
S298

San Marino
S258

Urbino
E78/S73bis
Fermignano

Fossombrone
Metauro
S3
E78
S423

Pesaro
S16
A14
Fano

Fabriano
S76
S3

Pergola
Cesano
Misa

Marotta
S424
Senigallia

Jesi
S76

Potenza

Macerata
Recanati
Loreto

Ancona

Numana

255

and Byzantine invasions over several centuries. But Umbria's towns are most apparently relics of the Middle Ages, when the region was torn apart by the Guelph-Ghibelline conflict (a scrap between supporters of the papacy and champions of the Holy Roman emperor). The towns reveal mazes of twisting alleys lined with somber, amply fortified palazzi.

Perugia is the lively provincial capital, a russet-color university town known for its cultural life and its chocolate. It is well situated to serve as a base for day excursions. The only hill town with heavy tourist traffic is Assisi, home of the mystic St. Francis (1181–1226) and an important pilgrimage site since medieval times. Also worth a visit are Orvieto, with its archaeological caverns and a mammoth cathedral; the elegant, austere towns of Todi and Spello; Spoleto, home of Europe's most celebrated international arts festival; and dour Gubbio, one of Italy's best-preserved medieval villages. Buses are usually the best way to get around, as trains often leave you and your luggage with a long uphill trudge to the town center. You might also consider springing for a small car (Italian car rental prices are shocking—do it stateside before you leave to get the best deal; a little over $200 a week should be possible). That way, you could also negotiate a weekly rate at a lodging in Perugia and easily cover all of Umbria in relaxed day-tripping.

You'll find beautiful traditional handicrafts here in superabundance, especially ceramics. Every sloping, cobbled byway in almost every town has its boutiques with colorful pottery spilling out into your path. Two of the most important ceramics towns with workshops still operating since medieval times are Gubbio and Orvieto. Gubbio has been famous since the Renaissance **SINCE "MEDIEVAL TIMES" OR SINCE "RENAISSANCE"; WHICH IS IT?**for its uniquely iridescent ruby-red glaze, Orvieto for its harmonious geometrics. But if you're an avid collector or gift-giver, the unprepossessing, easily-accessible town of Deruta (a stone's throw from Perugia and Assisi, right off the main highway between Perugia and Todi) is the place for a shopping pit-stop. It's practically nothing but pottery workshops and their adjoining showroom-warehouses (most open on Sundays in season), but it's authentic, with an 800-year tradition of Italy-wide importance. You'll find every sort of ancestral design and shape—along with useful contemporary adaptations—and if you buy more than one or two pieces, be sure to ask for *lo sconto,* the equally historic discount. Most stores also ship. Among the other time-honored handicrafts throughout the region are fancifully embroidered linens (unicorns, stags, wild boar, rampant lions, flowers, and so on), lace, wood carvings, and wrought iron.

PERUGIA

Much of Umbria's lifeblood courses through Perugia, its bustling capital. A 1,650-ft-high Etruscan hill town that has endured barbarian conquests and medieval chaos, Perugia—with its massive city gates and grand palaces and churches—still feels like a much-coveted spot. Its panoramic views are spectacular on all sides, and its importance as an intellectual and cultural center is long-standing. A thriving international student population and a world-renowned jazz festival make this town's joints really jump.

BASICS

MAIL AND PHONES • Perugia's **post office** (P. Matteotti 1, tel. 075/5720395; open Mon.–Sat. 8:10–7, Sun. 8:30–5:30) has a currency exchange machine (no commission) for use when the banks are closed. Self-service **Telecom** offices have phone-card-vending machines and phone books. There's one at the train station (P. Vittorio Veneto 8; open Mon.–Sat. 8 AM–10 PM) and two in the town center (C. Mazzini 26, next to post office; C. Vannucci, off P. della Repubblica; both open daily 8 AM–10 PM).

VISITOR INFORMATION • Perugia's **tourist office** (P. IV Novembre 3, in Palazzo dei Priori, tel. 075/5736458 or 075/5723327; English spoken; open daily 9:00–1:00 and 4:00–6:30, Sun. 9–1) hands out a rudimentary map, hotel listings, and transport schedules. Pick up a copy of *W Perugia What, Where, When* (L1,000) from a newsstand—its monthly calendar of events, printed in Italian with some English, is a gold mine of information.

COMING AND GOING

The **train station** is below the town, at the bottom of the hill (P. Vittorio Veneto). There is a nationwide train information **toll-free** number: 1478/88088, but you'll have to manage in Italian. Trains go to Rome (17 daily, 3 hrs, L18,000; change at Foligno), Florence (14 daily, 2 hrs, L16,000), Assisi (hourly, 30 min, L3,100), Spello (17 daily, 35 min, L3,900), and Spoleto (17 daily, 1 hr, L5,900). Six trains leave daily for Castiglione del Lago (1 hr 10 min, L5,900), Passignano (1½ hrs, L4,700), and Orvieto (2 hrs, L10,100). **Luggage storage** (L5,000 per piece for 12 hrs) is open daily 6:20 AM–8:20 PM.

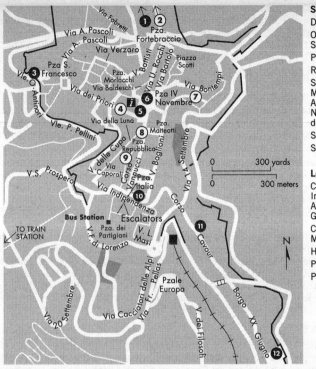

Sights ●
Duomo, **6**
Oratorio di
San Bernardino, **3**
Palazzo dei Priori, **5**
Rocca Paolina, **10**
San Domenico/
Museo
Archeologico
Nazionale
dell'Umbria, **11**
San Pietro, **12**
Sant'Angelo, **1**

Lodging ○
Centro
Internazionale di
Accoglienza per La
Gioventù Hostel, **7**
Convento di
Monteripido, **2**
Hotel Etruria, **8**
Pensione Anna, **4**
Piccolo Hotel, **9**

Long-distance buses depart from Piazza dei Partigiani, just beyond Piazza Italia (an escalator leads from Piazza Italia to Via Baglioni, which connects to Piazza dei Partigiani). Buy tickets from the **ASP** booth (P. dei Partigiani, tel. 075/5731707; open daily 6:15 AM–7:45 PM, on Sun. buy your ticket on board). Eight buses go to Gubbio (70 min, L7,400), six to Todi (1½ hrs, L9,200), five to Passignano (40 min, L5,000), and seven to Assisi (1 hr, L5,000). Service is limited on Sunday. A "green number" (*numero verde*) provides Umbrian public transport info in Italian, **toll-free** from anywhere in Italy: 1675/12141.

GETTING AROUND

City buses run frequently between 5:15 AM and 9:30 PM. Buy tickets (L1,000) at the **ATAM booths** outside the train station and in Piazza Italia. From the station, Buses 20, 26, 27, 28, 29, 33 or 36 will get you to **Piazza Italia,** though Buses 33 and 36 go first to Piazza Matteotti. Once you arrive up top, finding your way around is tricky, as the tourist office's map excludes many streets and gives no indication of how hilly the town is. **Corso Vannucci** runs through the center between Piazza Italia and **Piazza IV Novembre. Piazza Matteotti** is close to the hostel. Both universities lie north of the center; **Università per Stranieri** (University for Foreigners) is off Piazza Fortebraccio; **Università degli Studi** is farther northwest.

WHERE TO SLEEP

UNDER L60,000 • Convento di Monteripido. If you manage the major hike to this Franciscan monastery outside the city walls, you'll feel like you're one step closer to heaven. On the second-highest point in Perugia, it has a stunning view, beautiful gardens, a small church, a library, and a bar. Friars mill about and students from Perugia's universities come and go. Doubles, all with bath, go for L50,000. Unmarried couples sleep in separate rooms. *V. Monteripido 8, 06125, tel. 075/42210 or 075/40679. Reservations required: ask for Signora Vincenza, weekdays 7:30–noon and 3–6:30, Sat. 7:30–noon. From train station, take Bus CS or CD (last bus at 9:20) to P. Fortebraccio; from P. Italia, take C. Vannucci through P. IV Novembre and go down V. V. Rocchi (street farthest left) to P. Fortebraccio; walk northwest on C. Garibaldi; it's 1 km (½ mi) outside city gate; head up "steps" off V. Monteripido. 34 rooms with bath. Cash only.*

Pensione Anna. Well-worn antiques and solicitous proprietors make the Anna feel more like a home than a hotel. You get your own set of building keys, and you can hang out in the pleasantly decorated common rooms. Doubles (L60,000 without bath, L80,000 with bath) have glass doors with curtains and ample towels. The owners also run the Pensione Europa nearby. *V. dei Priori 48, off C. Vannucci, 06123, tel. and fax 075/5736304. 11 rooms, 7 with bath. Cash only.*

UNDER L90,000 • Hotel Etruria. Smack in the center of town, this small hotel with vaulted brick ceilings dating to the 14th century and comfy doubles (L86,000 with bath) offers medieval atmosphere and convenient access to Perugia's hot spots. *V. della Luna 21, off C. Vannucci, 06121, tel. 075/5723730. 8 rooms, 6 with bath. 1:15 AM curfew. Cash only.*

Piccolo Hotel. One block off central Corso Vannucci, this small hotel offers doubles for L75,000 with bath—two have a balcony over the quiet medieval street. *V. Bonazzi 25, 06123, tel. 075/5722987. 10 rooms, 8 with bath. Cash only. Closed Dec. 25–Jan. 25.*

HOSTEL • Centro Internazionale di Accoglienza per La Gioventù. Perugia's hostel is in a terrific location, minutes from the Duomo and Piazza IV Novembre, and has kitchen facilities, a library, large bathrooms, hot showers, a big TV lounge, and a terrace with a spectacular view. There are 20 rooms with bunks. Beds cost L18,000 a night, sheets L2,000 extra. A three-week maximum stay is imposed. *V. Bontempi 13, 06122, tel. and fax 075/5722880. 90 beds, 22 baths. Midnight curfew, lockout 9:30–4. Reception open 7:30–9:30 and 4–11. Cash only. Closed mid-Dec.–mid-Jan.*

CAMPING • Camping Il Rocolo. Campers here set up among rows of trees that line a terraced hillside. The trees are skinny and shade is scarce, but the spot is peaceful, and the odd, round indoor-outdoor bathrooms have hot water and toilet paper—scarce commodities in Italian campgrounds. You'll pay L8,500 per person and L7,000 per tent site July–August, slightly less in the off months. There are a market and a small bar that serves cold snacks. *V. della Trinità 1, 06100, tel. 075/5178550. From station or P. Matteotti (P. Italia on Sun.), Bus 36 to Colle della Trinità; follow yellow signs uphill about 1 km (½ mi). 100 spaces. Midnight curfew. Cash only. Closed mid-Sept.–mid-June.*

WHERE TO EAT

Regional specialties flood Perugia's markets and restaurants, including a plethora of pork products and the expensive *tartufo* (truffle), a wild fungus that has a cult following. Among Perugia's wines are the white Torre di Giano, the red Rubesco, and Vin Santo, a sweet dessert wine. Look also for bottles of *rosoli*, pastel-color liqueurs made in Umbrian monasteries (particularly Franciscan) that come in every fruit flavor imaginable—and even mushroom flavors.

For produce and fresh deli specialties, get it all done at once on **Piazza Matteotti.** At Number 18/A, the **Mercato Coperto** bustles weekdays 7–1:30, Saturday 7–1:30 and 4:30–7:30. Otherwise fill your cornucopia at Number 15, **Coop Le Delizie** (tel. 075/5722937; open Mon.–Sat. 9–8), with great wine and sausage; or hit the surprisingly affordable deli counter for a mouthwatering assortment of cheeses, quiches, stuffed vegetables, and salads. Pick up a pack of grains or legumes for someone back home at **Spezeria Bavicchi** (No. 32, tel. 075/5728314). Then follow your nose next door to the bakery **Ceccarini** (No. 16, tel. 075/5721960) for a huge selection of breads including whole wheat, flaky croissants, and incredible floral renditions in the window.

UNDER L10,000 • Pizzeria L'Era Nuova. This place makes the biggest pizzas in town and serves them in a small, crowded dining room where you're likely to sit at a long table with other guests. Pizzas cost L5,000–L10,000. Delve into a special creation like the *perla nera*, with mozzarella, Parmesan, and coveted Umbrian truffles (L9,500). *V. Baldo 6, off P. della Repubblica, no phone. Closed Fri.*

UNDER L15,000 • Brizi Ristorante. Perhaps the cheapest truffles you'll ever eat can be found atop Brizi's homespun cheese ravioli (L10,500). This small restaurant, brightly lighted with a low brick ceiling, is popular with students from both universities. It's no wonder, given its low-priced *piatti secondi* (around L7,000–L12,000). *V. Fabretti 77, tel. 075/5721386. From P. Danti, take V. Rocchi to P. Fortebraccio; turn left on V. Fabretti. Closed Tues.*

Osteria del Gambero. Ready for Umbrian cuisine in refined gourmet guise? This quiet restaurant will satisfy any longing for fancy garnishes and multiple courses. Try the *umbricelli* (squiggly spaghetti) with a puréed eggplant-and-porcini-mushroom sauce (L10,000) or the grilled pork with pine nuts and rosemary. *V. Baldeschi 17, tel. 075/5735461. From P. IV Novembre, take V. della Volte through P. Cavalotti to V. Baldeschi. Credit cards OK. Closed Mon. No lunch.*

UNDER L20,000 • Osteria Il Gufo. The best place in town to eat late into the night is this old-style osteria. Hearty local dishes are prepared in the open kitchen. *V. della Viola 18, tel. 075/5734126. Cash only. No lunch. Closed Sun., Mon. and Aug.*

Ristorante Vecchia Perusia. This is a nice little restaurant for a three- or four-course splurge. Specialties include tagliatelle *ai tartufi* (L16,000) or *agli asparagi* (with asparagus, L10,000). Cave in to your desire for full debauchery with the homemade *panna cotta* (custard). *V. U. Rocchi 9 (Arco Etrusco), farthest street left off P. Danti, just north of Duomo, tel. 075/5725900. Closed Sun.*

Enoteca Gio' Arte e Vini. This is a great place to sample local and national wines (more than 800 labels), with more than a few available by the glass. Attractive plates of local food—cheese ravioli with pumpkin cream sauce (all pastas and soups are L12,000) and lamb cubes (*bocconcini di agnello*) with dried tomatoes and artichokes (L17,000)—are served up, too. A daily menu, with choices, runs L34,000. A taste of several selected Italian wines is a deal at L8,000. *V. R. d'Andreotto 19, tel. 075/5731100. Closed Sun.*

WORTH SEEING

Wide, elegant, pedestrians-only Corso Vannucci runs from Piazza Italia up to the main square, **Piazza IV Novembre,** and its remarkable 13th-century **Fontana Maggiore.** Three nymphs decorate the head of this fountain (under what seems to be perpetual restoration) designed by Perugian Fra Bevignate and sculpted by Nicola and Giovanni Pisano. Water spills into a basin ringed by 24 figures; below it, panels depict the months of the year and scenes from the Bible and *Aesop's Fables.* Lining the piazza are the **Duomo** and the **Palazzo dei Priori.**

South of Corso Vannucci, the **Rocca Paolina** (open daily 8–7; admission free), a fortress partly destroyed and rebuilt three times, has been covered over in places by the city that sprouted up around it. The subterranean 15th-century **Via Baglioni** runs through the fortress; enter it from Via Marzia or by escalator from Piazza Italia—an oddly modern ride through ancient architecture. On one side of the fortress lies the **Porta Marzia,** a 2nd-century BC Etruscan city gate.

The famed chocolate-hazelnut Bacio (kiss) candies, wrapped in paper inscribed with multilingual love messages, are made at the Perugina factory and museum (V. San Sisto 207, tel. 075/52761), in nearby San Sisto. Chocoholics welcome.

Perugia's sprawling, hilly northern sector is home to two universities and allows unparalleled views. From the Duomo, take Via del Sole, which leads into Via delle Prome to reach Piazza Scotti. From here a staircase winds uphill to the picturesque **Vecchio Acquedotto,** an elevated walkway that soars over rooftops and offers unique views of otherwise hidden gardens. The aqueduct-turned-footpath was built to carry water to the Fontana Maggiore. Nearby Via Rocchi, which leads to Piazza Fortebraccio, dips under the huge **Arco Etrusco d'Augusto,** an Etruscan gate built in the 3rd century BC. At the end of Corso Garibaldi, **Porta Sant'Angelo** and its 14th-century tower mark the edge of the *centro storico* (historic center).

DUOMO • The facade of the 15th-century Gothic cathedral was never finished, but the marble design on the lower wall facing the piazza hints at how spectacular it might have looked. Inside, there's Federico Barocci's *Deposition*—his finest work—and a chapel containing the Virgin's wedding ring, a hunk of onyx Mary supposedly wore in her earthly marriage to Joseph. It's kept in an elaborate reliquary of 15 locked boxes (the keys are, of course, held by 15 different people), and it's removed twice a year, on the second-to-last Sunday in January and on July 30. *P. IV Novembre, tel. 075/5723832. Open Mon.–Sat. 7–noon and 4–6:45, Sun. 8–1 and 4–6:45.*

ORATORIO DI SAN BERNARDINO • Next to the church of San Francesco al Prato, now just a facade, shines the Oratorio di San Bernardino. Its marvelous 15th-century exterior of pink, gray, and white marble makes up for the faceless Duomo. It is the work of Florentine sculptor Agostino di Duccio, famous for the Tempio Malatestiano in Rimini (*see* Chapter 7). Duccio completed the oratorio in just 10 years and then stayed in Perugia for the rest of his life. *P. San Francesco, off V. dei Priori. Open daily 8–noon and 4–7.*

PALAZZO DEI PRIORI • This has been Perugia's town hall since the 13th century. The decorations on the white travertine facade symbolize the town's past power: the griffin is the mascot of the city; the lion denotes the city's allegiance to the Guelph (papal) cause. Both figures support the heavy chains of the gates of Siena, which fell to Perugian forces in 1358. To the right and above the tourist office is the striking and frescoed **Sala dei Notari** (admission free; open daily 9–11 and 3–7), once an assembly hall for lawyers.

Back on Corso Vannucci is the main entrance to Palazzo dei Priori. Go upstairs to the well-organized **Galleria Nazionale dell'Umbria.** The 33-room collection begins with gleaming medieval polyptychs and crucifixes, then segues into early Renaissance paintings by native Umbrian artists, including a multi-paneled Pinturicchio altarpiece. Works of Fra Angelico, Agostino di Duccio, Taddeo di Bartolo, and Piero della Francesca are also on display. *C. Vannucci 19, P. IV Novembre, tel. 075/5741247. Admission L8000. Open Mon.–Sat. 9–7, Sun. 9–1, closed 1st Mon. of month.*

The two buildings next door served as guild headquarters for centuries. The merchants met in the intricately paneled **Collegio della Mercanzia** (C. Vannucci 15), the bankers and money lenders in the especially impressive **Collegio del Cambio** (C. Vannucci 25). The latter contains masterful Renaissance frescoes by Perugino depicting not only the Nativity and the Transfiguration but also figures representing Classical virtues intended to inspire the bankers. On the right walls are the prophets and sibyls, thought to be in part painted by Perugino's most famous pupil, Raphael, whose hand, the experts say, is most apparent in the figure of Fortitude. Perugino's self-portrait is on the left wall (he's wearing the red cap). *Admission L6,000 for both rooms, or L2,000 for the Collegio del Mercanzia and L5,000 for the Collegio del Cambio. Open Mar.–Oct., Mon.–Sat. 9–12:30 and 2:30–5:30, Sun. 9–12:30; Nov.–Feb., Tues.–Sat. 8–2, Sun. 9–12:30.*

SAN DOMENICO • The church of San Domenico, Umbria's largest, has the same layout as the Duomo: a nave flanked by two aisles and ceilings that rise to impressive heights throughout. The Gothic exterior gives way to a spartan, remodeled interior, which has seen better days. The frescoes are peeling, but the apse, brightened by one of Italy's largest stained-glass windows (75 ft tall) is still in pretty good shape. San Domenico's claim to fame is the handsome tomb of Pope Benedict XI, who died in Perugia in 1304 after eating poisoned figs; it's in the first chapel to the right of the altar. The **Museo Archeologico Nazionale dell'Umbria,** inside the cloister to the left of the double staircase, displays a solid collection of local artifacts—funerary urns, bones, weapons, and jewelry—that reveal Perugia's roots as an Etruscan and then Roman town. There is also a display of prehistoric pieces found in the area. *P. Bruno, off C. Cavour. Museo Archeologico: tel. 075/5727141. Admission L4,000. Open Mon.–Sat. 9–1:30 and 2:30–7, Sun. 9–1.*

SAN PIETRO • You can't miss the spire of this church piercing Perugia's skyline in the south end of town. Three courtyards with porticoes link the various parts of the complex, which was started in the 10th century and finished about 700 years later. In the 16th century, the elaborate portal was sculpted by the school of Agostino di Duccio. Look at the paintings in the sacristy, to the right of the altar: you'll find works by Perugino, Algardi, and members of the school of Parmigianino. *Borgo XX Giugno, tel. 075/34770. Follow C. Cavour through Porta San Pietro. Open daily 7–noon and 3–6.*

SANT'ANGELO • The lawns in front of this 5th-century church, the oldest in Perugia, are good for napping or sunbathing. The large, round room inside—with mismatched columns taken from ruins of various pagan structures—deserves a look. *V. del Tempio off C. Garibaldi. Open Tues.–Sun. 9:30–noon and 3:30–7.*

FESTIVALS

In the second and third week of July, the whole city hums to the beat of the **Umbria Jazz Festival.** Such jazz heavies as Keith Jarrett, João Gilberto, Sonny Rollins, and Herbie Hancock roll into town. The piazzas, streets, clubs, and theaters brim with people gladly shelling out L15,000 to L50,000 per top-notch performance. A few events, like street parades with gospel groups and marching bands, and those performed in the Giardini Carducci, are free. For tickets call the festival organizers (tel. 075/5732432, fax 075/5722656; box office after May 5, 075/5730271). Pick up a pamphlet on who's playing at the tourist office (*see* Basics, *above*), or check out their Web site at www.krenet.it/uj. Beginning at the end of August, a week-long **International Puppet Festival** draws traditional and innovative masters from all over the world. And finally, if you're lucky enough to be in Perugia the third week of October, prepare to gorge at the annual **Chocolate Festival.** For information on either, contact the Perugia Tourist Office, tel. 075/5725341.

AFTER DARK

Nightlife is especially lively near the universities. The popular **Australian Pub** (V. del Verzaro 39, no phone; closed Mon.) serves L7,000 beers and is a good place to kick back with locals. Relax all day long at **Caffè Morlacchi** (P. Morlacchi 6, tel. 075/5721760; closed Sun.). For a wilder night out, head down the block to disco-pub **Domus Delirii** (V. Naspo 3, off P. Morlacchi, no phone), where DJs spin soul and hip-hop and students from both universities groove to live jazz. There's a cover charge (L5,000–L20,000 depending on the night), but flyers handed out around the universities will often get you in free. For late-night fun, grab a beer at **Asterix** (V. Guardabassi 4, off P. Morlacchi, tel. 075/5736827) or head to **La**

Terrazza (Mercato Coperto, P. Matteotti) for free music, films, theater, and lectures nightly in summer. If it's **cinema** you're after, check out films beneath the stars at the Giardini del Frontone (the EPT has the info) for everything from classic Italian art films to dubbed first-run American movies (L7,000–L8,000).

LAKE TRASIMENE

A low ring of mountains dotted with towns and castles surrounds Lake Trasimene (Lago Trasimeno), Perugino's birthplace (Pieve), and in ancient times where Hannibal's army massacred 16,000 Roman soldiers. Italy's fourth-largest lake spreads out amid the hazy hills of northwestern Umbria. Its fish-filled waters and a trio of islands in the center provide hiking, swimming and water sports, beaches, and excellent camping. **Isola Maggiore** is the most accessible island, and **Castiglione del Lago** and **Passignano sul Trasimeno** are the two main towns on the shore, both easily reached by train and bus. Buses stop closer to campgrounds than trains do and are the best way to get to the lake, but to go between the two towns, you'll have to hop on the ferry, as they're not connected by bus.

PASSIGNANO SUL TRASIMENO

Passignano makes a good base for exploring the lake—it's easy to reach and offers quick access to Isola Maggiore. The scenery may be better in Castiglione, but Passignano is plenty attractive, as it stretches along the lake with tree-lined streets and houses built into rugged cliffs. Like the rest of Lago Trasimeno, Passignano has avoided cultivating the slick air of a resort village, even though it's a popular tourist spot. Rent a **sailboat** at Sualzo (Lungolago L. Giappesi, L15,000 per hr). The friendly English-speaking **Pro Loco** folks (V. Roma 25, tel. 075/827635; open Tues.–Sat. 10–noon and 3–6, Sun. 10–noon) can answer questions about other beach activities and lodging options. To reach Pro Loco from the train station, go right on Via Giugno (the first street you hit), over the train tracks, and continue down Via Roma. To get to the beach, go farther down Via Roma, which becomes Via Pompili and will take you to the sandy shore.

COMING AND GOING • Passignano's **train station** (P. A. Buattini, tel. 1478/88088) has direct connections to Perugia (10–12 daily, 30 min, L3,400). Five **buses** come from Perugia Monday– Saturday (1 hr, L5,000). The bus stops on the waterfront near the ferry terminal (if you're headed for Isola Maggiore, this is the way to go). **Ferries** depart from the *imbarcadero* (loading dock) at the center of the waterfront off Via Pompili. Twelve ferries leave daily for Isola Maggiore (20 min, L8,500 round-trip) between 8:10 and 7:15. To reach Castiglione by boat, you must transfer at Isola Maggiore; buses don't run between the two coastal towns.

WHERE TO SLEEP AND EAT • Doubles go for L80,000 at **Albergo del Pescatore** (V. San Bernardino 5, tel. and fax 075/8296063), in the town center. Closer to the beach, **I Vecchi Tempi** (V. Europa 7, tel. 075/828095) has six clean rooms (doubles L60,000 with bath) and a restaurant serving fresh fish dishes, like spaghetti *allo scoglio* (with clams, mussels, and baby shrimp). Right on the beach, **Kursaal Campeggio** (V. Europa 41, tel. 075/828085; cash only; closed Nov.–Mar.) charges L9,000 per person and L14,500 per site; it has a restaurant, a private beach, hot showers, windsurfing, and paddle-boat rentals. There's also a three-star hotel, where a double costs L115,000. To get to the campsites and I Vecchi Tempi, follow Via Pompili out of town (it becomes Via Europa). For groceries hit **Sidis** (P. Trento e Trieste 3; open Mon.–Sat. 8–1 and 5–8).

CASTIGLIONE DEL LAGO

Castiglione, a walled town on a rocky promontory, is the most picturesque of the lakeside towns. The medieval **castle** and the Renaissance church of **Santa Maria Maddalena** create a stunning silhouette on hazy summer days. Castiglione's **tourist office** (P. Mazzini 10, tel. 075/9652484; open Mon.–Sat. 8:30–1 and 3:30–7, Sun. 9–1; closed Sun. off-season) will help with everything from getting a room to renting a Windsurfer for the day. **La Merangola** (Lido Arezzo, tel. 075/9652445) rents bikes (L10,000 per hr), canoes (L8,000 per hr), pedal boats (L10,000 per hr), and windsurfing equipment (L10,000 per hr) right alongside the lake from July through September. At night, groove to techno music at the beachside disco **La Sciaramada** (Lido Arezzo, no phone; cover L20,000).

COMING AND GOING • To reach Castiglione by train from Perugia (1 hr 10 min, L5,300), you must transfer in Terontola. Castiglione's **train station** (V. della Stazione, tel. 1478/88088) is outside the town center; there's no bus, so walk 25 minutes down Via Buozzi. **Buses** (call APM 075/5731707) run directly from Perugia (7 daily Mon.–Sat., L8,000), dropping you in Piazza Marconi. Castiglione's **ferry terminal** is next to the *lido comunale* (public beach) on Via Lungolago. Ferries leave daily between 8:50

SUPER 'SHROOMS

Tartufi *(truffles) are quite the culinary rage in Umbria, where they turn up in almost any course. The beloved fungi command an astronomical price—would you believe $300–$400 a pound?—but fortunately a little goes a long way, and you can sample the earthy, almost gamy delicacy without canceling the rest of your trip. Expect to pay about L15,000 extra to have a bit of truffle ever-so-thinly grated over your food.*

Most common in Umbria is the black variety (tartufo nero), and those found in winter are more prized than their summer equivalent. Out of season you can find truffles preserved in olive oil or ground into a paste. So pronounced is the truffle's emanation, you can have a truffle-flavored omelet without the truffle. Piled among eggs for a few hours, the truffle passes on its aroma through the shells.

Because truffles grow underground near oak tree roots, there is an art to finding the elusive lumps. Nowadays, specially trained dogs sniff out the gnarly goodies—and recently some dogs have been poisoned by rival truffle-hunters, so fierce is the competition—but according to tradition, sows in heat are the best sleuths. Whether truffles are rightly coveted for their pungent taste, exclusivity, or reputed powers as an aphrodisiac is up to you to sniff out.

and 5:25 for Isola Maggiore (30 min, L11,000 round-trip), where you can catch connections to other towns. For info call Passignano Tuoro (tel. 075/827157).

WHERE TO SLEEP AND EAT • On the same street as the train station, remodeled **Hotel Mona Lisa** (V. della Stazione 5/A, tel. and fax 075/951071) has sparkling doubles (L100,000), all with bath, balcony, and satellite TV. For a bit more there's also the **Duca della Corgna** (V. Bruno Buozzi 143, tel. 075/953238, fax 075/9652446); ask for one of the four rooms with a balcony. **Camping Listro** (V. Lungolago, Lido Arezzo, tel. 075/951193; cash only), a simple campground with a small beach, charges L7,000 per person and L7,000 per tent. It's a 25-minute walk to the imbarcadero and ferry terminal. Slide over to **Ristorante L'Acquario** (V. Vittorio Emanuele 69, off P. Mazzini, tel. 075/9652432; open noon–2:30 and 7–10:30; cash only; closed Wed. and Jan.–Feb.) for spaghetti or risotto with fresh fish from the lake (L8,500 each) or try *tegamaccio*, the local fish soup. If you'd rather shop for yourself, **Despar** (V. G. Leopardi 8, end of V. Buozzi) is close to the town center.

ISOLA MAGGIORE

Take an island vacation for a day in the heart of landlocked Umbria on Isola Maggiore. The charming forested island has a tiny "main street" and a large salamander population. You won't find any beaches, cars, or hip water sports—about 40 families make a living here from lace-making, fishing, and tourism. The winding footpath that circles the island will take you to the romantic, crumbling **Castello Guglielmi**, an ex-Franciscan monastery turned faux ancient castle by the Guglielmi family in the 19th century; thankfully, it's closed to the public. Climb to the Gothic church of **San Michele Arcangelo** atop the island to check out a cemetery and enjoy yet another gorgeous view. On your way up, look for the chapel erected on the spot where St. Francis prayed and fasted for 40 days during Lent in 1211. For transportation info, *see* Passignano sul Trasimeno *and* Castiglione del Lago, *above*.

GUBBIO

Despite its typically cataclysmic past, it's easy to see how Gubbio came to be called the "city of silence." Tucked into a mountainous corner of Umbria, the placid, walled city watches over green countryside. And despite some increased attention from tourists, the handsome gray buildings and narrow cobblestone streets preserve the town's medieval air. Just don't come looking for peace and quiet during the fast and furious festivals in May (*see below*).

Gubbio is an easy day trip from Perugia. When you get here, two tourist offices can help plan your visit: the privately owned **Easy Gubbio** (V. della Repubblica 11, tel. 075/9220066), open daily 8 AM–10 PM, and the regional **tourist office** (P. Oderisi 6, tel. 075/9220693 or 075/9220790) open weekdays 8–1 and 3:30–6:30 (3–6 in winter), Saturday 9–1 and 3:30–6:30 (3–6 in winter), and Sunday 9:30–12:30. To get to the latter from Piazza Quaranta Martiri, head up Via della Repubblica and turn right on Corso Garibaldi.

COMING AND GOING

Gubbio doesn't have a train station; you come and go by Perugia's **ASP** buses. Nine buses daily (four on Sunday) shuttle between Perugia's Piazza dei Partigiani (1 hr 10 min, L7,400) and Gubbio's **Piazza Quaranta Martiri,** a public garden named in remembrance of 40 citizens murdered by the Nazis in 1944. Buy tickets in advance at the Easy Gubbio office (*see above*) or at the newsstand in Piazza Quaranta Martiri. When you arrive, follow Via della Repubblica uphill to **Piazza della Signoria** (a.k.a. Piazza Grande) and take in the view.

According to tradition, Gubbio certifies as crazy anyone who runs circles around the fountain in Piazza Bargello (one block from Piazza della Signoria) while being splashed with its water.

WHERE TO SLEEP

You can easily explore Gubbio in a day, but if you want to hang around, reasonable accommodations are available. Two campgrounds, **Villa Ortoguidone** (L15,000 per person, L15,000 per tent) and **Città di Gubbio** (L10,000 per person, L10,000 per tent), occupy the same complex outside town (V. Perugina, tel. and fax 075/9272037) but are tough to reach without a car. The Gubbio–Perugia bus will drop you 1 km (½ mi) away; ask the driver. Central **Locanda del Duca** (V. Piccardi 1, off P. Quaranta Martiri, tel. 075/9277753) has simple doubles for L63,000 (L75,000 with bath), breakfast included. Even better is the **Hotel Dei Consoli** (V. dei Consoli 59, tel. 075/9273335), where a good-size double with bath will run you L75,000.

WHERE TO EAT

The specialty shop **Bartolini Produzione Propria di Prodotti Gastronomici** (V. Mastro Giorgio, tel. 075/9277579) serves stuffed to-go sandwiches for L4,000–L6,000. Get the lowdown on truffles here and find a vast array of picnic supplies, wine, honey, Franciscan liqueurs, marmalades, and pastas daily 9–1 and 2:30–8. **Ristorante Fabiani** (P. Quaranta Martiri 26/A, tel. 075/9274639; closed Tues.) is elegant yet accessible, with an outdoor patio and tremendous views of Gubbio. Try their risotto with basil and pecorino cheese, L13,000. **Trattoria San Martino** (P. Giordano Bruno 6, tel. 075/9273251; open 12:15–3 and 7–11; closed Tues.) serves gnocchi *ai funghi* (with mushrooms) and other *primi piatti* (first courses, L8,000 and up) on an ivy-canopied patio. You can get pizza *a taglio* (by the slice) on Via della Repubblica, near Piazza Quaranta Martiri.

WORTH SEEING

A large part of the city had to be rearranged in the first part of the 14th century to make way for the gargantuan **Palazzo dei Consoli.** This symbol of civic power and architectural elegance (admission L4,000) stands guard over the austere Piazza della Signoria. Outlaws were once hanged from the small opening on the upper right of the facade. Inside, the **Museo Civico** (P. della Signoria, tel. 075/9274298; open daily 10–1:30 and 3–6, reduced hrs Oct.–Mar.) houses coins, stone fragments from buildings, tombs, and the famous seven bronze **Eugubine Tablets**, discovered by a shepherd in 1444 outside the city walls. The tablets contain a phonetic transcription from Umbrii into Latin and Etruscan and shed light on the little-understood Umbrii and their language. A staircase climbs one wall of the museum to the **Loggietta,** with an amazing view of Gubbio, and the **Pinacoteca Comunale** (open daily 10–1:30 and 3–6, L4,000), containing works by local artists.

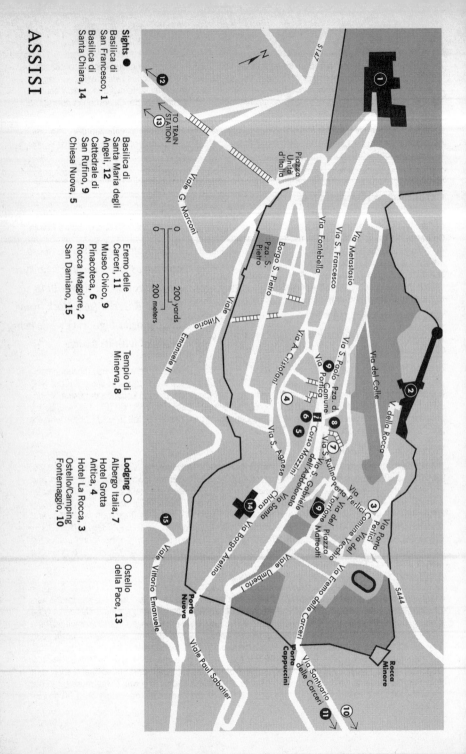

ASSISI

Sights ●
Basilica di
San Francesco, **1**
Basilica di
Santa Chiara, **14**

Basilica di
Santa Maria degli
Angeli, **12**
Cattedrale di
San Rufino, **9**
Chiesa Nuova, **5**

Eremo delle
Carceri, **11**
Museo Civico, **9**
Pinacoteca, **6**
Rocca Maggiore, **2**
San Damiano, **15**

Tempio di
Minerva, **8**

Lodging ○
Albergo Italia, **7**
Hotel Grotta
Antica, **4**
Hotel La Rocca, **3**
Ostello/Camping
Fontemaggio, **10**

Ostello
della Pace, **13**

TO TRAIN
STATION

0   200 yards
0   200 meters

Head up Via Ducale (off V. XX Settembre) to the top of town to see the recently restored **Palazzo Ducale** (V. Ducale, tel. 075/9275872; admission L4,000; open weekdays 9–1:30 and 2:30–7, weekends 9–1:30). Designed in 1470 by Luciano Laurana, it's a smaller version of another magnificent palace he built in Urbino for Duke Federico da Montefeltro. Across the way sits Gubbio's 13th-century **Duomo** (open daily 9–12:30 and 3:30–8:30). The exterior is relatively plain, but check inside for the small, elaborately decorated dome and apse, frescoed to look like a night sky and flanked by organ lofts that look like small theaters. Bring coins to illuminate the beautiful **Cappella del S.S. Sacramento,** to the right of the nave.

In the 13th century the Spadalonga family lived at the site now occupied by the late-Romanesque church of **San Francesco** (P. Quaranta Martiri, tel. 075/9273460). They were friends of St. Francis and hosted him here during his exile. Outside is a crumbling octagonal tower; inside are some of local artist Ottavio Nelli's best frescoes.

The funicular, more like a stand-up version of a ski lift, just off Via San Girolamo, takes you to the top of piney **Monte Ingino,** where you can wander around **Basilica di Sant'Ubaldo** and enjoy a view of the city. From Piazza della Signoria, follow the FUNIVIA signs on Via XX Settembre to reach the lift (L6,500 round-trip; operates daily Mar.–Oct. 10–1:15 and 2:30–5:30, longer hrs Sun. and June–Sept.; Nov.–Jan. 2:30–5, closed Wed.) The basilica, dedicated to Gubbio's patron saint, houses the three huge *ceri* (enormous contrivances in the form of candles, dating from pre-Christian times) used in the Corsa dei Ceri festival (*see below*).

Gubbian lore has it that when St. Francis of Assisi heard that a wolf was terrorizing the 'hood, he dropped by the beast's den to talk peace and love. Dissolving in tears, the wolf changed his evil ways and became a civic pet.

FESTIVALS

The silent town explodes with exuberance every May 15 during the **Corsa dei Ceri** (Race of the Candles), held every year since 1151 in honor of St. Ubaldo, Gubbio's patron saint. Rich in song, colors, and revelry, the festival is definitely something to see: three 16-ft-high constructions, elaborately decorated and crowned with statues of Saints Ubaldo, George, and Anthony (representing three medieval guilds) are carried by three teams as they race from Piazza della Signoria up the slope of Mt. Ingino to the Basilica di Sant'Ubaldo. Don't place any bets, though—Sant'Ubaldo always wins. Reserve ahead if you'll be in town at the time. The **Palio della Balestra** (Crossbow Contest), held each year on the last Sunday in May in Piazza della Signoria, began in the 12th century as a competition between Gubbio and Sansepolcro. The use of the crossbow, the most powerful of all feudal weapons, is still looked on as an art form in Gubbio.

ASSISI

The legacy of St. Francis, founder of the Franciscan order of monks, surrounds the rose-colored hill town of Assisi. Each year thousands of pilgrims make the trek here to pay homage to the man who made God accessible to commoners. But don't let that scare you away—not even a steady, massive flow of tourists and the shops and trinket sellers they support can spoil the singular beauty of one of Italy's most significant religious centers or its magnificent church, among the finest in the Christian world. No other town in Italy speaks so much of one person. Getting to know a bit about St. Francis, a remarkable individual who united asceticism and a tremendous love of nature together with Christian doctrine, is reason alone to stop.

BASICS

Everything you need to orient yourself, including the **tourist office** (P. del Comune 12, tel. 075/812534; open weekdays 8–2 and 3:30–6:30, Sat. 9–1 and 3:30–6:30, Sun. 9–1), is in Piazza del Comune. The **post office** (P. del Comune 23, tel. 075/812355; open Mon.–Sat. 8:30–5:30) has a **cambio** that charges no commission. **Agenzia Stoppini** (C. Mazzini 31, tel. 075/812597; open weekdays 9–12:30 and 3:30–7, Sat. 9–12:30) changes money and, unlike the post office, Visa traveler's checks. *Note: Some of these office locations may have temporarily changed due to earthquake damage.*

COMING AND GOING

Assisi lies on the Terontola–Foligno rail line. **Trains** run almost hourly between here and Perugia (30 min, L3,100). To get to Florence, transfer at Terontola; for Rome or Ancona, transfer at Foligno. The bus labeled ASSISI–SANTA MARIA DEGLI ANGELI travels back and forth (twice per hour) between the station and town, 4 km (2½ mi) away. Hop off at the end of the bus line in Piazza Matteotti; from there it's a down-

TONSURE, SACKCLOTH, ROPE BELT, & SANDALS

Born in Assisi in 1181, the rebellious Francis gave up the pleasures of the flesh and the merchant-class ways of his father, saying, "From now I shall serve only one father: God." His fervently poetic approach to poverty, asceticism, and the beauty of nature soon attracted a wide following. When reading the inscription CARRY NOTHING FOR THE JOURNEY, NEITHER PURSE NOR BAG NOR BREAD NOR MONEY amid the splendor of the Basilica di San Francesco, don't forget that large spaces were necessary for masses and that art and decoration were seen as homages to saintliness, aimed at elevating and intimidating the soul.

hill walk on Via del Torrione to the center, and you'll pass the Duomo on your way. For the hostel and campground **Fontemaggio,** follow Via Eremo delle Carceri uphill about 1½ km (1 mi).

Buses leave from Piazza Matteotti, Largo Properzio, and Piazza Unità d'Italia for Perugia (6 daily, 55 min, L5,000), Florence (1 daily, 2 hrs, L21,000), and Rome (1 daily, 2½ hrs, L23,500). Trains are a little less convenient; you have to catch a connecting bus from the station to the center. Schedules are posted outside the tourist office and the train station. Buy advance tickets for Perugia at the newsstand on Via Santa Chiara, between Piazza del Comune and the Basilica di Santa Chiara. For tickets to Florence and Rome, go to Agenzia Stoppini (*see* Basics, *above*).

GETTING AROUND

Getting around Assisi on foot isn't complicated, but the hills can be exhausting. You can walk almost everywhere, though some major sights are outside the walls. The isolated Eremo delle Carceri is 4 km (2½ mi) uphill, and the Basilica di Santa Maria degli Angeli is out by the train station (coming from Assisi, stay on the bus a few minutes after the station stop). Assisi's main square is **Piazza del Comune;** from here Via Portica runs toward the Basilica di San Francesco, Corso Mazzini leads to the Basilica di Santa Chiara, and the steep Via San Rufino goes to the Cattedrale di San Rufino.

WHERE TO SLEEP

Way back when, pilgrims who came to Assisi to worship slept under the simple portico of the Basilica di San Francesco, built especially for that purpose. Times have changed, and Assisi's pilgrims now have a huge selection of lodgings from which to choose. If you're coming to Assisi for meditation or a modern-day pilgrimage, the tourist office has a list of religious houses that offer lodging. Unless you come during Easter—when there's a weeklong celebration with music, dance, and processions—or during the **Festa di San Francesco** (October 3–4), finding a room should be no problem.

UNDER L50,000 • Albergo Italia. Up a flight of stairs from Piazza del Comune, the Italia offers spacious, clean doubles (L49,000–L69,000) with attractive wooden furniture and large bathrooms. Ask for a room with a view of the square. *P. del Comune, up steps above fountain, 06081, tel. 075/812625, fax 075/8043749. 13 rooms. Closed Jan.–Feb.*

UNDER L75,000 • Hotel Grotta Antica. The cheesy stone arches in the halls may not live up to the name "ancient grotto," but the cavelike restaurant downstairs with a decent L20,000 tourist menu does. Pleasant doubles a few paces from Piazza del Comune go for L70,000. *Vicolo Macelli Vecchi 1, 06081, tel. 075/813467. 7 rooms, all with bath.*

Hotel La Rocca. One of the cheapest hotels in Assisi, La Rocca sits on the town's upper terraces among alleys leading to the fortress. Spacious doubles, many with common balconies and mountain views, go for L72,000. There's also a restaurant. *V. Porta Perlici 27, 06081, tel. 075/816467, fax 075/812284. 29 rooms with bath.*

HOSTELS • Ostello/Camping Fontemaggio. A kilometer (half mile) above Assisi, this hostel is part of a compound that includes a campground, a restaurant, and a hotel. Of the hostel's two buildings, the Domus is the nicer. The other exemplifies the downside of communal living, with slimy bathrooms and grungy floors. Both have cooking facilities and showers, and there's a market to the right of the registration office. Beds cost L17,000 per night. There are also bungalows with kitchen and bath for four people (L120,000–L150,000). *V. Eremo delle Carceri 7, Fontemaggio 06081, tel. 075/813636, fax 075/813749. Follow V. Eremo delle Carceri (middle path at fork in road) 1 km (½ mi) uphill to Fontemaggio turnoff on right. 100 beds. Kitchen. Cash only.*

Ostello della Pace (HI). If the half-hour walk from the train station in Santa Maria degli Angeli makes this hostel less than ideal for you, at least buses shuttle between the station and town twice hourly. Della Pace is cleaner and better maintained than the hostel at Fontemaggio, and though it lacks the idyllic setting, it does have striking views. Beds are L22,000 (shared bath)–L28,000 (private bath), breakfast included. Complete dinner is served for L14,000. *V. Valecchie 177, 06081, tel. and fax 075/816767. Right out of train station, left on V. San Pietro (after hangarlike buildings); hostel's on left after you start up hill. 64 beds. Curfew midnight, lockout 9:30–3:30. Laundry. Cash only. Closed Jan.–Feb.*

WHERE TO EAT

For a rundown on regional goodies, stop at **La Bottega dei Sapori** (P. del Comune 34, tel. 075/812294; open daily 9–8), where proprietor Fabrizio will give you a mouthwatering tour of his wine shop/deli/market. You'll also find Franciscan liqueurs here, in flavors from rose petal to strawberry. Assisi's specialties include the inevitable truffles and porcini mushrooms, pecorino, and *strangozzi* (thick, chewy homemade noodles). In the main piazza is a **paninoteca** (P. del Comune 4), where you can grab a *panino* (sandwich) or a drink and pay just L1,000 extra to sit in the shade and check out the Temple of Minerva. Along Via Portica there are **pasticcerie** where you can get *torta della nonna* (pastry with cream and chocolate), *torta francescana* (a raisin pound cake made by monks), or *baci d'Assisi* (mini versions of the cake).

While Mussolini had control of the basilica during the 1920s, it was used as a home for abandoned boys. The upper church, believe it or not, was their gymnasium.

UNDER L10,000 • Osteria Piazzetta dell'Erba. Only the freshest herbs and veggies will do at this spot where daily specials are cheap and delicious. You can always get pasta with herbs (L8,000) or a large *insalata mista* (mixed salad; L5,000)—both delicious. Sit at the pastel-plaid tables, and you'll be breaking oven-fresh bread. *V. San Gabriele dell'Addolorata 15/B, off P. del Comune, up 1st ramp on left, tel. 075/815352. Closed Mon.*

Ristorante La Stalla. Even if you're not staying at the hostel or campground in Fontemaggio (*see* Where to Sleep, *above*), this restaurant in the compound is worth the 1-km (½-mi) trek from town. What are usually expensive local specialties are reasonably priced here and served in a rustic setting. In summer you can watch the chefs cook under an open portico as you order your meal at the *cassa* (cash register) and set your own table. Try the *assaggini di torta di testo* (cured pork, cheese, and vegetable sandwiches; L6,500) or strangozzi (L7,000). Homemade wine is L8,000 per bottle. *V. Eremo delle Carceri 8, tel. 075/812317. Follow directions to Ostello Camping Fontemaggio (see above).*

UNDER L15,000 • Ristorante Spadini. The pleasant decor and delicious cuisine here typify Assisi. Primi run L7,000 to L10,000, secondi L9,000 to L15,000. Try one of the Umbrian specialties such as pheasant with truffles (L16,000). *V. Sant'Agnese 6, off C. Mazzini, tel. 075/813005. Open Tues.–Sun. noon–2:30 and 7–9:30.*

WORTH SEEING

The **Pinacoteca** (Palazzo del Priori, tel. 075/812579) offers a survey of Umbrian art you can view daily 10–1 and 3–7 (2–5 in winter) for L4,000. A cumulative ticket valid for a month (L10,000) is good for entry to the Pinacoteca, Foro Romano, and Rocca Maggiore. The **Tempio di Minerva,** built in the 1st century BC, displays a classical facade and six columns supporting a tympanum. The **Museo Civico** (V. Portica; tel. 075/813053; open daily 10–1 and 3–7, 2–5 in winter; admission L4,000) houses a collection of remains found during ongoing excavations of the Roman Forum under the piazza. Stop by the little **Chiesa Nuova** and take Via Arco dei Priori to the enclosed alley to see the room where Francis's father "imprisoned" his son, hoping to rid him of his "silly ideas."

BASILICA DI SAN FRANCESCO • This celebration of Assisi's patron saint is a Gothic church built atop a Gothic-Romanesque basilica, each one remarkably beautiful and decorated floor to ceiling with perhaps the finest collection of frescoes in the world. Monks lead prescheduled group tours, so you might slyly attach yourself to an English-speaking group. Dress codes for entrance are strictly enforced here: tank tops, miniskirts, and shorts are no-no's. At press time, the lower church of Basilica di San Francesco was open and the upper church was to be reopened in November 1999, following restorations necessitated by the devastating 1997 earthquakes.

Start with the **lower church,** which feels a bit like a crypt and has stained-glass windows and low arches. The cross vaulting is decorated with allegories of the Three Virtues of St. Francis (poverty, chastity, and obedience) and *St. Francis's Triumph.* These frescoes, traditionally attributed to Giotto, are now credited to some of his followers. Stairs lead down into the crypt under the main altar, which holds the remains of St. Francis and four brother monks. The first chapel on the left contains a superb fresco cycle by Simone Martini depicting scenes from the life of St. Martin. In the left transept you'll find the Lorenzetti brothers' famous *Madonna of the Sunset,* which sparkles gold when the sun hits it. Notice Mary's pointing thumb; legend has it that Jesus is asking his mother which saint to bless, and she is pointing at St. Francis. In the right transept, Cimabue's *Madonna Enthroned Among Angels and St. Francis* is one of the most famous portraits of the saint. It is surrounded by scenes from the childhood of Christ, by assistants of Giotto, and a *Crucifixion* by the master himself. The five saints were painted by Simone Martini. Take the stairs up to the upper church.

The **upper church** was built just after the lower one, in then cutting-edge Gothic style. Pointed arches allow for greater height, and this basilica soars. Its stained-glass windows were the first in Italy; the windows in the lower church were a later addition. The frescoes in the apse and transepts were painted by the greatest Tuscan artists of the late 13th century. The upper registers in the nave—which have been variously attributed to Roman and Tuscan painters, including Cimabue—depict stories from the Old and New Testaments and are badly damaged. On the lower register, traditionally attributed to Giotto, are 28 frescoes portraying incidents in the life of St. Francis, now thought to be the work of Roman painter Pietro Cavallini. Here the artist broke away from the symbolic, non-naturalistic style of medieval art and moved toward a realism and grace that reached its peak during the Renaissance. The paintings are viewed left to right, starting in the transept. *P. San Francesco, tel. 075-819001. Lower church open daily 7–7; upper church scheduled to reopen Nov. 1999.*

BASILICA DI SANTA CHIARA • The pink-and-white 13th-century Santa Chiara (P. Santa Chiara, tel. 075/812216), supported by buttresses on one side, looks like it could fly away at any moment. The church's namesake, St. Clare, was inspired by her friend St. Francis to found the Order of the Poor Clares, one of the three Franciscan orders. Check out St. Clare's tomb downstairs, a grandiose copy of the one in San Francesco. In the chapel on the right is the painted crucifix that spoke to Francis, commanding him to "rebuild the church." He took the advice literally and rebuilt the Convent of **San Damiano** just outside town (V. San Damiano off V. Vittorio Emanuele, tel. 075/816668). San Damiano became the Poor Clares' first home and is where Francis composed *The Canticle of the Creatures,* which proclaims that man experiences God through His Creation. Only later did the humble Francis realize that the calling had been figurative rather than literal. *Basilica di Santa Chiara currently closed due to earthquake damage.*

BASILICA DI SANTA MARIA DEGLI ANGELI • The basilica (tel. 075/80511; open daily 9–noon and 2:30–6:30), outside town toward the train station, encloses and completely dwarfs the tiny frescoed chapel **Porziuncola,** first home of the Franciscan order. This is where Clare took her vows and had her hair ceremoniously cut off and where Francis died. To reach the basilica, take the bus marked SANTA MARIA DEGLI ANGELI from Piazza Matteotti, past the train station.

CATTEDRALE DI SAN RUFINO • The cathedral (P. San Rufino, tel. 075/812285) has one of the finest Romanesque facades in Umbria, with a rose window supported on the shoulders of stone figures. It was built in the 12th century on the foundation of an 11th-century structure, itself built over an 8th-century church (fragments of which can be seen in the church museum for L2,000), San Rufino is where Francis was baptized. *Cattedrale di San Rufino currently closed due to earthquake damage.*

ROCCA MAGGIORE • Uphill from the cathedral, the citadel offers breathtaking views of the city and valley below. The wonderfully preserved 14th-century fortress houses a torture and martyr museum (admission L2,500; open daily 10–noon and 2–6, 2–5 in winter). To get here, take Vicolo San Lorenzo, a staircase-alley off Via Porta Perlici.

EREMO DELLE CARCERI • The utterly tranquil Eremo delle Carceri (tel. 075/812301; open daily dawn–dusk) was one of St. Francis's favorite places for meditation. This collection of buildings at the top of a wooded grotto is where the holy man is reputed to have preached to the birds. To reach the site, exit Porta Cappuccini on Via Santuario delle Carceri and head uphill 4 km (2½ mi). From the site, climb down narrow staircases and through miniature doors to the **Grotta di San Francesco,** a series of little cavernous chapels.

SPELLO

"Spello, più che lo guardi, più è bello," the locals proudly intone ("Spello, the more you look at it, the more beautiful it is"). This ancient, perfectly preserved hill town offers one of the finest sweeping views of the Valle Umbria, all the way from Perugia down to Spoleto. Its walkways are for the most part an Escher-like honeycomb of stone arches and ramps and ancient brick stairways you can wander through delightfully lost for hours. A visit is especially enticing during the Feast of Corpus Christi, when the streets literally burst into bloom for the **Flower Festival** (*Infiorate,* see below).

BASICS

The **tourist office** (P. Matteotti, 3, tel. 0742/301009) is open every day 9:30–12:30 and 3:30–5:30.

COMING AND GOING

Spello is most easily reached from Perugia by train (17 daily, 35 minutes, L3,900). The **train station** is just outside the lower gates of the town. You can ask to leave your bags in the bar there. It's a five-minute walk to town.

Intercity buses connect Spello to Assisi (6 per day). For more info, contact the tourist office (*see above*).

WHERE TO SLEEP AND EAT

You can take in all of Spello's charms in an easy-going day, but if it casts its subtle spell over you and you want to stay a while, there's really only one budget-minded choice. Just outside the old town, in Spello borgo, at the **Hotel Paolucci** (V. G. Brodolini 21/23, 06038, tel. and fax 0742/301018; cash only) you'll find 30 clean, large doubles, all with bath, for L70,000. If you really feel you must be up in the old town, to soak up the medieval atmosphere round the clock, **Il Cacciatore** (V. Garibaldi 42, tel. 0742/651141, fax 0742/301603; closed Nov. and 1st ½ June) up near the top, offers 22 doubles with bath for L110,000, half with spectacular views of the valley and distant mountains. Plus it has its own trattoria (closed Mon.), where you can dig into hearty local fare on their pretty terrace and get away for as little as L20,000. For a great snack in an expansive, shaded garden terrace, go for Maurizio's **Bonci Bar** (V. Garibaldi 10, tel. 0742/651397; cash only; closed Wed.) just down the street; try their *schiacciata* for L6,000, toasted *pizza bianca* filled with grilled *scamorza* cheese, *melanzane* and *prosciutto,* and a cup of their incredibly sensuous homemade *gelato* topped with *frutti di bosco* (wild berries) for dessert.

WORTH SEEING

Spello is remarkable for its ancient city gates, two of which are particularly fine and date from the Augustan Age. At the lower end of town is the **Porta Consolare,** its triple archways now decorated with three Roman statues originally found near the ruined amphitheater. Halfway up and to the west edge of town stands the magnificent **Porta Venere,** flanked by twin dodecahedral towers, the **Torri di Properzio,** gleaming white and elegantly beautiful as they keep watch over the valley approach. The church of **Santa Maria Maggiore,** dating from the 13th century and built on the ruins of a temple to Juno and Vesta, is adorned with graceful frescoes by Pinturicchio and Perugino. The church of **Sant'Andrea,** a cool cavern of tomblike peace from the 11th century, is brightened by another heavenly vision of a large Pinturicchio oil on wood; and a typically surrealistic crucifix attributed to Giotto adds just the right touch of weirdness. The **Pinacoteca Civica** (former Palazzo dei Cononici, next to Santa Maria Maggiore; admission L5,000) houses a full range of cultural riches from the 12th century onward. A particular curiosity is a 17th-century painting of *Madonna and Child* by Marcantonio Grecchi, in which two saints hold a cunningly perfect little model of Spello.

FESTIVALS

The year's big event is the ancient *Infiorate* (**Flower Festival**), held 60 days after Easter, in May or June. Teams of artistic young people compete to create the most gorgeous pavement painting, usually on religious or historic themes, taking for their palette only millions upon millions of flower petals. Once the fragile works have been duly guarded, judged, and admired, a late Sunday morning religious procession passes over these tender carpets, followed by strollers, sightseers, and passersby. *Sic transit gloria mundi!*

SPOLETO

For a few weeks in June and July, Spoleto becomes Umbria's most happening town. If you are interested in attending the Festival dei Due Mondi—Europe's biggest arts celebration—make reservations and plans way ahead of time. If not, stay far, far away, as this is when the crowds descend and prices ascend. The rest of the year, however, Spoleto might be Umbria's most impressive town, with fine art and ruins that evoke its Roman origins and a few notable, pretty Romanesque churches.

BASICS

The **tourist office** (P. della Libertà 7, tel. 0743/220311) is open 9–1 (weekends 10–1) and 4:30–7:30. The office hands out a great city map, lodging listings, and info on monuments and festivals. The **post office** (P. della Libertà 12, tel. 0743/223198; open Mon.–Sat. 8–7) has a **cambio** (no commission).

COMING AND GOING

Spoleto is easily reached by rail from Rome (hourly, 1½ hrs, L12,100) and from Florence (hourly, 3 hrs, L20,000) by way of Perugia (1½ hrs, L5,900) and Assisi (1 hr, L4,900); some routes require a transfer at Foligno. The **train station** (P. Polvani, tel. 1478/88088) lies outside town, but Navetta and Circolare Buses A, B, C, and E run to Piazza della Libertà near the center every half hour. Buy bus tickets (L1,200) and find luggage storage (open 6 AM–11 PM) at the bar in the station.

Intercity buses connect Spoleto to nearby towns. Two buses leave in the morning from Piazza della Libertà for Perugia Monday–Saturday. Buy tickets (L7,500) at newsstands or tobacco shops (marked TABACCHI). **SIT** buses (tel. 0743/212211) for Rome leave twice daily from the corner of Via Flaminia and Strada di Monteluco; buy tickets on the bus. For more info, contact the tourist office (*see above*).

WHERE TO SLEEP

Most of Spoleto's hotels are on the pricey side. Camping offers sublime views, and the tourist office has a list of *affitacamere* (rooms for rent in private homes). If you're coming between late June and mid-July, the operative word is *reservations*.

At **Hotel Panciolle** (V. del Duomo 3, tel. 0743/45677; cash only), in the upper town near the Duomo, tidy doubles go for L90,000, with bath. Also central is **Dell'Angelo** (V. dell'Arco di Druso 25, tel. and fax 0743/222385) offering modern doubles (L90,000–L100,000) with bath. Note that prices drop about 30% for the above hotels off-season—nonsummer months. **Camping Monteluco** (Località San Pietro, off Strada di Monteluco, tel. 0743/220358; cash only; closed Oct.–Mar.), in the Sacred Forest of Monteluco (*see* Museo Archeologico *in* Worth Seeing, *below*), has magnificent views and modern facilities, hot showers, and a dinner-only restaurant. The Monteluco bus (eight daily, L2,400) runs by it, but the 15-minute walk is easy; from Piazza della Libertà go up Via Matteotti. The going rate is L8,000 per person and L8,000 per tent.

WHERE TO EAT

Spoleto is full of gourmet specialty shops. The area around **Piazza del Mercato** is particularly well stocked with stores selling truffles, liqueurs, cheese, honey, sausage, and wine. *Strangozzi* is the town's pasta of choice. Cheap options are found in the piazza as well, including the small **mercato** (open Mon.–Sat. 8:30–1) and the **Self Service del Mercato** (tel. 0743/221974), where tasty meals go for about L12,000. Toward the bridge at **La Portella** (V. del Ponte, tel. 0743/221574; closed Tues.), sample standard bar panini (L2,000–L5,000) while enjoying a spectacular view of the countryside from an outdoor table. Two solid restaurants stressing regional specialties such as *strangozzi alla spoletina* (with hot pepper, garlic, oil, and parsley; L9,000) or *al tartufo* (with truffles; L20,000) are the **Taverna dei Duchi** (V. Saffi 1, tel. 0743/40323; closed Wed. in winter) and*, a little higher, **Il Pentagramma** (V. Tommaso Martiani 4, tel. 0743/223141; closed Mon.). Have a glass of local vino and snack on *bruschette* (toast rubbed with garlic and drizzled with olive oil) or a full meal for about L20,000, down the street at **Enoteca Provinciale** (V. A. Saffi 7, tel. 0743/220484; closed Tues.). For an after-dinner drink, try stylish **Tric Trac** (P. del Duomo 10, tel. 075/44592; closed Wed.). You'll pay about L8,000 for a beer, but you'll really enjoy it as you sit outside and take in the Duomo's grand facade and rustic backdrop.

WORTH SEEING

From the churches set among silvery olive groves on the outskirts of town to the stately *rocca* (fortress) atop Spoleto's peak, the city radiates grandeur and hushed charm. Notable sights are clustered in the upper part of town, with the exception of a pair of exquisite churches east of the city. The first one, **San Ponziano** (V. della Basilica di San Salvatore, tel. 0743/40655; open daily 9–12:30 and 3:30–6), is dedicated to the city's patron saint; a painting above the altar depicts his decapitation. Wander down into the crypt, where you'll find well-preserved 14th-century frescoes. Farther along the same road, the alluring and deserted 4th-century **San Salvatore** adjoins the magnificent town cemetery. Modeled on a Roman temple, it has decrepit columns as its only decoration.

In the upper town, the Romanesque **Duomo** (P. del Duomo) is breathtaking against a backdrop of hill and castle silhouetted against the sky. The facade incorporates a graceful portico (added to the 12th-century structure in the 15th century), eight rose windows, and a tympanum with a gleaming 13th-century mosaic. The campanile was thrown together from stones and fragments stolen from Roman ruins around town. Inside the church are several precious works of art, including impressive restored frescoes by Filippo Lippi. The artist died shortly after completing them, and Spoleto hung on to Lippi's body instead of shipping it back to his native Florence. He's buried in the cathedral, in a tomb designed by his son Filippino. The first chapel on the right as you enter is Pinturicchio's frescoed **Eroli Chapel,** painted for Bishop Eroli in 1497. The nearby 12th-century church of **Sant'Eufemia** (V. Saffi; open daily 10–2:30 and 3:30–7) lacks the Duomo's allure and charges a L5,000 admission fee (Museo Diocesano included), but you may want to check out its "women's balconies"—the first of their kind in Umbria—where women had to sit, apart from the men. From the Duomo, head west on Via Saffi; it's under the arch to the right. *Church of Sant'Eufemia currently closed due to earthquake damage.*

Spoleto also has some great Roman ruins, including the 1st-century AD **Arco di Druso,** the arch that once marked the entrance to an ancient forum, and the **Teatro Romano** (P. della Libertà; admission L4,000). Reachable through a door in the theater's west portico, the **Museo Archeologico** (tel. 0743/223277) displays assorted artifacts and the *Lex Spoletina* (Spoleto Law) tablets dating from 315 BC. This ancient legal document prohibited the destruction of the Sacred Forest, a pagan prayer site later frequented by St. Francis. The **Casa Romana** (V. del Visiale 9, off V. Saffi), a house uncovered only in the last century, dates from the 1st century AD. The L5,000 admission fee also gets you into Spoleto's **Pinacoteca** (Palazzo

Make a beeline to the most spectacular sight in Spoleto: the skinny brick Ponte delle Torri, a 13th-century wonder designed by the architect Gattapone. A Roman aqueduct once spanned the same gap. Take Via Saffi north, which becomes Via del Ponte.

del Municipio, V. Saffi 14, tel. 0743/218270), a small collection of 12th- to 18th-century paintings. Both the Pinacoteca and the Casa are open Tuesday–Sunday 10–1 and 3–6.

FESTIVALS

Founded by composer Gian Carlo Menotti in 1958 and held every year from late June to mid-July, the internationally acclaimed **Festival dei Due Mondi** (Festival of Two Worlds) mixes opera, ballet, and theater talents. Enthusiasts from Italy and the rest of Europe and America turn out for a cultural exchange and a lot of cheek kissing. Ticket prices range from L10,000 to L150,000 plus a 15% "selling fee." To buy tickets, write to the Associazione Festival dei Due Mondi, Biglietteria Festival dei Due Mondi, Teatro Nuovo, 06049 Spoleto. To purchase tickets while in Spoleto, go to Teatro Nuovo (tel. 0743/40265 or 0743/44097) or try your luck at the theater box office one hour before the performance begins. Pick up a pamphlet on the festival with performance schedules at the tourist office.

TODI

Although most Umbrian hill towns are high enough to suggest an aerie, only Todi is literally that—at least according to legend. As the story goes, an eagle stole a tablecloth from an Umbrian dining table. Unable to eat without it, the Umbrii tracked the eagle down, and they liked its nest so much that they settled here for good. With spectacular views over unspoiled surrounding countryside, a handful of monuments, and some fine restaurants, Todi makes a great afternoon trip from Perugia. For the usual info hit the **tourist office** (P. del Popolo 38, tel. 075/8942526; open Mon.–Sat. 9–1 and 4–7, Sun. 9:30–12:30). From Piazza Jacopone (the bus stop) take Via Mazzini to Piazza del Popolo and look to the right for the office.

COMING AND GOING

Todi lies on a meager rail line between Sansepolcro in Tuscany and Terni in southern Umbria. Trains arrive in Todi's **Ponte Rio station** (about 3 km/2 mi below town, tel. 1478/88088) from Perugia (12 daily, 50 min, L5,700); take Bus C to Piazza Jacopone (every 30 min, L1,200) up to town. Buy bus tickets from the machine at the station, the tourist office, or newsstands. Schedules are posted in Piazza Jacopone. One bus per day goes to Orvieto, at 5:50 AM (1¼ hrs, L7,700), and returns to Todi at 1:55 PM. Seven **intercity buses** daily also run from Todi to Perugia's Piazza dei Partigiani (Mon.–Sat., 1½ hrs, L9,200). Buy tickets at the Mercato Margherita (P. Jacopone, tel. 075/8942201).

WHERE TO SLEEP AND EAT

Todi is really day-trip material, but for L100,000–L110,000 without bath, you'll get a good deal of charm out of **San Lorenzo Tre** (V. San Lorenzo 3, tel. 075/89445555; cash only; closed mid-Jan.–Feb.). Unless it's Tuesday, head straight for **Ristorante Umbria** (V. San Bonaventura 13, tel. 075/8942390; closed Tues.) and let the feast begin. The polenta *con funghi e tartufi* (with mushrooms and truffles) costs L20,000, but portions are ample, and the terrace view is sensational. Try regional wines right next door at **L'Enoteca dell'Accademia dei Convivanti** (V. San Bonaventura 11, tel. 075/8944400). For cheaper eats, there's **Pizzeria Ristorante Cavour** (C. Cavour 23, tel. 075/8943730; closed Wed.), which serves pizzas on an outdoor patio. **La Mulinella** (V. Pontenaia 2, tel. 075/8944779; cash only; closed Wed.) serves homemade pasta and simple grilled meats—a full meal costs about L20,000.

WORTH SEEING

Piazza del Popolo is figuratively and literally Todi's highest point, a model of spatial harmony with stunning views onto the surrounding countryside. On one end is the 12th-century Romanesque-Gothic Duomo, with a simple facade and a trapezoidal tower mirrored by the **Palazzo dei Priori** across the way. A staircase in the square leads to the **Palazzo del Popolo,** which dates from 1213 and has Ghibelline battlements (castellations with a swallow-tailed *V* cut into the top of each "tooth"), and **Palazzo del Capitano,** built in 1292. The palaces were once homes to civic leaders; now they hold shops, banks, and a *caffè*.

From Piazza del Popolo, head down Corso Cavour and turn left on Via del Vecchio Mercato to reach the old **Foro Romano,** barely visible among the buildings of the Piazza del Vecchio Mercato. Note the minimalist rose window at the nearby Romanesque church of **Sant'Ilario,** not open to the public. The church of **Santa Maria della Consolazione** (V. della Consolazione), with its elegant white dome, is a Renaissance masterpiece. It's just outside town, downhill from the **Parco della Rocca** (look for trail on right side of castle). The walk there is pleasant, the trek back arduous.

ORVIETO

Orvieto sits atop a circular table of tufa stone shoved up from the valley below by volcanic movements. Its natural defenses eliminated the need for medieval walls, making Orvieto something of an anomaly among Umbrian hill towns. The Etruscans were the first to take advantage of this and settle here. Excavations have revealed a subterranean network of more than 1,200 wells and storage caves, but it is the singular beauty of the Duomo that draws visitors from near and far. Shops along narrow streets sell the town's famous exports, ceramics, and the dry white Orvieto Classico, known in these parts as *oro liquido* (liquid gold). If you get the impression the town belongs to tourists, wait for the evening passeggiata to see how the locals look. The **tourist office** (P. del Duomo 24, tel. 0763/341772; open weekdays 8–2 and 4–7, weekends 10–1 and 3:30–6:30) has maps, bus, and train schedules, and info on sights.

COMING AND GOING

Orvieto lies on the Rome–Florence rail line. Eight trains leave daily for Florence (1½ hrs, L16,000), and 13 for Rome (1 hr 20 min, L12,100). For Perugia (2 hrs, L10,000), you have to switch trains in Terontola. A **funicular** (every 15 minutes, L1,400 ticket includes bus ride from Piazza Cahen to Piazza del Duomo) carries you between Orvieto's **train station** (P. Matteotti 14, tel. 1478/88088) and Piazza Cahen, at the eastern edge of the city plateau (last funicular 8:30 PM; afterward buy tickets for the bus up to town center at the train station's bar). From Piazza Cahen, orange **buses** (A and B) run to Piazza del Duomo. If you're not laden with luggage, the 10-minute walk up **Corso Cavour** to Piazza del Duomo is pleasant. Buses to nearby towns split from Piazza Cahen. Every weekday, one leaves at 1:55 PM for Todi (L7,700, one way), five head to Terni (L9,700), and one goes to Perugia (L10,700) at 5:45 AM. Buy tickets on the bus.

WHERE TO SLEEP

You'll find a few budget hotels in **Orvieto Scalo,** the area near the train station. Though the neighborhood is uninteresting, it's easy to reach town on the funicular. The clean, modern **Albergo Picchio** (V. Salvatori 17, tel. 0763/301144, fax 0763/301846) has some rooms with balcony views of the fortress overhead. Doubles with bath, phone, and TV are L75,000. From Piazza Matteotti in front of the station, head uphill on Via della Pesa, which becomes Via Salvatori. Another good choice is friendly **Hotel Centrale** (V. Sette Martiri 68, across from station, tel. 0763/305881), minutes from the funicular. Small doubles with bath go for L70,000.

If you want the atmosphere of the centro storico, you'll find a flower garden, large rooms (doubles L60,000 without bath), and a top floor with a view at **Hotel Duomo** (V. di Maurizio 7, down steps from P. del Duomo, tel. 0763/341887; cash only). **Hotel Posta** (V. L. Signorelli 18, in alley between P. del Duomo and C. Cavour, tel. 0763/341909; cash only) is purely medieval, with narrow hallways and campanile bells booming through the walls. The beds are huge, the ceilings high, and the furnishings antique. Bathless doubles run L70,000. The hotel closes in January or February, so call ahead.

WHERE TO EAT

Orvieto is budget dining nirvana—if only all hill towns in central Italy made you choose between three great restaurants serving excellent food at reasonable prices: **I Sette Consoli** (P. Sant'Angelo 1/A, tel. 0763/343911; closed Wed.), **La Grotta** (V. Luca Signorelli 5, tel. 0763/341348; closed Tues. and Jan.), and **La Volpe e L'Uva** (V. Ripa Corsica 1, tel. 0763/341612; closed Mon.).

In between meals, quaff local wines at **Enoteca Foresi** (P. del Duomo 2, tel. 0763/341611; open daily 9:30–8; closed winter afternoons). Then visit the cellar, where hundreds of bottles are stored in moist earth. If you need a snack, pick up some tasty pecorino and/or sandwiches made with *cinghiale* (wild boar) sausage (L6,000). **La Bottega del Buon Vino** (V. della Cava 26, tel. 0763/342373; lunch only; closed Tues.) serves affordable meals (primi L6,000–L10,000; secondi L8000–L10,000) on outdoor tables with a window in the floor that looks down into caves. They also sell wine, ceramics, and tickets (L3,000) to the Etruscan well and caverns below. From Piazza della Repubblica take Via Filippeschi, which becomes Via della Cava. For local specialties such as wild boar sausage (L38,000 per kilo) and 12 varieties of pecorino (sheep's milk) cheese, there's **Dai Fratelli** (V. del Duomo 11, tel. 0763/343965). Wonderful gelato in large scoops is to be had at **L'Archetto** (to the left of the Duomo), its outdoor tables shaded by ivy.

Beneath Orvieto is the ancient Etruscan city, with carefully engineered cisterns, long tunnels carved out of solid rock, and underground spaces used for everything from keeping animals to pressing olives. Stop by the tourist office for tour info.

WORTH SEEING

Orvieto's **Duomo** is one of the most dazzling in all of Italy, a triumph of Romanesque-Gothic architecture. A Bohemian priest on a pilgrimage from Prague to Rome claimed to witness blood dripping from the host onto an altar cloth during a mass in Bolsena in 1264. The pope seized the opportunity to proclaim a new religious holiday—the Feast of Corpus Christi—and the Duomo was built to celebrate the miracle and house the stained altar cloth. The church benefited from three centuries of work by some of Italy's finest builders and artists. Lorenzo Maitani of Siena, who became involved with the project 10 years after its inception, left the most indelible mark when he reworked the facade on a triple-gabled plan. Magnificent mosaics and intricate stonework adorn the facade, its central elements a sublime rose window and a monumental arched portal. The bronze doors are 20th-century additions by Emilio Greco.

The major works inside are the two chapels in the transepts. To the left is the **Cappella del Corporale,** where the famous altar cloth is kept in a golden reliquary modeled on the cathedral, inlaid with enamel images of the miracle. The cloth is removed for public viewing on Easter and on Corpus Christi (the ninth Sunday after Easter). A trio of local artists executed frescoes depicting the miracle on the chapel walls. More glorious is the **Cappella Nuova** (a.k.a. Cappella della Madonna di San Brizio) in the right transept. It contains Luca Signorelli's fresco cycle *Stories of the Antichrist,* among the most delightfully gruesome works in Italy. As the damned fall to hell, demons with green buttocks bite off ears, step on heads, and spirit away young girls. Dante would surely have approved; in the chapel, his portrait accompanies scenes from *Purgatorio.* Signorelli and Fra Angelico, who also worked on the chapel, witness the gory scene. *Admission L3,000; buy tickets at tourist office across piazza. Open Apr.–Sept., daily 7–1 and 2:30–7:30; Mar. and Oct., daily 7–1 and 2:30–6:30; Nov.–Feb., daily 7–1 and 2:30–5:30.*

Next door, the **Museo dell'Opera del Duomo** (tel. 0763/342477), to be re-opened after restoration by early 2000, contains original and later plans for the cathedral, as well as some painting and sculpture. Across the piazza, the **Museo Claudio Faina** (Palazzo Faina, tel. 0763/341511; admission L7,000) holds Etruscan and Roman artifacts; the museum is designed in a way that makes its Roman coins, bronze pieces, and sarcophagi accessible and interesting. On Piazza Cahen, the **Fortezza,** built in the mid-14th century, encloses a public park with grass, benches, shade, and an incredible view. The nearby **Pozzo di San Patrizio** (V. Sangallo, off P. Cahen, tel. 0763/343768), or Well of St. Patrick, was commissioned by Pope Clement VII in 1527 to ensure a plentiful water supply. Descend into the well (a steep L6,000) via a pair of zigzagging mule paths, designed to avoid animal traffic jams.

FESTIVALS

Orvieto hosts the winter half of the **Umbria Jazz Festival** during the week around New Year's. There's great music day and night, plus the special atmosphere of Italy's month-long Christmas-Epiphany season. Call the tourist office for details.

LE MARCHE

Until 1860, the region known as Le Marche belonged to the pope, and for centuries served as a shield against invading powers (*marca* means "boundary"). The Church's tax collectors were recruited from the region, resulting in the unfortunate adage, *Meglio una morte in casa che un marchigiano alla porta* ("Better a corpse in the house than a Marchigiano at the door"). You'll find a bit of everything here: a long coastline full of resorts, breathtaking mountain scenery, and hilltop villages packed with surprising art treasures. In summer the beaches are packed, too—don't bother trying to find undiscovered territory. The interior landscape, however, is relatively unspoiled. Urbino is Le Marche's most spectacular city, and one of Italy's as well. Virtually unknown to foreigners, Ascoli Piceno, in the south, offers access to the **Sibillini Mountains,** the most beautiful section of the Apennines.

URBINO

It's not hard to understand how Urbino is held by many to be the surviving example of the ideal Renaissance city, true in architecture and art to the harmony and balance exemplified in the mysterious *Città Ideale* (Ideal City), which hangs in the town's Galleria Nazionale. Isolated in the sharp foothills south of the magnificent Sibillini Mountains, with its skyline of towers and domes, Urbino has changed little since Castiglione based his *Libro del Cortegiano* (*Book of the Courtier*)—the definitive etiquette guide to 16th-century courtly life in Italy and abroad—on local duke Federico da Montefeltro and his court, who embodied the noble ideal of *sprezzatura* (nonchalant perfection). Federico hosted a dazzling group of painters in Urbino; the city's artistic heritage includes works by Piero della Francesca, Paolo Uccello, Titian, and, of course, native son Raphael. With a popular university and summer programs that attract students from all over the world, four centuries later lively little Urbino still feels almost as utopian as the city in the painting.

Urbino's **Jazz Festival** draws thousands of visitors each year during the second week of June. Also gaining recognition is the **Festival Internazionale di Musica Antica** during the second week of July, which sponsors outdoor performances and Renaissance music, theater, and dance. The **tourist office** (P. Rinascimento 1, tel. 0722/2613; open Mon.–Sat. 9–1 and 3–6, Sun. 9–1; in winter, Mon.–Sat. 9–1) will give you all the info on these festivals.

COMING AND GOING

There is no train service to Urbino. Get here by bus from Pesaro (12 daily, 50 min, L3,500) or Rimini (1 daily, 1 hr, L5,500). Buses arrive at Urbino's Borgo Mercatale, beneath the Palazzo Ducale. The "bus station" has a schedule posted (buy tickets on board), and an **info booth** (open July–Aug., daily 9–1 and 3–7) that passes out maps and hotel listings. To get to town, take the elevator or spiral staircase to Palazzo Ducale. Climb the two sets of brick steps on your right, go under the arch, and you'll hit Piazza Rinascimento, close to the major sights.

WHERE TO SLEEP

Urbino has several reasonably priced places to stay. If you can't find one that suits your needs, the tourist office has a long list of *affitacamere*, rooms available in private homes.

Albergo Italia (C. Garibaldi 32, off P. della Repubblica, tel. 0722/2701; cash only) has spacious lounges, sitting rooms, breakfast nooks, and panoramic views. Some rooms (L70,000 doubles, L90,000 with bath) have balconies. The hotel is closed for two weeks in September, depending on the university's schedule; call ahead. **Pensione Fosca** (V. Raffaello 67, tel. 0722/2542, fax 0722/329622; cash only), a few doors from Raphael's house, lets airy doubles with bathrooms down the hall for L60,000. **Hotel San Giovanni** (V. Barocci 13, tel. 0722/2827; cash only) is the third-cheapest choice in the center, offering large, clean doubles without bath for L60,000 (L90,000 with bath); it's closed in July.

Ultraserene **Camping Pineta,** in the hills overlooking Urbino, has amazing views of the city and the countryside below. Facilities are modest, but the forest provides a sense of privacy that most Italian campgrounds lack. There's a small market on the site (open 8 AM–11 PM). It'll cost you L9,000 per person; L18,500 (including car) per tent site. From central bus depot, take Bus 4 or 7 (L2000), and ask driver for Camping Pineta; a minibus will pick you up if you call ahead. *V. San Donato, Località Cesana 61029, tel. 0722/4710. Showers. Cash only. Closed mid-Sept.–Easter.*

WHERE TO EAT

Just like a university town, Urbino has a student cafeteria, plenty of cheap snack joints, and fine medium-range restaurants. Local specialties include *crescioni* (cheese and veggie-filled pastry pockets). Strangozzi *pasticciati* (with a sauce of tomatoes, cream, and sausage) is a local specialty. Find them and other tantalizing take-out at **Ristorante al Girarrosto** (P. San Francesco 3, off V. Raffaello, tel. 0722/4445; open daily 8–2:30 plus Thurs.–Sun. 5:30–7:30). A **macrobiotic grocery** (V. Battisti 19, tel. 0722/320193; open Mon.–Sat. 8–12:30 and 4:30–7:30) with a breakfast bar is around the corner from Morgana Pub (*see below*). **Gelateria Orchidea** (C. Garibaldi 70), three doors down from Albergo Italia, specializes in soy-milk flavors (L2,000)—the smooth gelato *di caffè* (coffee) is a winner.

UNDER L10,000 • Un Punto Macrobiotico. This inexpensive, wonderful restaurant serves Italian vegetarian and fish dishes with a flair. You can go for the L4,000 self-serve menu and get soup, rice, beans, and salad (add pasta for L2,000 more), but more exciting are the four-course L13,000–L18,000 daily lunch and dinner specials in which you might have deep-fried zucchini flowers or *maltagliati con borlotti* (homemade square pasta with beans). *V. Pozzo Nuovo 4, off V. Cesare Battisti, tel. 0722/329790. Closed Sun.*

UNDER L15,000 • Morgana Pub. A large wood-burning oven and young crowd keep the pizzas (L7,000–L15,000) coming and beer (L3,500) flowing. If you're up for something different, try the pizza *morgana* (with porcini mushrooms and truffles; L15,000) and end the evening with *tartufo bianco* (white chocolate ice cream truffle; L4,500). *V. Nuova 3, off V. Cesare Battisti, tel. 0722/2528.*

Ristorante Agripan. Get it straight from the farm at this little restaurant, where the proprietors serve what they grow chemical-free at a nearby farm, plus free-range chickens and local meat, with wine made from unsprayed grapes. Smoking is not permitted. *V. del Leone 11, tel. 0722/327448. Cash only. Closed Wed.*

Ristorante Pizzeria Tre Piante. Join the students on a canopied terrace overlooking rolling hills and enjoy *stossaprete* or rice salad with shrimp; any first course costs L10,000. *V. Volpaccia delle Vechie 1, tel. 0722/4863. From P. della Repubblica, take V. Vittorio Veneto, left on Vicolo San Filippo, right on V. F. Budassi, left on V. Foro Posterula. Closed Mon.*

WORTH SEEING

The most prominent site in town is Luciano Laurana's sublime **Palazzo Ducale,** built in the mid-15th century over the remains of Duke Federico's ancestral home. In no other palace of its era are the principles of the Renaissance stated quite so clearly. The stunning facade composed of two towers linked by a trilevel loggia gives way to a **courtyard,** a masterpiece of symmetry, with a white travertine portico. To the left is the door to Federico's **library,** which in his time held an extensive collection of books from all over Europe. All that remains is a ceiling painting of an eagle, the family symbol. To the right of the courtyard is the entrance to the palace's **subterranean chambers,** a system of baths, stables, heating and cooling systems, and laundry facilities.

Upstairs is the **Galleria Nazionale delle Marche,** filled with works by local painters, including Federico Barocci and Giovanni Santi, Raphael's father. The masterpiece *Città Ideal* has been attributed to Piero della Francesca, Luciano Laurana, and Bramante—no one knows for sure who should get credit. Also look for the bizarre *Flagellation* by Piero della Francesca, Titian's *Resurrection* and *Last Supper,* and Paolo Uccello's *Profanation of the Host.* Notice the many portraits of Federico, all done in profile to hide the eye he lost in a joust. The duke's study is itself an incredible trompe l'oeil, its walls done in wood inlay made to look like cupboards full of books and musical instruments, with doors half open and squirrels perched on window ledges. *P. Duca Federico, tel. 0722/2760. Admission L8,000. Open Tues.–Fri. 9–7, Sun.–Mon. 9–2.*

Pretty archways knit together the rest of the town, and just wandering around you're sure to run into a few of Urbino's other sites. The Renaissance **Oratorio di San Giovanni** (Scala di San Giovanni 31, off V. Mazzini, tel. 0722/320936; admission L3,000; open Mon.–Sat. 10–noon and 3–5:30, Sun. 10–12:30) is known for a 15th-century fresco cycle depicting the life of John the Baptist, painted by regional artists Giacomo and Lorenzo Salimbeni. The **Oratorio di San Giuseppe** (V. Barocci 42, tel. 0722/320936; admission L2,000; open Mon.–Sat. 10–noon and 3–5:30, Sun. 10–12:30), undergoing restoration at press time (although likely to be open for 2000), contains two chapels: one with elaborate tempera paintings and the other with a life-size stucco manger scene.

Raphael's house contains only a few of the artist's original works, including *Madonna col Bambino*, but the beautiful Renaissance home does look a lot like it did when he was born here in 1483. Check out the torqued-wood ceiling beams and the original kitchen equipment. *V. Raffaello 57, off P. della Repubblica, tel. 0722/320105. Admission L5,000. Open Mon.–Sat. 9–1 and 3–7, Sun. 9–1.*

The **Fortezza Albernoz** is surrounded by the **Parco della Resistenza,** open daily 8–7. The fortress is currently being restored (the work is scheduled for completion in 2000), but that doesn't mar the amazing views of the surrounding countryside. To reach this terrace atop the city, take the stairs (V. Androncello) off Via Raffaello and turn left on Via dei Maceri; it's about a 10-minute walk from Piazza della Repubblica.

AFTER DARK

Thanks to the students, there's plenty to do after dark—and you don't have to spend a lot of lire to do it. **Cagliostro** (V. San Domenico 1, tel. 0722/327463) has pool and live bands on Wednesday night. After 10 PM, head to rocking disco **Club J** (V. Nuova 4, tel. 0722/2512; closed Sun.); there's no cover July–August, but you'll pay L10,000–L15,000 the rest of the year. Or try **Osteria Gula** (V. Garibaldi 23, across from Albergo Italia) for a beer (L6,000) and some Italian rock tunes. **Underground** (V. Barocci 16, tel. 0722/350269) blasts pop tunes and ensures a steady flow of food and spirits.

PESARO

Roman-era relics in the local museum and a small centro storico notwithstanding, it was Gioacchino Rossini, composer of *The Barber of Seville,* who put Pesaro on the map. The town has grown into a popular beach resort, and every August welcomes the **Rossini Opera Festival,** billed as Europe's second-largest musical festival (after Salzburg's), with opera and concerts all over town. Tickets (L30,000–L210,000) can be reserved and purchased through the Biglietteria del Festival (V. Rossini 37, 61100 Pesaro, tel. 0721/33184, fax 0721/30979; open from July 1; tel. 0721/30161 for information rest of yr); the tourist office will give you a listing of festival performances. Celluloid junkies come out of the woodwork in the third week of June for the increasingly popular **Mostra Internazionale del Cinema Nuovo** (International Exhibition of New Cinema), debuting up-and-coming directors exploring diverse social issues. Contact the festival office (tel. 0721/4456643) for the lineup.

BASICS

You'll find the **tourist office** (V. Trieste 164, tel. 0721/69341; open daily 9–12:30 and 4–6:30, reduced hrs in winter) down by the beach; Viale Trieste is the last cross street on Viale della Repubblica before you hit water.

COMING AND GOING

Frequent trains take you south to Ancona (50 min, L5,100) and north to Rimini (25 min, L3,900) and Bologna (2 hrs, L12,000), where you can connect to faraway places. At the info office in the **train station** (V. Risorgimento, tel. 1478/88088; open daily 8–noon and 3–5), tickets can be purchased 5:45 AM–9 PM. If you get on a late train without a ticket, find the conductor before he finds you, and you might be lucky enough to avoid a fine.

The **bus station** (P. Matteotti, tel. 0721/34768), off Via San Francesco near Piazza del Popolo, sends buses to Urbino (10 daily, 50 min, L3,500) and Ancona (5 daily, 1 hr 15 min, L7,900). Local buses (L1,100) leave from outside the train station and from Piazza Matteotti, but everything is easily accessible on foot.

WHERE TO SLEEP

Unimpressive high-rises dominate Pesaro's waterfront, but some turn-of-the-century Art Deco villas remain, and a few of these former vacation homes have been converted into seaside hotels. One of the first pensions built in Pesaro, **Villa Olga** (V. C. Colombo 9, north of P. della Libertà, tel. 0721/35029; cash only) is as close to the water as you can get. Doubles with frescoed ceilings and ocean views run L60,000 with bath. Also close to the beach is **Guglielmo Tell** (V. Trento 195, tel. 0721/32445; cash only; closed Oct.–May) with 15 nice doubles (L80,000). Call ahead in winter, when many establishments close down.

WHERE TO EAT

Because it's on the coast, Pesaro has many restaurants that serve fresh seafood at reasonable prices. For a platter of assorted *pesce* (fish) and a true family-run restaurant, check out **Trattoria da Maria** (V. Mazzini 73, off C. XI Settembre, tel. 0721/32986; cash only; closed Wed.), where there's no menu, but you'll get tasty specials of the day (three courses around L35,000). If you'd rather try something different, **Charbonnade** (V. Mazzini 13, tel. 0721/31911; closed Wed.) will grill your choice of meat table-side; a very full dinner runs about L50,000, including appetizers, drinks, and coffee. Boardwalk snacks are easy to find, especially *piadine,* the local griddle bread stuffed with everything but the kitchen sink. For one with cheese and sautéed spinach, head over to **Polo** (V. Marco Polo, off P. della Libertà), where you can sit on the terrace and enjoy the sea view. For a quick bite and change of pace, the Chinese takeout at **Bella Cina** (V. Baviera 29, off P. del Popolo, tel. 0721/370248; open daily 10:30–3 and 5:30–11), including fried rice (L4,000) and shrimp with peas (L8,000), hits the spot.

Nightlife in Pesaro seems to revolve around gelato, especially in summer, when people clutching Herculean cups capped with whipped cream stroll along the lungomare. You'll need two agile hands to manage the gelato from **Bar Pasticceria Gelateria Germano** (in summer, P. della Libertà 9, tel. 0721/61963; year-round, P. Collenuccio 12, tel. 0721/64415). Their thirst-quenching *granita* made with fresh lemon juice packs a punch.

WORTH SEEING

Tired of the beach? The **Museo Civico** (P. T. Mosca 29, tel. 0721/67815; admission L8,000; open daily 9–7, Sun. 9–1; in winter, daily 8:30–1:30, Sun. 9–1) has a few Renaissance paintings—the highlight is Bellini's *Pala di Pesaro*—and a good collection of the ceramics for which the town was once renowned, but even so, it's hard to justify the L8000. It does, however, include admission to Rossini's house (*see below*) and the pleasant **Museo del Mare** (Villa Molaroni, V. Pola, tel. 0721/67815; open mornings by request). Serious relic hunters can also visit the **Museo Oliveriano** (V. Mazza 97, tel. 0721/33344; open by appointment only Mon.–Sat. 9:30–12:30), full of Italic, Greek, Etruscan, and Roman artifacts, and a separate **Museo delle Ceramiche** (P. Toschi Mosca 29, tel. 0721/31213). Opera devotees will get a kick out of **Casa di Rossini** (V. Rossini 34, tel. 0721/387357; same hrs as Musei Civici), but **Teatro Rossini** (V. Rossini 29, tel. 0721/69359) is more impressive. If there's not much going on, the doorman will let you have a peek at the grandiose opera house. The **Conservatorio di Musica G. Rossini** (P. Olivieri 30) is closed to the public, but from the entrance in the caffè-lined piazza, you can often hear practicing musicians.

Piazza del Popolo is the town's main square and gathering spot. On one side is the 15th-century **Palazzo Ducale.** The icily elegant cupid-adorned structure is now home to the Prefettura, but guided tours are sometimes offered; call the tourist office for info. The evening *passeggiata* goes along portico-lined Corso XI Settembre toward the church of **Sant'Agostino,** which contains lovely wooden choir stalls with inlaid landscapes. Though the surrounding medieval walls and doors have been taken down, the 15th-century castle, **Rocca Costanza,** off Piazza Matteotti, remains intact.

ANCONA

Ancona, named from the Greek word for elbow, for its akimbo coastal site, was founded as a port city by the Syracusans in the 4th century BC. Bombing during World War II destroyed almost all evidence of its past, and an earthquake in the 1970s leveled much of what the Allies missed. These days it seems like Ancona's main cargo is beach-bound backpackers on their way to the Greek isles. Still, there are certainly worse places to hang around; the archaeological museum and Duomo are worth a gander if there's time before your ship sails, and if it's hot, you can always join everyone else at the beach.

BASICS

In summer you'll find an **APT** booth (tel. 071/41703; open daily 9- -2 and 5–7) at the train station. Off-season, trek out to the **main tourist office** (V. Thaon de Revel 4, tel. 071/3329), accessible by Bus 1/4 (L1,200) from the station. The main **post office** (P. XXIV Maggio, tel. 071/201808) does its thing Monday– Saturday 8:15–7. The **phone office** (P. Rosselli 12) is open daily 8 AM–9:45 PM.

COMING AND GOING

Trains depart from Ancona's **train station** (P. Rosselli, tel. 1478/88088) for Milan (hourly, 4–5½ hrs, L35,500), Bari (6 daily, 5 hrs, L35,500), Rome (8 daily, 3–4 hrs, L25,500), Bologna (hourly, 2½ hrs, L18,000), and Pesaro (hourly, 50 min, L5,100). Bus 1/4 runs from the train station to the port and Piazza Cavour in town.

BY FERRY • If you're traveling through Ancona in summer, you're probably here to catch a ferry. The English-speaking information office at **Stazione Marittima** (Molo Santa Maria, tel. 071/201183) will give you the skinny on cheap eats and on sights. Luggage storage (L1,000 per day per bag) at the port is open daily 8–noon and 1–9.

Strintzis and Minoan Joint Service (Stazione Marittima, tel. 071/2071068) sends ferries daily to Greece's Corfu (24 hrs), Igoumenitsa (26 hrs), and Patras (36 hrs) from April to mid-October (off-season less often). *Poltrona* (reclining seat) tickets run L70,000 in low season, L124,000 in high season. **Anek** (Stazione Marittima, tel. 071/205999) plies the harbors of Corfu, Igoumenitsa, and Patras (mid-May–mid-Oct., Mon.–Tues. and Fri.–Sat.) for similar prices. **Marlines** (Stazione Marittima, tel. 071/202566) also does the same routes. Their prices are slightly lower, but their service is less frequent—sending ships on Tuesday and Saturday afternoons only. Buy tickets at the company booths at the harbor or at any travel agency. The boats have discos, bars, restaurants, and more, but they're no bargain. Before you board, load up on supplies.

WHERE TO SLEEP AND EAT

Across from the station is **Albergo Dorico** (V. Flaminia 8, tel. and fax 071/42761), where 22 doubles with bath start at L70,000. You'll pay L70,000 to L90,000 for a clean double with large windows and chenille bedspreads at **Pensione Centrale** (V. Marsala 10, off C. Stamira, tel. 071/54388; cash only), five minutes from the port and closer to the center. Among affordable trattorias in the centro storico, **La Cantineta** (V. Gramsci 1/C, tel. 071/201107; cash only; closed Sun. and Aug.) and **Osteria Teatro Strabacco** (V. Oberdan 2, tel. 071/54213; closed Mon.) all serve traditional fish and seafood dishes; a complete meal runs L25,000–45,000. If you are stocking up for a ferry ride, hit the **Standa** (V. Alcide 2; closed Sun.) three blocks from the train station.

WORTH SEEING

If you have the time, check out what remains of the old city, including the magnificent 11th-century Romanesque-Byzantine **Duomo** (P. del Duomo; Bus 11 if you don't want to climb the hill) and the 13th-century **Santa Maria della Piazza** (P. Santa Maria), its intricate facade composed of tiny decorative arches. You'll inevitably stumble upon Piazza del Plebiscito; not far away lies the **Pinacoteca Comunale Francesco Podesti** (V. Pizzecolli 17, tel. 071/2225040; admission L4,000; open Tues.–Sat. 9–7, Sun.–Mon. 9–1), a museum with works by Titian and Guercino, as well as a small modern-art collection. For L4,000 visit one of central Italy's best ancient-art exhibits at **Museo Archeologico Nazionale delle Marche** (V. Ferretti 1, above V. Pizzecolli, tel. 0721/202602; open daily 8:30–1:30), which showcases vases, bronze pieces, and two Roman ivory beds.

ASCOLI PICENO

When you've overdosed on hill towns, head for one of the few valley towns in central Italy, Ascoli Piceno in the southern Marches. It's said that a helpful *picchio* (woodpecker) guided a tribe of shepherds to this valley at the edge of the Sibillini foothills, encircled by the Tronto and Castellano rivers. Ascoli has some of Italy's best-preserved medieval walls, and though they didn't hinder various invaders over the centuries, perhaps they keep the tourists away today—prices are reasonable, and this pleasant town maintains a good museum and easy access to the Sibillini Mountains. The locals are genuinely friendly, too. The **tourist office** (P. del Popolo 17, tel. 0736/255250; open weekdays 8:30–1 and 3–6:30, Sat. 9–1 and 3–6:30, Sun. 9–1) has brochures in English and info on trains, buses, sights, and lodging.

COMING AND GOING

To go to Ascoli by train, you must change at the seaside town of San Benedetto del Tronto (11 daily, 40 min, L3,900), reachable from Ancona (1 hr, L10,100) or Pescara (40 min, L8,200). Ascoli's **train station** is in Piazza della Stazione, where Bus 2, 3, or 4 takes you to the town center. Otherwise it's a 20-minute walk; from the station follow Viale Indipendenza past the Duomo and baptistery and take a right on Via del Trivio to hit the main square, Piazza del Popolo. It's easier to hop a **bus** from San Benedetto del Tronto (2 per hr, 50 min, L3,100); this way you get dropped closer to the town center, at Viale Alcide. Buy tickets at the train station bar in San Benedetto; the bus leaves from in front of the station. In Ascoli buy tickets at the newsstand on Viale Alcide. Three buses daily (one on Sunday) go from Ascoli to Rome (3 hrs, L20,000). Buy tickets at **Cameli Tours** (V. Angelini 127, off P. Orlini, tel. 0736/261154). Fewer trains and buses run on Sunday, so plan accordingly.

WHERE TO SLEEP AND EAT

Ostello de Longobardi (Palazzetto Longobardo, V. dei Soderini 27, tel. 0736/259007) offers salvation from pricier hotels. Built into a medieval tower, the tidy hostel with hospitable management charges L18,000 per night (showers L1,000). Curfew is 11 PM, but the signora gives out a few keys, and there's no afternoon lockout. From Piazza Ventido Basso, take Via Soderini (street farthest left) to Rua Longobardo. On the off chance the hostel is full, another option is **Cantina dell'Arte** (Rua della Lupa 8, tel. 0736/255744; cash only), which rents comfortable doubles with modern baths for L65,000–70,000. Take Via Mazzini off Piazza del Popolo, go left on Via Afranio, left after the post office, right onto alleylike Rua della Lupa.

Affordable meals are definitely part of Ascoli's not-invaded-by- tourists appeal. Laid-back **Al Teatro** (V. del Teatro 3, tel. 0736/253549; closed Mon.) is a good trattoria with an outdoor patio. Talking birds will charm you as you dig into a great pizza with asparagus (L6,500) or tagliatelle with salmon (L8,000). Hike up Monte Annunziata to find **Incontri** (V. Fortezza Pia 3, 1 km/½ mi from town center, tel. 0736/252227; cash only; no lunch), where dinner is served on a terrace overlooking the town or inside by the fireplace in winter, often accompanied by live music. Sample the local specialty, *fritto all'ascolana* (olives stuffed with meat and Parmesan and fried), at the pension **Cantina dell'Arte** (*see above*; Rua della Lupa 9, tel. 0736/255744). Order the bountiful, cheap daily specials (three courses under L20,000), often fresh fish caught by the owner. Ascoli's oldest pizzeria, **Pizzeria Bella Napoli** (P. della Viola, tel. 0736/257030; cash only), has an outdoor patio filled with family folks munching pies for L5,000–L9,000; closed Thurs.; no lunch). In between meals, stop for some sustenance at **Panificio Tranquilli** (V. dei Conti 10, tel. 0736/261609).

WORTH SEEING

Social life centers around the exquisitely balanced and symmetrical **Piazza del Popolo,** crowded every night during the *passeggiata*. If you're in the mood, **Bar Centrale** (No. 9) is a good spot to try the anise spirits for which the town is renowned, or sample some local pastries at the **Pasticceria Angelini** (No. 55) across the way. The galleries lining two sides of the piazza were created early in the 16th century, around the same time the **Loggia dei Mercanti** was built against the side of the church of **San Francesco.** The **Palazzo dei Capitani del Popolo,** a medieval palace begun in the 13th century and remodeled throughout the Middle Ages and Renaissance, looms over the piazza. Its facade, with a statue of Pope Paul III, was designed by local artist Cola d'Amatrice. The church of **San Francesco** (open daily 8–noon and 3–6) was modified from a Romanesque to a Gothic structure. You see its side from the piazza; the simple square facade, graced by a beautiful Gothic portal, is to the left.

A collection spanning works by d'Amatrice, Titian, Tiepolo, Tintoretto, and Caracci, ceramics, musical instruments, and excellent contemporary sculpture make Ascoli's **Pinacoteca Civica** (Palazzo del Comune, P. Arringa, tel. 0736/298213; admission L2,500; open Mon.–Sat. 9–1, also 3–7 in summer) well worth your time. Next door, the overbearing **Duomo** (open daily 8–noon and 4- -7) has a blue ceiling with gold stars and one too many chandeliers.

OUTDOOR ACTIVITIES

The **Sibillini Mountains,** which cover more than 250 square mi, offer hikes through some of the most beautiful scenery in Italy. Many of the range's rocky faces extend above 6,600 ft and are surrounded by glacial basins, wooded valleys, and serene mountain communities. One of the easiest ways to enter the landscape is to take a bus to **Amandola** from Ascoli Piceno's train station (3 per day, 1 hr, L4,100), where you'll find a friendly, amply stocked **tourist office** (P. Risorgimento, tel. 0736/848037; open July–mid-Sept, daily 9:30–12:30 and 4–7), which provides maps, info on excursions, and lodging listings. From here make the trek (11 km/7 mi) to **Lago di Pilota.** From Montemonaco on the lake, catch a bus to Monte San Martino (4 daily, L6,000), a beautiful mountain village in **Parco Nazionale del Lago di San Ruffino.** A popular four-hour hike starts at Forca di Presta and leads up Monte Vettore, a long walk along the south ridge. The towns are truly breathtaking, their medieval stone buildings perched on mountainsides. Limited public transportation may mean you'll have to spend a night in a village or camping, though hikes generally aren't longer than five hours. Camping is an option almost anywhere; to reserve, inquire at the tourist office in Amandola. For less rustic digs, hike to **Rifugio Amandola** (V. Campolungo, tel. 0736/847512; closed Oct.–May, except Christmas and Easter), 15 km (9 mi) outside Amandola. It has eight beds (L25,000 per person), hot water, and a restaurant (L25,000–L35,000 for a meal).

ROME

BY VALERIE HAMILTON

REVISED BY JON ELDAN AND CARLA LIONELLO

he currents of time run deep in Rome: 2,500 years of history are piled on top of each other, a study in contrasts as the modern metropolis grows over them like a vine. Modern offices in Renaissance buildings with dirty and worn Baroque facades look out over ancient ruins at a bus stop, while proud Romans chat on cell phones while tracing the same paths their ancestors once walked. These layers are a large part of the city's enigmatic charm and make Rome a continually unfolding city. There's no doubt that the home of the Colosseum, the Trevi Fountain, the Pantheon, St. Peter's Basilica, *and* the Sistine Chapel demands a lot of sightseeing, but despite its cultural treasures, Rome is no museum. The city—and it is *definitely* a city—bears its history with what is at best an offhand grace, at worst an erratic carelessness. Careening motorists, blaring televisions, stylish café-goers, all manner of workers, politicians, tourists, and thieves keep modern Rome in constant, vibrant motion around, over, and through the decaying remains of civilizations gone by.

According to legend, Rome was founded in 753 BC by Romulus and Remus, twin brothers nursed by a she-wolf in a cave below the Capitoline Hill. The city prospered and grew, eventually defeating its Etruscan rulers, and for centuries was the heart and soul of the nation that bore its name, which reached across Europe to the British Isles and spanned the Mediterranean from Gibraltar to Constantinople. As Rome was rebuilt after the centuries of looting and sacking that befell it, medieval churches were constructed over ancient temples and early Christian basilicas. In the Renaissance (1350–1600) and Baroque (1600–1750) periods, the elite-sponsored papacy commissioned extravagant additions to existing structures, ensuring that by the modern era much of Rome's architecture bore the mark of one papal dynasty or another. In the early 20th century, Mussolini tried his hand at renovating the Eternal City, bulldozing neighborhoods to make way for neo-imperial boulevards intended, along with government reforms, to make Rome a model of efficiency and a city of the future.

In the last few years the city has begun to reap the rewards of ambitious restoration projects, with freshly cleaned facades emerging from behind the scaffolding. And there is much more to come as the city readies itself for the *Giubileo* (Jubilee) in the year 2000, when more than 30 million people are expected to visit.

TIME-HONORED TRADITION

Legend has it that a Gypsy made off with five of the intended nails at Christ's crucifixion. In return, he and his people were exempted from the Eighth Commandment. What this means to you: watch your wallet. Violent crime isn't common in Rome, but pickpockets are everywhere. Never carry wallets in back pockets or open bags, cover watches and jewelry, and be sure that people on crowded buses keep their hands to themselves. Children carrying newspapers or cardboard use it to distract you while your wallet is stolen. A modicum of awareness should keep your belongings where they belong.

BASICS

AMERICAN EXPRESS

The English-speaking staff offers travel services and currency exchange and will cash traveler's checks for no commission. Cardholders can cash personal checks and receive mail. After hours call toll-free 1678/72000 for lost or stolen traveler's checks, 1678/74333 for lost or stolen cards. *P. di Spagna 38, 00187, tel. 06/67641; open weekdays 9–5:30, Sat. 9–12:30 (Sat. 9–3 in summer).*

CHANGING MONEY

Rates are best at banks, which are typically open weekdays 8:30–1:30 and 2:45–3:45 and charge a flat fee of L5,000. ATMs are all over town. The rates at **Thomas Cook** (P. Barberini, 21A, tel. 06/4828082; V. della Conciliazione 23, near the Vatican, tel. 06/68300435) aren't great, but you can draw money from your Visa or MasterCard, and the Barberini office is open every day: Monday–Saturday 8:30–7 and Sunday 9–1:30.

CONSULATES

Australia (C. Trieste 25/C, tel. 06/852721; open Mon.–Thurs. 9– noon and 1:30–5, Fri. 9–noon). **Canada** (V. Zara 30, tel. 06/445981; open weekdays 8:30–12:30 and 1:30–4). **Ireland** (P. Campitelli 3, tel. 06/6979121; open weekdays 10–12:30 and 3–4:30). **New Zealand** (V. Zara 28, tel. 06/4402928; open weekdays 8:30–12:45 and 1:45–5). **South Africa** (V. Tanaro 14, tel. 06/852541; open weekdays 8:30–noon). **United Kingdom** (V. XX Settembre 80/A, tel. 06/4825441; open weekdays 9:30–1:30). **United States** (V. Veneto 121, tel. 06/46741; open weekdays 8:30– noon).

DISCOUNT TRAVEL AGENCIES

Transalpino (P. dell'Esquilino 102, tel. 06/4870870; open weekdays 9–6:30, Sat. 9–1:30) handles discounted tickets for train, air, and boat travel. **CTS** (Centro Turistico Studentesco; V. Genova 16, off V. Nazionale, tel. 06/4620431; C. Vittorio Emanuele II 297, tel. 06/6872672; open weekdays 9:30–1 and 3:30—6:30, Sat. 9:30–1) is a student travel office where you can buy discounted plane, ferry, and train tickets. See their web page at http://www.cts.it.

EMERGENCIES

The general emergency number for **first aid, fire,** and **police** is 113. If you need help and don't speak Italian, look for a police officer wearing a translator badge (a British, French, or German flag) on his or her left arm—it'll save you from having to play charades. If you have to file an all-too-routine theft report, an English speaker is usually on staff at the **main police station** (V. San Vitale 15, just north of V. Nazionale, tel. 06/4686). There are also English-speaking officers and English-language forms at the **Ufficio Stranieri** (Foreigners' Office; V. Genova 2, off V. Nazionale, tel. 06/46862702; open daily 8–8).

ENGLISH-LANGUAGE BOOKS AND NEWSPAPERS

Wanted in Rome (L1,500) is a biweekly English magazine with classifieds available at newsstands and English-language bookstores. The larger Italian bookstores have decent selections of books in English at reasonable prices; try **Feltrinelli International** (V. V. E. Orlando 84, tel. 06/4827878; open Mon.– Sat. 9– 8, Sun. 10–1:30 and 4–7:30) or **Rizzoli** (Largo Chigi, 15, tel. 06/6796641; open Mon.–Sat. 9–7:30, Sun. 10:30–1 and 4–8). Newspapers from many homelands are expensive but available from many *edicole* (newsstands) in the city center. The one on Via del Corso, opposite the Column of Marcus Aurelius, is open 24 hours. **Economy Book and Video Center** (V. Torino 136, 1 block south of V. Nazionale, tel. 06/4746877; open summer, weekdays 9–8, Sat. 9–2; winter, Mon. 3–8, Tues.–Sat. 9–8) carries a large selection of new and used books plus cards and English-language movies (L10,000). The well-stocked **Anglo-American Bookstore** (V. della Vite 102, near P. di Spagna, tel. 06/6795222; open Mon.–Sat. 9:30–1:30 and 3:30– 7:30) is the place to go if you need a cookbook, new novel, or some brushing-up on ancient history. Another centrally located option is the **Lion Bookshop** (V. dei Greci 33; open Tue.—Sat. 10–7:30, Mon 3:30–7:30; tel. 06/32650437). The tiny **Corner Bookshop** (V. del Moro 48, tel. 06/5836942; open daily 10–1:30 and 3:30–8; closed Mon. morning), in Trastevere, packs books in from floor to ceiling.

LAUNDRY

One of the few self-service *lavanderie* (laundromats) around is **Onda Blu** (V. Palestro 59/61, tel. 06/ 4465864; open daily 8 AM– 10 PM), four blocks northeast of Stazione Termini. Each load costs L6,000 to wash and L6,000 to dry. If dry cleaning is unavoidable, ask around for the nearest *lavasecco* (dry cleaner). Expect to pay about L3,500 per piece.

LUGGAGE STORAGE

Luggage depots (open 5:30 AM–midnight) at either end of **Stazione Termini,** near Tracks 1 and 22, are the most central places to stash your bags. The going rate is L5,000 per piece per 12-hour period.

MAIL

Post offices, conveniently positioned all over Rome, sell stamps and are open in the morning Monday– Saturday; some are also open in the afternoon. The **main post office** (P. San Silvestro, 1 block east of V. del Corso; open daily 9–6) handles currency exchange and has fax machines. Bring your passport to receive *fermo posta* (held mail addressed to: Fermo Posta San Silvestro, 00187 Roma). Stamps (*francobolli*) are also sold at tobacco shops (marked TABACCHI), and there's mail pickup from the red mailboxes all over the city (there are also some special blue letter boxes in the center of town reserved for international mail). Technically a separate country, the **Vatican** has an independent postal service that's reputedly more reliable than the Italian mails. Buy stamps and post personal scripture weekdays 8:30– 7 and Saturday 8:30–6 at the post office (tel. 06/69883406) on Piazza San Pietro, just inside the Vatican walls. Note that Vatican stamps are not accepted by the Italian postal service, and Vatican post office boxes are located only in and around Vatican City.

MEDICAL AID AND PHARMACIES

Dial 113 for all emergencies. **Pharmacies** are marked with an illuminated green cross or white signs bearing a red cross. **Farmacia Piram Omeopatia** (V. Nazionale 228, tel. 06/4880754) and **Farmacia della Stazione** (P. dei Cinquecento 51, tel. 06/4880019) are both open 24 hours; others are open all night on a rotating basis. Check listings posted outside pharmacy doors for current schedules. Expect to pay a flat surcharge of L7,500 on pharmacy purchases after midnight.

ON-LINE RESOURCES

The Internet Cafè (V. Cavour 213, tel. 06/47823051, near Metro Line B Cavour) is open 7 days a week and offers internet access at L2,500 per 15 minutes. Across town (near the Vatican) is **X. Plore Internet Café** (V. dei Gracchi 83/85, near Metro A Ottaviano station, tel. 06/3241757), with techno-chic bar tables and slick computers that rent for L8,000 per hour in the afternoon, L15,000 per hour at night.

PHONES

Ubiquitous orange phones charge L200 for approximately three-minute local calls. Since they gulp down metallic morsels like mad, a *scheda telefonica* (phone card), sold at newsstands or tobacco shops in denominations of L5,000, L10,000, or L15,000, is more practical for long-distance calling. It's a good idea to carry both coins and a card, as many phones accept one and not the other. Collect and calling-card calls to the United States are best placed through an American operator; dial 1721011 for AT&T,

1721022 for MCI, but keep in mind that it is much cheaper and easier to call home using the Italian phone system and a phone card (just dial 0 + your country code + the area code and phone number).

VISITOR INFORMATION

Tourist information offices are opposite Track 2 in **Stazione Termini** and at **Fiumicino Airport** (tel. 06/4824078 and 06/65953038; both open daily 8:15–7:15), or three blocks northwest of the station at Via Parigi 5 (tel. 06/48899255; open Mon.—Fri. 8:15–7:15, Sat 8:15–1:15). There are also several information kiosks (open daily 9–6) located around town, including at Castel Sant'Angelo, midway down Via del Corso, and at Piazza Sonnino in Trastevere. **Enjoy Rome** (V. Varese 39, tel. 06/4451843; open weekdays 8:30–2 and 3:30–6:30, Sat. 8:30–2), 3½ blocks from Stazione Termini, is a good stop for maps, hotel listings, events schedules, travelers' info, and friendly advice in English. They book rooms free of charge and offer a three-hour walking tour of the city for L30,000 (L25,000 for those under 26). In person and over the phone, the **Hotel Reservation Service** (Stazione Termini or Fiumicino Airport, tel. 06/6991000; open daily 7 AM–10 PM) provides free booking services at more than 300 hotels in Rome plus other cities in Italy—you tell them what you want, and they'll find it for you.

GAY AND LESBIAN RESOURCES • For current listings on gay Rome, including nightclubs, film screenings, and political discussions, call the English line at **Circolo di Cultura Omosessuale "Mario Mieli"** (V. Corinto 5, tel. 06/5413985; open weekdays 10–6). Also associated with the Circolo is the gay bookstore **Libreria Babele** (V. Paola 44, off C. Vittorio Emanuele II, tel. 06/6876628).

COMING AND GOING

BY PLANE

The international **Leonardo da Vinci Airport** (30 km/18½ mi southwest of city center, tel. 06/65951), also referred to as **Fiumicino,** is served by major airlines. Inside the terminal, there's currency exchange, luggage storage (L4,100 per bag per day), and an **information office** (*see above*). The airport is open 24 hours, but omnipresent *carabinieri* (Italian national police) frown on using it as a hotel.

AIRPORT TRANSIT • Roughly every 20 minutes from 6:28 AM to 12:15 AM, local trains connect the airport with Rome's Trastevere (23 min), Ostiense (26 min), and Tiburtina stations (40 min) for L7,000. Express trains to Rome's main station, Stazione Termini (30 min, L15,000), run hourly 7:38 AM–10:08 PM. For a taxi from the airport to the city center, expect to pay about L70,000.

BY TRAIN

Rome's principal rail depot is the gargantuan **Stazione Termini** (*see below*), named for the ruins of Roman baths nearby. Trains don't run to or from Stazione Termini between 12:30 AM and 5 AM, so if you need to skip town under cover of night, go to **Stazione Ostiense** (P. dei Partigiani, tel. 1478/88088), which has all-night service to Genoa, Naples, Palermo, and Nice. Take Bus 57 from Stazione Termini or Piazza Venezia, or Metro B to the Piramide stop.

STAZIONE TERMINI • Trains from **Stazione Termini** (V. Cavour at V. Marsala, P. dei Cinquecento, tel. 1478/88088 for ticket and general rail information for all of Italy) serve major Italian and European destinations. An info desk in front of the ticket windows exclusively serves EurailPass holders. Avoid the hassle of long lines at the station by purchasing train tickets and/or making reservations in advance from most travel agencies (*agenzie di viaggio*). Tickets for trips of fewer than 100 km (62 mi) are sold throughout Rome at tobacco shops, newspaper kiosks, and anywhere else you see the FS emblem. Finally, don't forget to validate your ticket by stamping the back side in the little machines by the tracks before getting on board.

Get maps and information from the **EPT** (*see* Visitor Information, *above*) near Track 2. The free **Hotel Reservation Service** (*see* Visitor Information, *above*) opposite Track 10 will help you arrange lodgings. Get money from the ATM near the information office or make local or long-distance phone calls from the **phone center** near the ticket windows daily 8 AM–9:45 PM. Downstairs, an **albergo diurno** (day hotel) charges L10,000 for showers; towels are included but not soap (L500) or shampoo (L1,000). Near the northernmost Metro entrance is **DrugStore Termini,** a 24-hour complex of stores offering everything from groceries to underwear to English-language books to eyeglass repair and the only 24-hour mini-supermarket in town. The pharmacy outside on the piazza is open all night.

A safe place to kick back at any hour is the **waiting room** near Track 1, open only to ticket holders; the guard runs a tight ship, and sleeping is frowned upon.

BY BUS

Rome doesn't have a central bus terminal. Instead, blue **COTRAL** (tel. 167/431784 toll-free) buses leave from different points around town for various destinations in Lazio province. Get the details from EPT offices (*see* Visitor Information, *above*), or try calling COTRAL directly. Private coaches—most with plush seats and air-conditioning—serve destinations throughout Italy. Get info and buy tickets at **Euro-jet Tours** (P. della Repubblica 54, tel. 06/4817455; open weekdays 9–7, Sat. 9–1).

BY CAR

There are much better ways to spend your time than braving Rome's hellish traffic, maze of one-way streets, restricted zones, and dismal lack of public parking. Leaving town is another, uniquely frustrating experience—and be prepared for some high auto rental rates. The main access routes from the north are the A1 (Autostrada del Sole) from Milan and Florence and the A12/E20 from Genoa. To go to Naples, hop on the A2. All highways that intersect Rome connect with the GRA (Grande Raccordo Anulare), a confusing beltway that funnels traffic into the center. To conquer the GRA, you'll need a good road map and a healthy dose of patience.

RENTAL CARS • Rentals cost around L100,000 per day for the cheapest compact, although better deals are often available on weekends. Rates include insurance but not gas, which can cost up to L80,000 per tankful. You'll need a credit card, a passport, and (of course) a driver's license. In most cases, you'll need to be 25 or older. Nerves of steel wouldn't hurt either. Procrastinators take note: renting in advance from an international company like **Avis** (tel. 06/4701400) or **Hertz** (tel. 167/234679 toll-free) can save you nearly 50% off what you'd pay renting locally (*see* Getting Around *in* Chapter 1). Both companies have offices in Fiumicino and Stazione Termini. If you are coming to Rome with a car (and you have no idea where to put it), keep in mind that the *centro storico* (historic center) is closed to cars without permits, and parking in the periphery can be tricky. A good place to start is the large garage under the Villa Borghese (*see* Exploring Rome, *below*).

GETTING AROUND

The maze of medieval streets in Rome's center can be more frustrating than charming until you figure it out. Buses and the two-line subway system are convenient for getting around, but Rome is really a walking city, and you'll see and do more on foot. The **Tiber River** runs north–south (more or less) through the middle of the city, making a backwards S-curve that separates the Vatican to the west from the **centro storico** to the east. Many city-center hotels, restaurants, and sights are accessible from the handy bus stop Largo di Torre Argentina (a.k.a. Largo Argentina), connected to Stazione Termini by Buses 64 or 170 during the day and Bus 78 at night. **Stazione Termini** to the east is also accessible from the city center by way of Via Nazionale, which meets Via del Corso and Via del Plebiscito at **Piazza Venezia** (recognizable by the enormous Vittorio Emanuele II monument). To the south of Piazza Venezia lies ancient Rome, to the north Via del Corso divides the town and ends in **Piazza del Popolo,** with the Spanish Steps and Trevi Fountain to the east and the centro storico—**Campo dei Fiori, Piazza Navona,** the **Pantheon,** and the Tiber—to the west. Signs in the centro storico direct you to major sights, which themselves serve as landmarks to help you orient yourself. Keep an eye out for uneven cobblestones, speeding mopeds, and flying Fiats.

BY BUS AND METRO

Most (orange) city buses run from 5:30 AM to midnight, with some late-night lines. Stops are marked by signs and labeled FERMATA, and most also list route numbers, the main destinations along each route, and lines with night service. A free map of main bus routes is available from the ATAC information kiosk in Piazza dei Cinquecento (tel. 06/46954444 for bus info or 06/5816040 for lost property). A long-awaited expansion of the Metro has begun, but for now you'll have to make do with the two existing routes. The red **Line A** runs between Ottaviano–San Pietro (walking distance to the Vatican) and Anagnina (far southeast), hitting piazzas Barberini, della Repubblica, and di Spagna. The blue **Line B** runs between Laurentina (EUR) and Rebibbia and is useful for reaching the Colosseum and the Ostiense train station. Entrances are marked by M signs above ground and in Stazione Termini, the only point where the two lines intersect. The Metro runs daily from 5:30 AM to 11:30 PM.

A one-time orange BIT ticket can be bought at cafés, tobacco shops, and newspaper kiosks displaying the ATAC emblem; it has three validation spaces and is good for bus rides or a combination of one Metro ride and multiple bus rides within 75 minutes. Stamp the ticket in the bus or Metro turnstile and again in the remaining two spaces if you make your connections. Beware: machines in Metro stations and at some bus stops hardly ever work, so play it safe and get your tickets ahead. If you're caught without a ticket, you'll get stuck with a L50,000 fine. Get on the bus at the back door and validate your ticket in the orange boxes (take the front door if you have a pass). Exit through the center doors and always keep your eyes out for those crafty pickpockets. The BIG (*biglietto integrato giornaliero*; L1,500) is an integrated bus-Metro ticket; the BIRG ticket is the regional version. If you plan on crossing town frequently, consider a day pass (L6,000) or the weekly *carta integrata settimanale* (CIS; L24,000). Both are good for unlimited Metro, bus, and urban train travel and only need to be validated the first time you use them. Month-long passes (*abbonamento mensile*; L50,000) are also sold.

BY CAR

Unless you're a race-car driver or related to Evel Knievel, don't even dream of braving Rome's hellish traffic. The historic center is closed to cars without residential permits, and parking elsewhere is expensive and difficult.

BY TAXI

The meter reads L4,500 at flag fall; add L1,300 every kilometer (L480 in slow traffic). You'll pay L5,000 extra between 10 PM and 7 AM, L2,000 extra on Sunday, and L2,000 per piece of luggage. There is a L14,000 supplemental charge to the airport and a L11,500 charge from the airport into town. Only take authorized taxis (they have certificates posted inside). Grab a cab at a taxi stand (don't bother trying to hail one; they rarely stop)—usually on main piazzas—or call **La Capitale Radio Taxi** (tel. 06/4994) or **Radio Taxi Romana** (tel. 06/3570). **Radio Taxi** (tel. 06/88177) accepts American Express if you let them know in advance. When you call a cab, you'll pay for the time it takes to get to you—up to L6,000 extra.

BY BIKE OR MOPED

The medieval streets and scary traffic in Rome don't make for smooth biking, but renting a bike is a good way to cover a lot of ground. For uninterrupted pedaling, take a leisurely ride through town on Sunday, when a long stretch of road (P. del Popolo to the Colosseum and out beyond the walls) is closed to cars, or any day along the bike path (*pista ciclabile*), which follows the river north out of town. Expect to pay about L6,000 per hour or L20,000 for the day, a bit more for mountain bikes and tandems.

In good weather, you'll find rental stands open from 10 to sunset on piazzas Popolo, San Silvestro, di Spagna, and Augusto Imperatore, and in the Villa Borghese on Viale dei Bambini. **Collalti Bici** (closed Mon.) is open year-round for rentals and repairs (V. del Pellegrino 80–82, near Campo dei Fiori, tel. 06/68801084). **I Bike Rome** (V. Vittorio Veneto 156, inside Villa Borghese parking garage, tel. 06/3225240) and **Scoot-a-Long** (V. Cavour 302, tel. 06/6780206) rent bicycles year-round at similar rates, as well mopeds and mandatory helmets, all for about L80,000 a day. A credit card or passport is required; a driver's license is not.

WHERE TO SLEEP

If you're not too picky, a clean double in a no-nonsense pension can be had for L60,000–L80,000. In the L90,000–L160,000 range, you'll get ambience, a private bath, and perhaps a more central address. Keep in mind that prices can vary considerably between high, low, and in-between seasons, so it's best to call ahead and be specific. If you want to let someone else handle the reservations for you, call the Hotel Reservation Service (*see* Visitor Information, *above*) for free bookings, or hit their booth at Stazione Termini or Fiumicino Airport. If you want to hunt on your own, the tourist office has the *Annuario degli Alberghi*, a booklet that lists everything from five-star hotels to one-star dives. All registered hotels have fixed prices, printed on cards on the back side of the door of each room. Stay clear of solicitors at Stazione Termini luring travelers to their establishments: They may not be legit and will likely charge twice the going rate.

Stick to the area around **Stazione Termini** if price is more important than setting. Hotels in the **centro storico** and **Trastevere** and near the **Vatican** are closer to what you'll want to see and do, but prices start in the L90,000 range. Campgrounds are inconveniently located on the city fringes, but sites are *cheap*—expect to pay around L13,000 for your spot on the grass.

NORTH OF STAZIONE TERMINI

Although a few blocks farther from the historic center of town, the area north of Stazione Termini is cleaner and more secure at night than its southern counterpart.

UNDER L90,000 • Pensione Monaco. At this simple, very clean family-run place between the train station and Villa Borghese, doubles without bath run L65,000. *V. Flavia 84, 00187, tel. 06/4744335. 12 rooms, 5 with bath. Cash only.*

Hotel Germano. This hotel is a diamond in the rough off Via Volturno. New, airy rooms with modern furniture, hair dryers, and phones suggest a more expensive hotel. Doubles run L75,000, with bathroom L90,000. *V. Calatafimi 14/A, 00185, tel. 06/486919. 15 rooms, 5 with bath.*

UNDER L140,000 • Hotel Cervia. These spartan rooms (L100,000–L140,000) may not be homey, but they're clean, and having 30 rooms means vacancies are common. Breakfast—an all-you-can-eat spread including coffee, OJ, and bread—is available for groups for L5,000 per person. *V. Palestro 55, 00185, tel. 06/491057, fax 06/491056. 30 rooms, 15 with bath.*

Pensione Piave. It's far enough from the station to be quiet and residential, but close enough to walk. Well-lighted doubles with phones, desks, and tiled bathrooms cost L110,000. The young managers will give you front-door keys. *V. Piave 14, 00187, tel. 06/4743447, fax 06/4873360. 12 rooms, 10 with bath. Laundry. Cash only.*

Pensione Katty 2. Recently renovated rooms with all the amenities are still at a budget price. The same owners run another pensione in the building with lower rates. Doubles with baths run L130,000. *V. Palestro 35, 00185, tel. 06/4441216. 9 rooms with bath. Cash only.*

Pensione Virginia. You'll find inexpensive rooms pleasantly decorated with faux frescoes. Doubles cost L80,000, with bathroom L130,000. *V. Montebello 94, 00185, tel. 06/4457689. 16 rooms, 2 with bath. Cash only.*

Hotel Cambridge. Rooms are deluxe for the neighborhood, most with showers, hair dryers, minibars, and TVs. The couple who run the place are eager to please, providing breakfast (L5,000) if you get up early and front-door keys if you stay out late. Doubles with bath cost L120,000–L180,000. *V. Palestro 87, 00185, tel. 06/4456821, fax 06/4959254. 34 rooms, 28 with bath. Cash only.*

SOUTH OF STAZIONE TERMINI

Rome's thickest concentration of budget lodging is in the relatively uncharming neighborhood south of Stazione Termini. Via Cavour, Via Manin, and Via Principe Amedeo aren't dangerous during the day, but when the sun sinks low, lone travelers—especially women—should be careful. The area is redeemed by its proximity to the station and because you get more for your money here than in more pleasant neighborhoods.

UNDER L100,000 • Hotel Giugiù. Up a marble staircase, the Giugiù boasts sunny and comfortable rooms (doubles L90,000–L100,000) big enough to pitch a tent in. The family that runs the place offers breakfast (L8,000). *V. del Viminale 8, 00184, tel. and fax 06/4827734. 9 rooms, 7 with bath. Cash only.*

Hotel Pensione Selene. The family-run Selene is bright and clean, and you should sleep well under cotton comforters in summer and down comforters in winter. Doubles have been redone with wooden furniture and TVs and run L90,000. *V. del Viminale 8, 00184, tel. 06/4744781, fax 06/47821977. 15 rooms with bath. Curfew 12:30 AM. Cash only.*

UNDER L130,000 • Hotel Perugia. The Perugia's location is a big draw for ancient-history aficionados; it's on an alleyway not more than two blocks from the Roman Forum and the Colosseum in a quiet neighborhood that's as close to the centro storico as it is to Stazione Termini. Doubles with bath cost L120,000–150,000. *V. del Colosseo 7, 00184, tel. 06/6797200, fax 06/6784635. 13 rooms, 11 with bath. Cash only.*

Pensione Stella Elsa. This airy third-floor hotel lies behind a courtyard away from the street and its unsavory characters. A hospitable couple makes sure that the rooms (doubles L60,000, with bath L120,000) are spotless; all have either a sink or a shower. *V. Principe Amedeo 79/A, 00185, tel. and fax 06/4460634. 9 rooms, 6 with bath. Cash only.*

UNDER L160,000 • Hotel Contilia. The personable, English- speaking owner is proud of his hotel, thoroughly modern from top to bottom. The shiny tile in the reception and breakfast room looks a bit slick, but the rooms themselves (doubles L120,000–L160,000) are hospitable. All have desks, TVs, and

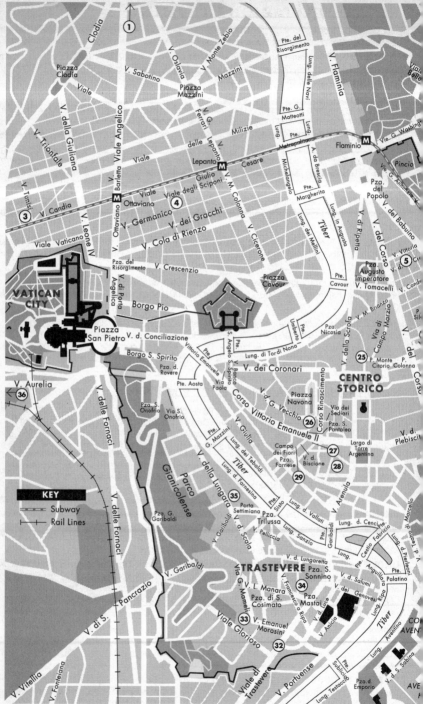

ROME LODGING

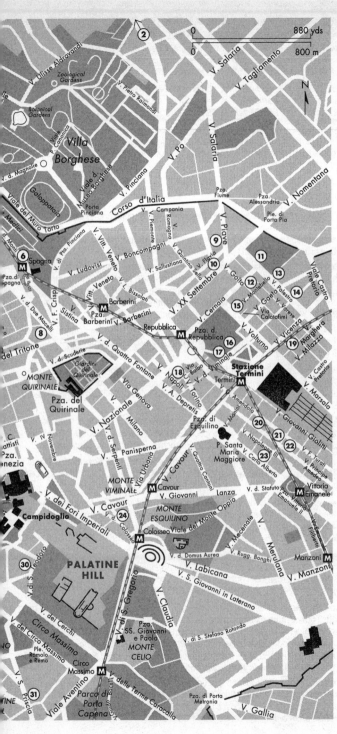

Albergo del Sole, **29**

Albergo
della Lunetta, **27**

Bed-and-Breakfast
Accademia dei
Licei, **35**

Casa Kolbe, **30**

Fawlty Towers, **19**

Giuggioli Hotel, **4**

Hotel Alimandi, **3**

Hotel
Cambridge, **13**

Hotel Cervia, **14**

Hotel Cisterna, **34**

Hotel Contilia, **22**

Hotel Erdarelli, **8**

Hotel Germano, **15**

Hotel Giugiù, **17**

Hotel Margutta, **6**

Hotel Montreal, **23**

Hotel Navona, **26**

Hotel Parlamento, **7**

Hotel Pensione
Selene, **16**

Hotel Perugia, **24**

Hotel Santa
Prisca, **31**

Hotel Smeraldo, **28**

Hotel Sweet
Home, **20**

Hotel Teti, **21**

Ostello del Foro
Italico, **1**

Pensione Campo
Marzio, **25**

Pensione
Carmel, **33**

Pensione Esty, **32**

Pensione Katty, **11**

Pensione
Monaco, **10**

Pensione Panda, **5**

Pensione Piave, **9**

Pensione Stella
Elsa, **22**

Pensione
Virginia, **12**

Roma Camping, **36**

Village Camping
Flaminio, **2**

YWCA, **18**

phones. The Contilia is in the same building as Pensione Stella Elsa (*see above*). *V. Principe Amedeo 79/D, 00185, tel. 06/4466942, fax 06/4466904. 30 rooms, 27 with bath.*

SPLURGE • Hotel Montreal. Another simple, cleaner-than-average hotel in the south-of-Termini area, this one is on a tree-lined street across from Santa Maria Maggiore. Doubles are billed at L150,000–200,000. *V. Carlo Alberto 4, 00185, tel. 06/4465522, fax 06/4457797. 16 rooms with bath or shower.*

Hotel Teti. This small, no-nonsense hotel between the station and Santa Maria Maggiore is clean and fresh-looking. Rooms have firm beds and ample closet space. Sinks are standard in all rooms. Doubles cost L185,000. *V. Principe Amedeo 76, 00185, tel. 06/4825240. 11 rooms with bath. Cash only.*

Hotel Sweet Home. Overrun with lively colors and floral prints, this place is cozy, pretty, and almost *too* cute. Thick doors with gilded molding open onto immaculate rooms (doubles L120,000–L180,000), all with TVs and phones. Six rooms face away from the noisy street. *V. Principe Amedeo 47, 00185, tel. 06/4880954, fax 06/4817613. 12 rooms with bath.*

CENTRO STORICO

The centro storico, Rome's heart and soul, is everyone's favorite place to stay, and hotel proprietors know it. Prices here are generally higher than in the rest of the city. Your money is buying prime location but not necessarily more amenities. The bottom line: if you're on a whirlwind tour and really want to savor the flavor of Rome, it's worth the extra cash.

UNDER L100,000 • Pensione Campo Marzio. Housed in a 17th-century palazzo just steps from the Pantheon, this pension's location compensates for Salvation Army–style furnishings and unreliable utilities. Rooms (doubles L90,000) are big if shabby and all overlook the piazza. Try to pay in advance, as there's no office and no guarantee that someone will be around when you want to leave. *P. Campo Marzio 7, 00186, tel. 06/68801486. 14 rooms without bath. Cash only.*

UNDER L140,000 • Casa Kolbe. On a tranquil street on the edge of the Forum, the Kolbe is a great deal at L135,000 for a double with a bathroom and access to a small garden. *V. San Teodoro 44, 00186, tel. 06/6794974. 64 rooms with bath. Cash only.*

Pensione Panda. Convenient to Piazza di Spagna and its evening *passeggiate* (strolls), this friendly pension has wrought-iron fixtures, terra-cotta tiles, and marble sinks throughout. Anti-noise windows keep street life in the street. Doubles range between L110,000 and L150,000 with superclean baths. *V. della Croce 35, 00187, tel. 06/6780179, fax 06/69942151. 20 rooms, 4 with bath.*

UNDER L190,000 • Albergo della Lunetta. Open walkways and a central courtyard with potted plants give this place a tropical feel in stark contrast to the gloomy rooms (doubles L120,000–L160,000). *P. del Paradiso 68, 00186, tel. 06/6861080, fax 06/6892028. 35 rooms, 20 with bath. Cash only.*

Hotel Margutta. This gem hidden away on a charming side street between Piazza di Spagna and Piazza del Popolo commands L175,000 for its double rooms. *V. Laurina 34, 00187, tel. 06/3223674, fax 06/3200395. 24 rooms with bath.*

Albergo del Sole. This is a worthwhile spot near the pubs, eateries, and open-air market centered around Campo dei Fiori. Read a book in the antiques-filled common rooms or watch the sun set over the dome of Sant'Andrea della Valle from the fifth-floor terrace. Doubles fetch L150,000–L170,000. Reservations are a must. *V. del Biscione 76, 00186, tel. 06/68806873, fax 06/6893787. 65 rooms, 50 with bath. Cash only.*

Hotel Smeraldo. This hotel occupies a narrow street between Largo Argentina and Campo dei Fiori. Doubles (L130,000–L180,000) are on the small side, but they are clean and pleasant and come with air-conditioning. *Vicolo dei Chiodaroli 9, 00186, tel. 06/6875929, fax 06/6545495. 35 rooms, most with bath.*

Hotel Navona. In classic Roman style, the building that houses this hotel has been under renovation on and off for 19 centuries. The 16th-century exterior hides a 13th-century frame into which is tucked a 1st-century doorway flanked by ancient columns. Inside, the brusque Australian who runs the show carries on the tradition, having added wooden beams here, fire alarms there, so that the place is eclectic and up to date. Doubles run L135,000–L185,000, breakfast included. *V. dei Sediari 8, 00186, tel. 06/6864203, fax 06/68803802. 25 rooms, 17 with bath. Cash only.*

SPLURGE • Hotel Parlamento. If this hotel just off the Corso had an elevator, you'd be paying a lot more. Schlep your bags up the stairs to the fourth floor and reap the rewards, including a roof terrace for breakfast and sunbathing. Doubles with bath cost L190,000. *V. delle Convertite 5, 00187, tel. 06/69921000. 23 rooms with bath. Cash only.*

Hotel Erdarelli. Halfway between the Spanish Steps and the Trevi Fountain, the Erdarelli has comfy doubles that go for L170,000, with bath L200,000. Ask for a room on the inner courtyard if you want to avoid street noise. *V. Due Macelli 28, 00187, tel. 06/6791265. 28 rooms, 20 with bath.*

Hotel Santa Prisca. Retreat from the noise and commotion of the busy city to your villa on the nearby, peaceful Aventine Hill. Well, sort of. Your share of the villa is a double room with bath for L209,000, but breakfast is included. *Largo Manilo Gelsomini 25, 00153, tel. 06/5741917. 50 rooms with bath.*

WEST OF THE TIBER

West of the Tiber, hotels are clustered in the area near the **Vatican** and in **Trastevere,** the former served by Buses 64 and 81 and Metro Line A (Ottaviano–San Pietro station), the latter by Buses 56 and 60. Both are good locations from which to explore the town.

UNDER L80,000 • Pensione Esty. The building housing this family-run pension is right on trafficky Viale di Trastevere. Convenient enough, sure, but the street din gets out of hand despite two layers of shutters; light sleepers should request one of the rooms facing the back courtyard. Doubles cost L75,000. *V. di Trastevere 108, 00153, tel. 06/5881201. Past V. Aurelio Saffi on V. di Trastevere; turn up driveway and enter 1st doorway on left, marked* SCALA A; *take elevator to 3rd floor. 11 rooms without bath.*

UNDER L130,000 • Bed-and-Breakfast Accademia dei Licei. This so-called B&B feels more like your own apartment—that is, if your apartment has 20-ft ceilings and a fountain in the hall. Each of the two enormous rooms has a loft that sleeps up to four people; living areas below are plushly appointed with real furniture, and you're welcome to use the kitchen. Prices (L85,000–L120,000 for a double) are almost too good to be true; be sure to call ahead. *V. della Lungara 18, 00153, tel. and fax 06/68806905. 2 rooms without bath.*

UNDER L140,000 • Giuggioli Hotel. The Victorian age meets the 1940s at this first-rate, time-warped joint. The same woman has run things for 40 years, and her stately furniture has accumulated in the grand high-ceilinged rooms (doubles L110,00–L130,000). Her four cats appreciate a good belly scratch. *V. Germanico 198, 00192, tel. 06/3242113. From P. Venezia, take Bus 70 to V. Germanico. 5 rooms, 1 with bath. Cash only.*

Pensione Carmel. The Carmel is on a quiet, tree-lined street near Trastevere's nightlife—the best of both worlds. Average-size doubles (L130,000) have a woody, mountain-lodge flair, some with patterned tiles in the bathroom. Soak up the sun on the greenery-filled terrace or relax in the reading room. *V. G. Mameli 11, 00153, tel. and fax 06/5809921. 7 double rooms with bath. Cash only.*

UNDER L190,000 • Hotel Cisterna. Night owls will find a roost in this comfortable hotel hidden on a winding street in lively Trastevere, with plenty of nearby restaurants and clubs. There's a small rooftop patio plus a courtyard in back with tables and umbrellas. Doubles cost L180,000. *V. della Cisterna 7–9, 00153, near P. San Calisto, tel. 06/5817212, fax 06/5810091. 18 rooms with bath.*

SPLURGE • Hotel Alimandi. The Alimandi's medieval-looking furniture and odd battle accessories liven up the TV room, saloon bar, dining room, and entranceway. By comparison, the clean doubles (L210,000) seem generic. Head to the rooftop garden for some sun. *V. Tunisi 8, 00192, 1 block from entrance to Vatican museums, tel. 06/39723948, fax 06/39723943. 35 rooms with bath.*

HOSTELS

Fawlty Towers. This hostel (affiliated with Enjoy Rome; *see* Visitor Information *in* Basics, *above*) just a few steps from Stazione Termini is staffed by helpful, English-speaking residents. Common areas include a terrace and lounge with satellite TV; beds in semiprivate rooms run L30,000–L35,000, sheets included. Doubles are L90,000–L100,000. Reserve ahead of time—Fawlty Towers is deservedly popular. Two other *pensioni*—Sandy and Ottaviano—are under the same management. There's free luggage storage. *V. Magenta 39, 00185, tel. 06/4450374, fax 06/4450743. 36 beds. 15 rooms, 4 private rooms with bath. Cash only.*

Ostello del Foro Italico (HI). This grim hostel's inconvenient location in Rome's northwest corner—and that it's a slab of cold, fascist architecture—doesn't keep away hordes of travelers. L25,000 per person includes sheets, hot showers, and breakfast. The barracks-inspired dorms each hold about a dozen bunk beds, and men and women are channeled into different wings. A basement cafeteria serves bland meals (from L14,000). Hostel cards are required but can be issued on the spot for L30,000. Luggage storage (L1,500) is available. *V. delle Olimpiadi 61, near Stadio Olimpico, 00194, tel. 06/3236267, fax 06/*

3242613. From Stazione Termini, take Metro Line A to Ottaviano, then Bus 32 to 7th stop (past V. Mares-ciallo Giardino); entrance is around building to right. 334 beds. Midnight curfew; lockout 9–2. Cash only.

YWCA. If you can handle the midnight curfew and gender imbalance, the YWCA south of Stazione Termini is unbelievably posh. Sexes mix in the TV room, the sitting room, and the peaceful library. The high-ceilinged bedrooms have twin beds, desks, and sinks; many face Via Cesare Balbo, the scene of a morning market. Priority is given to women, but occasionally they do allow men in small groups (ask nicely). Eat in the backyard garden or upstairs in the cafeteria (meals from L20,000). Doubles are L80,000, L100,000 with bathroom; breakfast is included. Photocopier and fax machines are available. *V. Cesare Balbo 4, 00184, tel. 06/4880460, fax 06/4871028. 78 beds. Reception open 7 AM–midnight. Cash only.*

CAMPING

Camping in Rome is predictably inconvenient; the only open spaces are outside the city, so camp-grounds are nowhere near where you want to be. It's a hassle to get to these sites without a car, but if you're so enamored of the great outdoors that you want to *camp* in a city of 3 million people, go for it.

Roma Camping. Separated from Via Aurelia by a walk up a grassy hill, this campground has clean, basic toilet facilities, a breakfast bar with outdoor seating, and a supermarket across the road. Stake your claim on Roman soil for L11,000 per person plus L5,500 for your tent and L500 for a hot-ish shower. *V. Aurelia 831, 00165. tel. 06/6623018, fax 06/66418147. From Largo Argentina, Bus 46 to P. Irnerio, then Bus 246 to Silos supermarket on V. Aurelia; cross on overpass. Flush toilets, showers. Cash only.*

Village Camping Flaminio. Acres of space mean there's room for you and 300 friends. It's geared more toward car camping and bungalow rentals, but you can pitch a tent for L13,000 per person. The Village offers a bar, restaurant, and grocery, which is a good thing since the walk from the entrance is so long you may never leave. *V. Flaminia Nuova 821, 00191. tel. 06/3332604, fax 06/3330653. Metro A to Flaminio; follow signs to Roma Nord COTRAL trains, take Prima Porta line past Tor di Quinto to Due Ponti stop; walk south along highway 600 ft to Bar Euclide and cross highway. Cash only.*

WHERE TO EAT

If you really want to eat on the cheap in Rome, the answer is pizza. But that means several different things in Rome. Here's the scoop: the simplest version is **pizza** from a bread bakery—it's basically bread dough stretched thin and baked quickly and should be enjoyed while still warm—and if it's not right out of the oven, it's probably not worth biting into. The choices are called pizza *bianca* if it's got just olive oil brushed on top, pizza *rossa* if they've slathered on a thin layer of (good) canned tomato sauce, and pizza *margherita*, dressed with sauce and mozzarella cheese, and it's always sold by weight, just like bread. An *etto* (100 grams, or about a quarter pound) is usually a modest portion. Busy bread bakers don't have time to get fancy with the toppings, so if you want cheese or anything else on your pizza, head for a specialist. **Pizza al taglio** (by the cut) shops are everywhere, generally open from mid-morning to late evening without an afternoon break. They sell pizza by weight with a large variety of toppings, such as potato and rosemary, mozzarella and zucchini, and even combinations like shrimp and artichoke. Finally there is pizza from the pizzeria, which in Rome means sitting down for a plate-size wafer-thin pizza, baked for a scant minute in a wood-burning oven.

Another budget option is to do it yourself: consider practicing your Italian while foraging for picnic ingre-dients at an open-air market. Then round out your feast by stepping into an *alimentari* for cheese and cured meats, bread, and a little bottle of wine, and *ecco fatto* (there you are)! Even if you are crazy about pizza and picnics, don't make the mistake of not sitting down to a meal in a restaurant or trattoria. A lazy dinner outside on a warm summer evening is as quintessentially Roman as you can get.

NEAR STAZIONE TERMINI AND COLOSSEUM

Stazione Termini is surrounded by cheap pizza al taglio shops and snack bars. A 15-minute walk will get you to the city's most crowded (hold on to your bag) open-air market, at Piazza Vittorio (Mon.–Sat. 8–1). **Caffè dell'Orologio** (V. Cavour 77–79, 3 blocks south of Stazione Termini, tel. 06/4740491), with outside tables and inexpensive sandwiches, is a good place to kill time if the waiting room at Termini isn't your style.

UNDER L10,000 • Alle Carrette. Tables and crowds spill out of this popular pizzeria, tucked into an alley at the bottom of Via Cavour, just around the corner from the Imperial Fora. First courses are available if you aren't hungry for pizza. *Vicolo delle Carrette 14, tel. 06/6792770. Closed Mon.*

Cavour 313. After tramping through the fora, pop into this casual wine bar for a glass of vino and some nibbles. A good variety of salads, cheeses, and salami hits the spot when you're not yearning for a full multi-*piatti* (courses) meal. *V. Cavour 313, tel. 06/6785496. Closed Aug. and Sun. in July and Sept.*

Da Bruno e Romana. Assorted pots, clocks, and keys adorn the walls of Bruno and Romana's country-style dining room three blocks from Stazione Termini. Feast on *stracciatella alla romana* (egg-drop soup) and cannelloni filled with spinach and ricotta cheese. Thursday is gnocchi day. The best reason to come here is the friendly atmosphere, a real rarity in this grimy, touristy neighborhood. *V. Varese 29, tel. 06/490403. From Stazione Termini, walk 3 blocks north on V. Milazzo to V. Varese. Cash only. Closed Sun.*

Ristorante Rossi. Grab your grub to go or pull up a chair at this Denny's look-alike restaurant. Try the *bruschetta* (garlic-rubbed toast with various toppings), especially the one piled high with mushrooms and mozzarella. Also tasty are pizzas, pastas, and a wide array of *insalate* (salads). *V. Vicenza 23, tel. 06/4957996. From Stazione Termini, take V. Vicenza north 4 blocks. Cash only.*

UNDER L15,000 • Aduliss. Although billed as a restaurant, Aduliss is more like a social club for Rome's African, Turkish, and Middle Eastern immigrants. Relax amid colorful murals while Pop Aduliss cooks up piles of Ethiopian food. A gargantuan plate of curried potatoes, lentils, and spiced beef with *injera* (Ethiopian bread) goes for L15,000. *V. Milazzo 1/C, 1 block north of Stazione Termini, tel. 06/4451695. Cash only. Closed Fri.–Mon.*

Donati. An anomaly this close to the station, you'll find a decidedly flashy look lent by pink tablecloths and polished granite tiles. *Uova strapazzate* (scrambled eggs) are served alongside the requisite pasta dishes. The street is quiet enough to enjoy sitting outside. *V. Magenta 20, tel. 06/491868. Corner of V. Marghera, 1 block north of Stazione Termini. Cash only. Closed Sat. in winter.*

Trimani. Founded more than a hundred years ago and still family run, the wine bar and wine shop have a decidedly updated feel, but the staff is friendly and the wide selection of wines—plus savory soups, quiches, and *crostini* ("little toasts" served warm, topped with a spread such as chicken liver)—will warm you up to the place. The set L25,000 menu is a good deal as long as you're not super hungry. *V. Cernaia 37/B. Closed Sun.*

UNDER L20,000 • Osteria Nerone. Halfway between the Colosseum and the church of San Pietro in Vincoli, this family-run trattoria has an irresistible antipasto table. The specialty is fettuccine *alla Nerone* (with peas, salami, and mushrooms), but other fresh pastas are good, too. A few outside tables have views of the Colosseum. *V. Terme di Tito 96, tel. 06/4745207. Cash only. Closed Sun. and mid-Aug.*

Pommidoro. Want to see where Romans really eat? The long walk or short ride is definitely rewarded at this most typical of Roman trattorias in the San Lorenzo neighborhood east of Stazione Termini. The menu is full of hearty pasta dishes and a great selection of grilled meat and game. Portions are big, prices fair. Tables are set outside in summer. Reservations are a good idea. *P. dei Sanniti, 44. tel. 06/4452692. Take Bus 492 from Stazione Termini. Cash only. Closed Sun. and Aug.*

UNDER L35,000 • Il Guru. It ain't cheap, but that's because the Indian dishes are first rate and served in large portions. Il Guru is owned by an ultrafriendly family that prepares—in addition to an à la carte menu—three set meals from scratch every day. One focuses on fish (L35,000), one on meats (L32,000), and one purely on vegetables (L27,000). *V. Cimarra 5–6, tel. 06/4744110. From Metro B Cavour station, turn left on V. Urbana and right on V. Boschetto, then left on V. Cimarra. No dinner Sun. Closed Mon.*

CENTRO STORICO

Even if there aren't cheap hotels in the centro storico, you can still eat on the cheap within view of a great church if you're choosy. Campo dei Fiori, home of the open-air market (Mon–Sat. 8–1) is unbeatable for raw materials, with bread and great pizza—rossa and bianca—at the **Forno** (Campo dei Fiori 22/22a, tel. 06/68806662; closed Thurs. afternoon in winter and Sun.). If more toppings are your thing, head around the corner to **Pizza alla Pala** (V. del Pellegrino 11, tel. 06/68804557; closed Sun.) or down to the Jewish Ghetto for tasty kosher pizza from **Zi' Fenizia** (V. Santa Maria del Pianto 64; closed sunset

Fri.–sunset Sat.). Fast, cheap, and light snacks can be put together at any *alimentari,* like **Roscioli** (end of V. Giubbonari), and even all- day Sunday at the **Antico Forno** (opposite Trevi Fountain).

UNDER L10,000 • Al Piccolo Arancio. Even though it's been written up in a dozen guidebooks, this back-alley trattoria continues to balance cheap, tasty meals with an unpretentious atmosphere. Topping the menu are curried noodles with zucchini flowers and fettuccine with rabbit or mushrooms. Grouse in wine sauce goes for L9,500. *Vicolo Scanderbeg 112, tel. 06/6786139. From Trevi Fountain, head 2 blocks uphill on V. Lavatore, turn right on Vicolo Scanderbeg. Closed Mon. and middle 2 wks of Aug.*

L'Ambramarina. Narrow, homey, and surprisingly stylish, this place stands apart from the carbon-copy pizzerias that ring Campo dei Fiori. The menu changes daily, but it's generally a mix of soups, salads, vegetarian tarts, and homemade desserts that you'll see displayed on a table among books and candles as you walk in—just choose and point. The young staff will give you tips on the nightlife scene, so this is a good place for starting a night out. *Campo dei Fiori 48, tel. 06/68802474. Cash only.*

Crêperie Damiano. The crepes at this take-out hole-in-the- wall can be sweet, savory, or anywhere in between. There's a long list to choose from, or create your own for L8,000. *V. Tor Millina 8, tel. 06/ 6861091. From P. Navona, walk 2 blocks west on V. Tor Millina. Cash only.*

Da Tonino. Tonino cooks a lot of things—spaghetti *alla carbonara* (with a light sauce of pancetta, egg yolks, and Parmesan), meatballs, roasted potatoes, and more—and charges very little: hence the crowds. Note that dinner is only from 8 to 10:30. *V. del Governo Vecchio 18, no phone. Cash only. Closed Sun.*

Insalata Ricca. This low-cal, low-budget restaurant offers a dozen meal-size salads and a jovial atmosphere. The *capricciosa* salad (with peppers, corn, olives, and feta cheese) is especially good, as is the mouthwatering *bruschetta al pomodoro* (with tomatoes). Pastas and main courses are also available. *Largo dei Chiavari 83, tel. 06/68803656. Off C. Vittorio Emanuele II, 2 blocks east of Largo Argentina. Cash only. Closed Wed.*

La Monte Carlo. Despite the high-roller name, this is one of Rome's more affordable wood-oven pizzerias and a popular hangout for the twentysomething crowd. Tables are decked with red-checked tablecloths, fake flowers, and potato *crocchette* (croquettes). Superthin pizzas come in small, medium, and large. *Vicolo Savelli 13, tel. 06/6861877. From P. della Chiesa Nuova, walk 3 blocks east on C. Vittorio Emanuele II, turn left on Vicolo Savelli. Cash only. Closed 1st 2 wks of Aug.*

UNDER L15,000 • Bottega del Vino da Bleve. At lunchtime, tables are set up in this cozy wine shop in the Ghetto with plenty of bottles all around to tempt you. You'll savor the good selection of salads, smoked fish, cheeses, and excellent pasta dishes. *V. Santa Maria del Pianto 11/12, tel. 06/6869570. No dinner. Closed Sun.*

Da Baffetto. The brief menu offers a variety of superthin pizzas and crunchy calzone, plus tasty appetizers like bruschetta dressed up with beans and mushrooms (L4,000). Vie for seating in the street-facing front room, or head to the back for cozy incognito dining. *V. del Governo Vecchio 114, tel. 06/ 6861617. From P. della Chiesa Nuova, walk west on C. Vittorio Emanuele II, turn left on V. Sora, right on V. del Governo Vecchio. Cash only. Closed Aug.*

Il Filettaro di Santa Barbara. The closest you can get to fish- and-chips in Rome, this is the place for *filetti di baccalá* (fillets of salt cod) fried to golden perfection. Wash 'em down with half a liter of Frascati. *Largo dei Librari 88, in a piazza just off of V. dei Giubbonari, tel. 06/6864018. Cash only. No lunch. Closed Sun.*

L'Isola. Take a break from another pasta meal and try the light vegetable and fish dishes from Liguria, carefully prepared in an open kitchen at the fourth-floor restaurant near Piazza di Spagna. *V. delle Vite 14, 4th floor, tel. 06/6792509. No lunch. Closed Sun.*

Margutta. A vegetarian institution since the '70s, Margutta had a face-lift in the '90s. Food is still a solid reworking of Italian standards in meatless fashion. Good desserts abound. *V. Margutta 119, tel. 06/ 36001912. Closed Sun.*

Orso 80. You'll be blown away by the spread on the antipasto table in this old-style trattoria near Piazza Navona. There's also a good selection of pasta dishes if you are still hungry. *V. dell'Orso 33, tel. 06/ 6864904. Closed Mon. and mid-Aug.*

Pizzeria Il Leoncino. Lines out the door on weekends attest to the popularity of this fluorescent-lighted pizzeria in the otherwise big-ticket neighborhood around Piazza di Spagna. It's also one of the few pizzerias open for lunch. *V. Leoncino 28, 1 block west of V. del Corso, off Largo Goldoni, tel. 06/6876306. Cash only. Closed Wed. and Aug.*

UNDER L25,000 • Il Bacaro. This tiny, pretty bistro close to the Pantheon prepares traditional dishes with a creative touch. Specialties include *orecchiette con ruchetta e patate* (ear-shaped pasta with arugula and potatoes) and stuffed homemade pasta. *V. degli Spagnoli 27, tel. 06/6864110. No lunch. Closed Sun. and Aug.*

Lounge del Roman Garden. One might not expect a relatively affordable lunch stop at the swanky Hotel d'Inghilterra, just down the road from Piazza di Spagna. Consider a peaceful respite here after a morning of fancy window-shopping. Salads served in the elegant, small dining room begin at L24,000. *V. Borgognona at side of Hotel d'Inghilterra. No dinner.*

TRASTEVERE

There's still an old-style **produce and fish market** held in Piazza San Cosimato 8 AM–1 PM, and if you miss it, the **Standa** on Viale Trastevere is open 8–8. Great *salsicce* (sausage) and cheese make for a tasty snack from **La Norcineria** (V. Natale del Grande 15). Also be sure to check out one of the city's oldest and best **bakeries**, at **Via del Moro** (no sign, opposite the Corner Bookstore), where you can get bread and pizza by the slice. At night the streets and restaurants of Trastevere fill with people—it could almost be a different place. After dinner head to **Vicolo del Cinque** (near P. Trilussa) for *cornetti caldi*—sweet, sugary croissants, either plain or filled with jam or pastry cream, hot from the oven. Take home a bit of everything your stomach could desire from **Frontoni** (V. di Trastevere 52, at V. Francesco a Ripa, tel. 06/5812436), a *torrefazione-gastronomia* (coffee roaster/specialty food shop) with more than 60 kinds of pizza.

UNDER L10,000 • Dar Poeta. The new pizzeria on the block gets rave reviews for a Roman pizza made with a lighter-than-usual dough. Bruschette are exemplary, and the pizza margherita is the cheapest in town at L6,000, and one of the best. *Vicolo del Bologna 45, just off of P. della Scala, tel. 06/5880516. No lunch. Closed Mon.*

Il Marchese del Grillo. The barrel-vaulted ceilings of this family-run pizzeria give it a quiet, churchlike feel that sets it apart from the boisterous beer halls in the neighborhood. Cheap wine, pizzas, and bruschette with delectable spreads like olive paste and baby artichokes make for an inexpensive feast, and the restaurant's proximity to Piazza Trilussa means you can get rowdy after supper. *V. Benedetta 23, tel. 06/5896985. From P. Trilussa, left 1 block to P. S. Giovanni della Malva; V. Benedetta is on south side of piazza. No lunch.*

Pizzeria Panattoni. Families, kids, and clubbers with the munchies consume huge helpings of fast food in this cafeterialike space with superfast service. Wood-oven pizzas and fried *filleti di baccalà* are popular choices, and you can sit outside on the sidewalk. *V. Trastevere 53/59, tel. 06/5800919. No lunch. Closed Wed.*

Il Vicolo. This intimate restaurant, hidden on a Trastevere backstreet, offers indoor and outdoor seating. Choose from a dozen variations of inspiring salads, meat dishes, pastas, and pizzas, or dig into a specialty like risotto with radicchio. Tarot readings are featured on Monday evening. *Vicolo dei Cinque 27, near P. Trilussa, tel. 06/5810250. Closed Tues.*

UNDER L15,000 • Da Lucia. Choose from a short list of Roman dishes, served inside in this old-style trattoria or outside on the quiet little street, with laundry hanging from the windows. Spaghetti *cacio e pepe* (with pecorino and black pepper) is a favorite. *Vicolo del Mattonato 2/B, tel. 06/5803601. Cash only. No lunch. Closed Mon. and Aug.*

Pizzeria da Ivo. This is the epitome of a Roman pizzeria, complete with boisterous Romans, sidewalk tables, exhaust fumes, and a busy street scene. Beer and pizza are where it's at: try individual pizza *normale* or pizza *gigante* to share (L11,000– L16,000). *V. Francesco a Ripa 158, tel. 06/5817082. From V. di Trastevere, walk 3 blocks north on V. Francesco a Ripa. No lunch. Closed Tues.*

Sorelle Ferrara. Good hearty soups and innovative Italian dishes accompanied by a great wine list are served up in this new and supercomfy restaurant. There's outside seating on a small patio. *V. del Moro 1/A, tel. 06/5803769. No lunch. Closed Tues.*

Trattoria da Augusto. The old man outside this family restaurant assures that "*qui si mangia bene e si paga poco* (here you'll eat well and pay little)," and it's true: the food is dependably authentic and without tourist frills. Fresh pastas start at just L5,000 and homemade ravioli at L9,000; meat dishes run L7,000–L12,000. On warm nights, dine outside on the calm piazza with a liter of Castelli wine. *P. de' Renzi 15, tel. 06/5803798. From P. Trilussa, walk 1 block on V. del Moro, turn right on V. de' Renzi (it ends at piazza). No dinner Sat. Closed Sun.*

UNDER L20,000 • Gianicolo 23. Among the concoctions here are the creamy *farfalle al radicchio* (bow-tie pasta with cream, tomato, radicchio, and bacon) and fettuccine *al Gianicolo* (with mixed mushrooms). If you're feeling meaty, try *straccetti con ruchetta* (beef fillet sautéed with arugula, Gorgonzola, and garlic). Even with sizable crowds, there's usually room inside or on the tree-lined street. *V. G. Mameli 23, tel. 06/5815438. From V. di Trastevere, take V. E. Morosini north for 2 blocks and turn right on V. G. Mameli. No lunch. Closed Wed.*

NEAR THE VATICAN

Most restaurants anywhere near the Vatican charge exorbitant prices for a meager bowl of yesterday's pasta. Stay away from the schlocky trattorias on **Borgo Pio** and concentrate instead on the small restaurants around **Viale Giulio Cesare,** just west of the Metro A Ottaviano station. For fresh stuff, head to the indoor **market** at Via Caio Mario, between Via dei Gracchi and Via Cola di Rienzo; it's held Monday–Saturday 7–7. If it's pizza you crave, try **Il Tempio del Bongustaio** (P. Risorgimento 50, tel. 06/6833709; closed Sun.), or head down to **Franchi** (V. Cola di Rienzo 200, tel. 06/6864576; closed Sun.) for the city's best deli-style takeout. Finish off with gelato or a yummy *granita di caffè* (an espresso slush topped with fresh whipped cream) from the **Cremeria Ottaviani** (V. Leone IV 83/85, tel. 06/37514774; closed Wed.).

UNDER L10,000 • Il Bersagliere. This is the place for hefty pizza and frosty beer. It's a little dingy and dim, but filled with jovial locals. Filling antipasto plates are feasible at L6,000. *V. Candia 24, tel. 06/39742253. From Ottaviano Metro station, walk west along V. Giulio Cesare, which becomes V. Candia. Cash only. No lunch. Closed Mon.*

UNDER L15,000 • Dal Toscano. This place has been serving honest Tuscan specialties for 60 years. *Ribollita* (vegetable and bread soup) and *pici* (handmade pasta with a wild hare sauce) are old-timers here, but Romans come for the *bistecca alla Fiorentina*, a thick grilled T-bone steak. Quaff a heady Tuscan red along with it. *V. Germanico 56, tel. 06/39725717. Closed Mon. and 2 wks in Aug.*

Zi' Gaetana. It's like King Arthur meets the Elks Lodge in this friendly, air-conditioned vault near the entrance to the Vatican museums. Hold court over *melanzane alla parmigiana* (eggplant Parmesan), *saltimbocca alla romana* (sautéed veal), and pizzas at banquet-style tables in the main hall or groovy Grotto Room (like being inside a fish tank, minus the fish). Croon along to Roman love songs with the regulars at night. *V. Cola di Rienzo 263, tel. 06/3212341. Closed Mon.*

TESTACCIO

Not too long ago, Testaccio, south of Trastevere, was home to Rome's great slaughterhouses, and simple restaurants in the neighborhood invented dishes to make use of the variety meats (read: innards) that were so readily available. A few of those restaurants are still around, but don't let that scare you away from Testaccio. It's home to one of Rome's better outdoor markets (in Piazza Testaccio) and several fantastic restaurants. One of Rome's finest and priciest *gastronomie* is **Volpetti** (V. Marmorata 47, tel. 06/5742352; open Mon.–Sat. 8:30–2 and 5–8), which procures superb cheeses and meat products from all over Italy. They are happy to give samples, but then ask you how much you want to buy.

UNDER L10,000 • Il Grottino I. Tremendously popular among young Romans, this no-frills pizzeria offers the standard treats like *supplì* and *olive ascolane* (green olives stuffed with meat, breaded, and fried) along with wafer-thin, supercheap pizzas. Sit outside or choose from three air-conditioned rooms, one reserved for nonsmokers. *V. Marmorata 165, tel. 06/5746232. From Stazione Termini, Bus 57 to V. Marmorata. Cash only. No lunch. Closed Wed.*

UNDER L15,000 • Osteria dei Tempi Nostri. Sip wine and nosh away the hours in this wine bar stocking labels from all over Italy including friendly budget suggestions, along with small plates of cured meats, cheeses, crepes, and salads. *V. Luca della Robbia 34, tel. 06/57300685. Closed Sun.*

Perilli. A bastion of authentic Roman cooking since 1913, this is the place to go and try rigatoni *con pagliata* (with baby lamb intestines), if you're into that sort of thing. Otherwise, the *all'amatriciana* (with a piquant sauce of tomato, unsmoked bacon, and hot red chiles called *peperoncini*) and carbonara are classics. Try the house wine, a golden nectar from the Castelli Romani. *V. Marmorata 39, tel. 06/5742415. Cash only. Closed Mon.*

CAFFÈS

Rome has a bar-café on every corner, so be choosy and find a place that suits your style and budget. If you stand at the bar, an espresso runs L1,000–L1,500, a cappuccino L1,500–L2,000, a cornetto L1,000–L1,200. Prices can swell more than 200% for the simple pleasure of sitting at a table, inside or out, so be sure to check. A few choice spots follow, but this is by no means an exhaustive list.

Bar San Callisto. Unassuming, with old soccer posters tacked up, this is the familiar haunt of local artists and theater people who come to order their morning cornetto and espresso, a bottle of beer, or some gelato. Even though it's steps from Piazza Santa Maria in Trastevere, there's only a tiny extra charge to sit outside. *P. San Callisto 3, off V. di Trastevere, tel. 06/5835869. Closed Sun.*

Caffè Greco. The red-velvet chairs and marble tables of the expensive, touristy Greco have hosted the likes of Byron, Shelley, Keats, Goethe, and Casanova. Go ahead and sit down if you've got tired feet and deep pockets—a coffee at the table will cost you L8,000. At the bar, without the attitude or silver tray service, you'll pay the regular price. *V. dei Condotti 86, 1 block west of P. di Spagna, tel. 06/6791700.*

Caffè Sant'Eustachio. This classy place, traditionally frequented by Rome's literati, vies with Tazza d'Oro (*see below*) for the city's best espresso. Fork over the extra lire for a *caffè speciale* (sweetened double espresso). *P. Sant'Eustachio 82, tel. 06/861309. Closed Mon.*

Tazza d'Oro. It's said that the Gold Cup makes 10,000 cups of coffee—from espressos and cappuccinos to granite de caffè— every morning in this prime location next to the Pantheon. To speed things up, Rome's best cup of coffee comes presweetened. If you want yours without sugar, ask for it *amaro*. The place closes at 8 PM. *V. degli Orfani, tel. 06/6792768. Closed Sun.*

Did Romans invent snow cones, too? Romans line up to beat summer heat with grattachecca, ice shaved by hand from a big block, topped with colorful sweetened syrups, sometimes spiked with a little alcohol. Look for street stands on the Tiber.

GELATERIE AND PASTICCERIE

Fiocco di Neve. This low-key place near the Pantheon has tons of flavors. Do as the Romans do and try several together; they charge L1,000 per scoop in a cone or cup. Add L500 if you want yours *con panna* (topped with unsweetened whipped cream). *V. del Pantheon 51, at northeast corner of P. della Rotonda.*

Forno del Ghetto. Surprised to find a Jewish bakery in Rome? This hole-in-the-wall—no sign, no tables, just a take-out counter—is an institution, preserving a tradition of Italian Jewish sweets that cannot be found anywhere else. The ricotta cake with sour cherry jam or chocolate is unforgettable. *V. di Portico d'Ottavia 2, tel. 06/6878637. Closed Sat.*

Gelateria Fragola e Limone. This mom-and-pop gelato shop specializes in all-natural, homemade fruit flavors—no artificial anything in their frozen fantasia. The circus-colored cones, however, are another story. *V. Giustiniani 18, tel. 06/6896670. 1 block north of Pantheon.*

Gelateria San Crispino. By a long shot, this place concocts the best gelato in Rome, in Italy, maybe in the world, and it's made without artificial anything. Nobody else makes flavors this balanced, ice cream this real. This is worth crossing town for. *V. della Paneteria 54, near the Trevi Fountain, tel. 06/70450412. Closed Tues.*

EXPLORING ROME

You've probably heard that Rome wasn't built in a day—and you'll soon figure out you can't see it all in a day, either. As if the sheer number of worthwhile and interesting sites and the distances between them were not enough, the well-intentioned traveler must inevitably contend with other impediments, like endless restoration or a closed door when the guidebook (and the sign out front) says the place should be open.

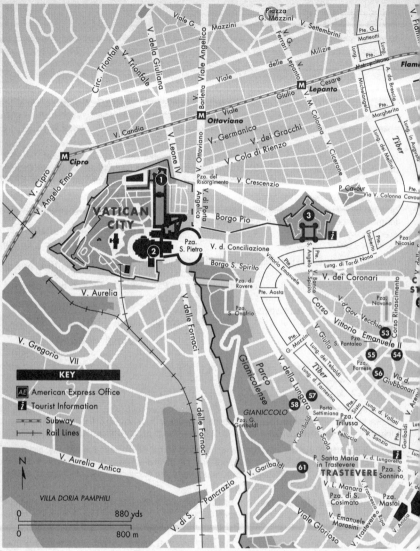

KEY

AE American Express Office

i Tourist Information

Subway

Rail Lines

N

VILLA DORIA PAMPHILI

0   880 yds
0   800 m

Beyond the list of postcard monuments, Rome is also home to a bevy of tiny neighborhood churches, quirky museums, and long-forgotten treasures. You could spend a month dashing from piazza to palazzo and still not see it all. What to do? Be a little flexible, have some alternatives, and call ahead if your heart is set on seeing a particular place. And don't try to do too much. After all, Rome wasn't built in. . .

ANCIENT RUINS

Most remnants of Roman antiquity lie south of chaotic Piazza Venezia—a dense concentration of ruins that once comprised the commercial, political, and religious epicenter of ancient Rome. From the city's legendary beginnings in 753 BC, the Capitoline and Palatine hills and the valleys between them were the center for Rome's steady growth. Beginning in 29 BC, Augustus, Rome's first emperor, is said to have transformed Rome from a city of brick to a city of marble: during his reign and that of his successors, the city center was laden with monumental displays of opulence and self-glorification.

So what happened to all the gold and marble? With the oft-cited decline and fall of the Roman Empire came centuries of successive lootings, sackings, natural disasters, and neglect. The result: crumbling ruins that barely hint at their previous grandeur. The Romans were excellent builders—the arch is basically a Roman thing—and highly ingenious at getting materials from far-off places. Consider that much of the marble you see today in the city was already in use in Roman times and that the emperors brought the obelisks all the way from Egypt. But in the dark centuries that followed Rome's golden age, it was easier to quarry raw materials from the abandoned Forum and Colosseum than to take them out of the side of a mountain. Where you see numerous woodpeckerlike holes in a facade of Roman brick, imagine the marble that once hung there. This practice was not perfected by the Goths and Vandals, but by Renaissance nobles and popes. On the bright side, some of the pieces were recycled into things we appreciate today. Where would Bernini's baldachin in St. Peter's Basilica be without its bronze taken from the roof of the Pantheon? In this way, the city has lived off itself for millennia and continues to do so, as even today we find modern uses for ancient sites.

Bring comfortable walking shoes, a good map, and a blind eye for the souvenir hawkers, tourist mobs, buses of schoolchildren, and very loud scooters. Be wary of pickpockets and carry plenty of water—roofless ruins don't lend much shade, and the nearby refreshment stands are rip-offs.

ARCO DI COSTANTINO

Back in ancient Rome, emperors built triumphal arches to commemorate great victories; this one celebrates Constantine's over rival Maxentius in 312 AD. The decorative reliefs were recycled from earlier structures—a frugal approach to ornamentation that was partly practical, partly political: Constantine wanted to show the link between Rome's past glories and those of the present. The four sculptures on top were swiped from the Forum of Trajan; the four medallions on the face, portraying hunting and sacrificial scenes, date from the reign of Hadrian. *Metro B to Colosseo.*

COLOSSEO

The single most evocative symbol of Rome, the Colosseum is equal parts glory and gore. At the end of the 1st century AD, the emperor Vespasian drained an artificial lake that Nero had dug for his gardens and built Rome a full-fledged amphitheater for its games, which had previously been staged in the Forum. Completed in AD 80 under his son Titus, the Flavian Amphitheater (named for the family, of course—the name *Colosseum* came from a colossal bronze statue of Nero that once stood nearby) was inaugurated with a 100-day festival in which 5,000 animals were slaughtered. The four-story structure had seats for 50,000 (patricians down front, women all the way up at the top), a movable canopy for sun protection, a safety net with elephant tusks to protect the audience from wild beasts, and a vast underground network of tunnels, chambers, and elevators to move creatures, prisoners, and other event paraphernalia. Looted continuously by passing barbarians until it was declared a holy shrine to Christian martyrs (and from then on, looted only by popes), the Colosseum has seen better days; yet its sheer size alone manages to astound even those with little imaginative powers. See what's left from the ground floor and view the upper level (including a small model of the Colosseum in its heyday) for L10,000. *P. del Colosseo, tel. 06/7004261. Open daily 9–7 (until 6 in winter). Metro B to Colosseo.*

PIAZZA DELLA BOCCA DELLA VERITÀ

The square now partially covers what was once the Forum Boarium, ancient Rome's cattle market. What remains are two of Rome's most intact ancient temples, built in the 2nd century BC: the rectangular **Temple** of **Portunus** and the round **Temple of Hercules Victor** (still undergoing restoration), originally misidentified as a Temple of Vesta because it resembles the one in the Roman Forum. If you can elbow your way through the lines of tourists outside the medieval church of Santa Maria in Cosmedin (across the street from the temples), take a minute to prove your honesty at the **Bocca della Verità** (Mouth of Truth). Legend had it that any liar who placed his hand in the mouth of this ancient sewer cover would have it chomped off.

FORI IMPERIALI

By the end of the Republic, the Forum could no longer accommodate all the civic and social functions of the sprawling city and capital of a rapidly expanding nation. To handle the overflow, in 54 BC Caesar paid a whopping 60 million sesterces for the land behind the Curia and built—surprise, surprise—the **Forum of Caesar.** It included the **Temple of Venus Genetrix,** dedicated to the goddess of love from whom Caesar claimed descent. Several emperors followed suit during the first and second centuries. Cross to the other side of Via dei Fori Imperiali, which partly covers the remains of the forums built, from left to right, by Trajan, Augustus, Nerva, and Vespasian.

If so far you've found it a bit difficult to imagine all those Roman buildings from a few remaining stones and columns, you might want to wander around ancient Rome's shopping mall, the semicircular **Markets of Trajan** (entrance in front of Trajan's Column; admission L3,750; open Tues.–Sat. 9–6, Sun. 9–1:30). Visually impressive and remarkably intact, these markets contained three levels of wholesale and retail outlets. Wandering through the halls, you can almost hear the din of pesky salespeople and toga-clad bargain hunters. Some of the market stalls are now used to display marble fragments of ancient statues found in the area. Climb up to the roof level for the view overlooking the Forum, then go down to ground level and find a comfy marble slab to lean against and admire the incredibly intricate **Column of Trajan.** The 650-ft-long relief, a series of violent battle scenes winding around the column, commemorates the expansion of the Roman Empire into Eastern Europe.

FORO ROMANO

As far back as the 10th century BC, wandering tribes gathered on Rome's hilltops and made use of the swampy lowland area, the present-day site of the Roman Forum, as a burial ground. In later years, the site's position between the Capitoline, Palatine, and Esquiline hills and its proximity to the commercial activity on the Tiber River made it an ideal spot for a marketplace and civic center. In the 7th century BC, the swamp was drained by a sophisticated sewer, the Cloaca Maxima, paved over, and divided in two: half was to be used as a marketplace and half for political purposes. By the time the Roman Republic emerged in the 6th century BC, this was already the city's core, full of shops and public buildings, as well as the spiritual center of ancient Rome, where priests and priestesses made offerings to the capricious gods who determined the fate of the Republic.

To your right as you enter the Forum from Via dei Fori Imperiali stands the **Basilica Emilia.** Built in 179 BC, this purely secular structure hosted judicial hearings and public meetings until it was destroyed by fire. There are still traces of ancient coins stuck in the floor tiles. Next door is the **Curia,** the seat of the Roman Senate, where, according to Shakespeare, Marc Antony gave his "Friends, Romans, countrymen" speech over the body of Julius Caesar. Orators gave speeches from the **Rostra,** the long platform perpendicular to the Curia. In front of the Rostra was the main square, where merchants hawked their wares, gladiators clashed, lovers lingered. Between the Curia and the Rostra lies the **Niger Lapis,** a flat black stone dating from the 8th century BC, one of the oldest objects in the Forum. Originally a shrine to Vulcan, god of metal, fire, and volcanoes, the stone is said to cover the final resting place of Romulus, mythical founder of Rome.

Towering above the Rostra is the **Arch of Septimus Severus,** constructed by Emperor Severus in AD 203 to celebrate a victory over the Parthians. To the left stand the eight remaining columns of the **Temple of Saturn,** the oldest in the Forum. It served as a treasury and was the site of the Saturnalia, a seven-day feast when slaves and masters sat at the same table, and everyone from children to elders feasted, drank, and exchanged gifts. In front of the Temple of Saturn lies a vast area that was once the site of the **Basilica Giulia.** Named for Julius Caesar, who began the project in 54 BC, the Basilica served as the Tribunal and was large enough to accommodate four proceedings simultaneously. You can still see how bystanders etched tic-tac-toe–like games into the pavement stones.

PALATINE HILL • To reach the Palatine Hill from the Forum, climb the path that leads from the Arch of Titus. Once you reach the top, surrounded by the trees and blossoms of the **Farnese Gardens,** you'll understand why the Palatine was prime real estate from the time shepherds first gathered here until Roman emperors made it their official residence. Today the shady lawns and incredible views make it a great spot for picnicking or collapsing after a long ramble through the Forum.

AUGUSTUS CAESAR was Rome's first emperor (27 BC–AD 14), and his rule began a 200-year period of peace known as the Pax Romana. Augustus expanded the empire as far as Scotland, Morocco, and Mesopotamia.

NERO (AD 54–68) was known for his violent persecution of Christians. Nero is also infamous for killing his mother, his wife, and countless others.

TRAJAN (AD 98–117) enlarged the boundaries of the Roman Empire in the east to include modern-day Romania, Armenia, and Upper Mesopotamia.

HADRIAN (AD 117–138) expanded the empire in Asia and the Middle East. He is best known in Rome for having designed and rebuilt the Pantheon in its present form. The British know him as the author of a wall across their country.

MARCUS AURELIUS (AD 161–180) was considered to be one of the more lenient and humanitarian emperors. Nonetheless, he was devoted to expansion and an aggressive leader of the empire.

CONSTANTINE I (AD 306–337) was the empire's first Christian emperor. His Edict of Milan granted universal religious tolerance and paved the way for the modern Roman Catholic papacy.

Beyond the garden, much of the hilltop is covered by the enormous **Domus Augustana,** the complex of rooms, halls, temples, and stadiums that served as the palace of the emperors. Among earlier ruins on the Palatine, don't miss the so-called **House of Livia,** with wall paintings and a layout typical of a 1st-century BC Roman home. The **Palatine Antiquarium,** an on-site museum, has modern, well-translated displays about the excavations on the hill. *Entrance to Roman Forum on V. dei Fori Imperiali and from Arch of Titus. Entrance to Palatine from Arch of Titus and on Via di San Gregorio. Metro B to Colosseo. Admission to Roman Forum free; to Palatine Hill L12,000 including Antiquarium. Open Mon.–Sat. 9–6, Sun. 9—1; tel. 06/6990110.*

On the other side of the Basilica Giulia are the **Temple of Castor and Pollux** and the remaining pillars of the small, round **Temple of Vesta.** Here the Vestal Virgins tended the sacred flame of Vesta, goddess of the hearth (*see box* Ain't Misbehavin', *below*). The **House of the Vestals,** which lies beyond the temple, still encloses a series of sculptures depicting the priestesses of this sacred order. The house was once their resplendent residence, which had bathrooms, central heating, and six secret state reception rooms.

The **Via Sacra,** or Sacred Way, the oldest street in Rome, runs the entire length of the Forum and leads past the massive **Basilica of Maxentius.** Begun by Emperor Maxentius in AD 306 and completed by Constantine, this is one of the best-preserved structures in the Roman Forum. The three remaining immense barrel vaults hint at the grand scale of this once richly decorated building—Michelangelo used the basilica as a model for the cupola of St. Peter's. The **Arch of Titus,** farther down the Via Sacra, was erected in AD 81 to celebrate the sacking of Jerusalem 10 years earlier and shows the menorah from the Jewish Temple being carried in triumph by Roman soldiers down the Via Sacra. The small **Antiquarium of the Forum,** in the ancient convent of Santa Francesca Romana (between the Basilica of Maxentius and the Arch of Titus), houses a small, dusty collection of archaeological finds from the area.

TERME DI CARACALLA

Maybe even more than the forums, the ruins of these gigantic thermal baths give some sense of the size, scope, and engineering genius of ancient Rome's civic architecture. The baths served an important social function for Romans of every class and position. The palatial structure once housed an extensive complex of gardens, libraries, and sports facilities. At the far end, enormous tanks once held millions of gallons of water; underground, a sophisticated system of heating and pumping equipment kept the water flowing. Bathers passed through several chambers elaborately decorated in marble, stucco, and mosaics: the *calidarium,* with very hot water; the *tepidarium,* kept lukewarm; and the *frigidarium,* for cooling off. Admission was free for both men and women, but visiting the baths today isn't. *V. Terme di Caracalla. Metro B to Circo Massimo; or from P. Venezia, Bus 160 to the baths. Admission L8,000. Open Tues.–Sun. 9–6 (until 3 in winter), Mon. 9–1.*

TEATRO DI MARCELLO

Near Piazza Venezia and the Jewish Ghetto, the Theater of Marcellus is a great example of how Roman structures have been recycled over the millennia. Begun by Caesar and completed by Augustus in 11 BC, the semicircular theater once held 15,000 spectators and hosted tragedies, comedies, and sporting events. Looted through the Middle Ages, it was subsequently fortified, reclaimed in the 16th century as a noble palace, and rebuilt several times. Though only a portion of the round theater wall remains, outdoor classical music concerts are staged in front of the facade on summer evenings. Good views can be had from the Via di Portico d'Ottavia side as well. *Closed to public.*

CAMPIDOGLIO

Once the political and religious center of ancient Rome, Il Campidoglio (Capitoline Hill) was home to the temple to the triad of Jupiter, Juno, and Minerva, as well as the state archives, treasury, and mint. Today you will find the city's municipal offices in the restored **Palazzo Senatorio** on the majestic **Piazza del Campidoglio.** In 1537 Michelangelo, called in to redesign the square and bordering palazzi, created here a miracle of Renaissance harmony and balance. Head to the top of Palazzo Senatorio's stairway to get a look at the symmetrical pavement, then down the roads on either side of the building for commanding views onto the Roman Forum and Palatine Hill. The equestrian statue of Emperor Marcus Aurelius in the middle of the square is a high-tech copy; the original stands just inside the Museo Capitolino.

BASILICA SANTA MARIA IN ARACOELI

This plain brick basilica looks impressive atop its daunting 124-step staircase; inside are colorful 16th-century frescoes—attributed to Pinturicchio—depicting scenes from the life of St. Bernard of Siena and an array of funerary sculptures, including one signed by Donatello. *V. del Teatro di Marcello, to left of steps to Campidoglio. Open daily 7–noon and 4–7; tel. 06/6798155.*

MUSEI CAPITOLINI

One ticket gets you into the museums in the matching buildings on either side of the Campidoglio. The **Museo Capitolino** is the older of the two—in fact it is the world's oldest museum, first opened to the public in 1734. Inside you'll see the original equestrian statue of Marcus Aurelius, once thought to be the Pagan-turned-Christian Emperor Constantine and thus not destroyed, as were most of the statues of his imperial predecessors. Upstairs you'll find one of the most extensive collections of Roman sculpture in the world. For the most part, Romans were better at copying Greek sculptures than creating their own; some of their best work includes the *Wounded Amazon, Laughing and Crying Centaurs,* and the *Capitoline Venus,* as well as the poignant 3rd-century BC sculpture of the *Dying Gaul.* You can also go hunting for familiar names and faces among the more than 100 busts of emperors, poets, and philosophers. If you decide to skip the museums, at least poke your head into the courtyard of the **Palazzo Dei Conservatori** across the way and size yourself up against the gigantic head and assorted body parts that remain from the mammoth sculpture of Constantine, which once stood in the Basilica of Maxentius—the toenail alone is as big as a human hand. Inside, the palazzo's frieze-decorated staircase, rich wall-paper, and gilded ceilings are as pleasant as the hodgepodge of works they surround. On the first floor are several fresco-filled rooms, including the **Salone degli Orazi e Curiazi,** with carved wooden doors and statues by Bernini. Its prize pieces are the 1st-century BC *Spinario,* a boy in bronze pulling a thorn from his foot, and the *Capitoline Wolf,* a 5th- century BC Etruscan bronze work to which, ironically, suckling figures of Remus and Romulus were added during the Renaissance to adapt the statue to the legend of Rome's founding. Upstairs in the **Capitoline Picture Gallery,** exhibits range from dark religious

AIN'T MISBEHAVIN'

Whoever said that bad girls have all the fun? In ancient Rome, the six physically perfect Vestal Virgins, chosen when they were prepubescent, lived a life of luxury in the serene and sumptuous Casa delle Vestali. As priestesses of Vesta and protectors of the Empire, the Virgins had to keep the sacred fire of Vesta lit (if it went out, the Empire would fall). In return, the fortunate femmes were free from paternal authority (unlike other Roman women), rode around in special chariots, knew the goings-on of the imperial house, and acted as ambassadors and judges. The catch: if they broke their 30-year vow of chastity, they were buried alive.

icons to paintings by Titian and Caravaggio. *P. del Campidoglio, tel. 06/67102071. Closed for restoration at press time.*

PIAZZA VENEZIA

You'll probably end up in chaotic Piazza Venezia again and again, as it's the hub of Rome's busiest thoroughfares, including **Via del Corso, Corso Vittorio Emanuele II,** and **Via Nazionale,** and site of a traffic symphony conducted every day during rush hour by an elegantly attired traffic cop atop a pedestal at the center of the intersection. Numerous bus lines stop at the piazza, but you can also reach it (and the concentration of nearby ruins and sights) by way of the Metro B Colosseo stop.

BASILICA SAN MARCO

On the south side of Palazzo Venezia, twin porticoes lead to this small but richly decorated parish church, frequent site of weddings, funerals, and baptisms. The basilica dates from the 4th century AD but was thoroughly renovated in the 15th century by Cardinal Pietro Barbo and again in the 18th century, which accounts for its purely Baroque interior. The interior can be taken in with a glance, though the wooden, coffered Renaissance ceiling and Byzantine mosaics near the altar deserve two. *P. San Marco 48, tel. 06/6755205. Open daily 9–noon and 4—7.*

MONUMENTO DI VITTORIO EMANUELE II

In 1862 Vittorio Emanuele II became the first king of a unified Italian state. Upon his death in 1878, a contest was held to construct a monument befitting this "Father of Italy." Thirty-three years later, the colossal creation of Giuseppe Sacconi was finally completed to the dismay (read: disgust) of most Romans. Nicknamed the "wedding cake" because of its massive white-marble facade, the monument is commonly thought of as pretentious and overbearing in comparison to the treasured remains of ancient Rome that surround it. Whatever your opinion, it makes an excellent navigational landmark, as you can see its unique outline from a surprising distance. The sprawling central staircase, guarded by uniformed sentinels—yes, they are real—leads to the **Tomb of the Unknown Soldier** (closed to the public).

PALAZZO VENEZIA

You may not notice Palazzo Venezia above the confusion of traffic on Piazza Venezia, but before it was overshadowed by the monument to Vittorio Emanuele II, the austere and commanding palace dominated the square. Built in 1455 for Cardinal Pietro Barbo (later Pope Paul II), the palazzo was one of Rome's first Renaissance creations. Today it serves as a **museum,** with permanent displays of silver and porcelain works; Flemish, German, and Italian tapestries; and colorful iconic art. It also hosts some of the most important visiting exhibitions. Mussolini used some of the rooms as offices, leaving the lights on 24 hours a day to give the idea that there was always someone working. The balcony over the main portal may be familiar to history buffs as the place where Il Duce addressed huge crowds. *V. del Plebiscito 118, tel. 06/6798865. Admission L8,000. Open Tues.–Sun. 9–1:30.*

SITES NEAR ANCIENT RUINS

PALAZZO DELLE ESPOSIZIONI

This giant neoclassical edifice houses Rome's most eclectic (and often highbrow) rotating exhibits of art, history, culture, and film (shown in their original languages), put together by artists and scholars. Check with the tourist office (*see* Visitor Information *in* Basics, *above*) for the latest goings-on. *V. Nazionale 194, tel. 06/4745903. Admission L12,000. Open Wed.–Mon. 10–9.*

SAN CLEMENTE

The 12th-century basilica is a gem on its own, with beautiful Cosmatesque (in the style of the work of the Cosmati) floors, apse mosaics, and a chapel frescoed by Masolino, but there is more than first meets the eye. Buy a ticket for the underground sections revealed by excavations just a hundred years ago: a stairway leads down to the nave and columns of a 4th-century AD church, with well-preserved frescoes depicting San Clemente himself. Then go down even deeper to the remains of a 1st-century AD temple used by the Mithraic cult and some adjacent Roman apartments. A well-written English guide sold at the entrance explains the fascinating story of the churches, as well as the significance of the frescoes. *V. San Giovanni in Laterano, no phone. 1 block southeast of Colosseum. Admission to underground: L3,000; guidebook L6,000. Ground floor open Mon.–Sat. 9–12:30 and 3–6, Sun. 10–12:30 and 3:30–6:30; tel. 06/70451018.*

SAN PIETRO IN VINCOLI

Although this church holds the very chains that bound the imprisoned St. Peter, the hordes of tourists who descend upon it every day are usually snapping pictures of Michelangelo's *Moses*. Originally intended for the top of a tall funerary monument planned for Pope Julius II but never finished, the powerful *Moses* sits at ground level, magnificent and a tiny bit out of proportion. *P. San Pietro in Vincoli, between Colosseum and V. Cavour. Open daily 7–12:30 and 3:30–7(Oct.–Mar. until 6 PM); tel. 06/4882865.*

Via dei Fori Imperiali was the result of Mussolini's ambitious urban renewal project. Il Duce razed a vast medieval quarter and an entire hill to connect his headquarters on Piazza Venezia with the Colosseum, the definitive symbol of ancient Rome.

CENTRO STORICO

Rome's historic center—basically the area from Via del Corso down to the Tiber River—encompasses the bulk of medieval and Renaissance Rome. It's not where Rome began—that's Capitoline Hill and the Forum—but it's where all the centuries come together—where many of the major historic sights are concentrated, and where narrow alleyways and outdoor cafés are alive with locals. If you only spend one day in Rome, this is the place to do it.

CAMPO DEI FIORI

The name of this neighborhood piazza means "field of flowers," which seems a bit sardonic considering that it was once used for public executions. In fact, the central statue commemorates the philosopher Giordano Bruno (1548–1600), burned to death after being tried for heresy during the Inquisition; he argued that the cosmos wasn't nearly as organized as the Church led its flock to believe. You will find flowers, as well as Rome's oldest outdoor produce and fish market (Mon.–Sat. 8–1). The streets around the square have always been alive with artisans and craftspeople, as the street names suggest: Via dei Chiavari (keys), Balestrari (crossbows), Cappellari (hats). Historically, the area was also filled with taverns, and there are still many in the area, which makes Campo dei Fiori a choice spot for bar-hoppers.

A block toward the river from Campo dei Fiori is **Piazza Farnese,** watched over by Michelangelo's impassive Palazzo Farnese, home of the French embassy (closed to the public). Walk around the back side to get a look at the gardens through the gate. The very strollable **Via Giulia,** old Rome's most gracious—and certainly its straightest—street, is lined with Renaissance palaces, antiques shops, and art galleries. Pope Julius II wanted the street to be an "imperial road" connecting the harbor with the Vatican, but when he died unexpectedly, so did the plans. In the other direction, Via Giulia ends at the pedestrian-only bridge **Ponte Sisto.** Cross over to the Tiber's west bank, and you're in Trastevere (*see below*).

CAVALLIERI DI MALTA

Atop the Aventine Hill lies the residence and headquarters of the Knights of Malta, a reclusive sect and a sovereign order. The public is not allowed past the huge wooden doors, but take a look through the keyhole, and you'll get an unusual view of St. Peter's dome. The knights intentionally designed the keyhole to afford a view of Rome's three independent states—the Knights of Malta, Italy, and Vatican City. To get here, take Metro B to Circo Massimo, walk down Via del Circo Massimo, left on Valle Murcia (which becomes Via Santa Sabina) to Piazza dei Cavallieri di Malta.

CHIESA DEL GESU

Excluding St. Peter's, Il Gesù is the most colorful church in Rome—every inch is covered with red, green, gold, and pink marble. The frescoed ceiling bordered by swirling figures flows over the pillars, creating a three-dimensional effect. The silver- and gold-lathered altar to St. Ignatius of Loyola (founder of the Jesuits) also gets a gasp from the crowd. *V. del Plebiscito, 2 blocks west of P. Venezia. Open daily 7–12:30 and 4–7:15; tel. 06/6786341.*

CIMITERO ACCATTOLICO

This atmospheric graveyard lies in the residential **Testaccio** district, on the east bank of the Tiber south of the Aventine Hill, opposite Trastevere. There are plenty of shady picnic spots, though most come to commune with the graves of Keats, Severin, Giacometti, Shelley, Edvard Munch, and Goethe's son. The macabre tone is softened by a huge colony of friendly cats and by groundskeepers who stay busy carving headstones and helping out visitors. *V. Caio Cestio 6, tel. 06/571900. Metro B to Piramide; walk northwest across plaza and turn left. Admission free. Open Thurs.–Tues. 8–11:30 and 3:20–4:30 (Mar.– Nov. until 5:30).*

GALLERIA DORIA PAMPHILI

With paintings and sculptures by Raphael, Titian, Bernini, Borromini, and Michelangelo, it's hard to believe this is a private collection—but then again family members like Andrea "Liberator of Genoa" Doria (1466–1560), Pope Innocent X, and Filippo Andrea V (1818–76) began acquiring art in the 15th century. The gallery has recently been restored to its 18th-century arrangement, so paintings are hung almost touching one another in a succession of stunning rooms with period furniture. A free handout is keyed to the paintings, numbered rather than labeled. If you want to get an idea of how these Doria-Pamphili lived, come before 12:30 and take a tour of the apartments, chock full of tapestries, more paintings, and porcelain and coral *oggetti d'arte. P. del Collegio Romano 2, off V. del Corso, tel. 06/ 6797323. Admission L12,000; tour L5,000. Open Fri.–Wed. 10–5. Closed last 2 wks of Aug.*

GALLERIA SPADA

Even if you don't go up to the picture gallery, Palazzo Spada is worth a look for the brilliant stucco decoration that makes this anything but another 16th-century Roman palazzo. Duck inside for a peek at Borromini's trompe l'oeil courtyard, visible through the library window or up close if the garden is open. Up a spiral staircase at the back of the building is the small gallery of mostly 17th-century portraits and religious scenes, with a few landscapes and still lifes. *P. Capodiferro 3, 1 block southeast of Campo dei Fiori, tel. 06/6861158. Admission L8,000. Open Tues.–Sat. 9–7, Sun. 9–1.*

GHETTO

Jews have lived in Rome continuously since the 1st century BC, and their living conditions have always been subject to the will of the city's rulers. One of the worst periods began in 1555, when Pope Paul II established a ghetto in Rome, the area bounded by the Portico d'Ottavia, the Tiber, and Via Arenula. The word comes from the Venetian name for the walled neighborhood in which Jews were forced to live and abide by restrictive laws. The area quickly became Rome's most squalid and densely populated quarter. At one point, the only trade Jews were permitted to engage in was selling used clothing. Dismantled around the time of the Risorgimento, the old ghetto has left only a few traces, but some of Rome's 15,000 Jews still live in the area and a few old Jewish families still run clothing shops on the Via di Portico d'Ottavia. Among the most interesting sights is the **Fontana delle Tartarughe** (Fountain of the Turtles) on Piazza Mattei, with turtles thought to have been added by Bernini.

German troops occupied Rome during World War II, and on October 16, 1943, many of Rome's Jews were rounded up and deported to Nazi concentration camps. In 1986 Pope John Paul II paid a visit to Rabbi Elio Toaff, becoming the first pope ever to pray in a Jewish synagogue; the synagogue had been bombed in 1982.

MUSEO EBRAICO AND SINAGOGA EBRAICO

The two-room Museum of the Jewish Community contains decorative torah shrouds, prayer books, holy chairs, and tapestries dating from the 17th century, most donated by prominent Jewish families whose ancestors once lived in the Ghetto. It's refreshing to see precious metals and marble crafted into something other than saints and angels. One of the more haunting displays is a prayer book that literally saved its owner's life during the 1982 attack on the synagogue—bullet holes and bloodstains tell the tale. The admission price includes entrance to both the museum and a brief guided tour in English of the synagogue. *Lungotevere Cenci, near Ponte Fabricio, tel. 06/68400661. Admission L8,000. Open Mon.–Thurs. 9–5, Fri. 9–2, Sun. 9–12:30. Closed Jewish holidays.*

LARGO DI TORRE ARGENTINA

At the intersection of Via di Torre Argentina and Corso Vittorio Emanuele II, Largo Argentina is more often referred to as a major bus stop than a tourist attraction. But while you're waiting for the bus on this busy square, check out the excavated remains of the four Republican temples. Each dates to the 3rd or 4th century BC, which makes them some of Rome's oldest identified ruins. More noticeable, perhaps, is the square's huge population of indigent felines, who've recently earned the square the nickname "Forum of Cats."

MUSEO BARRACCO

A little Renaissance palazzo holds a small but impressive collection of Egyptian, Phoenician, Greek, and Roman sculpture—mainly busts and funerary monuments—that date back as far as 2500 BC. In the basement are remains of the building's Roman foundations. *C. Vittorio Emanuele II 168, tel. 06/68806848. Admission L3750. Open Tues.–Sat. 9–7, Sun. 9–1:30.*

PANTHEON

If you go inside one building in Rome, make it the Pantheon. The effect of walking in through the massive front portico is breathtaking, and you will see why it is said to be the world's only architecturally perfect building.

This ancient temple-cum-church, the best-preserved ancient Roman structure, was built by Hadrian (AD 119–128), after a fire destroyed an earlier square version commissioned by Agrippa (whose name is visible on the facade). The dome measures 140 ft across and was the largest ever built until the 20th century (St. Peter's is a close second). The oculus at the top has always been open, allowing light and rain to pour in. The Pantheon avoided some of the looting and neglect suffered by other ancient monuments only because it was converted from a shrine to all the gods into a Catholic church in AD 608. Still, much of the roof was stripped of its bronze in 667, and the Barberini pope Urban VIII snatched what was left to recycle into the baldachin in St. Peter's Basilica. *P. della Rotonda, tel. 06/68300230. Admission free. Open Mon.–Sat. 9–6:30, Sun. 9–1.*

PIAZZA NAVONA

The queen of all piazzas and the crown jewel of the centro storico, Navona showcases the church of **Sant'Agnese in Agone** and Bernini's extravagant Fontana dei Quattro Fiumi, with statues representing the four corners of the world and, in turn, the world's great rivers: the Nile, the Ganges, the Río de la Plata, and the Danube. The piazza takes its unusual oval shape from the stadium built by the Emperor Domitian on this site in the first century AD. In more recent centuries, wealthy Romans imitated their ancient predecessors (who had staged boat battles in the stadium and Colosseum) by flooding the piazza and riding their carriages through the water for fun. Today Navona's attractions are more subdued: surrounding the piazza are flowered balconies, colored palazzi, the requisite sidewalk cafés, and every sort of street artist and musician. If you ever pull an all-nighter at Rome's discos, be sure to visit this normally packed piazza at dawn, when only the sound of your footsteps and the squawks of pigeons echo through the vast space.

SAN LUIGI DEI FRANCESI

A must-see for all Caravaggio fans, the last chapel on the left contains three of the artist's most important works, each depicting a scene from the life of St. Matthew: *The Calling of St. Matthew, St. Matthew and the Angel,* and *The Martyrdom of St. Matthew.* With his characteristically striking use of light and shadow (chiaroscuro), Caravaggio creates tension, drama, and extraordinary realism on these canvases. *P. San Luigi dei Francesi, 1 block east of Pantheon. Open Fri.–Wed. 7:30–12:30 and 3:30–7, Thurs. 7:30–12:30; tel. 06/688271.*

SANT'ANDREA DELLA VALLE

Because of its imposing size, Sant'Andrea's dome is sometimes mistaken for St. Peter's. Close but no cigar. The large basilica of Sant'Andrea was begun in the late 16th century by Giacomo della Porta and later altered by Carlo Maderno, responsible for both the dome and the Baroque **Barberini Chapel,** the first on the left as you enter. The church is richly decorated with frescoes, including the *Glory of Paradise,* which covers the dome. *P. Sant'Andrea della Valle between P. Navona and Campo dei Fiori. 4 blocks west of P. Venezia. Open daily 7–1 and 4:30–7:30; tel. 06/6861339.*

SANTA MARIA SOPRA MINERVA

Rome's only Gothic church has an exquisite, serene interior that's a pleasant contrast to the usual Baroque excesses. The church was built on the site of a Roman temple to Minerva (hence the name), and it is full of great art, including the **Carafa Chapel,** with a brilliant fresco cycle on the Annunciation by Filippino Lippi and Michelangelo's sculpture *The Redeemer.* The elephant supporting the obelisk in the piazza was designed by Bernini for Pope Alexander VII, as a symbol of wisdom supported by strength. *P. della Minerva, 1 block south of Pantheon. Open daily 8:30–1 and 4—7; tel. 06/6793926.*

VIA DEL CORSO

Traffic-clogged Via del Corso appears at first glance to be nothing more than a busy street connecting Piazza Venezia and Piazza del Popolo, marking the eastern edge of the centro storico. Between window-shopping and dodging Vespas, it's easy to overlook the enormous facades that line both sides of the street, masked as they are with 20th-century grime. Most of them were built in the 17th century by wealthy families who wanted front-row seats for the frantic antics of Carnevale. Halfway down the street is the **Column of Marcus Aurelius;** standing 100 ft above Piazza Colonna, this triumphal column (similar to the one in the Forum of Trajan) commemorates the Roman campaigns of AD 172–173.

NEAR STAZIONE TERMINI

PIAZZA BARBERINI

Get off at Piazza Barberini (Metro Line A, Bus 492, 56, or 60) if you want to walk up Via Veneto or down to the Trevi Fountain. On the heavily trafficked square stands Bernini's graceful **Tritone** (Fountain of the Triton), which depicts a manly sea god spouting water from a conch shell, designed in 1637 for Pope Urban VIII; a more modern touch is the self-appointed traffic director on roller skates in the middle of the piazza.

GALLERIA NAZIONALE D'ARTE ANTICA

The *Antica* here means 13th- to 18th-century Italian paintings, and the collection is one of Rome's best, with works by Fra Filippo Lippi, Raphael, Perugino, El Greco, and Caravaggio. The building, just emerged from a long restoration, isn't bad either: Palazzo Barberini was originally constructed as a Renaissance villa and once served as the official residence of the Pope's family. Credit Bernini, the ubiquitous Baroque master, for the construction of the central hall and the loggia facing Via delle Quattro Fontane, and Pietro da Cortona for the frescoed ceiling in the gallery. *V. delle Quattro Fontane 13, tel. 06/4814591. Admission L12,000. Open Tues.–Sat. 9–2 (Apr.–Sept. until 7), Sun. 9–1.*

SANTA MARIA DELLA CONCEZIONE

Stairs lead up to the 17th-century church of the Capucin order (the word *cappuccino* refers to the way in which the coffee- stained milk froth in the popular drink resembles the brown hood and white beards typically worn by Capucin monks) and the so-called cemetery here. The remains of 4,000 priests and monks were used to decorate the five-room crypt in the 18th century as a means to attract visitors and to inspire piety. Fluted arches made of collarbones, arabesques of shoulder blades, and spirals of dusty vertebrae are humorously gruesome. Note the eerie message: "What you are now we once were; what we are now, you will be." *V. Vittorio Veneto 27, tel. 06/462850. Small donation required. Open Fri.–Wed. 9–noon and 3–6.*

PIAZZA DELLA REPUBBLICA

Chances are you'll pass through Piazza della Repubblica on the way from Stazione Termini to the centro storico. The twin buildings that encircle half of the piazza were once home to fashionable hotels and cafés and now attest to the before-and-after effect of a face-lift. Now cars spin 'round as busty nymphs wrestle with buff sea monsters in the turn-of-the-century **Fountain of the Naiad**—recently restored with splendid results. Get here on Metro A (Repubblica station) or take Bus 64 or 492 from the centro storico.

MUSEO NAZIONALE ROMANO

Some of the best Roman sculpture in the world—mostly busts, funerary monuments, and sarcophagi—is on display in this museum, recently installed in this renovated palazzo across from Stazione Termini; but the highlights are the incredible wall frescoes brought from first-century AD Roman villas excavated on the outskirts of Rome and reassembled here as they were found. *Largo di Villa Peretti 1, opposite Stazione Termini. tel. 06/4815576. Admission L12,000. Open Tues.–Sat. 9–7, Sun. 9–2.*

SAN CARLO ALLE QUATTRO FONTANE

The small yet sumptuous church got its name from the four sculptured fountains—each representing a season—that stand on the corners of the adjacent intersection. Designed by Bernini's main rival, Francesco Borromini, it is one of the first experiments in pure Baroque style. Later Baroque works in Rome are indebted to Borromini's heavily curved walls and fluted decorations. *V. del Quirinale at V. delle Quattro Fontane, tel. 06/7676531. Closed for restoration at press time.*

The oldest Christian basilica within the city walls—and still the Cathedral of Rome—San Giovanni in Laterano was for centuries the seat of the papacy and the heart of Christianity.

SANTA MARIA DEGLI ANGELI

With its austere exterior and crumbly walls, this church looks like a Roman ruin from the outside. Step inside though, and you'll enter a gigantic light-filled space. If Santa Maria degli Angeli doesn't look like most churches, it's because Michelangelo (at age 86) designed the basilica within the ruins of the 4th-century Baths of Diocletian. His original work, with its lack of decoration, can only be seen in the vaulted ceiling—the rest of the interior has been covered by Baroque embellishments. Also of note is the church's art collection, including the *Martyrdom of San Sebastian* by Domenichino and the *Crucifixion of St. Peter* by Ricciolini. *P. della Repubblica, tel. 06/4880812. Open daily 8- -12:30 and 4–7 (Oct.–Mar. until 6:30).*

SOUTH OF STAZIONE TERMINI

MUSEO DI STRUMENTI MUSICALI

This isn't your average collection of flutes, horns, and drums. First of all, it's housed in an Art Nouveau building overlooking a shady park, perfect for an afternoon picnic. More to the point, the exhibits include sundry pipes, bells, and stringed instruments made of jawbones, armadillo-shell guitars, shaman drums, and a dozen bizarre long-forgotten instruments. Rounding things out are 15th-century harps, *spinettas*, cymbals, you name it—many of them elaborately painted, carved, and inlaid with semiprecious stones. *P. Santa Croce in Gerusalemme 9, tel. 06/7014796. Metro A to San Giovanni; walk northeast on V. Carlo Felice to P. Santa Croce. Admission L4,000. Open Tue.–Sat. 9–7, Sun 9–2.*

SAN GIOVANNI IN LATERANO

Originally built on land donated by Emperor Constantine to the newly sanctioned sect of Christians, San Giovanni soon attracted hordes of pilgrims as Christians everywhere wanted a firsthand view of the pope's pad. The church owes its present-day appearance to Borromini, who in 1646 rescued it from decay and successfully incorporated the elements of the ancient structure into a graceful new Baroque basilica. The chapels are big and rich enough to be churches themselves; if you linger at each one, plan on spending a few hours here. Under the Gothic tabernacle above the altar, look for the heads—yes, reputedly the actual skulls—of Saints Peter and Paul. A rest in the pleasant **cloister** is a better idea than the **Museo Laterano** in the Palazzo Laterano, once the pope's official residence. In any case, don't miss the stunning **baptistery:** follow the signs around the side of the church. *P. San Giovanni in Laterano. Metro A to Manzoni. Admission free; cloister L4,000; museum L4,000. Open daily 7–7; tel. 06/77207991.*

SANTA CROCE IN GERUSALEMME

Santa Croce's Chapel of the Holy Relics enshrines more early Christian souvenirs than you can shake a cross at. Besides two thorns from Jesus's crown and the grim and gangly finger with which Thomas poked Christ, the otherwise uninteresting church is the proud owner of a nail and part of the inscription from the one and true Cross. The Rosa d'Oro gift shop in front sells some mean liqueur (distilled by monks), tisanes, chocolates, and honey from the Lazio region. Next door, the Museo di Strumenti Musicali (*see above*) offers a diversion for the church-weary. *V. Santa Croce in Gerusalemme, tel. 06/7014769. Metro A to San Giovanni; walk northeast on V. Carlo Felice to Santa Croce. Open daily 7–noon and 4–7:15.*

SANTA MARIA MAGGIORE

In the 4th century, Pope Liberius had a dream in which he was instructed to build a great cathedral to St. Mary on the Esquiline Hill. Hesitant to shell out cash because of a sleep-induced fancy, he shelved the project—until St. Mary herself visited him in his sleep and then dumped a bunch of snow (in the middle of summer, mind you) on the spot where the church was destined to be built—an event reen-acted every August 5 (*see* Festivals, *below*). According to the legend, the pope put on his boots and traced the perimeter of the new basilica in the snow. Modern pilgrims can see a re-creation of the scene in a 13th-century exterior mosaic, which costs L5,000 to view close-up. Inside, the colorful apse mosaics aren't a bad consolation for those who'd rather not pay; they depict Mary as a Byzantine empress being crowned Queen of Heaven by Christ. Don't leave without seeing the vaulted ceiling (gilt with some of the first gold pillaged from the New World), the zany Cosmati floors, and Bernini's tomb, down the stairs just before the altar. *P. Santa Maria Maggiore, tel. 06/483195. Admission free; mosaics L5,000. Dress code enforced. Open daily 7–7.*

SCALA SANTA

Across the street from the Basilica di San Giovanni in Laterano, in the northeast corner of Piazza San Giovanni, faithful worshipers climb—on their knees—the 28 cold, hard steps of the Scala Santa (Holy Stairs). This is supposedly the original set, brought over from Jerusalem (covered in walnut for protection) that Jesus ascended after his trial by Pontius Pilate. At the end of it all, pilgrims are rewarded with a glimpse of the Sanctum Sanctorum (the pope's private chapel) and the *Acheropita*, a portrait of Jesus supposedly not painted by the hands of mere mortals. The less devout—or coordinated—should take the side stairs. *P. di Porta di San Giovanni, tel. 06/70494489. Open 6:15–12:15 and 3:30–7 (until 6 in winter).*

NEAR THE SPANISH STEPS

PIAZZA DEL POPOLO

At the end of three of the centro storico's most important streets—Via del Babuino, Via del Corso, and Via di Ripetta—the People's Square, as the name translates, was once the gateway to the city for foreign visitors. Today it's a meeting and mingling place for teenagers on scooters, grandmothers on park benches, and businesspeople on cell phones. Take in the commotion from the Egyptian obelisk of Ramses II (a mere 3,200 years old) at the center of the piazza, and check out the near-perfect symmetry of the twin 17th-century churches **Santa Maria dei Miracoli** and **Santa Maria di Montesanto.** For a view of the action from on high, walk up the steps (on the east side of the piazza) to the **Pincio.**

ARA PACIS AND AUGUSTEUM

Now housed in a modern glass structure (and visible even when the building is closed), the **Ara Pacis,** or Peace Altar, was originally erected in 13 BC to commemorate the peace won with Rome's military victories in Spain and Gaul under Emperor Augustus. The panels depict the members of his family, and also Romulus and Remus with the she-wolf. By hitching his wagon to the city's mythological heritage, Augustus underscored his divine right to rule. Across the street, the circular brick Augusteum (closed to the public) once held the emperor's glorified remains. The monument is now moss-covered and sits well below street level, a testament to the rising ground level of Rome over the last 2,000 years. Two huge obelisks that once stood at the mausoleum's entrance now adorn Piazza del Quirinale and Piazza dell'Esquilino. *V. di Ripetta. tel. 06/6711035. Admission L3,750. Open Tues.–Sat. 9–5, Sun. 9–1.*

SANTA MARIA DEL POPOLO

Snuggled against the 400-year-old **Porta del Popolo,** Rome's northern city gate, in the northeast corner of the piazza, Santa Maria del Popolo looks oddly plain at first glance. The interior artwork, however, makes up for any exterior decorative deficiency. Frescoes by Pinturicchio line the first chapel on the right and the vaulted room behind the altar. To the left of the altar are two Caravaggio canvases depicting the martyrdoms of St. Peter (left) and St. Paul (right). A big dose of color comes from the second chapel, designed by Fontana and decorated with all kinds of bright marble. None other than Bernini can take credit for the plump cherubs, ghastly saints, and sweeping angels that hang from the nave's ceiling. *P. del Popolo, tel. 06/3610836. Open Mon.–Sat. 7–12 and 4–7, Sun. 8–2 and 4:30–7:30.*

PIAZZA DI SPAGNA

Piazza di Spagna and its picture-postcard **Scalinata di Trinità dei Monti**—better known as the **Spanish Steps**—have been a magnet for sightseers and visitors for a few hundred years, ever since a diplomatic visit from the king of Spain inspired the glitzy makeover. The famous steps were constructed in 1723 by architect Francesco de Sanctis to link the Church of **Trinità dei Monti** at the top with the **Spanish Embassy** below. In the 1800s, expats and poets like Keats and Shelley made their homes in the neighborhood, and artists once combed the piazza for prospective models.

The Trevi Fountain had a conspicuous role in Fellini's film La Dolce Vita; it was the site of Anita Ekberg's midnight dip.

KEATS SHELLEY MUSEUM

John Keats (1795–1821) lived out the last months of his life in this cramped flat alongside the Spanish Steps. In the 19th century, this was the heart of bohemian Rome, especially frequented by American and British writers. The cluttered memorial house has a notable collection of Romantic-era relics. Three of the major figures of the time—Keats, Shelley, and Byron—left behind books, letters, pictures, locks of hair, and old furniture. *P. di Spagna 26, tel. 06/6784235. Admission L5,000. Open Mon.–Fri. 9–1 and 3–6, Sat. 11–2 and 3–6.*

PINCIO

Right above Piazza del Popolo and Piazza di Spagna, the shady Pincio is an extension of the Villa Borghese's gardens, lined with trees and benches, matrons, old men, and young nubile couples. Around 8 PM there's cheesy piano and electric beat-box accompaniment from the restaurant on Viale dell'Obelisco. On weekend afternoons, the scene turns frenetic with bikers and skaters. On summer afternoons, concession stands sell to the crowds gathered for puppet and mime shows.

FONTANA DI TREVI

From the narrow end of Piazza di Spagna, take Via due Macelli past Largo Tritone and turn right at Via in Arcione; follow the sound of crashing water, and there you have it—the Trevi Fountain. The fantastic Baroque arrangement of Neptune atop dolphins, sea creatures, boulders, and cascades flowing into a swimming-pool-size basin was conceived by Nicola Salvi in 1762. Water arrives via a 1st-century BC Roman aqueduct known as the Acqua Vergine, named after a virgin who led a group of thirsty soldiers to a spring outside the city. Legend had it that the water made men faithful, and women dragged their hubbies here by the thousands. Ironically, the area around the fountain is now a prime hunting ground for Italian men on the prowl. Brave the lechery long enough to toss a coin over your left shoulder, ensuring your return to the Eternal City.

VILLA BORGHESE

Rome's largest park is filled with playful fountains, sculptured gardens, and groves of shady pine trees. Stretches of green and plenty of leafy pathways encourage wandering, biking, or just hanging out. It is also home to several art museums, including the magnificent Galleria Borghese.

GALLERIA BORGHESE

With five of Bernini's most celebrated sculptures downstairs and paintings by Raphael, Caravaggio, Titian, and Caracci upstairs, this collection could be called the greatest hits of the 17th century. But

PASTA ON A PEDESTAL

The Museo Nazionale Storico degli Spaghetti e Paste Alimentari (National Pasta Museum) showcases Italy's most famous culinary item. Visit small galleries named the Wheat Room or the Ligurian Room and learn the compelling saga of pasta and its present-day production. P. Scanderbeg 117, tel. 06/6991120. From Trevi Fountain, take V. del Lavatore, right on Vicolo Scanderbeg to P. Scanderbeg. Admission L12,000, includes tour in English on CD. Open daily 9:30–7:30.

instead, just say Borghese. Relentlessly collected (even stolen) by Cardinal Scipione Borghese (the ruthless nephew of Pope Paul IV), it is on display again after a 14-year restoration of his stunning palace at the edge of his enormous villa. *P. Scipione Borghese 5, tel. 06/854–8577. Metro A to P. di Spagna; follow signs to park and then museum. Admission L12,000. Reservations mandatory, but last-minute tickets sometimes available. Open Tues.–Sat. 9–7, Sun. 9–1.*

GALLERIA NAZIONALE D'ARTE MODERNA

Rome's modern-art museum, in an immense neoclassical building on the northern fringe of Villa Borghese, houses a collection of Italian Impressionist and Romantic art. Highlights are a series of sculptures by Vincenzo Gemito and Giuseppe Pellizza's preparatory sketches for *Il Quarto Stato,* his statement about "humanity in the march for progress," inspired by the industrial revolution in Italy. Also displayed are works by Klimt, Degas, van Gogh, Cézanne, and Zorn. *V. delle Belle Arti 131, tel. 06/322981. Admission L12,000. Open Tues.–Sun. 9–7.*

MUSEO NAZIONALE DI VILLA GIULIA

The villa of Pope Julius III on the southwest edge of Villa Borghese displays one of the world's most important and exhaustive collections of Etruscan artifacts. The Etruscans dominated Lazio and Tuscany from the 8th to the 5th centuries BC, when their city-states were finally swallowed by the growing Roman republic. The villa's collection of sculpture, earthenware water jugs, terra-cotta bowls, bronze figures, and jewelry demonstrates the high artistry of the Etruscans. A highlight is the Sarcofago degli Sposi, a double tomb built so the deceased couple could cling eternally. *P. di Villa Giulia 9, tel. 06/3201951. Admission L8,000. Tues.–Sat. 9–7, Sun. 9–2.*

WEST OF THE TIBER

TRASTEVERE

So maybe it's not the neighborhood it once was, no longer full of working-class folks, no longer the city within a city. And so what if it's been discovered by tourists and guidebooks and real estate agents. There's still plenty of reasons to cross the river and enjoy charming and cool Trastevere: great walks day or night through narrow crumbling streets with little trattorias and bars at every turn.

ISOLA TIBERINA

This tiny island in the middle of the Tiber connects the Jewish Ghetto with Trastevere by two of the oldest bridges in Rome: Ponte Fabricio, built in 62 BC, and Ponte Cestio, dating from 42 BC. Legend has it that the island was created when the Romans dumped the crops of a defeated Etruscan town into the river. At the gods' behest, a temple was built to Aesculapius (god of medicine) on the pile of grain, and thus the Isola Tiberina has been the dominion of the healing arts ever since: because the island was ideally situated for quarantining the fatally contaminated, a hospital was erected here in the Middle Ages and still operates today.

SANTA CECILIA IN TRASTEVERE

Cecilia is the reputed inventor of the organ and the patron saint of music, and, like most martyrs, her death did not come quickly. The Romans, under orders of Emperor Marcus Aurelius, first tried to steam her in the baths of her own home under the now-Baroque church that bears her name, but she came out unharmed. Then came the sword, and it took the executioner three blows across her neck to finally do the deed. Her likeness on the altar, sculpted by Stefano Maderno in 1600, reproduces the exact pose of her body—sword marks and all—when it was exhumed in 1599, completely intact after 1,000 years in the tomb. *P. Santa Cecilia, off V. Anicia east of V. di Trastevere, tel. 06/5899289. Admission to ruins L2,000. Open daily 10–12 and 4–6 (Oct.–Apr., 3–5).*

SANTA MARIA IN TRASTEVERE

Once you've had enough of people-watching in Trastevere's most famous namesake piazza, step into the cool and serene interior of the 12th-century Santa Maria in Trastevere, one of the few churches in town that retains for the most part its medieval form and decoration. The Byzantine look to the dazzling series of mosaics surrounding the nave and apse is representative of the Eastern influences imported from Constantinople during the Middle Ages. *P. Santa Maria in Trastevere, tel. 06/5819443. Admission free. Open daily 7:30–1 and 4–7 (Oct.–Mar. until 6).*

VILLA FARNESINA

What would you do if you were Agostino "the Magnificent" Chigi, one of the wealthiest bankers in Renaissance Rome? You'd probably build a gaudy villa on a choice piece of land overlooking the Tiber River. You'd then call on the leading artist of the day, Raphael, to oversee the decoration of the walls and ceilings, hire a master of trompe l'oeil such as Peruzzi to make the second-floor walls disappear, and get Il Sodoma to put some rather steamy imagery on the bedroom walls. *V. della Lungara 230, tel. 06/68801767. Admission L8,000. Open Mon.–Sat. 9–1.*

ORTO BOTANICO

Twelve acres at the foot of the Janiculum Hill serve as the botanical gardens for the University of Rome. Come to see the formal gardens and greenhouses, teeming with exotic and medicinal plants, palm trees, lily-covered ponds, and pine groves. The **Garden for the Blind** includes a variety of aromatics and plants unusual to the touch. This is a serene refuge for lounging. *End of Largo Cristina di Svezia, just off of V. della Lungara opposite Villa Farnesina, tel. 06/6864193. Admission L4,000. Open Mon.–Sat. 9–1 hr before sunset.*

VATICAN CITY AND CASTEL SANT'ANGELO

The world's second-smallest nation, the Vatican is Europe's last absolute monarchy, currently ruled by Pope John Paul II. The Vatican has its own postal system, radio, newspaper, and military force (known as the Swiss Guards) and still exercises a great deal of influence over Italian politics, though you wouldn't know it in a country where abortion, contraception, and divorce are all unquestionably legal. From Ponte Vittorio Emanuele on the Tiber, **Via della Conciliazione** leads to the magnificent **Basilica di San Pietro** (St. Peter's Basilica), the Vatican's most visible landmark (the building code in Rome states that no structure can be taller than St. Peter's cupola). To reach St. Peter's, take Bus 64 from Stazione Termini or Largo Argentina; or take Metro A to Ottaviano station and walk 15 minutes south on Viale Ottaviano. A 10-minute walk toward the Tiber will deposit you at the hulking **Castel Sant'Angelo,** for centuries used as a fortress to guard the pope and his riches. The entrance to the **Vatican Museums** is a hike from Piazza San Pietro, or a quick ride on one of the Vatican's shuttles (*see below*).

CASTEL SANT'ANGELO

The unusual, imposing round structure was originally built in AD 135 as a mausoleum for the emperor Hadrian and his successors. The name Castel Sant'Angelo came about during the plague of AD 590, when Pope Gregory the Great had a vision of St. Michael the archangel on the mausoleum's rampart. Gregory immediately ordered that a temple to St. Michael be built on the site, whereupon, it is said, the plague magically ended. Gradually built up over the centuries, it was used alternatively as a fortress, prison, warehouse, and often as a hideout for the popes, since it is connected to the Vatican by a passageway inside the wall that runs between the two. Wandering around the many winding ramps and

ST. PETER'S FIT FOR A QUEEN

Queen Christina of Sweden abdicated her throne and came to Rome in the 1650s to bring herself closer to heaven, but legend has it she knew how to raise a little hell, too. Upon her arrival, she set about removing modestly placed leaves from public statuary, threw extravagant parties at the Villa Corsini, and carried on a not-so-secret affair with a cardinal. She held onto her reputation with good works at the Orto Botanico and today has the distinction of being the only woman buried in St. Peter's.

passageways is far more interesting than the art, armor, and cannonballs on display. The statue-lined **Ponte Sant'Angelo** spans the Tiber directly in front of the castle. *Lungotevere Castello 50, tel. 06/39080730. Admission L8,000. Open Tue.–Sun. 9–8 (shorter hours in winter).*

BASILICA DI SAN PIETRO

St. Peter's is the world's largest Christian church and an absolute must on any Roman itinerary, no matter what your religion. In AD 319, Constantine decided to bankroll a basilica for the newly legitimized Christian sect. Taking quite literally the passage in the Bible in which Jesus tells Peter, "You are the rock on which I shall build my church," Constantine ordered the church built directly above the grave of St. Peter. The original church stood for more than 1,000 years, undergoing all sorts of mutations and restorations until it was on the verge of collapse. Partial reconstruction began in 1452, though little was accomplished until 1506, when Pope Julius II instructed Donato Bramante to raze the site and completely redesign the basilica. Over the next 150 years, Italy's greatest artists and architects—ncluding Bramante himself, Bernini, Raphael, Peruzzi, Sangallo the Younger, and Michelangelo—had a hand in the design and decoration. If Bramante deserves the greatest part of the credit for the layout, Michelangelo gets the award for the most impressive artwork. Of these artists, only Bernini lived long enough to witness the completion of St. Peter's. Five days before his own death, Michelangelo inspected his pupils' progress on the dome's mosaics and, feeling the work was going according to his design, announced he could die (his plan was abandoned soon after his death).

If you're standing in front of St. Peter's, you lose some of the church's grandiosity, inasmuch as the enormous facade blocks a view of the dome. But climb the broad steps and enter the carved portico salvaged from the 4th-century structure, pass through Antonio Filarete's 15th-century bronze doors, and behold—the largest church in the world. Michelangelo's **Pietà,** behind lunatic-proof glass on the right (the sculpture was damaged in 1972 when a hammer-wielding viewer attacked it) depicts a very young Mary with the dead Jesus resting peacefully across her lap. To the right of the Pietà is the Holy Door, which the pope will open with a hammer to begin the Jubilee Year 2000. The door will remain open for the year and is to be closed again on the last day of the year. Heading toward the altar from the Pietà, look left for the **tomb of Queen Christina,** the sole woman buried in St. Peter's. She earned this honor by embracing Catholicism after having fled her native—and Lutheran—Sweden with the crown jewels in 1654 (*see box* St. Peter's Fit For a Queen, *above*).

People born on February 29 can pay homage at the **altar of Pope Gregory XIII** (up the right aisle), who in 1582 codified the formula for adding an extra day to the calendar every fourth year so as to keep it in sync with the Earth's movement around the sun. Behind Gregory's unadorned tomb is a bronze **statue of St. Peter,** saved from the original church. Pope Pius IX granted an indulgence to worshipers who kissed the statue's toes; after 140 years, there's not much toe left to kiss. At the center of things, where four massive piers support St. Peter's dome, Bernini's baldachin (canopy) rises 145 ft above the main altar; it was made from 20 tons of bronze stripped from the Pantheon by order of Pope Urban VIII. The canopy towers above the crypt, where remnants of the original church as well as the tombs of a few popes can be viewed. Below the crypt, under the foundations of the original church, the bones of St. Peter himself supposedly lie. If you have the time, it is definitely worth taking the special tour of the **Vatican Necropolis,** directly underneath the basilica and grotto, especially if you won't get a chance to see the catacombs. Apply in writing (Ufficio Scavi, Vatican City, tel. 06/69885318, fax 06/69885518; L15,000 for a 90-min English tour) including a local telephone number at which the office can confirm the reservation, or go in person at least a day in advance to the Excavations Office (on the right beyond the Arco delle Campane entrance to the Vatican, which is left of the basilica). Tell the Swiss guard you want the Ufficio Scavi, and he will let you by.

The sacristy hosts a small, dark **museum** (admission L5,000; open daily 9–3:30, until 4:30 in summer) with a hodgepodge of Vatican treasures, among them a remarkable 15th-century bronze of Pope Sixtus V by Antonio Pollaiuolo. As you leave St. Peter's, veer left toward the small courtyard and garden. If you want the view from the top of the cupola, buy your tickets, then take the long hike up to the top of the **dome** of St. Peter's, or take the elevator up halfway and walk the rest, (admission L6,000 via elevator, L5,000 via stairs; open daily 8–5, until 6 in summer). Either way there's a lot of stairs, but the reward is glorious, with unobstructed views over Vatican City and central Rome. *P. San Pietro. Dress code strictly enforced: No bare shoulders, no bare knees. Open daily 7–7 (Oct.–Apr. until 6).*

PIAZZA SAN PIETRO

These days the most common way to approach St. Peter's is from **Via della Conciliazione,** a road built to celebrate the agreement made in 1929 between Mussolini and the pope, which formally established the independent Vatican state. An old neighborhood was destroyed to make way for the road, which spoiled the grand effect the piazza once had on those who came upon it from a maze of dark, narrow streets. In any case, the entrance to **Piazza San Pietro** (St. Peter's Square) is impressive, unquestionably one of Bernini's masterpieces. It took him 11 years to design and oversee the construction of this massive square, capable of holding 400,000 people within its symmetrical arms. There's usually a stream of people moving around the piazza, but at the beginning or near the end of the day, the obelisk in the center of the piazza is a calm vantage point from which to take in the view. If you stand in one of the two stone disks in the pavement on either side of the obelisk, the colonnades will appear to be supported by a single row of columns. The balustrade above the quadruple colonnades is topped with more than 140 statues of saints and scholars, each one designed by Bernini. Looking toward St. Peter's Basilica, the peaked roof on the right belongs to the Sistine Chapel, out of which white smoke billows when the cardinals have selected a new pope.

You would have to walk about 7 km (4½ mi) just to cover all the gallery space in the Vatican Museums, where at least a dozen different museums contain artifacts and artwork from every corner of the world.

VATICAN MUSEUMS

The main entrance to the Vatican Museums is on **Viale Vaticano,** a long walk from Piazza San Pietro. Other options are Bus 49 from Piazza Cavour to the door of the Vatican Museums or Bus 81 to Piazza del Risorgimento, from which you can follow the signs or pick up the line. If the Metro suits you better, take Linea A to Ottaviano–San Pietro and walk southwest on Via dei Gracchi.

The museums are open for free on the last Sunday of every month, but the secret is out and crowds tend to be even more colossal than usual. If there is one morning that you get an early start, make it your Vatican day . . . the late-morning crowds—think tour buses—can be really overbearing.

You can explore the museums at will, but the pretaped English-language commentary is probably worth the rather steep L8,000 rental fee. You can start with the **Egyptian Museum,** filled with hieroglyphic tablets, jewelry, sculptures, and yes, mummies. The nearby **Pio Clementino Museum** holds some of the world's most notable ancient sculptures, among them the *Laocoön,* the *Belvedere Torso,* and *Apollo Belvedere,* all works of the 1st century BC that had a tremendous influence on Renaissance artists. Don't miss the lighter works in the **Sala degli Animali** (Animal Room) before moving on to the **Etruscan Museum,** full of terra-cottas, bronzes, and sarcophagi, many of which come from Cerveteri (*see below*). The superb **Gallery of Tapestries,** hung with dozens of comic, tragic, and purely decorative tapestries designed by Raphael, leads to the **Gallery of Maps,** a stunning display of late 16th- century cartographic ingenuity and accomplishment. Next are the **Raphael Stanze,** decorated with biblical scenes by the Urbino-born Raphael (1483–1520). One of these rooms, the Stanza della Segnatura, contains the artist's *School of Athens* (1511), a balance of geometric composition and harmonies of color exemplary of the Renaissance visual ideal. The faces of Plato, Aristotle, and other philosophers of antiquity are portraits of Raphael's contemporaries—note Leonardo da Vinci posing as Plato. The next stop is the cramped **Chapel of Nicholas V,** painted floor to ceiling with frescoes by Fra Angelico (1400–55), followed by the **Borgia Apartments,** with ceiling mosaics by Bernardino Pinturicchio (1454–1513).

Most of the museum's visitors (about 10,000 a day) rush straight through, wanting only to see the **Sistine Chapel,** which is just about always packed with neck-craning tourists—though some find it less painful to look down at the reflection of the ceiling in a hand mirror. Forget about personal space and dive in. If you have a romantic notion of wandering silently under Michelangelo's masterpiece, your only chance is to be there when they open the doors to the museum and sprint ahead and enjoy the room while it fills up. Just about every great Renaissance artist in Rome had a hand in its decoration—Pinturicchio, Signorelli, Botticelli, Cosimo Rosselli—before Michelangelo, much to his dismay, was cajoled by Pope Julius II into painting the ceiling, a barrel-vaulted artist's nightmare. Contrary to popular belief, Michelangelo's work on the Sistine Chapel was not spent on his back. He stood on his tiptoes and often painted freehand without any outlines. The result of Michelangelo's four years of labor, recently restored to (some say excessively) brilliant colors, has been called the most sublime example of artistry in the world. Biblical stories depicted on the ceiling include (from east to west) the Creation of Light, Creation of the Universe, Creation of Earth, Creation of Adam, Creation of Eve, the Fall from Paradise, the Sacrifice of Isaac, the Flood, and the Drunkenness of Noah. Around the sides are biblical prophets and Greek sibyls in poses that seem to support the ceiling. Twenty-four years after completing the Sistine Chapel, Michelangelo was commissioned to paint the *Last Judgment* on the wall behind the simple altar. A gruesome and tormented work, it articulates a very different version of the human condition. By this time the ideals of the Renaissance had been challenged by the upheavals of the Reformation and the Counter-Reformation. *V. Vaticano, tel. 06/6988-3333. Admission L18,000, free last Sun. of month. Open Nov.– Feb. and mid-June–Aug., Mon.–Sat. 8:45–1:45 (last admission at 1); Mar.–mid-June and Sept.–Oct., Mon.–Sat. 9–4:45 (last admission at 4); also last Sun. of every month 9–1:45 (last admission at 1).*

GIANICOLO

If you are crowd-weary from the Vatican or feeling overwhelmed by urban chaos, take a walk up the Gianicolo (Janiculum Hill) for a shady respite and a chance to view Rome from a quiet vantage point. Rising behind Trastevere and bordered by the Vatican gardens to the north, the hill offers plenty of good spots for a picnic. From Trastevere, **Via Garibaldi** winds up the hill, passing the church of San Pietro in Montorio and the **Acqua Paola,** a gushing early 17th-century fountain, to the **Porta di San Pancrazio.** Turning right here, the tree-lined **Passeggiata del Gianicolo** continues along the hillside to Piazza Garibaldi, where a column commemorates an important battle fought here in 1849. If you're approaching the Gianicolo from the Vatican side, go to Piazza della Rovere, and then up the Salita di Sant'Onofrio. Catch your breath at the **Chiesa di Sant'Onofrio,** the final resting place of the poet Tasso, before arriving at Piazza Garibaldi.

SAN PIETRO IN MONTORIO

The late-15th-century church of **San Pietro in Montorio** (V. Garibaldi, tel. 06/5813940; open daily 7:30–12 and 4–6) was built on the supposed site of the crucifixion of St. Peter. In the courtyard to the right of the church, Bramante built his celebrated Tempietto (Little Temple) over the exact spot. Inside the church are some beautifully decorated chapels, including the second on the right with del Piombo's *Flagellation*, based on sketches by Michelangelo.

VILLA DORIA PAMPHILI

Rome's largest and most picturesque park is home to relatively well-preserved 17th-century palaces, terraces, and gardens open to the public and free for all. Running trails are scenic and well marked; the less gung-ho can picnic on the grass. *Bus 72 from P. Venezia, or a short walk from Porta San Pancrazio.*

OUTER ROME

BASILICA SAN PAOLO FUORI LE MURE

The bulky Basilica of St. Paul Outside the Walls is second in size only to St. Peter's and was supposedly consecrated on the same day: November 18, AD 324. Originally a small affair commemorating Paul's martyrdom, it became the imposing fortress you see today due to an influx of funds from the likes of Charlemagne and Leo III. Although the building was damaged by a fire in 1823, much of the decoration was saved. The highlights are a candelabrum from 1170 that depicts scenes from Christ's life with human-faced monsters, a Gothic tabernacle studded with small statues of St. Paul, and a wooden crucifix (in the Chapel of the Sacrament, to the left of the altar) carved in a gruesomely realistic style. The meager light that comes through the dark windows makes it difficult to see the cycle of wall mosaics. If you can stand the crowd that jams the souvenir shop, check out the art on the walls—17th-century religious scenes that tend toward the provocative. *V. Ostiense. Metro B to San Paolo. Open daily 7—7 (Oct.–Mar. until 6), tel. 06/5410341.*

By then old and ornery, Michelangelo painted himelf into his "Last Judgment" on the altar wall of the Sistine Chapel. Look for his long, tired face on a body of sagging skin (all that was left of the great Renaissance master after the papacy and the times had bled his spirit dry), held in the hand of St. Bartholomew, below and to the right of Jesus.

EUR (ESPOSIZIONE UNIVERSALE DI ROMA)

Mussolini had big plans for Rome to host the 1942 World Exposition and had his cadre of fascist-era architects design a minicity from the ground up on the southern edge of town, complete with modern, wide avenues, artificial lakes, and tall buildings. Construction of EUR (pronounced ay-oor) for Esposizione Universale di Roma came to a halt during World War II but not before a few buildings had defined the area and the period by a style that is cold, monumental, and stark. Building resumed after the war and culminated with the construction of stadiums and a velodrome for the 1960 Olympics. The **Museo della Civiltà Romana** (P. Guglielmo Marconi, tel. 06/5448993; L5000; open Tues.–Sat. 9–7, Sun. 9–1) examines the history of the city through rooms devoted to catapults, emperors, and the glory of Roman engineering. The exhibit is tied together by a fascinating scale reproduction of ancient Rome in the time of Augustus, in the memory of whose reign Mussolini founded this museum in 1937. Finally, when museum-going has you feeling punchy, play hooky at **Luna Park** (V. Tre Fontane, tel. 06/5924747), a hokey amusement park full of rickety rides, trademark infringements, and other things you won't see at Disneyland. EUR Palasport on Metro B is the most convenient stop for downtown EUR. *Museo della Civiltà Romana: Walk up V. C. Colombo, turn right on V. Europa, left on V. dell'Arte, and right on V. della Civiltà Romana. Luna Park: Continue on V. dell'Arte to V. Tre Fontane.*

VIA APPIA AND CATACOMBS

Built in 312 BC, the Via Appia (Appian Way) was the most important of all Roman roads. As the chief campaign route during the conquest of southern Italy, it reached all the way to Brindisi on the Adriatic coast, a distance of 544 km (330 mi). Today it's best known for the miles of underground cemeteries along its first stretch. Since burial was forbidden within the city walls, residents buried their dead just outside, digging extensive, multilevel networks of tunnels in the soft tufa rock. Most of the remains are long gone, so you'll have to make do with eerie subterranean passageways and lots of Christian graffiti. Three sections of the catacombs along the Appia Antica can be visited, but unless you really have a fascination with spelunking, one will be enough. But then again, remember that on a hot summer day a catacomb is a very cool place indeed. Each charges L8,000 for a guided tour and is open 8:30–noon and 2:30–5.

The Catacombs of **San Callisto** (V. Appia Antica 110, tel. 06/5136725; closed Wed.) are the largest of the known catacombs and considered to have been the most important. The tour focuses on the second level and includes the crypt of St. Callisto, an early pope, as well as the crypt of St. Cecilia. The Catacombs of **Domitilla** (V. delle Sette Chiese 283, tel. 06/5548766; closed Tues.) are the oldest known and the least visited, although 1st-century jewelry and eating utensils were found here in 1985. **San Sebastiano** (V. Appia Antica 136, tel. 06/7887035; closed Thurs.) is the most famous, most interesting, and consequently the most heavily visited of the catacombs because of its Christ-era mausoleum. To reach the catacombs, take Bus 218 from San Giovanni in Laterano (*see above*) and follow the crowds. Rome's EPT office (*see* Visitor Information *in* Basics, *above*) has pamphlets on the catacombs and sometimes organizes cheap guided tours with transportation. Sunday is a good day to explore the Appia Antica, as the road is closed to car traffic.

Beyond San Callisto is the church **Domine Quo Vadis,** supposedly built on the spot where St. Peter, on his way out of Rome, met Jesus and asked him, "Where goest thou, Lord?" ("Domine quo vadis?") Jesus replied, "To be crucified a second time," hinting that Peter, too, should turn back and accept his death and eventual martyrdom. The church is run by a Polish order that speaks fair English and only half-heartedly believes in the authenticity of the footprints (supposedly Jesus's) in a piece of marble at the church entrance. *Bus 218 from San Giovanni in Laterano; ask driver to stop at church.*

FESTIVALS

Ask at EPT tourist offices (*see* Visitor Information *in* Basics, *above*) about festivals and seasonal events in the area.

JANUARY • On January 17, **dogs, cats,** and **canaries** are blessed on the steps of St. Eusebio at Piazza Vittorio.

FEBRUARY • **Carnevale** is hardly felt these days, in stark contrast to old days of processions and feasts.

MARCH • On March 9, cars are blessed—yes, cars—on Via dei Fori Imperiali, by the Church of Santa Francesca Romana. With Rome's gnarly traffic madness, it's no wonder that Italians show up in droves. The **Festa di San Giuseppe** (March 19) celebrates Jesus's secular dad, Joseph, with fried *bignè* (doughnuts filled with vanilla pastry cream) in streets and piazzas north of the Vatican.

APRIL • During Easter the city is mobbed with pilgrims, and the pope is one busy man: open-air mass in St. Peter's Square on **Palm Sunday,** nighttime mass in the Colosseum on **Good Friday,** and the celebrated **stations of the cross** procession on the Palatine Hill, as well as his Easter blessing at St. Peter's. Get there early. In late April, an **art show** on Via Margutta (between Via del Corso and the southwest edge of Villa Borghese) blankets this old and weathered street with paintings by semifamous local artists. There's a repeat engagement in the fall. At the Campidoglio, parades and parties celebrate **Festa di Roma** on the traditional anniversary of the city's founding (April 21, 753 BC) with spectacular floral and firework shows.

MAY • A month-long **rose show** adds color to Aventine Hill. From mid-May onward, an **antiques fair** on Via dei Coronari (two blocks north of Piazza Navona) keeps most shops open late; flaming torches line this normally dark and narrow road. The **Italian Open Tennis Tournament** and an **International Showjumping Competition** draw crowds to the Foro Italico and Villa Borghese at the end of May.

JUNE • On June 24, the **Festa di San Giovanni** (Feast of St. John the Baptist) is celebrated heartily in the neighborhood near the church of San Giovanni in Laterano (*see* South of Stazione Termini, *above*), with singing, dancing, games, and stewed-snail eating (don't ask). The best seats for the fireworks displays are Porta San Giovanni, Aventine Hill, and the Campidoglio. On June 29, the **Festa di San Pietro** honors Rome's patron saint in St. Peter's Basilica with candles and song presided over by the pope. **Estate Romana,** which runs June–September, has music, dance, theater, and films in venues throughout the city (primarily the Villa Medici, Massenzio, Villa Giulia, and Foro Italico). Events are listed in daily newspapers and *Roma c'è.*

AUGUST • Normally kept under glass, the **chains of St. Peter,** at San Pietro in Vincoli, are taken out for air and reverent kisses August 1. The **Festa della Madonna della Neve** (August 5) sees flurries of white rose petals whirling about Santa Maria Maggiore, at Via Cavour a few blocks southwest of Stazione Termini. The white petals, thrown from the roof of Santa Maria, are meant to re-create the legendary

August snow that marked the spot where the church was destined to be built. On **Ferragosto** (August 15), Romans skip town for picnics in the hills, but watermelon stands still do great business.

SEPTEMBER • A torchlighted **handicrafts fair** takes over Via dell'Orso, a few blocks north of Piazza Navona, from September to October.

DECEMBER • Much of the historic center gets dressed up for Christmas, with lights and decorations strung from every post and window, and Piazza Navona hosts a **Christmas toy fair** through Epiphany, when good children are awarded candies and sweets, bad children coal. **Capodanno** (New Year's) is predictably noisy, and fireworks supplies seem to last a week or two into January.

SHOPPING

Shopping and browsing are as much social pastimes in Rome as anywhere else in the country. Unfortunately, the designer shoes and clothes that Italy is famous for don't come cheaper here, especially at the celebrated shops on Via dei Condotti and Via Frattina. Lower-rent Roman fashion can be had along **Via del Corso, Via Nazionale,** and **Via Giubbonari** (off Campo dei Fiori), where clothes tend toward the trendy and funky and where good-quality shoes, miracle of miracles, cost less than in the United States. Clearly, however, Rome isn't just about clothes and shoes. Before you exhaust your credit limit on a whole new wardrobe, take a look at what else can be had in the stores and *botteghe* of modern Rome.

Street vendors animate busy thoroughfares and shopping areas, selling everything from hats to housewares at outdoor tables—no muss, no fuss, no receipts, and no guarantees. Caveat emptor.

MARKETS AND BARGAINS

The Sunday-morning **Porta Portese flea market** (7–2, along V. Portuense in Trastevere) has mainly used or second-rate new clothing, though there are still some deals to be had on old furniture and interesting junk. Bargaining is the rule here, as are pickpockets; beware. The market is immense and without official beginning or end. If you go, go early, while there's still a lot of choice and room to move around. To get here, hop on any bus going up Viale Trastevere and ask the driver to drop you at the market, or just follow the crowd. A less frenetic and crowded version of the Porta Portese market is the set of stands on **Via Sannio** (Mon.–Sat. 8–2, Metro Line A San Giovanni). Also in the realm of serious discount is the hilarious junk-filled **Mas** (V. dello Statuto 11, Metro Line A Vittorio), a three-story bargain "department store."

SPECIALTY STORES

ART SUPPLIES AND PAPER • A little like an artist's hardware store, **Ditta Poggi** (V. del Gesu' 74–75, tel. 06/6784477) has been selling art supplies for more than a century. Opposite is a shop that specializes in art paper and cardboard. If you are into serious pens (or need to get a gift for someone who is), **Stilofetti** (V. degli Orfani 82, near the Pantheon, tel. 06/6789662) has the distinguished brands, as well as replacement parts. Believe it or not, those cool notebooks and pads made with recycled paper can be found at **Feltrinelli** (opposite bus stop on Largo Argentina, tel. 06/68803248). For good writing paper, try **La Chiave** (Largo delle Stimmate 28, tel. 06/68308848).

CLOTHING • Bargains are few around Piazza di Spagna, but **Sermoneta** (P. di Spagna, tel. 06/6791960) sells a wide variety of leather gloves at reasonable prices. The best shops for new and vintage clothing are clustered along Via del Governo Vecchio and in the triangle made by Corso Vittorio Emanuele II, Piazza Navona, and Via dei Coronari. Specifically, check out the funky creations for women from **Maga Morgana** (V. del Governo Vecchio 27, tel. 06/6879995) and **Galleria di Orditi e Trame** (V. del Teatro Valle 54/B, tel. 06/6893372), where everything you see is made right there in the shop.

DEPARTMENT STORES • **Coin** (P. San Giovanni, tel. 06/7080020) and **La Rinascente** (V. del Tritone at V. del Corso, tel. 06/6797691) sell clothing and accessories seven days a week. **Standa** (V. Trastevere and V. Cola di Rienzo) and **UPIM** (V. del Tritone) are better for supplies and services—like while-you-wait shoe repair—than fashion.

MUSIC • **Metropoli Rock** (V. Cavour 72, tel. 06/4880443) has an astounding collection of vinyl and CDs. For a broad, traditional selection of CDs and records, try **Ricordi** (V. Giulio Cesare 88, tel. 06/3720215), near the Vatican.

SOMETHING IN PAPAL PURPLE?

If you've come to the Eternal City looking for ecclesiastical garb or religious doodads, you've hit gold. The shops on Via dei Cestari, north of Largo Argentina, specialize in ornate liturgical vestments with a sideline in Christian-theme knickknacks, and shops near the Vatican on Via Porta Angelica offer a celestial array of pope portraits, postcards, figurines, and even snow globes for low, low prices (but still many times what they're worth). The pious can have the loot blessed at a papal audience; blasphemers can put pope stickers on their cars. Lay shoppers may want to stick to the windows.

GIFT IDEAS • How about something in tin? The little **Lattoniere** shop (P. de' Renzi 22, in Trastevere, tel. 06/5806737) has tons of great tools and decorations all made right there by one of Rome's last tin-smiths, who might make something to order for you. Definitely worth a browse are the two coolest shops for designer household items and furniture: **Spazio Sette** (V. dei Barbieri 7, near Largo Argentina, tel. 06/6869708) and **Stock Market** (V. dei Banchi Vecchi 51, near P. Navona, tel. 06/6864238). Pottery and handicrafts at reasonable prices can be found at **Myricae** (V. Frattina 36, tel. 06/6795335). Furniture lovers should stroll Via Giulia, Via dei Coronari, Via del Babuino, Via del Pellegrino, Via dei Banchi Vecchi, and Via dei Banchi Nuovi. The **Alinari** shop (V. Aliberti 16A, near P. di Spagna, tel. 06/6792923) sells reprints from their vast collection of black-and-white photos. And stands in Piazza della Fontanella Borghese sell prints and old books. **Massimo Maria Melis** (V. dell'Orso 57, near the Pantheon, tel. 06/6869188) makes jewelry to order and can include fragments of Roman pottery or coins if you like. Of course nothing beats the streets around the Vatican—**Via della Conciliazione** and **Via della Porta Angelica**— for kitschy Catholic and papal gifts, knickknacks, votive candles, etc.

Consider bringing something to eat back from Italy. Cheeses and salamis will be thrown away (or eaten) at the airport by the customs folks, but there's no problem with most other things, and **Castroni** (V. Cola di Rienzo 196, near P. Risorgimento, tel. 06/6874383) is a great place to find that special something. Prices are on the high side, but then so is the quality. For fancy kitchen gadgets, hit stylish **C.U.C.I.N.A.** (V. del Babuino 118/A, off P. di Spagna, tel. 06/6791279), but you'll find more serious stuff at the store that caters to professionals, **Zucchi** (V. S. Antonio Esquilino 15, near S. M. Maggiore, tel. 06/4465871).

AFTER DARK

When Romans go out on the town, they literally head outside to the streets and piazzas, where so much of Italian social life takes place. As long as the weather is good, you'll find many Romans out on an after-dinner *passeggiata* (stroll), enjoying the night air and perhaps a cup of gelato (*see* Gelaterie and Pastic-cerie, *above*). If you have something a bit more active in mind, read on. **Campo dei Fiori** and the streets around **Piazza Navona** and the **Pantheon** are all good places to hang out, usually full of people and bars, pubs, *birrerie* (beer halls), and clubs to check out. **Trastevere** is home to dozens of nightspots, and nearby **Testaccio** is packed with discos for serious grooving. In summer the majority of discos literally move to the beach, so if you want to shake it to techno, your options will be better there.

Indispensable for anyone with an after-dark agenda is *Roma c'è*, a weekly guide to what's happening in town. It comes out every Thursday and is available from newsstands all week long. There is a short sum-mary in English at the back, but the lists in Italian of clubs, concerts, and events are easy to decipher.

Be prepared to pay for a *tessera* (membership card) at many clubs without public licenses, which are forced to operate as *associazioni culturali* (cultural associations). Membership lasts from a month to a year and costs L5,000–L20,000. Just think of it as a cover charge, which most real clubs charge anyway. If you want a simple beer and don't care about atmosphere (or even sitting down), head for one of Rome's innumerable cafés, where beer *alla spina* (on tap) or a glass of wine costs L2,500– L3,500.

BARS

By now you know that a *bar* in Italy is the place you go to get an espresso. For the other kind of bar, head for a pub, *birreria* (beer hall), or *vineria* (wine bar). Who would have guessed that nearly a hundred Irish pubs pour pints in Rome? A pint of Guinness will run you about L8,000 on average, so maybe it's worth starting earlier to catch happy hour, usually around 8 to 10 PM. Wine bars always have a good by-the-glass selection for about half off.

Antico Caffè della Pace. On an elegant, ivy-clad street behind Piazza Navona, this is perhaps Rome's most civilized caffè-bar. By day you can have tea. It's worth the price just to sit outside in the midst of it all. *V. della Pace 3, tel. 06/6861216.*

Bar del Fico. Decidedly hip and cool, this large bar has tables outside on the piazza even in winter. *P. del Fico 26/28, near P. Navona. tel. 06/6865205.*

Ciampini al Café du Jardin. At this intimate and romantic outdoor café, surrounded by creeper-filled trellises, you can get tasty sandwiches and snacks, cocktails, tea, and even breakfast. Especially pleasant for Sunday brunch and at sunset, it's right down the road from the Villa Borghese park. *V. Trinita dei Monti, tel. 06/6785678. Closed Nov.–Feb.*

Druid's Den. This cheerful bar occasionally hosts live Celtic music but always has plenty of gift-of-the-gab Guinness and Harp on tap. *V. San Martino ai Monti 27, near Metro B Cavour, tel. 06/48904781. Night buses 12N, 20N, 21N.*

Green Rose Pub. This cozy spot on a quiet street just a short walk from Piazza del Popolo is great for happy hour and throwing darts. It opens at 7 PM daily. *Passeggiata di Ripetta 33, tel. 06/3215584.*

Guinness Pub. The most elegant of Rome's Irish pubs, this place has an upscale interior, a laid-back clientele, live music downstairs, a full menu of munchies, and plenty of dark beer (Irish only) on tap. *V. Muzio Clementi 12, near P. Cavour, tel. 06/3218424. Cross Ponte Cavour onto V. V. Colonna, right on V. Muzio Clementi. Closed Aug.*

Jonathan's Angels. The bar is famous for its eclectic decoration, which includes murals and paintings, mirrors, statues, and yes . . . the grooviest toilet in town. *V. della Fossa 16, tel. 06/6893426.*

Miscellanea. During lunch and afternoon tea, this tavern fills with Italians of all ages who happily line up for generous salads and sandwiches. At night it's geared toward a coed crowd—a mix of Italians and expatriate internationals. *V. delle Paste 110/A, no phone. From northeast corner of P. della Rotonda, take V. de' Pastini to V. delle Paste.*

Oasi della Birra. As the name suggests, this is the oasis for beer; where else can you choose from a list of almost 600 different beers from all over the world? *V. Vespucci 42, tel. 06/5757894.*

Piedra del Sol. If you're craving a little south of the border, this somewhat pricey pseudo-Mexican restaurant has a lively bar where strawberry and lime margaritas sidle up to tortilla chips and salsa. *Vicolo Rosini 6, off the Corso, near P. del Parlamento, tel. 06/6873651.*

Trinity College. Enough to make you think you're back in Dublin, the accents here are authentic, as is the beer, of course. Lots of books, with cold and hot food served almost at all hours. *V. del Collegio Romano 6, just off the Corso., tel. 06/6786472.*

Victoria House. Happy hour runs from 6–9 at this English pub with a no-smoking room. *V. Gesu e Maria 18, tel. 06/3201698.*

Vineria. This so-so wine shop on Campo dei Fiori, with outdoor tables in summer, becomes a popular wine bar after hours as the day winds down. From 7 it's jammed with the after-work crowd, from 10 with youthful Romans. About 50 wines are available by the glass. Sandwiches are made upon request. *Campo de Fiori 15, tel. 06/68803268. Closed Sun.*

CLUBS

Serious club-goers should truck out to Testaccio (Bus 27 from Stazione Termini) and its main drag, **Via di Monte Testaccio,** off Via Nicola Zabaglia, where you can take your pick of blues, salsa, jazz, rock, or disco from the dozen or so clubs wrapped around the base of Monte Testaccio. Other clubs are scattered around the city, but especially concentrated in Trastevere. Contact Circolo di Culturale Omosessuale "Mario Mieli" (*see* Gay and Lesbian Resources *in* Basics, *above*) for a constantly changing list of gay-specific clubs and parties. One warning: Testaccio is on the seedy side, and women traveling solo should consider a cab.

DISCOS • Alibi. This venue has music on three levels. Thanks to a roof terrace, it's one of the few discos that doesn't move to the beach come summer. There are frequent gay and theme nights. *V. di Monte Testaccio 40, tel. 06/5743448. Admission L15,000. Free Thurs. and Sun. Closed Mon.–Tues.*

Angelo Azzurro. Take Bus 56 or 60 to this funky underground Trastevere disco awash in black lights and mirrors. It's women only Friday, men only Saturday. *V. C. Merry del Val 13, off V. di Trastevere, tel. 06/5800472. Cover: L10,000–L20,000, includes 1 drink. Closed Mon.*

Bossa Nova. Dance to live Brazilian music until way, way into the night in this simply decorated club. Tuesday is lesson night, well worth the L12,000 and one-drink minimum. *V. Orti di Trastevere 23, tel. 06/5816121. Closed Mon.*

Circolo degli Artisti. This warehouse space and bar blasts everything from ragamuffin and hip-hop to electrowave. It's the sort of place where you don't have to worry about offending anyone, no matter what you look like. In summer expect the occasional live band and performance art piece. The tessera costs L7,000. *V. Lamarmora 28, tel. 06/4464968. Metro A to Vittorio Emanuele; V. Lamarmora is 1 block south. Closed Mon.*

Club Picasso. Live or recorded? Rock, acid, reggae, or funk? The only way to find out what's playing is to call ahead or check the newspapers. Either way, count on frantic dancing in this dank, cavelike club. No hooligans or funky backpackers allowed, but grungy is okay if it looks intentional. Drinks start at L8,000. *V. Monte di Testaccio 63, tel. 06/5742975. Cover: Fri.–Sat. L15,000; Tues., Thurs., Sun. free. Closed Mon.*

LIVE MUSIC • Tickets for big-name shows are usually handled by **Orbis** (P. dell'Esquilino 37, tel. 06/4827403). If a big act is in town, chances are you will see the poster just by walking around.

Alexanderplatz. A must for serious jazz and blues fans, this is Rome's top jazz joint. There's Italian-creole food and a sushi bar. This is worth the trip, despite being off the beaten track, a few blocks from the entrance to the Vatican Museums, or a 15-minute walk from Metro A Ottaviano. Reservations are advisable. In summer the club stages outdoor concerts at the park in Villa Celimontana, just up from the Colosseum. If you can prove you're a tourist, you can forgo the tessera charge; otherwise most shows are free. *V. Ostia 9, tel. 06/39742171. Closed Sun.*

Big Mama. Rome's best small venue for rock and blues, Big Mama hosts more than 200 concerts a year. There is a bar with snack food and even a no-smoking section. *Vicolo San Francesco a Ripa 18, off V. Trastevere, tel. 06/5812551. L10,000 cover, plus ticket. Closed Mon.–Tues.*

Caffè Caruso. Rhumba, mambo, and salsa here with a mellow crowd of Italians and Latinos. The music is almost always live and always danceable. Fruity cocktails go for L12,000, beer L8,000. The one bummer is the L10,000 tessera, valid for a month. *V. di Monte Testaccio 36, tel. 06/5745019. Closed Mon.*

St. Louis Music City. Rome's favorite jazz spot attracts a young, well-dressed crowd with its *Casablanca*-esque setting—not to mention its Latin, Brazilian, swing, and blues shows. Bands start at 10 PM, but by 9:30 things are packed. The 8–9:30 happy hour is not only a bargain but a good way to ensure getting a seat. *V. del Cardello 13, south of V. Cavour, tel. 06/4745076. Metro B to Colosseo; walk northwest on V. del Colosseo to V. del Cardello. Closed Sun.*

CLASSICAL MUSIC

It's a good bet that on any given night there's a free (or almost free) concert somewhere in Rome, probably in a church. **Sant'Ignazio,** off Via del Corso, is a frequent venue. Look for posters around town advertising events, or stop by an EPT tourist office (*see* Visitor Information *in* Basics, *above*) for current listings.

Rome's main classical music associations are the **Accademia Nazionale di Santa Cecilia** (V. della Conciliazione 4, tel. 06/3611064), **Accademia Filarmonica Romana** (usually at Teatro Olimpico, V. Gentile da Fabriano 17, tel. 06/3234890), and the **Istituzione Universitaria dei Concerti** (Lungotevere Flaminio 50, tel. 06/3610051). Baroque music enthusiasts should check out the **Oratorio del Gonfalone** series (V. del Gonfalone 32/A, tel. 06/47709669). Both **Il Tempietto** (tel. 06/4814800) and **Associazione Musicale Romana** (tel. 06/6868441) produce concerts throughout the year. Ticket prices run L16,000–L45,000, depending on the locale and event.

MOVIE THEATERS

Check movie listings in newspapers or *Roma c'è,* and you'll see most major releases from English-speaking countries. The bad news is they are dubbed into Italian. Yes, Robert De Niro and Jack Nicholson have the same voice in Italy. Trastevere's **Pasquino** (P. Sant'Egidio 10, tel. 06/5803622) and the **Quirinetta** (V. Minghetti 4 , tel. 06/6790012) are the only theaters that show movies every day in their original version. You can also try the **Alcazar** (V. Mario del Val 14, off V. Trastevere, tel. 06/5880099), the **Cinema Majestic** (V. S. S. Apostoli 20, off V. del Corso, tel. 06/6794908), and the **Nuovo Sacher** (Largo Ascianghi 1, off V. Trastevere, tel. 06/5818116) on Mondays. Expect to pay about L10,000–L12,000.

OPERA AND BALLET

Rome's opera and ballet season runs November–May in the **Teatro dell'Opera** (P. B. Gigli 1, tel. 06/481601 or 06/48160255). Tickets run L20,000–L260,000. The Summer Opera Series, whch has been staged in recent years at the Stadio Olimpico (soccer stadium), is a treat with seats going for as little as L15,000.

THEATER

Unless you speak Italian, your theater choices here are severely limited. The Teatro Agora sometimes mounts English productions, but don't hold your breath waiting. Rome's theater season runs October–May; scan *Roma c'è* for the latest. Tickets generally run L15,000–L90,000.

NEAR ROME

If several days in the city have you screaming for pastoral relief, head for the hills, retreat to the mountains, or escape to the sea, as Romans have done for thousands of years. Once Rome had conquered its neighbors, the Roman countryside remained just that, and much of it swampland at that. In later centuries, Rome's emperors and nobles, and later popes and princes, chose Lazio's prime locales as sites for their villas and pleasure palaces, many of which are worth a daylong excursion from the chaotic capital. If you are looking for sun and sand, the coast near Rome ranks somewhere in the middle as Italian beaches go, between the finest and the filthiest. Be prepared to pay for the privilege of lying down, or at least for a folding chair and a shower. The nearest beaches to get to are at Ostia and Fregene, easily reachable by Metro or train. For smaller crowds and cleaner water, hop on a train to Santa Marinella (45 min) or take a COTRAL bus down to Tor Vaianica (1 hr).

FRASCATI

Perched on a steep hillside 40 km (25 mi) to the southeast of Rome, Frascati is like a balcony overlooking the city and its rural suburbs. If you need an excuse for a day trip, consider the sweeping views of Rome and the Alban Hills—and the Tyrrhenian Sea on exceptionally clear days. Frascati lacks the charm of a Tuscan or Umbrian hill town, and there are few historic sights; the reasons for coming here have always been to get out of the city, especially during sweltering summer months; drink the local wine; and eat yourself immobile. Take your pick from the cafés and trattorias fronting the central Piazzale Marconi, or do as the locals do—buy fruit from the market gallery at **Piazza del Mercato** (open Mon.–Sat. 8–1), then get a huge slice of *porchetta* (roast suckling pig) from one of the stalls, a hunk of *casareccio* bread, and a few *ciambelline frascatane* (ring-shape cookies made with wine), and take your picnic to any one of the numerous local cantine (homey wine bars). With wooden tables and folding chairs squeezed in between old vats, low ceilings, and dark corners, many cantine have the feel of a cluttered basement, with the fortunate addition of tasty and extremely cheap vino.

Frascati's 16th-century **Villa Aldobrandini,** designed by Giacomo della Porta and adorned with fountains by Bernini, Maderno, and Fontana, was once a weekend getaway house for Roman nobility but has now fallen into serious disrepair. You can ask for a free pass to wander around its rather overgrown gardens from the tourist office (*see* Basics, *below*).

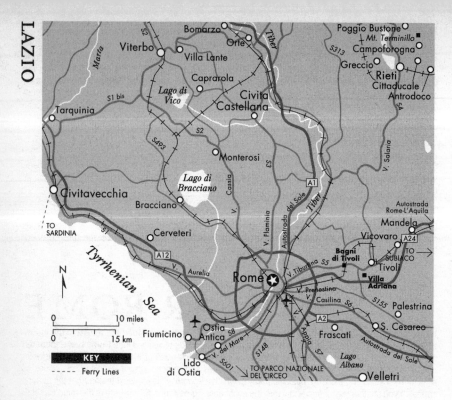

BASICS

The **AAST** tourist office (P. Marconi 1, tel. 06/9420331; open Mon.–Sat. 9–2 and 4–7:15, in winter 3:30–6:45) has detailed maps delineating wine-tasting spots in Frascati and nearby towns.

COMING AND GOING

Trains from Rome's Stazione Termini (16 per day, 26 min, L3,600) drop you off at Frascati's tiny depot and pick you up for the trip back until 10 PM. To reach the center, climb the hillside stairs to Piazza Marconi; Piazza San Pietro is two blocks to the left, and Villa Aldobrandini is straight ahead along Via Catone. **COTRAL buses** leave from Rome's Metro A Anagnina station (2 per hr, 20 min, L1,500) and drop you in Piazza Marconi; the last bus back to Rome leaves Frascati at 9:50 PM. It's a good idea to buy a return ticket or a BIRG, as tickets are sometimes hard to find in Frascati. Try **Toto Ricevitoria** near the bus stop at Piazza Marconi 16 (open Tues.–Sat. 8–1 and 4–8, Sun.–Mon. 8–1).

WHERE TO SLEEP AND EAT

Hotels in Frascati are no less expensive than in Rome, but if you overindulge to the degree that you can't make it back, stumble over to the **Albergo Panorama** (P. Carlo Casini 3, tel. 06/9421800). A double room with bath runs L100,000—now when did that last train leave?

Halfway up the stairs from the train station is the loud and chaotic **Cantina Comandini** (V. Emanuele Filiberto 1, tel. 06/9420307; open Mon.–Sat. 4–8), where long picnic tables nearly buckle under crowds of tourists. To toast Bacchus a bit more off the beaten track, pull up a chair and order a liter (L4,000 to stay, L2,500 to go) at **Cantina da Santino** (V. P. Campana 17, up the stairs from P. le Marconi, no phone).

There are tons of trattorias and pizzerias near Piazza San Pietro and Piazza Monte Grappa; try **Trattoria Piave** (V. Piave 6, tel. 06/9425596; closed Wed.) for its gorgeous antipasti and *melanzane alla Piave* (eggplant covered in anchovies, mozzarella, and tomato and roasted in the wood-burning oven). Indulge in homemade pasta at **Trattoria da Giselda** (P. Monte Grappa 7, tel. 06/9424161; no lunch; closed Wed.), where a set meal will run you L23,000, wine included (L30,000 on Sunday).

TIVOLI

In ancient times, just about anybody who was anybody had a villa in Tivoli, including Cassius, Trajan, Hadrian, Horace, and Catullus. Tivoli fell into obscurity in the medieval era until the Renaissance, when popes and cardinals came back to the town and built villas ostentatious enough to rival those of their extravagant predecessors. Nowadays, Tivoli is small but vibrant, with winding streets and views over the surrounding countryside. And its main attractions—the fountains and gardens of Villa d'Este and the dramatic waterfall at Villa Gregoriana—are easily accessible. Allow at least a half day to see the waterworks, and make it a full day if you want to see **Villa Adriana** as well.

BASICS

Tivoli's **AAST** tourist office (Largo Garibaldi, tel. 0774/311249 or 0774/334522; open daily 9–6, Sun. 9–1, shorter hrs off-season) has free maps and listings of the town's food and lodging options. However, Tivoli can and probably should be handled as a day trip from Rome.

COMING AND GOING

Buses are by far your best bet. From Rome's Metro B Rebibbia station, COTRAL buses run every 20 minutes (5 AM–midnight) to Tivoli (45 min, L6,000 round-trip, BIRG L8,500). You'll be dropped off at Piazza Garibaldi, a.k.a. Largo Garibaldi, across from the tourist office. **Trains** run from Stazione Tiburtina every hour or so, arriving at Tivoli's station (V. di Santa Agnese, tel. 0774/342495), on the eastern edge of town, about a 20-minute walk from the center.

If you like the Agro Pontino area, thank Benito Mussolini. In 1928 Il Duce carried out Julius Caesar's much-delayed plans for draining what was mostly a marshy swampland.

WHERE TO EAT

When hunger strikes, head to the pizza *al taglio* joint across from the bus stop (V. Manelli 27) for tasty pizza by the slice and beer. The usual pastas are served up at **Tre Fontane** (P. Garibaldi 12, tel. 0774/312207; cash only; closed Wed.), a sit-down place in the adjoining piazza.

WORTH SEEING

VILLA D'ESTE • In the late 16th century, Cardinal Ippolito d'Este, governor of Tivoli and one of the richest and most extravagant men of his time, built this estate. Inspired by the recent excavation of Villa Adriana and a devotee of the Renaissance celebration of human ingenuity over nature, Este paid architect Pirro an astronomical sum to create a mythical garden with water as its artistic centerpiece. To this day, several hundred fountains cascade, shoot skyward, imitate bird songs, simulate rain. Don't even touch the water—it is dangerously polluted. The fountains are occasionally shut off for maintenance, so call first. *Tel. 0774/312070. From Largo Garibaldi, take V. Boselli to P. Trento; entrance is right of the church. Admission L8,000. Open Tues.–Sun. 9–6:30 (until 4 in winter).*

VILLA GREGORIANA • This villa is really a large overgrown park on a steep hillside dotted with trails and shady picnic spots among ruined Roman pavilions and nymphaeums. The lush greenery and cool mists from the nearby Aniene River compensate for the sweaty, steep hike into the river gorge. The park itself is named for Pope Gregory XVI, who in 1831 saved Tivoli from chronic river damage by diverting the Aniene through a tunnel, weakening its flow. An unexpected (but not unappreciated) side effect was the creation of the **Grande Cascata** (Grand Cascade), which shoots a huge jet of water into the valley below. After entering the park, follow the footpath to the right to a small set of steps; at the bottom lies a terrace with views of the cascade and another terrace from which you can look into the tunnel itself. In rainy weather the park closes for safety reasons. *From bus stop on Largo Garibaldi, follow V. Pacifici (it changes names 6 times), veer left on V. Roma, and turn at Largo Sant'Angelo. Admission L2,500. Open daily 9–6 (until 3 in winter).*

Across the valley from Villa Gregoriana stand the 10 remaining columns of the round **Temple of Vesta** and the ruins of the rectangular **Temple of the Sibyl,** probably built earlier. The Sibyl was a direct channel to the gods, who could predict the future and reveal divine intentions. Like the Pantheon in Rome, these temples were preserved only because they were transformed into churches in the Middle Ages.

VILLA ADRIANA • If you loved the forum, don't go back to Rome without stopping at Villa Adriana, the astonishingly grand 2nd-century AD villa commissioned by the emperor Hadrian (he gets credit for the Pantheon, too). It took the best architects in Rome 13 years to build the temples, baths, living quarters, and gardens that made Hadrian's Villa the largest ever constructed by the Romans. Hadrian even had tunnels burrowed underground so that horse carts could haul supplies from end to end without being seen. Many of the structures are still visible, and signs label each section of the ruins, which are filled with scraps of statuary, sculpture, and mosaics. Don't miss the Canopus pool, a long reflecting pond modeled after a site in Egypt. Stop by the excellent **Museo Didattico** (open when there's enough personnel to staff it; call ahead) at the villa's entrance: its displays put the complex into perspective, as does the miniature model at the nearby snack bar. Before trekking into the unknown, consider bringing a sack lunch for a picnic and a blanket for a nap amid the ruins. In any case, fill up your water bottle at the spring by the entrance. Buses from Tivoli for Rebibbia, stopping at Villa Adriana, depart twice hourly between 6 AM and midnight from Piazza Garibaldi (15 min, L1200). *Tel. 0774/530203. Admission L8,000. Open daily 9–6:30 (until 4 in winter).*

SUBIACO

From high above a lush valley, Subiaco's serene vistas have provoked meditation and escapism since the town's inception in the 1st century AD. Probably founded by Nero, who built an opulent villa here, Subiaco is better known for its second founding father: at the end of the 5th century, a rich young man from Umbria's Norcia named Benedetto retreated into a cave in Subiaco's rocky hillside, rejecting the wicked ways of the world. He spent three years in total seclusion, became famous thoughout the region, and eventually amassed a group of disciples. In 529 St. Benedict went to Cassino and founded a new monastery that became the model in Europe for his Benedictine order, though some of his followers remained in Subiaco and eventually built 12 monasteries in the area. Today only two remain—excellent examples of medieval craftsmanship that can't help but evoke divine inspiration.

The largest of the two monasteries is **Santa Scolastica**, named after St. Benedict's twin sister, who continued to disseminate her brother's teachings even after the jealous local clergy ran him out of town. Don't miss the stunning cloisters, with delicately carved spiraling pillars and intricate gold mosaics. The library contains rare volumes as well as the first two books printed in Italy (photocopies on display). *Monastery tel. 0774/85525, library tel. 0774/85424. Admission free. Monastery open daily 9–noon and 4–6:30; library open weekdays 8:30–6:50, Sat. 8:30–1:30.*

A footpath climbs uphill from Santa Scolastica to the interesting monastery of **San Benedetto** (a.k.a. Sacro Speco), built over the grotto where St. Benedict lived in seclusion. Here he wrote his *Regola* (Rule), which formed the basis of the Benedictine order, a brotherhood of monks who forswore all material possessions. Wait around long enough—the stockpile of monastic home brew in the souvenir shop eases the pain—and one of the monks will fetch you for a guided tour; even if you don't understand Italian, it's an enjoyable way to get a feel for the monastery. Inside, the upper church is covered with brilliant frescoes done by 14th-century Sienese artists. In front of the main altar, a stairway leads to a chapel hewn from the rock, while a second stairway leads to the cave where St. Benedict once lived in blissful solitude. *Tel. 0774/85039. Admission free. Open daily 9–12:30 and 3–6.*

BASICS

One kilometer (½ mi) from Piazza della Resistenza along Via Cavour, southeast past Piazza San Andrea, is the **tourist office** (V. Cadorna 59, tel. 0774/822013), open Tuesday to Saturday 8–2 and 3:30–6:30, Sunday 9–noon.

COMING AND GOING

COTRAL buses (2 hrs, L6,000, BIRG L13,000) leave from Rome's Metro B Tiburtina station, stopping at Subiaco's Piazza della Resistenza; they return to Rome hourly up to 8:30 PM from the piazza. It is also possible to take the bus from Subiaco's Piazza della Resistenza to Tivoli, a 50-minute trip.

RIETI AND MONTE TERMINILLO

Rieti proudly claims the title of *ombelico italiano* (Italy's belly button) as the country's geographical center. Whether or not the calculations are truly valid, Rieti's attractions are many: ski resorts, castles, lakes, and a number of Franciscan sanctuaries accessible by bus. Rieti itself is a pleasant, well-maintained town, bordered by a daunting medieval wall and centered on the lively Piazza Vittorio Emanuele. Around the corner is Piazza Cesare Battisti and **Palazzo Vincentini,** which offers a peaceful though unspectacular garden and a view of the entire valley. The Romanesque **Cathedral of Santa Maria Assunta** is just next door.

Monte Terminillo rises 7,268 ft above the plain of Lazio, making it a popular day trip with skiers and hikers who clog the highways from Rome. A ski lift (L5,500 for a ride up in summertime) reaches Terminilletto, from which you can hike up to the windy summit, connected to the surrounding peaks by Club Alpinisti Italiani hiking trails. The towns of **Vallomina** and **Flamignano** also operate ski runs (though they're farther away) and the lakes of **Turano** and **Salto** all provide lush and scenic landscapes.

BASICS

The **AAST** tourist office (P. Vittorio Emanuele 17, tel. 0746/203220; open weekdays 9:30–1 and 4–6, Sat. 9:30–1) has great info on trails, outdoor activities, and accommodations.

COMING AND GOING

From Rome's Metro B Tiburtina station, **COTRAL** buses travel to Rieti every half hour or so (1 hr 45 min, L6,400, BIRG L13,000). COTRAL buses also connect Rieti to Monte Terminillo (10 daily, L3,500 round-trip).

WHERE TO SLEEP

The **Albergo Massimo d'Azeglio** (V. Ludovico Canali 4, tel. 0746/274250), half renovated, half grimy and trashed, has doubles with bathrooms for L70,000. Near Monte Terminillo lie three more-appealing options: the hostel **Ostello della Neve** (Località Anello di Campo Forogno, tel. 0746/261169), with a bed and breakfast for L18,000; the campground **Ski Caravan Club** (tel. 0746/261323), with charges of L8,000 per person plus L10,000 for a tent space; and the mountaintop **Rifugio Angelo Sebastiani** (tel. 0746/261184; beds L25,000), which is reachable by bus as far as Campo Forogno, then a 3-km (2-mi) hike up the hill.

CERVETERI

Narrow streets and alleyways atop a small hill retain some of Cerveteri's medieval character, but most people come for the nearby Etruscan necropolis. When you arrive, grab a sandwich and drink to take with you at the shop with "Panini—Bibite" on its awning in the yellow building opposite the bus stop.

From Piazza Aldo Moro it's a 20-minute walk along a narrow road shaded by umbrella pines to the **Banditaccia Necropolis.** This Etruscan city, originally called Caere, wielded formidable power over the Mediterranean and was a center for artistic and cultural activity in the 7th and 6th centuries BC. Having battled successfully against the Greeks, the Etruscans finally succumbed to the superior might of the Romans in the 4th century BC. The Etruscans' funerary architecture and elegant sculpture are some of the only remaining clues to their sophisticated culture. Most of the important artifacts were moved long ago to museums in Rome, but the circular hutlike tombs of various styles and sizes are nonetheless fascinating. Bring a flashlight to explore the chambers and carved stone beds, and don't miss the **Tomba dei Rilievi,** elaborately decorated in stucco reliefs. *Tel. 06/9940001. From P. Aldo Moro, walk down toward gardens and follow yellow signs. Admission L12,000. Open Tues.–Sun. 9–hr before sunset.*

Cerveteri's impressive **Museo Nazionale Cerite** provides explanations of the necropolis using diagrams and reconstructions and displays Etruscan vases, cups, terra-cotta statues, bronze jewelry, and even some ragged clothing. *Castello Orsini, P. Santa Maria, tel. 06/9941354. Admission free. Open Tues.–Sun. 9–7.*

BASICS

The closest EPT is in nearby Ladispoli, but all the info you need can be found at the private Caere Viaggi **tourist office** (P. Aldo Moro 17, tel. 06/9942860; open Mon.–Fri. 9–1 and 4:30–7:30, Sat. 9–1).

COMING AND GOING

COTRAL buses from Rome's Metro A Lepanto station (hourly, 45 min, L4,900, BIRG L8,500) will drop you in **Piazza Aldo Moro,** right by a shady park just outside the pedestrians-only centro storico.

WHERE TO EAT

If you don't want to picnic, stop at **Tuchulcha** (on right on way to necropolis, no telephone; no credit cards; closed Mon.). This trattoria serves wholesome country food on a terrace overlooking the town in fair weather or in a cozy paneled dining room with a fireplace in winter. *Fettucini ai boscoiolo* (mushrooms, sausage, fresh peas, garlic), plus a second course and some house wine averages L30,000 per person.

OSTIA ANTICA

Ostia Antica, like Pompeii, is an ancient city preserved in its entirety—only without the volcano and hordes of visitors. Even in summer it's possible to have the place to yourself, and with ivy-covered and pine-shaded theaters, apartment buildings, baths, temples, and even ancient pubs to explore, there's plenty to see. Plus, Ostia Antica's numerous rail and Metro connections make the site Rome's most convenient day trip—think picnic.

Ostia derives its name from *ostium* (Latin for river mouth), an appellation that reflects the city's position at the mouth of the Tiber River. Founded in about 335 BC, Ostia served as a crucial port connecting Rome to the sea. At its height, it was a bustling maritime town with a population of 80,000, boasting a potent middle class of traders, businessmen, and bureaucrats, united in efficient corporations. Ostia followed Rome into decline in the 4th and 5th centuries AD and was completely abandoned by the 9th. In 1557 the Tiber changed course, leaving the town high and dry, a full 3 km (2 mi) from the receding sea. Today the ruins still contain a number of murals, mosaics, and sculptures depicting daily life; the slightest bit of imagination can make it come alive again.

COMING AND GOING

From Rome, take Metro B to Magliana and transfer to a Lido train headed for the Ostia Antica stop. If you're returning to Rome in the same day, a BIRG (L8,500; *see* Getting Around *in* Basics, *above*) costs the same as a round-trip ticket but is valid for unlimited Metro-bus travel. To reach the site from the station, walk across the pedestrian overpass, continue straight, and follow the signs to the left.

WHERE TO EAT

There's no place to get food or drink within the site, so bring provisions, especially water. Near the site, an **alimentari** (grocery; P. Umberto 6; open 8–1 and 5–8) sells snacks and picnic supplies; walk toward the castle on Via Romagnoli and follow the road around the bend. There's also an overpriced snack bar connected to the restaurant called **Allo Sbarco di Enea** (V. Romagnoli 675, tel. 06/5650253; closed Mon.), between the train station and the ruins.

THE SITE

Decumano Massimo is the main street leading through the ancient city. As you enter the site, proceed down the Decumano; about 1,400 ft down on the right, the floor of the **Terme di Nettuno,** one of the largest of 18 bath complexes that served Ostia's ancient population, is ornately decorated with mosaics depicting the robust Neptune frolicking with all manner of sea creatures. Residents came to the **palaestra** for a workout, and for entertainment the **theater** once held 2,700 spectators. The **Piazzale delle Corporazioni** was once a porticoed gallery housing the offices of traders and merchants. The fascinating mosaic series encircling the piazzale depicts maritime scenes, Ostian daily life, and declarations of the titles of each office. Within the piazzale is a **temple,** probably dedicated to Ceres, goddess of grain and abundance, to whom Ostia owed a great deal of thanks for trade surpluses. On Via dei Molini you'll find an ancient **bakery,** with stone mills and ovens. The nearby **Casa di Diana** is a good example of ancient low-cost housing projects, with five-story apartments and communal toilets. On Via di Diana you'll see the **thermopolium,** a local bar where clients once ate, drank, and got merry. Note the huge wine vats and the menu painted on the wall.

The **Museum of Ostia** (V. dei Molini, admission included with ticket to site, same hrs) contains Ostia's sculptural treasures, including marble reliefs remarkable because they document scenes of town life rather than depicting gods or emperors. You'll also find beautifully preserved sarcophagi and an exquisite altar to the 12 gods of Olympus. Adjacent to the museum is a **bookstore,** with guidebooks, slides, and postcards.

The **Forum,** which served as the city's civic center, is dominated by the imposing **Capitolium,** dedicated to the triad of Juno, Jupiter, and Minerva. From the top of the Capitolium's stairs there is a great view of the city and the Forum's other structures, including the **Curia** (headquarters for the town council), the **Basilica** (seat of the tribunal), the **Forum Baths,** and **the Temple to Rome and Augustus** (opposite the Capitolium).

The last street off the Decumano leads to the opulent houses of Ostia's bourgeoisie. Turn right on the Via degli Aurighi and left on Vico delle Volte Dipinte, and you'll see the entrance to the **Casa delle Muse** (under restoration), once a single-family residence. Inside, the extensive wall paintings represent a style similar to that found at Pompeii. The nearby **Domus dei Dioscuri** showcases two striking mosaics dedicated to the divine twins Castor and Pollux, well loved in Ostia as the gods of commerce. Climb to the second-story terraces to catch a bird's-eye view. **Porta Marina** marks the western edge of the town. Just beyond on the left are more baths and the ruins of the oldest known **synagogue** in Europe, dating from the 1st century AD. *Tel. 06/5650022. Admission L10,000. Take Metro Line B to Ostia Antica. Open Tues.–Sun. 9–6 (until 5 in winter).*

CIVITAVECCHIA

Founded by Emperor Trajan to enhance Rome's Mediterranean trade base, Civitavecchia has a couple of Roman relics spread among the modern housing, oil-storage tanks, and port paraphernalia cluttering its shore. But let's be honest: the only reason to visit this bland industrial tragedy is to catch a **ferry to Sardinia.** If, as can happen, you end up trapped here waiting for your boat, rest assured that food is cheap and beds are plentiful. And if you're really bored, mosey through the free, peach-hued **Museo Nazionale** (Largo Plebiscito, tel. 0766/23604; open Tues.–Sun. 9–2), which has a skimpy collection of Etruscan and Roman trinkets.

Pilgrims flock to Sant'Agostino Church outside Civitavecchia to see the miraculous bloody tears said to have appeared on an image of the Virgin Mary. The statue was brought from a town in Bosnia, reportedly visited by an apparition of the Virgin herself.

BASICS

For the usual maps and accommodation listings, stop by **AAST** (V. Garibaldi 40–42, tel. 0766/25348; open weekdays 9–2 and 4–7, Sat. 9–1), on the waterfront between the station and the port.

COMING AND GOING

Trains leave frequently from Rome's Stazione Termini (1 hr, L6,000) for Civitavecchia's waterfront train station (V. della Repubblica), where you can also catch trains to Pisa, Turin, and Naples. From the station, it's a short walk downhill to the port. **COTRAL** buses (tel. 0766/35961) leave every 30 minutes from Viale Giulio Cesare, a few steps from Rome's Metro A Lepanto station (90 min, L6,000). In Civitavecchia, buses stop at both Via Cadorna, one block east of the FS ports, and at Piazza Vittorio Emanuele II, two blocks east of the dock for Tirrenia Lines (*see below*).

BY BOAT • Civitavecchia is Lazio's main port for ferries to Sardinia. **Tirrenia Lines** (tel. 0766/21703) serves both Olbia and Cagliari with sparkling white ferries that leave from two adjacent docks on Calata Cesare Laurenti, reached directly from Viale Garibaldi. Fares to Cagliari run L63,300–L88,000 (cabin) and L48,300–L70,300 (reclining chair), depending on the season. For Olbia, year-round fares are L51,600 (cabin), L35,600 (reclining chair). **FS** (tel. 0766/23273) has service to Golfo Aranci only, with fares equivalent to Tirrenia's. Ferries leave in the morning and late evening from the dock at the end of Via Cadorna, where there's a small terminal with grimy bathrooms and a limited snack bar. Tickets can be purchased on board, but be sure to reserve in advance in summer.

WHERE TO SLEEP AND EAT

If you somehow miss the last ferry, **Albergo Roma Nord** (V. Montegrappa 27, tel. 0766/22770), the cheapest option around and a few blocks east of the FS dock, has doubles from L35,000. The centrally located **La Palamite** (V. Aurelia Sud 6, tel. 0766/23657) has doubles at L50,000. For cheap, fresh sandwiches head to **Casa del Gelato** (Largo Plebiscito at V. Garibaldi). For more substantial eats, try **Santa Lucia** (V. Garibaldi 34, tel. 0766/25235; closed Wed.), with wood-oven pizzas (evenings only) from L10,000. At **STANDA** (V. Garibaldi, between the station and port), you can stock up on supplies.

VITERBO

The main attractions in Viterbo, 80 km (50 mi) northwest of Rome, are its 12th-century walls and towers and its perfectly preserved **Quartiere San Pellegrino**, a medieval labyrinth of enchanting architec-

MONSTER MASH

In the mid-16th century, a member of a junior branch of the Orsini family had constructed one of the strangest places in all Europe. The result is now called Il Parco dei Mostri (Park of the Monsters; tel. 0761/924029; admission L13,000; open daily 8:30–sunset), with stone monsters, figures from classical myth, topsy-turvey houses and architecture, and symbolic figures carved from rock outcroppings that together create the effect of an early—very early—theme park. From the ticket office it's a 1-km (½-mi) hike to the gardens. Postcards and replicas of the weird statues from the adjacent souvenir shop make excellent gifts. From Viterbo's depot on Viale Trento, catch a COTRAL bus to Bomarzo (about 18 km/11 mi, L4,000).

ture. Coming from Porta del Carmine, cross Ponte Paradiso and step into this eerie 13th-century time capsule, complete with dark, curving roads and a jumble of houses that tilt gracefully with age. Many more people than cars pass through the narrow streets of this part of town, which makes it a fine place to plant yourself in a café or piazza with a bottle of cheap wine and just relax. Viterbo's medieval churches, nearly all built of dark grey tufa, look squat and powerful, a defense against the earthquakes that have shaken the region periodically. At one time the papacy took refuge here, and the papal palace built then still exists. In the medieval fortress of **Rocca Albornoz,** an archaeological museum displays a not-to-be-missed collection of Etruscan finds from the excavations at Acquarossa and San Giuliano.

BASICS

The **EPT** office (P. San Carluccio, near Palazzo dei Papi, tel. 0761/304795; open Mon.–Sat. 9–1 and 1:30–3:30) has maps and info on accommodations throughout the area.

COMING AND GOING

Trains leave the Roma Ostiense station (1 hr 50 min, L8,000, Metro B to Piramide) every 20 minutes or so 5:30 AM–11 PM, returning on the same schedule. Viterbo has two train stations, each equally convenient to the center: **Stazione Porta Romana** is in the southwest corner of the city, about three blocks south of the centro storico's Porta Romana entrance; **Stazione Porta Fiorentina** is north of the centro storico on Viale Trento, a short walk from the COTRAL bus depot. Both stations have baggage storage for L5,000 per piece; for local train info call 0761/340955. **COTRAL** (tel. 0761/226592) buses (L6,400, BIRG L13,000) leave Rome's Saxa Rubra station (take Metro A to Flaminio and switch to a Roma Nord train) every 40 minutes or so (fewer on Sunday) from 6:30 AM until 7:40 PM, dropping you at the bus depot by the centro storico's northern wall and returning on the same schedule until 7:40.

WHERE TO SLEEP

The budget options in Viterbo are two: within a block or so of the COTRAL bus station and Stazione Porta Fiorentina is the depressing but fairly cheap **Pensione Trieste** (V. Nazario Sauro 32, tel. 0761/341882; doubles without bathroom L70,000), which sometimes has additional rooms to let a few blocks west on Viale Trieste. **Albergo Roma** (V. della Cava 26, tel. 0761/227274 or 0761/226474; 3 blocks southwest of Stazione Porta Fiorentina) has clean doubles without bath for L65,000, with bath L98,000.

TUSCANIA

Viterbo makes an excellent jumping-off point for a visit to the medieval town of **Tuscania.** When the town was flattened by an earthquake in 1971 the city fathers decided to reconstruct it as it was. The result is a 1000-year-old town in mint condition. The so-called pagan church of **San Pietro** has a frightening carved facade recycling Etruscan sculpture with mythological creatures from an unknown mythology.

The little church of **Santa Maria Maggiore** has 12th-century frescoes, including a *Last Judgment* to make your hair stand on end.

COMING AND GOING

There are frequent departures for Tuscania from the **COTRAL** station in Viterbo. Check the bus schedules when you get off at the local station near the main gate of the city.

WHERE TO EAT

Tuscania has several excellent trattorias. At **Sette Canale** you can get great country cooking with local wine for L30,000–35,000 per person for lunch.

PARCO NAZIONALE DEL CIRCEO

Back in junior high you read about the sorceress Circe, who turned men into pigs in Homer's *Odyssey*. Her namesake still retains some of the magic that seduced Odysseus and his crew. South of Rome along the Tyrrhenian Sea, 8,400 hectares of mountain, lake, and virgin forest have been set aside to form **Parco Nazionale del Circeo.** It's home to spoonbills, avocets, buffalo, and boar and offers opportunities for exploration, from day trails marked with educational signs to rough mountain hiking for access to the park's caves and lakes. The main entrance and **visitor information booth** with maps (L6,000) is in **Sabaudia** (8 km/5 mi north of San Felice Circeo, on Strada Migliaria 56). It's 15 additional minutes along the COTRAL bus route; ask the driver to stop. Once inside the park, you're on your own, so get a map before you start.

In the hilltop centro storico of **San Felice Circeo,** flowers spill out from villa windows overlooking lush, wild Monte Circeo and the sea. One kilometer (½ mi) downhill from the centro storico, the newer sector of San Felice Circeo has sugar-sand beaches that afford plenty of space for a lazy dip.

COMING AND GOING

COTRAL buses (1 hr, L8,500, BIRG L15,000) leave Rome's Metro B Fermi station hourly from 6:30 AM to 8 PM. They'll drop you in the new section of San Felice Circeo, near the beach on Via Domenichelli. (The last bus back to Rome is at 8 PM.) Every 15–20 minutes, orange buses (L700) connect the old and new parts of town; the main stops are at Piazza Vittorio Veneto, the centro storico's hub, and the COTRAL stop on Via Domenichelli. It's inconvenient to keep taking the bus up and down—try to cover the tourist office and the centro storico, then hit the beach.

WHERE TO SLEEP AND EAT

If you're planning a less rustic stop, Circeo is best as a day trip from Rome—resorty hotels are uniformly expensive. Room rentals, handled by the **Pro Loco** office (P. Vittorio Veneto, tel. 0773/547770; open Mon.–Sat. 9–noon) are cheap (L50,000) but unpredictable. If you're planning on taking the time to explore the park, there are a number of **campgrounds** in Sabaudia, where the park begins: try **Sabaudia** (V. S. Andrea 17, tel. 0773/593057; open Apr.–Oct.) or **S. Andrea** (V. S. Andrea 36B, tel. 0773/593105; open May–Sept.). San Felice Circeo has little to offer in the way of seafood; the real treat here is fresh mozzarella *di bufala,* made on local farms. Try it in *insalata caprese,* with tomatoes, basil, and olive oil. In the centro storico, **Grottino** (P. Vittorio Veneto, no phone) offers pastas and salads on a thatched-roof terrace with views of the hills. Beach-goers and hikers may want to do away with the formalities: **Via Tittori,** one street west of Via Domenichelli, has markets and snack bars where you can pack a picnic or grab a bite.

OUTDOOR ACTIVITIES

Between the mountain, the forest, the beach, and the lakes, you'd be hard-pressed to find something to do that's *not* outside. The most obvious summertime option is to head for San Felice Circeo's Viale Europa, a string of Italian-style **beach clubs,** where you pay a nominal fee (L2,000 or so) for use of the facilities, more for chairs or cabanas. This isn't as grim as it sounds—the clubs keep the powdery white beach clean, and the umbrellas and white buildings seem part and parcel of the thoroughly Mediterranean landscape of red-roof villas and green mountains sloping to the sea. For an adrenaline rush, locals head to the **Punta Rossa** on Monte Circeo for **cliff diving** into the deep water. Approaching the sea from the north in the park, you'll come upon a series of **caves,** including one reported to be that of Circe herself—explore at your own risk. Landlubbers and ornithologists can do some serious **bird-watching** at the park's lakes (get guides at the visitor center).

ABRUZZO AND MOLISE

BY SARAH ATTIA

UPDATED BY JON ELDAN

I n the overlooked center of Italy, mysterious Abruzzo and Molise conjure up an Italy of the past. Here, widows really wear all black (even when it's 100°F outside), the *mal'occhio* (evil eye) is still cast, and 2,000-year-old traditions are upheld fanatically. These regions also provide a variety of outdoor activities, from hiking in the **Gran Sasso** (Italy's highest mountain range) or exploring the wilderness of **Parco Nazionale d'Abruzzo** to soaking up the sun on the Adriatic coast. Buses will whiz you between the remote hill towns, craggy mountaintops, and wooded ravines that characterize the region's interior, and although prices of lodging and restaurants don't reflect the lack of tourism, camping is an option near most towns. On the downside, Abruzzo and Molise are among Italy's most economically depressed regions, as evidenced by drab cement-block buildings and downtrodden resorts.

The rich agricultural geography of this region is seen in the cuisine, which relies heavily on raw, fresh ingredients. The most typical dish is *maccheroni alla chitarra,* an egg pasta cut into strips by a chitarra, an instrument that looks like a guitar, and topped with various regional sauces such as pork, goose, or lamb *ragù.* Fish, fresh from the Adriatic, is also delectable. For dessert try *feratelle,* a type of waffle cookie.

ABRUZZO

Even with 113 km (70 mi) of coastline, the real jewels of Abruzzo are found deep inside the rugged interior. Few foreigners bother with the region's isolated mountain villages, and even fewer endeavor to see the still-thriving wildlife in the Parco Nazionale d'Abruzzo. Of course, the industrialized coast is another story altogether. Once-pristine beaches are declining every year, partly from pollution and partly from neglect. Some resorts are still worth a gander; in July and August, however, Italian city slickers bring the extended family for an extended vacation—call ahead to reserve a bed.

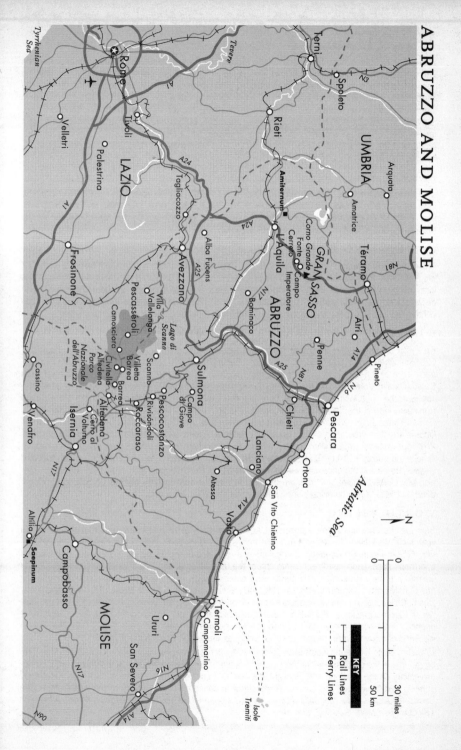

KEY

Rail Lines
Ferry Lines

N

0 miles 30

0 km 50

Adriatic Sea

Tyrrhenian Sea

UMBRIA

LAZIO

ABRUZZO

MOLISE

GRAN SASSO

Rome
Tivoli
Velletri
Palestrina
Frosinone
Cassino
Venafro
Isernia
Campobasso
San Severo
Ururi
Altilia Saepinum
Termoli
Campomarino
Isole Tremiti
San Vito Chietino
Ortona
Pescara
Pineto
Chieti
Lanciano
Vasto
Atessa
Sulmona
Campo di Giove
Pescocostanzo
Rivisóndoli
Roccaraso
Barrea
Scanno
Villetta Barrea
Civitella Alfedena
Alfedena
Cerro al Volturno
Camosciara
Parco Nazionale dell'Abruzzo
Pescasséroli
Vallelonga
Villa
Lago di Scanno
Avezzano
Alba Fucens
Tagliacozzo
Bominaco
L'Aquila
Corno Grande
Fonte Cerreto
Campo Imperatore
Amiternum
Téramo
Atri
Penne
Amatrice
Arquata
Rieti
Spoleto
Terni

A1
A24
A25
A14
A14
N3
N81
18N
N17
N17
N17
N16
N16
N90

Tevere

L'AQUILA

With a prime location high in the Gran Sasso Mountains, L'Aquila is convenient base for exploring the Parco Nazionale d'Abruzzo (*see below*). Compared to most Italian cities, L'Aquila's history, with no known Roman ties, is brief: the city was founded in the 13th century when Frederick II united the 99 surrounding kingdoms under one state and flag (bearing the eagle, or *l'aquila*). Unaccustomed to tourism, helpful locals seem more surprised than anything that you've taken the time to see their town. Sightseeing possibilities can be exhausted in an afternoon, but you may want to stay longer to admire a few snippets of beauty: ornate Renaissance architecture, stout medieval churches, and colorful fresh produce at the morning market in Piazza del Duomo. Unfortunately, food and lodging aren't cheap—head to the hills when you're low on lire.

BASICS

It's hard to miss the large **post office** (P. del Duomo, tel. 0862/410741; open Mon.–Sat. 8:15–7:30). The local tourist office is **AAST** (V. XX Settembre 8, tel. 0862/22306; open Mon.–Sat. 8–2 and 3:30—7; Sun. 9:30–12:30 in summer). For good area maps, head to L'Aquila's **Centro Alpino Italiano** (V. del Mulino, tel. 0862/24342) between 8 AM and 8:15 PM.

COMING AND GOING

The central **bus station** (P. Battaglione Alpini, tel. 0862/412808) sends hourly ARPA buses to Rome(1¾ hrs, L16,900), Pescara (1½ hrs, L13,000), and Avezzano (1 hr, L8,000). Buy tickets in the small ARPA kiosk on the piazza. Most trains to and from L'Aquila change at Sulmona, an hour southeast. Upon arrival at L'Aquila's **train station** (P. della Stazione, tel. 1478/88088), take Bus 79 or 11 to reach the city center. You can also reach the center by foot, but it's a 30-minute trek, mostly uphill.

WHERE TO SLEEP, EAT, AND BE MERRY

Except at the city-center **Pensione Maria Ausiliatrice** (P. Lauretana 2, tel. 0862/22057, fax 0862/ 62866)—where you'll pay L35,000 per person per night, L3,000 for breakfast, and L10,000 for dinner—there ain't a double in sight for less than L90,000. Your only other budget option is **Funivia Gran Sasso** (Località Fonte Cerreto, tel. 0862/606163). They charge L7,000 a head and L6,000 for a two-person tent; the price includes showers. Take Bus 6 (L1,500) from the central bus station to the *funivia* (funicular) stop at the base of the Gran Sasso. The best place for a cheap meal is **Pizzeria San Marco** (P. San Marco 1, tel. 0862/410015), with scads of freshly baked pizzas (L8,000–L18,000). Piazza del Duomo and its surrounding alleys also have a plethora of *rosticcerie* (rostisseries)—most offer samples to devour while you wait. If you've had it with pizza, try the homemade pasta called *strozzapreti* (literally, "choke the priests"; L14,000) at **Trattoria Da Rino** (V. S. Marciano 2, tel. 0862/25280). Fresh fruit and veggies are best at the enormous **outdoor market** (P. del Duomo; open Mon.–Sat. 6–1), where you can also buy clothes, shoes, and random trinkets. At night venture to lively **Mythos** (V. Sallustio 105, tel. 0862/412541), a nearby disco blaring house and cheesy Top 40 music.

WORTH SEEING

Baroque churches are a dime a dozen in L'Aquila, but many of the major sites require more purposeful searching. Walk five minutes east from the train station to reach Piazza San Vito and its famous fountain, **Fontana delle 99 Cannelle.** In the sunken three-sided basin, 93 carved heads drool water into the enormous base; each head represents one of the 99 villages united into a kingdom by Frederick II of Germany in the 13th century (six heads were never carved). Turn back toward the town center to see one of Italy's most peculiar churches: The 13th-century **Basilica di Santa Maria di Collemaggio** (Piazzale di Collemaggio) is a simple square box—no arching spires, no towering buttresses. Even the interior is barren save for a mismatched Baroque apse, altar, and the so-called Holy Doors, which are opened for 24 hours every August 28 to absolve the sins of those who pass through. On the second weekend of every month, L'Aquila hosts an **antiques market** (P. Santa Maria Paganica).

L'Aquila's austere **castello** looms above a dry moat, offering sweeping vistas of the Gran Sasso Mountain range. Inside the castle is the comprehensive but uninspired **Museo Nazionale d'Abruzzo,** with a modern gallery on the top floor. The highlight is a mammoth skeleton found in the early 1950s. From early June to mid-November, the castello hosts classical concerts; obtain info from the **AAST** office (*see* Basics, *above*). V. delle Medaglie d'Oro, near bus stop, tel. 0862/6331. Castello and Museo admission L8,000. Open Mon.–Sat. 9–2, Sun. 9–1.

NEAR L'AQUILA

GRAN SASSO

L'Aquila cowers beneath the towering Gran Sasso Mountains, home to one of Italy's tallest peaks, the **Corno Grande** (9,551 ft). The unforested Gran Sasso are steep, rocky, and largely untouched by the 20th century—that is if you ignore the nuclear test site and the nearby highway. Bus 6 runs every 20 minutes from L'Aquila to **Fonte Cerreto** (40 min, L1,500), at the foot of the Gran Sasso. This hamlet is little more than the sum of its parts—a bar and an overpriced hotel.

Fonte Cerreto is also the base station for the funivia (closed June and Oct.), which leaves every half hour 8:30–5 for the vast plain **Campo Imperatore** (7 min, L15,000), great for hiking. Mussolini was once held prisoner here. Anyone planning more than a one-hour jaunt should buy the map "Gran Sasso d'Italia: Carta dei Sentieri" (L12,000) at local hotels or at L'Aquila's Centro Alpino Italiano (*see* Basics *in* L'Aquila, *above*), which details campgrounds, *rifugi* (mountain lodges), and 22 different treks. Don't forget to pack something warm; it gets chilly up there, even in summer. In winter, hiking trails become fantastic ski runs that draw herds of Italians; full-day lift tickets (which include the funicular to Campo Imperatore) cost L28,000 (L40,000 on weekends).

Four-star hotel **Campo Imperatore** (tel. 0862/400000) charges L120,000 for a double room and has info on 10 nearby hikes ranging from easy to tough. At Campo Imperatore you'll also find a **hostel** (tel. 0862/411202; open June–Sept.); L25,000 will get you dorm-style accommodations; add another L30,000 and they'll serve you a square meal. The hostel is the last place to find hiking supplies, but it does rent skis and boots (L20,000).

SULMONA

Sulmona, with its majestic mountain setting and good rail connections, is an excellent gateway to the Parco Nazionale d'Abruzzo. Although travelers do pass through town, Sulmona is trying to retain visitors by cashing in on its history as a hotbed of Roman and medieval culture. In 1995 the Sulmona city council revived an ancient tradition: a horseback **jousting** competition in Piazza Garibaldi (July 30), followed by a week of theater, music, and art. Another testimony to Sulmona's Roman past dominates Piazza XX Settembre, the town's main plaza: a pensive bronze statue of Sulmona's famous love child, the poet Ovid.

Stick to the main street, Corso Ovidio, and you won't miss the main attractions. Start at **Santissima Annunziata** (C. Ovidio at V. dell'Ospedale, no phone), a large Baroque church attached to a 15th-century Gothic-Renaissance palazzo. For a view of Sulmona's mountains, continue past Piazza XX Settembre and numerous confection shops—Sulmona is famous throughout Italy for *confetti,* the candy-coated almonds typically given away as wedding favors—to **Piazza Garibaldi.** This stadium-size square, with arches from a 13th-century aqueduct, is also the site of a daily market in the morning. Get some figs and picnic in Sulmona's huge **Giardini Publicci.**

BASICS

If you're national park bound, get info at Sulmona's **AAST** tourist office (C. Ovidio 208, tel. 0864/53276; open Mon.–Fri. 8–2).

COMING AND GOING

Bus A (L1,500) runs from the **train station** (P. della Stazione, tel. 1478/88088) to the town center every 30 minutes, or you can walk (1½ km/1 mi) up tree-lined Viale Stazione. Buses operated by **ARPA** (tel. 0864/210469) stop at Piazza Tresca, near the Villa Comunale (in the town center). Buy tickets from any tobacconist for L'Aquila (9 daily, 1½ hrs, L9,800), Scanno (9 daily, 50 min, L5,000), and Pescasseroli (4 daily, 2 hrs, L11,100; change at Castel di Sangro).Sulmona has rail service to L'Aquila (11 daily, 1 hr, L5,900), Pescara (18 daily, 70 min, L5,900), and Rome (7 daily, 2 hrs, L14,000).

WHERE TO SLEEP, EAT, AND BE MERRY

Judging from the outside, **Hotel Italia** (P. Tommasi, off P. XX Settembre, tel. 0864/52308) is the most luxurious place in town. From the inside, it's a little less deluxe, but the doubles (L75,000) are spacious. **Albergo Stella** (Via P. Mazara 15, tel. 0864/52653), just up the road another block, has spartan doubles (L80,000). **Ristorante Italia** (P. XX Settembre 26, tel. 0864/33070; closed Mon.) is chock-full of regional specialties like the fettuccine *al Nicolò* (a white sauce with sausage; L13,000). For local atmosphere and cheap beer, head to **Black Bull** (P. Capograssi 14, tel. 0864/53829).

NEAR SULMONA

SCANNO

The bus ride between Sulmona and Scanno(9 daily, 50 min, L5,000), a dramatic route along the peaks of **Monte Genzana** (7,108 ft) and **Monte Miglio** (5,615 ft), is as exciting as the town itself. Besieged and exploited by gawking tourists in summer, Scanno is a culturally worthwhile trip year-round for the rich local costumes. The women's attire is the most noticeable: dark embroidered blouses, cream-colored dresses, and funky drum-shape caps (which supposedly originated in Asia). If the mood strikes, rent your own Scannese costume for L20,000 at **La Violetta** (Via Roma 14, tel. 0864/74473).

Below town lies the incredible **Lago di Scanno,** a cool, shimmering mountain lake. You can camp on its western shore at **I Lupi** (tel. 0864/740100), a friendly, grassy tent-camper and RV facility. Sites cost L7,500, plus L7,500 per person. You can rent horses next door for about L29,000 per hr and paddleboats about 8km (5 mi) away for L6,000 per hr. The campground is open daily May–September, weekends only off-season. Hotel options include the central **Belvedere** (P. Santa Maria della Valle 3, tel. 0864/74314), where L70,000 doubles come equipped with baths and views. Farther uphill is the well-kept **Albergo Seggiova** (Via D. Tanturri 42, tel. 0864/74371), where all doubles(L85,000)come with bath. If you're left bedless, or if you want info on lake activities, head to the **AAST** tourist office (P. Santa Maria della Valle 12, tel. 0864/74317; open Mon.–Sat. 8:30–1 and 4:30–6:30).

PARCO NAZIONALE D'ABRUZZO

The Parco Nazionale d'Abruzzo, central Italy's wild kingdom, combines lakes, streams, castle ruins, wildlife, and rocky terrain with myriad hiking trails and ski runs. Italians get back to nature here year-round, but for some inexplicable reason foreigners have yet to discover the park. Catering to an Italian sensibility, the park includes a number of stores, hotels, and restaurants.

BASICS

The park is open year-round, and information offices for hiking and camping are marked with UFFICIO DI ZONA signs and the park logo, a dopey bear. Park staffers will recommend the perfect hike. For this reason, it's worth shelling out L10,000 for the "Carta Turistica," an enormous topographical map that lists every trail, campsite, and wildlife refuge. Info offices in **Pescasseroli** (V. Piave, tel. 0863/91955) and **Civitella Alfedena** (about 10 km/6 mi southeast of Pescasseroli, tel. 0864/890141) are open daily 9–noon and 3–7. Lodging, skiing, and restaurant info is handled by the **Azienda Soggiorno** (V. Piave 1, tel. 0863/910461; open Mon.–Sat. 9–1 and 4:30–6:30) in Pescasseroli. In July and August, additional stations are open daily (same hours) in **Villetta Barrea** (corner of *vie* Barrea and Scanno, no phone), **Barrea** (V. Roma 7, no phone), and **Camosciara,** an area with waterfalls on the road to Pescasseroli, 3 km (2 mi) west of Villetta Barrea. On the main road, in front of the turn off to Camosciara, is the environmental center **Casone Antonucci** (no phone; open daily 10–1 and 3–6), with information in English, wildlife displays à la *National Geographic,* and a groovy film about animals.

COMING AND GOING

Take a train from Sulmona (11 daily, 1¼ hr, L5,900) or Rome (14 daily, 1¾ hrs, L12,100) or a bus from L'Aquila (20 daily, 1 hr, L8,000) to Avezzano. From Avezzano, nine buses daily make a slow, nausea-inducing circuit through the park, stopping along the way in Alfedena (1½ hrs, L3,000), Pescasseroli (2½ hrs, L3,600), and other villages. From Sulmona take one of four daily **ARPA** buses to Castel di Sangro and change to a coinciding bus to Pescasseroli (2 hrs, L11,100). The bus stops in all of the park's villages on its way to Pescasseroli. Because trains only stop at the fringes of the park and buses are slow and infrequent, you may want to rent a car. If you're driving from Rome (2½ hrs) or L'Aquila (1½ hrs), take A24 to the A25, get off at the Celano exit, and head south on the N83 toward Pescasseroli.

GETTING AROUND

ARPA buses travel six times daily (once on Sunday) between Avezzano, Pescasseroli, Barrea, and Alfedena (L1,500 from one town to the next). Even so, buses are unpredictable and unbearably slow. To avoid undue angst, get a photocopy of ARPA's bus schedule from any tourist office.

WHERE TO SLEEP AND EAT

There is no free legal camping in the park, but most regulated campgrounds are well maintained (with bars, showers, and cooking facilities) and open year-round; they run about L12,000–L16,000 per person. They're all far from public transport, so you'll have to walk or take a taxi from the nearest town. Some bus drivers are laid back, though, and will take you close to your campsite. The "Carta Turistica" map, available at park info offices, is invaluable for finding the perfect remote campsite.

BARREA • If you can stomach the crowds, Barrea is the cutest one-street town in the park and has keen views of Lago di Barrea from its hillside perch and one of the park's two youth hostels, **Ostello Le Vicenne** (V. Roma, tel. 0864/88362). Look for the green gate near Bar Il Chioschetto, off Barrea's main drag. Prices—L25,000 for space in a four-bed suite—are steep for a hostel, but the place is clean; book ahead in summer. Also, the park has many *affitacamere* (rooms for rent in private homes); a quiet, spotless, luxurious double at **Nora's** (V. Rimone Orientale 48, off V. Roma, tel. 0864/88215) costs L60,000. One kilometer (½ mi) east of town toward Civitella Alfedena is **Camping La Genziana** (tel. 0864/88101), a peaceful site close to hiking trails. The rates (L6,000 per person, L10,000 per tent) include showers. Barrea's **Pizzeria da Francesco** (V. Roma 159, tel. 0864/88144) has first-rate pizza and pasta (L8,000–L16,000).

Once a critically endangered species, the chamois, a goatlike deer, was saved from extinction by the Parco Nazionale d'Abruzzo.

CIVITELLA ALFEDENA • The newest and smallest of the park villages, Civitella Alfedena is a gateway to many trails and has two accessible campgrounds. **Camping Wolf** (V. Sotto I Cerri, tel. 0864/890222; closed Nov.–Apr.) is a hilly site with showers west of Alfedena; it charges L8,000 per person and L8,000 per tent site. Open between June and September, the shady **Campeggio Le Quite** campsite (near Lago di Barrea, tel. 0864/890141) charges identical prices for generally nicer facilities with showers and more trees. If you're tired of roughing it, the modern **Albergo La Torre** (V. Castello 3, tel. 0864/890121) charges L50,000 per double; tack on an additional L10,000 in summer.

PESCASSEROLI • This place is packed with hotels that cater to an upper-crust clientele, so steer clear if you're on a tight budget. In the center of town, spiffy **Locanda al Castello** (V. G. d'Annunzio 1, tel. 0863/910757) is one of the better deals around at L60,000 per double. **Camping La Panoramica** (Vialone della Cabinovia 19/B, tel. 0863/912257), spread beneath a sheep-freckled hill south of town, charges L11,000 per site, plus L9,000 per person. You can rent horses across from La Panoramica at **Le Foche** (V. Oppieto 1, tel. 0863/912863) for L19,000 per hour. For local cuisine such as penne *di orapi* (a bitter veggie that grows in these hills; L13,000), cross the bridge from Piazza San Antonio to **Peppe di Sora** (V. Benedetto Croce 1, tel. 0863/91908).

EXPLORING PARCO NAZIONALE D'ABRUZZO

With more than 150 nature and hiking trails—not to mention ski runs and horseback-riding and mountain-bike trails—you'll find plenty of action. There's no official sight here, but the "Carta Turistica" map (*see* Basics, *above*) shows every twist and turn of the park's many trails.

HIKING • "Carta Turistica," the mother of all maps, rescues you again with clear directions for all hiking trails plus approximate duration and level of difficulty. Hikes are marked **F** for *facile* (easy), **M** for moderate, and **D** for difficult. The park's most popular trails are **F1** (2 hrs, F), which starts near the town of Opi, and **I1** (3 hrs, M), which begins near Civitella Alfedena. Both meander through forests and valleys before moseying down some rocky hillsides. The only downside is that you must sign up one day in advance at the Ufficio di Zona in Camosciara; between July 15 and August 31 you must also pay L10,000 for the privilege of hiking with the masses on F1 and I1. On the other hand, it doesn't cost a single lira to hike **K6** (2½ hrs, M), although in summer you must get permission first from Barrea's Ufficio di Zona. K6 runs through wolf, mountain goat, and lynx breeding grounds; go early in the morning—in the afternoon, they're no longer in the mood. For a full-day hike from Barrea, try the challenging **K3** (5 hrs, D), which ends at photo-worthy Lago Vivo; for a gentler trip down, connect with **K4** (3 hrs, M). From Pescasseroli, the adventurous can make the trek leading to placid Lago di Scanno (*see* Scanno, *above*) on **D1** (2 hrs, M), **A9** (30 min, F), **A1** (1 hr, F), **A2** (1 hr, F), or **Y10** (2 hrs, M).

HORSEBACK RIDING • Horses are for hire at a dozen spots throughout the park—look for CENTRO IPPICO signs near towns and campsites. The going rate is about L28,000 per hour.

MOUNTAIN BIKING • When speed-crazed Italian drivers park their cars, they take to trails on their mountain bikes. One of the most popular areas for this reckless sport is **Altopiano di Macciarvana,** near the town of Opi, off trails C3 and C1. **Monte Tranquillo** is another good spot; check at the tourist office for degrees of difficulty. To rent a mountain bike (L6,500 per hr) or road bike (L5,000 per hr), go to **Nolo Bici** (P. Sant'Antonio, tel. 0863/912760) in Pescasseroli.

SKIING • For remarkably little money, you can spend the day tearing down the slopes outside Pescasseroli thanks to the **Società Impianti Funiviari** (tel. 0863/912839) ski lift. There's no public transportation, but it's so close to town you can hitch or call a cab. Ski-lift passes cost L25,000 a day (L18,000 for afternoon only); it's L20,000 to rent skis and boots, and lessons are available. The **Orsa Maggiore** chairlift nearby operates year-round (L11,000), whisking you up (and for nonskiers, back down) the steep mountain.

ABRUZZO COAST

Abruzzo does not have the prettiest stretch of coast in the world—some beaches are sandy and scenic, and many are marred by port facilities and heavy industry. Strangely enough, Italian vacationers don't seem to mind a little grime, nor do they seem to care that prices hardly reflect the region's mediocre reputation. Backpackers, however, do care, especially in a town like **Pescara,** Abruzzo's largest and most easily accessible coastal resort. Despite its downtrodden look, it's still easy to find pleasant beaches and take a refreshing swim in the Adriatic. Stick to smaller towns like **Pineto,** where you can avoid tourists and tourist prices but still savor the coast. If you're a bargain hunter and looking for the charm, bag the beach and head for **Atri.** There's no swimming or sunbathing, but this picturesque, historic town hovers peacefully above the coast and the hoi polloi.

PESCARA

The largest town on Abruzzo's coast, Pescara draws packs of teenagers and carloads of families in July and August. Pescara is also a major transportation hub; if forced to change trains or buses here, give yourself an hour or so to explore the sights—which means heading straight for the brown-sand beaches. The main drag, **Corso Umberto I,** accommodates slow-walking beach bums and fast-talking hustlers, plus anyone who wants to do time in a tacky bar. For the latest details on Pescara's renowned **jazz festival** (around July 20), contact the **Società del Teatro e della Musica** (V. Liguria 6, tel. 085/4221463).

BASICS

The efficient **UIT** tourist office (Stazione Centrale, tel. 085/4214626; open Mon.–Sat. 9–1 and 4–8) has information on outdoor concerts, plays, and jazz shows along the beach at **Teatro d'Annunzio** (V. C. Colombo 69, tel. 085/374198). The sole redeeming feature of Pescara's other **tourist office** (V. Fabrizi 171, tel. 085/429001; open Mon.–Sat. 9—noon, longer hours in summer) is that they sell tickets (L10,000–L25,000) to Teatro d'Annunzio.

COMING AND GOING

On Piazza della Repubblica is Pescara's **bus station** (tel. 085/4215099), with regular ARPA coaches to Sulmona (5 daily, 1¼ hrs, L9,800) and Atri (hourly, 1 hr, L4,000). Pescara is a major stop on the Bologna–Bari coastal line and has a multi-mirrored modern **train station** (P. della Repubblica, tel. 1478/88088) with luggage storage facilities. Trains run regularly to Rome (3½ hrs, L31,500) and Bologna (5 hrs, L41,000). To reach town, walk out of the station and head straight through the archway to Piazza della Repubblica.

WHERE TO SLEEP AND EAT

The **Hotel al Corso** (Corso V. Emanuele 252, tel. 085/4224210) offers the basic double with bath for about L60,000. Worlds apart in luxury and price, **Hotel Alba** (Via M. Forti 14, tel. 085/389145) has quiet, tidy doubles with TVs and phones for L90,000. Even if you don't stay at the Alba, nearby **Ristorante Gaetano** (V. M. Forti 21, P. della Repubblica, tel. 085/4217840) is a good bet for for heaps of spaghetti *al pescatore* (with fresh seafood; L18,000).

Finally, a travel companion that doesn't snore on the plane or eat all your peanuts.

When traveling, your MCI WorldCom Card is the best way to keep in touch. Our operators speak your language, so they'll be able to connect you back home—no matter where your travels take you. Plus, your MCI WorldCom Card is easy to use, and even earns you frequent flyer miles every time you use it. When you add in our great rates, you get something even more valuable: peace-of-mind. So go ahead. Travel the world. MCI WorldCom just brought it a whole lot closer.

You can even sign up today at www.mci.com/worldphone or ask your operator to make a collect call to 1-410-314-2938.

EASY TO CALL WORLDWIDE

1 Just dial the WorldPhone access number of the country you're calling from.
2 Dial or give the operator your MCI WorldCom Card number.
3 Dial or give the number you're calling.

France ◆	0-800-99-0019
Germany	0800-888-8000
Ireland	1-800-55-1001
Italy ◆	172-1022
Spain	900-99-0014
Sweden ◆	020-795-922
Switzerland ◆	0800-89-0222
United Kingdom	
To call using BT	0800-89-0222
To call using CWC	0500-89-0222

For your complete WorldPhone calling guide, dial the WorldPhone access number for the country you're in and ask the operator for Customer Service. In the U.S. call 1-800-431-5402.

◆ Public phones may require deposit of coin or phone card for dial tone.

EARN FREQUENT FLYER MILES

MCI WorldCom, its logo and the names of the products referred to herein are proprietary marks of MCI WorldCom, Inc. All airline names and logos are proprietary marks of the respective airlines. All airline program rules and conditions apply.

Distinctive guides packed with up-to-date expert advice and smart choices for every type of traveler.

Fodor's. For the world of ways you travel.

PINETO

Pescara may be a chaotic free-for-all, but the scene is more sedate 20 km (12½ mi) north in Pineto, where the beach is cooler, the scene calmer and less commercialized. Note that Italian families reserve hotels and campsites months in advance, making it difficult for budget types to sleuth out anything under L50,000 in summer. Adding insult to injury, nearly every hotel makes room and board mandatory in July and August.

BASICS

The **AAST** tourist office (Centro Polifunzionari on V. Mazzini, tel. 085/9491745; open Mon.–Sat. 8–12:30 and 4–7:30, Sun. 9—-noon; shorter hours in winter) has **affitacamere** listings in the area if you're left high and dry for a room.

COMING AND GOING

Pineto's **train station** (P. della Stazione, tel. 1478/88088) has luggage storage but serves only two destinations: Pescara (15 daily, 15 min, L3,900) and Ancona (10 daily, 1½ hrs, L12,100). ARPA buses do better, with service to Pescara (about every hour, 30 min, L2,000) and Atri (13 daily, 30 min, L2,000). The bus stop is on Via Gabriele d'Annunzio, one block north of the train station.

In search of wealth, the family of Madonna, America's very own "material girl," left its homeland of Abruzzo for America.

WHERE TO SLEEP AND EAT

Even the pricey hotels on waterfront Via Gabriele d'Annunzio, Pineto's main street, suffer from train noise. The cheap and friendly **Albergo Corallo** (V. Roma 74, tel. 085/9491563), only three blocks from the beach, has doubles with bath and balconies for L90,000 (including one meal in summer). Mega-sites **Camping Helipolis** (V. XXV Aprile, 2 km/1¼ mi north of town, tel. 085/9492720; open Apr.–Sept.) and **Camping Pineto Beach** (V. XXV Aprile, 1 km/½ mi north of town, tel. 085/9492724; open June–Sept.) sit on the same road along the beach and have swimming pools, game rooms, laundries, and markets. Sites start at L12,000, plus L8,000 per person. To reach the campgrounds, taxi it (L5,000) from the station or walk the short distance along the water. Fresh-fish pasta dishes (L11,000–L14,000) and pizza (L8,000–L15,000) are tasty at **Vecchia Londra** (tel. 085/9492850), in the town center.

ATRI

Tiny Atri, 10 km (6 mi) southwest of Pineto, is a welcome change from beach towns—replete with fresh air and country hospitality. Olive groves, steep Renaissance streets, Abruzzo's best frescoes (a 15th-century cycle by Andrea Delitio in the **Duomo**), ancient Roman baths surrounded by four Renaissance churches, and the interesting Atrian artifacts in **Museo Capitolare** (C. Adriano, tel. 085/87744; closed for renovation at press time) are all beautiful reasons to visit.

COMING AND GOING

Atri is only a short, scenic ride from Pineto (13 daily, 30 min, L2,000) or Pescara (hourly, 1 hr, L4,000), so you can be a beach bum by day and spend evenings in laid-back Atri. The **ARPA** bus stop is outside Atri's gates at Porta San Domenico, ½ km (¼ mi) uphill from Piazza del Duomo. Buy tickets at the bar next door.

WHERE TO SLEEP AND EAT

Atri's lone albergo is **Hotel San Francesco** (C. Adriano 38, tel. 085/87287), where L70,000 buys an airy double room and breakfast. The hotel bar, with MTV and cheap beer, is one of the town's hippest. Most local restaurants serve up that old standby, pizza, with the crucial exception of **Greentime** (V. Portico Pomenti 6, off P. Minzoni, tel. 085/8798125, closed Wed.), which serves up fresh seafood at wholesale prices: a gargantuan plate of spaghetti *al pescatore* costs a reasonable L12,000.

MOLISE

Separated from Abruzzo only 33 years ago, Molise is the least-known and possibly the oddest province in Italy. Within the region you'll find a large Albanian population, Europe's oldest human settlement, hardworking but impoverished people, and a fickle fault line that has regularly wreaked havoc on Molise's landscape. Geography and geology have blessed the province with beaches, lush hills, and postcard-perfect sunflower fields, but Molise hasn't succeeded in turning its assets into a roaring tourist industry yet. Still, if you're curious about what Italy was like when your great-grandmother lived here—or why she left—Molise merits exploration. For an inside look at this agricultural region, ask the local tourist office about *agriturismo,* which involves staying in a local farmhouse, sampling homemade cuisine, and spending long days in the country.

ISERNIA

Bloody hell, you're stuck in Isernia, possibly the most unfortunate town in Italy. Part of the problem is the earthquakes that regularly, continually, and perpetually thrash the city. Forced to rebuild from the ground up so many times, it's no wonder that Isernia's Old Town is now a maze of bricks and scaffolding. Even the old main square, **Piazza San Pietro Celestino,** has been largely abandoned. In the middle of all this rubble and cement lies the sole reason to visit: the **Museo Nazionale della Pentria e Isernia** (C. Marcelli, on P. Santa Maria 48, tel. 0865/415179; admission L4,000; open daily 9–1 and 3–7), which showcases Europe's oldest known human settlement, from 736,000 years ago. Workers laying Isernian streets discovered the site in 1979, and the museum's eerie display re-creates the painstaking hillside excavation, with the genuine artifacts positioned exactly where they were uncovered. Mysteriously, no human bones were found, although large mammal bones, weapons, body paint, and animal innards were discovered.

COMING AND GOING

The run-down **train station** (P. della Repubblica, tel. 1478/88088) serves Rome (4 daily, 3 hrs, L16,500), Naples (2 daily, 2 hrs, L11,100), and Campobasso (hourly, 1 hr, L5,200). Other rail routes are roundabout, so take either a **Cerella** (Campobasso, tel. 0874/91035; open 8–8) or **SATI** bus. These stop in front of the train station en route to Naples (6 daily, 3 hrs, L9,500) and Campobasso (hourly, 1 hr, L5,600), as well as a host of small towns in between. If you call Cerella's office, be prepared to use your Italian phrase book.

WHERE TO SLEEP AND EAT

If you're forced to spend the night in Isernia, **Hotel Sayonara** (V. G. Berta 131, tel. 0865/50992) has spotless doubles with bath for L80,000. To get here, take Via P. Patriarca from the piazza across from the train station and turn right on Via G. Berta. The **Taverna Maresca** (Corso Marcelli 186, tel. 0865/3976; closed Sun.) is a good bet for lamb and pork dishes; try the memorable *tagliatelle al sugo d'agnello* (thin pasta in lamb sauce; L14,000).

CAMPOBASSO

Only come to Molise's dreary capital city, full of concrete buildings, exhaust fumes, and depression, if you're planning to visit the Roman ruins at **Saepinum,** a one-hour bus ride away. The ancient Romans founded Saepinum as an administrative center and convenient stopover on the Abruzzo–Puglia road. Because later civilizations found this site neither beautiful nor strategic, the ruins were undisturbed, leaving them in a superbly preserved state. Enter through the **Porta Terravecchia,** one of four doors left standing, and follow the paved path, which will take you past ruined baths, a marketplace, and the foundations of the temple to Jove. You'll end up at the entrance to two small **museums** (closed for renovation at press time), which explain how the area was excavated. Admission to the site is free, but getting here is a real hassle: in Campobasso buy a bus ticket (L3,500) to **Altilia,** a one-café town next to Saepinum's walls. Otherwise, take the more frequent bus (8 daily, 30 min, L3,700) to **Sepino** and walk back 3 km (2 mi) to the site, or ask the driver to stop as close to the ruins as possible.

BASICS

For bus schedules and town info, contact the **EPT** office (P. della Vittoria 19, tel. 0874/415662; open Mon.–Sat. 8—2).

COMING AND GOING

Sandwiched between an abandoned stadium and a prison, Campobasso's crowded **bus station** (V. Mons Secondo Bologna) is best avoided at night. The **Cerella** (tel. 0874/91035) line has an information shed alongside the stadium, but you can buy tickets on board for Isernia (hourly, 1 hr, L5,600), Termoli (every 2 hrs, 1 hr, L6,000), and Altilia/Saepinum (2 daily, 1 hr, L3,500). The **train station** (P. Cuoco, tel. 1478/88088) has hourly trains to Isernia (1 hr, L5,100) and service every three hours to Termoli (1¾ hrs, L6,700). Two trains daily make the trek to Naples (3 hrs, L16,000).

WHERE TO SLEEP

The only cheap solution is to catch any bus from the train station labeled UNO NEGRO in the direction of the *zona industriale* (industrial zone). Be sure to ask the driver to stop at **Albergo Tricolore** (V. San Giovanni in Golfo 10, tel. 0874/63190), where good-size double rooms with bath and views cost L70,000 per person. The comparable **Albergo Belvedere** (V. Colle delle Api 32, tel. 0874/62724) lies on the same bus route and charges L50,000–L70,000 for a double with bath.

TERMOLI

Each year in early May, the town of Ururi, south of Termoli, stages a gladiator revival. Carts pulled by bulls and helmet-wearing horseback riders careen through the streets squirting blood, as hordes of horrified spectators applaud.

Termoli's long and clean sandy beaches and its mellow Adriatic feel are a welcome change from snootier Mediterranean towns. During July and August, though, Italians arrive in droves to bake in the sun, driving prices sky high. Make reservations in advance, or simply make Termoli an easy day trip on your way to Pescara or Bari. If you already have a sunburn, explore the town's historic quarter, Il Borgo Antico, which dates from the 4th century. Tiny streets wind around boutiques and gelaterias until you hit the 12th-century Norman **Duomo** (P. Duomo 31, tel. 0875/706237) and Frederick II's **castello** (ring for entry), which houses free modern art exhibits and has a great view of the town and beach. When the sun sets, watch a free marionette show in Termoli's central piazza. For information, festival dates, and bus schedules, try **AAST** (P. M. Bega, near the bus station, tel. 0875/706754; open Mon.–Sat. 8–12:30).

COMING AND GOING

The **bus station** (P. M. Bega) is hidden one block south of the train station. Major bus destinations include Campobasso (every 2 hrs, 1 hr, L6,500) and Pescara (3 daily, 1½ hrs, L11,500). Termoli's **train station** (P. Garibaldi, tel. 1478/88088) dominates the town center. Trains serve Pescara (hourly, 2 hrs, L7,200), Bari (15 daily, 2 hrs, L18,000), and Campobasso (8 daily, 1½ hrs, L7,400).

WHERE TO SLEEP AND EAT

In July and August, *any* room is hard to come by. The best of the budget bunch, **Villa Ida** (V. M. Milano 27, tel. 0875/706666, open Easter–Sept.) is within hearing distance of the ocean and a five-minute walk from the train station. Doubles are L95,000, all with bath. More expensive is the beachfront **Hotel Meridiano** (Lungomare Colombo, tel. 0875/705946), a huge resort-size hotel with comfy doubles (L130,000). One kilometer (½ mi) north of town lies **Campeggio Cala Saracena** (S. S. Europa 2, tel. 0875/52193; open May–Sept.), with tent sites for L12,700–14,700, plus L6,900–L8,900 per person. In the Old Town near the beach, get a huge plate of *tzatziki* (yogurt, cucumber, and garlic salad; L8,000) or a Greek salad at excellently priced **Il Battello Ebbro** (Vico VI Duomo, tel. 0875/703261).

NAPLES AND CAMPANIA

BY JAMES KWAK

UPDATED BY GREGORY BAILEY

ampania is the centerpiece of the Mezzogiorno (southern Italy), a region whose glorious past outshines its present problems. A land of myths—where Ulysses was tempted by the Sirens and the Cumaean Sibyl dispensed wisdom—it has archeological sites, from Pompeii to Paestum, that offer glimpses of Greek and Roman civilization. After a handful of hedonistic Greeks established the first colonies, their successors, the Romans, further "civilized" the region by building luxury palaces and brothels. In the 17th and 18th centuries the city of Naples became a requisite stop on every aristo's grand tour of Europe, and by the 19th and 20th centuries, exiled left-wing intellectuals and artists found refuge and inspiration on the region's islands and in its small coastal towns.

Today the islands of Ischia and Capri and the Amalfi coast—a combination of rocky cliffs, green mountainsides, and blue seas—still entice pleasure seekers. And of course there is Naples, the spectacular but chaotic city where a traffic signal is seen not as a command but as a suggestion. Naples is now one of the most densely populated cities in Europe, and much of it is controlled by the *cammorra* (the local organized crime faction). It's unemployment rate hovers at around 30%. But things are definitely on the upswing: the current mayor has cleaned up many parts of the city (particularly where tourists visit and overnight—even the notorious Stazione Centrale is now crawling with police); the city's dazzling Baroque art and architecture are being restored; and a whole new flock of young artists has settled near the Capodimonte museum. In the end, there may be things you will hate about Campania—in addition to its bus companies—but you won't be able to resist at least some of its innumerable fascinations.

NAPLES

Lifelong Neapolitans claim that theirs is the most beautiful city in the world. Approaching Naples (Napoli) from the water at sunset, as the moon rises over Mt. Vesuvius, or looking down from the Vomero Hills over the sweeping curve of the bay, you may be moved to agree. Once amid the swirling traffic of the city, however, you may think you have tumbled from *Paradiso* to *Inferno*. Naples's energy, chaos, and (seeming) lawlessness rival anything in Europe, and, until recently, little effort had been made to soften the city's hard edges for foreigners. Nevertheless, it only takes a little patience and an open mind

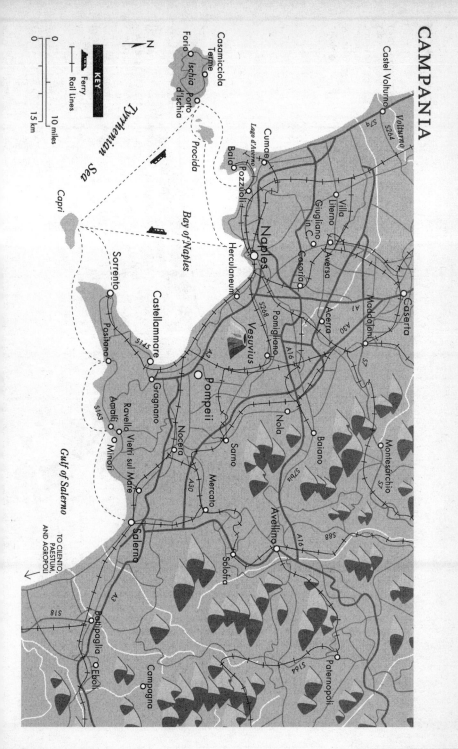

CAMPANIA

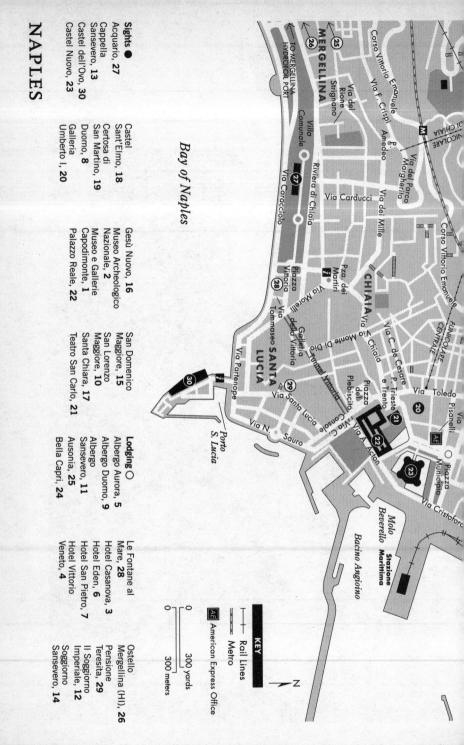

NAPLES

Sights ●
Acquario, **27**
Cappella
Sansevero, **13**
Castel dell'Ovo, **30**
Castel Nuovo, **23**

Castel
Sant'Elmo, **18**
Certosa di
San Martino, **19**
Duomo, **8**
Galleria
Umberto I, **20**

Gesù Nuovo, **16**
Museo Archeologico
Nazionale, **2**
Museo e Gallerie
Capodimonte, **1**
Palazzo Reale, **22**

San Domenico
Maggiore, **15**
San Lorenzo
Maggiore, **10**
Santa Chiara, **17**
Teatro San Carlo, **21**

Lodging ○
Albergo Aurora, **5**
Albergo Duomo, **9**
Albergo
Sansevero, **11**
Ausonia, **25**
Bella Capri, **24**

Le Fontane al
Mare, **28**
Mergellina (HI), **26**
Hotel Casanova, **3**
Hotel Eden, **6**
Hotel San Pietro, **7**
Hotel Vittorio
Veneto, **4**

Ostello
Mergellina (HI), **26**
Pensione
Teresita, **29**
Il Soggiorno
Imperiale, **12**
Soggiorno
Sansevero, **14**

Bay of Naples

MERGELLINA

Corso Vittorio Emanuele

Via F. Crispi

Via del
Rione
Strignano

TO MERGELLINA
HYDROFOIL PORT

Villa
Comunale

Via Caracciolo

Via del Parco
Margherita

Riviera di Chiaia

Via Carducci

Corso Vittorio Emanuele

Via dei Mille

CHIAIA

Pza. dei
Martiri

Via Morelli

Piazza
Vittoria

Galleria
della Vittoria

Via
della Vittoria

Via Monte Di Dio

Via C. de Cesare
e P. Trieste
e Trento

Via Toledo

Via Pisanelli

CENTRALE

FUNICOLARE

Piazza
del
Plebiscito

**SANTA
LUCIA**

Via Santa Lucia

Via Chiaia

Via Partenope

Via Console

Via A. Acton

*Porto
S. Lucia*

Via N.
Sauro

Piazza
Municipio

Via Cristoforo

Via Toledo

Via Tommaseo

*Molo
Beverello*

**Stazione
Marittima**

Bacino Angioino

KEY

Metro
Rail Lines
AE American Express Office

N

0 — 300 yards
0 — 300 meters

344

NAPLES

VOMERO

OLD NAPLES

345

to adapt to the pace of Neapolitan life—an effort well rewarded by the city's numerous monuments, churches, and museums, not to mention its world-renowned pizza and seafood. In time, Naples reveals its beautiful side: a deep-rooted tradition of closely knit families and neighborhoods set in the cosmopolitan cultural capital of the Mezzogiorno. So, don't let Naples's outsized reputation for poverty and petty crime scare you off. Relax: the genuinely warm and friendly people you meet will far outnumber the few who are after your wallet. Once you have learned to navigate the crowded streets like a native, you may never want to leave this ancient yet modern city by the sea.

BASICS

AMERICAN EXPRESS

Every Tour travel agency (P. Municipio 5–6, tel. 081/551–8564; open weekdays 9–1:30 and 3:30–7, Sat. 9–1) provides the entire range of **American Express** services.

CHANGING MONEY

If you want convenience and aren't changing a big wad, use the **Ufficio di Cambio** inside Stazione Centrale (*see* Coming and Going by Train, *below*); it's open daily 7:15 AM–8:30 PM. If you want to compare rates, go to the financial district around Piazza Municipio. Several major banks and many small exchange offices are spread along Via A. Depretis between Piazza Municipio and Piazza Bovio. You'll find other exchange offices just below on Via Cristoforo Colombo, one of which is open until 7 PM.

CONSULATES

United Kingdom (V. Francesco Crispi 122, off P. Amedeo, tel. 081/663511; open weekdays 9–12:30 and 2–4:30). **United States** (P. della Repubblica 2, at west end of Villa Comunale, tel. 081/5838111; open weekdays 8–1).

DISCOUNT TRAVEL AGENCIES

Dedicated to helping students, **Euro Study Travel** (Mezzocannone 119, tel. 081/5520947; open weekdays 9:30–1:30 and 3–6) is across from the central university building. The ticket office (V. Mezzocannone 87) is also open Saturday 9:30–12:30.

EMERGENCIES

For general emergencies call 113; for an **ambulance** call 081/7520696. To report a medical emergency after 8 PM, call 081/7613466 and ask for an English-speaking nurse. The main **police station** (V. Medina 75, tel. 081/7941111) has an *ufficio stranieri* (foreigners' office) that usually has an English speaker on staff. If the *farmacia* (pharmacy) in Stazione Centrale is closed, it will post the address of one that's open; the newspaper *Il Mattino* also prints a list of pharmacies that are open nights and weekends.

ENGLISH-LANGUAGE BOOKS

For romance, philosophy, or a handy thesaurus, head to **Universal Books** (V. Rione Sirignano I, just off Riviera di Chiaia, tel. 081/663217; open weekdays 9–1 and 4–7, Sat. 9–1).

MAIL AND PHONES

The best place to make long-distance calls is at **Telecom** (V. A. Depretis 40, between P. Bovio and P. Municipio; open Mon.–Sat. 9:30–1 and 2–5:30). The main **post office** (P. Matteotti off V. Diaz, tel. 081/5511456; open weekdays 8:15–7:20 and Sat. 8:15–1:30) has *fermo posta* (held mail). The postal code is 80100. Branch offices are usually open weekdays 8:15–1:30 and Saturday 8:15–12:10.

VISITOR INFORMATION

The numerous tourist offices in Naples aren't always open when they claim to be, but most are generally open Monday to Saturday 9–7 and Sunday 9–2 except where noted. There's an **EPT** office (tel. 081/268779) in Stazione Centrale; the main administrative center is in Piazza dei Martiri (P. dei Martiri 58, tel. 081/405311; open weekdays 8:30–2). Branches are at Stazione Mergellina (tel. 081/7612102) and at the airport (tel. 081/7805761). An **AACST** office (P. Gesù Nuovo, tel. 081/5523328) specializes in information on Old Naples. A second office is in front of the Castel dell'Ovo (tel. 081/7645688; closed Sun.).

COMING AND GOING

BY BUS

Medium- and long-distance buses out of Naples are handled by two companies. **ACTP** (tel. 081/7001111) buses usually leave from Piazza Garibaldi; **SITA** (tel. 081/5522176) buses leave from either Piazza Garibaldi or Via G. Pisanelli, just south of Piazza Municipio, for destinations that include Bari and the Amalfi Coast. Some major routes are listed in *Qui Napoli,* available free at EPT offices, but in general, avoid buses if you can take a train to the same place.

BY FERRY

If you're heading to the Aeolian Islands, other parts of Sicily, or Sardinia, Naples may be a convenient departure point. The major long-distance carriers are **Tirennia** (departs from Stazione Marittima, near P. Municipio, tel. 0147/899000 or 081/580–0340) and **Linee Lauro** (departs from Molo Belvedere below Castel Nuovo, tel. 081/5513352). Boats leave occasionally (not every day) for Tunis (18 hrs southwest, L120,000–L170,000), Sardinia (14 hrs west, L50,000—L100,000), Palermo (11 hrs southwest, L61,600–90,500), and the Aeolian Islands (8–14 hrs, L66,500–L75,500), among other places. Departure times and additional info on some routes, including the local ferry and hydrofoil lines listed below, can be found in *Qui Napoli* or in the newspaper *Il Mattino.*

For info on live performances, transportation schedules, and museum exhibits in Naples, pick up the free guide Qui Napoli at an EPT office.

For trips around the Bay of Naples, the main port is **Molo Beverello,** below Castel Nuovo. Many carriers send boats to the islands all day, until 7 or 8, though off-season service is less frequent. Carriers include **Linee Lauro** (tel. 081/5513352), **Caremar** (tel. 081/5513882), and **Navigazione Libera del Golfo** (tel. 081/5527209). Hydrofoils (but not ferries) also leave from the port at Mergellina, a short walk below the Mergellina train station; these are run by **SNAV** (tel. 081/7612348) and **Alilauro** (tel. 081/7614909). Major destinations from both ports include Capri (hydrofoils: 40 min southeast, L16,000; ferries: 1 hr 20 min, L9,800), Procida (hydrofoils: 30 min southeast, L14,500; ferries: 1 hr, L8,800), and Ischia (hydrofoils: 40 min south, L18,000; ferries: 1 hr 20 min, L10,000). Several hydrofoils also ply to Sorrento (25 min southeast, L12,000), Positano (1 hr southeast, L25,000), and Amalfi (1½ hrs southeast, L26,000).

BY PLANE

Capodichino Airport, 8 km (5 mi north of Naples, tel. 081/7896259) has many domestic and international connections. **Alitalia** (tel. 081/5425111), **Lufthansa** (tel. 081/5515440), and **British Airways** (tel. 081/7803087) all fly from here. Bus 14 runs from Piazza Garibaldi to the airport (hourly, 25 min) between 5:15 AM and 10:05 PM. A shuttle bus (tel. 081/5311706) also runs from 6 AM to midnight between the airport and Piazza Municipio (hourly, 30 min, L3,000), stopping in Piazza Garibaldi along the way. If you take a taxi from Piazza Garibaldi, expect to pay L40,000 (agree on a fare beforehand) for the 15-minute trip.

BY TRAIN

Stazione Centrale (tel. 1478/88088 toll-free) overflows onto Piazza Garibaldi, northeast of Old Naples and the port. Services in this hectic station include a pharmacy, a money exchange office, 24-hour luggage check (L5,000 every 12 hrs), a post office, and a visitor information office. A **Wasteels branch office** (tel. 081/201071) sells BIJ train tickets (*see* Getting Around *in* Chapter 1) Monday–Saturday 9–7:30. Trains leave at least hourly for Rome (2½ hrs northwest, L18,000) and several times daily for Milan (7 hrs northwest, L64,000) and Reggio di Calabria (4½ hrs southeast, L38,500). If you're staying at the youth hostel in Mergellina, many trains stop first at **Stazione Mergellina** (C. Vittorio Emanuele 4, tel. 1478/88088), also near a hydrofoil port. If you arrive at night, consider taking a taxi to your hotel, but be sure you and the driver agree on a price ahead of time—many Neapolitan taxi drivers like to pretend the meter doesn't work.

Naples has two sets of commuter rail lines, each with its own tickets. The **Ferrovia Circumvesuviana** leaves for points east from the Stazione Circumvesuviana (tel. 081/7792144) on Corso Garibaldi; all trains also stop on the lower level of **Stazione Centrale** (P. Garibaldi). Destinations include Herculaneum, Pompeii, and Sorrento. **SEPSA** (tel. 081/7354111) manages two railway lines that leave from the **Stazione Cumana** (near the Montesanto Metro station). Both end at Torregavata, at the west end of the Gulf of Naples; the Cumana line goes along the coast and stops at Pozzuoli and Baia, among other places.

GETTING AROUND

The heart of Naples stretches along the Bay of Naples from Piazza Garibaldi in the east to Mergellina in the west, with its back to the Vomero Hills. From Stazione Centrale, on Piazza Garibaldi, Corso Umberto I heads southwest to the downtown area of piazzas Bovio, Municipio, and Trieste e Trento. To the north are the historic districts of Old Naples; to the south is the port. Farther west along the bay are the more fashionable neighborhoods of **Santa Lucia** and **Chiaia,** and finally the waterfront district of Mergellina. The residential area of **Vomero** sits on the steep hills rising above Chiaia and downtown. **Via Toledo,** Naples's major north–south axis, begins at Piazza Trieste e Trento and heads up to Capodimonte. To the west are the narrow streets of the tiny **Quartieri Spagnoli** (Spanish Quarter). To the east is Naples's most picturesque quarter, **Spaccanapoli** (literally, "spine" of the medieval quarter), called the Decumano Inferiore in Roman times, a street that changes names several times on its way through the heart of Old Naples (it comprises Via Benedetto Croce and Via San Biagio dei Librai, among others). Just north on Via Toledo is the café-lined Piazza Dante, in the **university district.**

In Naples both walking and taking public transit can be confusing and inconvenient. Even the simple task of crossing a street can present a challenge, as most Neapolitan drivers don't follow traditional traffic laws. Essentially, it's a constant game of chicken: cross big streets one or two lanes at a time, and don't ever hesitate in the middle of a lane—keep moving so hurtling motorcycles can avoid you. A major saving grace in the city's transit system is the *Giranapoli* (L1,500), a 90-minute ticket that works for the *Metropolitana* (subway), tram, *funicolari* (funiculars), and **ATAN** city buses, as long as you are within the city limits. You can purchase tickets at most tobacco shops (look for the TABACCHI sign) or newsstands. If you buy a day pass (L4,500), remember to stamp it the first time you use it.

BY BUS

Bus routes in Naples change frequently, signs posted at bus stops aren't too helpful, and there is no bus map available. That said, the **R1** runs from Piazza Bovio up into the hills, the **R2** runs between Piazza Garibaldi and Piazza Municipio, and the **R3** runs between Piazza Dante and Mergellina; all three converge in the downtown areas at various transfer points. The **24** takes you from downtown (Via Monteoliveto) to Capodimonte. Otherwise, most buses go to the suburbs and may or may not get you where you want to go. As transfers are free, a few mistakes won't deplete your bank account.

BY METROPOLITANA

Naples's main urban metro line runs through the city from Gianturco, east of Stazione Centrale, through the lower level of Stazione Centrale, and tours as far west as Pozzuoli. Useful stops include **Piazza Cavour** (just up the street from the Museo Archeologico Nazionale), **Montesanto** (near the Cumana railway station), **Piazza Amedeo** (in the tony Chiaia district), and the **Stazione Mergellina.**

BY FUNICOLARE AND TRAM

If you're heading up to Vomero (*see* Cheap Thrills, *below*), **funicolari** make the trek from stations at Montesanto, Via Roma, and Piazza Amedeo. The city's **tram** system runs northeast– southwest; Tram 1 will take you from Piazza Garibaldi to Mergellina along the waterfront.

WHERE TO SLEEP

Considering how divey the dives can be in Naples, you may want to shell out the extra lire for a little cleanliness and security. In general, the farther you stray from Piazza Garibaldi, the more palatable (and pricey) the accommodations become. When possible reserve ahead and firmly settle on a final price over the phone or by fax. Many hotels have storage safes, so you can stash your valuables and walk around town worry-free.

PIAZZA GARIBALDI

If you stay in one of the many hotels near the train station, your perspective on the city will inevitably be skewed. This area is known for its prostitution; several of its hotels rent rooms out on an hourly basis. Just remember: all of Naples isn't this tawdry and threatening.

DIRT CHEAP • Albergo Aurora. It's a cut above most of the low-end places nearby, but you still have to withstand the noisy piazza, squishy beds, and a mangy atmosphere. Doubles go for L36,000. *P. Garibaldi 60, above Hotel Sayonara, 80142, tel. 081/201920. 9 rooms, 3 with bath.*

UNDER L75,000 • Hotel Vittorio Veneto. It's nothing spectacular, but this small hotel only charges L65,000 for doubles with TVs. The bathrooms are in decent shape, too. *V. Milano 96, 80142, tel. and fax 081/201539. Head straight out of Stazione Centrale, turn right on V. Milano. 13 rooms, 5 with bath. Laundry. Cash only.*

UNDER L90,000 • Hotel Casanova. This is the best deal near Piazza Garibaldi—just far enough from the square to be relatively quiet and secure but close enough for you to catch your morning train. Small but clean doubles, all with TV, cost L64,000, L87,000 with bath. *V. Venezia 2, 80139, tel. 081/ 268287, fax 081/269792. 18 rooms, 14 with bath.*

Hotel Eden. Three friendly brothers run this four-story hostelry with all the services of a major hotel. The tasteful rooms have firm beds and newly tiled bathrooms. Doubles, all with bath, are available at L80,000. If you call from the station, they'll come help with your bags. *C. Novara 9, 80142, tel. 081/ 285344, fax 081/285690. Go right leaving the station and walk 2 blocks. 43 rooms. Luggage storage.*

UNDER L130,000 • Hotel San Pietro. What this large, anonymous hotel lacks in character, it makes up for in reliability. The functional, clean rooms are equipped with TVs—those without bath include the use of a closetlike shower down the hall. Doubles cost L80,000, L130,000 with bath. *V. San Pietro ad Aram 18, 80139, tel. 081/5535914, fax 081/286040. 50 rooms, 22 with bath.*

SPACCANAPOLI

Spaccanapoli, the center of historic Naples, really beats Piazza Garibaldi by virtue of its antiquity and atmosphere, but it has surprisingly few hotels and pensioni. If you can find a place, you'll have the advantage of being near most of the important sights.

Naples has a reputation for petty theft, but if you're street-smart, you'll have a perfectly safe stay. Carry all cash, traveler's checks, and documents in a money belt. Women should take extra precautions, as they are more often victims of purse-snatching by people on mopeds.

UNDER L70,000 • Il Soggiorno Imperiale. This hotel provides tidy, secure budget accommodations in a great area near Piazza Dante. The friendly couple who run the place can tell you all about Old Naples. Doubles start from L60,000. *P. Miraglia 386, 3rd floor, 80138, tel. 081/459347. Metro: P. Cavour, walk south to V. Tribunali, turn right; V. Tribunali leads into P. Miraglia. 7 rooms without bath. Cash only.*

UNDER L95,000 • Soggiorno Sansevero. Set on the beautiful Piazza San Domenico in the the heart of Spaccanapoli and occupying one floor of the former palazzo of the princes di Sangro di San Severo (who built the Capella Sansevero just behind the palace), this pensione has clean, modest rooms with modern furniture, a delightfully friendly staff, and perhaps a few ghosts (composer Carlo Gesualdo, inventor of the madrigal, murdered his wife and her lover on the palace staircase on October 16, 1590). Doubles start at L80,000. *P. S. Domenico Maggiore 9 (Palazzo Sansevero), 2nd floor, 80138, tel. 081/ 555–5949, fax 081/211698. Bus 43 to Corso Umberto I, then walk six blocks north from Via Mezzacannone. 12 rooms with bath, 4 rooms with shared bath. Cash only.*

UNDER L130,000 • Albergo Duomo. This pension in the heart of Old Naples offers breezy, immaculate blue- and white-tiled rooms with clean bathrooms, firm beds, and TVs. Comfortable doubles cost L100,000–L110,000. *V. Duomo 228, 80138, south of Duomo, tel. 081/265988. Bus R2 to V. Duomo. 10 rooms with bath. Restaurant, laundry. Cash only.*

UNDER L150,000 • Albergo Sansevero. Run by the same folks as the Soggiorno Sansevero (*see above*), this is just off pretty, café-set Piazza Bellini on one of the grand avenues laid out by the Bourbons. You're just a few blocks from the heart of Spaccanapoli. Doubles start at L140,000. *V. S. Maria di Constantinopoli 101, 80138, tel. 081/210907, fax 081/211698. Bus 22 on Via E. Pessina to Piazza Dante, then walk on Via Port'Alba to Piazza Bellini. 11 rooms with bath. Cash only.*

WATERFRONT

Many of Naples's most expensive hotels are set on the waterfront, offering spectacular views and lavish rooms, but their prices can deplete any inheritance you want to pass along. The same district, however, offers a few budget options. The area is safer than Piazza Garibaldi, and some great seafood restaurants pop up in the streets around the bay.

PAZZO FOR PIZZA

Pizza was born in Naples. Despite similarities, the pizza of Naples is a different animal from the pizza of California (multinational), Chicago (overstuffed), New Haven (burnt to a crisp), and even of Northern Italy. Succulent tomatoes, creamy mozzarella, fresh basil, abundant olive oil, and a thin, slightly chewy crust baked in a wood-fired oven can be magical. The simplest Neapolitan pies are marinara (tomatoes, garlic, and oil) and margherita (tomatoes, mozzarella, and basil), and you won't find the massive multi-ingredient versions. People here know not to mess with a good thing.

UNDER L70,000 • Pensione Teresita. These clean rooms by the bay—some with balconies—are almost always full. If you get in, you can kick back in a large and airy TV room, along with the owners, the maids, and some nightclub dancers who siesta here. Doubles are L65,000, which includes the use of decent showers down the hall. *V. Santa Lucia 90, 2nd floor, 80132, tel. 081/7640105. From Stazione Centrale, Bus R2 to P. Trieste e Trento. 13 rooms without bath. Cash only.*

UNDER L125,000 • Bella Capri. Near Piazza Municipio with views over the bay, this place has doubles with bath for L120,000. *V. Melisurgo 4, tel. 081/5529494, fax 081/5529265. Tram 1 from Stazione Centrale. 10 rooms with bath.*

Le Fontane al Mare. Come here for luxury accommodations at a relatively low price, with doubles for L90,000, or L120,000 with bath. Most of the elegant rooms have balconies overlooking the sea, and you're a short walk from the Villa Comunale, a pleasant park on the bay. *V. Niccolò Tommaseo 14, 4th floor, 80121, tel. 081/7643811, fax 081/7643470. From Stazione Centrale, Tram 1 to P. Vittoria. 25 rooms, 5 with bath.*

UNDER L175,000 • Ausonia. On the waterfront near the Mergellina FS and Metro station and across from the Mergellina port, the Ausonia has clean and comfortable doubles with television and breakfast for L120,000 or L170,000 with bath. *V. Carracciolo 11, tel. 081/682278, fax 081/664536. 20 rooms. Bus 22 to Lungomare. 22 rooms with bath.*

HOSTEL • Ostello Mergellina (HI). Naples's only youth hostel may be on the western edge of town, but it also happens to be just below the tombs of Virgil and Leopardi, just above the Mergellina FS and Metro station, and a 10-minute walk from Mergellina's hydrofoil port. Most of the rooms (from two to six beds) have their own bath. HI members pay L24,000 to L30,000, which includes breakfast. Membership costs L30,000. You can take advantage of luggage storage and self-service dinner. Reservations are advised in summer. *V. Salita della Grotta 23, 80122, tel. 081/7612346, fax 081/7612391. Metro: Mergellina; leave station to the right, go back under tracks and follow signs. 250 beds. 12:30 AM curfew, lockout 9–4. Reception closed 9–2. Cash only.*

WHERE TO EAT

Neapolitans like their architecture Baroque but their cuisine classic and simple. Take part in Naples's lively street life by shopping in the **open-air food markets** that line Via Tribunali between Piazza Dante and the Duomo, or the narrow streets between Montesanto and Via Roma. Most of the restaurants around Piazza Garibaldi serve mediocre food in a rushed atmosphere; it's definitely worth it to venture into Spaccanapoli for the real thing, and things don't get much more real than at **Di Matteo** (V. Tribunali 94, tel. 081/294203, closed Sun.), one of the shrines of Neapolitan pizza. The slices here are so yummy even President Clinton came here to get his taste of Neapolitan fast-food during the G-7 Summit. Their great pizzas even have a great price: only L4,000 for a margherita. This is one reason why the place is often mobbed.

Usually pricier than pizza joints, Neapolitan trattorias also offer incredible deals. A local specialty is mozzarella *di bufala* (made from water-buffalo milk), a tangier, juicier version of the cheese we know. Try it fresh in an *insalata caprese* (with tomatoes and basil). *Frutti di mare* (seafood, primarily shellfish) mixed into pasta is a typical Neapolitan *primo piatto* (first course). Spaghetti *alle cozze,* with sweet tomatoes and mussels, and *zuppa di pesce* (fish stew) are other favorites, though these can cost up to L15,000. When you need to be frugal, you can usually find spaghetti *al pomodoro* (in tomato sauce) for L5,000.

PIZZERIAS

Naples is naturally a paradise of pizzerias, which are found all over town. The best include the only-five-tables **Sorbillo** in Spaccanapoli (V. Tribunali 35, closed Sun.) and **da Michele** (V. Sersale 1, tel. 081/5539204, closed Sun.) off Corso Umberto near the central station; this only offers two choices (with or without cheese) but remains one of the best deals in town. **Cibo** (P. del Gesù Nuovo 26, tel. 081/5518427), across from the Gesù, has a creative selection of pizzas and great sandwiches to take away. Near the parks of the Villa Comunale is **Salvatore alla Riviera** (Riviera di Chiaia 91, tel. 081/680490), while in the Mergellina area, **Da Pasqualino** (V. P. Sannazaro 77-78-79, tel. 081/681524, closed Tues.), is open until dawn and has sublime potato croquettes. Most of these places don't accept plastic—for that, head to the pricier pizzerias. Legendary **Brandi** (Salita Sant'Anna di Palazzo 1, tel. 081/416928) is where the pizza margherita was created in homage to the Bourbon queen; its tiny, wood-timbered rooms are so adorably picturesque you won't mind rubbing elbows with hoardes of Americans and Japanese. At **Lombardi a Santa Chiara** (V. Benedetto Croce 59, near P. Gesù Nuovo, tel. 081/552–0780), in the heart of Spaccanapoli, you'll battle with a long line of locals waiting to pick up take-out pizzas, such as their specialty, pizza *alla Lombardi.* A relative of the margherita, it's made with fresh chopped tomatoes.

If you work up an appetite walking along the bay in Naples, stop at any of the stands between Santa Lucia and Mergellina for a tarallo con mandorle e pepe, a savory almond pastry that makes a great quick snack.

OLD NAPLES AND CHIAIA

Competition for student lire has made eating around Piazza Dante and Via Tribunali the best deal in Naples. Restaurants are relaxed, with outdoor seating in a balmy, calm atmosphere—at least at night. West of Piazza del Plebiscito in the Chiaia district, you'll find an older crowd in spirited family-run trattorias.

UNDER L15,000 • Dante e Beatrice. From the outdoor patio, a gas station and parking lot hamper your view of Piazza Dante until dark, when the cars disappear. Justifiably one of the most famous spots in the city, this tasteful and elegant trattoria whips up Neapolitan specialties like pasta *e fagioli* (a hearty white bean and pasta soup) or *frittura mista del golfo* (mixed fried seafood). *P. Dante 44–45, tel. 081/5499438. Cash only. Closed Mon. and 3 wks in Aug. or Sept.*

La Cantina di Via Sapienza. This busy, friendly Spaccanapoli trattoria attracts the young and hip with its low prices (primi courses for L4,000–L5,000) and great selections for vegetarians. Lunch only. *V. Sapienza 40/41, tel. 081/459078.*

Ristorante 53. Some 300 years old, this restaurant lays claim to being the oldest in Naples. Sample their array of 10–15 different antipasti and enjoy the outdoor seating on Piazza Dante. *P. Dante 53, tel. 081/5499372.*

UNDER L20,000 • Amici Miei. On a quiet street above Via Chiaia, "Our Friends" isn't cheap, but it's well worth the money. The interior is artfully decorated, and the ever-changing selection of delicious Neapolitan fare and Northern cuisine is seemingly endless, with dishes like *fusilli con melanzane e mozzarella* (spiral pasta with eggplant and mozzarella). *V. Monte di Dio 78, tel. 081/7646063. Closed Sun. and Aug.*

WATERFRONT

Neapolitan seafood is excellent, and the restaurants near the water will indulge your cravings. Some are touristy and overpriced, especially the ones at the foot of the Castel dell'Ovo, but with perseverance you can find fresh fish or shellfish for about L10,000–L20,000. The waterfront area around Mergellina is also a good place to go hunting for dinner.

UNDER L15,000 • Da Ettore. Locals and travelers in the know come to this restaurant and pizzeria for its mouth-watering *pizzelle,* small pieces of fried dough topped with tomatoes and mozzarella, and, of course, traditional pizza. *V. Santa Lucia 56, tel. 081/7640498. Cash only. Closed Sun.*

Vino e Cucina. Owner Michele Moccia and his sons serve good cheap pasta and seafood across from the Megellina FS and Metro station. Don't pass up the excellent house wine. *Corso V. Emanuele 762, tel. 081/660302. Cash only. Closed Sun. (and Sat. in July).*

THE LEGACY OF IL DUCE

Although currently governed by a left-wing mayor, Naples has been a bastion of the Italian extreme right of the 1990s, having elected Alessandra Mussolini—granddaughter of Il Duce—to the national parliament three times. Previously a movie actress and television variety show host, Mussolini won her seat in 1992 as a member of the Italian Social Movement—a party founded in 1946 by her grandfather's supporters.

Mussolini symbolizes her party, rebaptized the National Alliance, in more than name alone. Although she has expressed admiration for her grandfather's policies and draws openly racist skinheads to her rallies, she also ran a campaign promising to fight corruption, reduce crime, and improve social services. Young and telegenic—she stole the cameras by making her first appearance in parliament wearing a miniskirt—she is also a bit of a wild card, speaking out in defense of gays and constantly at the forefront of women's rights in Italy, and has helped give the neofascists the more modern, well-dressed image that has brought them close to 20% of the vote in national elections.

UNDER L20,000 • Ristorante Marino. This ultratypical Neapolitan restaurant is always packed with loud natives and boisterous waiters. Primi include specialties like spaghetti *ai frutti di mare. V. Santa Lucia 118, tel. 081/7640280. Closed Mon.*

CAFFE AND PASTICCERIE

Neapolitans do the café scene right, making countless stops throughout the day for coffee, *tè freddo* (iced tea), and delicious pastries. Make it a point to try *sfogliatelle,* a crunchy, flaky triangular pastry filled with vanilla or chocolate pastry cream, or *frolle,* soft, round pastry shells filled with delicately flavored ricotta cheese and candied fruit. For dessert nothing is more Neapolitan than *babà,* a rum-soaked cake sometimes served with fresh fruit.

Priests and nuns from neighborhood churches gather at **Giovanni Scaturchio** (P. San Domenico Maggiore 19, tel. 081/5516944, closed Tues.) to anticipate what heaven will taste like. Just as popular, **Gran Bar Riviera** (Riviera di Chiaia 181–183, across from Villa Comunale, tel. 081/665026) overflows with every sweet concoction imaginable. **Pintauro** (V. Toledo 275, tel. 081/417339, closed Sun.) has justifiably famous *sfogliatelle.* If you want to feel like a turn-of-the-century boulevardier, treat yourself to a luxurious sit-down cappuccino and pastry under the chandeliers at historic **Caffè Gambrinus** across from the Teatro San Carlo on Piazza Trieste e Trento. If you don't fancy a pastry, gelaterias abound in Naples; one of the best is **Chalet Ciro** (V. F. Caracciolo, tel. 081/669928), one block west of the Mergellina hydrofoil port. Also, halfway up the Via Toledo is **Scimmia** (P. Carità 4).

WORTH SEEING

If you're only in town for the day, you can take a walking tour of the main sights around Spaccanapoli and down by the waterfront, but you'll really need more time if you want to fill up on the city's lively streets and excellent museums. If you're overwhelmed by the number of churches and the variety of architectural styles in Naples, head to the tourist office on Piazza Gesù Nuovo. Their color-coded free itineraries—delineating four different tours of medieval, Renaissance, Baroque, and Rococo churches—go a long way in helping you distinguish your apse from a flying buttress.

SPACCANAPOLI

Old Naples centers around the Spaccanapoli neighborhood, where already narrow streets are crowded by small shops, impromptu soccer matches, crisscrossing clotheslines, and motorcycles. You'll be surprised at how many of the abundant churches in the area are in constant use; others are undergoing eternal restoration. Besides the major sites, discussed below, other interesting churches include Gothic **San Domenico Maggiore** (P. San Domenico Maggiore 8/A, tel. 081/5573111), once frequented by St. Thomas Aquinas, and **San Lorenzo Maggiore** (V. Tribunali 316, at P. San Gaetano, tel. 081/290580), begun in the 13th century on top of newly discovered Greek and Roman remains; these are visible Mon. and Wed.–Sat. 9–1 and 3:30–5:30 (4–6:30 in summer), and Sun. 9–1:30 (tel. 081/454948, admission L5,000). Be aware that the opening hours of nearly all churches (except ones that are now museums) are approximate at best; most are open roughly 7:30–noon and 4 or 5–7. To see as many as possible, try to start out in the morning.

CAPPELLA SANSEVERO • For Neapolitan Baroque at its most phantasmagorical, head to this famous chapel overflowing with elaborate reliefs and richly colored frescoes. Creation of the notorious Prince Raimondo di Sangro—alchemist, "sorcerer," and who knows what else—this chapel was built between 1749 and 1771 and houses three celebrated sculptures. Veiled Modesty and Disillusionment are bravura depictions of allegorical figures, thanks to the chisel of sculptor Corradini which blithely tranformed marble into fishing nets and diaphonous veils. Most spectacular is the centerpiece sculpture by Sammartino, known as the Veiled Christ (1753). Christ's graceful figure lies under what looks like a creepy transparent cloth, though the whole piece is crafted from a single piece of marble. On display in the basement are two rather fake-looking cadavers with (supposedly) preserved cardiovascular systems resembling a tangle of blue and red wires, which hint at the sometimes lurid history of Prince Raimondo. *V. Francesco de Sanctis 19, near P. San Domenico Maggiore, tel. 081/5518470. Admission L8,000. Open Mon. and Wed.–Sat. 10–6 (until 5 in winter), Sun. 10–1:30.*

The main streets of Spaccanapoli are among the most ancient in Italy; Via Tribunali and Via S. Biaggio dei Librai were once the Decumano Maggiore and Inferiore of the old Greco-Roman city.

DUOMO (CATHEDRAL OF SAN GENNARO) • Though the Duomo's facade is nearly overshadowed by surrounding tenements, its interior is suitably vast and extravagant—one step beyond the front doors and you know that you are in the mother church of Naples. Charles II built this cathedral at the end of the 13th century, integrating parts of a 4th-century Christian church. For L5,000 you can visit the archaeological zone under the modern church (open Mon.–Sat. 9–noon and 4:30–7, Sun. 9–noon). The Duomo's big moment comes when it hosts the yearly celebration of San Gennaro, Naples's patron saint (*see* Festivals, *below*). The all- important blood is kept in the extravagantly opulent 17th-century **Chapel of San Gennaro,** lined with medieval reliquaries, Baroque marbles, and frescoes honoring the popular saint. *V. Duomo, tel. 081/449097. Open daily 7:30–noon and 5–7:30.*

MUSEO ARCHEOLOGICO NAZIONALE • This is nothing less than the most important museum of Greek and Roman antiquities in the world—although visitors might wonder at that description when looking at the museo's untranslated labels, closed-off wings, and dusty corridors. No matter that the ground floor holds hundreds of antique sculptures waiting for your identification (labels are scarce), this remains a must-see. Just one of the treasure troves here is the famous Farnese collection, which features the largest extant sculpture from antiquity, the *Farnese Bull* and the celebrated *Farnese Hercules,* whose awesome form makes even Schwartzenegger look puny. The first floor houses a stunning collection of bronzes, while the second level has all the most important mosaics and frescoes excavated from Pompeii and Herculaneum, including the world famous Alexander mosaic floor. Empty rooms in eternal restoration hint at even more treasures. To escape the endless corridors, catch some sun in the courtyard among the scattered tombstones. *P. Museo Nazionale 19, tel. 081/440166. Metro: P. Cavour. Admission L12,000. Open Wed.–Mon. 9–2, and perhaps (this is Naples) until 9 in the summer.*

PIAZZA GESU NUOVO • In the middle of the piazza, **Guglia dell'Immacolata,** a prickly looking Spanish spire covered with saints and cherubs, exemplifies the square's Baroque design. The column faces a Jesuit church known formally as Trinità Maggiore, but popularly referred to as the **Gesù Nuovo** (tel. 081/5518613). The facade, made up of rows of stones that jut out defensively from the wall, was originally part of a 15th-century palace. In 1601 the structure was converted into a church, with a brilliant Baroque interior that contrasts sharply with the grim exterior.

SANTA CHIARA • Locals come to this huge, lofty church to hear morning mass, usually beginning at 7:30 (V. Benedetto Croce, tel. 081/552–6209). Allied bombing in 1943 destroyed the roof and gutted the Angevin Gothic interior, but restoration work returned the church to its original sparse 14th-century design. As a stunning contrast, the church's **Chiostro delle Clarisse** is adorned with magnificently colorful Rococo majolica tiles, painted with fanciful 18th-century landscapes, roses, and grapevines (unfortunately, the pathways were once covered by arbors threaded with the real thing, but these are now under restoration). In frantic, noisy Spaccanapoli, this cloister remains an exquisite island of peace. Officially, the cloister is open 8:30–12:30 and 4–6:30, but ask politely and you can see it whenever the church is open. The **Museo dell'Opera di Santa Chiara** showcases excavated Roman artifacts and medieval religious art. *V. Benedetto Croce, tel. 081/5526209. Open Mon.–Tues. and Thurs.–Sat. 9:30– 1 and 3:30–5:30, Sun. 9:30—1. Admission L5,000.*

WATERFRONT

Right in between the traffic-filled Piazza Municipio and Piazza Trieste e Trento is the lofty, spacious **Galleria Umberto I,** a marble-and-glass ancestor of the modern shopping center, built in the 19th century. These days decked-out bridal parties cross its huge mosaic floor to take wedding photos. At Christmastime the galleria shelters an enormous crèche full of *pastori* and elaborate, suspiciously Neapolitan-looking scenes (like a pizzeria) surrounding Christ's manger. Farther south, the long walk along the bay between the Castel dell'Ovo and the Mergellina district gives a more romantic impression of this often harsh city. The bay shimmers, old *pescatori* (fishermen) fly-fish from the rocks, and sun worshipers bake themselves on the large, flat stones.

If you head west from Piazza Trieste e Trento toward the Riviera di Chiaia, you'll hit the bustling shopping streets of the chichi Chiaia district, starting at **Via Chiaia.** The shops get progressively more fashionable as you move toward **Piazza dei Martiri** and **Via Calabritto.**

CASTEL DELL'OVO • The Castel dell'Ovo (literally Egg Castle) juts into the Bay of Naples from the picturesque Santa Lucia port—a spectacular setting that remains the best spot to drink in the fabled view of Vesuvius across the water. This 12th-century beige monster sits atop the remains of a Roman villa; its eclectic appearance is the work of many occupants, including the Basilican monks, the Normans, and a few Swabians. These days the castle hosts art exhibits, concerts, and other cultural events, such as the Antiqua antique show held in mid-September. *V. Partenope, tel. 081/7648311. Open Mon.– Thurs. 10:30–8., Fri.–Sun. 10:30 AM–11 PM.*

CASTEL NUOVO (MASCHIO ANGIOINO) • Overlooking the bay, the giant Castel Nuovo in Piazza Municipio was built to protect Naples against sea invasions. Its dark turrets look like something from the Scottish highlands and contrast nicely with the castle's famous sculpted entryway, the Arch of the Triumph of Alfonso, a marble masterpiece partly designed by Francesco Laurana which heralded the beginnings of the Renaissance in late medieval art. Today the castle sits placidly in the middle of a swirling nexus of traffic and houses a museum of early Renaissance works and eerie 17th-century Neapolitan religious paintings. As you enter the fortress, cross the expansive courtyard to the exhibit room. Check *Qui Napoli* or posters for information on the castle's summer pop concert series. *V. Parco del Castello, tel. 081/7952003. Exhibit room admission L10,000. Castle open Mon.–Sat. 9–7.*

PALAZZO REALE • Huge, brick-red Palazzo Reale casts a heavy shadow on Piazza del Plebiscito. The facade is flanked by statues of some of the city's conquerors, demonstrating the variety of influences on Naples. Just past the entrance, the space is dominated by a sweeping marble stairway and Aragonese armaments sculpted into the walls. Upstairs, the living apartments stretch endlessly—all gold, mirrors, and countless paintings from the early Renaissance to the 19th century. The **Biblioteca Nazionale,** with its separate entrance at the rear of the palazzo (but no separate admission), has changing exhibitions of old books and manuscripts. *P. del Plebiscito, tel. 081/5808111. Admission L8,000. Open Sun.–Tues. and Thurs.—Fri. 9—2, Sat. 9–7.*

TEATRO SAN CARLO • Teatro San Carlo, across from Galleria Umberto I, is Italy's largest and acoustically finest opera house. Built in a frantic six months, just in time for King Charles's birthday in November 1737, it was then redone in neoclassical gilt stucco. Many premieres of great operas have taken place here, including that of Donizetti's Lucia di Lammermoor. Tours are given irregularly—ask at the gate, 40 ft to the left of the ticket office. You can catch performances of opera and ballet October– June (*see After Dark, below*). *V. San Carlo 93/F, tel. 081/7972330 (gate), 081/7972331, or 081/ 7972412 (ticket office), fax 081/7972309.*

THE HILLS

Naples sprawls, and you'll need to use public transportation to reach the hilly Vomero district to the west or Capodimonte to the north.

CASTEL SANT'ELMO • Broad switchback ramparts lead to this castle, built in the 14th century under the Bourbon king Robert of Anjou, who chose the site for its strategic vantage point. It was originally designed to look like a six-point star, but later additions ruined this plan. Ascend to the broad roof and check out the astounding view of the entire city at your feet (on smogless days, that is). *Entrance on V. Tito Angelini, tel. 081/5784030. From the top of Funicolare di Montesanto Vomero station, turn right on V. E. Dalbono, right again on V. Tito Angelini. Admission L4,000. Open Tues.–Sun. 9–2.*

CERTOSA DI SAN MARTINO • Just below Castel Sant'Elmo, the 17th-century Certosa di San Martino is a flowery Baroque building designed as a solemn residence for Carthusian monks. Inside, the **Museo Nazionale di San Martino** has some eye-catching landscape paintings, but the church's ornate interior, its peaceful garden, and views from its upstairs balconies are more rewarding. *Tel. 081/5781769. Admission L9,500. Open Tues.–Sun. 9–2.*

MUSEO E GALLERIE CAPODIMONTE • Set in a large wooded park (one of Naples's best), the 18th-century Capodimonte was built as a Bourbon homestead. It now houses a collection of big-name Renaissance paintings. Italian, Spanish, and Dutch works share space with over-the-top furnishings and portraits from its days as a royal residence. Don't miss Masaccio's *Crucifixion* and the wonderful drawings by Michelangelo. *Parco di Capodimonte, tel. 081/7441307. From Stazione Centrale, Bus 110 or 127R; or from. V. Monteoliveto, Bus 24. Admission L9,500. Open Tues.–Sat. 10–7, Sun. 9–2.*

If you want to take gifts home, stroll down Via San Gregorio Armeno in Old Naples, where artisans hand-carve and paint pastori, the terra-cotta figurines used in Christmas crèches that are known to shoppers worldwide.

CHEAP THRILLS

If negotiating Piazza Garibaldi and Via Toledo has stressed you out, lie in the shade in one of Naples's public parks and relax. Along the bay from Santa Lucia to Mergellina, the **Villa Comunale** is replete with palm trees and statues arranged in the style of an English garden—perfect for a sunset promenade. For an even better view of the sea, cross Via Caracciolo (carefully) and relax on the white rocks below. In the middle of the park, look for the **Acquario** (V. A. Dohrn, tel. 081/5833263; admission L3,000; open Mon.–Sat. 9–5, Sun. 9–2), one of the oldest in the world. To get here, take Tram 1 or any bus going to Mergellina from Stazione Centrale. For a choice view of the Bay of Naples, seek out overgrown **Parco Virgiliano;** from the Mergellina train and metro station, turn right and go under the tracks; the entrance will be on your left. Here, amid the hyacinths and near the (supposed) tomb of Virgil, Boccaccio was moved to declare himself a poet. Theoretically, the park is open daily 9–1, but sometimes it stays open later. A third option is to take any funicolare that goes to the Vomero district, where you can wander in the shady, rather weed-choked gardens of the **Villa Floridiana.** The entrance is on Via D. Cimarosa, west of the three funicolare stations.

FESTIVALS

Naples's most famous festival, the **Festa di San Gennaro,** occurs on September 19, when crowds gather at the Duomo to see if the saint's preserved blood will liquefy; if not, tradition dictates that the city is headed for disaster. In 1943, for instance, the blood didn't turn, and soon afterward Vesuvius erupted. Naples suffered a severe cholera outbreak in 1973 when it again remained congealed. In addition to the September 19 festival date, the miracle is scheduled to occur on May 5 and 19, with similar pomp and circumstance. July 16 welcomes the **Festa della Madonna del Carmine,** which combines traditional religious ceremonies with popular festivities. On a more secular note, the **Festa della Musica** celebrates the coming of summer on June 21, with free outdoor concerts of all genres throughout the city.

AFTER DARK

Naples is busy after dark, with outdoor bars in **Piazza Bellini,** plenty of live music clubs, and nocturnal Neapolitan theatrics on the streets. The American GIs stationed here during World War II introduced jazz to the already lively Neapolitan music scene, and the integration has been smooth. Look in *Qui*

Napoli and the local newspaper *Il Mattino* for info on free summertime concerts, club events, theater, and movies.

Opera productions at **Teatro San Carlo** (*see* Worth Seeing, *above*) run from December to June; economy seats go for L30,000, but everything's usually sold out months in advance. Occasional concerts and ballet performances find their way here, too. The box office is open Tuesday–Saturday 10–1 and 4:30–6:30. In iffy **Piazza Municipio,** near the docks, you can spot the famous *femminelli* (transvestites). They are usually dressed like runway models at a Paris fashion show and surrounded by young Neapolitans on mopeds.

Kiss Kiss (Via Sgambati 47, tel. 081/894533) is the largest disco in town and attracts the young and restless (10 PM–3 AM Tues., Thurs., and Fri.). **Piazza di Spagna** (Via Petrarca 101, tel. 081/467453) is the dance club favorite of the high style crowd, who hip-hop here till the wee hours on weekends. Outfitted in '50s Americana, **Le Rock** (V. Bellini 9, next to P. Dante) features U.S. rock and blues played by local musicians. The ghost of Elvis is said to haunt the place, and young Italians crowd the floor till closing time. Open weekends 9 PM–2 AM, the club has more sporadic hours in summer. A student crowd kicks back in outdoor **Club 1799** (P. Bellini 71, tel. 081/294483) and at the many other cafés on the square, where it doesn't cost much more for a table on the piazza than for an espresso at the bar. In Spaccanapoli, **Riot** (V. San Biagio dei Librai 39, up the staircase in the back of the courtyard, tel. 081/7663228) will give you insight into the Neapolitan avant-garde. Jazz groups jam throughout the evening in front of young leftist intellectual types. The club is open Wednesday–Sunday 9 PM–3 or 4 AM and closed in August. Via G. Paladino, also in Old Naples, is home to several popular bars, including **Il Mattone** and **La Vineria.** For techno music and a largely gay crowd, head to **Tongue** (V. Manzoni 207, tel. 081/7690800), open weekends 9 PM–3 AM.

NEAR NAPLES

CASERTA

The main reason to go to modern Caserta, 30 km (18½ mi) north of Naples, is to visit the **Reggia di Caserta,** or Palazzo Reale, a bombastic testament to aristocratic excess. Work began on the palace in 1751 for the Bourbon king Charles II, who commissioned architect Luigi Vanvitelli to design a palace that would match the courts at Versailles and Potsdam. Two kings, more than 30 years, and 1,200 rooms later, the palace was completed in all its Baroque grandeur. Hundreds of neoclassical windows peer out at you from enormous rectangular facades, and archways and interconnecting courtyards abound.

Your visit to the **Royal Apartments** will begin grandly enough: Vanvitelli designed a staircase of marble and inlaid stone that sweeps up to the royal digs. The rest, however, is unremarkable, consisting of gilt-caked rooms with huge chandeliers dangling a few feet from the ground. Take a right at the end of the long entrance hall to reach the royal boudoirs, where Bourbons washed their regal flesh with water from hot and cold taps (a novelty at the time). *V. Douet 2/a, tel. 0823/321127. Apartments admission L8,000. Open Mon.–Sat. 9–1:30, Sun. 9–1.*

When you leave the apartments, turn right at the bottom of the staircase to reach the huge **Royal Gardens,** a popular spot for family picnics. The park's main axis stretches 3½ km (2 mi) toward the **Fountain of Diana;** if you don't feel up to the walk, hop on a shuttle (L1,500 round-trip) that'll stop at various other fountains along the way. The Fountain of Diana depicts Actaeon turning into a deer (he's about to be devoured by his own hounds for spying on the goddess at her bath). *Admission to garden L4,000. Open daily 9–1 hr before sunset.*

Beyond the famed palazzo, about all there is to do in Caserta is take Bus 10 (hourly, L1,500) from the train station or walk about 50 minutes to the mostly abandoned medieval town of **Caserta Vecchia.** Its narrow cobblestone streets, lined with terra-cotta houses, are fun to explore, if a bit spooky, and you can get a plate of homemade pasta for L5,000–L6,000 at **Medievale** (V. della Valle 10, tel. 0823/371410, closed Fri.). From Naples's Stazione Centrale (P. Garibaldi), trains run frequently to Caserta (35–50 min, L3,400); the palace is visible from the train station.

BAY OF NAPLES

From the fascinating ruins of Herculaneum and Pompeii to the gorgeous cliffs of Capri, this narrow stretch of coastline dazzles even the most jaded traveler. Greeks came to Ischia and Cumae in the 8th century BC and eventually settled throughout modern-day southern Italy. Their successors, the Romans, built cities that you can still visit today, frozen by the eruption of Mt. Vesuvius in AD 79. West of Naples are the ancient settlements of Pozzuoli and Cumae—awash in mythical lore—and the Campi Flegrei, known in classical literature as the Phlegraean (burning) Fields because of all the sulfurous smoke that rises out of them. If you head south, you might be drawn to Sorrento and the islands of Capri, Ischia, and Procida, where despite the crowds, you can still travel 2,000 years back in time or just swim in the sea.

POZZUOLI

Once a major Mediterranean port, this ancient seaside city is notable for its Roman ruins, steaming volcano, and ferry connections to Ischia and Procida. One might expect the birthplace of Italian cinema's patron saint, Sophia Loren, to be a bit flashier, but the area by the harbor still has the look and feel of a Greek fishing village. Unfortunately, most of the Old Town—some of its buildings date from Roman times—is still being rebuilt after an earthquake in 1980. It now looms sadly over the port.

Many sites in the Campi Flegrei have been affected by a geological phenomenon known as bradyseism (a slow earthquake), which has even submerged an entire Roman port on the coast between Pozzuoli and Baia.

BASICS

In Piazza Matteoti you'll find the **tourist office** (P. Matteoti 1A, tel. 081/5266639; open weekdays 9–2). To reach Pozzuoli, take either the **Cumana train** line from Naples's Stazione Montesanto (25 min west, L2,000), which will drop you one block from the port, or the **Metro** from Stazione Centrale (30 min, L1,500), which leaves you just above the Anfiteatro Flavio. **Buses** to Cumae (L1,000) stop on Via Roma between the Cumana station and the port. **Ferries** leave all day until 7 PM for Procida (40 min southwest, L3,500) and Ischia (1 hr southwest, L12,000).

WHERE TO SLEEP AND EAT

If you have to stay overnight, your few choices include the **Hotel Flegreo** (V. Campi Flegrei 30, tel. 081/5261523), a 20-minute walk from the Metro station, which has doubles with bath for L65,000, and **Da Raffaelina** (L. Taverno 7, tel. 081/8661789) with doubles at L68,000. **Il Capitano** (Lungomare C. Colombo 13, tel. 081/5262283), a restaurant on the waterfront, rents newly refurbished rooms with bath for L100,000. Or choose the **Camping Internazionale Vulcano Solfatara** (V. Solfatara 161, tel. 081/5267413, fax 081/5263482), which borders the volcanic crater itself, a 10- to 15-minute walk up Via Solfatara (or take Bus M1) from the Metro station. For L11,000–L14,000 per person and L6,500–L9000 per tent, you also get free use of the natural saunas nearby. The campground is open April–October. You can pick up some fruit, cheese, and bread at the **open-air market** (open daily 7–2) on the dock. For a quick bite near the water, **Pizza e. . .** (V. Marino Boffa at V. Roma, no phone) has pizza slices and sandwiches.

WORTH SEEING

Built under Emperor Vespasian around AD 70, the still-impressive, easy-to-spot **Anfiteatro Flavio** (V. Anfiteatro, tel. 081/5266007; admission L4,000; open Tues.–Sun. 9–1 hr before sunset) once held more than 40,000 screaming fans, and its subterranean structures remain in near-perfect condition. Look for posters advertising concerts and other performances, held here in summer. Along the waterfront, the columned **Tempio di Serapide** stands in a well-maintained garden. Once thought to be a temple dedicated to the god Serapis, it was actually a bustling Roman market in the 1st century AD. The giant **Solfatara Crater** (tel. 081/5262341; admission L8,000; open daily 8:30—1 hr before sunset), a real live volcano, is a 15-minute walk above the Metro station uphill on Via Solfatara (or take Bus M1). Visitors with a good tolerance for the smell of rotten eggs can walk down chalky pumice paths streaked

ONE HELLISH LAKE

The ancient Greeks believed that the volcanic Lago d'Averno, between Cumae and Pozzuoli, was the entrance to Hades. Birds that flew over the lake would pass out from the sulfuric gases and fall in—proof positive of the lake's demonic powers. Today, as you watch water-skiers glide over its surface without getting sucked in, you may find this calm and deserted lake less menacing than Homer, Virgil, and Dante reported it to be. It's still spooky, though, and on Sunday you may find an ancient Pozzuolean who will be willing, for a few thousand of your lire, to lead you with torches through clammy tunnels to the underground waterway where boats headed for Hades supposedly disembarked.

At one end of the lake stand the lonely remains of the Tempio di Apollo, a reminder of Roman glories. To reach the lake, take the Cumana railway to Lucrino (three stops after Pozzuoli); leaving the station, turn right, then immediately left. At the fork, bear right. For the guided tour, walk around the left side of the lake about 750 ft from where the main road hits the water and look for a vine-covered path off to the left; the Tempio di Apollo is at the right-hand end of the lake.

with sulfuric stains, stomp their feet on the hollow ground to hear the echo, and stick their heads in steaming vents.

NEAR POZZUOLI

BAIA

Baia is home to some of the most impressive Roman ruins in the Campi Flegrei. Up a staircase from the train station, you'll find the entrance to the **Parco Archeologico di Baia** (tel. 081/8687592; admission L4,000; open daily 9–1 hr before sunset). This complex includes the baths used by Roman emperors from the 1st century BC to the 3rd century AD and two surprisingly intact Roman villas. Few frescoes and tiled floors remain, but you can walk through most of the rooms and tunnels and imagine how the elite lived 2,000 years ago. Baia is four stops (southwest) past Pozzuoli on the Cumana railway; from Naples the 35-minute trip on the Cumana railway costs L2,000.

CUMAE

Dating from the 8th century BC, Cumae (Cuma), the first Greek settlement on mainland Italy, was once the most powerful city in the region. In addition to some scattered Greek and Roman ruins and views of the sea, it's home to the **Parco Archeologico** (V. Fusaro 35, tel. 081/8543060; admission L4,000), open daily from 9 to two hours before sunset (last entry one hour before closing). The park is known for the mysterious **Antro della Sibilla** (Sibyl's Cave), a triangular tunnel carved into a rock beneath Cumae's acropolis, with vaulted chambers that allow light to stream through intermittently. The far end of the tunnel was tentatively identified by Virgil as the place where Aeneas came to hear the Sibyl's oracular pronouncements. You can try out the acoustics, which may have helped the Sibyl eavesdrop on approaching wisdom seekers and prepare her prophesies. To get here, don't take the Circumflegrea railway to the Cuma stop; it's nowhere near the site. Instead, take ACTP Bus 12 from Pozzuoli (15 min, L1,500) and follow the ACROPOLI DI CUMA signs.

HERCULANEUM

Named after its mythical founder, the strong man himself, Herculaneum (Ercolano) was a Roman resort town full of posh villas with great bay views. For more than 300 years the town quietly conducted its affairs until AD 79, when pitiless Vesuvius erupted and buried the town under massive lava mud flows. The volcanic mud hardened, eventually protecting and preserving the site better than the burning lava that destroyed so much of ancient Pompeii before petrifying it. The **Scavi di Ercolano** (Ruins of Herculaneum) were first explored in earnest in the 18th century, when foreigners, mostly British, began to take an interest in them. Herculaneum is smaller than Pompeii, but it's less crowded and closer to Naples, so coming here is a wise choice if you want to see ancient Roman houses but you're short on time. A visit to the site is best combined with a hike up Mt. Vesuvius (*see* Near Herculaneum, *below*) as a day trip from Naples.

BASICS

At the **tourist office** (V. IV Novembre 84, tel. 081/7881243; open Mon.–Sat. 8–2) you can get a free map of the ruins. For a succinct account of Herculaneum's history, get a copy of archaeologist Amedeo Maiuri's expert guide at the bookstore near the entrance. From Naples's Stazione Centrale or Stazione Vesuviana, take the **Circumvesuviana** railway to the Ercolano stop (5 per hr, 20 min east, L2,200). The ruins are a five-minute walk down Via IV Novembre toward the water.

THE SITE

You are largely free to wander, with the map you received at the entrance in hand, amid the ruins of Herculaneum and discover for yourself the intact colonnades, tiled floors, and two-story buildings that form a close approximation of the Roman city of 2,000 years ago. The columns and gardens of the **House of Argus** are the remains of what was once a lavish mansion. The **Forum Baths** are a series of intricately painted rooms that include a perfectly preserved floor mosaic of Neptune. Note the steam vents ingeniously built into the baths' benches and the small overhead cubbies in which members stashed their clothing. The **House of Neptune and Anfitrite** reveals two stunning, colorful mosaics, and in the **House of the Charred Furniture** you'll see the corner of a bed and some wine jugs more or less as they were before the eruption. The well-preserved **House of the Wooden Partition** displays a wooden screen carbonized by the eruption. The beautiful interior of the luxurious **House of Deer** contains large expanses of intact frescoes, with many fascinating details protected by glass panes. There's much more to see here if you have the time, and you'll see it all more clearly if you take a flashlight to explore the dark corners. *P. Museo 1, tel. 081/739–0963. Admission L12,000. Open daily 9–1 hr before sunset (last admission 1 hr before closing).*

NEAR HERCULANEUM

MT. VESUVIUS

Dark, towering Mt. Vesuvius (Monte Vesuvio) looks out over the entire Bay of Naples. It beckons to be climbed, but those who answer the call do so at their own risk. Since its first recorded eruption in AD 79, the hot-tempered volcano has blown its top roughly every 50 years, often with catastrophic results. The last eruption was on March 19, 1944, so the clock is ticking. There is a plan to evacuate the area in case of an eruption, but few expect it to work. Vesuvius *is* constantly monitored, so nothing should take you by surprise.

No public buses run from Naples to Vesuvius, but the **Vesuviobus** (5 per day, L4,000), taken from just outside the Herculaneum train station, will take you only 1 km (½ mi) from the volcano's crater. The ride is less than an hour; call the tourist office (*see* Basics *in* Herculaneum, *above*) in Herculaneum for departure times. At the top, you're supposed to pay L6,000 for a guided visit to the crater, perhaps because puffs of steam rise up from the core as you walk along the rim, which drops off steeply at each side and lacks guardrails in some places. If you'd prefer to hike up, ask to be let off at the base of the mountain (prepare for strange looks); from here, it's a good 1½-hour trek to the top up gravelly cinder paths. Trekkers should bring water, excellent climbing shoes, and shades. The roads become scorching hot during summer, so take serious precautions against sunstroke.

To descend, you might want to take the bus back, since there's no regular stop at the base. Or consider hiking all the way back to Herculaneum (2½ hrs); you'll pass interesting vegetation growing out of the lava flows, and there's a volcano-monitoring station partway down the mountain.

POMPEII

There is probably nothing in the world like the massive ghost town of Pompeii, an imposing and haunting testament to a long-vanished civilization. Here you can see richly colored frescoes, majestic colonnades, and all the architectural details of a thriving city. Pompeii was a Greek colony before it fell to the Romans in 200 BC, when the city really began to flourish. With more than 20,000 inhabitants, the city had everything: outdoor theaters, banks, bars, working-class and wealthy districts, public baths, health clinics, and brothels. It was a hub of commercial activity in the region until Mt. Vesuvius destroyed it all in the big bang of AD 79. Luckily, for the populace, Pompeii had been partially destroyed by an earthquake that preceded the eruption; many citizens fled the town then, leaving only 25% of the original population to be buried in the blast. Today tourists come in droves to peek into the incredibly well-preserved buildings, stare at the plaster casts of the eruption's victims, and ímagine life in the days of the Caesars. More than a place of astonishing beauty, Pompeii also has the power to suddenly transport you back into a strange and mysterious world.

Visiting Pompeii does have its frustrating aspects: Many buildings are blocked off by locked gates, and enormous group tours tend to clog up more popular attractions. But the site is so big that it's easy to lose yourself amid the quiet side streets. To really see the site, you'll need four or five hours. If you're short on time, consult the suggested itineraries posted by the entrance, but don't waste your money on the expensive guided tours. Occasionally you may find yourself wanting a flashlight, as many buildings aren't open to the sky. Since most of the mosaics and frescoes that once decorated Pompeii's homes—the ones that weren't looted, anyway—have been removed from the site for preservation, also visit the Museo Archeologico Nazionale in Naples (*see* Worth Seeing *in* Naples, *above*) for a fuller understanding of the culture of ancient Pompeii.

BASICS

Down the hill and across the main road from Porta Marina is a **small tourist office** (Porta Marina Inferiore, tel. 1670/13350 toll-free), where you can pick up a free map of the site. The **main tourist office** (V. Sacra 1, tel. 081/8507255, fax 081/8632401) is next to the east entrance; both are open weekdays 8–3 and 4–7 and Saturday 8–2.

COMING AND GOING

From Naples's Stazione Centrale or Vesuviana, the Sorrento line of the Circumvesuviana railway system runs trains to the Pompeii Scavi stop (2–3 per hr, 35 min southeast, L3,100), which is about halfway to Sorrento (do not go to any other stop named Pompeii). Leaving the station, walk 100 ft to the right and you'll see the **Porta Marina** entrance.

WHERE TO SLEEP

It's best to make it a day trip from Sorrento or Naples, since there's not much to do but visit the site. If you decide to stay anyway, leave the station to your left and walk five minutes up to **Motel Villa dei Misteri** (V. Villa dei Misteri 11, tel. 081/8613593, fax 081/8622983), where doubles with sparkling bathrooms and firm beds are only L80,000. Campers should walk over to **Camping Zeus** (tel. 081/8615320), slightly to the left of the train station. You'll pay L7,500 per person and L5,000 per tent all year long, and passably decent rooms are available for L65,000.

WHERE TO EAT

Avoid the restaurants by the train station or Villa dei Misteri entrance, and head out instead into modern Pompeii—use the Via del Pace entrance or ride from the station using the No. 4 bus (tickets purchased on board; tell them you want to get off near the church). **Trattoria "addù Mimì Donnarumma"** (Via Roma 61, tel. 0347/9550133; closed Fri.), near the entrance to Pompeii by the ancient ampitheater, has genuine homestyle food, and no sign at all outside, which is a good sign in Italy: this is where the locals go.

THE SITE

As you enter the ruins at Porta Marina, make your way to the **Forum,** which served as Pompeii's cultural, political, and religious center. You can still see some of the two stories of colonnades that used to line the square. Here vendors sold goodies from their reserved spots in the central market, politicians let rhetoric fly, and worshipers croweded the **Temple of Jupiter.** The **House of the Tragic Poet** is famous for the black-and-white mosaic of a dog at the entrance, with the message CAVE CANEM (beware of the dog). The

POMPEII

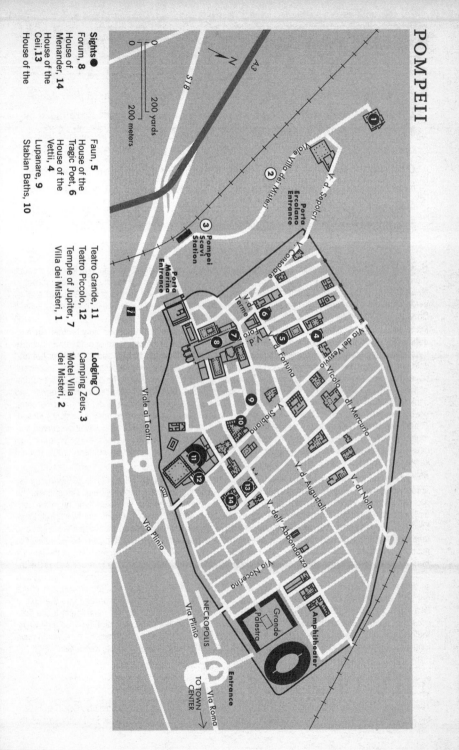

Sights ●
Forum, **8**
House of the
Menander, **14**
House of the
Ceii, **13**
House of the

Faun, **5**
House of the
Tragic Poet, **6**
House of the
Vettii, **4**

Teatro Grande, **11**
Teatro Piccolo, **12**
Temple of Jupiter, **7**
Villa dei Misteri, **1**

Lodging ○
Camping Zeus, **3**
Motel Villa
dei Misteri, **2**

Lupanare, **9**
Stabian Baths, **10**

200 yards
200 meters

POMPEIIAN REAL ESTATE DESIGN

By peeking into houses in Pompeii, you'll start to notice patterns in their design. Life revolved around the atrium, an uncovered inner courtyard surrounded by a colonnade, from which the occupants received air, sunlight, and rainwater, the latter caught by the Jacuzzi-shape receptacle under the sloped roof. Opposite the entrance was the living room/dining room; to the left and right were bedrooms and the hearth. Some families built a shop or bar on the street, with living quarters behind it. Interior floors and walls were covered with colorful marble tiles, mosaics, and frescoes.

House of the Faun was named for the bronze sculpture of a tiny but wild-looking faun in its central court; the original sculpture is in the Museo Archeologico Nazionale (*see* Worth Seeing *in* Naples, *above*) in Naples. Look for the traces of costly marble that once lined the walls. The **House of the Vettii** has a lovely garden and a small room of well-preserved Roman paintings, but most remember it for its depictions of Priapus, who shows off with absurdly swollen pride why he is the god of fertility.

For a gander at additional raunchy frescoes, head to the **Lupanare,** an intact two-story brothel. An illustration of a particular sexual act adorns the entry to each prostitute's room, large enough for an uncomfortable-looking stone bed. Pompeii's largest bathhouse, the **Stabian Baths,** had a variety of hot and cold baths, steam rooms, a swimming pool, courts for boccie ball, and even boxing rings. The rooms still have intact vaulted ceilings and elaborate floor mosaics. The **Teatro Grande** held 5,000 ancient Pompeiians, with box seats for bigwigs, and now hosts weekend music performances in the summer and early fall (ask at the tourist office for more info). The covered **Teatro Piccolo,** used for small concerts, poetry readings, and ballet, held 1,300 people. The luxurious **House of Menander** is currently closed. The **House of the Ceii** includes a large fresco showing hunting scenes with several well-preserved surrounding panels. The large *anfiteatro* seated 20,000 spectators in its day and was one of the most raucous (and egalitarian) social spots in town. From here you can meander west on a different route if you'd like to take a look at more of the ruins.

A bit out of the way, the amazingly intact, cryptic murals of the **Villa dei Misteri** (Villa of the Mysteries) are worth the walk as they are the most celebrated surviving frescoes from antiquity. Once inside the gates of Pompeii, look for the signs to the villa, which are everywhere, or just keep heading in the general northwest direction. The most direct way to get to the villa is through the ruins' northwest exit, Porta Ercolano; it was closed at press time (summer 1999), so you'll have to go out the Porta Marina exit and take a 10-minute walk up Viale Villa dei Misteri past the train station instead (you'll need your ticket to get in). Unearthed in 1909, this villa had more than 60 rooms painted with frescoes, many in the famous Pompeian red. At one end of the house, just in front of the back entrance to the Pompeii site, is the triclinium (or dining room) covered with the legendary fresco cycle representing the exotic, intriguing, and seductive Dionysian rites of initiation. The process, depicted in eight scenes starting from left of the entrance, has plenty of sexual overtones, including flagellation, a symbolic marriage into the cult, a Dionysian dance, and the unveiling of a phallus. Scholars endlessly debate the meaning of these frescoes, but anyone can tell they are the most beautiful paintings left to us by antiquity. In several ways, the eruption of Vesuvius was a blessing in disguise, for without it, these masterworks of art would have long ago perished. *Tel. 081/8575280. Admission L12,000. Open daily 9–1 hr before sunset.*

THE ISLANDS

The islands in the Bay of Naples offer a scene for everyone. Capri has chichi cafés and Gucci stores for the rich; the rest of us will have to settle for pathways running beside cactus-covered cliffs and whitewashed Arabian houses. Enormous Ischia offers sandy beaches, thermal spas, and a 2,600-ft dormant volcano. Meanwhile, tiny Procida is perfect for those seeking to escape the crowds and take in island life without shelling out exorbitant sums.

CAPRI

Capri has long been the life of the party in the Bay of Naples, frequented by emperors Augustus and Tiberius and later by artists and intellectuals such as Maxim Gorky, who headed a school for communist revolutionaries that was visited by both Lenin and Stalin. In summer a zillion tourists swarm over the island, and the towns of Capri and Anacapri and the port feel like ant farms, but you can still find yourself alone atop a cliff without a trace of humanity in sight. You can climb mountains that suddenly drop off into the sea, wander through Roman ruins, and swim in the clear blue water off beautiful, rocky beaches. The only real drawback to Capri is that it's much more expensive than the rest of the region. Taking the earliest hydrofoil and making Capri a day trip will save you money, but a midnight walk on the island's deserted pathways, with the smell of jasmine in the warm evening breeze, can be an unforgettable part of your trip through Campania.

BASICS

There are **AACST** information offices at the base of the main dock in Marina Grande (tel. 081/8370634), below the campanile in the center of Capri Town (P. Umberto I, tel. 081/8370686) and off Piazza Vittoria in Anacapri (V. Orlandi 59/A, tel. 081/8371524). All three offices offer a good map of the island for free. The **main post office** (V. Roma 50, tel. 081/8377240) is in Capri, off Piazza Umberto I. You can make calls from the **Telecom** center in Capri (P. Umberto I, above info office, tel. 081/8375550), open daily 9–1 and 3–10 (until 8 in winter) and in Anacapri (P. Vittoria 5, tel. 081/8373377; open daily 9–5). **Luggage storage** is available at the top of Capri's funicular or at Anacapri's Telecom office.

In summer you can buy and taste Vesuvian wine at stands scattered around the base of Mt. Vesuvius. Just be sure you drink it on the way down, not up.

COMING AND GOING

The carriers that serve Capri are **Alilauro** (tel. 081/8376965), **Caremar** (tel. 081/8370700), **SNAV** (tel. 081/8377577), and **Navigazione Libera del Golfo** (tel. 081/8370819). Frequent hydrofoils run to both of Naples's ports (40 min south, L16,000), Sorrento (20 min south, L13,000), and Amalfi (1 hr southeast, L19,000); service is less frequent to Positano (35 min southeast, L18,000), Salerno (1 hr 50 min southeast, L20,000), and Ischia (50 min southwest, L20,000). Ferries are cheaper than hydrofoils but take longer. They run to Naples (1 hr 20 min, L8,800) and Sorrento (40 min, L9,000). All the ticket offices are on the waterfront by the port. If you have cash to burn and you want to save time, from May to September there is direct helicopter service (tel. 081/7896273 or 081/5844355) between Capodichino Airport (*see* Basics *in* Naples, *above*) and Capri or Ischia.

GETTING AROUND

It's easy to get around on foot on most of the island, but because of the steep terrain, most people use public transportation between the Marina Grande (the main port), Capri Town, and Anacapri. You may have to wait in line for the cog railway (L3,400 round-trip) from Marina Grande to Capri town. Buses (L1,700) between towns run every 20 minutes; they also stop at the two main ports and some major points of interest. A funicular connects Marina Grande with Piazza Umberto I, the center of Capri Town, every 15 minutes (L3,000 round-trip).

WHERE TO SLEEP

Even the most spartan rooms are costly all over swank Capri, but you can try to talk down the price off-season, and several private residences offer furnished *affitacamere* (rooms for rent) at decent rates. Reserve your room weeks ahead for travel July through September.

CAPRI TOWN • Hotel Villa Certosa (Via Certosa 3/B, tel. and fax 081/8370005) is enchantingly homey and set just a stone's throw from Capri's spectacular Certosa monastery (now a museum); breakfast on the hotel's beautiful palm-shaded terrace, set below the hotel's veranda and double rooms (L170,000–L240,000), is a memorable way to start off your Capri day. **Stella Maris** (V. Roma 27, tel. 081/8370452, fax 081/8378662), a friendly family-run pension with sea views, has doubles (L100,000–

L120,000) right across from the main bus stop. **La Tosca** (V. D. Birago 5, tel. 081/8370989), run by a cheerful Italian-American couple, has doubles sharing impeccably clean hallway bathrooms for L95,000, and doubles with private bath for L135,000

ANACAPRI • Prices in Anacapri are significantly lower. The best deal is **Il Girasole** (V. Linciano 47, tel. 081/8372551, fax 081/8373880), where doubles begin at L90,000. The warm owners, Arnaldo and Silvana, also run a restaurant where you can get American breakfasts and inexpensive home-cooked Italian dinners. Call ahead, and they'll pick you up at the port. Recently featured in a May 1999 Travel & Leisure article on Capri, **Villa Eva** (V. La Fabbrica 8, tel. 081/8372040) charges L100,000–120,000 for comfortable doubles with bath and access to a garden and Mediterranean views, and L45,000 per person in their semi-private rooms. The Eva will pick you up from the bus stop in Anacapri.

MARINA GRANDE • A good bet is the modern **Hotel Belvedere e Tre Re** (V. Marina Grande 264, just west of the port, tel. and fax 081/8370345), where doubles (L140,000–L180,000) include bath and breakfast.

WHERE TO EAT

You'll pay high prices, even for the island's own products: wine, fish, fruits, and vegetables. Buying unprepared foods from bakeries and markets is the best way to eat cheaply. Especially in Capri, most restaurants are high on ambience, with patios and views, but unexceptional in quality. Watch out for high cover and service charges that tend to inflate your bill.

CAPRI TOWN • Head for **Scialapopolo** (V. Le Botteghe 31, tel. 081/8370246; open Tues.–Sun. 8–8), a cafeteria-style place where you can choose your own selection of antipasti and vegetables like grilled zucchini and eggplant. For dessert get the classic *capresina* (chocolate cake with almonds) at **Sfizi di Pane** (V. Le Botteghe 4).

ANACAPRI • You can eat cheap pizza and sandwiches at popular **Aumm Aumm** (V. Caprile 18, tel. 081/8372061, closed Mon.). Try the penne with tomatoes, mozzarella, and eggplant or local dishes like ravioli *alla caprese* (also with tomatoes and mozzarella). Prices are moderate though not cheap. Finally, if you want to splurge, take Via Migliera out of Anacapri to Belvedere Migliera to find **Da Gelsomina** (V. Migliera 72, tel. 081/8371499, lunch only in off-season, lunch and dinner in summer, closed Tues.), which serves excellent food at high but justified prices.

MARINA GRANDE • On the waterfront, the best option is **Buonocuore** (tel. 081/8370384), a *tavola calda* (cafeteria) just to the right of the funicular, where you can get a *panino caprese* (sandwich with tomatoes and mozzarella) for L4,000 and small pizzas for L3,000. The owners also run **Da Peppino,** a restaurant on the same block with pizzas from L5,000 and simple dishes like lasagna.

WORTH SEEING

CAPRI TOWN • In this silly little place, centered on **Piazza Umberto I,** you can burn half your daily budget on a gelato or beer. Chances are you'll want to escape this adult's Disneyland as soon as possible, especially as Capri's visiting celebs now hole up in their private villas and no longer grace the "piazzetta"—at least not during summer months. The flower-filled **Giardini di Augusto,** atop a cliff at the south end of Capri Town, has a stupendous view of the Faraglioni Rocks and the cliffs to the northwest. Even farther from the madding crowds is Capri's major attraction, the **Villa Jovis.** Seven thousand square meters and several stories high, the enormous palace of the Roman emperor Tiberius has been dismembered since its discovery in the 1930s, but you can still climb around its crumbling walls. Right near the entrance is Tiberius's Rock, a sheer cliff off which the manic tyrant supposedly threw unlucky subordinates—so the lurid legend goes, now believed by historians to be negative propaganda created by later scandalmongers. It turns out dear Tiberius was really a quiet homebody who spent most of his time indulging in his hobby——astronomy. *From P. Umberto I, head east on V. Le Botteghe and take V. Tiberio (45-min hike). Admission L4,000. Open daily 9–2 hrs before sunset.*

ANACAPRI • The island's most beautiful house is the **Villa San Michele** (V. Axel Munthe, tel. 081/8371401; open daily 9–6 in summer, 9:30–3:30 in winter; admission L8,000), built by the Swedish doctor and humanitarian Axel Munthe in the late 19th century. It houses an eclectic collection of ancient art, most of which he dug up from his own backyard (his villa was built on the ruins of one of Tiberius's) and incorporated into his whitewashed walls and shady arbor. Built on one of Capri's highest peaks, the villa's terraced gardens offer a Cinerama view of the entire Bay of Naples. The 18th-century octagonal **Chiesa di San Michele** (P. San Nicola, tel. 081/8372396; admission L2,000) has a hand-painted tile floor with a Neapolitan artist's rendition of earthly paradise. It's open daily 9–7 in summer (10–5:30 in winter). If you're lounging in Anacapri and not sure what to do, stop by **Capri in Miniature** (V. Orlandi

103–105; admission L6,000), a 40-ft-long model of the island by the artist Sergio Rubino that gives an introduction to Capri's sights and history.

Anacapri's most popular site is the celebrated **Grotta Azzurra** (Blue Lagoon), a large cavern lighted up from underwater by sunlight reflecting off the submerged limestone walls. It glows an eerie blue, but boatloads of tourists popping flashbulbs detract from the dazzle. Back when, Tiberius used this cool place as for summertime meals and frolics. The only way in is to pay L14,000 for a brief peek from a rowboat, which you can do from 9 until 5 (closing earlier in winter). To get there, you can take a boat from Marina Grande (L7,600 round-trip) or a 10-minute bus ride from Anacapri.

AFTER DARK

For many, the most tantalizing after-hours activity is to head for a private lookout point with a bottle of Capri wine, and it's probably your best response to Capri's uninspired nightlife. Streets like **Via Camerelle** and **Via Vittorio Emanuele** are full of formulaic clubs and/or piano bars, repeated endlessly. On weekends **Number 2** (V. Camerelle 1, tel. 081/8377078) becomes an expensive disco for the well-heeled. For a change, you can try **Guarracino** (V. Castello 7, tel. 081/8370514; closed Tues.) or **Anema e Core** (V. Sella Orta 1), which feature Neapolitan music. Anacapri is a more normal town, with less glitzy nightclubs like **Zeus** (V. Orlandi 103, tel. 081/8371169) and **Underground** (V. Orlandi 259, tel. 081/8372523). Prepare to part with a *bundle* for drinks.

OUTDOOR ACTIVITIES AND SPORTS

Despite the cutesiness of Capri Town, the island is blessed with tremendous natural beauty, its towering cliffs plunging into the sea on all sides. If you're here only for the day, take the *seggiovia* (chairlift; tel. 081/8371428) from Piazza Vittoria in Anacapri to the top of **Monte Solaro.** After the 12-minute ride, you'll be awestruck by the almost 90-degree drop and 360-degree view down the cliff to the water. Tickets cost L5,000 one-way, L7,000 round-trip, and the lift runs daily 9:30–6 (until 3:30 in winter).

BEACHES • A beach in Capri is a narrow strip of rocks from which you can swim without having to dive off a cliff. Most easily accessible is one just west of Marina Grande. If you take the bus to Marina Piccola and walk down to the water, there is a small beach to your right; continue straight ahead past the shops and climb out on the **Scoglio delle Sirene,** a rocky outcrop that the ancients believed was the place the Sirens lured Odysseus with their song. This has a good view of the island's southern cliffs and is next to some of Capri's prettiest beach clubs and cafés. A few minutes west of the Grotta Azzurra is **Giovanni a Gradola,** a tiny but popular beach. Finally, you can take the 10-minute bus ride from Anacapri all the way out to Faro. Below you on the right (facing the lighthouse) is a cove where you can swim; if you walk around the north side of the lighthouse, the rocks of the **Punta Carena,** the farthest tip of the island, beckon to be climbed.

HIKING • Capri is a novice hiker's paradise, with plenty of moderate hikes that lead to stunning vistas. One of the simplest routes is to take Anacapri's Via Caposcuro and Via Migliera south to the **Belvedere di Migliera,** a lookout point above a cliff on the island's south side. For another great hike, from Capri Town follow Via Camerelle–Via Tragara past ritzy hotels and villas to a terrific southward vista, within spitting distance of the Faraglioni Rocks. From here there's a path leading down to the secluded beaches under the Faraglioni; head here for lunch at the legendary Da Luigi (Via Faraglioni 2, tel. 081/837–0951). Back up on Via Tragara–Via Pizzolungo, climb the stairs to reach the dramatic cliffs. If you turn right on Via Arco Naturale and climb the bell, you'll reach the Arco Naturale, a large, twisted natural limestone arch that overlooks the sea. Here, too, is one of Capri's most idyllic places for lunch or dinner: Le Grotelle (Localitá Arco Naturale, tel. 081/837–5719), set under an arbor overlooking the Bay of Naples. To return to town, follow Via Arco Naturale to Via Matermania and head down the hill. A short but dizzying hike descends the cliff beneath the **Giardini di Agosto.** Via Matteotti is closed just beneath the gardens because of the risk of falling rocks, but some people climb around the gate and walk down the cliff's series of switchbacks. After the path straightens out, there's a path on your left; veer left where it divides, and you'll come to the **Grotta dell'Arsenale,** a large cave in the base of the cliff and one of Capri's most secluded beaches. Once you're back on the main path, you can go downhill to Marina Piccola.

WATER SPORTS • Head to **Sercomar** (Largo Fontana 64, tel. 081/8378781), in Marina Grande, if you're interested in snorkeling or scuba diving (L100,000 per dive) or want to rent an inflatable motorboat (from L75,000 per hr). Two-hour boat tours of the island, leaving from Marina Grande, cost L19,000, but they do show you some parts of Capri that are otherwise inaccessible.

ISCHIA

From sandy beaches to densely wooded hills, Ischia's natural beauty easily compares with that of the more cosmopolitan Capri across the bay. Even though much of the island's important natural resources—sand, ancient pine trees, and thermal mud—have been annexed by pricey resorts, the island is big enough so that you can get far away from the four-star hotels and their clientele and even escape the motorcycles that seem to have followed you from Naples. Outside of **Ischia Porto,** the touristy port area, the island is divided into six tiny towns, communities that have managed to maintain their identity despite the island's popularity with vacationing Germans. The natives are hoping for a new influx of visitors from all nations, thanks to the recent Anthony Minghella film version of Patricia High-smith's The Talented Mr. Ripley, in which Ischia's seductive locales share the screen with the likes of Matt Damon and Gwyneth Paltrow.

BASICS

The **AACST** office (hydrofoil dock, tel. 081/991464) gives out info on sights and lodging Monday–Saturday 8–1 and 4–7. Ferries (1½ hrs west, L10,000) and hydrofoils (45 min, L18,000) run all day until about 8 PM between Naples (Molo Beverollo or Mergellina) and Ischia (Ischia Porto or Casamicciola Terme). The two big carriers are **Caremar** (tel. 081/984818) and **Linee Lauro** (tel. 081/5522838). The main **bus station** is at Ischia Porto between the ferry and hydrofoil docks; the CD and CS lines both circle the island (clockwise and counterclockwise, respectively), but don't stop everywhere. Tickets valid for one hour cost L1,500; L4,500 tickets are valid for the entire day.

WHERE TO SLEEP, EAT, AND BE MERRY

Accommodations on Ischia are both plentiful and pricey. Your first choice should be **Locanda sul Mare** in Ischia Porto (V. Iasolino 90, tel. 081/981470, fax 081/981470), on the waterfront between the ferry and hydrofoil docks. Doubles cost L75,000–L90,000; the owner offers 20% discounts at the stunningly beautiful Negombo thermal resort as well as enthusiastic advice for your stay. If that's full, head up Via Quercia, to the left of the main bus station, to **Pensione Rosita** (V. Quercia 48, tel. 081/993875), where doubles, all with bath, go for L60,000–L70,000. **Camping Internazionale Isola d'Ischia** (V. Foschini 1, tel. 081/991449, fax 081/991472; closed mid-Oct.–mid-May.) costs L10,000–L15,000 for a space and L12,000–L18,000 per person. From Ischia Porto, take the main road east; at the fork (15 min) stay to the right (V. M. Mazzella); turn left on Via Foschini. When your stomach starts grumbling, visit Ischia Porto's **open-air market** at the port weekdays 11–2. Along the docks, **Ristorante da Emiddio** (V. Porto 30, tel. 081/992432) and **Da Scatoletta** (V. Iasolino 64, tel. 081/991389) both serve pizzas and classic dishes like risotto *alla pescatora* (seafood risotto). At night, the *riva destra* (the right side of the port, facing the water) teems with young Neapolitans, who dine well past midnight; you can join them at discos like **Disco Bambo** (V. Porto 54, tel. 081/992070).

OUTDOOR ACTIVITIES AND SPORTS

If you are tempted to climb Ischia's dormant volcano, **Mt. Epomeo,** take Bus CD or CS to Fontana. Allow an hour for the hike to the top, which has a spectacular view of, well, everything. For water sports, stop by the **Dimensione Blu** diving centers at Ischia Porto (V. Iasolino 106, tel. 081/985008) and Lacco Ameno (Baia di San Montano, tel. 081/986152), and check **Maronti** (Spiagga di Maronti, Camping Mirage, tel. 081/990551) for snorkeling (L10,000) or scuba diving (L45,000) equipment rentals.

WORTH SEEING

Just south of Ischia Porto in mellow **Ischia Ponte** (take Bus 7 or walk 30 min), a 15th-century cause-way leads to the **Castello Aragonese** (admission L8,000; open 9–sunset), an ancient fortress largely rebuilt in the 14th and 15th centuries. Inside the castle grounds you can see fortifications, several churches, and on a clear day a view of the entire Gulf of Naples. The white-sand cove of **Spiaggia dei Maronti** (take Bus 5 to the end) is Ischia's most picturesque beach; a steep 30-minute walk from the west end of the beach brings you to the tiny fishing port of **Sant'Angelo,** with colorful buildings built into the side of a cliff. If you're coming from the port, Bus 1 or CS to Cava Grado will also get you to Sant'Angelo; from where the bus deposits you, it's a 10-minute walk to the water. On the west coast, **Forio,** accessible by the same buses, has a stretch of sandy beach (to the north) and the whitewashed chapel of **Santa Maria del Soccorso** on a rocky cliff—an incredible sunset spot.

PROCIDA

In sharp contrast to its glitzy neighbors, Procida is a small and isolated island that offers a fairly realistic look into Campanian life. It doesn't look a lot different today than it did as the setting for that Oscar winning film *Il Postino* (*The Postman*), the story of Pablo Neruda in exile. The brightly painted fishing boats that crowd the main *porto* still generate the island's primary income, and the old *pescatori* (fishermen) repairing their nets would much rather see a fat morning's catch than a fat tourist. You can walk across the 4-km (2½-mi) island in about an hour, and the people you pass on your way will be sure to give you a once-over.

BASICS

At the port, you'll find the **AACST** info office (tel. 081/8101968; open daily 9–1 and 4–7). **Caremar** (tel. 081/8967280), in Naples, runs regular hydrofoils (30 min, L13,500) and ferries (1 hr, L7,200) to Procida. Two bus lines, the **L1** and the **L2,** make frequent trips from the port to Chiaiolella and back; buy tickets (L1,500 per trip) at tobacco shops by the port.

WHERE TO SLEEP

The **Riviera** (V. G. da Procida 36, tel. 081/8967197), near Chiaiolella, has doubles with bath for L95,000–L110,000. Take Bus L2 from the port and tell the driver where you're going. The **Savoia** (V. la Vatera 32, tel. 081/8967616) has doubles with shared bath for L70,000. **La Rosa dei Venti** (V. Vittorio Rinaldi 32, near the port, tel. 081/8968385) rents bungalows that sleep two to six people for L35,000 per person per night (L40,000 in July and August).

Visiting Ischia may give you the liberating feeling that the American invasion has come to an end; the island's second language— spoken constantly by most people in the tourist industry—is not English, but German.

WORTH SEEING

The **porto,** where ferries and hydrofoils dock and buildings are distinguished by different stages of fading pastel paint, lies on one end of the island; the small harbor community of **Chiaiolella,** with a few waterfront cafés and bars, occupies the other. Connected by bridge to Chiaiolella is the little island of **Vivano,** with good hiking and bird-watching terrain. Two long beaches bracket Procida: **Spiaggia Ciraccio,** on the north side and the less accessible **Spiaggia Chiaia,** at the foot of huge cliffs, on the south side.

About 1 km (½ mi) south of the port, the town of **Ponte Lingua** has most of the island's historical action, with a 14th- century **castello** (closed to the public) and a 16th-century **basilica** (open daily 11–2) perched atop the cliffs. The basilica gives you a good sense of the symbolism involved in southern Italian Catholicism: skulls adorn the walls, and the basement is filled with skeletons. There's a great view from the basilica's library (admission L2,000), which has antique furniture and medieval manuscripts.

SORRENTO

"Come Back to Sorrento" goes the famous song, and many visitors here do exactly that, enchanted by the town's setting on the Bay of Naples, its historic center—a Belle Epoque jewel—and the resort's legacy of English politesse, still palpable more than a century after the era of the Grand Tour. Most of Sorrento stretches across a plateau that ends abruptly at a steep tufa cliff 100 ft above the sea. Hotels and villas monopolize most of the cliff's edge and the bay views that inspired artists like Richard Wagner, Maxim Gorky, and Henrik Ibsen. At the base of the cliff are ports and wood-and-concrete beaches, where sunbathers deep-fry in coconut oil. Clean, quiet, and tourist-friendly, Sorrento in summer is overrun by foreigners who seek a base for exploring the region but are afraid to stay in Naples. You may hear more English (especially British English) and German than Italian.

BASICS

The **tourist information office** (V. Luigi de Maio 35, tel. 081/8074033; open summer 8–8; winter, Mon.–Sat. 8:30–2:30 and 3:30–6:30) is staffed by people with ample information on everything, as well as a decent map of the city. The **American Express** representative is Acampora Travel (P. Lauro 12, tel. 081/8072363), open weekdays 9–1 and 3–7, Saturday 9–1, Sunday 10–12:30. The **post office** (C. Italia 210/S–V, tel. 081/8781636) exchanges money and is open Monday–Saturday 8:15–7:20. You'll find **currency exchange** offices all over the central part of town, but they give consistently poor rates. You pay in cash to use the metered phones at the **Telecom** office (P. Tasso 37, tel. 081/8073317; open Mon.–Sat. 9–1 and 4–10, Sun. 10–1 and 5–10).

COMING AND GOING

Sorrento is small and well-mannered enough that **hitching** a ride isn't difficult. If you're heading south, try picking up a ride at the southern edge of town on Corso Italia, where it becomes the highway Via del Capo.

BY TRAIN • The private trains on the **Circumvesuviana** line (tel. 081/7792144, for what it's worth) make frequent trips between Sorrento and Naples's Stazione Centrale (1 hr southeast, L4,700), stopping along the way at Pompeii (30 min southeast, L3,500) and Herculaneum.

BY BUS • **SITA** (tel. 081/5522176) sends buses to the Amalfi Coast hourly, stopping at Positano (45 min east, L2,200) and Amalfi (1½ hrs, L4,400). Buses leave from the train station. Buy tickets at Mayflower Bar and Bar dei Fiori in Piazza Lauro, the newspaper stand in the train station, or Bar Tonino in Piazza Tasso.

BY BOAT • **Alilauro** (tel. 081/7871430) and **Caremar** (tel. 081/8073077) provide frequent hydrofoil service to Naples (30 min northwest, L12,000) and Capri (20 min southwest, L13,000); there are also a few departures for Ischia (40 min west, L18,000) and Amalfi (45 min east, L16,000). Five ferries a day go to Capri (50 min, L9,000).

GETTING AROUND

Sorrento's main street is **Corso Italia,** which runs parallel to the cliff above the port. From the train station, walk downhill one block to Corso Italia; **Piazza Tasso,** the main square, is two blocks to your left. From the port, take Via de Maio (the only street) toward the cliff. It's only a 10-minute walk to town, but if you have luggage, you may want to take the local Circumvesuviana buses (L1,700). For L60,000 a day, **Sorrento Rent a Scooter** (C. Italia 210/A, tel. 081/8781386) helps you buzz around town.

WHERE TO SLEEP

Many of Sorrento's hotels are open only from March or April through October and are generally packed; call in advance, or you may have a hard time finding a room. Every room in small **Hotel City** (C. Italia 221, tel. and fax 081/8772210) has a patio or a terrace, but all of them face busy Corso Italia, which almost never quiets down. Doubles cost L85,000–100,000, depending on the season. Comfortable and homey **Hotel del Corso** (C. Italia 134, tel. 081/8073157; closed Nov.–mid-Feb.), run by a laid-back family, has sunny doubles (L120,000 with bath) with colorful bedspreads and sparse wooden furniture. Closest to the station, **Hotel Nice** (C. Italia 257, tel. 081/8781650, fax 081/8071154, closed Dec.–Feb.) offers clean doubles (L90,000–L115,000 including breakfast) with modern furnishings and baths. **Pensione Linda** (V. degli Aranci 125, tel. 081/8782916) has an ugly exterior, uninspiring rooms, and does not take credit cards, but for L70,000–L90,000 a double, the beds are firm and the bathrooms are large.

CAMPING • **International Camping Nube d'Argento** (V. del Capo 21, tel. 081/8781344; closed Oct.–Mar.) costs L10,000–L14,000 per person, L7,000 per tent. To get here, take Corso Italia until it becomes Via del Capo. Farther out on Via del Capo, **Villaggio Campeggio Santa Fortunata** (V. del Capo 41, tel. 081/8073579, fax 081/8073590; closed Nov.–Mar.) has its own beach and hot showers and costs L10,000–L15,000 per person, L7,500–L9,500 per site, or L85,000–L125,000 for a two-person bungalow. Both campgrounds have washing machines.

WHERE TO EAT

For cheap eats, seek out the *rosticcerie* and produce stands along car-free **Via San Cesareo**, off Piazza Tasso. Corso Italia is a locus for cheap pizzerias; don't miss pizza *sorrentina* (with broccoli, sausage, and mozzarella). A **Standa** supermarket (C. Italia 223) provides basic food and sundries. Next door, **Bar Rita** (C. Italia 219, tel. 081/8781420) has delicious homemade pastries, thick pizza slices, and *arancini* (balls of rice, tomatoes, mushrooms, and meat, with melted mozzarella in the center). The center has some reasonably priced trattorias, but avoid eating right on touristy Piazza Tasso. **Gigino** (V. degli Archi 15, tel. 081/8781927; closed Tues.) serves excellent local specialties, with a fixed-price lunch menu. You can get specialties like gnocchi *alla sorrentina* (with tomatoes and mozzarella) or pizza with shellfish at **La Lanterna** (V. S. Cesareo 23, tel. 081/8781355). For an impressive gelato selection, drop by **Pollio** (C. Italia 172, tel. 081/8782190).

WORTH SEEING

There are no must-see sights in Sorrento—instead, the entire historic town is the main course: a three-dimensional stage set, full of picturesque alleys, sorbet-hued palazzi, and belvederes overlooking the

Bay of Naples. The 14th-century cloister of the **Chiesa di San Francesco** (tel. 081/8781269) reveals delicate archways covered in flowering vines, earning its nickname "del Paradiso." Take Via S. Francesco out of Piazza San Antonino. The richly adorned **cathedral** (C. Italia, tel. 081/8782248) is graced with everything from large ceiling paintings to inlaid woodwork (a Sorrentine artistic specialty); it's usually open in the morning and around 5–7 in the evening. **Via S. Cesareo** is the main pedestrian street running from Piazza Tasso through the historic core. Take this to the tiny square that's home to the 16th-century **Sedile Dominova**—a frescoed loggia that was once an assembly hall for nobles; opposite the loggia, take in the passing parade by enjoying a time-out at Caffé 2000, the most delightful of all Sorrento's delightful cafés. If it's raining, you may want to pay L8,000 to visit the **Museo Correale di Terranova** (V. Correale 48, tel. 081/8781846; open Wed.—Mon. 9–2), a former palace that displays a collection of ancient statues, Italian art, woodwork, and furniture. It's a five-minute walk from Piazza Tasso.

AFTER DARK

During warm months, residents and visitors take to the streets, spilling onto Corso Italia, crowding the seaside view spots, and gathering on the main piazzas. The youngest group collects on **Piazza Achille Lauro,** near the train station. British-style pubs are scattered around the center, providing English tourists' Guinness fixes. On weekends dance ensues at **Kam Kam** (P. Sant'Antonino 7, tel. 081/8781114). In July and August, the classical concerts of the **Estate Musicale Sorrentina** take over the cloister of the Chiesa di San Francesco. If you're under 27, you'll pay a reduced admission (L12,000–L15,000).

OUTDOOR ACTIVITIES AND SPORTS

BEACHES • Sorrento's beaches are concrete platforms and breakwaters of piled rocks, but it is possible to swim off them. **Marina Piccola** and **Marina San Francesco** are on either side of the hydrofoil and ferry port; in the summer, the latter can also be reached by an elevator near the Chiesa di San Francesco. To get to **Marina Grande,** take Bus D from Piazza Tasso.

HIKING • If you crave exercise, explore the green hills above Sorrento. Try to find *A Passeggio con Le Sirene,* a detailed hiking map with itineraries in four languages; three of the itineraries begin in Sorrento, and many other trails are marked. If the newspaper store at the train station doesn't have the map, ask to study the tourist office's copy.

GULF OF SALERNO

Just below the Bay of Naples, the massive Gulf of Salerno meets the most scenic stretch of waterfront in Italy. Towns sprang up in the most unlikely places on the **Amalfi Coast**; stacked between the cliffs and the sea, these tiny communities developed into great seafaring republics and later into vacation empires. In the last few centuries, their dramatic Mediterranean vistas and fragrant lemon trees have attracted politicians, artists, and expatriates. Although the coastal towns are loaded with beached vacationers in summer, just a few kilometers inland you will find farmers climbing up and down their terraced fields wielding hand tools. On the east end of the coast, the city of **Salerno** has grown into an important commercial center; along with the city of **Amalfi,** it's a logical base for exploring the area. Southeast of Salerno, the golden remains of **Paestum's** Doric temples stand only a cow chip's throw from buffalo pastures, country villas, and farms. Farther south lies **Cilento,** a land of fishing villages, rolling hills, and seemingly endless beaches.

AMALFI

Amalfi's chalk-color buildings are stacked high on the rocky base of Monte Lattari. In its glory days during the Byzantine era, Amalfi was a powerful maritime republic that minted its own money (called *tarì*), refined the compass, designed a constitution, and drew up codes for Mediterranean trade practices. Much of the ancient city was destroyed by the sea during an earthquake in 1343, and it declined in prominence thereafter, never even becoming a luxurious seaside resort. Accommodations and food are relatively cheap, making it a good base for exploring smaller, more expensive coastal towns. Amalfi's one street runs north from here to the central Piazza del Duomo and continues as Via L. d'Amalfi and Via P. Capuano; the majority of the town is made up of narrow alleys and staircases.

BASICS

The **AACST** office (C. Roma 19, tel. 089/871107; open Mon.—Fri. 8- 2, Sat. 8–1) is half a block from the port in a small courtyard. Near the port, the **post office** (C. delle Repubbliche Marinare 31- -35, tel. 089/871330) is open weekdays 8:15–6 and Saturday 8:15–1. To change money, go to one of Amalfi's three banks (on or around P. Duomo) or to the exchange office **Financial Tour** (V. L. d'Amalfi 31, tel. 089/872583; open Mon.–Sat. 8:30–1 and 3–8, Sun. 8:30–1). Amalfi doesn't have a regular phone office, but the **Bar della Valle** (Largo E. Marini 4, tel. 089/871265) has metered phone booths and phone books.

COMING AND GOING

BY BUS • SITA buses (tel. 089/871016) leave from Piazza Flavio Gioia. There are about one or two per hour to Minori (15 min east, L1,700) and Salerno (70 min, L3,100), and hourly buses to Ravello (30 min, L1,700), Positano (45 min, L2,200), and Sorrento (1 hr 35 min west, L3,900). Infrequent buses to Naples (2 hrs northwest, L5,700) leave in the early morning. Buy bus tickets (L1,700) at port-side bars, travel agencies, or tobacco shops. Schedules are posted on Piazza Flavio Gioia; service runs from dawn to around 9 or 10 PM.

BY BOAT • Several carriers, including **Alilauro** (tel. 089/871483) and **Cooperativa Sant'Andrea** (tel. 089/873190), sail throughout the day to Salerno (35 min east, L5,000), Positano (30 min west, L7,000), and Capri (70 min west, L15,000–L19,000). The ticket booths are on the docks and on Lungomare dei Cavalieri, parallel to the water. Be prepared for infrequent departures.

GETTING AROUND • Trains are nonexistent along the Amalfi Coast, so opt for the frequent, speedy, and cheap SITA buses whose coastal routes offer thrillingly beautiful vistas at nearly every curve of the road. Ferries and hydrofoils are the easiest way to travel between Positano, Amalfi, and Salerno, but most only operate in summer, and infrequently at that. Scooters are helpful, but vertigo may strike as you battle Neapolitan drivers for space on narrow, winding roads hundreds of feet above crashing sea and jagged rock. If you feel invincible, the **Divina Costiera** travel office (P. Gioia 3, tel. 081/871254) in Amalfi rents scooters for L65,000 per day. Just remember: in the peak days of summer, the main road of the Amalfi Coast, called the Via Smeraldo, can become a parking lot by high noon—so always get an early start to beat the traffic.

WHERE TO SLEEP

Accommodations in Amalfi are fairly standard and getting more expensive. The **Albergo Sant'Andrea** (P. Duomo 26, tel. 089/871145) has one of the most spectacular locations in town—directly opposite the square from Amalfi's cathedral; guns and velvet-swags deck the walls of the reception area, and cell-size doubles (L100,000) are cluttered with somewhat mismatched furniture. **Hotel Fontana** (P. Duomo, tel. 089/871530; closed Nov.–Mar.) has another great location offering large, bright doubles (L120,000) that overlook the marina or Piazza del Duomo. The **Lido Mare** (Largo Piccolomini 9, tel. 089/871332) has comfortable modern doubles with television and a terrace over the harbor for L130,000, or L100,000 in low season. Though it's a little worn around the edges and the hallway bathrooms aren't the greatest, **Pensione Proto** (Salita dei Curiali 4, tel. 089/871003) has doubles for L75,000–L95,000, or L100,00–L105,000 with bath. From Piazza del Duomo, walk up Via L. d'Amalfi and turn right on Salita dei Curiali.

ATRANI • In the tiny neighboring village of Atrani, **A' Scalinatella** (P. Umberto I 12, tel. 089/871492) sits just two blocks above the beach. Filippo and his family offer campsites at L15,000, hostel-style rooms at L20,000–L25,000 per person or doubles with bath for L50,000–L60,000 per person; demi-pensione (breakfast and dinner) at the family restaurant costs L35,000. Take the shore road east; before the tunnel, cut through the restaurant and go down the staircase; continue down on the road that turns left through an arch to A' Scalinatella. To avoid the 10-minute walk, get off at the Atrani bus stop (on the Amalfi–Salerno line) and walk down the steps and away from the water. They also have apartments and rooms in Amalfi.

WHERE TO EAT

In Amalfi you can feast on some of the freshest fruits and vegetables in the area, although most of the fish you'll see was likely frozen months ago. The bakery **Apicella** (V. L. d'Amalfi 27, tel. 089/871268; closed Sun.), on the north side of Piazza del Duomo, serves fresh, hot baguettes worthy of Paris.

If you want a hot meal and service, ditch the beach and venture through the whitewashed staircases and pathways off Piazza del Duomo. For cheap eats, grab a slice of pizza or a sandwich at **Porto Salvo,** just off Piazza del Duomo (Via Supportico Marina 8, tel. 089/872445; closed Wed. In winter). On Piazza del Duomo, **Ristorante-Pizzeria S. Andrea** has a large selection of good pizzas, wonderful *scialatielle ai frutti di mare* and a good local wine (Sanmarco) for L9,000 a bottle (Piazza Duomo 26, tel. 089/871023). The menu at **Trattoria San Giuseppe** (Salita Ruggero II 4, tel. 089/872640; closed Thurs.) is in three languages, but both the food and prices are reasonable (under L15,000). You can get penne *alla San Giuseppe* (with mushrooms, peas, tomatoes, and hot pepper), spaghetti with clams, and the usual pizza lineup. Up the main street, Antonio at **La Taverna del Duca** serves 19th-century Amalfitan cuisine and pizzas in a warm friendly atmosphere (P. Spirito Santo 26, tel. 089/872755). For dessert step into **Pasticceria Pansa** (P. Duomo 40, tel. 089/871065, daily in summer, closed Tues. in winter) for a small *torta di limone* (lemon cake).

WORTH SEEING

Earthquakes and other disasters have toppled Amalfi's really ancient stuff, but you can still get more than a glimpse of some of the city's glorious past. The ornate **Duomo** in the town center has greenish bronze doors from 1066—supposedly the first of their kind. You'll see the Duomo's colorful facade, on top of a long flight of steps, depicted on postcards throughout the region. To the left at the top of the stairs, a L4,000 ticket will let you visit the elegant flower garden at the **Chiostro del Paradiso** (currently under restoration) and the remains of the 6th-century **Chiesa del Crocefisso** (tel. 089/871059; open 8–6), as well as the cathedral's crypt and treasures. The free **Museo Civico** (P. Municipio, tel. 089/871001; open Mon.–Sat. 9–1), displays original manuscripts of the *Tavoliere Amalfitane,* the maritime codes that governed the whole Mediterranean until 1570.

A typical product of Amalfi is limoncello, a liqueur made from lemons along the coast from Capri down into Calabria. It'll be offered to you after almost every meal.

The **Grotta dello Smeraldo** (Emerald Cave), Amalfi's most famous coastline attraction, is actually a ways out of town in the idyllic hamlet of Conca dei Marini. Take a SITA bus toward Positano and ask to be let off at the Grotto entrance (10 min west, L1,700); then descend the stairs or pay for an elevator ride down the cliff. Guys with boats hang around from morning to late afternoon during high season (not as regularly off-season or in bad weather) to whisk you through the limestone caverns for L5,000 per person. It's a quick ride—over before you can cock your camera—but the surreal green light coming up through the water is chillingly beautiful. Alternatively, you can take a boat from the docks at Amalfi (L10,000 round-trip plus L5,000 for the grotto itself).

OUTDOOR ACTIVITIES AND SPORTS

BEACHES • To the left of the port (facing the water) is the large and public Marina Grande beach, in summer jammed with vacationers; to the right is a series of smaller beaches, some public and some owned by clubs and hotels. A 10-minute walk along the water to the east (*see below*), Atrani's beach is sandier and usually a little less crowded.

HIKING • Rather than dropping straight into the sea, the steep hills of the Amalfi Coast cascade in rows down toward the water, providing wonderful, arduous hiking terrain. If you'll be in the area for long, try to find a copy of *Walks in Amalfi* (*Amalfi e Ravello: Guida agli Antichi Sentieri*) at tourist offices, which provides detailed itineraries of hikes throughout the region. A difficult but highly satisfying hike is the ascent from the coast up two cliffs to **Ravello** (*see Near Amalfi, below*). The stairs begin in Piazza Umberto I in Atrani, a 10-minute walk along the coast east of Amalfi (take the stairs down on your right just before the tunnel). Leave the piazza on the staircase in the middle of the north side of the square (away from the water). Where the path divides, take the staircase on the right. At the top, the path levels off; before the steps start going down, take the staircase on your left, which soon leaves the town and starts up the side of the cliff. Halfway up the last cliff, you come to a dirt path that traverses the side of the cliff. Turn right and you'll approach the road to Ravello. The climb can be done in an hour, but you may want another half hour to rest and enjoy the views of the steep valleys with terraced rows of lemon and olive trees.

NEAR AMALFI

POSITANO

Climbing up a cove between steep, narrow cliffs, Positano looks more like a toy town or a giant wedding cake than a popular resort. It's a good place to go for a week and do nothing but lie on the beach and enjoy the unforgettable views of the sea, the cliffs, and the town itself. But besides the beach, Positano's maze of overpriced boutiques is probably its biggest attraction, which isn't terribly encouraging. Positano's main street, Via dei Mulini, is at the base of the cliffs and slopes down to the Spiaggia Grande, an almost sandy beach.

BASICS • Check out the **AACST** office (V. del Saracino, tel. 089/875067; open weekdays 8–2 and Sat. 8–noon) for info on sights and lodging.

COMING AND GOING • Getting in and out is difficult, so you should think twice about a quick trip. **Alilauro** (tel. 089/227979) in Salerno and **Cooperativa Sant'Andrea** (tel. 089/873190) in Amalfi run boats and hydrofoils to Positano from Amalfi (30 min east, L7,000–9,000) and Capri (40 min east, L14,000–L18,000). **SITA** buses run to and from Sorrento (1–2 per hr, 45 min east, L4,400), Amalfi (1–2 per hr, 45 min east, L2,200), and infrequently to Naples (2 hrs southeast, L5,700). From Salerno (L4,200) change in Amalfi. A local bus (L1,700) hits all of the SITA stops and loops through the town itself every 30 minutes.

WHERE TO SLEEP AND EAT • If you're seized by the desire to stay overnight, scramble for one of the six doubles with bath and terrace (L50,000–L70,000) rented out by the incredibly friendly **Pietro Pane** (V. Canovaccio 5, tel. 089/875360). If they're full, **Villa Verde** (V. Pasitea 338, tel. 089/875506) has a peaceful garden, and doubles with bath and breakfast for L120,000–L130,000. **Hotel Maria Luisa** (V. Fornillo 40, tel. and fax 089/875023) has doubles with bath and terrace over the sea for L90,000. The food situation in Positano is simple: the closer you are to the water, the more you'll pay. **La Zagara** (V. Mulini 8, tel. 089/875964) has a *tavola calda* that serves reasonable small pizzas and calzone. For a great meal at a low price, try the homemade pasta at **Grottino Azzurro** (V. G. Marconi, tel. 089/875466). Whatever you do, don't miss lunch at **Lo Guarracino,** which enjoys a magically scenic setting on the path to the Fornillo beach (Via Positanesi d'America 12, tel. 089/875794).

RAVELLO

You can practically kiss the clear blue sky from this hilltop city, naturally fortified on a precipitous tower of limestone. Views of the sea and the valley are broken only by citrus, fig, and cypress trees and stucco walls and cottages. A population of fewer than 3,000 enjoys Ravello's air of retreat and escape.

Ravello's seaside views are its primary draw, though there are some man-made sights. The 11th-century **Duomo** (P. Duomo; open daily 9–1 and 3–7) has bronze doors and a 13th-century campanile; inside, look for the elaborate mosaics of the Rufolo family pulpit, supported by spiral columns that rest on the backs of six white-marble lions. Follow the signs from Piazza del Duomo to the **Villa Cimbrone** (V. S. Chiara 26, tel. 089/857459); open daily 9–7 (until 4 in winter). The villa itself is a private residence, but for L6,000 you can peek into its beautiful Arab-influenced cloister and stroll in its stupendous gardens, whose paths lead to the Belvedere of Infinity, which breathtakingly overlooks the entire Gulf of Salerno. The crumbling Sicilian, Arabic, and 11th-century Norman buildings of **Villa Rufolo** (P. Duomo, tel. 089/857657; admission L5,000) can be visited daily 9–8 (until 5 in winter, until 10 in July and August). Wagner's 1880 visit to the villa inspired the Klingsor's garden scene in his opera *Parsifal*; in July and August, the gardens are the site of the **Festival Musicale Ravello** (tel. 167/213289). For info and a useful map, stop at the **AACST** office (P. Duomo, tel. 089/857096, fax 089/857977; open summer, Mon.–Sat. 8–8; winter, 8–7).

The pleasant 45- to 60-minute hike down to Minori takes you through quiet **Torello.** Descend the stairs from Piazza del Duomo to the left of the Villa Rufolo, and you'll be on your way, but consult a copy of *Walks in Amalfi* so you don't end up in Milan. A more rigorous hike is the trek to Amalfi (*see* Amalfi, Outdoor Activities and Sports, *above*).

COMING AND GOING • SITA's buses come from Amalfi almost hourly (20–30 min, L1,700) and stop just a few minutes from Piazza del Duomo (follow the signs).

WHERE TO SLEEP • Plan to splurge: no hotel here rates less than two stars. Cliff-side at **Hotel Garden** (V. Boccaccio 4, tel. 089/857226, fax 089/858110; open Apr.–Oct.), doubles with bath and breakfast cost L130,000 (L110,000 in low season). Doubles at **Hotel Toro** (V. Emanuele Filiberto 8, tel. and fax 089/857211) cost L125,000 (L113,000 in low season), including bath and breakfast.

MINORI

The beach is wide and sandy by Amalfi Coast standards (which isn't saying much), but otherwise there isn't much to this cute little town. Stucco buildings cover hills that lead down to the beach, where Minori's visitors congregate. You can visit the somewhat pedestrian remains of the local **Roman Villa** (Piazzetta P. Troiano, tel. 089/852893) and the adjoining collection of mundane relics for free. Stop at the **Pro Loco** office (P. Umberto I, tel. 089/877087), open Monday–Saturday 9–noon (also 4–8 in summer) for info on other sights. **SITA** buses pass through Minori on frequent runs between Amalfi (15 min, L1,700) and Salerno (55 min, L2,700), stopping on Via Roma, which runs along the beach. Minori's more affordable lodgings include the three-star **Hotel Caporal** (V. Nazionale 22, tel. 089/877408), which has doubles for L110,000 (L80,000 in winter), and **Hotel Europa** (V. Nazionale 65, tel. and fax 089/877512), where doubles cost L90,000; Europa is open only March–mid-October.

SALERNO

Salerno may be a rundown port town, but it's a serviceable Amalfi Coast depot. In the wake of heavy bombing during World War II and a destructive earthquake in 1954, long rows of architecturally redundant housing units were built around the new town center. The result is more an inexpensive commercial center than a tourist stop. Despite the lack of charm, Salerno offers beautiful views of the coast and a medieval quarter that was home to one of the first universities in Europe.

BASICS

The **EPT** office (P. Vittorio Veneto 1, tel. 089/231432) dispenses visitor information Monday–Saturday 9–2 and 3––8, and there is a second office (V. Velia 15, tel. 089/230411) which is open Mon.–Sat. 9–1 and 4:30–7. The central **post office** (C. Garibaldi 203, tel. 089/224154) is open weekdays 8:15–1:50 and Saturday 8:15–11:50. Salerno has few **exchange offices,** so you'll have to go to the information window at the train station (open 9–7) or to one of the banks along Corso Vittorio Emanuele. Make long-distance calls at the **Telecom** office (C. Garibaldi 31; open weekdays 9:30–1 and 2–5:30).

In July and August, the Estate Salernitana festival brings jazz concerts, dance performances, and theater to Salerno. For film lovers, the city hosts its Festival Internazionale del Cinema every October.

COMING AND GOING

BY TRAIN • Salerno's **train station** (P. V. Veneto, tel. 1478/88088) is a stop on the Milan–Reggio di Calabria line. Trains leave for Pompeii (1–2 per hr, 25 min northwest, L2,800), Naples (2 per hr, 45 min northwest, L5,500), Agropoli (1 per hr, 35 min southeast, L4,200), and Reggio di Calabria (9 per day, 4 hrs southeast, L34,500).

BY BUS • For long trips, blue **SITA** (tel. 089/226604) buses leave from Piazza della Concordia, south of the station near the port, or from the SITA office (V. Martiri Salernitani), three blocks west of the train station. Buy tickets at the office or at tobacco shops showing a SITA sticker. Buses run to Sorrento (hourly, 2 hrs 45 min west, L5,900), Naples (3 per hr, 1 hr northwest, L5,100) and Amalfi (1–2 per hr, 1 hr 10 min west, L3,100). ATACS (tel. 089/487286) Buses 4 and 41 run from the train station to Pompeii (3 per hr, 30–50 min northwest, L3,900). ATACS and SCAT send frequent buses to Paestum (30–45 min, L4,700) and Agropoli (35 min, L5,200); buses depart from Piazza della Concordia.

BY BOAT • Most boats leave Salerno for Amalfi and Positano from the main port at Piazza della Concordia; those that continue to Capri and Ischia leave from Molo Manfredi, at the west end of the waterfront. Departures are usually in the morning, with return trips in the late afternoon. The EPT office dispenses information, or you can call the **Cooperativa Sant'Andrea** (tel. 089/873190).

GETTING AROUND

The orange **ATACS** buses (L1,000) cover the city well, but walking will usually suffice.

WHERE TO SLEEP

Salerno's hotels cluster around Piazza V. Veneto, in front of the train station. As always, it's smart to call a week or so in advance in summer. Ask at the tourist office about affitacamere in private residences for about L25,000 per person. Just down the street from the train station, **Albergo Santa Rosa** (C. Vittorio Emanuele 14, tel. and fax 089/225346) offers the nicest budget digs in town, with clean, quiet doubles (L65,000). The hostel **Ostello Irno** (HI; V. Luigi Guercio 112, tel. 089/790251, fax 089/405792) organizes group excursions throughout the region as well as climbs with the local Alpine club. Rooms have from two to eight beds; baths in the hall are passable but could be cleaner. You'll pay L15,000 per night, breakfast included, and L10,000 for dinner in the restaurant. The 12:30 AM curfew really doesn't apply; there is a lockout 11–2.

WHERE TO EAT AND BE MERRY

Salerno's specialty is *baccalà* (dried cod with potatoes and fresh tomatoes). For fast, cheap eats, the pizzerias and tavole calde around the train station are your best bet. Most restaurants by the sea on Lungomare Trieste aren't worth the cost, though they do have nice views and late hours. A safe choice is **Pizzeria Il Cavatappi** (V. A. M. de Luca 8, tel. 089/239490; dinner only, closed Sun.), on a small street between Corso Garibaldi and Corso Vittorio Emanuele. Several moderately priced restaurants are lined up on the north side of Via Roma below the medieval quarter, including **Taverna del Pozzo** (V. Roma 220, tel. 089/253636; closed Sun.), which has a lunch menu for L15,000 and dishes like linguine *alla ionica* (with shrimp and tomatoes). This stretch of Via Roma also has a number of bars, for example **Mini Pub** (V. Roma 274; closed Sun.). In the medieval quarter, the **Peach Pit** (V. dei Mercanti 119) serves good beer. You'll find changing musical styles and occasional live performances at the bar-discotheque **Movida** (V. Generale Clark).

WORTH SEEING

West of the station, you'll find hotels and fancy stores along Corso Vittorio Emanuele. The street runs directly into Via dei Mercanti and to the narrow corridors of Salerno's medieval quarter, which surrounds the Duomo. One block south of Corso Vittorio Emanuele is Corso Garibaldi, which becomes Via Roma as it heads west. One block south of that is Lungomare Trieste, which runs along the water. Here you can begin a prime seaside stroll through a narrow park with palm trees.

The 11th-century **Cathedral of St. Matthew** (P. Alfano; open daily 10–noon and 4–6:30) dominates a section of the old quarter and displays a set of bronze doors made in Constantinople. Its courtyard, surrounded by marble columns (some lifted from the ruins at Paestum), is more interesting than the church's interior. A few blocks behind the cathedral sits the small **Museo Archeologico Provinciale** (V. San Benedetto, tel. 089/231135; open daily 9–7:30), housed in a Benedictine convent and chock-full of archaeological finds. A 15-minute ride on Bus 19 (L1,000), which begins at Teatro Verdi at the western end of Via Roma, takes you to the **Castello di Arechi** (tel. 089/227236; open Mon.–Fri. 9– 1), an uninteresting medieval castle with a spectacular view of the Amalfi Coast. Admission to all three sights is free.

PAESTUM

If you grow tired of greased bodies on the beach, a short trip south from Salerno will bring you to a slice of Greece at the archaeological site of Paestum. Founded in the 7th century BC, the former capital of Magna Graecia (the Greek colonies of southern Italy) is now a set of Greek and Roman ruins in the countryside just beyond Salerno's industrial tentacles. The site itself consists of a large plain strewn with flowers, the remains of a Roman town, and three stunning Greek temples, the best-preserved Doric temples in Europe. For information on accommodations and a simple brochure on the site, stop by the **AACST** office (V. Magna Grecia 151–155, tel. 0828/811016; open Mon.–Sat. 8—2, and also 4—7:30 in summer), slightly to the left of the museum.

COMING AND GOING

Paestum is best as a day trip, so plan your transportation carefully. It's easy to miss the last bus or train and get stranded. **Trains** (tel. 1478/88088) run about every two hours from Naples (1½ hrs northwest, L8,200) and Agropoli (10 min, L1,500), except in late morning. Service from Salerno (30–45 min, L4,200) is a bit more frequent. From the station, walk straight ahead (perpendicular to the tracks) for 10 minutes to get to Via Magna Grecia, near the entrance to the site. **Buses** between Salerno (1 hr, L4,700) and Agropoli (15 min south, L3,900), operated by any of four companies, stop on Via Magna Grecia both north and south of the site (the latter stop is a little more convenient) and at the train station. You can pay on the bus, which should run at least hourly—but don't count on it.

WHERE TO SLEEP AND EAT

Most hotels are between the Greek ruins and the beach, at least a half-hour walk from the station. Your best budget bet is to stay at the hostel in Agropoli (*see* Cilento, *below*), but the most convenient option is the threadbare **Pensione delle Rose** (V. Magna Grecia 193, tel. and fax 0828/811070), where the road from the station meets Via Magna Grecia. It has fairly clean doubles for L90,000 (you can bargain during the off-season). For an excellent alternative, spend a few days at **Pensione Arcobaleno** (V. Gaiarda 51, tel. 0828/722178), run by Dr. Daniele Nunzio—a well-regarded author and lecturer on Paestum—and his family. If you do stay here, try to observe the family in action, growing its own food, making wine, or tending to the livestock. Immaculate rooms with bath go for L50,000 per person, L70,000 with breakfast and dinner, and L80,000 with full pension. Meals here are regional homestyle food at its best. Call from the train station and someone will pick you up.

There are few places to eat near the ruins. For a quick, inexpensive snack, **Bar Anna** (V. Magna Grecia, tel. 0828/811196) has passable pizza slices and sandwiches. If you want a full meal, you may as well go to the elegant but unexciting **Ristorante Museo** (V. Magna Grecia 171, tel. 0828/811135) for reasonable risotto alla pescatore and grilled steak.

THE SITE

The visible ruins sprawl across a broad field but only comprise a fraction of the ancient city. At the south end lies the **Basilica,** Paestum's oldest temple, dating from the 6th century BC. Its 50 Doric columns were made up of heavy circular stone slabs stacked one on top of another. You'll see three pillars remaining from the inner sanctuary; only the temple priests were allowed in here, to perform sacred rituals. Built a century later and next to the Basilica, the magnificent **Temple of Neptune** still displays grand columns only partially pitted and aged. The inner columns supported a second row, some of which are still standing. At the north end of the site, the lonely **Temple of Ceres,** built around 500 BC, later served as an early Christian church. Both the Temple of Neptune and the Temple of Ceres have been popularly misnamed; the former actually was dedicated to Hera and the latter to Athena. *Admission to ruins and museum L8,000. Open daily 9–2 hrs before sunset.*

Wandering around the site of Paestum and munching grass are herds of water buffalo, whose milk is used to make the creamy mozzarella di bufala cheese. As the cheese does not travel well, be sure to try some while you're in the locale; the fresh product is amazing.

Between the magnificent temples, you can walk amid the still-impressive remains of the immense **Roman Forum,** an **amphitheater,** a onetime swimming pool, and many other buildings. To the west lie blocks and blocks of residential structures that are still being uncovered. Across Via Magna Grecia, the **National Archaeological Museum** (tel. 0828/811023; admission L8,000; open daily 9–7, closed 1st and 3rd Mon. of each month) houses Greek artifacts including painted vases, bronze sculptures, and largely intact frescoes taken from nearby tombs. The most famous fresco depicts a man diving over a row of columns, representing the world of mortals entering the unknown realm of death. A new single ticket price of L12,000 for the ruins and museum was set to take effect at press time (summer 1999). A simple 5th-century **Christian Basilica** (open summer, daily 8–8; winter, daily 8–7) is next to the AACST office. If you're here on a hot day, Paestum's broad sandy **beach** is a 35-minute walk west of the site.

CILENTO

Apparently Cilento was once the area between Agropoli and the Alento River, but the region has grown to encompass the entire southern part of Campania. First settled by the Greeks in the 7th and 6th centuries BC, the area has been a backwater for much of the last two millennia, although it is increasingly the vacation spot of choice for Italians from farther north. Almost the entire coastline is made up of sandy beaches broken by rocky outcrops and grottoes; inland, its rugged hillsides remain relatively underdeveloped. The **Parco Nazionale del Cilento,** which covers most of the region, is not a park in the usual sense—it also encompasses residential areas. Don't come expecting uninhabited wilderness, though the park is increasingly dedicated to environment-friendly tourism.

AGROPOLI

Agropoli sits at the northern end of Cilento, crowned by a medieval quarter atop a steep promontory that juts into the sea. Climb a bit higher to the **castello,** built in the 6th century and largely modified in the late medieval period. It's a private residence, but if you ring the bell between 5 and 8 PM, someone will usually let you in free of charge.

This big city can be difficult to navigate on foot; street signs and maps are almost nonexistent, and many signs have been twisted to point the wrong way. From the train station, walk away from the tracks for 20 minutes on Via A. de Gasperi and Via Piave to get to **Piazza V. Veneto,** the modern city center. To the right are the streets leading up to the Old City, flanked by small beaches. There is also a long, sandy beach stretching up the coastline to the north, tempting for evening strolls. The gorgeous beach along the southwestern **Baia di Trentova** is a scenic 35-minute walk from the city center on Via Trentova; in summer local buses run from Piazza V. Veneto to Baia di Trentova every hour or two.

COMING AND GOING

Trains (tel. 1478/88088) run hourly from Naples (1½ hrs northwest, L10,100) and Salerno (35 min northwest L4,200); an hourly service heads to close points south. **ATACS, SCAT, Giuliano, Lettieri, Stromillo,** and **Santa Claus** provide long- distance bus service. In principle, there are one or two buses per hour from Paestum (15 min, L3,900) and Salerno (1¼ hrs, L5,100); other destinations are served less frequently. Buses stop at either Piazza V. Veneto or Via delle Taverne, south of Via. A. de Gasperi. Schedules are posted nowhere; ask at your hotel or hostel or call **Pro Loco** (P. Umberto I, tel. 0974/827341) in the old city below the castle.

WHERE TO SLEEP AND EAT

Most of Agropoli's hotels are near the water and, hence, far from the train station. **Hotel Carola** (V. C. Pisacane 1, tel. 0974/823005), just above the marina, has well-kept doubles with bath for L85,000. The best place to stay in the entire region is the newish and clean **Ostello La Lanterna** (HI; V. Lanterna 8, tel. 0974/838003; closed Dec.–Feb.). With a day's notice they'll help arrange bicycle or walking tours of the countryside. A bed is L16,000 per night and groups of two to four (depending on the season) can have their own room for L17,000 each. It's five minutes from the beach, 20 from the station. Turn right and walk along the tracks; follow under the tracks and the highway through the intersection; V. Lanterna is the first left. For a budget meal surrounded by local fishermen, try **U'Sghizz** (P. Umberto I, tel. 0974/824582) in the old quarter. The tasty pasta e fagioli with mussels will stick to your ribs.

MARINA DI CAMEROTA

This is inconvenient as a day trip, but if the Grand Tour is wearing you down, Marina di Camerota is lovely for relaxation and exploration of the area. It fills up with vacationers in July and August, but you can practically have the run of the place the rest of the year.

BASICS

Count on **Pro Loco** (V. Porto 15, tel. 0974/932036; open daily 10:30–1 and 5–8:30; closed Oct.–Mar.). For a variety of hikes and guided tours, contact the environmentally conscious **Cooperativa Posidonia** (V. Lungomare Trieste 11, tel. 0974/939127). Walk down to the left-hand end of the marina and make a deal with a fisherman for a boat tour of the coastline and its many coves and grottoes.

COMING AND GOING

Buses come here from the Pisciotta train station (2 per hr, 40 min southeast, L2,000) and stop on the Lungomare Trieste just above the marina. From October to June, the last Pisciotta–Marina di Camerota bus runs in early afternoon. There's a schedule at the station, but the **Agenzia Infante** (V. N. Sauro 65, tel. 0974/939111) just above the bus stop is the area's most reliable source for bus info. Pisciotta, on the Salerno–Paola train line, has hourly **trains** from Agropoli (35 min, L3,400) and Salerno (1 hr 10 min, L7,200).

WHERE TO SLEEP

Call four weeks ahead if you plan to come here in August. Most hotels insist on at least *mezza pensione* (breakfast and dinner), especially in July and August. An exception is **Pensione Coppola** (V. S. Domenico 5, tel. 0974/932056; closed Oct.–May), where a clean, bright double with bath runs L55,000–L65,000. **Il Pinguino** (V. S. Domenico 18, tel. 0974/932115) has decent rooms with bath and charges L45,000–L55,000 per person for mezza pensione. At the pleasant **Al Capalluccio Marino** (V. Bolivar 48, tel. 0974/932270), a wonderful family will treat you like one of their own. Full pension is L70,000–L80,000 per person; if you're not staying there, meals are about L16,000.

PUGLIA, BASILICATA, AND CALABRIA

BY JAMES KWAK

UPDATED BY JON ELDAN

Surrounded by some of the most ancient seas known to human civilization, Puglia (Apulia), Basilicata, and Calabria occupy a forgotten corner of the Italian peninsula that is missing from most travelers' itineraries. Lacking the cosmopolitan splendor and hubbub of Naples and the romantic mystique of Sicily, this is the deep south, usually glimpsed on the way to the Greek islands or during a beachside vacation. Here life is balanced between the inviting waters and baking-hot sand of endless coastline and the rocky plateaus and mountain ranges of the interior. With its natural beauty, relative seclusion, and some of the friendliest, most outgoing people in the entire country, this remote end of Italy offers a welcome contrast to the crowded cities farther north.

In a less fortunate contrast, Puglia, Basilicata, and Calabria suffer from the economic and political problems that have beset the entire Mezzogiorno (southern Italy) for centuries. Italian immigrants throughout the world came largely from the underdeveloped, highly agricultural south, searching for jobs in the United States in the late 19th century and in northern Europe in the 1950s and '60s. Since World War II, repeated attempts to solve the "southern question" have brought increased prosperity but failed to provide economic independence.

As a traveler, however, you are more likely to notice and appreciate the many wonders of this corner of the continent. From the isolated Gargano peninsula to the mountainous coastline of Maratea, countless places will draw you to their largely unspoiled natural settings in relative peace and quiet. Although much has changed, these regions still offer an occasional window onto an ancient Mediterranean civilization not yet transformed by modern industry and commerce. Prices are among the lowest in Italy, both for accommodations and for a regional cuisine that embodies the best of simple Italian food. Here the hot sun pays dividends in plentiful olives and ripe red tomatoes, and the nearby waters provide seafood in abundance. Finally, the entire region, except for the beach resort areas, is well off the beaten path. Outside Brindisi and Bari, you are less likely to meet an American than, say, a water buffalo, and when you get home, you can tell people about the blue, blue water that no one else has seen before you.

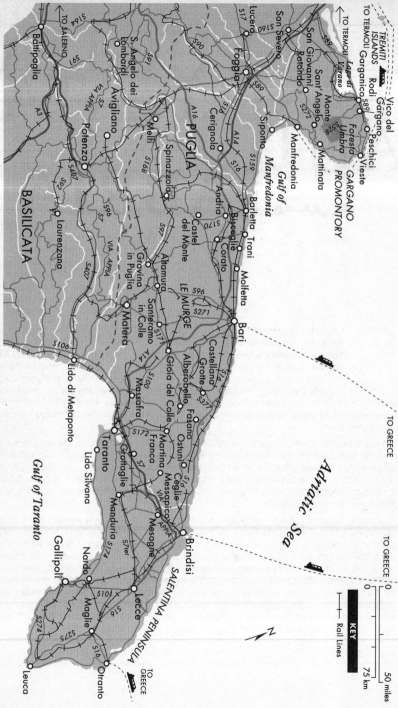

PUGLIA

PUGLIA

BASILICATA

GARGANO PROMONTORY

Gulf of Manfredonia

Adriatic Sea

Gulf of Taranto

SALENTINA PENINSULA

LE MURGE

TO TERMOLI
TO TERMOLI
TO TERMOLI Garganico
TREMITI ISLANDS
Vico del Gargano
Rodi Garganico
Peschici
Foresta Umbra
Vieste
Mattinata
Monte Sant'Angelo
Manfredonia
Siponto

TO GREECE

TO GREECE

TO GREECE

TO SALERNO
TO SALERNO

Battipaglia
Lucera
San Severo
San Giovanni Rotondo
Sant'Angelo
Foggia
S. Angelo dei Lombardi
Avigliano
Potenza
Melfi
Laurenzana
Spinazzola
Cerignola
Andria
Castel del Monte
Altamura
Gravina in Puglia
Barletta
Bisceglie
Trani
Corato
Molfetta
Bari
Matera
Lido di Metaponto
Santeramo in Colle
Gioia del Colle
Massafra
Alberobello
Castellana Grotte
Fasano
Ostuni
Taranto
Lido Silvana
Grottaglie
Martina Franca
Cisternino
Ceglie Messapico
Brindisi
Manduria
Mesagne
Gallipoli
Nardò
Maglie
Lecce
Leuca
Otranto

Lago di Varano

VIA APPIA
VIA APPIA
VIA APPIA

A16
A14
A3

S17
S160
S155
S89
S528
S272
S89
S273
S90
S91
S168
S655
S93
S407
S7
S96
S97
S407
S159
S16
S170
S96
S271
S170
S106
S100
S172
S7
S16
S377
S7ter
S174
S101
S275
S274
S16
S16

KEY
Rail Lines

0   50 miles
0   75 km

N

378

PUGLIA

Stretching along Italy's east coast all the way to the mouth of the Adriatic is Puglia, its history and culture shaped by its proximity to the sea. One of the oldest regions of Italy, with cities dating to ancient Greek settlements, Puglia has since seen Romans, Byzantines, Normans, Crusaders, Saracens, Swabians, Anjous, Aragons, and Bourbons all come and go. Its strategic location and major port cities made it a crossroads for commerce and conquest, resulting in an architecture and culture that combine the influences of East and West.

Today Puglia's coastline remains its chief livelihood. Most of the region's attractions are along the Adriatic, from the coastal villages of the Gargano Promontory to the fanciful Baroque facades of Lecce, on the Salento peninsula. In between you can find bustling port cities, sleepy hilltop towns, and countless beaches, all relatively well served by the FS train line. But Puglia is not just sun and sea. Inland, you'll find the bizarre houses known as *trulli* and the towering trees of the Foresta Umbra—vivid testaments to the diversity of the region's history and landscape.

FOGGIA

Wheat-covered hillsides brushed with green foliage level to flatness as you approach Foggia, the first major stop for trains heading to Puglia. The city has a history of tragedy, including a massacre of the townspeople in 1528, a serious earthquake in 1731, and extensive Allied bombing during World War II, all of which left little of Foggia's *centro storico* (historic center) intact. In more modern times, most of the city has been rebuilt in a decidedly Baroque fashion, with wide, clean boulevards and well-shaded parks. There's not much to see here other than the 13th-century **cattedrale** (P. F. de Sanctis), with its somewhat cluttered Romanesque and Baroque facade, but the town makes a good base for more interesting treks inland or along the coast. When residents disappear for the coast in summer, you can take advantage of Foggia's hospitable atmosphere and comprehensive train and bus systems to get you to the ancient towns of the Gargano Promontory.

BASICS

The **EPT** office (V. Perrone 17, tel. 0881/723650; open weekdays 8–1, also 3:30–7 in summer) is a bit out of the way, but the staff can give you a map of the city and some rosy brochures about attractions on the Gargano Promontory. From the train station, take Viale XXIV Maggio to Piazza Cavour; turn left on Via IV Novembre, which becomes Via Roma, and then go left on Via Bari and right on Via Perrone. Foggia has many banks, especially around Piazza Cavour. The main **post office** (V. XXIV Maggio 30, tel. 0881/724001; open Mon.–Sat. 8:15–7:10) also changes money weekdays 8:15–5:30, Saturday 8:15–1.

COMING AND GOING

Foggia's clean, efficient **train station** (P. Vittorio Veneto, tel. 1478/88088) is a central stop on the Bologna–Lecce line. The station has a helpful train and bus information office (open daily 7 AM–9 PM) and luggage storage (L5,000 per 12 hrs; open daily 6 AM–10 PM). Trains head for Naples (2 daily, 3 hrs, L16,000), Bari (hourly, 1½ hrs, L10,100), and Rome (7 daily, 3 ½ hrs, L55,500).

Travel within the province of Foggia is confusing in theory but manageable in practice. Two bus companies, **ATAF** and **SITA**, serve many of the same towns; ATAF buses also fill in for the FS train system to Lucera (hourly, 15 min, L2,200) and Manfredonia (hourly, 45 min, L3,500), so some appear on the FS timetable and not on the ATAF timetable. The manageable parts are that all buses and trains charge the same prices, you can buy all tickets in the train station, all the buses leave from front of the train station, and the information office in the station knows what's up. There is little or no bus service Sunday, except to Lucera; to reach Manfredonia on Sunday, take an hourly train (25 min, L3,500).

GETTING AROUND

Most places you'll want to go to are within easy walking distance of the train station. **Viale XXIV Maggio** runs from the station to **Piazza Cavour,** the closest thing to a center Foggia has. From here, Via Lanza will take you to **Piazza Giordano,** from which Corso Cairoli leads to **Piazza XX Settembre.** At this point, the cathedral and the old city are to your right; if you have time for sightseeing, various buildings of historical interest are labeled with large yellow signs. If you get an urge to explore the outer limits of the city, local buses (L1,200) congregate in front of the train station.

WHERE TO SLEEP

Rooms in Foggia are easy to come by except during the first week in May, when a huge agricultural fair takes place on the outskirts of town. The whole neighborhood in front of the train station is safe and clean, and it's filled with decent restaurants, markets, and shops. **Albergo Venezia** (V. Piave 40, tel. 0881/770903), has doubles for L50,000 (L70,000 with bath), but the rooms are pretty dreary, the bathrooms just tolerable, and there are no hallway showers. From the station, take Viale XXIV Maggio and turn right on Via Piave. **Albergo Centrale** (C. Cairoli 5, tel. 0881/771862) has high-ceilinged rooms (doubles L78,000) but a sometimes unreliable supply of hot water. From the train station, take Viale XXIV Maggio to Piazza Cavour, turn right on Via Lanza, and bear left at the fork onto Corso Cairoli.

WHERE TO EAT

It wouldn't last a week in New York, but for an alternative to Italian food, try **Ristorante Cinese Ton Fen** (V. Piave 60, tel. 0881/770212). The portions are small, but tasty noodle and fried-rice dishes sell for L3,000–L4,000 (other entrées run L6,000–L10,000). **Caffè Cairoli** (C. Cairoli 1, tel. 0881/772472; closed Wed.) is a great *tavola calda* (cafeteria) beneath Albergo Centrale (*see above*), where people in suits race through lunch. The menu changes daily, with first courses like *pennette alla crudaiola* (little penne with tomatoes and tuna) for L3,500 and second courses for L5,000.

AFTER DARK

Nightlife concentrates around Piazzale Italia and Corso Roma, near the university, where you'll find popular spots like **Kandinsky** (V. Tugini 44, tel. 0881/773543; closed Mon.), which stages blues and jazz concerts in the street on Friday and Sunday nights in summer; the rest of the year, performances are in the bar.

LUCERA

Eighteen kilometers (11 miles) northwest of Foggia, Lucera rises above the flatlands of the Tavoliere. Its commanding view of the Puglian plains made it a key strategic outpost for Frederick II, who relocated 20,000 loyal Saracen mercenaries to Lucera in 1224. In what was considered an enlightened gesture for the 13th century, he allowed the Saracens to build mosques so that they could practice their faith. When Charles I of Anjou captured the town, however, religious intolerance quickly resurfaced. The Arab community was wiped out, and its mosques were leveled. Although today's Lucera retains practically none of its original Arab architecture, some say signs of the Saracen settlement are apparent in the layout of the city, with its narrow alleyways and lively courtyards.

BASICS

The **tourist office** (V. San Domenico 66, tel. 0881/546878; open Mon.–Sat. 9–noon, also 5–7:30 and Sun 9–noon in summer) supplies maps and info and will help with hotel reservations. The first bank you'll see is **Banca di Roma** (C. Manfredi 8, tel. 0881/520013).

COMING AND GOING

The only way to reach Lucera is to hop on a blue **SITA** or **ATAF** bus outside Foggia's train station (hourly, 30 min, L2,200); note that there are only half as many on Sunday. You can buy tickets at Foggia's train station; get off in Piazza del Popolo just south of the city center, where there's an ATAF office.

WHERE TO SLEEP AND EAT

Lucera has only two hotels, but luckily they're reasonably priced, comfortable, and credit-card friendly. **Albergo al Passetto** (P. del Popolo, tel. and fax 0881/520998) is in a palazzo in the centro storico and consequently has more character than the competition across the street. Clean, cheap doubles with bath go for L80,000. The three stars at **Hotel La Balconata** (V. Ferrovia 15, tel. and fax 0881/520998) get you a TV with your nice but ordinary hotel room. Doubles with bath are L95,000. The restaurant downstairs from Hotel La Balconata serves standard Italian dinners for L30,000. Highly recommended for its local specialties, **La Cantina del Pozzo** (V. Giannone 1–5, tel. 0881/547373; closed Tue.) might be a better choice. A sprawling fruit and veggie **mercato** (market) takes over Piazza della Repubblica, near the Duomo, Monday–Saturday 7–1.

WORTH SEEING

After you've explored Lucera's cobblestone streets and narrow corridors, head for the 14th-century Byzantine-Gothic **Duomo** (P. del Duomo, no phone; open daily 7–noon and 4:30–8). The church was built on the site of the town's old Saracen mosque and salvaged several of its green marble columns. To learn more about Lucera's past, head to the **Museo Civico G. Fiorelli,** east of the cathedral. In the 17th-century mansion of the Baroness de Nicastri, the museum has a large store of Greek-influenced Puglian crafts and pottery, as well as bits of Roman sculpture, coins and jewelry, a few paintings, and the baroness's elegant furniture. *V. de Nicastri 36, tel. 0881/547041. Admission L1,500. Open Tues.–Sat. 9–1 and 4–7, Sun 9–1).*

You can walk around Lucera's partially reconstructed ancient Roman **amphitheater** (V. Augusto, tel. 0881/549214; admission free; open winter, Tues.–Sun. 9–1 and 3–5; summer daily 8 AM–9:30 PM), at the eastern edge of town. Lucera's most impressive site, however, is its free **Castello** (V. Castello, no phone; open daily 9–1; also 4–7 in summer). The massive defensive wall, completed in 1283 under Charles I of Anjou, was constructed around the already existing **Palatium,** a palace built in 1233 under Frederick II. Today only the lowest level of the original palace, called **La Cavalleria,** remains. The path around the castle provides a fantastic view of the miles and miles of checkerboard fields of the Tavoliere.

GARGANO PROMONTORY

Every August 14th, Lucera hosts the Corteo Storico, a grand festival that reenacts the defeat of the Saracens in 1300.

Until 20 years ago, the Gargano Promontory consisted of a collection of small fishing towns and wooded hills. The sandy beaches and often gorgeous coastline of the Gargano now lure Italian and German vacationers in profusion. Despite seasonal crowds, the villages of **Vieste** and **Peschici** are more appealing than your average beach town, for both their natural setting and their semi-urban character. The entire promontory is a national park, which doesn't mean much except for the majestic **Foresta Umbra,** a pocket of dense interior woods reached from the coast by bike. All in all, if you're looking for a brief vacation away from large cities and major tourist centers, this is one of the best escapes in southern Italy.

MANFREDONIA

The southern entry point into the Gargano Promontory, the large industrial city of Manfredonia moonlights as a vacation spot in summer. Though not particularly attractive, it has decent beaches and can serve as a starting point for exploring the interior of the Gargano. Manfredonia's cultural attraction is the large castle begun by Frederick II's son, Manfred—hence the town's name—which now serves as the **Museo Nazionale di Manfredonia** (C. Manfredi, tel. 0884/587838; admission L4,000; open Tues.–Sun. 8:30–1:30 and 3:30–7:30). The museum has a collection of objects from Stone Age villages in the area, but most striking are the Daunian stelae. These slabs of rock, decorated to look like human torsos and topped with eerie stone heads, are the principal testament to the Daunian civilization that developed from the 9th century BC, independent of the Greeks. You can swim in front of the castle or head to the beach town of Siponto (*see* Near Manfredonia, *below*).

BASICS

Manfredonia has an excellent **AAST office** (C. Manfredi 26, north of P. Marconi, tel. 0884/581998) that provides bus and ferry schedules and a booklet of bike tours in the Gargano. It's open Monday–Saturday 8:30–1:30, Monday and Tuesday also 3–7. Manfredonia's **banks** are mainly on Viale Aldo Moro and Corso Manfredi.

COMING AND GOING

Trains from Foggia (25 min, L3,,900) pull into Manfredonia's **train station** (P. Libertà, tel. 1478/88088) almost hourly. If you just want to hit the beach, you may as well get off at Siponto, just before Manfredonia. From the Manfredonia station, Viale Aldo Moro (right as you leave the station) heads north to Piazza Marconi, from which Corso Manfredi leads north to the castle. Heading south, Via Giuseppe di Vittorio leads to Siponto (*see* Near Manfredonia, *below*).

SITA and **ATAF** buses from Foggia (45 min, L3,500) take Via di Vittorio and Viale Moro on their way to Piazza Marconi, so they may be able to let you off closer to your hotel than the train does; there's one every hour or so, fewer on Sunday. Buses leave for Vieste (7 daily, 2 hrs, L8,000), Mattinata (16 daily, 20 min, L2,000), and Monte Sant'Angelo (17 daily, 30 min, L3,000); there are almost none on Sunday. Buy tickets at **Bar Impero** (P. Marconi 16). From June to September, an Adriatica **hydrofoil** (port, tel. 0884/582888) leaves for the Tremiti Islands (2 hrs, L62,000 round trip) every morning at 8 and returns at 5:30 in the evening. From Piazza Marconi, the entrance to the port is a three-minute walk south; buy tickets at the booth on the dock, which is open during boat arrival and departure times.

WHERE TO SLEEP, EAT, AND BE MERRY

During June and early July, you can find modestly priced rooms at the nondescript hotels along the strip in front of the train station. In late July and August, call well in advance. **Hotel Azzurro** (V. Giuseppe di Vittorio 56, tel. 0884/581498), 900 ft south of the train station toward Siponto, offers clean doubles with bath (L98,000). You can pick up pizza and cheap, thick slabs of focaccia bread with tomatoes at the bakeries on **Viale Aldo Moro** and **Via Giuseppe di Vittorio.** Most keep longer hours than regular pizzerias (7 AM or 8 AM until midnight is not uncommon), and you can stuff yourself for only L3,000–L5,000. Fruit stands and supermarkets also line Via Giuseppe di Vittorio, in case you want to stock up on beach supplies. For sit-down meals, check out the restaurants around Piazza Marconi, like **Trattoria Il Baracchio** (C. Roma 38, tel. 0884/583874; closed Thurs.), a tasteful little place that makes a divine spaghetti *con gli scampi* (with prawns) and fresh grilled fish (sold by weight; about L11,000–L16,000). **Bar delle Rose** (C. Manfredi 275, no phone) stages concerts of all types throughout the year, either in the street or in **Tunnel,** their basement club.

NEAR MANFREDONIA

SIPONTO

This beach town is a 25-minute walk south from Manfredonia's Piazza Marconi. Some of the buses to Foggia will take you to Siponto, and trains to Manfredonia stop here too. The beach is marginally less crowded than in Manfredonia, but almost all of the waterfront is broken off into private beaches, where you can expect to pay L13,000 for a spot. A kilometer (half mile) south of Siponto's train station is the 11th-century Romanesque **Basilica di Santa Maria Maggiore,** which was built atop the ruins of a 5th-century church. You can tour the hypogea and catacombs Monday through Saturday, between 9 and noon. **Hotel Sipontum** (V. Giuseppe di Vittorio 229, tel. 0884/542916) has decent doubles with bath (L86,000) and a friendly owner. It's a little closer to the Siponto station than the Manfredonia station; from Siponto walk away from the water to the main road and turn right.

MONTE SANT'ANGELO

If you've been staying in Manfredonia, you may think the Gargano Promontory is all housing projects and chemical factories. A bus trip to Monte Sant'Angelo, the highest hill town in the Gargano at almost a kilometer (half mile) above sea level, will expand your horizons. During the Crusades, the faithful made the arduous trek up narrow switchbacks to pray at the town's Sanctuary of San Michele. Today, SITA buses climb up from Manfredonia's Piazza Marconi (45 min, L3,000) hourly (five times on Sunday). The bus ride up the narrow, windy road provides you with a view of ashen mountains stitched in at their base by symmetrical rows of olive trees. As you climb, sun-bleached limestone rock gives way to natural caves and quarries of *carcaro* marble, and you can see how farmers made the most of the inhospitable terrain by building terraces into the hillsides.

The SITA bus drops you off in the **Piazza Duca d'Aosta.** If you still have an appetite after the bus ride, try local specialties like *capretto alla bracce* (grilled baby goat) or *agnello al forno* (baked lamb) at **La Caravella** (V. Reale Basilica 84, tel. 0884/561444). From the bus stop, walk straight ahead on Corso Vittorio Emanuele, which becomes Via Reale Basilica. Just past the restaurant on the right is the **Sanctuary of San Michele** (V. Reale Basilica, no phone; admission free; open Apr.–Sept., daily 7:30–12:30 and 2:30–5; Sept–Mar. daily 7:30–7), fronted by a tall hexagonal tower built by Charles I of Anjou in 1273. To reach the shrine itself, go through the archway to the left of the tower. Despite the crush of tourists, the dark cave with pews set before a sculpture of San Michele in white marble has a mystical atmosphere, reinforced by the fervently praying devotees who dip their hands in basins of holy water at the foot of the saint's shrine.

Continue past the sanctuary and take the first stairs on your right for the impressive, partially restored ruins of the **Norman-Swabian-Aragonese Castle** (admission L3,000). The Torre dei Giganti was built in 837, the adjoining sections in the 13th and 14th centuries, and the bulk of the fortifications in the

1490s. The ramparts offer a panoramic view of the Gulf of Manfredonia and the interior of the Gargano. If they're not too busy, the friendly members of the **Cooperativa ECO** (Largo R. Guiscardo 2, tel. 0884/565444), which administers the castle, will show you around and explain (in English) its history. The cooperative also offers information about the area and organizes occasional excursions and hikes; you can contact them at the office or at the castle.

On the southern slope of the hill is the medieval quarter, with neighborhoods of stark white houses stacked one atop another. Follow signs for the **Museo Tancredi**, with an exhibit of peasants' work tools and wine presses and a wonderful set of black-and-white photos that capture the townsfolk early in the century. *P. San Francesco d'Assisi, tel. 0884/562098. Admission L3,000. Open May–Sept., Mon. 8:30–2, Tues.–Sat. 8:30–2 and 2:30–8, Sun. 10–12:30 and 3:30–7; Oct.–Apr., Mon.–Sat. 8–2.*

VIESTE

Vieste, at the northeast tip of the Gargano Promontory, almost lives up to the airbrushed photos in its travel brochures. The whitewashed houses of the old city protrude into the sea on two rocky spurs, with miles of broad coves and sandy beaches to the west and a rockier, even *more* scenic coastline to the south. Despite a rush of Italian and German vacationers in July and August, Vieste never quite loses its charm—made up of equal parts natural scenery, refreshing sea breezes, and almost-urban conveniences. It's also a good place to access the Tremiti Islands, to begin a boat tour of the grottoes along the Gargano coast, or to use as a base for exploring the Foresta Umbra.

The 15th-century walls of Monte Sant'Angelo's castle were built by Francesco di Giorgio Martini, a military engineer and Renaissance man. The walls outline a human torso, the large phallus pointing east to discourage enemies from attacking at dawn.

BASICS

The helpful staff at the **AAST** office (P. Kennedy 1, tel. 0884/708806; open daily in winter 8–1 and 3–7, 4–8 in summer) speaks some English. They can answer all your questions and know the bus schedules backward and forward. Piazza Kennedy is at the end of Corso L. Fazzini. The most conveniently located bank is **Banco di Napoli** (V. XXIV Maggio 38, tel. 0884/708003).

COMING AND GOING

SITA and **ATAF buses** buzz between Vieste and Manfredonia (2 hrs, L6,000), and most continue on to Foggia. About six buses run daily except Sunday, when there is none or only one. The bus stop is in Piazzale Manzoni; the nearest place to buy tickets is **Blu Bar** (V. XXIV Maggio 76). If you're approaching Vieste from the north, the FS Bologna–Lecce line will take you to San Severo, where you can switch to the private train line **Ferrovie del Gargano;** this leaves you at Calanella (8 daily, 1¾ hrs, L6,700), 3 km (2 mi) outside Peschici (*see below*). From here you transfer to a Ferrovie del Gargano bus (40 min, L3,000), which brings you to the intersection of Via Rossini and Via Verdi in Vieste. The entire trip from San Severo takes about three hours, but the scenery is incredible.

From June to September, an **Adriatica** (Galli, tel. 0884/582888) hydrofoil departs for the Tremiti Islands at 9 AM and returns at 7 PM (1 hr, L40,000 round-trip).

GETTING AROUND

From the SITA/ATAF bus stop, **Viale XXIV Maggio,** which becomes Corso Fazzini, leads through the center of town and to the **centro storico** (on your right). To get to the port, follow Corso Fazzini as it curves left, becoming Viale Italia; where the road ends, continue on four blocks. For the hotels on **Lungomare Europa,** follow signs from the bus stop for Lungomare Europa or Peschici Litoranea and turn left at the water. The Ferrovie del Gargano bus stop is a few blocks down from the other stop, toward the water.

WHERE TO SLEEP

Accommodations in Vieste are expensive, especially during high season, but they're still cheaper than in Peschici or on the Tremiti Islands. Most hotels close down from the end of September until Easter and are fully booked in late July and August. Doubles, all with bath, at **Pensione Giada** (Lungomare Europa 18, 1 km/½ mi from bus station, tel. 0884/706593) go for L30,000–L80,000. Across from the beach, **Hotel Vela Velo** (Lungomare Europa 19, tel. 0884/706303) has clean doubles with bath (L35,000–L90,000); the price includes breakfast, an umbrella on the beach, and the use of a bike. Vela Velo also rents equipment for water sports (*see* Outdoor Activities, *below*). Centrally located **Pensione al Centro Storico** (V. Mafrolla 32, off V. Pola, tel. and fax 0884/707030) has clean and comfortable rooms (doubles with bath L60,000–L100,000, breakfast included). Check out the spectacular ocean view from the breakfast room.

Scores of **campgrounds** line the coast both west and south of Vieste. They're difficult to reach on foot, but those to the west are accessible in summer, when Ferrovie del Gargano buses follow the coastal road (the Litoranea) between Vieste and Peschici. The one campground that can be reached on foot is the modern **Baia degli Aranci** (Lungomare Europa, just past Pensione Giada, tel. 0884/706591; open May–mid-Oct.), on an attractive site sloping up a hill right above the beach. It costs L6,000–L14,500 per person and L9,000–L21,500 per tent.

WHERE TO EAT

The entire town of Vieste is crammed with places to eat, most serving moderately good food at moderate prices. There is also an **open market** near the bottom of Viale XXIV Maggio that is open daily from early morning to late evening in summer. For a sit-down meal, **Trattoria Rustichello** (V. Spina 23, tel. 0884/708698) makes a mean fresh grilled sole. **Il Fornaio** (C. Fazzini 1, tel. 0884/701895) and **Pizzeria Portofino** (V. Sante Naccarati, just past the info office, no phone) both have good, cheap pizza by the slice; the former is known for its *panzerotto* (basically a calzone), the latter for its 3-ft-long calzone. **Ristorante Box 19** (V. Santa Maria di Merino 19, tel. 0884/705229, closed Mon. in winter), which must be in every German guidebook, serves spaghetti *alle vongole* (with clams) in a silly oversize clam shell, but it tastes pretty good. The menu runs from homemade *orecchiette* (ear-shape pasta) to fish stew (L24,000). The family-run **Enoteca Vesta** (V. Duomo 14, tel. 0884/706411; closed Oct.–Apr.) features tasty dishes like *melanzane ripiene* (stuffed eggplant) and a huge selection of Puglian wines such as Bollina and Cerbinare (both dry whites), as well as a hearty helping of local hospitality.

WORTH SEEING

The call of Vieste's ocean is too strong and its monuments too few to inspire much sightseeing. But before you scamper down to the surf, climb around the **centro storico,** the neighborhood of whitewashed houses and stone archways, above and to the east of the downtown area. Every now and then you'll catch a glimpse of the blue sea framed by a narrow alleyway. The **Duomo** (off V. Duomo) is pretty ordinary, but you should climb the stairs to the 13th-century **castello** (closed to the public) for the views of the city, the green hills in the background, and the coastline to the south. Before you leave the centro storico, walk back down Via Duomo to Via Cimaglia and check out the **Chianca Amara** (Bitter Stone), where more than 5,000 townsfolk were beheaded when the Turks sacked and pillaged the town in 1554.

OUTDOOR ACTIVITIES

For simple beach lounging, you can choose between **Spiaggia di San Lorenzo** to the west of the center and **Spiaggia del Castello** to the south, both pleasant, sandy, and largely free. The most enticing beaches are along the rocky coast farther south; you can bike to them, but many are controlled by campgrounds. The large beaches farther west can be reached on the coastal bus toward Peschici. At most beaches, you can rent a pedal boat or lightweight canoe for L10,000 per hour. **Hotel Vela Velo** (*see* Where to Sleep, *above*), on the Spiaggio di San Lorenzo, usually rents Windsurfers (L20,000 per hr, L40,000 per half-day). For catamarans and sailboats (L30,000 per hr), you'll have to make the 5- to 7-km (3- to 4-mi) walk toward Peschici to **Camping Capo Vieste** (tel. 0884/706326) or **Camping Umbramare** (tel. 0884/706174).

If you don't want to climb up to the Foresta Umbra, the ride along the coastal road, the Litoranea, toward either Peschici or Mattinata is relatively easy and allows some spectacular views of the coast. You can rent a bike (L30,000 per day), moped (L70,000), or scooter (L90,000) at **Sol** (V. Trepiccioni, tel. 0884/7011558).

PESCHICI

The small fishing village of Peschici sits atop a ridge jutting out into the sea, with a rocky coastline to the east and the broad, sandy beach of the Baia di Peschici to the west. There are no significant sights here, though the centro storico poised directly above the water keeps some of its old-world charm. Most people come for the beach, framed by the town on one side and by green rolling hills on the other, but largely covered by the gaudy umbrellas of private entrepreneurs. Though overrun by Italian and German families in July and August (and correspondingly expensive), Peschici in the off-season remains a good place to relax and enjoy the coastline of the Gargano at its best.

BASICS

From June to September, the **tourist office** (C. Garibaldi 57, tel. 0884/962796) is open Monday–Saturday 10–12:30 and 6–10:30; it's closed the rest of the year.

COMING AND GOING

Ferrovie del Gargano (tel. 167/296247) buses run about every two hours to Vieste (40 min, L3,000) to the east and Peschici Calanella to the west, where you catch trains for San Severo. The bus stop is the parking lot of **Camping Sport** (V. Montesanto 34–40, tel. 0884/964015), where you can see the schedule and buy tickets; you can also buy tickets at several tobacco shops and newsstands in town.

WHERE TO SLEEP AND EAT

Many of Peschici's hotels are reasonably priced in theory but only accept guests paying full pension (three meals) in high season (June–Aug). **Locanda al Castello** (V. Castello 29, follow signs toward castle, tel. 0884/964038), in the old quarter overlooking the ocean, has a beautiful vista and cushy rooms (doubles with bath L95,000 not including full pension). Near the beach, try **Hotel Piccolo Paradiso** (Contrada Vignola, tel. 0884/963466; closed Oct.–Apr.) before and after high season, when doubles with bath cost L80,000, not including full pension; otherwise, you'll have to pay twice that for full pension. Take the street behind the beach, and you'll see the hotel on your left. The closest campground is **Camping Marina Piccola** (Baia di Peschici, tel. 0884/963424; closed Oct.–May), a third of the way down the beach. Tent spaces go for L12,000–L13,000, plus L7,500 per person, depending on the season. Cut across the sandy beach; the entrance is a white building fronted by orange-and-white umbrellas.

Around Piazza IV Novembre, you'll find a slew of eateries. The best restaurant is in Locanda al Castello (*see above*); try the homemade *orecchiette* or the *seppie ripiene* (stuffed squid; L14,000). The same people run the excellent **Pizzeria al Castello** (V. Recinto Baronale 1, behind Locanda al Castello, no phone), with pizzas for L7,000–L10,000. For some fruits and veggies, stop at the large **produce market,** open Monday–Saturday 7–1, in Piazza Trieste, off Via Solferino.

FORESTA UMBRA

Nestled in the heart of the Gargano, this secluded ancient forest is one of the most beautiful parks in southern Italy. Densely packed giant trees blanket steep valleys, home to flora and fauna sometimes found nowhere else. Only two roads cut through the forest. Apart from a few wildlife reserves, you can explore the rest of the forest on foot, though you should probably stick to the clear, well-marked paths. Some paths are okay for mountain bikes, but you should watch out for fallen branches. The time posted at the beginning of each path is for a round-trip hike.

You'll have to overcome numerous difficulties when visiting the Foresta Umbra. There is no lodging in the forest, and it is illegal to camp except in an RV or similarly equipped vehicle. No drinking water is available except at the **Punto di Ristoro** (tel. 0884/560980; bar closed Oct.–Easter, trattoria closed Sept.–May), at the top of the forest. Luckily, they stay open all day and charge nonmonopolistic prices (L3,000–L4,000 for a sandwich). Punto di Ristoro is the only place that sells maps of the forest (L2,500) or more detailed guides (L10,000), though you can get a serviceable photocopy at the tourist office in Vieste (*see above*), among other places. If the **information office** (300 ft past the Punto di Ristoro coming from Vieste) isn't open, continue another 500 ft to the park's **administrative offices** (tel. 0884/560944).

COMING AND GOING

This is the hardest part, but it's not impossible. **Agrifoglio** (P. Sant'Antonio, tel. 0884/962721) in Peschici will drive you to the forest and provide a guide for full day of hiking, exploring, and swimming, plus a picnic lunch, all for L65,000 per person. **S.O.L.** (V. Trepiccioni 5, tel. 0884/701558) in Vieste also organizes group hiking tours (L40,000 per person), jeep tours of the Foresta Umbra (L65,000), free-climbing expeditions, and other outdoor activities, all including transportation , equipment and lunch.

BY BUS • In summer there is one bus (tel. 167296247 for bus

schedules) per day from Rodi Garganico, on the **Ferrovie del Gargano** rail line from San Severo (*see* Coming and Going *in* Vieste, *above*); otherwise, the bus leaves from Vico del Gargano, which does not have a train station. The bus schedule leaves you about two hours to spend in the forest. Call the tourist office in Peschici (*see above*) for information about private agencies that organize day trips.

BY BIKE • The most challenging—and rewarding—option is to explore the forest by bike. S.O.L. (*see above*) rents bikes (L25,000/day) and organizes bike trips (L45,000, including the bike rental) from the coast, but you can also do it on your own with a map. In either case, you must be in good biking shape to reach the park, about a 15 km (9 mi) trip. From Vieste take Via Verdi, which becomes the road to Peschici (*not* the Litoranea). After the short but steep climb out of Vieste, you'll pedal along about 10 fairly flat km (6 mi), and then you take the clearly marked left turn for the Foresta Umbra. After going marginally uphill for 4 km (2½ mi), you suddenly leave the flat, sunny plain for the shade of the forest. This part of the forest is the lowest in altitude, so all the trails, which start about 1 km/½ mi from the entrance, are uphill. To reach the Punto di Ristoro—the only place for water—you'll need a bike with working gears, and you'll want to use all of them. Getting there requires 13 more km (8 mi) of uninterrupted climbing, at first moderate and then increasingly steep (the top is more than 2,600 ft above sea level). Resist the temptation to tear down the hill on the way back; you could hit a pothole and bruise more than your ego.

TREMITI ISLANDS

Billed as the "last paradise," the Tremiti Islands are a quiet refuge far from the bustling beach towns of Puglia's coast. The main islands are San Domino, Capraia, San Nicola, and far to the north, Pianosa; only verdant San Domino and historic San Nicola are inhabited. The islands aren't particularly clean, the beaches aren't too sandy, and the restaurants are overpriced and mediocre. The one thing you can expect from the islands, however, is peace and quiet. Even if you're on a rather expensive day trip, a short walk will get you away from the crowds to a place where you'll be disturbed only by waves and seagulls.

All hotels and most everything else are on **San Domino**, at 2½ km (1½ mi) long the largest of the islands. Day-trippers swarm the beach at **Cala delle Arene,** near the dock, but you can head off more or less alone to explore the coastline's coves and grottoes. Steep cliffs around much of the island make getting down to the water difficult if not impossible, but for long stretches on the west and south sides you can walk all the way down. The southern part of the island is covered with an overrated pine forest that at least serves to insulate you from civilization and the hot sun.

San Nicola, a flat-top, treeless island surrounded entirely by steep cliffs, has an annoying strip of restaurants and shops and the abbey of **Santa Maria a Mare,** once a powerful Benedictine monastery with territories on the mainland. Wily pirates tricked their way inside the fortress in 1321, slaughtering all but two of the monks and making off with the abbey's treasure. The church interior reveals a masterful mosaic floor and an early Byzantine wooden cross. If you continue straight through the complex, you'll come out on the desertlike main part of the island, where you can follow the narrow paths above the cliffs, hemmed by the rocks and water below.

BASICS

This is one place where you shouldn't depend on help from the tourist information office. A booth at the San Domino port is open somewhat erratically during high season (mid-July–late Aug., Mon.–Sat. around 10–2 and 4–6). Bring plenty of cash with you to the islands, where there is all of one bank; Cassa di Risparmio di Puglia (Piazzetta San Domino, tel. 0882/463406) changes money but does not give cash advances on credit cards. They do, however, have an ATM.

COMING AND GOING

The ferry lineup for the Tremiti Islands changes from year to year. In summer, **Adriatica** (tel. 0884/582888) runs two boats to and from Termoli (*see* Termoli *in* Chapter 11): a hydrofoil (50 min, L23,900), with one to three departures per day (in each direction), and a ferry (1 hr 40 min, L13,600), with one departure each day. **Navigazione Libera del Golfo** (tel. 0875/704859 or 0875/703937 in Termoli) has two fast boats per day from Termoli to the Tremiti (50 min, L23,000). In summer there's an Adriatica hydrofoil to Vieste (1 hr, L17,000) and Manfredonia (2 hrs, L30,900). There are also occasional boats to Ortona, Vasto, and Peschici. In general, boats come to the islands in the morning and leave in the late afternoon. They arrive either at San Domino or San Nicola; buy a ticket at the port before your departure.

GETTING AROUND

Boats shuttle back and forth every 15 minutes between San Domino and San Nicola for L2,000; buy your ticket at the booth on the dock or, for some companies, on board. Don't confuse these boats with the ones that provide tours of San Domino (45 min, L15,000) or the entire archipelago (2 hrs, L22,000), which are not really worth it. To reach San Domino's makeshift town center, with grocery stores, hotels, and bars, head up the steeper of the two streets leaving the port. There are no street signs, but if you go straight for ¾ km (½ mi), you'll reach the main square.

WHERE TO SLEEP AND EAT

From mid-July through August, most places only accept guests paying at least *mezza pensione* (half pension: room, breakfast and either lunch or dinner) for around L90,000 per person. **La Nassa** (V. Villagio Rurale, tel. 0882/463345) is the least expensive of the small pensions off San Domino's central square. Doubles with bath are L60,000 in low season, but in high season you'll have to fork over L85,000 for half pension at their mediocre restaurant. **Rossana** (V. Spiaggia, tel. 0882/463298) is just 150 ft above the port; doubles with bath are L65,000–L75,000, but with the obligatory half pension in July and August, they cost L85,000–L100,000 per person. At the **Villagio Internazionale Punta del Diamante** campsite (tel. 0882/463405; closed Oct.–mid-May), at the northern tip of San Domino (take the less steep road out of the port and make a sharp right at the sign), you can stay in a strange but functional aluminum hut in the pine woods next to a beautiful cove. Doubles are L120,000, but from late July to early September you have to tack on at least half pension (L110,000 per person). If you're just here for the day, pack a lunch from a market on the mainland; if you came unprepared, **Alimentari e Ortofrutta** (V. del Vecchio Forno 3, tel. 0882/463413; open Mon.–Sat. 7–1:30 and 5–8), on San Domino, has fresh *panini* (sandwiches, L4,000–L5,000).

OUTDOOR ACTIVITIES

On San Domino you can rent a mountain bike for L10,000 per hour (L35,000 per day) at **Da Gimmy** (P. Belvedere; open Easter–Sept., sporadically 9 AM–midnight). Stands along the beach at Cala delle Arene rent kayaks (L15,000 per hr). **Marlin Diving Center** (in Hotel Eden, Villaggio San Domino, tel. 0882/463211) charges L70,000 for a dive, including gear.

According to legend, both Augustus and Charlemagne used the Tremiti island of San Nicola as a place of exile, a tradition continued when the Bourbons turned the Abbey of Santa Maria a Mare into a prison.

HIKING • Despite its small size, you can spend hours in San Domino's pine forest, following the narrow paths that wind along the coastline, with frequent views of various grottoes and coves. For more seclusion and/or adventure, walk along the periphery of San Nicola and try to find a path down to the rocks 200 ft below. A number of nearly vertical paths go at least part of the way down the cliff, but use extreme caution: no one will even see you fall. The least dangerous way down to the water is to take the dirt road to the cemetery at the far end of the island and follow the path that skirts the cemetery's back (northern) wall. This leads to a narrow path that slowly meanders all the way to the bottom, where you can be completely alone and check out the desolate island of Capraia.

BARI

The thriving business and commercial center of Bari has been responsible for shuttling goods and tourists throughout the eastern Mediterranean for centuries. Just about every major European power, including the ancient Greeks, Romans, Ostrogoths, Byzantines, Lombards, and Saracens, made use of Bari's strategic position, turning the city into one of the most important ports in the Adriatic. During World War II, planes and ships left from Bari for attacks on Greece and Yugoslavia, making the city the object of heavy bombing by both the Allies and the Germans.

The Bari of today is broken up into the huge, neatly designed Città Nuova (New City), built in the early 19th century by the king of Naples, and the Città Vecchia (Old City), a bewildering array of cobblestone streets and medieval homes sticking out into the sea. The Old City holds what picturesque, premodern character Bari may have, as well as the remains of good ole St. Nick (*see* Worth Seeing, *below*). The New City, despite its lack of appeal to sightseers, is a prosperous, energetic, and diverse (by southern Italian standards) metropolis with broad boulevards, grand old apartment buildings, and first-class shops and restaurants.

BASICS

CHANGING MONEY • You can change money at the **FS information office** in the train station or at one of Bari's many, many banks. Most have an office in the New City between Via Dante and Corso Vittorio Emanuele.

DISCOUNT TRAVEL AGENCIES • Try Bari's **CTS** (V. Fornari 7, tel. 080/5213244; open weekdays 9:30–1 and 4:30–8, Sat. 9:30–1).

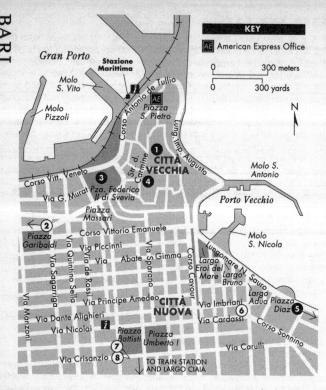

BARI

Gran Porto

Stazione Marittima

Molo S. Vito

Molo Pizzoli

Corso Antonio de Tullio

Lung. Imp. Augusto

Piazza S. Pietro

CITTÀ VECCHIA

Str. d. Carmine

Molo S. Antonio

Porto Vecchio

Molo S. Nicola

Corso Vitt. Veneto

Via G. Murat

Pza. Federico II di Svevia

Piazza Massari

Corso Vittorio Emanuele

Via Sparano

Via Quintino Sella

Via de Rossi

Via Piccinni

Via Abate Gimma

Piazza Garibaldi

Via Sagarriga

Via Manzoni

Via Principe Amedeo

CITTÀ NUOVA

Via Dante Alighieri

Via Nicolai

Piazza Battisti

Piazza Umberto I

Via Crisanzio

Corso Cavour

Lungomare N. Sauro

Largo Eroi del Mare

Largo Bruno

Largo Adua

Piazza Diaz

Via Imbriani

Via Cardassi

Corso Sonnino

Via Carulli

KEY

AE American Express Office

0   300 meters
0   300 yards

N

Sights ●
Basilica di San Nicola, **1**
Castello Normanno-Svevo, **3**
Cattedrale di San Sabino, **4**
Pinacoteca Provinciale, **5**

Lodging ○
Pensione Fiorini, **6**
Pensione Giulia, **8**
Pensione Romeo, **7**
Pineta San Francesco Park, **2**

TO TRAIN STATION AND LARGO CIAIA

EMERGENCIES AND MEDICAL AID • The central **police station** (V. G. Murat 4, tel. 080/5291111) has an *ufficio stranieri* (foreigners' office) to help you.

MAIL • The central **post office** (P. Battisti, tel. 080/5216426) is open Monday–Saturday 8:15–4:40.

VISITOR INFORMATION • There are four **Stop-Over in Bari** information centers (*see box, below*) that can tell you anything you could possibly need to know: the OTE office (V. Nicolai 47, tel. 080/5232716), the Magic Bus (in front of train station, tel. 080/5214211), at the Stazione Marittima, and at Stop-Over's Pineta San Francesco campsite. All are open daily 9:30–9 (except the OTE office, open Mon.–Fri. 9:30–1 and 4:30–8), and you can call the number at the campsite at any time. Outside of the Stop-Over season, June to September, only the OTE office and Magic Bus are open. No matter what you need, go here first. The **EPT** office (P. Aldo Moro 32/A, tel. 080/5242244; open Mon.–Sat. 8:30–1), to the right of the train station, is unhelpful by comparison, though their map of Bari is marginally better.

COMING AND GOING

Coming and going is Bari's main shtick. The city offers a plethora of train connections, and it's a better choice than overcrowded Brindisi for ferries to Greece. Unfortunately, ferries from Bari don't accept Eurailpasses, but some from Brindisi do.

BY TRAIN • Bari's many train systems include the **Ferrovie dello Stato** (tel. 1478/88088) and three private lines, **Ferrovie del Sud–Est** (FSE; tel. 080/5562111), **Ferrovie Bari–Nord** (FBN; tel. 080/5213577), and **Ferrovie Calabro–Lucane** (FCL; tel. 080/5244881). The FS railway, at the main station in **Piazza Aldo Moro,** handles most traffic, with service to Milan (7 daily, 8½ hrs, L91,000) and Rome (6 daily, 4½ hrs, L54,500). Trains on the **FS** line also leave hourly for Foggia (1½ hrs, L10,100), Lecce (2 hrs, L12,100), and Taranto (1½–2 hrs, L10,100). Luggage storage (L5,000 for 12 hrs) is available 6 AM–midnight. The **FSE** station is on the other side of the tracks, at the end of the underpass. Its trains head hourly to Grotte di Castellana Grotte (1 hr, L3,900) and Alberobello (1 hr 40 min, L5,900). Be fore-warned: private lines like this one move slowly, with long pauses and frequent stops. Outside the main station to the left, the **FBN** line has frequent trains (but almost none on Sunday) north to Bitonto (25 min, L2,000) and Barletta (1¼ hrs, L5,700). The **FAL** line next door runs every couple hours to Matera in Basilicata (1½ hrs, L5,700).

BY BUS • It is highly unlikely that you will need to take a bus anywhere, but if you do, four companies serve the area: **SITA** (tel. 080/341835) buses leave from the front of the train station, **AMET** (tel. 080/5793819) and **SPA** (tel. 080/5232202) from Largo Eroi del Mare, and **FSE** (tel. 080/5562111) from Largo Ciaia, south of the train station.

BY FERRY • Ferries to Greece cost roughly the same from Bari and Brindisi, but Bari is a more appealing place to spend a day or two. On the other hand, there are more boats from Brindisi, which may make a difference out of season. You can either buy your ticket directly from a ferry company at the **Stazione Marittima** or from a travel agent. Two of the cheaper companies are **Poseidon** (Stazione Marittima, Box 11–12, tel. 080/5241039) and **Lorusso** (Stazione Marittima, tel. 080/5217699). Fares to Corfu (10–12 hrs), Igoumenitsa (11–13 hrs), and Patras (16–18 hrs) should be about L41,000–L85,000 on the deck, L75,000–L115,000 for a reclining seat inside, and L90,000–L171,000 for the cheapest beds, including port taxes. There's a 10% discount on return tickets and a L5,000–L20,000 discount for students on some lines. Do some investivating when buying your tickets because prices vary widely. Except for a few days in peak season, you should be able to reserve a spot the same day you travel. About two hours before your departure, you are generally required to check in with the ferry company and the police at the Stazione Marittima.

BY PLANE • The **Bari Palese Airport** (tel. 080/5382370), 8 km (5 mi) west of Bari, has flights to major cities throughout Europe (with connections provided by **Alitalia** (V. Argiro 56, tel. 080/5216511), **Air France** (tel. 080/5213246), **British Airways** (tel. 080/5584944), and **Lufthansa** (tel. 06/46601). A shuttle bus (L6,000) leaves from the train station for the airport 80 minutes before each flight.

GETTING AROUND

Trains and buses drop you in Piazza Aldo Moro in Città Nuovo. From here Piazza Umberto I is one block north, the Città Vecchia is about 10 blocks north, and the port is around the left side of the Città Vecchia. The entire New City between Piazza Umberto I and Corso Vittorio Emanuele is filled with designer stores, chic *caffè*, and old apartment buildings; to the east is Bari's most pleasant walk along the sea. Bari is very walkable. The orange **local buses** (L1,000; buy tickets before you board) that hang out in Piazza Aldo Moro are useful in getting you around the city, particularly at night. To reach the ferries from the train station, take the infrequent Bus 20 to the port or the more frequent Buses 18, 21, and 22, which go to Piazza Massari, 10 minutes south of the port.

WHERE TO SLEEP

One of the wonders of the Stop-Over in Bari program is the free—yes, *free*—campsite at the edge of town, in the large **Pineta San Francesco Park** (take Bus 3 or 5 or 5/ from the station as late as 10:45 PM). The campground has showers and luggage storage; if you don't have a tent, they'll provide one for you. The campsite is open from mid-June to mid-September, and you have to be 30 or younger. If camping isn't your style, the people at the Magic Bus can also call around to find a hotel room for you.

There are a few decent hotels within walking distance of the train station.You get what you pay for at **Pensione Fiorini** (V. Imbriani 69, tel. 080/5540788)—a cramped room and a dismal bathroom (doubles L59,000). **Pensione Romeo** (V. Crisanzio 12, 1 block north of train station, tel. and fax 080/5237253) has passable doubles with bath for L90,000. **Pensione Giulia** (V. Crisanzio 12, tel. 080/5218271) has big, plain doubles for L90,000 (breakfast included).

WHERE TO EAT

Bari is known for its tasty and reasonably priced seafood, and good restaurants dot the city. Grab warm focaccia with tomatoes at **Panificio Signorile** (C. Sonnino 6, tel. 080/5540895). To try some fish without going broke (L25,000–L35,000 for a full meal), go to **Osteria delle Travi** (Largo Chiutla 12, tel. 0330/840438; closed Mon.) or **La Credenze** (Strada Arco di Sant'Onofrio 14, tel. 080/5244747; closed Wed.). **El Pedro** (V. Piccinni 152, 1 block from Città Vecchia, tel. 080/5211294; closed Sun.), a self-service restaurant, is always crammed with busy businesspeople eating a wide variety of *primi piatti* (first courses; L4,500), from *bucatini* (long, squiggly pasta) with tomatoes and green beans to *sartù di riso* (rice casserole), and *piatti secondi* (second courses; L5,500–L6,000), from roast squid to fried chicken. Everything is good.

To satisfy your sweet tooth, stop at **Portoghese** (Strada Palazzo di Città 55, in Città Vecchia, tel. 080/5241890) for *castagnedde* (sweets with almonds, sugar, and a touch of lemon zest). A tradition among

STOP-OVER IN BARI

From early June to early September, Stop-Over in Bari offers abundant information, free travel on urban (AMTAB) buses, free bike and skateboard usage (go to the campsite and leave your passport), and a daily newsletter. At the high-tech end, you can watch TV programs from all over the world from 4 PM to midnight at the Magic Bus or surf the Internet (and send and receive E-mail: StopOver£inmedia.it) at the main office on Via Nicolai whenever it's open. If you're under 30, you can take advantage of all this simply by showing your passport or identity card.

Bari's youth is to end an evening out by having a snack of warm *cornetti* (flaky pastry filled with pastry cream or jam). There are places all over that turn out these buttery pillows well into the wee hours, including **Il Dolcetto** (V. de Rossi 148, no phone), where everything is half price on Wednesday, and an unmarked shop (C. Benedetto Croce 63, no phone) south of the train station. Both bakeries stay open until midnight on weekdays, until 2 AM Saturday.

WORTH SEEING

The **Città Vecchia** neighborhood hasn't changed much in 500 years, except for the forest of television antennas—it's still a wonderful maze of crooked cobblestone alleyways, low-hanging arches, and the occasional whitewashed dwelling. A strong sense of community is fostered among the working-class folks and poor people who live here. But crime is a serious problem in the Città Vecchia, and women and solo travelers should avoid coming here at night. It's reasonably safe during the day, but be alert.

The remains of **St. Nicholas**—the patron saint of fishermen, Orthodox Russians, pawnbrokers, and greedy children the world over—were stolen from their original home in Asia Minor and brought to Bari by more than 60 boisterous sailors. The sailors built a wonderful crypt for him, with translucent marble and a colonnade of 28 stone columns. You can visit the crypt, in the **Basilica di San Nicola** (P. San Nicola, tel. 080/5211205; open daily 7:30–1 and 5–7), smack in the heart of the Old City. The simple A-frame centerpiece at the front gives the church a sturdy, barnlike look that exemplifies Lombardian and Norman siege-mentality design. To the right is a tower co-opted from an earlier Byzantine fortress; the tower on the left was added for balance. The roof is embroidered with Saracen-inspired arabesques, and the portal is laced with more arabesques and miniature gargoyles. The broad interior has a cavernous feel, with sunlight reflecting off the white stone walls.

Bari's **Cattedrale di San Sabino** (P. dell'Odegitria, tel. 080/5210605; open daily 8:30–1 and 5–7) was built at the end of the 12th century for Bari's original patron saint, before the more popular St. Nicholas came along and took the title. The crypt of this simple, hauntingly bare medieval church houses the Madonna Odegitria, a dark-skinned Madonna icon said to have been based on a sketch by the apostle Luke. Near the Duomo, the seaside **Castello Normanno-Svevo** (P. Federico II di Svevia, tel. 080/5214361) guards the perimeter of the Città Vecchia. The Normans built the castle on a Roman fort, and Frederick II, as he often did, rearranged and built on top of the original Norman design, finishing in 1290. If you cross the moat to the large courtyard, you can visit the **Gipsoteca** (admission L4,000; open Mon.–Sat. 9–1 and 3:30–7, Sun 9–1), a collection of casts of sculptures on churches throughout Puglia. Unless you're a connoisseur of late medieval church design, it's probably not for you. For more culture, head down Lungomare Nazario Sauro to the Palazzo della Provincia, which houses the **Pinacoteca Provinciale** (V. Spalato 19, tel. 080/5412431; open Mon.–Sat. 9:30–1 and 4–7, Sun. 9:30–1; admission L5,000), a fair-sized but rather humdrum collection of Italian art from the late medieval period to the present. Its major selling points are middling paintings by Bellini, Tintoretto, and Veronese (one each). For a change of pace, Bari's Aquario Provinciale is due to reopen in late 1999 after a renovation and should give you a close-up view of Adriatic fish and sea life. Check with the tourist office for opening times.

AFTER DARK

At night, Bari's youth spread out along the water from Largo Eroi del Mare to Piazza Armando Diaz, stopping for drinks at the bars in between, such as **Baraonda** (Largo G. Bruno 7, no phone; closed Sun.) and **Taverna del Maltese** (V. Nicolai 67, no phone; closed Tues.). Look for the jazz, blues, and hip-hop performances arranged by the cultural association **FEZ**, at various locations. For a touch of Americana, drink up at **Yankee Pub** (C. Vittorio Emanuele 98, no phone; closed Wed.).

FESTIVALS • There's plenty of music to listen to in Bari all summer long. During the last two weeks of June, concerts and other events of the **Festa d'Estate** take place almost every evening at the Fiera del Levante, just west of the port. In late July, the **Festa della Musica** hosts groups of all types in the streets for free concerts all day and into the night. And at the end of August, bands perform at Stop-Over's **Bari Rock Contest,** at the **Pineta San Francesco,** which is also the venue for Stop-Over's regular concert series.

NEAR BARI

ALBEROBELLO

In the heart of the Murge hills, between Bari and Taranto, Alberobello has a dense concentration of trulli, some of the oddest dwellings in all of Europe. One legend has them dating from the 13th century; yet another claims the trulli date from a 16th-century decree forbidding the use of mortar in building a roof, supposedly in order to exploit a tax loophole. The necessary result was the construction of squat, small one-story houses with steep conical roofs made of flat stones. You'll spot these curious buildings throughout the region all the way to the suburbs of Bari, but Alberobello's old sections are composed almost entirely of them. Many of the trulli are still inhabited, and most of the rest are in the business of foisting things onto tourists. Of course, the roofs have been sealed with plaster from the inside, but they still look the same from the outside, often decorated with Christian or pagan symbols. Wherever you see an ENTRATA LIBERA sign, feel free to have a peek inside, but there may be pressure to buy something. The free **Trullo Sovrano** (open daily 10–1 and 3–7), behind the church at the far end of Corso Vittorio Emanuele from Piazza del Popolo, is the only two-story trullo.

Bari leads all Italian cities in petty theft. The Old City is particularly unsafe at night. The streets of the New City, though safer, are neither well lighted nor heavily traveled at night.

BASICS • There are FSE trains to and from Bari (1 hr 40 min, L5,700) about every hour (every 2 hrs on Sun.). From the train station, take Via Mazzini, which becomes Via Garibaldi and leads to the central Piazza del Popolo. Turn left and go down to Largo Martellotta, and the trulli will rise in front of you on a gentle hill like something out of a Disney flick. The **tourist office** (P. Ferdinando IV, tel. 080/080/ 4321916) is off P. del Popolo. If you'll be in town more than a few hours, head to **EcoTurAm** (V. Aldo Moro 49, tel. 080/9325137), where you can rent a bike (L4,000 per hr, L20,000 per day) and get info on hikes, bike trips, and weeklong cooking classes. If you want to stay overnight, three-star doubles with luxurious bathrooms are L85,000 (breakfast included) at **Hotel Lanzilotta** (P. Ferdinando IV 31, tel. 080/721511, fax 080/721179). Sample typical Puglian dishes like *fave e cicorie* (bean purée with chicory; L7,000) or *brasciola alla barese* (veal or horsemeat roulades with tomato sauce; L9,000) at **Gli Ulivi** (Contrada Popoleto 15, tel. 080/9323796; closed Wed.).

GROTTE DI CASTELLANA

To cool off on a hot day, pay a visit to the **Grotte di Castellana** (tel. 080/4965511), a complex of spectacular underground caves and tunnels filled with enormous and varied stalagmites and stalactites. At the entrance, an elevator takes you down to **La Grave,** the largest of the caverns. From there a series of passageways—Corridor of the Serpent, Corridor of the Desert, and so on—leads through various caves to the **Grotta Bianca,** known for its brilliant off-white stalagmites. You can visit the grottoes only on guided tours (L20,000), which run hourly from 8:30 AM to midday and 2:30 to 5 PM (until 6 PM in summer). To get to the caves, take an FSE train from Bari (1 hr, L3,900) or Alberobello (40 min, L2,700) to the Grotte di Castellana Grotte stop; there's about one train per hour. And no matter how hot it is, take a sweater; the average underground temperature is only 59°F.

TARANTO

A major port and naval base with a touch of seediness, Taranto retains its own brand of charm. Perched on a narrow strip of land between two bays, the Mare Piccolo and the Mare Grande, Taranto offers quiet seaside walks on all sides, and beach towns like Lido Silvana are not far away. According to legend, the city was established by Tiras, son of Neptune, 1,200 years before the founding of Rome. Skeptics suggest that Taranto was actually established by the Spartans in 701 BC, chosen for its strategic position on the Ionian coast. Today Taranto is feeling the effects of economic restructuring. The city's high-tech steel industry seems to have produced more pollution than exportable steel, and the Italian navy, Taranto's other dominant economic force, is being scaled back. But you wouldn't know it from the broad streets, tree-lined squares, and expensive shops of the Città Nuova (New City). And if you come during Holy Week, the week before Easter, you'll be able to witness one of Italy's largest and most spectacular series of pre-Easter processions and parades.

BASICS

Taranto's **EPT** office (C. Umberto I 113, tel. 099/4532392; open Mon.–Fri. 9–12 and 4:30–6:30, Sat. 9–12) provides maps and information on accommodations; Corso Umberto I borders Piazza Garibaldi on the north side. The **post office** (P. Libertà, tel. 099/4709163; open Mon.–Sat. 8:15–7:40) is to the right as you exit the train station.

COMING AND GOING

Taranto is a main stop on the **FS** and **FSE train lines.** Trains leave hourly for Bari (1½ hrs, L10,100) and Metaponto (30 min, L4,700) and every two hours or so for Brindisi (1 hr, L5,900). Nine trains leave daily for Naples (4½ hrs, L22,000).

Three bus companies serve Taranto, all leaving from Piazza Castello at the east end of the old city. **FSE** sends buses to Bari about every two hours (1–2 hrs, L8,500). **SITA** buses head to Matera (5–6 daily, 2 hrs, L7,500). **CTP** buses go to Lido Silvana (3–4 daily, 35 min, L4,000). Purchase FS and CTP tickets at the nearby tobacco shop (P. Castello 4) and SITA tickets at the newsstand next door.

GETTING AROUND

Taranto extends from the train station in the northwest to the new city in the southeast, with the Mare Grande to the southwest. From the train station, walk 500 ft straight ahead to the bridge to the Città Vecchia (Old City). At the other end of the half-mile-long island are Piazza Castello and the bridge to the New City. One block into the New City is Piazza Garibaldi. Via d'Aquino, Taranto's most fashionable street, heads east from Piazza Garibaldi. All local orange **AMAT buses** (L1,000) connect the train station to the New City. Buses run until about 11 PM; buy tickets at tobacco shops, bars, and newsstands.

WHERE TO SLEEP

Catering primarily to families visiting their sons at Taranto's naval base, **Sorrentino** (P. Fontana 7, tel. 099/4707456) is a mom-and-pop budget hotel. Their doubles (L60,000) could use some modernizing, but they're passable for a night or two, and the bathrooms do sparkle. From the station, take Viale Duca d'Aosta to Piazza Fontana. Safely tucked away behind two locked gates, **Albergo Pisani** (V. Cavour 43, tel. 099/4534087, fax 099/4707593) has quiet, clean rooms (doubles L88,000) with reasonably firm beds.

WHERE TO EAT

Taranto has a few choice finds and a lot of mediocre restaurants offering a *menù militare* to sailors. At the entrance to the New City, **Panificio Due Mari** (V. Matteotti 16, tel. 099/4534584; closed Sun.) serves Neapolitan-style pizza. **Queen** (V. de Cesare 20–22, in the New City, tel. 099/4591011) has a decent tavola calda loaded with seafood dishes. A plate of *insalata di riso* (rice salad) is L4,000; *secondi* cost around L5,000. It's not cheap, but for its incredibly fresh seafood, **Gesù Cristo** (P. Ramellini 8, tel. 099/4526466) may in itself be worth a pilgrimage to Taranto for plates of squid, octopus, and mussels, and dishes like spaghetti with tomatoes and shellfish and whole grilled *spigola* (bass). A meal costs L30,000–L40,000, depending on how many dishes you are able to turn away. In the New City, walk about 1 km (½ mi) east on Via Mazzini, three blocks south of Via d'Aquino.

WORTH SEEING

Wander around the crumbling buildings of the **Città Vecchia** if you want to experience Taranto as it was before industrialization. Be as careful here as you would in the old quarters of Bari or Naples and avoid the area at night. After crossing over to Piazza Fontana from the station, take Via Cariati on your left; it has an occasional fish market filled with old *pescatori* (fishermen) who've been casting their nets in the surrounding Mare Piccolo and Mare Grande for years. If you leave Piazza Fontana on the second road on your right, you'll come to Via Duomo, which winds past the 13th-century **Chiesa di San Domenico Maggiore;** note the Gothic portal, Romanesque window, and Baroque double stairway. The road continues past the **Duomo,** with its **Chapel of San Cataldo,** a florid Baroque masterpiece created in honor of Taranto's Irish patron saint. If the church happens to be open, check out the crypt adorned with Byzantine frescoes. At the far end of the old quarter, the expansive **Aragonese Castle** (closed to the public) was built in 1480 by Ferdinand of Aragon; the Italian navy uses it today.

On Piazza Garibaldi in the New City you'll find the **Museo Archeologico Nazionale,** which documents civilization in Puglia from the Stone Age to Roman times. Highlights of the impressive collection include tiny ancient figurines, marble, bronze, and terra-cotta sculptures left behind by Greek and Roman settlers, and a huge assortment of painted vases that reveal various details about early Greek civilization. Be forewarned that a very long-term restoration project has certain sections of the museum closed off to visitors. *C. Umberto I, 41, tel. 099/4532112. Admission L8,000 (L4,000 while under restoration). Open daily 9–2, also Tue.–Sat. 3–7:30.*

BRINDISI

On summer afternoons, Brindisi's docks take on a surreal cast, as they are covered with immobile backpackers looking like they just washed ashore with the tide.

Brindisi might be considered the backpacker's rite of passage into the major league of budget travel. Exchange offices, ticket agents, and multilingual menus have multiplied like rabbits on the Americanized strip that leads from the train station to the docks, where ferries depart for Albania, Greece, and beyond. If you're going to Brindisi to cross the Adriatic, you can buy your ferry ticket ahead of time from a travel agency in another Italian city, though you may miss out on last-minute discounts or schedule changes. It's not difficult to buy a ticket in Brindisi. The free publication *Brindisi Agenda,* available at bars, lists most ferry lines and their representatives, although you can purchase tickets at the many ticket offices all over town. It's also a good idea to buy a warm shirt for the crossing and a cushion or mat to sit on while you wait . . . and wait, and wait.

You don't have to sit on your backpack and wish you had a deck of cards, though. Just a block or two from the main street, Brindisi is a nice, normal (though not tremendously exciting) Puglian city, and the **beaches** are only half an hour by bus (L1,000), which you can catch on Via Cristoforo Columbo, one block from the station. On Thursday morning there's a huge **market** hawking all kinds of things in the Sant'Elia district. And if that doesn't appeal to you, you can reach Ostuni or Lecce in 30 minutes by train. Wherever you go, exercise caution and common sense—Brindisi has acquired a reputation for petty crime, though some argue that it's not entirely deserved.

BASICS

The **AAST** office (Lungomare Regina Margherita 5, tel. 0831/523072; open Mon.-Fri. 8:30–2, also Tues. 2–6:30) has city maps and can help you find a place to sleep. There are myriad places to change money on and around Corso Umberto I and Corso Garibaldi on your way to the launch. Banks are usually open 8:30–1 and 2:30–4. The main **post office** (P. Vittoria 10, tel. 0831/517128; open Mon.–Sat. 8:15–7:40) also changes money.

COMING AND GOING

BY TRAIN • The **FS** (tel. 1478/88088) line serves the **main station** in Piazza Crispi, about a kilometer (½ mi) from the ferry port. In summer, two trains go all the way to the **Brindisi Marittima** station at the port. Luggage storage (L5,000 for 12 hrs) is available at the main station daily 6:40 AM–10:40 PM and in summer at the port daily 8:40 AM–10:40 PM. There is service to Rome (3 daily, 6½ hrs, L56,900) and Milan (6 daily, 9½ hrs, L81,000). Trains to Bari (1½ hrs, L9,800) and Lecce (30 min, L3,400) run about once an hour.

BY BUS • **FSE, Marozzi,** and **STP** buses leave from the main train station for smaller cities in the region. From the station, Corso Umberto I cuts through Piazza Cairoli and turns into Corso Garibaldi, which goes down to the port.

BY FERRY • You can buy your ticket directly from a ferry company's office, but the many **maritime agents** that line the street from the station to the port offer the same prices and a much broader range of options. Most agents represent more or less the same ferry companies, but it's still worth your while to shop around a little.

Adriatica (C. Garibaldi 85, tel. 0831/523825) and **Hellenic Mediterranean Lines** (C. Garibaldi 8, tel. 0831/528531) accept **Eurailpasses** and **InterRail** passes. Deck seats are free with a pass, but inside seating costs L29,000 and up. Everyone pays a L10,000 port tax, and Eurailpass holders pay a L19,000 surcharge in summer. You'll also have to take a boat that leaves late at night. If you don't have a pass, you can save up to 30% by buying a round-trip ticket. Depending on the season, the lowest one-way fare will be L30,000–L60,000 on the deck; inside seats will cost at least L35,000–L66,000. Prices are generally the same for Corfu (6–10 hrs), Igoumenitsa (7–10 hrs), and Patras (18–19 hrs); remember that posted fares never include the L10,000 port tax. Two of the cheaper companies are **Fragline** (C. Garibaldi 88, tel. 0831/590334) and **Minoan Lines** (C. Garibaldi 65, tel. 0831/562200). You should ask about the high-speed **Misano Alta Velocità** boat (C. Garibaldi 96, tel. 0831/590305). It can get you to Corfu in three hours for L95,000–L150,000 (L60,000–L100,000 if you're under 26), but there may be steep discounts off-season. After buying your ticket, check in at the ferry company's office and go to the **Stazione Marittima police station** to show your passport and have your boarding pass stamped. Remember: You must arrive at the terminal for check-in at least two hours before departure.

WHERE TO SLEEP AND EAT

Missed your ferrry? **Hotel Europa** (P. Cairoli 5, tel. 0831/528546, fax 0831/563351) has slightly dingy doubles (L60,000) with clean bathrooms. **Pensione Altair** (V. Tunisi 4, tel. 0831/524911) is a decent place to crash, with doubles for L60,000–L90,000. Via Tunisi is off Corso Garibaldi, three blocks above the port. The recently redone **ACLI Youth Hostel** (V. Nicola Brandi 2, tel. 0831/413123) is a short bus ride away, but if you call from the station, they'll come pick you up. A bed and breakfast cost L18,000; show up any time except 12:30–2:30. Stock up on food at either of the **Supermercato SIDIS** stores (P. Cairoli 30 or C. Garibaldi 106; the former closed Sun.) or at the fruit and vegetable **market** in Piazza Mercato, behind the central post office. The cheap restaurants on the side streets near the station are actually quite decent; look for freshly made orecchiette (about L6,000), the local specialty. For a touch more atmosphere, try **Bella Napoli** (V. Bastione Carlo V, tel. 0831/523885), on the first right leaving the station, where L30,000 will get you a feast of Neapolitan specialties.

WORTH SEEING

Since you'll probably have some time on your hands, you might as well take a look around; most of the sights are conveniently close to the port. From the train station, follow Corso Umberto I and Corso Garibaldi to the docks and go left on Lungomare Regina Margherita. Just beyond the tourist office on your left is the broad, steeply inclined **Scalinata Virgilio** (Virgil Stairway), near the place where Virgil purportedly died. At the top are the bases of the two columns that marked the end of Rome's Appian Way. One is now in Lecce, and the other is being restored because it threatened to topple over. A block inland from the columns, you'll pass the 12th-century **Duomo** and its small, free **Archaeological Museum** (P. del Duomo 8, tel. 0831/221111; open weekdays 9:30–1:30, Tues. also 3:30–6:30), which houses Roman remains and urns. If you follow Via Giovanni Tarentini from the Duomo and go left on Via San Giovanni al Sepolcro, you'll reach the crumbling **Church of San Giovanni al Sepolcro**, built by the Crusaders on their return from the Holy Land. It's leaning in several directions, apparently deciding which way to fall down.

NEAR BRINDISI

OSTUNI

Known as *la città bianca* (the white city), Ostuni has (mostly) chalk-white buildings that are visible for miles around, spread across three hills overlooking the coastal plain. Ostuni was an important Greek outpost, but it most obviously bears signs of medieval times. The 11th-century *borgo antico* (historic center), on the slopes of the highest hill, is the most interesting spot for a stroll. In Piazza della Libertà, the weather-stained **Colonna di Sant'Oronzo** (1771) supports a statue of the saint leaning unsteadily to his left. From the square, take Via Cattedral, which winds up through the centro storico to the 15th-century **Duomo.** The interior is decorated from floor to ceiling with elaborate designs in multicolored marble. Take some time to wander through the peaceful streets of the borgo antico, and be sure to walk down to the northern rim for the views over the fields of olive groves and the azure sea beyond.

Stop at the **AAST** office (P. della Libertà, tel. 0831/301268; open Mon.–Fri. 8:30–1:30, in summer Mon.–Sat. 8:30–1:30 and 6–9 for a map and information about the sights. Almost all trains between

Bari (1 hr, L5,900) and Brindisi (25 min, L3,900) stop at Ostuni; there's about one every hour. Local **Circolare buses** shuttle back and forth between the train station and town every half hour (10 min, L1,500), dropping you at **Piazza della Libertà,** on the edge of the centro storico.

WHERE TO SLEEP AND EAT • Though it's pricey, the most convenient hotel is the **Orchidea Nera** (C. Mazzini 118, tel. 0831/301366), with spartan doubles (L90,000) and minimalist bathrooms. It's a five-minute walk below Piazza della Libertà on the road from the station. Ostuni is packed with pizzerias and bars, especially near Piazza della Libertà, but the best eating takes place in the old quarter. Even if you're on a strict budget, you should splurge for a meal at **Osteria del Tempo Perso** (V. G. Tanzarella Vitale 47, not V. F. Tanzarella Vitale, tel. 0831/303320; closed Mon.). Try *fave e cicorielle selvatiche* (bean purée and wild chicory; L8,000) and creamy *cacio cavallo alla brace* (grilled local cheese; L9,000) while enjoying the comfort of air-conditioning. Take Via Cattedrale from Piazza della Libertà and turn right where two signs tell you both to turn right and to continue straight ahead.

LECCE

Known as the Florence of the Mezzogiorno, Lecce has lavish Baroque facades that can uphold the comparison for, well, a few hours. On its own merits, though, attractive Lecce still revolves around the old center with its richly decorated churches, and the city's university ensures a large population of young people. Besides Lecce's most famous sites, a walk through town will also reveal many other interesting Baroque churches, as well as several pleasant caffè for a late-afternoon drink.

BASICS

An **APT** office (tel. 0832/304443; open weekdays 9–1 and 5:30–7:30, Sat. 9–1) is just inside the Castello di Carlo V on Viale XXV Luglio, one block from the Piazza Sant'Oronzo. The central **post office** (Piazzetta Libertini, tel. 0832/243564) is open Monday–Saturday 8:15–7:30. A **CTS** budget travel office (V. Palmieri 91, tel. 0832/301862), near the university, is open weekdays 9–1 and 5–8, Saturday 9–12:30.

COMING AND GOING

Lecce is at the end of the **FS train line,** which means it's easy to get to Brindisi (hourly, 30 min, L3,900) and Bari (hourly, 2 hrs, L10,100), but to go east and south, you have to take the plodding **FSE line.** Several trains leave each day for Otranto (1½ hrs, L4,200; change at Maglie) and Gallipoli (1 hr 20 min, L5,000). For destinations not served by trains, **FSE** buses (tel. 0832/347634) leave from Viale Torre del Parco east of the station and **STP** buses (tel. 0832/302873) from Via Adua north of the station; you can get schedules for either at the APT office.

GETTING AROUND

Lecce's train station is about a kilometer (½ mi) from **Piazza Sant'Oronzo,** in the center of the old quarter. Streets in the old quarter are poorly marked, so it's a good idea to pick up a map at the APT office (*see* Basics, *above*) before wandering around. To reach the piazza, walk straight from the station on Via Oronzo Quarta, which becomes Via Cairoli, bear left onto Via Paladini, continue past the back of the Duomo, and turn right on Corso Vittorio Emanuele II. Lecce's main streets are Corso Vittorio Emanuele II and Via S. Trinchese, not only home to all three Benettons, but also the spot where half the city turns out on warm evenings for a *passeggiata* (social stroll). Via S. Trinchese leads from Piazza Sant'Oronzo to Piazza Mazzini, whose fountain gets circled by kids on roller and in-line skates.

WHERE TO SLEEP

Despite its attractions, Lecce is short on tourists and, consequently, budget accommodations. **Dolce Casa di Andreina Goffredo** (V. Taranto 31, tel. 0832/304654) rents doubles (L65,000, including breakfast), but there are only three rooms, so call well in advance. **Hotel Cappello** (V. Montegrappa 4, tel. 0832/308881) is everything you've been looking for in a hotel—clean, comfortable, even tasteful at L85,000 for a double with bath. This place fills up with workers from nearby towns during the week, so again, call ahead. From the station, take the first left and the first left again.

WHERE TO EAT

La Capannina (V. Cairoli 13, tel. 0832/304159; closed Mon.) has a tremendous buffet of 25–30 types of antipasti and classic dishes like spaghetti *alle cozze* (with mussels). The very popular **Carlo V** (P. Falconieri 1, tel. 0832/243509; open for dinner Tues.–Sun.) has outstanding *piatti speciali* (vegetarian dishes, but some have shrimp) and elaborate pizzas for L9,000–L14,000 (asparagus, smoked salmon, and so on). **La Rusticana** (C. Vittorio Emanuele II 31, tel. 0832/300544; closed Wed.) has a trattoria and pizzeria in back but does most of its business at the tavola calda in front, selling filling snacks like *arancini di riso* (fried stuffed rice balls; L1,500) to evening crowds. Students go to **Caffè Paisiello** (V. Palmieri 72, tel. 0832/301404) for drinks at the end of a long day. Later in the evening, continue at the more serious **Orient Express** (V. Palmieri 31) down the street.

WORTH SEEING

Begin your tour in **Piazza Sant'Oronzo,** where ancient, Baroque, and modern coexist harmoniously. The **Roman amphitheater** (currently under restoration) on the south side of the piazza, was completed during Hadrian's rule in the 2nd century AD, when it seated 20,000 bloodthirsty spectators. Nowadays, kids and old-timers hang out by the "bleachers" in front of the **Sedile** (former town hall), built in the comparatively restrained early Baroque style by the Venetian Pier Moceigo in the late 16th century. Across from the Sedile, a copper-coated wooden statue of Lecce's patron saint stands atop the **Colonna di Sant'Oronzo.** In 1686 Giuseppe Zimbalo, the master of Lecce Baroque, completed the column's base and the statue on top (though the current one is an 18th-century replacement).

From the piazza, walk up Via Templari to Via Umberto to see the **Basilica di Santa Croce** (V. Umberto 1). Architect Gabriele Riccardo started work on this bravura Baroque display in 1532. The church was completed 150 years later. You can spend lots of time noting the infinite details of the contorted, flowery facade, but also look for the statues of St. Benedict and St. Peter, appearing a bit troubled amid the dazzling architectural flora and fauna. The interior of the cathedral is laid out according to a simple Latin cross plan, but the severe Corinthian columns burst into flames of Baroque ornamentation at their capitals. The comparatively austere **Palazzo dei Celestini** stretches out beside the basilica. Originally a Celestine convent, the edifice was begun in 1659, the lower half of its facade designed by Zimbalo and the upper half by Cino.

Leaving Piazza Sant'Oronzo on Corso Vittorio Emanuele II, you'll pass the imposing facade of the **Church of St. Irene** before coming to the elegant **Piazza del Duomo** on your left. Designed for stately affairs, the square doubles as a great soccer field for young kids. From left to right, you'll see the campanile (closed to the public), Duomo, Palazzo Vescovile, and seminary. The **Duomo** was first built in the 12th century, but the ostentatious facade is a product of Giuseppe Zimbalo's renovations between 1655 and 1670. Inside, the chapels are luxuriant with decorations, and cherubs stare down at you from the tops of the columns. The bell tower stands 250 ft tall, with Sant'Oronzo topping off its fifth floor. The square is especially attractive at night, when artificial lights bathe its buildings in a warm glow.

The **Museo Provinciale** (V. Gallipoli 28, tel. 0832/307415; admission free; open weekdays 9–1:30 and 2:30–7:30, Sun. 9–1:30), near the train station, has a stylish modern interior but a rather lackluster collection of decapitated Roman sculptures, Greek vases, and other assorted archaeological finds.

NEAR LECCE

OTRANTO

Otranto really is the end of the line, the east end of the Salento Peninsula, which feels as much Greek as Italian. It's a quiet little backwater town with some interesting history and architecture, great seafood, and good campsites. In July and August, however, it fills up with vacationers who want some nature and culture side dishes along with their beach main course. Like most Puglian coastal towns, Otranto has seen a long succession of rulers, including the Greeks, Byzantines, Normans, and—most notoriously—Turks, who massacred the town's 800 citizens in 1480. A year later, things settled down when Duke Alfonso of Aragon came into power. Today, despite large stretches of not entirely unattractive concrete apartment buildings, Otranto looks more or less as it did centuries ago: the east is a sea of navy blue; the west is marked with verdant, rocky terrain. It's difficult to get around the scenic countryside if you don't have a car, but you get a good taste of the region in Otranto itself.

The interior of the Romanesque **Duomo** (P. Basilica), erected by the Normans in the 11th century, is covered with terrific floor mosaics crafted by the monk Pantaleone in the 12th century. The entire length of the nave is covered by the Albero della Vita (Tree of Life), and a great cast of characters hangs out in its limbs, including Alexander the Great ascending to heaven, King Arthur fighting the Cat of Losanna (but looking more like a wide-eyed kid waving to the crowd), Noah building his ark, and lots of pagan serpents, mermaids, and signs of the zodiac. To the right of the altar are the bones of the martyrs of 1480. The small Byzantine **Chiesa di San Pietro,** atop a small hill in the Old City, is decorated with a series of well-preserved frescoes dating from the 10th century.

BASICS • Otranto's **AAST** tourist office (V. Pantaleone Presbitero 12, tel. 0836/801436) is open July and August, Monday–Saturday 9–1 and 4:30–8. The rest of the year it's open Monday–Saturday 8–2.

COMING AND GOING • Trains depart regularly for Lecce (8 daily, 1½ hrs, L4,200), though you have to transfer at Maglie. **Linee Lauro** (tel. 0836/806061) sends ferries to Valona (3 hrs, L60,000) and Durazzo (7–10 hrs, L70,000) in Albania two or three times per week. In summer ferries go to Corfu (12 hrs) and Igoumenitsa (9 hrs), both for L40,000–L60,000, about four times a week. You can get a schedule at the AAST office or at **Ellade Viaggi** (V. Porto, at the port, tel. 0836/801578).

WHERE TO SLEEP • Staying in Otranto can get expensive, but **agriturismo** (staying in the countryside) is a good way to save money. Most farmhouses with agriturismo are within easy reach of the ocean, and if you pay full board, you'll eat very well. **Il Contadino** (Località Frassanito, tel. 0836/85065; open Easter–Sept.), one of the more popular farmhouses, charges L10,000 per person to camp or L65,000 for a double room with bath. Frassanito is 10 km (6 mi) north of Otranto and can be reached by a shuttle bus (L1,000) that runs every two to three hours throughout the day. A taxi from the station will cost about L20,000.

In town, **Idrusa** (tel. 0836/801255) is a wooded campsite and the cheapest place around. You'll pay L6,000–L8,000 per person, L3,500 per tent, and L2,000 for electricity. You can also go four to a bungalow for L90,000. From the station, walk down to the water, turn right, go straight up Via San Francesco, and bear left at the fork at Piazza A. de Gasperi—it'll be on your left. **Il Gabbiano** (V. Porto Craulo 13, tel. 0836/801251) has pleasant doubles near the water for L70,000–L84,000. **Hotel La Plancia** (V. Porto Craulo 13, tel. 0836/801217) is a bit farther out but just above the water; doubles with bath are L75,000–L85,000. For both hotels, turn left at the water, take the staircase up where the road turns inland, continue along the water, and bear left at the fork. If you're coming in August, call well in advance. Along the *lungomare* (seaside promenade) there are many generic restaurants with decent prices, but look in the Old City if you want more atmosphere. **Margaret** (Lungomare J. Kennedy 4, tel. 0836/801325; closed Tues.) often has fresh fish for about L15,000, though it's grilled a bit longer than necessary.

> *Lecce's sites are not frequented solely by tourists; at night teenagers and university students park their motorcycles all over Piazza Sant'Oronzo and gather around the Roman amphitheater or cluster on the steps of the Piazza del Duomo.*

AFTER DARK • In summer Otranto is well supplied with nightspots for the vacationing masses. If dancing's your thing, boogie down on Saturday night (after midnight) at **Nike** (Riviera degli Haethey, 2 km/1 mi north of Otranto, tel. 0836/801196), in a 16th-century country house with a private beach. Cover is L25,000. If you're staying at Il Contadino, head to **Country Club** (V. Alimini, tel. 0836/85221), with mainstream dance music, a swimming pool, and crepes to munch on. The cover is L25,000. If you'd rather have a mellow night out, head over to **Griffin's Pub** (V. Castello 10, near *cattedrale,* tel. 0836/801301).

BASILICATA

Basilicata is the most forgotten region of the Mezzogiorno, boasting two short strips of coastline but otherwise composed of a dry, mountainous interior. Although Basilicata has not achieved the standard of living of the north, today it suffers more from anonymity and poor transportation than anything else. If you make the considerable effort to visit the small villages of the interior, you may get a glimpse of traditional agrarian society, but otherwise you'll primarily be exposed to postwar urban development and a nascent tourist industry.

Because of the dearth of public transportation, it's difficult to visit the region in one fell swoop. Italians' preferred destinations are the mountainous coastline of Maratea and the unexceptional beach town of Metaponto, though the most rewarding place to visit is the strangely beautiful city of Matera, home of the *sassi* (caves). If you have a car and want to explore untouched forests and mountainsides, head to the **Parco Nazionale del Pollino,** on the Calabrian border.

Adriatic Sea

Andria
A14
Bari
Monópoli

Spinazzola
PUGLIA
Fasano
S16

A16
Melfi
Altamura
Gioia del Colle
Ostuni

Gravina in Puglia
Matera
Massafra
Francavilla
S7

CAMPANIA
Grassano
Via Appia
Taranto

Potenza
Auletta
BASILICATA
Pisticci
Metaponto

Sala
Consilina
Viggiano
Colobraro

Lagonegro
Parco
Nazionale
del Pollino
Gulf of
Taranto

Acquafredda
S106

Marina di
Camerota
Maratea

Marina di Maratea
Castrovillari
Sibari

Praia a Mare
Rossano

Scalea

Cirella
Parco
Nazionale
della Calabria

Diamante

N

Tyrrhenian Sea

Paola
Camigliatello
S107
San Giovanni
in Flore

Cosenza
Lorica
Crotone

Sila MASSIF

KEY

Rail Lines

Ferry Lines

Catanzaro

S280
Lamezia
Terme

0   30 miles

0   50 km

Pizzo

Tropea

Stromboli

Nicotera
Marina di
Monasterace

Panarea
A3
CALABRIA

Salina

Lipari
Rosarno

Vulcano
S106

Bagnara
Gerace

Villa
San Giovanni
Scilla
Locri

Milazzo
Reggio di
Calabria

Barcellona
Messina

SICILY
A18
Ionian Sea

MATERA

Set high on the rocky plateau of the eastern Basilicatan interior, Matera is one of the oddest and most enchanting cities in Italy. Its reputation rests on its dense neighborhoods of sassi—condemned by Carlo Levi in the 1930s as a symbol of southern Italian poverty, evacuated by the government in 1952, and now coming to life again as people move back into caves recently renovated with modern amenities. Walking around the periphery of the sassi—just a few minutes from the New City's heart—with the steep slopes of a lonely, winding canyon below, you may think yourself transported not only to another age but to another planet.

BASICS

The well-stocked **APT** office (V. de Viti de Marco 9, off V. Roma, tel. 0835/331983) has maps of Matera and info on Basilicata. The friendly English-speaking staff can answer your questions Monday–Saturday 9–1, also Mon. and Thurs. 4–6:30. The **Cooperativa Nuovi Amici dei Sassi** office (P. Sedile 20, tel. 0835/331011; open daily 9–1 and 3:30–6:30) is the most convenient place to get a decent map of the sassi (L6,000). Not only do they have fluctuating open hours, but **Cooperativa Tourservice** (P. V. Veneto 42, tel. 0835/334633) is also deep in the sassi, so you may have trouble finding it. Both offer guided tours, but the prices are set for large groups.

COMING AND GOING

The **Ferrovie Appulo-Lucane** serves the **Matera Centrale** station; there are trains to Bari (1½ hrs, L6,000) about every two hours and not much else. **SITA** buses (tel. 0835/385027) cover most of the region, with service to Taranto (5–6 daily, 2 hrs, L8,000) and Metaponto (4 daily, 50 min, L5,200), though there is none on Sunday. The ticket office (P. Matteotti 3–4) is open Mon.–Sat. 7:30–2 and 4–7. The main bus stop is in Piazza Matteotti, near the train station. For long-distance buses to destinations like Florence (9½ hrs, L82,000) and Bologna (9 hrs, L66,000), ask at the **Kronos Travel Agency** (P. Matteotti 8, tel. 0835/330291; open weekdays 9–1 and 4–8, Sat. 9–1); in general, you're better off taking the train and changing at Bari.

GETTING AROUND

Local buses (L1,000) cover all of Matera except for the sassi neighborhoods, though it's easy to get around on foot. Most buses come and go from Piazza Matteotti, and tickets can be purchased at newsstands and tobacco shops. From Piazza Matteotti, take Via Roma to get to the central Piazza Vittorio Veneto. From here the sassi are right in front of you; both Via San Biagio on the left and Via delle Beccherie on the right have turn-offs heading down among them. The latter leads to the centrally located Piazza del Duomo, with the **Sasso Barisano** neighborhood on your left and the **Sasso Caveoso** on your right.

WHERE TO SLEEP

Around festival time (late June and early July), call ahead to reserve a room. Matera only has one budget hotel: **Albergo Roma** (V. Roma 62, tel. 0835/333912) has been in business for more than 50 years, and the charming family that runs it keeps the aged rooms and beds immaculate. Doubles are L65,000. Fortunately, a modern, comfortable hotel and hostel have opened right in the sassi, just two minutes from Piazza Veneto in a recently renovated 18th-century complex carved into the rock. **Hotel Sassi** (V. S. Giovanni Vecchio 89, tel. 0835/331009, fax 0835/333733) is a splurge at L140,000 for a double, but the minibar, cable TV, and private balcony might soften the blow. Otherwise, continue along V. San Giovanni Vecchio to the **Sassi Hostel** (HI; V. S. Giovanni Vecchio 89, tel. 0835/331009, fax 0835/333733), where for L24,000 you'll get the same view, a bed in a dorm room, breakfast, and perhaps your only chance to sleep in a part of a UNESCO-designated World Heritage Site. You can buy a meal ticket for L15,000, which covers a full dinner at Il Terrazzino sui Sassi (*see* Where to Eat, *below*). Lockout is noon–3:30; curfew is 11:30 PM. From Piazza Veneto, take Via San Biagio to Piazza San Giovanni and follow the sassi sign.

WHERE TO EAT

Food here is generally fresh, excellent, and cheap. The town has two large **markets,** the most convenient of which is at Piazza Asconio Persio (open Mon.–Sat. 7–1). Hit **Bar Tripoli** (P. Vittorio Veneto 17, tel. 0835/333991, closed Mon.) for the best gelato. You'll find the best pizza at **Pizzeria La Panca** (V. Giolitti 39, tel. 0835/222159). Many young people gather at **Caffè Mulino** (P. Mulino) for drinks and tasty snacks, across the street at the town's new **Internet Cafè** (P. Mulino), and at **Speedway** (V. Roma 48–50; tel. 0835/331571, closed Mon.) for cheap panini and slices of pizza. For a more substantial

SHORT AND SASSI

Named by UNESCO as a World Cultural Heritage site, Matera's sassi might look like houses piled up on one another, but they are caves with walls and ceilings carved into the rocky hillsides. The oldest date back thousands of years, making Matera, in some anthropologists' eyes, the most ancient city in the world. As you watch birds swirl over their gaping empty windows, the sassi may look like part of a strange and mysterious ghost town. However, many of the sassi are currently inhabited, and some are being transformed into thoroughly modern houses, hotels, shops, and bars.

meal, **Il Terrazzino sui Sassi** (Vico San Giuseppe 7, tel. 0835/332503; closed Tues.) has great food and an amazing view of the sassi from its terrace. Try the orecchiette *tegamino* (with meatballs, tomatoes, and mozzarella). Deservedly, **Trattoria Lucana** (V. Lucana 48, tel. 0835/336117; closed Sun. and 1st 2 wks Sept.), off Via Roma, is always full. Although the antipasti *della casa* (L15,000) are a meal in themselves, other specialties include *cavatelli alla lucana* (fresh pasta with mushrooms and sausage) and orecchiette *alla materana* (with tomatoes, peppers, eggplant, zucchini, and arugula). For a casual evening drink, drop into **Café Hemingway** (V. Ridola 44, tel. 0835/310794).

WORTH SEEING

Most of the **sassi** are built into two valleys on either side of the hill on which the 13th-century Romanesque **Duomo** is perched. It's quite easy to explore the area on your own by following the marked *itinerari turistici* (tourist itineraries); the L6,000 map available at the information offices comes with descriptions of each of these itineraries. **Sasso Barisano,** to the north, is the newer and more complex of the two. Leave Piazza Veneto on Via San Biagio and turn down any side street, and you'll twist and wind through ancient homes built right on top of one another. When you reach the bottom of the valley, head away from the Duomo toward Via Madonna delle Virtù (alias Strada Panoramica dei Sassi), which winds around the periphery of the sassi at the top of the steep canyon of the Gravina di Matera. On the other side of the ravine you can make out some of the *chiese rupestri,* small churches carved into the rock off the cliff side. There are about 150 chiese rupestri, built between the 6th and 13th centuries, some in the sassi of Matera. Circling the sassi with the ravine on the left, you'll come to the church of **San Pietro Caveoso** and built into the top of a twisted rock above it, the church of **Santa Maria de Idris,** both of which contain Byzantine frescoes dating from the 12th to 16th centuries.

Past San Pietro, you enter **Sasso Caveoso,** the older of the two ancient quarters. Continuing along the edge of the ravine, you can peek into some of the smallest and oldest of the sassi, now uninhabited. Next you'll come to the church of **Santa Lucia alle Malve,** which contains spectacular frescoes from as far back as the 10th century. The last church on the canyon rim is the **Convicinio di Sant'Antonio,** a onetime monastery made from four chiese rupestri that tunnel down into the rock. The monastery is also adorned with nearly intact frescoes.

Back outside the sassi, the morbid church **Purgatorio** lies on Via Ridola (the continuation of V. del Corso). The entrance has a fantastically sinister door etched with skulls and crossbones and topped with a figure of the grim reaper. Near the church is the **Museo Nazionale Ridola,** the town's main museum, with a good collection of prehistoric artifacts and finely decorated ancient Greek vases. It is closed for restoration until early 2001.

FESTIVALS

During the last week of June and the first week of July, Matera celebrates the **Festa della Madonna della Bruna,** commemorating the return of a dark-skinned Madonna figure stolen by the Turks in the 8th century. Local artists compete to build ornate carriages to transport the Madonna through the streets. After a week of parades, fireworks, and religious ceremonies, the festival comes to a head on July 2, when the whole town turns out at dawn in Piazza del Duomo for the **Assalto al Carro** (Assault on the Cart). The main parade has turned into something of a media spectacle in recent years, but it's still amazing to behold. Try to hitch a ride from the square with one of the cars heading to the other side of the ravine. From the mountaintop perch you'll have a great view of the thunderous fireworks display, which lasts well into the evening.

METAPONTO

Founded in the 7th century BC by Greek colonists, Metaponto is home to the region's most important set of Magna Grecia ruins, which isn't necessarily saying a lot. Most visitors are content to let dead Greeks lie, and they head straight to Metaponto's prime Ionian beaches. Otherwise Metaponto has absolutely nothing of interest, and off-season the town barely exists, though you can have the run of the long, sandy beach then.

BASICS

There is currently no tourist information office in Metaponto. Check with the office in Matera for information.

COMING AND GOING

Metaponto makes a viable day trip by bus from Matera, with four to six daily buses (fewer on weekends) traveling the route (50 min, L5,200). The bus stops at the train station and in summer at Piazzale Nord near the beach. Metaponto is also an important rail junction, with train service to Taranto (hourly, 30 min, L4,700) and Cosenza (5 daily, 2½ hrs, L12,100).

Most travelers pass through Basilicata without even realizing it. The express train down the Tyrrhenian coast spends all of nine minutes in the region, most of it in tunnels.

WHERE TO SLEEP

Several hotels and a ton of campsites in Metaponto are close to, if not right on, the beach. A mere 650 ft from the water, on the street that connects the train station and town center, is **Hotel Kennedy** (V. Ionio 1, tel. 0835/741832). Ugly but clean doubles with bath go for L60,000–L80,000. Grab a tasty dinner or a cup of coffee in the bar/restaurant downstairs. **Hotel Oasi** (V. Olimpia 12; open mid-June–mid-Sept.), where plain doubles with bath cost L80,000, is owned by **Hotel Sacco** (P. Lido 7, tel. 0835/741930, fax 0835/741975), which has fancier doubles for L100,000. You have to go there to check in; where the road from the station divides into three, take the middle road all the way to the beach.

CAMPING • For a night under the stars, head to **Camping Magna Grecia** (V. Lido 1, tel. 0835/741855; closed Oct.–Mar.), Metaponto's most happening campground and one of its better spots for summertime nightlife. It has everything, including a swimming pool (L2,500 per half day), horseback riding (L20,000 per hr), tennis courts (L6,000 per hr), a cafeteria, a small market, a restaurant, a discotheque (always free to campers, free to noncampers except in Aug.), telephones, and clean, modern bathrooms. You'll pay L5,000–L12,000 per person, L6,000–L12,000 per tent site. They also send a free bus to and from the train station and to and from the beach.

WHERE TO EAT

You definitely won't confuse Metaponto with any of Italy's culinary capitals. Most restaurants serve mediocre food, albeit at reasonable prices. At **Le Sirene** (V. delle Sirene, near the beach, no phone; closed Sept.–May), at least the pizzas don't come out of the freezer, and the penne *all'arrabbiata* (with spicy tomato sauce) is seriously hot. Another place to try is **La Masseria** (V. Torremare, tel. 0835/741838, closed Mon.), with mostly fish specialties on the menu. Plan on spending about L30,000 for a full meal. Buy picnic food from the vendors who set up regularly in and around Piazzale Nord, or stop at **Mini Market da Lucia** (V. Ionio 18/A, no phone). For takeout, head to **Pommarolo** (V. Ionio at Strada Nazionale del Lido; closed Sept.–May) for roast chicken, panini, and *patatine* (french fries) L5000–L11,000.

WORTH SEEING

Metaponto is really two different towns. **Metaponto Borgo,** near the train station, is a tiny, utterly uninteresting town; **Lido di Metaponto,** by the water, is a small collection of hotels and campsites and a long, sandy beach. From the train station, head straight ahead to a four-way intersection. For Lido di

Metaponto, turn right and follow the road that curves over the train tracks (2½ km or 1½ mi); for Metaponto Borgo, go straight and look to your left. In summer a bus (L1,000) travels almost hourly between the station and Lido di Metaponto. Continuing straight through the first intersection, turn left at the next four-way intersection (1,350 ft) for the **Archaeological Museum** (open daily 9–7, admission L4,000, tel. 0835/745327), built a few years ago to display an increasing number of Magna Grecia finds, including ceramics, costumes, and the skeletal remains of the Sybarites and various Lucanian tribes.

If instead of turning left for the museum, you turn right, after 1½ km (1 mi) you'll come to Metaponto's **Parco Archeologico,** a vast field littered with the rather humble remains of the ancient city of Metapontum (open sunrise to sunset, admission free). The chief attractions are the 6th-century BC **Temple of Apollo Lykeios** and **Temple of Hera,** and the clever partial reconstruction of the **Greek theater.** Back on the main road from the station, another 2 km (1 mi) will bring you to the **Necropoli di Crucinia** (ancient burial grounds). This group of small stone huts isn't worth the hike unless you're continuing on to the beautiful Doric **Tavole Palatine,** the area's most impressive ruin. This was the temple of Hera, later turned into a school where mathematician-philosopher Pythagoras supposedly taught until his death in the late 6th century BC. However, this involves walking another kilometer (½ mi) and then turning right onto a major expressway (S.S. 106) and continuing along the expressway for yet another kilometer (½ mi).

MARATEA

Maratea, a dazzling 30-km (18½-mi) stretch of steep mountains and aquamarine ocean on the Tyrrhenian coast, is notable for its natural beauty more than its religious or cultural artifacts. Maratea is less a town than a region, encompassing the coastal villages of Acquafredda, Cersuta, Fiumicello, Porto di Maratea, Marina di Maratea, and Castrocucco and the old inland town of Maratea. There are no real sights of interest; Maratea's centro storico is worth a peek, but you'll have to take one of the few buses to get there. If you can't find an affordable room, you can make the town a day trip from Calabria's Praia a Mare (see below), but it may not be worth the trouble. Make sure you check bus and train schedules ahead of time, as transportation in this region is sparse. For info, the **AAST** office (V. Santavenere 40, Località Fiumicello, tel. 0973/876908) is open daily 8–2, also on Tuesday and Thursday 3–6; in summer, it's open daily 8 AM–9PM.

COMING AND GOING

Most **trains** stop at the Maratea train station, a fair walk above Fiumicello and Porto di Maratea and a long way below Maratea. From here hourly trains go north to Agropoli (1½ hrs, L7,400) and Naples (2 hrs 40 min, L18,000) and south to Paola, most continuing to Cosenza (1½ hrs, L10,100). Trains stop less often at Acquafredda and Marina di Maratea; from Maratea both take five minutes and cost L1,500. If you want to get in and out quickly, try to find a train that stops at Marina di Maratea.

Buses run between Porto di Maratea and Fiumicello up to Maratea's centro storico, passing by the Maratea train station. In summer there's roughly one per hour, but otherwise there's one every full moon. From Maratea station, follow the signs down to Fiumicello and Porto di Maratea (not Porto Scala). After 10–15 minutes, the road to Fiumicello becomes Via Santavenere and continues down another 10 minutes to a gravelly beach set in a rocky cove beneath the towering 3,300-ft-high peak of La Serra.

WHERE TO SLEEP

Most hotels in Maratea are strictly for the wealthy, and there are none near the Maratea station, but the tourist offices can help you find something within your budget from lists of hotels and private rooms. One affordable option is **Hotel Fiorella** (V. Santavenere 21, tel. 0973/876921), where doubles are L100,000. Instead of turning left on Via Santavenere for the Fiumicello beach, continue straight ahead, and it'll be on your left; check in at the bar across the street. Another option is the nearby **Hotel Calaficara** (Via S. Teresa 6, tel. 0973/87016; closed Oct.–Mar.), where a double with bath will cost you L130,000.

WHERE TO EAT

Maratea is one of the more expensive towns in southern Italy. In Fiumicello you can buy food at the **Trotta Supermarket** (V. Santavenere 112, tel. 0973/876491), almost always open. Next door, **L'Incontro** (V. Santavenere 116, no phone) serves snacks like *arancini* and pizza slices as well as simple dishes like lasagna. For more ambience, the docks at the *porto* are ringed by restaurants. Go to **Trattoria da**

Cesare (Contrada Cersuta 52, tel. 0973/871840; closed Thurs. Sept.–June) for the spaghetti *al nero di seppia* (with a black sauce of cuttlefish ink) and fresh grilled fish for around L25,000. You can still gorge yourself on local pastries without going broke at **L'Antica Pasticceria Iannini** (Vicoletto Rovita 18, in centro storico, tel. 0973/876697). Try regional desserts flavored with *pasta di mandorle* (almond paste), *cedro* (citron), or *noci* (walnuts).

CALABRIA

As the southernmost province on the Italian peninsula, Calabria might be expected to display the general impoverishment and *The Godfather*–like stereotypes foreigners associate with southern Italy. This poor agrarian region is controlled by the Mafia—known down here as the *'ndrangheta*—but if you've come looking for picturesque backwardness, you'll have to venture into the small agricultural villages of the interior, and good luck getting there. Calabria is trying to make itself over into a popular vacation destination, capitalizing on its considerable natural assets: a rugged interior of giant mountains, hilltop towns, and forests that drops off to a flat coastline along the Tyrrhenian and Ionian seas. Off-season, the coastal towns, especially along the Ionian coast, hardly merit a second glance unless you're looking for miles of sandy beach all to yourself. For those needing their urban fix, there are two major cities: Cosenza, a good stop for travelers on their way to the mountains, and Reggio di Calabria, where you can take a breather, congratulate yourself for having made it this far, and continue on to Sicily.

The sassi have seen two phases of modern urban development: first, the deterioration of lower-class living conditions after the industrial revolution; and second, the transformation of run-down areas into housing for the rich and artsy.

COSENZA

The first major Calabrian city you reach from the north, Cosenza sprawls across a plateau ringed by densely wooded mountains. Founded by Greek colonists and later an important city during Roman times and the Renaissance, Cosenza today bears the imprint of its most recent conquerors—the urban developers who built row after row of concrete slab apartment buildings in the 1960s. On Sunday afternoon the city is dead as a doornail, though most evenings it can rouse itself into a respectable metropolis. Beyond the crumbling centro storico, Cosenza's principal asset is its surrounding countryside, with its rugged mountains and narrow valleys. For a scenic tour, take the slow, winding train ride to Camigliatello.

BASICS

The **APT** tourist office (C. Mazzini 92, tel. 0984/27271) is open Monday to Friday 7:30–1:30, as well as Monday and Wednesday 2–5. Change money at the main **post office** (V. Vittorio Veneto, at end of V. Piave off C. Mazzini, tel. 0984/26435; open weekdays 8:15–5, Sat. 8:15–12:30) or at the banks on Corso Mazzini.

COMING AND GOING

COSENZA'S • train stations are on the fringes of the city. **Ferrovie dello Stato (FS)** trains run about once per hour toward Paola (25 min, L3,100), on the west coast, and Sibari (1 hr 20 min, L5,900), on the east coast. **Ferrovie della Calabria (FC)** trains head toward Catanzaro (2 hrs, L13,600) or San Giovanni in Fiore, stopping first at the old train station (Cosenza Centrale) in the downtown area. There are three departures per day to San Giovanni in Fiore (2 hrs, L3,500), stopping en route at Camigliatello (1 hr 20 min, L2,500). Luggage storage (L5,000 for 12 hrs) is at the FS ticket window. **Ferrovie della Calabria** (tel. 0984/36851) runs buses every two to three hours to the Sila Massif, stopping in Camigliatello (45 min, L2,800) and San Giovanni in Fiore (1½ hrs, L4,800). Buses leave from the **Autostazione** (V. delle Medaglie d_Oro, near P. Fera, tel. 0984/413124) and also stop at the main train station. Other long-distance buses leave from one or the other. You can get schedules at the information booth at the Autostazione.

SOUTHERN HOSPITALITY

Although tourists from all over the world flock to Capri and the Amalfi Coast, Italians often bypass that region for the endless beaches of the Calabrian coast, where the water is warm, the beaches broad and sandy. Weekends start heating up in June, but the chaos heightens from the end of June to mid-September, when lodging becomes a seller's market. Quiet towns like Maratea, Praia a Mare, and Locri suddenly come to life; hotels, restaurants, discos, and aquatic amusement parks open up, bus services become more regular, and miles of beaches are jammed from end to end.

GETTING AROUND

Cosenza is a large, modern city, but the downtown area and the centro storico are of manageable proportions. Orange **ATAC** buses run through town, but the only one you're likely to need is Bus 5, which begins at the new train station, stops at Piazza Fera just above the main bus depot, and ends at the old train station, one block from **Corso Mazzini,** Cosenza's main street. Buy tickets (L1,500) at tobacco shops. Bus 5 runs every 25 minutes 6 AM–9 PM and every 40 minutes 9 PM–11:30 PM.

WHERE TO SLEEP

For a city of its size, Cosenza has a disappointingly slim pickings in the budget lodging category. Your best bet is **Albergo Bruno** (C. Mazzini 27, 1 block from old train station, tel. 0984/73889), with cheap, clean, and more pleasant rooms (doubles L70,000 with bath) than the small, dilapidated sign in front suggests. The **Hotel Excelsior** (P. Matteotti 14, tel. and fax 0984/74383) has large, clean doubles with bath for L80,000 including breakfast. It's across from the old train station (where no trains pass at night). Also nearby is **Il Grisaro** (Viale Trieste 38, tel. 0984/26838), with doubles with bath for L90,000.

WHERE TO EAT

Cosenza doesn't overflow with places to eat, but you can easily live off the cream-filled cornetti that the townsfolk whip up with a passion. Aptly named **La Cornetteria** (P. dei Bruzi 6; open daily 7:30 AM–noon and 7 PM–2 AM) serves up cream, amaretto, peach, and chocolate cornetti to a late-night crowd. The cheapest option of all is the **open market,** held mornings Monday–Saturday on Via Asmara, near Piazza Riforma. **Ristorante da Giocondo** (V. Piave 53, off C. Mazzini, tel. 0984/29810; closed Sun.) is a favorite among locals, with traditional fare in a simple but elegant white-tablecloth setting. Primo of the day might be lasagna *con polpettine* (with meatballs); try one of the delicious grilled fish dishes as a secondo. **Al Vicoletto** (V. Simonetta 7–11, tel. 0984/29807), one block above Piazza Fera, serves local specialties like fusilli *alla consentina* (with tomatoes and spicy sausage), though the pizza isn't quite up to Neapolitan standards. For an appetizer, try the *fresina* (L4,000), a piece of stale bread doused with water and topped with mozzarella, tomatoes, and olives. In summer Vicoletto is open Monday–Saturday; the rest of the year it's open Saturday–Thursday. Most restaurants close in August, when residents split for the coast.

WORTH SEEING

Cosenza's centro storico merits a few hours of exploration. From the newer part of town, take the **Ponte Mario Martire** over the Busento River to the Old Town's **Piazza Valdesi.** From the square, Corso Telesio crosses the heart of the centro storico, running through Piazza del Duomo and passing Cosenza's **Duomo** (P. del Duomo, tel. 0984/77864; open daily 8–10:30 and 4–7). Built in the 12th and 13th centuries, the cathedral has the look of the Gothic style hailing from Provence. The interior was redone in full Baroque 600 years later. You can also visit the church of **San Francesco d'Assisi** (V. San Francesco d'Assisi, tel. 0984/26063; open daily 7:30–noon and 4:30–7:30), with its 13th-century doorway and elegant cloister. From Piazza Valdesi, take the right-hand staircase and keep going up. A short but steep hike from the bottom of the centro storico is the **Castello Normano** (tel. 0984/74165; open Mon.–Sat. 9–1:30 and 5–midnight or until sunset in winter, Sun. 3–1), seriously damaged by a series of earthquakes. Though the interior is bare and hardly worth the calories burned to reach it, the castle does offer a great view of the countryside. And admission is free.

NEAR COSENZA

When the sweltering summer heat descends upon Calabria's coast and sirocco winds blowing northward from Africa get you fiery, you can find relief in the mountains in the heart of this region. In the immense, largely unspoiled **Sila Massif,** you'll find southern Italy's best hiking, fishing, and camping amid swaths of pine-forested mountains. The massif consists of three sections: the **Sila Greca** to the north, the central **Sila Grande** (the largest of the three zones, including the most accessible and interesting villages and campsites), and the **Sila Piccola** to the south. The alpine countryside teems with tumbling brooks, mountains capped with snow in winter, and every brand of flora and fauna imaginable. As the Sila Massif gains recognition for its natural beauty, the villages are becoming increasingly touristed, but you can still spend quality bonding time with nature here. The best way to approach the Sila is to take the mountain train from Cosenza to the alpine villages in the Sila Grande, including Camigliatello and San Giovanni in Fiore. The train climbs through some of Italy's most amazing natural scenery—ravines, pine forests, and shimmering lakes—en route to the mountains. San Giovanni in Fiore is humdrum, but the train ride there and the unusual layout of the town make it a worthwhile day trip. West of Cosenza, the Tyrrhenian coast unapologetically offers surf, sun, and lots of beach towns like Praia a Mare, and train service makes travel here relatively easy.

Next door to Cosenza's APT office on Corso Mazzini, you'll find a candy store selling one of the city's specialties: decadent, delectable chocolate-covered figs.

CAMIGLIATELLO

The first alpine village that you reach on the train from Cosenza, Camigliatello is the Sila Grande's most heavily visited and most expensive town. It caters to a middle-aged crowd looking to be pampered in the upscale hotels that fill the town center. The town offers almost no organized fair-weather sports and is really hopping only during the winter ski season. Very little is accessible if you are without a car. However, if you enjoy aimless hikes and beautiful natural surroundings without intrusive crowds, Camigliatello beckons.

Once in town, stop at the **Casa del Forestiere** (*see* Basics, *below*) for info and maps, then get out and explore the countryside. The shores of Lake Cecita are 7 km (4½ mi) away on the continuation of Via Roma, a lightly traveled road heading east past the train station. The reservoir is almost overwhelmed by the towering hills and an abundance of masticating cows. Several signposted campsites just off the road to Lake Cecita are legal and relatively rustic. If you visit in winter, the **Complesso Monte Curcio** ski resort (V. Tasso, tel. 0984/578037 or 0984/578136) is 2 km (1 mi) west of Camigliatello; bear left at the fork at the edge of town. A day of skiing on the resort's three runs costs about L22,000–L30,000; another L20,000–L30,000 buys you skis and boots for the day. The skiing doesn't get any better in southern Italy, but it's hardly the Alps—or even Vermont, for that matter. On Sunday in summer you can take the chairlift up and down the mountain for L4,000 (round-trip).

BASICS • The Casa del Forestiere (V. Roma 3–7) is a poetically (though unjustifiably) named building that holds two information offices. The **Pro Loco** office (tel. 0984/578091; open daily 9–1 and 4–7) is not known to be terribly helpful.

COMING AND GOING • The most scenic route to Camigliatello is by **train** from Cosenza. Three trains (1 hr 20 min, L2,500) leave Cosenza daily and continue on east to San Giovanni in Fiore (40 min, L2,700). Buses also leave Cosenza every few hours for Camigliatello (45 min, L2,800); from Camigliatello, buses continue to San Giovanni in Fiore (30 min, L1,700). Camigliatello's bus stop and train station are at the bottom of **Via Roma;** the town is just up the road. You can buy train or bus tickets at the train station.

WHERE TO SLEEP AND EAT • Camigliatello has plenty of hotels, but most cater to the wealthy leisure crowd instead of the humble hiker. A cheap place in town is **Meranda** (V. del Turismo, parallel to V. Roma, tel. 0984/578022), with rather plain-looking doubles for L80,000–L100,000. **Leonetti** (V. Roma 44, tel. 0984/578075) has spick-and-span doubles with bath for L80,000.

You can camp legally at a designated campsite or slink off into the woods and sleep (this is illegal, but generally no one will bother you if you don't light a fire). The closest campground, **La Fattoria** (Contrada La Bonia, tel. 0984/578364), is about 3 km (1½ mi) outside Camigliatello. Double bungalows with bath go for L80,000–L120,000 a night, or you can pitch a tent on a wide-open field in front of a mountain range for L7,000–L9,000 per person, L7,000–L9,000 per tent. The bathrooms are clean, the showers are hot, and the place is rarely crowded. From the campground, it's a short hike to Lake Cecita. Take Via Roma west from town and turn right in tiny Moccone. If you're coming by train, get off at Moccone. One bus goes to the site off-season, and three go daily in summer; the people at the campground know the schedule.

Most restaurants in town are part of a lodging establishment. For fast meals, stop by the pub **Da Egidio** (V. Roma 10), where you can get cheap sandwiches, simple pasta dishes, and real American french fries with ketchup, as well as choose from a small but eclectic selection of international beers. Otherwise, pick up picnic supplies at one of the small markets on Via Roma.

PRAIA A MARE

A sleepy, unremarkable beach town most of the year, Praia a Mare, on the Tyrrhenian coast just south of Maratea, metamorphoses in July and August into a swinging, splashing, open-all-hours vacation spot. It's essentially a long, wide, reasonably nice beach with a reasonably nice town attached as an afterthought. Its approximation of a main street, Via L. Giugni/Via Turati, runs parallel to the water two blocks in. Farther back is a row of cliffs, impassable without a car or motorcycle.

The chapel of **Grotta del Santuario della Madonna** (open summer, daily 9–6; 9–1 and 3–6 off-season) is in a large, damp cave partway up a cliff. The short but steep staircase begins on the east (inland) side of the train tracks, about 10 minutes south of the station. The **Isola di Dino**, a squarish hunk of rock about 4 km (1½ mi) down the beach from the town center, has two grottoes high enough to explore in a small boat. The island is within swimming distance of shore, but for L13,000 an hour you can rent a pedal boat at one of the many stands on the beach. For information stop by the **Pro Loco** office (V. F. Crispi 15, tel. 0985/777030; open daily 9:30–12:30 and 5:30–8:30). You can rent scooters (L80,000 per day) and mountain bikes (L20,000 per day) at **Noleggio Praia '90** (V. F. Cilea 27–29, tel. 0985/73455).

COMING AND GOING • The **Praja** train station handles almost all public transport in and out of Praia a Mare. There are almost hourly trains north to Agropoli (1¼ hrs, L9,800) and Naples (2¾ hrs, L17,200) and south to Paola, most continuing to Cosenza (1½ hrs, L8,000). The station is just a few minutes from the town center.

WHERE TO SLEEP AND EAT • The cheapest place to sleep is **Pensione La Piedigrotta** (V. Majorana, tel. 0985/72192), with passable rooms, rudimentary bathrooms, and a good restaurant. Doubles with bath cost L60,000. Leaving the station, take a left on the first paved road and walk 10 minutes parallel to the tracks to where the road meets the tracks again. To get away from the noise of the trains, try **Le Arcate** (V. Turati 17, tel. and fax 0985/72297), where clean doubles with bath, TV, and breakfast are L70,000. Head away from the station and turn left on Via Longo, which becomes Via L. Giugni and then Via Turati.

You can buy fruit and vegetables at the **outdoor market** (V. Leonardo da Vinci, off main street toward water; open daily 7:30–1:30). At **Bar Scalzipenna** (P. Italia 9, tel. 0985/72458; open daily 7:30 AM–11 PM, later in summer), you can snack on pizzette, calzone, and arancini for L2,000 a pop. Should you crave fresh-from-the-oven cream-filled cornetti late at night, **Il Fornaio** (V. della Libertà 21) bakes 'em 7–7, July–mid-September (L1,200). By day you can get a wide selection of pastries at **Eburum** (V. L. Giugni 21, tel. 0985/72137).

AFTER DARK • A number of dance clubs around Praia a Mare rock in season, the most happening of which is **Harem** (Località Fiuzzi; open July weekends; Aug. daily), a 40-minute walk south along the lungomare. This open-air beachside disco has both techno and mainstream dance floors; the cover is L15,000–L20,000. Right next door, you can play late-night miniature golf at **Fiuzziland** (Località Fiuzzi), open nightly 9–4 in summer. In town, spend a mellow evening at **Bix Pub** (V. Turati 79, tel. 0985/74282), where you can down a few beers (L5,000) and snack on arancini while listening to cool jazz tunes.

ROSSANO

It takes some planning to get here, but Rossano, with its well-preserved medieval quarter, is one of the most attractive towns on the Ionian coast. Trains and buses drop you off near the ocean in the bustling New Town, **Rossano Scalo,** of little cultural interest. From the train station, exit onto Piazza Leonardo da

Vinci, where an orange city bus (every half hour, L1,000; last bus 8:20 PM) takes you 5 km (3 mi) up the winding hill to the centro storico. The historic center is a wonder of important churches and a museum overflowing with religious icons and treasures. Housed in the **Museo Diocesano d'Arte Sacra** (tel. 0983/520542; admission L2,000; open Tue.–Sat. 9:30–12 and 4–6, Sun. 10–12:30) is Rossano's prize cultural artifact—the Codex Purpureus (Purple Codex), a mint-condition manuscript of biblical stories dating to the Byzantine era. The nearby church of **San Marco,** built in the 9th century, is an elegant yet extremely simple example of the Byzantine style. Aside from the monuments, Rossano is a congenial place to spend a day hanging out in a piazza with the old-timers or wandering through winding streets.

COMING AND GOING • Rossano makes a good day trip from Cosenza by **train** (2 hrs, L8,000); you'll have to change at Sibari. Rossano is on the **FS** train line, which travels the length of the Ionian coast. The trip to Reggio di Calabria (L35,400) takes four hours by InterCity train; you can also come from Metaponto (2 hrs, L9,800). Buy your ticket on the train, as the station is entirely self-service. The **bus** (1 hr 40 min, L6,400) is faster and cheaper but has an inconvenient schedule; the last bus leaves Rossano in the early afternoon. Long-distance buses also stop in front of the train station; regional service is provided by **I.A.S. Scura** (V. Luca de Rosis 9, tel. 0983/511790; open Mon.–Sat. 8:30–12:40 and 4–7); buy your ticket on the bus. **SIMET** (V. Luca de Rosis 49, across from train station, tel. 0983/512793) handles northbound buses to cities such as Florence (10 hrs, L76,000). Their office is open weekdays 9–1 and 3:30–7:30, Saturday 9–1.

If you've been traveling through southern Italy in the summer, a stop in the mountains of the Sila Grande may be worth it just for the cool mountain air: temperatures are 10°F–20°F lower than on the coast. You'll need a sweater at night.

REGGIO DI CALABRIA

By the time you've reached Reggio di Calabria, it's hard to go much farther south without getting on a boat. It's hardly the end of the world, though; Reggio is Calabria's largest city, a bustling commercial center laid out along the Straits of Messina with a tempting view of Sicily. The bad news is that earthquakes at the turn of the century and heavy aerial bombing during World War II razed most of the historic buildings and destroyed cultural treasures. Still, it's a good place to visit for a day or two if you're tired of beach towns and multilingual menus or just want to do a little shopping.

BASICS

Reggio has three **IAT** tourist information offices: one in **Stazione Centrale** (tel. 1478/88088), one in the town center (C. Garibaldi 309, tel. 0965/892012), and one at the airport (tel. 0965/643291). All three are open Mon.–Sat. 8–8, with shorter hours in winter.

COMING AND GOING

From 7 AM to 8 PM, ferries and hydrofoils run regularly between Reggio's port, a half kilometer (¼ mi) north of Stazione Lido, and Messina (20 min, L4,000). They are operated by the **Ferrovie dello Stato** (tel. 1478/88088) and **SNAV** (tel. 0965/29568). You can get a copy of the schedule at an IAT office. If you are coming to Reggio solely to take the ferry to Sicily, you should get off the train at Villa San Giovanni, 15 minutes north of Reggio. The FS ferries are right in front of you as you leave the station, and there are one or two per hour 'round the clock.

BY TRAIN • Reggio's main train station is **Stazione Centrale** (P. Garibaldi, tel. 1478/88088), from which a train heads up the Ionian coast toward Taranto and Brindisi (1–2 per hr) and another travels up the Tyrrhenian coast toward Naples and Rome (2–3 per hr). Five daily InterCity trains head to Rome (7½–8 hrs, L60,400); for Cosenza (2½–3 hrs, L20,800), you'll probably have to switch at Lamezia Terme and/or Paola. Most trains on the Tyrrhenian coastal line also stop at **Stazione Lido,** 2 km (1 mi) north of Stazione Centrale and closer to the port. Neither station has luggage storage.

BY BUS • For any destination on either coast, it's best to go by train. The urban bus company **Azienda Municipale Autobus** (tel. 0965/620121) has frequent bus service to several regional towns. Otherwise, four private carriers handle medium- and long-distance service. You can peruse their schedules at the IAT office in Stazione Centrale or at the travel agency **Simonetta** (C. Garibaldi 521, tel. 0965/331444; open weekdays 9–1 and 4:30–8, Sat. 9–1). Local buses run frequently between Stazione Centrale and Stazione Lido along Corso Garibaldi. Tickets cost L800; purchase them at newsstands and tobacco shops.

BY PLANE • Reggio's small **Aeroporto Civile Minniti** (tel. 0965/642232) is served by **Alitalia** (tel. 0965/643095) and a few charter companies. Many local buses make the 20-minute trip (L800) from Stazione Centrale, or you can take a shuttle to the port. A taxi from the station to the airport will cost L20,000–L30,000.

WHERE TO SLEEP

Not many tourists spend the night here, though you might have to contend with the workers and immigrants who fill the budget hotels near both train stations. These places are simple and drab, but if you're willing to venture to the outskirts of town, you'll find a wonderful pension, the **Albergo Eremo** (V. Eremo Botte 12, tel. 0965/22433). Two kind, older Calabrian women have been running the hotel and tending its jasmine-scented garden since 1962. Quiet, immaculate, and affordable, this place is southern Italy at its best. Doubles with bath go for L70,000. Take Bus 7 (hourly, 20 min, L1,000; last bus 9 PM) from Stazione Centrale. If the Eremo is full, try **Albergo Noel** (V. Genoese Zerbi 13, tel. 0965/890965), 500 ft north of Stazione Lido along the water. It's on a heavily traveled street, but it's near the sea and a short walk from the town center. The rooms are ugly but clean, with strange closet-like bathrooms. Doubles (all with bath) go for L80,000. **Hotel Mundial** (V. Gaeta 9, tel. 0965/332255) has doubles with bath for L90,000.

WHERE TO EAT

Reggio has a decent selection of moderately priced restaurants near Stazione Centrale. Standard fare around here consists of an obligatory prima pasta, a secondo of grilled fish, and a bottle of Cirò, a regional red. On the same street as Albergo Eremo (*see* Where to Sleep, *above*) you'll find **Taverna degli Ulivi** (V. Eremo Botte 32, tel. 0965/891461; closed Sun.), dishing out Calabrian fare such as *maccaruni i casa* (homemade pasta with meat sauce) and *braciolette alla calabrese* (small broiled slices of mixed meats; L13,000). They're open for dinner only. For a quicker meal, stop by either of the stylish **Cordon Bleu** bars (C. Garibaldi 203, tel. 0965/332447; C. Vittorio Emanuele 39, tel. 0965/891161), which serve everything from cornetti to antipasti to fancy desserts. Prices range from L 1500 to L13,500.

WORTH SEEING

Reggio is a relatively easy town to negotiate, as most interesting things lie between the two train stations. Running north from Piazza Garibaldi parallel to the water is Corso Garibaldi, filled with banks and fancy stores—even a Body Shop. The city's main attraction is the world-famous **Museo Nazionale della Magna Grecia** (P. de Nava, tel. 0965/812255; admission L8,000; open daily 9–6:30; closed every 1st and 3rd Sun.), on Corso Garibaldi near Stazione Lido. The museum is dedicated mainly to archaeological finds from ancient Greek settlements in southern Italy. The Bronzi di Riace, two bronze statues dating to the 5th century BC, steal the show. They were discovered in 1972 when a diver off the coast of the small town of Riace caught a glimpse of an arm protruding from the ocean floor. Three blocks above Corso Garibaldi you'll find the defiantly anachronistic, asymmetric **Castello Aragonese** (P. Castello), built in the 15th century. Down toward the water, between Corso Vittorio Emanuele and Lungomare Matteotti, lie the rather humble remains of a **Greek wall** that circled the city in the 4th century BC, as well as ruins of some Roman baths. If you want to go for a swim, the beach is just below Stazione Lido. Reggio's most important festival, on the second or third Sunday in September, is the celebration of the Madonna della Consolazione, with a procession, concerts, and games.

AFTER DARK

On warm summer evenings, most of Reggio's population seems to gather first on Corso Garibaldi and later on Lungomare Matteotti, a street with a great view of the Sicilian coast. Heading in the direction of Stazione Lido, the street ends at **Piazza Independenza;** here legions of *ragazzi* (young people) gather in front of **Gelateria Cesare,** where you can get a mean *mela verde* (green apple). A good evening hangout is **Metrò** (V. Zecca 3, off V. Giudecca; closed Mon.), halfway between Stazione Centrale and Stazione Lido, with beers, sandwiches, and occasional live music of all types—from avant-garde jazz to bluegrass—until the wee hours.

NEAR REGGIO

The coast near Reggio broils during August, when temperatures climb as high as 105°F. Trains run up the Ionian coast as far as Taranto and along the Tyrrhenian coast, past old fishing villages like **Pizzo, Tropea,** and **Scilla,** which offer well-preserved castles and cliff-top views.

LOCRI

Only 100 km (62 mi) from Reggio along the Ionian coast, the small town of Locri is strung along its clean, sandy beach. Locri suffers from—or enjoys, depending on how you look at it—near-Saharan temperatures, which means you can swim in its waters almost any time of year. Beyond the beach-vacation throngs in July and August, the town itself has little to offer. If you're a Greek-ruins diehard, walk 4 km (2½ mi) south on the main road (just inland from the train tracks) to the remains of **Locri Epizefiri** (admission free; open 9–sunset), founded in the 7th century BC. For the most part, it's just the remnants of walls; the stump of a column marks a 5th-century BC temple with its altar. At the entrance to the site, the **Antiquarium** (admission L4,000; open daily 9–7, shorter hrs in winter) has a collection of sculptures, vases, and other objects found in the area; they're of more archaeological than artistic interest.

Trains run hourly to Locri from Reggio (1½ hrs, L8,000). The spartan but quiet **Hotel Orientale** (V. Tripoli 33, tel. 0964/20261) has doubles for L80,000 with bath, L60,000 without. From the station, walk straight ahead two blocks to Via Matteotti and turn right; Via Tripoli will be on your left.

PIZZO

Once a humble fishing village, Pizzo is now overrun in July and August by vacationing Italians. The old quarter still has its charm, though, and great beaches stretch along both sides of the marina. Pizzo is on the southern Tyrrhenian coast between Praia a Mare (1 hr 40 min, L13,600) and Reggio (1 hr 20 min, L8,000). Get off the train at the Vibo Valentia Pizzo station, 2 km (1 mi) south of town; from here occasional buses run to the center (Mon.–Sat.). For a schedule, call the **Pro Loco** office (tel. 0963/44318) in Vibo Valentia; buy tickets in the station's bar. The closest campground, **Villaggio Europa** (tel. 0963/534936; closed Oct.–late June), is on the beach 3 km (2 mi) from town. You'll pay L8,800 per person, L7,000 per tent. Whatever the duration of your stay, pay a visit to the quaint little **castello,** famous as the site where Joachim Murat, king of Naples, was executed in 1815 after fleeing to Pizzo when Napoléon was defeated. Supposedly, his last words were, *"Mirate al petto e salvate il viso"* (Aim for the body and save the face). Oh, the vanities of kings.

> *Don't miss Calabria's specialty, wild funghi (mushrooms) gathered from the nearby hills.*

SICILY

BY VALERIE HAMILTON

UPDATED BY JEFFREY KENNEDY

A land of beaches, volcanoes, fishermen, gangsters, temples, tenements, and open fields, Sicily (Sicilia) has so many different faces that it seems more like a separate country than the small island it is. Black-veiled widows and *The Godfather*-style villages contrast sharply with the relatively cosmopolitan Siracusa and teeming Palermo. Greek ruins and glitzy resorts are wedged between mountain peaks and long stretches of farmland. Italy tends to regard Sicily as a distant and unwelcome relation, and many cynics, most of them northern Italians, are ready to give the island up for lost. The commonly held belief is that the island's development is held back by the Mafia. But the truth about the island is that there is no one truth; Sicily is a varied place with a rich history and an uncertain future.

The roots of Sicily's diversity can be found in its tumultuous past. Over the centuries, the island's key position, fertile soil, and warm climate encouraged pretty much every great Mediterranean and European civilization to go to the trouble of invading it. The first conquerors to make a name for themselves were Hellenes from the Greek city-states and Phoenicians from Carthage—in the 8th century BC. These early travelers first colonized the Ionian coast, and one of their initial settlements, Siracusa, rapidly became one of the most powerful cities in antiquity. The ambitious Siracusi clashed with the Carthaginians stationed in the western part of the island, and after centuries of discord, Rome crushed them both. By the 3rd century BC, Sicily was little more than a big Roman Club Med (and major Empire bread-basket). The next major change came when the North Africans overran the island in the 9th century AD, introducing mathematics, couscous, and a third prophet. The island entered its golden period with the AD 1061 invasion of the Norman king Roger I. His son Roger II was crowned the first Norman king of Sicily in 1130 and turned Palermo into Europe's intellectual and cultural center for a time. A later Norman successor, Frederick II, managed to steer the kingdom with a strong system of law and order, building fortresses and patronizing the arts. After Frederick's death in 1250, countless European aristocrats made claims to the island, keeping Sicily in a repressive and backward state of feudalism.

The defining moment in Sicily's recent history came in 1860, when Garibaldi landed with his 1,000 Red Shirts, sending out Italy's first call for independence from foreign rule in the modern era. But when Garibaldi kicked out the Bourbons, he created a power vacuum that was quickly filled by an institution of *padrones* and their armed families, known as the Mafia (*see box* Sleeping with the Fishes, *above*). Just as troublesome as the medieval-minded nobles they replaced, La Cosa Nostra stifled the island's economic growth and creativity while the rest of Europe was soaring through the last stages of the industrial revolution. Since World War II, the Italian state has tried to modernize the island in spite of the

Mafia, but the campaign has been only partially successful, no matter how many shiny new highways and apartment blocks (often in open defiance of building codes) you'll see. Recent political campaigns once again raised the question of an independent Sicilian state, and although such a drastic change is unlikely, it's emblematic of the identity crisis from which Sicily has suffered for thousands of years.

Perhaps because of its centuries-long economic and political instability, much of Sicily retains its old-world flavor. The island's ancient colonies hold some of the best Greek ruins in the world: in addition to spectacular (but touristy) **Siracusa** and **Agrigento,** small and obscure Selinunte and Segesta to the west have some splendid and relatively undiscovered sites. History is equally alive in the capital of **Palermo,** where you visit Norman cathedrals and gardens, medieval alleys, and crumbling *palazzi*. And when you're not improving yourself in museums, you can enjoy the beaches in picture-perfect **Taormina** and the **Aeolian Islands,** or in lesser-known coastal beach towns. Or grab your hiking boots and flirt with destiny on the slopes of volatile **Mt. Etna.** But it's in the smaller cities—whether Baroqued-out Noto or colorful Caltagirone—that you'll experience a Sicily almost untouched by tourism. Best of all, after a long day in the sun, you'll have the chance to sample some of Italy's freshest fish and vegetables, prepared with Arab, Greek, and Spanish influences.

Sicily's food is dependably delicious and always affordable. As well as having access to all the fresh seafood it can pull out of the sea, Sicily is a major agricultural producer of oranges, lemons, olives, onions, grains, and nuts. Vegetarians will have no problem here. Regional specialties include *involtini di pesce spada* (swordfish roulades stuffed with spices and bread crumbs); Catania's pasta *alla Norma,* with a sauce of eggplant, fresh tomatoes, basil, and ricotta; Palermo's pasta *con le sarde,* with sardines and wild fennel; and Trapani's *busiate al pesto trapanese,* handmade squiggly pasta in a pesto of basil, tomato, eggplant, olive oil, garlic, and crushed almonds. Dive into huge plates of fresh *tonno* (tuna), more *pesce spada* (swordfish), *polpo* (octopus), *aragosta* (lobster), and *gamberetti* (shrimp), particularly on Sicily's fishing-oriented western shore, where you may also find couscous on the menu.

Over a million Sicilians emigrated to America around the turn of the century. If you have Sicilian blood, the Italian Cultural Institute (tel. 212/879–4242, New York) can help you trace your family history. Town halls in Sicily might let you nose through their records.

COMING AND GOING

Messina, on the northernmost tip of Sicily's eastern Ionian coast, is the main gateway to Sicily and is served by frequent trains, hydrofoils, and ferries (*see* Coming and Going *in* Messina, *below*). It's also possible but more expensive to ferry from Genoa and Naples to Palermo and from Reggio di Calabria to Siracusa. If you're traveling on somebody else's credit card, Catania and Palermo have airports served by national carriers. You'll need more than a few days to see the island—just traveling in between coasts is no easy task, as train service is limited and winding roads slow down buses. If you're heading to North Africa after trekking through Sicily, Trapani (*see* Coming and Going *in* Trapani, *below*) may be a convenient departure point.

SAFETY

Traveling in Sicily is for the most part safe, but you should always be alert, especially in port cities like Catania, Palermo, and Messina, where, sadly, the streets belong to a rougher element after dark. Women traveling alone, especially in the less-touristed interior, should try to cover legs and shoulders as much as possible to avoid unwanted attention and unsolicited invitations.

WHEN TO GO

When planning your trip, keep in mind that the climate here is more like Tunisia's than Rome's. The dry sirocco sweeps up from North Africa, and the Mediterranean sun glares relentlessly, which can cause dehydration and serious sunburn. Due to oppressive heat and crowds, July and August are not the greatest times to visit. June and September are less crowded and not quite so hot, but spring takes the prize: wildflowers abound, crowds are minimal, and the weather is mild enough that you can comfortably take a dip in the sea.

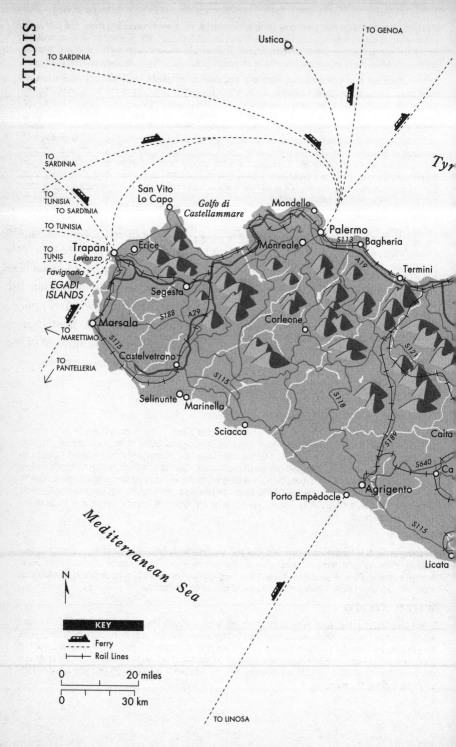

SICILY

TO GENOA

Ustica

TO SARDINIA

TO SARDINIA

TO SARDINIA

TO TUNISIA

TO SARDINIA

TO TUNISIA

San Vito
Lo Capo

Golfo di
Castellammare

Mondello

Palermo

Tyr

TO TUNIS
Trapani
Levanzo

Erice

Monreale

S113

Bagheria

Favignana

EGADI
ISLANDS

Segesta

A19

Termini

S188

A29

Corleone

TO MARETTIMO

Marsala

S115

S121

TO
PANTELLERIA

Castelvetrano

S115

S118

Selinunte

Marinella

Calta

Sciacca

S189

S640

Ca

Agrigento

Porto Empèdocle

Mediterranean Sea

N

Licata

KEY

Ferry

Rail Lines

0   20 miles

0   30 km

TO LINOSA

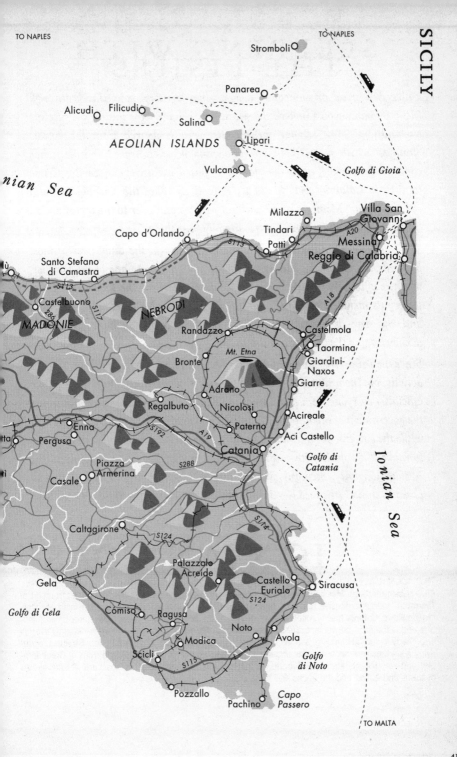

SLEEPING WITH THE FISHES

Unless you tread on someone's drug-dealing territory, your travels through Sicily probably won't involve the Mafia, an oblique term that defies succinct explanation. Some scholars believe the word is derived from the Arabic "muafa," which means both protection and perseverance. Over time it has come to denote the 90 or so "families" based exclusively in Sicily. Crime families in Calabria and Naples are respectively called the "indrugheta" and the "camorra." Members of the Sicilian Mafia never refer to the organization as such, preferring La Cosa Nostra, literally "our thing."

The modern-day Mafia is an influential presence in the daily lives of most Sicilians. Almost all businesses pay protection (pizzo) to one of the families, who are effectively hidden behind a cloak of "omertà," the lifelong pledge of secrecy its members commit to when first initiated. Until recently, omertà— and the fear of brutal retribution—has kept most Sicilians from even acknowledging the existence of the Mafia.

Since the 1960s, the Italian government has periodically cracked down on mob activity, but the primary effect has been to incite violent assassinations of public officials—everyone from prosecutors to liberal politicians. Many people accuse the government of intentionally losing the war against the Mafia, claiming that while the government maintains the facade of justice, corrupt officials continue to make illicit deals with mafiosi for huge profits. But when it comes to the Mafia's longevity, Sicilians cite an insightful local saying: "calati junco 'ca passa la china" (the reed lies down until the flood has passed).

IONIAN COAST

The ancient ruins and natural beauty of Sicily's east coast make it the island's most popular destination. After passing through **Messina**'s ferry ports, head south along the coast to the idyllic clifftop resort of **Taormina**—rather expensive and very touristy, but filled with hidden piazzas and stunning Mediterranean views. **Catania** has a limited dose of urban charm, but it's home to extensive Baroque architecture and is the most convenient passageway to nearby **Mt. Etna.** The volcano towers defiantly over all else, ready to spread clouds of ash far across the Mediterranean at a moment's notice. **Siracusa,** occupying a southeastern section of the Ionian coast, is noteworthy for its millennia-old ruins of Greek temples and amphitheaters and fine Baroque architecture. Most towns along the coast are well connected by trains and buses, and the tracks and roads often run right above the sea.

MESSINA

The best place to view Messina is from across the sea—when you can almost imagine that the squat buildings and sprawling streets still hold the mysteries a 3,000-year-old port should. Once you arrive, however, the illusion vanishes. Messina has had its share of invasions along with epidemics: like most of southern Italy and Sicily, the port town was taken by the Romans, Carthaginians, Arabs, Normans, Angevins, Aragonese, and Bourbons alike. But almost all traces of the town's complicated history were erased by the 1908 earthquake, when in the course of one day, 91% of Messina was flattened and 84,000 people were killed, two-thirds of the city's population .

Not surprisingly, there isn't much here to distract you from your wait between trains and ferries. If you have time, check out the elaborate ceiling and apse mosaic of the rebuilt **Duomo** (P. del Duomo), originally constructed by Norman king Roger II in the 12th century. The adjacent **campanile** (1933) boasts Europe's second-largest astrological clock, which twirls and dances every day at noon; the fetchingly Mannerist **Fontana di Orione,** by one of Michelangelo's students, is in the same piazza. To get to the piazza, walk west from the station on Via Primo Settembre. From the train station it's a 15-minute ride on Bus 47 to the tiny but interesting **Museo Nazionale** (V. della Libertà 465, tel. 090/361292; admission L2,000), which houses fragments of works salvaged from the earthquake, including Caravaggio's stunning *Resurrection of Lazarus.* If you happen to pass through town on June 3 or August 15 (at Ferragosto), the lively half-religious/half-social processions of the Madonna della Lettera and the Vara are worth a peek. Feast on Sicilian treats and forget about what Messina's like the other 363 days of the year.

BASICS

The main **tourist office** (P. della Repubblica, tel. 090/672944; open Mon.–Thurs. 8–6, Fri.–Sat. 8–2) is to the right as you exit the train station. An **information desk** (tel. 090/675234; open Mon.–Sat. 6 AM–8 PM) in the train station changes money at mediocre rates. The rates at **Banco di Sicilia** (V. Garibaldi 102, at V. Primo Settembre, tel. 090/77601; open weekdays 8:30–1:30 and 3–4) are much better. The **post office** (P. Antonello, 1 block northwest of the Duomo, tel. 090/774437; open Mon.–Sat. 8:10–6:30) is an outdoor postal unit.

COMING AND GOING

BY TRAIN • From **Messina Centrale** (P. della Repubblica, tel. 1478/88088 toll-free) there's frequent service to Palermo (19 daily, 5 hrs, L20,000), Catania (16 daily, 1½ hrs, L8,200), Siracusa (12 daily, 3 hrs, L16,000), and Milazzo (15 daily, 45 min, L5,000), as well as Rome (8 daily, 8 hrs, L53,000) and Naples (10 daily, 4 hrs, L40,000).

BY BUS • **SAIS** (P. della Repubblica 6, tel. 090/771914) has an office open daily 6 AM–8 PM and serves Taormina (9–19 daily, 1½ hrs, L5,100), Catania (18 daily, 1½ hrs, L9,500), and many small towns in between. Western Sicily is better served by **Giuntabus** (V. Terranova 8, tel. 090/673782), which travels to Milazzo—the port for the Aeolian Islands—(10 daily, 30 min, L5,500) and points west; buy tickets on the bus.

BY BOAT • Messina's ferry terminal, **Messina Marittima** (tel. 1478/88088) is an extension of the train station—to get from one to the other, walk on the platforms or Via Calabria. Ferry companies serve the mainland ports of Villa San Giovanni (15 daily, 20 min, L2,200) and Reggio di Calabria (10 daily, 35 min, L6,000). You can take a ferry to the Aeolian Islands from Messina, but you'll save upwards of 50% by departing from Milazzo (*see* Tyrrhenian Coast, *below*). Messina's hydrofoil station, **SNAV** (tel. 090/364044, 1 km/½ mi north of train station on C. Vittorio Emanuele), serves Naples (1 daily, 3 hrs, L147,000) and Reggio di Calabria (hourly, 15 min, L6,500).

WHERE TO SLEEP AND EAT

You'd do better spending the night elsewhere—not only are hotels in Messina uniformly overpriced, but you'll spend L15,000 on a taxi to get to them after dark because the streets are unsafe. If you do get stuck, try L100,000 doubles with bath at the clean and spare **Hotel Touring** (V. N. Scotto 17, tel. 090/2938851), two blocks south of the train station, but be wary of the walk at night. If the Touring is full, head next door to the **Hotel Mirage** (V. N. Scotto 3, tel. 090/2938844), where trim doubles with unfortunate speckled floors cost L70,000–L90,000. The large **Il Peloritano** campground (tel. 090/348496), in a beautiful setting about 20 km (12½ mi) north of Messina, has clean facilities and hot showers, but bring your own food. Sites cost L6,000 per person, and you can pitch a tent for L6,000 a double, L7,000 a quad. From the train station, take Bus 81 to the Rodia stop, a 30-minute ride, and follow the signs.

Inexpensive pizzerias abound around Corso Cavour and Via Cesare Battisti, which lie above and below the Duomo, respectively. In the morning, sidewalk fruit stands line Via Tommaso Canizzaro near the university. You can get a filling *pizza rustica* (meat-and-cheese stuffed pie) for L7,500 at **Pizzeria del Capitano** (V. dei Mille 88, no phone; closed Sun.) and wash it down afterward with a glass of vino for L1,500 from the neighboring wine bar **Fiaccetteria Vini** (V. dei Mille 74, no phone; closed Sun.).

TAORMINA

At the height of summer, Taormina's beauty is a double-edge sword. The city's meandering stairways, bougainvillea-covered palazzi, and dazzling vistas make the prospect of a trip here very appealing, but in July and August you can barely see the sights for all the video cameras. The city had its start in 358 BC when Siracusa's tyrannical ruler Dionysius crushed nearby Naxos, inducing the survivors to flee to the hills and form a new city. You can see the **Teatro Greco** they built, set against a seemingly airbrushed panorama of Mt. Etna, on any travel brochure, but it's worth it to visit in person. Obscure parts of town provide a glimpse of the Taormina that seduced Goethe, D. H. Lawrence, and a host of 19th- and 20th-century gay exiles and artistic types, and the scenery really is breathtaking. Even so, you might want to consider making Taormina a day trip, as lodging here is a fairly precious commodity, and your time and lire may be better spent delving deeper into the island.

BASICS

The folks at **AAST** (Palazzo Corvaja, C. Umberto I, tel. 0942/23243), near Porta Messina, hand out maps, post train schedules, and help you find lodging Monday–Saturday 8–2 and 4–7. **Monte dei Paschi di Siena** (P. del Duomo 5, tel. 0942/626010) has an ATM with credit card and Cirrus access, while **La Duca Viaggi** (V. Don Bosco 39, overlooking P. IX Aprile, tel. 0942/625255) runs a full-service AmEx office. You can do worse than to settle for the exchange rates at **Sicilcassa** (C. Umberto I 2, tel. 0942/23070; open weekdays 8:30–1:30), across from the AAST. Make calls at **Telecom** (V. S. Pancrazio 6, tel. 0942/24669; open Mon.–Sat. 8:30–12:30 and 4:30–8), in the Avis agency to the right of Porta Messina. The **post office** (P. Medaglia d'Oro, at C. Umberto I, tel. 0942/23010; open Mon.–Sat. 8:30–6:30) also changes money. **Internet services** are available at Computer Center (C. Umberto I 34, tel. 0942/625963).

COMING AND GOING

The **Taormina-Giardini** train (tel. 1478/88088; ticket office open daily 5:30 AM–9 PM) serves Catania (15 daily, 45 min, L4,200), Siracusa (12 daily, 2 hrs, L11,700), and Messina (17 daily, 1 hr, L4,200). It sits uncharitably far below town, so leave your luggage (L5,000) and hike 30 minutes uphill or take a taxi (L15,000). Buses make the trek sporadically 5 AM–9:25 PM (Sun. until 7:30 PM); buy tickets (L1,500) on board. The **SAIS** bus terminal on Via Pirandello—really just a glass booth with some schedules—has service to Messina (12–15 daily, 1½ hrs, L5,100), Catania (15 daily, 1 hr 45 min, L5,100), and Giardini-Naxos (26 daily, 20 min, L1,500). To reach town, take a left out of the terminal on Via Pirandello, which leads to Porta Messina.

GETTING AROUND

Taormina's streets cling to the rocky hillside in a crescent shape. Corso Umberto I is at the center of it all, passing east to west through Porta Messina, Piazza Vittorio Emanuele II, Piazza del Duomo, and Porta Catania. Downhill from Corso Umberto I spreads a tangle of stepped alleys that all somehow end at Via Roma or Via Bagnoli Croci, the lowest border of the city. To reach the Bay of Mazzarò and its ever-congested **beach,** take the *funivia* (funicular; L2,000–L2,500 one-way) from its station on Via Pirandello for the five-minute ride. From the lower funivia station follow the signs to the pebbly shore. If you want to cruise like the natives, **California Motonoleggio** (V. Bagnoli Croci 86, across from Giardini Pubblici, tel. 0942/23769) rents Vespas (L48,500 a day) daily 7–12:30 and 3:30–8 with a credit card deposit.

WHERE TO SLEEP

There are plenty of places to stay in Taormina, but few are cheap. Most places won't give you a room for less than two nights, and you must reserve ahead, although smaller hotels are more likely to take cash-in-hand over a promise made over the phone. In a pinch, try the musty **Hotel Moderno** (tel. 0942/51017; doubles L50,000), across from the train station, or head to Giardini-Naxos (*see* Near Taormina, *below*). For a cheap sleep under the stars, **Camping San Leo** (Capo Taormina, tel. 0942/24658) charges L8,000 per person; a tent L12,000. Set on the bay, the 156 sites fill up fast in summer, and the thundering traffic of Via Nazionale is never far away. Take any bus between the train station and town and ask the driver to drop you halfway at "il camping."

UNDER L65,000 • Locanda Diana. The best deal in Taormina is run by an older couple who rent out homey rooms just a heartbeat from Piazza Vittorio Emanuele II. Some doubles (L60,000) have obscured views of the sea over the city's rooftops. *V. di Giovanni 6, 90839, tel. 0942/23898. From P. Vittorio Emanuele II, walk downhill until street becomes V. di Giovanni. 4 rooms with bath. Cash only.*

UNDER L85,000 • Il Leone. Affable owner Salvatore Arrigo rents tiny and drafty but functional rooms above his restaurant (doubles L80,000), breakfast included. If your room is without a view, seek out the stunning rooftop terrace, shared by lucky Rooms 1, 2, and 3. Video games and a pool table are downstairs in a back room behind the restaurant. *V. Bagnoli Croci 126, 98039, tel. 0942/21182. 19 rooms, 17 with bath. Cash only.*

Casa Grazia. This small, spotless hotel on a narrow lane close to the town center was completely remodeled a few years ago. The rooms (doubles L70,000–L80,000) aren't large, but the big windows let in cool sea breezes. *V. Iallia Bassia 20, 98039, tel. 0942/24776. Down the block from steps near entrance to Greek Theater. 5 rooms, 3 with bath. Cash only. Closed Nov.–Dec.*

Villa Gaia. Up a wide stone staircase from Piazza del Duomo, this quiet pension is tucked into a lush garden full of fruit trees and hibiscus. For a L80,000–L100,000 double, you're paying for air-conditioning, a clean, well-appointed and spacious private bath, and a sunny terrace with breathtaking views of Mt. Etna and the ocean. Night owls can ask for a key to the front door. *V. Fazzello 34, 98039, tel. 0942/23185. 8 rooms with bath. Closed Nov.*

UNDER L105,000 • Villino Gallodoro. This pink, two-story hotel is down at Mazzarò, across from the base of the funivia, right on the water in a garden with a patio. Doubles are L100,000, breakfast included. *V. Nazionale 147, 98030, tel. 0942/23860. 15 rooms with bath.*

WHERE TO EAT

Dining in Taormina isn't as expensive as you might imagine, and the quality is consistently decent most everywhere. If you prefer to fend for yourself, avoid the gourmet markets on Corso Umberto I and head downtown to the fruit carts on the side streets leading to Via Roma. The *salumeria* (deli) **Bottega di Laganà** (V. di Giovanni 47, near C. Umberto I, tel. 0942/23040) won't rip you off, and the *panificio* (bakery) **Managò** (V. Giardinazzo 55, tel. 0942/24365) serves little pizzas. Don't miss Taormina's confectionery hometown hero, the *torrone bianco,* a flat, almond-filled nougat cake topped with candied fruit. They're in every pastry-shop window on Corso Umberto I.

Taormina's restaurants have a lot of self-conscious charm and quasi-authentic ambience with pleasant outdoor terraces. Scrappy old Salvatore boasts of his *pennette alla vecchia Taormina* (pasta with pesto, cream, mushrooms, and garlic, L11,000) at the restaurant below his hotel, **Il Leone** (*see* Where to Sleep, *above*). The best out of dozens of similar eateries, **La Botte** (P. Santa Domenica, tel. 0942/24198) serves up *pasta con sarde* on its lantern-lighted patio for L12,000. From Corso Umberto I, walk down Via di Giovanni to the piazza. **La Bougainville** (V. Bagnoli Croci 88, tel. 0942/625218) also has great prices and great food. Try *penne alla Bougainville* (with olive sugo), grilled fish, a mixed salad, fresh strawberry sorbet, and coffee, all for L20,000. Or for L12,000, try their super specialty, *spaghetti alla Diana,* pasta with seafood cognac sauce, served up in a conch shell. It's down from the Greek Theater, right across from the public park. For L22,000, you can get a great tourist menu at the **Bella Blu** (V. Pirandello 28, tel. 0942/24239), right near the funivia stop, topside. The menu options include every local specialty you could ask for, including lots of fresh fish. Or you can go for your choice of pizza and a drink for only L12,000.

WORTH SEEING

Although Taormina is chock-full of sights, half the fun is just wandering around. Before you go strolling, pick up a free map with information about the architecture of the city at the AAST, itself housed in the **Palazzo Corvaja,** former meeting place of the Sicilian parliament. Across from the tourist office, the comparatively uneventful 1st-century BC **Odeon Romano** (P. della Repubblica; admission free; open daily 9–1 hr before sunset) sits partially excavated, while the Hellenistic-era **Gymnasium** (or, Naumachiae) is still standing two streets downhill from Corso Umberto I, halfway between Porta Messina and Porta di Mezzo. The buildings on Corso Umberto I between **Porta di Mezzo** and **Porta Catania** date from the Middle Ages, though almost all have been rebuilt since World War II. The severe 13th-century **Duomo** (P. del Duomo, at C. Umberto I) sits opposite the Baroque **fountain,** topped by a two-tone two-footed female centaur, an odd rendition of the town's usual symbol, a conventional four-footed male centaur. Good spots to hang out during the empty siesta hours or the *passeggiata* (social stroll) are

Piazza IX Aprile, with its unrivaled view of Mt. Etna and the coast below, and the **Giardini Pubblici** (open daily 6–1 hr before sunset), whose shady paths, manicured hedges, and bizarre treehouse-style stone-and-wood terraces were pieced together by an eccentric British ornithologist.

First built in the 3rd century BC, the **Teatro Greco** (tel. 0942/23220; admission, L2,000; open daily 9–6:30) is Sicily's second-largest amphitheater. To suit the needs of ever-popular blood sports, the Romans added holding pens for animals and warriors and drainage gutters—for the innards of animals and warriors. What you see today is a 19th-century reconstruction. From June to August, the theater hosts an arts festival; call **Taormina Arte** (tel. 0942/21142) or AAST for info. Tickets run L15,000–L25,000. Perched above the city on Monte Tauro, **Castello di Taormina** (open daily 9–1 hr before sunset; admission free) was once a proud fortress but is now a jumble of ruinous walls and wildflowers. Even after the gates close, you can hop the wall to enjoy the best views in town. It's a 30-minute climb from Via Circonvallazione up a stepped path to the castle.

AFTER DARK

Taormina is no New York City, but there are a few places to go after the restaurants close. Sumptuous **Club Marrakech** (Piazzetta Garibaldi 2, tel. 0942/625692; open Thurs.–Tues. 7 PM–3 AM, Sat. until 5 AM) serves cocktails (from L8,000) in a Morocco-inspired, incense-filled room and outside under a spreading fig tree. To reach Marrakech from Corso Umberto I, walk downhill on Via S. Domenico de Guzman to the *piazzetta*. The disco of the moment is **Septimo** (V. San Pancrazio 50, tel. 0942/625522), where L20,000 brings you into the midst of fake marble columns, mirrors, and strobe lights. Head downhill to Giardini-Naxos (*see below*) for a more active dance club scene.

NEAR TAORMINA

For more spectacular aerial views, and a crisper climate even when it's roasting down below, make your way up to **Castelmola,** which probably feels like Taormina 100 years ago. You can have a drink and a snack on the upper terrace of the **Bar Turrisi,** with its famous collection of phalluses, right near the cathedral.

Also worth your time are the **Gole Alcantara,** where you can swim up dramatic gorges and under waterfalls and skitter along rapids—when it's sizzling, Sicilian hot, this icy water is just the antidote. Get info at the AAST Office (*see above*).

GIARDINI-NAXOS

If Taormina is the Cinderella of Sicily, the beach town of Giardini-Naxos—Giardini for short—is her ugly stepsister. This mess of concrete apartment blocks and garish waterfront eateries 2 km (1 mi) south rivals Taormina as a place to stay because of its abundance of cheap hotels, good—or better—restaurants, and dance clubs. When night falls, get down in the discos along Via Stracina, across from the Zona Archeologica. Both **Lady Godiva** (tel. 0942/53306) and **Marabù** (tel. 0942/54076) charge L15,000 for megabass sound; the price includes a watered-down drink.

The tacky nods to tourism obscure the town's historical significance. In the 8th century BC, a few Greek ships landed here and established Naxos, the first Greek colony in Sicily. Though the colony never amounted to much, it was a crucial first step to Hellenizing the island. All that's left of it—temple foundations, the harbor, and the city walls—is contained in the **Zona Archeologica** (admission free; open daily 9–2). The ruins aren't much to look at, but the site, with its eucalyptus trees and orange groves, is a pleasant place to spend an afternoon. The goods dug up from the site are displayed in the **Museo Archeologico** (V. Schisò 38, tel. 0942/51001; open Mon. 9–2, Tues.–Sat. 9–2 and 3–6). To reach Giardini-Naxos and the Zona Archeologica from Taormina, take the Giardini-Naxos bus (26 daily, 20 min, L1,500) to the Recanati stop.

WHERE TO SLEEP AND EAT • AAST (V. Tysandros 54, tel. 0942/51010; open weekdays 8–2 and 4–7, Sat. 8–2) can help you find lodging. In summer it may be easier to get a hotel room in Giardini-Naxos than Taormina, but be careful: many pensions charge 1½ times their list price when demand is high. Ugly duckling **Villa Collina** (V. Larunchi 34, tel. 0942/52448) is the cheapest sleep in town, with doubles for L60,000. Unfortunately, it's not exactly in town—it's north of Via Naxos and away from the water. Both **Hotel Otello** (V. Tysandros 62, tel. 0942/51009) and **Hotel Costa Azzura** (V. Naxos 35, tel. 0942/51458) have doubles for about L90,000, depending on the season, and most rooms have showers and balconies. Most hotels on Via Naxos have restaurants downstairs, but if you feel like venturing outside, you can dive into **Angelina** (V. Calcide Eubea 2, tel. 0942/51477, right on the port, where pasta dishes start at L8,000. **Taverna Naxos da Angelo** (V. Tissandros 108, tel. 0942/52251) is busy even off-season—Angelo's *cassata,* the traditional Sicilian rich sponge cake with candied fruit, marzipan, and icing, makes the rest of the meal forgettable. Macaroni with eggplant will run you L9,000.

CATANIA

With all the disasters that tend to plague eastern and southern Sicily, it's no surprise that Catania has had a hard time of it. But this city has its own built-in disadvantage—it sits within explosion range of Mt. Etna. For 122 days in 1669, hot lava inundated the town during the volcano's worst recorded eruption. Only 24 years later, an earthquake leveled everything left standing. With a stubbornness more characteristic of mules and university registrars, Catania set out to rebuild itself, entrusting the design of a new, grander city to architect Giovanni Vaccarini. The Baroque master tried to make the most out of Catania's situation by using gray lava stone in every building; the result is more than a little glum.

Catania's boutiques and caffè-lined boulevards may point to a certain sophistication, but the murky, twisting side streets are a part of a second city, an unknowable place of muffled conversations and children who stop playing to watch you pass by. Mysterious and estranged from itself, Catania is great for those who get their kicks from contradiction. It's also reputed to be Italy's most crime-ridden city. The two reasons you might come here are to see composer Vincenzo Bellini's birthplace and to bond with Mt. Etna (*see* Coming and Going, *below*).

In the sleepy town of Savoca, about 30 km (18 mi) north of Taormina, visit Bar Vitelli, the caffè where they shot the breakfast scene from "The Godfather." A picture of Don Brando vouches for it.

BASICS

AAPIT runs two helpful offices for info on Catania and Mt. Etna, the first of which is on Track 1 of the train station (tel. 095/531802 or 095/7306255; open daily 8–8). The **central office** (V. Cimarosa, tel. 095/7306233), just below Villa Bellini, is open weekdays 8–2 and 3–7, Saturday 8–2. **Open Mind** (V. Gargano 33, tel. 095/532685) is the local ARCI gay liaison—call for info or E-mail arcgayct£dimtel.nti.it. For local and international calls, head to **Telecom** (C. Sicilia 67; open Mon. 4- -7:30, Tues.–Sat. 9–1 and 4–7:30). The main **post office** (V. Etnea next to Villa Bellini) is open weekdays 8–6, Saturday 8–1.

La Duca Viaggi is the AmEx representative (V. Etnea 65, tel. 095/316155 or 095/316317; open weekdays 9–1 and 4–7:30, Sat. 9–noon). Elegant banks line Corso Sicilia, including **Banca Nazionale di Lavoro** (C. Sicilia 30; open weekdays 8:20–1:20 and 2:35–4). Pick up a classic from **English Book Vaults** (V. Umberto I 36, tel. 095/325385; open Mon. 4:30–8, Tues.–Fri. 9–1 and 4:30–8); a paperback costs around L15,000.

COMING AND GOING

Most trains and out-of-town buses depart from the unsavory Piazza Giovanni XXIII. If you arrive after nightfall, you'll want to take a cab downtown (L10,000). Some trains may stop first at Catania Acquicella, but don't get off until Catania Centrale.

BY TRAIN • At Catania's **Stazione Centrale** (P. Giovanni XXIII, tel. 1478/88088), catch hourly trains to Siracusa (1½ hrs, L7,400), Taormina-Giardini (1¼ hrs, L4,200), and Messina (2 hrs, L8,200), as well as trains to Palermo (6 daily, 4 hrs, L20,000), Enna (10 daily, 1½ hrs, L7,800), and Caltagirone (2 hrs, L9,000). You can store your luggage 6 AM–10:30 PM for L5,000. If you want to circumnavigate Mt. Etna by train (*see* Mt. Etna, *below*), head to the privately run **Ferrovia Circumetnea** depot (FCE; V. Jonio, tel. 095/374042 or 095/541240; ticket office open weekdays 6:55–2:10 and 3:30–8, Sat. 6:55–12:05 and 4:20–4:40), on the corner of Viale Vittorio Veneto and Corso Italia, which you can reach on Bus 448 from Piazza Giovanni XXIII to Corso Italia.

BY BUS • Long-distance **SAIS** buses (V. d'Amico 181, tel. 095/536168; open 5 AM–1:30 AM) leave for Messina (9 daily, 3¼ hrs, L9,500), Taormina (17 daily, 1¾ hrs, L5,100), Siracusa (11 daily, 1¼ hrs, L6,100), and Enna (8 daily, 1½ hrs, L8,500). Though the depot is on Piazza Giovanni XXIII, the waiting area is clean and safe.

BY PLANE • Catania's airport lies 5 km (3 mi) south of town and is a popular entry point for cheap flights into Sicily. To get into the city, take AMT's **Alibus,** which stops at Via Etnea on the way to the train station every 20 minutes 5 AM–midnight; buy your L1,300 ticket from a tobacco shop (marked TABACCHI) in the airport. A **taxi** to the airport should cost L20,000.

ROLY-POLY
FISH HEADS

Myriad open-air food markets and wholesalers make Catania one of Italy's most exhaustive market towns. The streets east of the Duomo are packed with bulk retailers—one block has only undies, another caskets, a third tuxedos. Every morning La Fiera fills Piazza Carlo Alberto with fruit stands. Head across town for La Pescheria, a market held every morning except Sunday on Piazza di Benedetto, with sights and odors you won't soon forget. There are piles of fruits, olives, meats, cheeses, useless trinkets, and, of course, squirming fish, squirting clams, and bloody swordfish heads.

GETTING AROUND

Vaccarini's broad, straight thoroughfares cut through the twisty Old Town streets, making Catania easy enough to navigate. Don't stray from the main thoroughfares at night—even think twice in daylight, especially if you're a woman or alone—or you'll find yourself in a mess of narrow alleys and empty, dead-end streets that invite exploration but smell of danger. Via Etnea, the main drag, slices north–south through most of the major piazzas and streets, culminating at **Piazza del Duomo** in the south, near the port. To reach Stazione Centrale from Piazza del Duomo, take Via A. di Sangiuliano. Buses run daily 5 AM–10 PM, and a 90-minute ticket costs L1,300 at any tobacco shop. Buses 129 and 136 go along Via Etnea, Bus 448 runs past the Ferrovia Circumetnea depot, and Bus 427 goes to the campgrounds and beaches south of the city.

WHERE TO SLEEP

It's wisest to stay in one of the hotels around Via Etnea—those around the station and port may be cheaper, but they are *dicey*. Hotels can fill up in summer, so reserve ahead. Kind owners run **Pensione Ferrara** (V. Umberto 66, tel. 095/316000), with comfortable doubles with bath for L78,000. It's three blocks east of Via Etnea near the main entrance to the Villa Bellini gardens. Funky **Holland International** (V. Vittorio Emanuele 8, tel. 095/533605) is run by an English-speaking Dutchman and his Catanese wife. Though it's in an iffy neighborhood, the showers are clean, a lot of the ceilings are frescoed, and it's cheap (doubles L60,000–L75,000). From the train station walk southwest on Via VI Aprile to Via Vittorio Emanuele. Also cheap, **Rubens** (V. Etnea 196, tel. 095/317073) looks like the home of someone's Italian grandparents, but it's in the middle of the action on Via Etnea. The spiffy owner speaks passable English and keeps the rooms clean and well maintained. Doubles are L55,000–L72,000, some with private bath; request the quieter rooms: 5, 6, or 7.

WHERE TO EAT

You shouldn't have difficulty eating well in Catania, especially if you like fresh seafood. Don't bypass the market (*see box* Roly- Poly Fish Heads, *above*), a great place to pick up a picnic *and* check out local color. The local pasta specialty is spaghetti *alla Norma*, with fresh basil, salted ricotta cheese, and eggplant. It's named after the opera by native son Vincenzo Bellini (what the romantic difficulties of a druid priestess have to do with eggplant is better left unexplored). To satisfy your sweet tooth, stop by the entirely unstylish **Savia** (corner of V. Etnea and V. Umberto, tel. 095/322335; closed Tues.), a local institution that has been serving cappuccinos and pastry delights for ages. **Trattoria di Fiore** (V. Coppola 24, tel. 095/316283; closed Mon.) attracts a local crowd for huge, lovingly prepared dinners. The spaghetti alla Norma is second to none, and the roast chicken (L8,000) is divine. From Piazza dell'Università, walk north one block on Via Etnea, turn right on Via A. di Sangiuliano, walk four blocks, and turn left. Watch yourself in this area after dark.

WORTH SEEING

Catania is unrelievedly gray, thanks to Mt. Etna. Vaccarini ensured that everything was lava-tinted and subsequent generations of Catanesi have expanded on this aesthetic, touching up buildings with ashen stucco and gray paint. However, within this monochromatic cityscape some engaging bits of architecture gleam through. A stroll on Via Etnea and into the side streets to the east of Piazza Università will get you in touch with most of Catania's sites. Sicily's largest church, the imposing **San Nicolò** (P. Dante), east of the Piazza del Duomo, remains closed to the public.

MUSEO BELLINIANO • The apartment where Vincenzo Bellini was born in 1801 now houses a cool collection of death masks, posters, period instruments, and original manuscripts. The composer layered frill upon frill in his popular operas and came to define the Neapolitan style before dying young, at the age of 34. *P. San Francesco d'Assisi 3, tel. 095/7150535. From P. del Duomo, follow V. Vittorio Emanuele II 2 blocks uphill. Admission free. Open Mon.–Sat. 9–1:30, Sun. 9–12:30.*

PIAZZA DEL DUOMO • This piazza, centered around the **Fontana dell'Elefante** (Elephant Fountain), epitomizes Vaccarini's 18th- century vision of a spacious municipal square. The fountain's friendly pachyderm carries an Egyptian obelisk with hieroglyphs relating to the cult of Isis, and his already elephantine testicles are exaggerated to celebrate Catanese virility. Of the impressive Baroque structures that line the piazza, the **Cattedrale di Sant'Agata** (tel. 095/312620; open daily 8–1 and 4–8) dominates the space with its ornate, towering facade. Inside on the right is **Bellini's tomb;** note the unchurchly crystal chandeliers.

In Homer's "Odyssey," the cannibal-infested Laestrygonian Fields surrounded Catania. Today in Catania beware of modern-day cannibals—pickpockets and con artists—near the train station and bus depot.

TEATRO ROMEO ED ODEON • Built in the 2nd century AD on the site of an earlier Greek stage, all that remains of this Roman theater is dirty, cracked lava blocks (the Normans pilfered the original marble facing to do up the cathedral). It's all a little gloomy, but the view of the city from the theater seats is possibly Catania's most interesting, although that's not saying much. If they're not flooded from recent rain, be sure to gather enough courage to burrow through the theater's dark underground passageways. *V. Vittorio Emanuele II 266, tel. 095/7150508. Admission free. Open daily 9–1 hr before sunset.*

VILLA BELLINI • When you need a break from Catania's grimy urban sprawl, head to the peaceful Villa Bellini Gardens. Check out the park's unique feature, near the duck pond at the main entrance: today's date spelled out in shrubs and flowers on the hillside (it's changed by a troop of gardeners every day at dawn). The garden also hosts free contemporary and classical music performances in the **Catania Musica Estate** festival (June– September); check with the tourist office or on posters around town for schedules. *Main Entrance: V. Pacini at V. Regina Margherita, just off V. Etnea. Admission free. Open daily dawn–1 hr before sunset.*

AFTER DARK

If you decide to wander at night in search of goings-on, stay out of the port area, where there's nothing to do but get mugged. Instead, pick up a copy of *Caffè Concerto* at the AAPIT office for a list of pubs in town and check out the handful of bars on Via Umberto, near Piazza Vittorio Emanuele II, or the student hangouts clustered in the streets east of Piazza Università. **La Collegiata** (V. Collegiata 3, at V. Etnea, no phone) is frequented by coeds from the nearby university. Check for posters at Via A. di Sangiuliano 256 for student events and current club happenings. **Teatro Massimo Bellini** (P. Bellini, 2 blocks north of V. Vittorio Emanuele II, tel. 095/7150921), which opened in 1890 with a performance of Bellini's *Norma,* can offer you an evening of high culture. Opera, ballet, and classical music performances run from September to mid-June. Tickets can be had for as little as L15,000 if you're under 26; contact the box office (open Mon.–Sat. 9–12:30 and 5–7) or the tourist office for details.

MT. ETNA

With soft ridges and gradual slopes, snowcapped Mt. Etna (Monte Etna) might seem to be sleeping. It's only pretending, though. A temperamental lout (the ancients personified it as Polyphemus, the Cyclops who almost ate Ulysses and his men), the one-eyed, boulder-tossing demigod has exploded more than 140 times in recorded history. Etna is the highest (11,257 ft) and most active volcano in Europe. Etna's craters continuously belch lava, and on a clear night these flows can be seen glowing from a distance of 250 km (155 mi). In 1979 six people died when an unexpected tremor flung them into the crater's bubbling cauldron. In the most recent eruption (summer 1992), several houses in Randazzo, at the northern foot of Etna, were engulfed by lava. The flip side of these dangerous eruptions is the mountain's fertile volcanic soil, which makes for a lush landscape.

Dangerous as it is, Mt. Etna can be conquered by anyone who dares. Along with a few hardy mountaineers, Etna is attacked daily by everyone from blissful babies carried on their parents' shoulders to unsure-footed septuagenarians. Their tour buses and garish orange warm-up suits won't spoil the fun, but you should be prepared to share the volcano. It may have nothing on Colorado, but Mt. Etna probably offers the best skiing in all of southern Italy. The lifts, at Nicolosi Nord, run December–March, and an all-day pass costs L35,000 on weekends (L25,000 on weekdays). Contact SITAS (see Basics, below) for more skiing info.

Nothing compares to gazing into the infernal abyss of Etna after a long day's hike, but if you're short on time or phobic about eruptions, the privately owned **Ferrovia Circumetnea** (FCE) runs a 105-km (65-mi) circuit around the base of the mountain. From the train, you'll be treated to views of the crater, rugged lava fields bearing prickly pear cactus, vineyards, olive and lemon groves, and clay-tiled cottages. If you've got the time, jump ship and check out some small towns along the way. Especially noteworthy are medieval **Randazzo,** built almost entirely of volcanic rock; **Paterno,** with its 13th-century Norman castle; and **Adrano,** named for the fire-god of the Siculi (the dominant pre-Greek tribe in this area) and home to one of the first archaeological museums in Sicily, the Museo Archeologico Etneo, with finds dating to the rule of Siracusan tyrant Dionysius I. The train makes a four-hour circuit between the FCE depot in Catania (see Coming and Going in Catania, above) and **Giarre-Riposto,** and you can start from either point. FCE is a private company, so rail passes are *not* accepted; a ticket for the whole trip costs L10,600.

BASICS

Getting atop Mt. Etna is a confusing process. Ask for guidance at the tourist offices in Catania (see above), at the **Grupo Guide Alpine** (tel. 095/914141) in Nicolosi, or the usually deserted **AAST** (V. Etnea 32, tel. 095/911505; open Tues. and Thurs.–Sat. 9–noon). There's also a **SITAS** office (tel. 095/914142) in Nicolosi Nord, which has erratic hours and posts information on the most expensive routes to the top.

COMING AND GOING

From Catania a single bus leaves every morning for **Nicolosi Nord.** From here you can reach the **Rifugio Montagnola** (8,200 ft) by foot, jeep, or cable car; the **Torre del Filosofo** (9,578 ft) by foot or jeep, or in winter by snowmobile; or the **Caldera** (cauldron; 10,938 ft), only accessible on your own two feet. One final option is to take a **ski lift** from Nicolosi Nord to the funivia.

BY BUS • A single blue **AST** bus (1 hr, L7300) leaves every morning at 8:15 AM from in front of Catania's train station, making a single return trip at 4:30 PM. The bus pauses at the pleasant mountain village of **Nicolosi** before stopping at **Nicolosi Nord,** where you can pick up a lava carving of Mary done up in blue glitter. Twelve additional AST buses leave Catania daily, only going as far as Nicolosi (1 hour, L2,500), so you could head to Nicolosi later in the day, stay overnight, and then catch the regular bus up the volcano the next morning. Buy your ticket at the bar across the street from the **bus station** (P. Giovanni XXII), adjacent to the train station's piazza.

BY FUNIVIA • The quickest way to reach Rifugio Montagnola from Nicolosi Nord is to hop on an efficient orange cable car, which will whisk you up in a few minutes. To soften the blow of the L15,000 one-way fare, they let you use your credit card.

BY TRUCK • Clunky Fiat four-wheel-drive vehicles, fondly called "Jeeps," will bring you to the Torre del Filosofo from either the SITAS office in Nicolosi Nord (45 min, L23,000) or Rifugio Montagnola (15 min, L10,000). The first option isn't posted at the SITAS office, so you must ask for it and pay there. The truck is driven by a mandatory guide, whose services (including walking you up toward the caldera) cost an additional L6,000 per person.

ON FOOT • Trudging up the mountain is the most honorable course to take—after all, you can't tell somebody you've climbed Mt. Etna unless you actually climbed it. Though possible, it is laborious and the little lava rocks on the path will pummel the soles of your feet no matter how tough your boots are. From Nicolosi Nord it's two hours (5 km/3 mi) to Rifugio Montagnola, then one hour (3 km/2 mi) to Torre del Filosofo, and then one more hour to the caldera. The easiest path follows the truck roads or ski-lift trails, both of which start behind the SITAS building. Though the folks back home may think of you as half mountain goat, half god, the actual trip doesn't get you very far from civilization, what with the cable cars looming overhead.

If you reach the Torre del Filosofo by truck, your guide will take you to a rope stretched some 820 unsatisfying ft below the caldera and tell you it's not safe to venture farther—remember those six people in 1979? If you choose to tempt fate, shrug off the crowd and head back down the truck track to the first curve, where you will see a rough footpath going off to the south. This trail is poorly marked—a pole here, a red rock there—but there are plenty of footprints. After climbing an hour, you can step over the gaping cracks in the soil and peer into the steaming crater, pondering mortality, mythology, geology, and the long hike back down.

WHERE TO SLEEP AND EAT

Its title *refugio* (refuge) was earned when a 1983 flow of lava stopped at its back wall (you can see the mark), but **Rifugio Sapienza** (Nicolosi Nord, tel. 095/911062; open year-round) is more like a Quality Inn with a great view. Doubles (L70,000) are plain and modern. Back down in Nicolosi, **Ostello per la Gioventu' Etna** (V. della Quercia 7, tel. 095/7914686, fax 095/7914701) costs L25,000 per night and another L3,000 for breakfast, L15,000 for dinner. You can get a grilled panino at the bar at the top of the funicular station or join the bus drivers at their hangout, **La Cantoniera** (P. Cantoniera, tel. 095/914155), where a full meal costs L25,000.

It will be cold no matter when you make it up Mt. Etna. If you only packed sandals and tank tops, Rifugio Montagnola will rent you a puffy down jacket and uncomfortable rubber boots.

SIRACUSA

During the glorious millennium of Greco-Roman domination, Siracusa (Syracuse) rivaled Athens as one of the most powerful and influential cities in the Western world. Some temples and amphitheaters built during this ancient age of splendor have survived, as have later masterful Baroque works. The combination of living history, beautiful architecture, and a temperate seaside climate draws hordes of archaeology buffs and shutterbugs, but even the crowds can't tarnish Siracusa, still reminiscent of the Greek cities that are its distant cousins.

Siracusa got its humble start in 734 BC, when Corinth, eager to keep up with the Joneses, packed up a group of Greek colonists and sent them off to establish a colony in Italy. The city quickly flourished as a center of art and culture under the rule of Heron, who brought the poet Pindar and the playwright Aeschylus to his court. Archimedes and the poet Theocritus were born here. The later ruler Dionysius, though brutal and unpopular, turned Siracusa into the preeminent city of Magna Graecia. Dionysius even invited Plato to be his teacher, but he soon found the chattering philosopher tiresome and threw him in prison until his buddies back in Athens could post bail. Siracusa's reign continued until 215 BC, when, having worn itself down with regional politicking, the city was crushed by Roman forces.

After Rome's pillaging, precious little happened here until about 1960, when Siracusa came into its own as a manufacturing center and provincial capital. Today most of the population (about 100,000, a third of the number who lived here in ancient times) live in bulky concrete apartment blocks, but cross the bridge to the island of **Ortigia**, and you'll find a picturesque maze of alleyways lined with Arab, Norman, Baroque, and 19th-century buildings with views looking out to the sea. This romantic neighborhood and the Greco-Roman site are the main reasons to visit. Locals also claim that Siracusa is Sicily's only major city without a Mafia—but watch your wallet anyway.

BASICS

The friendly staff at the **AAST** (V. Maestranza 33, tel. 0931/464255; open Mar.–Dec., weekdays 8:30–2 and 4:30–7:30, Sat. morning only), 1½ blocks east of Piazza Archimede, dole out excellent city maps and transport schedules. You can also get info on the mainland from the **APT** (tel. 0931/461477; open Mon.– Sat. 8–1) by the Parco Archeologico entrance or at the main office (V. San Sebastiano 45, tel. 0931/67710; open daily 9–1 and 3–6, Sun. 9–noon), across the street from the Basilica di San Giovanni and the catacombs.

You'll find **Telecom** (V. Teracati 46, tel. 0931/700111; open Mon.- -Sat. 8 AM–10 PM) across from Via Augusto, which leads to the Parco Archeologico. The **post office** (Riva delle Poste, tel. 0931/66995; open weekdays 8:30–5:30, Sat. 8:30–1) looms over the bus station to the left of the causeway as you enter Ortigia. **Monte dei Paschi di Siena** (P. Pancali 12, tel. 0931/691–0494; open Mon.–Sat. 8:20–

1:20), next to the bus depot on Ortigia, has a handy ATM, as does the **Banca Nazionale del Lavoro** (C. Umberto 29, tel. 0931/726294; open Mon.–Sat. 8:35–1:35 and 3–4) on the mainland.

COMING AND GOING

All trains to Siracusa arrive at **Stazione Centrale** (northwest of Ortigia on the mainland, tel. 1478/ 88088). Luggage storage (L5,000 per piece per day) is available 6 AM–10 PM. Rail service includes Messina (11 daily, 3 hrs, L16,500), Catania (15 daily, 1½ hrs, L7,400), Taormina (10 daily, 2¼ hrs, L13,000), Palermo (1 daily, 5 hrs, L28,000), Ragusa (4 daily, 2½ hrs, L10,300), and Noto (8 daily, 45 min, L4,200). **AST** (Riva delle Poste 13, tel. 0931/462711) buses generally make short trips, to Noto (14 daily, 45 min, L3,700), Ragusa (6 daily, 2 hrs, L7,500), and Catania (14 daily, 1½ hrs, L6,100). **SAIS** buses (V. Trieste 28, tel. 0931/66710) leave from one block behind Riva delle Poste, serving Palermo (5 daily, 4 hrs, L25,700) and Noto (13 daily, 1 hr, L3,900).

GETTING AROUND

Siracusa is comprised of two main areas connected by the causeway **Ponte Nuovo:** the older part of the living town is on the island of Ortigia; the modern city is on the mainland, the site of the major archaeological finds. The city is small, but the trek between sights can be exhausting. All **AST** city buses (L600) operate until 9 PM, and most run along Corso Umberto on their way to and from Piazza delle Poste on Ortigia. Bus 2 goes from the train station to Ortigia and takes a round-about route back, so take Bus 1 in the opposite direction. To make the 20-minute walk from the station to Ortigia, take a left on Via Francesco Crispi, which merges into Corso Umberto and leads to Ponte Nuovo.

WHERE TO SLEEP

The least expensive hotel on Ortigia is **Hotel Gran Bretagna** (V. Savoia 21, 2 blocks south of P. XXV Luglio, tel. 0931/68765), where you can pay in plastic for cutesy doubles (L87,000–L99,000). The mainland atmosphere certainly isn't as idyllic, but there are a bunch of decent, cheap beds near the train station.

UNDER L45,000 • Hotel Centrale. This is the consummate budget hotel: cheap, close to the station, and with rooms resembling a monk's cell. If you're nice, the nice woman who runs the place may give you a room with a window. Doubles run L40,000–L50,000. *C. Umberto 141, mainland, 96100, tel. 0931/60528. Head straight out of station, left on C. Umberto. 14 rooms, 4 with bath. Cash only.*

UNDER L55,000 • Bel Sit. It's like staying with friends-of-friends-of-the-family—the owner's kids are always watching TV, and you usually have to step over a toy truck to get out the door. In the heart of the mainland, doubles here cost L50,000–L65,000. *V. Oglio 5, mainland, 96100, tel. 0931/60245. Cross train tracks at V. Catania and follow C. Gelone 3 blocks, left on V. Tirso, right on V. Oglio. 15 rooms, 10 with bath. Cash only.*

UNDER L75,000 • Hotel Aretusa. This hotel, right near the train station, has large rooms and a friendly staff but not much else of interest. Doubles (L70,000–L80,000) offer 2-star amenities, but no breakfast is available. *V. F. Crispi 75, mainland, 96100, tel. and fax 0931/24211. 39 rooms, 22 with bath.*

Hotel Pantheon. Within walking distance of the station, the Pantheon charges L70,000–L80,000 for immaculate doubles with a shower and a sink in each room but with shared bath. *Foro Siracusano 22, mainland, 96100, tel. 0931/21010. 14 rooms without bath.*

HOSTEL • Ostello della Gioventù. This private, dorm-style hostel isn't terribly convenient—it's 6 km (4 mi) from Siracusa, in Belvedere—but the friendly proprietors can offer suggestions about what to do in the area. Castello Eurialo (*see* Worth Seeing, *below*) is nearby, as is an excellent pizzeria. Beds, in rooms of maximum 4 persons, cost L25,000 including breakfast and a sleep sheet; hot showers cost L2,000. *V. Siracusa 7, Belvedere 96100, tel. 0931/711118 or 0931/745157. 20-min ride from C. Umberto on Bus 11. 46 beds. Cash only.*

WHERE TO EAT

Corso Umberto has a handful of take-out pizza joints that are better and cheaper than any you'll find on Ortigia. Every day until 10:30 PM, the *salumeria* **Cassia Ionario** (southeast corner of P. Marconi, mainland) does a boisterous job of making sandwiches. The best gelateria in town is **Voglia Matta** (C. Umberto 34, mainland, tel. 0931/67118; closed Thurs.), with a delicious amaretto flavor.

UNDER L10,000 • Spaghetteria do Scogghiu. Friendly, chaotic, and authentic despite a dearth of Italian speakers, this is always the hot spot in Ortigia. The robust Russo brothers really know their spaghetti: choose from 20 varieties, each only L8,000. Don't miss the delicious pasta *puttanesca* (with hot peppers, black olives, tomatoes, and bacon) or the *tutto mare* (with shrimp, squid, and mussels). *V. Domenico Scina 11, Ortigia, no phone. Downhill from P. Archimede in center of island. Cash only. No dinner Sun. Closed Mon.*

UNDER L35,000 • La Foglia. This cozy Mediterranean restaurant would have a line out the door if it were in Los Angeles. Specialties include seasonal soups (L13,000) and stuffed pastas like spinach ravioli the size of small Frisbees (L15,000). Very little meat is served, and the cuisine verges on nouvelle, incorporating flavors and textures from all around the coast. A full meal may run you up to L40,000, but local hipsters deem it worthy. *V. Capodieci 29, Ortigia, tel. 0931/66233. Across from Museo Nazionale di Palazzo Bellomo.*

L'Orto di Epicuro. *Ragazzi* (young people) crowd this waterfront eatery not for the food—which is decent but nothing exceptional—but because of the large airy terrace and efficient, friendly service. On Tuesday and Thursday, you can gorge yourself on all-you-can-eat pasta or pizza for L20,000. *Largo della Gancia 5, Ortigia, tel. 0931/464222. Cash only.*

WORTH SEEING

The bulk of Greek Siracusa's ruins are hidden among the towering apartment blocks of the mainland. On Ortigia, in addition to the **Duomo** (*see below*), you can still see the goldfish-filled **Largo Aretusa** (the mythical origin of Siracusa) and, back by the causeway, the remaining columns of a **Temple of Apollo** in Piazza Pancali.

Catania's stony faces and mean streets can make even the toughest traveler feel tame. Luckily, you can buff up your image with a don't-touch-me tattoo or strategic piercing at the tattoo parlor on Via Etnea 183.

ORTIGIA • Museo Nazionale di Palazzo Bellomo. Though filled with the usual hodgepodge of Madonnas and period costumes, this museum is the unlikely home of two masterpieces. Antonello da Messina's 15th-century *Annunciation* still has enough Flemish- Mannerist bits sticking to it to demonstrate why he's regarded as Sicily's greatest painter. A world away is Caravaggio's 17th-century *Seppellimento di Santa Lucia*, one of his later works in which his chiaroscuro (use of light and shadow) is at its inky and melodramatic best. *V. Capodieci 16, tel. 0931/69511. From P. del Duomo, walk down V. Santa Lucia to V. Concilazione, 1st left on V. Capodieci. Admission L2,000. Open Mon.–Sat. 9–2, Sun. 9–1.*

Piazza del Duomo. Around Ortigia's oblong central piazza stand several fine Baroque palazzi, including the 17th-century **Palazzo Senatorio** (now the city hall) and the 18th-century **Palazzo Beneventano del Bosco,** with an inviting courtyard and elegant winding staircase, neither of which can be visited. The **Duomo,** an opulent concoction of Norman and Baroque buildings, is on the site of a 5th-century BC temple to Athena. Note the original Doric columns, now part of the church's walls. *From Ponte Nuovo, take C. G. Matteotti to P. Archimede; turn right on V. Amalfitania, left on V. Cavour.*

MAINLAND • Castello Eurialo. Running along several kilometers of seafront hills outside town are the ruins of a masterpiece of military architecture. Built by Dionysius the Elder in the 5th century BC, the 22-km (13½-mi) circuit of walls and towers stood impregnable until the tireless Romans breached them in 212 BC. The official entrance is by the castle proper, but a more interesting approach is to get off the bus as soon as you see the large white walls and walk north through the flower-covered ruins—bring a picnic and have an ancient feast among the crumbling stones. *V. Epipoli, near Belvedere, 7 km (4½ mi) northwest of Siracusa. Take Bus 9 or 11 from C. Gelone and ask to be let off at "il castello." Admission free.*

Catacombe di San Giovanni. The earthquake of 1693 cracked open the nave of Siracusa's first cathedral. Today flowers grow where early Christians once accepted communion. Still standing are three Norman walls, a Byzantine apse, and several Greek columns. Below ground, the damp **Cripta di San Marziano** contains a few faint frescoes. From the apse descend into the 4th-century **catacombs,** where thousands of niches once held the remains of thousands of Christians. *V. San Giovanni, tel. 0931/67955. 1 block east of Museo Archeologico and north of Santuario della Madonnina. Admission L4,000. Open daily 9–6; shorter hrs in winter.*

Museo Archeologico. Sicily's newest museum was opened in 1988 to hold the majority of the island's Hellenic and pre-Hellenic artifacts—major and obscure archaeological sites are documented in painstaking detail. Yet the museum isn't wholly academic: there are plenty of freakish gorgons as well. The landmark piece, a 1st-century AD Roman statue of Venus, is remarkably true to life, despite her missing head and right arm. *V. Teocrito 66, tel. 0931/464022. Admission L2,000. Open Tues.–Sat. 9–1; sometimes Sun. 9–1.*

Parco Archeologico. This site is the only swatch of the ancient city left uninhabited since Roman times, and even after centuries of looting, there are still enough petrified wheel ruts and blocky temple foundations to make for a good couple of hours of exploring. Unfortunately, you will never have the ruins to yourself—every package tour in Sicily stops here for snapshots of the blinding white ruins against the shadows of neighboring cypress groves. The most famous ruin is the **Ear of Dionysius,** a cave named for its lobe-shape entrance. It was none other than Caravaggio who decided that the tyrant must have stood at the mouth of the cave and eavesdropped, thanks to acoustics, on the conversations of his enemies incarcerated inside. Hold on to your ticket while exploring the site and use the stub to gain entrance to the adjacent **Anfiteatro Romano,** a 2nd-century arena built to satiate the Roman need to see blood flow. The arena is carved almost entirely out of rock, including the rooms that held the gladiators and beasts before they were disemboweled in front of the seething crowd. *Near intersection of V. Cavallari and V. E. Romagnoli. From C. Gelone or C. Umberto, Bus 1, 4, 5, 8, or 10 west to park entrance. Admission L2,000. Open daily 9–1 hr before sunset (ticket office open daily 9–6).*

Santuario della Madonnina. In August 1953, a 2-ft-tall plaster bust of the Virgin Mary started crying. Angelo and Antonietta Iannuso, over whose bed the Madonnina (little Madonna) had been displayed, ran out to tell the world, and the bishop of Palermo had the alleged teardrops tested. He declared a miracle, and Siracusa was soon overrun with pilgrims. A massive sanctuary—which looks like an upside-down 250-ft ice cream cone and can be seen from any point in the city—was constructed to hold the Madonnina and the half-poignant, half-gruesome collection of crutches and prosthetic limbs the faithful have left behind. Please remember to dress and behave decorously in the sanctuary—this is a special place for many people. *Tel. 0931/64077. Across V. Teocrito from Archaeological Museum. Admission free. Open daily 6–12:30 and 4–7:30 (until 8 in summer).*

AFTER DARK

At night, suave, stylish Siracusa feels like an arcane Milan-by-the-sea. Spotless piazzas and pedestrian streets illuminated by old-fashioned streetlights are the province of the young and good-looking. **Buio** (V. delle Vergini, no phone; closed Mon.) is the bar of the moment, attracting the droves that spill out onto the street. Expect to pay L4,000 per game at the regulation-size pool table. For a cozy watering hole, head to **The Hole** (V. Nizza 42, no phone). Iron that little black dress to join the city's nightclub scene at **La Nottola** (V. Gargallo 61, off V. Maestranza, tel. 0931/60009), an elegant megaplex that contains a disco, piano bar, jazz club, and restaurant in the former stables and courtyard of a centuries-old country estate. Entrance costs L15,000 there and at **Malibù** (V. Elorina 172, tel. 0931/721888), an even more gigantic seaside disco with room for 1,000 gyrating revelers. It's quite a walk from Ortigia—try to split the L20,000 cab fare with friends.

INTERIOR

If the Romans, Normans, and everyone in between had set sail for the States and colonized Vermont, the end result would probably look something like Sicily's interior. Mountains and narrow, winding roads punctuate rolling farmlands and rural towns. At night only crickets and the wind in the trees can be heard. This pastoral idyll combined with **Casale**'s mosaics and **Caltagirone**'s ceramics would seem to make the interior a low-key traveler's paradise, but in reality the area is visited by fewer tourists than any other region. Transportation can be frustrating, but trains and buses from Catania do make the region accessible. There's also a dearth of restaurants, and lodging—when you can find it—is often inconvenient without a car. This is the way to see the real Sicily, stripped of resorty trappings, in quiet hilltop towns where you may well be the only tourist for miles.

CALTAGIRONE

If it weren't for clay, Caltagirone might be just another Baroque reconstruction of a ruined hilltop village destined for quaint obscurity in Sicily's southeastern interior. But the city's majolica tradition gave it its name (from Qal'at Ghirân, or Hill of Vases), its look, and its raison d'être. Today Caltagirone is completely devoted to its industry. The town is home to a famous ceramics school and countless artisans who make and sell the characteristic yellow-and-blue plates, vases, and tiles that decorate everything from kitchen tables to bridges. The most photogenic of the ceramic monuments is also the newest: the risers of the 142 steps of the 11th-century **Santa Maria del Monte** (off P. Municipio) were tiled in the 1950s by local artists. Each row has a different design, and the entire work is meant as an homage to ceramicists from every era. Every year on July 24, 25, and 31 and August 15, the town turns out for the lighting of the **Luminaria,** a tapestrylike decoration of the steps made by arranging as many as 4,000 paper lanterns, which are lighted as the sun goes down. A 10-minute walk downhill on Via Roma will bring you to the brilliantly tiled **Teatrino** in the well-kept **Giardino Pubblico,** home to the national **Museo delle Ceramiche** (tel. 0933/21680; admission free; open daily 9–6:30), an exhaustive but well-organized collection of ceramic pots and tiles focusing on local works from prehistory to the 19th century.

BASICS

The **AAST** (Palazzo Libertini di San Marco, off P. Umberto, tel. 0933/53809; open weekdays 8:30–1:45, Tues. and Thurs. also 3:15–6:30, Sat. 10–1 and 3–6, Sun. 10–1) has maps, event calendars, and info on where to buy ceramics. Caltagirone's adjacent **train** (tel. 0933/24765) and **bus** stations are on Piazza della Repubblica. Frequent trains run to Catania (2 hrs, L9,000) and Gela (45 min, L5,000). By bus, **AST** and **Etna** (tel. 0933/54628 for both) serve Catania (14 daily, 1¼ hrs, L7,800), and AST goes to Piazza Armerina (7 daily, 1 hr, L4,000). **SAIS** (in Catania, tel. 095/536168) stops at Palermo (3 daily, 4 hrs, L11,500) and Enna (daily at 6:20 AM, 1¼ hrs, L6,100). Schedules for all three lines are posted upstairs.

WHERE TO SLEEP AND EAT

There's little in the way of budget lodging in town, but you can try **Hotel Monteverde** (V. delle Industrie 11, tel. 0933/53533 or 0933/53682), which has large clean doubles and huge tiled bathrooms for L96,000 a night. For true country living Sicilian style, stay at **La Casa degli Angeli** (S. P. Caltagirone-Niscemi 39, tel. 0933/25317). The working farmhouse amid olive trees and vineyards about 9 km (6 mi) south of Caltagirone rents doubles with bath for L75,000, breakfast included; your room might have an antique double bed and armoire or twin beds and the owners' son's soda and beer can collection. The bus from Catania to Niscemi stops just across the road. In Caltagirone's *centro storico* (historic center), there's a **produce stand** (V. L. Sturzo 43, off P. Municipio; open daily 8–2:30) and a sweet-smelling bakery, **Dal Fornaio** (tel. 0933/21588; open Mon.–Sat. 6:30–2:30), at the corner of Via Infermeria and Via Taranto.

PIAZZA ARMERINA

Enna (*see below*) founded the Norman town of Piazza Armerina to extend its influence over the mountains, and you'll find the two have everything from creamy sandstone palazzi to a tranquil pace in common. Piazza Armerina's winding spiral of streets ends at the 15th-century **Duomo** (tel. 0935/680214), which towers over the dull modern buildings on the lower slopes of the valley. The rough, warm-hued 17th-century facade contrasts brilliantly with the cool, whitewashed interior. To reach the **AAST** office (V. Cavour 15, tel. 0935/680201; open Mon.–Sat. 8–2), follow Via Garibaldi into town from Piazza Europa and turn right at Piazza Garibaldi onto Via Cavour. If you make the walk on Thursday, you'll go right through a huge **outdoor clothing market** (open 6–1) that takes over the streets west of the station. Before you bargain, be forewarned that the closest Cirrus ATM is in Enna.

From Piazza Armerina you're within striking distance of the village of **Casale,** home to stunning Roman mosaics that rank among the most complete and best preserved in the world. The **Villa Romana** (tel. 093/680063; admission L2,000; open daily 9–1 hr before sunset) was built in the early 3rd century AD and occupied by various people until it was covered by a landslide in the 12th century. The dry climate and the piles of dirt under which the villa was covered fended off 800 years of decay. It wasn't until the 1950s that local scholars discovered the location of the villa from ancient writings. Little is left of the superstructure (the steel columns and fiberglass roof approximate the dimensions of the original building), but there are plenty of mosaics: Some 37,673 square ft of brilliantly colored, painstakingly arranged tiles depict mythological figures, Circus Maximus races, hunts, games, and people going about their hedonistic imperial-era lives. You view the mosaics from suspended walkways, easily clogged by tour groups; try to avoid getting stuck by going through the site backwards.

COMING AND GOING

From Piazza Europa, buses head north to Enna (8 daily, 45 min, L3,700; change at Pergusa) and south to Caltagirone (3 daily, 1 hr, L7,200); stop by the AAST office for schedules. The local bus company, **ATAN,** runs shuttles to Casale (6–9 per hr, 15 min, L500) May–September. In the off-season you have two options for reaching Casale: take a Caltanissetta or Mazzarino bus and get off at the Casale turnoff (1 km/½ mi from Casale); or make the fairly flat 5-km (3-mi) hike yourself—just mind the cars and follow the yellow signs south out of town.

WHERE TO SLEEP AND EAT

Given the difficulty of getting around Sicily's interior, it's worth spending a night or two in beautiful Piazza Armerina. Renovations at the **Hotel Villa Roma** (V. Alcide de' Gasperi 18, tel. and fax 0935/682911) have catapulted this into the splurge category; at press time prices were swelling to around L130,000 for a double, breakfast included. Farther afield, the tidy **Hotel Mosaici** (Contrada Paratore, tel. and fax 0935/685453) was built over a popular restaurant on the turnoff to Casale, five minutes from the Villa Romana (L80,000 with bath). Just around the corner, **La Ruota** (at Casale turnoff, tel. 0935/680542) operates a small campground (L6,000 per person) next to their trattoria. Although it may seem odd to eat seafood in the mountains, try the fresh seafood selections at **La Tavernetta** (V. Cavour, tel. 0935/685883; closed Sun.). Expect to pay L10,000 for filling primi, or get cheaper eats at *paninoteche* (sandwich shops) clustered around Piazza Europa.

ENNA

Perched on a ridge in the center of Sicily, the small town of Enna has been mellowed by centuries of economic stagnation. Unable to compete with port towns for international trade, Enna has accepted its role as a humble agricultural center, despite being the provincial capital. You'll step off the bus at sand-color Piazza Vittorio Emanuele, where men mark the passage of time by following the sun as it changes the hue of the beautiful weathered church of **San Francesco d'Assisi.** From the piazza, Via Roma runs through several other piazzas, each with an accompanying church and caffè. The street continues past the looming 14th-century **Duomo** (V. Roma, tel. 0935/26293), whose basalt columns are decorated with sharply delineated Norman carvings. Via Roma ends at the 14th-century **Castello di Lombardia** (tel. 0935/500962; admission free; open daily 9–1 and 3–5), one of the most important military buildings of Norman Sicily. You can climb to the top of its reconstructed **Torre Pisana** for a commanding view of the valley. One of the castle's courtyards always has a pickup soccer game; the other has open-air concerts in summer.

BASICS

The local **AAPIT** (V. Roma 413, tel. 0935/500901; open Mon.–Sat. 9–1) has maps and info on surrounding towns. You can change money at the **post office** (V. Volta, behind Municipo on P. Garibaldi, tel. 0935/500950; open weekdays 8:10–5:30, Sat. 8:10–1:20). **Istituto Bancario San Paolo di Torino** (P. IV Dicembre) has the *only* Cirrus ATM in the area.

COMING AND GOING

Getting to Enna can be a hassle, but it's more accessible than other parts of Sicily's interior and can be a good jumping-off point from which to explore the area. The **train station** (tel. 1478/88088; open daily 6 AM–9 PM) sits at the foot of a very steep hill, so getting to town requires either an impossible one-hour hike or a 15-minute bus ride (12 daily, L1,500; last up 9:10 PM, last down 9:30 PM). The station's safe and well-guarded waiting room is open 24 hours, so if you miss a connection you can rough it here—just have some sort of ticket to flash at the police. Direct trains run to Catania (11 daily, 1¼ hrs, L7,800) and Palermo (6 daily, 2 hrs 20 min, L14,500); you can reach Agrigento and the west via Caltanissetta (11 daily, 30 min, L4,500).

Enna's **SAIS** bus station (V. Diaz, tel. 0935/500902; ticket office open Mon.–Sat. 6–2 and 3:30–7) is a 10-minute walk down Via Vittorio Emanuele from Via Roma, though most buses swing by the fountain on the northeast corner of Piazza Vittorio Emanuele. Buses travel to Catania (9 daily, 1½ hrs, L9,000), Palermo (3 daily, 2¼ hrs, L12,000), Piazza Armerina (7 daily, 45 min, L3,700), and Pergusa (8 daily, 20 min, L600). For connections to Ragusa and the south, go first to Caltagirone (1 daily, 1 hr 40 min, L5,800); for Agrigento and the west, go to Caltanissetta (5 daily, 55 min, L4,000). Orange (municipal) SAIS Bus 4 makes eight additional daily trips to Pergusa (last bus 10:30 PM) from Piazza Vittorio Emanuele.

WHERE TO SLEEP AND EAT

Unless you're willing to spend L155,000 for a room at Enna's only hotel, the **Grande Albergo Sicilia** (P. Colaianni 7, tel. 0935/500850, fax 0935/500488), catch the next bus to Pergusa (*see below*), about 5 km (3 mi) north. Accommodations in Enna may be sparse, but good eats are easy to find just off Via Roma. One good bet is the lively, popular **Da Marino** (V. Lombardia 2, near Castello, tel. 0935/25878; closed Mon.), which serves pizza (L5,000–10,000) until midnight.

NEAR ENNA

PERGUSA

Pergusa may be only a hair more than two blocks long, but the town boasts of amenities that nearby Enna can't—a selection of hotels, a nature reserve (with porcupines!), and a Formula One racetrack. Life in the town revolves around this asphalt ribbon, which encircles the waters of **Lago di Pergusa,** site of Persephone's mythical abduction by Pluto into the underworld. Next to the lake near the entrance to the racetrack, the free **Riserva Pergusina** park and animal sanctuary (open daily 9–1 hr before sunset) has easy walking trails and picnic facilities. Getting to Pergusa from Enna is easy (*see* Coming and Going *in* Enna, *above*). From Pergusa you can catch buses to Piazza Armerina (6 daily, 30 min, L2,900) and Caltagirone (1 daily, 1 hr 20 min, L8,800).

WHERE TO SLEEP AND EAT • Pergusa's hotels are always filled during race time (Sun., Mar.–Oct.), so call ahead. A 10-minute walk north, the **Miralago** (V. Nazionale, tel. 0953/541272) has sparkling doubles (L70,000) with showers and a disco downstairs. A 15-minute walk in the opposite direction will bring you to **Hotel Garden** (V. Nazionale, tel. 0935/541694, fax 0935/541690), which charges L120,000 for bungalow-style rooms that have balconies overlooking the lake. The bar-pizzeria **Da Carlo** (no phone) is hilarious—everybody from soldiers to racing pilgrims packs in for tasty pizzas such as the Da Carlo, with sausage and bell pepper (L7,500). The guy at the espresso machine claims to steam the worst cappuccino in Italy. He's probably right.

SOUTH

The rugged south of Sicily is full of surprises: quiet Baroque towns in the southeast, and, farther west, the well-preserved Greek ruins at **Agrigento.** In between are hillside farms with fields, thankfully not yet overrun by tourists. If you're coming from the packed Ionian resorts, you'll find relief in southern Sicily's tranquil beauty. Getting around in the south takes a bit more stamina, however: the trains are tiny and painfully slow, the bus service fragmented and disorganized. For this reason, the less adventurous skip this part of the island altogether—excellent news for the rest of us.

Sicily's entire southeast corner suffered terrible damage from a massive earthquake in 1693. This tragedy paved the way for a talented crew of architects—among them the renowned Rosario Gagliardi—

to rebuild in the flamboyant Baroque style, a profound contrast to Sicily's dry, stony landscape. These 18th-century time capsules abound in **Noto,** the southern *pasticceria* mecca not to be missed by those eating their way through Italy. The less photogenic **Ragusa** is a convenient base for day trips.

NOTO

At once luminescent and gloomy, Noto is a strange little place. Not only was the town entirely rebuilt after the 1693 earthquake as a showcase for Enlightenment-era architecture, but it was constructed out of a local beeswax-color sandstone that glows as if lighted from within. Though beautiful, Noto feels abandoned—many buildings are vacant or propped up by aging wooden braces in case another earthquake comes to town.

The rebuilding of Noto came at an interesting point in the history of architecture: when architects first realized that cities could be formally planned, but nobody had a clue about what worked best. Noto's solution is a little awkward—the narrow **Corso Vittorio Emanuele II** traverses the town starting at **Porta Reale,** the ancient city border, but the buildings on it are so big and the street so narrow that you feel the need for a little perspective. One of these buildings is the 17th-century **Duomo,** now just a shell due to an earthquake in 1990 and subsequent heavy rains in 1996, when all but the facade and lateral walls collapsed. Plans are to restore it to its original Baroque splendor, minus 18th–20th century accretions, over the next few years. Farther down the *corso* is one of Gagliardi's masterworks, the **Chiesa di San Domenico,** on the same square as the **APT** office (P. XVI Maggio, tel. 0931/836744; open Mon.–Sat. 8–2 and 3–5). In this town of 20,000 people, and 20% unemployment, no fewer than 18 other churches exist, each of them both strange and exquisite. If you're tired of the Baroque period, a dip in the sea is as easy as hopping on a bus from Noto's Giardini Pubblici to **Noto Marina,** 7 km (4½ mi) east. Four buses run Monday–Saturday, and the last returns to Noto about 6 PM.

COMING AND GOING

Buses are by far the best way to reach Noto. From Siracusa, **AST** buses (13 daily, 45 min, L3,700) and **SAIS** buses (12 daily, 1 hr, L3,900) drop passengers at the Giardini Pubblici. Nine buses continue to Ragusa (1½ hrs, L5,100). Buy tickets on board or at **Bar Efirmedio** (V. di Piemonte 6, just downhill from Giardini Pubblici), where they also have schedules. Noto's small **train station** (tel. 1478/88088; open daily 8:30–noon and 1–6) offers service to Siracusa (4 daily, 1 hr, L4,200) and Ragusa (8 daily, 1½ hrs, L6,000). There's no official luggage storage, but the guy in the office has been known to stash bags for free if he's around. Getting into town from the station requires either a 20-minute walk up Via Principe di Piemonte or a ride on the lone bus (L600).

WHERE TO SLEEP AND EAT

Noto's only hotel, **Albergo Stella** (V. F. Maiore 44, tel. 0931/835695), is run by a talkative self-touted world traveler. Clean rooms are still dull despite their trapezoidal shapes (doubles with bath L70,000). From Giardini Pubblici walk one block down Via Napoli. Be sure to call ahead in summer. Whatever you do in Noto, *do not* miss a visit to **Pasticceria Mandolfiore** (V. Ducezio 2, tel. 0931/836615), one of the greatest gastronomic experiences in Italy. The cannoli (L2,000) are delicious, as are the L1,000 *raviolini* (sweet ricotta-cheese–stuffed pastries) along with a cappuccino in the small caffè. **Trattoria del Carmine** (V. Ducezio 1/A, tel. 0931/838705; closed Mon.), next to the Chiesa del Carmine, serves outstanding home-style food at fair prices: *tagliatelle alla capricciosa,* L6,000, *coniglio* (rabbit) *alla cacciatora,* L11,000. Strangely enough, Noto has a natural/macrobiotic market, **Associazione Sapori Smarriti ed Altro** (V. Ducezio 85/A, tel. 0931/839066; closed Sun.).

NEAR NOTO

RAGUSA

Ragusa is just not going to make any overt attempts to entertain you. The town has few postcard sights, but it does offer a slice of provincial Sicilian life you won't find in more bustling towns. Devastated by the 1693 earthquake like the rest of the region, Ragusa was rebuilt by some of the rabble of the old town, called **Ragusa Ibla,** while the nouveaux riches migrated uphill and built a larger, grander district. The competition between the two was so intense that Ragusa Ibla willingly waited more than 15 years for the construction of the more impressive, Baroque **Duomo di San Giorgio** (1783), with its three-tiered facade, enormous cupola, and galloping horsemen statues. Today Ragusa Ibla is a walkable, quiet place of rustic buildings and stunning views of the countryside, especially from the **Giardino Ibleo** (downhill from P. del Duomo; open 8–8). Other than that, there's not much of interest for you. The city is strung across three hilltops, and you'll have to climb a lot of stairs and cross many gorge-spanning footbridges. Ignore the directional signs to the tourist office and Duomo—they're meant for cars with limited street access and might take you on major detours.

COMING AND GOING • The **train station** (P. del Popolo, tel. 0932/621239) serves Noto (8 daily, 1½ hrs, L6,000) and Siracusa (9 daily, 2½ hrs, L10,500); for Agrigento (3 daily, 3½ hrs, L16,500), change trains in Canicattì. **AST** (tel. 0932/621249) has the most frequent bus connections to Noto (9 daily, 1½ hrs, L5,100) and Siracusa (6 daily, 2 hrs, L7,500). All buses depart from Piazza Gramsci in front of the train station; schedules are posted, and you buy your tickets on board. Save your legs the 40-minute walk to Ragusa Ibla and take orange AST Bus 1 or 3 (L600) from the station to San Giorgio (P. del Polo, downhill from P. del Duomo).

WHERE TO SLEEP AND EAT • The **APT** (V. Capitano Bocchieri 33, in Palazzo Rocca, tel. 0932/621421; open Mon.–Sat. 9–1) makes lodging recommendations. You could do a lot worse than to stay at the quiet **Hotel San Giovanni** (V. Traspontino 3, tel. 0932/621013), which charges L90,000 for a double with bath. From the train station, take Via Leonardo da Vinci down and to the left, turn left on Via I. Migliorisi (which becomes V. Schinina), and continue through Piazza Cappuccini to Via Traspontino. If you're in Ragusa Ibla and want to treat yourself, **Ristorante U Saracinu** (V. del Convento 9, tel. 0932/246976; closed Wed.), at the lower end of Piazza del Duomo, has great atmosphere, friendly service, and top-notch food. Try the *ravioli di ricotta al sugo di maiale* (pork, L10,000) or *agnello arrosto* (roast lamb, L12,000). A complete menu goes for L23,000 and up. Down the hill one block off Piazza Pola is fancy **Ristorante Il Barocco** (V. Orfanotrofio 29, tel. 0932/652397; closed Wed.), still affordable for its *salsiccia ragusana* (local-style sausage), roasted locally grown vegetables, or *cavati* (a regional pasta) with broccoli and sausage, L8,000 each.

Noto's time-warp effect is amplified on the second Sunday in June, when the town turns out for the Procession of Corpus Domini, a combination religious parade and civic pride love-in executed in full ecclesiastical regalia.

AGRIGENTO

Built on a broad open field that slopes gently to the sun- simmered Mediterranean, the ancient city of Akragas was a showpiece of temples erected to flaunt a victory over Carthage. Despite a later sack by Carthage, mishandling by the Romans, and neglect by the Christians and Muslims, the eight or so monuments in the **Valle dei Templi** are considered to be, along with the Acropolis in Athens, the finest Greek ruins in all the world. What Greek poet Pindar called "the most beautiful city among mortals" was Akragas, not modern Agrigento, but the city—while lacking the splendor of its ancient past—still measures up nicely. Snazzy **Via Atenea** in the medieval center affords plenty of opportunities for people-watching, and San Leone's beaches, though hardly undeveloped, will cool you off after a morning of high culture.

BASICS

The most helpful **AAST** office (V. Cesare Battisti 15, just off V. Pirandello, tel. 0922/20454; open Mon.– Sat. 8:30–1:40 and 4–7) is in the town center. Change money at **Banco di Sicilia** (P. Aldo Moro I, tel. 0922/481111), across from the train station, weekdays 8:30–1:30 and 3–4; Saturday you'll have to make do with the rates at the post office. **Monte dei Paschi di Siena** has a Cirrus ATM in Piazza Vittorio Emanuele II. The fascist-era central **post office** (P. Vittorio Emanuele, tel. 0922/595150) changes money and does the postal thing Monday–Saturday 8:10–7. Make phone calls in relative comfort at **Telecom** (V. Atenea 96).

COMING AND GOING

Whether you go by bus or train, getting in and out of Agrigento is slow at best, agonizing at worst. To venture farther west, you must take a bus. Agrigento's **Stazione Centrale** (P. Marconi, tel. 1478/88088) sits just downhill from Piazzale Aldo Moro (the public park) and Piazza Vittorio Emanuele. Trains head to Palermo (10 daily, 2 hrs, L12,100), Enna (4 daily, 2 hrs, L10,800; change at Caltanisetta), and Ragusa (3 daily, 3½ hrs, L17,000; change at Canicattì). Store your bags here from 6 AM to 10 PM daily. Agrigento's long-distance **bus station** (P. Fratelli Rosselli) is just east of Piazza Vittorio Emanuele II. A confusing variety of bus companies departs from here, and the only agency with a nearby ticket office is **SAIS** (V. Ragazzi del '99 12, tel. 0922/595620), which offers sparse service to Catania (7 daily, 3 hrs, L16,500) and Caltanissetta (7 daily, 1 hr, L5,800). **Salvatore Lumia** (tel. 0922/20414) runs four daily buses to Trapani (3½ hrs, L17,600) and Castelvetrano (2¼ hrs, L11,000), where you can catch a local bus to take you the 8 km (5 mi) to Selinunte. For other companies and routes, check the schedules posted in Agrigento's **Bar Sprint** (V. Ragazzi del '99 2) or around the bus lot.

GETTING AROUND

From Stazione Centrale, the main street, **Via Atenea,** is reached by climbing the stairs to the left, and then making another left halfway through Piazzale Aldo Moro, also known as the public park. From the bus station, follow the huge post office building along Via Imera, then head right through the park for Via Atenea. The main drag winds westward through the city, intersected by Via Bac-Bac almost at its end. The Valle dei Templi, which you can see (sort of) from the train station, can be reached either by a 40-minute walk (start below the train station on Via Crispi, then follow the signs) or on **TUN** Bus 1, 1/, 2, 2/, or 3 (hourly, L1,000), all of which depart from Piazza Marconi. Buses marked SAN LEONE also embark from here for the **beach** and campgrounds.

WHERE TO SLEEP

Agrigento gets positively packed during summer, and budget choices are few and far between—you *must* call ahead for a room.

UNDER L75,000 • Hotel Concordia. This is the closest hotel to the train station, and though small, the rooms are clean and comfortable, with upscale dorm furniture. Doubles without bath cost L70,000. *P. San Francesco 11, 92100, tel. 0922/596266. Take V. Pirandello from P. Aldo Moro. 25 rooms, 22 with bath.*

UNDER L85,000 • Hotel Bella Napoli. French novelist Alexandre Dumas may once have slept at this hotel smack in Agrigento's medieval center, but he'd hardly stop by today. The few lovely rooms are L75,000 with bath. For L55,000 you can get a fairly drab room with communal bathrooms that are—dare we say—filthy. Unfortunately, with only three budget hotels in town, you might just get stuck here. If you do, confirm the price of your room *firmly* before checking in. *P. Lena 6, 92100, tel. 0922/20435. Walk up V. Bac-Bac from west end of V. Atenea. 46 rooms, 23 with bath.*

Hotel Belvedere. Big, clean bathrooms with Turkish tiles and vintage furniture await you at this modern-looking hotel, with spectacular views making good on its name. The manager is friendly and proud of his struggling though lovely garden, where you can watch the sun go down and drink a beer as evening rolls into dinnertime. Doubles are L68,000–L98,000 (breakfast L4,000). *V. San Vito 20, 92100, tel. 0922/20051. From northeast corner of P. Vittorio Emanuele II, follow V. Cicerone to V. San Vito and turn right. 34 rooms, 15 with bath.*

WHERE TO EAT

Most of the restaurants in the town center cater to tourists. The cheapest way to go is stocking up at affordable grocery stores and food stalls on the side streets below Via Atenea.

UNDER L15,000 • Trattoria Black Horse. Though you probably won't be the only tourist in here, the food is excellent and the service polite. Sit at a quiet outdoor table with an immense platter of roasted calamari (L13,000). *V. Celauro 8, tel. 0922/23223. Take V. Atenea from P. Aldo Moro. No dinner Sun.*

Trattoria La Forchetta. One son is in the kitchen, the other serves the wine, and Mamma Giuseppa sits in front and runs the whole operation. The menu changes according to what's fresh, and there's always bound to be penne with something good for under L10,000. Billing appears to be somewhat, er, flexible—double-check your check. *P. San Francesco, tel. 0922/596266 (shares phone with Hotel Concordia next door). Closed Sun.*

UNDER L20,000 • L'Ambasciata di Sicilia. The bright yellow walls and funky painted beams of this trattoria are reminiscent of a traditional painted ox cart, but don't be fooled—this is no country kitchen. Regional specialties comprise the menu, including a *fritto misto* (mixed fried seafood, L15,000) served Agrigento style with a twist: a lime instead of lemon wedge. The owner will probably tell you what to order—listen to him, and you may get to taste his almond wine. *V. Giambertoni 2, off V. Atenea, tel. 0922/20526. Closed Sun.*

WORTH SEEING

The main reason to come to Agrigento may be to meander through the Valle dei Templi, but that doesn't mean that the town is an uninteresting place to poke around. The steep, hilly neighborhood in the northwest corner of town has countless winding alleys in which to lose yourself and a few medieval churches worth finding. The 13th-century **Chiesa Santa Maria dei Greci** (V. Santa Maria dei Greci 31, in northwest corner of town), built by the Normans on the site of a 5th-century BC Doric temple, has some original columns as well as partially preserved 14th-century frescoes. Enter the underground tunnel from the courtyard to check out the *stereobate* (ground floor) and column remnants that form the church's foundation. To enter the tunnel, ring the bell or find the guardian at Via Santa Maria dei Greci 15. Farther up the hill, the perpetually closed **Duomo** (P. Minzoni) looms over the city with its huge sandstone belfry. On the first Sunday in February, the town turns out for the **Almond Festival,** a street fair of floats, games, and lots of sweet, nutty pastries made with guess what?

MUSEO NAZIONALE ARCHEOLOGICO • If you're heading to the Valle dei Templi by bus, get off at the Archaeological Museum first for a good overview of the site. Ignore the dull introductory exhibits and make a beeline for the displays of objects culled from the temples themselves. Among them a group of sculpted lion heads (once waterspouts) and a reassembled *telamone*—a 25-ft-high figure traditionally used as a decorative column on the sides of buildings. *Contrada San Nicola, tel. 0922/401565. Admission free. Open daily 8–12:30, Tues., Thurs., Sat. also 2–5:30.*

Across the road from the museum is the free **Quartiere Ellenistico-Romano** (Greco-Roman Quarter; open daily 9–1 hr before sunset), more than 107,639 sq ft of ruined houses, shops, and taverns that date from the 3rd century BC. Some excavated structures still have semi-intact mosaic floors, and the complex system of sidewalks and gutters is easy to make out—reminding you that the ancient world wasn't all temples and togas.

In 1996 Italian authorities in Agrigento apprehended Giovanni Brusca, the fugitive Mafia boss charged with orchestrating the murders of several prominent anti-Mafia crusaders. Brusca almost slipped the net again—his suitcases were at the door.

VALLE DEI TEMPLI • Though getting to, from, and around the dusty ruins of the Valle dei Templi is no great hassle, this important archaeological zone deserves several hours. Stock up on snacks and water in town, as the handful of bars around the site make Tokyo look cheap. Perhaps in atonement, admission to the Valle dei Templi is free. The site, which opens at 9 AM, is divided into a western and eastern section: the western section closes at dusk, the well-lighted eastern section at 11 PM. For instant aesthetic gratification, walk through the eastern zone; for a more comprehensive tour, start way out at the western end and work your way back uphill—the route described below.

Two of the original 34 columns are all that's standing of the **Tempio di Vulcano** (Temple of Vulcan, or Hephaestus), the last major Akragas project to be built, in 430 BC. The **Tempio dei Dioscuri** (Temple of Castor and Pollux) is a troublesome reconstruction of a 5th-century BC temple, pieced together by some enthusiastic if misguided 19th-century romantics. The four gently crumbling columns they came up with make up one of the postcard images of Sicily, but compare the slender columns of this temple to the roughly contemporary Temple of Concordia across the road—the Dioscuri Temple looks more Roman than Greek. Very little remains of the **Tempio di Giove** (Temple of Jove, or Zeus), which was once, appropriately, the biggest of the Akragas temples and one of the largest temples in the Greek world. Only the stereobate and one of the telamones were left behind; the latter is now in the museum (the telamone you see here is a reproduction).

Through the gate and across the modern road, you'll notice wheel ruts marking the ancient road to the temples. To the right, at the westernmost point overlooking the modern road, is the poorly named **Tomba di Terone** (Tomb of Theron)—the stout, squared building was more likely to have been a monument to Romans who died in the Punic Wars. Back up on the acropolis, the 6th-century BC **Tempio di Ercole** (Temple of Hercules), the oldest structure in the valley, was dedicated to the favorite god of the often-warring citizens of Akragas. Farther up Via Sacra past the visible cubicles of the necropolis is the 5th-century BC **Tempio di Concordia** (Temple of Concord), thought to be the best-preserved Greek temple around. Everything but the roof and treasury are still standing, thanks largely to the efforts of San Gregorio delle Rape (St. Gregory of the Turnips), Agrigento's 6th-century bishop who consecrated the pagan temple. For preservation, this temple is blocked off to the public, but you can still get close enough to

TASTING MARSALA

Marsala is known throughout Italy for the sweet dessert wine that bears its name. Sometimes flavored with berries or almonds, Marsala is traditionally made from the remnants of table wine pressings, and most vintages are still mixed and aged on the outskirts of the city. The oldest and most distinguished of the distilleries is Florio (Lungomare Florio 1, tel. 0923/781111). Call ahead for a free tour and to sample a few glasses. Enoteca Luminario (V. Lungomare Boeo 36, tel. 0923/713150) pours you five free glasses and always has an open package of biscotti.

appreciate how well it's withstood the past 2,400 years. The final and easternmost structure is the **Tempio di Giunone** (Temple of Juno, or Hera), a 5th-century BC temple.

CASA DI PIRANDELLO • This is the birthplace of innovative playwright Luigi Pirandello (1867–1936), who won the 1934 Nobel Prize for literature and is best known for his plays *Six Characters in Search of an Author* and *Enrico IV*. His house (just west of the temples) is now a small, free museum that contains his study, murals he painted, and random memorabilia. Pirandello's ashes lie beneath a lonely pine tree outside. In July or August Agrigento hosts performances of his works; contact the AAST (*see* Basics, *above*) for info. *Contrada Caos, near Valle dei Templi, tel. 0922/511102. Bus 1 from P. Marconi. Open daily 9–1 and 3–5.*

WEST

The western half of Sicily has always been poorer and less visited than the east. And though the west's social and economic situation has improved significantly over the past 50 years, there remains a visible lack of infrastructure and a less visible (and not unrelated) disparity of wealth. It's said that this region is completely controlled by the Mafia and that government money earmarked for development buys the incongruous luxury cars you might see. Whatever the reason, the west has been left behind to a certain extent by the rest of the island, and the past is tangible, making this one of the last remaining strongholds of a more traditional Sicily anywhere near the coast.

Facing North Africa, the west coast has been strongly influenced by Arab traders and invaders. Their traces can be found in the whitewashed buildings surrounded by palms and in culinary treasures such as couscous *con pesce in brodo* (with fish in broth), which is big in seaside **Trapani.** Towns like **Marsala** and Trapani have their own charms, but they're mostly springboards for treks to remote Mediterranean islands and the many beaches and fishing villages clinging to the rocky shoreline. If beach bumming isn't your thing, spooky, medieval **Erice** and the ancient ruins at **Selinunte** and **Segesta** merit the effort it takes to reach them.

MARSALA

Marsala is a clean, breezy port town where little happens. This wasn't always the case—in its ancient days, it was Carthage's main Sicilian stronghold, and the port, now an outpost for a handful of fiberglass yachts, was for 2,000 years one of the most important stops between Europe and North Africa. Arab influences are stronger here than in any other Sicilian town (its name means "port of Allah" in Arabic), from the *panini con pannelle* (ground chickpea sandwiches) in the marketplace to the narrow streets and whitewashed buildings. Marsala's 15 minutes of fame came in 1860, when Giuseppe Garibaldi landed with his "1,000 Red Shirts" (a band of revolutionaries) and somehow managed to wrench control of the island from the ruling Bourbons. Despite historical anecdotes and pleasant atmosphere, Marsala is more a place to pass through than to stay and visit, but do allow time for a casual stroll downtown and a taste of the sweet Marsala wine.

BASICS

The local **Pro Loco** tourist office (V. XI Maggio 100, tel. 0923/714097; open Mon.–Sat.8–2 and 3–6:30; sometimes open Sun.) has maps, bus and train schedules, and lodging info. The **post office** (V. Garibaldi 3–7) is a few doors down toward the water. Next door, **Banco Ambrosiano Veneto** (V. Garibaldi 9–13) has a Cirrus ATM.

COMING AND GOING

Marsala's **train station** (V. Fazio 9, tel. 1478/88088) has frequent connections to Palermo and Trapani. Check your bags (L5,000) Monday–Saturday 6 AM–8:15 PM. Piazza del Popolo is the main bus depot: **AST** serves Castelvetrano (4 daily, 40 min, L5,000), Palermo (13 daily, 2½ hrs, L14,100), and Trapani (18 daily, 30 min, L4,600); **Salvatore Lumia** serves Agrigento (4 daily, 3 hrs, L15,200).

WHERE TO SLEEP AND EAT

The only affordable hotel in town, **Hotel Garden** (V. Gambini 36, tel. 0923/982320) charges L85,000 for a clean, comfortable double with bath and TV; from the train station, head straight on Viale Fazio, hang a sharp right across the tracks on Corso Calatafimi, then a quick right on Via Cave, which ends at Via Gambini. For seafood priced under L10,000, locals heartily recommend **Trattoria de Marco** (V. Vaccari 6, tel. 0923/956718), right off Piazza Repubblica and up the tiny lane across from the **Duomo**'s front door. Vegetarians and carnivores alike will enjoy the inexpensive chickpea sandwiches sold at stands in the **market** (open Mon.–Sat. 6–2) next to Porta Garibaldi.

Selinunte is named after a local variety of wild celery that still grows profusely in spring among the ruined columns and overturned capitals. We don't suggest foraging for it for dinner.

WORTH SEEING

MUSEO CAPO LILYBAEUM • A museum in an old wine-making factory houses one of the few ancient ships ever recovered intact and the only surviving example of a Carthaginian warship. The ship's crew met its maker off the nearby Stagnone Islands, probably in 241 BC, during the First Punic War. The Phoenician inscriptions on some parts of the planking were put there by the original shipbuilders in Carthage. Display cases hold objects dredged from the ship, including some *Cannabis sativa* (a.k.a. kind bud), used to keep the 68 oarsmen "awake." The museum is 20 minutes west of downtown. *Lungomare Boeo 30, tel. 0923/952535. From P. Repubblica, take V. XI Maggio to P. della Vittoria, then follow V. Sauro to Lungomare Boeo and turn right. Admission free. Open daily 9–1 (Wed. and Sat. also 4–7).*

MUSEO DEGLI ARAZZI FIAMMINGHI • This tiny museum behind the Duomo has only one display: an impressive eight-part set of 16th-century tapestries. The tapestries were fashioned in Brussels and later given to Marsala-born Antonio Lombardo, the archbishop of Messina and ambassador to Spain. It's a good collection, but be forewarned that the curator will probably insist on showing you around himself. For a glimpse of the Marsala of old, look at the remnants of a doorway and storefronts from the 16th and 18th centuries, on the northeast side of the Duomo. *V. Garraffa 57, off V. Garibaldi, tel. 0923/712903. Admission L1,000. Open Tues.–Sun. 9–1 and 4–6.*

NEAR MARSALA

SELINUNTE AND MARINELLA

As a Greek colony, **Selinunte** was too close to Carthaginian territories to ever enjoy lasting peace, but now it's just remote enough to discourage most modern invaders. Stranded in the southwest corner of Sicily, Selinunte boasts 5th-century BC ruins strung across two hilltops overlooking a sandy beach and sparkling sea. Among the palms and wildflowers remain scraps of eight temples, about which so little is known that they're referred to by letter instead of by the names of gods. Temple E has been more or less reconstructed (some say in error). Temple G, although never completed and no more than a pile of rocks today, would have been one of the largest buildings of the ancient world. The plain between the two temple areas is thought to have been the site of the *agora* (market), but there's nothing to see there now except a shady picnic area where a daring camper might (discreetly) rough it. There is also a small museum on the site that contains other excavated pieces. *Ruins and museum admission L2,000. Open daily 9–1 hr before sunset.*

Selinunte's modern counterpart is the temple-free **Marinella,** a fishing-village-turned-middle-class-summer-resort just east of Selinunte, complete with the ubiquitous cheesy pizzerias and stores selling postcards. The town has no tourist office, despite i signs pointing hither and yon, but bus schedules are posted in **Ristorante Pierrot** (Vicolo Pierrot, off V. Marco Polo). You can change money at the **Cassa di Cambio Siciliano** (V. Marco Polo, across from L'Approdo; open Mon.–Sat. 8:30–8), then spend it at **Pensione Costa d'Avorio** (V. Stazione 10, tel. 0924/46207), which charges L75,000 per person for a room and full pension (three meals) and is a stone's throw from the ruins. Resorty **Albergo Lido Azzurro** (V. Marco Polo 98, tel. and fax 0924/46256) is the cheapest option by the beach at L95,000 for a renovated double with bath, breakfast included. **Camping Il Maggionlino** (tel. and fax 0924/46044) is on a beautiful site but rather far from the coast; it costs L5,000–L7,000 for a tent and L7,500 per person. Food in Marinella isn't cheap, but of the many pizza joints, **Ristorante Africa da Bruno** (V. Alceste 24, tel. 0924/46456, open every day, but closed from November to March) has famous antipasti, about L15,000 a plate, depending on quantity, and grilled fish in the evenings, L12,000.

COMING AND GOING • To reach Selinunte and Marinella, you must first travel to Castelvetrano by train from Marsala (4 daily, 40 min, L5,000) or by bus from Marsala (4 daily, 40 min, L4,800) or Agrigento (4 daily, 2¼ hrs, L9,600). If you arrive in Selinunte by train, walk to Piazza Regina Margherita—from here you can take one of six daily buses (20 min, L2,000) to Marinella. If you arrive by bus, ask to be let off at **Bar Selinus** (V. Marinella 13), where you can catch one of the Marinella-bound buses en route.

TRAPANI

Several kilometers long but only about a thousand feet at its widest, Trapani is a spindly finger of a city pointing westward into the sea. This relative isolation has kept the city's tourist flow to a trickle, and as a result, its buildings house weathered fishermen and bare barber shops instead of too many hotels, discos, and obnoxious *caffè.* But this is far from a backwater town—one lap on the evening passeggiata route of Corso Vittorio Emanuele will give you an eyeful of fashion that'll make you think twice about packing "practical" clothes on your next trip to Italy. This incongruous worldliness is due to the numerous Mafia bosses who call the city home—which may explain the preponderance of fancy cars and slick men with cellular phones.

The two main reasons to make the trek to Trapani are to visit the Egadi Islands and to witness the spectacle of Easter. Trapani takes the cake for intense Easter festivities, with elaborate processions, masses, statues, crowds, bonfires, hooded pallbearers—you name it. If you somehow manage to get a reservation during Easter week, you'll witness something you may never forget—not to mention never understand.

BASICS

Pick up brochures and lodging lists from the **EPT** (Piazzetta Saturno, off P. Sant'Agostino, tel. 0923/29000; open Mon.–Sat. 8–8, Sun. 9–noon). **Monte dei Paschi di Siena** (V. XXX Gennaio 80) has an ATM. The **post office** (P. Vittorio Veneto; open weekdays 8:30–7, Sat. 8:30–1) exchanges money at good rates.

COMING AND GOING

To reach the port or centro storico from the train station or bus depot (a 20-minute walk), cross the small park in front of the stations, walk right on Via Scontrino three blocks, turn left and walk ½ km (⅓ mi) through Piazza Vittorio Veneto down Via Garibaldi, and turn left on Via Torreasa to get to Corso Vittorio Emanuele. At Trapani's **train station** (P. Stazione, tel. 0923/28071), the attractive centro storico fades into the modern city. From Trapani there are trains to Palermo (19 daily, 2 hrs, L12,100) and Segesta (daily, 30 min, L4,000). Luggage storage (L5,000 per bag) is open daily 7 AM–9:30 PM. The main **bus station** (P. Montalto, tel. 0923/21021) is off Via Osorio, immediately south of the train station. From here **AST** serves Erice (10 daily, 1 hr, L2,500), Marsala (4 daily, 30 min, L3,700), and San Vito Lo Capo (6 daily, 45 min, L4,400). Buy tickets at the station or on board. Catch **Autolinee Segesta** buses to Palermo (15 daily, 2 hrs, L11,000) either from the bus station or from the Egatour office (V. Ammiraglio Staiti 13, tel. 0923/21956). **Tarantola** buses run to Segesta (7 daily, 45 min, L4,000) from Piazza Garibaldi.

BY BOAT • All ferries arrive and depart from **Molo di Sanità,** Trapani's main docks, which extend seaward from Piazza Garibaldi between Via Regina Elena and Via Ammiraglio Staiti. **Siremar** (V. Ammiraglio Staiti 63, tel. 0923/540515) runs *traghetti* (ferries) to Favignana (3 daily, 1 hr 20 min, L5,000), Levanzo (2 daily, 50 min, L4,800), and Marettimo (1 daily, 2½ hrs, L12,200); the company also runs *aliscafi* (hydrofoils) to Levanzo and Favignana (11 daily, 15 min, L10,000). **Alilauro** (V. Ammiraglio Staiti, tel. 0923/24073) runs hydrofoils to Favignana (7 daily, 20 min, L8,700) and Levanzo (7 daily, 20 min, L8,500). **Tirrenia** (V. Ammiraglio Staiti 55, tel. 0923/21896) offers ferries (L92,000) to Tunisia every Monday at 10 AM, arriving 8hours later; the return boat leaves Tunisia every Monday at 9 PM but takes 10hours to get to Trapani.

WHERE TO SLEEP

Reservations are imperative around Easter, when even the EPT (*see* Basics, *above*) has trouble arranging private rooms. If you want to visit during the trippy Easter processions, reserve at least one month in advance for a front-row seat at the **Nuovo Albergo Russo** (V. Tintori 4, tel. 0923/22166 or 0923/22163, fax 0923/26623), a comfortable three-star hotel where a L70,000–L110,000 double will get you a balcony overlooking the crowded, festive Corso Vittorio Emanuele. Half of **Albergo Moderno** (V. T. Genovese 20, tel. 0923/21247) has been refurbished, while the other half has saggy beds, barely functional bathrooms, and dirty floors. The less immaculate doubles cost L45,000–L70,000; the nice ones L67,000–L70,000. Heading away from the port on Via Torrearsa, take the second left past Corso Vittorio Emanuele. You'll get what you pay for at **Pensione Messina** (C. Vittorio Emanuele 71, tel. 0923/21198). For L40,000–L50,000 you won't find a cheaper double, but your home-away-from-home has been known to have dirty sheets and broken windows. On the up side, the location is unbeatable—an 18th-century apartment block with a private courtyard. One word of warning: the OSTELLO DELLA GIOVENTU sign near the train station might as well be pointing the way to Moscow (the youth hostel is actually 40 minutes away), so ignore it unless you have your own transport. The hostel is also expensive, making it worthwhile to stay in a more convenient hotel for almost the same price.

On Good Friday, Trapani commemorates the Passion and crucifixion of Christ with a chaotic 18-hour Easter procession, a blend of Catholic and pagan rituals. The centro storico is awash with painted icons, hooded figures, and weeping onlookers.

WHERE TO EAT

It's worth staying an extra day in Trapani for a few extra meals. Everything is prepared painstakingly, right down to the fennel-spiced bread served with every meal. If you're ready to splurge, sample scrumptious Trapanese specialties like couscous *con pesce in brodo* and *busiate al pesto trapanese* at **Ristorante Da Peppe** (V. Spalti 50, tel. 0923/28246; closed Mon.). Although this restaurant has been named one of the best in the country, a meal won't set you back more than L30,000. Late on a scorching afternoon, you can sidle over to the always-crowded **Pizzeria Calvino** (V. N. Nasi 71, near V. Giglio, tel. 0923/21464; closed Tues.) to appease your less carnal hungers with a generously sized pizza, averaging L9,000. Cozy little rooms in back have narrow peephole windows, which spawned the legend that Calvino was once a brothel (it wasn't). The *capricciosa* salad (L8,500) toppings are at the whim of the chef. What **Trattoria da Salvatore** (V. N. Nasi 19, near port, tel. 0923/546530; closed Sun. except in Aug.) lacks in ambience, it makes up for amply with good food—fresh fish pulled from local waters and well-executed classics like spaghetti *alle vongole veraci* (with small clams; L8,000) and *bucatini* (long, squiggly pasta) al pesto trapanese (L7,000). The friendly cook will be glad to give you recipes.

WORTH SEEING

All but one of Trapani's historical attractions are in the centro storico. The best way to explore this neighborhood is to get as lost as possible in the maze of narrow lanes and alleys. You're always bound to come upon something interesting.

CHIESA DEL PURGATORIO • If you don't make the pilgrimage to Trapani during Easter, stop by this 17th-century Baroque church to see *I Misteri*, the colorful life-size wooden statues that depict scenes from the Passion of Christ. Each group is cared for by a trade organization (such as the carpenters or fishermen) that's also responsible for carrying the icons during the procession. *V. Giglio, 2 blocks south of C. V. Emanuele. Admission free. Open daily 8–noon; Mon., Wed., and Fri. also 4–7.*

SANTUARIO DELL'ANNUNZIATA • It's worth trekking out to a blandly urban section of Trapani to visit this joint church and museum. The structure dates from 1315, but because of renovations in 1760, only the spectacular rose window and Gothic portal are original. Inside, the **Cappella della Madonna** houses a statue of the Virgin and Christ sculpted in the 1300s by Nino Pisano. The highlight, though, is the **Museo Nazionale Pepoli,** entered through the Villa Pepoli gardens next door. Seemingly random displays in this small museum include beautiful coral sculptures, medieval art, ancient coins, and a huge guillotine built in 1789. Especially evocative is the basket for you-know-what beneath the blade. *V. Conte A. Pepoli 198–200. Take SAU Bus 1, 10, or 11 (L1200) from P. Matteotti or P. Vittorio Emanuele. Museum admission L2,000. Church open daily 7–noon and 4–7; museum open Mon.–Sat. 9–1:30 (Tues. and Thurs. also 3–6:30).*

NEAR TRAPANI

SEGESTA

Little is known about the origins of this 8th-century BC colony except that it was probably founded by Trojans fleeing their sacked city. Today only two structures still stand—a nearly intact **theater** and an unidentified **temple** populated by hundreds of tiny birds whose music echoes off the columns and floor. Although the site isn't as spectacular as those in Agrigento or Selinunte, the hilltop ruins are less ruined and the surrounding landscape is lovely: pine trees, rocky gorges, distant vineyards, and hills dotted with wildflowers make this the most picturesque archaeological stop in Sicily. Admission to the archaeological park (open 9–1 hr before sunset) is free, and there's a blue Autolinee Segesta bus (every ½ hr, L2,000 round-trip) that will shuttle you up from the parking lot to the theater. While you're waiting, if you must, grab an overpriced drink or sandwich from the **Posto di Ristoro Segesta** (tel. 0924/951131), a combination bar, restaurant, and souvenir shop.

COMING AND GOING • There is only one daily train to the Segesta-Tempio station from either Palermo (1½ hrs, L9,000) or Trapani (30 min, L4,000), but there are 11 trains from Palermo and 10 from Trapani that stop daily at Calatafimi, a 2-km (1-mi) walk from the ruins (prices and times are the same). Or you can take an **Autoservizi Tarantola** bus from Trapani's Piazza Garibaldi (4 daily, 30 min, L4,000) straight to Segesta. From Segesta's train station it's a beautiful 20-minute walk uphill to the temple.

ERICE

Founded by the Phoenicians and dedicated to Astarte and later to Aphrodite by the Greeks, Erice is most famous for its medieval incarnation—a virtually impenetrable fortress preserved intact atop a steep mountain. The Goddess of Love (and her surrogates, sacred temple prostitutes) attracted countless invaders despite the tiny, triangular town's inconvenient location. Erice is still isolated and remote, with horizon-wide views of the Mediterranean and even Tunisia on a good day and a mysterious, almost spooky atmosphere you'll discover by wandering its stony alleys. The past comes alive at the **Castello di Venere** (at southeast end of V. Contepepoli), even more so when low clouds obscure the sweeping view of the valley and the misty clifftop courtyard could well serve as a stage set for *Hamlet*. Next door, the privately owned **Castello Pepoli** hosts courtyard honey tastings all summer long. The **Museo Comunale Cordini** (P. Umberto I; admission L2,000; open Mon.–Sat. 8:30–1:30) is home to a fine sculpture of the *Annunciation* by Antonello Gagini.

From Trapani's Piazza Montalto, buses to Erice (11 daily, 1 hr, L2,500) will drop you just outside Porta Trapani. Erice's main drag, Via Vittorio Emanuele, is straight ahead and will lead you to Piazza Umberto I. The helpful **AAST** tourist office (V. Conte Pepoli 11, tel. 0923/869388) is a bit east and has an excellent brochure and map of the town. As for lodgings, the **Ostello della Gioventù CSI** (V. delle Pinete, tel. 0923/869144; closed Oct.–late June) charges L20,000 a night. Even though it's just northwest of town, the hostel fills up with youth groups, so call ahead. In a pinch, **Affittacamere Italia** (V. A. Palma 7, tel. 0923/869185) arranges private rooms for about L25,000 per person. You can try all sorts of local treats at **La Vettu** (V. G. Fontana 5, tel. 0923/869404, closed Fri.), featuring *pasta al pesto trapanese* (with tomatoes) and *busiate con sarde,* L10,000, and in the evening they do pizzas for L7,000–13,000.

SAN VITO LO CAPO

The laid-back resort town of San Vito Lo Capo sits at the tip of a narrow peninsula on the edge of the Golfo di Castellammare. Its out-of-the-way location (arrivals are by bus only) will encourage you to linger, relaxing alongside clear, bottle-glass-green water on one of Sicily's largest sand beaches. The 7 km (4½ mi) of rough coast south of town are part of the **Riserva Naturale dello Zingaro,** a nature preserve with great hiking, biking, and swimming. You'll find the best swimming at **Tonnarella dell'Uzzo,** the abandoned tuna fishery in the northern part of the park. Head south along San Vito's beach to reach the park; maps are available at the **tourist office** (V. Immacolata 8, tel. 0924/974300; open weekdays 8–2).

In addition to its beach and nearby nature preserve, San Vito is a noted water-sports and diving center. At **Centro Mare Sport** (V. Faro, by the port, tel. 0923/974288; closed Oct.–Apr.) you can rent kayaks (L10,000 per hr), sailboards (L15,000 per hr), or a full set of scuba-diving equipment (L40,000 per day). No credit card deposit is required—any form of ID will do. Rock climbers eyeing the sharp peaks that encircle San Vito should contact the **Club Alpino Italiano** in Palermo (V. Agrigento 30, tel. 091/6254352) for info on the best and safest routes up—some of the rock in this area is not secure.

COMING AND GOING • Unless you have a car, public buses are the only way to reach San Vito Lo Capo. **AST** runs buses to and from Trapani's Piazza Montalto (9 daily, 1½ hrs, L4,600); buses arrive and depart on the upper stretch of Via Mattarella, near its intersection with Via Foritano. **Autoservizi Russo** (C. Garibaldi 55, Palermo, tel. 0924/31364) runs buses to and from Palermo's Piazza Marina (3 daily, 3 hrs, L11,400); wait at the corner near the port where Via Napoli becomes Via Faro.

WHERE TO SLEEP AND EAT • Because it is a popular beach resort, San Vito has cheap sleeps and eats clearly marked with signs. Two related pensions in the same building near the beach are **Sabbia d'Oro** (V. Santuario 49, tel. 0923/972508) and **Pensione Ocean View** (tel. 0923/972613), which both charge L60,000–L70,000 for modern doubles with bath, breakfast included. Private rooms at homey **Affittacamere Eden** are only L60,000 (V. Mulino 62, tel. 0923/972460). **Camping Soleado** (V. del Secco 40, tel. 0923/972166), on the east side of town near the beach, charges L6,000–L9,000 per person and L8,000–L10,000 for a small tent. For ocean views and couscous with a culinary history lesson, try **Riviera** (V. Lungomare, tel. 0923/972480), on the east end of San Vito's beachfront road. Like all respectable Italian beach towns, San Vito has a hot summer disco scene, and the open-air dance floor at **Discoteca Stardust** is packed with frenzied vacationing Sicilians. Women get in free, courtesy of machismo. The Stardust is east of town, about 15 minutes by foot along the coast road. In summer it's jammed Tuesday–Sunday from around 10:30 PM until 1 or 2 AM.

If you visit Segesta during the summer of an odd-numbered year, contact the EPT in Trapani for tickets to classical dramas performed in a theater under the auspices of the Istituto Nazionale del Dramma Antico. Special buses from Trapani are available.

EGADI ISLANDS

Arriving in the Egadi Islands (Isole Egadi) can be disorienting. Only 15 minutes on the hydrofoil from the dirty and decidedly urban port of Trapani, you'll see green mountains rising up out of the clear water, and the quiet gives no indication of the city practically within shouting distance of the beach. **Favignana** is the largest, most populated, and most touristed of the islands—it's not even remotely crowded—and its main draws are sandy beaches and services like restaurants and a bank. It's a five-minute (L4,000) hydrofoil hop from Favignana to **Levanzo,** where the port's deep turquoise waters are as enticingly swimmable as the ones off many pebbly beaches. Remote, wild **Marettimo** is 40 minutes farther out by hydrofoil (two hours by ferry) and virtually untouched by the touristy likes of you and me. In short, the trio makes up a Mediterranean island chain of brochure fantasies, and if you make it a day trip from Trapani, it's possible to visit, bask, and photo-op here all on the cheap.

Although lodging on the islands isn't outrageous (L70,000 for a resorty double with bath, L25,000 or so per person for a room in a private home), it's definitely cheaper to stay in Trapani and make day trips. You can also camp—officially on Favignana and discreetly on Levanzo and Marettimo. Ferries and hydrofoils leave for Favignana and Levanzo frequently from Trapani's Molo di Sanità docks (*see* Coming and Going *in* Trapani, *above*), and ticket booths for the four competing lines—Alilauro, Tirrenia, Ustica, and Volviamare—are right next to each other; just show up and buy a ticket for the next one out. The same general principle applies to distant Marettimo, but it takes a bit more planning—stop by the docks or EPT (*see* Basics *in* Trapani, *above*) for current schedules.

FAVIGNANA

It would be easy to spend your entire Egadian sojourn on Favignana. Most of the archipelago's services are concentrated here around **Piazza Europa,** to the right as you leave the port. If you're planning nothing more adventurous than a day trip, make a beeline for the sandy **Lido Burrone,** a quiet beach 3 km (2 mi) across the island from the port, on the south coast. Continue southeast along the rocky coast for Punta Panfalo and Cala Azzurra, headlands overlooking the calm Mediterranean. Farther along on the north coast is **Cala Rossa** (Red Cove), another good swimming spot with tufa-rock formations. In May or June, Favignana hosts its annual **Mattanza,** when schools of giant tuna are corralled by boats and then harpooned and heaved on deck by local fishermen. Animal lovers beware: the tuna run is more than a little bloody and gruesome.

BASICS

Biking is the best way to get around the island. **Noleggio da Rita** (P. Europa 11, tel. 0360/409965) charges L7,000 per day for bicycles and about L35,000 per day for mopeds. Ask around at the docks or in bars near Piazza Madrice, the port's main square, for private rooms, or ask the staff at **Pro Loco** (P. Madrice 7, tel. 0923/921647; open Mon.–Sat. 9–noon and 2–5) to arrange one for you. **Albergo Bouganville** (V. Cimabue 10, 8 blocks west of P. Europa, tel. 0923/922033) charges L80,000 for newish, quiet rooms with bath. The island has several campgrounds—the closest to town is **Villaggio Quattro Rose** (Località Mulino a Vento, tel. 0923/921223), which gets L7,000 per person. At **A & O Supermarket** (V. Florio), you can stock up on staples.

LEVANZO

The biggest debate in Levanzo is how many people live on the island—most agree that the population hovers around 120, though some—stubborn, elderly types—insist it is closer to 100. As you can imagine, there are limits to what can be done with such a small cast of characters, but there is quiet and peaceful beauty in the steeply sloped island with its sugar-cube houses. The island's port is clean and doubles as a swimming hole; for a bit more seclusion, it's a 15-minute walk (1 km) over a hill to the pebble beaches of **Cala Tramontana, Cala Fredda,** and **Cala Calcara.** In addition to one hotel, three restaurants, two caffès, a market, and a bakery, Levanzo is home to the **Grotta del Genovese,** a cave etched with 6,000-year-old Paleolithic animals and abstract designs and Neolithic human representations. The grotto is only accessible by contacting its official guardian, signore **Natale Castiglione** (V. Calvario 11, above the dock, tel. 0923/924032), who usually meets arriving ferries and hydrofoils. He charges about L15,000 per person for a guided, several-hour journey by car and foot to the cave. To stay the night here, you'll have to shell out L80,000–L90,000 at **Albergo dei Fenici** (V. Calvario 18, tel. 0923/924083).

MARETTIMO

Hardly any tourists visit Marettimo, which lies in the middle of nothin' some 40 km (25 mi) west of Trapani. This is bad news for overnight visitors (inquire at the docks for private rooms) but good news for isolationists and rugged hikers. The island's rocky terrain and coastline are ideal for solitary exploring, with several trails winding into its most secluded reaches. From the port, head south for an hour to **Cala Sarde,** a popular swimming spot. Another hour west, near Punta Libeccio, is **Cala Nera,** so isolated that you can skinny-dip undisturbed. For a long hike (4 km/2½ mi, 3 hrs each way), follow the northeast coast from the port for about 15 minutes, then turn inland to hook up with a major path that stretches along the entire shoreline. You'll eventually end up at some cement steps that lead to a hidden beach just below the ruins of **Castello di Punta Troia,** used by the Spanish as a prison in the 17th century.

PALERMO

Natives of Palermo like to say that their city has two faces: *la bella e la brutta* (the beautiful and the ugly). Crowded, crumbling, impoverished, and unwieldy, Palermo has been undergoing a steady decline since the 14th century, but historical and artistic attractions showcase the exotic influence of its Arab and Norman conquerors. Don't expect Palermo to charm you at first glance. Sicily's capital is a *city* in all senses

PALERMO

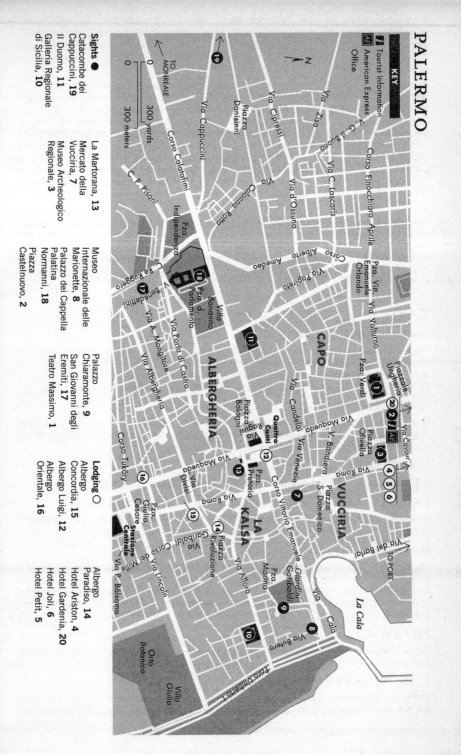

KEY

- *i* Tourist Information
- AE American Express Office

Sights ●

Catacombe dei Cappuccini, **19**
Il Duomo, **11**
Galleria Regionale di Sicilia, **10**
La Martorana, **13**
Mercato della Vucciria, **7**
Museo Archeologico Regionale, **3**
Museo Internazionale delle Marionette, **8**
Palazzo dei Cappella Palatina
Normanni, **18**
Piazza Castelnuovo, **2**
Palazzo Chiaramonte, **9**
San Giovanni degli Eremiti, **17**
Teatro Massimo, **1**

Lodging ○

Albergo Concordia, **15**
Albergo Luigi, **12**
Albergo Orientale, **16**
Albergo Paradiso, **14**
Hotel Ariston, **4**
Hotel Gardenia, **20**
Hotel Joli, **6**
Hotel Petit, **5**

of the word, and with every stride you take on the traffic- and people-infested streets, you push farther into a seemingly untamed metropolis of 800,000. That said, its rich heritage and patina make it too intriguing to ignore, and its winding medieval streets, with dilapidated but beautiful Baroque palaces, are fascinating.

Perched on a crescent-shape bay at the foot of Monte Pellegrino, Palermo was first colonized in the 6th century BC, during Carthage's control of northwestern Sicily. The Romans followed, and after a few centuries of dominance, Moorish princes from Spain conquered the city around the turn of the millennium. Over the next 700 years they refashioned Palermo in the manner of Cairo and Córdoba, with mosques, minarets, and palm trees. But the city's heyday really began in AD 1130, when the Norman king Frederick II named it the capital of his empire. One of the great intellectual leaders of the Middle Ages, Frederick II transformed Palermo into the most cosmopolitan and vibrant center of learning in all of Europe—many of the city's greatest monuments date from this period. For the next seven centuries, Palermo and Naples were in competition for domination of lower Italy, though almost all of the innovative spirit of the 12th century had been lost.

After Sicily slipped into the embryonic Italian state, the Mafia began to gain influence in Palermo, and today the city is known throughout the world as the home of Italy's most powerful dons. The images you've come to expect from movies—burly men kissing each other and exchanging suitcases, armor-plated Alfa Romeos, and police-turned-hit-men—are mostly based on reality, but you probably won't see any of it. The most sinister element you'll encounter is the less powerful but equally intimidating institution of adept pickpockets and Vespa-riding bag snatchers. But this petty crime shouldn't discourage you from a visit.

BASICS

AMERICAN EXPRESS

AmEx cardholders can cash personal checks, replace lost or stolen cards, and pick up mail at the travel agency **G. Ruggieri and Figli** (V. Emerico Amari 40, tel. 091/587144; open weekdays 9–1 and 4–7, Sat. 9–1). The rest of us can exchange money and replace lost or stolen traveler's checks. From Stazione Centrale, take Bus 101 or 107 to Piazza Castelnuovo, then follow Via Emerico Amari toward port.

CHANGING MONEY

In addition to the train info office, post office, and countless banks along Via Roma, you can change money at **Banca Nazionale di Lavoro** (V. Roma 291, tel. 091/6024111; open weekdays 8:25–1:30 and 2:50–4), with an outdoor ATM that accepts Plus and Cirrus cards.

CONSULATES

U.S. Consulate (V. Re Federico 18/B, tel. 091/6110020; open weekdays 9–noon).

ENGLISH-LANGUAGE BOOKS AND NEWSPAPERS

For reading material with substance, **Feltrinelli** (V. Maqueda 459, tel. 091/587785; open weekdays 9–8, Sat. 9–1) has an excellent selection of classics and modern fiction in English.

MAIL AND PHONES

The best place to make an international call is at one of **Telecom**'s two locations: across Via Cavour to the north of Teatro Massimo (P. Ungheria 22; open Mon.–Sat. 8–8) or on Via Lincoln across the street from the train station (open daily 8 AM–9:30 PM). At **Posta Centrale** (V. Roma 322, tel. 091/528155; open Mon.–Sat. 8:10–7:30) you can receive mail addressed to Fermo Posta, Posta Centrale, Via Roma 322, 90139 Palermo.

PHARMACY

Farmacia Inglese (V. Mariano Stabile 177, tel. 091/334482), to the port side of where Via Marino Stabile intersects Via Maqueda, is open 24 hours on weekdays, shorter hours on weekends.

VISITOR INFORMATION

APT offices (P. Castelnuovo 35, opposite Teatro Politeama Garibaldi, tel. 091/583847, open weekdays 8–8, Sat. 8–2; the train station; the airport) have maps and a rather hot-and-cold English-speaking staff.

GAY AND LESBIAN RESOURCE • Contact **ARCI Gay** (V. Trapani 3, tel. 091/324917; open weekdays 9:30 AM–11:30 PM).

COMING AND GOING

BY TRAIN

Stazione Centrale (V. Roma at P. Giulio Cesare, tel. 1478/88088) is at the south end of Via Roma near Palermo's medieval districts. Catch trains to Agrigento (12 daily, 2¼ hrs, L13,000), Catania (6 daily, 4 hrs, L20,000), Bagheria (16 daily, 10 min, L3,000), Cefalù (2–3 per hr, 1 hr, L7,000), Enna (6 daily, 2½ hrs, L14,500), Messina (18 daily, 3½ hrs, L20,000), Milazzo (19 daily, 3 hrs, L17,000), Marsala (7 daily, 2½ hrs, L14,100), and Trapani (7 daily, 3 hrs, L12,100). Palermo also has direct routes to Rome (7 daily, 13 hrs, L72,000) and Milan (3 daily, 19 hrs, L95,000). Inside the station, the **railway information office** (open daily 7 AM–9:10 PM) exchanges money and answers scheduling questions. **Luggage storage** (L5,000; open daily 6 AM–10 PM) is on the far right side of the tracks.

BY BUS

As there's no central bus station, Palermo's 18 privately owned companies usually make two stops before leaving town: one in front of their office and one at the train station. Ask the bus drivers themselves, preferably a day in advance at the actual stop, as the company offices tend to be of little help. **AST** (tel. 091/6167102) goes to Ragusa (4 daily, 3½ hrs, L17,900). **Cuffaro** (tel. 091/6161510) travels to Agrigento (3 daily, 2 hrs, L13,000). **Russo** (tel. 0924/31364) services San Vito Lo Capo (3 daily, 3 hrs, L11,400). **SAIS** (091/6166028) heads to Catania (10 daily, 2¾ hrs, L18,000) and Messina (15 daily, 5 hrs, L24,500). **Salemi** (tel. 091/6175411) runs to Marsala (13 daily, 2½ hrs, L14,600). **Segesta** (tel. 0924/6167919) buzzes to Trapani (15 daily, 2 hrs, L11,000) and Siracusa (5 daily, 4 hrs, L20,000).

The rugged western end of Sicily is reminiscent of the terrain in American westerns—as it well should be: many spaghetti westerns were filmed here.

BY BOAT

All ferries and hydrofoils dock at **Stazione Marittima** (V. Francesco Crispi 118). If you're going by boat to Sardinia, Ustica, Genoa, or Naples in high season, make reservations a few days in advance, especially if you want a cabin. The following agencies are usually open Saturday morning and during, er, normal weekday hours. **Tirrenia** (Calata Marinai d'Italia, tel. 091/333300) sends boats to Naples (daily, 9 hrs, L70,600) and Cagliari (1 weekly, 14 hrs, L66,500). **Siremar** (V. Francesco Crispi 118, tel. 091/582403 for info or 091/582403 for reservations) sails to Ustica by ferry (2 hrs 20 min, L21,100) and hydrofoil (2 daily, 1¼ hrs, L32,100).

GETTING AROUND

Stazione Centrale lies at the southern edge of the city at the foot of Palermo's two main drags: **Via Roma** and **Via Maqueda.** The equally busy **Corso Vittorio Emanuele** runs perpendicular to these two thoroughfares. The intersection of Corso Vittorio Emanuele and Via Maqueda is known as **Quattro Canti** (Four Corners) and is the axis of the centro storico's four traditional neighborhoods: Capo to the northwest, Vucciria to the northeast, La Kalsa to the southeast, and Albergheria to the southwest. Most of the major monuments and sites are scattered around these medieval quarters, characterized by a web of winding, narrow streets and alleys. As long as you keep the main streets in mind, it's easy to find your way.

BY BUS

Palermo's extensive **AMAT** bus system is amazingly convenient and well organized, although most buses run only until 11 PM. Some major routes are 101 and 102, which run from the train station along Via Roma to Piazza Castelnuovo (Bus 101 continues north along Via Libertà). Bus 109 goes from the train station to Piazza Indipendenza, at the west end of Corso Vittorio Emanuele—transfer here for Bus 389 to the outlying district of Monreale. Bus 139 takes you from the station to the port. Tickets (L1,500) are available at most newsstands, and route maps are posted at major stops.

WHERE TO SLEEP

Palermo's cheapest hotels are squashed between Via Maqueda, Via Roma, Corso Vittorio Emanuele, and Stazione Centrale. Hotels often share the same building, and the prices go down as the stairs go up. Traffic near the train station can be deafening, but things mellow out after 10 PM. Women, especially those traveling alone, should stay out of the medieval quarters after dark. If you're especially worried about crime, stay in the modern part of Palermo, near Piazza Castelnuovo—take Bus 101 or 107 from Stazione Centrale—and avoid La Kalsa. All of the places below will store your luggage. Beds fill up fast during Palermo's Festival of Santa Rosalia, July 11–15 (see Cheap Thrills, below).

NEAR STAZIONE CENTRALE

UNDER L65,000 • Albergo Concordia. You'd expect more for the price (doubles L50,000–60,000), but in this neighborhood, that it's clean is recommendation enough. Spartan tile-floored rooms have high ceilings and balconies. V. Roma 72, 4th floor, 90133, tel/fax 091/6171514. 13 rooms, 2 with bath. Credit cards OK.

Albergo Orientale. It's a toss-up for the prize for decaying grandeur—the sweeping pink marble steps of this 18th-century palace's courtyard or the high-ceilinged salon with views over Via Maqueda. Certainly not the rooms, which can only be described as decaying. Bathrooms are inexcusably dirty (doubles L75,000, with bath); haggle if you plan to stay more than three nights. This hotel forms a duo with the Alessandra (V. Divisi 99); they share telephone and fax numbers. V. Maqueda 26, 90134, tel. 091/6165727, fax 091/6165180. 45 rooms, 24 with bath.

Albergo Paradiso. Hardly paradise, it's still the best of the worst in La Kalsa. You make the call—bad neighborhood, good price (doubles L50,000). The rooms are small, the noise level high. On the plus side, everything is clean and some rooms overlook the piazza. V. Schiavuzzo 65, off P. della Rivoluzione, 90133, tel. 091/6172825. 10 rooms without bath. Cash only.

NEAR QUATTRO CANTI

UNDER L55,000 • Albergo Luigi. Clean if slightly seedy rooms matter less than the excellent location. The two rooms with views of Piazza Pretoria are a real score. Doubles start at L50,000–L60,000. Salita Santa Caterina 1, off C. Vittorio Emanuele, 90133, tel. 091/585085. 9 rooms, 5 with bath. Cash only.

NEAR PIAZZA CASTELNUOVO

UNDER L70,000 • Hotel Petit. This hotel is in the most congenial part of Palermo, on a pedestrians-only thoroughfare that is home to a few good caffès. The bathrooms sparkle, and many of the comfortable rooms have balconies. For comfort, quiet, and safety, it's worth the L65,000 for doubles. Reservations are advised. V. Principe di Belmonte 84, off V. Roma near P. Castelnuovo, 90139, tel. 091/323616. 7 rooms, 6 with bath.

UNDER L95,000 • Hotel Ariston. Rooms at the Ariston are boring but exceptionally clean (doubles L70,000–L80,000). The manager is a friendly fellow who might let you use his washing machine (for a small fee, naturally). V. Mariano Stabile 139, 90139, tel. 091/332434. 2 blocks off V. Roma toward V. Ruggero Settimo. 5 rooms with bath. Cash only.

UNDER L115,000 • Hotel Joli. A step up from your average budget hotel, Joli has air-conditioned doubles (L110,000) with wide, comfortable beds, phones, and commodious bathrooms with hot showers. It's in the safe and pleasant Castelnuovo district, yet within a few blocks of the rambling streets of old Palermo. Many rooms overlook quiet and grassy Piazza Florio. V. Michele Amari 11, 90139, tel. and fax 091/6111766 or 091/6111765. From P. Verdi, walk east on V. Cavour, north on V. Roma for 5 blocks, and right on V. Granatelli. 25 rooms with bath.

Hotel Gardenia. If traveling on the cheap has beaten you down, this hotel near Piazza Castelnuovo may be just what the doctor ordered. Each immaculately clean, air-conditioned room has its own balcony, color TV, and phone; feel free to kick back on the leather sofas in the American-style TV room. Doubles with bath are L120,000. V. Mariano Stabile 136, 90139, tel. 091/322761. 16 rooms with bath.

CAMPING • Camping Trinacria. Way out on the northern edge of the city, this is a semirustic, fairly luxurious year-round campground with a market. A site costs L6,500 per person; a tent is an additional L6,500. Località Sferracavallo, V. Barcarello 23–25, 90139, tel. 091/530590. Take Bus 101 for 20 min to Stadio stop; transfer to Bus 128 to V. Barcarello (ask driver for "Camping Trinacria"). Showers.

WHERE TO EAT

Try *pesce spada* (swordfish) and *polpo* (octopus), local specialties. If you're a vegetarian, look for *capunata di melanzane* (a sweet-and-sour eggplant relish), olives, and stuffed artichokes from the city's antipasti tables—reputed to be the best on the island. At the cheap end of the spectrum are markets like **Vucciria market** (*see* Worth Seeing, *below*) and **Standa** (V. Roma 59, near Stazione Centrale, tel. 091/6170600). Top off any meal with delectable pastries and marzipan from a local *pasticceria* (*see below*).

NEAR QUATTRO CANTI

UNDER L20,000 • Hostaria da Ciccio. Come for some of the best home-cooked food in Palermo, served up under local artwork in a bright and cheerful room. Try the mixed antipasti plate (L8,000). A complete meal runs L30,000–35,000, but you can get away for less. On warm summer evenings, linger over dinner at an outdoor table and watch various music shows in the piazza. *V. Firenze 6, tel. 091/329143. Off V. Roma, just before C. Vittorio Emanuele. Closed Sun.*

Osteria al Ferro di Cavallo. The atmosphere at this blue-collar lunch spot is hectic and lively. There's no menu, but the *polpo* and *sarde* dishes are dependable. A full lunch consists of salad, pasta, bread, meat or fish, and beer or wine, all for L7,000–L12,000. *V. Venezia 20, tel. 091/331835. Off V. Roma, 1 block north of C. Vittorio Emanuele. Cash only. Closed Sun.*

Trattoria Primavera. Primavera has received excellent reviews in New York and Italy, so it's downright shocking that the prices are still affordable. The food here lives up to its reputation; try spaghetti *alla nera di seppie* (in squid ink sauce; L8,000) or grilled tuna (L11,000). It's best to make reservations about two days in advance, but you can try your luck and just stop by. *P. Bologni 4, tel. 091/329408. From Quattro Canti, walk west down C. Vittorio Emanuele. Cash only. Closed Tues.*

In the austere '60s in Sicily, almond pastries were a source of income for convents; you would put your coins in the "wheel," a revolving hatch, and out came the delectable treats. Pastry production in convents is documented to the 16th century.

Trattoria Stella. In the courtyard of a seemingly abandoned palatial hotel, this is one of the best places to eat cheaply and well in the old district of Palermo. The penne *alla disgraziata* (with butter, ricotta, peppers, and eggplant, L10,000) is more than a full meal, but if you're hungry enough, try the delicious calamari *ripieni* (stuffed with a secret-recipe filling and roasted on the outdoor grill, L14,000). Reservations are imperative. *V. Alloro 104, tel. 091/6161136. From V. Roma, walk east on V. Divisi through P. Rivoluzione, turn right onto V. Alloro. Closed Sun. eve. and Mon.*

NEAR PIAZZA CASTELNUOVO

UNDER L20,000 • La Gondola–Da Pippo. This thoroughly funky restaurant has photographs of Bruce Lee and Telly Savalas on the wall, fresh fish in the cooler by the door, and a serve-yourself antipasti bar on a bookcase in back. Mamma Pippo runs the kitchen and turns out dishes like spinach- and ricotta-stuffed ravioli, fettucine with little shrimps and rucola, and succulent grilled squid. A complete meal is only L20,000 (meat)–L25,000 (fish). *V. Principe di Scordia 144, tel. 091/320488. From P. Castelnuovo, walk on V. Emerico Amari toward the port, right on V. Principe di Scordia. No dinner Sun. Closed Mon.*

Hosteria al Duar. Sample Tunisian delicacies (complete meal L16,000) like *merghes* (sausage) or *cebtia* (a dumpling of fried potatoes, greens, and spices) in this long, cozy dining room or outside at the sidewalk tables. *V. A. Gravina 31–33, near V. Emerico Amari, tel. 091/329560. Closed Mon.*

Osteria Fratelli Lo Bianco. This local joint has been going strong for more than 90 years, thanks to its simple, delicious Palermitan dishes like pasta *Tarantina* (with mussels and tomato sauce) and *sgombretti a beccafico:* fresh, cold fillets of fish wrapped around a paste of bread crumbs, lemon juice, oil, and pressed grapes. Dishes run from L5,000 to L10,000. The brusque waiters will tell you what's on for the day in rapid-fire Italian; pay attention, because they're not coming back. *V. Emerico Amari 104, tel. 091/585816. Walk toward port from P. Castelnuovo. Cash only. Closed Sun.*

Ristorante-Pizzeria Italia. It's considered the best pizzeria in Palermo, which explains the long lines of expectant locals. Sit outside in a shady alleyway and choose from 25 kinds of pizza (L5,000–L8,000). Don't miss the *Greca*, with fresh tomatoes, mushrooms, onions, eggplant, and Parmesan. *V. dell'Orologio 54, tel. 091/589885. From Quattro Canti, take V. Maqueda north and turn right just before Teatro Massimo. Cash only. Closed Mon. and mid-Aug.–early Sept.*

PASTICCERIE

The gastronomic world is forever indebted to Palermo for the invention of gelato, but other than its historical appeal, the gelato you'll find here is pretty darn similar to what you'll find all over Italy. Pastries are another matter—Palermo is known for having the nation's greatest sweet shops. Of these, two stand out. **Alba** (P. Don Bosco 7/C, tel. 091/309016; closed Mon.), in upper-middle-class suburban Palermo, is worth the trek to sample *babà* (cake soaked in sweet rum) or assorted *semifreddi* (cold mousses). Closer to the center, **Gran Café Nobel** (V. della Libertà 35, tel. 091/6110750) is an elegant tearoom specializing in seasonal fruit tarts and cannoli.

WORTH SEEING

Palermo's attractions are scattered among the labyrinthine streets and alleyways of its four medieval quarters. Although neighborhood identity is no longer as strong as in days past, the poorer La Kalsa and Vucciria quarters are associated with rubble and grime because of the still-unrepaired damage wrought during World War II. Many of these sooty tenement houses, some without running water, are actually crumbling villas of an earlier wealthy class. Traces of the buildings' original glamour come in snatches— a neoclassical window touched up with brown stucco, a Baroque pink staircase standing alone in a deserted courtyard. The four medieval quarters are notorious for pickpockets and purse snatchers. At night, Jekyll-and-Hyde Palermo puts on its ugly face: watch your belongings, put away jewelry and watches, and stick to main streets. During the day, however, it's quite safe to wander the narrow, mainly pedestrian streets of the city center.

LA KALSA

GALLERIA REGIONALE DELLA SICILIA • Housed in the 15th-century Palazzo Abatellis, this spectacular art gallery contains paintings and sculpture from the 11th through the 17th centuries. The most striking piece is the massive, pock-marked, 16th-century fresco *Trionfo della Morte,* in which the Angel of Death gallops through a crowd of wealthy folk and turns them stiff and blue with his arrows. *V. Alloro 4, near waterfront, tel. 091/6164317. Admission L2,000. Open Mon.–Sat. 9–1:30 (Tues. and Thurs. also 3–5:30), Sun. 9–12:30.*

LA MARTORANA (SANTA MARIA DELL'AMMIRAGLIO) • Originally founded in 1143 by the Norman admiral George of Antioch, this chapel later became part of a convent established by a Spanish noblewoman, Eloisa Martorana. The Baroque exterior was refurbished in 1688, but the interior still houses some 12th-century Byzantine mosaics. The political meets the spiritual in two mosaics near the entrance. One shows the admiral offering the church to the Madonna, and the other has Christ crowning King Roger de Hauteville, who conquered Palermo in 1061. *P. Bellini 3, off V. Maqueda near Quattro Canti, tel. 091/6161692. Admission free. Open Mon.–Sat. 9:30–1 and 3:30–5:30.*

MUSEO INTERNAZIONALE DELLE MARIONETTE • Palermo has succeeded in the difficult task of taking an almost-lost tradition and making it spooky and vibrant. It's hard to overstate the cultural importance of puppets in Sicily: The lengthy and often brutal history of the island was handed down through generations by the dolls' violent and comical antics. The displays—illuminated by eerie, undulating lights—feature the local hero Orlando and his archenemy Saladino, but they aren't limited to Sicilian puppets—it's like Disneyland's "It's a Small World" without the annoying singing. *V. Butera 1, tel. 091/328060. Admission L5,000. Open weekdays 9–1 and 4–7, Sat. 9–1.*

PALAZZO CHIARAMONTE • This imposing Arabic-Norman structure, built in 1307 by the influential Chiaramonte family, is the second-largest palace in Palermo. More to the point, in the late 17th and 18th centuries it served as the seat of the Inquisition in Sicily. Today the palazzo can be viewed only from the outside. *P. Marina 61, near Giardini Garibaldi.*

ALBERGHERIA

PALAZZO DEI NORMANNI • On a slight hill above the gardens of the palm-filled Villa Bonanno, this former Saracen castle was transformed into a royal palace by Sicily's 11th-century Norman king, Roger de Hauteville. During the next century, in the reign of Roger II, it became famous throughout medieval Europe as a center of culture and the arts. Today it houses the Sicilian Parliament and is closed to the public (thanks to a spate of political bombings in 1992). Fortunately, the **Cappella Palatina** remains open. The French writer Guy de Maupassant called the chapel "the finest religious jewel dreamt of by human thought," and it's hard to disagree. Constructed between 1130 and 1143, every inch of the chapel's interior is covered with brilliant Byzantine mosaics, except for its honeycomb wooden ceiling, itself ornate. Upstairs are the royal apartments, including the **Sala di Ruggero** (King Roger's Hall), which has some outstanding mosaics of hunters and their prey. You'll need a simple authorization from the Ufficio di Questura for a *visita di Palazzo* (tel. 091/6561737) to visit the apartments—call a day in advance. Come early to avoid crowds. *P. Indipendenza, tel. 091/6961111. Admission free. Open weekdays 9–noon and 3–5, Sat. 9–noon, Sun. 9–10 and noon–1.*

SAN GIOVANNI DEGLI EREMITI • This 12th-century church, topped with five pink domes, was designed by Norman-employed Arab architects and built on the foundations of a mosque. The real attraction, however, isn't the exotic architecture. It's the ruined 13th-century cloisters and peaceful gardens—wild masses of flowering vines, roses, and drooping palms—that surround the building. *V. dei Benedettini 3, across from Palazzo dei Normanni, to right of royal palace entrance, tel. 091/6515019. Admission free. Open Mon.–Sat. 9–1 (Mon. and Thurs. also 3–6), Sun. 9– 12:30.*

CAPO

DUOMO • This imposing 12th-century cathedral is a grab bag of architectural styles. Of the original church, only the twin towers, gigantic cupola, and triple apse remain, appearing as if they were transplanted from a completely different structure. The interior, often renovated and now uninteresting, has an inlaid-marble astrological clock stretching diagonally from the altar toward the right aisle. Every day at noon, a dusty shaft of light indicates the position of the sun in relation to the signs of the zodiac. The **treasury,** to the right of the altar, displays the gold tiara of Constance of Aragon and a variety of fine jewelry, among other things. *C. Vittorio Emanuele. Cathedral open Mon.– Sat. 7–noon and 4–7 (in summer 7–7), Sun. 8–1:30 and 4–7. Treasury admission L1,000. Treasury open daily 9–noon and 4–5:30.*

TEATRO MASSIMO • This monumental neoclassical theater was the second-largest opera house in the world—only Paris's was bigger—when it was built at the turn of the century. Its lion-flanked staircase was the backdrop for one of the cinema's worst-delivered lines: Sophia Coppola's "Dad?" from the death scene in *The Godfather III.* The theater finally reopened in May 1997 after undergoing years of restoration. A program of concerts and operas is presented throughout the year. *P. Verdi, at intersection of V. Maqueda and V. Cavour, tel. 091/6053111.*

VUCCIRIA

MERCATO DELLA VUCCIRIA • Palermo's Vucciria market is known throughout Sicily for its animated merchants and congested alleyways. Everywhere you turn there's some boisterous thug holding aloft a head of lettuce, a slab of meat, or the bloody head of a freshly butchered swordfish. Come in the morning—after lunch things really die down—and snack on olives while you shop for contraband cigarettes. Watch your wallet *carefully* lest it fall into the hands of resident thieves. After a morning of hectic shopping, you can sample market-bought fish and vegetables in one of the restaurants on nearby Vicolo Mezzani. *Off V. Roma, between C. Vittorio Emanuele and P. San Domenico. Open daily early morning– early afternoon.*

MUSEO ARCHEOLOGICO REGIONALE • A 16th-century convent houses Palermo's vast archaeological museum. Artifacts dredged from the Mediterranean—including Roman and Phoenician anchors—are on display in the cloisters, and in an adjacent hall you'll see 5th-century BC lion-headed drip stones from Himera (the gaping mouths and curved tongues were used to drain water from rooftops). The most famous exhibits are in the **Salone di Selinunte,** which has blocky but beautiful 5th- and 6th-century BC metopes from Selinunte. The friezes displayed here (also taken from the temples) illustrate Greek myths. *P. Olivella 4, off V. Roma behind main post office, tel. 091/6620220. Take Bus 101, 107, or 122. Admission L2,000. Open Mon.–Sat. 9–2 (Tues. and Fri. also 3–7), Sun. 9–1.*

CHEAP THRILLS

FESTIVALS

Palermo honors its patron saint during the **Festino di Santa Rosalia** (Festival of St. Rosalia), which begins every July 11 with a raucous parade down Corso Vittorio Emanuele. The parade highlight is the 65-ft-long, 82-ft-high flower- and musician-bedecked float of St. Rosalia. On the final day, July 15, the saint's relics are carried through the city and a massive fireworks display follows. In between, Palermo goes on a five-day eating and drinking binge. In November the **Festività dei Morti,** on Via Bara all'Olivella, brings children and other greedy souls to the outdoor fair of toys and marzipan fruit where everyone (traditionally) gets a gift.

LA VECCHIA DELL'ACETO

In the early 18th century, a woman in Palermo known as La Vecchia dell'Aceto (The Old Lady of the Vinegar) sold different types of vinegar—red, balsamic, fruit scented, even medicinal—at the Vucciria market. One toxic blend was used for scalp lice. It was also used by young matrons to kill pests of a different kind: their husbands. After years, somebody finally ratted, and La Vecchia was arrested. At her trial, she claimed to have done in 350 husbands, a quantity that so infuriated the local (male) authorities that they skinned her alive and had her drawn and quartered in Piazza Marina.

AFTER DARK

The city of Palermo sponsors a toll-free info line (tel. 1670/14196) with tips on restaurants, bars, live music, and other cultural activities. It's staffed weekdays 6 PM–11 PM, weekends 3–midnight.

BARS

Palermitan nightlife is complicated by the historical center's seedy air—if you're looking for a friendly dive bar, you're going to be looking for a long time. Instead, head to more upscale neighborhoods—try the fashionable spots along Via Principe di Belmonte (off Via Roma). **Liberty Pub** (V. N. Cozzo 20, tel. 091/329385; closed Wed.), off Via Maqueda just past Teatro Massimo, is a cool place to grab a cheeseburger (that's right) and a beer while contemplating the latest Italian disco hits. On warm summer nights, all of Palermo heads out to drink and stroll along the strand at **Mondello,** a dirty little beach to the north of the city. To get here, hop on Bus 327 from the train station. If you plan to return to the city after 11 PM, you're pretty much stuck with the L20,000 taxi fare.

BALLET, OPERA, AND THEATER

You've missed the point if you're in Palermo and don't check out a puppet performance, however unappealing that may sound to you. Most are held at the Museo Internazionale delle Marionette (*see* Worth Seeing, *above*). Other show spots include the **Opera dei Pupi** (V. Bara all'Olivella 95, tel. 091/323400), across from the Museo Archeologico Regionale; the **Teatro Marionette Ippogrifo** (Vicolo Ragusi 6), off Corso Vittorio Emanuele just past Quattro Canti heading west; or the very reputable **Compagnia Bradamante di Anna Cuticchio** (V. Lombardia 25, tel. 091/6259223), past the Giardino Inglese off Via della Libertà. Tickets start at L10,000 and peak at L30,000; box offices open one hour before show time. Palermo's opera and ballet season runs January–June. The primary venue is the massive fresco-smothered **Teatro Politeama Garibaldi** (P. Ruggero Settimo), where tickets start at L35,000. Contact the box office (tel. 091/6053321; open Tues.–Sat. 10–1 and 5–7) for info.

NEAR PALERMO

MONTE PELLEGRINO

Rising almost 2,000 ft above Palermo, Monte Pellegrino is a famous city landmark and the place to come for panoramic views of the coast. Bus 106 (L1,500) from Piazza Castelnuovo climbs the winding road up the mountain to **Santuario di Santa Rosalia** (open Mon.–Sat. 7–12:30 and 2–7, Sun. 7 AM–8 PM), a limestone cave in which Palermo's patron saint, St. Rosalia, is said to have once lived in hermetic seclusion. Today the grotto houses a chapel where ailing pilgrims come to pray and cleanse their sins with the waters from what they believe is the miraculous underground spring.

MONREALE

If you have time for only one day trip from Palermo, head 9 km (5½ mi) southwest to Monreale, a small medieval town with some first-rate architecture. Positioned on a flat spot in the hills above Palermo, the town is eminently wanderable, with public fountains, small pedestrian piazzas, and quiet caffè-lined streets. The only real sightseeing attraction is the stupendous **Duomo,** but what an attraction it is. The cathedral's original facade—comprised of blind arches and an 18th-century portico—pales in comparison to what lies behind the large 12th-century bronze doors: mosaics that rank among the most beautiful in the world. These were composed between 1174 and 1176 by Islamic artisans commissioned by the Norman king William II. All told there are 130 panels covering some 6,000 square yards. The most striking mosaic is reserved for the Messiah—a huge and gorgeous Christ Pantocrator (Master of the Universe) figure, whose right hand alone is 6½ ft tall. Don't overlook the cloisters, the world's most resplendent in the Romanesque style, replete with Islamic mosaic zig-zags, squiggly arabesque carvings, and a Moorish fountain. *P. del Duomo, tel. 091/6404413. From P. della Indipendenza, take Bus 389; end of the line is right in front of cathedral. Admission free. Open daily 8:30–noon and 3:30–6.*

BAGHERIA

During the 17th and 18th centuries, tiny Bagheria became a summer hideaway for Palermo's noblest families, who subsequently endowed the town and the surrounding countryside with grand Baroque villas. Right in the town center is **Villa Palagonia,** the most famous one, decorated with a bizarre array of grotesque statues commissioned by the crippled prince of Palagonia; the statues, it seems, are caricatures of his wife's many lovers. From Palermo there are several rail connections (17 daily, 10 min, L3,000) to Bagheria. *Villa Palagonia, P. Garibaldi 3, 10 min from station along C. Umberto I, tel. 091/ 932088. Admission L1,000. Open daily 9–12:30 and 4–7.*

USTICA

It's only 60 km (37 mi) north of Palermo, but this volcanic island feels light-years away from the chaos of the capital. The main town, up a steep hill from the port, is charming enough, with its whitewashed houses and ubiquitous wall murals—contributed by the artists who use the island as a retreat. The real attraction here is the sea—Ustica is Italy's largest marine reserve and one of the best diving spots in the Mediterranean. Numerous dive outfits will take you down and show you around for similar prices (L50,000 per person, plus L30,000 for full equipment rental). No beaches hug the shores, but you can take a dip off **Punta Spalmatore,** on the west coast, accessible from town via the minibus (L1,000) that circles the island hourly.

BASICS • Ferries and hydrofoils from Palermo (*see* Coming and Going, *above*) dock downhill from **Piazza Vito Longo,** the port's main plaza. From Palermo, **Siremar** (V. Francesco Crispi 120, tel. 091/ 582403) serves Ustica by ferry (Mon.–Sat., 2 hrs 20 min, L16,700) and hydrofoil (2 daily, 1¼ hrs, L32,100). If you miss the last boat to Palermo, spend the night at **Hotel Patrice** (V. Rifugio 23, tel. 091/ 8449053), where a large double costs L85,000. The Centro Accoglienza della Riserva Naturale Marina (P. Vito Longo, tel. 091/8449456), which doubles as a **visitor information center,** can also arrange accommodations and diving expeditions.

TYRRHENIAN COAST

The Tyrrhenian coast stretches between Palermo and Milazzo, encompassing rocky coves, sandy beaches, ancient ruins, and—sorry to say—upscale resort communities. A train runs the length of the coast, making it easy to jump off at less touristed nooks. **Cefalù** is not one of these; it's the best-known and most crowded seaside town, worth a day or so if only for its photogenic jumble of medieval streets. The curving beaches of **Capo d'Orlando** are less crowded (and cheaper). The only reason to go to the dull port town of **Milazzo** is to catch ferries to the volcanically active archipelago of the **Aeolian Islands,** a refuge offering mud baths, pristine snorkeling waters, and hikes to fiery cauldrons of lava. Throughout the region, lodging is difficult to find only in July and August, when throngs from mainland Italy and France drive prices up and availability down.

CREEPY CAPPUCCINI

Entombed within Palermo's Catacombe dei Cappuccini (V. Cappuccini, Bus 389 from C. Vittorio Emanuele; donation L1,000; open daily 9–noon and 3–5) are more than 8,000 ghostly mummies displayed behind flimsy mesh screens. From the early 16th to late 19th centuries, the Capuchin monks dried and embalmed cadavers, which were then dressed and inserted upright into individual wall niches. The Capuchins took their job pretty seriously, dividing the mummies according to earthly occupation, gender, and social class. You'll need a strong stomach to view the glass-encased, mummified small children.

CEFALU

This fishing-village-turned-resort is the Tyrrhenian coast's main attraction, not least because it's only an hour by train from Palermo—and also because there's a Club Med resort within 3 km (2 mi). Cefalù's cheesy beachfront is easily forgotten amid the well-tended decay of the centro storico—a labyrinth of medieval streets pressed between the sea and an immense granite cliff, which locals call **La Rocca**. Number one on your to-do list is a sunset hike up La Rocca, followed by a drink or gelato on **Piazza del Duomo**. The highlight of the busy square is Cefalù's **Duomo** (open daily 8–noon and 3:30–6:30; no shorts allowed), founded in 1131 by Roger II, ostensibly in gratitude for having survived a nasty shipwreck. Roger didn't skimp on decorations, and inside you'll find some of the finest mosaics in Sicily, in a Byzantine tradition similar to that of Monreale's Duomo, with a Christ Pantocrator in the center.

At the end of Corso Ruggero, a left turn onto Via Porto Salvo and then onto Via Vittorio Emanuele will bring you past the **Porta Pescara**, one of four original city gates still standing. It's currently draped in fishnets, with various other tools of the fisherman's trade hanging from the ceiling in an informal homage to Cefalù's humbler origins. Keep walking north to reach Cefalù's **beach**—a long, narrow strip of pale sand.

BASICS

The main tourist office, **AAST** (C. Ruggero 77, tel. 0921/421050; open weekdays 8–2 and 4–7; Sat. 8–2, Sun. 9–1), is equipped with maps and lists of accommodations. The **post office** (V. Vazzana 2, tel. 0921/921703) is between the train station and the beach in the new part of town.

COMING AND GOING

Stazione Ferroviaria (P. Stazione, tel. 1478/88088) doubles as the train and bus terminal and is within walking distance of both the old and the new parts of town. Hourly trains run to Milazzo (2 hrs, L14,000) and Palermo (1 hr, L7,000). **SAIS** buses connect Cefalù with Castelbuono (7 daily, 40 min, L4,000). You'll notice that few streets in Cefalù have signs, and if you spend your time poring over a map, there's a good chance you'll get run down by a scooter. Just remember that when you're facing the ocean (north), the new part of town is west, the old part of town and La Rocca east. One street you'll encounter is **Viale Lungomare**, which runs along the beach before becoming **Via Vittorio Emanuele** in the old part of town. Via Matteotti runs in front of the post office, Via Umberto behind it; they meet at **Piazza Garibaldi** and continue east under the name **Corso Ruggero**, the old part of town's main drag.

WHERE TO SLEEP

Cefalù's Club Med status means that three- and four-star hotels abound. Skip 'em and head for **Pensione La Giara** (V. Veterani 40, north of C. Ruggero, tel. and fax 0921/22518), which keeps big, clean rooms, all with private baths. Doubles are L55,000–L115,000 depending on season, and credit cards are accepted. **Locanda Cangelosi** (V. Umberto 28, tel. 0921/21591) is on a second story overlooking busy Via Umberto. Large doubles—plus a douse in the communal bathroom's strong, hot water—cost L65,000.

CAMPING • Cefalù's two campgrounds are actually 3 km (2 mi) to the west in Località Ogliastrillo. Fortunately, it's an easy bus ride: take any bus labeled LASCARI from Stazione Ferroviaria. At **Camping Costa**

Ponente (tel. 0921/20085; closed Oct.–Apr.) you can sleep in a citrus grove that keeps things cool, sitting on a cliff overlooking the sea. Perks include a pizzeria, a swimming pool, almost clean bathrooms, and beach access. The rates are L7,500 per person and L7,000 per tent; prices increase by L1,000 from mid-June to mid-August. Adjacent **Camping Sanfilippo** (tel. 0921/20181; L6,000 per tent, L6,500 per person) has beach access but is shabbier.

WHERE TO EAT

There are plenty of markets along Corso Ruggero, and the fruit stand at the east end of Viale Lungomare has reasonably priced produce. **Ristorante da Nino** (V. Bagni 11, tel. 0921/422582; closed Tues.) is among the cheapest spots on the *lungomare*. Pizza and pasta start at L5,000, the antipasti buffet at L8,000. For a splurge, head to **Gabbiano** (V. Lungomare Giardina 17, tel. 0921/4211495) for seafood specialties that range from L15,000 to L30,000.

NEAR CEFALÙ

CASTELBUONO

The winding streets of Castelbuono, 25 km (15 mi) south of Cefalù, are spread on a steep hill under the watch of the town's weather-beaten 14th-century **castello** (tel. 0921/76268). Castelbuono's relaxed, mountainous atmosphere makes a fine change from the resort culture on the coast, and there are plenty of hiking trails to tackle in the surrounding Madonie Mountains—at least for those equipped with more than just Teva shoes. A topographic map is available from the **Ufficio Tecnico** (open weekdays 8:30–1:30 and 4:30–7:30) in the town hall. A favorite hike is the five-hour climb to Piano Battaglia and **Rifugio Marini** (tel. 0921/649994), where dorm beds fetch L25,000 a night. Less strenuous is the two-hour climb from Castelbuono to **Rifugio Francesco Crispi** (tel. 0921/672279), where full pension is required at L58,000–L64,000 per person per day. Catch buses to Castelbuono (5 daily, 1 hr, L6,100) from Cefalù's train station.

CAPO D'ORLANDO

With tree-lined streets, lively piazzas, and uncrowded sand-and-pebble beaches, Capo d'Orlando is the perfect vacation spot, even if the atmosphere is un-Sicilian—you could just as well be in southern California or the south of France. The **AAST tourist office** (V. Pave 71, at V. Crispi, tel. 0941/912784; open weekdays 8–1 and 4:30–7:30) tries to bill Capo d'Orlando as a the "city of history and culture," and glossy brochures tout the town's 3,000-year history. But Capo d'Orlando is a beach town first and foremost. It borders a long sweep of deep, sandy shore that becomes more rocky and inexplicably more popular 1½ km (1 mi) to the east, at **Baio San Gregorio**. It's also an alternative gateway to the Aeolian Islands; hydrofoils make daily trips (1 hr, L11,000) to Vulcano and Lipari from Capo d'Orlando mid-June–September.

At least during Capo d'Orlando's two annual religious festivals you can discover a bit of local color. The protectress of fishermen is celebrated every August 15 during the **Feast of Maria Santissima di Porto Salvo,** with a unique boat parade on Capo d'Orlando's waters. A weeklong landlocked party at the end of October toasts the **Madonna of Capo d'Orlando.**

WHERE TO SLEEP, EAT, AND BE MERRY • Especially during festival season, book in advance at the spruced-up **Nuovo Hotel Faro** (V. Libertà 7, east end of Lungomare, tel. 0941/902466), the town's only remotely affordable hotel (doubles L85,000). The beachside **Camping Santa Rosa** (tel. 0941/901723, fax 094/912384), 3 km (2 mi) west of town, charges L10,000 per tent and L8,000 per person. Most of Capo d'Orlando's restaurants are outdoor-pizzeria clones where a pizza will run you L5,000–L12,000. In summer you can get down and boogie until the wee hours at **La Tartaruga** (Lido San Gregorio, tel. 0941/955012), reputed to be the hottest disco in the province. Covers are steep (L10,000–L20,000), so consider doing what the locals do and cross the street to **Bar Mami Papi** (Lido San Gregorio, no phone), where you can listen to music for free.

MILAZZO

With all the spots along the Tyrrhenian coast, Milazzo should not top your list. It's little more than the most convenient jumping-off point for the Aeolian Islands, but you could do far worse than sleep here for a night if you are stranded. As for the beaches and the town's 13th-century **castello** (V. Duomo Antico, no phone), which doubles as an open-air theater in summer, both are overshadowed by Milazzo's massive oil refinery and gloomy industrial port.

BASICS

The well-stocked **tourist office** (P. Duilio 20, north of port, tel. 090/9222865; open Mon.–Sat. 8–2 and 4–7) has an outdoor bulletin board with information about the surrounding archaeological sites, timetables for Aeolian-bound ferries and hydrofoils, and a nifty pocket-size map of the town. The **post office** (P. Duilio 2, tel. 090/9281200; open weekdays 8:10–6:30, Sat. 8:10–1:20), a stone's throw from the tourist office, cashes AmEx traveler's checks. **Monte dei Paschi di Siena** (V. M. Regis 2, tel. 090/9283288; open weekdays 8:30–1:30) is one of the many banks near the post office where you can change money and use a Cirrus ATM. The local Telecom phone center is in the multiservice **Pro Milazzo** shop (P. Quilio; open Mon.–Sat. 8:30–noon and 4–7:30).

COMING AND GOING

Milazzo's **train station,** 5 km (3 mi) southeast of town, has service to Messina (27 daily, 45 min, L5,000), Cefalù (17 daily, 1¾ hrs, L14,000), and Palermo (18 daily, 3 hrs, L17,000). **Giuntabus** (V. Terranova 8, tel. 090/673782) runs hourly to Messina (45 min, L5,500). **AST** city buses (L600) run every 30 minutes or so from the train station to the town center; tickets and schedules are available at the station's bar.

BY BOAT • Making sense of Milazzo's various *traghetto* and *aliscafo* schedules can be maddening— departure times change every two weeks. The main routes are Milazzo–Lipari and Milazzo–Vulcano; from Lipari boats generally go Salina–Panarea–Stromboli or Salina–Filicudi–Alicudi. In summer, ferries run every 40 minutes between 6 AM and 9 PM, and the much quicker and more expensive hydrofoils leave about every 20 minutes; the frequency drops to every two hours in winter. Numerous traghetto and aliscafo lines serve the islands, and the only noticeable differences between them are departure times. For aliscafi to the islands, try **SNAV** (V. Luciano Rizzo 14, tel. 090/9284509) or **Siremar** (V. dei Mille 33, tel. 090/9283242), which also runs a few traghetti. **Navigazione Generale Italiana** (V. dei Mille 26, tel. 090/9283415) runs three daily traghetti that ply between all of the islands.

In high season, **Aliscafi** run to Vulcano (18 daily, 1 hr, L20,000), Lipari (19 daily, 1 hr, L21,500), Salina (10 daily, 1½ hrs, L25,000), Panarea (5 daily, 2 hrs, L25,800), Stromboli (daily, 1½ hrs, L31,300), Filicudi (3 daily, 2 hrs, L33,800), and Alicudi (3 daily, 2½ hrs, L41,700). **Traghetti** prices and times are about half as much and twice as long in high season: Vulcano (6 daily, 1½ hrs, L11,700), Lipari (6 daily, 2 hrs, L12,600), Salina (3 daily, 3½ hrs, L16,000), Panarea (2 daily, 5 hrs, L15,100), Stromboli (2 daily, 5 hrs, L20,100), Filicudi (2 daily, 5 hrs, L26,300), and Alicudi (daily, 5½ hrs, L24,300).

WHERE TO SLEEP AND EAT

Prepare for a barrage of HOTEL signs near the ferry docks. The good news is that with so many choices, you shouldn't have to pay more than L60,000 for a double. If you want *any* peace and quiet, ask for a room off the street. There's plenty of room at the **Hotel California** (V. del Sole 9, 3 blocks west of ferry dock, tel. 090/9221389), where clean, simple doubles with bath go for L70,000. If you loathe The Eagles, cross the street to **Hotel Central** (V. del Sole 8, tel. 090/9281043), a smaller—but no less respectable— hotel. Doubles without bath cost L75,000 in July and August. **Hotel Cosenz** (V. E. Cosenz 5, 1 block west of V. Umberto I, tel. 090/9282996) has a handful of doubles (L60,000) away from the madness of the port area yet still within walking distance of Milazzo's bars and restaurants. The American-style **Punta Convenienza** market (V. del Sole 34; closed Sun.) is a cheap place to stock up on groceries.

AEOLIAN ISLANDS

The seven Aeolian Islands (Isole Eolie) have been inhabited continuously for more than 3,000 years, and Aeolian natives have understandably developed a fearful reverence for their temperamental, volcanic homeland. Ancient legends speak of the islands as the "mouths of hell," the home of fire-breathing gods and goddesses who guarded the gateway to a fiery netherworld. No doubt these tales grew in recognition of the smoldering volcanoes that even today belch steam and ash over the Mediterranean. Then as now, the islands and their inhabitants face the constant threat of extermination—be it from a raging lava flow or a volcanic quake.

Of course, this hasn't stemmed the flood of tourists, nor has it hindered the development of resorts and exclusive health spas, the islands' economic mainstays. To some, it seems, the Aeolian Islands mean little more than radioactive mud baths and package tours. But the islands are still wild enough to seem indifferent to the tourists approaching their shores.

With its health resorts and hiking, **Vulcano** is a fun but expensive island—a definite easy day trip unless you're loaded with cash. Cheaper **Lipari** is a lot more developed and crowded, so you may have to fight for bed space in summer—at least it hosts the island chain's only youth hostel. There's not much to do on **Salina, Filicudi,** or **Alicudi** except hike or bask in the sun— good news if you hate crowds, bad news if you're looking for something to do after dark. Of all the Aeolian Islands, posh **Panarea** is the most Grecian, with whitewashed houses and smooth black-sand beaches. If you're a snorkeling or scuba diving enthusiast, come hither. Lonely, dramatic **Stromboli** is an active volcano that you can climb or observe from the sea, depending on your thrill threshold. On nearly all the islands, windsurfing equipment and boats are available for rent.

BASICS

Vulcano and Lipari have their own tourist offices, and other islands sometimes open AAST branches in summer, but most of the info you'll need is in the free, superhelpful booklet *Ospitalità in Blu* (*Hospitality in Blue*), available at the tourist offices in Milazzo and the islands. Transportation between and to the Aeolian Islands is efficient and easy, and most island life revolves around the ferry ports, so you're usually near lodging, food, and tourist info upon arrival. You can buy boat tickets at travel agencies and at the dockside ticket kiosks in Milazzo, a jumping-off point in Sicily (*see* Coming and Going *in* Milazzo, *above*). Ferries also leave from the eastern **Messina Marittima** (tel. 1478/88088), but fares are cheaper from Milazzo. Interisland traghetto trips are generally an hour long and cost L7,000–L11,000. Aliscafi take about half as long and cost twice as much.

In winter, a thick haze envelops the Aeolian Islands, adding to their mystery and driving out sun worshipers. In summer, the intense Mediterranean sun brings things to a halt, brightening the white houses against a sparkling blue sea.

LIPARI

Lipari is the largest and most heavily visited of the Aeolian Islands and the chain's economic focal point: the large-scale pumice and obsidian quarries in the north shore's **Aquacalda** make it the richest and most influential of the islands. And because of the island's many tourist facilities—including cheap lodgings and restaurants—it makes a good base for exploring the Aeolian chain. The port's pastel-colored houses and sunny piazzas are enchanting, but if you're looking for isolation and quiet beaches, head someplace else.

Local buses (L1,500) circle Lipari every half hour in summer and give good views of Sicily and of a 17th-century cliff-top **Castello** (V. Castello), Lipari's grand attraction south of the ferry docks and just north of the hydrofoil port. Inside the castle is Lipari's lone youth hostel (*see below*) and surprisingly one of the best archaeological museums in Europe, the **Museo Archeologico Regionale di Lipari** (tel. 090/9880174; admission free; open Mon.–Sat. 9–2), with archaeological finds from various sites in the archipelago. As this particular site was occupied continuously from Neolithic times to the Roman Age, archaeologists have been able to use the layers of artifacts as a time line to date other Mediterranean finds.

BASICS

Virtually all of Lipari's tourist services are clustered together on the port's main drag, Via Vittorio Emanuele. **AAST** (V. Vittorio Emanuele 202, tel. 090/9880095; open June–Oct., Mon.–Sat. 8–2 and 4–10, Sun. 8–2; Sept.–May, Mon.–Sat. 9–2) will give you the skinny on all the islands with their ever-so-handy brochure, *Ospitalità in Blu*. **Banca del Sud** (open weekdays 8:30–1:30) has the best exchange rate and handles Visa cash advances; after hours, head to **Menalda Tours** (open daily 9–1 and 3–9). The **post office** (tel. 090/9811270; open weekdays 8:30–6, Sat. 8:30–1) also exchanges money.

WHERE TO SLEEP

Locanda Salina (V. Garibaldi 18, just north of hydrofoil dock, tel. 090/9812332) has big, comfy rooms in the heart of town. Doubles go for L60,000–L70,000. At **Hotel Europeo** (V. Vittorio Emanuele 98, tel. 090/9811589) doubles cost L70,000–L100,000. **Augustus** (V. Ausonia 16, off north end of V. Vittorio Emanuele, tel. 090/9811232) is a steal in the off-season, when doubles—all with baths and TVs—are L90,000. From May to September, though, prices double. For low-budget but decent lodging, inquire at the port—you may be met by locals as well—about *affitacamere* (rooms in private homes).

HOSTEL • Ostello della Gioventù. The setting for the archipelago's only hostel couldn't be better; it's in the Castello above Lipari's port, with sweeping views of the sea. Beds cost L15,000 per night, sheets and cold shower included. Breakfast costs L3,000, but use of the kitchen is free, or dinner is available for L15,000. *Castello, V. Castello, tel. 090/9811540. 100 beds in summer, closed in winter. Cash only. Midnight curfew, lockout 10–1. Reception open daily 7–9 and noon–midnight. Showers.*

CAMPING • The town of Cannetto, 3 km (2 mi) north of Lipari's port, has long pebble beaches, a host of waterfront bars and restaurants, and the island's only campground, **Campeggio Baia Unci** (Località Cannetto, tel. 090/9811909; closed Dec.–Feb.). You'll pay L12,000 per person, plus L7,000–L19,000 per tent, depending on the season.

WHERE TO EAT

On restaurant-lined Via Vittorio Emanuele you'll find the best bargains at the fruit vendors, the well-stocked market **Upim Supermercato** (V. Vittorio Emanuele 202; closed Sun.), and the handful of pizzerias that sell slices by weight. The best real restaurant is **Ristorante Pizzeria Pescecane** (V. Vittorio Emanuele 223, 090/9812706; closed Thurs. off-season), where an eggplant-parmesan pizza costs L9,000. Across the street at **Ritrovo Sottomonastero** (V. Vittorio Emanuele 232, tel. 090/9880720), sample marinated octopus salad (L9,000) or whatever the temperamental chef feels like preparing for you.

OUTDOOR ACTIVITIES

Rent a bike or a moped and explore via the well-surfaced road that circles Lipari. Small motorized numbers are available from **Roberto Foti** (V. F. Crispi 31, 150 ft north of ferry port, no phone), where full-day rentals start at L35,000, plus a L100,000 deposit on a credit card and your passport. Informal bike rentals (L5,000–L10,000 a day) can be arranged with the many eager entrepreneurs at the hydrofoil port. **Cannetto,** 20 minutes north of town, is the most popular beach spot, while the **Spiaggia Bianca** is the most photographed; both are accessible via Urso buses (V. Cappuccini 29, tel. 090/9811262), which also run L5,000 tours of the island in summer. Diving excursions can be organized through various competing diving centers—expect to pay L70,000 for a guided dive, L40,000–L50,000 for equipment rental.

VULCANO

Closest to the Sicilian "mainland," Vulcano is named for the god of fire and metallurgy, who supposedly keeps his smithy in the depths of the island's volcano. Although he hasn't reared his head in the past century—the last eruption was in 1890—the ominous sulfur clouds that billow from the *gran cratere* (large crater) suggest he's still in residence. Even so, the smell of rotten eggs doesn't keep Vulcano from being one of the most exclusive Aeolian destinations, a paradise where Europeans soak in mud baths and turn pink on black-sand beaches. The drawback is that Vulcano's main town takes advantage of its resort status with exorbitant prices, so stick to day trips.

Besides lying in mud or on sand, the prime island activity is hiking. The 3-km (2-mi) hour-long climb to the 1,300-ft-high crater of the island's volcano packs in awesome views into the mountain's murky depths and sweeping Mediterranean panoramas. The path starts ¾ km (½ mi) southwest of the ferry dock and is accessed via the only road leading from town. Although hiking boots aren't necessary, the sharp stones are murder on sandals.

Vulcanello, a once-distinct island that merged with Vulcano after an eruption in the 1st century AD, also has easy-to-explore hiking trails. On the west side of the spit that joins the two, there's a black-sand beach with placid emerald water. Nearby, Vulcano's *fanghi* (mud baths) are heated by breathtakingly stinky sulfuric springs believed to cure rheumatism, arthritis, and skin ailments. Four caveats: don't step where the scalding-hot gas comes bubbling up; don't get your clothes near the stuff, unless what you're wearing is expendable; don't wear jewelry unless you'd like it permanently discolored; and rinse off in the warm sea, also heated by natural springs, next to the mud pool.

BASICS

Vulcano's **tourist information office** (tel. 090/9852028) is open from mid-June to mid-October; it changes location every year, so follow signs from the port. Autolinea Scaffaldi (tel. 090/9853017) runs a **bus line** (L2,000) all over the island daily until late afternoon—get specific route and schedule info from their bulletin board at the port. Rent **bikes** (L5,000–L10,000 daily) and mopeds (L35,000 daily) from **Noleggio da Paolo** (V. Porto Levante 31, tel. 090/9852112). **Pensione La Giara** (V. Provinciale 18, tel. 090/9852229), at the low end of the lodging scale, will rent you an air-conditioned room with bath and mini-refrigerator for L70,000–L140,000 in summer.

SALINA

The second-largest Aeolian island is also the most fertile: Fields of capers and Malvasia grapes (used to make Malvasia wine—strong, sweet, and smoky, like port) are a welcome change from the barren volcanic hills of Salina's neighbors. Five communities lie along the mountainous roads that straddle **Monte Fossa delle Felci** (3,155 ft), the highest mountain in the Aeolian chain. An 8-km (5-mi) trail runs around the mountain's base, joining the port, **Santa Marina**, with the small village of **Santuario Madonna del Terzito**. A less strenuous way to see Salina is by bus; a L1,500 ticket covers the entire island.

Besides Santa Marina, check out **Lingua**, 3 km (2 mi) south. It has a seaside boardwalk, a saltwater lagoon, and several trattorias with great views. **Malfa**, 8 km (5 mi) northwest of Santa Marina, perches high above a sandy beach and is peppered with vineyards and caper fields. The small mountain town of **Leni** harbors several Baroque churches. Salina's secondary traghetto and aliscafo port, **Rinella**, lies on the southwest side of the island. Hop off the bus at Rinella's black beach, which snuggles up against old fishermen's houses at the base of Monte Fossa.

WHERE TO SLEEP AND EAT

Santa Marina is the most convenient place to crash. Try **Iacono Giovanni** (V. Francesco Crispi 13, uphill and right from the port, tel. 090/9843096), with doubles from L60,000. Off-season, Santa Marina's **Punta Barone** (V. Lungomare Notar Giuffré, north end of town, tel. 090/9843172) has oceanfront doubles with bath for L90,000 (L100,000 in high season). In Rinella there's a terraced campsite, **Campeggio Tre Pini** (tel. 090/9809155), with tent spots for L20,000 plus L8,000 per person (L12,000 in July and Aug.). Also in Rinella, **L'Ariana** (V. Rotabile 11, uphill from dock, tel. 090/9809075) charges L90,000 for off-season doubles, L160,000 otherwise. Amazingly, Salina actually has a hip restaurant, with good, cheap food and ambience to spare. The virtually unpronounceable **Pub 'nni Lausta** (V. Risorgimento 188, no phone; closed Nov.–Mar.; no dinner) serves pastas with crazy sauces like the fennel, nut, and anchovy combo, and be sure to try something with the famous local capers (L9,000).

Markets along Stromboli's impossible-to-miss main street sell food and such hiking provisions as flashlights and canteens.

PANAREA

It's fitting that archaeological digs on Panarea have turned up links between the archipelago's Bronze Age culture and the Minoans of Crete. Desert hues and bright bougainvillea dapple the smallest island in the Aeolian chain, with blue-trimmed whitewashed houses tumbling down to the sea in the most Greek-island-like landscape you'll find in Italy. Lush, ritzy Panarea is the vacation home of choice for Italy's rich and famous—nearly all of the houses have names, and you're unlikely to find budget anything.

WHERE TO SLEEP AND EAT

Lodging and food can cost a pretty penny here. The locals are friendly, but they know how to milk those willing to pay to escape the chain's more touristed islands. For lodging, one possibility is **Da Francesco** (V. San Pietro, just north of the dock, tel. 090/983023), where off-season doubles are L100,000 (L150,000 May–Aug.); they also serve hearty pasta dishes for under L10,000. **Rodà Pensione** (V. San Pietro, tel. 090/983023, fax 090/983006) charges L90,000 for an amenity-packed double all year except July and August, when the price goes up to L120,000. Deli snacks, fresh sandwiches, and drinks are available at **Supermarket Bruno** (V. San Pietro, tel. 090/983002).

OUTDOOR ACTIVITIES

Even more appealing are snorkeling and diving on Panarea. Head 3 km (2 mi) south of town via the villa-lined road (go to the back of town and turn left) and look for a black-sand beach that curves to meet a steep switchback trail. This leads to the **Punta Milazzese** headlands; the west side is prime snorkeling territory. **Panarea Sub Diving Center** (Drautto Beach, at end of lina drautto SIGNS, TEL. 090/983288) RENTS COMPLETE DIVING EQUIPMENT FOR L50,000 AND LEADS GUIDED RESORT DIVES FOR L70,000 (TANK REFILLS L15,000). IF YOU'D PREFER NOT TO SUBMERGE, BOAT RENTALS CAN BE ARRANGED INFORMALLY NEAR THE FERRY-HYDROFOIL LANDING. YOU ASK HOW MUCH, THEY SIZE YOU UP, AND THEN THE NEGOTIATING BEGINS. TYPICALLY YOU'LL PAY L50,000 PER DAY PLUS L25,000 FOR GAS.

STROMBOLI

It's hard to imagine how locals get any sleep living at the base of an active volcano. Yet they ramble around their flat whitewashed homes in relative disregard for the nightly displays of spurting lava and gaseous belches. Perhaps they're soothed by loot: the port survives on tourists who come to tackle the relentlessly steep trail to the crater. Although it's illegal to climb without an authorized guide, the path is well marked and manageable on your own. That said, the volcano is notoriously unpredictable, and you should check in advance with the tourist office to be sure that the trail is indeed open. Guides charge L20,000; ask at the various stands set up near the ferry-hydrofoil dock or contact the **Club Alpinisti Italiani** (tel. 090/986093 or 090/986263). If you decide to go it alone, head north through town to **Piscità**, Stromboli's finest black beach. From here the road climbs through tall grass and up the side of the mountain (follow the red-and-white markers). The 5-km (3-mi), 3,031-ft ascent to the caldera takes about three hours; sturdy walking shoes, plenty of water, and lots of energy are essential—this is a *tough* hike. To experience the volcano in all its lava-belching glory, you'll want to remain at the caldera after dark—in which case camping gear and a flashlight are absolute necessities. If you do remain up top, do not—repeat: *do not*— hike up or down in the dark. The path is way too tricky, and the red-and-white markers are hard to find. Another option is to tour Stromboli by boat (L20,000), which gives the best views of the **Sciara del Fuoco** (Slope of Fire), where the lava flows into the sea. At the port, the Stromboliana rental office (V. Marina, tel. 090/986390) does double duty from April to October as an unofficial **tourist office.**

WHERE TO SLEEP AND EAT

Locals with affitacamere to spare meet incoming ferries, or try **Locanda Stella** (V. F. Filzi 14, tel. 090/986020), 1 km (½ mi) north of the dock past the church. Its breezy doubles with bath start at L66,000. Bathless doubles are L55,000, but the communal toilet is a pit. Much more appealing is **Pensione La Nassa** (V. Michele Bianchi, tel. 090/986033), where renovated, terraced doubles with bath run you about L80,000–L120,000. For a posthike beer and pizza (L8,500) or grilled swordfish (L12,000), head to **La Lampara** (V. Vittorio Emanuele 27, tel. 090/986009; closed Dec.–Apr.).

FILICUDI AND ALICUDI

Off in their own little world, Filicudi and Alicudi are the wildest and least-touristed islands. Their small villages depend more on fishing than tourism because neither island has any beaches to speak of. All the activity on Filicudi, the larger of the two, takes place in **Peccorino**, the main port. If you decide to spend the night, **La Canna** (V. Rosa 43, tel. 090/9889956) has L70,000 doubles with views of Salina, Panarea, and Stromboli; from the port, follow the path that starts to the left of Hotel Phenicusa. The hike up to **Fossa Felci**, the island's highest peak, extends good views of Filicudi's rock terrace. If you have an extra L15,000 to rent a boat from **Filicudi SNC** (V. Porto, tel. 090/9889984), circle the rugged coastline for a firsthand look at the numerous grottoes, cliffs, and rock formations.

Alicudi can be easily summed up: one place to sleep, one place to eat, and two things to do—explore the steep slopes and caves at the water's edge or climb past a crumbly old castle to the island's highest point. In spring, purple heather explodes in profusion on Alicudi's volcanic cone, which explains the island's ancient name, Ericusa (roughly translated as "heather color"). Nowadays it's the namesake for the island's lone hotel-restaurant, **Ericusa** (V. Regina Elena, tel. 090/9889902, 20 rooms, open June–Sept.), just above the port. Doubles with bath are L105,000 and full pension L130,000 per person.

SARDINIA

BY SARAH ATTIA

UPDATED BY MARY JANE CRYAN

O n the island-continent of Sardegna (Sardinia), in the Mediterranean west of Rome and Naples, nature is still untouched, with turquoise water and beaches of powdery sand or fantastic rocks. Many city-dwelling Italians faithfully return year after year for month-long summer holidays here. Though officially part of Italy, Sardinia is almost nothing like its motherland on the continent. Its culture, landscape, cuisine—even the music and language—are worlds apart from both Europe and Africa. Sardinia lures visitors with seven months of summer (from April to October), 1,850 km (800 mi) of pristine and dramatic coastline, dusty olive groves, wild mountain landscapes, fascinating towns, and culture. Although the island has a history of foreign domination, colonization by the Phoenicians, Romans, Pisans, Genoese, and Aragonese has strengthened rather than destroyed Sardinia's identity. If you come to explore the land and culture you'll experience both warmth and wariness from Sardinians—a people who have always been on their guard against invaders.

Sardinia's tumultuous history reaches back to the Neolithic Age, with extant prehistoric remains dating from as early as 6000 BC. The rugged interior of the island is dotted with more than 7,000 towering *nuraghi*, Bronze Age (1800 BC–AD 500) volcanic stone structures used as defense towers and fortified villages. The architectural ingenuity of the nuraghi, as well as that of numerous sacred wells, giants' tombs, and enigmatic necropolises (burial places), attest to the sophisticated and mysterious culture of Sardinia's original inhabitants.

Due to the island's strategic position in the central Mediterranean, its rich mineral resources, and the agricultural abundance provided by its volcanic soil, control of Sardinia has been sought by every major sea power since the beginning of time. With each successive wave of invaders, new languages, customs, and architectural styles washed up on Sardinia's shores, forming the distinct culture you witness today. Even in the face of extensive development on the north coast, the Sardinians have held steadfastly to their unique culture, maintaining a largely agricultural way of life—one rich in folklore, crafts, traditions, and festivals. In addition to this cultural heritage, the island forms the habitat for more than 50% of Italy's rare and endangered species, so exotic pink flamingos, miniature horses, wild pigs, mouflon, hawks, and vultures may cross your hiking path as often as sheep. To really see Sardinia, sometimes you have to take a flying leap into the unknown. Your risk-taking, however, is rewarded by the possibility of experiencing rural hospitality, exquisite blue waters, and a variety of gastronomic treats.

SARDINIA

CORSICA
(FRANCE)

Mediterranean Sea

KEY
Rail Lines
Ferry Lines

0   30 miles
0   45 km

BASICS

COMING AND GOING

BY FERRY • Sardinia is connected by *traghetto* (ferry) to Genoa, Livorno, Civitavecchia, Naples, Palermo, and Trapani. The cheapest option, *posto ponte* (deck class), will either get you an uncomfortable, not-meant-for-sleeping chair in the bar (if you can scrounge one) or else an even less comfortable plot on deck. Considering most ferry trips to Sardinia are 8- to 20-hour journeys, you should probably spring for a *poltrona* (reclining seat), about 50% more expensive. A second- or first-class cabin with bunk beds and private WC costs L40,000 to L60,000 more. Though there are snack bars and a restaurant on board, you'll save money by bringing your own eats. To avoid being harassed, solo female travelers should get a reclining seat and stick to it. Ferry prices vary according to the time of year, time of day, and any other reason the reservation agents can think of, but you should expect to pay poltrona prices of about L35,000–L70,000 for a trip from Civitavecchia or Naples; L70,000–L90,000 for a trip from Genoa. High season runs June–September. If you wait around until just before the boat leaves, you can maybe get a ticket for half the normal cost, assuming there are still tickets left.

From Livorno to Olbia a *posto ponte* costs L36,000 in low season and L83,000 in high season. Other ferries from Genoa to Porto Torres start from L61,000. Sardinia Ferries even has some day-time crossings on cruise ships with swimming pools . Check the Web sites (www.tirrenia.it and www.sardiniaferries.it) for up-to-date hours, costs.

Tirrenia (toll-free tel. 1478/99000 or 010/5958629 from abroad; www.tirrenia.it) is the largest and cheapest ferry line, with offices in Cagliari (V. Campidano 1, tel. 070/666065), Olbia (Stazione Marittima, Isola Bianca, tel. 0789/24691 or 0789/24692), and Porto Torres (Stazione Marittima, tel. 079/514107 or 079/514108) on Sardinia. Tirrenia has a fast ferry during high season that takes you from Civitavecchia to Olbia in only 3½ hours, but it leaves at midnight from Civitavecchia and has only reclining seats from L40,000. **Corsica Elba Sardinia Ferries** links Livorno (Nuova Stazione Marittima Calata Carrara, tel. 0586/898979) with Golfo Aranci (tel. 0789/46780). **Moby Lines** has service between Livorno and Olbia and between Santa Teresa di Gallura and Bonifacio (on the island of Corsica). The major Moby Lines reservation centers are in Olbia (Stazione Marittima, Isola Bianca, tel. 0789/27927), Cagliari (V. Campidano 28, tel. 070/655359), Livorno (V. V. Veneto 24, tel. 0586/890325), and Santa Teresa di Gallura (Porto di Santa Teresa di Gallura, tel. 0789/751449).

> As the producer of 50% of Italy's pecorino sheep's-milk cheese, Sardinia arguably does it best: this is one of the only areas where the little guys can roam freely and grub on aromatic plants and herbs. Forget about Parmesan— pecorino's where it's at.

BY PLANE • **Alitalia** flies between mainland cities like Rome, Milan, Genoa, and Naples and the airports in Fertilia (near Alghero), Olbia, and Cagliari (Elmas airport, tel. 070/241014 or 070/240640). **Meridiana** flies from Rome, Milan, Bologna, Florence, Pisa, Verona, and Catania to Olbia and Cagliari. Flights take about an hour, but they usually cost well over L100,000.

GETTING AROUND

Provided you stick to major towns, Sardinia is a relatively easy place to get around by reliable public buses such as **ARST** and **FDS** and by private **PANI** buses. Trains are useful if sometimes slow-moving, with limited coverage, for there are only 1,000 km of track covering the entire island. If you really want to explore the island's nooks and crannies, a car is essential. There are only two *superstrade* (highways)—the SS131, also known as the Carlo Felice highway, connecting Cagliari with Sassari, and the SS130 from Cagliari to Sulcis—but there is a good network of smaller roads, delving deep into the mountains and crossed by the occasional flock of sheep. Car rental is available in bigger towns and resorts, but prices can be steep (L125,000–L180,000 per day) unless you cut a deal on a long-term rental—like L400,000 for five days.

WHEN TO GO

The touristy towns along the north coast swell in the summer months, when boatloads of Italian vacationers invade. If you visit the north coast during this time, expect packed hotels, higher prices for food and lodging, and body-to-body beaches. Luckily, you can still find unspoiled beaches with fewer people along the **Costa Verde** (the west coast) as well as towns that are relatively tourist-free in the cultural heart of the **La Barbagia** east coast region, even in summer. During the "mid" seasons of May, June, and September everything is cheaper. In winter, when the weather stays mild, the whole island is peaceful and cheap, but many hotels, campgrounds, and restaurants close down until Easter or May. Three-star hotels often host noisy school groups in late April and May.

WHERE TO SLEEP

Like everything else in the summer, hotels are often prohibitively expensive in Sardinia; in coastal towns expect to pay L80,000–L120,000 for a nondescript double. But cheap sleeps are still possible and easy to find. If you've got a tent, campsites are everywhere and are sometimes luxuriously equipped, reasonably priced, and often right on the beach. Another option is **agriturismo,** a farmhouse holidays program in which owners of private homes and farms rent rooms and serve meals based on local produce. Out in the countryside, they can be problematic if you don't have wheels, but if you can get out to one, it's usually worth the effort. Rooms run L30,000–L50,000 per person for B&B or L55,000–L80,000 per person for half or full pension (3 meals per day); you're usually expected to stay for a week and you should book a few days in advance. Most tourist information offices have brochures and phone numbers and will often check availability. You can also call or fax the following participating organizations directly: **Agriturist** (V. Bottego 7, 09123 Cagliari, tel. 070/303486, fax 070/303485), **Turismo Verde** (V. Libeccio 31, 09126 Cagliari, tel. 070/373733, fax 070/6754301), **Cooperativa Agriturismo di Sardegna** (Via Duomo 17, 09170 Oristano, tel. 0783/73954, fax 0783/73924), **Consorzio Ekoturist Sardinia** (Via S. Benedetto 2/d, tel. 070/229047, fax 070/22125), **Terra Nostra,** (Viale Trieste 124, 09123 Cagliari, tel. 070/280537, fax 070/20260301), **Cooperativa Agrituristica Dulcamara** (località S. Maria La Palma, 07040 Alghero, tel. 079/999197, fax 079/9999250). The bible for agritourism fans is the 200+-page guide *Agriturismo in Sardegna—guida alle Aziende Agrituristiche della Sardegna e al loro territorio,* published by the Assessorato dell'Agricultura e della Riforma Agro Pastorale and available from ESIT (Via Mameli 95, 09124 Cagliari, fax 070/664636) and tourist offices

CUCINA

Although you'll find pizza and pasta with tomato sauce all over Sardinia, you should try some of the scrumptious regional specialties that are an integral part of Sard culture. Food here is a mixture of Spanish, Italian, North African, and uniquely Sardinian elements. The spit-roasted suckling pig known as *porceddu* is a regional speciality and all kinds of seafood including *aragosta* (lobsters, but smaller than Maine's and served with lemon) are particularly enticing. Perfect first dishes are spaghetti *alle arselle* (with clams) or with *bottarga,* dried, orange-colored fish eggs ("poor man's caviar"). Also keep your eyes peeled for *malloreddus* (little dumplings), often served with sausage and a spicy tomato sauce. The special Sardinian bread, sometimes brushed with olive oil and salt, is a flat, crisp, dry cracker called *pane carasau* or *carta da musica.* Sardinian wines such as Cannonau, Vermentino, and Vernaccia are justly famous and can be purchased directly from the producers at their *Cantine Sociale* (*see* text *below*). The Sardinians love beer; the local brew is *Ichnusa,* which is also the ancient name of the island. For an aperitif ask for ice-cold *mirto,* (either white or red), a deceptively strong, perfumed drink made from myrtle berries. For an after-dinner *digestivo* try *filu ferru,* literally "iron string," much like grappa. Every town has its special sweet: *suspiros* ("sighs"—almond paste biscuits) from Ozieri, or *pirichittus,* lemon-scented bignè with sugar coating, typical of Cagliari. Some, made with *mandorle* (almonds), figs, and *miele* (honey), are reminders of the island's Moorish legacy. If you are lucky you will be offered mouthwatering *seadas,* home-made pastry filled with fresh creamy cheese, fried in olive oil, then dusted with orange or lemon peel and doused with honey.

LANGUAGE

Although the influx of foreign and Italian tourists means you probably won't have much trouble making yourself understood in English and broken Italian, there are actually several dialects and even other languages spoken on Sardinia. Most of the local dialects are bunched together under the term *la lingua sarda* as they all share a mumbling fluidity that sounds like Arabic and passionate rolls of the *r* resembling Spanish. Currently the autonomous Sardinian government is attempting the impossible task of imposing a single dialect on the entire island and integrating the study and use of this common language in the schools. Students of old Catalan Spanish come to Alghero (where "adios" is "goodbye") to hear it still being spoken, while an ancient Genoese dialect that sounds like Portuguese is spoken on the southwestern islands of S. Antioco and S. Pietro, which were colonized by Ligurians in the 18th century.

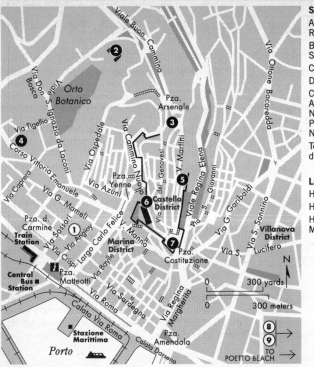

Sights ●
Anfiteatro
Romano, **2**
Bastione di
San Remy, **7**
Casa di Tigellio, **4**
Duomo, **5**
Cittadella dei Musei
Archeologico
Nazionale/
Pinacoteca
Nazionale, **3**
Torre
dell'Elefante, **6**

Lodging ○
Hotel Calamosca, **8**
Hotel Califfo, **9**
Hotel Quattro
Mori, **1**

CAGLIARI

Originally called Karalis (rocky place) by the Phoenicians in the 9th century BC, Cagliari struggles to strike a balance between the conservation of its natural and historic splendor and the encroachment of modern amenities. Sardinia's capital city—its population hovering around 250,000—has always been a center for commerce and export. During the Middle Ages, Cagliari became one of the Mediterranean's most important trading ports for cheese, minerals, and wool. When Pisa gained control of the city in 1326, construction began on the castle, towers, walls, palaces, and churches that now constitute the looming *centro storico* (historic center), which is now in disrepair or under renovation. But Cagliari—one of the few places on the island where you can get back in touch with semi-modern urban reality—is still thriving today. The city makes a convenient base for visiting nearby archaeological sites and beaches.

BASICS

The **currency exchange/information booth** (P. Matteotti, tel. 070/656293; open Mon.–Sat. 7:30–7:25) in the main train station charges a L2,000 commission. Money can be changed also at the main **post office** (P. del Carmine, tel. 070/663356), which provides the usual services, including *fermo posta* (held mail) for L300 a letter (postal code 09100). For long-distance calls, go to **Telecom** (V. Angioy 4, off P. Matteotti, tel. 070/668012; open daily 8 AM–9:30 PM). **Farmacia Schlich** (V. Francesco Crispi 12, tel. 070/658761; open Mon.–Sat. 9–1 and 4:30–7:50), convenient to both the train and bus stations, posts a list of pharmacies that rotate 24-hour service.

VISITOR INFORMATION

Plunked conveniently in the middle of Piazza Matteotti, where all the bus, train, and ship lines converge, is the **AAST information center** (P. Matteotti, in front of Comune di Cagliari, tel. 070/ 664195 or 070/

I THINK I CAN

The trenino verde is still the best way to see the real Sardinia and the humble attractions of tiny farm towns. The Cagliari–Sorgono line (4¼ hrs) takes you from Cagliari directly to Parco del Gennargentu, the largest national park in Sardinia. The Sorso–Sassari line takes you to Galluresi mountain towns, typified by 16th- and 17th-century granite houses. Check out nearby Valle della Luna, the most provocative of the Galluresi granite formations. For trenino info, call Gestione Governativa Ferrovie della Sardegna in Cagliari (tel. 070/580246).

658200; open Mon.–Sat. 8–2, June–Sept. also 4–8), where you can pick up information, brochures, and itineraries. The **EPT** office (P. Deffenu 9, at other end of V. Roma, tel. 070/654811, 167/013153 toll-free; Elmas airport, tel. 070/240200) is open weekdays 11 to 1:30.

COMING AND GOING

BY TRAIN

Train service is more reliable in Cagliari than in any other city on Sardinia, and there's a helpful info booth in the train station (P. Matteotti, tel. 1478/88088 toll-free; open daily 7 AM–9 PM). Trains run regularly to Sassari (3½ hrs, change at Ozieri Chilivani, L22,800), and Olbia (4 hrs, L24,000). Luggage storage (L5,000 for 12 hrs) is available 6 AM–9 PM.

BY BUS

ARST (P. Matteotti, next to train station, tel. 070/40981, 167/865042 toll-free) is the most reliable means of transportation. One daily bus leaves Piazza Matteotti for Nuoro (2½ hrs, L18,400) and Barùmini (1½ hrs, L8,000), and two leave daily for Santa Maria Navarrese (3½ hrs, L14,800). **PANI** (Calata Darsena 4, tel. 070/52526), a private bus service with unpredictable hours, runs buses to many of the same places for slightly higher prices.

BY FERRY

Tirrenia (V. Campidano 1, tel. 070/666065) has a virtual monopoly on ferry travel because it's the cheapest ferry line. You can purchase ferry tickets at literally hundreds of travel agencies along the *lungomare* (boardwalk) or go directly to **Stazione Marittima** (V. Roma, tel. 070/663328); plan to arrive at least half an hour before departure. In July and August, you must make reservations at least three days in advance. Ferries from Cagliari to Civitavecchia (12 hrs, L48,300) leave daily at 6 PM year-round. Ferries travel to and from Genoa late June to early September only (Wed. and Sun., 18 hrs, L90,000). Ferries leave for Naples Wednesday at 6:30 PM; mid-July to mid-September they also leave on Friday (13 hrs, L49,000–L67,000). A ferry goes to Palermo (13 hrs, L47,000–L65,000) every Friday at 7 PM year-round. A ferry to Tunisia leaves Cagliari 7 PM Sunday, arriving the following afternoon at 4 (21 hrs, L95,000–L110,000).

BY PLANE

Aeroporto Elmas (Località Elmas, tel. 070/240079), served primarily by **Alitalia** (V. Carlo Bacco 3, tel. 070/240526), handles domestic and some European flights. Many of the major car-rental companies (Hertz, Avis, Europe-Car, Maggiore) here have comparable rates (*see* Getting Around, *below*). Buses (15 min, L1,100) leave the airport hourly for the ARST station.

GETTING AROUND

Cagliari's four main districts are best explored on foot: The Marina District is between Via Roma (the central lungomare) and Via Manno; the Castello District is up above and to the west of Viale Regina

Elena; Stampace 's old streets meander at the west of Largo Carlo Felice; and the Villanova District, a newer section of town, is east of Piazza Costituzione. If you need to ride the local orange buses, the **ACT** office (tel. 070/20081; open daily 7:15–6:30), across from the ARST station (*see* Coming and Going, *above*), gives out information and sells tickets. You can also buy bus tickets from any newsstand or tobacco shop on Via Roma. Buses run until 10 PM or midnight. To get to nearby **Poetto Beach,** a 6-km (4-mi) stretch of turquoise water and talcum-powder sand, take Bus P (every 10 min, 15 min, L1,100) from Piazza Matteotti. For day-tripping or increased mobility, **Hertz** car rental has an office next to the ARST station on Piazza Matteotti (tel. 070/240037 or 070/668105) and another location at Aeroporto Elmas (where you'll also find Avis, Europ-Car, and Maggiore). Rentals cost L150,000–L180,000 per day plus tax; discounts are offered on rentals of two days or more.

WHERE TO SLEEP

You should call at least a day in advance to get a room in one of Cagliari's few inexpensive places, which are concentrated in the noisy but conveniently located Marina area. The sign of the **Pensione Vittoria** (V. Roma 75, 09100, across from Stazione Marittima, tel. 070/657970, fax/667970) is visible from the ferry. Despite the dingy entrance and squeaky cage of an elevator, the rooms are immaculate and each different from the others. If the rooms with views over the port (doubles are L80,000–L100,000) are noisy at night ask for one at the rear. There's air-conditioning and the baths are modern. Another central hotel is **Quattro Mori** (Via A. M. Angioy 27, tel. 070/668535, fax 070/666087), with double rooms at L120,000 furnished in wood and wicker, air-conditioning, and garage. To combine the city with a beach setting try the **Hotel Calamosca** (Viale Calamosca 50, tel. 070/371628, fax 070/370346), at the end of the 11 bus line from Cagliari center. The double rooms, each with its small sea-facing terrace, cost L120,000 including breakfast. There is also a cactus and palm-filled garden, a restaurant, and a beach. Nine kilometers (6 mi) out of town on the road to Villasimius is the sports complex and **Hotel Califfo** (Viale Leonardo da Vinci 118, Quartu Sant'Elena Foxi, bus PF or 2Q from Cagliari center, tel. 070/890131, fax 070/890134) with a pool, sports, and comfortable doubles with large baths for L100,000–L160,000.

Come May 1, Cagliari celebrates its patron saint's feast day, the Festa di Sant'Efisio. Every province in Sardinia is represented in the procession of costumes that starts in Cagliari and ends 30 km (19 mi) away in a little chapel in Nora, where Sant'Efisio was beheaded.

WHERE TO EAT

Cagliari's restaurants stay open late, and great, inexpensive meals abound; midnight snackers can find pizza by the slice or even fresh fish. Local specialties include spaghetti *all'arselle* (with small clams), *malloreddus,* and fresh seafood. For basic food supplies go to **Econo Market** (V. Angioy 56, near P. Matteotti, tel. 070/663046) or the small supermarket on Via Sardegna. For quintessential Sardinian specialties, also to ship abroad, try **Bonu Prodotti Sarde Alimentari** (Via Sassari 86). Next door is **Trattoria da Umberto,** which promises typical first courses of pasta at about L6,000 and *secondi piatti,* main dishes, at L12,000. Quick snacks and panini are available at all bars, but those frequented by locals are on Via Mameli. **Il Baretto** (V. Mameli 42, tel. 070/653700) has outdoor tables in a tiny garden. Cagliari's historic caffès are **Caffè dell'Arte** (Via San Lucifero 71, tel. 070/666399) and **Caffè Libarium Nostrum** (Via Santa Croce 33/35, tel. 070/650943) for a drink or tea in decorative surroundings. **Ristorante Italia** (Via Sardegna 26, tel. 070/657987) is a historic restaurant that has been restored. Try the antipasti or the 6-course menus (L35,000, meat menu; L65,000, fish menu). The area of Via Sardegna and Via dei Mille abounds with **pizzerie** and **paninocoteche** offering giant sandwiches and prepared foods.

Tucked away in a tiny back room, elegant but reasonably priced **Trattoria Gennargentù** (V. Sardegna 60/C, tel. 070/658247; closed Sun.) serves spaghetti *all'arselle* with *bottarga. Secondi piatti* (second courses) are reasonable, at L8000–L12,000. Their *maccaruin terra e mare* (huge potato dumplings with mint) are insanely good. At **Piper** (Viale Diaz 152, tel. 070/301195) you can have a salad and giant steak of beef or horsemeat as well as a large selection of pizzas. Next to the train station, **744** (V. Roma 744, tel. 070/666626) serves *spaghetti al cartoccio* with *bottarga* or clams. Just out of town on the Capoterra road is **Su Cardigu e Su Schironi** ("on the grill and on the skewer"; SS. 195 at SS. 91 for Teulada, tel. 070/71652, closed Mon.) for a memorable meal of Sardinian specialities at about L60,000.

WORTH SEEING

In the late Middle Ages, Pisan administrators set up shop in what is now the **Castello District** to regulate port trade and commerce down south. The Genoese, however, were constantly trying to take control of Cagliari, so the Pisans constructed the white **stone walls** that encircle the Castello District and descend all the way to the Marina District below. Despite such military fortifications, it was the Aragonese invading from mainland Spain in the 14th century that the Pisans couldn't fend off. Under the iron-fisted Aragonese rule, the people of Cagliari were forced out of the Castello District to make room for foreign nobles. A bastion of Spanish rules and customs, this district was virtually off-limits to non-Spaniards. Jews were tolerated because of their financial expertise and could live, worship, and set up shop here, but Sardinians had to leave at the sound of a warning trumpet every evening at sunset or be thrown off the walls. It wasn't until the end of the 18th century that the area finally became accessible to the city's indigenous population.

The buildings of the Castello District alternate between being under renovation or run-down, emitting either the aroma of freshly baked bread or that of *"Casteddaius piscia arrenconis"* ("Castellani who piss in the corner"). In Piazza Costituzione, the stairs of the monumental **Bastione di San Remy** form an entrance to the whole Castello District and are the seat of weekend collectors' fairs and art exhibits. You can reach the 14th-century **Torre dell'Elefante** (open Tues.–Sun. 9–4:30) by heading left on Via Università from the top of the Bastione di San Remy stairs. Looking up from under the tower, you'll see a small marble elephant, symbolizing strength. The tower was used by the Spanish as a prison, and you can still see the rusty iron gates where Spaniards hung the heads of executed prisoners. A few blocks to the north, beyond Piazza Palazzo, **Piazza Indipendenza** leads directly to the **Cittadella dei Musei.** This museum complex is home to four separate collections. The **Museo Archeologico Nazionale** (tel. 070/655911; admission L4,000; open summer, Tues.–Sun. 9–2 and 3–8; winter, Tues.–Sun. 9–7) documents Sardinia's prehistoric civilizations. The **Pinacoteca Nazionale** (tel. 070/674054; admission L4000; open Tues.–Sun. 8:30–7) has 15th-century Catalan art. In the **Museo Siamese Cardu** (tel. 070/2002410, admission free) you'll find 11th- to 19th-century objects from Asia. Finally, the **Mostra di Cere Anatomici** (tel. 070/664783; open only by appointment) is a 19th-century anatomical wax collection by Florentine wax model maker Clemente Susini.

Perched on the hill above the Castello District are the remains of Cagliari's Roman era (238 BC–AD 450): the ruins of the **Anfiteatro Romano** (no phone; admission free, open summer, Tues.–Sun. 9–1 and 5–8; winter, Tues.–Sun. 8:30–5:30). South of the amphitheater, through the botanic garden, explore the **Casa di Tigellio** (V. Tigellio; admission free; always open), the remains of a 2nd-century imperial Roman housing project. To reach both sites, follow Viale Buon Camino from Piazza Indipendenza.

Though constructed by Pisans in the 13th and 14th centuries, the **Cattedrale di Santa Maria** bears the signature of ensuing foreign rulers, with its Romanesque style, Gothic influences, and Baroque embellishments. Pulpits on either side of the main door display scenes by the Pisan master Guglielmo. Note the 17th-century organ hidden inside its red wooden case and ask the sacristan to let you see the Flemish masterpiece and rare Spanish leather benches in the sacristy. The crypt, with 292 funerary niches and bas-reliefs, holds two Romanesque sarcophagi bearing the remains of early Christian martyrs: saints Saturno, Bonifacio, and Claudio. The crypt's ceiling is decorated with 584 different baroque rosettes. *Piazza Palazzo 4, tel. 070/663837. Open daily 8–12:30 and 4–8.*

Other important sights are visible in the old Stampace quarter: the Baroque jewel of **San Michele** church, and the crypts and churches of **Santa Restituta** and **Sant' Efisio.**

AFTER DARK

Cagliari has heaps of bars and cafés that stay open until 2 AM. Due to escalating temperatures in summer, locals flock like lemmings to nearby beach towns to party. The closest discotheque is in a bar-disco-café complex called **Lido** (V. Poetto 41, 5 km/3 mi outside Cagliari, tel. 070/380846). The cover is L20,000; take Bus P from Piazza Matteotti along the lungomare and get off at the second stop.

NEAR CAGLIARI

BARUMINI

Sardinia's biggest and best-preserved nuraghi complex—Su Nuraxi—is just outside the small town of Barùmini, about 50 km (31 mi) north of Cagliari. Before you head straight for the nuraghi, spend a little time in Barùmini itself, a charmingly lazy town amid golden fields and rolling hills. Follow the signs to **Parrocchiale della Beata Vergine Immacolata,** a pretty 15th-century church with a late-Gothic interior and a 17th-century bell tower and cupola. Peek into the garden and courtyard of **Casa Zappata,** facing the church, for an idea of how 15th-century Sards lived, then wander past the low stone houses with tiny windows and doors that characterize this rustic, well-preserved little town.

COMING AND GOING • A 2 PM bus from Cagliari's Piazza Matteotti runs to Barùmini (1 daily, 1½ hrs, L7,800). To return, take the 6 PM bus to Sanluri (40 min, about L5,000) and change to the 7 PM train to Cagliari (45 min, L4,300). Double-check these times. Buses run year-round, but in winter be sure to check schedules. To reach Su Nuraxi from the bus stop in Barùmini, follow the TUILI and NURAGHI signs left and continue for about 10 minutes (1 km, or ½ mi).

WORTH SEEING • The fascinating **Su Nuraxi** nuraghi complex offers a glimpse into a mysterious unknown culture dating from 4,000 years ago (predating the Punics and Romans). The initial building (1400 BC) was expanded by the addition of concentric walls and towers for grain and livestock storage. You could spend all afternoon exploring this unusual stone structure, with dark chambers and passageways that once were living quarters. The deep well in the interior courtyard and the peaked domes—carved out of volcanic rock using no mortar—show the inhabitants' amazing ingenuity. The smaller dwellings comprising the surrounding village contain the remains of grinding stones, ovèns, and altars for water purification rites (water was scarce and sacred in these parts). The visit is not recommended during hot mid-day hours. On the bus ride over, don't miss the intricate murals along all the concrete walls of the town of Villamar, 20 minutes south of Barùmini; the fascinating artwork depicts Sardinia's political protests over the past 20 years. *Tel. 0337/ 813087. Admission L7,000. Open June–Sept., daily 8:30– 7:30; Oct.–May, daily 9–5.*

Centuries ago, inhabitants of the west coast were driven into the hinterland as they fled the malaria-ridden coastline. Even today locals manage to avoid the modern-day scourge on the coast— tourism—and maintain an agricultural existence.

NORA

Founded by the Phoenicians in the 7th and 8th centuries BC, Nora is the oldest city on the island. Although the narrow peninsula was inhabited for 16 centuries and was once home to 5,000 people, the city is now in ruins and partially submerged in water due to rising sea levels. What remains is the city center, mostly the work of imperial Roman artists and architects from the 2nd to 4th centuries AD: mosaic floors, vestiges of roads and pillars, baths complete with ancient heating systems, and a small semicircular theater with ancient versions of box seats. If the sea is calm, look under the water along the shore for more ruins. Adjacent to the archaeological zone, a crescent-shape beach offers white sand, clear water, and good swimming. Rejoin the modern world with a drink or gelato at **L'Approdo,** a friendly restaurant right on the beach. *Excavations: tel. 070/929138. Admission L5,000. Open May–Sept., daily 9–8; Oct.–Apr., daily 9–5 or 9–6.*

To reach Nora, take the **ARST** bus (hourly, 45 min, L3,900) from Piazza Matteotti in Cagliari to Pula. From Pula take local Bus 1 (7 daily, L1,000) to Nora, the beach, or the archaeological zone. Near Pula, the large beachside campground **Cala d'Ostia** (Località Cala d'Ostia, 09010, tel.& fax 070/921470; cash only; closed Oct.–Mar.) charges L12,000 per person and L14,000 for a tent in high season. To get here from Pula, follow the CALA D'OSTIA or HOTEL FLAMINGO signs from the intersection.

WEST COAST

Along the rural west coast, rare species of wildlife such as pink flamingos, falcons, and hawks share the rocky uplands with sturdy medieval churches and endless scatterings of ever-enduring nuraghi. Unlike resort towns in the north, which lure visitors with their fun-in-the-sun pleasure packages, west coast towns attract those looking for a taste of unspoiled nature and the persevering Sardinian spirit. Western culture, however, does not come at the price of precious lounging time; Alghero, with its distinct Spanish flair and Catalan dialect, has plenty of the island's prime beaches. Keep in mind, however, that since tourism is in its beginning stages, middle-level accomodations will be hard to come by, they may range from very grungy to very fancy and pricey. An exception are the farmhouses that offer bed & breakfast, meals, and an open window on Sardinian family life. Public transportation is also sorely lacking once you get away from the coast.

THE SOUTHWESTERN ISLANDS

Off the southwestern coast of Sardinia lie a group of islands that still breathe of times long past. The town of **Sant'Antioco** (Pro-Loco, tel. 0781/82031) on the island of the same name, is a layer-cake of history, the site of **Sulcis**, a Phoenician city founded in 750 BC, which has a necropolis, a 2nd-century Roman amphitheater, catacombs, and the church of St. Antioco dating from 1089, as well as a modern tourist port. The small port of **Calasetta** was founded by Ligurian coral fishermen whose descendants, after 250 years of isolation, still preserve their original dialect and customs. The town was built on a checkerboard grid plan in 1769 by the Piedmontese and is the sleepy embarcation port for **San Pietro island** (tickets at Saremar office, 50 minutes, 16 times a day, L6,000 round-trip). Here, too, the population's ancestors were Ligurian coral fishermen who immigrated in the 1700s to San Pietro. On the island, in the town of Carloporte, the church of S. Pietro was built on the ruins of an earlier one dedicated to "The Holy Innocents," children shipwrecked off San Pietro in 1212 while participating in the semi-legendary Childrens' Crusade.

WHERE TO SLEEP AND EAT

L'Eden (Pza. Parrocchia 15, 09017 S. Antioco, tel. 0781/840768, fax 0781/840769) is in the center of town with doubles at L100,000–L120,000. On the mainland nearby, the modern rooms at **Punta Giara** (on main road at Sant'Anna Arresi, tel. 0781/966105, fax 0781/966151) have a frigobar and a TV; doubles go from L95,000 to L130,000. For campers there are **Le Saline** (Via Le Saline, Calasetta, tel. 0781/88615, fax 0781/88489), with shady campsites and bungalows, and **Tonnara** (Loc. Calasapone, S. Antioco, tel. 0781/809058, fax 0781/809036). On San Pietro island, **Hotel Galman** (loc. Bellavista, tel. 0781/852088, fax 0781/852077), on a hilltop overlooking the island's main beaches, has well-appointed doubles for L85,000–L150,000, as well as a multi-lingual staff and a panoramic restaurant, **Ai Pescetti,** where the locals come to celebrate special occasions. In the old town of Carloforte you'll find the classic fish restaurant **Al Tonno di Corsa** (Via Marconi 47, tel. 0781/855106), where *zuppa di pesce, gamberi in guazzetto,* and locally caught tuna are the stars for memorable meals at about L40,000.

IGLESIAS

The castles, cathedral, and city walls are reminders of the city's Pisan past when Count Ugolino della Gherardesca was lord here and in the 13th century built the Villa di Chiesa in the image of his hometown, Pisa. By 1324 the Spanish were dominating the town they renamed Iglesias. The center of a once-important mining area, it was a depressed zone after the mines were abandoned, but the city has now restored them as tourist attractions.

BASICS

The **Pro Loco** in the town hall has brochures, and **Cooperativa La Gherardesca** (Via Don Minzoni 62, tel. & fax 0781/33850) has a multilingual staff who conduct tours to the mining sites and museums.

WHERE TO SLEEP AND EAT

Il Sillibario Hotel (SS 130, km. 47.400, tel. 0781/33833, fax 0781/33790) has 15 rooms decorated in vague country-cottage style. The restaurant is reached through a tunnel decorated with old photos and bits of local history. Doubles go for L100,000–L120,000. **Ristorante Gazebo Il Medioevale** (Via Musio 21, tel. 0360/620098) has a medieval atmosphere and first courses at L8,000–L10,000, while *secondi,* including lobster, will run about L12,000–L15,000.

WORTH SEEING

The cathedral of **Santa Chiara,** the town's patron saint, is in Piazza del Municipio, the main square, along with the town hall and Pisan-style houses. The compact, neat city center buzzes around Piazza Sella and its park and cafés, where traffic jams happen twice a day during the *passeggiata.* The local beach is **Funtanamare** (6 km/3½ mi south of Iglesias) on the way to the mines at Masùa and Nèbida along a coastal road that puts the Amalfi Drive to shame: not for the faint-of-heart.

PENISOLA DI SINIS

A lone finger dipping into the Gulf of Oristano, the Sinis Peninsula is home to rare species of birds such as pink flamingos and pilgrim falcons, as well as several ancient temples and tombs. The peninsula's **San Giovanni di Sinis** is a one-church town with one great church—Chiesa San Giovanni di Sinis, part of which dates from the 5th century. In summer it's open 9–6 daily; off-season, when buses arrive less frequently, you'll have to find the nun—the keeper of the key—to let you in. On both sides of the peninsula lie gorgeous isolated beaches where you can frolic in the same waters the Romans did. Also take note of the town's archaic *barralas de crucuris* (fishermen's huts), made of wood and straw.

Established by Phoenicians in 800 BC, **Tharros** is an intriguing ancient ruin at the tip of the peninsula. Protected by the San Marco Promontory, it was a perfect natural port used by Carthaginians and Romans, fortified in the Byzantine era, and deserted in the 8th and 9th centuries. Free tours of the Phoenician temples, Phoenician and Roman dwellings, and Roman aqueduct vats are conducted in Italian only. The site is open daily 9–7, but call **La Zona Archeologica di Tharros** (tel. 0783/370019) before making the trip off-season. *Admission L8,000. Free guided tours of site (1 hr) June–Sept., daily 9–2 and 4–8; Oct.–May, daily 9–2 and 4–5:30 (last tour 1 hr before closing).*

To the right of Tharros's entrance, a path leads up to the **Torre di San Giovanni** (tel. 0783/370019; admission L3,000). Built by Filippo II during the Saracen invasions, the tower provides an amazing view of the sea and ruins. You can also follow a path down to one of the beautiful but crowded beaches.

Oristano is the scene of livestock fairs and a rousing series of horse races and cross-dressing, called Sa Sartiglia, marking the end of February's Carnevale.

COMING AND GOING • Unfortunately, buses run here only in July and August; the rest of the year you'll have to hitch a ride. From Oristano buses run to San Giovanni and Tharros (3 daily, 20 min, L2,500); it's a few minutes' walk between Tharros and San Giovanni.

WHERE TO SLEEP, EAT, AND BE MERRY • A good sandy stretch is at **Marina di Torre Grande,** just 7 km (4 mi) from Oristano. The nightlife hops along its pizzeria-lined lungomare. If you prefer to stay here, you have two alternatives: **Del Sole Hotel** (V. Duca degli Abruzzi, 09170, tel. 0783/22000, fax 0783/22217), where a double will put you back L140,000–L180,000, or **Camping Torregrande** (Via Stella Maris, 09170, tel. 0783/22228), with 133 sites. Bungalows for two with kitchens go for L12,000 per person and you can rent a tent or trailer. The surrounding countryside abounds in agritourism properties like **Le Mimose** (Strada 24 Ovest, Arborea, tel. 0783/800587), just a mile from the beach with eight large rooms and a campground. Half-board (bed, breakfast, and dinner) costs L50,000–L62,000. It looks like it would be touristy, but **L'Oasi** (P. della Torre 6, tel. 0783/22062) is surprisingly authentic. There's an enormous selection of scrumptious antipasti (L12,000), and you can pile the plate yourself.

SANTA CRISTINA

Twenty-five kilometers (15 miles) northeast of Oristano, Santa Cristina's archaeological zone has the highest concentration of nuraghic architecture on the island. Relics include **Bronze Age towers** (18th–10th centuries BC) and the **well temple,** the site of age-old sacred-water rituals. Most remarkable is the **Ipogeo,** a 4,000-year-old underground church. On the other side of Santa Cristina's information office-bar are the remains of a nuraghic village re-used by the Carthaginians and the Romans. You can climb up the single-tower structure, dating from 1500–1200 BC, and look out over the sacred olive groves. *Complesso Nuragico Santa Cristina, Località Paulilatino, tel. 0785/55438. Admission L4,000; includes Ethnographic Museum. Open summer daily 9–1 and 5–8; winter daily 9–1 and 3–5:30; tours daily 9–1 and 2:30–6.*

COMING AND GOING • Four buses leave daily from Oristano's **ARST** station for the 40-minute ride to Paulilatino (L3,400), a few kilometers from the archaeological sites. Ask the driver to let you off at the archaeological zone before you reach Paulilatino, or you'll have to walk from town. Returning to Oristano is tricky: Only a couple of early morning buses leave Paulilatino for Oristano (currently at 7:20 and 8:20). The **train station** is several kilometers outside town and 6 km (4 mi) or so from the site, with sporadic service (call ESIT, tel. 167/013153 toll-free, for current hrs).

BOSA

The historically captivating yet humble town of Bosa, in the province of Nuoro, lies on the right bank of the **Temo,** Sardinia's only navigable river. Even with its succulent seafood, sandy beaches, and small-town hospitality—the town has only 8,000 inhabitants—beautiful Bosa somehow remains virtually unscathed by tourism. Spend an afternoon winding through the mazes of the Old Town, called **Sa Costa,** where merchants hawking reasonably priced antique Sard jewelry and coral mingle with hole-in-the wall caffè and adobe buildings. The staff at the **Pro Loco** tourist office (C. Vittorio Emanuele 56, tel. 0785/376107; open summer, daily 10–1 and 6–9) speaks little English, but at least they're friendly.

Nearly every side street from the Sa Costa leads up a cactus-lined, stone-stepped path to the free ruins of the **Serra Valle Castello** (open daily), built by the Malaspina family in 1122. From here you can get a panoramic view of the town, the river, and surrounding hills. Wend your way back down the stairs to view the Baroque interior of the **Chiesa Santa Maria Immacolata** (P. del Duomo, tel. 0785/373286), constructed in the 13th and 14th centuries. Two kilometers (1 mi) across the Temo's bridge on Via San Pietro is the **Chiesa San Pietro,** an authentic display of Romanesque architecture. Medieval Spanish **watchtowers** prowl along the coastal Via Lungo Temo, which leads to **Bosa Marina,** where you can relax on sandy beaches. Between applications of sunscreen, try to catch a glimpse of the griffon vulture, an endangered species found in the surrounding hills.

COMING AND GOING

FDS buses connect Bosa to Alghero (4 daily, 1 hr 10 min, L5,600), Màcomer (2–3 daily, 1 hr, L5,000), Nuoro (3 hrs, L11,000; change at Màcomer), and Sassari (1 daily, 2 hrs, L10,000). Buses leave from either Piazza Bosa Marina or from the main piazza in the Sa Costa, a 15-minute walk along the river. Buy bus tickets on board or at tobacco shops.

During summer months, the **trenino verde** (*see box* I Think I Can, *above*) runs on weekends between Bosa Marina and Màcomer, a town accessible by bus from Alghero, Sassari, or Cagliari. The trenino trip begins at 9 in Màcomer, stops briefly in several small towns, and then continues to the beach in Bosa. Call the Ufficio Turistico Ferrovie della Sardegna (tel & fax 070/580246) or the Màcomer information office (tel. 0785/70001) for details and tickets.

WHERE TO SLEEP AND EAT

In the town center is the family-run 1870s **Hotel Sa Pischedda** (V. Roma 2, 08013, tel. 0785/373065), where L90,000 will get you a double with bath. If you want to stay near the beach in Bosa Marina, about 3 km (2 mi) away via local bus, **Hotel Bassu** (V. G. Deledda 15, 08013, tel. & fax 0785/373456) has 27 rooms; doubles cost L80,000–L100,000. The 64-bed **hostel** (V. Sardegna 1, 08013, tel. 0785/375009; cash only), also in Bosa Marina, is modern and clean, and out of season you'll probably be alone. Beds in dorms go for L16,000. Bosa's specialty is seafood, and it's always fresh. In Bosa Marina, **La Griglia d'Oro** (V. Genova 19, tel. 0785/373157) is terraced and surrounded by flowers and olive trees. It offers fish specialties and delicious homemade ravioli di ricotta.

ALGHERO

Irresistible Alghero caters to travelers with taste and integrity, managing to strike the perfect balance between modern conveniences and the preservation of a pristine medieval core. More than any other town on the island, Alghero maintains a distinctively Spanish air; years under Catalan dominion earned it the nickname Little Barcelona. With endless sandy beaches, the famous Grotto of Neptune, and a number of nuraghi, Alghero makes the perfect base for day excursions. Though the efficient buses will get you to and from neighboring towns, the best way to do it all is by *motorino* (moped) or bike (*see* Getting Around, *below*). When you're back in town at the end of the day, the piano-bar-lined lungomare looks like an international bazaar, with people of all nationalities selling handmade arts and crafts.

BASICS

AAST (P. Porta Terra 9, tel. 079/979054; open June–Sept., Mon.–Sat. 8–8, Sun. 9–noon; Oct.–May, Mon.–Sat. 8–2) gives out bus schedules, glossy brochures, and maps galore, but the staff can't make reservations.

COMING AND GOING

BY TRAIN • A 50-minute train ride takes you to Sassari (L3,500), where you can catch other trains, including ones to Olbia, Oristano, and Cagliari. To reach the **train station** (V. Don Minzoni, tel. 1478/88088), walk from the town center along the port on Via Garibaldi or ride on an AP or AF city bus (L1,100).

BY BUS • A booth on the Via Catalogna side of the Giardini Pubblici (Public Gardens) sells tickets and provides information for **ARST/PANI** and **FDS** bus lines (tel. 079/950179). Buses connect Alghero to Sassari (hourly, 50 min, L5,000) and Bosa (2 daily, 1¼ hrs, L5,600), and one goes directly to Olbia's port at 8 PM (1 daily, 2 hrs, L14,100). You have to connect with buses in Sassari (*see below*), a bigger transport hub, to reach Cagliari and other destinations. Buses to Fertilia Airport leave from Piazza Mercede, in the new part of town (5 daily, 15 min, tel. 079/950458).

BY CAR • **Avis** (V. P. Nedda N. 16/A, tel. 079/979577 or 079/935064 at Fertilia airport) will make your life a lot easier if you're determined to reach the most secluded beaches. However, prices are painful— at least L125,000 a day, not including gas. You'll find comparable rates at **Nolauto Alghero** (V. Vittorio Veneto 11, tel. 079/953047), **Auto Express** (V. Sebastiano Satta N. 48, tel. 079/951505 or 079/935054 at the airport), and **Maggiore** (tel. 1678/935045). If you want to rent for a longer period, most places have five-day deals starting at L380,000.

GETTING AROUND

All major streets converge at the *centro storico*, which juts out at the westernmost point of Alghero. The Giardini Pubblici are flanked by the tourist information office to the west and the bus terminal and port to the north. The **lungomare** runs south from the southern entrance of the centro storico and changes names from Dante to Valencia as it winds toward Bosa, 45 km (28 mi) to the south. Orange local buses are marked by initials according to their destination: **AF** (Alghero Fertilia) runs hourly, **AP** (Alghero Pertraia Maria Pia) runs every 20 minutes, and **AO** (Alghero Ospedale Marino) runs every 30 minutes. Tickets (L1,100) must be purchased beforehand from tobacco shops or newsstands.

After the 1354 overthrow of Italy's powerful Doria family, Pedro IV of Aragon took over Sardinia. The influence of Spanish rule through the 18th century can be seen today in Alghero's Catalan-style Gothic cathedral, street names, and local language.

The hostel (*see below*) rents bikes for L15,000 per day—a convenient option if you're staying there. Otherwise, **Cicloexpress** (V. Garibaldi Porto, tel. 079/986950; open Mon.–Sat. 9–1 and 4–8:30) rents street bikes (L12,000 a day), mountain bikes (L18,000 a day), mopeds (L25,000 a day), and scooters (L50,000 a day). Their main booth is at the port.

WHERE TO SLEEP

Family-run **Pensione Normandie** (V. Enrico Mattei 6, 07041, tel. 079/975302; cash only) is the cheapest hotel around; reservations are advised. Small, clean doubles (sharing baths) run L80,000 and fill up quickly in July and August. From the Giardini Pubblici, take Via Cagliari, which becomes V. Giovanni XXIII, away from the port and bus station; turn right on Via Enrico Mattei. **San Francesco** (Via A. Machin 2, 07041, tel & fax 079/980330), has doubles at L80,000–L110,000. **Hotel San Giuan** (V. Angioy 2, off V. Garibaldi, 07041, tel & fax 079/951073), has a bar, a garden, and 19 modern doubles for L100,000–L120,000.

AGRITURISMO • With the overwhelming demand for cheap sleeps in high season, agriturismo becomes an increasingly attractive option. The chance to experience (and *taste*) Sard farm life is worth the minor inconvenience of having to commute in and out of town. For agriturismo stays near Alghero, contact **Cooperativa Agrituristica Dulcamara** (07040 Santa Maria La Palma, Alghero province, tel. 079/999197; cash only), which offers a variety of room and pension plans ranging from L30,000 to L65,000 per person, plus a small booking fee. One of the best is **Correddu** (Podere 3, 07040 Fertilia, tel.079/999024), with its two guest rooms (B&B L35,000) and a large restaurant that serves specialities like asparagus and mushrooms.

HOSTEL • Ostello della Gioventù "Dei Giuliani" (HI). In Fertilia, a short bus ride from both the airport and Alghero, this 70-bed hostel has been run since 1975 by friendly Mamma Margherita. The staff will point you in the direction of nearby beaches and pizzerias, though a delicious three-course lunch or dinner is served at the hostel for L14,000. Beds are also L14,000, breakfast L2,500. *V. Zara 1, Località Fertilia 07040, tel. 079/930353. Take orange Bus AF to Fertilia; from Fertilia's P. Giulia, take V. Parenzo, right on V. Zara. Showers. Cash only.*

CAMPING • Seaside **Camping Calik** (Località Fertilia, tel. 079/930111, fax 079/930031; closed Oct.–May) is L15,000–L20,000 per person, but it's shaded by eucalyptus trees and equipped with a bar, a self-service restaurant, and a market. Take Bus AF toward Fertilia and ask the driver when to get off. **Camping La Mariposa** (V. Lido 22, 07041, tel. 079/950360, fax 079/950480; closed Nov.–Mar.) charges L13,000–L21,000 per person, but it's just 2 km (1 mi) from the town center. It has the same amenities as Calik, plus bungalows (L45,000–L60,000). Tent sites cost L7,500–L12,000. From the train station, turn right on Via Minzoni, left on Via Malta, and right on Via Lido; or take Bus AP.

WHERE TO EAT

Nothing in Alghero is untapped by tourism, so don't be daunted by TOURIST MENU signs and credit-card stickers. For an excellent outdoor fruit and veggie market (open daily 8–noon), go to Via Cagliari past the public gardens. For mouth-watering made-to-order *panini* (sandwiches), head to **El Bocadillo** (V. Kennedy 12, tel. 079/982443), open daily, except Tuesday, beginning at 9:30 AM and "as long as there are people around."

Under an alley archway, colorful **Ristorante Dieci Metri** (Vicolo Adami 47, tel. 079/979023; closed Wed. in winter) has outdoor tables incorporated into the stone structure. The spaghetti *alle vongole* (with clams) is cooked to garlicky perfection. A large meal that includes spaghetti, fried calamari, and a drink is about L30,000. From Torre di Porta Terra, walk down Via Roma, left on Carrer del Barcelonetta, and right on Vicolo Adami. Even though **Ristorante da Pietro** (V. Machin 20, tel. 079/979645; closed Wed.) is in the middle of the touristy town, this hole-in-the-wall restaurant is a favorite among locals. A three-course lunch of grilled sea bass or spicy Sardinian sausage costs L35,000. From the Giardini Pubblici, head down Via di Porta Terra and go right on Via Machin.

WORTH SEEING

Alghero is home to a graceful medieval center glutted with goldsmith workshops and jewelry stores specializing in every shade of coral from Sardinia's coral-reefed coast. Stocky medieval and Renaissance towers spring up in spots along the Old Town's circular fortified wall.

On Via Carlo Alberto at Vicolo Teatro, the **Chiesa di San Francesco**'s soberly majestic 14th-century stone facade constitutes one side of a small, triangular piazza. Take a close look at the church's beautifully carved wooden doors. The severe vaulted ceiling is juxtaposed with delicate ornamentation on the capitals and gold-inlaid Baroque altars and sculptures. From a higher vantage point you can see San Francesco's multicolor cupola-topped tower—a signature image of Alghero. From the church, turn right (north) toward the water on Via Carlo Alberto to **Cattedrale di Santa Maria** (V. Manno). The cathedral's best feature is its late-Gothic octagonal bell tower.

AFTER DARK

Summer nightlife happens along the lungomare, where artists and artisans compete for attention with piano bar musicians playing covers of bad American soft rock. All the while, scantily dressed nymphs show off their tans, elderly couples stroll arm in arm, and children waddle around with dripping ice cream cones. During the summer the lungomare hosts an impressive outdoor carnival with rides and more of the above. Piano bar **Opera** (V. Don Minzoni, tel. 079/977633) is a good place to hear live music and watch all the action along the port. The popular discos **Il Ruscello** (Strada Alghero-Sassari, tel. 079/953168) and **La Siesta** (Strada Alghero-Vilanova) are only accessible by car. Check the daily newspaper *La Nuova Sardegna* for other club listings. Cover charges for discos run L20,000–L25,000. Also during the summer months top-name world artists such as South Africa's Miriam Makeba perform weekly at **World Music Al Porto** (Teatro Paladino, Molo Rizzi, tel. 079/985344). To purchase tickets, go to **Tot Per La Musica** (V. Lo Frasso 10, tel. 079/976137) or to the theater early on the night of a performance. Tickets start at L20,000; the tourist office has current listings for shows.

OUTDOOR ACTIVITIES

The charm of Alghero's Old Town is still intact, but the nearby beaches are where it's really at. The closest sandy stretches lie along the **Lido di Alghero**, an umbrella-lined arc leading from the marina to Fertilia. Boat, jet ski, and kayak rentals are available along its Spiaggia di San Giovanni and Maria Pià, starting at around L50,000 per hour; contact **Base Nautica Usai** (tel. 079/930233) for specifics. Farther away from the screaming toddlers and prowling lifeguards, **La Spiaggia delle Bombarde** is a white-sand beach bordered by pine trees and the insanely beautiful sea. The neighboring **Spiaggia del Lazzaretto** is protected by an 18th-century tower and known for its swift current and cold waters. Both are accessible by taking a bus from the Giardini Pubblici toward Porto Conte (6 daily, 30 min, L1,700).

Porto Conte itself is one of the Mediterranean's largest natural harbors; with very calm waters, it's great for swimming and snorkeling. Certified divers interested in exploring the area's coral reefs and grottoes should contact **Porto Conte Marine Diving Center** (tel. 079/942205), at Maristella in Porto Conte. L60,000 will rent you diving equipment for half a day, and instruction is available; reserve one day in advance. Inland, you can explore the rocky terrain on **horseback** (L30,000 per hr) by contacting **Il Grifone** (Centro d'Equitazione, tel. 079/986294).

NEAR ALGHERO

NEPTUNE'S GROTTO

About 15 km (9 mi) north of Alghero, the promontory culminates at Capo Caccia, a uniquely wild, rocky nature reserve where a motley crew of birds holds court among crops of rosemary, asparagus, and fennel. Here you can take the scenic, 654-step Escala del Cabirol into semisubmerged Neptune's Grotto, a mysterious den where monk seals hung out until 25 years ago, when they were driven away by the noise of boat traffic. Nowadays, groups are led through the stalagmite-filled cave compartments called *sale* (rooms), each with spectacular rock formations in which you might recognize familiar shapes—anything from grand organs to Christmas trees to piles of spaghetti. The oldest stalagmite is believed to be 120 million years young. Three FDS buses (one in winter) leave daily from the Alghero bus terminal for Capo Caccia (50 min, L3,400), and three return. Otherwise, you can go by boat to avoid the long staircase up from the grotto. By boat, **Compagnia Navisarda** (at marina, tel. 079/ 950603 or 079/ 976202) charges L16,000 for a 2½-hour excursion. The fare does not include admission to the grotto, but takes you only to and from it, allowing two hours at the grotto; boats leave hourly 9–5 in summer and four times daily (9, 10, 3, and 4) in April, May, and October. *Località Capo Caccia, tel. 079/946540. Admission L13,000. Open Apr.–Oct., daily 9–7 or dusk; Nov.–Mar., daily 9–2.*

> *In winter, families in Sardinia have running water for only four hours a day. After that, the bare necessity flows from a 50-liter tank each household cherishes.*

On the way to Porto Conte and Capo Caccia, yet another stony structure, **Nuraghi Palmavera** (admission L4,000; open Apr.–Oct., daily 9–7 or 9–8), is worth a quick look. The main tower and "palace" complex, dating from 1100 BC, is surrounded by 50 circular huts that made up the living quarters of the village. **Cooperative Silt** (tel. 079/980750) offers guided tours in English on request for L5,000 per person (L4,000 per person for groups). To get here, catch the bus to Capo Caccia and ask the bus driver to drop you off at the Nuraghi Palmavera. To return, jump on any bus from Porto Conte or Capo Caccia for Alghero.

NORTH COAST

An incredible coastline leads from Olbia to Sassari, but you'll sacrifice true Sardinian culture for your golden days in the sand. Of Sardinia's drop-dead-gorgeous coastal towns, cast your sights on Santa Teresa di Gallura and ignore the astronomically expensive Costa Smeralda, the northeast part of the coast that billionaire Aga Khan developed as a playground for the yacht-owning jet set. The islands of Caprera and La Maddalena are equally beautiful, but prepare for the shock of encountering flocks of corn-fed gringos in red-and-white-striped tube socks who reside at the U.S. naval base on La Maddalena.

SASSARI

The intrepid Sassarese spirit, characterized by feistiness and independence, dates from 1236, when local rebels killed foreign tyrant Barrione III, who foolishly tried to control the city's commercial activity. Though reminders of Genovese and Pisan occupation remain here, the Sard dialect determinedly persists—as does an air of self-sufficiency that borders on the antisocial. Sassari, Sardinia's second-largest city after Cagliari and the capital of Sardinia's largest province, is primarily a transportation hub. The town does offer a few excellent ways to spend an afternoon: a stroll through the centro storico with its

WAXING MEDIEVAL

La Faradda de li Candareri, or Festa dei Candelieri, happens August 14 in Sassari. Local guilds design huge, stunning candlesticks—actually large columns—in honor of the Madonna and parade in extravagant traditional costumes. Each sculpted column represents an individual guild's insignia and is carried by eight men through the centro storico, Piazza Castello, and Corso Vittorio Emanuele, ending at Santa Maria di Betlem. Dating from the Middle Ages, the festival has been celebrated annually since a devastating plague ended here on the eve of Assumption Day in 1582.

tiny medieval living quarters that open onto grand neoclassical piazzas, or a cappuccino at one of the old porticoed bars off Piazza Italia.

BASICS

The staff at **AAST** (V. Umberto 72, tel. 079/233534; open weekdays 8–2 and 4–6, Sat. 8–noon) provides hotel and agriturismo listings and will even help you make a reservation if you're desperate. You can also get information at the EPT office (Viale Caprera 36, tel. 079/299544). Show your ISIC card at **CTS** (V. Costa 48, tel. 079/234585; open weekdays 9:30–1 and 4:30–7, Sat. 9:30–noon) for various travel packages.

COMING AND GOING

The **train station** (P. Stazione 12–15, tel. 1478/88088 toll-free; ticket/information office open daily 5:30 AM–8:30 PM), at the northeast end of town, has four daily trains to Oristano (3 hrs, L14,000) and Cagliari (4 hrs, L22,000), five to Porto Torres (20 min, L2,000), eight to Olbia (2 hrs, L10,100), and 10 to Alghero (1 hr, L3,500). The station has luggage storage (L5,000 for 12 hrs); retrieve your bags before 8:45 PM.

PANI (V. Bellieni 25, off V. Roma, tel. 079/236983 or 079/234782), the long-distance bus carrier, offers three nonstop daily buses to Cagliari (3¾ hrs, L26,000) at 6 AM, 2:15 PM, and 6 PM. Other buses to Cagliari pass through Màcomer (1½ hrs, L7,800) and Oristano (2 hrs 20 min, L13,900). Six buses leave daily for Nuoro (2 hrs 25 min, L13,100), and two go to Porto Torres (30 min, L2,300). The **ARST** station (Emiciclo Garibaldi 23, tel. 079/2639220; open daily 5 AM–8:30 PM), off Corso Margherita in the town center, has five daily buses to Alghero (1 hr, L5,000) and Santa Teresa di Gallura (2 hrs, L12,200) and 13 to Castelsardo (1 hr, L3,900). Tickets can usually be bought on board the bus but cost 10%–20% less if you buy them ahead of time.

GETTING AROUND

The city center extends southeast and uphill from the train station. Although Sassari is Sardinia's second-largest city, it is still surprisingly walkable. The main drag, **Corso Vittorio Emanuele,** runs northwest–southeast through **Piazza Castello** and **Piazza Italia,** after which it becomes **Via Roma.** Orange APT buses (L1,500) stop frequently in front of the train station and at the public gardens. Bus 8 runs from the station to the south end of town, passing through Piazza Castello and Piazza Italia. Buses start running at approximately 6 AM and head for the barn around 8 PM–10 PM.

WHERE TO SLEEP

Accommodations in Sassari are less than inspiring and fill up fast in high season, even though it may seem like no one's around. There are no campgrounds within the city and police are very strict—you can't even take a nap in the city's central parks. Agriturismo is popular on the outskirts of town; **Azienda Agrituristica Terrosa Giuseppa** (Località Agliado, Platamona, 07046, tel. 079/310070) has listings for the area, but most places are not accessible without a car.

If you get a room on the piazza (street side) you'll think screaming teenagers on Vespas are driving across your bed at **Hotel Giusy** (P. Sant'Antonio 21, 07100, tel. 079/233327, fax 079/2394910; cash only). Charmless but clean, all rooms (L75,000 for a double including breakfast) have a bathroom, phone, and '60s furniture. From the train station, turn left and make a right at Piazza Sant'Antonio. Though more expensive, **Hotel Marini Due** (V. Pietro Nenni 2, 07100, tel. 079/277282, fax 079/280300) is a big leap into the realm of quasi-luxury. The rooms (doubles with bath L110,000, including breakfast) have TVs, phones, air-conditioning, and bathrooms. From the train station, take Bus 5, 7, or 8 and ask the driver when to get off (after about 10 min). Just outside town in Ottava is **Hotel Marini** (S.S.131, Loc. Ottava, 07100 Sassari, tel. & fax 079/390716) with modern rooms with TV, air-conditioning, and phones at L95,000 per double.

WHERE TO EAT

Though Sassari is big on excellent restaurants, most are rather expensive. Still, even at these places you can always find a big bowl of Sardo-style *gnocchetti* (little gnocchi, or potato dumplings) cooked with sausage, basil, and tomato for L7,000–L9,000. Buy produce at the Piazza Tola **outdoor market** (open Mon.–Sat. 8:30–1:30) and groceries at **Multi Markets** (V. Cavour 66, tel. 079/234736).

Marini (P. Italia 10, tel. 079/234250), right in the heart of town, has an unbeatable tourist menu—four courses for about L20,000. Their *cozze alla marinara* (mussels in tomato sauce) are incredible; for dessert try the fresh fruit salad, which is soaked in a light liqueur. At the semi-elegant family-run **Trattoria Gesuino** (V. Torres 17g, tel. 079/273392), locals meet for late lunches. The house special is tricolor gnocchetti made of spinach, squash, and potato with a cheesy sausage, tomato, and basil sauce (L13,000). From the museum (*see below*), continue up Via Roma and make a right on Via Alghero. **L'Antica Hostaria** (V. Mazzini 27, tel. 079/200066) is the yuppiest, most gourmet restaurant in town. Their menus are handwritten and always evolving, but if they're offering the scrumptious North African couscous with fresh fish (L18,000), order it. All their dishes are innovative and original and yet retain a distinct Sard flair. Their tiramisu (L5,000), made with *mirto,* is mouthwatering. Late-night snacks can be had at **Bar Daniele** (6 P. Tola, no phone).

WORTH SEEING

Between **Piazza Italia,** Sassari's heart, and the train station lies the tangle of streets that make up the centro storico, where most of Sassari's sights are. A walk through the centro storico in the shade of the medieval Pisan walls along **Corso Trinità** highlights some of the best parts of the city. Though many of the town's historic structures have fallen into irreparable decay, this area still bustles and is filled with shops and the strong scents of bread and garlic. Under the porticoes off Piazza Italia, one of Sassari's oldest caffè, **Café Rau** (P. Italia), is still a popular hangout, even on Sunday, when everything else in town seems dead. The next piazza down from Italia, Piazza Castello, has not survived the modern era's aesthetic decline unscathed; the towering '60s Banco di Sassari eclipses the disheveled though lovely 16th-century **Chiesa della Madonna del Rosario** (P. del Rosario). Via Turritana, running northeast from behind Chiesa della Madonna del Rosario, takes you to the **Duomo,** which has a richly carved Baroque facade superimposed on a much older structure. Closer to the train station is the **Chiesa Extra-Muros di Santa Maria di Betlem** (P. Santa Maria, corner V. XXV Aprile and V. Copino). The 16th- and 17th-century renovations have spoiled much of its original beauty, though, and today it is most famous for the huge candle-shape columns kept here for the Festa dei Candelieri (*see box* Waxing Medieval, *above*).

If you want to get a handle on Sardinia's complex history don't miss the **Museo Archeologico Etnografico G.A.Sanna.** The display labels are written in Italian, but the museum is well organized and arranged chronologically, so it's easy to understand. Fragments, utensils, jewels, and coins from the Paleolithic, pre-nuraghic, Bronze, and Roman eras round out the displays. The nuraghic reconstructions are particularly fascinating. A small *pinacoteca* (picture gallery) contains Sardinian paintings from the 14th to early 20th centuries. *V. Roma 64, tel. 079/272203. From P. Italia, follow V. Roma 4 blocks. Admission L4,000. Open Tues.–Sat. 9–2, Sun. 9–1, also 2nd Wed. of month 4–7.*

NEAR SASSARI

CASTELSARDO

Precariously perched above the Mediterranean, medieval Castelsardo was an impenetrable fortress and stronghold of the Genovese Republic in the 12th century, when it was called Castelgenovese. Its name changed depending on who was in charge; it was also known as Castelaragonese under Spanish rule. Its fortified wall is completely integrated with the town's naturally protective setting of rocks and hills—a harmonious union that is only interrupted by the subtle beauty of the campanile's cupola.

You can skip the hotel- and restaurant-lined boardwalk, but a trip to the town and its eponymous castle is essential.

Though Castelsardo thrives on tourism, a walk through the old part of town reveals unexpected authenticity: the artisan workshops, jewelry shops, and boutiques in the lower part of town might unearth a few treasures, but the real reason to be here is the higher, older section, where the lofty **castello** now houses a small museum of Sard handicrafts, **Museo dell'Intreccio** (Coop Il Cigno, tel. 079/471380; admission to castle and museum L3,000; open July–Aug. daily 9–1 and 2–midnight; closed Mon. winter). Note the woven baskets just like those still being made by the local artisans, and the raft made entirely of straw. The explanations in English offer a glimpse into the tumultuous and difficult lives of the townspeople. From here don't miss the striking rooftop view of the town, the surrounding hillside, and rough waters. For another astounding view, follow the signs to the beautiful 16th-century **Cattedrale Sant'Antonio Abate,** one side of which faces onto the sea and the reefs. Inside are beautifully carved wooden choir stalls and a painting behind the altar of the Madonna and child with angels by the Maestro di Castelsardo, one of the area's hidden treasures. The island's most ancient statue is probably the Crucifix of the Black Christ housed in the church of **Santa Maria** (V. Vittorio Emanuele I) in the highest part of town. Don't miss the **Mostra Mercato dell'Artiginato** (Via Roma 17, tel. 079/471061; Via Sedini 14, tel. 079/470253), huge exhibtion spaces with the best of crafts that have made Castelsardo famous: baskets, carpets, coral, and ceramics.

COMING AND GOING • Buy bus tickets at the tobacco shop just past the *pescheria* (fish shop) on your left as you head up Via Roma from the lungomare; or get them at the newsstand in the town's sole piazza. From Sassari, **ARST** runs 13 daily buses (1 hr, L3,900) to Castelsardo. If you are taking a day trip, get off at the town's second stop, in the piazza just below the *Borgo* (old part of town). Otherwise, if you're headed for a hotel, get off at the first stop along the lungomare when you see the castle in the distance. The last returning bus to Sassari is at 9:20 PM.

WHERE TO SLEEP AND EAT • Though the Borgo has no hotels, you'll find plenty of accommodations if you take a two-minute walk along the lungomare. Doubles go for L70,000–L80,000 at the cozy, family-run **Pensione Pinna** (Lungomare Anglona 7, 07031, tel. 079/470168), or try **Hotel Cinzia** (V. Colle di Frigiano 1, 07031, tel. 079/470134, fax 474273; cash only; closed Oct.–Mar.), which offers pleasant, quiet doubles (L70,000–L90,000) with terraces and views. Breakfast is included. **La Aragona** (V. Manganella, tel. 079/470488) is a great place for panini, savory specialties like *melanzane alla parmigiana* (eggplant Parmesan), and a view of the sunset from its large patio overlooking the sea. From the main piazza, take the stairs on Via Trieste, turn right on Via Piave, and head to the top.

NURAGHI SANTU ANTINE

An hour south of Sassari lies the **Valley of the Nuraghi,** a rural area with a high concentration of nuraghic complexes dating from Sardinia's Bronze Age (1800 BC–500 BC). Call the Pro Loco (tel. 079/847010) for a guided visit. Unfortunately, many of Sardinia's 7,000-odd crumbling stone towers have not been excavated but lie neglected along the rocky hilltops or amid wheat fields overgrown with olive trees. The most sophisticated of the nuraghic villages, the excavated Nuraghi Santu Antine, outside the village of **Torralba,** offers a look at one of the most advanced and best-preserved of these fascinating structures. The main tower, three stories high, is nearly 4,000 years old; its bastions, staircases, internal corridors, and chambers were all constructed out of enormous blocks of volcanic rock using no mortar. A number of bronze figurines representing hunters, mothers with infants, and suppliants with votive offerings were found at the site; they now reside in museums in Cagliari and Sassari. In Torralba, the **Museo della Valle dei Nuraghi** (V. Carlo Felice, tel. 079/847298; open May–Sept. daily 9–8, Oct.–Apr. daily NVI 9–5) displays reconstructions of the nuraghi, remains of pottery and jewelry, and illuminating chronicles of Sardinian culture. To reach the nuraghi, take an ARST bus from Sassari (4 daily, 1 hr, L4,500) and ask the driver to let you off after the town of Torralba; it's a short walk to the site (follow the MUSEO signs). Returning to town, walk the 35 minutes back to Torralba. The last bus goes back to Sassari from Torralba at 4:50 PM. *Admission to site and museum L5,000. Site open summer, daily 8–8; winter, daily 8–sunset.*

SANTA TERESA DI GALLURA

Don't bother asking people for directions in Santa Teresa di Gallura; nobody actually lives here, and summer never ends in this tourist-packed village by the sea. But comfortable Santa Teresa, which can practically kiss Corsica, just across the Strait of Bonifacio, is blessed with having each panorama more awesome than the last. The closest beach, **Spiaggia Rena Bianca,** is a bun-to-bun rotisserie of scantily clad, tanner-than-thou sunseekers who lounge on the sands and splash around in an endless shallow stretch of turquoise Mediterranean sea. Though not the place to get a real dose of Sard culture, this town has an undeniable allure that is surpassed only by another nearby beach (Spiaggia di Rena Maiore), the breathtaking Capo Testa Promontory and beaches, and Isola Monica (*see* Outdoor Activities, *below*)—all accessible on foot with a little motivation. With a youthful spirit, affordable accommodations, and four campgrounds in the vicinity, Santa Teresa may be the only refuge for budget travelers on this gorgeous but prohibitively expensive coast.

BASICS

The **tourist office** (P. Vittorio Emanuele 24, tel. 0789/754127, fax 0789/754185, open weekdays 8:30–1 and 3:30–6:30, Sat. 8:30–1, June–Oct. also Sun. 8:30–1; Porto Pozzo, tel. 0789/752121, open June–Aug. weekdays 8:30–1 and 3:30–6:30, weekends 8:30–1) will hand you scads of listings and brochures.

COMING AND GOING

Bus service is sorely lacking and often requires you to transfer in Sassari or Olbia. All buses leave from Via Eleonora d'Arborea off Via Nazionale. Seven **ARST** buses leave daily for Olbia (1¾ hrs, L7,200), passing through Palau (40 min, L3,900), and five go to Sassari (2 hrs, L12,200). Get tickets and information at **Bar Black and White** (V. Nazionale, no phone; open daily 7 AM–midnight), near Via del Porto, around the corner from the bus stop. Copies of the bus schedule are available at the tourist office (*see above*).

WHERE TO SLEEP

The few budget hotels, mostly near the port, fill up fast in July and August, but they generally maintain high standards. Unfortunately, many hotels (including all the ones listed below) are open only June 20–September 15. On the plus side, they all accept credit cards. Agriturismo is nearly unheard of here and requires a car. Inquire at the tourist information office about families who rent rooms and at **Agriturismo Saltara** (Località Saltara, 07028, tel. 0789/755597).

Albergo Miramare (P. della Libertà 6, 07028, tel. 0789/754103, fax 754675; closed mid-Oct.–mid-May) has airy doubles (L100,000–L160,000) with a view of the sea. From Piazza Vittorio Emanuele, take Via XX Settembre to Piazza Libertà. **Hotel Moderno** (V. Umberto 39, 07028, tel. 0789/754233) has comfortable, quiet doubles (L70,000–L80,000) that are filled with light and with heavenly aromas from the restaurant downstairs. From the bus stop, go right on Via Eleonora d'Arborea and left on Via Umberto. Friendly, clean, family-run **Pensione Scano** (V. Lazio 4, 07028, tel. 0789/754447) is housed in a cozy old building redone in the '60s. Small, tidy doubles—some with sea views—run L65,000–L85,000; meals are also available. Walk toward the water on Via Nazionale, turn left on Via Capo Testa, and right on Via Lazio.

CAMPING • Campeggio La Liccia (Strada per Castelsardo Km 66, 07028, tel./fax 0789/755190; closed Oct.–May) offers numerous amenities including beach access and a restaurant and is reachable on the bus to Castelsardo (30 min). The charge is L17,500 per person, showers included, and there are also bungalows for two (L45,000–L90,000). **Camping Gallura Village** (Località Li Luccianeddi, 07028, tel. 0789/755580) runs a free shuttle service to and from Santa Teresa three to four times daily from mid-May through mid-October; the rate is L12,000–L20,000 per person, including showers, plus L3,000 for the site. On the water, **Campeggio Arcobaleno** (Località Porto Pozzo, 07028, tel. 0789/752040; closed Oct.–Apr.) has every amenity you can imagine; it can accommodate as many as 1,600 people at L15,000 per person in high season (L11,000 in low season), including tent and electricity. Take the bus toward Olbia and ask the driver to let you off at the campsite (20 min).

WHERE TO EAT

Good, authentic Sard cuisine can be very expensive, and you'll spend L20,000–L40,000 for meals that are merely adequate. If you are willing to drop L35,000–L50,000 on a full meal, try **Canne al Vento** (V. Nazionale 23, tel. 0789/754219), reputed to be the best joint in town for home-style seafood dishes. Rooms are also available here (L75,000–L95,000). At **Gastronomia Artigiana del Corso** (V. XX Settembre 15, tel. 0789/755725), you can choose from an amazing selection of delicious pastas, salads, and seafood dishes. Try one of their seven kinds of fresh seafood salads (L4,000–L7,000 for a huge dish). Undoubtedly, **Pape Satan** (V. La Marmora 24, tel. 0789/755048) serves the best Neapolitan-style pizza in town. Sit outside in their terraced, circular adobe booths near the huge wood-burning oven. The

COSTA SMERALDA

The drop-dead beautiful Costa Smeralda (Emerald Coast) along Sardinia's east coast south of Porto Cervo has only been developed over the last 30 years or so. Legend has it that the rich Saudi Arabian prince Aga Khan stepped off his yacht, was dumbstruck by the coast's beauty, and offered Sardo farmers a total of $2 million. With the help of foreign investors, the area has undergone a major make-over, and the little fishing villages have all been turned into ritzy resorts. It goes to show that money can buy a lot, but it can't buy back the original rustic beauty of these towns.

salmon pizza (about L13,000) is devilishly good. From Piazza Italia, head down Via Capo Testa and left on Via La Marmora. To make a picnic of your own or to pick up some knickknacks, browse through the huge coral-laden **flea market** (open Thurs. 8–noon) encompassing three blocks of Via Eleonora d'Arborea. Wind your way through snazzy threads and footwear and end up in fresh fruits and veggies.

AFTER DARK

After sundown, Piazza Vittorio Emanuele fills with tourists of all ages comparing tan lines and clutching gelati and slick guys with snazzy 'dos handing out passes to the latest and greatest clubs. Unfortunately, many hot spots, including the new and tacky **Estasi's Disco** (100 Buoncammino, tel. 0789/755570), are outside town. A great alternative for night music and munchies until 8 AM is the hopping **Poldo's Pub** (V. Garibaldi 4, near P. Vittorio Emanuele, tel. 0789/755860), where a crew of jovial bartenders serve up panini, hamburgers, and beer. Friday and Saturday nights bring live jazz. You can kick back at **Groove Café**, right on Piazza Vittorio Emanuele, with live music from jazz to cheesy pop. It's worth the trip to Santa Teresa just to catch a show in the amazing ivy-covered **outdoor cinema** (V. Capotesta 9, no phone), which presents international films (L10,000) in Italian every summer night at 9:15 and 11:30.

OUTDOOR ACTIVITIES

From Spiaggia Rena Bianca, trails (about 2½ km, or 1 mi) heading west into the hills will take you to **Isola Monica**, an isolated grass clearing surrounded by large rock formations—a kind of psychedelic Stonehenge. Other amazing rock formations are at Valle della Luna. Trails aren't marked, but the footpaths are visible. From the hilltop overlooking both the sea and Santa Teresa, head 4 km (2½ mi) west (the sea is north) down Via Nazionale to **Capo Testa,** a weather-beaten promontory with striking panoramic views and gorgeous sandy beaches on both sides. **Spiaggia di Rena Maiore** is farther away than Spiaggia Rena Bianca, but it has the clearest water and views of islands and rock formations. Surprisingly, it is also the most isolated beach nearby. Hop on a bus toward Sassari or Tempio (L2,000) and ask the driver to let you off at the beach. Getting back means a rather dispiriting 6-km (4-mi) trek homeward, but you can avoid all that if you rent some wheels at **Gulp** (V. Nazionale 58, tel. 0789/755689; open weekdays 9–1 and 3:30–7:30, Sat. 9–1; in summer also weekend afternoons). Mountain bikes go for L25,000 a day or L60,000 for three days (10% less in July and Sept., 20% less Oct.–June), and scooters cost L50,000 a day with the same discounts.

Several boat excursions leave daily from the port at the east side of town. One of the private companies, **Consorzio delle Bocche** (P. Vittorio Emanuele, tel. 0789/755850), runs boat tours to **Budelli (Spiaggia Rossa), Spargi, Cala Corsara,** and **Cala Azzurra** from 9:15 to 5. The boats stop for swimming breaks at each of these isolated bays, with their pink coral beaches and breathtaking water, as well as for photo-ops at each and every vaguely phallic rock formation en route. The L50,000 fare includes a four-course lunch. Reservations should be made the day before at one of many offices scattered around the central piazza.

NEAR SANTA TERESA DI GALLURA

Though the port town of Palau and the nearby islands of La Maddalena and Caprera have suffered from hasty development in recent years (not to mention overly aggressive tourists), they still offer campgrounds, relatively affordable accommodations, and access to perfect beaches.

LA MADDALENA AND CAPRERA

The seven islands of the Caprera–La Maddalena archipelago became a National Marine Park in 1996. La Maddalena remains enchanting despite having sold its peaceful soul to the U.S. Navy and a number of loud boys in blue. Some of Sardinia's best beaches and rocky ruins are here, but you have to share them with a host of enthusiastic beach bums in high season.

Even if you're depending on the buses (*see* Coming and Going, *below*) you can still reach some stunning beaches; just get off when the pull of the turquoise water gets too much for you, perhaps at **Monti da Rena** or **Baia Trinità,** both with water as clear and calm as a swimming pool. On the bus from La Maddalena's port across the bridge to Caprera, ask the driver to let you off near the postcard-perfect beach **Cala Coticcio,** also known as Tahiti.

Caprera, La Maddalena's smaller and less inhabited neighbor, is lined with countless clearwater coves begging to be explored; unfortunately you won't be the only explorer—the nearby Club Med ensures omnipresent flocks of errant beachcombers. Italians come to Caprera to pay homage to Giuseppe Garibaldi, the Risorgimento figure and "hero of two worlds" who retired to be a farmer here. There is a continuous procession of visitors at **Casa Garibaldi,** the Italian equivalent of George Washington's Mt. Vernon. In the humble red-roofed home of Italy's unification hero (*see box* Espresso Shot Heard 'Round the World *in* Chapter 5) personal objects, locks of hair, portraits, crutches, clothes (the famous Red Shirts were worn with the first blue jeans), and furniture, are all well displayed; you can progress from the hero's deathbed to his grave outside. *Località Caprera, tel. 0789/727162. Take Cherchi bus from Maddalena port to stop ½ km/¼ mi from museum. Admission L4,000. Open daily 9–1:30.*

COMING AND GOING • Ferries run to La Maddalena from Palau every 30 minutes (10 min, L1,500 one-way). For info and tickets in Palau, head to Stazione Marittima's bar/tobacco shop (P. del Molo, tel. 0789/709689; open daily 5 AM–11:45 PM). Once you reach La Maddalena, you might want to rent a moped for L35,000 a day to check out some of the island's impressive beaches; stop in at **Cuccu** bothers (V. Amendola 30, tel. 0789/738528). At **Nicol Sport** (Viale A. Moro, tel. 0789/736168), you can also rent bicycles for L20,000 a day. You can arrange boat excursions at **Nico d'Aquila Sail Charter** (Porto Massimo, tel. 0338/6596450). **Cherchi** buses (La Maddalena Port, tel. 0789/737392) run hourly (L1,200) from La Maddalena to Caprera (15–20 min) and to La Maddalena's beaches (15–30 min).

WHERE TO SLEEP • The closest thing to a budget hotel is the simple but clean **Arcipelago** (V. Indipendenza Traversa 2, 07024, tel. 0789/727328, fax 0789/728100), where the cheapest double room is L120,000 in high season, L100,000 at other times. **Il Gabbiano** (V. Giulio Cesare 20, tel. 0789/722507, fax 0789/722456), near the town and Cala Gavetta, has doubles for L115,000–L140,000 that have views over the bay to the island of Santo Stefano. Due to the lack of inexpensive accommodations on the island, many families unofficially rent their homes or offer rooms to visitors. Ask at the tourist office (Via Nizza 1, tel. 0789/736321). La Maddalena's many campgrounds are cheap, but they're also packed and are only open mid-June–mid-September. **Campeggio L'Abbatoggia** (Località Abbatoggia, 07024, tel. 0789/739173) is the only one on the water, but it has little shade and is not the best. It does have a great restaurant with delicious seafood like *cozze alla marinara,* a bar, a market, and hot showers. Camping costs L15,000 per person in the high season. Take the Panoramic bus from the port and ask to be let off at Abbatoggia; the campground is a short walk down a dirt road. **Campeggio Il Sole** (V. Indipendenza 17, 07024, tel. 0789/727727, fax 0789/663630) is inland, with modest facilities, including a bar and restaurant, and modest prices to match (L7,000). From La Maddalena, take the bus to Caprera and ask to be let off at the campground.

WHERE TO EAT • Restaurants and outdoor cafés are concentrated around La Maddalena's port and the nearby streets, Via Garibaldi and Via XX Settembre. For a morning cappuccino and cornetto (L5000) try **Sabatini** (V. Amendola 14, tel. 0789/738015) with its veranda overlooking the boats at Cala Gavetta. In the central Piazza Garibaldi, **Gran Caffè Garibaldi** (P. Garibaldi 8, tel. 0789/737003), facing the town hall, is the place for pastries (from L1500) and fantastic ice cream (L2000). Here you will also find a covered market every morning for vegetables, fruit, and picnic fixings. Italians rarely eat breakfast, especially when they're on vacation, so a mid-morning snack is the rule; join them at **Casa del Pane** (V. V. Emanuele 5) for a piece of focaccia with olive oil, salt, and maybe anchovies and onions. Pick up supplies for a beach picnic at **Market Ginetto** (V. Amendola 6, on waterfront, tel. 0789/737541; closed Sun.). After the day-trippers leave on the last ferries, the port still offers a good time. **Bar Milano** (P. Umberto Primo 8, tel. 0789/76646) has pool tables (L13,000 per hr), video, and pinball machines. **Re Artù** (V. Principe di Napoli, tel. 0789/738270), at the end of the port, is the young crowd hang-out.

EAST COAST

The harsh, mountainous terrain south of Nuoro has been notoriously impenetrable since ancient times. In Roman times it earned the name La Barbagia (land of the barbarians), as it was the only region that managed to resist Roman occupation. Ironically, this part of Sardinia was populated long before anywhere else on the island—in 6000 BC—when mysterious and still relatively unknown nuraghic civilizations found refuge in mountain grottoes. These days, La Barbagia is proud of its title, remaining stubbornly indomitable and secluded. People here are still bound to the old ways of farming, shepherding, and even folk dancing. Sustained by *pane carasau* and strong red wine, these natives won't miss an opportunity to share their bounty or extend their hospitality.

OLBIA

The nearby Golfo Aranci beaches are beautiful, but undistinguished Olbia itself is a major ferry hub that you're likely to pass through quickly. As soon as you arrive, head for the **tourist office** (V. Catello Piro 1, off C. Umberto, tel. 0789/21453; open summer, Mon.–Sat. 8–8, Sun. 9–noon; winter, weekdays 8–2 and 3:30–6:30, Sat. 9–noon), where the efficient employees will supply you with maps, glossy brochures, and travel info. From the port, take Bus 3 (hourly, 10 min, L1,100) to the town center. The multilingual staff at the **American Express** office (c/o Avitur, C. Umberto 142/B, tel. 0789/24327; open weekdays 9–1 and 4–7, Sat. 9–12:30) handles checks, sells tickets, and offers tourist info.

COMING AND GOING

BY FERRY • All the ferry lines have representatives at **Olbia Marittima Port,** where you can get ferry info for all of Sardinia. **Tirrenia** (Stazione Marittima, Isola Bianca, tel. 0789/24691) runs a frequent Civitavecchia–Olbia ferry (8 hrs, L36,000 year-round), with daily trips even in the lowest of seasons and as many as four daily trips mid-June–early September, as well as a new, quick 3 ½-hour run. Tirrenia ferries from Olbia to Genoa run every day during the summer at 8:30 PM (13 hrs, L70,000). **Moby Lines** (Stazione Marittima, Isola Bianca, tel. 0789/27927, or c/o Unimare, V. Principe Umberto 1, tel. 0789/23572) chugs between Olbia and Livorno (10 hrs, L42,000–L86,000) about twice a day during the summer, daily mid-March–May, and three times a week mid-October–mid-January.

BY TRAIN • The **train station** (V. Pala, tel. 1478/88088) is off Corso Umberto in the town center. Arriving trains coincide with departing ferries. Eleven daily trains run to Golfo Aranci (25 min, L2,800), and 10 to Chilivani (1 hr, L6,800), where you catch connecting trains to Sassari, Oristano, and Cagliari. One daily train heads to Cagliari (4¼ hrs, L25,000) at 7:05 AM. Luggage storage is available (L5,000 for 12 hrs) 8 AM–9 PM.

BY BUS • Blue **ARST** buses are scheduled to take arriving boat passengers from the ferry station (just outside Olbia Marittima) to the ARST station (C. Umberto, tel. 0789/21197) in town. Direct buses to Nuoro (9 daily) take 2½ hours; they cost L12,200–L14,000, depending on whether or not they're direct. Buses leave for Sassari (2 daily, 1 hr 40 min, L11,300) at 6:25 AM and 8:20 PM. Buy tickets at Mokà Bar, next to the station.

WHERE TO SLEEP AND EAT

Budget accommodations are scarce in Olbia; in July and August reservations are recommended. The clean, cheap doubles at **Hotel Minerva** (V. Mazzini 7, 07026, tel. 0789/21190; cash only) are L80,000–L90,000. **Albergo Terranova** (V. Garibaldi 6, 07026, tel. 0789/22395, fax 0789/25008), on two floors with no elevator, has doubles costing L95,000–L145,000. In front of the station, with tastefully done rooms and an excellent restaurant is **Hotel Gallura** (Corso Umberto 145, 07026, tel. 0789/24548, fax 0789/24629). The most convenient campground is 20 minutes out of town by bus: From the ARST station, take any bus headed for Costa Smeralda, Palau, and Santa Teresa and ask the driver to let you off at the campground **Cugnana** (Località Cugnana, 07026, tel. 0789/33184, fax 0789/33057), where camping costs L12,500–L22,500 per person. Set off from the sea, the large site holds a restaurant, pizzeria, and market. The nearest sites south of Olbia are **San Teodoro** (V. del Tirreno, tel. 0784/865777) and **Cala d'Ambra** (Località Cala d'Ambra, tel. 0784/865650), both with similar buses and easily accessible from Olbia.

Most restaurants have tourist menus that start at about L30,000. Your best bet is one of the pizza-by-the-slice places or *paninoteche* (sandwich shops) along Corso Umberto. Try **Il Golosone** (C. Umberto 41, tel. 0789/26475; cash only) for delicious crepes. Off Piazza Principale, go right onto Via Porta Romano to the popular and palm-tree-filled **Tre Dollari Ristorante** (V. Porta Romano 8, no phone). Their extensive, cheap menu includes great gnocchi (L9,000) and eggplant pizza (L8,000).

NEAR OLBIA

Thirty miles southwest is **Ozieri,** which became famous when remnants of the late-neolithic Ozieri culture (c. 3500 to 2500 BC) were discovered in the Grotta di San Michele in 1914. The **Museo Archeologico** (Archaeological Museum; P. S. Francesco, tel. 079/787638, open Tues.–Sat. 9–1 and 4–7, Sun. 9:30–12:30) is housed in a wing of the old Franciscan convent.

NUORO

Nuoro's position amid monochromatic mountains kept it safe from Saracen attacks in the late Middle Ages but couldn't protect it from aesthetic attacks by 20th-century architects. Although Nuoro was once cluttered with traditional rural stone houses, postwar construction has ruined much of its harmony with the rocky landscape. The only portion of the original town remaining is the tiny centro storico, around San Pietro. Despite the modern eyesores, Nuoro attracts travelers with its

Members of Nuoro's younger generation seem determined to rid themselves of the simple agricultural lifestyle that makes up their heritage. It's just another example of how modernity and conformity are swallowing up some of Sardinia's rural towns.

two unique museums and its proximity to several amazing villages and sites. Unfortunately, public transportation to neighboring towns is minimal; the best way to get around is to rent a car.

BASICS

Hotel listings and info on mountain excursions are available at the **EPT** (P. Italia 19, tel. 0784/30083, fax 0784/33432; open weekdays 8–2, Tues.–Wed. also 4–7), but they're all hopelessly vague. If you simply must, walk east on Via La Marmora, turn left on Via IV Novembre to Piazza Italia.

COMING AND GOING

Nuoro's **train station** (P. della Stazione, tel. 1478/88088) is almost useless. Nuoro is Italy's only province without direct or quasi-reliable train service. **Buses** are a better way of getting around. The people working at the **ARST** bus ticket counter (tel. 0784/32201) in the train station are helpful, but they keep irregular hours; when the counter is abandoned, buy tickets at the snack bar in the station. Most buses stop across the street from the train station in Piazza della Stazione, but ask at the ticket counter for the most recent information. Two buses a day leave for Cagliari, one direct (7:10 AM, 2½ hrs, L20,000), one with numerous stops (2 PM, 5 hrs, L20,000); eight for Dorgali (40 min, L3,500); nine for Olbia (2½ hrs, L12,000); four for Orgòsolo (40 min, L2,800); two for Sassari (4:10 AM and 7 AM, 3 hrs, L16,000); and eight for Siniscola (50 min, L4,500). Otherwise you can rent a car at **Maggiore** (V. Convento 32, tel. 0784/30461), but they charge a steep L138,000 for one day, L92,000 a day for three days, or L550,000 per week.

WHERE TO SLEEP

Accommodations here are generally acceptable but certainly not luxurious. The **Grazia Deledda Hotel** (V. Lamarmora, 08100, tel. 0784/31257, fax 0784/31258) charges L90,000–L140,000 for doubles and has a restaurant and air-conditioning. For L100,000–L120,000 there are doubles at **Hotel Sandalia** (V. Einaudi, 08100, tel 0784/38353, fax 0784/38353). The **Fratelli Sacchi** (Monte Ortobene, 08100, tel. 0784/31200, fax 0784/34030) gives you a double room and breakfast for L110,000–L120,000. If you've got gear, the best camping is in nearby Cala Gonone (*see below*), connected to Nuoro by frequent buses (1 hr, L5,000).

WHERE TO EAT

Affordable food is scarce in Nuoro, though some hotels have good restaurants, and fast-food pizza joints are always a backup. **Trattoria Il Rifugio** (Vicolo del Pozzo 4, tel. 0784/232355), the best and most reasonable place to eat in Nuoro, is a meeting ground for yuppies and Sardinian locals. Try the spaghetti *alle cozze*, redolent of wine and garlic, or tasty pizzas. From the train station, turn left down Via La Marmora to the church, make a U-turn around the gelato caffè, walk straight and turn right on Via Mughina, and then right again on Vicolo del Pozzo. **Trattoria Il Gabbiano** (V. Mughina 11, tel. 0784/32919; cash only), a local hangout on the way out of town, serves delicious fish and homemade ravioli. From the station, follow Via La Marmora to Piazza della Grazie, then turn right on Via Manzoni; it's across from Piazza Mameli, to the right of the Agip gas station.

WORTH SEEING

The building housing the **Museo della Vita e delle Tradizioni Popolari Sarde** (Museum of Sardinian Life and Traditions) is itself an example of traditional Sardinian architecture, with wooden balconies and black stone portals. Each room is dedicated to a different aspect of Sardinian culture, such as traditional clothing and accessories, for example; intricate turquoise buttons used to fasten shirts. Also check out the phallic *munifica*, a pendant used to cast the evil eye, and the displays of petrified *turtichedda durchicheddos de malde*, traditional decorative pastries filled with dried fruit and honey. *V. Mereu 56, tel. 0784/31426. From P. Vittorio Emanuele, head downhill and follow signs. Admission L3,000. Open mid-June–Sept., daily 9–7; mid-Mar.–mid-June and Oct., daily 9–1 and 3–7; Nov.–mid-Mar., Tues.–Sat. 9–1 and 3–7.*

NEAR NUORO

If you're looking for a little adventure and isolation, the mountains surrounding Nuoro offer plenty of hiking and spelunking opportunities on rocky heights and in water-filled grottoes. You'll also discover some of the oldest archaeological finds on the island here and some of the best beaches. Down the coast, **Santa Maria Navarrese** is a good hub for taking boat trips and seeing the area. Two buses daily leave Nuoro for Arbatax, at 8 AM and 2 PM (2 hrs, L11,300) and stop in Santa Maria Navarrese. One stop prior to Santa Maria Navarrese on the Nuoro–Arbatax bus is **Baunei**, where footpaths connect mountainous goat turf with the sea. Here parched mountain terrain punctuated by ghost-town churches opens onto marvelous turquoise bays accessible only by unmarked paths or by boat. Seek navigational help at the **Cooperativa Turistica Il Golgo** (08040 Baunei, tel. 0337/811828; open daily 8 AM– 11 PM), run by a group of friends in their thirties who lead excursions and have a fantastically authentic (albeit fantastically remote) restaurant.

DORGALI

Perched on the cliffs above Cala Gonone, Dorgali is a touristy but excellent shopping town, with endless handcrafted pottery, leather, and local wine. Though essentially a one-street village, Dorgali is an easy pit stop on your way to Cala Gonone, if only to sample *il pistidu* (a dessert made with cooked wine) at one of the many pastry shops or to take advantage of the town's efficient tourist office. The **Pro Loco** (V. Lamarmora 1, tel. 0784/96243; open weekdays 9–1 and 3:30–7) will give you a map and explicit directions in English to nearby caves, nuraghi, and tombs. The area is rich in scattered nuraghic remains, including the **Giants' Tomb,** a mysterious burial ground covered with massive monoliths. Also worth a visit—if you have a car—are the nuraghic villages of **Serra Orrios** and **Su Casteddu.** Pro Loco also conducts guided tours of the **Grotto di Ispinigoli,** a chasm—thought to be the site of ancient Phoenician sacrifice rituals—that includes the tallest stalagmite in the world (125 ft). If you want to stay the night in Dorgali, a L65,000 double (L60,000 in low season) at **San Pietro** (V. Lamarmora 29, 08020, tel. 0784/96142; cash only) is the cheapest in town. Doubles cost L95,000–L120,000 at the nearby **Hotel Querceto** (V. Lamarmora, tel. 0784/96509, fax 0784/95254). Six **ARST** buses travel daily from Nuoro to Dorgali (40 min, L3,500), and seven daily buses journey back to Nuoro.

CALA GONONE

The big attraction at cheerful Cala Gonone, a touristy seaside village, is the boat excursion to the **Grotto Bue Marino,** the spectacular monk-seal caves, although seals haven't been spotted since 1983. Formed by an underground spring, this extensive grotto includes 15 km (9 mi) of extraordinary stalactite and stalagmite formations, but only the first kilometer (half mile) is accessible to the public. Four boat excursions (tel. 0784/93305), increasing to hourly departures in high season, leave daily from the marina in Cala Gonone and include a guided walking tour of the grotto (2 hrs, L17,000). For L9000–L13,000 extra (depending on season) you can also see the beautiful beach of **Cala Luna** and stay for up to four hours. Other daylong excursions run along the cave-dotted coast, stopping at dramatic beaches accessible only by boat. **Cala Mariolu** is one beach that will leave you *con bocca aperta* (with mouth agape); it is strewn with white polished boulders, and its cliffs and caves end in dreamlike aquamarine depths. For more details on boat excursions, contact the **Nuovo Consorzio di Trasporti Marittimi** (tel. 0784/93305) at the port. To reach Cala Gonone, take one of the eight daily buses (1 hr 10 min, L3,700) from the ARST station in Nuoro.

WHERE TO SLEEP AND EAT • Plenty of hotels and campgrounds make Cala Gonone a good place to settle in for a while. **Piccolo Hotel** (V. C. Colombo, 08022, tel. 0784/93232; cash only off-season) has the cheapest private doubles, L80,000 in low season, L99,000 in high. Prices include breakfast, and you'll pay a little more if you want a sea view. The tiny hotel **La Conchiglia** (V. Lungomare, 08022, tel. 0784/93448) has doubles for L100,000–L120,000. For some reason many hotels here only accept credit-card payments in high season. **Camping Cala Gonone** (V. Collodi 1, 08020, tel. 0784/93165; closed mid-Oct.–Mar.) is a well-rated setup in the middle of town, with free hot showers and laundry, as well as a bar, restaurant, barbecue, and sports facilities. If you're hungry, Cala Gonone has numerous beachside trattorias where you can gorge on pasta and seafood while enjoying the picturesque backdrop. Or save some bucks and eat just as well at **Snoopy** (Lungomare Palmavera, at V. Caio Duilio), where you can pick and choose from a variety of prepared dishes, like fresh marinated seafood salad or a huge slab of eggplant pizza.

ITALIAN GLOSSARY

PRONUNCIATION

Lucky for you, Italian is pronounced almost exactly as it is written. If you learn just a few rules, you'll be able to pronounce most Italian words. Best of all, Italians, unlike many of their neighbors to the north, will appreciate your efforts to speak their language.

VOWELS

A is always pronounced **ah** (as in pasta), **i** sounds like **ee** (as in police), and **u** is always pronounced **oo** (as in blue). **E** sometimes sounds like **eh** (as in memory), sometimes like **ay** (as in weigh). **O** can sound like **oh** (as in most), or like **ah** (as in cost). When you see two vowels right next to each other, pronounce each one individually. For example, *paura* (fear) is pronounced pa-OO-ra. To accomplish this, you may have to stretch your mouth in directions it's never gone before, but if you didn't make a few faces, you wouldn't be speaking Italian.

CONSONANTS

In Italian **ch** is always pronounced like a **k**, so *chiesa* (church) is pronounced kee-AY-za. A **c** followed by an **i** or an **e** is pronounced like the English **ch**, so *città* (city) is pronounced chee-TAH. A **c** followed by anything else sounds like a **k**; *cambio* (change) is pronounced KAHM-bee-oh. Both **g** and **gg** are pronounced as **j** when followed by **i** or **e**, so Luigi sounds like Loo-EE-jee. **Qu** always sounds like kw, so *qui* (here) is pronounced KWEE.

The sound that is most likely to trip up English speakers is the **gl**, which is pronounced sort of like **ly**, much like the sound in million. Gli, the masculine plural for the word "the" is thus pronounced LYEE; try to resist the temptation to say GLEE. Similarly, **gn** is pronounced like **ny**. If you know how to pronounce gnocchi (NYO-kee), you've got it made. Finally, **double consonants** are pronounced differently than single ones, so *fato* (fate) is pronounced differently than *fatto* (made). Pronounce the double letter twice, once at the end of the first syllable and once at the beginning of the second.

English	Italian
GETTING BY	
Yes/no	Sì/no
Okay	Va bene
Please/You're welcome	Per favore/Prego
Thank you	Grazie
Excuse me/I'm sorry	Scusi/Mi dispiace
Good morning/afternoon	Buon giorno
Good evening	Buona sera
Goodbye	Arrivederci/ciao
How are you?	Come sta?
Fine, and you?	Bene, e Lei?

Do you speak English?	Parla inglese?
I don't speak Italian.	Non parlo italiano.
I don't understand.	Non capisco.
How do you say. . . ?	Come si dice. . . ?
I don't know.	Non lo so.
What's your name?	Come si chiama?
My name is. . .	Mi chiamo. . .
Where is. . . ?	Dov'è. . . ?
What time is it?	Che ore sono?
How?	Come?
When?	Quando?
What?	Che cosa?
Where is the bathroom?	Dov'è il bagno?
This/That	Questo/Quello
Is there a bank nearby?	C'è una banca qui vicino?
An exchange bureau	Una cassa di cambio
Is there a charge?	C'è una tariffa?
Can I use my credit card?	Posso usare la carta di credito?

EMERGENCIES

I am sick.	Sto male.
Hospital	L'ospedale
First aid	Il pronto soccorso
Call a doctor.	Chiami un medico.
Help!	Aiuto!
Call the police!	Telefoni la polizia!

NUMBERS

One	Uno
Two	Due
Three	Tre
Four	Quattro
Five	Cinque
Six	Sei
Seven	Sette
Eight	Otto
Nine	Nove
Ten	Dieci
Eleven	Undici
Twelve	Dodici
Twenty	Venti
Thirty	Trenta
Forty	Quaranta
Fifty	Cinquanta
Sixty	Sessanta
Seventy	Settanta
Eighty	Ottanta
Ninety	Novanta
One hundred	Cento
One thousand	Mille
Ten thousand	Diecimila
One hundred thousand	Centomila

DAYS OF THE WEEK

Sunday	Domenica
Monday	Lunedì
Tuesday	Martedì

Wednesday	Mercoledì
Thursday	Giovedì
Friday	Venerdì
Saturday	Sabato

COMING AND GOING

The train station	La stazione/ferrovia
A ticket	Un biglietto
Round-trip	Andata e ritorno
Arrival/departure	Arrivo/partenza
Platform	Il binario
First/second class	Prima/seconda classe
Bus (long-distance)	Pullman
City bus	L'autobus
Bus stop	La fermata dell'autobus/del pullman
A city map	Una pianta della città
Here/there	Qui/là
Left/right	A sinistra/destra
Straight ahead	Sempre diritto

WHERE TO SLEEP

Where can I find a cheap hotel?	Dove potrei trovare un albergo a buon prezzo?
Hostel	Un ostello
A room	Una camera
I would like to make a reservation.	Vorrei fare una prenotazione.
Is there a private bathroom?	C'è un bagno privato?
For one person/two people	Per una persona/due persone
A key	Una chiave
Campground	Campeggio
Can I leave my bags here?	Posso lasciare qui i miei bagagli?

FOOD

Breakfast	La prima colazione
Lunch/dinner	Il pranzo/la cena
A bottle of...	Una bottiglia di...
A glass of...	Un bicchiere di...
Cheese/bread	Formaggio/il pane
The bill/check	Il conto
I'd like to order...	Vorrei ordinare...
Cheers!	Cin cin!
I am a diabetic.	Ho il diabete.
I am a vegetarian.	Sono vegetariano/a.

MORE USEFUL PHRASES

Cover charge	Coperto
Will you walk me home?	Mi accompagni a casa?
Grocery store	Alimentari
Tampons/pads	Tamponi/assorbente
How much is it?	Quanto costa?
Too much	Troppo
Leave me alone.	Lasciami in pace.
I already have a boyfriend/girlfriend	Ho già un ragazzo/una ragazza

INDEX

Villa Melzi, *120*
Villa Napoleonica, *251*
Villa of Catullus, *113*
Villa Palagonia, *449*
Villa rentals, *14–15*
Villa Romana, *428*
Villa Rotonda, *56*
Villa San Michele, *364*
Villa Serbelloni, *120*
Villa Valmarana ai Nana, *56*
Violin-making, *104, 105*
Virgil, *111, 394*
Visas, *18*
Visitor information, *23*

Viterbo, *329–330*
Vivano, *367*
Volgalonga (festival), *46*
Volcanoes, *357–358, 359, 366, 411, 414, 421–423, 454*
Volgalonga (festival), *46*
Volterra, *234–235*
Volunteering, *23*
Vulcano, *453, 454*

W

Walser Museum, *136*
Watchtowers, *468*

Water sports, *365*
Weather, *22, 24*
Web sites, *23–24*
Well temple, *467*
Wildlife preserves, *137, 139–140, 331, 336–338, 429, 471*
Wineries, *236, 238, 245, 424*
Working in Italy, *24*

Z

Zone, *118, 119*